Proceedings

Ninth IEEE International Conference on Tools with Artificial Intelligence

Proceedings

Ninth IEEE International Conference on Tools with Artificial Intelligence

November 3–8, 1997
Newport Beach, California

Sponsored by

IEEE Computer Society
Technical Committee on PAMI

In cooperation with

Pan American Center for Earth and Environmental Studies

IEEE COMPUTER SOCIETY

Los Alamitos, California

Washington • Brussels • Tokyo

IEEE Computer Society Order Number PR08203
ISBN 0-8186-8203-5
ISBN 0-8186-8204-3 (case)
ISBN 0-8186-8205-1 (microfiche)
IEEE Order Plan Catalog Number 97CB36147
ISSN 1082-3409

Additional copies may be ordered from:

IEEE Computer Society
Customer Service Center
10662 Los Vaqueros Circle
P.O. Box 3014
Los Alamitos, CA 90720-1314
Tel: + 1-714-821-8380
Fax: + 1-714-821-4641
E-mail: cs.books@computer.org

IEEE Service Center
445 Hoes Lane
P.O. Box 1331
Piscataway, NJ 08855-1331
Tel: + 1-908-981-1393
Fax: + 1-908-981-9667
mis.custserv@computer.org

IEEE Computer Society
13, Avenue de l'Aquilon
B-1200 Brussels
BELGIUM
Tel: + 32-2-770-2198
Fax: + 32-2-770-8505
euro.ofc@computer.org

IEEE Computer Society
Ooshima Building
2-19-1 Minami-Aoyama
Minato-ku, Tokyo 107
JAPAN
Tel: + 81-3-3408-3118
Fax: + 81-3-3408-3553
tokyo.ofc@computer.org

Editorial production by Penny Storms

Cover art production by Joe Daigle/Studio Productions

Printed in the United States of America by Technical Communication Services

IEEE COMPUTER SOCIETY

IEEE

Table of Contents

Message from the General Chair

On behalf of the Tools with Artificial Intelligence Committees, I welcome you to the Ninth International Conference on Tools with Artificial Intelligence. I believe you will find that this year's conference will provide an excellent insight into the currently significant areas of artificial intelligence.

Many people have devoted a great deal of their effort during the past year to ensure the quality and excellence of this conference. I greatly appreciate the efforts of the authors and the reviewers. Special thanks are due the Program Chairs: Phillip Sheu and Robert Reynolds. The Vice Chairs of the Program Committee also did an excellent job in developing the content of this conference.

The Steering Committee provided excellent guidance for the conference committees and me. The continuity, intelligence, and experience provided by this group of outstanding individuals cannot be overstated.

Thanks is also due to the staff of the IEEE Computer Society. I especially thank Ms. Penny Storms for her efforts in helping us organize this year's conference.

Finally, I thank the outstanding group of keynote speakers who will, no doubt, set the tone for an excellent 1997 IEEE Tools with Artificial Intelligence Conference.

Daniel E. Cooke

General Chair TAI '97

Message from the Program Chairs

Following in the footsteps of its successful predecessors, the Ninth International Conference on Tools with Artificial Intelligence (TAI '97) continues to emphasize both theoretical and applied frameworks that can serve as tools for the development of intelligent systems and artificial intelligence applications.

The variety of papers present in the proceedings strongly reflect the current themes in the field of artificial intelligence today. The papers fall into ten basic tracks that include: Intelligent Agents, Artificial Intelligence in Software Engineering, Knowledge Discovery and Data Mining, Evolutionary Computation and Genetic Algorithms, Neural Networks, Knowledge Representation and Reasoning, Machine Vision and Pattern Recognition, Machine Learning, Problem Solving, and Natural Language Processing.

This year 108 papers were submitted to the conference from over 20 countries. Approximately 70% of all submissions were from overseas which reflects the truly international scope of the conference. Each submitted paper was reviewed by three referees under the guidance of a technical area chair. The program committee accepted 50% of the papers as regular papers, 11% as short papers, and 8% as poster papers as shown in the following table.

Table of Submissions

Geographical Area	Submitted	Accepted Regular	Accepted Short	Accepted Poster
USA	35	21	2	2
EUROPE	29	15	4	2
CANADA	8	2	3	1
JAPAN	8	4	1	1
ASIA	18	7	2	2
AUSTRALIA	7	4	0	1
SOUTH AMERICA	3	1	0	0
TOTAL	**108**	**54**	**12**	**9**

The success of TAI '97 is due to the efforts of a number of individuals. In particular, we would like to thank Dan Cooke (General Chair) and Nick Bourbakis (Treasurer) as well as the program vice chairs and the entire program committee for their tireless efforts on behalf of the conference.

We are pleased that TAI '97 has provided a forum for researchers and professionals from around the world to discuss their work in the relaxing and friendly atmosphere of Newport Beach, California. In closing, we wish to thank most of all each of the attendees. Your striving for excellence has helped us produce an excellent conference program this year.

Robert Reynolds **Phillip Sheu**

Program Co-Chairs TAI '97

ICTAI '97 Committees

Steering Committee

Farokh Bastani, *University of Texas. Dallas, USA*
Nikolaos G. Bourbakis (Chair), *SUNY at Binghamton, USA*
Rüdiger Brause, *J.W. Goethe-University, Germany*
Bill Manaris, *University of Southwestern Louisiana, USA*
Pierre Marquis, *INRIA, France*
C.V. Ramamoorthy, *University of California, Berkeley, USA*
Jeffrey J.P. Tsai, *University of Illinois at Chicago, USA*

General Chair

Daniel Cooke, *The University of Texas, El Paso, USA*

Publicity Chair

Raymond Paul, *The Pentagon, USA*

Registration Chair

D. Kavraki, *AIS, NY, USA, USA*

Local Arrangement Chairs

Kane Kim, *University of California, Irvine, USA*
Demetri Michalopolos, *California State University, Fullerton, USA*

Award Chair

Nikolaos G. Bourbakis, *SUNY Binghamton, USA*

Program Chairs

Robert Reynolds, *Wayne State University, USA*
Phillip C.-Y. Sheu, *University of California, Irvine, USA*

Program Vice Chairs

David Dampier, *Army Research Laboratory, USA*
Sven Dickenson, *Rutgers University, USA*
Tharam Dillon, *La Trobe University, Australia*
Vijay Garg, *University of Texas, Austin, USA*
Jim Gattiker, *Los Alamos National Laboratory, USA*
Ioannis Hatzilygeroudis, *CTI, Greece*
Seth Hutchinson, *University of Illinois, Urbana Champaign, USA*
Mike Pazzani, *University of California, Irvine, USA*
Isidore Rigoutsos, *IBM Watson Research Center, USA*
Ishwar Sethi, *Wayne State University, USA*
Bharghavan Vaduvur, *University of Illinois, Urbana Champaign, USA*
Sachio Watanabe, *NEC, Japan*
Radu-Popescu Zeletin, *GMD, Germany*

Program Committee Members

Kamal Ali, *IBM Almaden, USA*
R. Andel, *SUNY at Binghamton, USA*
Nikolaos Avouris, *University of Patras, Greece*
A. Bansal, *Kent State University, USA*
B. Bhargava, *Purdue University, USA*
Sourav Bhattacharya, *Arizona State University, USA*
Nikolaos Bourbakis, *SUNY at Binghamton, USA*
Clifford Brunk, *Silicon Graphics, USA*
Ronald Byrnes, *U.S. Military Academy, USA*
Chye Lin Chee, *National University of Singapore*
Stefan Covaci, *GMD-Fokus, Germany*
Alex Delis, *Polytech University of New York, USA*
Arif Ghafoor, *Purdue University, USA*
Christos Faloutsos, *University of Maryland, USA*
A. Hall, *Air Force Research Lab at Rome, USA*
Robert Hammell, *Army Research Laboratory, USA*
Jean Paul Haton, *INRIA, France*
Caroline Hayes, *Beckman Institute, USA*
Susan Hruska, *Florida State University, USA*
Moon Kim, *Konkuk University, Korea*
B. Mahr, *Technical University of Berlin, Germany*
Abe Mamdani, *Imperial College, UK*
S. Mertoguno, *Fujitsu, USA*
Roman Neruda, *Czech Academy of Sciences, Czech Republic*
Atul Prakash, *Univsersity of Michigan at Ann Arbor, USA*
Han Reichgelt, *University of West Indies, Jamaica*
Sudeep Sarkar, *University of South Florida, Tampa, USA*
Rajeev Sharma, *Pennsylvania State University, USA*
Shashi Shekhar, *University of Minnesota, USA*
Kaleem Siddiqi, *Yale University, USA*
Jaideep Srivastava, *University of Minnesota, USA*
Jeffrey Tsai, *University of Illinois, USA*
Joseph Urban, *Arizona State University, USA*
Ramasamy Uthurusamy, *General Motors Research, USA*
Jason Wang, *NJIT, USA*
I-Ling Yen, *Michigan State University, USA*

Keynote Addresses

Keynote Address

"Cognitive Prostheses"

Kenneth M. Ford

Associate Center Director of NASA Ames Research Center
and Director of the NASA Center of Excellence for Information Technology

---

Banquet - Keynote Address

"Looking from Outside of the Box"

Raymond Yeh

CEO of ISSS

Keynote Address

"Knowledge Representation Based Upon Models of Human Cognition"

Peter Chen

Professor of Computer Science, LSU
and President of Chen and Associates

Keynote Address

"Content-based Interactivity"

Dr. Ramesh Jain

University of California at San Diego
and Virage Inc. San Diego

Session A.1

Intelligent Agents and Applications I

Session Chair:
Raymond Paul, The Pentagon, USA

W-ACE: A Logic Language for Intelligent Internet Programming

Enrico Pontelli & Gopal Gupta
Lab. for Logic and Databases
New Mexico State University
{epontell,gupta}@cs.nmsu.edu

Abstract

The development of the World Wide Web (WWW) *has been considerably delayed due to the excessive complexity of developing advanced and intelligent applications for the Internet. An average application may require the use of different languages, an in-depth understanding of various communication protocols and low-level communication mechanisms, etc. In this paper we propose a logic programming system, called* W-ACE, *extended with various features to support natural and efficient development of Internet tools. The nature of the constructs introduced makes it particularly suitable to support* intelligent *Internet applications (knowledge-based systems, agents, etc.). W-ACE covers various issues in supporting knowledge-based handling of the World Wide Web, allowing structured and constraint-based management of WWW information, passive and active view of WWW, as well as a powerful support for concurrent applications. Various examples of complex intelligent applications are presented, to underline the simplicity and the power of the proposed ideas.*

1 Introduction

The growth of the *Internet* and the *World Wide Web (WWW)* has lead the computer science community to focus a great deal of research effort within this application field. This has produced notable results in development of fast and reliable communication systems, and sophisticate, user-friendly WWW browsers. On the other hand, this trend of research shows that the focus has been mainly on the lowest and highest level issues for supporting Internet software (communication and high-level applications). It is a growing concern in the community [1, 4] that not enough effort has been placed in filling the gap between these two levels. This gap is mainly caused by the lack of an adequate programming support for the development of Internet related applications. Thus, the task of developing and maintaining this sort of applications is complex and not accessible to average programmers.

The large majority of programs operating on the Internet—e.g., browsers, servers, agents—have been developed by mixing a variety of different languages (e.g., C, Perl, Java), as there is no single language which offers all the adequate features for developing Internet tools. This leads to applications composed of a variety of modules in different languages, interacting through complex and unnatural interfaces. Furthermore, traditional languages lack some basic features that we deem fundamental for the next generation of Internet applications, specifically *concurrency*, *data structuring* (i.e., most of the data currently obtained from the Internet (e.g., Web pages) are just seen as unstructured sequences of characters), *dynamicity* (most existing Web-related applications are seen as programs manipulating static collections of information), and *statefulness* (i.e., the life-span of an execution is typically limited to a single interaction),

In this project we propose to develop a complete framework aimed at supporting the efficient development and execution of complex Web-based applications. The system, named *W-ACE*, is based on one of the most efficient parallel logic programming systems available, the *ACE* system [16] and takes advantage of the search and symbolic manipulation facilities offered by logic programming. W-ACE combines some original ideas (specific data domains and data structuring, modality-based operations, both server and client side active view) with other ideas proposed in various separate proposals (client side computation, HTML interfaces), to produce a complete and uniform programming framework. The use of a logic-based language and the choice of operators makes W-ACE an ideal choice for the development of agents and knowledge-based systems. Furthermore, the parallel capabilities of the underlying ACE system allow the exploitation of the concurrency inherent in Web-applications.

2 Problem Description

The current view of the WWW is that of a giant, highly disorganized database. Retrieval of information is realized in the large majority of the cases using browsers (e.g., Netscape, Mosaic) with fixed capabilities. The need for more sophisticated tools can be easily justified with a simple analogy: the current status of the WWW is analogous to that of a purely extensional database, that lacks any mechanism to perform inferences and extract intensional knowledge. Thus, there is an emerging need to give to both programmers and final users the ability to easily manipulate this source of knowledge. The number of tools for *Network Information Retrieval (NIR)* is constantly growing [8], confirming the need for this sort of applications.

In the current setting, developing applications which deal with the WWW requires considerable skills. We can distinguish two classes of applications: *Direct Access Applications (DAA)* are independent applications which perform a direct access to Internet via any of the basic protocols—e.g., HTTP—*Agents/Softbots* and *browsers* are typical examples. *HTML-based Applications (HA)* rely on the use of HTML-based interfaces—i.e., input and output of the applications is realized through HTML pages and via standard browsers. These applications require support for

1082-3409/97 $10.00 © 1997 IEEE

HTML-like [17] interfacing (hyperlinks, forms), interfacing of external applications (e.g., CGI scripting [9]), and developing intelligent connected applications (e.g., communicating via CGI scripts).

Thus, a typical Web-based application requires the use of three different programming languages: HTML for the web pages, Perl (Javascript, etc.) for CGIs, and a traditional language for the "real" computing application. Even if the interfaces between the different components are well-defined and standardized (which is not the case), the issue of communication between different components is delicate, and the design of the interfaces represents a considerable part of the whole development process. This whole system places a considerable burden on the developer, and calls for a *unified* framework which would allow to *effectively*, and *efficiently* tackle all the issues described above.

Very limited support has been offered by the current tools in trying to hide the complex issues of communication and data structures, with few exceptions like Java (support for networking and HTTP) and libraries like PiLLoW [4] (HTML structuring) and LibWWW [22] (HTTP interface). Internet data (e.g., HTML documents) are required to show a dynamic behaviour, either in their content or in their structure; adequate mechanisms to structure and manipulate them are needed. This data structuring organization should allow a closer interaction between clients and servers, allowing the management of multiple interacting components. This is the direction of Java's *Applets* (server-initiated executions on client's side), Common Gateway Interface (CGI) scripts [9] (client-initiated executions on server's side), and Server Side Includes (SSI) (server-initiated executions on server's side). These schemes are very limited and do not offer sufficient control to the programmer. Last but not least, very little consideration has been given to the issue of efficiency of Internet applications—expected to become a major issue in the near future. To tackle these issues concurrency and parallelism are required. Logic programming [16] is a viable paradigm to handle these sorts of requirements.

Various proposals have recently emerged which extend logic programming to support Internet Programming, demonstrating the distinct advantage of this programming paradigm for WWW-applications [11, 4, 21, 20, 1]; similar attempts are also present in the functional programming community [3]. Nevertheless, most of these schemes are limited to abstracting some of the interfaces, without tackling the more general problem of developing an actual Internet programming paradigm. The only exceptions are LogicWeb [11] (which supports a view similar to that of client-side active layer) and Fox [3].

3 W-ACE

W-ACE is a constraint logic programming language [10] embedding a variety of constraint domains—some general purpose (e.g., Sets), some specifically designed to handle Internet-related information. The general idea is to offer 2 layers in the computational model. The *Object Layer* deals with Internet information as data for the execution; The *Active Layer* views Internet data as active computations (along the lines of lightweight databases [5] and LogicWeb [11]). Furthermore, the two layers above are not separate, but they have to be seen as alternative points of view of the same reality. Thus additional mechanisms must be supplied to allow switching from one level to the other. This is equivalent to the concept of *meta-programming*, for which logic programming has been recognized as one of the best paradigms.

3.1 The Object Layer

The object layer is related to developing applications which manipulate information obtained from Internet as *data*. Most current proposals in the literature regarding tools for WWW/Internet programming are within this layer of operation. The power of using logic programming to handle object layer applications has already been pointed out in some recent proposals [4, 1, 20]. W-ACE aims to provide the user with a language which allows a more natural management of the structured information deriving from web processing.

Messages: At the lowest level, information is exchanged in the form of messages which are communicated using TCP/IP protocol. W-ACE supports direct access to this level, encoding messages as appropriate terms. Socket based TCP connections are used to support also HTTP communications.

HTML: Various existing proposals do not supply any representation for HTML documents. E.g., Eclipse server [1] and Amzi WebServer [20] require the user to deal with explicit HTML, typically coded as a string of characters. PiLLoW [4] proposed (to our knowledge) for the first time the idea of handling HTML documents as Prolog structures. W-ACE represents (part of an) HTML document as a tree structure (or, equivalently, as a logic term). Each node is labeled with a special identifier indicating the nature of the entities at the next immediate level. The root of the tree for a page is labeled html. Figure 1 illustrates the tree for a fragment of a document, describing a simple enumeration; on the side the corresponding HTML code is reported. The translation of the the tree into a W-ACE

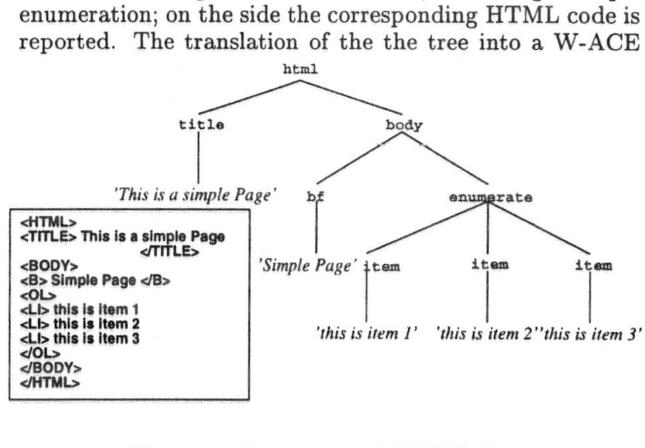

Figure 1: Fragment of HTML Tree

terms follows the traditional syntax of logic (each logical term *is* a tree). Hyperlinks can be either *external*, i.e. they contain an actual URL, or *internal*, identifying another tree. Each HTML tree is *named*, and the name is associated to the instance of the html functor.

Additionally, the W-ACE language provides very powerful mechanisms for symbolic management of HTML documents. The final aim is that of developing W-ACE as a *CLP(HTML)*, i.e., a constraint programming language (CLP) capable of dealing with equations and inequations over W-ACE HTML trees. This allows us to perform in a very natural way very sophisticated operations on trees.

Equality (=) can be used to easily extract components from a page; the constraint nature of the schema allows also to view equality as a constraint on the *possible* structure of the pages created/accessed. $\preceq$ is used to represent the *subtree* relation. This allows, for example to easily identify the presence of a certain structure in a page (without having to "dismantle" the whole page—as required in any other proposed schemes); a W-ACE goal like: Links = { X : ref(X) $\preceq$ Page } allows to extract in the set Links all the the HTML links which appear in the document Page.

Collection of Pages: HTML trees are themselves organized into *HTML graphs*. In fact, HTML pages on the Web are not separate and independent entities, but are more commonly tightly coupled collections of interdependent information. To our knowledge the concept has not been extensively explored within the framework of languages for Internet/WWW-development. The concept has been successfully used in some domain-specific applications [18]. In W-ACE, pages (i.e., W-ACE HTML trees) are organized into active graphs. Each node of the graph is an HTML document. An edge between two nodes denotes the accessibility relation between the two documents (existence of a link from one page to the other). This allows for immediate verification of various properties (connectivity between two nodes, degree of nodes, etc.). HTML graphs themselves can be treated as nodes which are part of a higher level graph, and so on. This imposes a hierarchical structure on the HTML documents, controlling at the same time the accessibility of documents (e.g., security).

3.1.1 Semantic Features

In the same spirit as Java, W-ACE also provides an extensive collection of built-ins for performing a variety of Internet-related operations.

Web-Pages Development: The structure representation given for HTML documents and their organization as HTML graphs can be directly used to develop web pages using W-ACE. Two predicates are available to perform conversion between internal (structured) and external (byte stream/string): html_page and html_graph. The two predicates are bidirectional. Furthermore, a predicate html_io is available to store an HTML structure into external files and vice versa. This approach also offers to the programmer an easy mechanism to design programs which generate HTML documents (e.g., an HTML editor) or which perform symbolic manipulation of HTML documents (e.g., filters from/to HTML).

Generic Access: An additional layer is built on top of the HTTP access, supplying a high level programmable interface to the Internet (through HTTP). The generic predicate is called get_url, taking as argument the URL to access. The simple clauses below expand the current HTML graph by adding all the HTML documents linked by a certain page.

```
update(Page,GraphIn,GraphOut) :-
            Links = { X : ref(X) ⪯ Page},
            verify_link(Links,Page,GraphIn,GraphOut).
verify_link(∅,_,GraphIn,GraphOut) :-
            GraphIn = GraphOut.
verify_link(X less Rest,Page,GraphIn,GraphOut) :-
            get_url(X,Tree),!,
            GraphTemp = {(Page,Tree)} ∪ GraphIn,
            verify_link(Rest,Page,GraphTemp,GraphOut).
verify_link(X less Rest,Page,GraphIn,GraphOut) :-
            GraphTemp = {(Page,dead)} ∪ GraphIn,
            verify_link(Rest,Page,GraphTemp,GraphOut).
```

CGI Scripting: Scripting languages, like Perl and Javascript, are commonly employed for CGI scripts, as they are very simple to debug and allow to write simple CGI scripts in few lines. Scripting languages are notoriously slow, inherently sequential, and unsuitable for activities more complex than simple file and data filtering. For these and other reasons [15], we decided to continue the proposals made by various researchers [4, 3] aiming at integrating CGI scripting with main applications written in high-level languages. Any W-ACE program can be used as a CGI script. The entry point of a CGI script can be an arbitrary predicate with a single argument. Whenever the script is executed (called by a client session), the indicated entry point will be started, and the argument supplied will be initially instantiated to a structure:

cgi_info(*remote_host,remote_adr,*
*server_port,request_method,*Pairs)

where Pairs is a list of name-value pairs passed as input to the CGI script. For example, the input from a form with a single field named client will be coded as

cgi_info('joe.nmsu.edu','128.123.3.4',80,'GET',[client(1)])

The decoding of the input string is performed automatically and transparently. The output of the CGI script is produced using the predicate cgi_output(*type, data*). HTML documents developed using the HTML tree structure can encode calls to CGI scripts by a simple reference to the entry point of the script (assuming, of course, that the CGI script in part of the same program used to develop the HTML tree). For example, the encoding of an HTML tree fragment aimed at obtaining an input from the user is shown below:

```
...
Tree = html(title(X),body(
   input(text,25,name,cgiscript))),
...
cgiscript(X) :-
...
```

where cgiscript is the entry point of the script.

3.1.2 Applications

The Web Tourist Advisor: The HTML graph can be used to generalize the limited notion of browsing history offered by traditional Web browsers (e.g., the *Window History* menu of NCSA Mosaic). During browsing, it is quite common that the user accessing a new page has the desire to explore all the links emanating from such page in a systematic way. Using traditional browsers this becomes a quite cumbersome activity, involving repeated backtracking steps to get back to the root page. W-ACE has been developed as a *Common Client Interface (CCI)* [12] compliant application. This allows W-ACE to exchange information with NCSA Mosaic. This feature can be used to create a simple interface which allows to maintain a graphical representation of the current HTML graph, which changes in sync with the browsing actions performed during a Mosaic session. The graphical representation will represent pages as nodes and connect them with edges whenever there is a link between them. The user will be able to detect its current position and move directly to the desired pages.

Stateful Servers CGI scripts have a lifetime that spans a single interaction; as such they do not allow to retain (at least in a simple and *efficient* way) a state across different interactions with the user. The problem can be tackled by storing information in the exchanged documents (using hidden fields)—but this may dramatically increase the amount of information exchanged at every interaction, with consequent impact on the system efficiency. Furthermore, since CGI scripts are restarted at every interaction, this implies having to pay at every interaction the price for starting up the whole system. The use of CGI scripts only as communication scripts to allow interaction between a browsing session and an external server (different from the HTTP server) is becoming more widespread. The external server has a lifetime which spans multiple interactions, thus maintaining a state across them. Figure 2(i) describes intuitively the structure of the system, while figure 2(ii) illustrates the lifetimes of the different components.

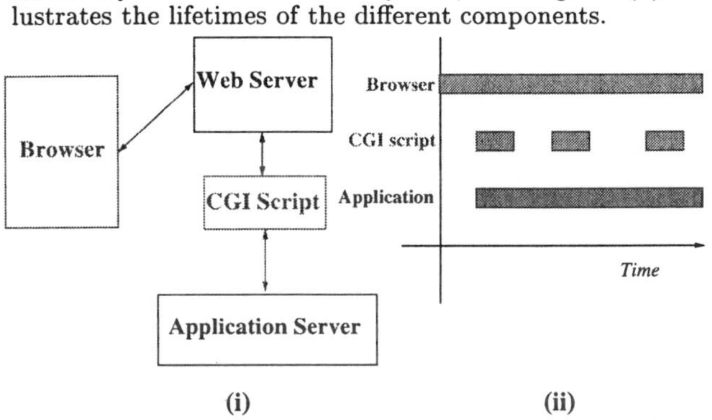

Figure 2: Stateful Servers

Interactions between the application server and the CGI scripts in W-ACE are simple. W-ACE is an inherently concurrent system (based on the ACE parallel system [16]). This allows to spawn server computations which support the state of one interaction with a client. Communication between client and server is transparent and (syntactically) realized via standard read operations (the underlying implementation takes care of the CGI-based communication).

3.2 The Active Layer

The second layer offers the possibility of handling Web pages as *programs*. The use of forms, CGI scripts, and Java Applets represent one first step towards a more dynamic notion of browsing. In the active layer we make one step further, viewing HTML information as *programs*, which can be both executed and manipulated. This can be structured in two possible ways: *(1.)* the *active server* scheme, where client is mainly a simple browsing scheme and the server is a "smart" program capable of following the browsing on the execution of a program (tight connection). *(2.) active client*: where servers are just supplying pages and the pages are interpreted at the client site as programs to be executed. The encoding of WWW documents as active entities enables implementation of some unique facilities that cannot be offered at the level of object layer.

Dynamicity: logic programming allows self-modifying programs—i.e., programs can change during their execution. Encoding HTML documents as part of programs, and allowing self-modification translates to the possibility of having HTML documents that can adapt themselves depending on the course of action. This is of primary importance to effectively tackle issues like adaptive navigation [6], user modeling, automatic learning. The principle of dynamic programs can be applied as well to arbitrary computing components of the Internet applications. Thus we can envision servers that can modify their structure during execution (e.g., by learning user's characteristics and appropriately customizing their services), and clients that use the information received to change their own behaviour. The dynamicity can be either:

- *compositional:* the component is parameterized on some modules, which are meant to be generated during the computation (as in lightweight databases [5]);
- *interactive:* the component is instantiated during a session (e.g., during one interactive session with a browsing client) and self-modifies itself during such session (e.g., a server which learns information from the client and consequently modifies its output).
- *permanent:* the component get *permanently* modified during an execution. The best example of this is given by automatic code patching (applications which automatically connect to servers to download upgrades and patches).

Stateful Computations: WWW servers maintain a minimal amount of information about a session (the current page, eventually some information about security access); even their dynamically generated executions (CGI scripts) have a bounded lifespan and as such cannot maintain a state. Analogously, the state kept by the client is limited to the sequence of accessed pages. This problem is evident, for example, in game playing applications. In an interactive game of chess on the Web, the description of the board has to be *explicitly* passed back and forth, and the board have to be explicitly reconstructed every time the server is contacted. This slows-down the execution, makes playing more sensitive to broken connections, and dramatically increases the traffic on the network.

The ability of W-ACE to describe the backbone of an HTML tree as a W-ACE program allows a simple way to maintain a stateful server. Each browser connection can be mapped to a new instance of execution of the corresponding program. Arguments can be passed around during the execution maintaining a tight interaction between server and browser.

In addition, W-ACE allows the creation of *Intelligent Browsers (IB)*. This a simple meta-interpreter layer, written in W-ACE, which filters all the interactions between the browser and the user. The intelligent layer's main task is to replace the dumb caching of traditional browsers with the intelligent local creation of the HTML backbone. The IB generates a W-ACE program during the browsing session, which represents the current session, as well as maintaining information relative to the connection with the correct instances of the server. This interaction can be made more efficient using a *code-shipping* mechanism (see figure 3).

3.2.1 Active Servers

In the active servers scheme the code associated to dynamic Web pages is executed on the server side. This

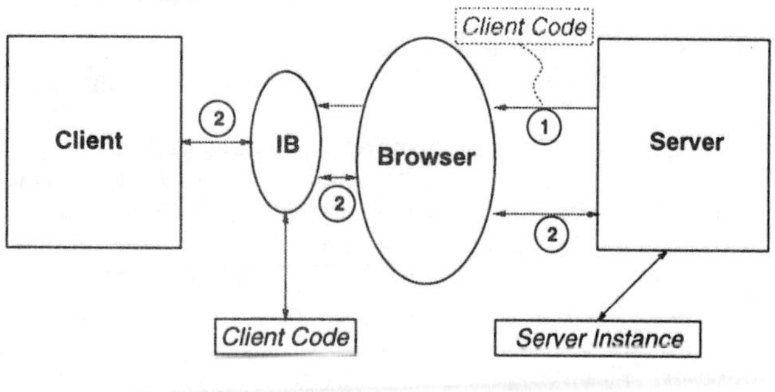

Figure 3: Intelligent Browsing

is consistent with the trend of research shown in various works [9].

Mechanism: W-ACE support for active servers originates from a modified notion of HTML tree and HTML graph. In active layer, the nodes of the HTML graph are goals to be executed in a W-ACE program; intuitively, each "page" is now represented by a fragment of code in the program. The activity of producing a Web page to the client is replaced by the action of executing the corresponding fragment of code.

Observe that this approach is deeply different from both CGI scripting and Applets. In active servers we introduce the concept of *connection* between client and server. A connection is realized when the browser (client) performs the first request to the server. This corresponds, from a "logical" point of view, to generating a server instance dedicated to serve the specific client. Thus client and server instance will proceed in a close lock-step; the server instance will maintain the control, occasionally sending information (e.g., in the form of traditional HTML documents) back to the client for further interaction. Control actions (e.g., selecting an hyperlink, pressing the *Back* button in the browser) correspond closely to actions in the server instance (call to a new predicate, failure and activation of backtracking). Data actions by the client (input of data) are translated into arguments for predicates call in the server instance (e.g., the input of a form becomes the argument for the subgoal associated to the form). The client structure is unchanged, i.e. the activity of the server is transparent to the client.

At the implementation level, concurrency is needed in the language to realize the multiple instances of the server, as well as an efficient parallel implementation.

Applications: In the active server, the server at every moment in time knows what the client is doing.
Monitoring: the active server can keep track of every action that the client is taking. It knows which pages are accessed (i.e., which procedures of the HTML program have been executed), and which data have been communicated. This allows to create statistics about accesses, as well as implement security policies. For example, the user can communicate to its server instance a password and obtain a validation that allows him to access certain protected documents.
Fault Tolerance: the server can monitor the communication with the client. If the Internet connection fails during a session, the server instance may save a trace of the execution, and eventually generate an e-mail message to the client, communicating that the session was interrupted. The message may also contain a password used to restore the session once the connection is re-established. A sketch of the W-ACE code for this problem has been described elsewhere [15].

3.2.2 Active Clients

Active clients allows the client to treat information coming from the Internet as programs to be executed, instead of data to be displayed.
In this framework, we are assuming that

- the client (e.g., a browser) has been developed using W-ACE—this doesn't mean that the whole client need to be a W-ACE application, as GUI can be "borrowed" from existing browsers, as long as the they allow to plug in the necessary reasoning component. This is possible, for example, by using NCSA Mosaic as browser.
- The client is a parametric application which is capable of accepting additional modules and perform execution against them;
- a mechanism is used to encode and decode program information (clauses, goals) into HTML documents transmitted by the server.

Traditional programming paradigms (e.g., imperative paradigms) do not allow modification of the structure of a program during the execution. Logic programming languages embed operators that allow to add/remove clauses during the execution. Nevertheless, these program modifying operators (e.g., assert and retract in Prolog), are not the ideal solution, as they are typically rather inefficient and they can operate only one clause at the time.

What we would really like to achieve is extending the logic language with a set of operators that allow various *operations on programs* [2]. Logic programs are treated as sets of clauses, and operators to perform union, intersection, etc. of programs are defined. Thus, for example, the task of "extending" the client with a new module can be coded as the *union* of the client with the module obtained from the server.

W-ACE Logical Theories: At the active layer, in order to support active clients, we need to design a scheme to encode W-ACE programs within HTML documents. Each HTML document is viewed as the definition of a logical theory (collection of clauses). Each HTML document is uniquely identified by its URL; thus, the URL is used as identifier for the theory described by the page. The HTML page is parsed to construct the usual HTML tree. The main difference is that the occurrences of the tag script are used to detect the parts of the document that have been used to encode the W-ACE active module. The parsing process, that builds the HTML tree of the page, will take care of generating the correct internal representation of the logic theory. A set of basic facts is also collected in the theory corresponding to each HTML document, containing the description of the page, its location, etc. The notation *theory*(⟨URL⟩) allows to access the theory which has been obtained from accessing the URL *URL*. From the syntactic point of view, logical theories can be thought of as *modules*. Each module is named, and the access to a module through its name is realized as indicated above.

W-ACE Composition of Theories: Logic theories obtained from the various HTML documents obtained from the Internet can be manipulated by W-ACE programs, using powerful meta-level operations:

(i) the meta-predicate *theory* is available to access the definition of a theory from its name.

(ii) logic theories can be combined either by taking their simple union ($\cup$), or by using an *overriding union* ($\lhd$) [2], where, in presence of definitions of the same predicate in different theories, one of them is kept as preferred definition, while the others are discarded.

(iii) the operator ($*$) is used to protect a theory's predicates from being affected by the definitions coming from other theories (i.e., we want to create a closed local scope).

Each theory is, by definition, a *set of closed clauses.* The same predicate names can be present in different theories, and their handling will depend on the combination approach chosen (e.g., $\cup$, $\lhd$). Observe that these operators for combining logic theories are sufficient to cover most of the foreseeable cases. For example, $\lhd$ can be used to implement both dynamic and static inheritance.

W-ACE Dynamic Use of Theories: The next step is to provide the language with adequate mechanisms to allow the use of these logical theories. In this section we explore how to embed the use of theories in W-ACE programs and the specification of executions which are *local* to a given theory. Execution of a goal using a different theory is expressed using the notation $\mathcal{G}@\mathcal{T}$, indicating that the execution of the goal $\mathcal{G}$ has to be performed taking into account the content of the theory $\mathcal{T}$. This is very similar to the notion of *embedded implication* which has been studied in the context of modular programming [2]. The interpretation given to $\mathcal{G}@\mathcal{T}$ is simply that of attempting a proof of $\mathcal{G}$ in a the current *logical context* enriched with the content of the theory $\mathcal{T}$. The way in which the content of $\mathcal{G}$ has to be used is expressed through the use of a prefix operator: if the current context is $\mathcal{P}$, then $\mathcal{G}@\oplus\mathcal{T}$ implies proving $\mathcal{P}\oplus\mathcal{T}\models\mathcal{G}$ (where $\oplus$ is either $\cup$, $\lhd$ or $\rhd$). Observe that, in order to guarantee flexibility in the language, we need to allow nesting of the @ operator—i.e., composition of multiple theories. W-ACE supports [2] a *dynamic* scoping of predicates.

W-ACE Meta-Engine: The approach of the previous section requires the client program to *constructively* use the logical theories, combining them and executing goals in the resulting set of clauses—e.g., if an HTML document contains the extension of a database, then the best way of handling it is to add it to an intensional component and perform the desired queries. W-ACE also supports expressive manipulation mechanisms, which simplify the task of moving across different logical theories. The HTML graph is in fact seen as the description of the *accessibility* relation between *possible worlds.* This well matches the semantic structure offered by traditional forms of modal logic [13]. A typical modal logic programming language extends the traditional logic language with two new components: *(1)* modal interpretations are composed by a set of standard models, called *worlds*, connected via an *accessibility relation.* Truth of a goal is not absolute, as it can change across different worlds; *(2)* some high-order operators are added to the language, in order to relate goals validity with the underlying worlds structure—e.g., $\Box G$ expresses the fact that G is valid in all the worlds accessible from the present one.

The intuition is that the logical theories obtained from the HTML documents represent different worlds and the HTML graph is used to supply the accessibility relation. In W-ACE, the accessibility relation, originating from the HTML graph, is assumed to be *reflexive* (self-accessible), *direct* (i.e., in general non-symmetrical), and *transitive.* Each possible world is obtained from one of the logical theories $\mathcal{T}$ combined with the main program ($\mathcal{T}\oplus\mathcal{P}$). The operator for the combination is by default $\cup$, but can be modified ($\lhd$ or $\rhd$) with appropriate declarations. The HTML graph present in the W-ACE execution is typically only a finite window over the potentially infinite branching of links over the Internet. For this reason, W-ACE supports two classes of operators, *local operators* in which the logical theories belonging to the current HTML graph represent the possible worlds, and *global operators* in which the set of possible worlds is represented by all the pages (also unexplored) that are reachable from a given entry point. The programmer will be responsible to guarantee a correct usage of global operators. The following modal operators are supported in W-ACE: $\Box$ (validity of a goal in all accessible worlds), $\Diamond$ (existence of an accessible world in which the goal is valid), and $\bigcirc$ (validity of the goal in all the worlds accessible in one step from the present one). Each operator can be parameterized as follows:

- $\oplus^{\uparrow}$ and $\oplus^{\downarrow}$ representing respectively the global and local versions of the operator $\oplus$;
- $\oplus_i$ representing the fact that the operator is meant to be restricted on all the worlds that are reachable within i steps from the current one.

Additionally, the computation can be placed in a specific world by using the above mentioned @ notation.

Using these operators various applications can be expressed in a few lines of code. For example, in a diagnosis program, each HTML page represents different assumptions about the values of certain laboratory results. Starting from a page, we can enquire whether the current symptoms can lead to the diagnosis of a certain illness, with a simple application of $\Diamond$.

Applications:

Lightweight Databases: HTML documents are seen as small databases, and allow clients to act as intelligent (e.g., deductive) query solver over these databases. The concept, introduced by Dobson [5] and generalized by others [11, 4], can be implemented with extreme ease in the active client model offered by W-ACE. The database information are stored in HTML documents, as a sequence of facts (for example). Once a page is loaded, it is turned into a W-ACE theory, against which the client can pose queries. The same can be generalized to include complex knowledge-bases within HTML documents (e.g., part of rule-bases for an expert system).

Active Programs e.g. normal programs that at the beginning of their execution accesses some URL to update themselves. This would allow, for example, to solve the problem of distributing patches for software—the program itself will connect to the appropriate Web server before starting execution and eventually download and apply automatically the patches.

Adaptive Browsing The idea is to allow the structure of the document to change due to the interaction with the user.

This can range from changing the structure of the HTML tree during the browsing process (e.g., collapse the HTML tree), to performing more extensive modifications, like in the *Adaptive Hypermedia Systems* [6]. We can distinguish between:

- adaptive presentation: the *content* of the HTML tree is changed depending on the user model. This is easy to model in W-ACE, thanks to the possibility of parameterizing (with a simple selector argument) the execution of the HTML program that has been downloaded, producing "alternative" pages.
- adaptive navigation: the *structure* of the HTML tree is modified depending on the user model.

The adaptivity of the scheme can be varied also by accessing separate *databases of links*. Adaptation can be performed by keeping a *user model* [14]. Limited applications of these ideas have been realized in some AI projects [6], capable of performing automatic generation of Web pages.

3.3 Concurrency and Parallelism

Parallelism indicates ability of performing parallel execution of different components of the computation. Thus, its main aim is *efficiency*. *Concurrency* indicates the ability to express concurrent execution of different components of the program. This is a *semantic* issue. Both the issues are of primary importance in the context of Internet-based applications. Management of multiple agents can take considerable advantage from parallelism, while interacting sessions or managing multiple connections represent concurrency issues. Web-related applications are going to become, in our opinion, one of the major areas of application of techniques for parallel execution. In W-ACE we distinguish between two forms of parallelism, *Intra-Parallelism* and *Inter-Parallelism*.

3.3.1 Intra-Parallelism

The concept of intra-parallelism originates from the exploitation of parallelism within a single browsing/serving activity. This form of parallelism can be obtained by using the basic support for parallel execution which is supplied by the ACE parallel system. The ACE system supports both and-parallelism and or-parallelism in logic programs. *And-parallelism* attempts parallel execution of different subgoals belonging to the current query. It is common [16] to distinguish two flavors of and-parallelism: *independent parallelism* which originates when the parallel subgoals are not allowed to affect each other's executions, and *dependent and-parallelism* where [16] subgoals executed in parallel are allowed to share variables and compete for their bindings. *Or-Parallelism* allows parallel execution of the alternatives associated to a resolution step—i.e., allows to explore in parallel the different clauses that can be used to reduce the selected subgoal. Thus or-parallelism is a mechanism to speedup the exploration of the search space generated by a logic program. ACE provides efficient exploitation of parallelism, as well as a collection of constructs to specify concurrency in the programs. The concurrent language supported by ACE consists of the following components:

- *and-concurrency:* the notation $p(X)\&q(Y)$ is used to denote conjunctions of subgoals in which the two subgoals can be run in parallel. The notation becomes slightly more complex if we allow dependences between the concurrent subgoals. Dependent execution in ACE is structured in such a way to respect the sequential semantics of the language [16]. Nevertheless, W-ACE allows us to specify for each argument position in a concurrent subgoal whether such position should be treated as a producer or consumer position. This can be supplied simply as mode declarations (in the same fashion as in Parlog), or by explicitly describing the dependence graph to be used during execution. This feature is extremely powerful, as it allows to create separate computations and to use variables as unidirectional communication channels.
- *or-concurrency:* ACE admits the declaration parallel to indicate which procedures of the program have to be considered for or-parallel execution. W-ACE admits the possibility of declaring a procedure to be reactive. This is aimed at capturing the behaviour typical of guarded commands. A reactive procedure implies that, at the moment of clause selection, the selection process will not consider one clause at the time, in their textual order, but it will loop through the different clauses in the procedure until a successful head unification will be completed. This, combined with the use of dependent and-parallelism, allows the development of servers which can react to different kinds of stimuli coming from the clients.

And-Parallelism in Web Applications: Executions over recursive data structures, data-parallel computations, producer/consumer pipelined computations are all examples of executions which are very likely to offer large amounts of and-parallelism [16].

More specific to the case of W-ACE, the explicit use of notations to indicate concurrency can be directly translated to parallel executions. This is typical, for example, of multiple agents which are exploring different set of HTML documents searching for certain patterns/keywords. Another example is represented by efficient servers which are implementing various forms of "distributed" management of data. Queries arriving from client applications can be *(a)* partitioned between different servers that are maintaining different databases; *(b)* processed through a pipelined organization of multiple servers—this requires communication between different active entities, i.e., a form of dependent and-concurrency; and *(c)* assigned to independent instances of servers, to allow overlapping of requests handling.

Or-Parallelism in Web Applications: Most of the applications which involve a sufficiently complex search are suitable to this form of parallelization. Typical examples are: *(a)* agents which are performing a search over the nodes of the HTML graph; alternative paths emanating from a given node can be explored in parallel; *(b)* analysis of data often requires non-deterministic steps—e.g., parsing data to identify their structure with respect to a given structural description (e.g., a grammar, a finite state automata); *(c)* searching for an element from a given set which satisfies a certain property (e.g., looking for dead links between the set of all links in an HTML document).

Modal Parallelism: An additional form of parallelism emerges from the introduction of modality in the language. The operations to be performed across different worlds can be easily cast into parallel executions. *Necessity* modal operators (□) require the verification of a goal across all the worlds belonging to a certain modal interpretation (e.g., all the logical theories currently accessible through the HTML graph); this verification can be done in parallel (exploring concurrently different worlds). This is a generalization of and-parallelism, and the W-ACE system can be easily extended to accommodate for it. *Possibility* modal operators (◇) are required to verify whether a given goal holds in at least one of the accessible worlds; this can also be attempted in parallel, by considering alternative accessible worlds in parallel. This can be seen as a generalization of or-parallelism.

3.3.2 Inter-Parallelism

The possibility of expressing parallel computations and communication assumes extreme importance when dealing with different interacting executions. The mechanisms required for this sort of computations are the same described in the previous section. W-ACE goals represents the different concurrent computations while *shared* variables are used as communication channels between them. These mechanisms are sufficient to cover most of the interesting cases arising in Web-related applications. Nevertheless, there are some new issues which require more sophisticated mechanisms. In particular, the notion of a single server supplying HTML documents to the various clients is progressively overcome by the notion of servers providing more comprehensive services (e.g., access to knowledge bases). The need to perform complex computations as answers to client requests may require the need to allow servers to distribute computations across different connected hosts. Analogously, client themselves can use HTTP protocol to distribute a computation between different computing resources. This may require assigning execution of certain computations to specific resources.

3.3.3 Serving HTML Clients

The problem of having a server handling multiple clients through Web-connections has been largely underestimated. The issue, as pointed out by Szeredi [21], is of extreme importance: modern "intelligent" servers are AI-like applications, which are large and expensive; maintaining a separate running copy of the server for each client connection may not be a suitable solution, since the impact of the multiple running computations on the server's side may be unbearable. Furthermore, keeping separate server processes makes interactions between them (if necessary, e.g., accessing and modifying a common database) extremely challenging to program. On the other hand, the ideal situation of handling the different connections within the scope of a single server can be as difficult to realize within a sequential programming framework—and can easily lead to inefficient systems (which may force an unnatural sequentiality between clients' requests).

The potential of using parallelism to serve different browsing sessions has already been pointed out in the literature. The serious problem in this context is serving multiple clients. The different sessions are *separate threads* of computation. Furthermore, in order to make possible an efficient usage of resources, the different threads should *share* the same resources as much as possible (thus, spawning a new process for each client connection is not a viable solution). In [21] a solution to a similar problem is proposed using an *or-parallel* Prolog system (Aurora). The solution suffers of various drawbacks. Different client connections have to be encoded as separate "alternatives" of a choice point (which is unnatural). Alternatives of a choice point are *necessarily* independent, and cannot directly communicate. Communications can only be realized in a very unnatural (and *expensive*) fashion through the use of unsynchronized side-effect predicates. Additionally, or-parallelism does not gracefully offer ways of suspending branches (e.g., while waiting for some input from the client). Aurora's developer solved the problem by introducing new explicit built-ins to suspend and resume branches. The solution in W-ACE is very natural. Multiple client sessions can be easily handled as separate subgoals, which are executed in and-parallel—which better capture the "coexisting" nature of client sessions, instead of the unnatural "alternative" nature attributed in the Aurora scheme. A loop like:

```
main(Sockets,Args) :-
   wait_connection(Sockets,Inst),
   ( client_execution(Sockets,Inst,Args) &
     main(Sockets,Args)
   ).
```

is used. Suspensions are automatically obtained thanks to the suspension mechanism used by dependent and-parallelism [16]. In the specific case of the diagnosis application, the different client sessions are independent—thus the `Args` argument is actually empty. Communication with the browser is through separate sockets (one per worker) and is completely transparent to the programmer.

Interacting Clients (Example): In the previous example client sessions are non-interacting and independent (same assumption as in [21]).

There are many cases in which it is desirable to allow clients to interact with each others. This may range from the simple *indirect* interaction caused by accessing and modifying a common database, to the more complex case of a *direct* client interaction, as in a multi-players game. Traditional languages (e.g., Java) require complex and explicit communication mechanisms (sockets, IPC messages). On the other hand, the scheme adopted in W-ACE allows to avoid any additional complexity. Since each separate client connection is represented by a separate recursive subgoal, they can directly interact via shared variables [16]. We have tested this feature in a simple server application which allows two client sessions to play tic-tac-toe one against the other.

3.3.4 Applications

Communicating Agents: Interacting agents has been for long an actively researched topic in the AI community; within the framework of the WWW, this concept assumes a great importance; the search space for agents traveling on the Web is extremely large, and concurrent, interacting agents may lead to drastic reductions in search time. Using traditional programming languages, the practical development of communicating agents is a very challenging task (e.g., dealing with threads, communication, etc.).

W-ACE offers a framework where managing communicating agents is extremely simple. Each agent is represented by a goal (i.e., a call to a predicate defining the agent); parallel execution is readily available through the and-concurrent support; communication is directly available through shared variables. For example, a W-ACE top-level call to generate two communicating agents will be as follows:

```
... mark([Ch1,Ch2]), In1=Ch1,In2=Ch2,
  Out1=Ch2,Out2=Ch1,
   (agent(1,In1,Out1) & agent(2,In2,Out2)),...
```

The two unidirectional communication channels (`Ch1,Ch2`) are set between the two agents. For example, agent 1 will send a message to agent 2 by instantiating its Out channel in the following way: `Out = [Message | NewOut]`, where `Message` is the message to be sent and `NewOut` is a new variable (representing the "new" access to the output channel).

Generalized Browsing: The browsing activity is strictly a single user-single step execution. The user moves from one page to the other, but at any time he is focused on only one document. Availability of concurrency allows for various extensions:

1. Concurrent browsing: allows a single user to concurrently explore different paths of the HTML graph. This is easily realized by having a client spawning separate processes to carry on the navigation of the documents. The separate sessions may be independent (i.e., they separately report results in different parts of the user interface), or the may interact during the navigation—for example, one of the navigation sessions may attempt to explore a document which has been explored previously by another session—this can be avoided by having a shared representation of the HTML graph between the different navigations.

2. Cooperative browsing: it is also important to allow separate navigation sessions, eventually initiated by different users, to interact. A good example of this is represented by the principle of *annotating* HTML documents [18, 15]. Members of a working team may be separately operating via different browsing sessions (e.g., they are browsing the Web in search of information on a given topic). The members of the team, even if they are carrying on independent activities, need to interact, in order to avoid re-visiting twice the same document and to allow a member of the team to gather information regarding documents visited by other members. This can be realized using communicating browsers (e.g., shared database of annotations, shared representation of the visited HTML graph, etc.)

4 Conclusions

This project aims at investigating and developing a unified programming framework for Internet programming. The key is to support an environment in which the programmer does not need virtually any knowledge of the complex details of the communication protocols involved, as well as he is provided with a set of domains and computational tools allowing communication and processing of WWW data at a very high level of abstraction. We strongly believe that our approach will produce a relevant advance in the state-of-the-art for Internet-based programming, yielding an efficient programming environment, usable by average programmers. We also aim at showing how various techniques proposed in different frameworks can have a substantial impact in helping developing Internet related applications (e.g., modal logic, modularization, constraint management). We also provide what we believe is a novel view of the WWW—no more simple linked collections of static data, but active and interactive computations. Various researchers approximated this notion, without accomplishing it in its full generality. It is our intention to show that this is the best direction in which WWW research should move to tackle the new computational requirements. The ability of W-ACE to take full advantage of this computing power (converting the inherent concurrency present in Internet applications into actual parallelism) represent an ideal solution to a serious issue in Internet computing, the bottleneck of servers unable to adequately serve a large number of requests.

References

[1] P. Bonnet et al. Towards ECLiPSe Agents on the Internet. *Workshop on Logic Progr. Tools for Internet*, 1996.

[2] M. Bugliesi et al. Modularity in Logic Programming. *Journal of Logic Programming*, Vol. 19/20, 1994.

[3] J. Buhler. A Language-structured Approach to Networking Software. Tech. Rep., Carnegie Mellon University, 1996.

[4] D. Cabeza et al. The PiLLoW/CIAO Library for Internet Programming. *Logic Progr. Tools for Internet*, 1996.

[5] S. Dobson et al. *Towards Improving Automation in the WWW.* Tech. Rep., Rutherford Appleton Lab., 1995.

[6] F. Espinoza et al. An Interactive WWW Interface to an Adaptive Information System. *User Modeling*, 1996.

[7] R. Fielding et al. *Hypertext Transfer Protocol – HTTP/1.1.* Request for Comment: 2068, January 1997.

[8] J. Foster. *A Status Report on Networked Information Retrieval: Tools and Groups.* RFC-1689, 1994.

[9] M. Gleeson et al. Beyond Hypertext: using the WWW for Interactive Applications. *AusWeb Conference*, 1997.

[10] J. Jaffar and M. Maher. Constraint Logic Programming. *Journal of Logic Programming*, Vol. 19/20, 1994.

[11] S. Loke et al. Lightweight Deductive Databases on the WWW. *Logic Progr. Tools for Internet*, 1996.

[12] NCSA. *Application Programmer's Interface for the NCSA Mosaic CCI.* Technical Report, 1995.

[13] M.A. Orgun et al. An Overview of Temporal and Modal Logic Programming. *Conf. on Temporal Logic*, 1994.

[14] A. Paiva, J. Self, R. Hartley. Externalising Learner Models. In *Proc. of AIED95*, AACE Publications, 1995.

[15] E. Pontelli and G. Gupta. *Using ACE as a Parallel Engine for WWW Applications.* Internal Report, NMSU, 1996.

[16] E. Pontelli and G. Gupta. Parallel Symbolic Computing in ACE. *Annals of Mathematics and AI*, (to appear).

[17] D. Raggett. *HTML 3.2 Reference Specification.* W3C Recommendation, January 1997.

[18] M. Röscheisen et al. Beyond Browsing: Shared Comments, SOAPs, Trails, and On-line Communities. Tech. Rep., Stanford University, 1996.

[19] S. Sato. Dynamic Rewriting of HTML Documents. *First International WWW Conference*, 1994.

[20] A. Sehmi, M. Kroening. WebLS: A Custom Prolog Rule Engine for Providing Web-Based Tech Support. *Logic Progr. Tools for Internet*, 1996.

[21] P. Szeredi et al. Serving Multiple HTML Clients from a Prolog Application. *Logic Progr. Tools for Internet*, 1996.

[22] World Wide Web Consortium. *LibWWW User Documentation.* Technical Report, 1997.

A Generic Tool for Distributed AI with Matching as Message Passing [‡]

Eugene Eberbach
Jodrey School of Computer Science, Acadia University
Wolfville, NS B0P 1X0, Canada
eugene.eberbach@acadiau.ca, eberbache@acm.org
and
Information Systems Department, Applied Research Laboratory
The Pennsylvania State University
State College, PA 16804, USA

Abstract

The paper concentrates on the problem how to integrate genetic programming, neural networks, autonomous agents with some symbolic AI techniques. For this purpose, it introduces and employs the $-calculus, which is a general model of computation with a quantitative aspect (cost) allowing naturally to express optimization and modification in dynamic parallel AI systems. The papers presents basic operators of the calculus, and a basic inference engine, so called modifying algorithm, used for problem solving. Next the approach is illustrated through a series of examples from various domains, including symbolic and subsymbolic systems.

1 Introduction

The paper presents a unifying effort which allows to investigate and implement symbolic and subsymbolic systems. It concentrates on three areas: genetic programming, neural networks and expert systems. Genetic programming, derived from subsymbolic genetic algorithms and using symbolic S-expression-based representation, is a new approach to automatic program synthesis, which tries to build algorithms from fixed elements where the length of programs vary. On the other hand, subsymbolic neural networks have a fixed algorithm (network) structure, but their elementary elements are modified. Expert systems use symbolic knowledge representation and various types of logic inferences to solve a problem using, usually fixed, production rules or clauses.

The typical approach of symbolic artificial intelligence to problem solving is the application of various types of if-then rules (for instance, in the form of production rules or clauses) to move the program from the initial state to the goal state. The process of logic deduction is employed (by matching or unification) to efficiently navigate through the search space of tes. The search is automatized then by the inference engine of the expert system or logic language by constructing appropriate inference trees - sequences of actions solving the problem. To deal with program abstraction, the divide-and-conquer strategy is applied, i.e. if the inference engine cannot find applicable rules to a current state, it may replace goal by its subgoal, and try to find matching rules again. The job of the programmer is to provide building blocks (if-then rules and facts), plus the initial and/or goal states. Additionally, the user is responsible to decompose explicitly problem into subproblems, to allow the inference engine to generate subgoals.

Genetic Programming (GP) [7] provides a new way of thinking about automatic program synthesis. The programmer has to specify basic building blocks (terminals and functions) which she/he thinks are sufficient to write a program and genetic algorithms techniques do the rest by joggling/building the sequences (parse trees) composed of terminals and functions. Instead of matching and means-ends analysis, genetic programming explores the search of programs by crossover and fitness function, which can be considered as a special case of the generate-and-test strategy. The key issue is the proper guess (or, rather intelligent deduction) of building blocks, and the hope that genetic algorithms techniques will do the rest using properly feedback from the fitness directed search. Because control mechanism of genetic programming is not directly based on inferences, the onus of the programmer is a precise definition of the fitness function, which provides the only measure how well "simulated inferences"- generated parse trees are built. In genetic programming, dissimilar to symbolic AI, because no inference techniques are employed, building blocks do not have to have the if-then form. However, instead of that, functions and terminals have to be designed to fulfill the requirement for syntactic closure, to allow unrestricted (i.e., without the need for some kind of repair or penalty functions) use of crossover and secondary genetic operators. For program abstraction, genetic programming uses ADFs (Automatically Defined Functions), where the responsibility of the pro-

[‡]Research partially supported by a grant from NSERC No. OGP0046501

1082-3409/97 $10.00 © 1997 IEEE

grammer is to find the number of ADFs and to specify their corresponding terminal and function sets, and return values. Once again, the appropriate trees of ADFs will be evolved automatically by joggling ADFs functions and terminals using genetic algorithms techniques.

In the case of Neural Networks (NN), the designer has to choose the fixed structure of the network (the number of neurons, layers), to choose the type of the neuron transfer function and the learning algorithm to modify the weights. Next he/she initializes the weights, and the learning algorithm does the rest trying to find a correct input/output relation using a feedback from the classification error directed search, trying to minimize the classification error - an implicit goal of computation. This corresponds to the program which has the fixed number of instructions, but we do know which ones (and in fact, we may never know, because they might be not expressible in symbolic terms), although the neural network "black-box" may learn correctly or approximately the appropriate input-output mapping. For program abstraction, neural networks may use specialized subnetworks working, for instance, as associative memories, performing appropriate mapping, or responsible for weight modification of other subnetwork.

All GP, NN and symbolic AI require proper specification of building blocks and the explicit hints how to deal with program abstraction. Additionally, symbolic AI requires explicitly specification of the initial and/or the goal states, whereas GP and NN - implicitly, by the fitness function, or the classification error.

In the paper we try to combine the best of subsymbolic and symbolic worlds. Despite the differences, it is not a hopeless task. But for this purpose, it was necessary to turn to the model which is more general than evolutionary algorithms or neural nets. Such a model is the $-calculus, which is a process algebra with a quantitative aspect (cost) in which one can naturally express optimization and modification in dynamic parallel AI systems. The project on $-calculus aims at investigation, design and implementation of hybrid AI symbolic, connectionist, fuzzy, and evolutionary systems. The obtained results allowed not only to integrate to some extent both symbolic and subsymbolic AI, but additionally, allowed to obtain an enlightment on design of the neural network structure, and on several GP open questions, including fitness calculation, length of generated trees, choice of terminals/functions. More details can be found in the main part of the paper.

In Section 2 we define the constructions of the $-calculus, including cost expressions, cost functions, and the inference engine. In Section 3, experts systems, logic programming, communication and synchronization in dynamic parallel systems, genetic programming and neural networks are presented in terms of $-calculus. Section 4 presents conclusions.

2 The $-calculus

The *$-calculus (read: cost calculus)* is a *process algebra* with a quantitative aspect (called *cost*) allowing to capture adaptability (usually involving optimization) in dynamic parallel, distributed and interactive AI systems. It has been designed to specify, investigate, and implement systems exhibiting meta-computation (self-modification) and optimization, including adaptive expert systems, neural networks, evolutionary computation and artificial life, adaptive autonomous agents, plan generation, fault-tolerant systems, distributed and concurrent computing, machine learning, and new generation computer architectures and languages. The $-calculus is a simplified and clarified version of *CSA (Calculus of Self-modifiable Algorithms)* [2, 3] preserving its basic properties, i.e. *self-modification* and *cost-optimization*. The work is related to other general models for sequential and parallel computation, including Church's λ-calculus [1] and Milner's π-calculus [9], which is believed to be the most general approach to concurrency, subsuming the λ-calculus. A main difference to other models of computation is the inclusion of the quantitative aspect (cost) as a fundamental feature of the calculus to allow to capture optimization behavior typical for many AI systems. The uniform approach to data, code and meta-code is somehow similar to that in Lisp, and this together with cost optimization, is believed to be crucial for the work of the approach.

2.1 Cost expressions

Let T be a set of *terminals*, which correspond to the inputs (can be constants, variables, data structures, or suppressed functions). They are called terminals because they are last (they terminate/suppress) evaluation of expressions. Let F be a set of functions, which may be standard arithmetic operations, standard programming operations, standard mathematical/logical functions, user or automatically defined functions. Functions are executed by evaluation. Terminals are input data for functions. Functions are dynamic, in the sense that they take as their input terminals (perhaps, returned by other functions), and modify them, producing as the output new terminals. Let M be a set of modifications, which are higher-order functions taking as the input or returning as the output other suppressed functions, or function definitions. Modifications and costs are the two unique and the most important features of the $-calculus.

Throughout the paper we will use mostly a prefix notation, i.e., we will write function $f(x)$ as $(f\ x)$, where f is a function name (label) and x is its parameter (variable). Sometimes if it is understable from the context, we will omit parameter(s), and we will write simply f.

Let $a, b, c, ...$ be *names* over sets T, F and M, and each with an arity - an integer ≥ 0 (representing number of parameters) for each terminal, function and modification. Let P, Q, R, ... range over the $-expressions $\mathcal{P}$ (read: cost expressions, also can be called agents, programs, processes, objects). Then the set $\mathcal{P}$ of cost expressions is the smallest set, which includes the following kinds of cost expressions (assuming that $P, P_1, P_2, ...$ are already in $\mathcal{P}$):

1. A *simple cost expression*.

   These are predefined elements of T, F, and M, i.e., possible to evaluate immediately. Simple cost expressions will identify atomic actions which may be performed by a process or atomic data, and which are treated as indivisible. The structure of simple cost expressions is neglected, and they are considered as possible to evaluate in one indivisible step. Simple cost expressions have the form $(f\ y_1\ ...\ y_n)$, where f is a name of the expression, $y_1, ..., y_n$, $n \geq 0$ are its parameters. For $n = 0$ we will write simply f. Evaluation of simple cost expressions may return other cost expressions. In particular, there are two distinguished elements $\perp$ and ε. A *zero* terminal $\perp$ simply blocks and does (returns) nothing (degenerate process or inaction with blocking), and a *silent* zero-argument function ε, unlike zero never blocks, but executes silently returning nothing (thus its effects are considered to be unobservable, i.e. uncontrollable by the environment). Zero $\perp$ fulfills function of the logical false, and any value not explicitly $\perp$ is taken to mean true.

2. A *sequential composition* $(\circ\ P_1\ P_2)$.

   This function means that if P_1 does not block, then P_1 is avaluated first, next P_2; otherwise it blocks. To generalize, we write $\circ_{i \in I} P_i$ for an indexed sequential composition, where the index set I is possibly countably infinite. A sequential composition behaves like ε for the empty sequential composition (for $I = \emptyset$). P_1 will be called prefix (the first element to evaluate) and P_2 postfix of $(\circ\ P_1\ P_2)$, and will be denoted as $pre(\circ\ P_1\ P_2)$ and $post(\circ\ P_1\ P_2)$ respectively.

3. A *parallel composition* $(\parallel\ P_1\ P_2)$.

   This function evaluates both P_1 and P_2 simultaneously. P_1 or P_2 may block, then only P_2 or P_1 are evaluated. If both P_1 and P_2 block, then parallel composition blocks (deadlocks). To generalize, we write $\parallel_{i \in I} P_i$ for an indexed parallel composition. In particular, the empty parallel composition behaves like $\perp$.

4. A *nondeterministic choice* $(\uplus\ P_1\ P_2)$.

   The nondeterministic choice means that if both $pre(P_1)$ and $pre(P_2)$ do not block (are evaluated to true), then the function evaluates one of P_1 or P_2; otherwise it blocks. As a generalization, we write $\uplus_{i \in I} P_i$. An empty nondeterministic choice (for $I = \emptyset$) behaves like $\perp$.

5. A *general choice* $(\sqcup\ P_1\ P_2)$.

   The general choice means that if $pre(P_1)$ or $pre(P_2)$ does not block, then the function evaluates that corresponding P_1 or P_2; otherwise it blocks. If both $pre(P_1)$ and $pre(P_2)$ do not block, a general choice behaves like nondeterministic choice. As a generalization, we write $\sqcup_{i \in I} P_i$. An empty general choice $\sqcup_{i \in I} P_i$ behaves like $\perp$.

1

6. A *(recursive) definition* $(:=\ (f\ x_1\ ...\ x_n)\ P)$ and its call $(f\ y_1\ ...\ y_n)$.

   The definition creates or redefines a template object (without execution) named f, with formal input parameters $x_1\ ...\ x_n$, and with the body P. f can be executed (evaluated) by its associated call $(f\ y_1\ ...\ y_n)$ returning new (calculated) values. For a call f (different than a simple cost expression and having arity $n \geq 0$) to be evaluated, there must be a current unique defining equation $(:=\ (f\ x_1\ ...\ x_n)\ P)$, where the names $x_1, ..., x_n$ are distinct and are the only names which may occur free in P. Then $(f\ y_1\ ...\ y_n)$ behaves like $P\{y_1/x_1, ..., y_n/x_n\}$, where y_i/x_i means the simultaneous substitution of y_i for all occurrences of x_i (for $1 \leq i \leq n$) in P. The definition provides recursion, since P may contain any identifier, even f itself. If associated definition does not exist, and the function call is not a simple cost expression, then it blocks. In particular, $(:=\ (f\ x_1\ ...\ x_n)\ \perp)$ defines an empty object or destroys an existing object f. Formally, we will treat definitions as simple \$-expressions not returning any value, but their associated calls do not belong to simple cost expressions.

As the special cases of simple \$-expressions, we define toggling, cost, negation, forward matching, backward matching, mutation and crossover constructors as follows:

1(a) A *toggling (suppression/evaluation)* $'P$.

   If P is not suppressed, this function simply returns $'P$ suppressing evaluation of P, i.e. it treats P as data (terminals). If P is suppressed, i.e. $P = 'P_1$, then toggling cancels suppression and returns P_1 for evaluation. Suppression and evaluation cancel each other, i.e. $''P = P$. Toggling temporarily changes status of functions/modifications into data to allow their modifications, or allows to restore functions/modifications their active status.

1(b) A *cost* $(\$\ P)$.

   This function calculates a *cost* (the value of the objective function) associated with P. The return value of the cost function \$ is another cost expression for which linear (or at least partial) order is defined. Usually, the return value is a vector of component costs $(v_1\ ...\ v_k)$, $k \geq 1$, where $\{v_i\}_{1 \leq i \leq k}$ typically take values in the domain of real numbers $\mathcal{R}$, or in the real interval $[0, 1]$. Some component return values can be used for optimization, other - to express complexity, probability, possibility, belief, error, or fitness.

1(c) A *negation* $(\neg\ (f\ y_1 ... y_k))$.

   For each simple or defined cost expression call $(f\ \ y_1 ... y_k)$ there is associated its negation $(\neg\ (f\ y_1 ... y_k))$ with the following property: if $(f\ y_1 ... y_k)$ blocks then $(\neg\ (f\ y_1 ... y_k))$ evaluates to true, and if $(f\ y_1 ... y_k)$ evaluates to true then

$(\neg\ (f\ y_1...y_k))$ blocks (evaluates to false $\perp$). Of course, $(f\ y_1...y_k) \neq (\neg\ (f\ y_1...y_k))$, and we declare $(\neg\ (\neg\ (f\ y_1...y_k))) = (f\ y_1...y_k)$.

1(d) A *forward matching (send)* $(\rightarrow\ P_1\ P_2)$.

This function assumes that P_1 is equal $P_1\{x_1, ..., x_k\}$, and P_2 is equal $P_2\{y_1, ..., y_k\}$. If after simultaneous substitution of names in $P_2\{x_1/y_1, ..., x_k/y_k\}$ by names from $P_1\{x_1, ..., x_k\}$, it can be inferred from all smallest subexpressions P_j from $post(P_1)$ that if they were executed and did not block, then $pre(P_2)$ was executed without any blocking. Then forward matching evaluates $P_{12}\{x_1, ..., x_k\}$, which is a result of substitution of all P_j from $post(P_1)$ by P_2'. P_2' is a subexpression of P_2, which would be executed if P_j was executed. In other words, P_1 tries to communicate (send) appropriate names to P_2 (by substitution), "glues" and synchronizes P_1 and P_2 by executing P_{12}. An unsuccessful result of matching (caused by send to a full variable $y_i \neq \perp$ or $x_i \neq y_i$, when y_i is a constant, or failure of an inference process) blocks. There is possible matching without execution: $'(P_1\ \rightarrow\ P_2)$ will perform matching, but execution of P_{12} will be suppressed.

As a generalization for multiple matching (multicasting/broadcasting), for $(\rightarrow\ P_1\ (P_i)_{i\in I})$ if after substitution of names, from all smallest P_j from $post(P_1)$ executed without blocking, it can be inferred $pre(op_{i\in I}\ P_i)$ could be executed without any blocking (where op can be, for instance, $\|$, or $\uplus$, or $\sqcup$), then forward matching evaluates $P_{12}\{x_1, ..., x_k\}$, which is a result of substitution of all P_j from $post(P_1)$ by $(op_{i\in I}\ P_i)$.

1(e) A *backward matching (receive)* $(\leftarrow\ P_1\ P_2)$.

This function assumes that P_1 is equal $P_1\{x_1, ..., x_k\}$, and P_2 is equal $P_2\{y_1, ..., y_k\}$. If after simultaneous substitution of names in $P_1\{y_1/x_1, ..., y_k/x_k\}$ by names from $P_2\{y_1, ..., y_k\}$, it can be inferred from all smallest subexpressions P_j from $post(P_1)$ that if they were executed and did not block, then $pre(P_2)$ was executed without any blocking. Then backward matching evaluates $P_{21}\{y_1, ..., y_k\}$, which is a result of substitution of all P_j from $post(P_1)$ by P_2'. P_2' is a subexpression of P_2, which would be executed if P_j was executed. In other words, P_1 tries to communicate (receive) appropriate names from P_2 (by substitution), glues and synchronizes P_1 and P_2 by executing P_{21}. After substitution $y_1, ..., y_k$ become equal $\perp$ (are "consumed"). An unsuccessful result of matching (caused by receive from an empty variable $y_i = \perp$ or $x_i \neq y_i$, when x_i is a constant, or failure of an inference process) blocks. $'(P_1\ \leftarrow\ P_2)$ will perform matching but suppresses execution of P_{21}. To generalize, instead of a single P_1, there is possible to have a multicast backward matching with indexed set of receivers.

1(f) A *mutation* $(\rightharpoondown\ P)$.

This function assumes that $P = (lR\ R\ rR)$, where lR is a left, and rR is a right context of cost subexpression R, then negation/mutation replaces R by another cost expression R', returning $P' = (lR\ R'\ rR)$. Left and right contexts may not be syntactically valid cost expressions.

If P is not suppressed, then the negation function substitutes $R = pre(P)$ by $R' = (\neg R)$ returning a modified P, i.e. P' with the following property: if P blocks then P' evaluates to true, and if P evaluates to true then P' blocks (evaluates to false $\perp$).

1(g) A *crossover* $(\rightleftharpoons\ P_1\ P_2)$.

This function assumes P_1 is equal $(lR_1\ R_1\ rR_1)$, P_2 is equal $(lR_2\ R_2\ rR_2)$, where lR_1, lR_2 are left, and rR_1, rR_2 are right contexts of selected cost subexpressions R_1 and R_2, respectively. Contexts may not be syntactically valid cost expressions. Then the crossover performs the exchange of subexpressions returning $(lR_1\ R_2\ rR_1)$ and $(lR_2\ R_1\ rR_2)$. Crossover can be considered as very closely related to parallel composition (simultaneous substitution), but also to matching (two subexpressions are communicated).

Toggling, cost, negation, choices, compositions, matchings, crossover, mutation, and primitive arithmetic, logical and relational functions are examples of built-in functions, other functions, including data structures, can be specified using definition. Forward and backward matching perform function of send and receive from message passing. In \$-calculus everything is a cost expression: agents, environment, communication/interaction links, inference engines, modified structures, data, code, and meta-code.

2.2 Cost functions

Cost (objective) functions represent a uniform criterion of adaptation (control). Cost functions may have many possible interpretations and formulas. For this reason we do not assign one particular definition to be used within the calculus - a user may specify his/her own cost functions. Nevertheless, a few typical examples of costs include functions representing time, money, fitness, error, probability, possibility, complexity, distance, energy, entropy, the number of resources, etc. For instance, the costs representing probabilities of cost expressions lead to the ***probabilistic \$-calculus***, and the costs interpreted as the fuzzy set characteristic function - lead to the ***fuzzy-logic \$-calculus***.

Costs can be explicit or implicit (endogenous like in Echo system [6]). Explicit costs can be understood as an abstraction of the measure how well the system (agent, program, process) performs in the environment. In implicit costs, the environment provides the direct feedback, fulfilling as the result a similar function as explicit costs.

Costs expressing performance of multiple agents or evaluating several factors can be combined in one cost to express multiobjective optimization (using, for instance the weighted sum of component costs), or in multimodal optimization they can be kept separately as a vector of component costs (this can be useful, for instance, for autonomous adaptive agents or co-evolutionary systems).

Dissimilar to the GA fitness measure, the costs can be both positive, and negative (i.e., profits, or fitness from GA). This extension is more natural in many applications, and not necessary violates Holland's schema theorem [4] (if cost values do not include $-\infty$, then they always can be shifted to be nonnegative numbers by subtracting their overall minimum). For taking a decision, important is the relative order, rather than a sign of the number. Another advantage having both positive and negative costs, is that all optimization problems (minimization and maximization) can be expressed uniformly in $-calculus by minimization of costs only (i.e., maximization of fitness - by minimization of negative costs, and minimization problems - by minimization of positive costs).

To compute the cost, the most important is the compositionality principle: *the cost of the problem consisting of subproblems is the function of costs of subproblems.* Sometimes this function is difficult to find and easier is assign fitness to the program as the whole.

2.3 The Inference Engine: A Modifying Algorithm

The inference engine is the control structure of the $-calculus responsible for problem solving. Formally, it is a *cost expression* where modifications work upon functions and terminals, producing a new program or algorithm, or an architecture (in the form of another cost expression - a modified algorithm). Together, a *modifying algorithm* and a *modified algorithm* form a *self-modifiable algorithm.* The typical example of the inference engine, so called *simple modifying algorithm* is used almost without changes in expert systems, neural networks, or genetic programming, and is the following:

```
(∘ (init T F)            /* initialize P from
                            {T, F} */
   ($ P)                 /* find cost of P */
   (loop P)              /* basic cycle: select,
)                           examine, execute */
(:= (loop P)             /* loop recursive def.*/
   (⊔ (∘ (¬ (goal P))    /* goal not satisfied */
         (sel P)         /* select: select subexp-
                            ressions & perform
                            modifications */
         (exam P)        /* examine: optimize P
                            using laws of progra-
                            mming, and resolve
                            nondeterminism in
                            ⊎ by taking the
                            cheapest branches */
         (exec P)        /* execute: run P and
                            find its cost */
         (loop P))       /* return to loop*/
      (∘ (goal P) ε))    /* goal satisfied*/
)
```

The Inference Engine of the $-calculus can, however, take the form of more complex algorithms (as a basic structure of an evolutionary algorithm, applicable practically without changes to genetic programming, genetic algorithms, evolution strategies, evolutionary programming, and classifier systems, may lead to a more complex form of the cultural algorithm, or the genocop algorithm [8]).

3 $-calculus as a Unifying Tool for Symbolic and Subsymbolic Computation

The examples in this section illustrate application of $-calculus to three completely different areas: conventional symbolic AI, communication and synchronization in computer systems, and to emerging or well established distributed AI, including genetic algorithms, neural networks, cellular automata and intelligent autonomous agents.

3.1 Classical Symbolic AI: Maching as an Inference

Example 1 *Rule-based Expert Systems with crisp, probabilistic and fuzzy rules*
The set of terminals T these are Expert System facts, the set of functions F these are production rules or clauses. The modifications form the Expert System inference engine. The *init* modification selects the initial state (or terminal state), the *goal* modification verifies whether terminal (or initial) state has been achieved (depending whether the Inference Engine works forward or backward). In the select phase *sel*, a current state is matched using forward or backward matching with the set of rules F and T. The examine phase is empty. The execute phase runs matched rules and calculates new costs. If the rules are crisp, the cost function is not used. For uncertain or vague rules, the probabilistic or fuzzy set characteristic functions are used to express costs. Adaptive expert systems employ modifications changing rules/clauses.

Each production rule *if* $(a_1 \wedge \ldots \wedge a_n)$ *then* $(b_1 \wedge \ldots \wedge b_k)$, in $-calculus has the form $(\circ\ (\uplus_{i=1,\ldots,n} a_i)\ (\uplus_{j=1,\ldots,k} b_j))$. Additionally, with each production can be associated its cost (\$ *rule*): probability for Bayesian ES or possibility for fuzzy ES. Because facts can be considered as a special case of production rules, where one of *if* or *then* part is replaced by ε, thus they will be omitted. Formally, a forward expert system can be described as consisting of 3 elements: the definition of productions rules, the definition of the Inference Engine ES, and the starting cost expression calling ES with the initial state parameter.

A simple modifying algorithm (Inference Engine of ES) plus a modified algorithm (Knowledge Base)

```
/* the list of production rules */
((:= rules (
    (∘ (⊎ i=1,...,n1 a1i)(⊎ j=1,...,k1 b1j))
    ...
    (∘ (⊎ i=1,...,nm ami)(⊎ j=1,...,km bmj))
))
/* ES inference engine recursive definition */
(:= (ES state) (⊔
/* if state does not match goal continue */
    (∘ (¬(→ state goal))
/* redefining state after firing production rule */
            (:= state' (→ state rules))
            (ES state') /* recursive call of ES */
    )
/* stop if state matches goal */
    (∘ (→ state goal) ε)
))
(ES σ)) /* calling ES with the initial state σ*/
```

For backward expert system, the backward matching operator ← should be used, and start should be from the goal, and termination should be checked against an initial state.

Dissimilar to conventional expert systems, \$-calculus allows to look for the optimal solution, to employ parallelism, and by use of meta-rules (cost calculus modifications) with cost optimization to allow for learning.

Example 2 *Logic programming: Prolog.*
Without loss of generality, we can consider that Prolog program is a set of clauses of the form $a : -b_1, ..., b_n.$, which in \$-calculus takes the form of definition $(:= a\ (\circ\ b_1 ... b_n))$, and of facts (clauses only with heads). The rest will be somehow similar to rule-based expert systems.

A simple modifying algorithm (Inference Engine of Prolog) plus a modified algorithm (Prolog's program)

```
((:= clauses (                      /* clauses def. */
    (:= a1 (∘ j=1,...,k1 b1j))
    ...
    (:= am (∘ j=1,...,km bmj))
))
(:= facts (c1 ... cl))              /* facts */
(:= (Prolog term) (⊔                /*Prolog inf.eng.
                                    recursive def. */
    (∘ (¬(→ term facts))            /*if term doesn't
                                    match fact cont.*/
            (:= term'               /* redef. term
              (→ term clauses))     after eval.clause */
            (Prolog term')          /* recursive call
    )                               of Prolog */
    (∘ (→ term facts) ε)            /* stop if term
))                                  matches fact */
(∘ i=1,...,p (Prolog di)))          /*initial query*/
```

As we see, the simulation of the Prolog-like work in \$-calculus is straightforward, although the cost calculus operators resemble rather temporal/modal logic operators.

3.2 Communication and Synchronization in Dynamic Parallel Systems: Matching as Message Passing

Example 3 *Mobility in the style of π-calculus.*
One of the advantages of the π-calculus [9], compared to CSP [5] or CCS [9] is its ability to express processes which have changing structure. In [9] as the basic example of such a mobility is presented the solution to the following problem: Originally, agent P sends 5 to agent R along a link named a, and after that P executes P', and R continues with R'.

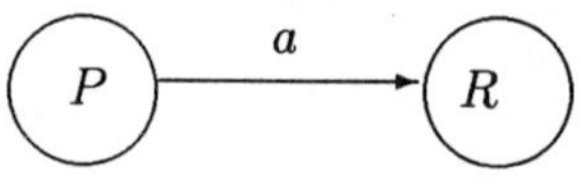

In \$-calculus, we solve this problem in the following way:

$$(\parallel\ (\circ\ (\rightarrow\ (a\ 5)\ (a\ x))\ P')\ (\circ\ (\leftarrow\ (a\ y)\ (a\ x))\ R'))\ \overset{\{(a\ 5),(a\ 5)\}}{\longrightarrow}\ (\parallel\ P'\ R')$$

Note that this resembles a typical handshaking communication from Hoare's zero-buffered channels from CSP/OCCAM/Transputers, or Milner's CCS. Initially $x = \perp$, and send $\rightarrow$ is blocked when x is full (different than $\perp$), and receive $\leftarrow$ is blocked when x is empty (equal $\perp$).

Now, let's assume that P delegates a new agent Q, to transmit 5 to R. However, Q does not have a communication link to R. Such a link is moved from P and R pair to Q and R pair, i.e., we have a changeable communication topology.

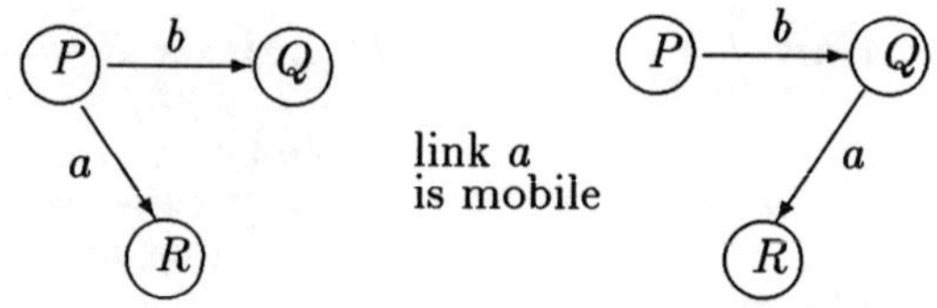

This takes the following form in \$-calculus (where initially $x = y = z = v = \perp$):

$$(\parallel\ (\circ\ ((\rightarrow\ (b\ a)\ (b\ x))\ (\rightarrow\ (b\ 5)\ (b\ x))\ P')\ (\circ\ (\leftarrow\ (b\ y)\ (b\ x))\ (\leftarrow\ (b\ z)\ (b\ x))\ (\rightarrow\ (y\ z)\ (y\ x))\ Q')\ (\circ\ (\leftarrow\ (a\ v)\ (a\ x))\ R')).$$

In the first step P sends by matching link a to Q (mobile link a) through link b, and after that 5 to Q through link b giving $(\parallel\ P'\ (\rightarrow\ (a\ 5)\ (a\ x))\ Q')\ (\circ\ (\leftarrow\ (a\ v)\ (a\ x))\ R'))$.
In the final step $(a\ 5)$ from Q forward matches $(a\ x)$, and $(a\ v)$ from R backward matches $(a\ x)$ (Q sends 5 to R) giving the final result $(\parallel\ P'\ Q'\ R')$.

Compared to the π-calculus, in \$-calculus the change of expressions P and Q could be expressed explicitly as the result of action of another modification cost expression.

3.3 Subsymbolic and Distributed AI

Example 4 *Genetic programming.*
A Genetic programming procedure is the following simple modifying algorithm with modifications *loop*, *sel*, *exam*, $\rightleftharpoons$, and user specified \$ and *goal*, working upon population of imperative/functional (sequential and deterministic) programs P constructed of user selected terminals and functions. Terminals are limited to atoms: constants, variables, and zero-argument functions. User selected functions may include analogues of $\circ$ (PROGN from Lisp), $\sqcup$ (IF-THEN-ELSE), and $:=$ (ADFs). Automatically Defined Functions (ADFs) take the form: $(:= (f\ x_1\ ...\ x_n)\ (\circ\ P_1\ (val\ P_2))$, where, as the standard, crossover (and other modifications - secondary GP operations) are limited to body P_1, return values $(val P_2)$ are fixed, and no recursive definitions are allowed. The cost function is a standardized GP fitness, calculated from raw fitness provided by the user and specifying, how well the program as the whole solves the problem. The best program is with minimal standardized fitness (nonnegative reals). *init* generates randomly population of programs P, The select phase *sel* consists of the selection based on cost/fitness, and crossover and reproduction modifications ($\rightleftharpoons$ and ε). The examine phase *exam* is limited to editing modification simplifying programs using laws of programming. The execute phase \$ consists of running programs and calculating their costs.

An arbitrary evolutionary algorithm (which subsumes genetic algorithms, evolutionary programming, evolution strategies, and genetic programming) is very similar to a simple modifying algorithm:

```
(∘ (init T F)                  /* init.population P
                                  of chromosomes*/
   (eval P)                    /* run P and find
                                  its cost/fitness */
   (loop P)                    /*basic cycle:select
                                  ,alter, evaluate */
)
(:= (loop P)                   /* loop rec.def. */
  (⊔ (∘ (¬ (term_cond P))      /* termination cond.
                                  not satisfied */
        (sel P)                /* select surviving
                                  individuals based
                                  on fitness */
        (alter P)              /* apply crossover
                                  and mutation */
        (eval P)               /* run P and find
                                  its cost/fitness */
        (loop P))              /* back to loop */
     (∘ (term_cond P) ε))      /* the termination
)                                 cond. satisfied */
```

Example 5 *Neural networks.*
An artificial neuron f can be defined simply as the function:

$$(:= (f\ x_1 ... x_n)\ (\sigma\ (\Sigma_{i=1}^{n}\ w_i x_i)))$$

and called (evaluated) by the function call $(f\ y_1 ... y_n)$, where σ is the neuron activation function (usually, in the form of the threshold, piecewise-linear, or sigmoid function) with inputs $x_1, ..., x_n$ and weights $w_1, ..., w_n$. The definition provides recursion, i.e. f can occur in any place of one or more inputs $x_1, ..., x_n$. Note that the \$-calculus is not limited to symbolic terms, i.e. it allows to express a general neuron (including nondeterministic ones and spiking ones - simply function f will return one from set of possible values, or function f will have a spiking shape in time domain).

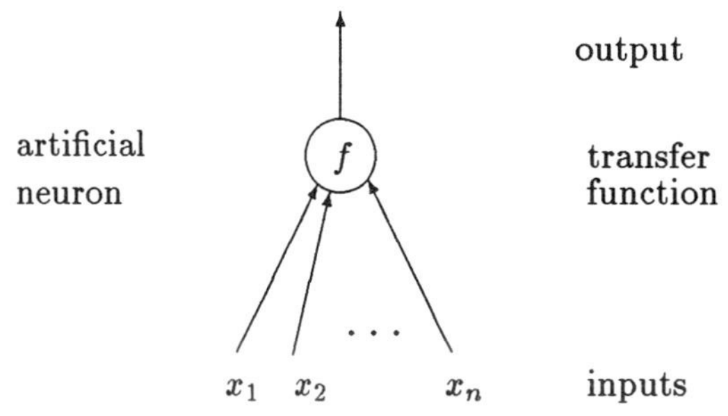

Neural networks take the form of the possibly countably infinite number of interconnected neurons.

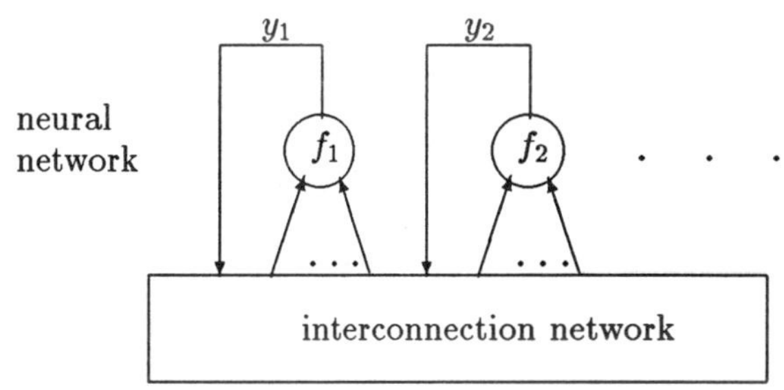

In terms of \$-calculus a (recurrent) neural network can be defined as a possibly infinite set of neuron definitions:

$$(:= (f_1\ x_{11}\ ...\ x_{1n_1})\ ...)$$
$$(:= (f_2\ x_{21}\ ...\ x_{2n_2})\ ...)$$
$$...$$

and called, in a general case, by a parallel composition of neurons $(\ \|\ _{i=1,2,...}\ (f_i\ y_{i1}\ ...\ y_{in_i}))$.

An arbitrary neural network can be expressed in terms of \$-calculus.

The above means that a computational power of \$-calculus is at least equal to neural nets [4], i.e., the \$-calculus can solve the halting problem of the Turing machine.

Neural networks very often undergo process of modification of weights, which is a basis of various types of neural nets learning algorithms. Then a neural network forms a modified algorithm, and its learning procedure this is a modifying algorithm. A typical neural network learning procedure is the simple modifying algorithm working on population of neurons P, with modifications *init* initializing neuron weights, *goal* being the classification error, *sel* selecting the group of neurons and performing weight updating modification, empty examine phase *exam*, and execute modification propagating new output signals and calculating the cost function $. The cost function calculates the classification error of neural net. A universal neural network [4], i.e., where modification of weights is done by other fixed weight neurons, takes the form of the self-modifying algorithm.

4 Conclusions

The paper shows the approach which could be considered as the proposal of the formal model for a wide class of symbolic and subsymbolic systems.

We propose to extend the use of cost function in expert systems. The costs are proposed to consist of two elements: the first one used for optimization, and being the sum of the complexity of found so far solution, and the goodness - the estimated distance to the goal (something similar like in the original A* algorithm [10]), and the second component expressing uncertainty or vagueness of rules (in the form, for instance, of probabilities, or fuzzy set characteristic functions. In the examine phase *exam*, the number of next states is reduced based on costs. Then the expert system will look not for any solution satisfying (or approximately satisfying) the goal, but rather for the optimal solution.

A cost programming paradigm allows to enhance genetic programming by generating nondeterministic and parallel programs. It allows to integrate both symbolic AI inferences and GP operators, and to generate production rules/logic/procedural programs. A majority of programs are built using standard components: compositions, choices, iterations. This is not a case in GP: each program has to have it own terminals and functions. It is proposed that the GP function set included $\circ$, $\|$, $\uplus$ and $\sqcup$ by default, and the user will add his/her own functions, and eventually will remove some defaults (for instance, if the program should not allow parallelism). Genetic programming could also benefit from the library of standard fitness functions. Probably, the most important contribution to genetic programming is to propose to calculate fitness of programs as the function of program components. More precisely, we propose to keep the GP standardized fitness $\$_h$, (better programs have lower costs) estimating how far the program is from the goal, to which we add the cost of component functions used to solve the problem $\$_g$ (i.e., $\$ = \$_g + \$_h$ - so far, GP uses only estimates $\$_h$, $\$_g$ can be calculated). It solves the problem of too long GP trees, i.e., longer trees will be more expensive - this means less fit and less likely to be selected for reproduction. It may also allow to treat correctness of generated programs as cost optimization problems (infinite programs will have infinite cost, and programs further apart from the goal will have a higher estimate part of costs).

For neural networks, we propose for costs to be the sum of the neural network complexity $\$_g$ plus the classification error $\$_h$. The best neural network would be the network with the minimal cost (smallest complexity and minimal error). By analogy with symbolic A* algorithm we obtain the following result: for the NN design search tree, if the classification error $\$_h$ is not overestimated (in particular, computed exactly), the designed neural network will be with the least complexity, i.e. the cost function $\$ = \$_g + \$_h$ will be minimal. The A*-like search for NN and GP convergence, requires further studies.

References

[1] Church A., *The Calculi of Lambda Conversion*, Princeton, N.J., Princeton University Press, 1941.

[2] Eberbach E., "Neural Networks and Adaptive Expert Systems in the CSA Approach", *Intern. Journal of Intelligent Systems*, Special Issue on Artificial Neural Networks, vol.8, no.4, pp.569-602, 1993.

[3] Eberbach E., "SEMAL: A Cost Language Based on the Calculus of Self-modifiable Algorithms", *Intern. Journal of Software Engineering and Knowledge Engineering*, vol.4, no.3, pp.391-408, 1994.

[4] Garzon M., *Models of Massive Parallelism: Analysis of Cellular Automata and Neural Networks*, Springer-Verlag, 1995.

[5] Hoare C.A.R., *Communicating Sequential Processes*, Prentice-Hall, 1985.

[6] Holland J., *Adaptation in Natural and Artificial Systems*, second edition, The MIT Press, 1992.

[7] Koza J., *Genetic Programming: On the Programming of Computers by Means of Natural Selection* and *Genetic Programming II: Automatic Discovery of Reusable Programs*, The MIT Press, 1992 and 1994.

[8] Michalewicz Z., *Genetic Algorithms + Data Structures = Evolution Programs*, third edition, Springer-Verlag, 1996.

[9] Milner R., Parrow J., Walker D., "A Calculus of Mobile Processes, I & II", Information and Computation 100, pp.1-77, 1992.

[10] Nilsson N.J., *Principles of Artificial Intelligence*, Morgan Kaufmann, 1980.

Two Approaches of Human Behavior Anticipation

Christophe Meyer, Irina Akoulchina, Jean-Gabriel Ganascia

Université Paris VI - LIP6-CNRS
e-mail: {meyer, akoul, ganascia}@poleia.lip6.fr

Abstract

This article presents an in-depth look at the different aspects of anticipation and describes two intelligent agents which are able to learn human behavior, to anticipate next actions and then act accordingly. The first agent is intended to predict and to anticipate, with good accuracy, evolutive (indeed adaptive) observed behavior of a game player. The second is an adaptive interface agent for a particular Web-based application. It is an active browser, interactively assisting and guiding the user by proposing right navigation ways.

1. Introduction

The intelligence of an individual is commonly evaluated according to some particular abilities: *Learning, Adaptation, Anticipation*. An artificial intelligent system ought to be judged on the same criteria. Most of the « intelligent » realizations on computers are concerned with *Learning* (problem solving, games, etc.) or *Adaptation* (Adaptive systems, robots, etc.). Only a few of these systems deal with *Anticipation* and when they do, they rarely take into account its whole complexity.
Broadly speaking, Anticipation can be defined as the combination of forecasting and action. Different researches tackled with prediction have been carried out in the several domains: Mathematics, Economy, Games theory, Cybernetics, Robotics, Software Science, etc. These prediction applications require various methods : statistics, simulation, fuzzy logic, Learning or « cognitive » methods. The various applications using all these methods are mostly prediction systems and not anticipation ones. An anticipating system must take into account not only the forecasting aspect, but the action shape also. Such anticipating systems have been elaborated only in certain domains - robotics, interface agents, animats. In our scientific group we develop two intelligent learning agents that are capable to analyze user's behavior and to anticipate his or her next actions. Our applications have two important particularities : they are *auto-adaptive* and evaluate their performances in *real time*. When the anticipation takes into account these two features : adaptability and real time work, it becomes « reflective ». In order to build such a "reflective" system, we tried to specify an anticipating agent which is not only observing and acting according to its observations but which is also considering the effects of its own behavior.

2. The S.A.G.A.C.E. method

2.1. Presentation

SAGACE is a method intended to create agents performing such reflective anticipating behavior. SAGACE is the French translation for Sagacious and the French acronym for Genetic Algorithmic Solution for Evolving Behaviors' Anticipation.
To evaluate SAGACE, we used Games as an experimental testbed. More precisely we considered games with complete but imperfect information, such as the famous *Rock / scissors / paper* game, in which you have to be able to anticipate your opponent's next action to be efficient [10].
Our method calls upon an original architecture. We use a first Learning Classifier System (L.C.S.) [6] in a classical way. It takes information from the environment (typically, the game state) and then creates associated messages. These messages are then used to activate appropriate classifiers that deliver an action message corresponding to the next action for the game. This L.C.S. uses reinforcement Learning to improve its performances and Genetic algorithms for rules creations [7], [5].
The point is that we added a second L.C.S. to complete the information provided to the first one. In fact, this 2nd L.C.S. takes information from the environment and uses modeling to forecast the opponent next action and then to refine the messages of the 1st L.C.S. New classifiers are created on-line for modeling the opponent's behavior. For each new behavior observed, a new classifier is created according to the situation and to the opponent's action. Also, some coefficients are added to the action messages of this L.C.S. according to the results of the corresponding opponent's behavior. For example, if the opponent has just made an action that maked him lose, a classifier is created according to this action and a coefficient corresponding to a selective value is added and this coefficient indicates that

this action was not successful for the opponent. These coefficients are useful for the first L.C.S. to forecast with good accuracy the opponent next actions. (See Figure 1.).

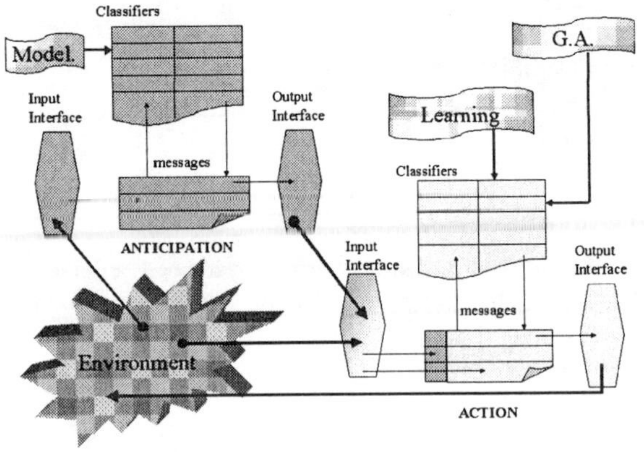

Figure 1. SAGACE's Architecture

2.2 Evaluation

To evaluate our method, we designed a very simple game called ALESIA.

Alesia is a game between two players who have to try and push the marker across the board to the other one's citadel. At best this can be done in three consecutive winning moves. At the beginning of the game each player receives a capital of 50 points. The players decide in secret and announce simultaneously how many points (at least one and at most their capital) they have decided to play during a given move. The player who announces the highest number pushes the marker (initially at the center) one slot towards the adversary's citadel. If they both announce the same number, the marker remains where it is. In both cases the number of played points is deducted from the players' capital. A player wins if he manages to move the marker to the adversary's citadel. Otherwise it is a draw.

This game contains a number of interesting features. The rules are very easy and can very quickly be understood by a human, the information is complete and imperfect and there is no general non-mixed winning strategy (this has been proved mathematically). We have implemented a system that allows different players (human or artificial) to play Alesia against each other. We developed five particular programs to compare against the SAGACE one. They are more and more sophisticated. For each different adversary, SAGACE will build, from scratch, a specific model to anticipate its behavior.

The first opponent was a uniform probabilistic adversary. That means that at each time, it chooses a bid randomly between 1 and its capital. Only 10 games are necessary for SAGACE to construct an efficient model of this opponent and then to win all the next games.

The second one is different. It is randomly choosing a bid always between 1 and 50. That means that if it chooses a bid greater than its capital, it plays all its remaining points. In this case, there is no equiprobability in the choices of action as the higher moves are naturally favored. Anticipation is more tricky with this kind of adversaries, but, after 50 games, the model is reliable and the results are very good (90% of won games for the SAGACE player).

The third adversary simulates an expert theoretician and is able to compute mathematically when a situation allows a winning strategy. Otherwise, it uses a set of probabilistic rules introduced according to a games expert. SAGACE needs at least 150 games in order to produce a reliable model of this player. At the end, the percentage reaches the limit of 85% as the model becomes quite good.

The fourth adversary is an adaptive one. It has been implemented in the form of a classical L.C.S. but it doesn't build any model of its adversaries. It learns trough the traditional method of positive and negative retribution of its rules. It is also allowed to create new rules, using Genetic Algorithms. At the beginning, SAGACE manages to model this opponent relatively well, then the adaptive adversary adapts ! After, SAGACE manages to determine a new consistent model. After a certain number of these "adaptations", the percentage of games won stabilizes (60% for SAGACE and 40% for the adaptive player).

Then we developed the best adversary we could think of. This one uses a kind of adaptive MinMax algorithm. It is not possible here to explain in details its functioning but just notice that it knows all the winning strategies when they exist and that it is able to adjust on-line the probabilistic coefficients of its strategies according to their results. This player beats easily all the previous adversaries (for example, it wins more than 80% of the games against the classical L.C.S. one) but it is defeated by SAGACE, winning only 30% of the games against 50% (20% draw).

We also engaged series of tests against human players and the graph illustrates the typical aspect of the resulting curves (Figure 2.). The progression is not monotonic as can be seen. The two players adapt continually their way of playing to the other. After 85 games, the human player no longer seems to be able of imagining new strategies adapted to SAGACE. At the end, the percentage is in general around the same values (55% for SAGACE and 45% for the human player). Notice that if the system uses exactly the same components with the same classifiers when the adversary modeling component is disabled, the human wins more than 80% of the games. This result proves the importance of modeling and anticipating.

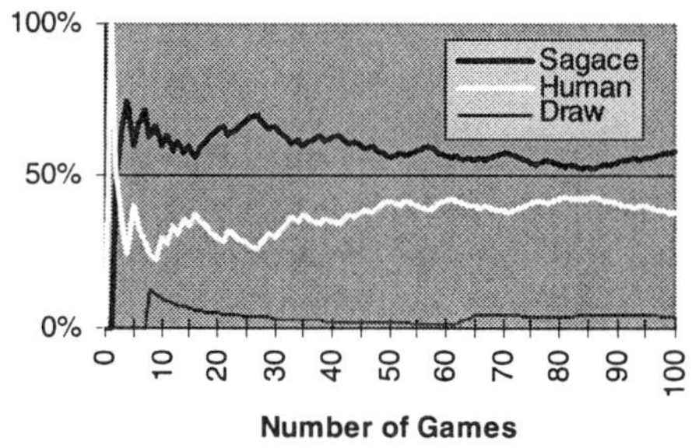

Figure 2. SAGACE Vs human.

The results are very good and prove that our approach for a cognitive Anticipation is quite efficient. The architecture used in this method is devoted to any cognitive Anticipation. However, in the context of games, anticipation is commonly used to counter opponents. But anticipation can useful also in other kind of applications in which it may improve cooperation between different agents. For instance it is the case for interface agents or to bootstrap an evolutive distributed artificial intelligence system by anticipating the actions of an expert [9]. In the next section, we shall present an application of anticipation to *intelligent interface agents*.

3. SAGE Agent Web-Browsing Anticipation

Now, with the enormous growing of hypermedia information networks like the Internet, the problem of efficient « browsing » and « getting lost » in the global hyper-space draws more and more attention. The anticipation of next browsing action on the Web and the construction of adapted interfaces become an essential task. The *learning intelligent interface agents* have been developed in order to resolve these problems. Such agents can learn user profile and guide him or her in the multi-value network space, remember user's preferences and propose « interesting » Web pages to visit and so on.
Existing Web agents are developed for « active browsing » of all pages available on the Web. They combine machine learning techniques with information filtering methods. They track user's behaviour and attempt to anticipate his next browsing actions by doing concurrent, autonomous exploration of links starting from the user's current position. These agents are distinguished by the level of the « browsing autonomy », the feedback from the user and the machine learning technique used. For example, the *WebWatcher* agent [2] requires the user to state explicitely a « browsing goal ». On the contrary, *Letizia* [8] works completely independently from the user, it does not use any feedback in the response to its predictions. These agents do not use the previously acquired knowledge about domain application. By contrast, the agents which use knowledge about a particular domain, have been created for the environment of local systems with a limited number of users (for instance, *Active Browser* [3]).
The principal idea of the development of SAGE agent [1] is to combine the advantages of these two types of agents. SAGE (SATELIT AGENT ; « sage » stands for « wise » in French) is dedicated to support an adaptive interface of the Web-based SATELIT system. SATELIT allows the acquisition of a knowledge base and the automatic indexing of Web documents according to the contents of this base in order to facilitate information access [4]. The application domains of SATELIT are the natural sciences. In those domains, objects are clustered according to their similarities to make up classes, called taxa, organised in hierarchical structures, called taxonomies. An appropriate knowledge representation formalism here the Conceptual Graphs model [11]. The textual information represented by taxa is held in several Web pages in the HTML format. The special SATELIT's tools relying on the domain knowledge and developed in the JAVA language, manage these Web pages.
SAGE plays a role of intelligent browsing assistant that learns a search goal from user's ordinary browsing actions and can anticipate his next actions. SAGE is applied not to all Web pages, but to a *subset* of pages containing SATELIT information. In addition, it is based on a precise model of the SATELIT knowledge about application field. In this way it integrates the methods of the user's behaviour analysis and the knowledge based systems techniques (figure 3).

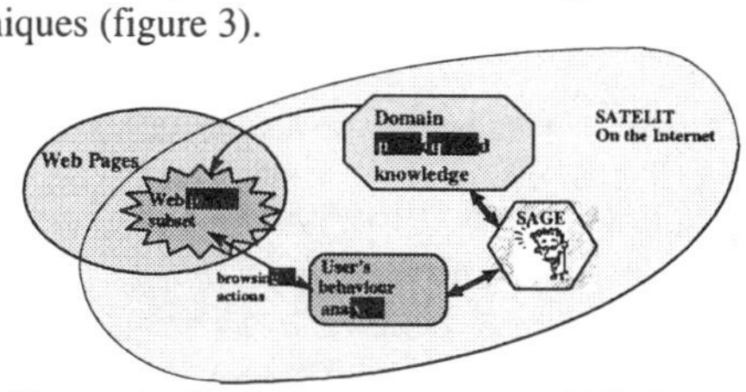

Figure 3. SAGE : a new type of WEB agent

During the SATELIT session, the user operates with two types of tools : the ordinary Web browser kit and a set of some appropriate SATELIT's tools : that allow the user to browse the taxonomy and conceptual graphs, or to compose requests for information search. The user consulting a SATELIT application tries to identify an object with certain known properties. Such a search in the large and complex SATELIT bases is a very difficult process. The user has always difficulties with describing directly and precisely his search goal. The system proposes certain tools that help him, but in the waste set of concepts, references, characteristics and taxa names, the user may easily get lost. Browsing is seen as a more natural process when the user is uncertain about the target's description.

The user repeats interactively browsing process to skim at a glance the results and refines the search goal at each step. Our approach proposes to infer the user's search goal from learning his repetitive browsing actions, to anticipate the next browsing action and, consequently, to decrease the risk of user « disorientation ».

The user's interactions with SATELIT's interface consist of a set of actions including *feedback actions* with SAGE. An action and a suggestion of SAGE adopt the same representation : « to select an argument of the certain type in a certain tool ». Thus, in order to compose a suggestion, SAGE has to find the responses to two principal questions : *Which tool should I propose ?* and *Which argument in this tool can I suggest ?*

SAGE analyses a user's action, extracts the terms describing a tool *T* and an argument *A*, and places them in the Working Memory. A special SAGE's engine searches the *relative arguments* $\{A_1,...A_n\}$ for the chosen *argument A* and, with the help of the rule base, it associates with them the weights. The relative arguments are those having common links in the conceptual graphs or in the Taxonomy. The closeness of a relative argument A_i to a direct argument *A* is estimated by a relativity measure, also called *importance* $(Imp(A_i))$, varied from 0 to 1. The importance of relative arguments increase with lower (more specific) levels of the conceptual graphs, and of the taxonomy.

For each argument A_i SAGE calculates its weight :

$$W(A_i, M(T,A_i)) = (frequency(A_i)/n) * Imp(A_i) * Reinf(A_i) + \sum_{j}^{k} W(A_i, m_j(T, A_i)),$$

where $W(A_i, M(T, A_i))$ is the weight of an argument A_i connected to an action M, *n* is a number of arguments in the Working Memory, *Imp* (A_i) is the current importance of this argument, *Reinf* (A_i) is its reinforcement coefficient, and $\{m_1,...m_k\}$ are the other actions, to whose the argument A_i has been connected. SAGE uses a technique of learning by reinforcement inspired by SAGACE's : the default importance values are changing gradually depending on the user's feedback. If the user does not accept some SAGE's advises, the importance of the proposed arguments are decreased by 20% ; otherwise the importance of the chosen argument and all relative arguments are increased by 20%. Thus, on reinforcing certain propositions about the worthiness of an argument, SAGE infers a search's goal and anticipates next browsing actions.

It is evident that at the beginning of a browsing session when working memory has no a lot of information, the agent can not make strong suggestions about next browsing actions. But with the time SAGE accumulates more learned knowledge and becomes more skillful for anticipation. The user's actions implicitly carry information about his or her search goal because they have been deliberately chosen to serve the user's interests. However this facility of choice poses some principal problems that tie up with noisiness of learned information. One solution to reduce the ambiguousness is to present less information at each browsing stage. We make our agent sensitive to « misleading » actions by decreasing the importance (and consequently the weight) of old information. Our current experiments show that SAGE accelerates the search process by 40%.

4. Conclusion

Now, work will be done to improve the SAGE agent by giving it means to use the 'reflective' anticipating aspect of the SAGACE method. Using it, SAGE will be able to tell when it has been efficient and what has been the consequences of its proposals for the user. Then SAGE will be able to change behavior accordingly without disturbing the user. As for the SAGE agent, the proposed approach may be used to design tools for other artificial intelligence systems that deal with anticipation.

References

[1] Akoulchina I., Ganascia J.-G. SATELIT-agent : An Adaptive Interface Based on Learning Interface Agents Technology. *In Proc. of the Sixth International Conference User Modeling (UM'97),* SpringerWienNewYork, Chia Laguna, Italy, 1997.

[2] Armstrong R., Freitag D., Joachims T. and Mitchell T. WebWatcher: A Learning Apprentice for the World Wide Web. *Proc. of AAAI Spring Symposium on Information Gathering from Heterogeneous, Distributed Environments*, March, 1995.

[3] Drummond C. Automatic goal extraction from user actions to accelerate the browsing of software libraries. *M.A.Sc. Thesis, University of Ottawa,* December, 1992

[4] Faron C., Akoulchina I., Ganascia J.-G. Integrating Knowledge in Hypermedias: the system SATELIT. In *Proc. Of CESA'96 IMACS Multiconference*, Lille, France, July 1996

[5] Goldberg E.D. *Genetic Algorithms in Search, Optimization, and Machine learning*. Addison-Wesley, 1989.

[6] Holland J. *Adaptation in Natural and Artificial Systems.* University of Michigan Press, 1975.

[7] Holland J., Holyoak K-J., Tagard, and Nisbet. *Induction : Processes of Inference, Learning and Discovery*. MITpress 1986.

[8] Lieberman H. Letizia : An Agent that assists Web browsing, In Proc. of International Joint Conference on Artificial Intelligence, Montreal, Canada, August, 1995

[9] Meyer C. and Ganascia J-G. *Utilization of imitation and anticipation mechanisms to bootstrap an evolutive distributed artificial intelligence system.* Animal Societies as an Alternative Metaphorical Basis for DAI - ICMAS, 1996.

[10] Meyer C.,Ganascia J-G, Zucker J-D. Learning Strategies in Games by Anticipation. *Proc of the fifteenth International Joint Conference on Artificial Intelligence, IJCAI'97.* Morgan Kaufman editor 1997.

[11] Sowa J.F. Conceptual structures: Information Processing in Mind and Machine, Addison Wesley, 1984.

CoMeMo: Constructing and Sharing Everyday Memory

H.Maeda, T.Hirata and T.Nishida
Graduate School of Information Science
Nara Institute of Science and Technology
8916-5, Takayama, Ikoma, Nara, 630-01, JAPAN

Abstract

This paper describes the CoMeMo project which aims to develop systems which articulate, organize and utilize everyday memory in a group or in a community. The basic hypothesis is that connecting information without defining the semantics using the weak information structures is effective to deal with a large amount of diverse information. The CoMeMo architecture consists of (a) CoMeMo Workbench, (b) CoMeMo Incorporator, (c) CoMeMo Mobile Terminal, (d) CoMeMo Server, (e) CoMeMo Protocol and (f) CoMeMo Agent. We have implemented the CoMeMo Workbench, the CoMeMo Incorporator and a prototype of the CoMeMo Mobile Terminal. We have developed applications based on the CoMeMo architecture: (a) Information Gathering and Reorganization from WWW pages, (b) Ontology development, (c) Education Support and (d) Conference Support.

1 Introduction

Most of events in everyday life are forgotten. It is difficult to utilize ideas and thoughts which we hit on when watching TV or strolling at street corners, unless we make note of them. We call such ideas and thoughts in everyday life "everyday memory." We believe that it is significant to construct and utilize everyday memory. Everyday memory plays a critical role to facilitate human-human interaction. Sharing everyday memory and creating common background knowledge facilitates efficient message exchanges.

The CoMeMo[1] project aims to develop systems which articulate, organize and utilize everyday memory in a group or in a community. We propose the *weak information structures* to gather incomplete everyday events and gradually reorganize them. The CoMeMo project is a part of the Knowledgeable Community project[8] which aims to develop an environment of creating knowledge by humans and computers. The CoMeMo project is to assist human memory, in the light of human information processing.

There are some research topics in constructing and sharing everyday memory.

1. **Memory Representation**: how to represent memory
2. **Recall**: how to recall from clues
3. **Utilizing Memory**: how to utilize memory stored in different situations or from different viewpoints.
4. **Cooperative Construction of Memory**: how to support the process of cooperation to construct memory
5. **Presentation of Memory**: how to present memory to be comprehensible to humans

In computer knowledge sharing[8, 9, 10] which aims to implement interoperability of virtual knowledge base, the role of (1) formal common languages which define the semantics of information, (2) facilitators which mediate between agents has been emphasized. The protocol design between agents is important in multi-agent systems.

On the other hand, in order to support human interactions, we aim to make use of tacit background knowledge or contexts shared with humans. We believe it important to investigate tacit knowledge and contexts in real world problems, in the light of information science to design systems which construct and share everyday memory.

In the CoMeMo project, we attempt to explain the mechanisms of (a) interaction between tacit and explicit knowledge and (b) cognition and generation of contexts and situations by studying human interaction systems.

2 CoMeMo Architecture

We set a hypothesis that connecting information without defining the semantics using the weak information structures is effective to deal with a large amount of diverse information. *Associations* are one of such information representations we are investigating (Figure 1); each of which is a many-to-many mapping of memory units. Associations connect a collection of key *units* (hereafter *keys*) with a collection of units (hereafter *values*) which are normally reminded by the given keys. Units are basic entities of associations which represent concepts, texts, or image files.

We call a set of associations collected from a particular point of view *workspaces*. The CoMeMo information base is a collection of workspaces (Figure 2).

[1] "CoMeMo" represents "Common Memory", "Continuous Memory", "Computer-enhanced Memorandum", formerly called CM-2 [1, 2, 3, 4, 5, 6, 7].

1082-3409/97 $10.00 © 1997 IEEE

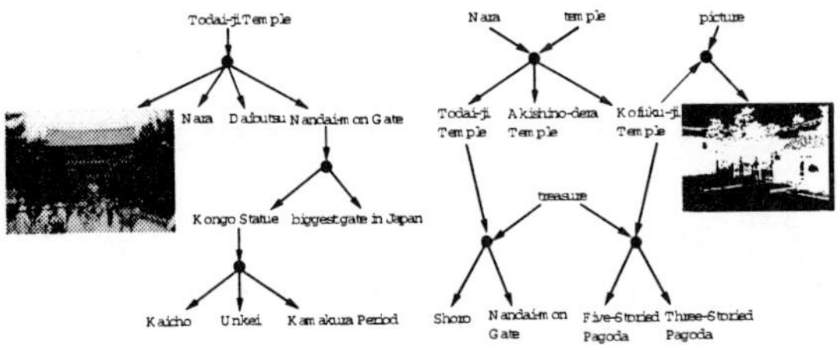

Figure 1: Example Associations

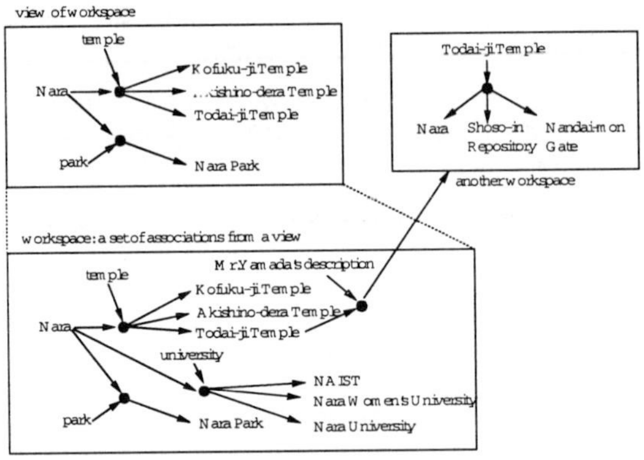

Figure 2: Workspaces

In our approach, the semantics of the associations is not defined rigorously. Instead, we leave the interpretation of the semantics to tacit human background knowledge. This facilitates information acquisition from a variety of data (e.g. images, texts, ideas, memoranda). The CoMeMo architecture helps sharing and reuse of fragmented information.

The CoMeMo architecture consists of following components (Figure 3).

1. **CoMeMo Workbench** helps users explore, browse and edit associations in the CoMeMo information bases.
2. **CoMeMo Incorporator** gathers and converts a wide variety of information into information representations which CoMeMo can deal with.
3. **CoMeMo Mobile Terminal** enables users ubiquitous use of CoMeMo information.
4. **CoMeMo Server** articulates and serves associations on demand, and mediates between information users and developers.
5. **CoMeMo Protocol** exchanges information between each component.
6. **CoMeMo Agent** (a) executes user tasks, (b) negotiates common problems with other agents or humans, and (c) presents the contents of CoMeMo information bases to users.

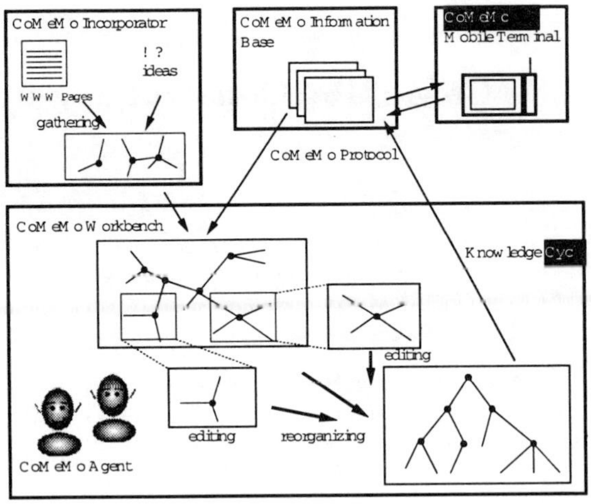

Figure 3: CoMeMo Architecture

We have implemented the CoMeMo Workbench and the CoMeMo Incorporator. We have implemented a prototype of the CoMeMo Mobile Terminal. The CoMeMo Server, the CoMeMo Protocol and the CoMeMo Agent are under construction. We will describe the CoMeMo Workbench and the CoMeMo Incorporator in next two sections.

3 CoMeMo Workbench

The CoMeMo Workbench helps users explore, browse and edit associations in the CoMeMo information bases.

3.1 Information Exploration

In addition to basic input, edit functions, following functions help users to edit and reorganize information bases.

1. **Focus**: to hide units which are unrelated to selected units
2. **Neighbor Search**: to display units which are linked to selected units
3. **Path Finding**: to display relations between selected units
4. **Unit Search**: to display units by keyword search

In what follows, we concentrate on the path finding. Path finding is based on the idea of "spreading activation" on semantic networks [11]. Path finding with distance n searches a set of units which are linked by associations with distance n. Distance 1 denotes an extent between keys and values. Figure 4 illustrates how the algorithm works to answer a question;

> "Is there any temple related to Prince Shotoku?"

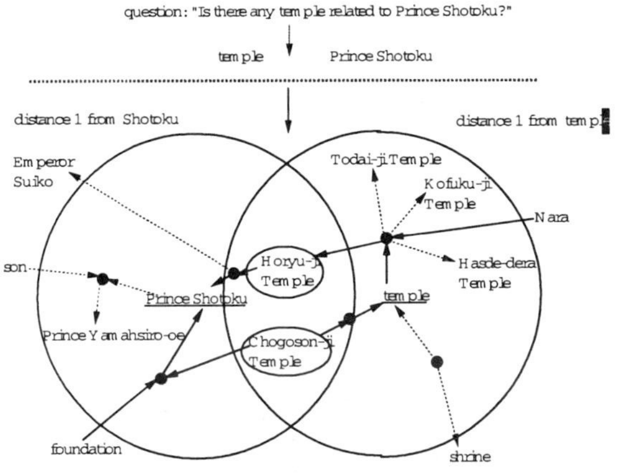

Figure 4: Path Finding

Table 1: Experimental Results of Path Finding

Distance	Precision	Recall
Distance 1	64%	64%
Distance 1 + 2	76%	92%

Precision: $\frac{\textit{answers whose results are all appropriate}}{\textit{questions}} \times 100\ (\%)$

Recall: $\frac{\textit{answers which contain appropriate results}}{\textit{questions}} \times 100\ (\%)$

As preliminary experiments (10 questions) had shown that (a) when appropriate answers are obtained by nearest path, far more search is in vain and (b) many unnecessary answers are obtained in distance 3 search, we decided to evaluate distance 1 search and distance 1 + 2 search. Distance 1 +2 search means that if no answers are obtained in distance 1 search, distance 2 search is performed.

We manually constructed an information base referring a sightseeing guidebook of Nara. It contains 1,286 units and 862 associations. We tested path finding against this information base. We obtained appropriate 38 answers out of 50 queries (76% at precision rate, distance 1 + 2; See Table.1). In distance 1 + 2 search, units which cannot be found in distance 1 are found. This is why it improves both of precision and recall rate.

3.2 Information Unification

Information unification unifies various associations such as generated from WWW pages and those created by humans into new associations and remove unnecessary associations using heuristics.

Figure 5 shows an example of information unification: information in the right 2 workspaces are unified onto the left workspace.

This facility helps users to utilize information bases possessed by himself/herself or other members in his/her small group. When it is used in bigger societies, ontology and background knowledge bases may be necessary to supply the deficit of the contexts.

Another example is shown in Figure 6. Members of our lab have constructed information bases of slides, survey and so on. User A wrote a plot to write a paper

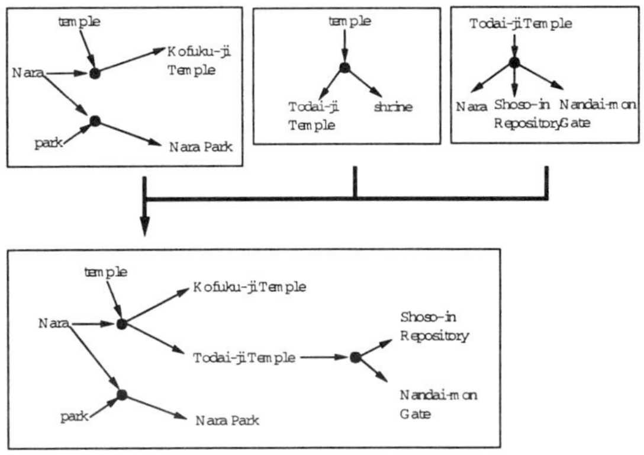

Figure 5: An Example of Information Unification

Table 2: Experimental Results of the CoMeMo Incorporator

Information Sources	Test	Precision	Recall
Nara Sightseeing Guidebook	*Test*1	92%	–
	*Test*2	86%	–
Nikkei Newspaper Full-text Database	*Test*1	63%	91%
	*Test*2	83%	71%
HTML Documents on WWW	*Test*1	90%	83%
	*Test*2	68%	73%

Precision: $\frac{\textit{appropriate units}}{\textit{generated units}} \times 100\ (\%)$

Recall: $\frac{\textit{appropriate units}}{\textit{units which should be extracted}} \times 100\ (\%)$

(Figure 6(a)) and then unified information bases in the lab. As a result, a piece of slides or papers contained in User B's survey information base and User A's slide information base are integrated through the workspace (Figure 6(b)).

4 CoMeMo Incorporator

The CoMeMo Incorporator gathers and converts a wide variety of information into information representations which CoMeMo can deal with. For example, information is gathered from HTML documents on WWW and newspaper databases[2, 3, 4, 5]. The current algorithm is quite simple; extracting keywords by morphological analysis[12] and generating associations by analyzing HTML structures (Figure 7). Figure 8 shows an example of associations generated from WWW Pages concerning Kyoto sightseeing information.

To evaluate the effectiveness of the methods, we tested several cases to generate associations from full-text newspaper database, HTML documents and so on. The number of units was around 1000 – 2000. Table 2 shows the results. See [2, 3, 4, 5] for details.

5 Applications

We have developed some applications based on the CoMeMo Architecture. The first three systems con-

(a)Workspace Before Information Unification

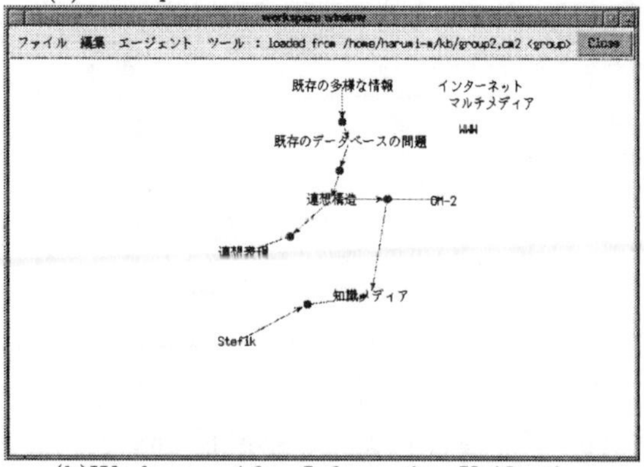

(b)Workspace After Information Unification

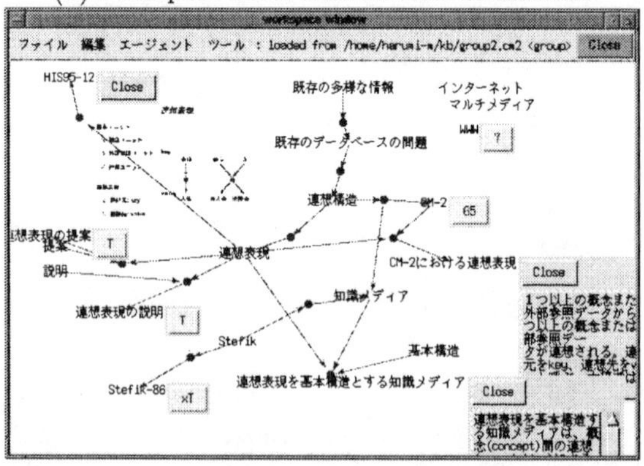

Figure 6: Unifying CoMeMo Information Bases

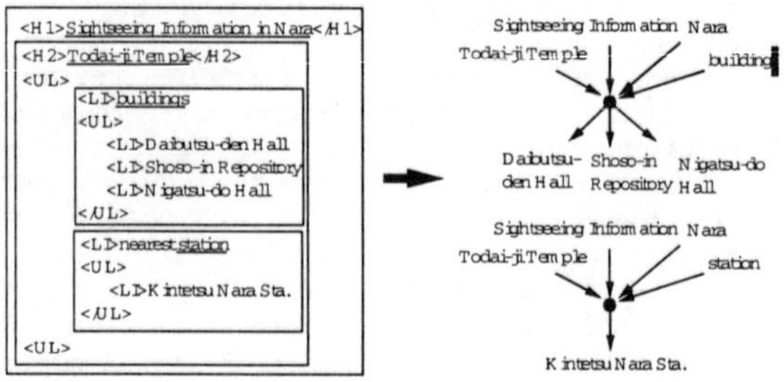

Figure 7: Generating Associations from Mark-up Documents

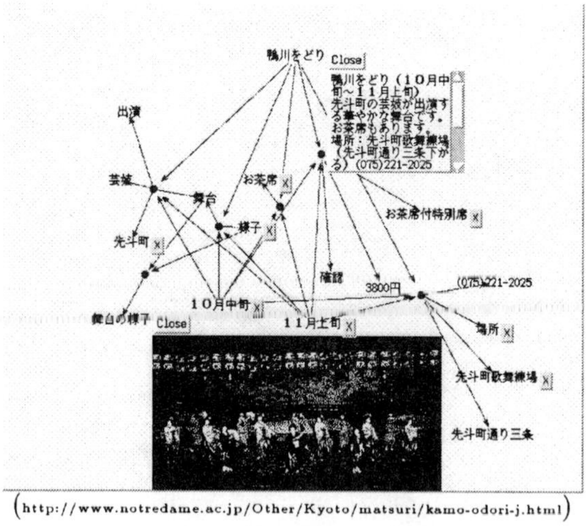

(http://www.notredame.ac.jp/Other/Kyoto/matsuri/kamo-odori-j.html)

Figure 8: An Example of Associations Generated from WWW Pages

cerns the CoMeMo Workbench and Incorporator, and the last one is a prototype of the CoMeMo Mobile Terminal.

5.1 Information Gathering and Reorganization from WWW Pages

Recently the World Wide Web has become very popular for human information sharing. Although a number of search tools available, it is difficult to extract useful information and reorganize it according to user's point of view.

We have developed an application to gather WWW pages, extract information and reorganize it according to user's input.

We gave 100 WWW pages concerning AI researchers to CoMeMo Incorporator for organizing AI directories. The CoMeMo Incorporator extracted units about 7 classes (researchers, projects, e-mail, topics, universities, departments and laboratories), and generated associations. It then reorganized these units and associations to display various lists according to user's input.

The overview of the process is illustrated in Figure 9. The algorithm is as follows; (1) to generate units and associations by morphological analysis and analyzing HTML structure, (2) to identify class of the generated units using heuristics, (3) to unify units and associations using heuristics, and (4) to reorganize associations by path-finding according to user's input.

Figure 9(a) shows an example result when a user input "reasoning","researcher","e-mail","project" and "university". For example, researchers such as Adam Farquhar, Alon Levy, Edward Feigenbaum and James Allen are extracted first, because the word "reasoning" and their names are written near in WWW pages, and then their related information is reorganized. The experimental results are shown in Table 2. See [3, 4] for details.

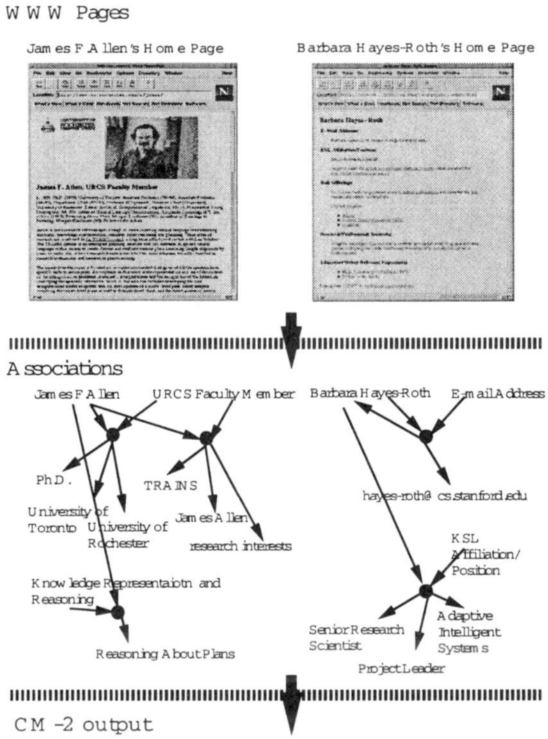

(a) Test 1 (researcher)

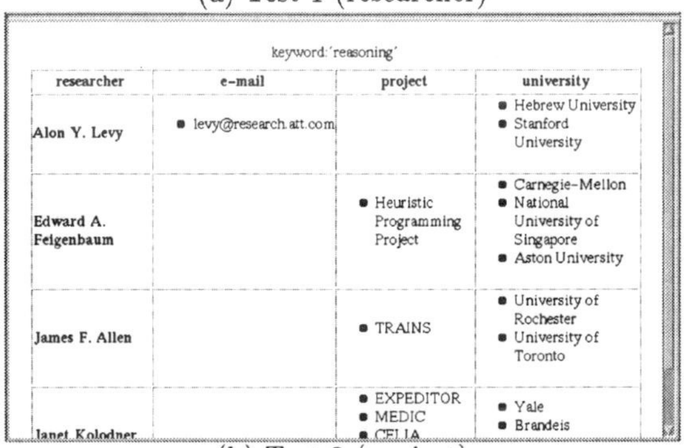

keyword: 'reasoning'

researcher	e-mail	project	university
Alon Y. Levy	• levy@research.att.com		• Hebrew University • Stanford University
Edward A. Feigenbaum		• Heuristic Programming Project	• Carnegie-Mellon • National University of Singapore • Aston University
James F. Allen		• TRAINS	• University of Rochester • University of Toronto
Janet Kolodner		• EXPEDITOR • MEDIC • CELIA	• Yale • Brandeis

(b) Test 2 (project)

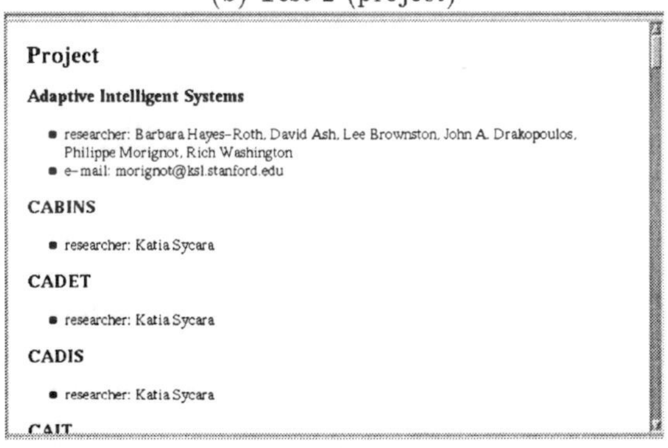

Project

Adaptive Intelligent Systems

- researcher: Barbara Hayes-Roth, David Ash, Lee Brownston, John A. Drakopoulos, Philippe Morignot, Rich Washington
- e-mail: morignot@ksl.stanford.edu

CABINS

- researcher: Katia Sycara

CADET

- researcher: Katia Sycara

CADIS

- researcher: Katia Sycara

CAIT

Figure 9: Information Gathering and Reorganization from WWW Pages

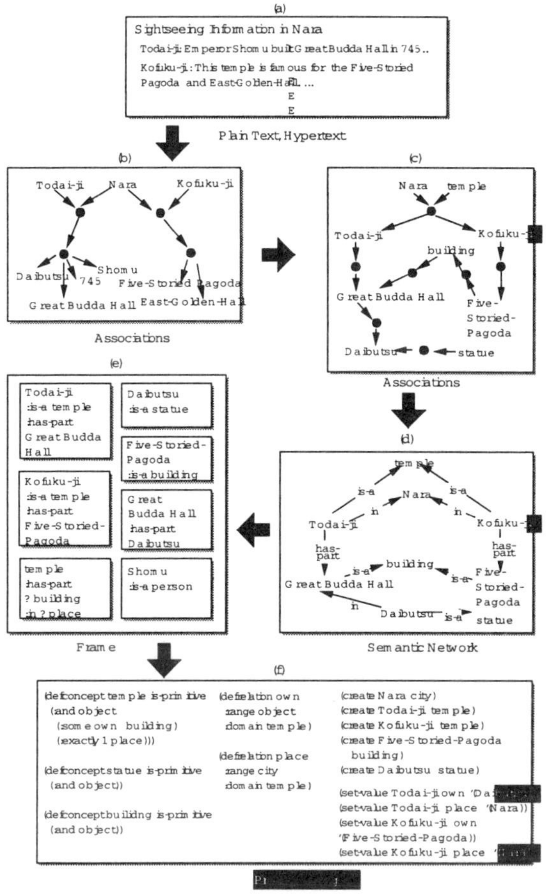

Figure 10: Ontology Development

5.2 Ontology Development

Ontology plays a central role in achieving large scale knowledge sharing. Unfortunately, development of ontology is often a quite painstaking and time consuming task, because it needs much effort to collect and select terms through task analysis. We have applied our approach based on the weak information structures to ontology development. It allows for data-driven ontology development, by accumulating raw data and incrementally creating the structure of concepts through human-computer collaboration (raw data → associations → refined associations → semantic networks → frames → predicate logic) . The overall process of our approach is shown in Figure 10.

We gave 30 WWW pages concerning ARPA Intelligent Integration of Information (I3) Initiative [2] to CoMeMo Incorporator. Each page contains overview of projects which belong to the I3 Initiative. The CoMeMo Incorporator generated associations. Generated associations themselves are incoherent and can-

[2] http://dc.isx.com/I3/

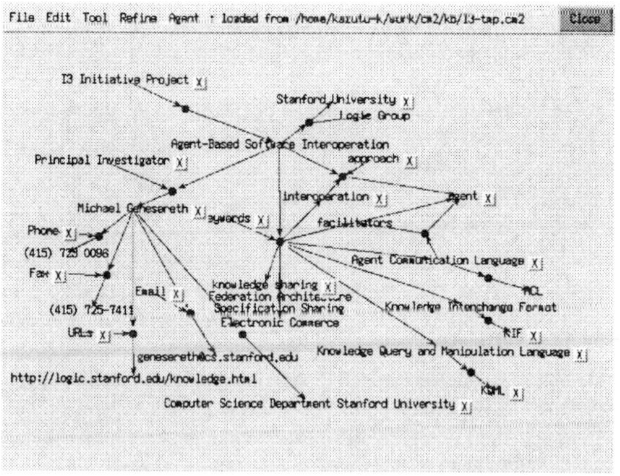

Figure 11: An Example Result of Refined Associations

not be used as ontology as they are. Users and computers collaborated to form these associations into more coherent structure on the CoMeMo Workbench. Figure 11 shows an example result of refined associations concerning the project "Agent-Based Software Interoperation". It corresponds to level c ontology (refined associations) in Figure 10. See [6] for details.

5.3 Education Support

A high school teacher Mr.Moriyama has developed a system called **CALON** based on the CoMeMo Workbench which helps high school students learn Japanese history. He used the system at the classroom for one year and evaluated it.

CALON allows teachers to express their knowledge and students to access the contents of textbooks.

He evaluated how students understand the semantics of associations written by himself. He created associations from historical facts. 41 students tried to convert these associations into natural language texts. He found that 90% students could do the above tasks.

Next, he examined how students create associations from natural language texts in textbooks. From this experiment, he found how students understand the historical facts. See [7] for details.

5.4 Conference Support

We have implemented a shared-card information system to support community information sharing called **InfoCommon**, which is a prototype of the CoMeMo Mobile Terminal.

We evaluated the usefulness of **InfoCommon** at the ICMAS'96 (Second International Conference on Multiagent Systems) Mobile Assistant Project[13], which is the world first experiment in applying mobile computing systems to community support. 100 personal intelligent communicators with handy phones were loaned to conference participants to actually try out the system. Figure 12 is a photo taken in the Nara Park where an excursion was held, which shows how a user actually used **InfoCommon**.

Figure 12: **InfoCommon** in Use

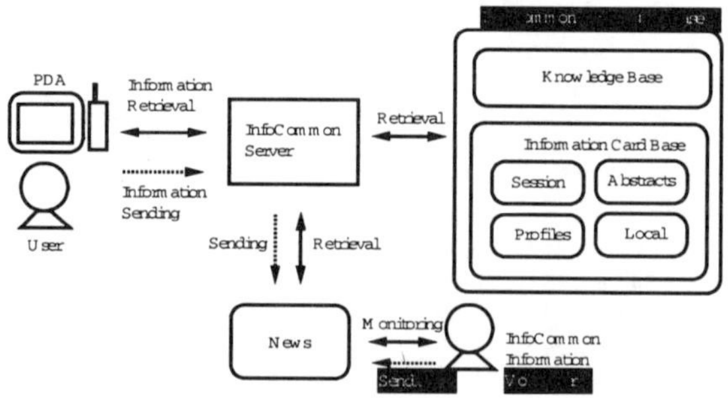

Figure 13: Overview of **InfoCommon**

InfoCommon provides visual interface for retrieving and sending information cards. Figure 14 shows a screen image of **InfoCommon**. The relation between two information cards is displayed by a link. **InfoCommon** information base consists of (a) a knowledge base which links keywords and information cards using the weak information structure and (b) an information card base as shown in Figure 13.

InfoCommon information bases store static information such as abstracts of papers, session, local information and profiles to share information among participants.

InfoCommon supports the following functions.

Content-based Information Retrieval Given a set of keywords, InfoCommon will respond with the set of information cards connected to the keywords. The result of retrieval is stored in the user's local information base where the user can re-arrange the collection of information cards, and add/remove nodes/ links as desired.

Information Sending (Posting News) **InfoCommon** is built on a conventional News service. Users can add information cards on their local information base and send them to a News server.

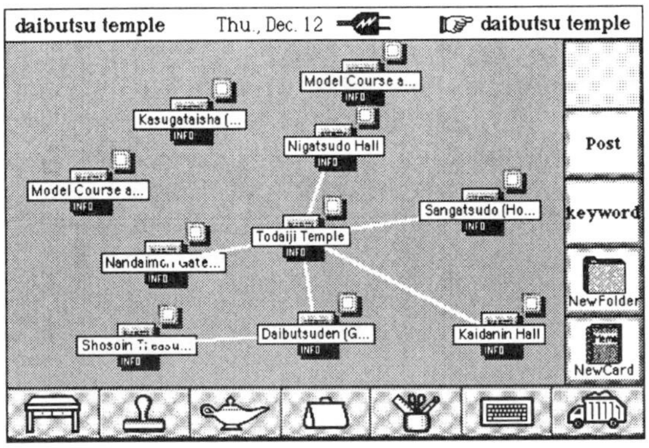

Figure 14: Screen Image of InfoCommon

The following results indicate the system's usefulness for information sharing in community: (a) 51% of users were satisfied of the system, (b) 81% felt search results were fine and (c) 55% answered that the system was useful for getting information they need. We consider the results are supporting evidence of the effectiveness of the weak information structure for information sharing in community. See [14] for details.

6 Related Work

Our work is related to recent work on information gathering from heterogeneous sources on Internet ([16],[17],[18],[19],[20]). Instead of focusing on the strategies and heuristics for information gathering, we concentrate on how to classify information obtained from multiple information sources and integrate it into personal information spaces.

CYC[21] and ARPA Knowledge Sharing Effort[10] have made a significant contribution in the sense they shed light on the importance of knowledge and information sharing and that they have presented a self-completed computational model. Their approach orients computer information sharing while ours is for human information sharing.

Gaines uses semantic networks as information representation for group knowledge sharing[22]. Our approach is based on much weaker information representation than semantic networks.

Kautz studied the use of agents in assisting and simplifying person-to-person communication for information gathering tasks[23]. They focus on the use of a software agent. We concentrate on the process of how humans create knowledge and information.

Sumi[24], Hori[25] and Kunifuji claim the importance of knowledge and information in the field of creative thinking support.

The basic recognition behind this research is a trade-off between the benefit from conceptually well-structured information representation and the cost for organizing information space. The more well-structured information representation becomes, the more useful it is for computational manipulation, however, the more expensive the cost of information acquisition and integration becomes.

Our approach is to provide a framework of collaborations between humans and computers to construct and share everyday memory with a low structural facilities and to facilitate raw information from vast information sources to be incorporated without much labor and gradually refined and elaborated as more insights are obtained.

7 Future Work

As information systems spread into human societies, supporting human interaction in community becomes more important. We think that one direction of future work is to support communication directly, such as matchmaking proposed by Ishida[26]. Other direction may be indirect support based on information sharing to find people who has information one needs.

The CoMeMo architecture supports to send and receive information produced in everyday life. We attempt to study knowledge creation on social networks which is proposed by Imai, Nonaka[27], and Hori[25] and so on.

8 Concluding Remarks

We described the CoMeMo project for constructing and sharing everyday memory in a group or in a community. The basic hypothesis is that connecting information without defining the semantics using the weak information structures is effective to deal with a large amount of diverse information. We implemented the CoMeMo Workbench, the CoMeMo Incorporator and a prototype of the CoMeMo Mobile Terminal. We evaluated applications based on the CoMeMo architecture.

In addition to experiments stated in this paper, we are currently investigating cognitive modeling on how humans create the weak information structures and how humans understand the semantics of the weak information structures using their tacit knowledge.

References

[1] T. Nishida, H. Takeda, K. Iino and M. Nishiki, "A knowledge media approach to ontology development," *Towards Very Large Knowledge Bases: Knowledge Building & Knowledge Sharing 1995*, (Editor N.J.I. Mars), IOS Press, pp. 84-94, 1995.

[2] H. Maeda, K. Koujitani and T. Nishida, "A Proposal of Associative Structures for User-Friendly Interface in Information Bases," *Progress in Human Interface*, Vol.5, No.1, pp.49–56, 1996, (in Japanese).

[3] H. Maeda, K. Koujitani and T. Nishida, "A Knowledge Media Approach Using Associative Representation for Constructing Information Bases," *Proceedings of The Ninth International Conference on Industrial and Artificial Intelligence and Expert Systems (IEA/AIE-96)*, pp.117–126, 1996.

[4] H. Maeda, K. Koujitani and T. Nishida, "Information Reorganization using Associative Structures," *Transactions of Information Processing Society of Japan*, Vol.38, No.3, pp.616–625, 1997, (in Japanese).

[5] K. Koujitani, H. Maeda and T. Nishida, "Constructing Information Bases with a Weekly-Structured Medium," *Progress in Human Interface*, Vol.5, No.2, pp.69–76, 1996, (in Japanese).

[6] K. Koujitani. "Constructing Ontologics Based on Real Data," Master's Thesis, Graduate School of Information Science, Nara Institute of Science and Technology, 1996, (in Japanese)

[7] A. Moriyama,"Construction of Computer Aided Learning System Using Weakly-Structured Knowledge Representation and its Application in Education of History of Japan in High School", Master's Thesis, Graduate School of Information Science, Nara Institute of Science and Technology, 1997, (in Japanese).

[8] T. Nishida, "Very Large Scale Knowledge Base Systems," *Journal of Information Processing Society of Japan*, Vol. 35, No. 2, pp. 130-139, 1994, (in Japanese).

[9] R. Neches, et al., "Enabling Technology for Knowledge Sharing," *AI Magazine*, Vol. 12, No. 3, pp. 36–56, 1991.

[10] R. S. Patil et al. "The DARPA Knowledge Sharing Effort: Progress report, Principles of Knowledge Representation and Reasoning," *Proceedings of the Third International Conference*, (eds. C. Rich, B. Nebel and W. Swartout), Morgan Kaufmann, 1992.

[11] M. R. Quillian, "Semantic memory," In Marvin Minsky edition, *Semantic Information Processing*, MIT Press, 1968.

[12] E. Brill, "Some Advance in Transformation-Based Part of Speech Tagging," In *Proceedings of the Twelfth National Conference on Artificial Intelligence (AAAI-94)*, 1994.

[13] Y. Nishibe, H. Waki, I. Morihara and F. Hattori, "Analyzing Social Interactions in Massive Mobile Computing - Experiments of ICMAS'96 Mobile Assistant Project-," IJCAI-97 International Workshop on Social Interaction and CommunityWare, pp.19-24, 1997.

[14] H. Maeda, M. Kajihara, H. Adachi, A. Sawada, H. Takeda and T. Nishida, "Weak Information Structure for Human Information Sharing," IJCAI-97 International Workshop on Social Interaction and CommunityWare, pp.7-12, 1997.

[15] T. Nishida and H. Takeda, "Towards the knowledgeable community," *Knowledge Building and Knowledge Sharing*, IOS Press, pp. 155–164, 1994.

[16] A. Y. Levy, Y. S. Sagiv and D. Srivasava, "Towards efficient information gathering agents," *Working Notes of the AAAI Spring Symposium on Software Agents*, pp. 64–70, 1994.

[17] R. Armstrong, D. Freitag, T. Joachims and T. Mitchell. "A learning apprentice for the World Wide Web," *Working Notes of the AAAI Spring Symposium on Information Gathering from Heterogeneous, Distributed Environments*, pp. 6–12, 1995.

[18] M. Balabanovi'c and Y. Shoham. "Learning information retrieval agents: Experiments with automated web browsing," *Working Notes of the AAAI Spring Symposium on Information Gathering from Heterogeneous, Distributed Environments*, pp. 13–18, 1995.

[19] W-S Li. "Knowledge gathering and matching in heterogeneous databases," *Working Notes of the AAAI Spring Symposium on Information Gathering from Heterogeneous, Distributed Environments*, pp. 116–121, 1995.

[20] M. Iwazume, H. Takeda and T. Nishida, "Ontology-Based Information Gathering and Text Categorization from the Internet," *Proceedings of the Ninth International Conference in Industrial and Engineering Applications of Artificial Intelligence and Expert Systems* pp. 305–314, 1996.

[21] R. V. Guha and D. B. Lenat, "Enabling Agents to Work Together," *Communications of ACM*, Vol. 37, No. 7, pp. 127–142, 1994.

[22] B. R. Gaines and M. L. G. Shaw, "Using Knowledge Acquisition and Representation Tools to Support Scientific Communities," *AAAI-94*, 1994.

[23] H. Kautz and B. Selman and A. Milewski, "Agent Amplified Communication," *Proceedings of the Thirteen National Conference on Artificial Intelligence (AAAI-96)*, pp. 3–9, 1996.

[24] Y. Sumi and K. Hori and S. Ohsuga, "Computer-Aided Thinking Based on Mapping Text-Objects into Metric Spaces," *Proc. of The 2nd Pacific Rim International Conference on Artificial Intelligence*, 1992.

[25] K. Hori, "A System for Aiding Creative Concept Formation," *IEEE Transactions on Systems, Man, and Cybernetics*, Vol. 24, No. 6, pp. 882–894, 1994.

[26] T. Ishida and T. Nishimura, "Global Information Network for Community Support," *Journal of Information Processing Society of Japan*, Vol. 38, No. 1, pp. 48–53, 1997 (in Japanese).

[27] I. Nonaka and H. Takeuchi, "The Knowledge-Creating Company: How Japanese Companies Create the Dynamics of Innovation," Oxford University Press, 1995.

Session A.2

Neural Network Applications

Session Chair:
Benjamin Wah, University of Illinois, USA

A New Hybrid Neural-Genetic Methodology for Improving Learning

A. Likartsis[‡] I. Vlachavas[*‡] L. H. Tsoukalas[*]

[‡]Aristotle University, Computer Science, Thessaloniki, GREECE

[*]Purdue University, W. Lafayette, IN 47907-1290

Abstract

A new hybrid neural-genetic methodology is presented that exploits the optimization advantages of genetic algorithms for the purpose of accelerating neural network training. The choice of fitness function is addressed and experimental findings are shown where neural network training is improved through the proposed approach. The results suggest that genetic algorithms can be a powerful tool for improving learning in neural networks.

Keywords: *Neural Systems, Genetic Algorithms, Learning*

1. Introduction

A principal challenge in neural computing is adjusting the set of internal parameters known as weights in order to encode an underlying relation assumed to exist amongst various data sets. The optimization strength of genetic computing provides a new tool for speeding the process of weight adjustment (which is broadly referred to as *learning* in neural network terminology). Genetic algorithms (GA) were initiated and developed in the early 1970's by John Holland (Holland, 1975) as a tool for solving optimization problems. Although, there is no theoretical guarantee that a genetic algorithm will give an optimal solution or arrangement, an appropriate choice of specific fitness functions has been shown to lead to near optimal solutions in many practical problems and the connection with neural networks has been elucidated by a number of researchers in several high quality investigations (Holland, 1992), (Harp, 1989; 1990; 1994), (Koza, 1990), (Moricic, 1990), (Whitely; 1989; 1990).

GA's mimic some of the processes of natural evolution and use two key notions, *chromosomes* and *genes,* which are computational metaphors that are based on evolutionary systems. *Chromosomes* are composed of *genes* which define the characteristics of the *chromosomes* and may take on several values called *alleles*. The position of a *gene* (its *locus*) is identified separately from the gene's function. Hence we can have a particular gene with a *locus* of position 12 whose *allele* value is brown. Generally, the *strings* of artificial genetic systems are analogous to chromosomes in biological systems and are also called *chromosomes.*

Natural selection involves creation of many chromosomes by *reproduction, mating (crossover), mutation* and the survival of the chromosomes with the better characteristics. Successive generations of chromosomes improve in quality, provided the criteria used for survival are appropriate. This process is often referred to as Darwinian natural selection or "survival of the fittest." In nature, this process of evolution occurs over many years, even hundreds or thousands of years. In computers, the representations of chromosomes can undergo literally thousands of generations of change in a few seconds.

Historically, the characteristics of the chromosomes in genetic algorithms have been represented by 0's and 1's. All of Holland's work used this representation, and we will use it here too. However, chromosomes can be represented by real numbers, permutations of elements, a list of rules, or other symbols. Binary representation is still the most common representation because the behavior of bit strings is better understood.

Evolution takes place through the process of reproduction which involves mutations and recombination after mixing of the parent's chromosomes to produce a creature that may have entirely different characteristics from the previous generation. The chromosomes of the two parents are mixed by a process called *crossover* in which two new chromosomes are produced, each having some of the characteristics of the two parents. The two parent chromosomes split at some point, and one part of one parent chromosome is exchanged for the corresponding part of the other parent chromosome. The location of the crossover point at which the parents' chromosomes divide is apparently a uniform random process. If one of the new chromosomes obtains 75 percent of its characteristics from one parent and 25 percent from the other, the second new chromosome gets 25 percent from the first parent and 75 percent from the second parent.

Both resultant chromosomes go into the gene pool (where all the alleles reside) where they either replace poorer quality chromosomes or are discarded. Once a chromosome is discarded, its unique features (good or bad) are lost forever. It is only through the processes of mutation that such a chromosome might possibly be recreated.

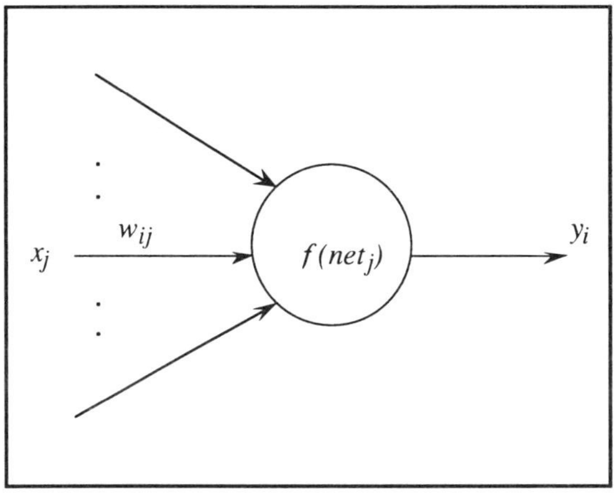

Figure 1. A typical processing unit of a neural network.

The function on which an optimization algorithm operates, i.e., seeking its maximum or minimum, is called the *objective function.* In neural networks, the objective function to be minimized is the mean square error over the entire training set. In genetic algorithms, the "fitness" is the quantity that determines the quality of a chromosome, from which a determination can be made as to whether it is better or worse than other chromosomes in the gene pool. The fitness is evaluated by a "fitness function" that must be established for each specific problem. This fitness function is chosen so that its maximum value is the desired value of the quantity to be optimized. Its importance cannot be overemphasized, because it is the only real connection between the genetic algorithm and the problems in the real world.

A fitness function must reward the desired behavior; otherwise the genetic algorithm may solve the wrong problem. Fitness functions should be informative and have regularities. However, they need not be low-dimensional, continuous, differentiable, or unimodal.

A neural network is composed of fundamental processing elements called neurons such as the one shown in figure 1. Each neuron performs a local computation that involves the incoming signals x_j (coming from previous neurons) with their weighted sum minus a threshold $[net_j = \sum_j^N w_{ij}x_j - \vartheta_j]$ undergoing a nonlinear transformation $f(net_j)$ before producing output y_i propagated through its outgoing connections to other neurons in the network. During training a number of input-output pairs, called *examples*, are presented to a network of such neurons and the connection weights are adjusted until the network has "learned" the underlying relationship that the examples represent. This is called *supervised learning* and the process of weight adjustment is referred to as *learning* or *training.* The most widely used algorithm for this kind of training is *back-propagation* (Tsoukalas, 1997). Figure 2 shows a typical neural network composed of three layers of neurons: *input, hidden (i.e., middle)* and, *output.*

Although back propagation training of neural networks is a rather universal option, there is considerable demand for approaches that can optimize faster. In this paper we propose and investigate for this purpose a new GA approach called Single-Offspring Technique (SOFT). We will show in Section 4 that SOFT offers significant improvements in terms of quality and speed of learning.

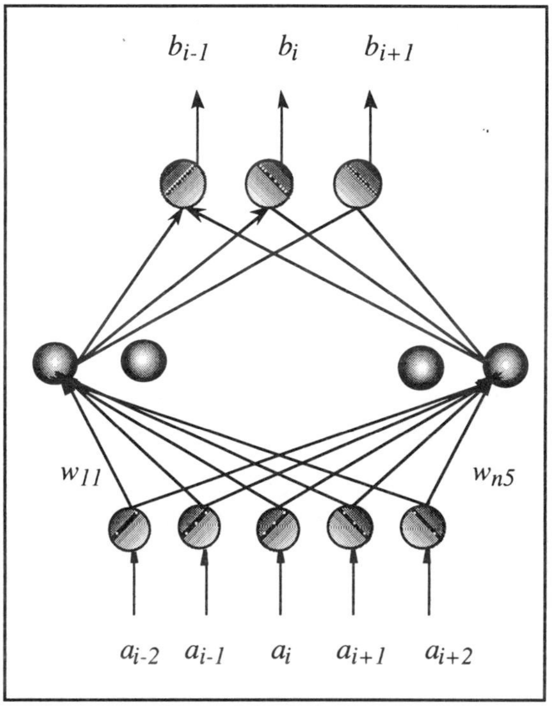

Figure 2. A neural network maps a number of inputs from the neighborhood of a_i onto a number of outputs in the neighborhood of b_i having learned the underlying relation.

2. Application of Genetic Algorithms to Accelerating Neural Network Training

To illustrate the proposed approach let us consider an arbitrary function *f(x)* for which we want to find the global maximum and where the independent variables x is a vector of the form [x_1 $x_2 ... x_n$], with $x_i \in \mathbf{B} = \{0, 1\}$.

The *fitness function* takes real values in the range [0, 1] while the variable x is a *bitstring.*

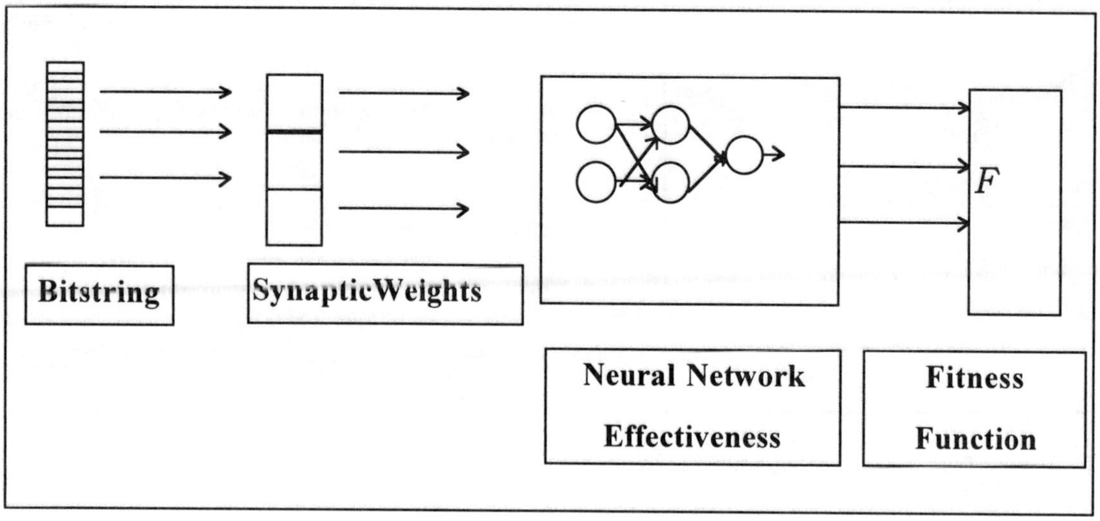

Figure 3. Schematic representation of the hybrid neural-genetic approach.

The optimization problem implies that we are looking for the vector $\mathbf{x}^0 = [\,x^0_1\, x^0_2 \ldots x^0_n\,]$, i.e.,

$$f(x^0) \geq f(x), \quad \text{for every } \mathbf{x} \in \mathbf{A} \subseteq \mathbf{B}^n$$

Making a *small* change in $\mathbf{x}^0$ produces the bitstring $\mathbf{x}^1 = [\,x^0_1\, x^0_2 \ldots < x^0_k > .. \, x^0_n\,]$ where $< x^0_k >$ is the complement of x^0_k in **B**, and we will observe a minor or major variation in the value of the function f, i.e.,

$$f(\mathbf{x}^1) < f(\mathbf{x}^0)$$

Testing all the possible replacements of the bits with their complement, results in different decrements in the function values. Thus, in relation to the bitstring $\mathbf{x}^0$, towards which we want to converge, the replacement of a bit results in a different change (always a decrement) in the function's value. As a consequence, we can consider that every bit has a weight which can determined as:

$$W_i = f(\mathbf{x}^0) - f(\mathbf{x}^0_i)$$

where $\mathbf{x}^0_i = [\,x^0_1\, x^0_2 \ldots <x^0_i> \ldots \, x^0_n\,]$, $i = 1 \ldots n$

The bit p with $W_p = max\,(\,W_i\,)$ is obviously the factor with determining significance in the solution of the problem. Thus, an algorithm that would converge to the desired bitstring, should find the correct value in the bit p, only if the gradient descent in the error function (e.g. $1/\,(1 + f(x))$) would produce local minima for each wrong value of the particular bit p. The entire hybrid neural-genetic approach is schematically shown in figure 3.

3. The SOFT Algorithm

Local optimisation is a straightforward problem. After finding the first definite factor for the particular problem, we can go on with a bitstring of size n-1. Following the same procedure, we decrease the problem size until it is adequately solved. In most optimisation problems, the definitive factors are less than 10% of the total implying that for finding the definitive factors of a problem the value of $f(x)$ is better that the acceptable limit, irrespective of the values of the other bits. Nevertheless, we usually continue the procedure until convergence is reached.

Replacing one or more bits we obtain several variations of the algorithm. SOFT using *1-replacement* only is as follows:

1. A random initial bitstring of length n is chosen.
2. All the bitstrings that differ from the initial one, in exactly one bit are produced (obviously there are n bitstrings).
3. The fitness values of these bitstrings are evaluated.
4. If there is no bitstring with greater fitness value than the initial one, the algorithm has converged to this bitstring. Otherwise the bitstring with the biggest fitness value is selected as the new offspring and the steps 2 to 4 are repeated until final convergence or until a member with acceptable performance is found.

The main features of this algorithm are:

- It is a local optimisation algorithm.

- Convergence is guaranteed due to the fact that it continuously leads to improved offsprings.
- It is deterministic, except for the randomly chosen initial ancestor.

The algorithm SOFT with *k-replacements* is as follows:

1. A random initial bitstring of length n is chosen.
2. All the bitstrings that differ from the initial one in k bits, are produced (obviously there are $\binom{n}{k}$ bitstrings).
3. The fitness values of these bitstrings are evaluated.
4. If there is no bitstring with greater fitness value than the initial one, the algorithm has converged to this bitstring. Otherwise the bitstring with the biggest fitness value is selected as the new offspring and the steps 2 to 4 are repeated until the final convergence or until a member with sufficient performance is found.

The main features of this algorithm are:

- As k increases and leads to n, the possibility for global optimisation increases. So, the 3-replacement algorithm, is more probable to find the global maxima (minima) than the 2-replacement algorithm, but it requires more computational time.
- In the case of $k = n$ the algorithm evaluates the fitness values of all strings.
- Convergence is guaranteed since it is always driven to better offsprings.
- It is deterministic, except the random initial ancestor.

Illustrative Example: The XOR Problem

In order to illustrate the methodology let us apply the SOFT algorithms described above to selecting weights for a neural network which is used to solve the XOR problem. The network has 2 inputs, 1 output and one hidden layer with 2 neurons. Consequently, there will be 9 weights, including the neuron thresholds. The required output is either 0 or 1. Thus, we transform (round) the output of the neuron with a threshold of 0.5. Each weight of the neural network is represented by an 8-bit string.

Selecting the appropriate fitness function is a rather complicated task. A bitstring which represents a set of weights, is evaluated in terms of the effectiveness of the neural net. Thus, the fitness function must transform the bitstring in decimals, put them as weights in the net, test the net with the total set of inputs and finally return a value indicating the effectiveness of the net, under these weights. Although the method appears to be complicated and slow, the experimental results in fact suggest that it is much faster than the back propagation algorithm.

The procedure is repeated, optimizing the weights. As the number of bits (72) is big, its better to use the SOFT with 2-replacements. Performance results, show that this is the best choice as far as speed is concerned.

4. Experimental Results

The gradient descent training algorithm used in back propagation neural networks although it is simple it seems to be inefficient in terms of quality and speed. In complicated problems, it usually fails to find the best or at least a satisfactory solution. In addition, the training timing is prohibitive for large scale problems like, for example, in identification-classification problems in computer vision.

The training of a neural net is actually a global optimization problem. As a consequence, we can apply alternative optimization methods. From this perspective, genetic algorithms in general and the SOFT methodology in particular, prove to be much more efficient in terms of quality and speed. An alternative technique, is a hybrid form of a genetic algorithm and back propagation. Under this scheme, the genetic algorithm is applied first, finding an efficient solution (probably the best) and then the back propagation method is used to improve precision.

Tables 1, 2 and 3, show the efficiency of the proposed technique in comparison with the back propagation algorithm in three types of neural nets. SOFT-1, 2, 3 refers to the SOFT algorithm with 1, 2 and 3 replacements respectively. The mean time is the average of the network training times. Actual time is the sum of the training time and the time needed for the instantiation of parameters with proper values. The success ratio is the rate of the correct function approximations without restarting.

5. Conclusions

We have shown a method for neural network acceleration of training using SOFT (single-offspring technique) which is a rather simple Genetic Algorithm operation. Experiments with several neural architectures have been performed involving three different variations of the SOFT algorithm. From the experimental results we have found that the SOFT with *2-replacements* algorithm, provides the best, that is the fastest solution to the training problem. We also notice, that in general the technique doesn't increase the actual time. This is because no parameter adjustment is needed. In addition, we must mention that in large scale problems, the actual time is not much more than the mean time, as it has been observed in the sample example presented in this paper.

6. References

Harp, S., T. Samad, and A. Guha, "Designing Application Specific Neural Networks Using the Genetic Algorithm," *Advances in Neural Information Processing Systems 2*, D. S. Touretzky, Editor, San Mateo, CA, Morgan Kaufmann, 1990.

Harp, S., T. Samad, and A. Guha, "Towards the Genetic Synthesis of Neural Networks," *Proceedings of the Third International Conference on Genetic Algorithms*, San Mateo, CA, Morgan Kaufmann, 1989.

Harp, S., Tariq Samad, "Genetic Optimization of Neural Network Architectures for electric Utility Applications," Final Report, Electric Power Research Institute, Research Project No. 8016-04, Palo Alto, CA March 1994.

Holland J.H., "Genetic Algorithms," *Scientific America*, Vol. 267, pp. 66-72, July 1992.

Holland J.H., *Adaptation in Natural and Artificial Systems*, University of Michigan Press, Ann Arbor, MI, 1975.

Koza, J.R., Keane, M.A., "Cart Centering and Broom Balancing by Genetically Breeding Populations of Control Strategy Programs," *Proc. of IJCNN-90-Wash.-DC*, Washington, DC, January 1990.

Moricic, B., Nikolov, Z., "GENNET - System for Computer Aided Neural Network Design Using Genetic Algorithms," *Proc. of IJCNN-90-Wash.-DC*, Washington, DC, January 1990.

Tsoukalas, L.H. and Uhrig, R.E., Fuzzy and Neural Approaches in Engineering, John Wiley & Sons, New York, 1997.

Welstead, S.T., *Neural Network and Fuzzy Logic Applications in C/C++*, John Wiley and Sons, New York, NY, 1994.

Whitely, D., Bogart, C., "Optimizing Neural Networks using Faster, More Accurate Genetic Search," *Proc. of the Third International Conference on Genetic Algorithms*, Morgan Kaufmann, 1989.

Whitely, D., Bogart, C., "The Evolution of Connectivity: Pruning Neural Networks using Genetic Algorithms," *Proc. of IJCNN-90-Wash.-DC*, Washington, DC, January 1990.

Table 1 Results of applying SOFT to a 2x2x1 neural network.

	BP	SOFT-1	SOFT-2	SOFT-3
Mean Time	10 sec	28 sec	4 sec	8 sec
Real Time	78 sec	28 sec	4 sec	8 sec
Success Ratio	25 %	8 %	25 %	85 %

Table 2 Results of applying SOFT to a 2x3x1 neural network.

	BP	SOFT-1	SOFT-2	SOFT-3
Mean Time	8 sec	17 sec	3 sec	14 sec
Real Time	47 sec	17 sec	3 sec	14 sec
Success Ratio	85 %	8 %	92 %	100 %

Table 3 Results of applying SOFT to a 2x5x1 neural network.

	BP	SOFT-1	SOFT-2	SOFT-3
Mean Time	5 sec	11 sec	4 sec	19 sec
Real Time	45 sec	11 sec	4 sec	19 sec
Success Ratio	98 %	86 %	100 %	100 %

A Scalable Distributed Heterogeneous Associative Logic Programming System

Stephen W. Ryan and Arvind K. Bansal
Department of Mathematics and Computer Science
Kent State University, Kent, OH 44242 - 0001, USA
E-mail: sryan@mcs.kent.edu and arvind@mcs.kent.edu

Abstract

This paper describes a distributed implementation of a scalable heterogeneous associative logic programming model, and describes an abstract instruction set for the distributed version of the model. Associative computation exploits data parallel computation. The implementation uses PVM for architecture independence, and uses object oriented programming for modularity and portability. Performance results on a cluster of IBM RS 6000 are presented.

Keywords: Artificial intelligence, Associative computing, Data-parallel computing, Distributed Computing, Heterogeneous computing, Logic programming, Knowledge base, Scalable high performance computing, Symbolic computing

1. Introduction

The advent of fast distributed networks has made it possible to distribute large knowledge bases over multiple computer systems, and to partition complex computing tasks by distributing sub-tasks over multiple processors. Different types of sub-tasks, a symbolic versus a numeric task for example, can be mapped onto processors of different architectures according to their capability. This is known as heterogeneous distributed computing.

In this paper, we describe an architecture and a distributed implementation of a heterogeneous distributed associative logic programming model based upon the theory developed in [4]. In this model, the Logic programming paradigm, heterogeneous computing, the associative computing paradigm, and the object oriented paradigm have been integrated. Logic programming provides a declarative programming model, the PVM message passing library provides architecture independence, the low level implementation using the object oriented paradigm provides modularity, and associative computing integrates data parallel computing with associative search by content.

The distributed heterogeneous associative model distributes knowledge on multiple servers either based upon the different domains or to exploit data parallelism. A coordinator is used for coordinating and collecting data from servers, while major processing is done within the servers.

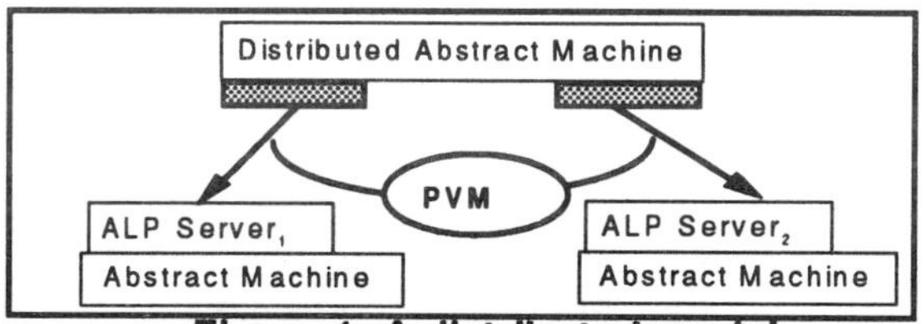

Figure 1: A distributed model

We believe that the model is suited for complex computation involving knowledge retrieval from distributed sources and the integration of symbolic and numeric computing. The distributed model consists of multiple cells each executing a sub-component of a complex computation. Each cell consists of a coordinator and multiple servers where the servers could be suited either for knowledge retrieval, symbolic computing or numeric computing.

The main contributions of this paper are as follows:

1. The model is mapped to a heterogeneous set of architectures in a user transparent manner.
2. The model supports modularity, and is scalable to any number of machines.

2. Background and Definitions

In this section, we briefly describe the related concepts of four paradigms: associative computing, heterogeneous computing, logic programming, and object-oriented paradigm.

Associative Computing searches and selects data elements for processing according to their contents [9, 10]. Data records are distributed among the processors, forming a table of parallel fields or *associated vectors* such that the data elements in associated vectors are accessed using the same index value. Vectors are processed simultaneously by broadcasting a single instruction to all processors. The results of the computation forms a new associated vector. A *filter vector* is an associated vector of Boolean values resulting from a data parallel logical operation. Filter vectors are used to select records for further processing.

Data parallel computing refers to simultaneous execution of some abstract computation on multiple data elements. Distributed computing refers to the distribution of computation over multiple computer systems and encompasses both the data parallel and process parallel computing models. In the absence of data dependency, distributing a computation can result in a near linear speed up.

The object-oriented programming paradigm is well suited to distributed computing using message passing between objects. The sub-components of a computation are isolated and encapsulated in 'objects'. An object acts as a client by making a request to another object for some data or for some function to be performed. The receiving object acts as a server by replying to the client with the requested information.

Parallel Virtual Machine (PVM) [12] is a library of message passing functions which allows processes on a heterogeneous network of computer systems to communicate and exchange data. The use of PVM makes the data transfer and network communication transparent to the user.

Logic programming [8] is a popular declarative paradigm suitable for high-level reasoning and knowledge representation. In a logic program, knowledge is represented by a set of facts and rules which describe relationships between data objects.

2.1. The Heterogeneous Associative Model

The heterogeneous associative logic programming model [4] exploits associative search to match the clause-heads with the query in a data parallel manner, and exploits compiled execution of clause bodies.

The data structures in this model are: the program representation — an associative table with parallel fields for the names and arguments in the clause heads, a data parallel environment associated with the program representation, a set of global registers, an associative control stack, and an associative table to handle aliasing of logical variables. The global registers are analogous to those in the Warren Abstract Machine [13], and are used to store pointers to variable bindings. The control stack contains information about the current state of execution and uses associative vectors to facilitate fast backtracking. Variable aliases are indicated by filter vectors and are tracked by the alias management table. A detailed explanation of this model and the corresponding abstract instructions is given in [2, 3, 4].

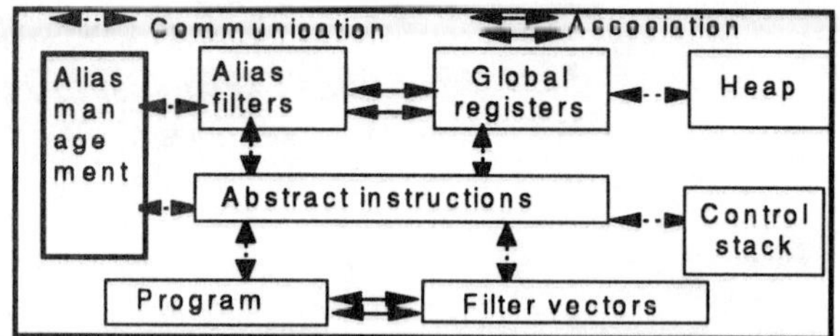

Figure 2: A heterogeneous associative model

Example 1:

p(1, 2). p(2, 3). p(3, 4). p(X, Y) :- q(Y, X).

q(2, 1). q(3, 2). q(4, 3). q(5, 4).

r(2, 2). r(X, Y) :- p(X, X1), q(X2, Y).

Example 1 illustrates a simple logic program. The corresponding compiled abstract instruction code is given in Figure 3. A symbol <P_n> denotes a procedure, a symbol <U_n> denotes a universal filter vector, a symbol <L_n> or <DP_n> denotes a program label, a symbol <B_n> denotes the binding filter vector, a symbol <C_n> denotes a clause filter vector, and a symbol <A_n> denotes the *nth* argument of the current predicate.

```
DP0:  match_register_arg       A0, U0
      test_and_backtrack       U0
      match_register_arg       A1, U0
      test_and_backtrack       U0
      and_bit_vectors          F0,U0, B0
      store_vector_id          B0, A0
      store_vector_id          B0, A1
      compliment_bit_vector    F0, T1
      and_bit_vectors          T1, U0, C0
      test_and_return          B0, L10
L10:  try_me_else              C0
R3:   copy_logical_register    A1, A0, P1
      copy_logical_register    A0, A1, P1
      call                     DP0, P1
      return
DP1:  match_register_arg       A0, U0
      test_and_backtrack       U0
      match_register_arg       A1, U0
      test_and_backtrack       U0
      and_bit_vectors          F0, U0, B0
      store_vector_id          B0, A0
      store_vector_id          B0, A1
      compliment_bit_vector    F0, T1
```

	and_bit_vectors	T_1, U_0, C_0
	test_and_return	B_0, L_{25}
L25:	try_me_else	C_0
DP_2:	match_register_arg	A_0, U_0
	test_and_backtrack	U_0
	match_register_arg	A_1, U_0
	test_and_backtrack	U_0
	and_bit_vectors	F_0, U_0, B_0
	store_vector_id	B_0, A_0
	store_vector_id	B_0, A_1
	compliment_bit_vector	F_0, T_1
	and_bit_vectors	T_1, U_0, C_0
	test_and_return	B_0, L_{36}
L_{36}:	try_me_else	C_0
R_1:	copy_logical_register	A_0, A_0, P_0
	load_new_variable	A_1, V_4, P_0
	call	DP_0, P_0
	continue	L_{40}
L_{41}:	load_new_variable	A_0, V_5, P_1
	copy_logical_register	A_1, A_1, P_1
	call	DP_0, P_1
	return	
LD:	load_program	PR_2
	load_program	PR_2
	load_program	PR_2

Figure 3: The compiled code for Example 1

We describe the general behavior of the instructions as follows.

There is one entry point in the code for each procedure in the logic program. First the goal arguments are matched with the arguments of the clause heads in a data parallel manner. The resulting filter-vector U_0 is ANDed with the filter-vector F_0 which annotates the ground facts. The resulting binding filter vector B_0 indicates the bindings of the goal arguments. The clause heads of rules are annotated by a clause filter-vector C_0. If facts were found, then control is returned. In the absence of matching facts or upon a request for more solutions, the compiled code for the rules is executed.

The compiled code for rules copies the goal arguments in global registers [3, 4] and calls the subgoals. The three *load_program* instructions load the three procedures in the program representation.

3. Object Oriented Implementation

This section describes an object model needed to provide modularity in the distributed execution of the heterogeneous associative logic program system

3.1. Class Hierarchy

There are two primary classes in the object model: the *abstract-machine* class and the *program* class. The *abstract-machine* class represents an abstract machine, and the *program* class encapsulates the associative representation of a logic program. Figure 4 illustrates the overall class structure.

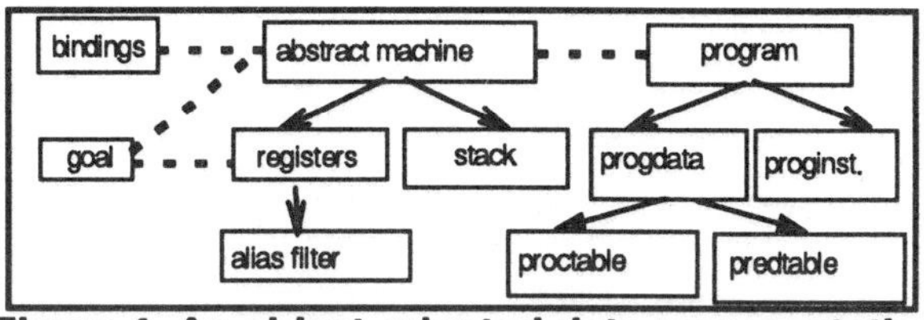

Figure 4: An object-oriented data representation

The public interface of the *abstract-machine* class allows for loading a program, solving a goal, requesting alternate solutions, and retrieving binding information for the goal arguments. The private member functions of the *abstract-machine* class include functions for executing the instruction code of the program, including the implementation of the abstract instruction set, and functions for backtracking and controlling the flow of the program. The two major subclasses of the *abstract-machine* class encapsulate the *registers* and the control *stack.*

The *program* class has two subclasses: *progdata* and *proginst*. The subclass *progdata* represents an associative table of clause-heads. The subclass *proginst* represents the compiled code for the clause bodies. The subclass *progdata* has two subclasses: *predtable* and *proctable*. The subclass *predtable* maps predicate names to a numeric predicate-id. The subclass *proctable* is used for fast lookup of the predicate and the entry point in the compiled code for each procedure. All of the components of the *program* class are public and manipulated directly by the abstract machine.

The associative data types are encapsulated in the two classes *associative-filter* and *associative-vector*. The *associative-filter* class represents an associative filter vector. It supports logical operations and assignment. The *associative-vector* class is used to represent associative data vectors. It is implemented using the C++ template facility to support arbitrary data types. Functions are provided to manipulate the associative vector using associative techniques.

4. The Distributed Heterogeneous System

The Distributed system consists of two types of abstract machines: a *coordinator* abstract machine and a *server abstract machine* (see Figure 5). The coordinator launches the server processes on a local or remote host. Each server has a heterogeneous associative abstract machine as described in Subsection 2.1, with the additional ability to receive goals and send solutions to the coordinator via a message passing paradigm. In addition, all servers share a procedure table with the coordinator.

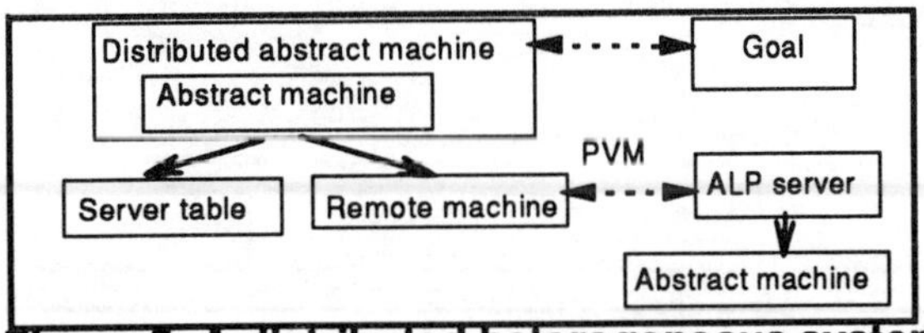

Figure 5: A distributed heterogeneous system

4.1. Abstract Data Structures

Two additional data structures — an associative server table and an associative binding area — are needed in the distributed model.

The *associative server table* stores the information about the predicates processed by the servers. For each server/procedure pair there is an entry of the form (*server-id, procedure-id, clause-count*) in the server table. The *server-id* uniquely identifies a server process. The *procedure-id* is a reference to the entry in the procedure table which describes a goal. The *clause-count* is the number of clauses the server has that match the goal.

The *associative binding area* stores the bindings incrementally as they are received from the servers. The data elements in associative binding area are *server-id, time-stamp, variable-id,* and the *value* and *type* of each bound argument. A filter vector associated to this table is used to identify the vectors bound to a register at a given time-stamp.

4.2. The Execution Model

A schema file prepared by the user specifies a list of remote hosts and the file names of the logic programs to be loaded onto the various hosts. The coordinator reads the schema file and initiates the server processes. After each server process has been successfully initialized and has loaded its program, it reports back to the coordinator with a list of the procedures it is able to serve. The coordinator builds up the server table from these reports.

To solve a goal, the coordinator performs an associative search on the server table to obtain a filter vector identifying all servers which have clauses that match the goal. The goal is broadcast to these servers. Upon receiving the message, each server first searches its facts and then its rules for a solution. After finding a set of solutions, the server waits for further instructions from the coordinator.

After broadcasting the goal, the coordinator queries each matching server for solutions. Each server, when prompted, transmits the bindings for the goal arguments to the coordinator. Anticipating further requests, the servers backtrack to find additional solutions. Meanwhile, the coordinator stores the received bindings in the associative binding area along with the current time-stamp and the server-id.

After collecting the solutions from all of the matching servers, the coordinator reports the solutions to the user. Upon further request from the user, the coordinator requests a new set of solutions from the matching servers. Additional bindings received from the servers are added to the associative binding area. A server sends *a failure* in the absence of additional solutions. After receiving a *failure*, the coordinator removes that server from the list of matching servers. This process is repeated until the list of servers is empty. When this occurs, the coordinating process backtracks and tries other rules.

4.3. Serving Multiple Subgoals

At a particular instance, a server might have solutions for more than one subgoal. After receiving a request to solve a subgoal, a server generates initial solutions. Upon request, the server sends the resulting bindings to the coordinator, and proceeds to generate alternate solutions. However, the coordinator's next request may be to solve the next subgoal instead of requesting the alternate solutions. The server then saves its state, including the alternate solutions to the first subgoal, and proceeds to solve the second subgoal. If the coordinator backtracks, it first requests more solutions to the second subgoal. After reporting *failure* to the coordinator, the server reverts back to its previous state with the alternate solutions to the first subgoal. The coordinator receives the *failure* message and removes this server from the list of servers for the second subgoal. If the list of servers becomes empty for the second subgoal, the coordinator backtracks and requests the alternate solutions to the first subgoal.

4.4. Distributed Abstract Instructions

There are four new abstract instructions in the coordinating abstract machine [12]: *get_servers, broadcast_goal, receive_binding,* and *repeat_else_try* that facilitate distributed processing.

The *get-servers* instruction takes a procedure-id as an argument and returns a filter vector which identifies the servers that can solve that goal.

The *broadcast_goal* instruction broadcasts a goal to the servers indicated by a server filter vector.

The *receive_binding* instruction is executed repeatedly to retrieve the bindings from the servers. The arguments for a *receive-bindings* instruction are a server vector and a binding vector. The bindings from each server in the server table are added to the associative binding area. The binding filter vector points to the new binding vectors. If all the matching servers transmit *failure*, this instruction releases the repeat label from the control stack, and the coordinator backtracks.

The abstract instruction *repeat_else_try* enables the repeated execution of the *receive_bindings* instruction with the capability to backtrack in the absence of bindings. It puts a repeat label and *try_me_else* label on the control stack which control the execution of the *receive_bindings* instruction.

5. A Distributed Logic Program Example

In this section, we present the execution trace of a simple logic program distributed over two servers.

Server 1	Server 2
p(1, 2). p(2, 3). p(3, 4).	p(1, 4). p(2, 5). p(3, 6).
p(X,Y) :- q(Y,X).	same as server 1.
q(2, 1). q(3, 2).	q(4, 3). q(5, 4).
q(2, 6). q(3, 7).	q(4, 8). q(5, 9).
r(2,2).	r(2, 3).
r(X, Y) :- p(X, X1), q(X2, Y).	same as server 1.

To simplify the trace, the programs in both servers have the same structure and differ only in their facts. The distributed compiled code is given in Figure 7.

```
DP0:  get_servers            P0, U0
      test_and_backtrack     U0
      broadcast_goal         P0, U0
      repeat_else_try        L4, L9
L4:   receive_bindings       U0, B0
      store_vector_id        B0, Arg0
      store_vector_id        B0, A1
      test_and_backtrack     B0
      return
L9:   try_me_else            R0
R3:   copy_logical_register  A1, A0, P1
      copy_logical_register  A0, A1, P1
      call                   DP0, P1
      return
DP1:  get_servers            P1, U0
      test_and_backtrack     U0
      broadcast_goal         P1, U0
      repeat_else_try        L18, L23
L18:  receive_bindings       U0, B0
      store_vector_id        B0, A0
      store_vector_id        B0, A1
      test_and_backtrack     B0
      return
L23:  try_me_else            R0
DP2:  get_servers            P2, U0
      test_and_backtrack     U0
      broadcast_goal         P2, U0
      repeat_else_try        L28, L33
L28:  receive_bindings       U0, B0
      store_vector_id        B0, A0
      store_vector_id        B0, A1
      test_and_backtrack     B0
      return
L33:  try_me_else            R0
R1:   copy_logical_register  A0, A0, P0
      load_new_variable      A1, V4, P0
      call                   DP0, P0
      continue               L37
L38:  load_new_variable      A0, V5, P1
      copy_logical_register  A1, A1, P1
      call                   DP0, P1
      return
LD:   load_program           PR2
      load_program           PR2
      load_program           PR2
```

Figure 7: The distributed compiled code

5.1. The Distributed Abstract Machine

To create a distributed abstract machine, a schema file with the host and path-name for each program is prepared as follows:

host1.domain1 /path/on/host1/program1
host2.domain2 /path/on/host2/program2

The command "dalps program schema" initiates the coordinator process. The first argument (the file name of the coordinator's program) is used to create a program object. A distributed abstract machine is then instantiated to execute the program. The coordinator process reads the schema file, and creates a server process for each entry.

Every server is implemented individually as a remote abstract machine object. The remote abstract machine spawns a server process on the specified host using PVM, loads the specified program into the server, and then acts as a communication interface between the coordinator and the server.

After creating the remote abstract machines, the distributed abstract machine requests each server to transmit a list of its procedures. This information is inserted into the server table as shown in Table 1.

Table 1. The server table for Example 2

Server	Procedure-list
1	0, 1, 2
2	0, 1, 2

5.2. An Execution Trace of the Coordinator

Let us suppose that the user enters the goal *p(X, Y)*. The distributed abstract machine initializes registers for the arguments *X* and *Y*, and starts executing the instructions from the label DP_0.

The *get_servers* instruction performs an associative match against the server table with the procedure P_0. The resulting universal filter vector U_0 represents matching servers. The *test_and_backtrack* instruction tests U_0. In the absence of servers, this instruction triggers a backtrack of the coordinator. In this example, the filter vector U_0 identifies two servers.

The *broadcast_goal* instruction builds a goal consisting of procedure P_0 and the two unbound arguments, and broadcasts the goal to the servers indicated by the universal filter vector U_0.

The *repeat_else_try* instruction puts the repeat label L_4 on the control stack. After the return instruction sees the label L_4 on the stack, the program counter is reset to L_4, and the execution of the following code is repeated. A *try_me_else* label is also placed on the stack to handle failure. Upon backtracking, the control is transferred to the location given by the *try_me_else* label. The *receive_bindings* instruction is used to report the bindings for the goal arguments from each eligible server. The initial set of received bindings corresponds to the ground facts. In this example, server 1 returns the bindings *p(1,2)*, *p(2,3)* and *p(3,4)*; and server 2 returns the bindings *p(1,4)*, *p(2,5)* and *p(3,6)*. The distributed abstract machine adds these bindings to its associative binding area as illustrated in Table 2.

Table 2: The binding area (first bindings)

Index	Server	Time-stamp	Argument 1	Argument 2
0	1	0	1	2
1	1	0	2	3
2	1	0	1	4
3	2	0	1	4
4	2	0	2	5
5	2	0	3	6

The distributed abstract machine builds a binding vector B_0 against the associative binding area by matching against the current timestamp *0*. The next two *store_vector_id* instructions store a pointer to the binding vector B_0 in the registers for both the arguments. The *test_and_backtrack* instruction would backtrack for empty binding vector B_0; and the control would be transferred to the *try_me_else* label L_9. Since B_0 is not empty, the return instruction places the repeat label L_4 in the program counter and returns. The distributed abstract machine reports the current bindings to the user and waits. Upon further request from the user, the distributed abstract machine resumes execution at label L_4, and requests bindings from the servers. The bindings for the rule *p(X, Y) :- q(Y, X)* are added to the associative binding area at timestamp *1* as illustrated in Table 3.

Table 3. The binding area (second bindings)

Index	Server	Time-stamp	Argument1	Argument2
0	1	0	1	2
1	1	0	2	3
2	1	0	3	4
3	2	0	1	4
4	2	0	2	5
5	2	0	3	6
6	1	1	1	2
7	1	1	2	3
8	1	1	3	4
9	1	1	4	5
10	2	1	6	2
11	2	1	7	3
12	2	1	8	4

The distributed abstract machine again builds a new binding vector B_0 by matching against the timestamp 1. The instructions *store_vector_id*, *test_and_backtrack* and *return* are executed as before, and the new bindings are reported to the user. Upon further request from the user, the control is transferred to the repeat label L_4. This time the *receive_bindings* instruction fails in the absence of additional solution for p/2 from the servers. The repeat label is removed from the control stack, and control is transferred to the *try_me_else* label L_9. The *try_me_else* instruction transfers control to the code for the rule at the label R_3. The *copy_logical_register* instructions allocate new registers for the arguments to the subgoal *q(Y, X)*. The *call* instruction then transfers control to the label DP_1 — the entry point for the compiled code of the procedure *q/2*. Both the servers are requested to solve the goal *q/2*. The bindings from their ground facts are added to the associative binding area. Requests for further bindings result in *failure*, and the execution terminates.

5.3. An Execution Trace of the Servers

Here we trace the execution of the servers. The code executed by the servers is illustrated in Figure 3, and the various states of the servers are illustrated in Table 4.

Let us assume that a user gives the goal *r(X, Y)* to the coordinating process. The distributed abstract machine broadcasts the goal to the matching servers. Upon receiving the goal, the servers load their registers with the given arguments and start executing their instruction code at label DP_2. First the *match_register_arg* instruction identifies all of the matching clauses. For the first server, the filter vector points to the fact *r(2, 2)* and the rule *r(X, Y) :- p(X, X1), q(X2, Y)*. The resulting filter vector is AND'ed with the fact filter, F0, and the result is stored as the binding for the two arguments. The complement of this filter vector, which represents the matching rules, is saved for further processing. The binding filter vector is then tested. Since the binding vector is not empty, the program returns the control. The server waits in state 1 for further instructions.

Table 4: Different states of the servers

State	Time	Description
1	1	bindings from r/2 ground facts
2	2	bindings from r/2 - first solution
3	3	bindings from r/2 - second solution
4	4	no more solution for r/2
5	4	bindings from p/2 ground facts
6	5	bindings from p/2 rule
7	5	solution from p/2 rule
7	6	solution from q/2
8	5	second solution from p/2 rule
8	7	no more solution of q/2
9	5	second solution from p/2 rule
10	6	no more solution for p/2
11	6	no more solution for p/2
11	7	solution from q/2 ground facts
12	6	no more solutions for p/2
12	7	no more solution for q/2
13	6	no more solution for p/2

Upon receiving the next request for bindings from the coordinator, the server extracts the bindings from the registers to get the vector of values. After transmitting the bindings (*2* and *2* in this example), the server looks for additional solutions. In this example, the server returns control to the *try_me_else* instruction at label L_{36}. The control is transferred to the code of the only rule for the procedure *r/2*, at label R_1. The server sets up the arguments and calls the procedures *p/2* and *q/2*. The server finds another set of bindings for r/2, and waits in State 2 for further instructions from the coordinator.

After receiving a request for the second set of bindings, the server sends the bindings to the coordinator. As before, the server resumes search for additional solutions. This time the server backtracks, and picks up the additional solutions derived from the rule *p(X, Y) :- q(Y, X)* as given by State 3.

The server sends the requested bindings, and tries for additional solutions. This time the server (in State 4) replies with *failure*. Upon receiving this message, the coordinator uses the rule for the procedure *r/2*, and requests the server to solve the subgoal *p(X, Y)*. The server complies with the request and waits on state 5.

When requested, the server sends the bindings corresponding to its ground facts for the procedure *p/2*, and searches for additional solutions given by the rule *p(X, Y) :- q(X, Y)*.

Since the coordinator is working on the rule *r(X, Y) :- p(X, X1), q(X2, Y)*, its next request is to solve the goal *q/2*. Upon receiving this request, the server increments its register and control stack pointers and begins working on the new goal. The second set of bindings for the previous goal *p/2* is unreported but is not overwritten due to the incrementing of the pointers. The bindings corresponding to the ground facts for the procedure *q/2* become the new current bindings as shown by State 7. Upon request from the coordinator, the servers report the current bindings for *q/2*. Since there are no additional solutions, the query fails as shown in State 8.

The coordinator reports the solutions of *p/2* and *q/2* to the user. On a request for additional solutions, the coordinator backtracks to the rule *r(X, Y) :- p(X, X1), q(X2, Y)*, and requests additional solutions to the subgoal *q/2*. The server reports *failure* upon the coordinator's request. The abstract machine of the server backtracks to the state prior to receiving the request to solve the goal *q/2*, and awaits the next request from the coordinator (see State 9). The current bindings are now the second solution previously determined for the goal *p/2*. The coordinator backtracks to the subgoal *p/2*, and broadcasts a request for additional bindings for *p/2*. After receiving the new solutions to the subgoal p/2, the coordinator continues execution of the rule and requests the servers for solutions to the subgoal q/2. The servers save the current state of the goal p/2, and compute solutions for the goal q/2 (see State 11).

On request, the server returns the solutions for q/2. The server *fails* to find additional solutions for the goal *q/2* (see State 12).

When the coordinator backtracks and requests more solutions to the subgoal *q/2*, the server responds with *failure* and decrements its register and control pointers (see State 13). The coordinator continues to backtrack, and asks the server for additional solutions for the first subgoal *p/2*. The server again responds with *failure*, and empties it's control stack. The coordinator finally fails.

6. Performance Evaluation

We tested the non-distributed (single processor) version of the abstract machine against the distributed version using a knowledge base of 20,000 facts. For the distributed version, we tested configurations of two, four, six, and eight IBM RS/6000 processors (with the facts distributed evenly on each) to study the overhead in going to a distributed paradigm. The results are summarized in

Table 5. We conclude that there is definitely a speedup to be gained by distributing the data. The break-even point, where the communication costs negate any further distribution of the data, seems to be at six processors with a granularity of 3,333 facts.

Table 5: Performance results

Processors	Facts	Time
1	20000	230 ms
2	10000	130 ms
4	5000	90 ms
6	3333	90 ms
8	2500	120 ms

These tests show that the granularity of the data (for this test environment) should be more than 3,000 facts per processor. The model is thus appropriate for distributing large knowledge bases. Allowing processors to perform more local computation will further reduce the communication overhead.

7. Current Limitations and Future Work

It would be desirable to automate the distribution of data and the creation of servers based on run-time requirements.

The template-based implementation of associative vectors has made it possible to handle complex data types. However, implementation of complex data-types is still underway.

It is possible to have access to a vast and widely distributed knowledge base using loose communication between multiple coordinators since the servers report to their coordinator about their capabilities. The formal model of communication between coordinators of different cells still has to be developed.

With the addition of complex data types and further refinement of the communication model, it will be possible to integrate other types of servers (specializing in numerical computation, for example).

8. Conclusion

In this paper, we have discussed a generic architecture independent abstract machine for the distributed execution of logic programs on a heterogeneous collection of architectures. The object oriented implementation is portable, flexible and extensible. The use of the PVM message passing library provides scalability and architecture independence. The performance results show that distributing the data provides significant performance improvement. More local processing will reduce overhead due to data transfer and can further improve performance.

Acknowledgments

The first author was supported by the summer internship program at the NASA Lewis Research Center in Cleveland, Ohio. We thank Greg Follen at NASA for that support and for providing the equipment and facilities to run the benchmarks. This work provides the basis for further research supported by a NASA GSRP grant from the NASA Lewis Research Center.

References

1. A. K. Bansal, and J. L. Potter, "An Associative Model to Minimize Matching and Backtracking Overhead in Logic Programs with Large Knowledge Bases," *The International Journal of Engineering Applications of Artificial Intelligence, Volume 5, Number 3,* (1992) pp. 247-262
2. A. K. Bansal, "An Associative Model to Integrate Knowledge Retrieval and Data-parallel Computation," *International Journal on Artificial Intelligence Tools, Volume 3, Number 1,* (1994), pp. 97 - 125.
3. A. K. Bansal, L. Prasad, and M. Ghandikota, "A Formal Associative Model of Logic Programming and its Abstract Instruction Set," *Proceedings of the International Conference of Tools with Artificial Intelligence,* (1994), pp. 145--151.
4. A. K. Bansal, "A Framework of Heterogeneous Associative Logic Programming," *International Journal of Artificial Intelligence Tools, Vol. 4, Nos. 1 & 2,* (1995), pp. 33 - 53.
5. J. A. Feldman, and D. Rovner, "An Algol Based Associative Language," *Communications of the ACM, Volume 12, Number 8,* (1969) pp. 439 - 449.
6. D. Gries, *The Science of Programming*, Monograph, Springer Verlag, New York, 1987.
7. K. Hwang, and F. A. Briggs, *Computer Architecture and Parallel Processing*, Mcgraw Hill Book Company, New york, USA, (1984).
8. R. Kowalski, *Logic for Problem Solving*, Elsevier-North Holland, (1979).
9. J. L. Potter, *Associative Computing*, Plenum Publishers, New York, (1992).
10. J. Potter, J. Baker, A. K. Bansal, S. Scott, C. Ashtagiri, "Associative Model of Computing," *IEEE Computer*, November 1994, 19 - 25
11. S. Ryan, "Scalable High Performance Distributed Execution of Heterogeneous Associative Model of Logic Programming," *MS Thesis,* Department of Mathematics and Computer Science, Kent State University, Kent, OH 44242, January 1996, 83 pages.
12. V. S. Sunderam et. al., "PVM: A Framework for Parallel Distributed Computing," *Concurrency: Practice and Experience, No. 2,* (1990), pp. 315 - 339.
13. D. H. D. Warren, "An Abstract Prolog Instruction Set," *Technical Report 309*, SRI International, (1983).

Using the Particle Swarm Optimization Technique to train a Recurrent Neural Model

John Salerno
Rome Laboratory, Rome NY

Abstract

This paper discusses the results of implementing an evolutionary learning technique entitled "Particle Swarm Optimization" as described by Kennedy and Eberhart [3]. We present a number of results using this technique on a number of neural model architectures using the XOR problem and then conclude applying it to a "real" problem - parsing natural language phrases.

1. Introduction

Researchers involved in the implementation of neural models are very familiar with the Backpropagation (BP) Learning Algorithm as defined by Rumelhart, Williams and Hinton [4] and the problems encountered with its use. Among these problems are: (1) the speed of convergence and (2) getting stuck in a local minimum. There have been many techniques introduced in an attempt to resolve these issues.

In the following paragraphs we will look at two different neural models and two different learning techniques to solve the XOR problem. We first look at a simple multi-layered feed forward model using both the BP Learning Algorithm and the Particle Swarm Optimization Technique. We varied the gain values associated with this algorithm and compared the results with that of the BP Algorithm.

After looking at the first model, we turned our attention to a recurrent model as presented by Elman [1] and again implemented both learning techniques and compare the results. We conclude our discussion by applying this technique to solve a "real" problem - the parsing of natural language phrases into a fixed size mapping.

2. The Multi-Layered Feed Forward Model

The Multi-Layered Feed Forward Model, shown in Fig. 1, was trained using the BP Learning Algorithm. We have extended this algorithm by adding a momentum term (also used by Rumelhart, etal) and a noise term. The noise term is introduced as part of the error calculation of the output errors and was first used by Fahlman [2]. This term, referred in this paper as the Fahlman Constant (FC), can reduce the overall number of epochs and in some cases, the error to learn the training set.

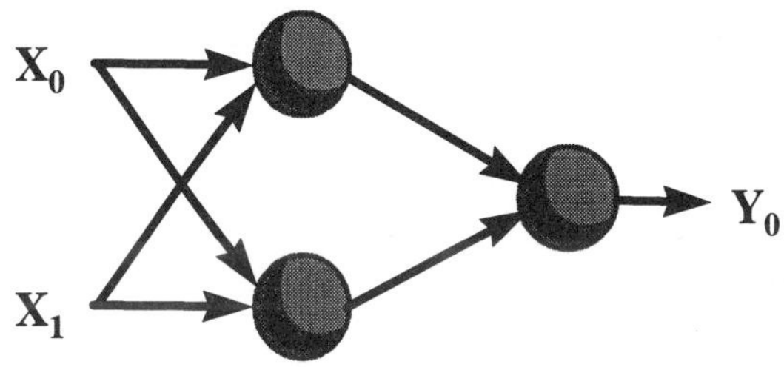

Figure 1. XOR Multi-Layer Feed Forward Model

The program was next modified to use the Particle Swarm Algorithm. The algorithm begins by randomly creating a number of models and then finding which one produces the best results (referred to as the global best). Each model is then updated based upon its previous best and the global best. The first question we needed to address was "How many models do we use?". To answer this question we fixed our initial set of weights and varied the number of models (5, 10, 20, 40, 50, 80). The results of this set of runs indicated that we achieved the optimum results with 40 models.

The initial state for each model for each run (i.e., weights) was varied. Two runs were made: (1) restricting the initial weights to be between -.1 and +.1 and (2) relaxing the initial weights between -1 and +1. Each model was run for each variable set until we successfully learned the training set 10 times. The lowest and highest values were then thrown out and the remaining eight averaged. To compare our results we look at the total number of epochs required to successfully learn the training set and the percent number of runs that resulted in the model unable to learn the problem.

1082-3409/97 $10.00 © 1997 IEEE

2.1 Training Results

Our first set of runs used the Backpropagation Learning Algorithm to learn the XOR problem. We varied the gain (or learning rate) in increments of .1. We then took the "best" value and added a momentum term. We again took the "best" value and added a noise constant.

The best that our Backpropagation Algorithm achieved (when the initial weights were restricted between -.1 and .1) was to learn the XOR problem in 2,250 epochs (Learning Rate (LR) = .6 and the Momentum Gain (MG) = .1), however not without the network getting stuck in a local minimum 29% of the time. The best overall was found with LR = .4 and MG = 0. This resulted in the model learning our problem in 4,638 epochs and the model not getting into a local minimum. When we relaxed the initial weight constraints such that they may fall within the interval of -1 and 1, our model was able to learn the XOR problem within 83 epochs, but with a 29% chance of getting into a local minimum. The overall best we could achieve was 388 epochs when we set the LR = .7 and MG = .6.

We next implemented the Particle Swarm Technique and ran each set of values for 10 runs and averaged them in a similar manner as before. Fig. 2 provides the results of varying both the local gain and global gain.

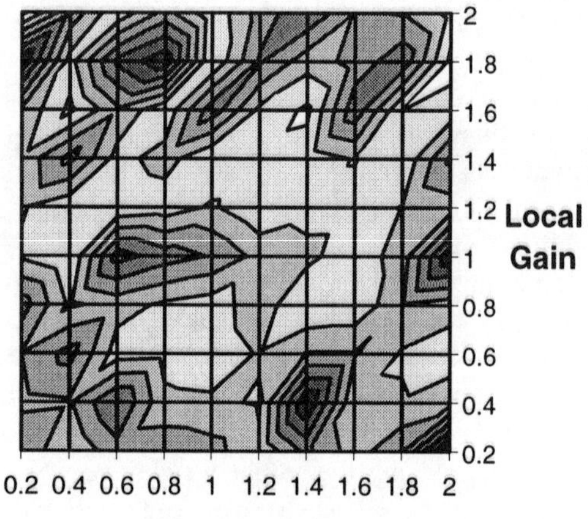

Figure 2. Varying Global and Local Gains for Particle Swarm

Using the Particle Swarm Algorithm we were able to learn the XOR problem in 29 epochs with a 9% chance of not learning. The best overall was achieved when the local gain was set to 1.6 and the global gain set to 1.4. These values resulted in the model learning the problem in 40 epochs and every run reaching a solution. Fig. 3 shows the results when we relaxed our initial weights within interval of (-1, +1). In this case we were able to train the model in 9 epochs (local gain set to 1.0 and the global gain set to 1.6) without getting stuck in a local minimum.

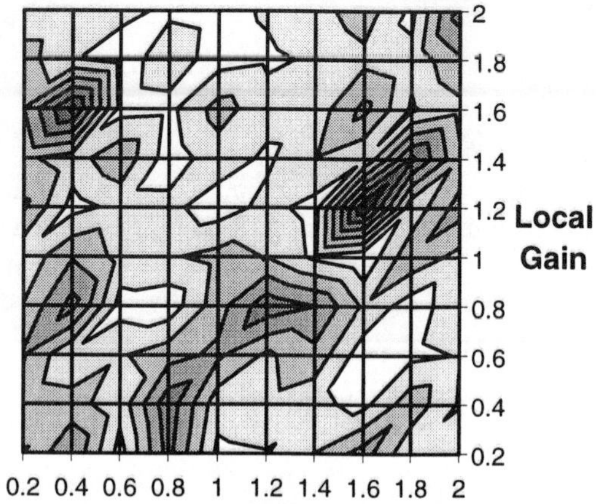

Figure 3. Varying Global and Local Gains for Particle Swarm

2.2 Comparison of Techniques

Let us consider the Particle Swarm Technique first. When the initial weights were initially set between -.1 and +.1, the overall average across all values was 135 epochs with 61 values being below the average and 39 above. When the initial weights were relaxed, the overall average decreased to a value of 95 with 62 of these values being below and 38 above.

We next took the values obtained for each of the gain pairs for the percent of runs that resulted in a local minimum and plotted them in the histogram shown in Fig. 4.

As we can see, using a larger interval had very little impact on whether a run successfully trained or not. For the XOR problem using a multi-layered feed forward model, the Particle Swarm Technique provided significantly better results. Relaxing the initial weights yielded the best results. The total number of epochs for the Backpropagation Algorithm was reduced from 83 epochs to 9 for the Particle Swarm Technique - an 89% reduction. Fahlman (1986) reported that Quickprop was able to learn the training set on average in 24 epochs.

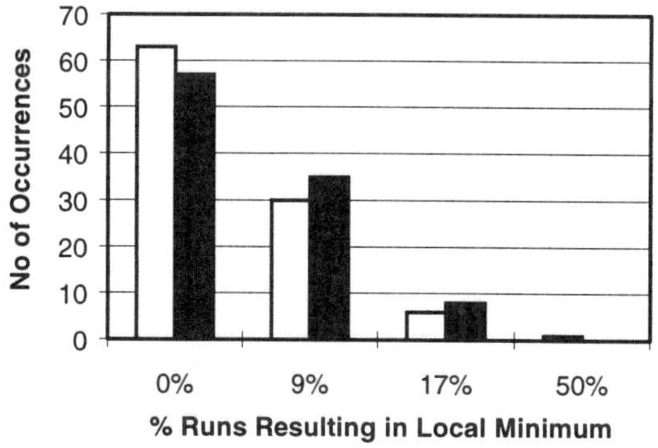

Figure 4. Comparison of Results

3. The Recurrent Model

We next followed a similar process with our recurrent model. Elman developed a neural model which was designed to take into account temporal information. Many of his experiments dealt with prediction and attempted to learn a time series function. Latter work (Miikkulainen [5]) used Elman's model to develop a temporal to spatial mapping. To further explain this difference in philosophy let us use the XOR problem. In his experiments, Elman presented his model with a continuous binary input stream such that after presenting the model with two inputs (one at a time), the output of the model would be the answer to the XOR problem. With only one input the network had a 50% chance of providing the correct results.

Miikkulainen used this model to take a temporal variable input (English phrase) and map it into a fixed size case frame representation. Thus this problem can be said to be a temporal to spatial mapping. Using Elman's model and the way in which he trained his model, there is no way to just provide the model with a set of discrete inputs and expect the model to learn the correct answer. This is due to the nature of the patterns. The output of the model is the probability of what the output will be. Since the training set contains two patterns ((0,0), (1,1)) which result in an output of a 0 and two ((0,1), (1,0)) with an output of 1, the model will continuously get stuck at the value of .5 for all training patterns. To overcome this problem we must provide a terminator value. In the case for Miikkulainen or parsing phrases, the terminator is a period. In our problem (XOR) we used the value of .5.

Fig. 5 provides the model used to solve the XOR problem using Elman's recurrent model.

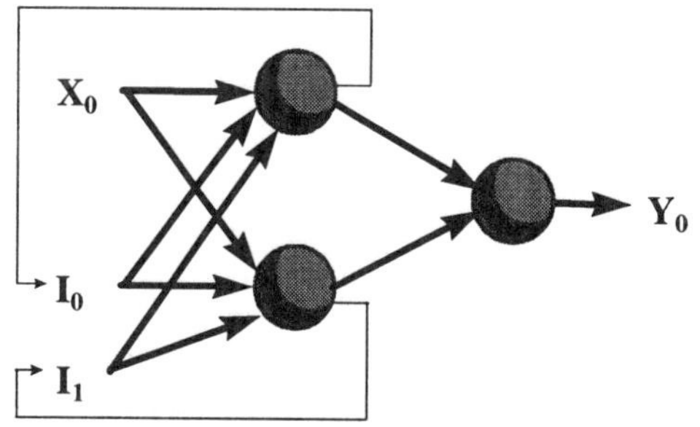

Figure 5. Recurrent XOR Model

Each input is presented one at a time and the output is read after the terminator is propagated through the model.

3.1 Results

The model was trained using the BP Algorithm with both a momentum term and the addition of a noise. When we allowed the initial weights to fall within the interval of -.1 and +.1, the best we were able to obtain was to learn the problem in 10,623 epochs (when LR = .6, MG = 0 and FC = .05). Relaxing the initial weights (between -1 and +1) yielded marginal returns. The best we were able to obtain was 10,263 epochs, when LR = .5, MG = 0 and FC = 0.

We next implemented the Particle Swarm Technique with the recurrent model to learn our XOR problem using an initial interval between -.1 and +.1. Fig. 6 provides these results. The best our model did was to learn the problem in 983 epochs (local gain set to 1.2 and global gain set to 1.4), with a 17% chance of getting stuck in a local minimum.

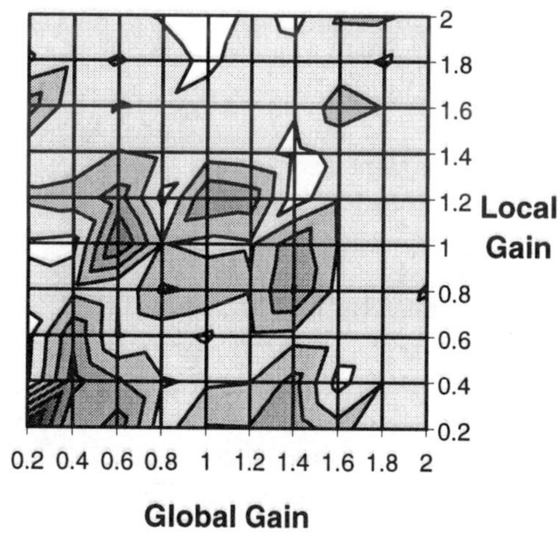

Figure 6. Results of Recurrent XOR Learning with PS

Fig. 7 provides the results when we relaxed the interval of our initial weights.

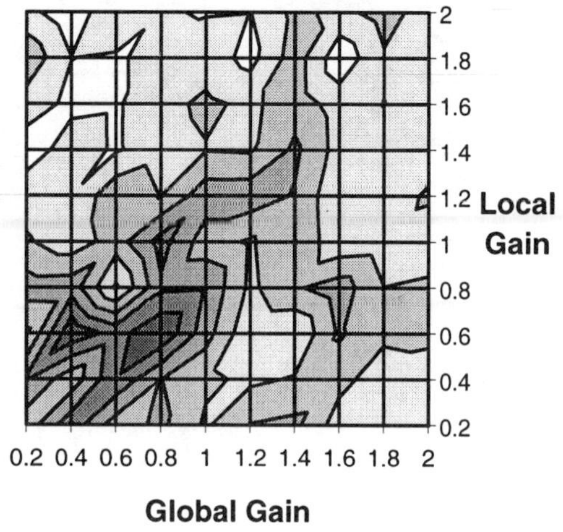

Figure 7. Results of Recurrent XOR Learning with PS

Unlike our earlier results, using a larger interval had very little impact on whether a run successfully trained or not. In this case the best we did was 529 epochs when the local gain was set to 2.0 and the global gain set to .4, and with a 62% chance of getting stuck in a local minimum.

3.2 Comparison of Techniques

Let us again consider our two implementations of the Particle Swarm Technique. When the initial weights were initially set between -.1 and +.1 the overall average across all values was 3,812 epochs with 64 values being below the average and 36 above. When the initial weights were relaxed, the overall average increased to a value of 4,296 with 58 of these values being below and 42 above.

We again took the values obtained for each of the gain pairs for the percent of runs that resulted in a local minimum and plotted them in the histogram shown in Fig. 8. As we can see, using a larger interval had very little impact on whether a run successfully trained or not.

For the XOR problem using a recurrent model, the Particle Swarm Technique provided significantly better results. Similar to our earlier runs with the multi-layered feed forward model, relaxing the initial weights did yield the best results (529 epochs). The total number of epochs for the BP Algorithm was reduced from 10,263 epochs to 529 for the Particle Swarm - a 95% reduction.

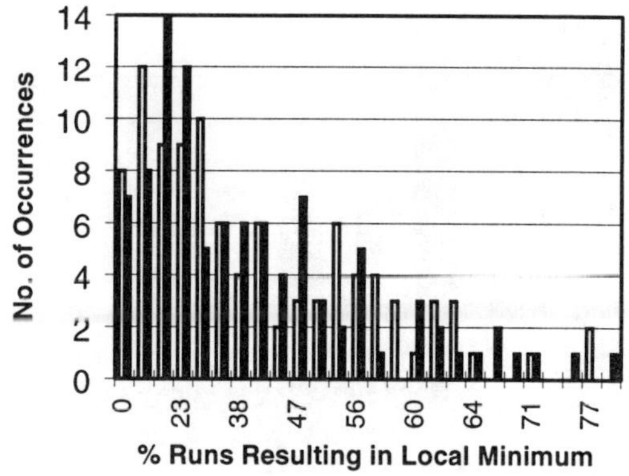

Figure 8. Comparison of PS

4. Applying the Particle Swarm Technique

We next applied the Particle Swarm Technique to our parsing problem, hoping to achieve similar results as with our recurrent XOR problem. Much to our amazement, the algorithm could not learn the problem. We first tried a learning scenario similar to the recurrent XOR problem, i.e., we propagated each training pattern completely through each of the 40 models, found the global best and updated the weights of each model. This scenario did not learn the training set and the time to train for one epoch was 15-18 times greater than the BP solution. Further analysis revealed that the algorithm could not learn the portion of the frame that involved the words found in the first part of the phrase.

We then attempted to learn after every word similar to the way in which we implemented BP. This approach also did not work and in fact, it took 35-38 times longer per epoch. Based on these results we decided it would not be fruitful to proceed any further with this technique.

5. Conclusion

The Particle Swarm Optimization Technique is a superior learning technique for the XOR problems that we have investigated in this paper. It is much simpler to implement then many of the other techniques that have been developed over the past decades and yield overall better results. This was the case not only for the simple multi-layered feed forward model but also for more complex recurrent models. However, when it came to our problem, the Particle Swarm Technique was unable to learn the problem.

References

[1] Jeffery Elman, "Finding Structure in Time", Cognitive Science, Vol 14, 1990, pgs. 179-211.

[2] Scott E. Fahlman, "An Empirical Study of Learning Speed in Backpropagation Networks", CMU-CS-88-162, September 1988.'

[3] James Kennedy and Russell Eberhart, "Particle Swarm Optimization", 1995.

[4] David E. Rumelhart, Geoffrey E. Hinton and Ronald J. Williams, "Learning Internal Representations By Error Prpagation", in Parallel Distributed Processing: Explorations in the Microstructures of Cognition, Volume 1, D. E. Rumelhart and J. L. McClelland (eds), Cambridge, MA: MIT Press, pgs. 318-362.

[5] Risto Miikkulainen, "Natural Language Processing with Modular PDP Networks and Distributed Lexicon", Cognitive Science, Vol 15 Number 3, 1991, pgs. 343-399.

FUSING LASER AND IMAGE DATA FOR 3D PERCEIVED SPACE REPRESENTATIONS

N. Bourbakis and Rich Andel
Binghamton University
Center for Intelligent Systems
Thomas J. Watson School of Engineering
Binghamton, NY 13902

ABSTRACT

In this paper a fusion technique is presented for 3-D representation of space. The technique is based on a fusion process which involves laser range data and segmented image data with human expertise related with the surrounding environment. In particular, the range data may contain noise due to reflections on sloped surfaces or long distance open corridors, thus the proposed fusion approach removes the noise by using human expertise from 3-D environments. This method could be utilized either by an autonomous robot in an unknown environment, or by an inspection machine in a complex manufacturing environment, or by a visual navigation device used by blind people. Additional applications for this technique are the ability to correct measurement deficiencies in a laser-scan and to provide a true color and 3-D perceived shape representation for a given object in a modeling environment

KEYWORDS: *Fusion, Image Segmentation, Laser Scanning, 3-D Images*

1. INTRODUCTION

Since recent advances in technology have resulted in robotics usage in specialized environments, such as manufacturing, the next milestone will be when robots are able to function in unknown and unfamiliar environments. Once this happens, robots will be able to perform many of the tasks that are now done by humans. In order for robots to function in these unknown environments they will have to have the capability to visualize and comprehend their new surroundings. In essence, the robot must be able to see and make inferences to its surroundings just as a human does. To reach this point, the robot will likely need to see the world in color and in three-dimensions as we do, to fully understand and function accordingly. Currently there is no such as a robust sensor that can generate a 3-D model to achieve this goal. A solution to this problem proposed here is to fuse data from multiple sensors. We intend on using the fusion of a color segmented image and a laser range finder to develop a working model of the space.

The idea of fusing two different sensory signals to formulate a 3-D image is not new. Extensive work has been done in the research field of machine vision [1,2]. In particular, a method of fusion between range data and intensity data is presented in [3]. The major goal of this approach is to minimize the extensive amount of time required to sense the range data. Using potential points of interest from the intensity data as directors for the range sensor, the range sensor collects the range data and combines it with the intensity data to form a graph. Another method is discussed in [4]. This method uses the most dominant sensor at one time (range or intensity) for seed segmentation. This segmented area then again uses the data from the range and intensity for merging. The authors use this method to minimize the lighting difficulties and color variance (intensity image segmentation), and the difficulties with sloped surfaces (range image segmentation). In [10], the authors present a method for fusing an range image and an intensity image for 3-D shape recognition. They selected planar and cylindrical regions and applied fusion of range and image data. In this method the range data were selected by laser sensors of short range. In [11], the authors used a fusion methodology based on range data and image segmented data to detect certain color regions and navigate an autonomous robot in a known industrial space. In [12], the authors use radar data for the representation of the outside space for navigation of an autonomous vehicle. In [14], the authors combine sonar and laser range data for navigation in unknown space. Also, in [16], the author generate 3-D sensing for a robot by combining sonar and vision.

By adding the ability to fuse a color image with depth data obtained from a laser scan a better understanding of the environment can be deduced. Having color information in conjunction with depth data will allow laser scan errors caused by refraction and reflection and illumination to be corrected. Additionally, color information will be extremely useful in the

1082-3409/97 $10.00 © 1997 IEEE

classification of objects encountered whether they are in the robots database or not, since the color fused image can be helpful in recognizing new objects as well.

This paper presents a method, which combines a methodology for fuzzy segmentation of color images with range images obtained by a long range laser sensor and human expertise related with the 3-D representation of the surrounding environment. It is assumed the laser device has a poor resolution compared to the camera image and discrepancies in the range data occur which will require correction by our proposed method. In addition, the range data will contain noise due to reflection on sloped surfaces and long distance open corridors. As a solution of this type of problem, the fuzzy segmentation and the human expertise are used to remove the noise from the final 3-D image.

2. LASER RANGE DATA

An ideal laser scanning system would provide a 2-D array of distance values with a resolution equivalent to a cameras (512 x 400). However, such a system is not feasible due to the diffusion characteristics of light.

Laser scanners have continued to improve in their resolution characteristics but their high cost (several thousand dollars) makes them impractical for widespread use. Since a laser scanner is still financially beyond our reach, we provide a basis for a theoretical laser scanning system for our work.

The theoretical laser system consists of a single semi-conductor laser mounted on a biaxial rotary mount. Using two motors the biaxal rotary manipulates the laser to scan 80 degrees horizontally and 62.5 degrees vertically. Motor movements provide a laser scan every 2.5 degrees. This setup results in a 2-D matrix with a resolution of 32 x 25.

Several problems must be addressed when using the theoretical design. A laser's beam width is measured in mrad. For example one mrad corresponds to 10cm beam width at 100m. Our laser mrad reading is higher due to an effort to limit cost. The laser scan sample will vary according to the distance measured. Closer samples will result in a larger mrad value than points farther away from the laser unit (this is depicted in figure 1a). Output will also be affected by uneven surfaces and the environments characteristics (fig 1b). These problems can result in overlapping measurements. Another problem is with a larger beam width a bigger portion of the scanned area will not be analyzed (fig. 2). To alleviate both these problems the laser system will scan the area several times and take the average of the values. Figure 3a, represents a laser scan with a differing number of columns in the matrix output.

Fig. 1a Sample Diameter decreases as distance increases

Fig. 1b Sample of uneven surface scan

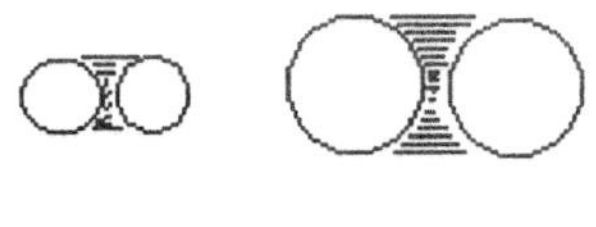

Fig. 2, Horizontal lines represent missed scan areas

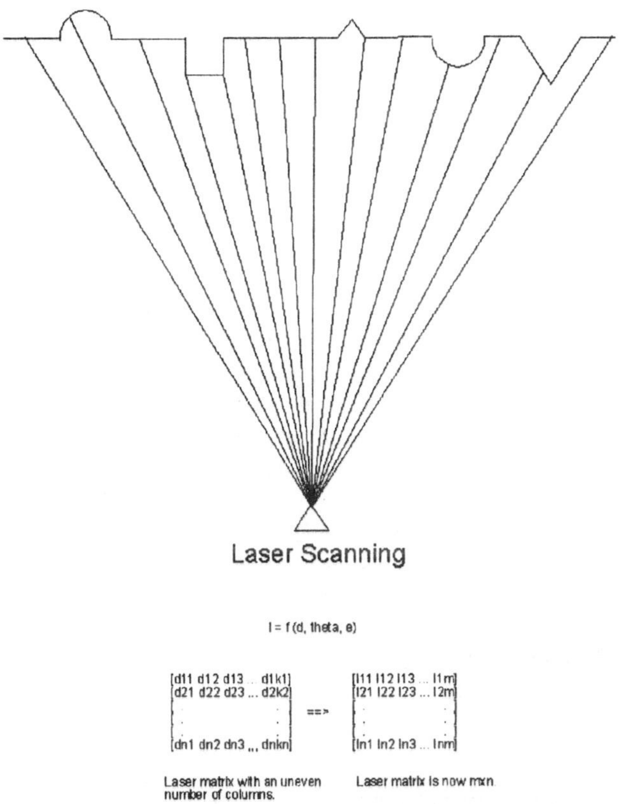

Fig. 3a Laser scan with uniform matrix conversion

Another problem with the laser system is as the distance being measured increases, larger areas will be missed by the scan (figure 3b). For our experiment this problem is ignored. It will be addressed when a real laser system is available.

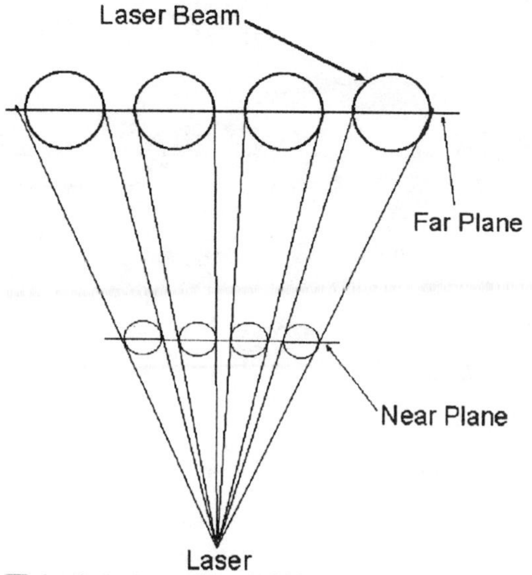

Fig. 3b: Missed Scan Areas

In order to generate the laser output we have modified a ray-tracer (which models the physics of light and object interactions within a virtual 3-D environment). Our ray-tracer just considers ray-object intersections (without reflection and refraction components) and it is analogous to an ideal laser scanner. The ray-tracer is similar to the laser scanner in that the virtual scene is traced in a biaxal fashion and it returns the distance from the rays origin to the point on the surface of the object where the ray object intersection occurs. A plane object was used to represent the floor plane in our scene and the scanner was positioned above a scene consisting of cube objects. The results obtained are a 2-D distance array as would have been obtained if an actual laser was used. An example from a simple scene and a close up view is represented in figures 4a and 4b. Figure 4c, represents the initial laser matrix and its expansion. The area containing three different patterns in figure 4a represents objects at three different heights.

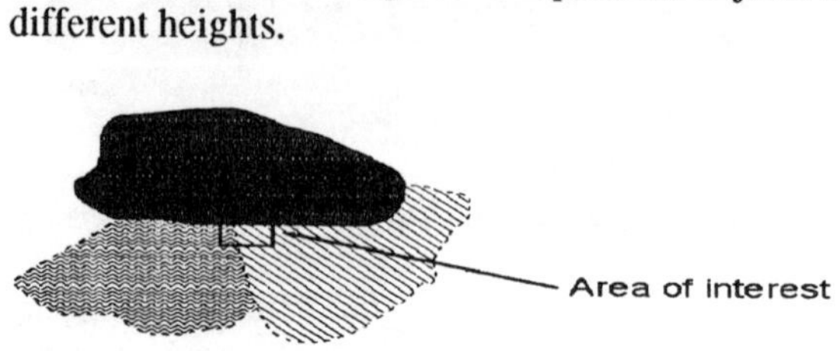

Fig. 4a: Simple Scene

The 3 surfaces are at different heights

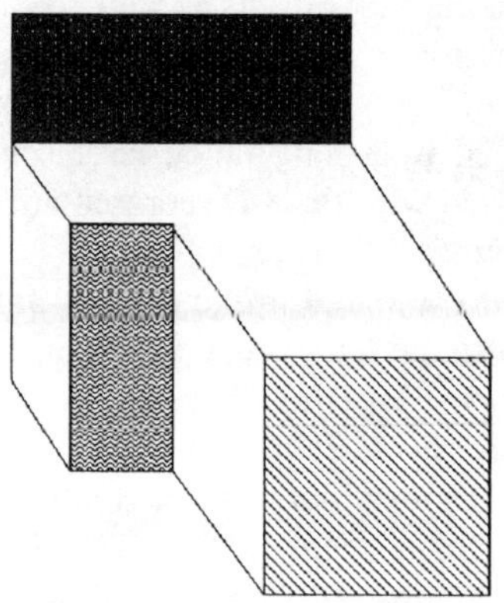

Fig. 4b: Close view of the area of interest

Laser Matrix Data

Original laser matrix (4x4)

10	3	2	2
10	3	2	2
10	3	2	2
10	5	3.5	3.5
10	6	4	4

$$\text{Ratio} = \frac{\text{Image Dimension}}{\text{Laser Dimension}} = \frac{16x16}{4x4} = 4x5$$

Expanded matrix (16x20)

10	10	10	10	3	3	3	3	2	2	2	2	2	2	2	2
10	10	10	10	3	3	3	3	2	2	2	2	2	2	2	2
10	10	10	10	3	3	3	3	2	2	2	2	2	2	2	2
10	10	10	10	3	3	3	3	2	2	2	2	2	2	2	2
10	10	10	10	3	3	3	3	2	2	2	2	2	2	2	2
10	10	10	10	3	3	3	3	2	2	2	2	2	2	2	2
10	10	10	10	3	3	3	3	2	2	2	2	2	2	2	2
10	10	10	10	3	3	3	3	2	2	2	2	2	2	2	2
10	10	10	10	3	3	3	3	2	2	2	2	2	2	2	2
10	10	10	10	3	3	3	3	2	2	2	2	2	2	2	2
10	10	10	10	3	3	3	3	2	2	2	2	2	2	2	2
10	10	10	10	3	3	3	3	2	2	2	2	2	2	2	2
10	10	10	10	5	5	5	5	3.5	3.5	3.5	3.5	3.5	3.5	3.5	3.5
10	10	10	10	5	5	5	5	3.5	3.5	3.5	3.5	3.5	3.5	3.5	3.5
10	10	10	10	5	5	5	5	3.5	3.5	3.5	3.5	3.5	3.5	3.5	3.5
10	10	10	10	5	5	5	5	3.5	3.5	3.5	3.5	3.5	3.5	3.5	3.5
10	10	10	10	6	6	6	6	4	4	4	4	4	4	4	4
10	10	10	10	6	6	6	6	4	4	4	4	4	4	4	4
10	10	10	10	6	6	6	6	4	4	4	4	4	4	4	4
10	10	10	10	6	6	6	6	4	4	4	4	4	4	4	4

Fig. 4c: Initial laser matrix &expansion

Corrected Laser Matrix

Observe that the distance measurements (from the intial expanded matrix) have been corrected with the color information and the fusion process.

Expanded matrix (16x20)

10	10	10	10	10	2	2	2	2	2	2	2	2	2	2	2
10	10	10	10	10	2	2	2	2	2	2	2	2	2	2	2
10	10	10	10	10	2	2	2	2	2	2	2	2	2	2	2
10	10	10	10	10	2	2	2	2	2	2	2	2	2	2	2
10	10	10	10	10	2	2	2	2	2	2	2	2	2	2	2
10	10	10	10	10	2	2	2	2	2	2	2	2	2	2	2
10	10	10	10	10	2	2	2	2	2	2	2	2	2	2	2
10	10	10	10	10	2	2	2	2	2	2	2	2	2	2	2
10	10	10	10	10	2	2	2	2	2	2	2	2	2	2	2
10	10	10	10	10	2	2	2	2	2	2	2	2	2	2	2
10	10	10	10	10	2	2	2	2	2	2	2	2	2	2	2
10	10	10	10	10	2	2	2	2	2	2	2	2	2	2	2
10	10	10	10	10	2	2	2	2	2	2	2	2	2	2	2
10	10	10	10	10	4	4	4	4	4	4	4	4	4	4	4
10	10	10	10	10	4	4	4	4	4	4	4	4	4	4	4
10	10	10	10	10	4	4	4	4	4	4	4	4	4	4	4
10	10	10	10	10	4	4	4	4	4	4	4	4	4	4	4
10	10	10	10	10	4	4	4	4	4	4	4	4	4	4	4
10	10	10	10	10	4	4	4	4	4	4	4	4	4	4	4
10	10	10	10	10	4	4	4	4	4	4	4	4	4	4	4

Fig. 4d: Corrected sample matrix (corresponds to fig 4c)

3. FUZZY IMAGE SEGMENTATION

A color image taken from the same point that the laser scanner resides will be useful in correcting discrepancies in the laser scan. This relies on the fact that the color image can be segmented resulting in a series of clusters which will reinforce and correct the scan measurements. Not much research has been done for color images with regards to distinguishing object from the background. The methodologies which segregate the red, green, and blue (RGB) components and examine them on an individual basis are not very accurate. First of all the relationship between the pixel being inspected and the surrounding pixels is lost. Second, the task of reuniting the three color values to recreate the original is complicated. These techniques, therefore, are only useful for images with few variations in color. The fuzzy image segmentation procedure in [8] resolves these problems and limitations.

Beginning with an edge detection algorithm which can detect most edges, the segmentation process can start. A histogram table is developed containing the RGB values and the number of pixels with those components. From this table various clusters, sections having contiguous pixels with the identical color or a slight variation in color, can be ascertained. These clusters are recreated using the edges previously determined and filling the area with the most dominant color from the image.

Clusters are separated into three categories based on size. A big cluster contains a number of B pixels, a medium cluster has a number of M pixels, and a small cluster must be greater than a number of S pixels. These numbers (B,M,S) are determined by using the histogram of the examined image [15]. First all the big clusters should be found and processed. Second the medium clusters need to be analyzed. Third, the small clusters are examined. Lastly, the pixels which did not fit into any of the previous classifications must be evaluated.

In order to determine which clusters fall into the big category a seed color and location need to be found. To start, the first value in the histogram is used as the seed color. Once a location is known, an evaluation of the growth of the seed within the edges of that segments is made. At that location where a big cluster is detected and the most seed colors are used, a seed is grown. All the values in the histogram table pertaining to this cluster are removed. This process continues until all the big clusters are located.

The value of the edges of the big clusters need to be evaluated to determine if they belong to this cluster. Fuzzy logic rules based on variance in color are utilized to determine where a pixel along the edge belongs. If a pixel's color is within a specified tolerance to be considered part of that cluster, then it belongs to that cluster. This compensates for a slight variation in color.

Now that all the big clusters have been found and the edges examined, the medium and small clusters can be found. Following the same procedure as before, all the medium clusters are evaluated before the small ones. Small clusters are then formed if the pixel has the proper characteristics and is drastically different from the surrounding clusters. After the completion of growing small clusters, those pixels not yet assigned to a cluster, are then attached to the cluster with the closest color and proximity.

4. LASER DATA CONVERSION

The output from the laser scanner is a 2-D array of values regarding how far the laser is from the environment that had been scanned. In order to arrive at the height or depth of objects, several conversion steps are necessary [Data may also require multiple scans of the scene to compensate for the problems described in section 2.]

Once the final matrix is complete several pre-processing steps are required before a 3-D representation may be displayed:

- Height Adjustment for Proper Distances
- Depth Compensation (sample smoothing)
- Matrix Expansion (if necessary)
- Polygon Surface Definition

Height adjustment is necessary because the actual laser measurements represent distances from the laser unit to a point on the object surface. For example, if we are working with objects on the floor plane the furthest distance measured would be the furthest point located on the floor plane. The sample data must be adjusted by subtracting all point from this furthest distance which results in the objects true height being determined.

Depth compensation (sample smoothing) involves adjusting the laser range data to compensate for the effects of increasing laser measurements for areas on the same plane. If a scan of a cube object is performed which is directly below the laser (on the ground plane), the closest point would be the center of the cube and measurements would continually increase toward the extents of the cube. This would result in the cube object having a rounded top plane, since the nearest point would be it's apex and this would result in a rounded surface which is not correct. The laser measurements can be corrected if we allow for a slight tolerance among successive sample points thereby insuring a smooth flat surface is generated when a level plane is encountered.

Matrix expansion may be necessary since the resolution of the lasers output is usually much less than that of the image produced by a camera. If the matrix resolution is 32x32 and the camera image is 128 x 128, this would result in a matrix expansion by a factor of 4 for proper alignment.

Note: If the resolutions do not factor into one another evenly, interpolation must be performed to achieve a 1:1 mapping.

Once the previous steps are complete, we are ready to actually define the surface as a series of adjoining polygons for display. Each of the 2-D points of an NxN matrix represents a vertex edge and then an edge list is generated which represents the surface contour among the (n-1)*(n-1) polygons. The amount of memory necessary for object representation is substantial. Assuming we have a 32 x 32 laser matrix and expand it by four, we then have a 128 x 128 matrix which has 16,384 points (vertices) and 16,129 polygons. Note: On polygon conversion, the number of sample points from the laser output always results in each row having one less polygon than the number of sample points and also one complete row of values missing. For instance, with the 128 x 128 sample, upon conversion we have only a 127 x 127 polygon representation not an ideal 1:1 laser to image mapping we desire. To compensate for this scale-down effect, during pre-processing we add one additional sample at the right end of each column and an entire additional row at the bottom of our sample. The sample values at these additional points are assumed to have an identical value as their predecessor. This allows a true 1:1 mapping since a 129 x 129 sample scales to a 128 x 128 polygon surface.

5. FUSION METHODOLOGY

The fusion methodology presented here uses the more accurate fuzzy segmented data to improve the resolution of the range data.

The method involves combining polygon surface definition derived from the laser output and applying the segmented camera image. Several steps are necessary before the fusion process can occur:

For the Laser Scan

- Obtain laser range data [section 1]
- Conversion of range data to height or depth data (depth compensation/sample smoothing)
- Generating an index matrix
- Expansion of index matrix (if necessary)
- Generation of polygon surface definition

For the Camera Image:

- Generating a Histogram
- Segmenting the Camera Image

Finally, *Fusing the index matrix and the segmented camera image.*

Acquisition of the range data was explained in the laser section. Range data provides information regarding how far the laser is from the environment it is scanning. It does not directly give the height or depth of the object which is necessary to create a 3-D model of the space. Therefore, several steps are needed to convert the range data to depth or height. First, the range data is used to identify potential objects. Second, the object under investigation must be classified as being on the floor plane or on the wall plane. Objects on the floor plane have a height whereas objects on the wall plane have a depth.

The laser range data is used to give a rough approximation of an object by subtracting a trigonometrically calculated reference matrix from the range data to form the object matrix. The reference matrix is generated by using the largest value in the range data (excluding the laser maximum measuring distance). Rapid value changes in the object matrix indicate potential edges of objects. In addition sloped or flat surfaces are determined with the range data. In figure 5a, the difference (e) between adjacent range values is small. By setting a threshold (h) the flat objects area is determined. Figure 5b shows that the difference (e') between adjacent range values is larger. This will be the case for sloped surfaces with the threshold (h') dependent on the angle of the slope.

An object on the floor plane is any object whose height does not exceed the scanning view of the laser. The height of an object in this plane can be determined by using simple geometry. An object on the wall plane is any object on the wall or any object that does not have a flat uniform vertical surface. For these objects depth is calculated by using the closest background value as a reference. In figure 6 h1 is the height of the laser from the floor, θ is the tilt angle of the laser, h0 is the height of the object, rn is the distance measured by the laser if no object is present, and r0 is the distance that the laser measured to the object. On flat surfaces the floor and h1 are perpendicular and a right triangle is formed. The height of the object can now be determined using simple trigonometry. Note that figure 6 is two dimensional and has to be corrected when the laser is off center to avoid rounding flat surfaces.

An index matrix is generated once the height and depth values are calculated. An index matrix eliminates the slight measurement and truncation errors by grouping

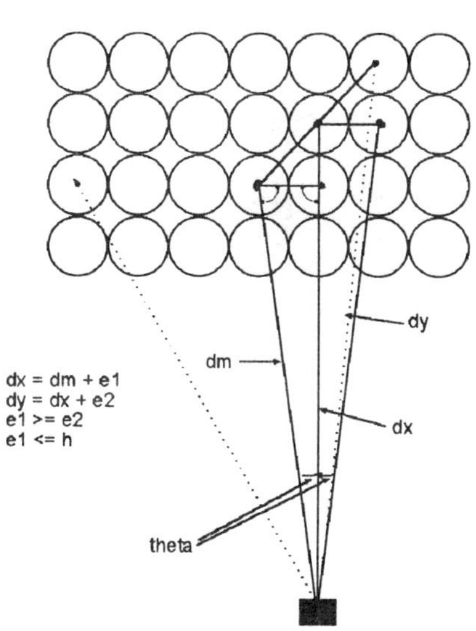

Fig. 5a Flat Surface

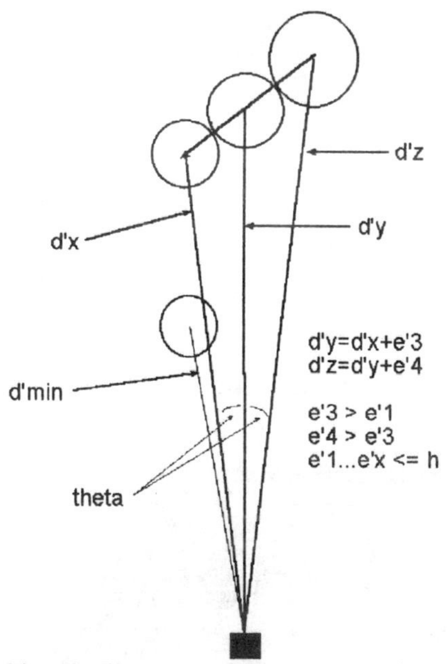

Fig. 5b Sloped Surfaces

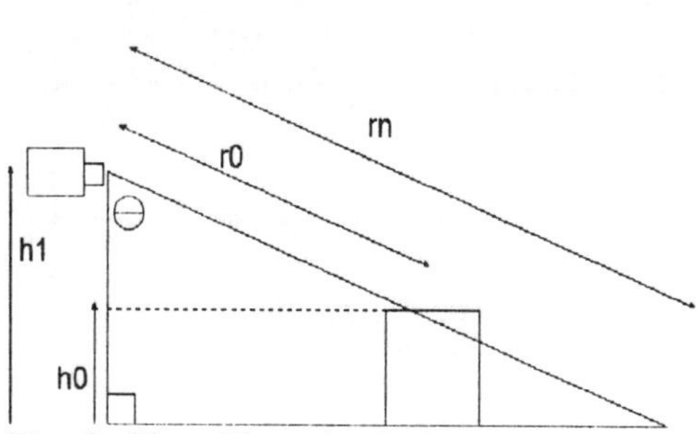

Fig. 6: Floor Plane Analysis

values that are very close in magnitude and assigning the groups the average of their values. Note that with flat objects this will be a single value. For sloping objects the index value will change in a step like fashion.

Once the index matrix is developed and the color image is segmented, a resolution ratio (Ri) is produced. The resolution ratio is the color image matrix size (Rc) over the index matrix size (Ri). In the example to follow Rc equals 128 x 128 and Ri is 32 x 32. These values yield an expansion factor, Rf, equal to 4. Obviously the resolution ratio will not be an ideal whole number every time. This difficulty will be addressed in a later paper. The index matrix is expanded to the size of the color image matrix based on Rf.

Next the values of the index matrix are adjusted by the color segmented image. An assumption in this process is that the color changes at different heights. With flat surfaces the color will dictate how the data is changed. For flat objects, if two adjacent index values are different and they both have the same color value, this indicates an edge. Then the adjacent index values with the same color are evaluated to determine the new index value at the boundaries. If the object is determined to have a slope, then the procedure is nearly the same as the flat surface method. However, fewer adjacent index values are evaluated because the local index changes too rapidly. Since the color changes may not be evident on gradually sloping surfaces the color is only used to determine the edges of the object. Once all the index values have been adjusted the color segmented matrix and the index values are combine to get the final 3-D model.

6. SIMULATED EXAMPLES

This subsection graphically presents the fusion of the laser and camera image segmented data. Both the color image and laser data were simulated with a computer. The range data matrices are 32 x 32 and the camera images are 128 x 128. These values were chosen so that the resolution ratio ended in a whole number. We have created a 3-D object viewer for Windows95/NT which is useful in the visualization process since our scene may be rotated, scaled and transformed as necessary. Figure 7a represents the initial 3-D representation of a range matrix with the addition of noise or "spikes". The "spikes" appear as sharp points protruding upward and may be considered inaccuracies of the laser scanner. Figure 7b is the expansion of the index matrix, notice that upon expansion the error (spikes) in the laser scan is compounded. Figure 7c shows the original image used in this example. Figure 7d is the final fused image, notice that the error in the laser measurements was corrected by the fusion process. In this simulation only the floor plane was evaluated. The vertical plane has not been simulated at this time. Figure 8 shows the fusion results from a range matrix and a different original color image.

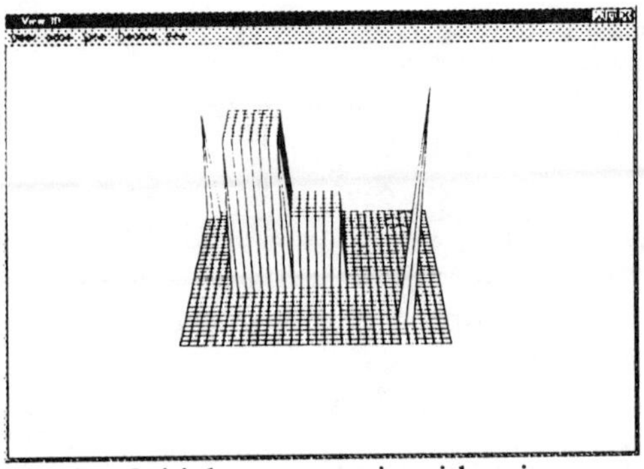

Fig. 7a. Initial range matrix with noise

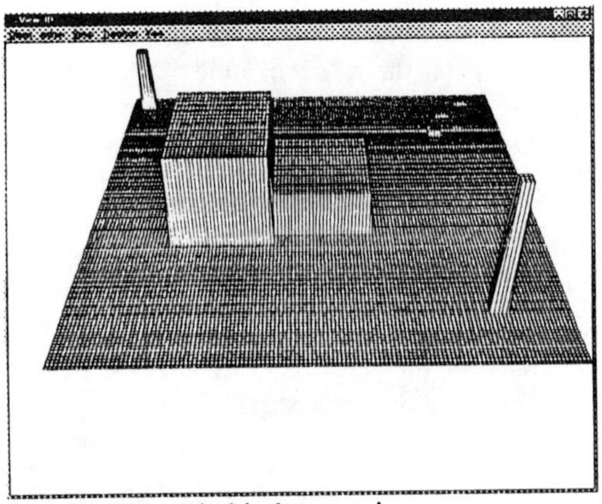

Fig. 7b: Expanded index matrix

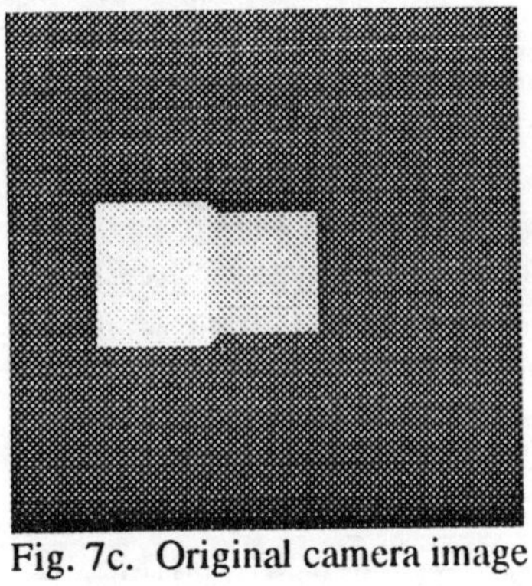

Fig. 7c. Original camera image

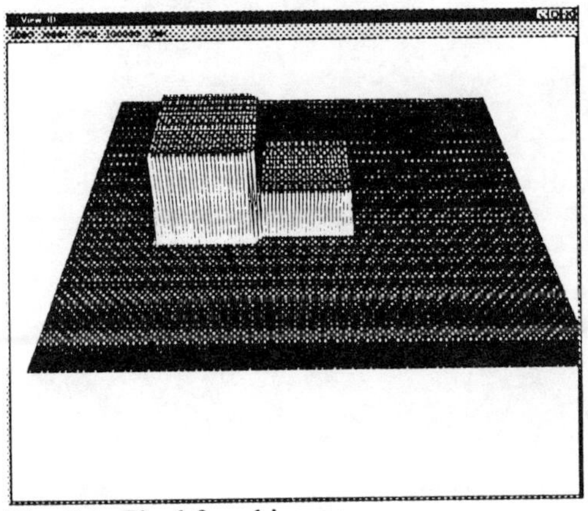

Fig. 7d: Final fused image

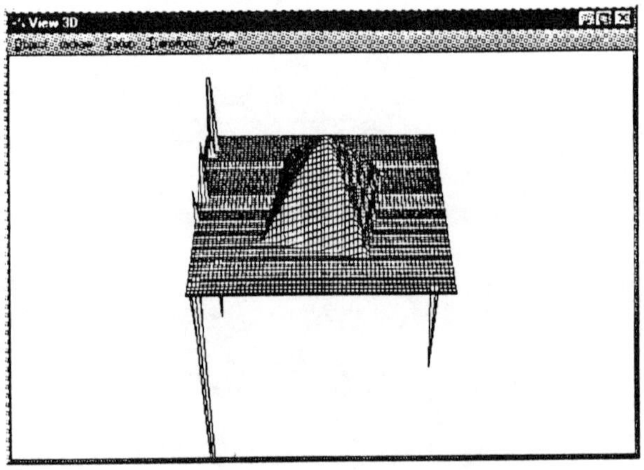

Fig. 8a. Initial range matrix with noise

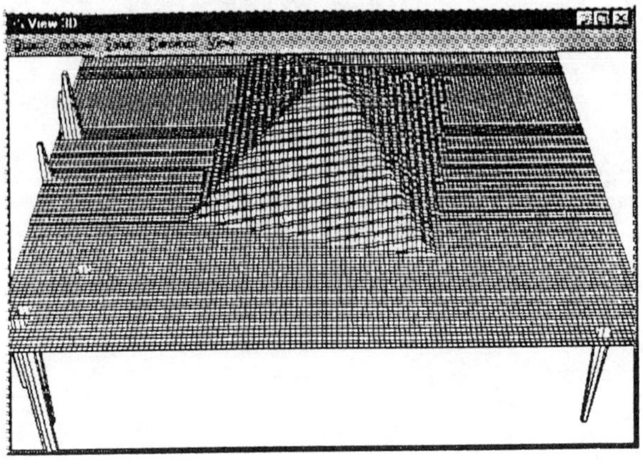

Fig. 8b: Expanded index matrix

Fig. 8c. Original camera image

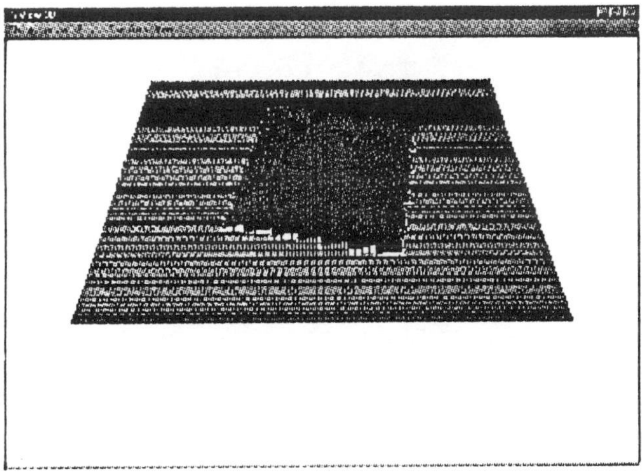

Fig. 8d: Final fused image

7. DISCUSSION

Several matters have yet to be addressed. The model of the vertical plane is complex due to the inability to define a reference point. Our method to determine a reference plane is still being investigated. Also, the resolution ratio will not always be a whole number which will affect the expansion process. Interpolation will be necessary to compensate for the non-whole resolution ratio. Additionally, in the evaluation of sloped surfaces steps are generated. We intend to use fuzzy logic to correct this error.

One of the problems that has been encountered deals with the large amount of memory required for the exceptionally large matrices. Additionally, since the number of point in a 128 x 128 matrix corresponds to 127 x 127 polygons (always one less polygon than point across or down) we need to compensate to achieve our desired 1:1 mapping between index matrix and the segmented camera image. Currently, we have added another row and column (making the matrix 129 x 129), the values of the previous point are used for these additional points. This allows the 1:1 mapping thereby giving us 16,384 polygons for the 128 x 128 index matrix.

When a real laser system is acquired specular reflection will have to be compensated for as well as any incorrect assumptions made in the theoretical model.

8. CONCLUSION

This paper presents a new method for 3-D modeling. Data from a camera image and a laser scanning system is fused to accomplish this task. Laser data is converted to a depth and height representation of the scanned scene. The problems of different resolutions between the two sensory devices is handled by expanding the lower resolution laser data to the dimensions of the color image. Fusion is accomplished by merging the fuzzy segmented image with the expanded index matrix. Based on our example, the deficiencies and incorrect measurement by the laser scanner (noise & spikes) were corrected with the fusion of the segmented camera image. Since a laser scanning system was not yet available for this work all results were simulated on a computer.

REFERENCES

[1] J.K. Hackett and M. Shah, "Multi-Sensor Fusion: A Perspective," *IEEE International Conference on Robotics and Automation*, pp. 1324-1339, 1990.

[2] J.K. Aggarwal and A, Mitiche, "Multiple Sensor Integration/Fusion Through Image Processing: A Review," *Optical Engineering*, 25:380-6, March 1986

[3] M.J. Magee, B.A. Boyter, C.H Chien, and J.K. Aggarwal, "Experiments in Intensity Guided Range Sensing Recognition of Three-Dimensional Objects," *IEEE Trans. Pattern Anal. Machine Intell.*, vol. PAMI-7, pp. 629-637, Nov. 1985.
[4] J.K. Hackett and M. Shah, "Segmentation Using Intensity and Range Data," *Optical Engineering*, 28:667-674, June 1989.
[5] B. Gill, A. Mitiche, and J.K. Aggarwal, "Experiments in combining intensity and range edge maps," *Comp. Graph. Image Pro.* 21, pp. 395-411 (1983)
[6] M. Heckbert, "Outdoor scene analysis using range data," *IEEE Conf. on Robotics and Automation 3*, pp. 1426-1432, 1986.
[7] R.O. Duda, D. Nitzan, and P. Barrett, "Use of range and reflectance data to find planar surface regions," *IEEE Trans. Pattern Anal. Machine Intell.*, PAMI-1, pp. 259-271, 1979.
[8] A. Moghaddanzadeh and N. Bourbakis, "Image segmentation using fuzzy region growing image" IAPR Society Journal of Pattern Recognition, vol.30,1997
[9] N.Bourbakis and M.Maas, "A methodology for the fusion of laser and image data for 3-D modeling of an unknown space", TR-1993, AAAI Research Lab, EE,BU
[10] K.Umeda, K.Ikushima and T.Arai, "Fusion of range image and intensity image for 3-D shape recognition", Int. IEEE Conf. On Robotics and Automation, MN 1996, vol. I, pp. 680-685
[11] S.Nickersa et. al.,"ARK: an autonomous mobile robot in an industrial known environment", Proc. Int. NASA Conf. on Intelligent Robotics, March 1994, Houston, TX
[12] R.Chatila, et. al."Perception system and functions for autonomous navigation in natural environments", Proc. Int. NASA conf. on Intelligent Robotics, March 1994, Houston, TX
[13] Riegl Laser Measurement Systems, RIEGL USA Inc., 4419 Parkbreeze Court, Orlando, FL 32808
[14]G.Dudek et.al."Just in line sensing :combining sonar and laser range data for for exploring unknown worlds" Proc. IEEE ICRA, 1, 667-672,1996
[15] A.Mogxadeh and N.Bourbakis, Segmentation of color images with lighting and shadows", PRL
[16] H.Akburally and L.Kleeman, 3-D robot sensing from sonar and vision ", Proc. IEEE ICRA,I,681-685, 1996

Session A.3

Knowledge Representation and Reasoning

Session Chair:
Jim Gattiker, Los Alamos National Laboratory, USA

Anytime Reasoning with Probabilistic Inequalities

Laila Khreisat and Mukesh Dalal

Department of Computer Science
Columbia University
New York, NY 10027
{laila,dalal}@cs.columbia.edu

Abstract

We present a novel approach for anytime reasoning with probabilistic inequalities. In our anytime approach, the accuracy of results improve gradually as computation time increases, providing a trade-off between resource consumption and output quality. Our approach can be used for computing probabilities of arbitrary propositional clauses, is tractable in providing the initial approximate answers, and provides exact answers in the limiting case. Reasoning is made tractable by restricting it to a set of clauses in a control set that can be gradually enlarged as more resources are made available. We present three strategies that differ in the way constraints are generated from the clauses in the control set. We provide examples of our approach using an ignorant belief network.

1 Introduction

Starting with probabilistic logic [17], several formalisms have been developed for representation and reasoning with uncertain information. However, the intractability of probabilistic reasoning [2] is a serious problem in most applications, specially for real-world tasks requiring time-critical responses. In this paper, we present a novel approach, based on anytime reasoning, for solving this problem. Anytime reasoning uses algorithms whose accuracy of results improve gradually as computation time increases, providing a trade-off between resource consumption and output quality [13]. Although interesting anytime algorithms for probabilistic reasoning have been published previously [20, 12, 19, 10], they are either incomplete, compute probabilities of only atomic formulas, are not known to be tractable, or are not general-purpose. In contrast, our anytime approach, which can be used for computing probabilities of arbitrary propositional clauses, is tractable in providing the initial answers, as well as complete in the limiting case. Our approach is similar in spirit to some anytime reasoning techniques for propositional reasoning [4, 5, 6, 8, 7, 9].

We restrict our attention to probabilistic theories consisting of linear weight inequalities over propositional clauses [11], that can be used to represent several other probabilistic formalisms, for example, belief networks [18]. Any given probabilistic theory is converted into a system of linear inequalities [14] that explicitly represent the constraints among the probabilities of propositional clauses present in the theory. Solutions of this linear programming problem provide the probabilities of any propositional clause posed as a query. Instead of the exact answer consisting of tight bounds defining a probability interval, our method usually provides wider bounds defining a larger interval. In general, tighter bounds defining smaller intervals represent more accurate answers.

In addition to the propositional theory and the query, we allow the user to specify a set of propositional clauses, called the *control set*; the clauses in the control set are also used in generating the linear inequalities. For anytime reasoning, the control set, which is initially set to the clauses in the input theory and query, is gradually expanded by adding new clauses to it. The accuracy of the answer increases with the increase in the control set, and the exact answer is guaranteed in the limiting case when the control set contains all propositional clauses.

We use three different strategies in generating the linear inequalities. In the first strategy, called BASIC, standard probability axioms are used in generating only equalities over the probabilities of only the clauses in the control set. In the second strategy, called INEQS, clauses that are not in the control set also are used to generate inequalities among the probabilities of clauses in the control set. In the third strategy, called EXPSN, the clauses missing from the control set are recursively substituted by constraints over clauses in the control set. Note that INEQS and EXPSN generates at least all the constraints that are generated by BASIC. As is expected, while BASIC is the most efficient strategy, it provides the widest intervals in the answers. However, the results provided by INEQS and EXPSN are incomparable, in general. Since we are dealing with probabilistic theories consisting of linear weight inequalities over propositional clauses, whose soundness was proved by [11], the linear inequalities generated by our method are guaranteed to be sound.

As an example, consider the ignorant belief network [1] shown in Figure 1, where "?" indicates missing information [21]. Informally, somebody reports (R) people leaving (L) a building because the fire alarm (A) went off, which could be either because of tampering

1082-3409/97 $10.00

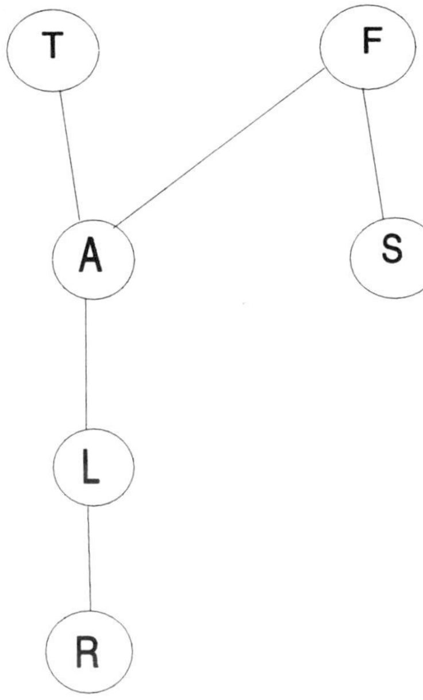

$P(T) = 0.02$
$P(F) = 0.01$

P(A)	F	¬F
T	?	0.85
¬T	0.99	0.0001

P(S)	F	¬F
	0.90	0.01

P(L)	A	¬A
	0.88	0.001

P(R)	L	¬L
	0.75	0.01

Figure 1: **The Alarm Belief Network**

$$
\begin{aligned}
P(T) &= 0.02 \\
P(F) &= 0.01 \\
P(S \wedge F) &= 0.90 * P(F) \\
P(S \wedge \neg F) &= 0.01 * P(\neg F) \\
P(L \wedge A) &= 0.88 * P(A) \\
P(L \wedge \neg A) &= .001 * P(\neg A) \\
P(R \wedge L) &= 0.75 * P(L) \\
P(R \wedge \neg L) &= 0.01 * P(\neg L) \\
P(A \wedge \neg T \wedge F) &= 0.99 * P(\neg T \wedge F) \\
P(A \wedge T \wedge \neg F) &= 0.85 * P(T \wedge \neg F) \\
P(A \wedge \neg T \wedge \neg F) &= 0.0001 * P(\neg T \wedge \neg F)
\end{aligned}
$$

Figure 2: **Translated Probabilistic Theory (Z_1)**

(T) or because of fire (F) that causes smoke (S). The probabilistic theory (Z_1) obtained by translating the belief net is given in Figure 2.

Suppose the system is asked to determine the probability of the query $Q_1 = T \vee F$. The initial control set (C_1) consists of only the clauses present in the theory and the query. Both BASIC and EXPSN provide the answer [0.02,1], while INEQS provides a tighter interval [0.02,0.03]. For the control set C_1' obtained by adding $T \wedge F$ to C_1, all the strategies provide the answer [0.02,0.03]. Section 3 provides the inequalities used in obtaining the above answers.

Consider another query $Q_2 = A$ posed to the theory Z_1. For the initial control set, C_2 consisting of the clauses in C_1 plus the two clauses $A \vee T \vee F$, $A \wedge F$, both BASIC and INEQS provide the answer [0,1], while EXPSN provides the answer [0,0.027]. For the control set C_2' obtained by adding $T \wedge F$ to C_2, both BASIC and INEQS provide the answer [0.0085,1], while EXPSN provides the answer [0.0085,0.027].

The rest of the paper is organized as follows: In Section 2 we define the basic terminology and concepts. In Section 3, we present the three strategies. In Sections 4 and 5, we present our algorithms and discuss the computational complexity of our approach, respectively. In Section 6, we compare our approach with related approaches, before concluding in Section 8.

2 Probabilistic Logic

Although probabilistic logic was first introduced in the AI community by [17], we use a simplified variant of the more general framework presented in [11]. We start with a propositional language $\mathcal{L}$ whose *formulas* are finitely constructed in the usual way from a denumerable set of *primitive propositions* (atoms), and logical connectives $\wedge$ (conjunction), $\vee$ (disjunction), and $\neg$ (negation) [16]. A *probabilistic formula* is a statement of the form $a_1 P(\psi_1) + \cdots + a_k P(\psi_k) \geq a$, where k is a positive integer, a's are reals, and ψ's are propositional formulas. For example, $2.0 * P(p_1 \vee p_2) - 7.5 * P(p_3) \geq 3.9$ is a probabilistic formula. A *proba-*

bilistic theory is a finite set of probabilistic formulas.

A semantics for probabilistic formulas is obtained by considering probabilistic interpretations, that is, probability distributions over the set of all possible worlds obtained by assigning truth-values (either *true* or *false*) to the atoms occurring in the formulas. The probability $P(\psi)$ of a propositional formula ψ in a probabilistic interpretation is the sum of probabilities of the possible worlds in which ψ is *true* . The probabilistic models of a probabilistic formula are exactly those probabilistic interpretation in which the inequality of the formula holds (that is, *true*). As usual, a probabilistic theory entails ($\models$) a probabilistic formula iff the formula is *true* in each model of the theory.

Since probabilistic formulas are linear mappings, each probabilistic theory entails a convex hull of consistent probabilities for each propositional formula. In other words, for any probabilistic theory Γ and for any propositional formula ψ, there is a tightest closed interval $[a, b]$ of reals such that $\Gamma \models a \leq P(\psi) \leq b$. Given any Γ and ψ, determining the tightest interval $[a, b]$ is the probabilistic reasoning problem that we focus in this paper. Since the tightest interval $[a, b]$ gives the exact answer, any wider interval $[a', b']$ (where $a' \leq a \leq b \leq b'$) is considered an approximate answer.

For convenience, we will omit the qualifier "probabilistic" while referring to all concepts except for clauses. For example, we will use "clause" to mean "propositional clause", "formula" to mean "probabilistic formula", and "theory" to mean "probabilistic theory".

3 Anytime Probabilistic Reasoning

In this section, we describe the three strategies for generating linear inequalities. We use Z to denote the input probabilistic theory, Q to denote the query, and D to denote the control set. Recall that the initial control set D is the set of clauses in theory Z and query Q.

To illustrate our approach, we continue to use the example theory Z_1, query Q_1, control set C_1, etc. given in Section 1. Figure 5 shows the graphical structures of the control sets C_1 (solid lines only) and C_1' (both solid and dotted lines). The nodes indicate conjunctive and disjunctive clauses in the control set, while the edges indicate subsumption of clauses: informally, $\alpha \vee \beta$ subsumes α subsumes $\alpha \wedge \beta$.

For a disjunctive clause, any maximal proper subclause is said to be a *child*. A conjunctive clause is said to be a *child* of any maximal proper conjunctive subclause. Two children of a clause are said to be *compatible* iff they differ in only one literal, which occurs positively in one and negatively in the other. The children relation can be extended to the *descendant* relation in the usual way. For example, T is a child of $T \vee F$, $T \wedge F$ and $T \wedge \neg F$ are compatible children of T, and $A \wedge T \wedge F$ is a descendant of $T \vee F$.

3.1 Strategy BASIC

In strategy BASIC, three kinds of linear equalities are generated from the clauses in the control set D:

$$\begin{aligned} P(L) &= P(L \wedge A) + P(L \wedge \neg A) \\ P(S) &= P(S \wedge F) + P(S \wedge \neg F) \\ P(R) &= P(R \wedge L) + P(R \wedge \neg L) \end{aligned}$$

Figure 3: **Equalities generated by BASIC for Z_1, Q_1, and C_1**

1. For each disjunctive clause $\psi = \alpha_1 \vee \cdots \vee \alpha_m$ ($m > 1$) such that D contains ψ, each non-conjunctive descendant of ψ, and $\alpha_1 \wedge \cdots \wedge \alpha_m$, the following linear equality is generated:

$$\begin{aligned} P(\psi) &= \sum\{P(\varphi) \mid \varphi \text{ is a child of } \psi\} \\ &\quad -\sum\{P(\varphi) \mid \varphi \text{ is a grandchild of } \psi\} \\ &\quad \cdots \\ &\quad +(-1)^{m+1} P(\alpha_1 \wedge \cdots \wedge \alpha_m) \end{aligned}$$

   For example, the equality $P(T \vee F) = P(T) + P(F) - P(T \wedge F)$ is generated for the control set C_1'. This equality is not generated for C_1 because the conjunctive clause $T \wedge F$ is not in C_1.

2. For each conjunctive clause $\psi = \alpha_1 \wedge \cdots \wedge \alpha_m$ ($m > 1$) such that D contains ψ, each non-disjunctive ancestor of ψ, and $\alpha_1 \vee \cdots \vee \alpha_m$, the following linear equality is generated:

$$\begin{aligned} P(\alpha_1 \vee \cdots \vee \alpha_m) &= \sum_{i=1}^{m} P(\alpha_i) \\ -\sum\{P(\varphi) \mid \varphi &\text{ is a non-disjunctive ancestor of } \psi\} \\ &\cdots \\ &+(-1)^{m+1} P(\alpha_1 \wedge \cdots \wedge \alpha_m) \end{aligned}$$

   For example, if $A \wedge T$ and $T \wedge F$ are added to the control set C_2', then the following equality is generated:

$$\begin{aligned} P(A \vee T \vee F) = P(A) + P(T) + P(F) - \\ P(A \wedge T) - P(A \wedge F) - P(T \wedge F) \\ +P(A \wedge T \wedge F) \end{aligned}$$

3. For each non-disjunctive clause ψ and its compatible children φ and φ' in D, the following linear equality is generated:

$$P(\psi) = P(\varphi) + P(\varphi')$$

   For example, the following equality is generated in C_1:

$$P(L) = P(L \wedge \neg A) + P(L \wedge A)$$

Figure 3 shows all the equalities generated by BASIC for Z_1, Q_1, and C_1, while Figure 4 shows the additional equalities that are generated when the control set is expanded to C_1'.

$$
\begin{aligned}
P(T \vee F) &= P(F) + P(T) - P(T \wedge F) \\
P(F) &= P(T \wedge F) + P(\neg T \wedge F) \\
P(T) &= P(T \wedge F) + P(T \wedge \neg F)
\end{aligned}
$$

Figure 4: **Additional equalities generated by BASIC for Z_1, Q_1, and C_1'**

3.2 Strategy INEQS

Strategy INEQS extends the BASIC strategy in the sense that if some descendant of a clause is missing from the control set, then instead of discarding the linear equality altogether a linear inequality is generated. For a disjunctive clause $\psi = \alpha_1 \vee \cdots \vee \alpha_m$ ($m > 1$) such that D contains ψ, and some of ψ's descendants, a $\geq$ inequality is generated if the probability of the missing descendant(s) was to be added if it was in the control set D. Otherwise a $\leq$ inequality is generated. For atomic and conjunctive clauses a $\geq$ inequality is generated if a child is missing.

For example, the inequalities $P(T \vee F) \leq P(T) + P(F)$ and $P(T) \geq P(T \wedge \neg F)$ are generated for C_1, since $T \wedge F$ is not in C_1.

3.3 Strategy EXPSN

EXPSN is the most sophisticated of the three strategies because it expands missing clauses whenever possible. Again it is based on the BASIC strategy, but if some descendant ψ_i (direct or not) of a clause ψ is missing it tries to replace it by its expansion, meaning, it tries to generate the linear equality corresponding to the ψ_i and replace ψ_i by its expansion in the original linear equality that is being constructed. The expansion procedure is recursive in the sense that if one or more of ψ_i's descendants are missing, then EXPSN tries to expand these clauses too. If a clause cannot be expanded (because some of its descendants are missing, and cannot be expanded), then the linear equality is not generated. An important restriction on EXPSN is that, when trying to expand a disjunctive clause of size m, and its conjunctive descendant ψ_m of size m is missing, EXPSN does not try to expand ψ_m as this would result in an infinite loop. For example, suppose EXPSN is trying to generate a linear equality for the clause $\alpha_1 \vee \alpha_2$, and the following descendants are available in the control set: α_1, α_2, in other words the clause $\alpha_1 \wedge \alpha_2$ is missing. Now if EXPSN were to expand the missing clause $\alpha_1 \wedge \alpha_2$, we would get $P(\alpha_1 \wedge \alpha_2) = P(\alpha_1) + P(\alpha_2) - P(\alpha_1 \vee \alpha_2)$, resulting in an infinite loop.

As an example of EXPSN, the following equality is generated in C_2': $P(A) = P(A \wedge F) + P(A \wedge T \wedge \neg F) + P(A \wedge \neg T \wedge \neg F)$, where $P(A \wedge T \wedge \neg F) + P(A \wedge \neg T \wedge \neg F)$ represents the expansion for the missing clause $A \wedge \neg F$.

4 Anytime Algorithms

This section lists our algorithm for anytime probabilistic reasoning. Prob-reasoning is the top-level algorithm.

Algorithm Prob-Reasoning(D,Z,Q,S,n):

Inputs:
```
   D: a set of clauses called the control set
   Z: the input probabilistic theory
   Q: the query
   S: the strategy to be used
   n:  the number of literals
```
Global variables:
```
   cl:  list of all clauses
   rules:  list of rules generated
begin
   cl = list of clauses in D ,Z and Q;
   Special-sort(cl); i=0;
   repeat
      if Check-clause(cl[i]) then
         S(i);
      i=i+1;
   until first clause of size n found;
   return(rules);
end (Prob-Reasoning).
```

Procedure S(k) for each strategy S generates the appropriate rules for the clause cl[k].

Procedure Basic(k):
```
begin
   c = cl[k]; i = k+1;
   m = No-desc(c);
   clist = (c);
   for j = i to length(cl) do
      if Desc(cl(j),c) then
         add cl(j) to clist;
   if length(clist) = m then
      Special-sort(clist);
      append (list = clist) to rules;
      return(rules);
   else Return(nil);
end (Basic).
```

Procedure Ineqs(k):
```
begin
   c = cl[k]; i = k+1;
   m = No-desc(c);
   clist = (c);
   for j = i to length(cl) do
      if Desc(cl(j),c) then
         add cl(j) to clist;
   Special-sort(clist);
   if length(clist) = 0 then
      return(nil);
   if length(clist) = m then
      op = ''='';
   else op= ''>='' or ''<=''
      depending on missing clauses;
   append (list op clist) to rules;
   return(rules);
end (Ineqs).
```

Procedure Exps(k):
```
begin
   c = cl[k]; i = k+1;
   m = No-desc(c);
   clist = (c);
   for j = i to length(cl) do
```

```
      if Desc(cl(j),c) then
         add cl(j) to clist;
   Special-sort(clist);
   if (length(clist) != m) then
      missing = Find-des(c, clist);
      i = 0;
      repeat
         mc = missing[i];
         result = Exps(mc);
         if result = nil then return(nil);
         add result to clist;
         i = i+1;
            until i > length(missing);
         append (list = clist) to rules;
         return (list = clist);
      end (Exps).
```

The above algorithm uses several procedures that are described below:

Special-sort(cl): sorts its argument cl in such a way that all the disjunctive clauses come first in decreasing order of size, followed by the atoms, which are followed by the conjunctive clauses in increasing order of size. As an example, $\alpha_1 \vee \alpha_2 \vee \alpha_3$, $\alpha_1 \vee \alpha_2$, α_1, α_2, $\alpha_2 \wedge \alpha_3$, and $\alpha_1 \wedge \alpha_2 \wedge \alpha_3$.

Check-clause(c): returns true if c is in the list cl, has not been expanded, and its complementary and counterpart clauses have not been expanded.

No-desc(c): returns the number of descendants of clause c.

Desc(x,y): returns true if x is a descendant of y.

Find-des(c,clist): returns the missing descendants for clause c.

length(x): returns the number of elements in x.

5 Computational Complexity

The computational complexity of probabilistic reasoning is a major concern for researchers in this field, since the number of clauses needed to specify a complete probabilistic model grows exponentially with the number of propositions. Exact probabilistic inference using general belief networks is NP-hard [2], and approximating probabilistic inference in belief networks is also NP-hard [3]. The method developed by [10] is $2n^2\log(n)$ in the most optimistic case, under the assumptions of skewed probability distributions and sufficiently sparse belief networks, and no worst case complexity results are provided. The reasoner of [20] runs in a time linear over a space of clauses of exponential size. The decision-problem version of the problem that we are dealing with is to determine whether a system of inequalities of the form $a \leq P(\psi_i) \leq b$ is feasible or not, where ψ_i is an arbitrary propositional clause and a and b are between 0 and 1 inclusive.

The special ordering in our algorithm of the list of clauses and traversal insures that the method runs in a time that is polynomial in the size of the control set D. Furthermore, specific techniques are used to reduce the size of D, to the extent that in the limiting case, where D contains all the clauses over the n atoms, the size is reduced in half. The first technique is *not to expand a clause if its complementary clause* has been expanded, i.e if a constraint has been generated for $P(\psi_i)$ then do not generate a constraint for $P(\neg\psi_i)$. As an example, if a constraint has been generated for $P(\alpha_1 \vee \alpha_2)$ and D contains $(\neg\alpha_1 \wedge \neg\alpha_2)$, then no constraint will be generated for $P(\neg\alpha_1 \wedge \neg\alpha_2)$ since $P(\alpha_1 \vee \alpha_2) = 1 - P(\neg\alpha_1 \wedge \neg\alpha_2)$. The second technique, is *not to expand a clause if its counterpart clause* has been expanded. The counterpart of a clause ψ_i is the clause ψ_j that is of the same type as ψ_i, but where its positive literals are negated in ψ_i and its negative literals are positive in ψ_i. For example, the counterpart clause of $(\alpha_1 \vee \neg\alpha_2)$ is $(\neg\alpha_1 \vee \alpha_2)$.

After generating the constraints that capture the probabilistic dependencies among the clauses in D, they are combined with those in Z to form a linear programming problem, which is then solved to provide probabilities of arbitrary clauses. Solving a linear programming problem is known to be $O(m^{3.5}E^2)$ [14], where m in our case is the size of the control set D (which is equivalent to the number of variables in the corresponding linear program) and E is the sum of the lengths of the constraint set, which is equal to $(3 * Size(D) - 1 + Size(Z)) * (Size(D) + f(n))$, where $f(n)$ is a polynomial in n of degree 3.

6 Other Related Approaches

There has been a lot of interesting work in the area of anytime probabilistic reasoning [20, 12, 19, 10]. However, these methods are either incomplete, compute probabilities of only atomic formulas, are not known to be tractable, or are not general-purpose. Ramoni [20] presents a method for anytime reasoning that extends the BCP algorithm [15] of Logic-Based truth maintenance systems from propositional calculus to probabilistic logic. The main weakness of his method is that it is incomplete due to the fact that only a specific set of clauses, called homogeneous clauses, is used when computing the probabilities. As an example, suppose that $P(\alpha_1 \vee \alpha_2 \vee \alpha_3) = [0.9, 0.9]$, $P(\neg\alpha_1 \vee \neg\alpha_2) = [0.8, 0.8]$, $P(\neg\alpha_1 \vee \neg\alpha_3) = [0.7, 0.7]$, $P(\neg\alpha_2 \vee \neg\alpha_3) = [0.7, 0.7]$, $P(\neg\alpha_1 \vee \neg\alpha_2 \vee \neg\alpha_3) = [0.9, 0.9]$, $P(\alpha_1) = [0.5, 0.5]$, and $P(\alpha_2) = [0.5, 0.5]$. Ramoni's method gives $P(\alpha_3) = [0.3, 0.8]$, whereas, our method yields the correct answer [0.6,0.6]. Another restriction of Ramoni's method is that it only computes probabilities for atomic clauses. D'Ambrosio in [10], presents an incremental reasoner for belief networks by constructing evaluation poly-trees. A restrictive assumption made by his method is that it requires the distributions in the belief net to be skewed. No worst case complexity result is provided. [12] presents a set of inference rules for deriving increasingly accurate conclusions, however, no tractability claims are made and no efficient procedure for applying the rules is provided. These inference rules were used in [19] to develop anytime decision methods for probabilistic databases.

7 Conclusions

We presented a novel approach for anytime reasoning with probabilistic inequalities. Our approach can be used for computing probabilities of arbitrary propositional clauses, is tractable in providing the initial approximate answers, and provides exact answers in the limiting case. Reasoning is made tractable by restricting it to a set of clauses in a control set that can be gradually enlarged as more resources become available. We presented three strategies that differ in the way constraints are generated from the clauses in the control set.

Our techniques can be extended to conditional probabilities using the Chain rule: $P(\alpha_1 \wedge \alpha_2) = P(\alpha_2) * P(\alpha_1|\alpha_2)$. This allows us to handle ignorant belief networks [21], where some conditional probabilities are missing.

References

[1] I. Beinlich, H.J. Suemondt, R.M. Chavez, and G.F. Cooper. The ALARM monitoring system : A case study with two probabilistic inference techniques for belief networks. In *Proceedings Second European Conference on Artificial Intelligence in Medicine*, pages 247–256, London, August 1989. http://www.norsys.com/networklibrary.html.

[2] G. Cooper. The computational complexity of probabilistic inference using bayesian belief networks. *Artificial Intelligence*, 42:393–406, 1990.

[3] P. Dagum and M. Luby. Approximating probabilistic inference in bayesian belief networks is NP-hard. *Artificial Intelligence*, 60:141–153, 1993.

[4] M. Dalal. Efficient propositional constraint propagation. In *Proceedings Tenth National Conference on Artificial Intelligence (AAAI-92)*, pages 409–414, San Jose, California, 1992. American Association for Artificial Intelligence.

[5] M. Dalal. Tractable deduction in knowledge representation systems. In B. Nebel, C. Rich, and W. Swartout, editors, *Principles of Knowledge Representation and Reasoning: Proceedings of the Third International Conference (KR'92)*, pages 393–402, Cambridge, Massachusetts, 1992. Morgan Kaufmann Publishers.

[6] M. Dalal. Tractable reasoning in knowledge representation systems. Technical Report CUCS-017-95, Department of Computer Science, Columbia University, New York, NY, July 1995. file://ftp.cs.columbia.edu/reports/reports-1995/cucs-017-95.ps.gz.

[7] M. Dalal. Anytime families of tractable propositional reasoners. In *Fourth International Symposium on Artificial Intelligence and Mathematics (AI/MATH-96)*, pages 42–45, Florida, 1996.

[8] M. Dalal. Semantics of an anytime family of reasoners. In W. Wahlster, editor, *Proceedings Twelveth European Conference on Artificial Intelligence (ECAI 96)*, pages 360–364, Budapest, Hungary, 1996. John Wiley and Sons, Ltd.

[9] M. Dalal and Y. Feng. Anytime temporal reasoning based on propositional satisfiability (extended abstract). In E. C. Freuder, editor, *Proceedings of Second International Conference on Principles and Practice of Constraint Programming (CP96)*, pages 535–536, Cambridge, Massachusetts, Aug 1996. Springer.

[10] B. D'Ambrosio. Incremental probabilistic inference. In *Proceedings of the Ninth Annual Conference on Uncertainty in Artificial Intelligence (UAI-93)*, 1993.

[11] R. Fagin, J.Y. Halpern, and N. Megiddo. A logic for reasoning about probabilities. *Information and Control*, 87:78–128, 1990.

[12] P. Haddawy and A.M. Frisch. Anytime deduction for probabilistic logic. *Artificial Intelligence*, 69(1–2):93, 1994.

[13] E.J. Horvitz. Reasoning under varying and uncertain resource constraints. In *Proceedings Eleventh International Joint Conference on Artificial Intelligence (IJCAI-89)*, pages 1121–1127. Morgan Kaufmann, 1989.

[14] N. Karmarkar. A new polynomial-time algorithm for linear programming. *Combinatorica*, 4:302–311, 1984.

[15] D. McAllester. Truth maintenance. In *Proceedings Eighth National Conference on Artificial Intelligence (AAAI-90)*, pages 1109–1116, 1990.

[16] E. Mendelson. *Introduction to Mathematical Logic*. Van Nostrand, Princeton, N.J., 1964.

[17] N. J. Nilsson. Probabilistic logic. *Artificial Intelligence*, 28(1):71–87, 1986.

[18] J. Pearl. *Probabilistic Reasoning in Intelligent Systems*. Morgan Kaufmann, 1988.

[19] M. Pittarelli. Anytime decision making with imprecise probabilities. In *Proceedings of the Tenth Annual Conference on Uncertainty in Artificial Intelligence (UAI-94)*, 1994.

[20] M. Ramoni and A. Riva. Belief maintenance in bayesian networks. In *Proceedings of the Tenth Annual Conference on Uncertainty in Artificial Intelligence (UAI-94)*, pages 204–212, 1994.

[21] M. Ramoni, A. Riva, and V. Patel. Probabilistic reasoning under ignorance. In *16th annual conference of the Cognitive Society. Atlanta, Georgia*, 1994.

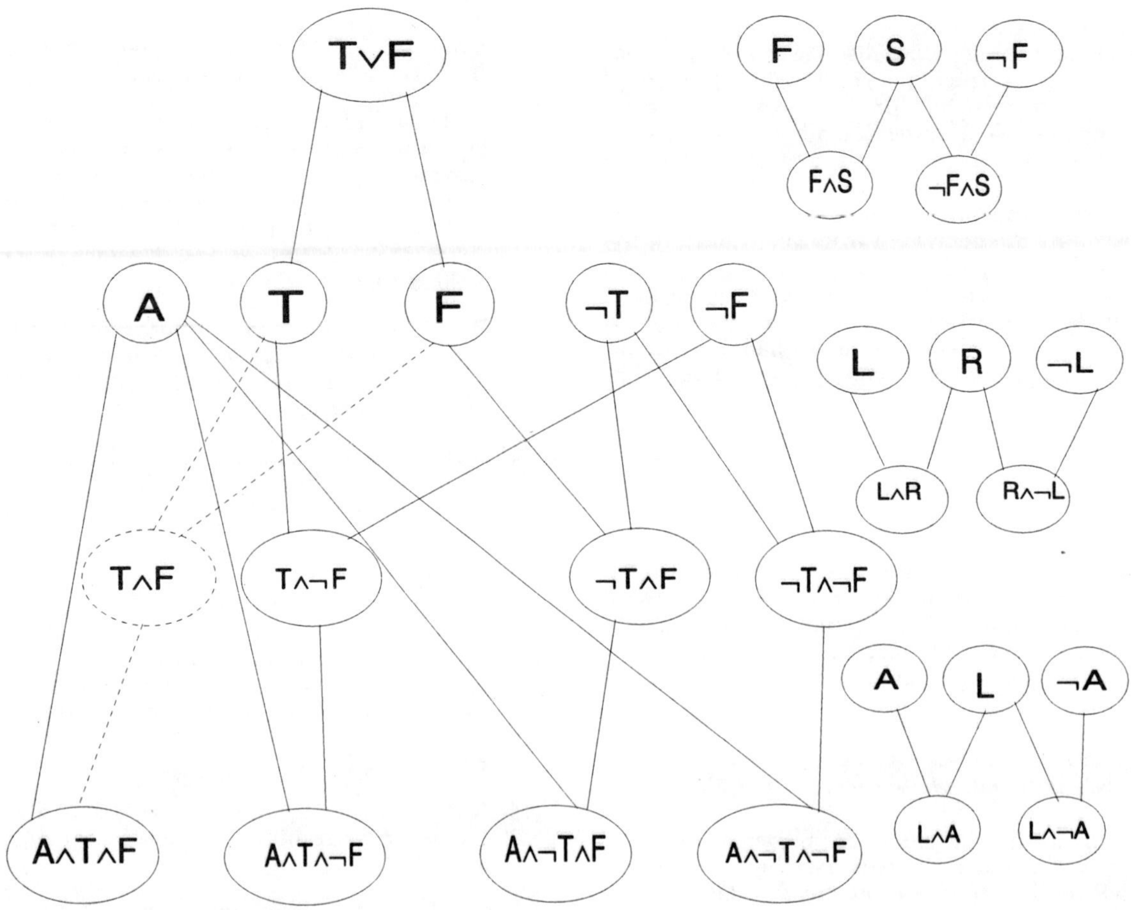

Figure 5: **Graphical structures of the control sets C_1 (solid lines only) and C_1' (both solid and dotted lines)**

The Space Algebra: Spatial Reasoning without Composition Tables

Baher A. El-Geresy
Dept. of Computer Studies, University of Glamorgan,
Treforest, Mid Glamorgan, CF37 1DL, Wales, U.K.
bageresy@glam.ac.uk

Abstract

In this paper we propose a general approach for reasoning with incomplete topological knowledge in space without the need for composition tables. The approach builds on and generalizes our earlier formalism where spatial relations are represented by the intersection of object and space components. The reasoning method is applicable to objects of arbitrary complexity. One general equation is proposed here for the propagation of intersections between object components and the derivation of the result of spatial composition. Hence, a general algebra for reasoning in space is proposed. A major advantage of this method is that reasoning with incomplete knowledge can be done by direct application of the equation and the algebra on any spatial objects considered, and thus eliminates the need for utilizing the inordinate number of composition tables which must be built for specific object types and topology. The method is applied on spatial objects of arbitrary complexity and in a finite definite number of steps controlled by the complexity needed in the representation of objects and the granularity of the spatial relations required.

1. Introduction

Spatial reasoning is the field of AI which studies formalisms for encoding qualitative spatial knowledge [5]. The ability to handle a certain level of indeterminacy makes techniques of spatial reasoning attractive to many application domains, such as computer vision, image processing, medical and geographic information systems (GIS). Qualitative treatment of the temporal knowledge is an established research area where different approaches exist for the representation of temporal entities (intervals, point) and their relations (interval and point algebra) [3, 17]. A similar general treatment of spatial knowledge is still lacking. While most of the temporal reasoning tasks are based on convex intervals, the situation is more complex in spatial reasoning. An inordinate number of possibilities exist considering the variations in the objects topology, shape and dimension of the embedding space.

Recently, a considerable body of research work has been devoted to studying and identifying the problem of spatial reasoning. Most of the work presented considered the reasoning problem with specific spatial objects. While dealing with specific object topologies may be of benefit for some applications [8, 9, 10], it is not practical in general. For example, in a GIS there is no limit on the object types, dimensions and topologies used. New composition tables need to be built for every new type of objects considered [16].

In [11], we presented a spatial reasoning formalism which was shown to derive composition tables for objects of arbitrary complexity in any space dimension. In earlier works, spatial reasoning was only possible for either convex [9, 15, 14, 13, 2, 1] or concave [8, 4] simple regions, since composition tables for those shapes were successfully derived. For a general spatial reasoner, all such tables have to be either stored initially or derived on the fly. Given the inordinate number of spatial objects, both options are not practically feasible for storage and computational costs.

Also since the incomplete or uncertain knowledge is usually represented by a disjunctive set of relation, one reasoning step will involve more than one look up operation in the table and a summation operation. For example, if for convex regions A, B and C, we have the relations $touch(A, B) \vee overlap(A, B)$ and $inside(B, C) \vee overlap(B, C)$, then the relations between A and C shall involve four look up operations in the composition table for each alternative combination with a summation operation in the end. Using the composition tables in this way slows the reasoning process [16].

In this paper, a general algebra for space is presented which completely eliminates the need for composition tables and which also allows the application of spatial reasoning with incomplete or uncertain knowledge of topological relations. The approach builds upon that proposed in [11] and inherits its generality in dealing with topological relations between objects of arbitrary complexity. It is also shown how the algebra is general and can be used for propagating spatial relations given an incomplete set of spatial knowledge, an important issue in many spatial applications.

The paper is organized as follows. In section 2, the approach used for the representation of topological relations is given. The space algebra is then presented in section 3. Several examples are given in section 4 to demonstrate the generality of the approach and some conclusions are derived in section 5.

2. The Approach

2.1. The Underlying Representation

Objects of interest and their embedding space are divided into components according to a required resolution. The connectivity of those components is explicitly represented. The representation of the spatial relations uses a similar approach to that used in [11] where relationships are described by the intersection of the objects components.

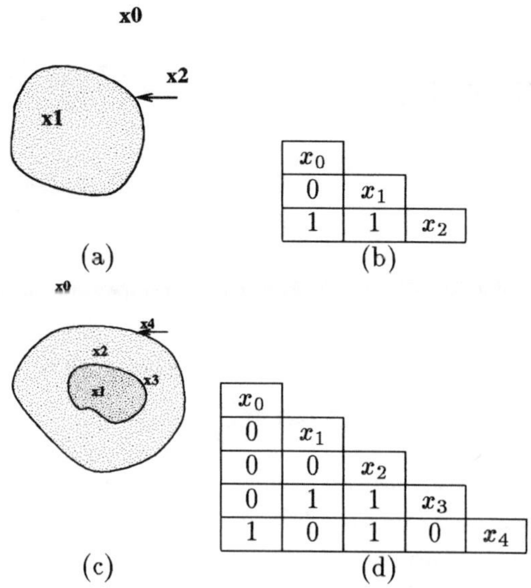

Figure 1. (a) Possible decomposition of a convex-shaped object and its embedding space. (b) Adjacency structure for the shape in (a). (c) Possible decomposition of a region with a hole. (d) Adjacency structure for the shape in (c).

2.1.1 The Underlying Representation of Object Topology

Let S be the space in which the object is embedded. The object and its embedding space are assumed to be *dense* and *connected*. The embedding space is also assumed to be infinite. The object and its embedding space are decomposed into components which reflects the objects and space topology such that,

1. No overlap exist between any of the representative components.
2. The union of the components is equal to the embedding space.

The topology of the object and the embedding space can then be described by a matrix whose elements represent the connectivity relations between its components, denoted *adjacency matrix*. Only half the matrix is sufficient for the representation of the object's topology. In figure 1(a) a possible decomposition of a convex object and its embedding space is shown and in 1(b) the adjacency structure for its components is presented. The example in figure 1(c) demonstrates the flexibility of the adjacency matrix in representing different topologies. In 1(c), a convex region with a hole is shown (which may represent an island with a lake) with two areal component x_1 and x_2 and two linear components x_3 and x_4. The adjacency matrix is shown in 1(d). The example can also be used to demonstrate the representations of regions with indeterminate boundaries. If the figure represents an oil tanker (x_1 and x_3) with an oil leakage around it represented by the region x_2, then the component x_4 and its corresponding row can be omitted from the matrix. If the figure represents a region with indeterminate boundaries (or non-crisp regions as investigated by Cohn et al [7] and Clementini et al [6]), then both the rows corresponding to x_3 and x_4 must be omitted, and the connectivity of x_0 changed in the matrix for both cases. Hence the decomposition of the space can be carried out according to the specific application at hand with no restrictions. The above example also shows the flexibility of the adjacency matrix for representing virtual components which facilitates the qualitative representation of physical phenomena.

2.1.2 The Underlying Representation of Spatial Relations

Topological relations are represented through the intersection of objects components. The distinction of

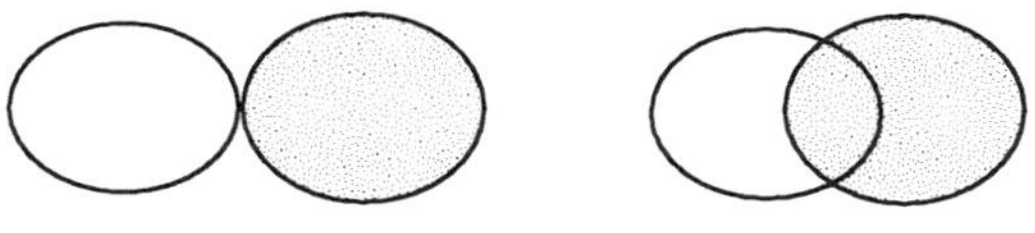

touch(x,y) (T(x,y))

	y_0	y_1	y_2
x_0	1	1	1
x_1	1	0	0
x_2	1	0	1

(a)

overlap(x,y) (O(x,y))

	y_0	y_1	y_2
x_0	1	1	1
x_1	1	1	1
x_2	1	1	1

(b)

Figure 2. Different qualitative spatial relationships distinguished by identifying the appropriate intersection of components of the objects and the space, and their corresponding intersection matrices respectively.

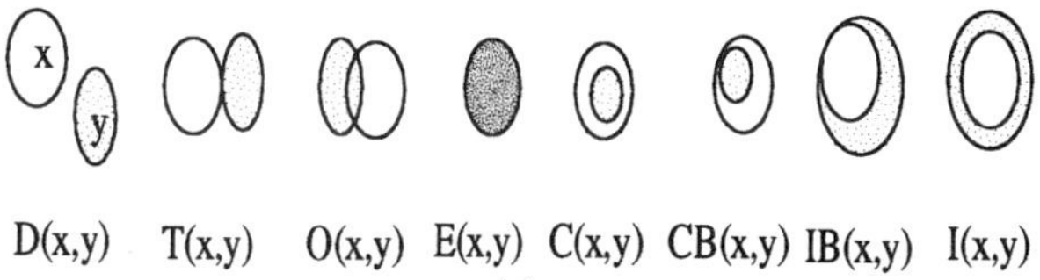

(a)

	y_0	y_1	y_2
x_0	ALL	$(D \vee T \vee O \vee I \vee IB)$	$(D \vee T \vee O \vee I \vee IB)$
x_1	$(D \vee T \vee O \vee C \vee CB)$	$(O \vee I \vee IB \vee C \vee CB \vee E)$	$(O \vee C \vee CB)$
x_2	$(D \vee T \vee O \vee C \vee CB)$	$(I \vee IB \vee O)$	$(T \vee O \vee IB \vee CB \vee E)$

(b)

Figure 3. (a) Set of possible relations between two convex areal objects. (b) Mapping the non-empty intersection of object components into a disjunctive set of possible relations.

topological relations is dependent on the strategy used in the decomposition of the objects and their related spaces.

The complete set of spatial relationships are represented by combinatorial intersection of the components of one space with those of the other space.

If $R(x,y)$ is a relation of interest between object x and object y, and X and Y are the spaces associated with the objects respectively such that m is the number of components in X and l is the number of components in Y, then a spatial relation $R(x,y)$ can be represented by one state of the following equation:

$$\begin{aligned} R(x,y) &= X \cap Y \\ &= \left(\bigcup_{i=1}^{m} x_i\right) \cap \left(\bigcup_{j=1}^{l} y_j\right) \\ &= (x_1 \cap y_1, \cdots, x_1 \cap y_m, x_2 \cap y_1, \cdots, x_n \cap y_m) \end{aligned}$$

The intersection $x_i \cap y_j$ can be an empty or a non-empty intersection. The above set of intersections shall be represented by an intersection matrix, as follows,

$R(x,y) =$

	y_0	y_1	y_2	$\cdots$
x_0				
x_1				
x_2				
$\vdots$				

For example, spatial relationships and their corresponding intersection matrices are shown in figure 2. The component x_2 have a non-empty intersection with y_1 in 2(a) and an empty intersection in 2(b).

2.1.3 Mapping Component Intersections into Relations

The intersection matrix is in fact a set of intersection constraints whose values identifies specific spatial relationships. Figure 3 represents the mapping between intersection constraints and whole set of spatial relations in the case of two convex areal objects. Table entries represent the resulting set of possible relations if the result of the intersection of the corresponding components is non-empty (or (1)). For example, if $x_0 \cap y_2 = 1$ is the only intersection known then the relationship between objects x and y is $D \vee T \vee O \vee I \vee IB$, and so on. If the result of the intersection is the empty set (or (0)), then the possible set of relations will be the complement of the sets shown. If $x_0 \cap y_2 = 0$, then the corresponding table entry will be $E \vee C \vee CB$. The possible relations between objects x and y can therefore be derived from the combination (set intersection) of all the table entries. An example is given in figure 4 where in 4(a) the intersection matrix for objects x and y is shown (with unknown value for $x_2 \cap y_2$). In 4(b) the mapping of the intersections into possible relations is given using the table (and its complement) in figure 3(b). The spatial relations between objects x and y is then derived from the set intersection of all table entries to be $I(x,y) \vee IB(x,y)$ shown in 4(c).

2.1.4 General Constraints

A subset of the set of constraints defining all spatial relations are general and are applicable to any relationship between any objects. These general constraints

	y_0	y_1	y_2
x_0	1	1	1
x_1	0	1	0
x_2	0	1	$0 \vee 1$

(a)

I(x,y) $\vee$ IB(x,y)

(c)

	y_0	y_1	y_2
x_0	ALL	$(D \vee T \vee O \vee I \vee IB)$	$(D \vee T \vee O \vee I \vee IB)$
x_1	$(I \vee IB \vee E)$	$(O \vee I \vee IB \vee C \vee CB \vee E)$	$(I \vee IB \vee O \vee T \vee E)$
x_2	$(I \vee IB \vee E)$	$(I \vee IB \vee O)$	$(T \vee O \vee IB \vee CB \vee E)$ OR $(D \vee I \vee C)$

(b)

Figure 4. (a) An example intersection matrix with unknown value for $x_2 \cap y_2$. (b) Mapping intersections of individual components to possible relations. (c) Possible relations between objects as the common subset in all the table entries.

are a consequence of the initial assumptions used in the definition of the object and space topology.

The two general intersection constraints are:

1. Every unbounded (infinite) component of one space must intersect with at least one unbounded (infinite) component of the other space.

2. Every component from one space must intersect with at least one component from the other space.

2.2. The Space Algebra

The process of spatial reasoning can be defined as the process of propagating the intersection constraints of two spatial relations (for example, $R_1(A,B)$ and $R_2(B,C)$), to derive a new set of intersections between objects. The derived constraints can then be mapped to a specific spatial relation (i.e. the relation $R_3(A,C)$).

Let $X = \bigcup_{i=1}^{m} x_i$ and $Z = \bigcup_{k=1}^{n} z_k$ represent the spaces X and Z associated with objects x and z respectively. m and n are the total number of components in those spaces. If $y_j \subset Y$ and Y is the embedding space for the common object in the composition relation and since $X = Y = Z$, it follows that $(X \supset y_j) \wedge (y_j \subset Z)$.

In general the intersection of two components can take one of three values: 0 or 1 or ? where 0 indicates an empty intersection, 1 a non-empty intersection and ? indicates either a 0 or a 1. (unknown value). Hence, if $P = \{0, 1, ?\}$ then $y_j \subset X \rightarrow \forall x_i \in X(y_j \cap x_i = P_q)$ where $P_q \in P$. Similarly, $y_j \subset Z \rightarrow \forall z_k \in Z(y_j \cap z_k = P_q)$

The reasoning process can be carried in two steps, namely:

1. **Multiplication Operation:** on the intersection relations between every component from the intermediate space and every component of the other two spaces.

2. **Addition Operation:** on the results of multiplication for all the components of the intermediate space.

The multiplication operation can be expressed as follows:

$$(X \cap Z)_{y_j} = \left(\bigcup_{i=1}^{m} x_i \cap y_j \right) \star \left(\bigcup_{k=1}^{n} z_k \cap y_j \right) \quad (1)$$

where $X \cap Z)_{y_j}$ are the propagated intersection relations between components of the spaces X and Y based on their intersection with the component y_j of space Y. The addition operation can be expressed as follows:

$$(X \cap Z) = \Sigma_{j=1}^{l} (X \cap Z)_{y_j} \quad (2)$$

where l is the total number of components of space Y.

Substituting 1 in 2 we get the general reasoning equation.

<u>**General Reasoning Equation**</u>

$$X \cap Z = \Sigma_{j=1}^{l} \left(\left(\bigcup_{i=1}^{m} x_i \cap y_j \right) \star \left(\bigcup_{k=1}^{n} z_k \cap y_j \right) \right) \quad (3)$$

Note that there is no restriction on the application of equation 1 to a single or a set of components of the intermediate space, hence a general form for equation 1 can be stated as follows.

$$(X \cap Z)_{y_j} = \left(\bigcup_{i=1}^{m} x_i \cap y' \right) \star \left(\bigcup_{k=1}^{n} z_k \cap y' \right) \quad (4)$$

where $y' \subseteq Y$, for example $y' = y_1 \cup y_2$..

The two equations 3 and 4 are the two general equation for spatial reasoning with incomplete or uncertain knowledge. Equation 3 shall always be applied in all cases. Equation 4 is only needed to be applied with equation 3 whenever a constraint exist of the following form:

$$x_i \cap y_j = ? \wedge x_i \cap y_{j+1} = ? \wedge x_i \cap (y_j \cup y_{j+1}) = 1 \quad (5)$$

i.e. the intersection of x_i with both y_j and y_{j+1} cannot be empty, then using $y' = (y_j \cup y_{j+1})$ will give $x_i \cap y' = 1$.

To distinguish the constraint in 5 from a non related constraint of the form: $x_i \cap y_j \ = ? \wedge x_i \cap y_{j+1} \ = ? \wedge x_i \cap (y_j \cup y_{j+1}) =?$, a label will be used and equation 5 can be rewritten as: $x_i \cap y_j \ = ?_a \ \wedge \ x_i \cap y_{j+1} \ = ?_a$ The added letter a indicates that the two constraints are related.

A constraint of the type 5 can be either an input to the reasoning task or an output of it.

2.2.1 Conditions for Related Constraints ($?_\alpha$)

In the previous section we showed how to deal with a related condition of the form $x_i \cap y_j \ =? \ \wedge \ x_i \cap y_{j+1} =? \ \wedge \ x_i \cap (y_j \cup y_{j+1}) = 1$ In this section the conditions under which such a constraint can result from the reasoning process are identified.

If x'' is the set of components of space X with all its components having a non-empty intersection with the component y_j of space Y. If x' is the set of components of space X with all its components having intersection values with component y_j of space Y as either 1 or ?. If m'' is the number of components of x'' and m' is the number of components of x', i.e. $x'' \subseteq x' \subset X$ and $m'' \subseteq m' \subseteq m$. Similarly, $z'' \subseteq z' \subset Z$ and $n'' \subseteq n' \subseteq n$.

Then the condition under which a related constraint will result from the reasoning process is as follows,

$$m'' > 0 \ \wedge \ n'' > 0 \ \wedge \ m' > 1 \ \wedge \ n' > 1 \qquad (6)$$

For example, if $(x_1 \cap y_1 =? \wedge x_2 \cap y_1 = 1) \wedge (z_1 \cap y_1 = 1 \wedge z_2 \cap y_1 =?)$, where $m'' = n'' = 1$ and $m' = n' = 2$. then the result of the composition can be expressed as either:

- $x_1 \cap z_1 =? \wedge x_1 \cap z_2 =? \wedge x_2 \cap z_1 =? \wedge x_2 \cap z_2 =?$ with $x_2 \cap (z_1 \cup z_2) = 1 \wedge z_1 \cap (x_1 \cup x_2) = 1$, or,
- $(x_2 \cap z_1 =?_\alpha \wedge x_2 \cap z_2 =?_\alpha) \ \wedge \ (z_1 \cap x_1 =?_\beta \wedge z_1 \cap x_2 =?_\beta$.

Note that if $m'' = m' = 1 \vee n'' = n' = 1$, such that $x_1 \cap y_1 = 1 \wedge z_1 \cap yl = 1 \wedge z_2 \cap y_1 =?$, then the result of the composition is $x_1 \cap z_1 = 1 \wedge x_1 \cap z_2 =?$.

Hence, there is a need to distinguish the relations where $m'' > 0 \wedge m' > 1$ and $n'' > 0 \wedge n' > 1$. We shall use the notations 1^+ and $?^+$ for values under the later condition.

Also note that the condition where $m = (m'' \vee m') \wedge n = (m'' \vee n')$ will result in a propagation of ? for all elements since it is an expression of the second general constraint.

$\star$	0	?	1	$?^+$	1^+
0	0	0	0	0	0
?	0	?	?	?	?
1	0	?	1	?	1
$?^+$	0	?	?	?	$?_\alpha$
1^+	0	?	1	?	$?_\alpha$

Table 1. Multiplication Table for incomplete knowledge.

+	0	?	1	$?_\beta$
0	0	?	1	$?_\beta$
?	?	?	1	$?_\beta$
1	1	1	1	1
$?_\alpha$	$?_\alpha$	$?_\alpha$	1	$?_\alpha \wedge ?_\beta$

Table 2. Addition Table for incomplete knowledge.

Accordingly the multiplication and addition tables of our space algebra are as shown in figure 1 and 2.

Note that in the addition table, we used $?_\alpha$ and $?_\beta$ since we add results for different components of space Y, i.e. $?_\alpha + ?_\beta = ?_\alpha \wedge ?_\beta$.

Equations 3 and 4 and the multiplication and addition tables represent the general space algebra for reasoning with incomplete or uncertain knowledge. The algebra makes no restriction on the complexity of the objects used or the completeness or uncertainty of the knowledge of the topological relations involved.

3. Example of Spatial Reasoning with Incomplete Knowledge

Consider the reasoning problem where the relations between simple convex areal objects x, y and z are: $C(x, y)$ *or* $CB(x, y)$ between x and y and $D(y, z)$ *or* $T(y, z)$ between y and z, as shown in figure 5(a). This indefiniteness is reflected in the intersection matrices in the figure where $x_2 \cap y_2 =?$ and $y_2 \cap z_2 =?$.

It is required to derive the possible relationships between objects x and z.

Applying the general topological reasoning equation 3 on y_0, y_1 and y_2 using the multiplication table, we get the following,

- y_0 intersections: ($n'' = n$ and $m'' = m$ - second

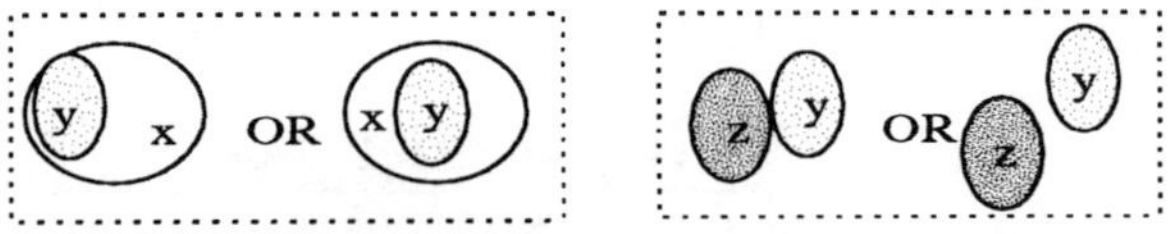

x_2	x_1	x_0		z_0	z_1	z_2
1	1	1	y_0	1	1	1
0	1	0	y_1	1	0	0
?	1	0	y_2	1	0	?

(a)

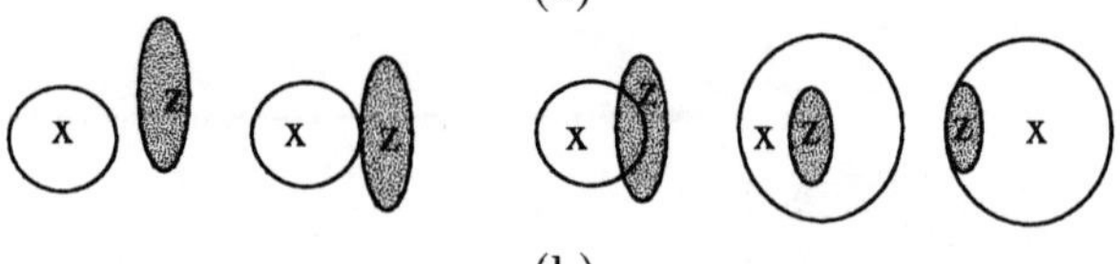

(b)

Figure 5. (a) Example reasoning problem with incomplete knowledge. (b) Resulting possible set of relations between x and z.

general constraint)

$$(X \cap Z)_{y_0} \quad \rightarrow \quad \{x_0, x_1, x_2\} \cap \{z_0, z_1, z_2\} =?$$

- y_1 intersections: $x_1 \cap z_0 = 1$ and $(X - x_2) \cap (Z - z_0) = \phi$.
- y_2 intersections: $(n'' > 0 \wedge n' > 1 \wedge m'' > 0 \wedge m' > 1$, i.e. a constraint of the type described in section 2.2.1(6) above.

  $x_1 \cap z_0 =?_a$
  $x_1 \cap z_2 =?_a$
  $z_0 \cap x_1 =?_b$
  $z_0 \cap x_2 =?_b$
  $x_0 \cap (z_0 \cup z_1 \cup z_2) = 0$
  $x_2 \cap z_2 =?$
  $z_1 \cap (x_0 \cup x_1 \cup x_2) = 0$

Using the addition table we get the following:

	y_0	y_1	y_2	$\Sigma_{j=1}^{3} y_j$
$x_0 \cap z_0$	?	0	0	?
$x_0 \cap z_1$	?	0	0	?
$x_0 \cap z_2$	?	0	0	?
$x_1 \cap z_0$	?	1	$?_a \wedge ?_b$	1
$x_1 \cap z_1$	?	0	0	?
$x_1 \cap z_2$	?	0	$?_a$	$?_a$
$x_2 \cap z_0$	?	0	$?_b$	$?_b$
$x_2 \cap z_1$	?	0	0	?
$x_2 \cap z_2$	?	0	?	?

Also from the first general constraint $x_0 \cap z_0 = 1$. Compiling the above intersection we get the following resulting intersection matrix,

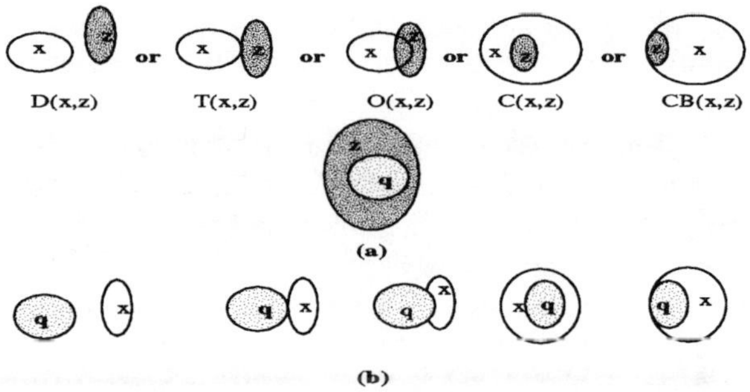

Figure 6. (a) Further composition of the spatial relations between x and z from the previous example with the relation $C(z, q)$ to get the possible relations between x and q in (b).

	z_0	z_1	z_2
x_0	1	?	?
x_1	1	?	?
x_2	?	?	?

Mapping the above matrix into spatial relations, as shown earlier in table 3(b), gives the disjunctive set: $R(X, Z) = D \vee T \vee O \vee C \vee CB$ as shown in figure 5(b).

3.1. Example 2

The resulting relationships in the above example gave the intersection of x_2 as $x_2 \cap \{z_0, z_1, z_2\} =?$, i.e. no constraints are propagated for the component x_2. If a new fact is added such that $x_2 \cap \{z_0, z_2\} = 1$, i.e. $x_2 \cap z_0 =?_a$ and $x_2 \cap z_2 =?_a$ and in this case the relationships between objects x and z are to be further composed with a relationship $C(z, q)$ between objects z and q as shown in figure 6.

Applying the general topological reasoning equation 3 on z_0, z_1 and z_2 and using the multiplication table, we get the following,

- z_0 intersections:

$$\begin{aligned}(X \cap Q)_{z_0} = \quad \rightarrow & \quad (x_0 \cap q_0 = 1) \wedge (x_1 \cap q_0 = 1) \\ \wedge & \quad (x_2 \cap q_0 =?) \\ \wedge & \quad \{q_1, q_2\} \cap \{x_0, x_1, x_2\} = \phi\end{aligned}$$

- z_1 intersections:

$$\{q_0, q_1, q_2\} \cap \{x_0, x_1, x_2\} =?$$

- z_2 intersections:

$$(q_0 \cap \{x_0, x_1, x_2\} =?) \wedge \{q_1, q_2\} \cap \{x_0, x_1, x_2\} = \phi$$

From the previous example we have that $x_2 \cap z_0 =?_a$ and $x_2 \cap z_2 =?_a$.

Applying equation 4 for x_2 only, we get the following,

- x_2 intersections:

$$x_2 \cap (z_0 \cup z_2) = 1 \wedge (z_0 \cup z_1) \cap q_0 = 1 \rightarrow x_2 \cap q_0 = 1$$

Compiling the above intersection we get the following resulting intersection matrix,

	q_0	q_1	q_2
x_0	1	?	?
x_1	1	?	?
x_2	?	?	?

Mapping the above matrix into spatial relations, as shown earlier in table 3(b), gives the disjunctive set: $R(X, Q) = D \vee T \vee O \vee C \vee CB$ as shown in figure 6(b).

3.2. Example 3: Composition with non-conceptual neighbours

In this example the space algebra is applied on incomplete knowledge which forms a disjunctive set of disjoint relations, i.e. non-conceptual neighbour relations, where conceptual neighbourhood is a phenomena defined by Freksa [12] in the temporal domain as "Two relations between pairs of events are conceptual neighbours if they can be directly transformed into one another by continuously deformation (i.e., shortening or lengthening) of the events topologically". In the spatial domain the same definition is valid by replacing "events" by "spatial objects".

Consider the relations between objects x and y and z as shown in figure 7 ($R(x, y) = T(x, y) \vee IB(x, y)$ and $R(y, z) = D(y, z) \vee C(y, z)$). Their representative intersection matrices are as follows:

x_2	x_1	x_0		z_0	z_1	z_2
1	1	1	y_0	1	?	?
?	?	?	y_1	1	?	?
1	?	?	y_2	1	0	0

Applying the general topological reasoning equation 3 on y_0, y_1 and y_2 and using the multiplication table, we get the following,

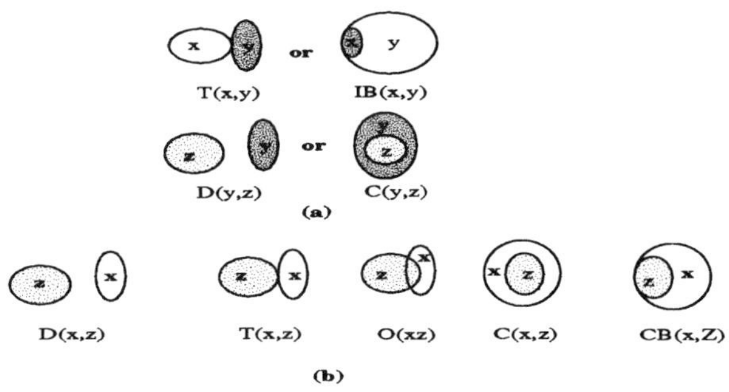

Figure 7. (a) Composition of relations which are non-conceptual neighbours, (b) the result of the composition between objects x and z.

- y_0 intersections: ($n' = n$ and $m' = m$) - second general constraint

$$(X \cap Z)_{y_0} \quad \rightarrow \quad \{x_0, x_1, x_2\} \cap \{z_0, z_1, z_2\} =?$$

  i.e. no constraints are propagated.

- y_1 intersections: ($m' = m$ and $n' = n$) since the intersection of all the components of X with y_1 are all ? ($X \cap y_1 =?$, equation 3 will propagate no new constraints, i.e.

$$(X \cap Z)_{y_1} \quad \rightarrow \quad \{x_0, x_1, x_2\} \cap \{z_0, z_1, z_2\} =?$$

- y_2 intersections: ($m'' = m' = 1$ and $n'' > 0$) then $x_2 \cap z_0 = 1$.

Also from the first general constraint $x_0 \cap z_0 = 1$. Compiling the above intersection we get the following resulting intersection matrix,

	z_0	z_1	z_2
x_0	1	?	?
x_1	?	?	?
x_2	1	?	?

Mapping the above matrix into spatial relations, as shown earlier in table 3(b) gives the disjunctive set: $R(X, Z) = D \vee T \vee O \vee C \vee CB$ as shown in figure 7(b).

While in the case of a simple convex object the use of composition table seems simple (8 relations with 64 entries in the table), a slightly more complex object such as a convex region with indeterminate boundaries produces 44 relations giving rise to a table with 1936 entries (a table never developed). Hence, using composition tables for objects with random complexity is practically not feasible. The method presented in this paper is a practical alternative to the use of composition tables.

4. Conclusions

A general approach to spatial reasoning over topological relations is proposed. The approach is applicable to objects with random complexity and handles incomplete spatial knowledge. The method builds on and genarlises previous work in [11] where spatial relations are represented by the intersection of object and space components. The following conclusions can be drawn:

- The spatial reasoning problem is reduced to the direct application of the proposed general space governing equation.
- The application of the equation is done in a finite defined number of steps which allows its implementation in many applications.
- A general algebra for space is proposed which eliminates the need for developing or utilising spatial composition tables.
- The proposed intersection algebra was shown to handle incomplete spatial knowledge.

We are currently pursuing the application of the proposed method for handling different types of spatial relations including orientation and size. The representation method used can represent temporal intervals [11]. The application of the proposed reasoning method in the temporal domain (e.g. reasoning with non-convex intervals) shall be investigated in future work.

References

[1] A. I. Abdelmoty and E.-G. B.A. A General Method for Spatial Reasoning in Spatial Databases. In *Proceedings of the Fourth Int. Conference on Information and Knowledge Management (CIKM'95)*. ACM, 1995.

[2] A. I. Abdelmoty and B. El-Geresy. An Intersection-based Formalism for Representing Orientation Relations in a Geographic Database. In *2nd ACM Workshop On Advances In Geographic Information Systems*. ACM press, December 1994.

[3] J. Allen. Maintaining Knowledge about Temporal Intervals. *Artificial Intelligence and Language Processing, Communications of the ACM*, 26:832–843, 1983.

[4] B. Bennett. Spatial Reasoning with Propositional Logics. In *Principles of Knowledge Representation and Reasoning (KR94)*, pages 51–62. Morgan Kaufmann, 1994.

[5] S. Chen. *Advances in Spatial Reasoning.* Ablex, 1990.

[6] E. Clementini and P. Di Felice. An Algebraic Model for Spatial Objects with Indeterminate Boundaries. In P. Burrough and A. Frank, editors, *Geographic Objects with Indeterminate Boundaries, GISDATA*, pages 155–169. Taylor & Francis, 1996.

[7] A. Cohn and N. Gotts. The "Egg-Yolk" Representation of Regions with Indeterminate Boundaries. In P. Burrough and A. Frank, editors, *Geographic Objects with Indeterminate Boundaries, GIS DATA*, pages 171–187. Taylor & Francis, 1996.

[8] A. Cohn, D. Randell, Z. Cui, and B. Bennet. Qualitative Spatial Reasoning and Representation. In P. Carrete and M. Singh, editors, *Qualitative Reasoning and Decision Technologies*, 1993.

[9] M. Egenhofer. Deriving the composition of Binary Topological Relations. *Journal of Visual Languages and Computing*, 5:133–149, 1994.

[10] M. Egenhofer, E. Clementini, and D. F. P. Topological Relations Between Regions With Holes. *IJGIS*, 8(2):129–142, 1994.

[11] B. El-Geresy and A. Abdelmoty. Order in Space: A General Formalism for Spatial Reasoning. In *Proc. of the Eighth International Conference on Tools with Artificial Intelligence, TAI'96*, pages 183–193, Toulouse, France, 1996. IEEE Computer Society.

[12] C. Freksa. Conceptual neighborhood and its role in temporal and spatial reasoning. In *Decision Support Systems and Qualitative Reasoning*, pages 181–187. Elsevier Science Publishers, (North Holland), 1991.

[13] C. Freksa. Qualitative Spatial Reasoning. In *Cognitive and Linguistic Aspects of Geographic Space.* Kluwer Academic Publishers, Dordrecht, 1991.

[14] Guesgen, H.W. Spatial reasoning based on allen's temporal logic. Technical Report TR-89-049, International Computer Science Institute, Berkeley, 1989.

[15] D. Hernandez. *Qualitative Representation of Spatial Knowledge*, volume 804. Springer Verlag, 1994.

[16] D. Randell, A. Cohn, and Z. Cui. Computing Transitivity Tables: A Challenge for Automated Theorem Provers. In *CADE*, Lecture Notes In Computer Science, 1992.

[17] M. Vilain, H. Kautz, and P. Van Beek. Constraint Propagation Algorithms for Temporal Reasoning: A revised Report. In D. S. Weld and J. de Kleer, editors, *Readings in Qualitative Reasoning about Physical Systems*, pages 373–381. Morgan Kaufmann, 1990.

IGLUE : An Instance-based Learning System over Lattice Theory

Patrick Njiwoua
C.R.I.L. - I.U.T. de Lens
Université d'Artois
Rue de l'Université SP 16
62307 Lens cedex, FRANCE
njiwoua@cril.univ-artois.fr

Engelbert Mephu Nguifo
C.R.I.L. - I.U.T. de Lens
Université d'Artois
Rue de l'Université SP 16
62307 Lens cedex, FRANCE
mephu@cril.univ-artois.fr

Abstract

Concept learning is one of the most studied areas in machine learning. A lot of work in this domain deals with decision trees. In this paper, we are concerned with a different kind of technique based on Galois lattices *or* concept lattices. *We present a new semi-lattice based system, IGLUE, that uses the entropy function with a top-down approach to select concepts during the lattice construction. Then IGLUE generates new relevant numerical features by transforming initial boolean features over these concepts. IGLUE uses the new features to redescribe examples. Finally, IGLUE applies the Mahanalobis distance as a similarity measure between examples.*

Keywords : Multistrategy Learning, Instance-Based Learning, Galois lattice, Feature transformation

1 Introduction

The past few years have witnessed the development of some lattice-based machine learning (ML) systems, including GALOIS [CR93], LEGAL [MN94] and RULEARNER [Sah95]. These papers come out with an experimental complexity that is quadratic in the number of instances, and therefore demonstrate that concept lattice systems can work as well as other sophisticated ML techniques. This paper deals with one of these systems, namely LEGAL [MN94], and focuses on such system in order to improve both its efficiency and its computational complexity in case of real-world applications, and to facilitate its usage in practice. LEGAL needs two user-specified learning parameters to achieve the concept formation process. These parameters have two major drawbacks.

First their choice in practice by a user, even familiar with the system, is always difficult in the case of a new problem. Secondly, through these parameters, LEGAL selects relevant nodes of the lattice on the basis of a majority principle over the set of examples. Thus when dealing with domains that contain some isolated positive instances as it may be the case in practice, the derived knowledge could not recognize such instances.

To avoid such limitations, this paper presents a new ML system called IGLUE that combines lattice technique (See Figure 1) and nearest neighbor (NN) algorithm.

$O\backslash A$	a	b	c	Class
1	1	1		+
2	1	1		+
3		1	1	-

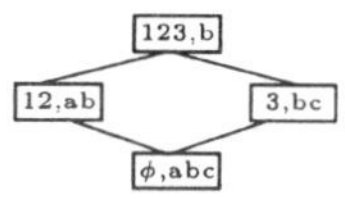

Figure 1: *A matrix context $C = (O, A, I)$ and its concept lattice [Wil82]. O is a set of objects, A is a set of attributes and I describes a relation between O and A. A rectangle represents a concept node and lines between rectangles denote the top-down order relation.*

2 IGLUE

IGLUE uses the entropy function to select relevant nodes at the h-first levels of the join-semi-lattice (see Figure 2). This function has one advantage over the previous empirical process of LEGAL, since it selects all *regularities* (i.e. a conjunction of attributes of a lattice node) that characterize a subset of significant examples.

Let A^* be the set of attributes of A which appears in at least one relevant regularity (its corresponding node is relevant). If an attribute a_i never appears in a regularity, then it is not relevant. Such an attribute would not be used again by the system when it generates new features. A feature a_k is more relevant than a_h if the number of regularities in which a_k appears is greater than the number of regularities containing a_h. We associate to each attribute a_k of A^*, a new descriptor, d_k which is defined by the following relation J. Let D be the set of those new descriptors, $d_1, \cdots, d_m$, where m is the number of attributes of the set A^*.

1082-3409/97 $10.00

Let $P_i \subseteq P$ be the set of pertinent regularities which holds for the object o_i. For an object o_i and a descriptor $d_k \in D$, we define a new relation J between O and D, where $d_{ik} = J(o_i, d_k)$ is the number of appearances of attribute a_k in all regularities $r \in P_i$, and thus, $0 \leq J(o_i, d_k) \leq |P|$. This relation is then extended to examples of the test set.

Each descriptor d_k is a quantitative variable and has a correspondence a_k in A^*. It is important to have a strong dependency between new descriptors and the set of built regularities due to their future use. They are built by the following scheme:

1. *Initially,* $d_{ik} = 0$ *for all objects* o_i *and all* $d_k \in D$.
2. *Repeat step* 3 *for each object* o_i
3. *Repeat step* 4 *for each regularity* $r \in P_i$
4. *Add* 1 *to* d_{ik} *for each attribute* a_k *of the regularity* r.

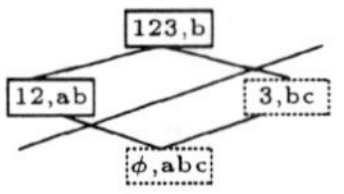

$O \backslash D$	d_1	d_2	Class
1	1	2	+
2	1	2	+
3	0	1	-

Figure 2: *The continuous-valued features obtained after redescribing the previous example context (see Figure 1). Solid rectangles denote relevant nodes while dashed rectangles are not generated by IGLUE since they are irrelevant.*

Methods of numerical taxonomy express similarity as a numerical value, and they appear to implicitly assume that objects can be represented naturally in terms of continuously valued variables. The similarity between two objects is the value of a numeric function applied to the descriptions of the two objects. Here we are interested in classifying a test example by using the training ones. IGLUE applies the Mahanalobis distance between the unseen example and the training set in order to achieve the classification.

3 Experimentations

We assembled four data sets (Monk, Breast Cancer, Small Soybean and Votes) from the UC/Irvine Repository. C4.5 and K* are tested with their default parameters values within the Waikato Environment for Knowledge Analysis, WEKA. We apply five time a 1-cross validation method and take the mean of the results. Each time, we make a random selection of the training subset and the remaining data was used for test. The size of the partition used for training was less than 70% of the total number of examples. The different system codes are executed on a Pentium 166 machine with $32M_o$ of RAM.

Results of experimentations performed to date show that classification accuracy obtained with IGLUE are comparable to those of some symbolic systems such as $C4.5$ and $K*$. When referring to other reported results in literature, IGLUE outperformed other lattice-based ML systems such as RULEARNER or GALOIS.

4 Conclusion

The Galois lattice framework is the *concisely* largest search space when constructing regularities among objects. The entropy function allows to take into account isolated examples when building the semi-lattice. The redescription of examples allows to suppress irrelevant features which are sometimes introduced by mistake in the initial description of examples. This preprocess generates new relevant features on the basis of similarity between initial examples. Thus difficulty that comes out from the application of NN similarity measures are avoided by the redescription of initial data.

The principal drawback of lattice representation of concepts is the lattice construction complexity. A first response is given in IGLUE by limiting the lattice depth to its first three levels. Therefore the time and space complexities of the system are reduced. It is obvious that regularities obtained at this stage are best suited for prediction since they represent more general knowledge. Our next work will deal with the lattice width by limiting the number of sub-nodes in the concept hierarchy to the *best* ones.

Ongoing research is also dealing with the selection of pertinent examples in the training set for the classification process.

Acknowledgments

Financial support for this work has been partially made available by the Ganymede project of the Contrat de Plan Etat Nord-Pas-de-Calais and the Association Internationale pour le Développement Intégré de l'Afrique (AIDIA).

References

[CR93] C. Carpineto and G. Romano. Galois: An order-theoretic approach to conceptual clustering. In *ICML-93 Proceedings*, pages 33–40, Amherst, July 1993.

[MN94] E. Mephu Nguifo. Galois Lattice: A framework for Concept Learning. Design, Evaluation and Refinement. In *Proc. of the sixth International Conf. on Tools with Artificial Intelligence*, pages 461–467, New Orleans, Louisiana, LA, November 6-9 1994. IEEE Press.

[Sah95] M. Sahami. Learning Classification Rules Using Lattices. In *Machine Learning: ECML-95*, pages 343–346, Heraclion, Crete, Greece, April 1995. Nada Lavrac and Stefan Wrobel eds.

[Wil82] R. Wille. Restructuring Lattice Theory. In Ivan Rival, editor, *Symposium on Ordered Sets*, pages 445–470. University of Calgary, Boston, 1982.

Empirical Results on Anytime Propositional Reasoning

Li Yang and Mukesh Dalal

Department of Computer Science
Columbia University
New York, NY 10027
{lyang,dalal}@cs.columbia.edu

Abstract

An anytime family of propositional reasoners is a sequence $\vdash_0, \vdash_1, \ldots$ of inference relations such that each $\vdash_k$ is sound, tractable, and makes more inferences than $\vdash_{k-1}$, and each theory has a complete reasoner in the family. Anytime families are useful for resource-bounded reasoning in knowledge representation systems. We describe implementations of an anytime family $\{\vdash_k\}$ of clausal propositional reasoners using three different strategies. We present empirical results comparing the three strategies, the completeness of reasoning, the time for making inferences, and the space used for reasoning. Our results show that the reasoners with higher values of k infer significantly more formulas than reasoners with lower values of k, and the time for inferencing decreases significantly as k is increased from 0 to 2.

1 Introduction

Since deductive reasoning is intractable for propositional knowledge representation systems, several tractable approaches for making incomplete inferences have been proposed [3]. The incompleteness of these reasoners make them unsuitable for several tasks where more inferences are needed [9]. An attractive approach that is tractable as well as complete in the limit is based on the notion of *anytime reasoners* [1]. They are complete reasoners that provide partial answers even if stopped prematurely; the degree of completeness of the answer improves with the time used in computing the answer. They are often used for providing a quick "first cut" to a problem, which can be later improved. In [5, 4], we presented a family $\vdash_0, \vdash_1, \ldots$ of reasoners such that each $\vdash_k$ is sound and tractable, each $\vdash_{k+1}$ is at least as complete as $\vdash_k$, and each theory has a complete reasoner $\vdash_k$ for reasoning with it. Such a family is called an *anytime family* of reasoners, since given any reasoning task, one can presumably start with $\vdash_0$, and successively proceed to the next reasoner if more time is available. In contrast to some other resource-bounded approaches (for example, see [17]) for dealing with limited computational resources, our anytime approach does not provide explicit quality measures with the answers, but instead provides semantic justifications [6]. In particular, each reasoner $\vdash_k$ is also characterized by a model-theoretic semantics. Since our family $\{\vdash_k\}$ is defined using boolean constraint propagation (BCP) [12], the semantics of each $\vdash_k$ is based on the semantics of BCP [7]. In this document, we describe implementations of our anytime family $\{\vdash_k\}$ of reasoners using three different strategies. We present empirical results comparing the three strategies, the completeness of reasoning, the time for making inferences, and the space used for reasoning. We show that (1) one particular strategies consistently outperforms the others; (2) reasoners with higher values of k infer significantly more formulas than reasoners with lower values of k; (3) the time for inferencing decreases significantly as k is increased from 0 to 2; and (4) the space required grows with the increase in k. Although BCP is an efficient linear-time method, it does not make all inferences that are logically entailed. For example, it cannot detect the inconsistency in the theory $\{(P \vee Q), (P \vee \neg Q), (\neg P \vee Q), (\neg P \vee \neg Q)\}$. We have shown that any theory can be transformed into a logically equivalent theory from which BCP can make all allowed inferences — such theories are called *vivid*. The term vivid is inspired by [11], where vivid theories are ones where an answer can be "read off" quickly. For a knowledge base that is accessed frequently, it might be useful to compile its theory into an equivalent vivid theory [14, 2]. This process of ***vivification*** was defined using a fixed-point construction based on inferences made by BCP. By suitably restricting this construction, we also defined notions of partial vivification, which provides yet another complete characterization of the anytime reasoners in the family $\{\vdash_k\}$. Our algorithms for anytime reasoning are based on partial vivification.

2 A Family of Anytime Reasoners

In this section, we review the definitions of the anytime family and vivification [5, 6]. For this, we restrict our attention to clausal propositional theories [13], that is, a theory is a set of propositional clauses. The empty clause is denoted by $\mathbf{f}$. Clausal boolean constraint propagation (BCP) is a variant of unit resolution. Given any theory Γ, BCP monotonically expands it by adding literals as follows: in each step, if any single clause in Γ and all the literals in Γ taken together logically entail any other literal (or $\mathbf{f}$), then

1082-3409/97 $10.00 © 1997 IEEE

this literal (or $\mathbf{f}$) is added to the theory Γ. This step is repeated until $\mathbf{f}$ is obtained or no new literal can be added to the theory. For example, starting with the theory $\{\neg P, P \vee \neg Q, P \vee Q \vee \neg R, P \vee Q \vee R\}$, BCP first obtains $\neg Q$ from $\neg P$ and $P \vee \neg Q$, then $\neg R$ from $\neg P$ and $\neg Q$ and $P \vee Q \vee \neg R$, and finally $\mathbf{f}$ from $\neg P$ and $\neg Q$ and $\neg R$ and $P \vee Q \vee R$. The *complement*, $\sim(\psi)$, of a clause $\psi = \alpha_1 \vee \ldots \vee \ldots \alpha_n$ is defined to be the theory $\{\sim\alpha_1, \ldots, \sim\alpha_n\}$. A clause ψ is BCP-inferable (or inferable using BCP) from a theory Γ, denoted by $\Gamma \vdash_{\text{BCP}} \psi$, iff BCP obtains $\mathbf{f}$ from the theory $\Gamma \cup \{\sim(\psi)\}$. Although $\vdash_{\text{BCP}}$ is sound, it is complete only for restricted classes of theories, for example, Horn theories. A common source of incompleteness in $\vdash_{\text{BCP}}$ is its inability to use previously inferred clauses for inferring new clauses. For example, for the theory $\Gamma_0 = \{P \vee Q, P \vee \neg Q, \neg P \vee S \vee T, \neg P \vee S \vee \neg T\}$, both $\Gamma_0 \vdash_{\text{BCP}} P$ and $\Gamma_0 \cup \{P\} \vdash_{\text{BCP}} S$, but $\Gamma_0 \not\vdash_{\text{BCP}} S$. A theory Γ is called *vivid* if for any clause ψ: $\Gamma \models \psi$ iff $\Gamma \vdash_{\text{BCP}} \psi$. If $\vdash_{\text{BCP}}$ is extended by allowing chaining on arbitrary formulas, the resulting entailment will be sound, complete, and intractable. So, we allow chaining on only a restricted set of formulas for defining the anytime family $\vdash$: For any natural number k, the consequence relation $\vdash_k$ is defined using the following two inference rules:

$$1. \quad \frac{\Gamma \vdash_{\text{BCP}} \varphi}{\Gamma \vdash_k \varphi}$$

$$2. \quad \frac{\Gamma \vdash_k \psi; \quad \Gamma, \psi \vdash_k \varphi}{\Gamma \vdash_k \varphi} \quad \text{for } |\psi| \leq k;$$

where Γ is any theory, ψ is any formula, and φ is any formula. We now define the vivification process. For any theory Γ, we restrict our attention to only those clauses that are built from the atoms in Γ such that all literals in a clause have distinct atoms; these clauses are called ***basic clauses.*** A basic clause with at most k literals is called a k-clause. The *extended Herbrand base*, $E(\Gamma)$, of a theory Γ is the the set of all basic clauses, and the *k-extended Herbrand base*, $E(\Gamma, k)$, is the the set of all k-clauses in $E(\Gamma)$. The operator $T_{\Gamma,k}$ on any set S of k-clauses produces the set of k-clauses that can be BCP-inferred from $\Gamma \cup S$, that is:

$$T_{\Gamma,k}(S) = \{\mu \in E(\Gamma, k) \mid \Gamma \cup S \vdash_{\text{BCP}} \mu\}.$$

Since $T_{\Gamma,k}$ is a monotonic operator over a finite lattice, it has a least fixpoint [15], which we denote by $\text{lfp}(T_{\Gamma,k})$. We will refer to $\text{lfp}(T_{\Gamma,k})$ as the kth fixpoint of Γ; k is said to be the *index* of this fixpoint. For example, if $\Gamma = \{(P \vee Q), (\neg P \vee Q), (P \vee \neg Q)\}$ then $\text{lfp}(T_{\Gamma,0}) = \emptyset$ and $\text{lfp}(T_{\Gamma,k}) = \{(P), (Q)\}$ for each $k > 0$. For any theory Γ and any number k, $\text{Viv}(\Gamma, k)$ is defined to be the theory $\Gamma \cup \text{lfp}(T_{\Gamma,k})$. Note that $\text{Viv}(\Gamma, k)$ augments the theory Γ, rather than replacing it, by the theory $\text{lfp}(T_{\Gamma,k})$, since this allows more clauses to be inferred from it using $\vdash_{\text{BCP}}$. In [6], we show that for any theory Γ, any clause ψ, and any number k: $\text{Viv}(\Gamma, k) \equiv \Gamma$ and $\text{Viv}(\Gamma, k) \vdash_{\text{BCP}} \psi$ iff $\Gamma \vdash_k \psi$. Thus, vivification can be used for anytime reasoning using the family $\{\vdash_k\}$ of reasoners.

3 Algorithms and Strategies

Algorithm `Vivify(k)` reads in a theory Γ and produces the theory $\text{Viv}(\Gamma, k)$ by possibly adding several basic clauses with at most k literals each.

Algorithm Vivify(k)

```
ReadTheory();
for size = 1 to k do
   Round(size);
   if (UNSAT) return(f);
return(t);
```

end (Vivify).

The exception UNSAT is trigerred anytime $\mathbf{f}$ is inferred from the theory. Procedure `Round(size)` iterates over basic clauses with at most `size` literals. It restarts enumerating clauses of size 1 onwards (`repeat` loop) as soon as any new clause is added to the theory. The intuition is that adding a new clause may cause the theory to entail new smaller size clauses, and adding smaller size clauses should speed up the vivification process. In Section 4, we provide empirical evidence that this strategy is faster than the one that does not reset the enumeration.

Procedure Round(max-size)

```
start-size = max-size;
repeat
   for size = start-size to max-size do
       start a new clause (pos=1);
       while (pos > 0) do
           pos = NextPos(pos, size);
           if (UNSAT) return;
       if (pos < 0) break {for};
   if (pos = 0) return;
   if (pos < 0)
       start-size = 1;
```

end(Round).

A new clause in `Round(size)` is usually created from the current clause by adding a new literal at position `pos`. Procedure `NextPos(pos, size)` generates the new literal by considering literals whose truth values are not yet determined. If such a literal is found, it tests whether the current clause can be BCP-inferred from the current theory (using `Ask-Lit(lit)`); if yes, the clause is added to the theory and the enumeration is reset by returning a negative flag. The next position is otherwise returned if the current clause hasn't exceeded the `size` bounds. If the current clause has `size` literals or no new literal can be found for the current position, it backtracks and removes the last literal that was added. If `pos` falls to 0, it means that no new clause of current `size` can be generated. Among all possible choices at any position, the literal which occurs most often is chosen. We have tried another strategy [10] that uses the weighted counts of both the literal and its negation. In Section 4, we provide empirical evidence that our strategy is faster than the one with weighted counts. Procedure `Ask-Lit(lit)` determines whether `lit` is entailed using BCP from the current theory. It does this by adding the complement of `lit` as a unit clause to the current theory and invokes Procedure `BCP`. Any unit clause added to the

Name	Theories	Atoms	Clauses	Sat	Unsat
aim1	8	100	160	4	4
aim2	4	200	320	0	4
jnh1	16	100	800	7	9
jnh2	18	100	850	2	16
jnh3	9	100	900	0	9
bf	2	1000	3500	0	2

Table 1: Groups of benchmark theories

Name	No Reset			Weighted Count			Reset		
	Min	Aver	Max	Min	Aver	Max	Min	Aver	Max
aim1	1.12	6.10	14.35	2.33	4.36	9.17	1.12	2.01	2.85
aim2	5.80	990.80	3744.13	4.22	859.13	3340.12	1.95	53.80	198.50
jnh1	0.08	1.87	6.43	0.07	0.74	4.00	0.08	1.85	6.00
jnh2	0.12	115.28	1827.57	0.05	7.52	114.05	0.08	57.12	894.92
jnh3	0.03	0.90	5.28	0.01	1.06	8.32	0.02	0.91	5.46
bf	7967.33	11371.64	14775.95	2565.82	4288.54	6011.27	603.18	1167.43	1731.68

Table 2: Comparison of three strategies on benchmark theories (CPU time in secs)

theory is also added to the `Stack` of unprocessed unit clauses.

Procedure BCP

```
while Stack is not empty do
    lit = pop(Stack);
    for all cls in Head(lit) do
        ShortenHead(cls);
    for all cls in Tail(lit) do
        ShortenTail(cls);
```

end (BCP).

For each literal popped from the *Stack*, BCP (see [16]) unit-resolves on the clauses having the negation of the literal either as the first (*head*) or the last atom (*tail*). Procedure `ShortenHead(cls)` examines the clause `cls` from its second literal to the last one. When encountering a literal set to TRUE, it returns because the clause is already satisfied. Literals set to FALSE are skipped because of unit-propagation. If all literals in the clauses are set to FALSE, the UNSAT flag is set because the clause can not be satisfied. Otherwise, the first unset literal becomes the new head of the clause. Whenever head of a clause meets its tail, the clause should be added again as unit clause by using Procedure `Add-Unit`. Procedure `ShortenTail` is identical to `Shortenhead`, except that it works from the second last literal back to the first one and determines the new tail of the clause.

4 Empirical Results

We have implemented our vivification algorithm using the three strategies described in Section 3. We ran the vivification algorithms and anytime reasoners based on them on several propositional theories taken from benchmarks archived at DIMACS web site (http://dimacs.rutgers.edu/), and on several randomly generated propositional theories. In this section, we present the results of these experiments. Table 1 lists some information about the benchmark theories which are clustered into 6 named groups. It presents the number of theories, satisfiable theories, and unsatisfiable theories in each group. The number of atoms and number of clauses in each theory (identical within a group, except for the last where the numbers are approximate) are also provided.

Table 2 shows a comparison of the three strategies we have implemented so far on all the unsatisfiable theories. The algorithm `Vivify` in Section 3 describes the *Reset* strategy. The *No Reset* strategy does not reset the enumeration of clauses after adding a new clause, while the *Weighted Count* strategy uses a different strategy for selecting the next literal. The numbers in the table give the CPU times (in seconds) used for inferring that the theories are unsatisfiable (minimum, average, and maximum for each group). The data shows that *Weighted Count* is faster than *No Reset* in most cases, while the *Reset* shows tremendous improvements over the other two strategies in all cases, except for some *jnh* cases where the absolute time difference is slight.

The rest of the tables focus only on the satisfiable theories. Table 3 gives the fraction of number of basic clauses (with at most 3 literals) that can inferred using BCP from Viv(Γ, *level*) but not from Γ. For example, about 87% of all basic clauses were inferable from Viv(Γ, 2) but not from an *aim1* theory Γ. The data shows that the completeness of reasoning with BCP increases with the level of vivification. Although there is a significant increase in completeness in going from Level 1 to Level 2, there is only a little increase in then going to Level 3.

Name	Level 1			Level 2			Level 3		
	Min	Aver	Max	Min	Aver	Max	Min	Aver	Max
aim1	0.000000	0.000000	0.000000	0.870078	0.870325	0.870805	0.870078	0.870325	0.870805
jnh1	0.000000	0.073649	0.351922	0.327409	0.586764	0.793308	0.327632	0.586940	0.793308
jnh2	0.053111	0.313945	0.574778	0.453137	0.513958	0.574778	0.453150	0.513964	0.574778

Table 3: Fraction of clauses inferable from benchmark theories after each level

Name	Level 1			Level 2			Level 3		
	Min	Aver	Max	Min	Aver	Max	Min	Aver	Max
aim1	0.743	1.066	1.457	5.647	15.190	34.250	4.576	14.090	34.250
jnh1	1.001	3.238	8.687	1.031	42.890	131.814	0.862	41.512	131.814
jnh2	8.735	94.233	179.730	11.741	99.330	186.920	11.334	92.204	173.074

Table 4: Time improvement (factor) in inference after each level

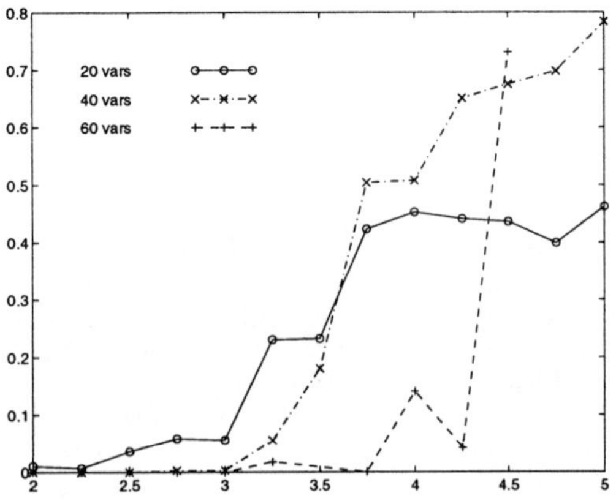

Figure 1: Fraction of additional clauses inferable after vivification at Level 2

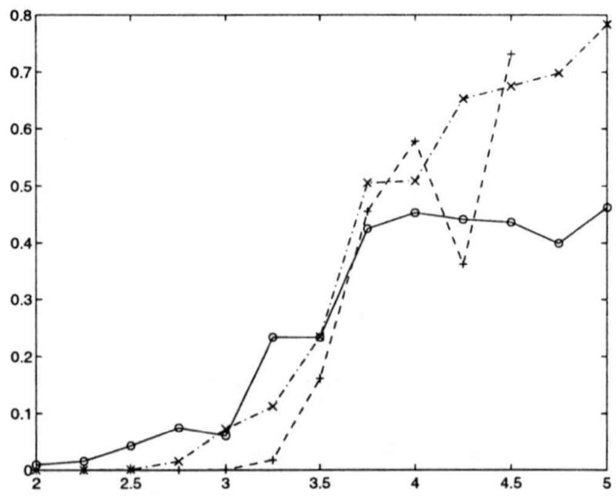

Figure 2: Fraction of additional clauses inferable after vivification at Level 3

Table 4 shows the time improvement in inferring basic clauses that are inferable using BCP from both Γ and $\text{Viv}(\Gamma, \textit{level})$. In particular, it shows the improvement factor due to vivification. For example, it is about 15 times faster to infer clauses from $\text{Viv}(\Gamma, 2)$ than from an *aim1* theory Γ. The data shows that efficiency increases as we move from Level 0 (that is, Γ) to Level 2, and then often decreases to Level 3. Table 5 shows the increase in size of the theory because of vivification. For example, $\text{Viv}(\Gamma, 2)$ is about 1.148 times the size of an *aim1* theory Γ. The data shows that the sizes increase with increase in level, as expected.

5 Conclusions

We presented some empirical results demonstrating that vivification using BCP increases the completeness as well as efficiency of reasoning, at least until Level 2. We have used vivification for anytime temporal

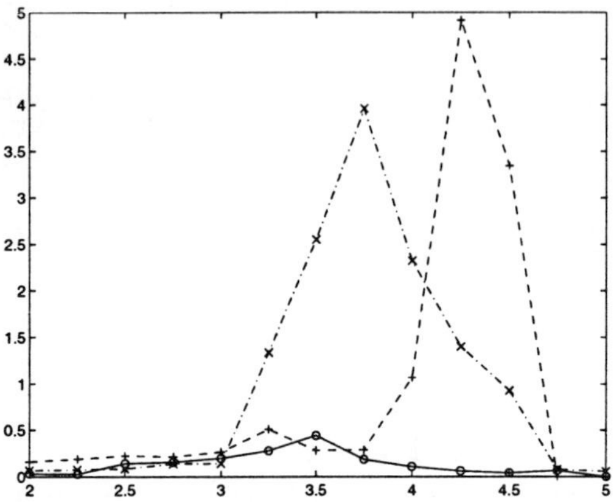

Figure 3: CPU time (in seconds) for vivification at Level 2

Name	Level 1			Level 2			Level 3		
	Min	Aver	Max	Min	Aver	Max	Min	Aver	Max
aim1	1.000	1.000	1.000	1.033	1.148	1.250	1.033	1.148	1.250
jnh1	1.000	1.001	1.006	1.041	1.123	1.353	1.044	1.218	1.589
jnh2	1.002	1.004	1.005	1.005	1.099	1.192	1.005	1.544	2.083

Table 5: Size of theory after each level (as fraction of initial size)

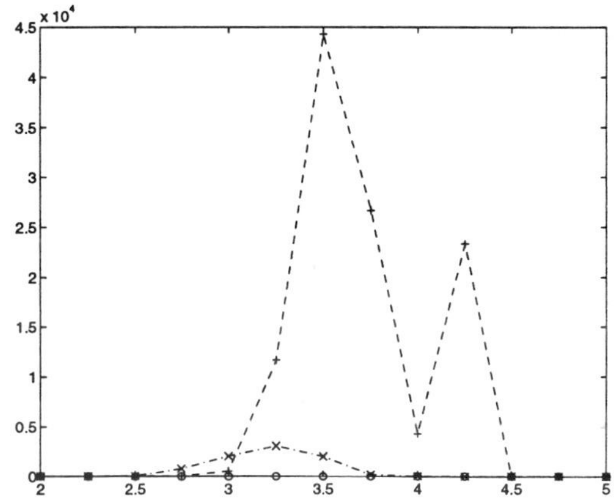

Figure 4: CPU time (in seconds) for vivification at Level 3

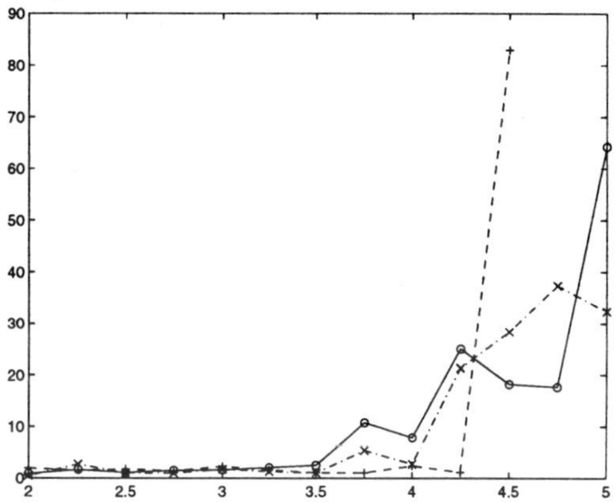

Figure 6: Time improvement (factor) in inference after vivification at Level 2

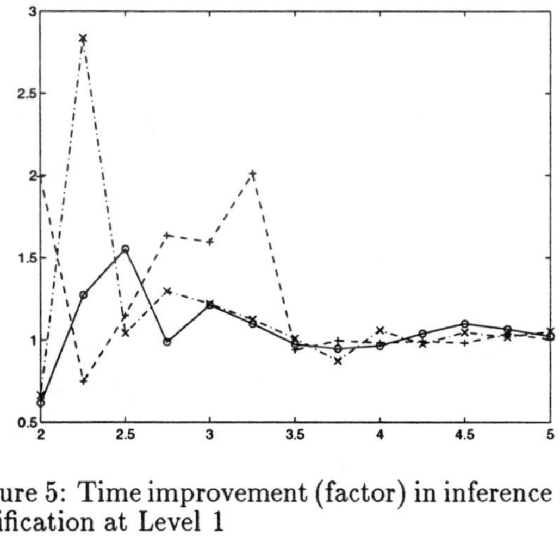

Figure 5: Time improvement (factor) in inference after vivification at Level 1

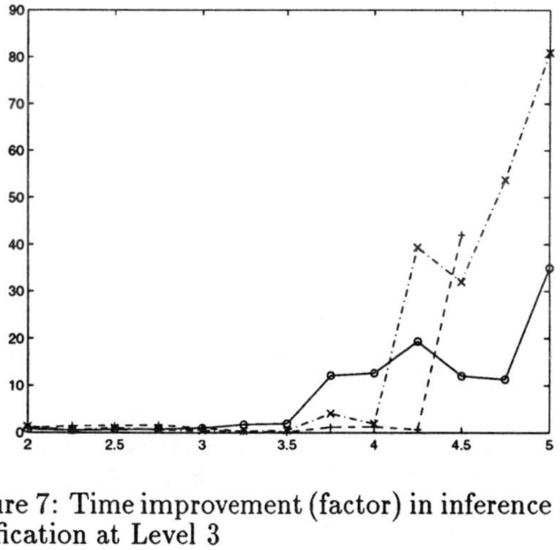

Figure 7: Time improvement (factor) in inference after vivification at Level 3

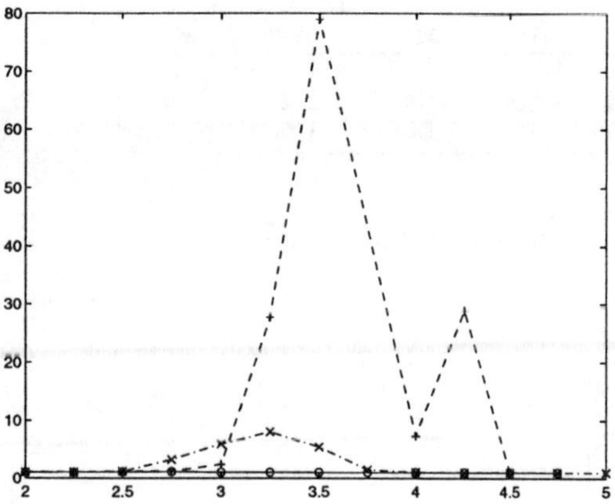

Figure 8: Size of the theory (as fraction of initial size) after vivification at Level 3

reasoning [8]. Our current work involves removing redundant clauses to offset the increases in sizes of the theories.

References

[1] M. Boddy and T. Dean. Solving time dependent planning problems. Technical report, Dept. of Computer Science, Brown University, 1988.

[2] M. Cadoli. Panel on knowledge compilation and approximations: terminology, questions, and references. In *Fourth International Symposium on Artificial Intelligence and Mathematics (AI/MATH-96)*, pages 183–186, Florida, 1996.

[3] J. Crawford, editor. *Proceedings of the AAAI Workshop on Tractable Reasoning.* American Association for Artificial Intelligence, San Jose, California, 1992.

[4] M. Dalal. Anytime clausal reasoning. Submitted to Annals of Mathematics and Artificial Intelligence, 1996.

[5] M. Dalal. Anytime families of tractable propositional reasoners. In *Fourth International Symposium on Artificial Intelligence and Mathematics (AI/MATH-96)*, pages 42–45, Florida, 1996.

[6] M. Dalal. Semantics of an anytime family of reasoners. In W. Wahlster, editor, *Proceedings Twelveth European Conference on Artificial Intelligence (ECAI 96)*, pages 360–364, Budapest, Hungary, 1996. John Wiley and Sons, Ltd.

[7] M. Dalal. Semantics of an efficient propositional reasoner: Preliminary report. In J. H. Stewman, editor, *Proceedings Ninth Florida AI Research Symposium (FLAIRS-96)*, pages 101–105, Florida, USA, 1996.

[8] M. Dalal and Y. Feng. Anytime temporal reasoning based on propositional satisfiability (extended abstract). In E. C. Freuder, editor, *Proceedings of Second International Conference on Principles and Practice of Constraint Programming (CP96)*, pages 535–536, Cambridge, Massachusetts, Aug 1996. Springer.

[9] J. Doyle and R. Patil. Two theses of knowledge representation: language restrictions, taxanomic classification, and the utility of representation services. *Artificial Intelligence*, 48(3):261–297, 1991.

[10] O. Dubois, P. Andre, Y. Boufkhad, and J. Carlier. SAT versus UNSAT. *DIMACS series in Discrete MAthematics and Theoretical Computer Science*, 24, 1995.

[11] H.J. Levesque. Making believers out of computers. *Artificial Intelligence*, 30:81–108, 1986.

[12] D. McAllester. Truth maintenance. In *Proceedings Eighth National Conference on Artificial Intelligence (AAAI-90)*, pages 1109–1116, 1990.

[13] E. Mendelson. *Introduction to Mathematical Logic.* Van Nostrand, Princeton, N.J., 1964.

[14] B. Selman, H. Levesque, and D. Mitchell. A new method for solving hard satisfiability problems. In *Proceedings Tenth National Conference on Artificial Intelligence (AAAI-92)*, pages 440–446, 1992.

[15] A. Tarski. A lattice-theoretical fixpoint theorem and its applications. *Pacific J. Math.*, 5:285–309, 1955.

[16] H. Zhang and M. E. Stickel. An efficient algorithm for unit propagation. In *Fourth International Symposium on Artificial Intelligence and Mathematics (AI/MATH-96)*, pages 166–169, Florida, 1996.

[17] Shlomo Zilberstein. *Operational Rationality through Compilation of Anytime Algorithms.* PhD thesis, University of California, Berkeley, California, 1993.

Session B.1

AI and Software Engineering I

Session Chair:
Jeffrey Tsai, University of Illinois, USA

A Performance Analysis of Hierarchical Shortest Path Algorithms

A. Fetterer

Oracle Corporation
500 Oracle Parkway
Redwood Shores, CA 94065

S. Shekhar

Department of Computer Science
University of Minnesota
Minneapolis, MN, 55455

Abstract

The shortest-path problem is an essential component of many applications including Advanced Traveler Information Systems (ATIS), computer networks, etc. A hierarchical routing algorithm decomposes the original graph into a set of fragment graphs and also into a boundary graph which summarizes the fragment graphs. A fully memoized hierarchical routing algorithm pre-computes and stores the shortest-path data structure and the shortest-path-cost data structure for the graph fragments, as well as for the boundary graph [8]. The storage cost of the fully memoized approach can be reduced by a virtual or a hybrid memoization approach, where few or none of the relevant data structures have been pre-computed. This paper achieves two firsts. We use a real graph with 123,000 nodes and 313,000 edges, which is two orders of magnitude larger than the graphs used in related work [8, 14]. Second, the paper analyzes the effect of memoizing individual data structures for the storage overhead and computation time of A-based hierarchical routing algorithms. Analysis and experiments with the Twin Cities metropolitan road-map show that memoizing the shortest-path-cost data structure for the boundary graph provides the best savings in computation time, for a given amount of storage and a small number of fragments. Memoizing the relevant part of the shortest-path-cost data structure for the fragment graphs provides the next best savings, followed by memoizing the shortest-path data structure for the boundary graph.*

1 Introduction

Spatial graphs [15] form the kernel of many important applications, including: transportation; water, electric, and gas utilities; telephone networks; urban management; sewer maintenance, and irrigation canal management. The phenomena of interest for these applications are structured as spatial graphs which consist of a finite collection of points (i.e. nodes), the line-segments (i.e. edges) connecting the points, the location of the points, and the attributes of the points and line segments. For example, a spatial graph for transportation applications may store road-intersection points and road segments connecting the intersections. Spatial graphs for large cities (e.g. road-maps) contain millions of nodes and edges. Shortest-path computations retrieve a sequence of nodes and edges that form an optimal path (e.g. shortest distance or shortest travel time) between the given node-pair (source,destination). The shortest-path-cost computation computes the aggregate cost (e.g. distance) of the shortest-path. Pre-computation and hierarchical algorithms are becoming important in processing shortest-path computations in time-critical applications such as Intelligent Transportation Systems [2]. Hierarchical algorithms decompose a large spatial graph into a boundary graph and a collection of fragment graphs, each of which is smaller than the original graph. The shortest-path computation on the large graph is decomposed into a collection of shortest-path-cost computations and shortest-path computations on the smaller graphs.

1.1 Related Work and Our Contributions

The single-pair path-computation problem is a special case of single-source path computation and all-pair path computation. Traditional research in database-query languages [13], transitive closure [6, 5], and recursive query processing [1, 11] has approached single-pair path-computation as a special case of more general problems. For example, partial-transitive-closure computation [7] and transitive-closures have been used for single-pair path computations. Previous evaluation of the transitive-closure algorithms examined the iterative, logarithmic, Warren's, Depth-first search (DFS), hybrid, and spanning-tree-based algorithms [12].

Hierarchical path-finding has been explored in the context of computer networks in [10] and in the context of planar graphs [3]. Researchers have investi-

1082-3409/97 $10.00

gated a hierarchical routing algorithm in ATIS called HEPV [8, 4] that guarantees optimal solutions. HEPV divides the base graph into a boundary graph and a set of fragment graphs. It memoizes (pre-computes and stores) the shortest-path and shortest-path-cost for the fragments and the boundary graph. The storage of these memoizations can reach gigabytes for a graph with 100,000 nodes and may become prohibitively large for ATIS maps with millions of nodes. However, selective memoization can be used to manage storage costs. The work on HEPV also explored the effect on performance of the decomposition of graphs into fragments, the number of levels in the hierarchy and the maintenance of memoized data in the face of updates.

In this work, we investigate memoizing different intermediate data structures for the hierarchical algorithm. Three types of intermediate data structure implementations are possible [17]. The *fully memoized* intermediate data structure stores all relevant information; i.e: all of the shortest paths, the cost of the shortest paths, or both. A *virtual memoization* relies on on-line computation, storing neither the shortest paths nor their cost. The *hybrid memoization* stores part of the relevant information: for example, storing the costs of the shortest paths but not the shortest path itself.

This paper explores hybrid memoization with the intent of analyzing the storage / computation-time trade-offs involved in memoizing the individual data structures needed for processing shortest-path computations. Analytical models show the CPU and storage trade-offs for the different memoizations. Experiments with the Twin Cities metropolitan road-map show that memoizing the shortest-path-cost data structure for the boundary graph provides the best savings in computation time, for a given amount of storage and a small number of fragments. Memoizing the relevant part of the shortest-path-cost data structure for the fragment graphs provides the next-best savings, followed by memoizing the shortest-path data structure for the boundary graph.

1.2 Scope of Paper and Outline

This paper focuses primarily on describing different memoizations for the hierarchical algorithm and their dynamic execution costs. We make simple choices for resolving other issues. For this study, the hierarchical algorithm has a two-level hierarchy. The issue of maintenance in the face of updates, etc., will be addressed in future work. Min-cut [9] partitioning is used to decompose the base graph into fragments. Memoized data structures are stored in main memory.

Section 2 describes the basic concepts in hierarchical routing. Section 3 introduces the concept of and describes the choices in, data structure memoization and gives analytical models describing execution time and storage costs. In section 4, we present experimental results for the memoizations in terms of CPU operations. Section 5 summarizes our work and presents future challenges in hierarchical routing.

2 Basic Concepts

2.1 Flat-Graph Definitions

Graph $G = (N, E, C)$ is a flat graph consisting of a node set N, a cost set C, and an edge set E. The edge set E is a subset of the cross product $N \times N$. Each element (i, j) in E is an edge that joins node i to node j. Each edge (i, j) is associated with a cost $c_{i,j}$. Cost $c_{i,j}$ takes values from the set of positive real numbers. A node i is a neighbor of node j if $E_{i,j} \in E$. The degree of a node is the number of neighboring nodes. A path $P_{s,d}$ in a graph from a source node s to a destination node d is a sequence of nodes (N_0, N_1, N_2, ..., N_k), where s = N_0, d = N_k, and the edges $E_{0,1}, E_{1,2}, ..., E_{k-1,k} \in E$. The cost of the path is the sum of the cost of the edges, i.e. $\sum_{i=1}^{k} c_{i-1,i}$. An optimal path from node i to node j is the path with the smallest cost.

2.2 Hierarchical Graph Definitions

The hierarchical graph has a 2-level representation of the original graph G. The lower level is composed of a set of fragments $F_1 \ldots F_k$ in G. The higher-level graph is composed of the boundary nodes (BN) and is called the boundary graph (BG). Boundary nodes are defined as the set of nodes that have a neighbor in more than one fragment, i.e. $N_i \in BN \iff \exists E_{i,j}, E_{i,k} | FRAG(k) \neq FRAG(j)$. Edges in the boundary graph are called boundary edges, and the boundary nodes of a fragment form a clique, i.e. are completely connected. The cost associated with the boundary edge is the shortest-path cost through the fragment between the boundary nodes. A boundary edge is associated with a fragment identifier. A boundary path is the shortest path through the boundary graph.

Figure 1 gives a template algorithm for finding a path in a hierarchical graph. The following functions are used to compute the optimal path:

- **SP(s,d)** : This function returns the shortest path between node s and d.
- **SPC(s,d)** : Function to find the cost of the shortest path from a source s to a destination d.
- **BoundaryNodes(f)** : Function that returns the set of boundary nodes for fragment f.

- **Fragment(n)** : This function returns the fragment identifier for interior node n.
- **ExpandBoundaryPath(boundaryPath)** : This function expands the path through the boundary graph and returns the corresponding path in G by using the **ExpandBoundaryEdge(boundaryEdge)** function for each edge in the boundary path.
- **ExpandBoundaryEdge(boundaryEdge)** : This function expands a boundary edge and returns a corresponding path in G by computing the shortest path between the endpoints of the edge in the fragment.

The hierarchical algorithm is composed of three steps: finding the relevant boundary-node pair in the boundary graph, computing the boundary path, and expanding the boundary path. The first step in determining the shortest path is to compute the boundary node through which the shortest path leaves the source's fragment and enters the destination's fragment. If both the source and destination are boundary nodes, then the solution is trivial. If the source is an internal node and the destination is a boundary node, the boundary node through which the shortest path leaves the source's fragment is found by computing the cost of the path from the source to all the boundary nodes of that fragment, and by computing the cost of the shortest path from all the boundary nodes of the source's fragment to the destination. The source-boundary-destination triple with the lowest aggregate cost determines the appropriate boundary node. The third case occurs when the source is a boundary node and the destination is an internal node. This case is similar to the second case, but the roles of the source and destination are reversed. When both the source and destination are internal nodes, the appropriate boundary-node pair is found by running computations on the fragment graphs to determine the cost of the shortest path from the internal nodes to all of the boundary nodes of the fragment. Next, computation is performed in the boundary graph to determine the shortest-path cost between all boundary-node pairs. The path with the lowest aggregate cost determines the boundary-node pair. Once the appropriate boundary-node pair has been determined, additional computation on the boundary graph is done to determine the shortest path between those boundary nodes. The final step is to expand the boundary path by computing the shortest path through individual fragments. Adjacent nodes in the boundary path form source/destination pairs on which the shortest-path computations are run in a fragment. This follows the following lemma:

Lemma 1 *The hierarchical routing algorithm finds an optimal path from s to d.*

Proof 1 *See [8].*

3 Degree of Memoization

Lengthy computations such as the shortest-path query and the shortest-path-cost query whose results are frequently accessed can reduce their computation time to a memory lookup by precomputing the result of the computation and memoizing (storing) it.

A cost memoization (*CM*) on a graph memoizes the cost of the shortest path between all of the node pairs in the graph. It does not store any path information. A compressed path memoization *CPM* stores the set of optimal paths between all of the points on the graph as a series of "hops". For a fragment graph, a partial memoization of the *CM*, the *C2B* or a cost-to-boundary-nodes memoization stores the cost of the shortest path from the interior nodes of the fragment to the boundary nodes of the fragment.

Figure 2 shows *CM* and *CPM* for an example graph with 5 nodes and 8 edges. Each node is associated with a table, with one entry for all of the other nodes. The node table in *CM* contains the costs of the shortest paths between two nodes. For example, the cost from node C to node A is given as 3. To find the shortest path between those two nodes, the algorithm uses the *CPM* table. Starting at the table for node C, the algorithm looks up the destination to get the next node on the path. In this case, the next destination is node E, and the algorithm uses the *CPM* table for node E. From that table, node A is found to be the next hop and the destination is reached.

Figure 3 shows the possible hybrid memoizations for the hierarchical algorithm. Memoization choices may be made for both the boundary graph and the fragment graph. The horizontal axis refers to the memoization possible for the fragmented graph, and the vertical axis refers to the memoization possible for the boundary graph. The axis labels are in lattice form, to indicate that a partial ordering exists among the memoization choices. The first choice in memoization for the fragment graph is to not pre-compute any data structures (column 1 in Figure 3). Thus, all computation is performed on-line. The next set of choices involves memoizing only a single data structure (columns 2-4 in Figure 3) in the fragment graph, the *C2B* and the *CPM* tables. If the *C2B* data structure is memoized, then the calls to frag[i].SPC(in,bn)

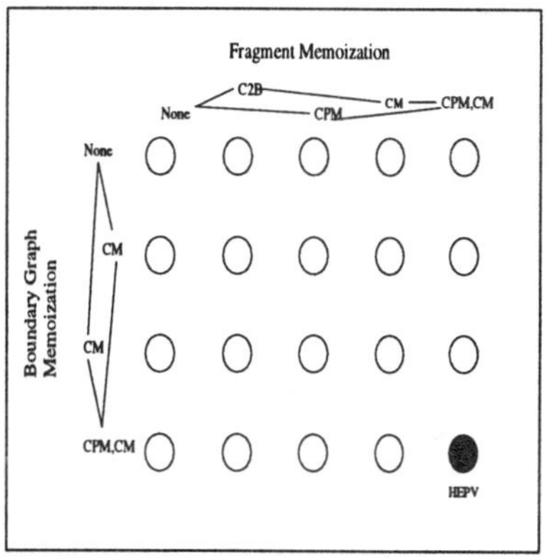

Figure 3: Memoization Matrix

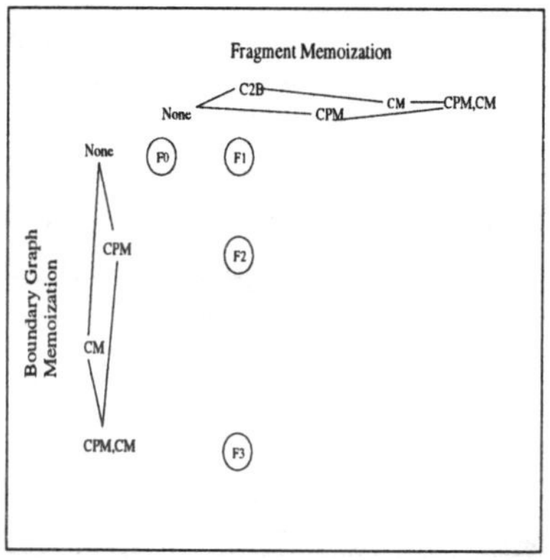

Figure 4: Candidate Hybrid Memoizations for Experiments

in the algorithm template correspond to lookups in main memory instead of to on-line computation. The *C2B* data structure is a subset of the *CM* data structure for the fragment graph, but memoizing the full *CM* is not interesting, since the algorithm does not use any of the extra information. If the *CPM* is memoized, computing the shortest path inside of a fragment corresponds to a series of lookups to the data structure instead of to on-line computation. It is also possible to memoize both the *CM* and *CPM* of the fragment graph (column 5 in Figure 3), so that no computation is done on-line. Memoization choices for the boundary graph proceed similarly. If the boundary graph has no memoization (row 1 in Figure 3), all computation in the boundary graph is done on-line. Likewise, any of the data structures for the boundary graph can be memoized independently (rows 2-3 in Figure 3). In addition, all boundary-graph data structures can be memoized (row 4 in Figure 3). Thus, the overall degree of hybrid memoization for the algorithm is defined as the amount of memoization in the boundary graph and the fragment graph. Hybrid memoization can exist in any circle in Figure 3. For our experiments, we focus on the hybrid memoization shown in Figure 4.

4 Hybrid Memoization Candidates

We chose four candidate hybrid memoizations for direct comparison, as shown in Figure 4. These candidates are chosen to facilitate studying the effects of memoizing individual data structures on the fragment graph and the boundary graph. F0 has no memoization in either the boundary graph or the fragment graphs. F1 only memoizes the *C2B* table in the fragment graph. F2 memoizes the *C2B* table of the fragment graph and the *CM* table of the boundary graph. F3 memoizes the *C2B* table in the fragment graph and both the *CPM* and *CM* tables in the boundary graph. We compare the candidates to determine the effect of memoization on the hierarchical algorithm. We compare F0 and F1 to determine the effect of memoizing the *C2B* table in the fragment graph. By comparing F1 and F2, we determine the effect of memoizing the *CM* table in the boundary graph. By comparing F2 and F3, we determine the effect of memoizing the *CPM* data structure in the boundary graph.

4.1 Execution Cost Models

Symbol	Explanation
L	Length of path in the original graph
M	Length of path through boundary graph
N	Number of nodes in the original graph
E	Number of edges in the original graph
K	Number of boundary nodes per fragment
F	Number of fragments
B	Total Number of Boundary Nodes
D	Average node degree
T_l	Lookup time
T_{A*}	Time to run A* on the complete graph
T^f_{A*}	Time to run $A*$ on a fragment
T^b_{A*}	Time to run $A*$ on the boundary graph

Table 1: Notations Used in the Cost Formulas

This subsection contains the execution-cost models for the different hybrid memoization levels. Table 1 lists the parameter names. The line numbers refer to the generic algorithm in Figure 1.

In F0, there will be K^2 A*s run in the boundary graph to compute the cross-fragment paths. In the fragment graph, there are $2K$ A*s run to determine the cost to the boundary nodes, $M + 2$ A*s run to expand the boundary path, and 1 A* run in the boundary graph to compute the boundary path.

In F0, computing the costs from the source/destination to the border nodes is computationally expensive. In F1, the $2K$ A*s used to determine the cost to the border nodes are replaced with 2 accesses to the *C2B* memoization.

Computing the boundary-graph costs between K^2 pairs of boundary nodes is also computationally expensive. Candidate F2 is identical to F1, but the K^2 A*s are replaced with K lookups in the *CM* for the boundary graph.

In candidate F3, all of the data structures for the boundary graph are memoized. Thus, both computing the boundary-graph costs and determining the shortest path through the boundary graph correspond to look-ups of memoized data structures (*CM, CPM*).

4.2 Analytical Modeling Using a Grid Graph

A summary of the parameters used in the remainder of the paper is given in Table 1. A square grid-graph of N nodes is an undirected planar graph. If $\sqrt{N}$ is an integer, the square grid-graph can be embedded in a Cartesian space with nodes at coordinates $(i * \sqrt{N}, j * \sqrt{N})$ with $i, j \in 0, 1, 2, ..., \sqrt{N} - 1$. Edges connect nodes $(i\sqrt{N}, j\sqrt{N})$ to nodes $((i+1)\sqrt{N}, j\sqrt{N})$ and $(i\sqrt{N}, (j+1)\sqrt{N})$. A grid-graph is often used in complexity analysis for transportation algorithms because of its regular structure and similarity to urban road-maps.

By decomposing the base graph into F fragments, each individual fragment will have $O(\frac{N}{F})$ nodes. The average number of boundary nodes per fragment is $K = O(\sqrt{\frac{N}{F}})$ since in a grid graph, each side of a fragment has $\sqrt{\frac{N}{F}}$ nodes along it. Since each fragment has $O(\sqrt{\frac{N}{F}})$ boundary nodes, the total number of boundary nodes in the boundary graph is $B = O(\sqrt{NF})$. A boundary edge exists in the boundary graph for each pair of boundary nodes in a fragment. Since there are K boundary nodes per fragment, there will be $O(K^2)$ or $O(\frac{N}{F})$ boundary edges per fragment. Since the base graph is partitioned into F fragments, the total number of boundary edges is $O(N)$.

The CPU execution cost depends on the number of edges expanded by the search algorithm and the cost of handling each edge. In the best case (perfect search), only the edges that appear on the optimal path are expanded. In the worst case, each search looks at all the relevant edges in the boundary graph and in the fragment graphs. In this analysis, we derive the asymptotic worst-case average heap size for the grid-graph example. We look at the worst-case asymptotic cost for the number of heap operations and of the average heap size for each version of the algorithm. Example derivations are given, and the results for this analysis are summarized in Table 3. For the analysis, we assume the most general source/destination pairing and use the cost models given in [16]. The number of fragments used in the analysis is chosen to minimize the total storage required: $F = O(N^{1/3})$. The length of the boundary path used is $M = O(\sqrt{F}) = O(N^{1/6})$.

The number of heap operations is a function of the number of nodes that the search algorithm visits. In the worst case, the search algorithm must visit every node once (the effects of backtracking are not discussed). For example, in F0 the execution time for Case 4 is $O(2KN^f_{A*} + K^2 N^b_{A*} + (M+2)N^f_{A*})$. Placing the variables in terms of N simplifies the CPU execution cost to $O(N^{5/6} + N^{17/12} + N^{3/4}) = O(N^{17/12})$. Row 2 of Table 3 shows the asymptotic number of heap operations required for a search on a grid graph.

To derive the worst case average heap size, we need to determine the total number of edges looked at by the search and the total number of searches required to find the optimal path. In F0, there are K^2 A*s run in the boundary graph and $M + 3$ A*s run in the fragments. If $F = O(N^{1/3})$ [16], there will be $E_f = O(\sqrt{\frac{N}{F}}) = O(\sqrt{\frac{N}{N^{1/3}}}) = O(N^{2/3})$ edges per fragment. The total number of edges expanded is thus $O(N^{1/3}N^{2/3}) + O(N^{2/3}N) + O(N^{1/6}N^{2/3})$. The average heap size can be found by looking at the total number of searches run. Two searches are required to determine the cost from the interior source and destination nodes to their respective border nodes. $O(N^{2/3})$ searches in the boundary graph are required to compute cross-fragment path costs. Finally, there are $O(N^{1/6})$ searches required to compute the actual path through the fragments. Dividing the total number of edges expanded by the total number of searches performed gives the average heap size as $O(N)$. Row 1 of Table 3 gives the asymptotic average heap size for searching a grid graph using the hierarchical algorithm.

The accesses to the memoized data structures required by each version of the algorithm are deterministic. F0 and A* do not access any memoized data structures. The number of data structure accesses for F1 is constant at $O(1)$, since it looks up the costs to the boundary nodes. In F2 and F3, the $O(K)$ lookups to the CM dominate the IO for an IO cost of $O(N^{1/6})$. Row 3 of Table 3 shows the asymptotic accesses to the memoized data structures.

Storage costs were calculated by creating the necessary views for the candidate hybrid materializations. The graph was fragmented using a min-cut [9] technique, with values of F ranging from 10 to 400. Our notations are summarized in Table 1. All candidates store the base and fragment graphs, whose storage requirements are similar to those of the base graph. The storage for the *C2B* view is $(N - B)K(S_c + S_{id})$ bytes. Each of the $(N - B)$ internal nodes have information on the cost to the border node for each of the K boundary nodes of their fragment. The *CPV* requires $B(B - 1)3S_{id}$ bytes of storage. Each of the B boundary nodes stores the boundary-node identifier as well as the source- and destination-identifiers for the $(B - 1)$ boundary nodes. Storing the *CV* takes $B(B - 1)(S_c + S_{id})$ bytes. Each of the B boundary nodes stored the cost to the $(B - 1)$ other boundary nodes. On our system, S_{id} was 4 bytes, and S_c was 8 bytes. Storage was measured using the UNIX 'ls -l' command. Table 2 shows the storage requirements for the different memoized data structures for both the boundary graph and the fragment graphs. Asymptotic storage requirements are given in terms of N. Actual storage requirements were derived from a base graph decomposed into 100 fragments.

5 Experimental Evaluation

The goal of these experiments is to ask: "What are the effects of memoizing individual data structures for fragments and for the boundary graph on the computation cost of the hierarchical routing algorithm." Computation cost is measured by the on-line computation effort in terms of heap operations and heap size. We also measure how the path length affects the on-line computation.

We report the CPU-costs of the candidate hybrid memoization strategies in our experiments, using the Twin Cities metropolitan road map with 123,000 nodes and 313,000 edges. These costs are analyzed to deduce the effect of memoizing individual data structures on the performance of the hierarchical routing algorithm.

5.1 CPU Cost Comparison

We measure the average heap size and average number of heap operations for the hierarchical routing algorithm, using alternative memoizations. A set of 500 randomly chosen (source,destination) pairs are used for the experiments. The number of heap operations includes inserts and deletes only. A count of these operations is measured for each path, and an average is reported in Figure 6. For each path, the heap-manager

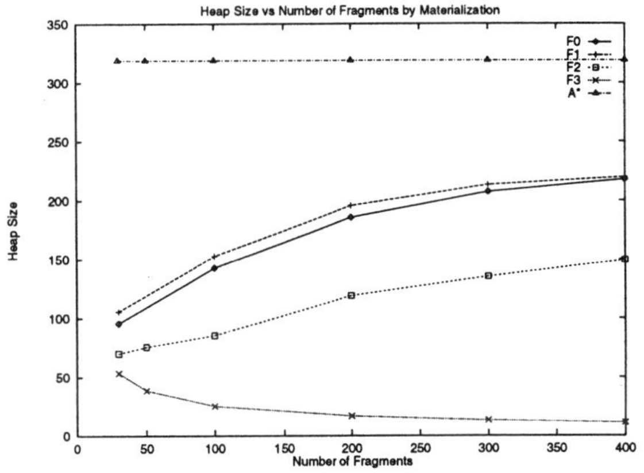

Figure 5: Average Heap Size per Heap Operation vs. Number of Fragments

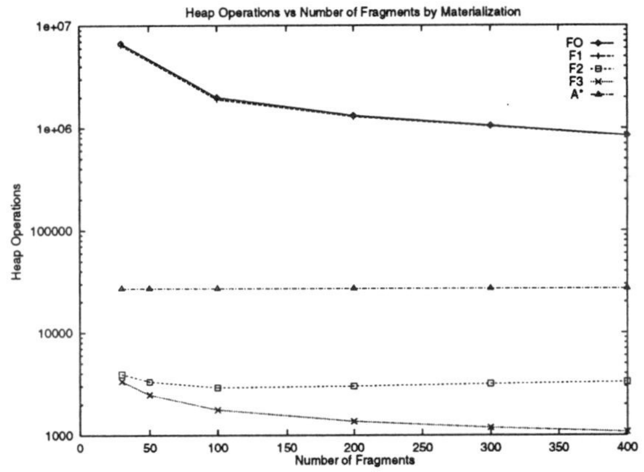

Figure 6: Average Number of Heap Operations per Path vs Number of Fragments

measures the heap-size at every (insert/delete) operation and produces an average heap size for a given (source,destination) pair. We report the average size of these for 500 paths in Figure 5.

To get a baseline performance measurement, we compare the heap results against running A* on the base graph . The effect of creating a hierarchy of graphs is apparent, as all of the hierarchical algorithms produce a smaller average heap size than when we ran A* on the base graph, as shown in Figure 5. A* produces a large average heap size, since it searches the entire breadth of the graph, while the hierarchical algorithms are focused on the fragments or boundary graph. If the *C2B* table is memoized as in F1, the average heap size increases, since $2K$ fewer A*s are run in the fragment graphs, but the same number of A*s are run in the boundary graph. The effect of memoizing the *CM* in the boundary graph is apparent in F2. In this case, the average heap size decreases dramatically,

	Adjacency list information		Compressed Path Memoization		Cost Memoization		Cost2-Boundary-Nodes
	per fragment graph	boundary graph	per fragment graph	boundary graph	per fragment graph	boundary graph	
Raw Storage	$F{*}G_f$	G_b	$N(\frac{N}{F}-1){*}$ $2S_{id}$	$B(B-1){*}$ $3S_{id}$	$N(\frac{N}{F}-1){*}$ (S_c+S_{id})	$B(B-1){*}$ (S_c+S_{id})	$(N-B)K{*}$ (S_c+S_{id})
Asymptotic Storage	$O(N)$	$O(N)$	$O(N^{5/3})$	$O(N^{4/3})$	$O(N^{5/3})$	$O(N^{4/3})$	$O(N^{4/3})$
Real Size F=100	4M	3M	2.3G	32M	2.3G	32M	40M

Table 2: Asymptotic Size and Complexity of the Memoized Data Structures

since the K^2 A*s in the boundary graph are replaced with lookups. The cost of running A* in the boundary graph is further highlighted by memoizing the *CPM* for the boundary graph (F3), which replaces the A*s and finds the path through the boundary graph with a lookup. The average heap size is small, because the only A*s run are in the fragments. The average heap size increases as the number of fragments increases when there is no memoization, or when the *C2B* and *CM* are memoized, since the number of nodes in the boundary graph grows. When the *CPM* in the boundary graph is memoized, the average heap size decreases, because no A*s are run in the boundary graph, and thus the size of the fragments decreases.

The number of heap operations is a count of the number of inserts into and deletes from the heap data-structure, and is shown in Figure 6. Memoizing the hierarchical graph (F0) causes the number of heap operations to increase due to running the K^2 A*s in the boundary graph as compared to running A* on the base graph. Memoizing the *C2B* data structure (F1) decreases the number of heap operations slightly, but the K^2 factor still dominates. The hierarchical algorithm will produce fewer heap operations than A* only when the *CM* is memoized (F2), since the K^2 boundary graph A*s are replaced with lookups. Memoizing the *CPM* minimizes the heap operations, since all of the computation is done in the fragment graphs. The number of fragments inversely affects the number of heap operations for two reasons. With a greater number of fragments, the number of boundary nodes per fragment decreases, lowering the K^2 term. Also, having more fragments means that individual fragments will be smaller, thus requiring fewer heap operations to search them. In summary, the number of heap operations decreases as more data structures are memoized, since each memoized data structure results in less dynamic computation.

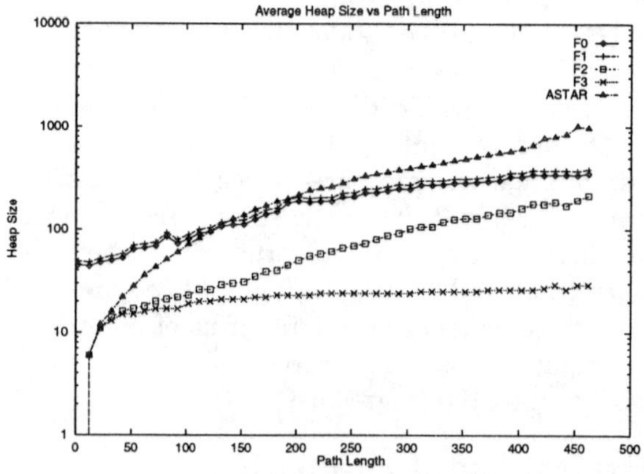

Figure 7: Heap Size vs. Path Length

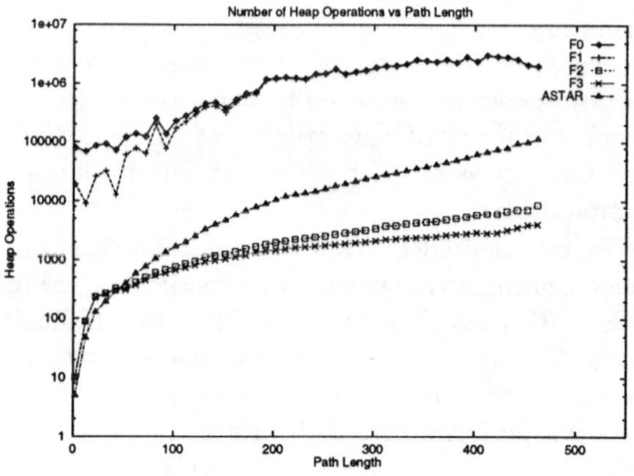

Figure 8: Heap Operations vs. Path Length

5.2 The Effect of Path Length

The length of the shortest path determines the amount of computation each version of the algorithm must perform. In these experiments, we measure how path length affects the number of heap operations, the average heap size, and the IO cost for each version of the algorithm. Candidate paths were chosen

Measure	Hybrid Memoization Candidate				
	F0	F1	F2	F3	A*
Average Heap Size	$O(N)$	$O(N)$	$O(N^{5/6})$	$O(N^{2/3})$	$O(N)$
Heap Operations	$O(N^{17/12})$	$O(N^{17/12})$	$O(N^{3/4})$	$O(N^{3/4})$	$O(N)$
Data Structure Accesses	0	$O(1)$	$O(N^{1/6})$	$O(N^{1/6})$	0

Table 3: Asymptotic Analysis of Hybrid-Memoization Candidates

based on the criteria that their length be greater than 400 nodes. The candidate paths were then split into multiple sub-paths, starting at the source and incrementing every ten nodes until the final destination was reached. Using this formulation, we were able to eliminate randomness in performance due to selecting different length paths, and we could concentrate instead on the effects of incrementally expanding the length of the path. In order to achieve statistical significance, the average of 100 candidate paths was used. In all of the experiments, 100 partitions were used.

Figure 7 shows the average heap size per path length. F0 and F1 again produce a larger initial average heap size than A* does, due to the extensive boundary-graph searching. The average heap size for F1 is larger than that for F0 since F1 uses the $C2B$ data structure instead of having to search fragments. As the length of the boundary path increases, the effect of running multiple A* s in the boundary graph increases the average heap size, since the size of the heap when searching the boundary graph is larger than when searching a fragment. The average heap size for F2 is less than that for F0 or F1, since only a single search takes place in the boundary graph. For F0, F1 and F2, it is interesting to note that the effect of increasing the boundary-path length (increasing the number of searches in the boundary graph) overcomes the effect of increasing the number of fragments traversed (increasing the number of searches in fragments). In F3, the average heap size is asymptotic with the average heap size for a fragment. The difference between F2 and F3 is thus attributed to the effects of performing a single search on the boundary graph. The heap size for the searches grows in proportion to the diameter of the search space. For F0 and F1, the numerous searches in the boundary graph make the average heap size large for all path lengths. The heap size for F2 increases in proportion to the length of the boundary path. The average heap size for F3 is stable for paths of all lengths.

Figure 8 shows the number of heap operations per path length. In all algorithms, the number of heap operations increases as the length of the path increases. F0 has a large number of initial heap operations due to running multiple A*s in the boundary graph. As the path length increases, the number of heap operations increases for F0, F1, and F2, due to running multiple A*s in the boundary graph for increasingly long boundary paths. F2 and F3 have a similar number of heap operations for small paths, because for short paths, the search diameter in the boundary graph is small. As the diameter of the search in the boundary graph increases, the difference between F2 and F3 becomes greater. For short paths, running A* alone produces the fewest heap operations for two reasons. First, it does not use the boundary graph. This helps because the connectivity of the boundary graph is high, which adds to the number of heap operations. Second, the search diameter for short paths is relatively narrow. For paths with a length greater than about 60, the number of heap operations increases rapidly as the search space increases. In fragments, the diameter of the graph is small, and thus even exhaustive searches are limited to the scope of the fragment. The lack of monotonicity for F1 is due to the K^2 A*s required to find the path through the boundary graph. As the path length increases, the destination fragment changes, changing the value of K for that fragment.

6 Conclusion

In this paper, we have described hybrid memoizations for the hierarchical routing algorithm and addressed two important issues regarding the hierarchical routing algorithm. Cost models were developed for executing the memoization in a main memory environment. Experiments showed that memoizing the shortest-path-cost data structure for the boundary graph provides the greatest computational savings, followed by memoizing the cost-to-boundary-nodes data structure for the fragments and then memoizing the shortest-path data structure for the boundary graph. We also showed that the hierarchical algorithm can provide a greater scalability than traditional dynamic searches. In this case, memoizing the shortest-path-cost data structure for the boundary graph provides the greatest computational savings, followed by memoizing the shortest-path data structure for the boundary graph and then the cost-to-boundary-nodes data structure for the fragments. In our future work, we plan on exploring the effect of multi-level hierarchies and implementing a parallel version of the hierarchical routing algorithm.

This work is sponsored in part by the Army High Performance Computing Research Center under the auspices of the Department of the Army, Army Research Laboratory cooperative agreement number DAAH04-95-2-0003/contract number DAAH04-95-C-0008, the content of which does not necessarily reflect the position or the policy of the government, and no official endorsement should be inferred. This work was also supported in part by NSF grant #9631539 We would like to thank Siva Ravada for his technical editing and Christiane McCarthy for improving the overall readability of the paper.

References

[1] F. Banchillon and R. Ramakrishnan. "An Amateur's Introduction to Recursive Query Processing Strategies". In *Proc. of SIGMOD Intl Conference on Management of Data.* ACM, 1986.

[2] W.C. Collier and R.J. Weiland. "Smart Cars, Smart Highways". *IEEE Spectrum*, pages 27–33, April 1994.

[3] Greg Frederickson. "Searching Among Intervals and Compact Routing Tables". *Algorithmica*, pages 448–466, 1996.

[4] Y.W. Huang, N. Jing, and E.A. Rundensteiner. Hierarchical Path Views: A Model Based on Fragmentation and Transportation Road Types. In *Proc. of the 3th ACM Workshop on Geographic Information Systems*, 1995.

[5] Y. Ioannidis, R. Ramakrishnan, and L. Winger. "Transitive Closure Algorithms Based on Graph Traversal". *ACM Trans. on Database Systems*, 18(3), September 1993.

[6] H.V. Jagadish, R. Agrawal, and L. Ness. "A Study of Transitive Closure As a Recursion Mechanism". In *Proc. of SIGMOD Intl. Conference on Management of Data.* ACM, 1987.

[7] B. Jiang. "I/O Efficiency of Shortest Path Algorithms: An Analysis". In *Proc. of the Intl. Conference on Data Engineering.* IEEE, 1992.

[8] Ning Jing, Yun-Wu Huang, and Elke Rudensteiner. "Hierarchical Optimization of Optimal Path Finding for Transportation Applications". In Proc. of ACM Conference on Information and Knowledge Management, 1996.

[9] George Karypis and Vipin Kumar. "Analysis of Multilevel Graph Partitioning". Technical Report 95-037 see also http://www.cs.umn.edu/~karypis, University of Minnesota, Department of Computer Science, Minneapolis, MN 55455, August 1995.

[10] Leonard Kleinrock and Farouk Kamoun. "Hierarchical Routing for Large Networks". *Computer Networks*, 1:154–174, 1977.

[11] Y. Kusumi, S. Nishio, and T. Hasegawa. "File Access Level Optimization Using Page Access Graph on Recursive Query Evaluation". In *Proc. Conference on Extending Database Technology.* EDTB, 1988.

[12] H. Lu, K. Mikkilineni, and J.P. Richardson. "Design and Evaluation of Algorithms to Compute the Transitive Closure of a Database Relation". In *Proc. of Intl Conference on Data Engineering.* IEEE, 1987.

[13] M. Mannio and L.D. Shapiro. "Extensions to Query Languages for Graph Traversal Problems". *IEEE Trans. on Knowledge and Data Engineering*, 2(3), Sept. 1990.

[14] S. Shekhar, A. Kohli, and M. Coyle. Path Computation Algorithms for Advanced Traveler Information Systems. In *Proc. of the 9th Intl. Conference on Data Engineering*, 1993.

[15] S. Shekhar and D. R. Liu. "A Connectivity-Clustered Access Method for Networks and Network Computation". In *Proc. Intl. Conf. on Data Engineering*, 1995. Complete version to appear in IEEE Transactions on Knowledge and Data Engineering.

[16] Shashi Shekhar, Andrew Fetterer, and Brajesh Goyal. A Comparison of Hierarchical Algorithms for Shortest Path Computation in Advanced Travel Information Systems. Technical Report 96-046, University of Minnesota, 1996.

[17] Gang Zhou, Richard Hull, Roger King, and Jean-Claude Franhitti. "Data Integration and Warehousing Using H20". *Bulletin of the Technical Committee of Data Engineering*, 18(2):29–40, June 1995.

```
//BG = boundary graph
//CASE 1: Both Source s and Destination d are boundary nodes

boundaryPath = BG.GetPath(s,d);
path = ExpandBoundaryPath(boundaryPath);

//CASE 2: Source s is a local node and destination d is a
//        boundary node

c = INFINITY;
for each bN in BoundaryNodes(Fragment(s)) do
        if ((cpc = Fragment(s).SPC(s, bN) + BG.(bN,d)) < c) {
               c = cpc;
               minB = i;
        }
path = Fragment(s).SP(s, minB)
       + ExpandBoundaryPath(BG.SP(minB, d);

//CASE 3: Destination is a local node and source is a boundary
//        node
//Similar to CASE 2, but with source and destination reversed

//CASE 4: Both source and destination are local nodes
c = INFINITY;
for each sBN in BoundaryNodes(Fragment(s)) do
        for each dBN in BoundaryNodes(Fragment(d)) do
               if ((cpc=Fragment(s).SPC(s,sBN)
                    + BG.SPC(sBN,dBN)
                    + Fragment(d).SPC(dBN,d))< c) {
                          c = cpc;
                          minSB = sBN;
                          minDB = dBN;
               }
if (Fragment(s) == Fragment(d) && c > Fragment(s).SPC(s,d))
        path = Fragment(s).SP(s,d);
else
        path = Fragment(s).SP(s, minSB)
               + ExpandBoundaryPath(BG.SP(minSB, minDB))
        + Fragment(d).SP(minDB, d);
```

Figure 1: Hierarchical Routing Algorithm Template

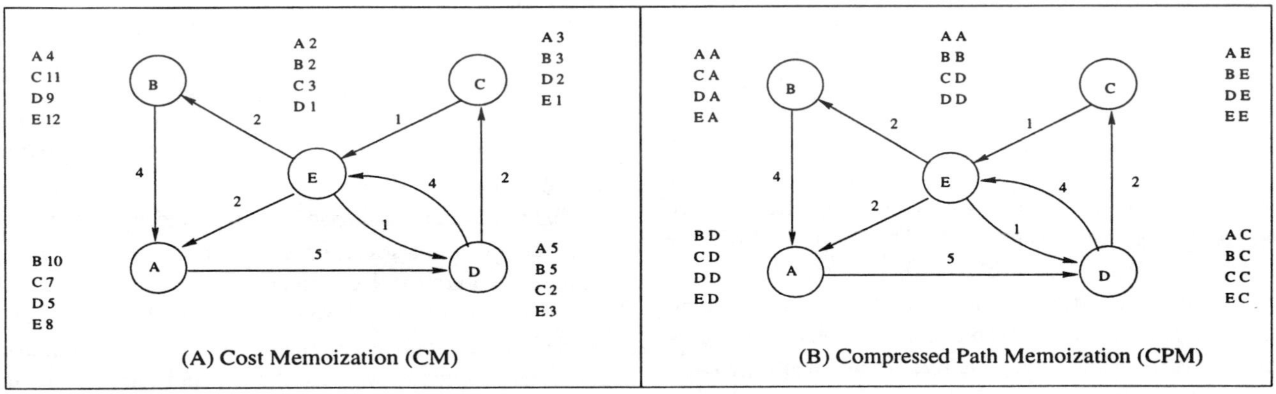

(A) Cost Memoization (CM)

(B) Compressed Path Memoization (CPM)

Figure 2: Path Memoization and Cost Memoization Examples

Formalizing and Automating Component Reuse*

Yonghao Chen and Betty H. C. Cheng†
Department of Computer Science
Michigan State University
East Lansing, MI 48824
email: {chenyong, chengb}@cps.msu.edu

Abstract

Using existing components to construct software systems has significant potential to improving software productivity and quality. A key problem in software component reuse is the selection of appropriate components for satisfying a given requirement. In this paper, we define a component interface generality relation that provides a foundation for component selection. This generality relation, represented in terms of formal specifications, precisely captures the semantic obligations for an existing component to satisfy the requirements of a target system. The formal specifications facilitate the (semi-) automatic determination of the generality relation. We show how this generality relation has been used to determine the reusability of software components in a software architecture-based reuse and integration environment.

1. Introduction

The use of existing software components to construct new systems is recognized as having significant potential to improving software development productivity and software quality [2, 6, 11]. Recently, a great deal of effort has been directed towards an architecture-driven, component-based software development paradigm. A software architecture is a collection of components, connectors, and a configuration of how the components should be connected via connectors. By specifying the interfaces of constituent components and connectors of a target system, software architectures serve as frameworks for assembling existing components. Given an architecture specification, the assembly process of software components consists of two phases: First, the existing components are retrieved, evaluated, and matched to the interfaces in the architecture specification. Then a packaging process is invoked to integrate these components, generating code as necessary for adapting components and/or implementing connections.

A key step in the assembly process is the component selection. Given an interface specification, the objective of component selection is to locate the most appropriate components that satisfy the interface. The criteria necessary for a component to satisfy an interface is usually implicit and not precisely captured. For example, a simple, but widely used, criterion is name (keyword) matching. However, keywords cannot convey significantly useful information, unless they are widely accepted terminology, such as mathematical functions, for example, *sin*, *cos*, etc.. A more informative criterion may be based on signatures (syntax and type information). Although signatures encapsulate type information, they still fail to capture the behavior of a component precisely. Natural language descriptions may document semantic information of components. However, the inherent ambiguity of natural languages (together with possible inconsistencies in the documentation) may make it difficult to locate the "right" component.

Recent work in formal methods has produced rich formalisms for use in software development. Among others is the Larch family of specification languages [7] used to specify programs written in C, C++, Modula-3, Smalltalk, Ada, and CLU. This paper describes an approach to software reuse that takes advantage of the logical reasoning and automated processing enabled by formal specifications of software components to determine which existing components can be used to satisfy the requirements of a new (target) system.

The remainder of this paper is organized as follows. The next section discusses the specification of software components. A Larch-styled formalism is presented to specify component interfaces. Based on the formal specifications, we define a component interface generality relation in Section 3. In Section 4, we describe the application of the interface generality relation in a software architecture-based reuse and integration environment. We discuss the use of the Larch theorem prover LP to determine the interface generality relation. Related work is described in Section 5. We

*This work is supported in part by National Science Foundation grants CCR-9633391, CCR-9407318 and CCR-9209873.

†Please contact this author for all correspondences.

conclude this paper with a summary and a brief description of future investigations.

2. Component Specification

In simplistic terms, a component is a computational unit. As a part of a system, each component provides certain services to its environment, as well as requires some services from its environment. The services provided by a component represent the *capabilities* of the component, and the services required by a component constitute the *assumptions* that the component requires of its environment. A service may be in a variety of forms, for example, an event in event-based systems, or a data stream in a pipeline system. In this paper, we consider components that have either data or functions (procedures) as their services. These components are also termed modules, since they have the same properties as those described in a conventional module interconnection language (MIL) [12].

The specification of the capabilities and assumptions of a module is encapsulated in the interface of the module. A module may or may not have an implementation. A component without an implementation is also termed an abstract component or simply an interface. Each existing component must have an implementation. The implementation of a module should conform to its interface.

Definition 1 (*Conformance of modules to interfaces*) A module M conforms to an interface I (denoted as $M \models I$) iff (1) M implements all of the capabilities of I, and (2) in order to implement the capabilities of I, M must use and only use all of the assumptions stated in I. M is called a conforming module of I, and I is a conformed interface of M.[1]

The conformance definition makes it possible to systematically check the reusability of a component solely based on its conformed interface. It should be noted that an existing module may conform to multiple interfaces, each of which describes a collection of possible behaviors (providing services and/or requiring services) that the module may exhibit in constructing a system.

Example 1 Consider a simple data access system. The system has three components that are organized into layers, where a given layer uses services provided by the layer below it. At the top is the user interface that accepts user data access requests, and handles them by calling data access functions provided in the middle layer. The middle layer component, in turn, uses an abstract data type (ADT) object defined in the bottom layer of the system. Figure 1 describes the interface of the middle layer component, where functions *read* and *write* are used by the top layer component, and the data object *x* of type *dtModel* is defined by the bottom layer component.

This example will be referenced and refined in the following discussions.

```
comp dataAccess is
    assumptions
        dtModel x;
    capabilities
        bool read(... ...);
        bool write(... ...);
end dataAccess
```

Figure 1. An example component interface specification

[1] In this context, module refers to the implementation of the module.

2.1. Refining Interface Specifications

In this section, we refine the definition of interfaces. In addition to the capabilities and assumptions of a component, we also include dependence information among capabilities and assumptions in an interface specification. We use Larch-styled formal specifications [7] to specify interfaces. Formal specifications of interfaces precisely capture the functionalities and provide a rigorous foundation to reason about the relations between interfaces. We choose Larch as the target specification language for several reasons. Larch has a simple syntax and provides support for commonly used programming languages, including C, C++, Smalltalk, Modula-3, and ML [7]. Second, Larch has support for libraries of specifications, thus promoting the reuse of specifications. Finally, there is good tool support for developing and analyzing Larch specifications, including a graphically-based browser and editor [9], syntax checker [7], and theorem prover [7].

2.1.1. Specifying Domain Theories

Larch specifications consist of two tiers: one tier specifies domain theories, and the other tier specifies module interfaces in terms of the problem domain. A domain theory is an algebraic model of a problem domain. It defines a set of abstract types (sorts) and operations over those sorts. The Larch Shared Language (LSL) is used to specify a domain theory termed a *trait.* An LSL specification for a table is shown in Figure 2.

The specification starts with the inclusion of another trait, *Integer*. The *Integer* trait defines the theory of integer, including constants 0, 1, and operator +, and so on. The *Integer* trait is specified in the LSL handbook [7], which is a collection (library) of many useful LSL specifications. The **introduces** clause declares a set of operators, each with

```
// LSL specification for Table
Table: trait
 includes Integer
 Entry tuple of index: Ind, value: Val
 introduces
   φ: → Tab
   add: Tab, Entry → Tab
   lookup: Tab, Ind → Val
   __ ∈ __: Ind, Tab → bool
   size:   Tab  → Int
 asserts
   Tab generated by φ, add
   Tab partitioned by ∈, lookup
   ∀i, i1: Ind, v, v1: Val, t: Tab, e: Entry
   ~(i ∈ φ);
   i ∈ add(t, e) == i = e.index ∨  i ∈ t;
   lookup(add(t, e), i1) == if e.index = i1
            then e.value else lookup(t, i1);
   size(φ) = 0;
   size(add(t, e)) == if e.index ∈ t
            then size(t) else size(t)+1;
```

Figure 2. LSL specification for a table

its own signature. The body of a trait contains, following the keyword **asserts**, equations between terms containing operators and variables. The theory of a trait is the set of all logical consequences of its assertions. The **generated by** clause asserts that each value of the sort Tab is generated by applying ϕ and *add* a finite number of times. And the **partitioned by** clause asserts that all distinct values of Tab can be distinguished by using only the *lookup* and $\in$ operators.

2.1.2. Interface Specifications

In Larch, an interface specification defines an interface between program components. Interface specifications are written in Larch Interface Languages (LILs), which are programming language dependent. For instance, LCL [7] is designed to specify C programs, whereas LM3 [7] is a Larch interface language for Modula-3. The components specified by these LILs are usually programming units, such as procedures, classes, and packages. In the following discussion, we present a Larch style interface specification for architectural components that not only provides services, but also requires services. The interface specification includes two sections, one for specifying the capabilities, the other for specifying the assumptions. In addition, we also specify the dependencies among capabilities and assumptions.

A template for an interface specification is given in Figure 3. The **uses** clause integrates the domain theory specifications and the interface specifications. Interface specifications are written using sorts and values defined in LSL traits. The **assumptions** clause declares the services required by the conforming module, whereas the **capabilities** clause specifies the services provided by the conforming

```
interface interfaceName is
   uses LSL traits
   assumptions
      {dataSpec; | functionSpec;}*
   capabilities
      {dataSpec; | functionSpec;}*
end interfaceName
```

Figure 3. Template for interface specification

module. A service can be prefixed with the keyword **virtual**, indicating that the service is not an actual capability or assumption, but it is needed for the purposes of specifying other services. A service is either a piece of data or a function.

A function is formally specified by giving its precondition and postcondition, as depicted in Figure 4. A precon-

```
functionSpec = function typeName  functionName (argList)
               [ depends on  dependencyList] {
      [ requires  logicalFormula ]
      [ modifies  dataNames ]
      ensures    logicalFormula
   }
```

Figure 4. Function specification

dition (specified in the **requires** clause) specifies when the function is applicable, whereas a postcondition (specified in the **ensures** clause) states what should be established by the execution of the function. In addition, the **modifies** clause specifies what data will be modified by the function. The dependencyList in the **depends on** section is used to list the specific assumptions for a given capability. An assumption specific for a capability is either an assumption of the interface or another capability that is required by the interface in order to provide the capability. By default (if not explicitly specified), the assumptions specific for a capability are those assumptions specified in the **assumptions** clause of the interface. By introducing the dependency list of a capability, we have a finer-grained description of the relations between capabilities and assumptions, rather than just a description of the assumptions of an interface as a single entity.

Data is specified by simply declaring it as shown in Figure 5. The behavioral specification for a complex data type (such as an ADT) is attached using the **with behavior** keywords. A behavioral specification consists of a set of function (method) specifications that each specify externally observable behavior of an object of the type.

Figure 6 is the refined interface specification for the component *dataAccess* from the previously presented example,

```
dataSpec = data typeName dataName
               [ depends on dependencyList]
               with behavior  behavioralSpec
```

Figure 5. Data specification

where within a function specification, *result* represents the return value of the function, $x^\wedge$ and x' represent the values of data (variable) x before and after the function is executed, respectively. The specification states that the component *dataAccess* has two capabilities, *read* and *write*, that depend on a data assumption, x. x is a table with behavior specified for checking the existence of a record in the table, inserting a record into the table, querying and updating the table.

```
comp dataAccess is
  uses Table(dtModel for Tab, int for Ind, int for Val)
  assumptions
    data dtModel x with behavior {
       bool exists(int recNo) {
          ensures result = recNo ∈ x;
       }
       void insert(int recNo, int val) {
          requires ~(recNo ∈ x^);
          modifies x;
          ensures  recNo ∈ x' ∧ lookup(x', recNo) = val;
       }
       int query(int recNo) {
          requires recNo ∈ x;
          ensures  result = lookup(x, recNo);
       }
       void update(int recNo, int newVal) {
          requires recNo ∈ x^;
          modifies x;
          ensures  lookup(x', recNo) = newVal;
       }
    }
  capabilities
    function bool read(int recNo, int recVal) depends on x {
      modifies recVal;
      ensures result = recNo ∈ x
         ∧ (if result then recVal' = lookup(x,recNo));
    }
    function void write(int recNo,int recVal) depends on x {
      modifies x;
      ensures  recNo ∈ x' ∧ recVal = lookup(x', recNo)
    }
end dataAccess
```

Figure 6. dataAccess interface specification

3. Interface Generality Relation

In this section, based on the formal specifications of component interfaces, we define a logic-based generality relation between interfaces. This generality relation provides a rigorous basis, amenable to automation, to determine the reusability of an existing component for satisfying a given requirement.

3.1. Generality Relation of Function Specifications

Since the provided and required services of an interface are a set of functions or data items, we first define the generality relation of two function specifications.

Definition 2 (*Generality relation of function specifications*) Given two function specifications, g and h, g is more general than h, denoted as $h \preceq_f g$, if the following rules hold:

- **Signature matching**
  - *Arguments rule.* g and h have the same number of arguments. Let the list of argument types of g be (T_g^1, T_g^2, ..., T_g^n), and that of h be (T_h^1, T_h^2, ..., T_h^n), then there exists a permutation of the list (T_h^1, T_h^2, ..., T_h^n), denoted as ($T_h^{1'}$, $T_h^{2'}$, ..., $T_h^{n'}$), such that for all i, $1 \leq i \leq n$, $T_h^{i'}$ is the same as T_g^i.
  - *Result rule.* Either both g and h have a result or neither has one. If there is a result, then h's result type is the same as g's result type.
- **Specification rule** [2]
  Let *pre*(f) and *post*(f) be the precondition and postcondition of function specification f, respectively.
  - *Precondition rule.* $pre(g) \rightarrow pre(h)$, the precondition of g implies the precondition of h.
  - *Postcondition rule.* $post(h) \rightarrow post(g)$, the postcondition of h implies the postcondition of g.

The signature matching requires that the two functions' range types match and their domain types match after permutation. The specification rule requires that a more general function have a stronger precondition and a weaker postcondition.

Intuitively, the generality relation between function specifications captures the following implementation property: *let H be a function implementing function specification h, then H also implements the function specification g that is more general than h.* In other words, whenever a function implementing g is needed, the function H implementing h can be used.

3.2. Generality Relation of Data Specifications

The generality relation of data items is determined based on their behavioral specifications.

[2] Parameter renaming has been conducted based on signature matching so that the specifications of function g and h are consistent.

Definition 3 (*Generality relation of data specifications*) Given two data specifications d_1 and d_2, let $SPEC_i$ be the set of function specifications of d_i's behavioral specification (where i is 1 or 2), d_2 is more general than d_1, denoted as $d_1 \preceq_d d_2$, if there exists a map π from $SPEC_2$ to $SPEC_1$, such that for any function (method) specification $m \in SPEC_2$, there exists a function specification $\pi(m)$ in $SPEC_1$, and m is more general than $\pi(m)$, i.e., $\pi(m) \preceq_f m$.[3]

The above definition captures the behavioral property that a data specification should provide all the behavior provided by a more general data specification. In terms of implementation, the generality relation between data specifications implies that *a data object that implements a data specification also implements any more general data specifications*.

3.3. Generality Relation of Interfaces

An interface specification contains a set of provided services (capabilities) and a set of required services (assumptions) that are needed for providing all of the capabilities. The assumptions for a specific capability are specified in the dependency list of the capability specification. An assumption for a specific capability is either an assumption of the interface or another capability of the interface. The relations among the services (both provided and required) of an interface can be depicted using a *directed acyclic graph* (DAG), called a dependence DAG. For instance, Figure 7 contains the dependence DAG of the interface *dataAccess* depicted in Figure 6.

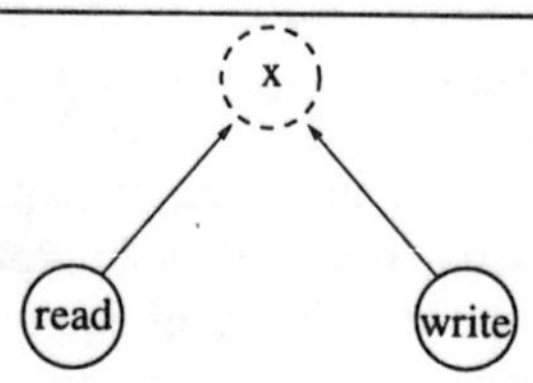

Figure 7. Dependence DAG of dataAccess interface

In Figure 7, there are three nodes, each of which corresponds to a service. The dashed circle (node) represents an assumption, whereas the solid circle (node) represents a capability. The directed edge $\overrightarrow{\langle u, v\rangle}$ means that u depends on v (v is an assumption needed for providing u).

[3]There should be an abstraction function that maps the value space (described in terms of the Larch Shared Language) of d_1 to that of d_2. We omit it here for simplicity. For details please see [1, 10].

Definition 4 (*Dependence DAG of interfaces*) Given an interface I, the dependence DAG of I, denoted as $G_I = \langle V, E\rangle$, is derived from the interface specification for I. Specifically, each service of I defined both in terms of the capabilities and the assumptions corresponds to a node in V (we name the node using its service name). If a service u depends on another service v, then directed edge $\overrightarrow{\langle u, v\rangle} \in E$.

In the following discussion, C_I and A_I represent the set of capabilities and the set of assumptions specified in interface I, respectively.

Definition 5 (*Assumptions specific to a single capability*) In an interface I, let A_I^c denote the set of assumptions upon which a capability c depends, then

$$A_I^c = \{t \mid t \in A_I \text{ and } t \text{ is reachable from } c \text{ in } G_I\}.$$

where G_I is the dependence DAG of interface I. A node u is reachable from a node v in a directed acyclic graph (DAG), if there exists a directed path from v to u.

For example, in the *dataAccess* interface, $A_I^{read} = \{x\}$ and $A_I^{write} = \{x\}$.

Definition 6 (*Assumptions specific to a set of capabilities*) For a set of capabilities, K, of interface I, let A_I^K be the set of assumptions upon which capabilities of K depend, then

$$A_I^K = \bigcup_{c \in K} A_I^c$$

According to the above definition, it is true that $A_I^{C_I} \subseteq A_I$ for any interface I. However, a correctly specified interface should not have the case where $A_I^{C_I} \subset A_I$, because this would mean that stronger assumptions than needed have been imposed over the interface.

Definition 7 (*Interface generality relation*) Given two interfaces I_1 and I_2, I_2 is more general than I_1, i.e., $I_1 \preceq I_2$, if there exists a map $\pi_c : C_{I_2} \to C_{I_1}$, such that the following rules hold:

- **Capabilities rule.** $\forall s_2 \in C_{I_2}$, there exists a s_1, $s_1 \in C_{I_1}$, such that $s_1 = \pi_c(s_2)$, and s_1 and s_2 are both data specifications or function specifications, and s_2 is more general than s_1, that is,
  - $s_1 \preceq_d s_2$, if s_1 and s_2 are both data specifications
  - $s_1 \preceq_f s_2$, if s_1 and s_2 are both function specifications

- **Assumptions rule.**
  There exists an onto map $\pi_{\mathbf{a}} : A_{I_1}^{\pi_c(C_{I_2})} \rightarrow A_{I_2}$, such that, $\forall s_1 \in A_{I_1}^{\pi_c(C_{I_2})}$, let $s_2 = \pi_{\mathbf{a}}(s_1)$, s_1 and s_2 are both data specifications or function specifications, and s_1 is more general than s_2, that is,
  - $s_2 \preceq_d s_1$, if s_1 and s_2 are both data specifications
  - $s_2 \preceq_f s_1$, if s_1 and s_2 are both function specifications

The capabilities rule states that a more specific interface I_1 should provide a corresponding capability for each capability specified in a more general interface I_2, and the corresponding capability in I_1 should be more specific than that in I_2. The assumptions rule states that every assumption required by the more specific interface I_1 needed to provide the specified capabilities should have a corresponding assumption in I_2 that is more specific. Moreover, the corresponding relation between the assumptions should be onto.

We claim that the interface generality relation defined in Definition 7 has the following property: (An informal justification for this claim is given in [4].)

Property 1 Given two interfaces I_1 and I_2, if $I_1 \preceq I_2$, i.e., I_2 is more general than I_1, then any module M conforming to I_1 also conforms to I_2.

Based on the generality relation, we can define the reusability of an existing module for fulfilling a given requirement, either for the construction of new systems or in the maintenance of existing systems.

Definition 8 (*Reusability*) Given a requirement, represented as an abstract component (interface) I, an existing component M (with conformed interface I_m) is reusable for fulfilling I if $I_m \preceq I$.

According to Property 1, it is easy to see $M \models I$, that is, M conforms to I. Therefore, we can use M to implement I. More specifically, we can map every capability c in I to $\pi_{\mathbf{c}}(c)$ of I_m, and every assumption a in $A_{I_m}^{\pi_c(C_I)}$ to $\pi_{\mathbf{a}}(a)$ of I.

4. ABRIE: A Software Architecture-Based Reuse and Integration Environment

ABRIE is an experimental system designed to explore the use of software architectures as a framework for assembling software components. The design objective is to provide an integrated environment to address various reuse issues: composition specification, component management and evaluation, and component integration. Three characteristics are particularly emphasized in the ABRIE design: visualization, multilevel abstractions, and automation. In addition to the textual form, visual representation and manipulation of components, connections, and architectures are supported. ABRIE uses three levels of abstraction in determining the reusability of existing components: types, signatures, and formal (logic-based) specifications. Automation is one main potential benefit of architecture-based reuse. In ABRIE, the component integration (packaging) process is fully automated. Based on the formal (logic-based) specifications, (semi-)automatic support in component evaluation is provided by integrating the Larch Theorem Prover (LP) to assist in the determination of the interface generality relation between components.

In ABRIE, a component has a set of ports, each of which describes a service that the component provides or requires. Connectors are encapsulations for interactions among components. A connector consists of a collection of roles for the participants of the interaction specified by the connector. Components and connectors are put together to describe an architecture by configuring the ports of components to roles of connectors. Components, connectors, and ports are typed. The type of a component is intended to capture the architectural properties, that is, the way the component may be used. Connector types capture recurring component interaction styles. Finally, port types encapsulate information about services provided or required by a component.

In the following discussion, we focus on the integration and use of LP in ABRIE. We illustrate how LP can facilitate the determination of interface generality relation, and thus automate the component evaluation process. More detailed discussions on ABRIE regarding its features and development can be found in [3].

The main working area of ABRIE is a canvas that provides a graphical representation and manipulation for architectural elements. Figure 8 shows a main program/subroutine style architecture for an example system *pwr* for recognizing palindrome words.

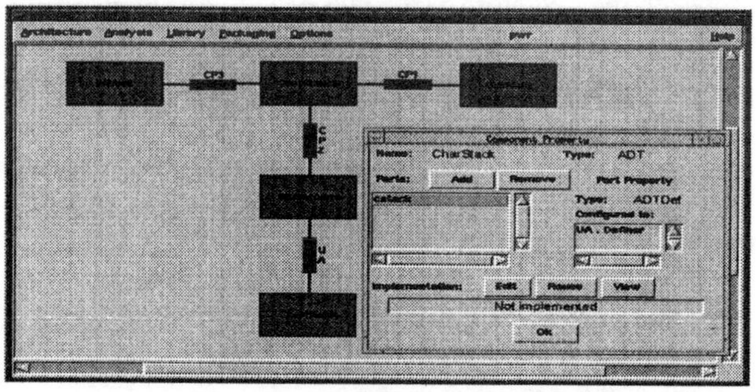

Figure 8. ABRIE Architecture Design

In *pwr*, *Coordinator* is the main control component that calls procedures defined in components *InWord*, *OutWord*, and *Recognizer*. *InWord* inputs words from an *InFile* port that is configured to the standard input. *OutWord* writes words to a port that is configured to the standard output. *Recognizer* defines and exports a procedure *isPalindrome* that checks if a word is a palindrome word. *Recognizer* imports and uses a character stack through a connector UA. Component *CharStack* defines and exports an ADT *cstack*.

In order to illustrate the process of evaluating and reusing existing components in ABRIE, let us consider the implementation of component *CharStack*. The "Component Property" window in Figure 8 shows the properties of component *CharStack*. By clicking the "Reuse" button in the "Component Property" window, the user instructs ABRIE to search its component library and return all the candidate components that are of the same type as *CharStack*. Based on their specifications, the user selects one candidate for further evaluation. Figure 9 shows the scenario of matching a library component *List* for satisfying *CharStack*, where *B* and *C* represent behavior and constructor, respectively.

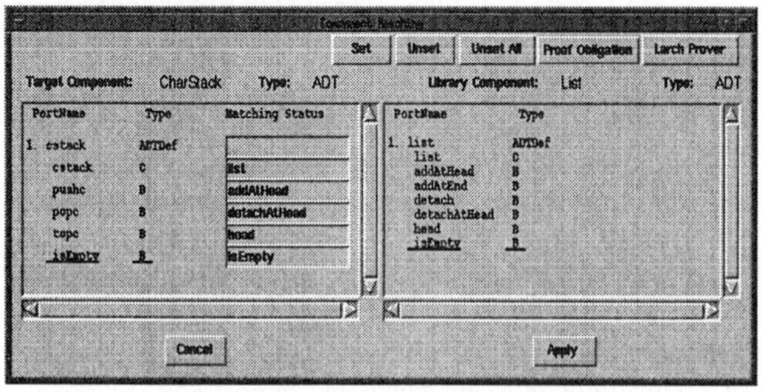

Figure 9. Component Matching

Both *List* and *CharStack* have only a provided service: a data item specified with a set of operations and their respective behavior. In order to determine the reusability of component *List*, we need to establish whether the ADT *cstack* defined in component *CharStack* is more general than *list* in component *List*. We proceed by assigning a mapping between the operators of the two ADTs. As shown in Figure 9, we assume that the constructor *cstack* is more general than constructor *list*, *pushc* than *addAtHead*, *popc* than *detachAtHead*, and etc.. Given the mapping, ABRIE will automatically generate the proof obligations for justifying the mapping. Figure 10 depicts the proof obligations generated for the mapping shown in Figure 9.

The proof obligations are generated based on the Larch specifications of the two components. In order to facilitate the application of the Larch Prover (LP) for analyzing them, the proof obligations are represented in terms of LSL specifications. After preprocessing the proof obligations, we can invoke the Larch Prover (LP) from the "Component Matching" window to assist in proving these obligations. If all these obligations are successfully resolved, then the user-assigned mapping is justified, and thereby establishing the

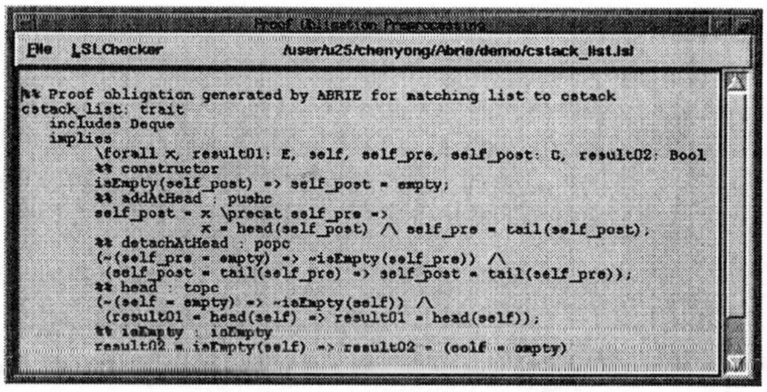

Figure 10. Proof Obligations

reusability of the library component. Figure 11 shows a snapshot of LP while it is discharging the proof obligations for our example. LP is an interactive theorem proving system for multi-sorted first-order logic. In certain cases, user interaction may be required in proving/disproving a conjecture. However, for our example, all the proof obligations are automatically proved by LP. Therefore the assumed mapping is justified and we can reuse the *List* component for satisfying component *CharStack*.

```
LP1.15: prove
  (isEmpty(self_post) => self_post = empty)
  ..
Attempting to prove conjecture cstack_listTheorem.1:
  isEmpty(self_post) => self_post = empty
Conjecture cstack_listTheorem.1
[] Proved by normalization.
Deleted formula cstack_listTheorem.1, which reduced
to 'true'.

LP1.16: prove
  (self_post = (x:E \precat self_pre) =>
  (x:E = head(self_post) /\ self_pre = tail(self_post)))
  ..
Attempting to prove conjecture cstack_listTheorem.2:
  self_post = x \precat self_pre =>
  x = head(self_post) /\ self_pre = tail(self_post)
Conjecture cstack_listTheorem.2
[] Proved by normalization.
Deleted formula cstack_listTheorem.2, which reduced
to 'true'.
```

Figure 11. A Snapshot of LP in resolving proof obligations

Based on the justified mapping between ports (and behavior of ports), ABRIE will automatically generate code necessary for resolving naming conflicts between the library component and the target component during the system packaging process [3].

5. Related Work

Jeng and Cheng [8] proposed specification matching for reuse based on order-sorted predicate logic (OSPL). They defined both exact and relaxed matches. Zaremski and Wing [13] summarized several types of specification matchings to capture different behavioral relations. Both approaches discussed module specification matching, where a module simply refers to a collection of individual functions, rather than an architectural unit such as those that we considered in this paper. In both approaches, there is no support for capturing assumptions that a module requires of its environment, nor are the dependence relations of the functions within a module considered.

Several behavioral notions of subtyping in object-oriented design have recently been proposed [1, 5, 10]. These notions capture the substitutability property of subtypes: Given a program P, when an object o of type T in P is substituted by o' of type S, where S is a subtype of T, the behavior of P will remain unchanged. Similar to our notion for interface generality relation, these definitions for behavioral subtyping not only consider syntactic constraints (such as matches between signatures), but also emphasize the semantic obligations. The main difference between our work and these projects lies in the granularity of components: their components (objects or object types) are relatively fine-grained, whereas we consider architectural units that have structural constraints imposed by *requiring* or *providing* services. In addition to theoretical investigations, we also explored the use of the interface generality relation as a basis for component evaluation and selection in ABRIE. ABRIE integrates tools to facilitate the determination of the interface generality relation.

6. Summary and Future Investigations

In this paper, we addressed an important issue in software component reuse: determining the reusability of an existing component for fulfilling a requirement. We first presented a formalism for describing component interfaces, and then we defined a component interface generality relation that explicitly captures the semantic obligations for an existing component to satisfy a requirement. We also showed how this interface generality relation can be used in automating the evaluation and selection of reusable components in a software architecture-based reuse and integration environment.

The interface generality relation defined in this paper is applicable to components that have data or procedures as their services. However, an actual system may consist of other kinds of components, such as filters that interact with their environment through pipes. We are currently investigating the generality relation for these kinds of components.

References

[1] P. America. Designing an object-oriented programming language with behavioral subtyping. In J. W. de Bakker, W. P. de Roever, and G. Rozenberg, editors, *LNCS*, volume 489, pages 60–90. Springer-Verlag, 1991.

[2] V. R. Basili, L. C. Briand, and W. L. Melo. Measuring the impact of reuse on quality and productivity in object-oriented systems. Technical Report UMIACS-TR-95-2, University of Maryland, Computer Science Department, 1995.

[3] Y. Chen and B. Cheng. Facilitating an automated approach to architecture-based software reuse. In *Proc. of 12th IEEE Intl. Conference on Automated Software Engineering (to appear)*, November 1997.

[4] Y. Chen and B. H. C. Cheng. Formalizing and automating component reuse. Technical Report MSU-CPS-97-15, Michigan State University, Computer Science Department, May 1997.

[5] K. K. Dhara and G. T. Leavens. Forcing behavioral subtyping through specification inheritance. In *Proceedings of the 18th International Conference on Software Engineering (ICSE'18)*, Berlin, Germany, March 1996.

[6] W. B. Frakes and S. Isoda. Success factors of systematic reuse. *IEEE Software*, 11, September 1994.

[7] J. V. Guttag and J. Horning. *Larch: Languages and Tools for Formal Specification*. Springer-Verlag, 1993.

[8] J.-J. Jeng and B. H. C. Cheng. Specification matching for software reuse: A foundation. In *SSR'95*. ACM SIGSOFT, ACM Press, April 1995.

[9] M. R. Laux, R. H. Bourdeau, and B. H. C. Cheng. An integrated development environment for formal specifications. In *Proc. of the IEEE 5th Intl. Conf. on Software Engineering and Knowledge Engineering*, June 1993.

[10] B. H. Liskov and J. M. Wing. A behavioral notion of subtyping. *ACM Transactions on Programming Languages*, 16(10), November 1994.

[11] H. Mili, F. Mili, and A. Mili. Reusing software: Issues and research directions. *IEEE Transactions on Software Engineering*, 21(6):528–561, June 1995.

[12] R. Prieto-Diaz and J. M. Neighbors. Module interconnection languages. *J. Systems and Software*, 6(4), Nov 1986.

[13] A. M. Zaremski and J. M. Wing. Specification matching of software components. In *3rd ACM SIGSOFT Symposium on the Foundations of Software Engineering*, October 1995.

A Role for Chunking and Fuzzy Reasoning in a Program Comprehension and Debugging Tool

Ilene Burnstein, Katherine Roberson, Floyd Saner, Abdul Mirza, Abdallah Tubaishat
Computer Science Department
Illinois Institute of Technology
Chicago, IL 60616
csburnstein@minna.iit.edu

Abstract

We are applying artificial intelligence techniques to develop a tool called BUG-DOCTOR that assists software engineers with program comprehension and debugging. In this paper we describe two of BUG-DOCTOR's knowledge sources, the Chunker and the Plan Processor. The Chunker identifies candidate chunks in the target code using program analysis techniques and a set of heuristics. Candidate chunks map to higher level concepts, and have a signature which captures their major identifying characteristics. The Plan Processor uses a signature to retrieve a set of program plans from a Plan Library with features that are similar to those of the candidate chunk. Its fuzzy reasoner then ranks the retrieved plans. The plan chosen as most similar to the candidate chunk is used for program comprehension and debugging tasks that follow. We believe that this approach could lead to more scalable tools for program comprehension and debugging.

1.0 Introduction

We are developing an automated tool for program comprehension-debugging called BUG-DOCTOR. To build this tool we have borrowed techniques from the artificial intelligence community. For example, BUG-DOCTOR's architecture is based on the blackboard model. Its overall design is based on cognitive models for program understanding/debugging. System knowledge sources use "if/then" rules, fuzzy reasoners, and heuristics to reason about code concepts and to locate faults. Several of these knowledge sources have been implemented and described in our previous work [1-4].

In this paper we report on a knowledge source called the Chunker that produces a set of abstractions called candidate chunks from the target code. We show that candidate chunks map to programming and problem domain concepts that programmers might identify. We describe a chunk signature which is derived from a subset of attributes of the candidate chunks. It encapsulates a candidate chunk's major identifying characteristics and plays a major role in a signature matching process we call ***M(sig)***.

We also report on a Plan Processor knowledge source that uses **M*(sig)*** to retrieve a set of program plans from our Plan Library with signatures similar to those of the target chunks. The Plan Processor's fuzzy reasoning component evaluates the closeness of the signature match. The retrieved plan that is most similar to the target code chunk is applied in a subsequent matching procedure involving the entire set of chunk and plan attributes. The latter procedure called ***M(plan),*** is essential for deep reasoning about the program's intentions and for fault identification. We believe that our approach eliminates the need for exhaustive searches of a plan library to find a match for the target code, and could lead to more efficient program comprehension/debugging tools that scale up for the analysis of large software systems.

2.0 Program recognition and fault localization processes

Our conceptual model for program recognition/fault localization provides the underpinnings for the design of the BUG-DOCTOR system [1-3]. The model identifies program comprehension as a major sub-task of debugging. Studies show that in order to locate all but the most trivial faults, programmers build a complex mental model of the buggy code that we call the ***actual code model***. [5]. A chunking process is used to simplify model construction during program comprehension. The chunking process produces identifiable code partitions that can be stored, used as building blocks for higher level concepts, and analyzed for faults. The partitions usually represent units that are simple functional entities; for example, "swap values",

1082-3409/97 $10.00 © 1997 IEEE

"calculate average" [5-7]. Recognition triggers such as variable names and control structures support chunking and comprehension. They help to partition the code, and stimulate the retrieval of stereotypical patterns known as program plans or clichés stored in the programmer's memory. A synthesis process takes place during recognition that maps the code partitions to elements in the plan in order to build the ***actual code model***. An analysis process takes place during debugging. Its goal is to identify the differences between the ***actual code model*** and the plan [1-3]. These differences represent potential faults. BUG-DOCTOR's knowledge sources cooperate to model the processes described above.

In the following section of this paper we give a brief description of BUG-DOCTOR's architecture. We then discuss two of its critical knowledge sources, the Chunker, and the Plan Processor.

3.0 System architecture

BUG-DOCTOR is a set of interacting components that assist a software engineer with the processes of code comprehension and debugging. The system architecture is based on the blackboard model. Using this architectural paradigm has enabled us to assemble a set of independent knowledge sources, knowledge bases, and controllers, that can be used for building and analyzing representations of the mental models necessary for code comprehension and debugging [1,2]. The knowledge sources we have designed and implemented are as follows:

Program State Monitor -Traces program behavior during execution of documented test cases, saves system states and actual output for inspection and queries. Monitors assertions statements inserted by the user [1].
Output Analyzer- Analyzes differences, and establishes relationships between the expected and actual outputs produced by the target code [1].
Protran Group -Identifies non-stereotypical code segments, applies transformations to "normalize" the target code while preserving the original code semantics [3].
Chunker-Identifies candidate chunks that map to programming and/or problem domain concepts. Generates chunk signature information [2-4].
Plan Processor (design stage only) -Uses candidate chunk signatures to select programming plans from a Plan Library. Retrieved plans are ranked in order of their similarity to target code candidate chunks by a fuzzy reasoner [2,3].

BUG-DOCTOR also requires several knowledge bases to support its reasoning processes. One of these is a Plan Library that contains representations of stereotypical program fragments called program plans. Others include a fault model data base, and a test case repository [1-4].

4.0 The role of chunk-like structures

Chunk-like structures have been used by computer scientists to support the development of program recognition and debugging tools. Most of the systems reported are knowledge-based, and use the concept of a chunk/plan/cliché as the fundamental unit of their knowledge-bases. For example, Johnson and Soloway describe units of comprehension as chunk-like program plans that represent stereotypical programming sequences within a framework of task-related goals. The plans were used in the context of their debugging system called PROUST [8]. Hartman, the developer of UNPROG, a program comprehension system, discusses a "programming concept" that can be taught to novices and is understood by most programmers [9]. Rich and Waters describe a concept called a program cliché which is proposed as a unit used by programmers to build and recognize code [6]. The cliché is the basic knowledge unit for the Programmer's Apprentice, a support tool for software maintainers. Kozaczynski, and Ning [10] describe a concept hierarchy of chunk-like structures to support their concept recognizer. Quilici's hybrid recognition system is also based on a chunk-like knowledge unit called a plan that is stored in an indexed plan library [11].

In the following sections of this paper we describe our approach to the development of the Chunker. The Chunker produces abstractions called candidate chunks that are used by BUG-DOCTOR for the following two knowledge-based matching processes:

1. A chunk signature derived from a subset of attributes of the candidate chunks is matched against program plan signatures to retrieve those plans whose signatures indicate they are closely related to the candidate chunks. We call this matching process ***M(sig)***.

2. The full set of attributes from the candidate chunks and the most closely related retrieved plans are matched for concept recognition and debugging. We call this matching process $\boldsymbol{M_{(plan)}}$.

The Chunker design and implementation is based on the pair of definitions for the term chunk that we have developed, and on program analysis techniques such as control flow and data dependency analysis. It is supported by an extendible knowledge base of heuristics derived from our definitions of a chunk.

5.0 Defining a program chunk

The Chunkers' goal is to help BUG-DOCTOR build an internal model of the target code by producing a set of abstractions called candidate chunks. The candidate chunks:

•are simple, but cohesive code patterns

•are groups of statements related by control and data dependencies

•can be mapped by software engineers to programming/problem domain concepts

•can be mapped to program plans in a plan library

•can be arranged in chunks hierarchies

•are abstractions that reduce the level of detail needed to reason about the structure and functionality of the code.

Candidate chunks are produced by the chunking process. We begin a discussion of the chunking process by defining the term chunk. In the literature it has been compared to a cliché, a plan, a schema, a slice and a prime. An intuitive definition of a program chunk is [2-4]:

Definition 1: A chunk is a sequence of software instructions that achieves a coherent purpose and that can be understood outside of the context in which it is used.

The key points in this definition are that the chunk has a purpose, and that it can be understood independently from the program in which it is found. The purpose is extracted from the syntactic/semantic representation in the code through a mapping to the problem domain. The definition also implies a cohesiveness property and the existence of a set attributes that help to identify the chunk and define its purpose.

A programming language-oriented definition of a chunk is stated below [2-4]. It is based on language semantics and the concept of a programming prime. Primes are the fundamental units from which all structured programs can be built. Prime types are: sequential, iterative, and conditional. For example, an assignment statement is a sequential prime, a "while" loop is an iterative prime, and an "if" statement is a conditional prime.

Definition 2: A chunk is either a prime, including all primes contained within it, or a sequence of primes that exist within the same programming scope, where for each pair of primes either one prime is data dependent on the other, or both primes are data dependent on a third prime within the sequence.

The property of cohesiveness in the intuitive definition 1 is supported by control and data dependency attributes in the less abstract definition 2.

Our approach to automation began with the application of definition 2. We wanted to group statements together within the same control level and analyze their data flow and data dependencies. The definition implies that all primes within a chunk work on common data elements. One would want to designate chunk boundaries at locations where the fewest data elements are shared; the statement grouping would occur where many data elements are shared. Using this approach, we cannot guarantee that the Chunker will find all the logical chunks, but one would assume from the intuitive and language-oriented definitions of a chunk that multiple statements in the same level of program scope working on a common set of variables probably implement a single concept or achieve some intended purpose that relates to the data. We decided that a good representation for a program that would allow us to achieve our goals would be the data dependency graph; a graph could be generated for each control level. We could build a chunk hierarchy from the set of levels and the chunks we find within them [3,4].

6.0 Implementation of the Chunker

The Chunker consists of seven components that implement a chunking algorithm as we have previously reported in the literature [3,4]. The components are briefly described below.

Tagger: This component is responsible for tagging the code primes with a unique identification tag that reflects the position of the primes in the control hierarchy.

Data Flow Analyzer: The data flow analyzer produces a list of nodes in the program uniquely identified by an integer, a list of tagged variables, a program control flow graph, and a data flow graph. The latter consists of definition-use sets for each node in the graph.

Data Dependency Graph Generator: The Chunker needs to examine data flow between nodes that are at the same control level. The net results of data flow to subordinate nodes must be propagated up to the node that encompasses them. This is done by a recursive algorithm that propagates definition-use sets up through the program control flow graph. A dependency graph for each level is then generated.

Transformation Component: This component attempts to reduce the number of nodes in the data dependency graphs to improve performance and reduce memory requirements.

Potential Chunk Generator: This component identifies potential chunks at a given control level based on a process that attempts all possible node combinations at that level. The generation of potential chunks is highly memory intensive. In the next section we describe an approach used to make the process more efficient.

Candidate Chunk Generator: The potential chunks generated represent a first pass at partitioning the code. However, many of these node combinations would not map to concepts identified by software engineers, nor to plans in our Plan Library. We prune the set of potential chunks using a knowledge base of heuristics and a weighting process to increase the likelihood that the selected chunks will match plans in our Plan Library.

In our experiments, we used the heuristics shown on Table 1. Each heuristic tends to favor potential chunks with specific types of attributes that could support mapping to a single independent concept. We currently use chunk size and connectivity as the principle attributes. Size depends on the number of nodes. Connectivity is related to the internal and external data connections a potential chunk has within itself and with the outside world. This gives an indication of the cohesiveness property implied in our intuitive definition. The first heuristic favors potential chunks that produce a single output. These chunks tend to be highly cohesive since many inputs may collapse to a single output indicating a single function. The second heuristic selects candidate chunks from those potential chunks that have a large number of nodes and have minimum external connectivity. This implies they have a minimum number of input/output data connections to other nodes and could stand alone as a unit. Choosing potential chunks with minimal external, but maximal internal connectivity is a refinement of heuristic II and indicates an internal connectedness among the nodes with minimal connections to the outside world. Heuristic IV uses a variable scope as an indication of cohesiveness.

Heuristic	Description
I	Find smallest chunks that produce single output
II	Find chunks with minimal external connectivity and choose the largest ones
III	Find chunks with minimal external but maximal internal connectivity
IV	Find smallest potential chunks that encompass the scope of a variable.

Table 1. Current Chunker Heuristics

The knowledge base of heuristics adds intelligence and flexibility to the Chunker. We add intelligence by supplementing the programming language oriented approach that produces potential chunks, with the higher level knowledge embedded in the heuristics. We gain flexibility by allowing BUG-DOCTOR to select from the heuristic set and generate alternative lists of candidate chunks for its subsequent matching processes. In addition, the knowledge base of heuristics can be modified to derive a set that is closer to optimal.

6.1 Working through an example

We will illustrate the workings of the Chunker with the standard deviation example in Figure 1. It has

```
Source Code                                          Data Access

real std(int a[],int n) {                            a:L,n:L
real average, deviation, sqrDev
A     int i = 0                                      i: W,L
B     real sum = 0                                   sum: W,L
C     while(i<n) {                                   i:R,n:R
C1              sum = sum + a[i]
                                                     sum:R,W,a:R,i:R
C2              i = i+1                              i:R,W
C               }                                    i:D
D     average = sum/n                                average:W,L,
                                                     sum:R,D,n:R
E     i = 0                                          i:W,L
F     sum = 0                                        sum:W,L
G     while(i > n)        {                          i:R, n:R
G1              deviation = a[i] - average
                                                     deviation:W,L,a:R,
                                                     average:R
G2              sqrDev = deviation*deviation
                                                     sqrDev:W,L,
                                                     deviation:R,D
G3              sum = sum + sqrDev
                                                     sum:W,sqrDev:R,D
G4              i = i+1                              i:R,W
G               }                                    i:D,average:D
H     average = sum/n
                                                     average:W,L,
                                                     sum:R,D,n:R
I     deviation = sqrt((average)
                                                     deviation:W,L,
                                                     average:R,D
J     return(deviation)                              deviation:R,D
      }                                              a:R,n:R,result:W
```

Figure 1. Tagged Source Code with Data Access

several interesting features including loop carried dependencies, variable reuse, and multiple logical chunks found in different scoping levels. In Figure 1 we see the tagged code and the results of data flow analysis that shows how the variables are accessed.

Data dependency graphs are generated for each control level. These can be simplified by reduction rules. Some of the 19 potential chunks that are generated from the reduced graph at the top level are shown in Figure 2. A much larger number would have been generated if the transformations had not occurred [4].

We then select and apply one of the heuristics previously discussed. In this example we apply the heuristic "the smallest chunk to produce a single output variable". It partitions the code in a functional way; a chunk is a unit that produces a single result. To apply this heuristic we must examine the code to find all output variables produced by the potential chunks.

The resulting list of candidate chunks includes two chunks that produce "sum", two that produce "average", one that produces "deviation" and one that produces a result. These candidate chunks are shown in Figure 3. They parallel those that might be chosen by a programmer and could also map to components in our Plan Library. We also use the same techniques to generate the lower level dependency graphs to find the candidate chunks at the lower levels of control. In this way we build a chunk hierarchy [3,4].

7.0 Challenges for the Chunker

The most challenging problem for the current version of the Chunker is to control the space complexity inherent in the algorithm. As the number of nodes in the dependency graph increases, the number of potential chunks at a given level increases along with memory and processing requirements. The relationship between the number of nodes and resource requirements is exponential. To improve the scalability of the Chunker we used the following strategies which have given promising results.

1. Control Level Grouping: We limit the production of potential chunks to the same control level. Even programs with thousands of lines of code can be segmented into control level dependency graphs with a dozen nodes or less in each segment provided the code uses standard nested control structures and excludes or restricts "goto" statements.
2. Graph Reduction Techniques: We reduce the number of nodes in the dependency graph at each level. We combine nodes that initialize data into the nodes that use that data. We also evaluate disjoint subgraphs for potential chunks separately; these are likely to be independent concepts since they do not share any data elements.
3. Limit Maximum Number of Nodes in Potential Chunks: If the number of nodes in a disjoint subgraph is very large, its memory requirements will become impractical. If the Chunker detects this situation, it limits the maximum number of nodes in a potential chunk.
4. Eliminate Potential Chunks at the Earliest Opportunity: This could be done with a set of additional heuristics we call Exclusion Heuristics. For example, the Chunker could eliminate from consideration a potential chunk that produces no output, or one that produces more than five output variables.

Potential Chunks	Input Variables	Output Variables
{D}	sum,n	average
{I}	average'	deviation
{J}	deviation	result
{H,I}	sum',n	deviation
{A,B,C}	a,n	sum
{E,F,G}	a,n,average	sum'
{A,B,C,D}	a,n	average
{D,E,F,G}	a,n,sum	sum'
{A,B,C,D,E,F,G}	a,n	sum'

Figure 2. Examples of Potential Chunks from the Top Level Graph of Standard Deviation

8.0 Experimental results

The experimental runs of the Chunker were performed on a 33 megahertz 80486 processor with 8 megabytes of memory. We used six programs from various problem domains [4]. The largest piece of code was about 300 lines in length. We also gave the same code samples to a group of professional programmers to chunk so that we could compare results. For each sample program we applied the four heuristics in our knowledge base. We also experimented with the space control strategies to determine their impact on the system. Not surprisingly, the graph reduction strategies worked well for those programs that had a large number of nodes that could be collapsed. The number of collapsible nodes depends on the structure and characteristics of the code. For the largest program the number of potential chunks dropped dramatically from approximately 2700 to 400.

We wanted to see which of the heuristics was better at selecting candidate chunks that could be mapped to concepts that programmers would identify. These concepts are typical of those represented by plans in a plan library. The results from applying each heuristic to the standard deviation example are shown in Table II.

Candidate Chunk	Input Variables	Output Variables
{D}	sum,n	average
{H}	sum',n	average'
{I}	average'	deviation
{J}	deviation	result
{A,B,C}	a,n	sum
{E,F,G}	a,n,average	sum'

Figure 3. Candidate Chunks at Top Level of Standard Deviation

The table shows the candidate chunks found by each heuristic, the logical concepts they represent, and their

Candidate Chunks	Concept	Position in Candidate Chunk List for Heuristic I	II	III	IV
{A,B,C}	sum	4	4	8	-
{D}	average	2	5	6	-
{E,F,G}	sum	5	14	10	-
{H}	average	3	6	7	-
{I}	deviation	6	1	2	-
{J}	result	1	2	3	-

Table II. Heuristic Results for Standard Deviation

position in the list of candidate chunks output by the Chunker. We expected six logical concepts to be found, and the list of candidate chunks found using heuristics I, II, and III all identified these concepts. Heuristic I performed the best, with the six logical chunks being in the top six of the sorted list of candidate chunks. Heuristic II found all of them in the top fourteen, and heuristic III found them in the top ten. Heuristic IV did not find any of the expected logical chunks.

In general we found that heuristics II and III did the best in selecting candidate chunks. Heuristic I was too limited in that it only chose potential chunks to be candidate chunks if they had a single output. Heuristic IV did poorly in general. Since we used a limited number of samples it is difficult to make a generalization about how the heuristics will perform for all programs, and whether or not this set of heuristics is optimal. It may be that certain heuristics work well for certain types of problem domains, or perhaps combination of heuristics would work best.

Our experiments with the Chunker included a study to compare the candidate chunks produced by the Chunker to chunks identified by programmers in the same programs [4]. No two programmers produced identical chunks, however overall the chunks identified were similar from programmer to programmer and also similar to the top ranking candidate chunks output by the Chunker.

9.0 Finding the right plan

Once the candidate chunks are generated they must be matched against program plans. Plans are representations of stereotypical programming concepts [6, 8-11]. Matching is necessary to identify code and problem domain concepts in the target code. A plan or a set of plans must be retrieved from the Plan Library in order to carry out the matching process. When a match between a candidate chunk and a plan is "successful", we say that the concepts in the chunk have been identified. These concepts can be added to the ***actual code model*** posted on BUG-DOCTOR's blackboard. Identifying efficient ways to handle plan retrieval and matching is a difficult problem associated with the development of knowledge-based program comprehension and debugging systems. A plan library could conceivably consist of thousands of plan instances that could be matched against the target code in an exhaustive search that is exponential in time requirements [6,11]. "Smart" tools should be able to break this barrier making it more feasible to scale them up for analysis of large software systems. We propose to address this issue by applying a procedure that precedes the actual concept recognition process $M_{(plan)}$. The procedure has two steps: 1) search and retrieval, and 2) ranking and selection. Chunk/plan attributes are used in both steps. Search and retrieval results in a set of plans that are possible matches. Ranking and selection ranks the retrieved plans in order of similarity to the target code chunk. The most similar plan(s) is then used for the more detailed concept recognition processes with $M_{(plan)}$.

These steps are not as straight forward as they may initially appear due to: 1) the nature of the attributes that are to be considered in each of the steps, 2) the question of whether the attributes should be weighted with respect to each other, 3) the question as to whether plan similarity can be quantified in an absolute sense, and 4) the question of how to best express similarity - as a number, or as a linguistic term.

We address these issues by proposing a signature matching procedure for search and retrieval, and a fuzzy reasoning procedure to support ranking and selection. These are discussed in the following sections of this paper.

10.0 Search and retrieval

A good approach to applying the computationally intense $M_{(plan)}$ is to find a plan from the library that is most similar to the target code. As a first step towards achieving this goal we propose to do a rapid search of the Plan Library to retrieve a subset of plans whose signatures closely match the signature of the target candidate chunk. The search is efficient because it is based on a small number of surface features of the plans and chunks which are easily compared. We have developed the groundwork for this approach by introducing the concept of a chunk signature in our previous work [2,3].

A signature consists of a subset of attributes that represent the most recognizable qualities of a chunk. Signatures are easily extracted during the process of producing candidate chunks. Plan signatures can be stored as components of each plan header [2,3]. We argue that a proper signature should be a good predictor of similarity between a chunk and a program plan, and can therefore be useful in retrieving a pertinent subset of plans from a plan library.

The signature approach for plan retrieval is supported by work in code reuse where signatures have been used to retrieve components from a reuse library [13]. Support also comes from the work of Quilici who uses an index (a kind of signature) as a plan retrieval mechanism in his program recognition system [11]. We have extended his work by: 1) introducing the candidate chunk as the unit to initiate the signature-based search for a matching plan, 2) adding a domain vocabulary component to the signature to facilitate the search, and 3) proposing the fuzzy reasoner to rank the plans resulting from the initial signature match, $M_{(sig)}$.

The requirements for a chunk signature are: **1)** it must be simple enough to support a rapid search through the plan library, **2)** it must contain a subset of attributes that most readily identify the problem and programming task domain of the chunk, **3)** it must be applicable at different levels of abstraction, and **4)** for compound chunks, a top level signature must be expressible as a combination of the component signatures of all its included chunks. Empirical studies suggests attributes such as: domain vocabulary items, control structures, control flow patterns, and data flow patterns [5,7]. Figure 4 illustrates an example signature for the standard deviation code shown in figure 1.

11.0 Ranking and selection

Use of $M_{(sig)}$ by the Plan Processor will most likely result in several candidate plans being retrieved whose signature indicates their surface characteristics resemble those of a target code candidate chunk. We call this set of plans the retrieved data set (RDS). The reason the RDS is likely to contain several members is that an exact match on $M_{(sig)}$ cannot be assumed. The target code chunk may contain an error, the target code or the retrieved plan may be a subcomponent of another unit, or there may be some idiosyncrasies in programming style in the target code that BUG-DOCTOR has not be able to normalize [3]. We propose to apply a fuzzy reasoner to the RDS to rank the plans in order to identify the plan most similar to the target code. That plan is selected for the computationally expensive $M_{(plan)}$. Lower ranked plans may be selected in rank order if $M_{(plan)}$ is not initially successful.

1. Deepest level of nesting regardless of control structure type = {0}. (All iterators and selectors in this code example occur at the outermost level)
2. Type of control structure present = {iterator}
3. Number of instances of control structures = {iterator, 2}
4. Complete control structure description = {iterator, level 0}, {iterator, level 0}
5. Domain vocabulary = {sum, deviation, average, sqrDev, sqrt, real}

Figure 4. Signature for Standard Deviation

We are building a fuzzy reasoner as a component of the Plan Processor to rank the program plans in the RDS with respect to similarity with target code chunks. The fuzzy reasoner will quantify a "similarity" factor that indicates the "degree of sameness" of the target code chunk and each of the retrieved plans. Its role is shown in Figure 5. A fuzzy reasoner seems ideal for this application, particularly since the human approach to determining similarity is a fuzzy process. Zadeh, the founder of the fuzzy reasoning approach, argues that to a large extent human communication, understanding and reasoning occurs within a fuzzy domain, and that fuzzy sets can be used to model human reasoning processes [14]. We believe that a Bayesain system is not a suitable solution to the similarity problem we face since we are not able to assign a fixed value to each attribute that indicates the degree to which it contributes to similarity.

Similarity will be measured using a set of code attributes we have begun to assemble called the "similarity set". These attributes have been identified by researchers such as Jankowitz as significant indicators of similarity in the software domain [14]. The similarity attributes we are currently considering include: total number of unique operands, number of assignment statements, and type and number of instances of control structures.

We postulate that several iterations of search and retrieval may be required to ensure that BUG-DOCTOR has obtained those plans in the RDS with the best promise of similarity for the fuzzy reasoner. The iteration approaches for $M_{(sig)}$ could be described as follows: 1) start with a loose set of search criteria in the signature and in each subsequent iteration use a tighter set of selection criteria to narrow the field of choices, or, 2) start with a tight set of search criteria and use a less tight set of search criteria for subsequent iterations (widening the field of choices). We are leaning towards the second approach since we believe that it will allow us to retrieve the least number of plans, and expand the search criteria only when necessary. Experiments with the Plan Processor will show which approach works best. We are planning to generate a large number of simulated program plans. The plans will only contain a header with a signature component. We will use a random process to create variations in the signature attributes. It will be important to have plans that are very similar as well as those that are dissimilar to the candidate chunks. The effectiveness of our approach will be evaluated using the following criteria: 1) the timing requirements for the search and retrieval, ranking and selection processes, 2) the usefulness of the selected attributes in predicting similarity, and 3) the accuracy of the plan ranking by the fuzzy reasoner.

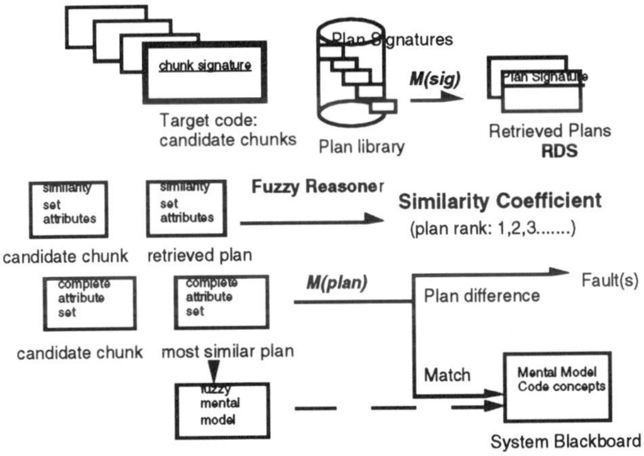

Figure 5. The Role of the Fuzzy Reasoner in the BUG-DOCTOR system

12.0 Summary and future research plans

We believe that the design of tools to assist software engineers should be supported by using artificial intelligence techniques. We have followed this philosophy in the development of the BUG-DOCTOR system. In this paper we report on two of BUG-DOCTOR's knowledge sources, the Chunker and the Plan Processor. Experiments with the Chunker show that it can partition code into candidate chunks that represent simple programming concepts. The Plan Processor design proposes signature matching and a fuzzy reasoner to retrieve, rank and select the plans to match against the candidate chunks. We believe that our approach will eliminate the need for exhaustive searches of a plan library to find a match for the target code, and could lead to more efficient program comprehension and debugging tools that scale up for the analysis of large software systems.

13.0 References

[1] I. Burnstein, N. Jani, S. Mannina, J. Tamsevicious, "The Development of a Knowledge-Based Software Fault Localization Tool", Proc. IEEE Internatl. Conf. of Systems, Man and Cybernetics, Chicago, IL, Oct., 1992, pp. 317-322 .

[2] I. Burnstein, F. Saner, K. Roberson, "Generating Chunks and Chunk Signatures for Program Recognition and Fault Localization", Proc. of the Midwest Artificial Intelligence and Cognitive Society Conf., Bloomington, IN, April, 1996. pp. 123-127.

[3] I. Burnstein, A. Mirza, K. Roberson, F. Saner, A. Tubaishat, "Knowledge Engineering for Automated Program Recognition and Fault Localization", Proc. of the Eighth Internatl. Conf. on Software Engineering and Knowledge Engineering, Lake Tahoe NV, June, 1996, pp. 85-91.

[4] I. Burnstein, K. Roberson, "Automated Chunking to Support Program Comprehension", Proc. Fifth Internatl. Workshop on Program Comprehension", Dearborn, Michigan, May, 1997, pp. 40-49.

[5] N. Pennington, B. Grabowski, "The Tasks of Programming", Psychology of Programming, J. Hoc, T. Greene, R. Samurcay, D. Gilmore, eds., London, Academic Press, 1990, pp. 45-62.

[6] C. Rich, R. Waters, The Programmer's Apprentice, Addison-Wesley, Reading, MA, 1990.

[7] E. Soloway, K. Ehrlich, "Empirical Studies of Programming Knowledge", IEEE Transactions on Software Engineering, SE-10, 1984, pp. 595-609.

[8] W. Johnson, E. Soloway, "PROUST: Knowledge-Based Program Understanding", IEEE Transactions on Software Engineering, Vol. SE-11, No. 3, 1985, pp. 267-275.

[9] J. Hartman, "Understanding Natural Programs Using Proper Decomposition" , Proc. IEEE Internatl. Conf. on Software Engineering, Austin, TX, May 1991, pp. 62-73.

[10] W. Kozaczynski, J. Ning, "Automated Program Recognition by Concept Recognition", Automated Software Engineering, Vol. 1, 1994, pp. 61-78.

[11] A. Quilici, "A Memory-Based Approach to Recognizing Program Plans", Comm. ACM, Vol. 37, No. 5, 1994, pp. 84-93.

[12] E. Ostertag, J. Hendler, R. Diaz, C. Braun, "Computing Similarity in a Reuse Library System: An AI-Based Approach", ACM Transactions on Software Eng. and Methodology, Vol. 1, No. 3, 1992, pp. 205-228.

[13] L. Zadeh, "Fuzzy Logic", IEEE Computer, Vol. 21, pp. 83-93, April, 1988.

[14] Jankowitz, "Detecting Plagiarism in Student Pascal Programs", The Computer Journal, Vol. 31, No. 1, 1988, pp 1-8.

Session B.2

Genetic Algorithms and Applications I

Session Chair:
Sachio Watanabe, NEC, Japan

Using a Genetic Algorithm for Multi-Hypothesis Tracking

David B. Hillis, Army Research Laboratory

Abstract

A technique has been devised that uses a genetic algorithm (GA) to address the multi-scan assignment problem in multi-target tracking. The problem is recast in the form of a scheduling problem, where the GA searches the space of possible orderings of detections, and a greedy heuristic is used to make the associations for a particular ordering. The resulting tracker can operate in either batch or continuous mode. In the continuous mode, a single population of hypotheses evolves on a fitness landscape that changes with each new scan of data.

1: Introduction

In a typical multi-target tracking application, a tracker receives a stream of reports over time from one or more sensors (such as a radar), each of which may indicate either the detection of an actual object of interest (or closely spaced group of such objects) or a false alarm. The objects of interest may include, for example, aircraft, missiles, ships, or land vehicles. The tracker may also be used to track particular points on an object (such as an organ in medical imaging applications).

The problem of assigning reports is to determine which reports correspond to which objects. A tracker may deal with many reports collected across some time period (which may be long enough that each real object may have generated two or more reports from observations at different times). Under these circumstances, the number of different ways of combining reports into tracks (or tracks and false alarms) can grow exponentially. Each possible combination is called a hypothesis.

The problem of assigning reports involves searching for an optimal or near-optimal hypothesis according to a metric specific to the tracker in question. In the general case, it is impractical to find the optimal hypothesis for more than a small number of objects observed over time, because of the high computational expense required. Therefore, suboptimal search techniques are usually employed.

Without loss of generality, we may describe the problem of assigning reports as if the sensor reports arrived in groups where each report in the group was collected over the same time period (called a "scan"). The problem of searching for an optimal or near-optimal hypothesis across multiple scans is different in character from searching for the best hypothesis for the associations between reports from one scan and a set of tracks. In general, finding the local optimal assignment of objects (targets) to tracks for each scan does not guarantee that the global assignment across many scans is optimal.

Multi-scan, multiple-target algorithms commonly used include multi-hypothesis trackers (MHTs) [1–3], joint probabilistic data association (JPDA) [3], artificial neural networks [4], integer programming [5], Lagrangian relaxation algorithms [6], and simulated annealing [7,8]. Angus et al [9] and Carrier et al [10] have described methods for using genetic algorithms (GAs) for data association within a single scan.

I describe how a GA using an order-based representation can be applied to the multi-scan data association problem. (I have developed a similar tracker that uses a GA with an edge-based representation and have tested it, in simulation, against other algorithms; the results are described elsewhere [11].) In this paper, the emphasis is on describing a range of configurations for a GA-based tracker, rather than characterizing the performance of any particular one.

2: Single-Hypothesis Tracker

Figure 1 shows a simple scenario in which three detections are reported in scan 0 and two detections in scan 1. At scan 0, there is only one possible hypothesis: each of the three detections represents the start of a new track. At scan 1, there are 13 possible hypotheses under the model described above (including the hypothesis where no detections are associated). All are continuations of the single hypothesis from scan one. Six hypotheses contain three tracks (both new detections are associated with one of the three original tracks), six contain four tracks (one detection is associated with an existing track and one is the start of a new track), and one (with no detections associated) has five tracks. Figure 1 shows three of the 13 hypotheses.

The single-hypothesis tracker must calculate the cost of some or all of the possible hypotheses, at scan 1, and choose one. For purposes of discussion, assume that all 13 hypotheses are tested, and that the hypothesis in figure 1a has the lowest cost and is selected. Figure 2 shows the same scenario with two more detections reported at scan 2. The hypothesis shown in figure 2 cannot be reached, even though it may have the lowest cost, because the tracker is constrained to look only at hypotheses containing the associations of figure 1a.

3: Multiple Hypothesis Tracker

An MHT operates roughly as follows [1–3]. For the first scan, in figure 1, there is only one possible hypothesis, and none of the detections can be associated with any other; thus the hypothesis contains three tracks with one detection each. With the next scan of data, there are 13 possible hypotheses. The tracker calculates and saves all of them, declares the lowest cost hypothesis as the (tentative) winner, and continues. With the third scan of data, the MHT calculates and saves all the hypotheses that can be formed as extensions of each of the 13 previously saved hypotheses.

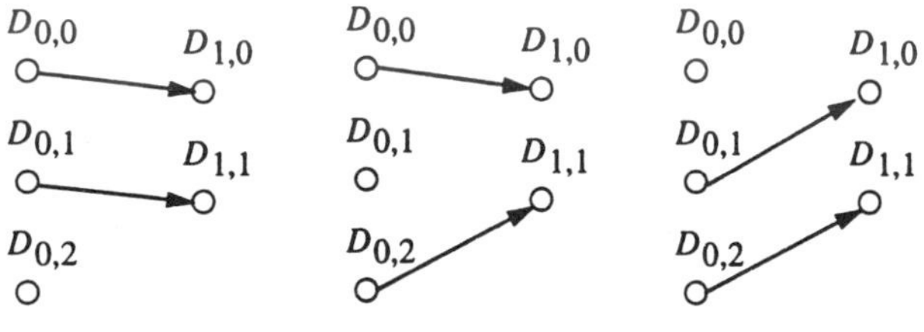

(a) (b) (c)

Figure 1. Some of possible hypotheses for a simple scenario with five detections in 2 scans. $D_{i,j}$ indicates jth detection in scan i, circles represent detections, and arrows indicate associations between them.

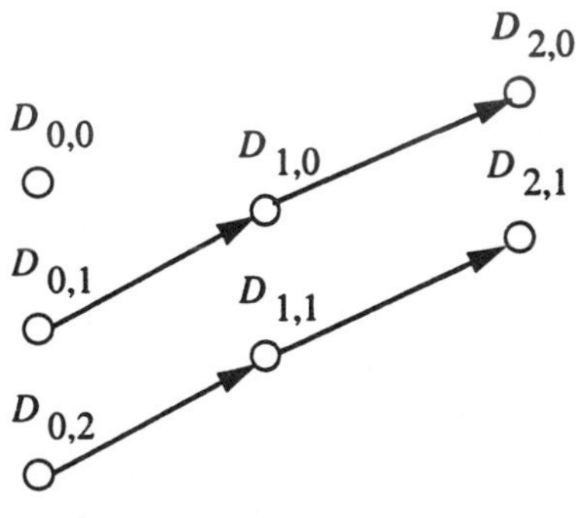

Figure 2. A single hypothesis (extension of hypothesis in figure 1c) for same scenario with one more scan.

If left unchecked, as more scans are added, the number of tracks and hypotheses will very quickly expand beyond the resources of processing time or memory available. Some method of "pruning out" the most expendable hypotheses must be regularly applied. One method is to periodically eliminate the highest cost hypotheses until only a predetermined number of hypotheses remain. If a track does not belong to any remaining hypothesis, it is eliminated as well.

For example, assume that the maximum number of hypotheses allowed is three, with no limit on tracks. The tracker builds and evaluates all 13 hypotheses. The three hypotheses shown in figure 1 have the lowest costs and are retained, while the other hypotheses are pruned away. The tracker declares the hypothesis in figure 1a to be the best at that time.

With the new detections from scan 2, the tracker calculates all the possible hypotheses that are continuations of the three remaining hypotheses (shown in figure 1). The hypothesis shown in figure 2 is among those tested and is selected as the best. It and two other hypotheses are retained, while the others are pruned away. For the hypothesis of figure 2 to be true at scan 2, the hypothesis of figure 1c must have been true at scan 1. Thus the tracker has "changed its mind" about the best hypothesis at scan 1.

If, however, the hypothesis in figure 1c were not one of the three best at scan 1, it would have been pruned away, and the hypothesis of figure 2 would never be examined at scan 2.

4: Genetic Algorithm

A genetic algorithm is an artificial intelligence technique based loosely on the process of natural selection in evolutionary biology [12–14]. It has wide applications in optimization, intelligent search, and machine learning.

To apply a GA, one generally expresses the problem in such a way that potential solutions can be encoded as character strings over some alphabet. (Most commonly, these are binary strings, but other representations can be applied.) Then, a population of potential solutions (called "individuals") is formed. Each individual is decoded, tested against some metric, and scored. A new population is then formed by mutation (small random changes) and recombination (formation of a new individual out of material from a pair of parent individuals). Individuals with relatively high scores or fitnesses are more likely to be selected, as parents, than others. The new population is then decoded and scored, and the process repeated until some end condition is reached.

4.1: Implementation

The GA developed for this tracker uses order-based strings, described below. Similar implementations are found in the literature, sometimes applied to scheduling, traveling salesman, or graph partitioning problems [13–17]. It uses the "elite" model and has nonoverlapping generations: at each generation the new population completely replaces the old, except for the best individual, which lives on.

Each individual is a string of integers in the form of a permutation of length N. Mutation consists of taking a random point in the string and moving it to a random location. In crossover, parts of two parents are combined to form two children. To be valid individuals, the children must also be permutations. A random crosspoint on the string is chosen, and all points before it are copied over from the first parent into the first child. All points in the second parent whose values do not already exist in the child are copied into the remaining half of the child, in the order in which they are found in the second parent. For the second child, the roles of the two parents are reversed.

For example, given parent1 = [1 2 3 4 5 6], parent2 = [3 4 1 2 6 5], and a crosspoint between the third and fourth points, we can determine the structure of the children:

The first part of child1 = [1 2 3]. The remaining numbers (4, 5, and 6) are in the order 4, ... 6, 5 in the second parent. So child1 = [1 2 3 4 6 5]. The first part of the child2 = [3 4 1]. The remaining numbers (2, 5, and 6) are in the order 2, ... 5, 6 in the second parent. So child2 = [3 4 1 2 5 6].

5: Genetic Algorithm Tracker

The tracker is of the batch-processing class [1,3]: it uses an optimizing algorithm, a GA, to search for the best hypothesis over a window of time, S scans deep. By applying the search across multiple windows, it produces a hypothesis for all the detections.

5.1: Search Across One Window

A single fixed hypothesis holds the track estimates up to the start of the current window. This hypothesis, the "starting hypothesis," cannot be changed during the search. The GA searches the space of extensions of this fixed hypothesis across the window. To search across this window, the tracker forms hypotheses by taking each detection in order and assigning it to the track (possibly a new track) that produces the best association (lowest cost) available for that detection. The GA searches for the best order in which to process the detections.

The process starts by creating a population of M randomly generated individuals. An individual is encoded as a permutation of the N sensor detections reported in the window. Each individual is then decoded and scored by being run through the decoding module, which uses a greedy heuristic to produce a hypothesis.

Every hypothesis inherits the associations in the starting hypothesis, so every hypothesis (implicitly) includes an association for every detection from the beginning of time. The cost of the starting hypothesis is also inherited.

The decoding module could serve as a crude single-hypothesis tracker itself. As each point is received (in the order described by the individual), the module calculates the cost of associating that detection with each of the active tracks that it has already formed for that individual (including those inherited from the starting hypothesis), as well as the cost of assigning the detection as a new track. (Track associations that would require a target to move backwards in time, occupy two places at once, or violate other constraints are given prohibitively high costs.) The lowest cost option is taken; the track's state is updated by a track filter such as those described by Blackman [2] (in this case, an alpha/beta filter is used for simplicity); and the next detection is considered until all points have been assigned. The fitness of the individual is inversely related to the cost of the resulting hypothesis: in this case, the sum of the costs of the associations made for each detection.

It is worth noting that there is no restriction on how the cost of a hypothesis is calculated, other than that it must be a nonnegative function of all the associations encountered, including those before the present window. It might be desirable in this example, for instance, to add a cost term for tracks not updated in a scan to account for the probability of detection.

With this model, the hypothesis in figure 1a could be encoded by the string $[D_{0,0}\ D_{1,0}\ D_{0,1}\ D_{1,1}\ D_{0,2}]$. The hypothesis in figure 2 could be encoded by the string $[D_{0,1}\ D_{1,0}\ D_{2,0}\ D_{0,2}\ D_{1,1}\ D_{2,1}\ D_{0,0}]$.

The mapping of strings to hypotheses is not one to one. Strings with detections in different orders may or may not decode into different hypotheses, depending on whether the detections could be associated with the same tracks.

At the end of the time available, the best solution found so far is used to construct a new "best" hypothesis for all the detections up to the end of the window. If the GA has a population size of M and runs for T generations, the number of hypotheses tested will be the product of M and T. Because a GA naturally produces exact copies of some individuals, and because different permutations of detections may decode into identical hypotheses, the number of unique hypotheses tested will be lower.

The above treatment has a weakness that is illustrated by the simple example of a single target detected on each of S scans in the window. The association problem should be solved trivially by association of all the N detections (in this case, $N = S$) into a single track. But there is only one of $N!$ permutations that can be decoded to produce this result. Using randomly formed permutations as the starting population for the GA is extremely inefficient, especially for large S.

The "random" permutations discussed in this paper are actually biased so that the detections are more likely to be listed in time order, from earliest to latest. One method of forming such a biased initial population is to form each individual as a random permutation of the detections in the first scan, followed by a random permutation of the detections in the second scan, and so on. These individuals are then subjected to several iterations of the mutation operator, described above, to provide some mixing between scans.

5.2: Continuous Tracking

The above section describes how a GA can search for a low-cost hypothesis across a single window S scans deep. Many typical tracker applications require the calculation of a best hypothesis after each scan of data for an indefinite number of scans. A tracker program could be created to produce periodic updates to the best hypothesis by invoking the search across one window every S scans and using the best hypothesis of the previous window as the starting hypothesis of the new window. Since these windows would not overlap, such a tracker would produce an undesirable bottleneck every S scans, by reducing the number of hypotheses carried forward to one. An additional drawback is that this tracker would not produce a hypothesis after receiving each scan of data.

5.2.1: Siding Window. An alternative approach would be to use a sliding window. A starting hypothesis holds the hypothesis (track estimates) up to the start of the window. The GA searches the space of extensions of this fixed hypothesis across the window (but does not modify the starting hypothesis). At the end of the time available, the best solution found so far is used to construct a new fixed hypothesis, one scan further in time from the beginning. The window slides forward to include the next scan of data. The new window overlaps the old, offset by one scan. The GA is called again to find the best hypothesis (with the new fixed hypothesis as its starting hypothesis) for the new window, and the process continues.

The siding window approach can be illustrated by the following example, in which a window size of five scans is used. When the tracker is first turned on, there are no prior points to consider, there are no points in the window, and there is nothing for the tracker to do. At some scan in the future, scan 0, some points are reported. A population is formed from random permutations. Each individual is decoded into a hypothesis and scored. In our simple model, since all the points have time tags from the same scan, none of the points is allowed to associate with any point other than itself, in which case the population represents many identical hypotheses in which all points are the start of new tracks. The GA is called to operate on the population until some stopping criterion is reached. (Typical stopping criteria might include the completion of a fixed number of generations, the difference in fitness between the fittest individual and the average for the population falling below a threshold, or an interrupt signalling the arrival of a new scan of data.) The hypothesis of the fittest individual is reported as the hypothesis for that scan (although later hypotheses could, in principle, amend it, based on additional data). If the next scan contains more reports, then a new population is formed from random permutations of all the points in the window. This new population is operated on by the GA once more.

After five scans, the window is full and must slide forward to include the next scan. The individual with the highest score (the best hypothesis at scan 4) is used to calculate the fixed hypothesis for scan 0. The fixed hypothesis for scan 0 is constructed from the assignments in the best hypothesis for points with times before the end of scan 1. This hypothesis will be the "starting hypothesis" for scan 0.

This individual has the highest score for scan 4 but may or may not have the hypothesis with the highest score at scan 0. The starting hypothesis for scan 0 may be different from the original hypothesis reported by the tracker and may in fact have a worse score at scan 0. The possibility that selecting a hypothesis with a relatively poor score at an early scan may lead to a hypothesis with a better score at a later scan is the reason for performing multi-scan optimization.

The new points from scan 5 are then added to the window containing the reports from scans 1 to 4, and the GA is invoked once more. While the associations for points before the start of the window may not be changed, points within the window may have associations with points outside.

The tracker continues in this manner indefinitely. The strings of the individuals will be longer or shorter from one window to the next, depending on how many points were generated over the scans in the window. At the start of each new scan, the tracker produces an output hypothesis for all the detections before that scan, which may or may not amend some of the associations in hypotheses output at previous scans.

This approach has the advantage that the bottleneck of a single unchangeable hypothesis is made $S-1$ scans in the past and is therefore more likely to be correct. It has the disadvantage that it requires S times as much computation as the nonoverlapping technique. A more serious disadvantage is that, when the new fixed hypothesis is used to start a new window, it might be impossible to recreate the winning hypothesis that gave rise to it in the first place. There might be no permutation of the remaining detections (plus those from the next scan) that can result in the original associations.

5.2.2: Overlapping Windows. An alternative approach is similar to the sliding window, except that the starting hypothesis for a window is chosen to be the hypothesis with the lowest cost, for that time, found by the program. While this choice might appear, at first, to result in the equivalent of a single-hypothesis tracker, it does not, because the lowest cost hypothesis for scan K is not constrained to have the same associations for the same points as the lowest cost hypothesis for scan $K-1$.

As the program is forming and evaluating each hypothesis for all the points in the window, it is simultaneously calculating the cost for S subhypotheses: the subset of the hypothesis' associations up to the end of each scan within the window. These costs include the cost inherited from the window's starting hypothesis. If one of the subhypotheses evaluated results in the lowest cost encountered for that scan for any of the scans within the window, then that subhypothesis (including all the associations inherited from its starting hypothesis) is saved as the tentative starting hypothesis.

5.3: GA Multi-Hypothesis Tracker

Only a few changes are needed to transform the batch mode tracker described above into a continuous mode tracker analogous to an MHT. When a new scan of data arrives, instead of the GA being restarted, the strings of the individuals in the existing population are extended by a random permutation of the new detections being appended to the end of them; the process of decoding and scoring of hypotheses and forming successive generations by crossover and mutation continues uninterrupted.

The process can be visualized as one in which the window size is infinite, and the lengths of the individual's strings grow forever, but the crossover and mutation operators are forced to pick points within N points of the end. Since manipulating and decoding these ever-growing strings would quickly prove impractical, some shortcuts are employed. Each new individual formed by the GA will inherit all but the last N detections of its string, intact, from one of its parents. This string of ordered detections can be decoded into a hypothesis (set of tracks) just once, and they can be included by reference thereafter.

The GA still operates across a sliding window, but the window is based on number of detections, not time, and each individual includes its own starting hypothesis. The crossover operator is still constrained to pick a crossover point within a sliding window equal to the number of detections in the last S scans, and the mutation operator is still constrained to pick a detection within the window and move it to a location that is also within the window. However, the hypotheses are not constrained to have the same associations for detections before the start of the window.

When a new scan of data containing D detections arrives, the starting hypothesis and the first D detections for each individual are decoded to produce a new starting hypothesis (including a state for all tracks) for that individual. The number of starting hypotheses is equal to the number of individuals in the population. The D detections are removed from the front of the individuals' strings, shortening them. (The ordering of the detections is not lost, because it is included in the new starting hypothesis.) The string for each individual is then extended by the addition of a random permutation of the new detections onto the end. The mutation operator will mix these detections with those from other scans during subsequent generations.

Each individual is encoded as an ordered list of detections plus a number (pointer) indicating which starting hypothesis it owns. When a new individual is formed, it inherits a pointer to the starting hypothesis of one of its parents. This tracker is similar to a traditional MHT, in that the starting hypotheses form a pool of hypotheses that can theoretically contain different associations for detections that are arbitrarily far back in time.

GA applications typically require some care to prevent premature convergence. The GA tracker is somewhat unusual in that it should never converge. Each new scan of detections changes not only the fitness landscape on which the GA must operate, but the lengths of the strings as well.

6: Complexity

The quality of the solutions found by a GA-based tracker can be improved if we increase the number of scans in the window, the size of the population, and the number of generations. Analogous gains may be obtained from most multi-scan algorithms, also at the cost of increased processing time.

Table 1 shows the results of increasing the window size, for a simulated data set (also used in Winkler et al [11]), for a GA tracker with overlapping windows. There are 16 maneuvering targets observed over 30 scans. For each window, the population size is, dynamically, set to be equal to N, where N is the number of detections occurring within the window. The number of generations, per window, is also set to be N, so that N^2 hypotheses are examined for each window. Since the decoding module has a processing cost that is proportional to N^2, the complexity of this particular implementation should be on the order of N^4. The memory requirements grow only as the square of N.

Table 1. Performance of a GA tracker using overlapping windows for different window sizes (in scans). Results from 10 independent trials for each window size.

Window size	Avg. cost
1	26087
2	24972
3	24389
4	23493

The cost obtained by use of the Munkres algorithm (a single-hypothesis algorithm described in Blackman [2]) was 25530. The GA has a relatively poor performance with a window size of one scan, but improves with larger windows.

7: Discussion

The GA based approach has a number of attractive features:

1. GAs (and hybrids between GAs and other algorithms such as local search techniques and simulated annealing) have been used successfully in a number of similar problem domains [15–23].

2. GAs can be very efficiently implemented on parallel processors via an island model with a subpopulation on each processor [13], or a parallel GA [15] where each individual interacts asynchronously with only a few neighbors. Such parallel implementations can be highly scalable, so that the number of processors can be changed without the need for significant modification to the code.

3. The performance vs. computation trade-off can be adjusted smoothly by changes in the depth of the window, the size of the population, and the number of generations. These changes can be made adaptively during run time.

4. After the first generation, the search process may be interrupted at any time and the best hypothesis found so far will be available. This leads to graceful degradation.

8: References

1. D. B. Reid, "An Algorithm for Tracking Multiple Targets," IEEE Trans. Autom. Control **AC-24** (December 1979), 843–854.
2. S. Blackman, "Multiple Target Tracking with Radar Applications" (Artech House, Dedham, MA, 1986).
3. Y. Bar-Shalom, ed., "Multitarget-Multisensor Tracking: Applications and Advances," Vol. II (Artech House, MA, 1992).
4. S. Shams, "Neural Network Optimization for Multi-Target Multi-Sensor Passive Tracking," Proc. IEE **84**, No. 10 (October 1996), 1442–1457.
5. C. Morefield, "Application of 0-1 Integer Programming to Multitarget Tracking Problems," IEEE Trans. Autom. Control **AC-22** No. 3 (June 1977), 302–312.
6. K. Pattipati, S. Deb, Y. Bar-Shalom, and R. Washb[illegible] New Relaxation Algorithm and Passive Sensor Data As[illegible]ciation," IEEE Trans. Autom. Control **AC-37** (1992), 198–213.
7. P. Ting and R. Iltis, "Multi-target Motion Analysis in a DSN," IEEE Trans. Syst. Man Cybern. **21** (1991), 1125–1139.
8. R. Iltis and K. Anderson, "A Consistent Estimation Criterion for Multi-Sensor Bearings-Only Tracking," IEEE Trans. Aerosp. Electron. Syst. **32** (January 1996), 108–120.
9. J. Angus, H. Zhou, C. Bea, L. Becket-Lemus, J. Klose, and S. Tubbs, "Genetic Algorithms in Passive Tracking," Claremont Grad. School, Math Clinic Rep. (May 1993).
10. J. Carrier, J. Litva, H. Leung, and T. To, "Genetic Algorithm for Multiple Target Tracking Data Association," Proc. SPIE **2739**, Acquisition, Tracking and Pointing, 180–190 (April 1996).
11. R. Winkler, P. David, and D. Hillis, "An Empirical Comparison of the Accuracy of Data Association Algorithms for Multi-Target Tracking," 19th Army Science Conference (June 1994).
12. J. Holland, "Adaptation in Natural and Artificial Systems" (University of Michigan Press, 1975).
13. D. Goldberg, "Genetic Algorithms in Search, Optimization, and Machine Learning" (Addison-Wesley, Reading, MA, 1989).
14. Z. Michalkawicz, "Genetic Algorithms + Data Structures = Evolution Programs" (Springer-Verlag, Berlin, 1992).
15. N. Ulder, E. Aarts, H. Bandelt, P. van Laarhoven, and E. Pesch, "Genetic Local Search Algorithms for the Traveling Salesman," Parallel Problem Solving from Nature, 1st Workshop (Springer-Verlag, Oct. 1990), 109–116.
16. H. C. Braun, "On Solving Travelling Salesman Problems by Genetic Algorithms," Parallel Problem Solving from Nature, 1st Workshop (Springer-Verlag, Oct. 1990), 129–133.
17. G. von Lawszewski and H. Muhlenbein, "Partitioning a Graph with a Parallel Genetic Algorithm," Parallel Problem Solving from Nature, 1st Workshop (Springer-Verlag, Oct. 1990), 165–169.
18. G. Lawton, "Genetic Algorithms for Schedule Optimization," AI Expert, (May 1992), 23–27.
19. S. Ucken, S. Bagchi, and K. Kawamura, "Managing Genetic Search in Job Shop Scheduling," IEEE Expert **8**, Issue 5, (October 1993), 15–24.
20. K. Maekawa, N. Mori, H. Tamaki, H. Kita, and Y. Nishikawa, "A Genetic Solution for the Traveling Salesman Problem by Means of a Thermodynamical Selection Rule," Proc. IEEE International Conference on Evolutionary Computation (1996), 529–53.
21. K. Wong and Y. Wong, "Combined Genetic Algorithm/Simulated Annealing/Fuzzy Set Approach to Short-Term Gener. Scheduling with Take-Or-Pay Fuel Contract," IEEE Trans. Power Syst. **11** (1996), 128–136.
22. T. Murata, H. Tshibuchi, "Performance Evaluation of Genetic Algorithms for Flowshop Scheduling Problems," Proc. First IEEE Conference on Evolutionary Computation. IEEE World Congress on Computational Intelligence (1994), 812–817.
23. C. Holsapple, V. Jacob, R. Pakath, and J. Zaveri, "A Genetics-Based Hybrid Scheduler for Generating Static Schedules in Flexible Manufacturing Contexts," IEEE Trans. Syst. Man Cybern. **23** (1993), 953–972.

sed Performance Analysis of Network Protocols

M. Baldi, F. Corno, M. Rebaudengo, G. Squillero

Politecnico di Torino
Dipartimento di Automatica e Informatica
Torino, Italy

Abstract

This paper tackles the problem of analyzing the correctness and performance of a computer network protocol. Given the complexity of the problem, no currently used technique is able to achieve good results: formal techniques can discover some bugs but can be applied to over-simplified models, only; on the other hand, statistical techniques relying on simulation often fail to find some critical cases for the protocol. Our proposed approach relies on coupling a Genetic Algorithm with a simulator of the system under verification. Genetic Algorithms recently proved themselves excellent tools for giving good, yet approximate, solution to hard-to-solve problems. To prove the effectiveness of our approach, we applied it to the quantitative verification of a network protocol: the complexity of this problem prevents the application of exact techniques, while experimental results show that the verification results we obtained are better than one can achieve with traditional statistical methods. As an example, the approach is applied to the verification of the TCP protocol operating on a given network. A Genetic Algorithm is able to find a configuration of the traffic over the network that sensitizes a critical problem in the TCP protocol.

1. Introduction[1]

Computer networks are gaining an increasing importance as they penetrate business and everyday-life. Technological evolution results in increased computational power and transmission capacity. These two phenomena open the way to the development and exploitation of new applications (e.g., video-conferencing) which require demanding services from the network. As a result computer networks are in continuous evolution and the protocols regulating their operation must be assessed for their (1) suitability to new technologies and (2) ability to support the new applications. This assessment is particularly important since new technologies and applications often differ from the ones the protocol has been designed for.

The effectiveness of a network solution depends on both the specification of the protocols and their software and hardware implementations. Given leading hardware and software technologies, the protocol specification thus plays a crucial role in the overall network performance. Some aspects are of utmost importance: the *correctness* of the protocol, i.e., the warranty of showing the intended behavior in any specific situation, its *performance*, i.e., the utilization of the available bandwidth it is able to achieve over the physical medium, and its *robustness*, i.e., the property of being able to work correctly under abnormal conditions.

The analysis of these different aspects of communication protocols is usually done according to the following techniques:

- *formal modeling*, to verify some properties of the protocol. This requires to model the protocol behavior according to some formal description language, such as LOTOS [ISO88], and to run some formal verification tool. Description languages are nowadays powerful enough to capture most of the protocol semantics, however, verification tools are often very limited in the size and complexity of the descriptions they can deal with. Some important aspects of a network protocol that are difficult to verify are those related with different timeout counters, message queues, and transmission strategies based on message contents.
- *simulation*, to check the protocol in its entire complex behavior and explore the dependencies among the various hardware and software components of a computer network. A typical simulator allows the actions taken by a protocol to be monitored while operating over a computer network with a specified topology and traffic load. The simulator models a number of sources that can be programmed to generate traffic according to statistical models defined after real sources. One or more sources

[1] This work is partially funded by EU-funded FOST and CHARME projects.

1082-3409/97 $10.00 © 1997 IEEE

behave according to the protocol under study; the others are considered *background traffic* generators. Poisson statistical processes [Hui90] are often adopted as a model of background traffic.

We feel that neither approach is sufficient to give a reliable information about the protocol performance. While the formal approach delivers a mathematically proven answer, it is forced to work on an over-simplified view of the protocol. Simulation techniques, on the other hand, rely on a clever choice of the traffic pattern to yield useful results, and worst-case analysis is often performed by hand-designing the traffic.

We propose the adoption of *simulation-based* techniques that rely on a *Genetic Algorithm* (GA) [Holl75] to explore the solution space and look for an inconsistency in the verification goal. As a case study problem, we chose the correctness and performance verification of the Transmission Control Protocol (TCP) [Post81], a widely used computer network protocol.

In this work, we show how to integrate a GA with a network simulator to drive the generation of background traffic. The GA therefore aims at generating the worst-case traffic for the protocol under analysis, given some constraints on the traffic bandwidth. Errors and weaknesses in the network protocol can therefore be discovered via simulation of this worst-case traffic. We expect the GA to drive the network to conditions where the protocol performance (e.g., the effective transfer rate) is low, and we can study the behavior of the protocol under extreme load conditions.

In a previous work [AlTr96] GAs were applied to the analysis of communication protocols by checking the correctness of their finite state machine (FSM). Communicating protocol entities are expressed as a pair of communicating FSMs, a GA generates communication traces between the two protocol entities, and a FSM simulator executes them. The GA aims at detecting deadlocks and useless states.

By contrast, our approach, being based on a network simulator, is able to model most of the aspects of the protocol stack and the network on which it is employed: not just the state machine, but also counters, message queues, routing tables, different re-transmission speeds, and so on. While the GA generates the worst operating conditions of the protocol (by defining the load in the network) and finds the traffic configuration that minimizes its performance, the protocol is stressed enough that we can say that both its functionality and its performance are verified. Some preliminary experimental results we gathered show that traffic generated by the GA is able to expose protocol shortcomings that were impossible to reveal with formal techniques, and that were not found by means of statistical simulation.

Section 2 describes the adopted verification approach and outlines the tool architecture. Details about the GA are given in section 3, and section 4 reports some experimental results on the verification of the TCP protocol over a packet switched network. Some conclusions are drawn in section 3.

2. The Approach

In this work we choose to examine the TCP protocol, whose characteristics and behavior are already well known to the computer network research community, in order to better focus on the verification methodology and exploitation of the GA, and not on the protocol itself. Hence, we do not expect to discover any new information about TCP behavior and performance, but to find in an automated way well known data that, with traditional approaches, requires skills and in-depth knowledge of the protocol.

We aim at studying the TCP protocol in real operating conditions. We set up an IP (Internet Protocol) network [Stev94] and a number of TCP sender-receiver pairs into it. The GA is not allowed to control such connections directly, but it monitors their activity, hence, we will refer to them as *probe connections*. The network is loaded with an additional *background traffic* generated by UDP (User Datagram Protocol, [Post80]) sender-receiver pairs controlled by the GA. We choose the UDP protocol for the sake of simplicity, but other kinds of background traffic sources can be modeled as well.

During the analysis process, the GA provides a *pattern* of the traffic generated by background sources and a network simulation is run on the given topology. During this simulation relevant data are gathered on the probe connections by the simulator program and provided to the GA, which uses them to estimate the "damage" that the background traffic did to the probe connections. Such information is then used to drive the generation of traffic patterns to be used in subsequent steps of the algorithm.

As for statistical methods, our analysis requires a large number of simulation runs to obtain a significant result, therefore the choice of the simulation program is critical in order to keep the computational time small. In our work, simulations were run using a publicly available simulator called *insane* (Internet Simulated ATM Networking Environment) [Mah96]. *Insane* adopts an event-driven mechanism for the simulation, thus being reasonably fast. Moreover, it is able to deal with an arbitrary network topology described as a TCL [Welc95] script and many characteristics of network nodes and links (such as processing speed, buffering capacity, bandwidth and latency) can be controlled.

Figure 1 shows the architecture of the proposed verification environment, called Nepal (Network Protocol Analysis Algorithm), which integrates the GA and the simulator. The approach is quite general and can be applied to different protocols using different simulators with limited effort.

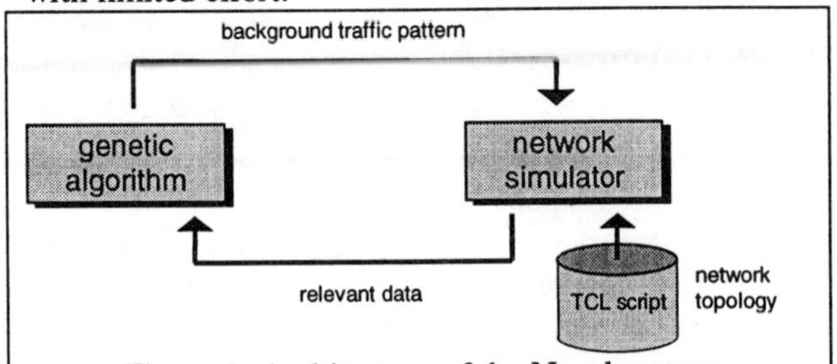

Figure 1: Architecture of the Nepal system

3. Genetic Algorithm Definition

The pseudocode of the GA adopted within Nepal is shown in Figure 2. When the GA starts, N_p individuals are randomly generated. In our approach an individual represents a background traffic pattern. Due to the encoding of the delay values in genes, which will be explained in section 3.1, the initial background traffic is generated according to a Poisson process whose inter-arrival time between packets is exponentially distributed.

At each generation the GA creates N_o new individuals by applying a crossover operator to two parents. Parents are randomly chosen with a probability linearly increasing from the worst individual (smallest fitness) to the best one (highest fitness). A mutation operator is applied over each new individual with a probability p_m.

At the end of each generation, the N_p individuals with higher fitness are selected for survival (*elitism*), and the worst N_o ones are deleted from the population. The fitness function measures the probe connections' throughput, i.e., the performance of the probe TCP connections perceived by end-users during the simulation experiment. All bytes successfully received at the TCP level, but not delivered to end-users, like duplicated packets received due to the retransmission mechanism of the protocol, are therefore not considered.

Since the fitness function should increase with the increasing goodness of a solution, and being in Nepal a solution good when the background traffic pattern is critical, the fitness function we defined is *inversely proportional* to the total number of bytes perceived by the end-users.

fitness = 1/(*total bytes delivered to the TCP users on all probe connection*)

This simple measure already delivers satisfactory results on simple network topologies. We are currently experimenting Nepal on more complex topologies, and we are considering the inclusion of additional parameters into the fitness function.

```
P0 = random_population();
compute_fitness(P0);
i=0; /* current generation number */
while (i < max_generation)
{
A = Pi;
for j=0 to No
{/* new element generation */
I' = select_an_individual();
I" = select_an_individual();
Ij = cross_over_operator(I', I");
if(rand()≤pm)
Ij = mutation_operator(Ij);
A = A ∪ Ij;
}
compute_fitness(A);
i++;
 Pi = {the Np best individuals ∈ A };
}
return( best_individual(Pi) )
```

Figure 2: Pseudocode of the genetic algorithm

3.1. Encoding

Each individual encodes the description of the traffic generated by all the background connections for the whole duration of the simulation. A connection is specified by a UDP source and destination pair, while the route followed by packets depends on the network topology and on the routing mechanism. We assume that all the packets sent on the network are of the same size, hence individuals do not need to encode this information for each packet.

Individuals are encoded as strings of N genes, where each gene represents a single background packet. Genes are composed of two parts: a TAG that indicates which background connection the packet will be sent on and a DELAY that represents how long the given source will wait before sending a new packet after sending the current one.

A model for background traffic commonly adopted in statistical network analysis is a Poisson process with negative exponentially distributed arrival times [Hui90]. In order to ensure that delays given by a randomly generated individual are exponentially distributed, the DELAY field is an index in an array of values exponentially distributed from 0 to K seconds with an average value of $0.4*K$. We make no assumptions on the number of genes with a given TAG; however, N is usually large enough to make the initial random background traffic almost equally distributed between sources.

To ensure that a given background traffic is determined by an unique individual, genes are sorted within an individual to guarantee that the packet associated to gene $i+1$ is never sent before the packet associated with gene i. Otherwise, it would be possible to exchange adjacent genes with different TAGs without modifying the represented background traffic. We say that genes in the individual are "sorted in time".

The crossover operators must have the ability to combine *good* schemata from different individuals and in Nepal each individual embeds two kinds of different schemata: the background traffic as a function of time (*time domain*) and the background traffic as a function of the background connection (*space domain*). It is important to maintain the conceptual separation of these two schemata, because, for instance, an individual could represent *good* background traffic during a given period of a simulation experiment, or it can represent a *good* traffic for a given background connection, or both.

Some crossover operators (explained in section 3.2) aim at combining good schemata in the *time domain*. If an individual do not fulfill the *sorted in time* property, it would be hard for such operators to preserve schemata related to such domain, and they would act almost like the well known *uniform* crossover. Our experiments show that the performance of the GA would be significantly reduced.

It is possible that the genes with a given TAG are not enough to generate traffic for the whole experiment, in this case the connection remains idle in the final part of the experiment. On the other hand, it is also possible that the simulation ends before all the packets are sent, and final genes are ignored.

Figure 3 shows, on the left hand side, a possible individual and, on the right hand side, the corresponding background traffic generated during the simulation experiment. The table mapping the DELAY field to exponential delays is reported in the middle of the figure.

In the individual shown in Figure 3 packet number 9 is not sent because the simulation is over before the delay associated with gene number 6 expires. On the other hand, one gene with tag ⊠ is missing, since the delay associated with the last packet on that connection (packet number 7) expires before simulation's end.

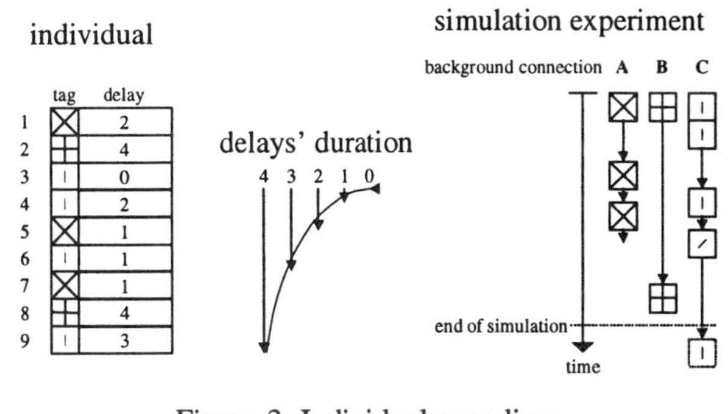

Figure 3: Individual encoding

3.2. Crossover Operators

Nepal implements 4 types of crossover: the well known *one-cut*, *two-cuts* and *uniform*, plus a peculiar one called *mix-source* (Figure 4). After crossover, genes of the offspring need to be *sorted in time*.

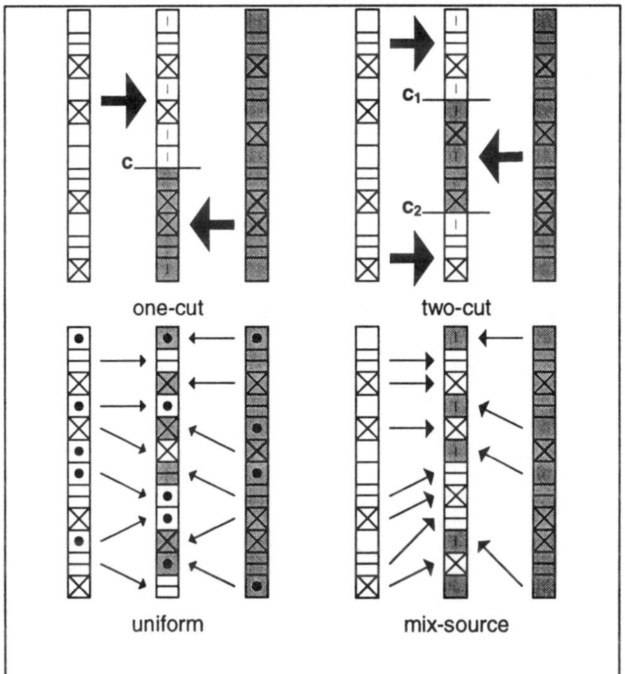

Figure 4: Crossover operators

In the **one-cut crossover** Nepal randomly selects a cut point c between 1 and N and generates a new individual copying the first c genes from the first parent and the subsequent N-c ones from the second parent.

The **two-cuts crossover** acts in a similar way, but it selects two cut points c_1, c_2 and genes are taken from the first parent at both the beginning and the end.

These two crossover operators generate a background traffic that is equal to the traffic generated by one parent for a given time and then suddenly changes and follows the traffic generated by the other parent (strictly speaking, it is possible that the cut points do not correspond exactly to the same time instants in the two parents, however, N is big enough for this to be neglected).

The **uniform crossover** generates an offspring taking each gene from the first or the second parent with the same probability.

In the **mix-source crossover**, Nepal first randomly associates each tag (i.e., each background source) with one of the two parents, then copies all the genes with the same tag from that parent. The new individual can be longer or shorter than N: in the former case the exceeding genes are dropped; in the latter one the individual is filled with random genes. The *mix-source* crossover aims at putting together good background sources from different individuals.

We can say that the *mix-source* crossover acts in the space (or source) domain while the *one-cut* and *two-cut* ones act in the time domain. The *uniform* crossover is hybrid and acts in both domains.

3.3. Mutations

Nepal implements three different mutation operators: *speed-up*, *slow-down* and *random*. Mutation applies on $N_m<N$ contiguous genes, where N_m is a constant. The first gene is randomly selected between 1 and N and the gene list is considered circular.

The **speed-up mutation** decreases the DELAY field by one without modifying the tag. DELAY values are considered circular.

The **slow-down mutation** increases the DELAY field by one without modifying the tag. DELAY values are considered circular.

The **random mutation** substitutes each gene with a new random one.

After each mutation, genes in the individual need to be sorted to fulfill the "sorted in time" property.

4. Experimental Results

We developed a prototypical implementation of the algorithm using the `perl 5` [WaCR96] language. The implementation of the GA is less than 500 lines long and, with a limited effort, can be ported to different simulators and different platforms.

The source of the simulator consists of 38,370 lines of C++ code. We needed to modify *insane* to handle an externally generated background traffic; modifications of the original code are limited to about 100 lines. Such modifications allow the user to define a traffic source taking the list of packets to be sent from a file or a Unix pipe.

4.1. Network topology

Figure 5 shows the topology of the IP network exploited in the experiments. 3 TCP connections span from the transmitters TXi to the receivers RXi through 3 IP routers. Each TCP connection performs long file transfers generating a series of 1024 Kbyte messages at a maximum average rate of 1.33 Mb/s. Thus, the 3 TCP sources can generate an overall load of 4 Mb/s, if they are allowed by the TCP flow control mechanism. Acknowledgments from each TCP transmitter are carried by control messages flowing in the reverse direction. These 3 TCP connections represent the *probe connections* of the experiment.

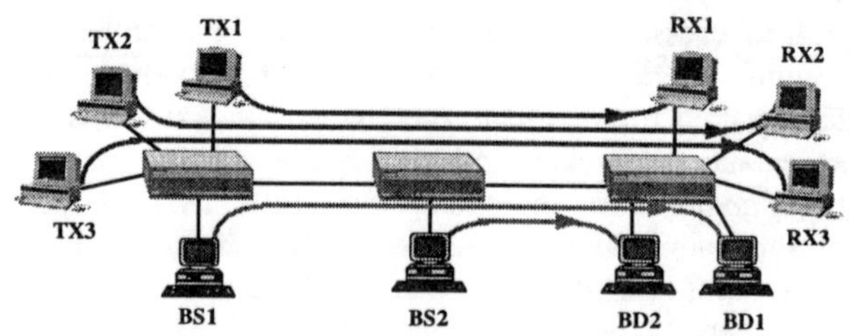

Figure 5: Topology of the network

Two sources (BSi) generate *background* UDP traffic directed to their respective destinations (BDi) over the same links traversed by the TCP connections. The timing of background packets is controlled by the GA, as described in section 3. The background traffic is generated only in the forward direction of the TCP connections and thus only data messages can be delayed and discarded due to network overload, not acknowledgments.

In this topology, the link between the rightmost two routers represents a bottleneck for the network since it is traversed by all the traffic generated by both the background sources and the TCP connections.

Each link shown in Figure 5 has a capacity of 10 Mb/s in each direction and introduces a fixed 10 μs delay. E.g., such links can be considered as dedicated 10 Mb/s Ethernet trunks, the 10 μs latency accounting for the propagation delay on the wires and the switching delay introduced by an Ethernet switch.

Routers introduce a fixed 0.1 ms delay component which accounts for the processing required on each packet and adds to the queuing delay. The size of output queues modeled by *insane* is given in terms of number of packets (we used 64 packet queues in our experiments). The buffering capacity of real routers is given in terms of byte volume, i.e., the number of packets that can be stored in a buffer depends on their size. We choose to deal with fixed size packets to work around this limitation of the simulator program.

4.2. Parameters values

All the parameters used by the GA are summarized in Table 1, and the value used in our experiments is reported.

PARAMETER	Name	Value
simulation duration [s]	T	3
population size	N_p	50
offspring size	N_o	20
number of genes in each individual	N	4,500
Poisson distribution's parameter [ms]	K	6.67
mutation's probability	p_m	50%
number of genes affected by a mutation	N_m	100

Table 1: Parameter values

The parameters K, N, and T are tuned in order to model a 6 Mb/s background traffic level, because, in this situation, the probe connections' traffic (4 Mb/s) plus the background traffic is nearly equal to the links' bandwidth (10 Mb/s). With a smaller load, the background traffic would be unable to interfere significantly with probe connections; while with a larger one, the whole network would be congestioned and the TCP throughput would be very small even with a completely random traffic.

4.3. Results

We let the GA run for 500 generations on a Sun SPARC Station 5 with 64 MByte of memory. The GA required about 17,000 seconds of CPU time (mainly spent for sorting in time genes of newly generated individuals) and *insane* employed about 53,000 seconds of CPU time for running all the required simulations.

Figure 6 shows the throughput of the probe connections, i.e., the connection bandwidth delivered to users. The X axis reports the generation number of the GA. These values are compared to the ones of a standard statistical approach, where the background traffic is randomly generated according an equivalent Poisson process. For the statistical approach, we report the lowest throughput obtained after simulating a number of random patterns equal to the number of simulations required by Nepal until the given generation. This value does not change significantly as new traffic patterns are randomly generated.

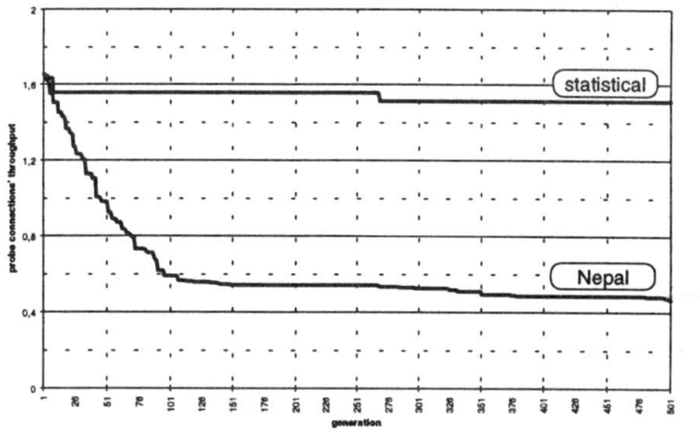

Figure 6: Throughput of probe connections

During the experiment, Nepal managed to dramatically degrade the probe connections' throughput from 1.66 Mb/s to 0.48 Mb/s with a small increment of the background traffic bandwidth. Thus, the genetic algorithm leads the background traffic sources to generating a traffic pattern that the TCP protocol cannot easily deal with.

Due to the fact that some genes may result unuseful at the end of the simulation run, the bandwidth of a critical background traffic pattern generated by Nepal is slightly bigger than the starting one. Thus, in order to eliminate this bias from the results, we defined a *disturbance efficacy* parameter at generation i as $DE_i = \dfrac{T^* - T_i}{B_i}$, where T^* is throughput of the TCP probe connections without the background noise traffic, T_i is the lowest throughput of the TCP probe connections archived until generation i and B_i is the corresponding background traffic bandwidth. In DE_i, the effects of the traffic are normalized with respect to the varying background traffic bandwidth B_i. We experimentally examined the DE of the statistical approach with different background traffic loads, and we found that the GA reaches the higher DE even when tuning the statistical traffic in order to provide the same load as the GA.

Figure 8 plots DE_i as a function of the GA generation i and clearly shows that a critical traffic pattern is identified by the genetic evolution, and cannot be easily found with standard statistical methods. I.e., the performance evaluated with statistical methods can be much larger than the one experienced on the field in equivalent operating conditions. Thus, the GA allows the performances of the protocol to be assessed without making unrealistic assumptions on the probabilistic distribution of the traffic generated by background sources.

Moreover, the GA proofs itself able to find a critical pattern examining the whole network almost as a black box, with very few information of what is happening inside, and few *control knobs* for influencing the system. This is an important point, because Nepal does not rely on the knowledge of a specific problem, but on the strength of a potentially generic GA.

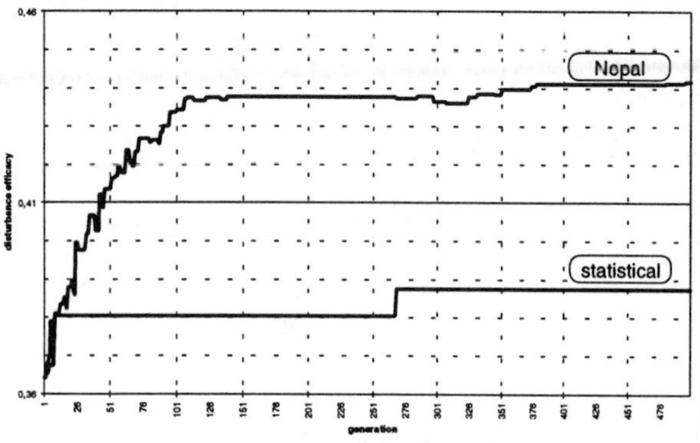

Figure 7: Disturbance efficacy

5. Conclusions

We presented a new heuristic methodology based on a Genetic Algorithm, for evaluating the performance of a communication protocol in a realistic environment and possibly finding its weaknesses. We developed a prototypical implementation of the tool called Nepal and we ran some experiments, examining TCP connections in a simple IP network topology.

The results proved that, when the background traffic generation is driven by the genetic algorithm, the TCP performance is much lower than when traffic is generated by statistical methods: Nepal is able to identify traffic patterns particularly critical to the protocol that were not found by means of traditional techniques, such as statistical simulation.

Moreover, Nepal is able to deal with real network topologies and with the real implementation of protocols, instead of a mathematical approximated model. Thus, it can discover problems related to all the features of protocols, including those features that were impossible to model with formal techniques.

We feel that our approximate methodology could be effectively used in conjunction with traditional methods of verification, giving useful information about the behavior of a transmission protocol when used with a given network topology.

6. References

[AlTr96] E. Alba, J. M. Troya, "Genetic Algorithms for Protocol Validation", Proceedings of the 4th conference on Parallel Problem Solving (PPSN IV), Berlin, Germany, September, 1996

[DeJo75] K. A. DeJong, "An analysis of the behavior of a class of genetic adaptive systems'', *Doctoral Dissertion*, University of Michigan, 1975

[Holl75] J. H. Holland, *Adaption in Natural and Artificial Systems*, University of Michigan Press, Ann Arbor, MC (USA), 1975

[Hui90] J. Hui, *Switching and Traffic Theory for Integrated Broadband Networks*, Kluwer Academic Publishers, 1990.

[ISO88] ISO - Information Processing Systems - Open Systems Interconnection - *LOTOS, A Formal Description Technique Based on the Temporal Ordering of Observational Behaviour*. IS 8807, 1988.

[LTWW95] Leland, Taqqu, Willinger, Wilson, "On the Self-Similar Nature of Ethernet Traffic (Extended Version)", IEEE/ACM Transactions On Networking, V2 N1, Feb 95, p. 1-15

[Mah96] B. A. Mah, "INSANE - An Internet Simulated ATM Networking Environment", available at **http://HTTP.CS.Berkeley.EDU/~bmah/Software/Insane/**

[Post80] J. Postel, *User Datagram Protocol (UDP)*, RFC 768. August 1980.

[Post81] J. Postel, *Transmission Control Protocol (TCP)*, RFC 793. Internet Engineering Task Force. Gennaio 1981.

[Stev94] W. R. Stevens, *TCP/IP Illustrated: the protocols*, Reading, Mass., Addison-Wesley Pub. Co., 1994

[WaCR96] L. Wall, T. Christiansen, R. L. Schwartz, *Programming Perl, 2nd Edition*, O'Reilly, September 1996

[Welc95] B. B. Welch, *Practical Programming in TCL and TK*, Prentice Hall Professional Technical Reference, May, 1995

Time Dependent Optimization with a Folding Genetic Algorithm

Alessio Gaspar **Philippe Collard**
University of Nice Sophia-Antipolis, I3S Laboratory — CNRS
250 av. A. Einstein, Sophia Antipolis, 06560 Valbonne FRANCE
Fax : (33-1) 04-92-94-28-98
e-mail : {gaspar, pc}@alto.unice.fr
Web : http://wwwi3s.unice.fr/mage.html

Abstract

Time dependent optimization has revealed to be a promising gap for the entire Genetic Algorithms community since it has numerous applications. This paper extends previous work related to the use of metagenes ([5]) in the so-called Dual Genetic Algorithms (DGAs). A more generic framework, involving a variable number of genes, is introduced. Folding Genetic Algorithms are thus proposed as a new class of genetic algorithms which effectiveness is investigated on two well known models of dynamical environments and compared to Simple Genetic Algorithms and DGAs.

Eventually, further analysis of these results enlightens the ability of FGAs to evolve a metrics over the search space (i.e. a kind of encoding scheme) along with potential solutions. These particularly encouraging results open us interesting perspectives as FGAs should be applied to to other fundamental problems investigated by the GA community in order to measure the benefits of this really meta level of evolution.

1 Evolutionist Approach

This paper considers time dependent optimization by Genetic Algorithms. At first, we precisely define what both of these terms correspond to providing a characterization of dynamical environments difficulty. We also link this particular issue to most fundamental ones addressed by the Evolutionary Community.

1.1 Genetic Algorithms

Genetic Algorithms ([9, 11]) have been introduced in the sixties by professor John Holland at university of Michigan as models of an Artificial Evolution. In the thirty past years, they have been successfully applied to a wide range of problems such as Natural Systems Modeling (e.g. Artificial Life environments [11], immune system modeling [7]), Machine Learning by the way of classifier systems, and optimization.

GAs basically handle a population of chromosomes (Individuals) often modeled by λ long vector of binary genes. Each one encodes a potential solution to the considered problem and is rewarded by a so-called *Fitness value* which is directly correlated to how good it is to solve the problem. Starting with a random initial population, we iteratively apply a so-called *Genetic Transformation* which consists of three genetic-like operators such as *crossover*, *mutation* and *selection*each having the following specific role ;

- *Selection* exponentially spreads, over generations, above average fitted chromosomes by allowing them more offsprings in next generation.
- *Crossover* exploits genetic material of the current populations by breeding most interesting strings.
- *Mutation* introduces diversity in population by flipping randomly chosen genes.

As a result, this overall non linear dynamics leads to an homogeneous final population only featuring instances of the best chromosome found so far.

Simple Genetic Algorithms (SGA) have shown a robustness in fitness landscapes featuring local optima, being able most of the time to find the global optimum. Nevertheless, *deceptive functions* or *Dynamical* ones revealed theirs limitations.

1.2 On Dynamical Environments

Fitness values changing over time define what we should call *Fitness Dynamics*. From this generic definition, we can distinguish between fitness values changing due to the Genetic Algorithm own dynamics (endogenous causes) or due to environmental causes (exogenous). The first case concerns average schemata values during hyperplane sampling as well as chromosomes fitnesses when using *scaling* or *sharing* methods.

The second defines *Dynamical Environments* that is functions fitness changing over time.

In both cases, the Genetic Algorithms are expected to be able to track the optimum over time after it has changed during a *Transition* separating two *Periods* of static behavior. By addressing the time dependent optimization issues, one obviously also addresses most of intrinsic weaknesses of Genetic Algorithms. Clearly, adapting a GA to such a context is nothing else than improving its exploration-exploitation tradeoff in order to enhance *diversity* management. Indeed, in natural as artificial ecosystems, *Polymorphic Populations* are a key to reactiveness as well as robustness to perturbations for species. In a Genetic search, maintaining diversity is central in order to be able to react to sudden environmental change as well as to escape local misleading optima leading to premature convergences.

This paper will focus on time dependent optimization in order to address both classes of issues. Without entering into details, a dynamical environment, at least in the unimodal case, may be fully characterized by its transitions parameters. Among all parameters that can be measured, this paper will focus on the *Transition Distance* (δ_d) and the *Period*. The first measure is defined as the hamming distance separating two consecutive optima in an unimodal context. The second measure, noticed δ_p, stands for the length, expressed in generations, of periods during which fitness is stationary (*Transition Speed*).

Both parameters have already been proved to be significative of a dynamical environment's difficulties.

1.3 The Pattern-Tracking Model

The first model of Dynamical Environments consists in experimenting with fixed values for δ_d and δ_p. The fitness value $\mathcal{F}_x$ is the hamming distance between x and an arbitrary chosen optimum. At each transition, optimum is changed to a random one located at distance δ_d from it. Such a model has been first experimented by Pettit and Swigger ([15]) and then Vavak and Fogarty ([17]). We will work on 40 genes long chromosomes for 250 generations with $\delta_s = 50$ and 3 different values for δ_d (5, 20, 35). The second model we used is more complex as it features a greater diversity of transitions within the same experiment.

1.4 The MD-Gaussian Model

This Dynamical Environment relies on a multidimensional gaussian-like function defined by :

$$\frac{1}{n}\sum_{i=1}^{n} e^{-\pi*\left(\frac{x_i}{2^{\lambda}/2}-t\right)^2}$$

Where t locates the optimum, λ represents the chromosome's length and π a *Peakness* coefficient parameterizing the gaussian top's shape (here $\pi = 3$). By increasing t over time the gaussian slides on the search space's diagonal, each of its n variables changing uniformly. We are going to encode 8 dimensions variables each 8 genes long. As a result, this 64 gene long chromosome will take 2^8 different values during the experiment. Each run will be 5000 generations long, this leads to a transition speed $\delta_s = 5000/2^8 = 19.53$. We use a binary coding to enumerate the search space, sliding on it will lead to every possible δ_d ranging from 1 when passing from $< 00000000 >$ to $< 00000001 >$ for example, to λ for the ***middle transition*** between $< 01111111 >$ and $< 10000000 >$. It's worth noticing that, in the case of DGAs and FGAs, population size was not increased despite of the growth of the search space[1]. Following results may thus be interpreted as a lower bound for the abilities of these meta approaches.

Moreover, a Multidimensional function avoid the Genetic Algorithm to only optimize most significant genes when processing long chromosomes with binary encoding (i.e leftmost ones traditionally). When considering Dynamical Environments, this would leads us to ignore transitions affecting low weighted genes.

1.5 GAs in dynamical environments

Our previous definition of a Simple Genetic Algorithm straightforwardly implies that it is not able, once having converged to a uniform population, to converge to a new optimum if fitness function changes. This is due to the fact that crossover and selection can not provide new chromosomes when applied to a uniform population. The SGA thus only relies on mutation to provide the required diversity to converge toward the new optimum. The issue thus becomes how to adapt GAs for time dependent optimization ?

A brief state of the art of Genetic approaches in this area enlightens some relevant entry points of the evolutionist paradigmto enhance significantly GA's adaptiveness to environmental changes. For instance, we classify them in 3 main classes;

- *Operational Diversity* i.e. adapting the mutation rate by increasing it when a change is detected in the fitness landscape ([10, 1]) or by making it emerge by the use of an implicit mutation rate (see Dual Genetic Algorithms below for an illustration of this principle).

- *Fitness Evaluation* : By changing the way to evaluate individuals by the use of sharing methods for example, polymorphic population can emerge from the GA dynamics. Therefore diversity can

[1] which is doubled for the DGAs and multiplied by a factor of 2^{λ} for the FGAs.

be enhanced by this method providing relevant enhancement of the diversity management.

- *Using Introns* : under this generic term we group all attempts to use genes non directly coding for a given solution. These genes are either ignored ([12, 13]) or used to influence other ones during a *transcription* like process.

Now that we have defined what is the problem we want to address, we describe, next section, the several steps leading to the approach we propose to address the intrinsic limit of SGAs through the third entry point previously presented.

2 Folding Genetic Algorithms

At first, we summarize previous work on the introduction of a meta-gene in chromosomes. Next, we extend this primary model and generalize it to the use of an arbitrary number of meta-genes. In order to valid this approach we eventually lead an empirical study on dynamical environments.

2.1 Dualism as a first step

Dual Genetic Algorithms (DGA) ([2, 6]) have been proved to be particularly efficient genetic algorithms which offer an improved robustness against most intrinsic weaknesses of SGA. DGAs work on chromosomes with a head-bit *meta-gene* in front of them. The search space Ω is thus doubled as the DGA considers $\lambda+1$ gene long chromosomes. So,this new search space $<\Omega>$ contains all possible $\lambda+1$ gene long strings (*genotypes*). As a result, the basic space Ω contains *phenotypes*, i.e. normal λ genes long chromosomes directly evaluated by user defined fitness function.

Thus, in order to evaluate a genotype, the DGA to maps it back to the phenotypic space through a so-called *Transcription* step[2] which is stated as follow;

$$\begin{array}{rcl} T: \ <\Omega> & \rightarrow & \Omega \\ T(\dot{0}\omega) & = & \omega \\ T(\dot{1}\omega) & = & \overline{\omega} \end{array}$$

In other words, if the meta-gene is active ($\dot{1}$) the phenotype is taken as the complement of the following λ genes of the genotype. Otherwise, the phenotype is the remaining genes themselves. This mechanism clearly leads complementary genotypes to encode for similar phenotypes, $<\Omega>$ wcan be therefore viewed as a doubled, symmetrically unfolded version of Ω. For instance, the phenotype $[011] \in \Omega$; can be transcripted from both $[\dot{0}\,011]$ or $[\dot{1}\,100] \in <\Omega>$.

[2]In analogy to tnatural genetics mRNA transcription phase.

Previous work ([6]) enlightened the ability of DGAs to take advantage of these two different levels (genotype and phenotype). A so-called *mirrorring operator* has been used. It stochastically maps, with rate τ, a chromosome from $<\Omega>$ into its dual counterpart by complementing it. This results in a genotypical diversity not affecting phenotypical uniformity.

In other words, DGAs can converge to a single phenotype while keeping in the current population complementary genotypes. Indeed, it is also worth noticing that both offsprings resulting from a crossover between two complementary genotypes (*dual pair*) will be complementary too. But, they will encode a different phenotype than their parents. So, by maintaining with mirrorring a minimal amount of dual pairs in a population, even when having converged, we offer to DGAs an opportunity to perform such crossovers and thus to introduce diversity without any explicit mutation or randomness in order to enhance the capability to react to its environment.

This property is central to explain why, despite of the growth of the size of the search space, DGAs are efficient Genetic Algorithms that have already been successfully applied to a wide range of areas including optimization [2], machine learning [3], Genetic Programming [16] and Dynamical Environments [5].

The Following section introduces *Folding Genetic Algorithms* as a new class of Genetic Algorithms extending and generalizing the use of meta-genes.

2.2 Multiple Meta-Genes

In comparison to the previous approach, chromosomes handled by FGAs are now composed of λ *exons* (i.e. genes coding for a chromosome in Ω), and of $\lambda \in [0..\lambda]$ meta-genes (*Introns*) at least separated by one exon. Each meta-gene will have influence over all exons following it until the next intron. In order to illustrate this structure, let us take some examples of transcriptions over a $\lambda = 3$ basic search space;

$$\begin{array}{rcl} T([\dot{1}01\dot{0}0]) & = & [100] \\ T([10\dot{1}1]) & = & [100] \\ T([\dot{1}0\dot{0}0\dot{0}0]) & = & [100] \end{array}$$

This mechanism clearly generalize DGA's ability to symmetrically unfold the basic space Ω by increasing the number of meta-genes used.

2.3 Partial Mirroring Operator

As Mirroring introduces diversity at the genotypic level while preserving the phenotypic homogeneity of the DGAs populations, FGAs use a *Partial Mirroring Operator* which complement, with rate $\tau_P = 0.01$, each meta-gene and all exons influenced by it.

By introducing *clones*[3] in the population *Partial Mirroring* is functionally equivalent to Mirroring in DGAs. Contrary to DGA, the number of clones potentially available is far higher ($\sum_{i=1}^{\lambda} 2^i = (2^{n+1} - 2)$ vs 2 for a DGA). This leads to an improvement of the diversity potentially available in the population.

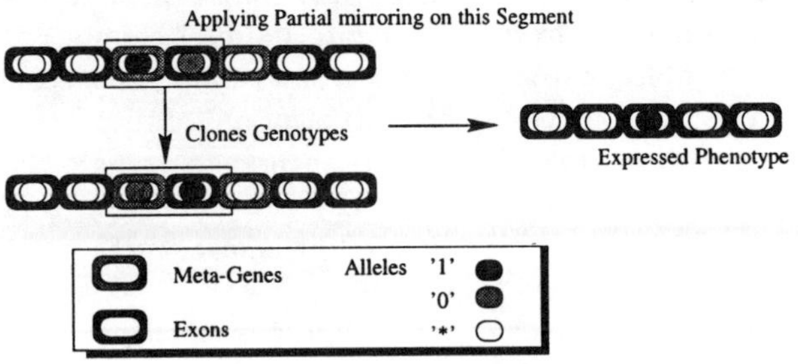

Figure 1: Partial Mirroring Operator.

2.4 Folding the search Space

The *Folding Operator* operates on exons with rate Φ and acts differently according to the presence of a meta-gene on the previous locus.

- If the previous gene is an exon, Folding inserts a meta-gene thus partially unfolding Ω.
- If previous gene is a meta-gene, Folding deletes it and thus partially folds the search space.

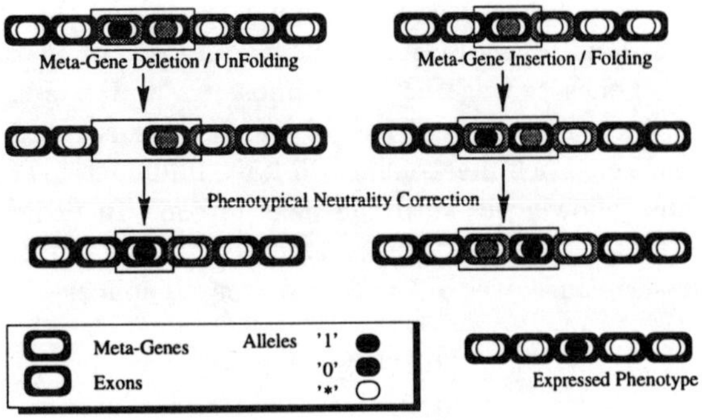

Figure 2: Folding with Active Meta-genes

If folding or unfolding concerns an active meta-gene, the phenotype is altered. Therefore, in such cases, we stochastically complement the concerned exons in order to keep this genetic operator *phenotypically neutral.* This repair process is applied with rate Φ_n, n standing for neutrality. Thus, it allows the exploration of all possible locations for meta-genes over chromosome. Figure 2 illustrates manipulation of an active meta-gene in both folding and unfolding cases.

We now test this new approach on two different models of dynamical environments previously defined.

3 Empirical Study

In this section, results obtained on both environments are presented and analyzed.

3.1 Experimental Parameters

The experimental conditions are the following; average on 10 runs with different seed values, mutation rate $\mu = 0.001$, crossover rate at $\mathcal{X}_c = 0.7$, population size is 100. We run the genetic algorithm each time for 5000 generations on MD-Gaussian and only 250 on Pattern Tracking as transitions are all identical. Tracked optimum is at respective constant fitness value 1.0 and 40 for gaussian and pattern tracking environments. Eventually, we used one point crossover and selection is assumed by a stochastic sampling method without elitism. FGA's specific parameters were tuned to respectively $\Phi_n = 0.7$ and $\tau_P = \Phi = 0.001$ in both dynamical environments. We introduced DGA-n, as a method featuring a fixed amount n of meta-genes (a hand designed meta-mask) dispatched over the chromosome. We conjecture that such fixed meta-mask may give particularly good results when especially designed for a given environment. In following experiments, we chose to use one meta-gene by function dimension in Md-gaussians. Mirroring rate was $\tau = 0.01$ for both kind of DGAs.

3.2 Pattern-Tracking Experiments

First Results obtained on this simple model are illustrated in figure 3 which plots best Fitness vs generations. This kind of analysis criterion involves an expected best fitness of $\lambda = 40.0$ corresponding to a Genetic Algorithm having tracked the optimum all the time. On the plottings, such a behavior would correspond to an horizontal line. Instead of this, one can see (fig. 3) that, at each transition, the GA may unhook even if its convergence to the optimum is quick because of the GA-easiness of this function within periods. Results clearly show;

- For $\delta_d = 5$ (Fig 3.A) :
  Problem is too easy, little transitions does not allow to distinguish between all four GAs.
- For $\delta_d = 20$ (Fig 3.B) :
  For reasons detailed latter and in [5], this was the worst case for DGAs even if they nevertheless performed better comparing to a SGA.

[3] i.e. different genotypes encoding a similar phenotype

- For $\delta_d = 35$ (fig 3.C) :
  Here DGA revealed to be better than any other GAs as they naturally handle dual structures.

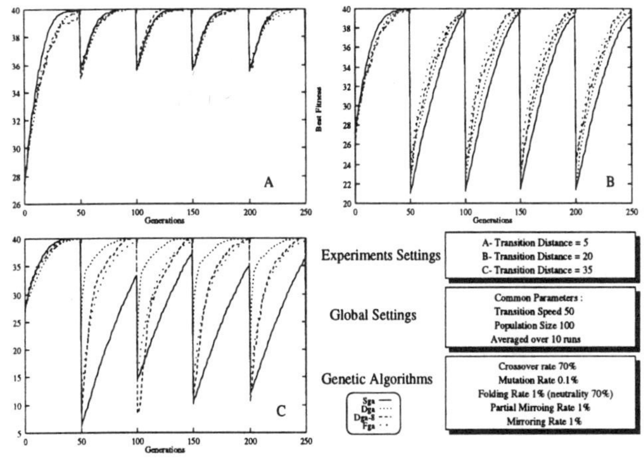

Figure 3: Pattern Tracking Results

In all cases, FGA revealed to keep very close to DGA results and even overtook it in some case despite of the considerably increased difficulty (especially in terms of search space growth). In a real complex environment, transitions are about to be somewhat unpredictable and irregular. According to these experiments FGAs seem more able to adapt to a wider range of perturbations without significant lost in their overall efficiency comparing to DGAs. For this reason, They seem more about to be applied to arbitrary unknown environments as featuring an enhanced adaptiveness. These results must nevertheless be completed in order to conclude on FGA efficiency as we have chosen to keep the population size identical. The following MD-Gaussian model features more complex transitions which difficulty changes over time. Such an environment is thus more realistic as we also decided to make continuous alterations of the fitness landscape.

3.3 MD-Gaussian Model Experiments

Results are presented in figure 4; the curve plots best fitness versus time and we detailed overall averaged values of both best and average fitness. Concerning the Average Best fitness, the ideal behavior is not straightforward. It may consist in a quasi perfect convergence characterized by an average value as close as possible to the best one. Or, in the other hand, as we have to keep diversity in population, the difference between best and average fitness should be a proper indicator of the phenotypical diversity quality. Even if, when using meta-genes, genotypical diversity is sufficient, this would nevertheless indicate that the system features an improved reactiveness against transitions through *Polymorphic Populations*.

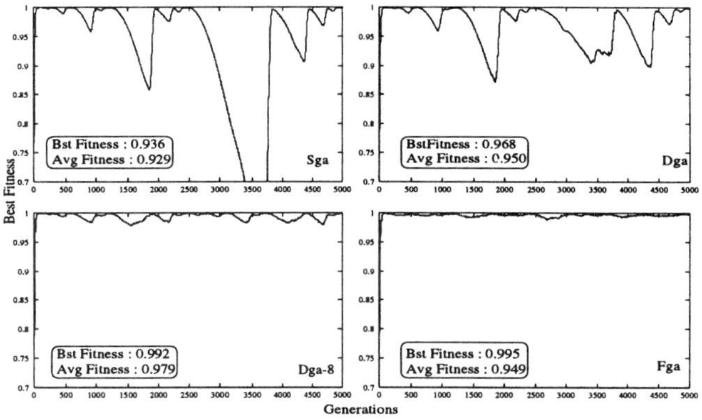

Figure 4: MD-Gaussian Results.

Regarding to these criteria, we can say that FGAs have revealed to be the most efficient approach both in terms of overall best fitness value and unhooking phenomena in the plottings. DGA already performed better than SGA as analyzed in previous work ([5]), this experiment enlighten the advantage of locating several meta-genes in the chromosome, and to use a method to evolve their number and location automatically. DGA-n were settled for this environment with one meta-genes per dimension, indeed FGAs revealed to be able to design (evolve) even a more efficient meta-mask. Moreover, we may also notice that they managed to increase the difference between their average best and average fitness. As the function is easy to optimize during periods (i.e. from a static point of view), average and best fitness values are very close in all cases, characterizing a particularly good convergence. With FGA, we find the larger difference among the four methods tested. This is interesting as it shows that FGAs easily feature diversity, even at a phenotypical level, without significant lost of effectiveness. This diversity plays a central role during transitions.

FGAs effectiveness is more than encouraging; as they achieved the design of both solution and coding while being more efficient than traditional approaches. We are thus facing a meta-system having itself chosen which meta-mask to use in order to optimize its own effectiveness. This characterizes, from our own point of view, the ***Artificial Life approach*** which tends to realize the transition between systems externally controlled or heavily parameterized to fit a particular task and ***adaptive***, ***autonomous*** ones behaving well without any expertise on their working (black box).

Comparing to the work realized by FGAs, DGA-8's

effectiveness is very poor and does not justify in any way their need of external parameters as specific as a meta-mask.

4 Explaining FGA's efficiency

This section explains previous experimental results by underlining FGA's ability to evolve metrics over the search space. At first we present the link between meta-genes and metrics and then consider cases study enlightening advantage of introducing several meta-genes (DGA-n). We eventually discuss in details why FGA is more efficient than other approaches on the basis of the different metrics it can feature.

4.1 Metrics and Search Spaces

What is a metrics over a search space ? Basically it's a distance relation between two points. In Simple Genetic Algorithms, mutation on one gene represents the canonical move in the search space. It is strongly correlated to the hamming distance that is the number of genes different between two chromosomes. In the context of DGAs, we have defined in previous work ([4]) *Dual Distance* between two points of $< \Omega >$. This measure takes into account the possibility to flip the meta-gene instead of exons. By doing so, one can "jump" of λ bits at the cost of only one flip. The distance between two chromosomes can thus be measured by either the hamming distance (δ_h) or its complementary *Dual Distance* ($\delta_{\overline{h}} = \lambda - \delta + 1$). Moreover, DGAs have been conjectured to be able to dynamically choose, according to a fitness criterion, the most interesting distance for exploring the search space ([4]). Here we simply define the *Effective Distance*[4] as an optimal choice between the two metrics available i.e $\delta_{Dga} = Min(\delta_h, \delta_{\overline{h}})$.

4.2 Case Study with DGA-n

Before to provide an analysis of the effective distance featured by FGAs (noticed δ_{Fga}), in order to fully explain obtained empirical results, we first enlighten the advantages of using several meta-genes with DGA-n. For display convenience, we restrict to examples involving small number of genes.

Our first example consists in 6 genes long chromosomes. We consider, for all GAs investigated (SGA, DGA and DGA-2[5]), the *Effective Distance*. This distance is defined as the best distance we can feature between two consecutive chromosomes in a binary enumeration of the search space similar to the one provided by multi-dimensional gaussians (see fig. 5). It

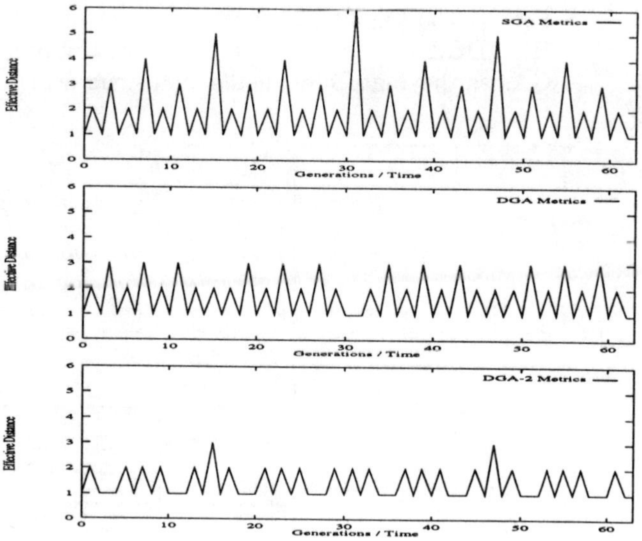

Figure 5: Metrics during Transitions.

is obvious, on this example, that increasing the number of meta-genes leads to a more convenient metrics over the search space as it allows to reduce the effective distance between two successive optima. Because they feature diversified values for δ_d, multidimensional gaussians and more generally such enumerations are good candidates to evaluate the adaptiveness of a particular GA.

Nevertheless, in order to precisely quantify the effects of a particular metrics, we may average the Effective Distance value over *all* possible transitions and not only consider the ones resulting from a binary enumeration. If previous method allows to feature all possible values for δ, it lack in considering every possible transitions (i.e. pairs of chromosomes). We now consider, for all possible hamming distances between two arbitrary chromosomes, all locations of the genes different from one chromosome to the other. By doing so, we consider all cases and thus provide more reliable and relevant results, especially for FGAs which, contrary to SGAs and DGAs, are able to feature different optimal distances for a similar value of δ_d according to differing genes location relatively to meta-genes. FGAs thus provide a more accurate metrics over the search space taking into account differences ignored by previous models.

We consider a second simple problem featuring 12 genes long chromosomes. We average the *Effective Distance* over all possible pairs of chromosomes for SGAs ($\delta_{Sga} = 6.001$), DGAs ($\delta_{Dga} = 5.03$) and DGA-n (for respective values $n = 1, 2, 3, 4, 6, 12$ we have

[4]The effective distance, for a SGA, is the only one it can use i.e. the hamming one. DGAs can use both Hamming or Dual ones.

[5]Which replace DGA-8 by considering 2 segments each 3 genes long.

$\delta_{Dga-n} = 6.001, 4.501, 5.00, 4.68, 4.81, 5.03$).

The later being evaluated with various number of meta-genes ($\dot{n}$). In all cases, DGA-n feature better average distances than SGAs and even DGAs. All this clearly advocates the hypothesis that the metrics used is strongly correlated with the easiness featured by the Genetic Algorithm to adapt to successive transitions. It is thus relevant to analyze which kind of metrics do FGAs induce over the search spaces.

4.3 Evolved Metrics

Previous section enlightened the advantage of multiples meta-genes as well as the relevance of their positions in chromosome. FGAs addresses both issues by evolving the meta-genes and consequently the metrics being in use for this individual. In order to characterize the metrics induced by a FGA, we may consider the fact that it emulates any of the previous metrics.

The optimal metrics δ_{Fga} is then taken as the minima among the ones associated to each of the 2^λ meta-mask available. From an informal point of view, δ_{Fga} can also be viewed as the number of isolated segments of consecutive alleles '1' in the x-or vector between the two considered chromosomes. This comes from the fact that, for each segment representing an isolated region of adjacent differing genes between two chromosomes, we can delimit it by two meta-genes and then get its bitwise complement in one step only (meta-gene flipping). This clearly confirms and explains how that FGAs take into account, beyond the distance, the location of differing genes between the two considered chromosomes.

As a result, we can no more consider the plotting of their effective distance according to δ_d only. We may rather, for each value of δ_h, average the effective distance value δ_{Fga} over all possible pairs of chromosomes located at this hamming distance from each other. Figure 6 shows this average value compared to δ_{Sga} and δ_{Dga}, for a 20 genes long chromosomes. This clearly enlightens the average quantitative improvement. The average has been done by choosing, for each pair of chromosomes being distant of δ_d genes, the metrics providing best results as we did for all GAs. This leads us to consider the qualitative improvement provided, not at the previous global and averaged level, but rather for each possible distance δ. More formally, let us note $\#_n^\delta$ the number of chromosomes being δ genes different and having these different genes located such as they form n isolated (i.e. separated by at least one gene identical in both chromosomes) segments on the λ long chromosome. Informally, this corresponds to the number of pairs of chromosomes over the search space having $\delta_{Fga} = n$.

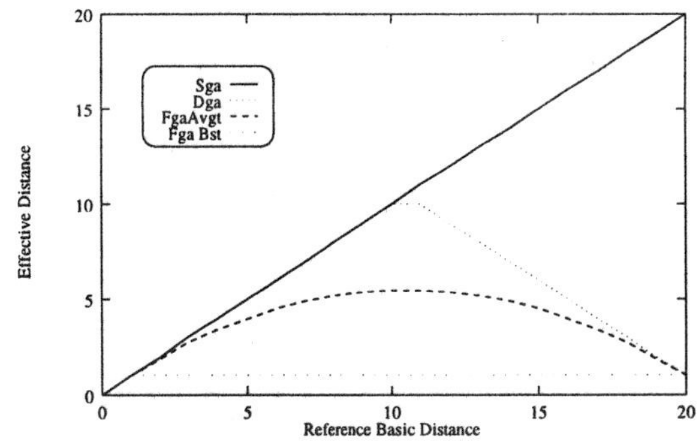

Figure 6: Effectives Distances.

The number of isolated segments of adjacent differing genes being an informal expression of the Effective δ_{Fga}.

Beyond the comparison with other effective distances, we now quantify the qualitative improvement provided by FGAs; Figure 7 plots the density of cases where ($\delta_{Fga} < \delta_{Dga}$) vs Effective Distances featured by the FGAs over this Search Space. In other words, this plotting considers for each value of δ (x axis on the curve) ranging from 0 to λ ($\lambda = 20$ in our example), the number of chromosomes pairs featuring $\delta_{Fga} < \delta_{Dga}$ among the C_δ^λ possible ones which have δ distant chromosomes. This density is evaluated given λ and δ and represents in fact the density of cases, given any pair of arbitrary chromosomes, where FGAs lead to an improvement via a metrics comparing to DGAs. This density is computed by summing $\#_i^\delta$ whereas $\delta_{Fga} \geq \delta_{Dga}$ for all number of isolated segments of adjacent differing genes that can be formed.

We can see clearly that, even if extrema distances (near 0 or λ) are moderately advantageous, FGAs are outstanding in most of cases at a rate close to 100 percent. Hence, there remains very little probability to

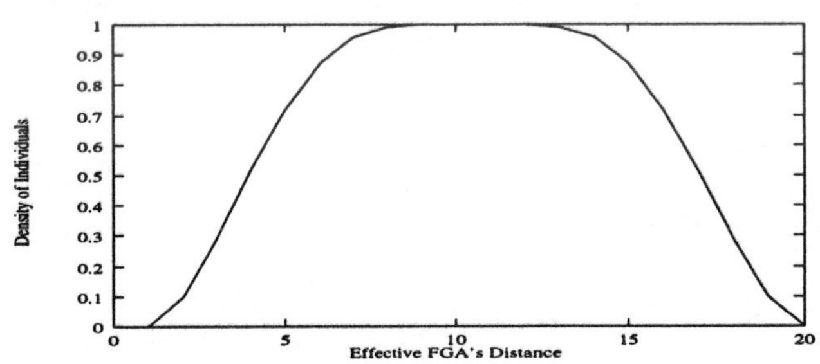

Figure 7: Density of Distances for fixed distance δ.

face worst cases. This leads to a qualitative improvement (and moreover adaptation) of the metrics over

Ω. This may be particularly relevant against encoding dependency related issues which are central to the Genetic Algorithms community.

Moreover it is worth noticing that altering metrics can improve the adaptiveness without large amounts of diversity in the populations. Individuals having good meta-masks are just potentially able to move quicker than other to interesting areas of the search space. At a low cost in terms of distance, meta-masks can allow them to reach any other area quicker. When evolving a good meta-mask they thus become able to have in their close neighboring, particularly fitted areas of the search space. In opposition to explicit diversity given by genotypes, we will refer to this potential diversity corresponding to potential quick moves over the search space as *Kinetic Diversity*.

5 Perspectives and further work

This paper has presented *Folding Genetic Algorithms* as a new efficient class of Genetic Algorithms based on real meta-level evolution of a suitable metrics over the search space. From an empirical point of view, Dynamical Environments have revealed to be of a great help in characterizing metrics properties. Such Adaptive Metrics explains the effectiveness of FGAs in Dynamical Environments which opened this new field to evolutionist tools. Further work will consist in studying in more details how can such an optimal meta-mask be evolved and what properties it must feature thus enlightening us on FGAs dynamics.

References

[1] H.C. Cobb and J.J. Grefenstette. Genetic algorithms for tracking changing environments. In *Icga-5*, 1993.

[2] P. Collard and J.P. Aurand. Dga: An efficient genetic algorithm. In *ECAI'94*, Amsterdam, 1994.

[3] P. Collard and C. Escazut. Relational schemata: A way to improve expressiveness of classifiers. In *Icga'95* [8], pages 397–404.

[4] P. Collard and C. Escazut. Fitness distance correlation in a dual genetic algorithm. In *Ecai'96*, 1996.

[5] P. Collard, C. Escazut, and A. Gaspar. An evolutionary approach for time dependant optimization. In IEEE Computer Society Press, editor, *IcTai96*, pages 2–9, November 1996.

[6] P. Collard and A. Gaspar. Royal road landscapes for a dual genetic algorithm. In *ECAI-96*, Budapest, 1996.

[7] P. D'haeseleer, S. Forrest, and P. Helman. An immunological approach to change detection : algorithms, analysis and implications. In *Proceedings of the 1996 IEEE Symposium on Computer Security and Privacy*, 1996.

[8] L.J. Eschelman, editor. *Sixth International Conference on Genetic Algorithms*, San Francisco, California, July 1995. Morgan Kaufmann.

[9] D.E. Goldberg. *Genetic Learning in optimization, search and machine learning.* Addisson Wesley, 1994.

[10] J.J. Grefenstette. Genetic algorithms for changing environments. In R. Manner abd B. Manderick, editor, *Parallel Problem Solving from Nature 2*, pages 465–501. Elsevier Science Publishers B.V., 1992.

[11] J. H. Holland. *Adaptation in Natural and Artificial Systems.* MIT Press, 2nd edition, 1992.

[12] J.R. Levenick. Inserting introns improves genetic algorithms success rate: Taking a cue from biology. In R.K. Belew and L.B. Booker, editors, *Fourth International Conference on Genetic Algorithms*, pages 123–127, San Francisco California, July 1991. Morgan Kaufmann.

[13] J.R. Levenick. Metabits: Generic endogenous crossover control. In Eschelman [8], pages 88–95.

[14] K. Peow NG and K.C. Wong. A new diploid scheme and dominance change mechanism for non-stationary function optimization. In Eschelman [8].

[15] K. Pettit and E. Swigger. An analysis of genetic based pattern tracking and cognitive based component tracking models of adaptation. In *Proceedings of National Conference on AI (AAAI-83).* Morgan Kaufmann, 1983.

[16] J.-L Segapeli, C. Escazut, and P. Collard. Dgp: How to improve genetic programming with duals. In *Proceedings of the 3rd International Conference on Artificial Neural Networks and Genetic Algorithms (ICANNGA'97)*, 1997.

[17] F. Vavak and T.C. Fogarty. A comparative study of steady state and generational genetic algorithms for use in nonstationary environments. In *Proceedings of the Society for the Study of Artificial Intelligence and Simulation of Behavior, workshop on Evolutionnary Computation'96*, pages 301–307. University of Sussex, 1996.

Exploiting Symbolic Techniques within Genetic Algorithms for Power Optimization

S. Chiusano, F. Corno, P. Prinetto, M. Rebaudengo, M. Sonza Reorda

Politecnico di Torino
Dipartimento di Automatica e Informatica
Torino, Italy

Abstract

This paper proposes an optimization algorithm for reducing the power dissipation in a sequential circuit. The encoding of the different states in a Finite State Machine is modified to obtain a functionally equivalent circuit that exhibits a reduced power dissipation. The algorithm is based on a newly proposed power estimation function, that is able to quickly give an accurate estimate of the dissipated power without actually synthesizing the circuit. Given this estimate, a Genetic Algorithm provides a state re-encoding for the circuit. The estimation function is computed in a very efficient way by exploiting some symbolic computations with Binary Decision Diagrams. The algorithm is experimentally shown to provide good results from the power optimization point of view, at a limited cost in terms of area increase, when compared with similar approaches.

1. Introduction

In modern VLSI circuits, due to a wide range of critical applications, the design task no longer concentrates on the area/speed trade-off, only. Currently, a new variable is becoming of primary concern: power consumption. In fact, the control of *power dissipation* is compulsory in mobile computing devices, but also allows desk-top systems to save energy and to increase their reliability.

Among different optimization possibilities [MoDe97], one of the often used power minimization techniques lies in a clever choice of the *state encoding* for a Finite State Machine (FSM). Intuitively, a low power circuit should reduce the number of transitions of gate outputs for each input switch. Therefore, state encoding for low power aims at reducing the average number of gate switches in each transition of the state transition graph. Most recent approaches take into account state probabilities and estimates of the combinational logic attached to each of the changing flip-flops in order to improve the accuracy of the algorithms. Some proposed approaches to state re-encoding for low power can be found in [HHPP94] [VTRa95] [OlKa94] [TPCD94] [WWHW94].

When the re-encoding problem for low power is considered, two main aspects have to be analyzed. First of all, the size of the search space, since the set of possible state encodings is factorial in the number of circuit states, that are exponential in the number of the flip flops of the circuit. Second, when a given state encoding is considered, it is not so easy to accurately estimate the power consumption for the corresponding circuit.

This paper aims at attacking both issues. For dealing with the former problem we propose to integrate Genetic Algorithms with Symbolic manipulation techniques, aiming at exploiting the main properties of each of them. For the latter, we propose a novel *power estimation function* able to take into account both state probabilities and the complexity of combinational logic; such function will be shown to significantly decrease power consumption and, as a beneficial side-effect, area occupation, for the analyzed benchmarks. Experimental results prove that our approach is able to significantly reduce the power consumption on the considered benchmarks, in an acceptable CPU time.

Genetic Algorithms (GAs) [Holl75] have been long investigated as a possible solution for many combinatorial problem. Since their structure is basically independent from the problem to be solved, Genetic Algorithms are usually applied in fields very far from each other.

The main quality of Genetic Algorithms is that they exploit the combined power of randomness and evolution to explore large solution spaces. Therefore, they are particularly suitable for dealing with problems where the search space is so large that an exact approach is not applicable, or at least not convenient. For this reason, GAs are good candidates to be applied to the state re-encoding problem for power minimization.

Usually, one most critical aspect of Genetic Algorithms is represented by the computation of the fitness function. In fact, depending on the problem, the required CPU time can grow so much, that the genetic approach becomes not applicable. To overcome this

1082-3409/97 $10.00 © 1997 IEEE

limitation, we propose to exploit some effective properties of Symbolic Techniques in fitness computation.

In recent years, very efficient techniques for representing and manipulating Boolean functions have been developed by using Binary Decision Diagrams (BDDs) [Brya92]. Symbolic Techniques exploit BDD properties to efficiently handle Boolean function of a large number of variables with an acceptable memory and CPU time requirement. In the fields of formal verification, test pattern generation, automated synthesis, BDDs are used to represent and manipulate the combinational network of digital circuits, their state transition graphs, or other information related to them.

The contribution of this paper is composed of three novel proposals. First, we devise a new power estimation function that is also able to control the area occupation of a circuit prior to synthesizing it. Second, we develop a Genetic Algorithm for exploring the space of the state re-encodings and finding the one minimizing power dissipation. Third, we integrate in the fitness function computation some Boolean computations based on Symbolic Techniques that boost the performance of power estimation computation. This last contribution is particularly valuable since we integrate some intrinsically approximated techniques, such as GAs, with exact Boolean computations based on state-of-the art exact symbolic function manipulation techniques.

The outline of this paper is as follows. Section 2 briefly reviews the definitions and notations used for representing FSMs. In Section 3 we define and review the techniques adopted for state re-encoding and propose our estimation of power consumption for sequential circuits. Section 4 details the re-encoding algorithm. Experimental results are given in Section 5 over standard benchmarks, while some conclusions are drawn in Section 6.

2. Definitions

A synchronous sequential circuit can be modeled as a Finite State Machine. The behavior of an FSM is completely specified once are defined:

- the set of Primary Inputs (PI) of the circuit. The set of admissible input values is $I=2^{\#PI}$.
- the set of Primary Outputs (PO) of the circuit. The set of admissible output values is $O=2^{\#PO}$.
- a set S of *symbolic states* $s \in S$.
- the set of possible *transitions*. Each transition indicates the state that is reachable starting from a given state. Every transition is performed according to a value assumed on the primary inputs and sets a value on the primary outputs.

A state probability $\mathbf{P}(s)$ [MDLT94] [VTRa95] can be computed from the above quantities, that expresses the steady-state probability of the circuit to be in a state s, given some statistical assumptions over the distribution of input patterns.

The listed properties are valid for a given circuit, independently from its logical implementation. A State Transition Graph (STG), such as in Fig. 1(a), is usually adopted to represent the behavior of the circuit at this level of abstraction.

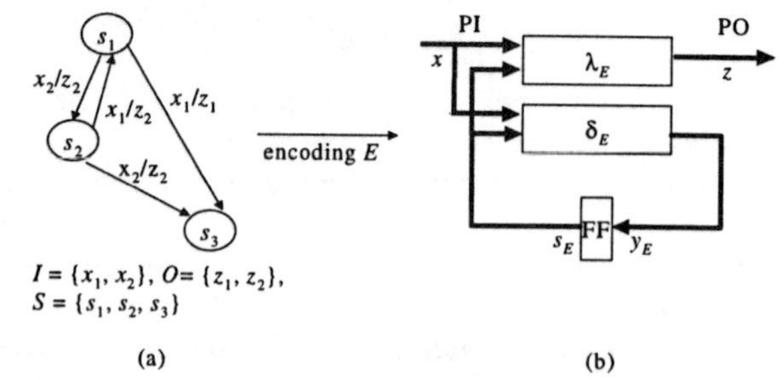

Figure 1: *a Finite State Machine*

An alternative representation may be obtained at lower abstraction levels by assigning Boolean labels to each symbolic state (Fig. 1(b)). This labeling operation is usually called *encoding* of symbolic states as binary configurations s_E representing the values of the set of state flip flops (FF) in the circuit. Formally, a *state encoding function E* is defined, such that:

$$E: S \rightarrow S_E, \text{ and } s_E=E(s),\ s_E \in S_E$$

and the following relations may be used to describe the circuit behavior:

- a state transition function, δ_E, that computes, for each input $x \in I$ and for each encoded state $s_E \in S_E$, the next state $y_E \in S_E$, $y_E=\delta_E(s_E,x)$.
- an output function, λ_E, that computes for each input $x \in I$ and for each encoded state $s_E \in S_E$, the output value $z \in O$: $z=\lambda_E(s_E,x)$.

Thanks to these functions, it is possible to formalize the relation between states, primary inputs and primary outputs of the circuit as Boolean functions.

Depending on the chosen encoding function E, different logical implementations of a same STG may be obtained. In this context, we consider only encodings on the minimum number of flip flops, that is, we have $\#FF=\lceil \log_2|S| \rceil$ and $S_E=2^{\#FF}$ possible states.

We want to stress that by changing the encoding function, only the dependencies among flip flops, and between each flip flop and primary input and outputs are modified. Every relation between inputs and outputs, on the other hand, is independent from E.

3. State Re-encoding for Low Power

As we previously mentioned, the choice of the state encoding function E does not influence the functional behavior of the circuit. One can therefore exploit this degree of freedom to pursue additional goals. In traditional logic-level synthesis environments [SSMS92], state encoding usually aims at minimizing the area of the multi-level combinational network subject to timing constraints [LiNe89].

Some recent research works exploited the state encoding function E for reducing the power dissipation in the circuit. In these cases, rather than devising an encoding starting from scratch, one can start from a given encoding, and try to improve it by obtaining a new encoding satisfying some additional goals. The problem is therefore expressed as a *re-encoding* one, and can be stated as follows: given an initial encoding E, generated for pursuing some specific goals (i.e., area and/or speed), devise a new encoding E' that optimizes some additional variable (i.e., power consumption) while maintaining acceptable values for the initial goals.

Although very accurate power estimation algorithms exist [MDLT94], they are too CPU-intensive to be used within optimization algorithms, and approximate solutions must be devised. This is especially true if one wants to exploit the degrée of freedom given by state encoding in sequential circuits, where, given a state encoding, a full logic synthesis and optimization is needed to estimate the power consumed by each logic gate. The proposed approaches vary in the adopted approximations, and on the choice of the algorithm. They have power minimization as their main goal, and they usually also provide an acceptable area occupation: in fact, area minimization and power minimization are compatible constraints. A summary of recent works and our proposed power consumption measure are reported in the next sub-section.

3.1. Power Consumption Measure

Power Consumption in a CMOS circuit is mainly due to *dynamic dissipation*, i.e., the one caused by the changes of values of the different logic gates. The power consumed by each logic gate [GDKW92] is given by the equation $P = ½ V_{dd}^2 C_{load} f_{CLK} N_{sw}$, where V_{dd} is the supply voltage, C_{load} is the output load capacitance of the gate, f_{CLK} is the clock frequency and N_{sw} is called the *switching activity* of the gate, and measures the *average* number of transitions per clock cycle. The switching activity of each gate can be computed [GDKW92] starting from the statistical distribution of input patterns and the circuit netlist.

For combinational circuits, input patterns are usually considered as uniformly distributed. In sequential circuits, the basic power estimation techniques of [GDKW92] are no longer sufficient, since the statistical distribution of present state inputs s_E is far from being uniform. Furthermore, the gate level netlist is not known until after logic synthesis and optimization, and in particular not at the state encoding step. Alternative, more approximate, solutions have therefore been developed for sequential circuits.

A first approximation considers the average number of flip flop changes over the whole state transition graph. Given the encoded state transition functions, one can count, for each state s_E and for each input x, the number of bits in which the next state y_E differs from the present one s_E. This measure is usually called the Hamming distance of the states, and has been adopted as an estimate of the global circuit switching activities in early re-encoding works [HHPP94]. The resulting switching activity measure can be written as:

$$N_{swFF} = \Sigma_{s_E x} |s_E \oplus y_E|. \quad (1)$$

We use the notation $|s_E \oplus y_E|$ to indicate the number of bits in which the binary vectors s_E and y_E differ, i.e., $|s_E \oplus y_E| = \text{count}_i(s_E[i] \neq y_E[i])$. The summation ranges over all the transitions in the state transition graph.

The Hamming distance implicitly assumes that all the states of the FSM are equally probable. In the reality, some states are visited more often than others. This effect can be taken into account by the *steady state probability* $\mathbf{P}(s)$ for the FSM to be in state s. This probability is dependent on the state transition graph, only, and is therefore not influenced by the encoding function E. The Hamming distance may therefore be weighted by using the steady state probability, so that the total number of flip flop changes is correctly measured. The switching estimation equation therefore becomes:

$$N_{swFF} = \Sigma_{s_E x} [\mathbf{P}(E^{(-1)}(s_E))\, |s_E \oplus y_E|]. \quad (2)$$

Power estimation measures analyzed so far implicitly assume that, for each flip flop change, the number of changes of the combinational logic is constant. In practice, even if we neglect the variation of C_{load} with fanout, some flip flops are fed by more complex or more active combinational cones, and feed a different portion of the circuit [TPCD94] [OlKa94]. The results of [VTRa95], for instance, show that, although N_{swFF} is reduced, the total power consumption can increase due to a different combinational network. They attribute this phenomenon to the increase in area of the combinational part, leading to a larger number of gates that dissipate power.

To estimate the combinational network size in a simple way, without making any hypothesis on the logic synthesis tool, we propose to compute the *support* of the input and output cones of each flip flop *i*. Given a flip flop *i*, we define as support of its input cone the number of combinational inputs (NCI(i)) that influence the flip flop ,and as support of its output cone the number of combinational outputs (NCO(i)) that are influenced by the flip flop (Fig. 3). Such measures do not need a synthesized netlist, and can be very easily computed with a BDD representation [Brya92] of the Boolean functions δ_E and λ_E. The size of the cones is then used as a weight associated to each flip flop that switches in each transition. The power estimation measure used within our algorithm is therefore:

$$PowEst = \Sigma_{s_E,x} \{ \mathbf{P}(E^{(-1)}(s_E)) \cdot \Sigma_i [(\mathrm{NCI}(i)+\mathrm{NCO}(i)) \cdot (s_E[i] \oplus y_E[i])] \} \quad (3)$$

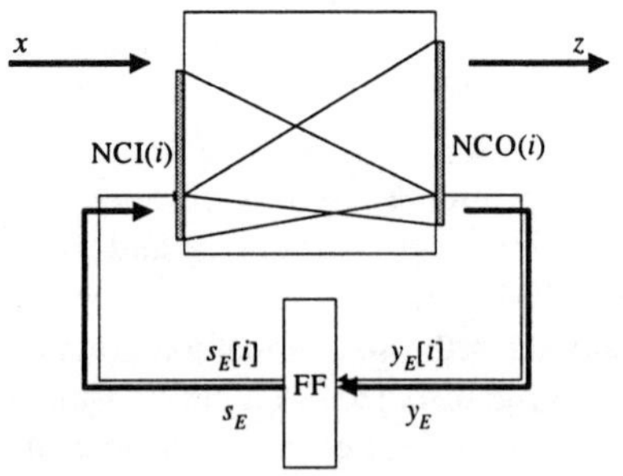

Figure 3: *definition of NCI and NCO*

The optimization algorithm presented in Section 4 uses equation (3) as a goal function to be minimized. Since we take into account the size of the cones, the power minimization algorithm will also aim at reducing the area occupation, as the experimental results will show. The accuracy of the estimate given by (3) will be proven by computing, on the final result, a precise power dissipation figure based on [MDLT94].

4. The Re-encoding Algorithm

In order to experimentally evaluate the effectiveness of the power estimation function (3), we devised an optimization algorithm able to find a good re-encoding for a Finite State Machine.

Fig. 4 reports the general structure of the algorithm. Our idea is to exploit a Genetic Algorithm, in order to explore the possible state encodings; then, for each of them, we estimate the power consumption of the related circuit by resorting to Symbolic Techniques. A first state encoding, computed as in [LiNe89], is used to initialize, at the beginning, both the genetic and the symbolic tools. Such encoding is generated to minimize area occupation of a multi-level logic implementation with no regards to power consumption.

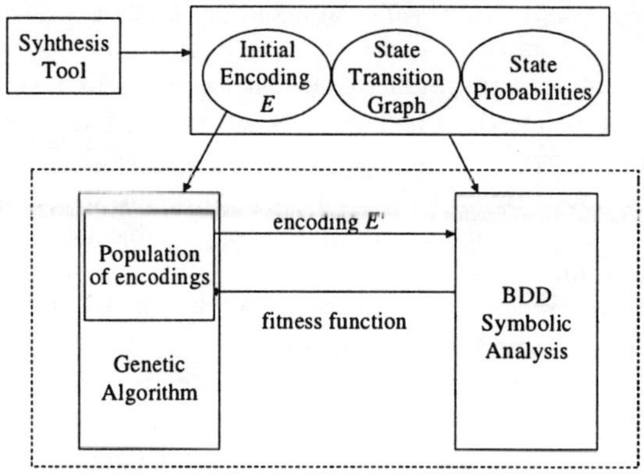

Figure 4: *Algorithm Architecture*

4.1. Genetic Tool

In our implementation, each *individual* of the *population* represents a particular state encoding function. Each *gene* corresponds to a given symbolic state, and the relevant gene values is the binary encoding associated to that state.

Starting from a set of binary encodings, the re-encoding problem consists of finding a different assignment of each binary encoding to the symbolic states of the STG. In our algorithm, the first population is generated by starting from the initial encoding *E* [LiNe89], and then repeatedly applying random perturbations to it.

Since we are looking for the best state encoding, we do not restrict the algorithm to the binary codes initially chosen by JEDI [LiNe89]; rather, we allow it to explore the whole $2^{\#FF}$ space.

The *evolution* mechanism inside the GA is performed by means of cross-over and mutation operators. The *selection* of individuals for reproduction is proportional to their ranking in the population. Once selected, two individuals generate a new encoding via a *cross-over* operator. It takes a random-length subset of codes from the first parent, the remaining ones from the second, and ensures that no code duplication occurs (one-cut order-based cross-over). A *mutation* operator is probabilistically applied, and consists in swapping two codes. If the newly generated individual has a higher fitness than the current worst one, it replaces it. To avoid losing the optimal solutions once they are generated, we use an *elitary* mechanism, by defining the number of best individuals in a generation that are copied to the new one.

The *fitness function* associated with each individual is obtained by estimating the power consumption for the circuit related to the given state encoding. The power dissipation evaluation is performed according to equation (3), and a symbolic manipulation library, developed at our institution, is used to compute the parameters of the equation.

4.2. Symbolic Tool

Whenever a GA is developed, its run-time effectiveness may be improved principally by reducing the computational cost of the fitness function.

In this context, since every new solution is a different state encoding, we need to estimate the power consumption of the corresponding circuit. A naive solution would be to re-synthesize the circuit down to the gate level whenever a new encoding was provided, and then extract the information on the input and output cones for each flip flop. However, experimental evidence demonstrates that this approach is not applicable, since too much CPU time is required. Besides, most information provided by re-synthesis is redundant in this application. In fact, we just need to estimate the dependencies between each flip flop and primary inputs and outputs, and no information on the internal structure of the combinational network of the circuit is needed.

To overcome the above limitation, we choose to compute the fitness function by exploiting Symbolic Techniques. A Symbolic approach consists in encoding of sets and relations as Boolean functions. The most efficient representation for Boolean function currently used is based on Binary Decision Diagrams (BDDs). In particular the class of BDDs known as Reduced Ordered BDDs are a very compact canonical representation and the time complexity for computing most Boolean operator is polynomial in the number of BDD nodes of the operands.

In the developed algorithm, the symbolic tool is initialized with both a initial state encoding E and the description of the combinational network corresponding to that encoding.

Then, from the structure of the circuit, for each flip flop i we extract the Boolean function representing the state transition function $\delta_E(s_E, x)[i]$, and, for each output j, the Boolean function representing the output function $\lambda_E(s_E, x)[j]$. A Boolean variable is assigned to each primary input and to each flip flop of the circuit, and we use BDDs to represent δ_E and λ_E. In the following, whenever a new state encoding is considered, the related state transition and output functions are computed by means of a re-encoding function: thanks to BDDs, we are able to completely avoid the re-synthesis of the circuit.

The procedure *compute_fitness*, sketched in Fig 5, is called by the genetic tool by passing as a parameter an individual of the population, i.e., a new state encoding E'. The first operation of the procedure consists in building a re-encoding function $RE{:}E \rightarrow E'$ (line 1). This is a Boolean function that maps every state of the STG, initially encoded as s_E, to a state encoded as $s_{E'}$. The function RE is invertible, with inverse function $RE^{-1}(s_{E'}, s_E){:}E' \rightarrow E$.

Once the re-encoding function RE is computed, for each flip flop i the new state transition is obtained as (line 3):

$$\delta_{E'}(s_{E'}, x)[i] = RE(\delta_E(RE^{-1}(s_{E'}), x)[i], x), \qquad (4)$$

and, similarly, for each primary output j the new output function is (line 5):

$$\lambda_{E'}(s_{E'}, x)[j] = \lambda_E(RE^{-1}(s_{E'}), x)[j]. \qquad (5)$$

Both computations are performed by resorting to the BDD operator *compose*.

At this point, all the information necessary to compute the support of the input and output cones of each flip flop is available. For each flip flop i, the procedures (line 6) and (line 7) count the number $NCI[i]$ of combinational inputs that influence it and the number $NCO[i]$ of combinational output that are influenced by it. Therefore, for a given flip flop i, we reason as follows:

- all the primary inputs and the flip flops that influence the value of the function $\delta_{E'}(s_{E'}, x)[i]$, belong to the input cone of the flip flop i;
- if a flip flop j is in the input cone of the flip flop i, then the flip flop i belongs to the output cone of the flip flop j;
- if a flip flop i influences the function $\lambda_{E'}(s_{E'}, x)[j]$, then the primary output j is in the output cone of the flip flop i.

To check whether a Boolean variable influences a function, i.e., whether it belongs to the support of a Boolean function, the BDD operator *smooth* is used.

Finally, once all the flip flops have been analyzed, the fitness function is obtained (line 8) according to equation (3) and the value is returned to the genetic tools (line 9).

5. Experimental results

We implemented the Re-Encoding Algorithm described in Section 4 as a prototypical tool consisting of two different Unix processes: the former containing the GA kernel and the latter executing symbolic computations, that communicate via Unix *named pipes*. The GA has been implemented in about 2,500 lines of C++. The Symbolic part has been implemented in about 800 lines of ANSI C, linking the BDD package developed at our institution and consisting of about 2,000 C code lines.

```
fitness_value compute_fitness(encoding E')
{
   re_encoding_function RE(sE, sE');
   vector_of_ functions δE(sE, x), δE'(sE', x);
   vector_of_functions λE'(sE', x), λE(sE, x);
   int NCI[#flip flops], NCO[#flip flops];
   int power_consumption;

1: RE(sE, sE') = compute_re_encoding (E,E');
2: for each flip flop i {
3:    δE'(sE', x)[i] = compute_new_δi
         (δE(sE, x)[i], RE(sE, sE'));
   }
4: for each primary output j {
      λE'(sE', x)[j] = compute_new_λj
         (λE(sE, x)[j], RE(sE,sE'));
   }
5: for each flip flop i {
6:    NCI[i] = compute_NCI(δE'(sE', x)[i]);
7:    NCO[i] = compute_NCO
         (δE'(sE', x)[i],λE'(sE', x));
   }
8: power_consumption =
      compute_power (NCI, NCO);
9: return( power_consumption - 1);
}
```

Figure 5: *Fitness Computation*

The experiments have been run on a Sun Sparcstation 5/110 with 64 MB of RAM and have been performed following the flow described in Fig. 6.

Initially, a first state encoding has generated with a synthesis tool. Our tool is integrated in the SIS [SSMS92] environment, since SIS is a synthesis tool widely used in the CAD field. SIS takes as an input the State Transition Graph of a circuit, assigns to it a state encoding, synthesizes it, and finally obtains its gate level description. Different programs are available in SIS environment to perform the state assignment. Among them, we selected JEDI [LiNe89], that looks for a state-encoding able to minimize the area of the circuit.

Starting from the JEDI encoding (computed in SIS with the script of Fig. 7), we run our Genetic-Symbolic algorithm, and compare the power and area of the final solution with the initial ones. The GA parameters, as they were set for experiments, are shown in Tab. 4.

Fig. 8 reports the sequence of SIS commands for power and area evaluation, once a state encoding is given. We use an internal library, named **pdt.genlib**, to perform the mapping operation. It contains D-type flip flops and simple single-output combinational gates (and, or, xor, ...) with up to 5 inputs, and for each of them attributes such as area, delay and so on are specified. Due to this customized library, we obtain slightly different values of area occupation and power consumption than other authors; therefore, we will base the assessment of our results on the relative improvement that we obtain, rather than absolute values. We gathered experimental data on a subset of the MCNC and ISCAS benchmarks whose characteristics are reported in Tab. 1. These circuits are typically used as reference for comparing different works in the automated synthesis and power optimization fields, among others.

As far as the effectiveness of our approach is concerned, Tab. 2 shows that the obtained results are very satisfactory, since significant improvements are attained in power consumption. Besides, for many examples, area occupation is reduced. In general, when power optimization drives the synthesis process, the area of the circuit is expected to grow, since area and power optimizations are contrasting requirements. However, thanks to the cone size parameters NCI and NCO, experimental results proved that we are often able to reduce the area occupation of the circuits.

To better understand the achieved results, the last two columns of Tab. 2 report some comparison data: all figures are in percent and measure the reduction of the reported quantity (power, area). In these columns, positive numbers indicate improvements. Our improvements with respect to the solution found by JEDI are in the average better than [VTRa95]: we have an average area increase of just 0.63% with respect to 4.45% and we feature a 16.61% reduction in power consumption with respect to 10.06%.

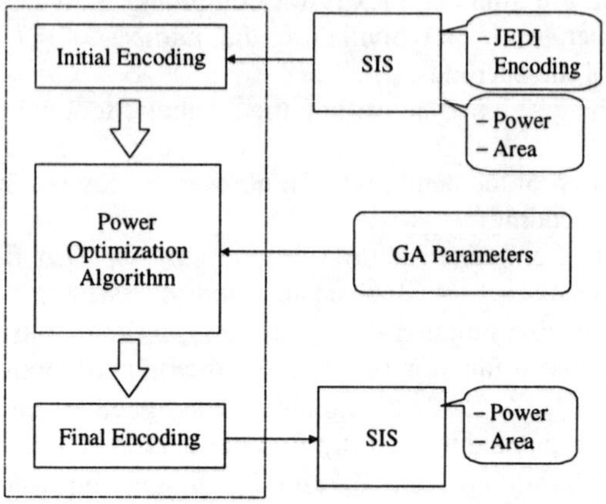

Figure 6: *Evaluation Flow*

```
read_kiss circuit.kiss
state_assign JEDI
write_blif circuit.blif
```

Figure 7: *SIS script for State Encoding*

```
read_blif circuit.blif
stg_to_network
source script.algebraic
power_estimate -t SEQUENTIAL \
               -s EXACT
read_library pdt.genlib
map -m 0
print_gate -s
```

Figure 8: *SIS script for Power Consumption and Area computation*

Tab. 3 reports the CPU time for the BDD manipulations and the GA, respectively. We want to stress that even on largest circuits, the required CPU time is acceptable. Therefore, by avoiding the re-synthesis step thanks to our Symbolic computations, we increase the run-time effectiveness of the algorithm, without reducing the quality of the results. By tuning the GA parameters, it is possible to suitably drive the trade-off among power consumption, area occupation and CPU time.

Circuit	#PI	#PO	states	#FF
pma	8	8	24	5
ex1	9	19	20	5
s386	7	7	13	4
keyb	7	2	19	5
dk16	2	3	27	5
styr	9	10	30	5
planet	7	19	48	6
s820	18	19	25	5
s1494	8	19	48	6
bbara	4	2	10	4

Table 1: *Benchmark Characteristics*

Circuit	Initial solution (JEDI)		Final solution (Our approach)		Decrease [%]	
	Area	Power [μW]	Area	Power [μW]	Area	Power [μW]
pma	374	946.8	323	628.8	13.64	33.59
ex1	427	862.9	426	721.8	0.23	16.35
s386	253	532.7	231	444.5	8.70	16.56
keyb	385	637.7	420	597.0	-9.09	6.38
dk16	459	1433.5	476	1417.8	-3.70	1.10
styr	826	1341.8	859	1238.0	-4.00	7.74
planet	987	2822.3	971	1625.0	1.62	42.42
s820	528	1220.9	508	819.4	3.79	32.89
s1494	1022	1168.8	1047	1016.3	-2.45	13.05
bbara	133	177.8	153	184.9	-15.04	-3.99
AVG.					*-0.63*	*16.61*

Table 2: *Power Consumption Optimization*

Circuit	CPU [s]	
	BDD	GA
pma	2574	42
ex1	3940	48
s386	1612	48
keyb	5185	36
dk16	992	48
styr	4226	42
planet	6577	32
s820	22507	40
s1494	12090	55
bbara	172	39

Table 3: *Run Time*

Parameter	Value
Maximum Number of Generations	170
Population Size	70
Elite size	4
Mutation activation frequency	50%
Crossover activation frequency	100%

Table 4: *GA Parameters*

6. Conclusions

This paper presents an optimization algorithm for reducing the power dissipation in sequential circuits, exploiting a Genetic Algorithm.

We propose the adoption of a novel power dissipation estimation measure to be used for sequential circuits. The measure is used within an optimization algorithm, based on Genetic Algorithms and symbolic BDD manipulations, to find the best re-encoding of the FSM states according to the desired trade-off point.

Experimental results show that the algorithm is able to provide better or comparable results than other, less flexible, approaches. The effectiveness of our approach also comes from the integration of symbolic techniques, that allow fast and exact Boolean computation to be integrated within the framework of Genetic Algorithms, thus exploiting the advantages of both exact and approximate algorithmic approaches.

Acknowledgments

The authors wish to thank R. Vietti for his contribution in the implementation of the Genetic Algorithm and in gathering the experimental results.

References

[Brya92] R. E. Bryant: *Symbolic Boolean Manipulation with Ordered Binary Decision Diagrams*, ACM Computing Surveys, Vol. 24, Nr. 3, 1992, pp. 293-318

[DeMi94] G. De Micheli, *Synthesis and Optimization of Digital Circuits*, McGraw-Hill, Princeton NJ, USA, 1994

[GDKW92] A. Ghosh, S. Devadas, K. Keutzer, J. White, *Estimation of Average Switching Activity in Combinational and Sequential Circuits*, proc. IEEE/ACM Design Automation Conference, June 1992, pp. 253-259

[HHPP94] G.D. Hachtel, M. Hermida, A. Pardo, M. Poncino, F. Somenzi, *Re-Encoding Sequential Circuits to Reduce Power Dissipation*, proc. IEEE/ACM Intl. Conf. on CAD, 1994, pp. 70-73

[Holl75] J.H. Holland, "Adaption in Natural and Artificial Systems," University of Michigan Press, Ann Arbor (USA), 1975

[LiNe89] B. Lin, A.R. Newton, *Synthesis fo Multiple-level Logic from Symbolic High-level Description Languages*, proc. IFIP Intl. Conference on Very Large Scale Integration, August 1989, pp. 187-196

[MDLT94] J. Monteiro, S. Devadas, B. Lin, C-.Y. Tsui, M. Pedram, A.M. Despain, *Exact and Approximate Methods for Switching Activity Estimation in Sequential Logic Circuits*, proc. IEEE Intl. Workshop on Low Power Design, April 1994, pp. 117-122

[MoDe97] J. Monteiro, S. Devadas, *Computer-Aided Design Techniques for Low Power Sequential Logic Circuits*, Kluwer Academic Publishers, Norwell MA, USA, 1997

[OlKa94] E. Olson, S.M. Kang, *Low-Power State Assignment for Finite State Machines*, proc. IEEE Intl. Workshop on Low Power Design, April 1995, pp. 63-68

[SSMS92] E.M. Sentovich, K.J. Singh, C. Moon, H. Savoj, R.K. Brayton, A. Sangiovanni-Vincentelli, *Sequential Circuit Design using Synthesis and Optimization*, proc. IEEE Intl. Conference on Computer Design, October 1992, pp. 238-333

[TPCD94] C.-Y. Tsui, M. Pedram, C.-A. Chen, A.M. Despain, *Low Power State Assignment Targeting Two- and Multi-level Logic Implementations*, proc. IEEE/ACM Intl. Conf. on CAD, 1994, pp. 82-87

[VTRa95] V. Veeramachaneni, A. Tyagi, S. Rajgopal, *Reencoding for Low Power State Assignment of FSMs*, proc. IEEE Intl. Symposium on Low Power Design, April 1995, pp. 173-178

[WWHW94] K. Wang, W. Wang, T. Hwang, A.C.H. Wu, Y. Lin, *State Assignment for Power and Area Minimization*, proc. IEEE/ACM Intl. Conf. on CAD, 1994, pp. 250-254

Session B.3

Logic Based Reasoning Systems

Session Chair:
Farokh Bastani, University of Houston, USA

Anytime Reasoning in First-Order Logic

Keith B. Vanderveen and C.V. Ramamoorthy *

Abstract

We propose a class of algorithms which gives best-efforts answers to problems in first-order logic given a bound on the resources available for reasoning. The algorithms in this class generate and attempt to solve S_1 *and* S_3 *approximations to the input problem, then use the results to determine the most likely solution to the input problem. We show that an algorithm in this class outperforms theorem provers which attempt to solve the problem directly.*

1 Introduction

First-order logic is used today in a variety of applications such as verification of hardware and software, solving resource allocation and scheduling problems [1], and answering queries posed to knowledge bases. However, the use of first-order logical reasoning in applications requiring real-time decision making has been inhibited because of the inability to give bounds on the resources needed to solve even very small problems.

For many real-time decision-making applications, it is necessary to make the best decision possible with limited resources for reasoning (usually the limited resource is time). For example, in content-based routing of messages between distributed intelligent agents, it is important to route the messages quickly, even if this means that some messages are misdelivered. Some errors can be tolerated in content-based routing, since it is commonly assumed that the routing process is unreliable anyway due to network problems [6].

*Keith B. Vanderveen and C.V. Ramamoorthy are with the Computer Science Division of the Department of Electrical Engineering and Computer Science at the University of California at Berkeley, Berkeley, CA 94024.

Algorithms which give best-efforts solutions to problems given bounds on the resources available for reasoning are known as anytime algorithms [10]. Such algorithms have the property that their best-efforts solutions to the problem improve by some metric as the resources for reasoning increase.

We propose a class of anytime algorithms for reasoning in first-order logic. Given a problem in first-order logic, an algorithm of this class generates and tries to solve approximations to the problem. A solution to the input problem may emerge during the process of solving the approximations. If no solution emerges, the algorithm uses the results of its attempts to solve the approximations to the input problem to determine the likelihood that the problem is satisfiable. The types of approximations which we use are S_1 and S_3 approximations, due to Schaerf and Cadoli [9].

The rest of this paper is organized as follows: Section 2 describes the problem which our algorithms solve, Section 3 describes S_1 and S_3 approximations and our extensions to them, Section 4 describes our class of algorithms and the particular algorithm which we have implemented, Section 5 describes our results, Section 6 presents our conclusions and ideas for future work, and Section 7 discusses related work.

2 Logical Reasoning and Satisfiability

In first-order logic, a domain is described in terms of *predicates* (also known as *relations*) on ordered tuples of *objects* in the domain. Objects are denoted by constant symbols or *variables*, and quantification is permitted over variables so that the expression $\forall x R(x)$, for example, means that the relation R holds for all objects in the domain. The logical connectives $\wedge, \vee, \rightarrow$ and the negation operator $\neg$ from propositional logic are used in the same manner in first-order logic. A *sentence* in first-order logic is an

1082-3409/97 $10.00 © 1997 IEEE

expression in which all of the variables are quantified over. For a more thorough explanation of first-order logic, see [8]. Throughout the rest of the paper, we will regard all variables appearing in sentences as being implicitly universally quantified and omit the quantifiers to improve readability.

Given a sentence in first-order logic, our algorithm attempts to determine whether or not the sentence is satisfiable. By satisfiable, we mean that there exists a model in which the sentence is true under some assignment of variables to objects in the model. All reasoning in first-order logic can be reduced to determining the satisfiability of sentences, since we can prove that a set of sentences T entails a sentence q ($T \models q$) by showing that $\wedge T \wedge \neg q$ is unsatisfiable, where $\wedge T$ is the conjunction of the sentences in T [8]. This method of proof is known as proof by refutation, and is the basis of most automated theorem proving techniques including resolution [8].

We say that sentence A is *weaker* than B if B is satisfiable only if A is, i.e. all models for B are also models for A. We say that sentence C is *stronger* than B if and only if B is weaker than C, i.e. all models for C are also models for B.

3 S_1 and S_3 Approximations

Schaerf and Cadoli introduced simple techniques of generating weaker and stronger approximations of sentences in propositional logic, modal logic, and fragments of first-order logic [9]. The weaker approximations are known as S_3 approximations, and the stronger approximations as S_1 approximations. We have extended S_1 and S_3 approximations to all sentences in first-order logic.

To understand S_1 and S_3 approximations for sentences in first-order logic, it is helpful to first consider these approximations for propositional sentences. The process of computing S_1 and S_3 approximations is particularly easy to describe for sentences which are in negated normal form (NNF), which means that all negations occur at the level of literals (propositions for propositional logic and occurrences of predicates for first-order logic). Any sentence can be converted to NNF in $O(nd)$ steps, where n is the number of literals and d is the maximum depth of nested conjunctions, disjunctions, or implications, by applying De Morgan's Laws [9].

An S_3 approximation is formed for a propositional sentence P in NNF by replacing all positive and negative occurrences of some set of propositional letters S by the truth value 'true'. For example, if P is the sentence $((p \vee q) \wedge r \wedge \neg q)$, then there is one positive and one negative occurrence of q in P. If $S = \{q\}$, then the S_3 approximation of P for the set S would be r, since both q and $\neg q$ would be set to 'true'. S_1 approximations are formed similarly, except that the occurrences of propositional letters in the set S are replaced by the truth value 'false' instead of 'true'. Thus, the S_1 approximation of P for the set S would be 'false' (since we replace both q and $\neg q$ with 'false', which renders the whole conjunction 'false').

Determining S_1 or S_3 approximations for a sentence in first-order logic is greatly simplified if, in addition to being in NNF, the sentence has only universal quantifiers which have the entire sentence as their scope. Any sentence can be put in this form, see [8] for details. S_1 and S_3 approximations for first-order sentences are computed in a fashion similar to that for propositional sentences, except that instead of replacing occurrences of propositional letters with 'true' or 'false', we replace occurrences of predicates. For example, consider the following sentence in which x and y are variables (implicitly universally quantified) and a and b are constants:

$$(P(x, y) \vee Q(a, x)) \wedge \neg R(y, b) \wedge Q(a, y) \wedge P(a, x)$$

If $S = \{R(y, b)\}$, then the S_3 approximation of the sentence would be 'true' and the S_1 approximation would be 'false'.

A complication with which we must deal in the case of approximations to first-order sentences concerns *variants*, which are occurrences of predicates which have the same arguments except for a change of variables. $Q(a, x)$ and $Q(a, y)$ in the above sentence are variants; $P(x, y)$ and $P(a, x)$ are not. Since all of the variables are universally quantified, variants of a literal must have exactly the same truth value as the literal. Therefore, we must treat all variants the same when we do S_1 or S_3 approximation. For example, if $S = \{Q(a, x)\}$, then the S_3 approximation for the above sentence becomes

$$P(x, y) \wedge \neg R(y, b) \wedge P(a, x)$$

because $Q(a, y)$ is also replaced by 'true'.

We have said that S_1 and S_3 approximations are respectively stronger and weaker sentences than the original sentence. This means that if we can prove that an S_1 approximation of a sentence is satisfiable, then the sentence itself must be satisfiable. Likewise if we can prove that an S_3 approximation is unsatisfiable, the sentence itself must be unsatisfiable. Because S_1 and S_3 approximations are strictly smaller than the original sentence, the hope is that they can be solved more quickly.

The intuition behind reasoning with S_1 and S_3 approximations is that certain information is ignored in the reasoning process. The ignored information is precisely that contained in the set S of literals which are set to 'true' or 'false' [9].

4 Algorithm

We have implemented an algorithm which attempts to determine the satisfiability of a sentence by analyzing S_1 and S_3 approximations to gather evidence. If the algorithm has not proved the sentence to be satisfiable or unsatisfiable when the time given for a solution has expired, it makes a guess based on the evidence it has gathered. Our present implementation takes input sentences which are in conjunctive normal form (CNF), in which a sentence is a conjunction of disjunctions of literals (the disjunctions are called *clauses*). Any sentence can be transformed into an equivalent CNF sentence [8].

The overall algorithm uses a theorem prover to attempt to determine the satisfiability of the S_1 and S_3 approximations it considers. We have chosen to use a theorem prover based on the partial instantiation technique [11], but any theorem prover for first-order logic would be suitable.

Obviously, if the algorithm finds an S_3 approximation that is unsatisfiable or an S_1 approximation that is satisfiable, it will have solved the problem immediately, so our concern is how to interpret an S_1 approximation that is unsatisfiable or an S_3 approximation that is satisfiable. Our approach is to treat such an event, which we call a *partial result*, as evidence pointing to the problem being satisfiable (if an S_3 approximation is found satisfiable) or unsatisfiable (if an S_1 approximation is found unsatisfiable). The algorithm assigns weights to partial results according to the size of the set S of literals which were ignored, weighting partial results with smaller S more highly than those with larger S. The algorithm keeps track of the weights accumulated in favor of satisfiability and unsatisfiability as it proceeds, and it guesses according to which possibility has accumulated more weight when time has expired.

To decide how much weight to assign to a partial result, we observed that S_1 and S_3 approximations form partially ordered sets above and below the original sentence, where 'is stronger than' is the ordering relation. Two S_1 approximations or two S_3 approximations can be compared with this relation if the set S of ignored literals used to generate one approximation is contained in the set S of the other. Knowing the status of an S_3 approximation is worth more than knowing the status of all the approximations which are weaker than it, since these are all S_3 approximations to it. Similarly, knowing the status of an S_1 approximation is worth more than knowing the status of all approximations stronger than it. To reflect this fact, we chose to set the weight of a partial result of an approximation with $\mid S \mid= d$ to be $\frac{(k-d)!}{(k-1)!}$, where k is the number of literals in the original sentence. This results in a slight overestimation of the value of an approximation relative to an approximation which is closer to the original sentence by one literal, but it seems intuitively to be close to being correct.

The search strategy of the algorithm is a form of bounded depth-first search, where the depth is the size of S. The search is bounded both in terms of depth and in terms of time: the algorithm considers an approximation in which only one literal is ignored, then ignores other literals one at a time until either the maximum depth is reached or the time for exploring the branch is exhausted. The algorithm calculates the time to spend exploring each branch by dividing the total time given to solve the problem by the number of literals (exclusive of variants) in the input sentence. Equal time is given to exploring S_1 and S_3 approximations.

The algorithm explores every approximation in which only one literal is ignored, except in cases where it is obvious that the result would be unhelpful (such as setting a literal to 'false' which appears in a clause containing only that literal). If the algorithm proceeds to explore deeper beneath a one-literal approximation, it chooses other literals to ignore in a manner which gives preference to literals which haven't participated in partial results yet. This is accomplished by weighting the literals using the same magnitudes of weights as is used to weight the partial results, and choosing literals with low weights in the selection process. This keeps the algorithm from exploring S_3 approximations which are weaker, or S_1 approximations which are stronger, than those which have already been solved.

There are two types of sentences which cause difficulty for the algorithm. The first type of sentence is one where there are clauses with very few literals, such as a unit clause (i.e. a clause which consists of just one literal). Such a sentence may be satisfiable, but most S_1 approximations will be trivially unsatisfiable because some small clause will be set to 'false' because all of its literals have been set to 'false'. Fortunately, we can easily detect when a small clause is set to 'false' in an S_1 approximation, and the algorithm doesn't count such trivially unsatisfiable approximations in accumulating evidence for the input sentence's status.

A more difficult problem is posed by unsatisfiable sentences for which a contradiction is derivable from a large set of clauses, but for which no contradiction can be derived if any one clause in the set is missing. For such a sentence, it is possible for every S_3 approximation to be satisfiable (because an S_3 approximation always replaces at least one clause with the value 'true', which would break up the contradiction), but every S_1 approximation would be unsatisfiable. Thus, no useful information would be gained from examining the S_1 or S_3 approximations of such a sentence. We do not have a solution to this problem at present.

To cope with the two kinds of pathological sentences mentioned above, our algorithm as currently implemented reserves a portion of the time given to solve a problem for direct consideration of the input sentence.

5 Results

We tested the anytime first-order reasoning algorithm on a set of 108 first-order logic problems from the Thousands of Problems for Theorem Provers (TPTP) problem library, v1.2.1 [2]. The 108 problems were chosen to provide balance in the number of satisfiable and unsatisfiable problems, with 54 of each. There are 59 known satisfiable problems in v1.2.1 of the TPTP, and our parser for the problem representation language broke down for 5 of them, so we included the 54 others in our test set. The 54 unsatisfiable problems were chosen at random from the 1590 known unsatisfiable problems in v1.2.1 of the TPTP.

Figure 1 shows the fraction of problems in the test set which the anytime algorithm classifed correctly as a function of time. For comparison, we also show the fraction classified correctly by using the theorem prover used in the anytime algorithm to try to solve the problem directly. The anytime algorithm examines approximations as described in section 4 for 90given to solve the problem, then it tries to solve the problem directly in the remaining 10problem already. If the problem is still unsolved when time has expired, the anytime algorithm makes an educated guess on the basis of the results of testing approximations, as described in section 4. If no evidence has been accumulated, the anytime algorithm guesses randomly. The direct algorithm spends all of the given time trying to solve the problem directly, and if the problem is still unsolved when time expires, it guesses randomly.

We see from Figure 1 that the anytime algorithm classifies more problems correctly throughout the range of times examined except for the intervals of 3-15s and 20-25s. The curve for the anytime algorithm is also much more jagged than the curve for the direct algorithm. We believe that the greater jaggedness of the anytime curve is due to the fact that it examines many approximations for each problem, and the solution of just one approximation can tip the balance of evidence from one status for the problem to the other in a short interval of additional computing time. The curve for the direct algorithm is more steady, by contrast, because a small increment of additional computing time is less likely to make a difference in whether a problem can be solved.

Figure 2 shows the fraction of random guesses made by the anytime algorithm and the direct algorithm. We see from this figure that the anytime algorithm is able to avoid guesing randomly very quickly compared to the direct algorithm. Figure 3 shows the fraction of the problem set which each algorithm was able to prove as

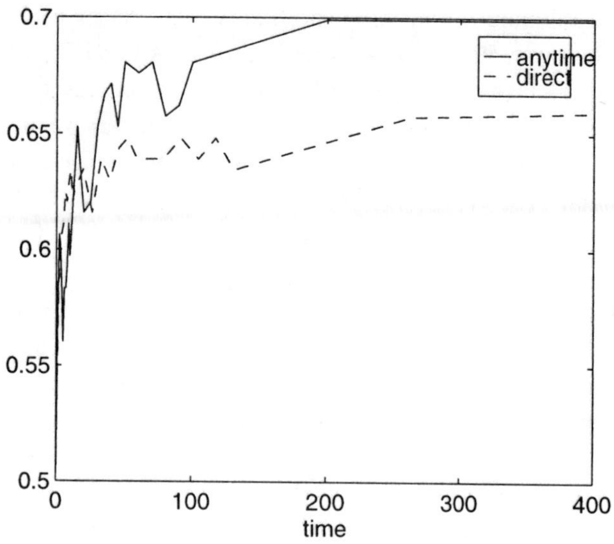

Figure 1. Fraction of problems classified correctly by anytime and direct algorithms

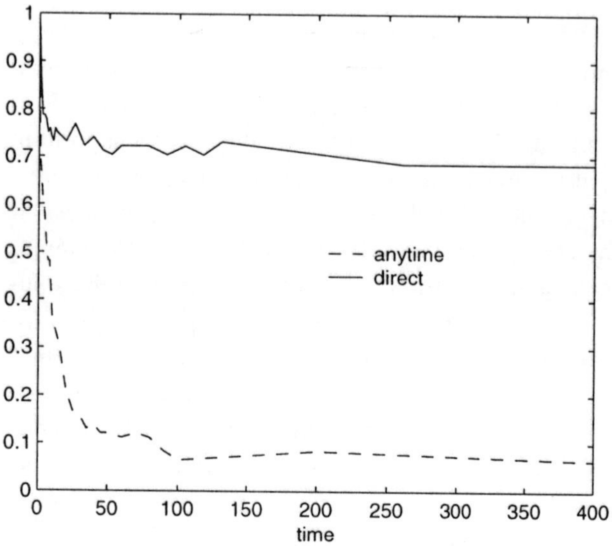

Figure 2. Fraction of random guesses made by anytime and direct algorithms

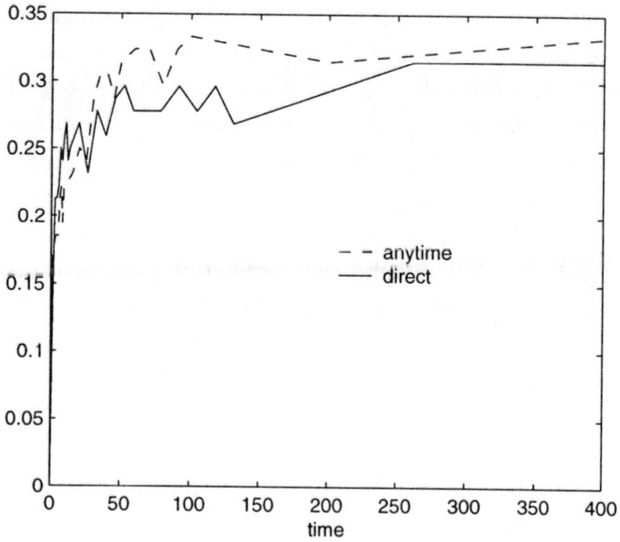

Figure 3. Fraction of proofs by anytime and direct algorithms

a function of time. After about 30s or so, the anytime algorithm is actually able to prove more problems by considering approximations than the direct algorithm is by attacking the problems directly. However, the overall fraction of proofs found by the anytime algorithm remains below .35, so the reduction in random guesses seen in Figure 2 is due mostly to an increase in educated guesses.

Figure 4 shows the fraction of educated guesses made by the anytime algorithm which were correct as a function of time. For times less than about 20s, the evidence is of such poor quality that the educated guesses are little better than random, and their correctness gyrates wildly. After 20s, however, the educated guesses tend to be right more than half the time. The educated guesses tend to be biased in favor of unsatisfiability by a ratio of 6 to 1 for all times greater than 100, but whether this is a bias of the algorithm or an artifact of the problem set hasn't been determined yet.

6 Conclusions

The results show that algorithms which examine S_1 and S_3 approximations can outperform algorithms using the same theorem prover which directly attack the problem, at least for some problem sets. We believe these results should generalize for all theorem provers,

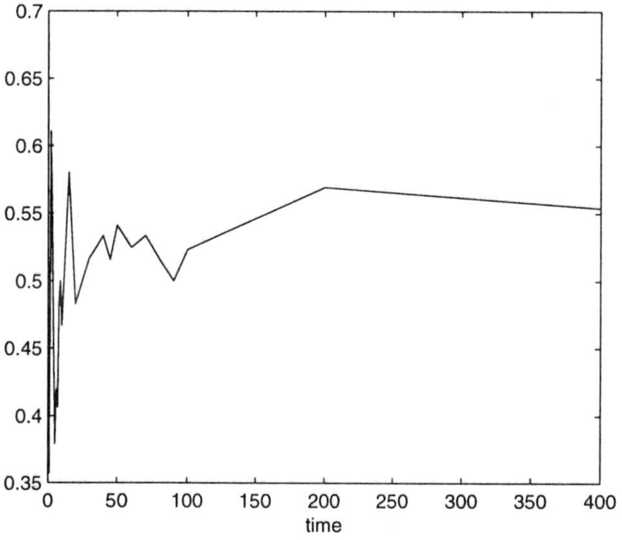

Figure 4. Fraction of correct educated guesses for anytime algorithm

because S_1 and S_3 approximations have fewer literals than the original sentence and all theorem provers of which we are aware would solve them faster than the original sentence most of the time.

We believe that the performance of the educated guesses made by the anytime algorithm can be improved. One possible improvement would be to reduce the weight given to partial results of unsatisfiability relative to the weight given to partial results of satisfiability, so as to eliminate the bias in the educated guesses in favor of unsatisfiability. The relative weights for partial results of different types could be adjusted by the algorithm itself by comparing the results of problems it has solved with the educated guesses it would have made for such problems. This would allow the algorithm to tune itself to perform better for different problem sets.

Other parameters of the anytime algorithm can be adjusted as well, such as the bound on the depth of approximations explored (the size of the set S of ignored literals) and the proportion of time reserved for direct consideration of input sentences. We are currently exploring these possibilities.

We see broad applicability for algorithms of this type in many time- or resource-constrained applications in which theorem provers are currently used. For example, semantic routing of messages by matchmakers or facilitators is currently accomplished using theorem provers [7]. As we noted in the introduction, this is a time-sensitive application. Other potential applications include time-sensitive scheduling and resource allocation, and real-time planning.

7 Related Work

Horvitz and Klein have explored theorem proving for propositional logic with limited resources [3]. If their algorithm has failed to find to prove that a sentence is satisfiable after the time allotted to solve the problem has expired, the algorithm determines the probabilities that the sentence is satisfiable or unsatisfiable from the portion of the search space explored. Horvitz and Klein have suggested that a simliar approach could be fruitful for first-order logic.

The term "anytime algorithm" was introduced by Dean and Boddy in the context of their study of time-dependent planning algorithms [10]. Work on reasoning about beliefs and actions under resource constraints was done by Horvitz [5]. Horvitz and others have also studied the tradeoff between action and continued reasoning in time-critical systems [4].

References

[1] D.B.Sturgill A.M.Segre. Using hundreds of workstations to solve first-order logic problems. In *Twelfth National Conference on Artifical Intelligence*, Cambridge, Massachussets, July-August 1994.

[2] C.B.Suttner and G.Sutcliffe. ATP system results for the TPTP problem library. Technical Report AR-96-02,96/09, Institut fur Informatik,Munchen and Dept. of Computer Science, James Cook University, Australia, 1996.

[3] A. Klein E. Horvitz. Reasoning, metareasoning, and mathematical truth: Studies of theorem proving under limited resources. In *Proceedings of the Eleventh Conference on Uncertainty in Artificial Intelligence*, Montreal, Canada, August 1995.

[4] G. Rutledge E. Horvitz. Time-dependent utility and action under uncertainty. In *Proceedings of*

Seventh Conference on Uncertainty in Artificial Intelligence, Los Angeles, CA, 1991.

[5] E. Horvitz. Reasoning about beliefs and actions under computational resource constraints. In *Proceedings of the Third Workshop on Uncertainty in Artificial Intelligence*, Seattle, WA, 1987.

[6] D. Kuokka and L. Harada. A communication infrastructure for concurrent engineering. *Journal of Artificial Intelligence in Engineering, Design, Analysis, and Manufacturing*, 1995.

[7] M.A.Syed M.R.Genesereth, N.P.Singh. A distributed and anonymous knowledge sharing approach to software interoperation. In *International Symposium on Fifth Generation Compution Systems*, pages 125–139, 1994.

[8] S. Russell and P. Norvig. *Artificial Intelligence: A Modern Approach*. Prentice-Hall, 1995.

[9] M. Schaerf and M. Cadoli. Tractable reasoning via approximation. *Artificial Intelligence*, 74:249–310, 1995.

[10] M. Boddy T. Dean. An analysis of time-dependent planning. In *Proceedings AAAI-88 Seventh National Conference on Artificial Intelligence*, 1988.

[11] M. Yamamoto, T. Ohyanagi, and A. Ohuchi. Theorem proving based on the partial instantiation technique. *Transactions of the Institute of Electronics, Information and Communication Engineers A*, J78-A(7):864–71, July 1995.

An Automatic Partial Deduction System for Constraint Logic Programs

Yi Tao and William I. Grosky
Department of Computer Science
Wayne State University
Detroit, MI 48202
(e-mail: yit, grosky@cs.wayne.edu)

Chunnian Liu
Department of Computer Science
Beijing Polytechnic University
Beijing 100022, P.R. China
(e-mail: bpvliu@public.bta.net.cn)

Abstract

This paper presents a new procedure of partial deduction of various constraint logic programs. The procedure takes a program-goal pair (P_0, Q_0) as input and outputs a resultant program-goal pair (P_n, Q_n). The procedure always terminates and the computational equivalence of the program-goal pairs (P_0, Q_0) and (P_n, Q_n) is preserved. P_n is more efficient in solving Q_n than P_0 in solving Q_0. Our procedure is based on the idea of program transformation, using transformation rules such as unfolding, constraint simplification, code deletion with respect to a goal, introduction of a newly defined clause, *and* folding. *We have implemented the procedure in an integrated partial deduction system, which can work with Prolog, CLP(Bool), and CLP(R) programs. Our results are compared with those resulting from other partial deduction methods, and it is shown that our method generates more succinct and efficient resultant programs in general.*

1 Introduction

Constraint logic programming (CLP) and partial deduction (PD) or partial evaluation (PE) are relatively new and active research fields in logic programming. In 1987, J.Jaffar and J.-L.Lassez [1] developed the constraint logic programming scheme CLP(D), which defines a class of languages based on the paradigm of rule-based constraint programming. Each instance of this scheme is a programming language and is obtained by the specification of the structure of the computation domain. The outstanding aspect of this class is that all the languages are soundly based within a single framework of formal semantics. For example, if the structure R is such that the constraints are relations over real arithmetic terms with uninterpreted functors, we get an instance of the CLP(R) language. Similarly, we can get other constraint logic programming languages such as CLP(Bool), if the domain is Boolean, and CLP(FD), if the domain is finite. In fact, Prolog is also an instance of this scheme, which restricts the domain to the Herbrand universe. In 1981, Komorowski first introduced partial evaluation into the area of logic programming. Lloyd and Shepherdson [2] developed the theoretical foundation of partial deduction for Prolog programs, and some implemented partial evaluators have been reported [4-7]. On the other hand, research on partial deduction of other constraint logic programs has just begun. As far as we know, there is only one paper concerning the partial deduction of CLP [3] besides our own work [8, 9].

With respect to (wrt) problem solving, partial deduction produces a specialized resultant program with respect to the input program and goal. With respect to program transformation, given an input program-goal pair (P_0, Q_0), partial deduction produces a series of program-goal pairs (P_1, Q_1), ..., (P_n, Q_n), with (P_n, Q_n) called the *resultant program-goal pair.* Partial deduction should guarantee termination and the computational equivalence of the program-goal pairs (P_0, Q_0) and (P_n, Q_n) should be preserved. Also, P_n is more efficient in solving Q_n than P_0 in solving Q_0.

The partial deduction procedure for constraint logic programs we present in this paper is based on the idea of program transformation. It is a natural extension of our new method of partial deduction of Prolog programs [10]. We have implemented the procedure on a Sun SPARC workstation for three languages: Prolog, CLP(Bool), and CLP(R), and the integrated partial evaluator is called CLP-PE, which provides our Constraint Logic Programming System [11] with a tool of optimizing programs.

The outline of this paper is as follows. In the next section, we briefly introduce the concepts of partial

1082-3409/97 $10.00

deduction and computational equivalence. Section 3 gives the formal definitions of the program transformation rules employed in our partial deduction procedure. In Section 4 we present the core algorithm of our partial deduction procedure for constraint logic programs and discuss its computational equivalence and termination issues. Section 5 shows running examples of partial deduction of CLP(Bool) and CLP(R) programs, and the partially evaluated results are compared with those resulting from other partial deduction methods. Finally, we give some conclusions and topics for further research.

2 PD(PE) and Computational Equivalence

Lloyd and Shepherdson in [2] describe partial evaluation as follows: "Given a program P and a goal G, partial evaluation produces a new program P', which is P 'specialized' to the goal G. The intention is that G should have the same (correct and computed) answers wrt P and P', and that G should run more efficiently for P' than for P. The basic technique for obtaining P' from P is to construct 'partial' search trees for P and suitably chosen atoms as goals, and then extract P' from the definitions associated with the leaves of these trees."

The computational equivalence of the original program P and partially evaluated program P' with respect to the goal G means that any answer computed by P with respect to G is also correctly computed by P' with respect to G (completeness) and conversely (soundness).

In [2], it is concluded that partial evaluation for definite programs and goals is always sound, but may not be complete, and for normal programs (i.e., those in which negation is allowed), partial evaluation is generally not only incomplete, but also unsound. However, for normal programs and goals, if the coveredness (Let **P** be a normal program, **G** a normal goal, **A** a finite set of atoms, **P'** a partial deduction of **P** with respect to **A**, and **P*** the subprogram of **P'** consisting of the definitions of predicate symbols in **P'** on which **G** depends. We say that **P'** $\cup$ {G} is *A-covered* if **P*** $\cup$ {G} is A-closed.) and independence (Let **S** be a finite set of atoms. We say that **S** is *independent* if no pair of atoms in **S** have a common instance.) conditions are satisfied, the computational equivalence of the original and partially evaluated programs will be ensured. The detailed theorems and their proofs can also be found in [2].

3 Transformation Rules for CLP Programs

In this section a brief introduction of the syntax and semantics of CLP languages is given, and then we present the formal definitions of the program transformation rules employed in our partial deduction procedure.

Constraint logic programming languages, similar to Prolog, comply with the syntax of Horn clauses. The CLP program and goal have the following forms:

fact clause:	**a(...).**
rule clause:	**a(...) :- b_1(...), ..., b_n(...).**
query clause:	**?- b_1(...), ..., b_n(...).**

where **a(...)**, which is called the *head* of the clause, is an atom. b_i ($1 \le i \le n$), which is called a *subgoal*, is an atom or a constraint. **b_1(...),...,b_n(...)** is called the *body* of the clause. An atom with predicate symbol **p** of arity m has the form of **p(X_1,...,X_m)**, and **X_1,...,X_m** are terms. Constraints depend on the constraint domain D and the operations on D. For example, **X = false .or. Y** is a boolean constraint; **X > 3+Y+7** is an arithmetic constraint.

A CLP program is a finite set of fact and rule clauses. A CLP goal is a query clause. The CLP scheme adopts the resolution theorem proving which is similar to Prolog, but it replaces syntactic unification over the Herbrand universe in Prolog with semantic unification over the intended domain of discourse. A complete description of the syntax and semantics of CLP languages can be found in [1].

3.1 Unfolding

Let CLP program $\mathbf{P_k}$ be a set of clauses $\{\mathbf{E_1,...,E_r, C, D_1,...,D_n}\}$, where clause **C** is of the form **H :- Before, A, After.**, for **A** an atom, and **Before** and **After** the conjunction of possibly empty subgoals. Assume that:

a) **A** is unifiable with any head hd($\mathbf{D_i}$), $1 \le i \le n$, of $\mathbf{D_1,...,D_n}$, and θ_i is the most general unifier (mgu) of **A** and hd($\mathbf{D_i}$).
b) Clause $\mathbf{C_i}$ is **(H :- Before, bd($\mathbf{D_i}$), After)**θ_i., where **bd($\mathbf{D_i}$)** is the body of $\mathbf{D_i}$, for $1 \le i \le n$.

Then we say that $\mathbf{C_1,...,C_n}$ results from *unfolding* **A** in **C** wrt $\mathbf{D_1,...,D_n}$. CLP program $\mathbf{P_{k+1}} = \{\mathbf{E_1,...,E_r, C_1,...,C_n, D_1,...,D_n}\}$ is the result of this unfolding of $\mathbf{P_k}$.

3.2 Constraint Simplification

Let CLP program $\mathbf{P_k}$ be a set of clauses $\{\mathbf{E_1,...,E_r, C}\}$, where clause **C** is of the form **H :– Before, A, After.**, for **A** a constraint, and **Before** and **After** the conjunction of possibly empty subgoals. Assume that:

a) **A** can be simplified to **A'**. For example, **X=false .xor. Y** can be simplified to **X = Y**, and **X > 3+Y+7** can be simplified to **X > Y+10**.
b) Clause **C'** is **H :– Before, A', After**.

Then we say that **C'** results from *simplifying* **A** in **C**. CLP program $\mathbf{P_{k+1}}$ = {$\mathbf{E_1,...,E_r}$, **C'**} is the result of this simplification of $\mathbf{P_k}$.

We note that if the constraint is the form **X=Y**, in which **X** is a variable and **Y** is either a constant or a variable, the simplified clause **C'** will be **(H :– Before, After){X/Y}.**. In this case, the transformation is a special form of constraint simplification, called *instantiation broadcasting*.

3.3 Code Deletion with Respect to a Goal

Let CLP program $\mathbf{P_k}$ be a set of clauses {$\mathbf{E_1,...,E_r,C_1,...,C_s}$}, and goal $\mathbf{Q_k}$ of the form **?-**$\mathbf{G_1,...,G_n}$**.**. Assume that:

a) The dependency graph of $\mathbf{P_k}$ is the same as that of the program resulting from omitting the constraints in $\mathbf{P_k}$.
b) According to $\mathbf{P_k}$'s dependency graph, $\mathbf{E_1,...,E_r}$ are all of the clauses on which $\mathbf{Q_k}$ depends.

Then we say that $\mathbf{C_1,...,C_s}$ are useless in computing answers by $\mathbf{P_k}$ with respect to $\mathbf{Q_k}$. CLP program $\mathbf{P_{k+1}}$ = {$\mathbf{E_1,...,E_r}$} is the result of deleting code $\mathbf{C_1,...,C_s}$ with respect to $\mathbf{Q_k}$ from program $\mathbf{P_k}$.

3.4 Introduction of a Newly Defined Clause

Let CLP program $\mathbf{P_k}$ be a set of clauses {$\mathbf{E_1,...,E_r}$, **C**}, where **C** is of the form **H :-** $\mathbf{B_1,...,B_m}$**.**, and goal $\mathbf{Q_k}$ of the form **?-** $\mathbf{G_1,...,G_n}$**.**. For Case 1, assume that:

a) $\mathbf{X_1,...,X_w}$ are all the distinct variables in $\mathbf{Q_k}$.
b) Clause **N** is **new**($\mathbf{X_1,...,X_w}$) **:-** $\mathbf{G_1,...,G_n}$**.**.

Then we say that introducing the newly defined clause with respect to $\mathbf{Q_k}$ results in **N**. CLP program $\mathbf{P_{k+1}}$ = {$\mathbf{E_1,...,E_r}$, **C**, **N**} is the result of introducing the newly defined clause into $\mathbf{P_k}$. $\mathbf{Q_{k+1}}$ is **new**($\mathbf{X_1,...,X_w}$).

For Case 2, assume that:

a) $\mathbf{X_1,...,X_w}$ are all the distinct variables in $\mathbf{B_i,...,B_j}$, for $1 \le i \le j \le m$.
b) Clause **N** is **new**($\mathbf{X_1,...,X_w}$) **:-** $\mathbf{B_i,...,B_j}$**.**.

Then we say that introducing newly defined clause with respect to $\mathbf{B_i,...,B_j}$ of **C** results in **N**. CLP program $\mathbf{P_{k+1}}$ = {$\mathbf{E_1,...,E_r}$, **C**, **N**} is the result of introducing the newly defined clause into $\mathbf{P_k}$.

We note that in our implemented partial evaluator, all of the predicate symbols of the heads (atoms) of these newly defined clauses are introduced dynamically as distinct names, e.g., new_1, new_2,....

3.5 Folding

Let CLP program $\mathbf{P_k}$ be a set of clauses {$\mathbf{E_1,...,E_r}$, **C**, **D**}, where **C** is of the form **H :-** $\mathbf{B_1,...,B_m}$**.**, and **D** is of the form $\mathbf{F_q}$ **:-** $\mathbf{S_1,...,S_w}$**.**. Assume that:

a) $\mathbf{B_i,...,B_j}$, for $1 \le i \le j \le m$, and $j-i+1 = w$, is an instance of $\mathbf{S_1,...,S_w}$. That is, a substitution θ exists such that {$\mathbf{S_1,...,S_w}$}θ = {$\mathbf{B_i,...,B_j}$}.
b) **D** is the only clause in $\mathbf{P_k}$.
c) All the distinct variables of $\mathbf{S_1,...,S_w}$ appear in $\mathbf{F_q}$.
d) Clause **C'** is **H :-** $\mathbf{B_1,...,B_{i-1}}$, {$\mathbf{F_q}$}θ , $\mathbf{B_{j+1},...,B_m}$.

Then we say that **C'** results from *folding* $\mathbf{B_i,...,B_j}$ of **C** by **D**. CLP program $\mathbf{P_{k+1}}$ = {$\mathbf{E_1,...,E_r}$, **D**, **C'**} is the result of this folding of P_k.

4 The Partial Deduction Procedure

We present a new and general partial deduction procedure for constraint logic programs in this section. This procedure is based on the idea of program transformation, employing the transformation rules introduced in Section 3. It inputs a program-goal pair ($\mathbf{P_0}$, $\mathbf{Q_0}$), outputs a resultant program-goal pair ($\mathbf{P_n}$, $\mathbf{Q_n}$), and always terminates. The computational equivalence of the program-goal pairs ($\mathbf{P_0}$, $\mathbf{Q_0}$) and ($\mathbf{P_n}$, $\mathbf{Q_n}$) is preserved. $\mathbf{P_n}$ is more efficient in solving $\mathbf{Q_n}$ than $\mathbf{P_0}$ in solving $\mathbf{Q_0}$. We have implemented this procedure for three languages: Prolog, CLP(Bool), and CLP(R), and the integrated partial evaluator is called CLP-PE.

4.1 Core Algorithm of CLP-PE

Main Procedure CLP_PE($\mathbf{P_0}$, $\mathbf{Q_0}$, $\mathbf{P_n}$, $\mathbf{Q_n}$**)**
% Input Parameters: a program-goal pair ($\mathbf{P_0}$, $\mathbf{Q_0}$).
%Output Parameters: a resultant program-goal pair ($\mathbf{P_n}$, $\mathbf{Q_n}$).
% Local Procedure: gen_resultant($\mathbf{P_n}$, **A**, $\mathbf{\Phi_R}$).

BEGIN_CLP_PE
{
1.Introduce newly defined clause N wrt Q_n:
1.1. **n := 0;**
% **n** is the subscript of program-goal pairs and its initial value is **0**.
1.2. ($\mathbf{P_n}$,$\mathbf{Q_n}$) is transformed by introducing newly defined clause **N** wrt $\mathbf{Q_n}$ to obtain ($\mathbf{P_{n++}}$,$\mathbf{Q_{n++}}$);
1.3. Establish a well-structured set $\mathbf{\Phi_L}$ of predicate symbols wrt $\mathbf{P_n}$ and the user;

% Φ_L is well-structured wrt P_n if, whenever $r \in \Phi_L$ and there exists a clause in P_n with the form of **q(...) :- ..., r(...), ...,** then $q \in \Phi_L$.

1.4. Φ_F := {N}; % Φ_F is a set of clauses resulting from the transformation of introducing the newly defined clause.

1.5. Φ_A := {**the head of clause N**}; % Φ_A is a set of atoms which are the heads of the clauses in Φ_F.

2. Partially deduce each atom in Φ_A by the transformation rules of unfolding, constraint simplification, folding, and introducing newly defined clauses wrt the clause body:

while $\Phi_A \neq \varnothing$ *do*

2.1. **A** is some atom in Φ_A; $\Phi_A := \Phi_A - \{A\}$;

2.2. **gen_resultant**(P_n, **A**, Φ_R);

% Φ_R is returned by unfolding and simplifying clause **A :- A.** wrt program P_n, similar to the set of resultants resulting from partially deducting pure Prolog in [2]. Its complete description will be given later in this section.

2.3. Transform Φ_R to Φ_R';

% Each clause C_i in Φ_R is transformed to clause C_i' in Φ_R' by folding subgoals of the clause body and then introducing the new clause if needed. The head of C_i' is the same as that of C_i, but each subgoal G_j of the clause body is transformed to G_j' as follows:

if G_j is an atom and G_j is foldable by some clause of the form **F:-G.** in Φ_F

then

$G_j' := F\theta$ (θ is the substitution from the folding.);

else if G_j is an atom and the predicate symbol of $G_j \in \Phi_L$

then

Introduce the newly defined clause **C** wrt G_j of C_i, and let **C** be of the form of **new(...) :-** G_j.;

G_j' := the head of clause **C**;

% Enlarge the following global sets:

$\Phi_A := \Phi_A \cup \{G_j'\}$; $\Phi_F := \Phi_F \cup \{C\}$;

$\Phi_L := \Phi_L \cup$ {**the predicate symbol of** G_j'};

$P_{n++} := P_n \cup \{C\}$; $Q_{n++} := Q_n$;

else

$G_j' := G_j$;

2.4. $\Phi_P := \Phi_P \cup \Phi_R'$;

% Φ_R' results from transformations wrt atom **A**.

end_of_while

3. $Q_{n++} := Q_n$;

% Replace Φ_F in P_n with Φ_P to obtain P_{n++}.

$P_{n++} := (P_n - \Phi_F) \cup \Phi_P$;

4. Delete useless code from P_n wrt Q_n to obtain resultant program-goal pair (P_{n++},Q_{n++});

}

END_CLP_PE

Local Procedure: **gen_resultant**(**P**, **A**, Φ_R)

% Purpose: clause **A :- A.** is transformed in finite times via unfolding and constraint simplification to obtain clause set Φ_R wrt program **P**.

% Input: **P** is a program; **A** is an atom.

% Output: Φ_R is a set of clauses.

Two functions used in **gen_resultant** are as follows:

i. **set**(**C**), called by **separate**(**C**), returns a set of unfolded atoms which are chosen during the transformations of unfolding and constraint simplification from **A :- A.** to clause **C**.

ii. **separate**(**C**), called by gen_resultant(P, **A**, Φ_R), returns null, an atom, or a constraint. It scans the subgoals in the body of clause **C** from left to right. If B_i is the current subgoal, then acts as follows:

1. If the body of **C** is scanned to the end, then return **null**;
2. If B_i is an atom having its predicate symbol belong to Φ_L, and there exists only one fact clause in **P** which is unifiable with B_i, then return B_i;
3. If B_i is an atom, its predicate symbol belongs to Φ_L, and an argument in B_i exists such that the length of the argument is more than the predefined constant **maxlength**, then scan B_{i+1}, and return;
4. If B_i is an atom having its predicate symbol belong to Φ_L, and B_i is not a variant of, nor an instance of, nor more general than, nor has a common instance with, any atom in **set**(**C**), then return B_i;
   (Note: These 4 conditions are analogous to the computation rules of R_v, R_i, R_g, and R_{ci}, respectively, in [4]. Users are prompted to choose only one out of them while running the partial deduction system.)
5. If B_i is a constraint which can be further simplified, then return B_i;
6. If conditions 1, 2, 3, 4 and 5 do not hold, then scan B_{i+1}, and return;

BEGIN_gen_resultant(**P**, **A**, Φ_R)

{

1. $\Phi_R := \varnothing$; Φ_S := {**A :- A.**};
2. *while* $\Phi_S \neq \varnothing$ *do*

2.1. **C** := some clause in the set Φ_S of clauses;

2.2. **G** := **separate**(**C**);

2.3. Process **G** as follows:

if **G** is null

```
            then
                  ΦS := ΦS - {C};
                  ΦR := ΦR ∪ {C};
                  % C is one of the resultants
            else if G is an atom
            then
                  Unfold atom G in clause C wrt
                  program Pn to obtain a set ΦN of
                  clauses;
                  ΦS := (ΦS - {C}) ∪ ΦN;
            else if G is a constraint which can be
                        furtherly simplified
                  then
                        Simplify constraint G in clause
                        C to obtain a new clause B;
                        ΦS := (ΦS - {C}) ∪ {B};
}
END_gen_resultant
```

4.2 Some Remarks on CLP-PE

In [6], it is indicated that "for the most important class of programs to be partially evaluated, the metainterpreters, folding for composite goals does not seem to be required for getting satisfactory results." In our partial deduction procedure, the transformations of *folding* and *introducing a newly defined clause* with respect to the atoms in the body of some clause are imposed on a single atom. Thus, our partial evaluator does not need users' information to direct the transformation process; it is automatic. In fact, the procedure we present can be easily extended to the case of folding and introducing a newly defined clause with respect to multiple atoms, as long as we can find a complete set of rules to guide the process of partial deduction.

It is worth noting that the following two points are very effective in leading to well partially-evaluated resultant programs. First, our partial deduction procedure always removes those instantiated variables from the atom that needs to be partially evaluated using the transformation rule of *introducing a newly defined clause*. Second, the procedure employs *instantiation broadcasting* in the transformation rule of *constraint simplification*.

Finally, in the partial evaluator for CLP(R) programs that we have implemented, constraint simplification is limited to single linear arithmetic constraints and some special cases such as 3*X=12 and 5*X-2.01*Y=0, in which, for example, we will remove the constraint 3*X=12 by substituting any variable X in the clause containing 3*X=12 with 4. Now we are working to deal with a group of arithmetic constraints as a unit in our partial evaluator.

4.3 Termination Problem of CLP-PE

We can prove that the above partial deduction procedure for constraint logic programs always terminates within a finite number of steps. An informal argument for this is as follows.

1. It can be proved that subprocedure **gen_resultant(P, A, Φ_R)** always terminates. Let us consider the loop statement *'while* ($\Phi_S \neq \emptyset$) *do'*. Because the function **separate(C)** is limited by a predefined constant **maxlength**, after being called a finite number of times, it will always return **null**. Each time the loop is executed, the set Φ_S (loop variable) will strictly decrease down to $\emptyset$ finally. Therefore the loop will terminate.
2. It can be proved that the partial deduction procedure **CLP_PE(P_0, Q_0, P_n, Q_n)** always terminates. First of all, consider the loop statement *'while* ($\Phi_A \neq \emptyset$) *do'*. The loop body deals with the head (an atom) of one newly defined clause each time, but it may introduce more newly defined clauses. If we can put a limit on the number of these newly defined clauses, the loop will terminate. In fact, there exists a predefined constant **maxlength** in the partial deduction procedure, so the length of any argument of the subgoals (atoms) of the clauses in Φ_R is no more than the threshold set by the predefined constant **maxlength** owing the fact that Φ_R is returned by the subprocedure **gen_resultant(P,A,Φ_R)**. Therefore, if variants are not considered, the number of existing atoms with one predicate symbol is limited. Therefore only a finite number of newly defined clauses can be introduced.

The predefined constant **maxlength** is only one of the methods to guarantee the termination of the partial deduction procedure. Actually, the termination problem itself is an active area of research in partial deduction. Interested readers can also refer to [2, 4-7], for other methods of dealing with this problem.

4.4 Computational Equivalence of CLP-PE

The computational equivalence of the resultant program-goal pair (**P_n, Q_n**) and the input program-goal pair (**P_0, Q_0**) means that any answer computed by **P_0** with respect to **Q_0** is also correctly computed by **P_n** with respect to **Q_n**, and conversely [2, 4-7].

In the partial deduction procedure for constraint logic programs **CLP_PE(P_0, Q_0, P_n, Q_n)** we present, variable Φ_A is a set of atoms which consists of the heads of the clauses resulting from the transformation of *introducing a newly defined clause*. Thus, Φ_A is finite and independent. Furthermore, any atom in Φ_A is the most general form of **new**($X_1,...,X_n$) in which the arguments $X_1,...,X_n$, for $n \geq 0$, are distinct variables, so we can also conclude that $P_n \cup \{Q_n\}$ is Φ_A-covered. Thus, since our procedure satisfies the independence and coveredness conditions, it preserves the computational equivalence of program-goal pairs (P_0, Q_0) and (P_n, Q_n).

5 Partial Deduction of CLP Programs

This section gives running examples of the partial deduction of CLP programs to show that our partial evaluator CLP-PE is effective. First of all, we partially evaluate a CLP(Bool) program appearing in [3]. Then we briefly compare the partial deduction method in [4] with ours. Finally the partial deduction of a CLP(R) program is given.

5.1 CLP(BOOL) Program

Let us consider the following program P1.

1. **add([A], [B], [C], D) :-**
   adder(A, B, false, C, D).
2. **add([A|As], [B|Bs], [C|Cs], D) :-**
   add(As, Bs, Cs, E), adder(A, B, E, C, D).
3. **adder(A, B, C, D, E) :- half(A, B, AB, C1),**
   half(AB, C, D, C2), E = C1 .or. C2.
4. **half(A, B, C, D) :-**
   C = A .xor. B, D = A .and. B.

In P1, predicate **half(A, B, C, D)** defines a half adder in which bit **A** plus bit **B** is sum **C** with a carry bit **D**. A full adder is defined by **adder(A, B, C, D, E)**, in which the sum of bit **A**, bit **B**, and low carry bit **C** is bit **D** with high carry bit **E**. The clauses defining predicate symbol **add** compute the sum of two binary numbers which are expressed by the lists of boolean values with the lowest order bit at the end of the list. If we want to double the binary number **X** to form a sum, the goal **Q1** is **?- add(X, X, Y, C).**, in which **C** is the highest order bit and **Y** is the list consisting of the left bits of the sum.

According to our procedure, the process of partial deduction is as follows:

Step 1: Introduce a newly defined clause with respect to the goal **?- add(X, X, Y, C).** to obtain the new goal **Q1' ?- new(X, Y, C).**, and the introduced new clause is the following,

5. **new(X, Y, C) :- add(X, X, Y, C).**

Step 2: Φ_R is a set of clauses consisting of clause 6 and clause 7 after the first execution of subprocedure **gen_resultant(P1, new(X,Y,C),** Φ_R**).**

6. **new([A], [false], A).**
7. **new([A|As], [C|Cs], A) :-**
   add(As, As, Cs, C).

Step 3: Fold **add(As, As, Cs, C)** in the body of clause 7 by clause 5 to obtain clause 8.

8. **new([A|As], [C|Cs], A) :- new(As, Cs, C).**

Step 4: Execute the transformation of code deletion with respect to new goal **Q1' ?- new(X, Y, C).** to obtain the resultant program **P1'** = {**clause**$_6$, **clause**$_8$}.

Obviously program-goal pairs (**P1,Q1**) and (**P1',Q1'**) are computationally equivalent. **P1'** is more efficient in solving **Q1'** than **P1** in solving **Q1**, because the resultant program **P1'** is only a bit shift program which does not contain any boolean constraints. Program **P1** was originally presented in [3], which also gave a partial deduction method which preserves breadth-first equivalence. The algorithm in [3] employs the 5 transformations of constraint simplification, failure elimination, unfolding, partial specialization, procedure factorization and dead code elimination, and produced the following program and goal as the result.

```
P1'':  query([X|Xs], [X|Ys]) :- add_1(Xs, Ys).
       add_1([ ], false).
       add_1([A|As], [A|Bs]) :- add_1(As, Bs).
Q1'':  ?- query(X,Y).
```

Program **P1''** contains one more clause than program **P1'**. This shows that our partial deduction procedure is better than that in [3] for partially evaluating program-goal pair (**P1,Q1**).

5.2 Prolog Program

Benkerimi and Lloyd [4] developed a partial deduction procedure for logic programs in [4] based on the definitions of partial deduction and the notion of computational equivalence. In their algorithm, the initial value of Φ_A consists those L-selectable atoms in the goal. After each atom in Φ_A is partially evaluated, all of the L-selectable atoms in the bodies of the resultants resulting from the corresponding partial deduction are added to Φ_A to be partially evaluated. In order to preserve the computational equivalence of partial deduction, Φ_A has to be finite and independent.

The partial deduction procedure we present is different from that in [4]. The main difference is that our procedure is based on the idea of program transformation [10]. In the process of partial deduction of Prolog programs, we employ the 4 transformation rules of *unfolding*, *folding*, *introducing a newly defined clause*, and *deleting code with respect to a goal*. The procedure in [4], however, depends on the definitions of partial deduction and the two conditions of computational equivalence. In Benkerimi and Lloyd's procedure, unfolding is the only means of partial deduction. Since we adopt the transformations of introducing a newly defined clause and folding to build the set Φ_A of atoms, the set Φ_A is finite and independent. Our procedure avoids the computation of the msg of the pair of atoms which have a common instance and replacing this pair with their msg. Thus, it generally produces a more efficient resultant program than the procedure in [4]. In addition, our procedure generally produces more succinct resultant programs since it employs the transformation of code deletion with respect to a goal.

5.3 CLP(R) Program

Partial deduction of CLP(R) programs is a new field of research on partial deduction. The partial evaluator CLP-PE we have implemented can solve a single arithmetic constraint and make special form of constraint simplification, *instantiation broadcasting*, in some cases. Consider CLP(R) program P2 containing some arithmetic constraints,

1. **mortgage(P, 1, I, MP, B)** :- **Interest = P*I/1200, B = P + Interest - MP.**
2. **mortgage(P, Time, I, MP, B)** :- **Time > 1, Interest = P*I/1200, Newp = P + Interest - MP, Newt = Time - 1, mortgage(Newp, Newt, I, MP, B).**

In program **P2**, the parameters considered above are the principal, life of mortgage in months, interest rate, monthly payment, and the balance. If we know that the interest rate is 12%, and the balance is finally 0, the relation of the other three variables forms the goal **Q2 ?- mortgage(P, T, 12, MP, 0).**.

According to our procedure, the process of partial deduction is as follows:

Step 1: Introduce newly defined clause wrt goal **?- mortgage(P,T,12,MP,0).** to obtain new goal Q2' **?- new(P, T, MP).**, and the introduced new clause is the following.

3. **new(P ,T, MP) :- mortgage(P, T, 12, MP, 0).**

From step 2 to step 8, we describe the first execution of subprocedure **gen_resultant(P, A, Φ_R)**.

Step 2: Unfold **mortgage(P, T, 12, MP, 0)** in the body of clause 3 by clauses 1, 2 to obtain clauses 4, 5.

4. **new(P, 1, MP) :- Interest = P*12/1200, 0=P + Interest - MP.**
5. **new(P, T, MP) :- Time > 1, Interest = P*12/1200, Newp = P + Interest - MP, Newt = T - 1, mortgage(Newp, Newt, 12, MP, 0).**

Step 3: Simplify the constraint **Interest=P*12/1200** in the body of clause 4 to obtain clause 6.

6. **new(P, 1, MP) :- Interest = 0.01*P, 0 = P + Interest - MP.**

Step 4: According to the constraint **Interest = 0.01*P** in the body of clause 6, we substitute any occurrence of the variable **Interest** in clause 6 with the arithmetic term **0.01*P**, and **Interest = 0.01*P** is then removed from this clause. (This is a special case of the transformation of constraint simplification.)

7. **new(P, 1, MP) :- 0 = P + 0.01*P - MP.**

Step 5: Simplify the constraint **0 = P + 0.01*P - MP** in the body of clause 7 to obtain clause 8.

8. **new(P,1,MP) :- 0 = MP - 1.01*P.**

Step 6: Simplify the constraint **Interest=P*12/1200** in the body of clause 5 to obtain clause 9, too.

9. **new(P,T,MP) :- Time > 1, Interest = 0.01*P, Newp = P + Interest - MP, Newt = T - 1, mortgage(Newp, Newt, 12, MP, 0).**

Step 7: Using the constraint **Interest = 0.01*P** in the body of clause 9, we substitute any occurrence of variable Interest in clause 9 with the arithmetic term **0.01*P**, and **Interest = 0.01*P** is then removed from this clause. (This is a special case of the transformation of constraint simplification.)

10. **new(P, T, MP) :- Time > 1, Newp = P + 0.01*P - MP, Newt = T - 1, mortgage(Newp, Newt, 12, MP, 0).**

Step 8: Simplify the constraint **Newp = P + 0.01*P - MP** in the body of clause 10 to obtain clause 11.

11. **new(P, T, MP) :- Time > 1, Newp + MP - 1.01*P = 0, Newt = T - 1, mortgage(Newp, Newt, 12, MP, 0).**

Up to this point, the first execution of subprocedure **gen_resultant(P, A, Φ_R)** is finished. The returned value of variable Φ_R is the set of clauses 8, 11.

Step 9: Fold mortgage(Newp, Newt, 12, MP, 0) in the body of clause 11 by clause 3 to obtain clause 12.

12. **new(P, T, MP) :- Time > 1, Newp + MP - 1.01*P = 0, Newt = T - 1, new(P, T, MP).**

Step 10: Make the transformation of code deletion with respect to the new goal **Q2' ?- new(P, T, MP).** to obtain the resultant program **P2'** = {$\mathbf{clause_8}$, $\mathbf{clause_{12}}$}.

Obviously, the resultant program **P2'** is more efficient than the original program **P2** because **P2'** contains less arithmetic constraints than **P2**.

6 Conclusion

Recently, constraint logic programming and partial deduction have attracted the increasing interests of researchers. Although current research activities are relatively active in both fields, few papers are concerned with the combination of these areas. Our paper gives a new and general partial deduction procedure for constraint logic programs. Based on this procedure, we have implemented an integrated partial deduction system to optimize Prolog, CLP(Bool) and CLR(R) programs. The partial evaluator is written in the logic programming language supported by our self-developed multi-domain CLP system [11], and consists of approximately 2000 lines of code. Since the domain of real numbers is much more complex than the boolean domain, we are still involved in extending our partial deduction system to CLR(R).

As far as we know, no papers besides our own [8,9] have discussed the partial deduction of CLP(R) programs. Although our partial evaluator CLP-PE simplifies only individual arithmetic constraints at this moment, our continuing work in this direction is trying to develop systematic theories and adequate techniques to deal with general arithmetic constraints.

Most of the implemented partial deduction systems reported as we know are not automatic. That is, human assistance is needed in the process of partial deduction in one way or another. Therefore, the users of these partial evaluators are limited to experienced researchers. This situation exists because it is very hard to find a completely automatic method that can satisfactorily partially evaluate all kinds of program-goal pairs. In our paper, we employ explicit program transformation rules to design and develop a fully automatic partial deduction system. As of now, we put some limitations on folding in our partial deduction procedure to achieve automation. That is, the newly defined clause is introduced only with respect to a single atom in the clause body, and folding is also done with respect to a single atom. Our current research goal is to find the solution to introducing newly defined clauses with respect to multiple atoms in the clause body and to make folding multiple atoms together possible.

References

[1] J. Jaffar and J.-L. Lassez, Constraint Logic Programming, *Proceedings of the 14th ACM Symposium on Principles of Programming Languages*, Munich, Germany, pp. 111-119, 1987.

[2] J.W. Lloyd and J.C. Shepherdson, Partial Evaluation in Logic Programming, *Journal of Logic Programming*, Vol. 11, No. 3&4, pp. 217-242, 1991.

[3] T.J. Hickey and D.A. Smith, Towards The Partial Evaluation of CLP Languages, *Proceedings of PEPM'91*, New Haven, Connecticut, pp.43-51, 1991.

[4] K.Benkerimi and J.W. Lloyd, A Partial Evaluation Procedure for Logic Programs, *Proceedings of the 1990 North American Conference on Logic*, Austin, Texas, pp. 343-358, 1990.

[5] J. Komorowski, Synthesis of Programs in the Partial Deduction Framework, In *Automating Software Design*, (Eds.), pp. 377-403, 1991.

[6] D. Sahlin, Mixtus: An Automatic Partial Evaluator for Full Prolog, *New Generation Computing*, Vol. 12, No. 1, pp. 7-51, 1993.

[7] Y. Tao, The Design and Implementation of a Partial Evaluator of Logic Programs, *Journal of Beijing Polytechnic University*, Vol. 20, No. 3 pp. 109-118, 1994.

[8] X. Zhang and C. Liu, Partial Evaluation of CLP(R) Programs, *Journal of Computer Research and Development*, Vol. 33, No. 5, pp. 347-354, 1996.

[9] Y. Tao and C. Liu, A Partial Deduction Procedure for Constraint Logic Programs, *Chinese Journal of Computers*, Vol. 20, No. 3, pp. 238-244, 1997.

[10] Y. Tao and C. Liu, A New Method of Partial Deduction of Prolog, To appear in *Journal of Beijing Polytechnic University*, Vol. 32, No. 3, 1997.

[11] C. Liu, X. Zhang, K. Yang, Y. Tao, and Zhiyang Wang, A Multi-domain CLP and its Partial Deduction, *Journal of Software*, Vol. 28, No 10, pp. 303-309, 1996.

Inducing Theorem Provers from Proofs

Raul H.C. Lopes
raul@scs.leeds.ac.uk
School of Computer Studies
University of Leeds
Leeds, England

Mark Tarver
mark@scs.leeds.ac.uk
School of Computer Studies
University of Leeds
Leeds, England

Abstract

A methodology is introduced for the automatic generation of theorem provers from sets of proof examples. As an example, this methodology was used to generate a theorem prover for Intuitionistic Propositional Calculus which proves any theorem for this logic found in [13], using depth-first search strategy without loop detection.

1 Introduction

In this work, we introduce a new methodology for *Machine Learning*, through inductive generalization. We start from an idea explored in [12] for generating theorem provers from proof steps by using randomized algorithms. Though the criteria and methods of evaluation used in that paper were too simple to allow very sophisticated theorem provers to be generated, the idea was developed in [6] to produce a template for a family of randomized algorithms (called **P**$\star$), which we defend as an adequate methodology for the automatic generation of provers from proof steps. A **P**$\star$ algorithm receives as input a set of proof steps in a given logic and it produces a logic program, defining a proof search strategy for that logic. The relevance of this work is related to the importance of the automatic generation of proof search strategies in automated theorem proving. In most of the modern logical frameworks, the inference rules for a given logic can be automatically generated from very high level specifications. However, the generation of proof search strategies is still a process depending on error-prone hand-coding of hundreds or even thousands of lines. A **P**$\star$ algorithm is a tool which can be used in conjunction with a framework to completely automate the task of generating theorem provers. Besides, since **P**$\star$ is not specifically connected to any logic, it can be used as well to generate problem-solving strategies in the domain of expert systems. We will show that **P**$\star$ algorithms have a wider range of application and are more effective than, for example, the *Version Spaces* methodology.

In this paper, we will start from **P**$\star$ (in the next section), and then will introduce a series of successive refinements (through definitions) for each of the procedures used in this template. Those refinements will lead us to three algorithms, each one intended as an improvement of its predecessor. Each one of them was experimentally evaluated and we cite results from Intuitionistic Propositional Calculus (**IPC**) and modal logic S5 to support our claim that the algorithms we introduce can be used for the automatic generation of efficient theorem provers. For **IPC** in particular, we compare the provers generated by our algorithms with provers based on the best formalizations found in the literature ([2], for example), showing that our machine generated-provers are in general more efficient, while still preserving the important characteristic of equivalence of derivation with Gentzen's **LJ**-calculus([7]). We also present some problems which are not amenable for depth-first provers (even using loop detection) that are, however, solved straightforwardly by one of our machine-generated provers.

2 The P$\star$ template

P$\star$ (figure 1) defines a family of algorithms for the generation of proof search strategies from proofs. We assume that logics are formalized in sequent calculus (see figure 2 for Dragalin's formalization of **IPC**), a *sequent* being an ordered pair of sets of formulas (the hypotheses and the conclusion, respectively). The standard notation is used to display sequents, as in the example below:

$$\neg(p \wedge q), \neg q \rightarrow \bot, q, \neg p \rightarrow \bot, p \vdash p, q$$

Proofs are produced by (automatic or assisted) tactical provers in a goal-oriented fashion. In this report, we assume that, for each inference rule in the formalization of **IPC**, there is a tactic mapping the conclusion of the rule to its premisses.

A **P**$\star$ algorithm receives as inputs a set (W in figure 1) of proof *steps* and a set of fixed terms ($\mathcal{F}$ in figure 1) of the formal language, and it generates schematizations (called *methods* and represented by M in figure 1) of those steps. As in [11], we assume without discussion that the symbols

Algorithm P⋆
Input: W: set of steps; $\mathcal{F}$: set of fixed terms
Output: set of methods
$M \leftarrow \{$*P⋆-schematization of* x *w.r.t.* $\mathcal{F} : x \in W\}$;
$M \leftarrow \{x \in M : x$ is not *P⋆-redundant* in M w.r.t. $W\}$;
do n times
  for each x in M
    for each y *P⋆-generated* from x
      if y is *P⋆-acceptable*
        in comparison with x w.r.t. M and W
      then insert y in M;
  endfor;
  $M \leftarrow \{x \in M : x$ is not *P⋆-redundant* in M w.r.t. $W\}$;
enddo;
return M;

end

Figure 1: The **P⋆** template

$(\to\vdash)\ \frac{(\varphi\to\psi),\Gamma\vdash\varphi;\ \ \psi,\Gamma\vdash\Delta}{(\varphi\to\psi),\Gamma\vdash\Delta}$

$(\vdash\to)\ \frac{\varphi,\Gamma\vdash\psi}{\Gamma\vdash(\varphi\to\psi),\Delta}$

$(\wedge\vdash)\ \frac{\varphi,\psi,\Gamma\vdash\Delta}{(\varphi\wedge\psi),\Gamma\vdash\Delta}$

$(\vdash\wedge)\ \frac{\Gamma\vdash\varphi;\ \ \Gamma\vdash\psi,\Delta}{\Gamma\vdash(\varphi\wedge\psi),\Delta}$

$(\vee\vdash)\ \frac{\varphi,\Gamma\vdash\Delta;\ \ \psi,\Gamma\vdash\Delta}{(\varphi\vee\psi),\Gamma\vdash\Delta}$

$(\vdash\vee)\ \frac{\Gamma\vdash\varphi,\psi,\Delta}{\Gamma\vdash(\varphi\vee\psi),\Delta}$

$(\neg\vdash)\ \frac{(\varphi\to\bot),\Gamma\vdash\Delta}{\neg\varphi,\Gamma\vdash\Delta}$

$(\vdash\neg)\ \frac{\Gamma\vdash(\varphi\to\bot),\Delta}{\Gamma\vdash\neg\varphi,\Delta}$

(axiom) $\alpha,\Gamma\vdash\alpha,\Delta$

$(\bot\vdash)\ \bot,\Gamma\vdash\Delta$

Figure 2: Dragalin's formalization for **IPC**

of a formal language are partitioned into two sets of fixed (logical constants like ∧ or ∨) and variable terms. A *step* is an ordered pair containing a sequent and the name of the tactic used to solve the sequent. A *method* is an ordered pair, containing a *meta-sequent* (a sequent with occurrences of meta-variables ranging over formulas or sets of formulas) and the name of a tactic. A *method* is generated from a *step* by a procedure of **Schematization**, which uniformly replaces each variable term in the step by a meta-variable.

Definitions will be introduced using the form "... $=_{\text{Def}}$ —", meaning that "..." abbreviates "—". We define now **Schematization**.

Definition 1 ***Schematization of a sequent*** *$\mathcal{S}$ w.r.t. to $\mathcal{F}$ $=_{\text{Def}}$ a meta-sequent obtained from $\mathcal{S}$ by replacing each term of $\mathcal{S}$ not occurring in $\mathcal{F}$ with a new meta-variable, assuring that all occurrences of one term are replaced by the same meta-variable.*

Definition 2 ***Schematization of a step*** *$\mathfrak{S}$ w.r.t. to $\mathcal{F}$$=_{\text{Def}}$ a method, which names the same tactic as $\mathfrak{S}$ and whose meta-sequent is a* schematization *of the sequent in $\mathfrak{S}$ w.r.t. to $\mathcal{F}$.*

We follow [1] and we consider a method as an assertion in the meta-language about the use of a tactic: in a proof, when a sequent is matched by its meta-sequent, the designated tactic should be applied. $\mathfrak{M}_0$, below, represents a method which is a *Schematization* of the step represented by < $p \vdash p \Longrightarrow$ **(axiom)**>:

$\mathfrak{M}_0$: [$\alpha \vdash \alpha$ ::> **(axiom)**]

$\mathfrak{M}_0$ asserts that any sequent which contains occurrences of the same formula both in the hypotheses and in the conclusion should be solved by **(axiom)**. We say that **(axiom)** is the tactic *named* (or recommended) by $\mathfrak{M}_0$. In this paper, Greek letters are used as names for meta-variables: lowercase letters range over formulas, and uppercase letters range over sets of formulas.

The algorithms in the family **P⋆** are differentiated by the definitions they give to the procedures **P⋆-schematization, P⋆-generated** (which generates methods from methods), **P⋆-acceptable** and **P⋆-redundant** (which are used to discard methods). In this paper, **P⋆-schematization** is always identified with **Schematization** (defined above).

3 P0

The first algorithm to be derived from **P⋆** is **P0**. **P0** introduces procedures for the generation of methods which are used in the other algorithms, but it is quite simple in its policy of method evaluation.

3.1 P0-generation

Two procedures, *thinning* and *lifting*, are used to generate methods from methods and they reflect, respectively, structural properties of the sequent calculus and of the composition of formulas.

Definition 3 ***Thinning*** *of method $\mathfrak{S}$ $=_{\text{Def}}$ any method obtained from $\mathfrak{S}$ by dropping some arbitrarily chosen for-*

mula in its meta-sequent.

For example, from $\mathfrak{M}_0$, $\mathfrak{M}_1$ and $\mathfrak{M}_2$ could be generated by *thinning*:

$\mathfrak{M}_0$: $[\alpha, (\alpha \rightarrow \bot) \vdash \alpha$ ::> **(axiom)**]
$\mathfrak{M}_1$: $[\alpha, (\alpha \rightarrow \bot) \vdash$ ::> **(axiom)**]
$\mathfrak{M}_2$: $[\alpha \vdash \alpha$ ::> **(axiom)**]

Definition 4 ***Lifting*** *of a method* $\mathfrak{M} =_{\text{Def}}$ *any method generated from* $\mathfrak{M}$ *by substituting a new meta-variable for an arbitrarily chosen sub-formula in an arbitrarily chosen formula of its sequent.*

Lifting could generate $\mathfrak{M}_3$ (below) from $\mathfrak{M}_0$:

$\mathfrak{M}_3$: $[\alpha, (\beta \rightarrow \bot) \vdash \alpha$ ::> **(axiom)**]

Thinning and *Lifting* give to our algorithms the characteristic of randomized search: the formulas to be dropped (in *thinning*) or replaced (in *lifting*) are chosen at random. They are very simple procedures which can be used to produce a procedure of randomized generalization of methods. However, when freely applied, they can generate lots of "silly" ($\mathfrak{M}_1$ above, for example) and redundant methods. Procedures for discarding nonsensical and redundant methods are necessary and they will be distinguishing points between our algorithms.

3.2 P0-acceptability

Methods must be validated against the steps from which they are produced and there is no way out of this, given the nature of our task: learning through inductive generalization. **P0** evaluates a method based on its *fitness*, which is the difference between the numbers of its *confirmations* and *contradictions* in a set of steps. *Fitness* can then be used to label a method as acceptable (or unacceptable).

Definition 5 *Meta-sequent S* ***subsumes*** *(meta-) sequent $\mathcal{T}$ $=_{\text{Def}}$ there is a substitution for the meta-variables in S which makes the first and second components of S (after substitution) respectively subsets of the first and second components of $\mathcal{T}$. We say $\mathcal{T}$ is an* ***instance*** *of S.*

Definition 6 *A Step $\mathfrak{S}$* ***confirms*** *a method $\mathfrak{M} =_{\text{Def}}$ $\mathfrak{S}$ and $\mathfrak{M}$ name the same tactic and the sequent in $\mathfrak{S}$ is an instance of the meta-sequent in $\mathfrak{M}$. In that case, we call $\mathfrak{S}$ a* ***confirmation*** *of $\mathfrak{M}$.*

Definition 7 *A Step $\mathfrak{S}$* ***contradicts*** *a method $\mathfrak{M} =_{\text{Def}}$ The sequent in $\mathfrak{S}$ is an instance of the meta-sequent in $\mathfrak{M}$, but $\mathfrak{S}$ and $\mathfrak{M}$ name different tactics. In that case, we call $\mathfrak{S}$ a* ***contradiction*** *for $\mathfrak{M}$.*

Definition 8 *$\mathfrak{M}$ is* ***P0-acceptable*** *in comparison with $\mathfrak{R}$ w.r.t. a set of steps W $=_{\text{Def}}$ the* fitness *of $\mathfrak{M}$ is not less than the fitness of $\mathfrak{R}$.*

1. $\vdash (p \wedge q) \leftrightarrow (q \wedge p)$
2. $\vdash (p \vee q) \leftrightarrow (q \vee p)$
3. $\vdash p \rightarrow (\neg p \rightarrow q)$
4. $\vdash \neg p \leftrightarrow \neg\neg\neg p$
5. $\vdash \neg(p \wedge \neg p)$
6. $\vdash \neg\neg(p \vee \neg p)$
7. $\vdash (p \vee \neg p) \rightarrow (\neg\neg p \rightarrow p)$
8. $\vdash ((p \wedge q) \rightarrow r) \rightarrow (p \rightarrow (q \rightarrow r))$
9. $\vdash p \wedge (q \vee r) \leftrightarrow (p \wedge q) \vee (p \wedge r)$
10. $\vdash (p \rightarrow q) \rightarrow (\neg\neg p \rightarrow \neg\neg q)$
11. $\vdash (p \rightarrow q) \rightarrow ((q \rightarrow r) \rightarrow (p \rightarrow r))$
12. $\vdash (\neg\neg p \wedge \neg\neg q) \leftrightarrow (\neg\neg(p \wedge q))$
13. $\vdash (\neg\neg p \rightarrow q) \rightarrow (\neg q \rightarrow \neg p)$
14. $\vdash \neg(p \vee q) \leftrightarrow \neg p \wedge \neg q$

Figure 3: Training set for **IPC**

3.3 P0-redundancy

The randomized generalization produces methods which are immediately discarded due to low *fitness*. Many methods, however, are generated (with an acceptable *fitness*) which are redundant when compared with other previously generated methods.

Definition 9 *$\mathfrak{M}$ is* ***P0-redundant*** *in a set of methods M $=_{\text{Def}}$ there is some $\mathfrak{R} \in M$ such that the meta-sequent in $\mathfrak{R}$ subsumes the meta-sequent in $\mathfrak{M}$ and $\mathfrak{R}$ and $\mathfrak{M}$ name both the same tactic.*

The property of being **P0-redundant** leaves open the possibility of two methods being redundant when compared to each other. In that case, we assume they are equivalent and we make an arbitrary choice for discarding only one.

3.4 Assessing P0

The methods generated by **P0** can be ordered by *fitness* (giving priority to the ones with higher fitness) and compiled into a logic program. Each clause would have the following pattern:

recommend$(< M, R >, S, R)$ **if** M *subsumes* S,

where $< M, R >$ is a pair sequent-rule from a method and S is intended to be the input parameter, accepting the sequent to solved.

1. $\vdash ((p \to q) \to \neg(p \wedge \neg q))$
2. $\vdash ((p \vee (q \wedge r)) \leftrightarrow ((p \vee q) \wedge (p \vee r)))$
3. $\vdash ((\neg p \vee \neg q) \to \neg(p \wedge q))$
4. $\vdash ((\neg p \vee q) \to (p \to q))$
5. $\vdash ((p \wedge \neg q) \to \neg(p \to q))$
6. $\vdash ((p \to q) \to (\neg q \to \neg p))$
7. $\vdash (p \to \neg\neg p)$
8. $\vdash ((p \to q) \to ((q \to r) \to ((r \to s) \to (p \to s))))$
9. $\vdash ((p \to \neg q) \leftrightarrow \neg(p \wedge q))$
10. $\vdash (((p \vee q) \vee r) \leftrightarrow (p \vee (q \vee r)))$
11. $\vdash \neg\neg(p \vee \neg p)$
12. $\vdash (\neg p \to (\neg\neg p \to q))$
13. $\vdash ((p \wedge (q \vee r)) \leftrightarrow ((p \wedge q) \vee (p \wedge r)))$
14. $\vdash ((\neg\neg p \wedge \neg\neg q) \leftrightarrow \neg\neg(p \wedge q))$
15. $\vdash (\neg(p \vee q) \leftrightarrow (\neg p \wedge \neg q))$

Figure 4: Problem set for **IPC**

Though [12] presents good results for the application of **P0** to the classical propositional calculus, we found much worse results for applying **P0** to **IPC**. **P0** was given a training set of proofs for the theorems exhibited in figure 3. The resulting **P0**-generated theorem prover was able to prove only 2 of the theorems in figure 4.

4 Method interference

The first problem with **P0** is one we call method interference. We identify in this section two types of interference: fitness interference, and subsumption interference.

Fitness interference occurs when one method has, among its confirmations, contradictions of another method. Since **P0** keeps all methods in the same bundle, the second method will have its fitness reduced and can even be eliminated. This kind of interference is associated, for example, with the following methods:

$\mathfrak{M}_0$: $[\bot \vdash \Delta ::> (\bot\vdash)]$
$\mathfrak{M}_1$: $[\alpha \vdash \alpha ::>$ **(axiom)**$]$.

Any solution for instances of the meta-sequent below will produce a case of *fitness interference*:

$\mathcal{S}_0$:$\bot, \Gamma \vdash \bot, \Delta$.

If an instance of $\mathcal{S}_0$ is solved by $(\bot\vdash)$, it will constitute a contradiction for $\mathfrak{M}_1$. If, in a given set of steps, instances of $\mathcal{S}_0$ are sometimes solved by $(\bot\vdash)$ and sometimes by **(axiom)**, both $\mathfrak{M}_0$ and $\mathfrak{M}_1$ will have their fitnesses reduced. Any of these conditions can lead to the elimination (due to low *fitness*) of at least $\mathfrak{M}_1$.

Subsumption interference is related to **P0**'s inability to balance between the generalized and the specialized knowledge.

P0 assumes that the method $\mathfrak{M}_2$, below,

$\mathfrak{M}_2$: $[(\alpha \to \beta) \vdash \Delta ::> (\to\vdash)]$

cannot coexist in the same set as, for example,

$\mathfrak{M}_3$: $[(\alpha \to \beta), \alpha, \Gamma \vdash \Delta ::> (\to\vdash)]$.

$\mathfrak{M}_2$, if it is not discarded due to low *fitness*, will "discard" $\mathfrak{M}_3$ (as redundant). However, the latter is an interesting expression of **Modus Ponens**, which should be kept, and $\mathfrak{M}_2$ is a default for implication on the left of the sequent which should be kept as a last resource. The algorithm we are searching for should generate a hierarchy of methods where $\mathfrak{M}_3$ would be kept with a higher priority than $\mathfrak{M}_2$.

4.1 Assigning priorities to methods

We are going to assign priorities to methods by observing that some of them express proof obligations. A method which is not contradicted imposes the use of the tactic it recommends as an obligation, at least, in face of the evidence we have, which is the set of input steps: we call it *valid* w.r.t. that set of steps.

Definition 10 *$\mathfrak{M}$ is **valid** w.r.t. a set of steps $W =_{\text{Def}}$ there is no $\mathfrak{S} \in W$ such that $\mathfrak{S}$* contradicts *$\mathfrak{M}$. We will write valid($\mathfrak{M}, W$).*

If $\mathfrak{M}$ is valid w.r.t. W and $\mathfrak{N}$ is not valid w.r.t. to W, we will assume that, when $\mathfrak{M}$ and $\mathfrak{N}$ both match a sequent, $\mathfrak{M}$ has the priority, and $\mathfrak{N}$ will be used only if $\mathfrak{M}$ fails. In this case, the priority is given to $\mathfrak{M}$ independent of whether it has a great number of confirmations or not. This observation can be used to define the validity of one method w.r.t. a set of steps and (in the presence of) a set of methods confirming all of its contradictions.

Definition 11 *$\mathfrak{M}$ is **valid**$*$ w.r.t. a set of steps W and a set of methods $M =_{\text{Def}}$ valid($\mathfrak{M}, W'$), where $W' = W - A$ and A is the set containing all (and only) the steps in W which are confirmations for methods in M.*

We will write valid$*$($\mathfrak{M}, W, M$).

We can now define a relation of precedence for methods, which will partition a set of methods w.r.t. a set of steps.

Definition 12 $\mathfrak{M}$ *is* ***weakly superior*** *to* $\mathfrak{N}$ *in* M *w.r.t.* W $=_{\rm Def}$ *for any set of methods* $A \subseteq M$ *if* $valid*(\mathfrak{N}, W, A)$ *then* $\mathfrak{M} \in A$.

We will write: $\mathfrak{M} \preceq_{M,W} \mathfrak{N}$.

The transitive closure of $\preceq$ is $\preceq^*$.

Definition 13 $\mathfrak{M} \preceq^*_{M,W} \mathfrak{N} =_{\rm Def} \mathfrak{M} \preceq_{M,W} \mathfrak{N}$ *or there is a method L such that:* $\mathfrak{M} \preceq_{M,W} \mathfrak{L}$ *and* $\mathfrak{L} \preceq_{M,W} \mathfrak{N}$.

Definition 14 $\mathfrak{M}$ *is* ***superior*** *to* $\mathfrak{N}$ *in* M *w.r.t.* $W =_{\rm Def}$ $\mathfrak{M} \preceq_{M,W} \mathfrak{N}$ *and it is not the case that* $\mathfrak{N} \preceq_{M,W} \mathfrak{M}$.

We will write: $\mathfrak{N} \prec_{M,W} \mathfrak{M}$.

A special kind of method is that which is confirmed by all steps that name the same tactic as it does. We will call a method with this characteristic *total.*

Definition 15 $\mathfrak{M}$ *is* ***total*** *w.r.t. a set of steps* $W =_{\rm Def}$ *if R is the tactic recommended by* $\mathfrak{M}$ *then every step in W which names R confirms* $\mathfrak{M}$.

The graph defined below establishes a pre-ordering of methods, which will be used to avoid method interference.

Definition 16 *An* ***ordering graph*** *for a set methods M w.r.t. to a set of steps W is the directed graph whose edges are defined below:* $d =_{\rm Def}$ *directed graph (called the* ***ordering graph*** *of M w.r.t. W) where the set of vertices are the elements of M and the directed edges denote* prece-dence *and are constructed as follows:*

1. *there is an edge from* $\mathfrak{M}$ *to* $\mathfrak{N}$ *when* $\mathfrak{M} \prec_{M,W} \mathfrak{N}$.
2. *the only edges are given by 1.*

The property of being *total* can be used to define order between two methods when they are at the same level and only one of them is *total.*

As usual in graph theory we define the *level* of a method in an *ordering graph.*

Definition 17 ***Level*** *of* $\mathfrak{M}$ *in an* ordering graph $G =_{\rm Def}$ *the length of the greatest path ending in* $\mathfrak{M}$.

A useful concept is that of a step being locked by a method. This method would be the first tried on the sequent contained in that step.

Definition 18 *Step* $\mathfrak{S}$ is locked *by method* $\mathfrak{M}$ *in the* order-ing graph $G =_{\rm Def}$ $\mathfrak{S}$ confirms $\mathfrak{M}$ *and there is no* $\mathfrak{N}$ *in G such that* $\mathfrak{S}$ confirms $\mathfrak{N}$ *and there is an arrow from* $\mathfrak{N}$ *to* $\mathfrak{M}$.

4.2 The definition of P1

We can introduce now a new algorithm (**P1**), by defining ***P1****-redundancy*, and ***P1****-acceptability*.

Definition 19 *Method* $\mathfrak{M}$ *is* ***P1-acceptable*** *in comparison with method* $\mathfrak{N}$ *w.r.t. set of methods M and set of steps W* $=_{\rm Def}$ *the* level *of* $\mathfrak{M}$ *in the ordering graph G of M w.r.t. W is less than the* level *of* $\mathfrak{N}$ *plus a fixed parameter k.*

The parameter k above was set by experiment as equal to 2.

A concept of method dominance is now introduced. One method should dominate another when the latter is not prior to the former and the former subsumes the latter.

Definition 20 *Method* $\mathfrak{M}$ ***P1-subsumes*** *method* $\mathfrak{N} =_{\rm Def} \mathfrak{M}$ *and* $\mathfrak{N}$ *name the same tactic and the sequent in* $\mathfrak{M}$ subsumes *the sequent in* $\mathfrak{N}$.

Definition 21 $\mathfrak{M}$ ***P1-dominates*** $\mathfrak{N}$ *w.r.t. a set of methods M and a set of steps* $W =_{\rm Def}$ *there is no arrow from* $\mathfrak{N}$ *to* $\mathfrak{M}$ *in the* ordering graph *G of M w.r.t. W and* $\mathfrak{M}$ **P1**-subsumes $\mathfrak{N}$.

The *redundancy* of one method will now happen only if the method is dominated by another. A method can only "discard" another method if it has a level less than or equal to the level of the latter.

Definition 22 *Method* $\mathfrak{M}$ *is* ***P1-redundant*** *in a set of methods M w.r.t. a set of steps* $W =_{\rm Def}$ *there is another method* $\mathfrak{N}$ *in the ordering graph G of M w.r.t. W such that* $\mathfrak{N}$ ***P1****-dominates* $\mathfrak{M}$ *in G.*

Fitness is not a fundamental concept anymore. A method can be preserved and be attributed a high priority (low level in the graph), even if it has only one confirmation, or even if it would have by **P0** standards a negative fitness. Methods in the same level in the graph have the same priority and this represents the fact that there is no "good" criterion to give priority to one of them. A prover could even use the number of confirmations to make a decision, but it could also use a parallel search among conflicting methods with same priority.

4.3 Assessing P1

P1 was used to generate successful provers for **IPC** and modal logic S5. In one experiment with **IPC, P1** generated a prover from the the same training set used with **P0**, which was able to prove all theorems contained in the training and the problem set (figure 4).

In another set of experiments, a formalization taken from [3] was used for modal logic *S5*. A training set of 16 problems was used to generate a prover using **P1**. The resulting prover proved the theorems *T1* to *T34* contained in the chapters 2 and 3 of [5].

It is important to observe that those two provers required loop detection and backtracking to drive the proof search.

5 Inserting negative conditions

The performance of **P1** can be improved by enriching methods with negative conditions — patterns that must not be matched if the method is to be applied. For example, the step $\mathfrak{S}_0$ below

$\mathfrak{S}_0$:< $\neg(p \wedge q), \neg q \rightarrow \bot, q, \neg p \rightarrow \bot, p \vdash \bot \Longrightarrow (\neg\vdash)$>, is contradiction to $\mathfrak{M}_0$:
$\mathfrak{M}_0$:$[(\neg\alpha \rightarrow \bot) \vdash \Delta$ ::> $(\rightarrow\vdash)]$.

It does not make sense to apply $(\rightarrow\vdash)$ to the sequent in $\mathfrak{S}_0$: this only generates (with the consecutive application of $(\vdash\neg)$ and $(\vdash\rightarrow)$) p or q (depending on the chosen formula) in the hypothesis of this sequent, and they are already in there. This observation can be used to strengthen $\mathfrak{M}_0$, using its contradiction $\mathfrak{S}_0$, to produce a new method ($\mathfrak{M}_1$), which includes a restriction that $\mathfrak{M}_1$ only matches a sequent which does *not* contain α among its hypotheses.

We extend now the definition of method to include negative conditions for matching of hypotheses and conclusion of its sequent.

Definition 23 *A* method *is a quadruple,represented as* $[\Gamma \vdash \Delta;\ \Lambda_l;\ \Lambda_r$ ::> **(R)**], *where* $\Gamma \vdash \Delta$ *is a meta-sequent,* Λ_l *and* Λ_r *are sets of meta-formulas, and R is the name of a tactic.*

Λ_l *is a set of negative conditions for the hypotheses and* Λ_r *is a set of negative conditions for the conclusion of any sequent matched by* $\Gamma \vdash \Delta$.

The method $\mathfrak{M}_1$ would have the form:

$\mathfrak{M}_1$:$[(\neg\alpha \rightarrow \bot) \vdash \Delta;\ \{\alpha\};\ \{\}$ ::> $(\rightarrow\vdash)]$.

The definition for a method matching a sequent must now include the restriction of the negative conditions. We start by redefining sequent matching.

Definition 24 *Meta-sequent* $\mathcal{S}$ $(\Gamma_s \vdash \Delta_s)$ ***i-matches*** *(meta-)sequent* $\mathcal{T}$ $(\Gamma_t \vdash \Delta_t)$ *with substitution* $\theta =_{\mathrm{Def}} \theta$ *is a substitution for the meta-variables in* $\mathcal{S}$ *which establishes an injection from* Γ_s *to* Γ_t *and from* Δ_s *to* Δ_t*: for each formula* α *in* Γ_s (Δ_s) *there is an associated formula* β *in* Γ_t (Δ_t)*, such that* α *is equal to* $\theta(\beta)$*. The formulas of* $\mathcal{T}$ *which have no correspondent in* $\mathcal{S}$ *are called* ***unmatched.***

Definition 25 *Method* $[\Gamma \vdash \Delta;\ \Lambda_l;\ \Lambda_r$ ::> **(R)**] matches sequent $\mathcal{S} =_{\mathrm{Def}} \Gamma \vdash \Delta$ i-matches $\mathcal{S}$ *under substitution* θ *and no formula of* Λ_l *or* Λ_r *(after the application of* θ*) matches any unmatched formula in the hypotheses or conclusion (respectively) of* $\mathcal{S}$.

$\mathfrak{M}_1$ does not match anymore the sequents

$\mathcal{S}_0$: $\neg(p \wedge q), \neg q \rightarrow \bot, p, \neg p \rightarrow \bot \vdash \bot,$
$\mathcal{S}_1$: $(p \wedge q) \rightarrow \bot, \neg q \rightarrow \bot, q, \neg p \rightarrow \bot, p \vdash \bot.$

No step containing those sequents is contradiction for $\mathfrak{M}_1$. In addition, $\mathfrak{M}_1$ avoids a non-determinism which arises if $\mathfrak{M}_0$ is applied to $\mathcal{S}_1$: $\mathfrak{M}_0$ does not carry enough information to permit a decision on to which formula the named tactic should be applied.

5.1 Generating negative conditions

Negative strengthening can be used to strengthen a method through one of its negative conditions (as it was done above to generate $\mathfrak{M}_1$ from $\mathfrak{M}_0$). *Negative weakening* generalizes a method by dropping one of its negative conditions — a *thinning* of the negative conditions.

Definition 26 *Negative strengthening of method* $\mathfrak{M}$ $([\Gamma_M \vdash \Delta_M;\ \Lambda_{Ml};\ \Lambda_{Mr}$ ::> $(R_M)])$ $=_{\mathrm{Def}}$ *the method* $[\Gamma \vdash \Delta;\ \Lambda_l \cup \Lambda_{Ml};\ \Lambda_r \cup \Lambda_{Mr}$ ::> $(R_M)]$ *obtained from the* i-match *of* $\Gamma_M \vdash \Delta_M$ *with* $\Gamma_T \vdash \Delta_T$*, where:* $\Gamma_T \vdash \Delta_T$ *is the sequent in the* Schematization *of one of* $\mathfrak{M}$*'s contradictions;* Γ *and* Δ *are the matched formulas in* Γ_T *and* Δ_T*, respectively; and* Λ_l *and* Λ_r *are the unmatched formulas in* $\Gamma_T \vdash \Delta_T$.

Definition 27 *Method* $\mathfrak{M}$ *is **P1+-generated*** $=_{\mathrm{Def}}$ $\mathfrak{M}$ *is generated by* thinning, lifting, negative strengthening, *or* negative weakening.

In our experiments with **P1+**, **P1+**-acceptable and **P1+**-redundant were given respectivelly the same definitions as **P1**-acceptable and **P1**-redundant.

6 Experiments with P1+

P1+ was used to generate a prover from the training set given to **P0**. Unlike the **P1**-generated prover, this new prover did *not* use either loop detection, or backtracking. It proved all theorems in the training and problem sets (figure 4). This prover proved any theorem for **IPC** present in [13].

In a new experiment, we compared three theorem provers: a **P1**-generated prover, a **P1+**-generated prover and a hand-coded prover based on Dyckhoff's formalization of **IPC**(see figure 4 of [2]). Dyckhoff's formalization is one of the best, possibly equaled only by the algorithm of [14]. It is a contraction-free calculus which admits an efficient depth-first search decision procedure for **IPC**, and this is an important feature since until only a few years ago no efficient decision procedure was known for this calculus. The provers were implemented in Lisp (Clisp under Linux) sharing as much code as possible. None of them used loop detection. The timings for the theorems

Theorem	P1	P1+	Dyckhoff
1	0.494034	0.532597	0.464764
2	0.766162	0.806845	0.915223
3	0.580895	0.351249	0.803779
4	0.668199	0.347451	0.376642
5	0.423688	0.935561	0.522327
6	0.571399	0.350279	0.62339
7	0.155708	0.138074	0.279215
8	*NO*	0.437343	0.435562
9	0.876126	0.846568	1.343198
10	0.750321	0.520904	0.695443
11	0.328181	0.465532	0.458652
12	*NO*	0.272739	0.473832
13	0.492477	0.567572	0.646535
14	2.424954	1.697075	2.381186
15	1.977125	1.157893	1.464697

Figure 5: Times for Problem Set (in seconds)

in our problem set are presented in figure 5 (using a PC-486, 66 MHz), showing that the **P1+**-prover is faster than the Dyckhoff-based prover in 11 out of 15 problems.

At least as important as this comparison is the analysis of some theorems proved. An interesting example is problem **8**. It can be proved using depth-first search on Dragalin's rules and loop detection, in **24** inferences (**P1+**-prover itself needed only 11 inferences). It's easy to check that without loop detection, however, it can only be proved using breadth-first or iterative-deepening search. A prover implementing Dragalin's rules and using iterative-deepening needed **476** inferences to find a proof. Much harder is problem **14**, which is not amenable even for a depth-first prover using loop detection. Its proof generates a tree with 15 levels, and every node after the second level has a branch factor of at least **3**. The proof has many cycles with many alternatives for backtracking between the antecedent and the repeating descendant node. An analysis of search tree with Dragalin's formalization, using iterative-deepening (or breadth-first) search (without loop detection), shows that more than 3^{12} nodes are generated.

7 Properties of P1+ provers

We can discuss now some properties of the provers generated by the **P**$\star$ algorithms, *soundness* and *completeness* being the most important. The *soundness* of any **P1+**-generated prover depends only on the formalization of the given logic. A **P1+**-generated prover does not change the rules of inference of any logic: it just drives the application of the given rules.

P1+-generated provers are not necessarily complete. However, this is an intrinsic property of the process of inductive generalization and of intelligent search, which necessarily involves failure.

An important property of **P1+**-generated provers is the fact that they preserve the equivalence of derivations when compared with the formalizations of the given logics. This is a crucial point in **IPC** because, as [7] shows, in general this fact is not verified for the formulations presented by [2] and [14]: in general, it is not possible to transform a derivation in one of those calculi to LJ, whilst preserving equivalence of proofs.

8 Related works

Inductive generalization has been widely applied to problem-solving. Connections can be found between **P0** and *Version Spaces* ([8]), which can be expressed as an instance of **P**$\star$. The use of randomized generalization, fundamental in *Version Spaces*, goes further back to genetic algorithms. However, experiments in [10] show that *Version Spaces* produces over-generalization when applied to theorem proving, producing very general schemata which cannot be used to drive search. We understand that this is a result of the naive policy for fitness evaluation used in that methodology (and in conventional genetic algorithms as well), a methodology which is in essence similar to that used in our **P0**. [4] advocates a combination randomized generalization and the construction of default hierarchies of knowledge to escape what they call "brittleness in randomized search." Our *ordering graph* seems to be a viable alternative to default hierarchies.

9 Conclusion

The **P**$\star$ algorithms show that randomized search and machine learning techniques can be fruitfully applied to automated deduction. We have experimentally demonstrated that one of its refinements (**P1+**) is capable of generating provers which outperform hand-written theorem provers. We do not treat this as a conclusive demonstration of the superiority of our methodology compared to traditional techniques. We think, however, that it is a significant and interesting result.

References

[1] Alan Bundy, Andrew Stevens, Frank van Harmelen, Andrew Ireland, and Alan Smaill. Rippling: a heuristic for guiding inductive proofs. *Artificial Intelligence*, 62:185–253, 1993.

[2] Roy Dyckhoff. Contraction-free sequent calculi for intuitionistic logic. *Journal of Symbolic Logic*, 57(3):795–807, 1992.

[3] Melvin C. Fitting. *Proof Methods for Modal and Intuitionistic Logics*. D.Reidel Publishing Company, 1983.

[4] John H. Holland, Keith J. Holyoak, Richard E. Nisbett, and Paul R. Thagard. *Induction: Processes of Inference, Learning, and Discovery*. MIT Press, London, 1986.

[5] G.E. Hughes and M.J. Cresswell. *An Introduction to Modal Logic*. Methuen and Co., 1968.

[6] Raul H.C. Lopes. Inducing search methods from proofs. Technical report, Technical Report, School of Computer Studies, University of Leeds, 1996.

[7] Gregory Mints. Normal form for sequent derivations. In Odifreddi [9], pages 469–492.

[8] Tom M. Mitchell. Generalization as search. *Artificial Intelligence*, 18:203–226, 1982.

[9] Piergiorgio Odifreddi, editor. *Kreiseliana : about and around Georg Kreisel*. Wellesley: A.K. Peters, 1996.

[10] Stephen Owen. *Analogy for Automated Reasoning*. Academic Press, 1990.

[11] Alfred Tarski. The concept of logical consequence. In *Logic, Semantics, Metamathematics*. Oxford: Clarendon Press, 1956.

[12] Mark Tarver. An algorithm for inducing tactics from proofs. Available by ftp on *agora.scs.leeds.ac.uk/scs/doc*, 1992.

[13] Dirk van Dalen. *Logic and Structure*. Springer-Verlag, 1994.

[14] N. Vorob'ev. A new algorithm for derivability in a constructive propositional calculus. *American Mathematical Society Translations*, 94:37–71, 1971.

Stratification: the computational base of a system for default reasoning

Grigoris Antoniou
Griffith University, CIT
Nathan, QLD 4111, Australia
ga@cit.gu.edu.au

Abstract

Default reasoning is computationally expensive. One of the most promising ways of easing this problem and developing powerful implementations is to split a default theory into smaller parts and compute extensions in a modular, "local" way. Up to now this idea was only followed for Reiter's default logic, yet it is also relevant to other variants of default logic which have found increasing recognition in the past years. This paper shows how it can be modified to work for several popular, alternative approaches of default reasoning: Justified, Constrained and Rational Default Logic. This work defines the formal basis for a Web-based default reasoning system which is under development at our institution.

1 Introduction

Default logic [14] is one of the most prominent approaches of nonmonotonic reasoning, since it provides a formal theory of reasoning based on default rules. One of the main problems with its applicability is that it is computationally harder than classical logic [12, 10], which makes the implementation of powerful systems difficult. A possible solution to this problem might be to split the available knowledge into smaller parts, and to apply default reasoning in a local way. This idea has been around for quite a while, but it is only quite recently that formal approaches were proposed to achieve this goal. Etherington and Crawford [9] propose restriction of the search space to a "relevant portion" of the knowledge base; their approach will usually deliver different results than the classical default logic applied to the entire knowledge base.

In contrast to this, an alternative approach was introduced which splits a default theory in a way that preserves extensions. In a series of papers [4, 5, 6] Cholewinski introduced and studied stratification of default theories. His idea was to take up the notion of stratification known from logic programming [3] and expand it to suit the necessities of default logic (it needs to treat negation, too). Essentially, his approach is based on the following idea: If the consequent of a default δ may be used by another default δ', then we should seek to apply δ before δ', but certainly not after δ'. This way we obtain information about potential orderings of defaults. Based on this idea, a powerful system for default reasoning was developed at the University of Kentucky [7]. A similar idea was presented in [16].

This paper will show how the approach of stratification can be adopted to work properly for some important variants of default logic that were proposed to overcome limitations of Reiter's original approach. We have chosen to study Justified Default Logic [11], Constrained Default Logic [8] and Rational Default Logic [13]. We show that the adaption of stratification to each of these logics reflects clearly the properties that characterize the difference between each of them and Reiter's original logic.

The results reported in this paper are straightforward adaptions of Cholewinski's original work to several important approaches to default reasoning. But it is necessary to establish and prove these results, if one wishes to follow the scientifically valid approach of developing *tools based on sound theory*.

The reported results build the sound theoretical foundation for the default reasoning system which is under development in the CIN Project. The project's aim is to build an integrated, domain-independent tool for default reasoning and belief revision which will be fully accessible on the WWW. The system is designed to be extendable, since it is being developed in an object-oriented language (Java). We intend to apply the system in various applications which require reasoning with incomplete and changing information. Such forms of reasoning are typically required in decision making. Also, representations using default rules are well suited as a compact representation language for program specifications, and as a language for requirements engineering (since representation of conflicting information is supported).

2 Basics of default logics

This section provides a forward chaining presentation of the default logics that will be studied in this paper.

2.1 Reiter's default logic

We assume that the reader is familiar with notation and basic notions of classical logic. In this paper we restrict attention to propositional default theories, as does Cholewinski; a generalization to closed defaults in first-order logic is straightforward. A propositional *signature* is determined by a set of propositional atoms U. For a formula φ, the set of propositional atoms occurring in φ is denoted by $Prop(\varphi)$. This notion extends to sets of formulae in a natural way.

A *default* δ has the form $\frac{\varphi:\psi_1,\ldots,\psi_n}{\chi}$ with propositional formulae φ, $\psi_1,\ldots,\psi_n$, χ $(n \geq 1)$. φ is the *prerequisite* $pre(\delta)$, $\psi_1,\ldots,\psi_n$ the *justifications* $just(\delta)$, and χ the *consequent* $cons(\delta)$ of δ. A *default theory* T is a pair (W, D) consisting of a set of formulae W (the set of *facts*) and a countable set D of defaults. In this paper we consider finite sets D of defaults (which is acceptable from the practical viewpoint, of course).

A *preconstrained default theory* has the form (W, D, PC), where (W, D) is a default theory and PC a set of formulae, the *constraints* of this theory.

Let $\delta = \frac{\varphi:\psi_1,\ldots,\psi_n}{\chi}$ be a default, and E a deductively closed set of formulae. We say that δ *is applicable to* E iff $\varphi \in E$, and $\neg\psi_1,\ldots,\neg\psi_n \notin E$.

Let $T = (W, D)$ be a default theory and $\Pi = (\delta_0,\ldots,\delta_m)$ a finite sequence of defaults from D without multiple occurrences (modelling an application order of defaults from D). We denote by $\Pi[k]$ the initial segment of Π of length k $(k \leq m+1)$, and by $Def(\Pi)$ the set of defaults occurring in Π.

- $In(\Pi) = Th(W \cup \{cons(\delta) \mid \delta \text{ occurs in } \Pi\})$[1].
- $Out(\Pi) = \{\neg\psi \mid \psi \in just(\delta), \delta \text{ occurs in } \Pi\}$.
- Π is called a *process of* T iff δ_k is applicable to $In(\Pi[k])$, for every $k \leq m$.
- Π is *successful* iff $In(\Pi) \cap Out(\Pi) = \emptyset$, otherwise it is *failed*. Note that in case Π is successful, every justification ψ of a default in Π is consistent with $In(\Pi)$.
- Π is *closed* iff every default that is applicable to $In(\Pi)$ already occurs in Π.

[1] shows that Reiter's original definition of extensions is equivalent to the following one: A set of formulae E is an *extension* of a default theory T iff there is a closed and successful process Π of T such that $E = In(\Pi)$.

2.2 Justified default logic

Lukaszewicz considered the possible nonexistence of extensions to be a representational shortcoming of the original default logic, and presented a variant, Justified Default Logic (JDL) [11] which avoids this problem. The essence of his approach is to avoid applying a default if it will lead to a contradiction, a posteriori.

For example, consider the default theory T consisting of the defaults $\delta_1 = \frac{true:p}{q}$, $\delta_2 = \frac{true:\neg p}{\neg p}$. In Reiter's default logic it has the single extension $Th(\{\neg p\})$, but in JDL there is the additional extension $Th(\{q\})$. The reason is the following: By applying the first default we get the information q. Subsequently we can apply δ_2 and then get failure, a posteriori. In JDL we do not carry out this "fatal" step, thus accepting $Th(\{q\})$ as an additional extension.

[1] shows that Lukaszewicz' original definition is equivalent to the following process based one: E is an extension of T in JDL iff $E = In(\Pi)$ for a maximally successful process Π of T. A process Π is called *maximally successful* iff Π is successful, and there doesn't exist a successful process Π' of T such that $Def(\Pi) \subset Def(\Pi')$.

In the example above, $\Pi_1 = (\delta_1)$ is maximally successful, since (δ_1, δ_2) is not a successful process (and (δ_2, δ_1) is not even a process, since δ_1 cannot be applied after δ_2). On the other hand, Π_1 is not closed. Therefore $Th(\{q\}) = In(\Pi_1)$ is an extension of T in JDL, but not in Reiter's default logic.

2.3 Rational default logic

It is easy to see that the default theory consisting of the defaults $\frac{true:p}{q}$ and $\frac{true:\neg p}{r}$ has the single extension $Th(\{q,r\})$ in Reiter's default logic. This shows that the *joint consistency* of justifications of defaults involved in an extension is not required. Justifications are *not* supposed to form a set of beliefs, rather they are used to sanction "jumping" to conclusions.

This design decision is natural and makes sense for many cases, but there are situations where this can lead to unintuitive results. Rational Default Logic (RDL) modifies Reiter's approach by requiring joint consistency. In the example above we would have two extensions in RDL, $Th(\{q\})$ and $Th(\{r\})$. The new

[1] where $Th(M)$ denotes the deductive closure of the set M of formulae.

element is that application of one default blocks a subsequent application of the other, therefore they cannot both contribute to the same extension.

Technically we have to maintain additionally the set of beliefs supporting the conclusions made. So for a sequence of defaults $\Pi = (\delta_0, \ldots, \delta_m)$ without multiple occurrences we define

- $Bel(\Pi) = Th(\{\psi_1 \wedge \ldots \wedge \psi_n \mid \{\psi_1, \ldots, \psi_n\} = just(\delta)$ for some $\delta \in Def(\Pi)\})$. In case the default theory T is preconstrained, we additionally require that $PC \subseteq Bel(\Pi)$.

A default δ is *rationally applicable* to a pair of deductively closed sets of formulae (E, C) iff $pre(\delta) \in E$ and $just(\delta) \cup C \cup E$ is consistent. Then we define the following:

- Π is a *rational process* iff δ_k is rationally applicable to $(In(\Pi[k]), Bel(\Pi[k]))$, for every $k \leq m$.
- Π is *successful* iff $In(\Pi) \cup Bel(\Pi)$ is consistent, otherwise it is *failed.*
- Π is *closed* iff every default rationally applicable to $(In(\Pi), Bel(\Pi))$ already occurs in Π.

The following definition [1] is equivalent to the original presentation of Mikitiuk and Truszczynski. E is an extension of T in RDL iff $E = In(\Pi)$ for a closed and successful rational process Π of T. In that case we say that E is *based* on the set of beliefs $Bel(\Pi)$

2.4 Constrained default logic

Constrained Default Logic (CDL) combines the idea of RDL (joint consistency of justifications) with the main idea of JDL (avoid running into failure). It is interesting to note that CDL was introduced before RDL; so RDL was the missing link that completed the picture of the default logics according to Figure 1 (founmd at the end of the paper).

Technically CDL works as RDL, with the only difference that the consequent of a default is included in the consistency check associated with default applicability. This assures that there are no failed situations. Therefore in the following we don't need to define success of a constrained process.

Let $\delta = \frac{\varphi:\psi_1,\ldots,\psi_n}{\chi}$ be a default, and E and C deductively closed sets of formulae. δ *is constrained applicable to* (E, C) iff $\varphi \in E$, and $\{\psi_1, \ldots, \psi_n, \chi\} \cup C$ is consistent. For a sequence of defaults $\Pi = (\delta_0, \ldots, \delta_m)$ without multiple occurrences we define

- $Con(\Pi) = Th(\{\psi_1 \wedge \ldots \wedge \psi_n \wedge \chi \mid \{\psi_1, \ldots, \psi_n\} = just(\delta)$ and $\chi = cons(\delta)$, for a default δ occurring in $\Pi\})$. If T is preconstrained, then additionally $PC \subseteq Con(\Pi)$.
- Π is a *constrained process* iff δ_k is constrained applicable to $(In(\Pi[k]), Con(\Pi[k]))$, for all $k \leq m$.
- Π is *closed* iff every $\delta \in D$ which is constrained applicable to the pair $(In(\Pi), Con(\Pi))$ already occurs in Π.

[1] shows that the original definition of extensions in CDL is equivalent to the following one: A set of formulae (E, C) is an *extension* of a default theory T in CDL iff there is a closed constrained process Π of T such that $E = In(\Pi)$ and $C = Con(\Pi)$. Slightly abusing the notation we often call E an extension of T, if we are not interested in the set of supporting beliefs.

We conclude this section with a comparative example which illustrates well the difference between default logic approaches. Consider the default theory $T = (W, D)$ with $W = \emptyset$ and

$$D = \{\frac{true : p}{q}, \frac{true : \neg p}{r}, \frac{true : \neg q, \neg r}{s}\}.$$

T has the single Reiter extension

$Th(\{q, r\})$,

two extensions in JDL,

$Th(\{q, r\})$
$Th(\{s\})$,

two extensions in RDL,

$Th(\{q\})$
$Th(\{r\})$,

and three extensions in CDL,

$(Th(\{q\}), Th(\{q, p\}))$
$(Th(\{r\}), Th(\{r, \neg p\}))$
$(Th(\{s\}), Th(\{s, \neg q, \neg r\}))$.

3 Stratification for Reiter's default logic

Let D be a finite set of defaults. A function ρ assigning a natural number to every default from D is a *stratification function*, iff for any defaults $\delta, \delta' \in D$ the following condition holds:

If $Prop(cons(\delta)) \cap Prop(\delta') \neq \emptyset$ then $\rho(\delta) \leq \rho(\delta')$[2]. (1)

[2]where $Prop(\delta)$ denotes the set of all propositional atoms occurring in δ.

An alternative, equivalent description of this property, which allows a more detailed referencing to aspects of condition (1), is the following:

If $Prop(cons(\delta)) \cap Prop(pre(\delta')) \neq \emptyset$ then $\rho(\delta) \leq \rho(\delta')$. (A)

If $Prop(cons(\delta)) \cap Prop(just(\delta')) \neq \emptyset$ then $\rho(\delta) \leq \rho(\delta')$. (B)

If $Prop(cons(\delta)) \cap Prop(cons(\delta')) \neq \emptyset$ then $\rho(\delta) = \rho(\delta')$. (C)

By assigning a number to each default, ρ decomposes D into layers (strata) $D_1, \ldots, D_k$ of ascending value under ρ. We denote by $Stratum_{\rho=k}(D)$ the stratum D_i such that $\rho(\delta) = k$ for all $\delta \in D_i$. A default theory $T = (W, D)$ is called *stratified* iff W is consistent, $Prop(W) \cap Prop(cons(D) \cup just(D)) = \emptyset$, and there exists a stratification function for D.

Essentially, this definition follows the idea that in case the information provided by the default δ may be used by the default δ', we should seek to apply δ before δ'. The following result from [4] shows that decomposition of a set of defaults according to a stratification function preserves the extensions.

Theorem 3.1 *Let $T = (W, D)$ be a stratified default theory, ρ an associated stratification function, and $D_1, \ldots, D_k$ the decomposition of D into strata. Then E is a Reiter extension of T iff for all $0 \leq i \leq k$ there exists E_i such that $E_k = E$, $E_0 = Th(W)$, and for all $1 \leq i \leq k$, E_i is a Reiter extension of $T_i = (E_{i-1}, D_i)$.*

For example, consider the following defaults:

$$\delta_1 = \frac{true : p}{p}, \delta_2 = \frac{p : q}{q}, \delta_3 = \frac{r : \neg p}{s}, \delta_4 = \frac{true : true}{\neg p}.$$

According to the definition of a stratification function, δ_2 and δ_3 make use of information in the consequent of δ_1 and δ_4 (because of the propositional atom p), but not vice versa. So, $\rho(\delta_2)$ and $\rho(\delta_3)$ may be strictly greater than $\rho(\delta_1)$ and $\rho(\delta_4)$, but certainly not less. On the other hand, by definition, $\rho(\delta_1)$ must equal $\rho(\delta_4)$. Thus one possible stratification function is:

$$\rho(\delta_1) = \rho(\delta_4) = 1, \rho(\delta_2) = \rho(\delta_3) = 2.$$

This function creates two strata. Another stratification function is

$$\rho'(\delta_1) = \rho'(\delta_4) = 1, \rho'(\delta_2) = 2, \rho'(\delta_3) = 3$$

which creates three strata. The algorithms used in implementations seek to decompose a default theory into as fine strata as possible. In our example, ρ' is preferable to ρ. The discussion of these algorithms is beyond the scope of this paper (but see section 6 for more information).

4 Stratification for variants of default logic

4.1 Justified default logic

Must the definition of a stratification function be modified to work properly in JDL? Let us reconsider the default theory T consisting of the defaults $\delta_1 = \frac{true:p}{q}, \delta_2 = \frac{true:\neg p}{\neg p}$, which was discussed in subsection 2.2.

If we adopt the definition of a stratification function without any changes, then $\rho(\delta_2) \leq \rho(\delta_1)$ is the only condition that must be satisfied. So a possible stratification function would be $\rho(\delta_2) = 1$ and $\rho(\delta_1) = 2$. In that case δ_2 is included in the lower stratum and δ_1 in the higher stratum. Using the method of theorem 3.1 we would compute all extensions of the lower stratum, in our case $Th(\{\neg p\})$, and then pass it over to the next stratum. But in this case δ_1 can never be applied, so we lose $Th(\{q\})$ which is one of the two extensions of T in JDL.

What went wrong is that in JDL there is a new way of interaction among defaults. In the example above, default δ_1 blocks the application of δ_2 *through its justification.* In that sense, δ_2 uses information provided by δ_1. Therefore, in addition to (1), we impose on stratification functions in JDL the following condition:

If $Prop(just(\delta)) \cap Prop(cons(\delta')) \neq \emptyset$ then $\rho(\delta) \leq \rho(\delta')$ (2).

An alternative, equivalent characterization of properties (1) and (2) is the following:

If $Prop(cons(\delta)) \cap Prop(pre(\delta')) \neq \emptyset$ then $\rho(\delta) \leq \rho(\delta')$. (A)

If $Prop(cons(\delta)) \cap Prop(just(\delta')) \neq \emptyset$ then $\rho(\delta) = \rho(\delta')$. (B')

If $Prop(cons(\delta)) \cap Prop(cons(\delta')) \neq \emptyset$ then $\rho(\delta) = \rho(\delta')$. (C)

With this addition, a result similar to Theorem 3.1 can be proven for JDL. A proof outline can be found in section 5.

Theorem 4.1 *Let $T = (W, D)$ be a stratified default theory, ρ an associated stratification function satisfying conditions* (1) *and* (2), *and $D_1, \ldots, D_k$ the decomposition of D into strata. Then E is an extension of T in JDL iff for all $0 \leq i \leq k$ there exists E_i such that $E_k = E$, $E_0 = Th(W)$, and for all $1 \leq i \leq k$, E_i is an extension of $T_i = (E_{i-1}, D_i)$ in JDL.*

One of the main advantages of Cholewinski's stratification in Reiter's default logic is that it suggests an application order for defaults which guarantees that an extension will be computed (of course, this is only possible if a non-trivial stratification function exists; for details see [4]). While this advantage is also valid for Rational Default Logic, it is not so relevant to Justified Default Logic and CDL, since in these logics extensions can be computed incrementally.

But we argue that stratification is still important in JDL and CDL for computational reasons. Theorem 4.1 defines essentially a reduction of the forward chaining search space in our quest to determine *all* extensions of a default theory (of course we could use backward chaining instead, in which case we would have to test all 2^n sets of defaults, if n defaults are given, e.g. [15]).

4.2 Rational default logic

As we said in subsection 2.3, the default theory consisting of the defaults $\frac{true:p}{q}$ and $\frac{true:\neg p}{r}$ has one Reiter extension but two extensions in RDL, since the justifications of the two defaults contradict one another.

This shows that we have a new kind of interaction among defaults not present in Reiter's approach. Therefore we have to modify the definition of a stratification function accordingly. If not, then in the example above ρ could assign any values to each of the defaults. As in JDL, if we would put the first default in the lower stratum, then it would always be applied first (adopting the technique from theorem 3.1), and we would lose one extension in RDL. Formally we have to impose the following condition in addition to (1):

If $Prop(just(\delta)) \cap Prop(just(\delta')) \neq \emptyset$ then $\rho(\delta) = \rho(\delta')$. (3)

An alternative, equivalent characterization of properties (1) and (3) is given by the following collection of conditions.

If $Prop(cons(\delta)) \cap Prop(pre(\delta')) \neq \emptyset$ then $\rho(\delta) \leq \rho(\delta')$. (A)

If $Prop(cons(\delta)) \cap Prop(just(\delta')) \neq \emptyset$ then $\rho(\delta) \leq \rho(\delta')$. (B)

If $Prop(cons(\delta)) \cap Prop(cons(\delta')) \neq \emptyset$ then $\rho(\delta) = \rho(\delta')$. (C)

If $Prop(just(\delta)) \cap Prop(just(\delta')) \neq \emptyset$ then $\rho(\delta) = \rho(\delta')$. (3)

With this modification a result similar to that of Theorem 3.1 can be shown.

Theorem 4.2 *Let ρ be a stratification function for a finite set of defaults D which satisfies conditions* (1) *and* (3), *$D_1 \cup \ldots \cup D_l$ the decomposition of D according to ρ. Let W be a consistent set of formulae such that $Prop(W) \cap Prop(cons(D) \cup just(D)) = \emptyset$. Then E is an extension of $T = (W, D)$ in RDL, iff for all $0 \leq i \leq l$ there exists (E_i, C_i) such that $E_l = E$, $(E_0, C_0) = (Th(W), Th(W))$, and for all $1 \leq i \leq l$, E_i is an extension of the preconstrained default theory $T_i = (E_{i-1}, D_i, C_{i-1})$ in RDL, based on the set of beliefs C_i.*

4.3 Constrained default logic

Essentially Constrained Default Logic (CDL) combines the features of the approaches in the two previous subsections. It adopts joint consistency from RDL, and avoidance of running into failure from JDL. Therefore the definition of a stratification function has to include the conditions (1), (2) and (3). An alternative way of describing a stratification function in CDL would be the following: A function ρ assigning a natural number to every default from D is a *stratification function*, iff for any defaults $\delta, \delta' \in D$ the following condition holds:

If $Prop(cons(\delta)) \cap Prop(\delta') \neq \emptyset$ then $\rho(\delta) \leq \rho(\delta')$ (A).

If $Prop(just(\delta) \cup \{cons(\delta)\}) \cap Prop(just(\delta') \cup \{cons(\delta')\}) \neq \emptyset$
then $\rho(\delta) = \rho(\delta')$. (E)

With this modification a result similar to that of Theorem 3.1 can be shown.

Theorem 4.3 *Let ρ be a stratification function for a finite set of defaults D, $D_1 \cup \ldots \cup D_l$ the decomposition of D according to ρ. Let W be a consistent set of formulae such that $Prop(W) \cap Prop(cons(D) \cup just(D)) = \emptyset$. Then (E, C) is an extension of $T = (W, D)$ in CDL, iff for all $0 \leq i \leq l$ there exists (E_i, C_i) such that $(E_l, C_l) = (E, C)$, $(E_0, C_0) = (Th(W), Th(W))$, and for all $1 \leq i \leq l$, (E_i, C_i) is an extension of the preconstrained default theory $T_i = (E_{i-1}, D_i, C_{i-1})$ in CDL.*

4.4 Comparison of the stratification concepts

In section 2 we discussed the relationships and differences between the default logics considered in this paper. Essentially, JDL and RDL introduce new kinds of default interactions, with CDL adopting both of them.

The stratification concepts presented in this section clearly reflect these conditions: Condition (2) and (3) is added to (1) in JDL and RDL respectively, with both conditions being used in CDL. So stratification is not only computationally beneficial, but it also reflects the properties of each logic in a natural way. The stratification concepts follow closely the situation in Figure 1 (at the end of the paper).

5 Discussion and conclusion

The main contribution of this paper is that it shows how stratification works for several important variants of default logic. We also explained that the basic idea of each logic determines the modifications that must be made to Cholewinski's original definition so that it works for the respective default logic variant. We pointed out that for RDL, as for Reiter's default logic, stratification defines an application order which leads to the computation of an extension. But even for JDL and CDL, in which incremental extension computation is inherently possible, stratification leads to a reduction of the search space, and thus to more efficient default reasoning.

Regarding implementation, Cholewinski proposed a more sophisticated way of computing extensions than the linear order provided by a stratification function [5]. Instead, he used the precedence information provided by the definition of stratification to define a partially ordered set. This way, the extensions of some strata can be computed in parallel, and this can lead to a drastic improvement. For example, if we consider Reiter's default logic and take T to consist of the defaults $\delta_1 = \frac{true:p}{p}, \delta_2 = \frac{p:q}{q}, \delta_3 = \frac{r:\neg p}{s}, \delta_4 = \frac{true:true}{\neg p}$, then δ_1 and δ_4 must be applied and in the same stratum, but there are no further constraints on the application of δ_2 and δ_3. Therefore they should be treated independently from one another, essentially in parallel.

Exactly the same idea and algorithm can be used for each of the default logic variant discussed in this paper; the only thing that changes every time is the precedence relation (since there are other conditions to be respected by a stratification function). In other words, we have a two-stage procedure. In stage 1 we determine the precedence relation using the definition of a stratification function according to the respective logic. In stage 2 we build a partially ordered set according to Cholewinski's algorithm [5], and use it to compute the extensions.

Stratification is the main underlying principle in our implementation of a default reasoning system. A prototype has already been implemented in C++. Currently we are developing a more mature system in Java, and are working on the integration with belief revision techniques.

References

[1] G. Antoniou. *Nonmonotonic Reasoning.* MIT Press 1997.

[2] G. Antoniou, A. Courtney, J. Ernst and M.A. Williams. A System for Computing Constrained Default Logic Extensions. In *Proc. 5th European Workshop on Logics in AI (JELIA'96)*, Springer LNAI.

[3] K.R. Apt and R.N. Bol. Logic programming and negation: a survey. *Journal of Logic Programming* 19/20 (1994), 9–72.

[4] P. Cholewinski. Stratified Default Logic. In *Proc. Computer Science Logic 1994*, Springer LNCS 933, 456-470.

[5] P. Cholewinski. Reasoning with Stratified Default Theories. In *Proc. 3rd International Conference on Logic Programming and Nonmonotonic Reasoning,* 1995.

[6] P. Cholewinski. Seminormal stratified default theories. *Annals of Mathematics and Artificial Intelligence* 1995.

[7] P. Cholewinski, W. Marek, A. Mikitiuk and M. Truszczynski. Experimenting with default logic. In *Proc. International Conference on Logic Programming,* MIT Press 1995.

[8] J.P. Delgrande, T. Schaub and W.K. Jackson. Alternative approaches to default logic. *Artificial Intelligence* 70(1994): 167–237.

[9] D.W. Etherington and J.M. Crawford. Towards Efficient Default Reasoning. In *Proc. AAAI-96,* 627–632.

[10] G. Gottlob. Complexity results for nonmonotonic logics. *Journal of Logic and Computation* 2(1992): 397–425.

[11] W. Lukaszewicz. Considerations on Default Logic. *Computational Intelligence* 4(1988): 1–16.

[12] W. Marek and M. Truszczynski. *Nonmonotonic Logic*. Springer 1993.

[13] A. Mikitiuk and M. Truszczynski. Constrained and rational default logics. In *Proc. International Joint Conference on Artificial Intelligence* 1995

[14] R. Reiter. A Logic for Default Reasoning. *Artificial Intelligence* 13(1980): 81–132.

[15] V. Risch and C. Schwind. Tableau-Based Characterization and Theorem Proving for Default Logic. *Journal of Automated Reasoning* 13(1994): 223–242.

[16] H. Turner. Splitting a Default Theory. In *Proc. AAAI-96*, 645–651.

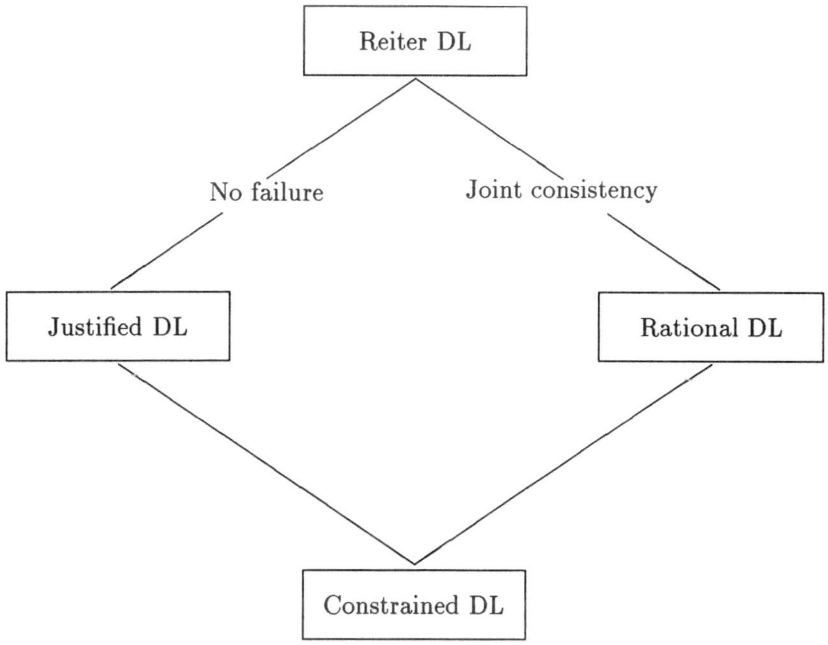

Figure 1: Relationship between default logics

Session C.1

Natural Language Processing and Applications

Session Chair:
David Dampier, Army Research Laboratory, USA

Automatic Generation of Portable Parallel Natural Language Parsers

A. G. Manousopoulou, G. Manis, P. Tsanakas and G. Papakonstantinou
National Technical University of Athens
Dept. of Electrical and Computer Engineering
Zografou Campus, Zografou 15773
e-mail: papakon@dsclab.ece.ntua.gr

Abstract

Since natural language parsing is a computationally intensive task, the parallel parsing of natural language seems a promising choice. This work describes both the Eu-PAGE meta-compiler for the Eurotra formalism, a tool that automatically generates parallel natural language parsers, and the Dialogos[†] *parser, a parallel parser for the Greek language generated by Eu-PAGE. Parallel parsers generated by Eu-PAGE are based on finite state machines, employ coarse grained parallelism, and are portably implemented on top of two parallel software platforms: PVM and Orchid. Orchid uses light weight processes as the basic unit of parallelism, enhanced with advanced operating system facilities. The collected experimental results so far demonstrate satisfactory speed-ups of the parallel implementations compared to the sequential one.*

1. Introduction

Natural language is a very dense and complicated encoding of information, much of which is implicit and heavily depending upon the real world context in which it is uttered; it encompasses several cooperating levels of structured knowledge, be it lexical, syntactic, semantic, or pragmatic. All these compose a complicated problem, which requires significant computational time to be challenged in a satisfactory way.

Parallel processing may contribute as a springboard to overcome the hurdle of complexity. The strength of parallel processing is the significant reduction of computation time requirements for a wide variety of applications from diverse scientific fields. The research related to parallel natural language processing is substantial; a review on distinct approaches to parallel natural language processing is given in [1].

Our contribution is presented in this paper: a tool for the automatic generation of parallel natural language parsers (Eu-PAGE), our parallel software platform on which parsers are built (Orchid), and their application to the Greek language (Dialogos). The Eu-PAGE (Eurotra PArser GEnerator) parser generator was motivated by the need for the incorporation of parallel processing techniques with a rich and expressive grammar formalism such as the Eurotra formalism ([2], [3]). Its purpose is to deviate from context-free techniques and move towards language representations a computational linguist would be more apt to. The Dialogos parser has been generated by Eu-PAGE, using as input the Eurotra description of the Greek language.

The rest of this paper will first make an introductory presentation of the Eurotra formalism; next, the tools we have built for the automatic generation of parsers will be described: Eu-PAGE and the Orchid platform. Then, the Greek language parser will be illustrated as an example of the generation of a parser, and finally, some experimental results will be presented.

2. The Eurotra formalism

The Eurotra formalism, a theory independent, unification-based formalism, gives a declarative description of the parse trees pertaining to correct natural language utterances; nodes of these trees carry feature sets, sets of atomically valued attributes.

There are two basic categories of rules in a Eurotra grammar: rules that build the parse tree(s) from an input sentence, and rules that operate on the -already built- trees. Tree building rules (b-rules) perform the main task of parsing and carry most of the computational load. The rules of the other category, although important for the linguistic adequacy of the grammar, are much cheaper computationally, as they operate on and alter already structured data. Our further discussion will be concentrated on b-rules and the parsing procedure that applies them to build parse trees of sentences.

A b-rule describes a parse tree node and its children,

[†] This work is partially funded by the Greek Secretariat of Research and Technology

1082-3409/97 $10.00 © 1997 IEEE

the latter given in the form of a regular expression over feature set descriptions. These descriptions contain "attribute=value" or "attribute=variable" pairs. Variables are entities local within a rule that can be either unbound or have a value; they are used as means of unification across the children nodes, as it is necessary that all attributes associated with a variable inside a rule have the same value. They are also used to transfer values from the children to the parent. The rules are applied to node sequences by means of simple unification (since all attributes are atomically valued).

An example of a b-rule is given in Figure 1. This rule identifies a noun phrase consisting of the optional word "all", an article, a series of adjectives and then a noun. Restrictions on the nodes are imposed by explicit values or by value unification through the variable N, which also copies its value to the newly created parent.

```
{ cat=np, number=N,
  person=third } [
   ^{ cat=special_adj,
      spadj_type=all },
    { cat=article, type=def,
      number=N },
   *{ cat=adj, number=N },
    { cat=noun, number=N }
].
```

Figure 1: Example of a b-rule

The other types of rules in a Eurotra grammar, which examine, enrich and modify the parse tree(s) built by b-rules are:

- *f-rules*, which add new values to the feature sets of the tree
- *i-rules*, which insert new leaf nodes in the tree
- *s-rules*, which select the viable parse trees among the ones produced
- *k-rules*, which reject trees of a specific form; these rules together with s-rules are countermeasures against the possible overgeneration introduced by b-rules for the sake of grammar simplicity and brevity
- *p-rules*, which classify the resulting parse trees to produce the most possible interpretation of the sentence
- *l-rules* and *dl-rules*, which test the new nodes introduced by other rules.

3. A parser generator for Eurotra grammars: the procedural approach

It is a tradition in the AI community to use more or less declarative languages, such as Lisp and Prolog; this work is an attempt towards a procedural approach to natural language parsing. Procedural languages lack the immediate correspondence between problem and program of declarative languages, but offer flexibility to the implementers of the parser, as they are not black boxes.

Eu-PAGE is a parser generator for Eurotra grammars [4] which produces portable C/C++ code. The generator itself is written in C++ and runs under Windows NT/95 environments.

The generator parses the Eurotra grammar and transforms the regular expression on the right hand side of each b-rule into the corresponding finite state machine (FSM) using the standard technique described in [5]; a transition of a FSM depends upon unification of the input tree node with the current rule node. Each rule is transformed into a recognizing routine, with accompanying data types, variables and transition tables. The corresponding information is encoded in a global rule table, which is used by the parsing algorithm to test and apply the rules.

The "naïve", exhaustive bottom-up approach to parsing with b-rules is not efficient, especially with simple and unambiguous grammars; for this reason the generator performs analysis of the grammar in order to produce more efficient code. In most grammars there is an attribute that plays the role of syntactic category; this attribute (hereafter the *basic attribute*) is present in all the rule nodes, paired with a value. The name of this attribute is supplied by the user; the generator calculates the First and Next sets for the grammar. These sets are different from the sets defined for context free grammars -e.g. in [5]-, as the right hand sides of rules are regular expressions.

The set Next(V, R) for the value V of the basic attribute in the context of rule R contains all the values of the basic attribute that may appear immediately after V in a node sequence that matches with R. If V can be the last in such a node sequence, ε (the empty string) is added to V's Next set. The set Next(V) is the union of the Next(V,R) sets for all the rules. The set First(R) for each rule R contains the values of the basic attribute that can be first in a node sequence matching the rule. Table 1 shows the Next(V,R) sets for the rule in Figure 1.

V	Next(V,R)
special_adj	article
article	adj, noun
adj	adj, noun
noun	ε

Table 1: Next(V,R) sets

The enhanced parse algorithm attempts to apply a rule R on a node sequence only when the value V of the basic attribute for the first node of the sequence belongs to First(R). It also defers the application of the rule, if the node that it will add is not immediately usable.

Let us consider the parse tree fragment in Figure 2, where a rule matches with the node sequence $V_1...V_k$; the new node that will be added is V_P. If the node V_N does not belong to the set Next(V_P), there is no rule which matches a sequence that contains the two nodes V_P and V_N. If ε does not belong to Next(V_P) either, no rule can match any sequence containing V_P at the present state of the parse tree. Thus, there is no reason to apply the rule and create the new node; application will be deferred. In the enhanced parse algorithm that follows in Figure 3, Parent(R) is the parent node of the rule R (V_P

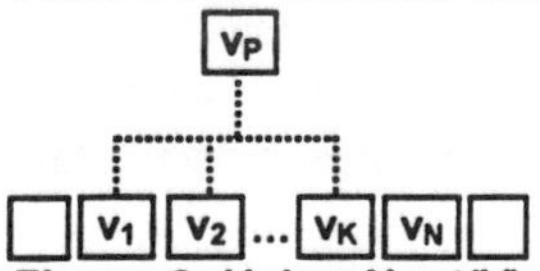

Figure 2: Using Next(V)

in Figure 2).

```
procedure Parse(var T: tree)
begin
for each parentless node V1 of T and
    for each rule R such that V1 ∈ First(R) do
   if R matches a sequence (V1...VK),VN in T then
      if Next(Parent(R))∩{ε,VN} ≠ ∅ then begin
         create the parent node VP of R;
         add P to T as the parent of
         (V1...VK) producing T';
         if T' is a full parse tree then
            insert T' into the solution list;
         else Parse(T');
      end
end
```

Figure 3: The enhanced parsing algorithm

4. Parallel programming platforms

The plethora of parallel computer architectures and the lack of a widely accepted model for parallel computation result into dependencies between the implementation of the application and the underlying machine (hardware and operating system). However, portability is a very essential issue. Parallel software platforms decouple the cycle of application development from the underlying hardware and operating systems. They mask the network topology and provide simple and system independent calls, but nonetheless adequate for the development of a wide variety of applications. The most widely used parallel software platforms are PVM [6] and MPI [7]; our choices were PVM and Orchid [8][9].

PVM unifies a collection of heterogeneous computer systems to a virtual parallel machine. Most of today's computer systems support PVM, while a large number of applications have been developed on top of it. PVM supplies functions for process management, transparent communication, load balancing, etc.

Orchid is a new portable and scaleable platform for parallel programming, suitable for any type of distributed memory architecture or heterogeneous systems emphasizing on portability; applications do not require changes when ported from a parallel machine to another, or are upgraded to a larger machine of the same type. The basic unit of parallelism in Orchid is the *light weight process*. Fast context switching, small creation time and low memory requirements enable the programmer to open a large number of concurrent light weight processes with minimal overhead.

Orchid provides a simple, system independent user interface, facilitating parallel application development with asynchronous process-to-process and group communication. New light weight processes are allocated to processors in a dynamic way, according to simple embedded allocation strategies or user defined ones. Global synchronization mechanisms enable synchronization of light weight processes running on the same or different processor. The distributed shared memory system of Orchid incorporates a set of flexible mechanisms for the implementation of customized distributed shared memory paradigms, rather than providing a general fixed DSM system with embedded policies.

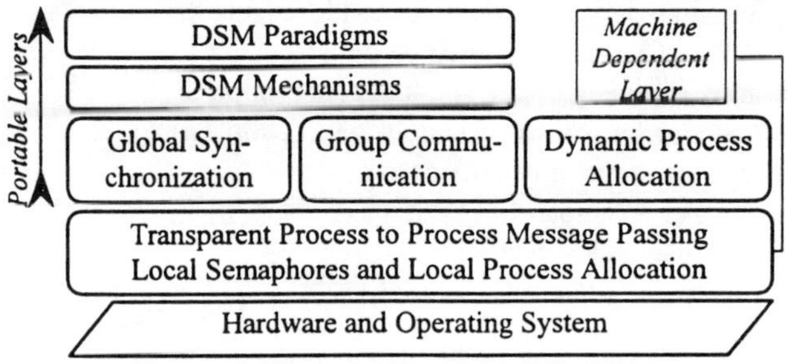

Figure 4: The architecture of Orchid

Orchid has been implemented and evaluated on various architectures, since its layered structure ensures portability. It has been successfully used for the development of parallel applications from the fields of signal processing, logic programming and attribute grammars. The first pilot implementation was developed on Multicluster 2 running the operating system Helios. Now, Orchid runs on top of SunOS 4 and Solaris operating systems, on top of Parix and Windows NT/95, while one version runs on PVM, enhancing PVM with light weight processes and the facilities of Orchid. The architecture of Orchid is depicted on Figure 4.

5. Generating code for parallel execution

Eu-PAGE, the parser generator described above, has been used for the automatic generation of two parsers. The first is a pilot parser for geographical descriptions in Greek. The second, the Dialogos parser, is a full blown parallel parser for the Greek language. The Eurotra grammar for Greek, which was the input to Eu-PAGE, was developed by the Greek Institute for Language and Speech Processing during the Eurotra project ([10]) and consists of 143 rules, 55 of which are b-rules; the parser is accompanied by a 5000 word sample lexicon.

To address the issue of full portability, the best solution appeared to be the generation of the same code for both platforms that would run on top of a platform dependent software layer responsible for the parallel execution. Only this layer, called "coordinator of parallel execution", has been implemented once separately for each platform.

The implementation exploits coarse-grained parallelism, the unit of parallelism being the syntactic analysis of single interpretations. Interpretations appear due to multiple entries of the same word in the lexicon (different word sense or features). The coordinator of parallel execution takes over after the lexical analysis is complete, giving as output the set of possible interpretations for the input phase. One process is created per processor, assigned with an interpretation. Syntactic analysis is performed on this interpretation using code generated by Eu-PAGE. When each analysis is complete, a new task is assigned to this process by the coordinator until all tasks have been performed. This strategy is a dynamic load balancing technique and ensures optimal processor utilization contrary to a static, pre-defined task allocation strategy.

A finer-grained parallelism could be achieved by running the four stages of syntactic analysis (one for the parse tree and three for the enhancement, selections and classification of parse trees) in a pipeline. However, the cost of the first stage is significantly greater than the total cost of the other three, making the expected benefit too small to outbalance the increased complexity, the communication overhead and the possible under-utilization of processors. An experience of finer-grained parallelism applied in an NLP application was acquired by our team with the development and evaluation of PAGE [9] (Parallel Attribute Grammar Evaluator) which was used for the development of a pilot syntactic analyzer of the Greek language.

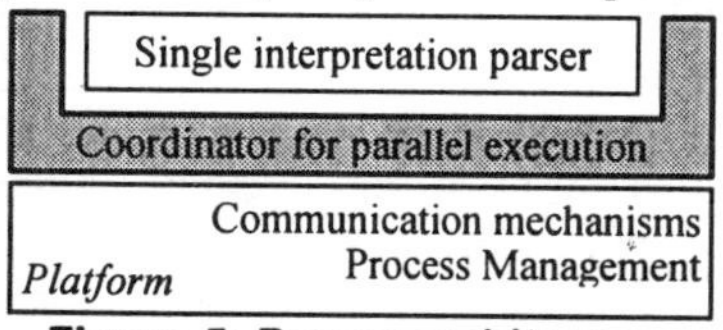

Figure 5: Parser architecture

6. Experimental results

This section presents evaluation results for Eu-PAGE and Dialogos. However, it is difficult to collect experimental data that give an objective image of them, especially Eu-PAGE since: (i) the efficiency of the parser depends on the nature of the specific language; Greek is a difficult language with free word order and inflectional morphology (ii) the generation of the parser is affected by the Eurotra grammar given as input; an unsuitably written grammar may lead to sub-optimal parser generation.

The graph in Figure 6 presents experimental results collected on a local area network of seven equally powered workstations running the Solaris operating system, using PVM as the parallel programming platform. The two sentences selected are the Greek equivalent of "the prices in the market are high", and "his/its office will organize experiments" (an ambiguous sentence in Greek).

Real execution times are not meaningful, since they depend on the processor power; faster workstations in our lab achieved much better execution times. What is more interesting is the speed-up, presented in the graph, where:

$$\text{speedup} = \frac{\text{executionTimeOnOneProcessor}}{\text{executionTimeOnNProcessors}}$$

The figure illustrates almost linear speedups showing that natural language parsing can benefit a lot from the application of parallelism. However, speedups are not equally good for all sentences, especially for simple ones with a small number of interpretations, while more complicated sentences are usually the ones that are amend to parallelism. This is not a disappointing conclusion since the processing of complicated sentences is the time consuming task, and the one that needs improvement in performance.

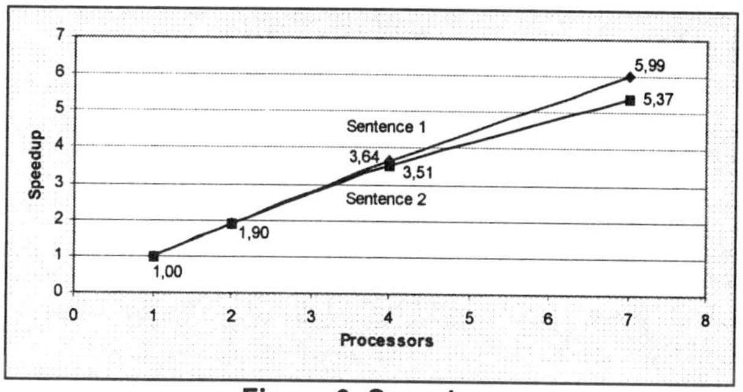

Figure 6: Speedup

References

[1] Gert Adriaens and Udo Hahn, eds., *Parallel Natural Language Processing*, Ablex Publishing Corp., 1994

[2] The User Language, *Eurotra Reference Manual 7.0*, Commission of the European Communities, Luxembourg

[3] D.J. Arnold, Louis des Tombe, "Basic theory and methodology in Eurotra," in Sergei Nirenburg, ed., *Machine Translation: Theoretical and Methodological Issues*, pp.114-135, Cambridge University Press, Cambridge, 1987

[4] A. G. Manousopoulou, "Natural Language Parsing with the Eurotra formalism," NTUA Diploma thesis (in Greek), 1995

[5] A. V. Aho, R. Sethi, J. D. Ullman, *Compilers: Principles, techniques and tools*, Addison Wesley, 1985

[6] Al Geist, A. Beguelin, J. Dongarra, W. Jiang, R. Manchek, V. S. Sunderam, *PVM (Parallel Virtual Machine): A Users' Guide and Tutorial for Network Parallel Computing*, MIT Press, Cambridge, MA, 1994

[7] W. Gropp, E. Lusk, A. Skjellum, "*Using MPI: Portable Parallel Programming with the Message Passing Interface*," MIT Press, Cambridge, MA, 1994

[8] C. Voliotis, G. Manis, Ch. Lekatsas, P. Tsanakas and G. Papakonstantinou, "ORCHID: A Portable Platform for Parallel Programming," *Euromicro Journal of Systems Architecture*, vol.43, no.6-7, April 1997

[9] C. Voliotis, G. Manis, A. Thanos, P. Tsanakas, G. Papakonstantinou, "Facilitating the Development of Portable Parallel Applications on Distributed Memory Systems," *Massively Parallel Programming Models 95*, Berlin, October 1995

[10] http://www.ilsp.gr/GBPROGS.HTM#eurotra

An Integrating Clues Method based on Syntactic Relations for Korean Verb Sense Disambiguation

Kwon Yang Kim
Dept. of Computer Science
Kyungil University
Republic of Korea
kykim@bear.kyungil.ac.kr

Se Young Park
Dept. of Computer Technology
ETRI
Republic of Korea
sypark@com.etri.re.kr

Sang Jo Lee
Dept. of Computer Engineering
Kyungpook National University
Republic of Korea
sjlee@bh.kyungpook.ac.kr

Abstract

We present a new approach for word sense disambiguation, specially for Korean transitive verb, based on supervised method. This approach integrates a set of clues based on syntactic relations for word sense disambiguation. Instead of using unordered set of surrounding words of a given ambiguous verb, we use co-occurrences as a clue for disambiguation based on some syntactic relations such as predicate-argument, modified-modified, adjacency, or mixture of them. The experimental results show that the accuracy of our disambiguation method on highly ambiguous verbs with fine-grained sense distinctions is always better than the default strategy of assigning all occurrences to the most frequent sense.

1: Introduction

Words can have several meanings or senses, and a use of the word out of context is ambiguous between these senses. The problem of disambiguation, determines which of the senses of an ambiguous word is invoked in a particular context, is of clear importance in a wide range of natural language applications such as machine translation, information retrieval, and so on. Whenever a system's action depends on the meaning of the context, disambiguation is beneficial or even necessary.

Much of recent work in lexical ambiguity resolution offers the prospect that a disambiguation system might be able to receive as input unrestricted text and tag each word with the most likely sense with fairly reasonable accuracy and efficiency [2, 3, 4, 5, 6]. In the methods of using a context as a classifier for sense disambiguation, the reason for poor performance may just be that the limited contextual representations are not very informative. So that even humans would not be able to disambiguate very well based on the same information. In this paper, we present a new approach that integrates a set of clues based on syntactic relations as a context representation.

2: Motivation

Our sense disambiguation method is based on the relatedness between contexts and possible senses. For a multiple sense word in a context, the sense in the context is chosen as the sense which has the highest relatedness to the context among all senses of the word. We used the surrounding word entry itself as a context representation that is a classifier for the sense disambiguation instead of using a sum of word vectors constructed from definition of entry [3] or similar neighbors [4]. If it is possible to collect the occurrence of clues sufficiently for disambiguating a given verb during the training, these clues themselves are the most informative knowledge source for a fine-grained sense disambiguation.

For example, verb '쓰다/ssuda' can mean 'write' or 'wear' depending on the different context. To decide which sense of '쓰다/ssuda' is used, we must look at the surrounding words in the context. The context of a word can provide good clues to decide which sense the word has in the context. On the one hand, '쓰다/ssuda(wear)' verb co-occurs with words such as "모자/moja(hat)', '안경/angung(glasses)', '머리/muri(head)', and so forth. On the other hand, we find '쓰다/ssuda(write)' verb co-occurring with '편지/punji(letter)', '연필/yunpil(pencil)', '칠판/chilpan(blackboard)', and so forth.

For disambiguation of two clearly distinct senses such as 'write' and 'wear' sense of verb '쓰다/ssuda', the surrounding words set can be used as a classifier for disambiguation. However, some senses of an ambiguous verb are interrelated and overlapping in many cases. Take the following examples for the fine-grained sense disambiguation of verb '쓰다/ssuda'.

1082-3409/97 $10.00 © 1997 IEEE

(a) 머리에 모자를 쓰다.
/muri-ae/ /moja-rul/ /ssuda/
on head hat put on
(put a hat on head)

(b) 그 일에 머리를 쓰다.
/gu il-ae/ /muri-rul/ /ssuda/
on that work head(brain) exercise
(exercise brain on that work)

(c) 영어를 유창하게 쓰다.
/youngu-lul/ /yuchangha-ge/ /ssuda/
English fluently speak
(speak English fluently)

(c) 영어로 일기를 쓰다.
/youngu-ro/ /ilgi-lul/ /ssuda/
in English diary write
(write a diary in English)

A noun '머리/muri(head)' was co-occurred with a verb '쓰다/ssuda' in (a) and (b), but a verb '쓰다/ssuda' has different sense ("put a hat on" and "exercise brain") according to its grammatical role (locative and object derived from postposition '에/ae' and '를/lul') of noun in each context. A noun '영어/youngu(English)' was co-occurred with a verb '쓰다/ssuda' in (c) and (d). A verb '쓰다/ssuda' has different sense ('speak' and 'write') according to its surface case (object and instrument derived from postposition '를/lul' and '로/ro')of noun '영어/youngu(English)'.

Therefore, we will focus on the difference of syntactic relations instead of unordered set of surrounding words in the context and propose to build clues based on each relation. This approach is based on the fact that some word behaves differently depending on its syntactic relation. Therefore, the sense of a verb in context should be classified according to its syntactic relation of surrounding words.

3: Word sense disambiguation

We present a new approach for word sense disambiguation, specially for Korean transitive verb, based on supervised method. This approach integrates a set of clues based on syntactic relations for word sense disambiguation. All clues for sense disambiguation are summed up and taken into account in word sense disambiguation process. Instead of using unordered set of surrounding words of a given ambiguous verb, we used co-occurrences as a clue for disambiguation based on some relations such as predicate-argument, modifier-modified, adjacency, or mixture of them.

At first, a set of sentences in training corpus manually sense tagged occurrences of verb v is given. EXTR-Clue (Clue extract program) extracts all clues for each training example with an occurrence of verb v and records all clues with a sense tag of a verb into the each clue library. These clues make word sense disambiguation possible by capturing semantic characteristics of the corresponding context and sense respectively.

In test, EXTR-Clue extracts all clues from new unseen sentences with an occurrence of verb v. These instances of clues are then compared to clue library which was constructed in training step. For instance of a clue, possible senses of verb v and its occurrence number are extracted from clue library by the simple matching. The evidence of all clues are summed up and taken into account for disambiguation of verb v. We infer that the sense of verb v in the test set is the sense has the highest score of its sense. Figure 1 shows the flow of training and test step in our experiments.

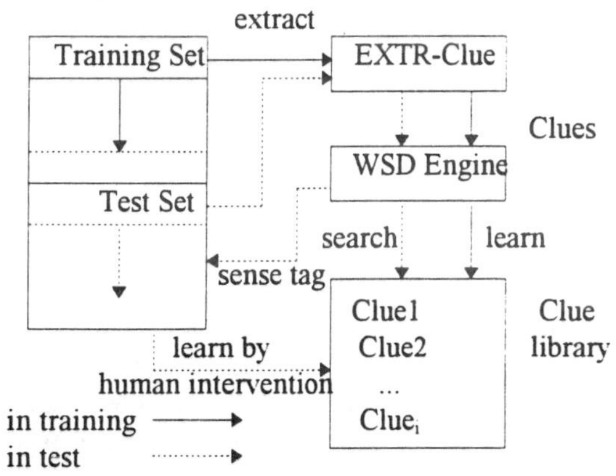

Figure 1: The flow of training and test step

3.1: Syntactic clues

For sense disambiguation of a verb, we exploit the nine clues based on syntactic relations between the surrounding words in the context and a given ambiguous verb. We deal three major verb-noun relations such as object-verb, locative-verb, and instrument-verb relations. The postpositions attached to the nouns are either '을/를(ul/lul)', '에(ae)' or '로/으로(ro/uro)', that represent the object, locative or instrument, respectively. Korean is a flexible word order language and the postposition attached to noun represents the syntactic relations between the noun and the verb. The verb-ending represents the relation such as verb-noun, verb-verb and adverb-verb. The verb(adjective form)-noun, verb-verb, and adverb-verb relations represent modifier-modified relation between each word.

The left context and right context supplement the

above seven clues as the remaining surrounding words in the context. EXTR-Clue program automatically extracts each clue for a given sentence. All the common function words such as postposition, determiner, numeral, conjunction are removed. The remaining words after stop list are stemmed in order to match the derived or inflected form of same word together.

<Clue-1> Noun+'을/ul' or '를/lul' ... Verb
<Clue-2> Noun+ '에/ae' ... Verb
<Clue-3> Noun+'로/ro' or '으로/uro' ... Verb
<Clue-4> Verb(adjective) - Noun+postposition Relation
<Clue-5> Adverb(or Adverbial form) - Verb Relation
<Clue-6> Vt(Left)-Verb Relation
<Clue-7> Verb-Vt(Right) Relation
<Clue-8> Lcontext-Verb
<Clue-9> Rcontext-Verb

Our disambiguation method also makes use of the unordered surrounding words to the left (Clue-8) or right (Clue-9) of a given verb in the sentence. These clues represent the other relations between surrounding words and a given verb, and supplement the seven clues previously defined by selecting the remaining surrounding words in the sentence. Some clues represent the relation between the noun attached by auxiliary postposition (such as '는/nun', '도/do', '만/man' that usually mean topic and emphasis) and verb. The grammatical relation for these auxiliary postpositions depends on the context, hence it is difficult to decide the correct relation whether it is used as a subject, object or locative. Therefore, we combine these clues into Clue-8 and Clue-9 according to the left or right of the given verb in the sentence.

3.2: Training and test

In training step, clue EXTR-Clue extracts all clues with a manually tagged sense of verb for each training examples. These clues are newly recorded into clue library as the form of "clue-instance/sense-number/occurrence-number" if the instance of clue and its sense is unique in each clue library. Otherwise, it only increments the occurrence number of the clue in the clue library.

In test step, all clues for a test sentence are extracted by the EXTR-Clue, and compared to clue library extracted in the training step according to the clue type. The score that the sense of verb v is likely to be v_j for a given clue $clue_i$ is defined as the following conditional probability, where $N(clue_i v_j)$ is the number of sentences in which $clue_i$ co-occurs with verb v where v has sense v_j. The n is the number of senses for a given verb.

$$score(v_j / clue_i) = N(clue_i v_j) / \sum_{j=1}^{n} N(clue_i v_j)$$

To compute the score for all clues in the context with an occurrence of a verb v, each clue is weighted according to its discriminating potential. With weighting, the equation for total score of all clues in the context where verb v has sense v_j becomes:

$$score(v_j / clues) = \sum_{i=1}^{m} score(v_j / clue_i) * W_i$$

W_i denotes weight for a $clue_i$ which is relative contribution of each clue. The m is the number of clues for a given sentence. W_i is likely to be lower if there are many instances which have multiple senses of a verb in a clue library. W_i is given by following equation.

$$W_i = \frac{1}{N_i} \sum_{clue \in clue-i} (1 / number\_of\_verb\_senses)$$

N_i denotes the number of clue instances in *clue-i* library. We infer that the sense of verb v in the test example is v_j, if the total score of v_j for some j is maximum among possible senses of verb v.

4: Experiments

In order to evaluate the performance of our sense disambiguation method, it was applied to the disambiguation of two highly ambiguous verbs. Two verbs have a large number of refined senses of word and some senses are interrelated and overlapping. The 1.4 M words Gemong encyclopedia corpus is used as a training and a test date set. Sentences containing two verbs were automatically extracted from the corpus and manually assigned a single sense tag corresponding to the Korean dictionary definition. Table 1 shows the sense distribution of the two verbs in the corpus and the average accuracy.

We conducted 100 random trails on a separate training and test set in order to measure average performance. At first, the performance of our disambiguation method was compared with the baseline performance that is achieved by assigning all occurrences to the most frequent sense [1]. Secondly, it was compared with the method which use an unordered surrounding words (that is only clue-8 and clue-9) as a context. The experimental results show that the accuracy of our disambiguation method is always better than the default strategy of assigning all occurrences to the most frequent sense. Moreover, it is better than a method which use only clue-8 and clue-9 as a left context and right context, respectively.

Transitive senses of '쓰다/ssuda' : Total set: 2025 Training Set : 1519 Test Set : 506		
Sense Distribution		
Sense Definition	frequency	percent
S1:write (character,number) on	243	12%
S2: write,compose (poet,letter)	324	16%
S3:put on (hat,glasses,wig)	142	7%
S4:use-1 (material)	425	21%
S5:use-2 (instrument)	446	22%
S6:employ (person,animal)	20	1%
S7:adopt (means,method)	304	15%
S8:spend (time,money)	61	3%
S9:speak (English,slangy term)	21	1%
S10:exert;exercise(brain,power)	25	1%
S11:administer (medicine)	7	<1%
S12:lend (money,house)	6	<1%
S13:be falsely charged	1	<1%
Accuracy		
Baseline	Clue-8 and Clue-9	All Clues
22%	62%	66%
Transitive senses of '막다/makda' : Total set: 818 Training Set : 614 Test Set : 204		
Sense Distribution		
Sense Definition	frequency	percent
S1:stop up (hole,bottle)	25	3%
S2:enclose (house,mountain)	16	2%
S3:stop/check(growth)	188	23%
S4:prevent (inflation)	311	38%
S5:defend (enemy,attack)	115	14%
S6:block (street,river)	155	19%
S7:partition (room)	8	<1%
Accuracy		
Baseline	Clue-8 and Clue-9	All Clues
38%	67%	70%

Table 1: Sense distribution of two verbs in Gemong corpus and accuracy

The second goal is to extract almost all of the clues needed for the disambiguation of a verb in the given corpus. If it is possible to collect the occurrence of clues sufficiently for disambiguating a given verb, we can employ these clues extracted from a training set for disambiguating the verb in an unseen sentence.

In order to show how many clues should be extracted and learned for the disambiguation of five verbs, we have gathered a large 30 M words corpus (different size for each verb) which consists of a wide variety of text from newspaper report.

With respect to verb '막다/makda', the accuracy curve increases fairly rapidly and then increases slowly around 400 training examples. At near 1000 examples, the accuracy curve levels off (85% accuracy). However, in the case of verb '쓰다/ssuda', it is not clear whether the accuracy curve is leveling or still increasing around 1000 examples. Up to near 2200 training examples (about 40 M words corpus), the accuracy curve for a verb '쓰다/ssuda' doesn't level off and increases. One probable cause that the accuracy curve of verb '쓰다/ssuda' levels off around the higher training examples is that the sense of verb '쓰다/ssuda' is more comprehensive than a verb '막다/makda' and then it needs a variety of words entry as a clue for the disambiguation. For example, the 'use' sense of '쓰다/ssuda' can co-occur with all of the material noun as an object case. With respect to other three verbs such as '쏘다/ssoda', '젓다/jutda', and '엎다/upda' that have two or three clearly distinct senses, the accuracy curves level off around a fairly small number of training examples.

5: Conclusion

This paper has presented that a method of integrating clues based on syntactic relations for Korean transitive verb sense disambiguation performs better than a baseline performance and alternative method which exploits only left and right context.

We also presented a variation of accuracy performance with varying amounts of training data on a larger corpus. On this task, we found that the accuracy curves for four verbs level off on a half sized training data in the larger corpus.

References

[1] Gale, William, Kenneth Ward Church, and David Yarowsky, Estimating upper and lowe bounds on the performance of word sense disambiguation programs, In the Proceedings of the 30th Annual Meeting of the Association for Computational Linguistics, 1992

[2] Hwee, Tou Ng and Hian Beng Lee, Integrating Multiple Knowledge Sources to Disambiguate Word Sense: An Examplar-based Approach, In the Proceedings of the 34th Annual Meeting of the Association for Computational Linguistics, 1996

[3] Niwa, Yoshiki and Yoshihiko Nitta,Co-occurrence Vectors from Corpora vs. Distance Vectors from Dictionaries, COLING94, p.304-309

[4] Schutze, Hinrich, Ambiguity in Natural Language Learning Computational and Cognitive Models, Ph.D. Dissertation, 1995, Stanford University

[5] Yarowsky, David, Unsupervised word sense disambiguation rivaling supervised methods, In the Proceedings of the 33rd Annual Meeting of the Association for Computational Linguistics, 1995

[6] Yarowsky, David, Word Sense Disambiguation using statistical models of roget's categories trained on large corpora, In Proceedings of the 14th Conference on Computational Linguistics, COLING92, p.454-460

A User-Assisted Business Letter Generator Dealing with Text's Stylistic Variations

E. Stamatatos, S. Michos, N. Fakotakis and G. Kokkinakis
Dept. of Electrical and Computer Engineering
University of Patras
stamatatos@wcl.ee.upatras.gr

Abstract

This paper describes a user-assisted business letter generator that meets the ever-increasing demand for more flexible and modular letter generators which draw on explicit thematic models and are easily adaptable to specific user needs. Based on a detailed analysis of requirements and taking full advantage of the end users feedback, the presented generator not only creates a business letter according to the user choices, but also refines it taking into consideration stylistic aspects like written style and tone.

1. Motivation

Correspondence is essential in establishing and confirming transactions in commerce. Although there are several competing forms of communications in the modern world (e.g., telephone, fax, telex, e-mail), an old-fashioned letter is still the most formal way to get the message across, since correspondence that's prompt, accurate, and professional looking, creates a sense of responsiveness, dependability, and trust [10].

The creation of business letters is an important activity in office environment applications. Taking into consideration the large amount of such common and stereotyped letters produced daily in an office, it is easy to understand that considerable losses in productivity as well as fruitless wastes in time and money are observed for such a trivial, but necessary, activity. Therefore, it is obvious that the automation of this procedure would help companies achieve better correspondence quality and avoid a time-consuming and expensive task.

The vast majority of business letters is a short (up to one page) standardized text. In many cases, similar letters must be produced several times with slight alterations. For any business a finite number of pre-written letters and paragraphs can cover virtually all situations. Additionally, a business letter often has to be composed in two or more languages [2]. Therefore, providing this possibility automatically could considerably facilitate the task of composing a letter, particularly for a non-native speaker of a language.

Moreover, commercial correspondence style obeys to some specific rules. There are specific expressions that set the tone of the letter and modify the addressee's reactions. Business letters are often written in an old-fashioned, pompous style which usually complicates the message [2]. Hence, setting automatically the interpersonal and situation aspects that affect the form and content of a business letter would help in establishing some simple and clear stylistic variations in a text that will convey the useful information without misunderstandings.

This paper presents an approach to the automation of business letter composition emphasizing on the above points. The next section contains a description of relevant work in natural language generation (NLG). Section 3 comprises the results of the analysis of a medium-sized business letter corpus and section 4 describes our approach in detail. Section 5 includes two examples of the system output together with some comments. Finally, in section 6 a brief discussion on system's performance is given and some conclusions are drawn.

2. Relevant work

During the last twenty years research in NLG has managed to offer robust general-purpose single-sentence generators and limited-purpose multisentence generators [8]. Some fruitful areas for application have been investigated. Particular promising areas seem to be situations where data change quickly, or where large amounts of data have to be extracted from a knowledge base and presented in a standardized way. So, the most popular and successful NLG applications to date are the generation of stock market reports [9], weather forecasts [6], technical reports [13] and business letters [14], [5].

Text generation as it is used in the vast majority of up-to-date software is limited to **canned text**. This technique, as opposed to linguistically founded text generation, has the following shortcomings:

1082-3409/97 $10.00 © 1997 IEEE

- the range of texts and the stylistic variations these systems can produce are very limited;
- the texts are not context sensitive. They are not tailored to the user. Therefore, the information conveyed or the form used may be inadequate for a specific user;
- extending and updating these systems is hard, if not impossible.

Template systems are used as soon as a message must be produced several times with slight alterations. They are the most robust approach for generating multisentence texts [9]. Form letters are a typical template application, in which a few open fields are filled in specified constrained ways. More sophisticated template systems fill template slots with linguistically-generated fragments [13]. In such systems, low-level phenomena (i.e., agreement, morphology, punctuation reduction, etc.) as well as more sophisticated ones (i.e., ellipsis, relative-clause introduction, etc.) cannot be easily handled. Moreover, if the number of templates becomes large, then it is hard to maintain and update these systems. Nevertheless, it seems that they are the most suitable approach for an application that requires the composition of standardized texts.

Linguistically based systems such as **phrase-based systems** [7] and **feature-based systems** [3] are not yet able to operate beyond the experimental level, especially for generating multisentence texts. These systems produce higher-quality output but building them is an expensive task that requires a large amount of computational effort. Additionally, they need some kind of representation of the information included in the text [6]. Such representations do not exist in the great majority of today's application systems.

On the other hand, style is the main factor besides the propositional content that modifies the listener's reactions. There are some approaches that try to take advantage of **stylistic aspects** in order to improve the quality of a text generator output [7]. Though stylistic aspects are too vague in their nature, it is obvious that stylistic variations depending on the topic of the text, the interlocutor, and the communication instance, are crucial for giving the reader the sense that (s)he doesn't read a machine-generated text. The main problem is that it is not yet possible to obtain a formal description of style that could be used in both style identification in text understanding and style generation in NLG. Furthermore, it is not yet clear how we can apply the results of our previous work in style identification to NLG [11]. Previous approaches to automatic generation of commercial correspondence did not pay special attention to stylistic variations of the produced texts, despite the fact that style is considered by them to be one of the most important factors for producing high quality letters [14].

Finally, the development of text plan libraries, that is representational paradigms for characterizing stereotypical texts, seems to be the crucial point in NLG research [8]. Such libraries would lead to reliable text planners capable of coping with real-world domains and planing texts of several paragraphs. So far no such text planner exists.

For all the above reasons, we decided to utilize template-based generation in the composition of business letters and take advantage of stylistic aspects, like written style and tone, in order to improve the quality of our text generator output. In the next sections, we will see how close to this initial goal are the output results.

3. Analysis of business letters

3.1. Sections of a business letter body

It is common ground that the quality of the output of a text generator depends on how well the text parameters (i.e., language, theme, written style, tone, etc.) have been analyzed and taken into consideration during its implementation phase. Towards this end, we analyzed manually a corpus of business letters that were collected from companies, organizations, institutions, and books written by experts on this field. This medium-sized corpus (about 1500 business letters) comprises common letters in Greek referring mainly to commercial transactions and announcements.

A business letter is composed of several fields: *the addresser's name, the addressee's name, the current date and place, a salutation, the body of the letter, a complimentary close, a list of enclosures* (optional), etc. [4]. In this work we deal with the **generation of the body of a letter**, that is the field conveying the important information.

In general, a well-formed business letter consists of three main sections [2], [10], [4]:

1. Cause: a statement of why the addresser was prompted to edit the letter. It is usually located at the beginning of the letter (i.e., the first paragraph). For instance, the addresser may want to reply to a previous letter sent by the correspondent.
2. Purpose: it concerns the basic points that need to be stated. For instance, the addresser may want to place an order for a product.
3. Conclusions: it comprises wishes and proposals which the addresser usually ends the letter with (i.e., the last paragraph).

Each one of the above sections consists of a set of *components*, that is the primary conceptual elements that compose the letter [4]. For example, the *conclusions* section of a letter may include the components: *further_inquiry_encouragement, thanks_for_writing,* etc. It has to be underlined here that a concrete component may be common in two or more letters belonging to different categories.

3.2. Extraction of letter plans

In order to extract general models for business letters, that is **letter plans**, we used the aforementioned business letter corpus. The first step was **the classification of this corpus into thematic categories**. Then, we focused on the most important categories. In particular, we chose to deal with the following general thematic categories:

- purchase and sale of products: it comprises catalogues, price-lists, samples, inquiries and replies, orders, complaints and adjustments on an order, etc.
- quotations: it comprises quotation of products, new products announcements, etc.
- payment settlements: it comprises invoices and statements, advice and acknowledgment of payment, etc.

The above categories were selected as they cover an important portion of the business letters spectrum [2]. In particular, over 80% of the aforementioned business letter corpus contained letters of these categories. Moreover, the letters that belong to these categories are stereotypical and it is possible to extract simple models that encode their structure.

These categories can be subcategorized further into **primitive thematic categories** that correspond to a specific theme. In other words, these sub-categories cover all the possible instances of the main category (as it was previously shown). For instance, concerning the *purchase_and_sale_of_products* category: consider that company-1 inquires catalogues, price-lists, etc., from company-2 (i.e., *inquiring_catalogues* letters) which, in turn, could reply to company-1 by sending catalogues, price-lists, etc., (i.e., *replying_inquiry* letters). Then, company-1 may want to place an order (i.e., *placing_an_order* letters) and company-2 either acknowledges this order (i.e., *acknowledging_an_order* letters) or refuses it (i.e., *refusing_an_order* letters), and so on [4].

The next step of the analysis of the corpus was **the extraction of the letter plans** that represent the structure of every primitive thematic category. Such a model describes what components may be included in each one of the aforementioned letter sections, what the correct order of these components is, and whether they are mandatory or not. In other words, a model represents a characteristic paradigm of a primitive thematic category that is composed of all the possible components in the right order. The set of these models forms our letter plan library and is language-independent since it is based on conceptual entities [12]. The initial structure we used in Prolog for a letter plan is:

plan(Thematic_Category,
[new_section,component(CodeNo,TYPE),...])

where the constant *new_section* states the starting of a new section (i.e., normally, each letter plan has three sections), and *TYPE* defines whether the component can be placed in a sentence containing other components or has to be placed in its own sentence (see the description of the sentence planning module in section 4.2).

3.3. Stylistic analysis

We processed the aforementioned corpus linguistically (i.e., by hand) in order to **identify all the possible linguistic expressions**, that is, canned phrases or sentences, that fit each one of the components of a section of a letter. It was found that each component may be generated by certain phrases. Furthermore, a sentence may consist of several phrases that correspond to several components. It was observed, however, that in the most formal and well-written letters each sentence included up to two components. In particular, about 60% of the sentences of these letters included two components and over 30% of the sentences included only one component.

Finally, the linguistic expressions extracted with this process were analyzed stylistically (i.e., by hand), in order to **identify their stylistic impact** on the letter. Since business letters is a restricted domain of texts, the stylistic variations were not clear. Nevertheless, slight alterations in terms of written style and tone have been detected. Hence, each phrase that generates a component has been analyzed in two dimensions:

- written style: *elegant*, *typical* and *official*
- tone: *friendly*, *usual*, *severe* and *offensive*

The written style of a text is characterized in a high degree by a set of words/phrases, that is mainly adjectives, adverbs, adverbial phrases, and prepositional phrases [11]. We call these words/phrases **style modulators**, and they can usually be removed from the text without the lack of any important propositional information. So, the more style modulators a phrase includes, the more elegant the phrase is. Furthermore, there are certain stereotypical phrases that set the letter tone as friendly, usual, severe and offensive. This can be seen easily in *complaints* letters where the addresser's tone may vary from very friendly to rude. For example, consider the stylistic distinctions between the following phrases taken from *payment_settlement* letters:

i) *we will sue you if your debt is not cleared within the next ten days* (offensive tone)
ii) *we are reluctant to place the matter in the hands of solicitors and are offering you a further ten days to settle the account* (friendly tone)

Certainly, there are thematic categories that such tone variations are of no practical use. For instance, in *placing_an_order* letters the addresser can't be rude [2].

4. Our approach

4.1. Basic characteristics of the system

During the design phase of our generator the user requirements as well as the types of reader characteristics and goals were taken into account. The presented generator is a **semi-automatic multisentence** generator that is based on templates. Template slots are filled by linguistically-processed fragments. In other words, the user determines the content of the letter by selecting the components that will be included in it and by filling in the appropriate templates, where it is necessary. This procedure is simplified via a simple and **user-friendly** interface designed and implemented in Visual Prolog that guides the user and helps him obtain the letter (s)he wishes for.

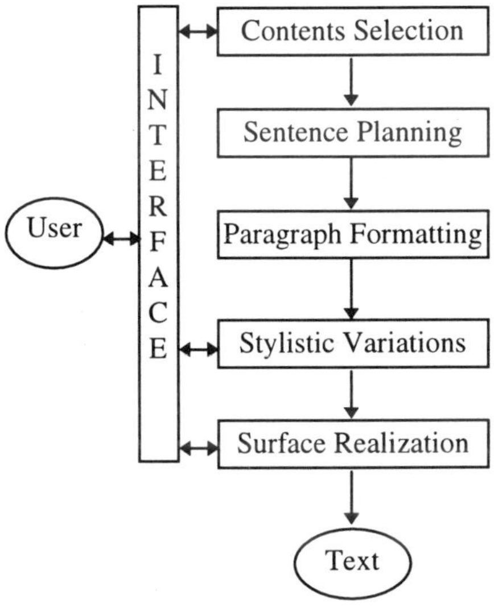

Figure 1. Overview of the generator

Although our system currently generates Greek business letters, the generation procedure has been designed with the view of achieving as much **language-independent** results as possible. Hence, our generator could be easily extended to another language (e.g., English) with least additional effort.

Moreover, the presented approach is based on a **pseudo-non-deterministic** generation procedure, that is, the same input can lead to different outputs. Of course, these outputs will have the same characteristics regarding the content of the letter, but they may differ either in the linguistic expressions used in the letter, or in the stylistic variations. Regarding these **stylistic variations**, the user is able to set the desired kind of written style and tone for the letter.

An overview of our generator is depicted in figure 1. The following paragraph describes analytically the generator modules.

4.2. Description of the system modules

The function of the system modules is as follows:

- **Contents selection**

As it has been mentioned earlier, each primitive thematic category possess a conceptual model that is composed of a **set of ordered components**. Additionally, a component may be **mandatory** or **optional**. So, after the selection of a thematic category by the user, the set of components that constitute the corresponding model is available and the user can select the optional component(s) that will be included in the letter. Hence, the user determines the contents of the produced letter according to his requests. Furthermore, the user also determines the size of the letter, since the less selected components the shorter the letter is. The internal structure we used for representing a component in Prolog is:

component(CodeNo,[phrase(PHRASE,TONE),...])

where *PHRASE* is a canned phrase string containing some possible open template slots together with some possible style modulators and *TONE* is the tone category of the phrase.

- **Sentence planning**

The next step in the generation procedure is the determination of the contents of each sentence, that is, the components that form each sentence. As it has been already noted, in a well-written letter each sentence includes up to two components. Additionally, there are certain components that have to be placed in their own sentence (e.g., for the sake of emphasis). Taking all these into account, the selected components are formed so as each sentence includes two components, if possible, or only one, otherwise. This procedure is performed automatically (i.e., it requires no interaction with the user).

- **Paragraph formatting**

Normally, the body of the letter is composed of three paragraphs, that is, one for each section (i.e., cause, purpose, conclusions). Nevertheless, according to the selected components and the sentence planning, two or even all three paragraphs may be unified into one. Additionally, if a section contains only one selected component, it can be included in the paragraph of the

Example Output 1

Stylistic Settings: Written Style = *elegant*, Tone = *friendly*

Κύριε,

Σας γνωρίζουμε ότι δεν έχουμε παραλάβει ακόμη την υπ' αριθμόν 107/1997 παραγγελία μας αν και ως κανονική ημερομηνία παραλαβής των εμπορευμάτων είχε οριστεί η 21/3/1997.

Σας παρακαλούμε να ενεργήσετε για την άμεση παράδοση όλων των ειδών που αναφέρονται στην παραγγελία μας. Παρακαλούμε επίσης να μας γνωρίσετε το συντομότερο αν είστε σε θέση να εκτελέσετε την παραγγελία μας, διαφορετικά θα βρεθούμε στην δυσάρεστη θέση να ακυρώσουμε την συμφωνία μας.

Περιμένουμε νέα σας.

Με ιδιαίτερη τιμή

Translation:

Dear Sir,

We would like to inform you that we have not yet to date received our order No. 107/1997 though the regular date of delivery of our merchandise was the 21/3/1997.

Would you please take the necessary steps so that all the items listed in our order be delivered immediately. Please let us know as soon as possible if you are in a position to deliver our order, otherwise to our regret we will have to cancel our agreement.

We look forward to hearing from you.

Yours sincerely

Figure 2. An example of the system output: *friendly tone.*

previous section. Hence, the produced letter may be consisted by less than three paragraphs. This procedure is also performed automatically, that is, it requests no interaction with the user as it is shown in figure 1.

- **Stylistic variations**

The user is able to select the tone (s)he wishes for the letter among three alternatives: friendly, usual, severe or offensive. For each component there is an appropriate set of phrases that realize it. Each phrase of this set belongs to one of the above tone categories. Hence, by setting the tone of the letter the user selects a subset of phrases that can realize each component. Furthermore, as it has already been mentioned style modulators contained in a phrase determine in a high degree how elegant the letter is. The user can set the degree of elegance for the phrases belonging to the selected tone category by selecting one of the following prompted alternatives:

- elegant: the maximum possible set of style modulators are inserted to the phrases.
- typical: a normal number style modulators is inserted to the phrases (up to one adjective or adverb for every phrase, if possible).
- official: no style modulators are inserted to the phrases.

- **Surface realization**

Each component is generated by a phrase that may be either a simple canned phrase or a canned phrase with a template slot. In the latter case, the user has to fill in properly the template. The surface realization module processes the user's input in order to form as linguistically-correct phrases as possible. For instance, if

Example Output 2

Stylistic Settings: Written Style = *elegant*, Tone = *offensive*

Κύριε,

Σας γνωρίζουμε ότι βρισκόμαστε σε εξαιρετικά δύσκολη θέση εξαιτίας σας δεδομένου ότι δεν έχουμε παραλάβει ακόμη την υπ' αριθμόν 107/1997 παραγγελία μας παρά τις διαβεβαιώσεις σας ότι θα είχαμε στα χέρια μας τα εμπορεύματα όχι αργότερα από την 21/3/1997.

Απαιτούμε την άμεση παράδοση όλων των ειδών που αναφέρονται στην παραγγελία μας. Σε περίπτωση που δεν είστε σε θέση να ανταποκριθείτε στις ανειλημένες υποχρεώσεις σας ειδοποιήστε μας σχετικώς, διαφορετικά θα μας αναγκάσετε να ακυρώσουμε την συμφωνία μας.

Περιμένουμε απάντησή σας το συντομότερο δυνατόν.

Με τιμή

Translation:

Dear Sir,

We would like to inform you that we are in an extremely difficult position because you have not delivered our order No. 107/1997 despite your assurances that we would receive our merchandise no later than 21/3/1997.

We demand immediate delivery of all the items listed in our order. If you are not in a position to fulfill your obligations you should notify us immediately, otherwise we will be obliged to cancel our agreement.

We expect your answer as soon as possible.

Yours sincerely

Figure 3. An example of the system output: *offensive tone.*

the user has to insert a list of products by typing a string for each product, then this module produces the concatenation of these strings taking into account punctuation and conjunction aggregation. According to the user's selection about the tone of the letter, there may be many phrases that generate a certain component. This module selects one phrase from this set **randomly**. Therefore, it is possible different letters to be produced by the same input settings. Moreover, this module deals with **low-level linguistic phenomena** such as punctuation checking, conjunction aggregation between two phrases and capitalization of the first letter for each sentence.

5. Two examples of the system output

Figure 2 and figure 3 show two examples of the system output in Greek (there are also their translations in English) as well as the stylistic settings selected by the user for each one of them. In order to illustrate the stylistic variations of the produced letters, we chose the *complaints for the delay of an order delivery* thematic category. This category includes the following components according to its letter plan:

(a) Mandatory components

1. Notification of non delivery of the order
2. Request for immediate delivery of the order
3. Request for notification about a possible inability for delivering the order
4. Determination of the regular delivery date
5. Exhortation to reply

(b) Optional components

6. Request for contact
7. Threat of possible order cancellation
8. Notification of subsequent problems (i.e., due to the delay of the delivery)

The user is able to select which of the optional components will be included in the letter. In the examples shown in figure 2 we chose to include components 6 and

7. Hence, the produced letters include the components 1, 2, 3, 4, 5, 6 and 7. The correct order of the above components is following:

Section	Components
Cause:	1-4
Purpose:	2-3-6-7-8
Conclusions:	5

Therefore, the final order of the produced letter will be 1-4-2-3-6-7-5 (i.e., omitting component 8), as it can be seen in the examples. Note that besides the choice for letter tone, the examples have been generated based on the same input settings by the user. Example 1 could be the first complaint letter for a delivery delay whereas example 2 could be the last letter of a series of similar letters that have not been replied.

6. Performance-conclusions

The presented system is fully-implemented. It has been developed in Visual Prolog and runs on a Pentium PC. Currently, it supports a user-interface in Greek and composition of business letters in Greek, as well as over 30 primitive thematic categories. The system produces letters in Rich Text Format encoding, that is a wide spread text formatting compatible with the vast majority of word-processors.

It has been tested on the basis of the black box evaluation technique, that is evaluating system output without looking inside to see how it works [1]. 15 people that write business letters on a daily basis have been used it for a week. About 90% of the produced letters was absolutely correct (i.e., without a single error). Moreover, all the users faced no problems on dealing with the system and considered the letter composition procedure whether fast or satisfying. On the other hand, it was observed that the end users considered the selection of a thematic category whether difficult or not suitable for their particular needs.

Regarding the quality of the produced letters, it has to be noted that despite the lack of pronouns and referring expressions, the generated text is pleasant to read and manages to give the sense of a human-composed text due to the careful selection of canned phrases and the creation of stylistic variations that differentiate the produced letters.

The main strength of the presented generator lies in the ability to handle stylistic variations on one hand and in the possibility of producing different letters from the same input settings on the other hand. As a more or less template system, it is able to produce letters by manipulating efficiently canned phrases and strings inserted by the user but it really doesn't know what is the meaning of this process.

As it has been mentioned previously, one of the most important activities in the NLG research is the construction of text plan libraries. We constructed such a library that includes the representation of several categories of business letters with the view of achieving as much abstraction as possible. Furthermore, the user is able to select what (s)he wishes to be included in the letter by guiding the system to generate short or long letters.

Additionally, our generator is based on a language-independent procedure and it can be ported easily to another language since we haven't used any intrinsic element of the Greek language. Actually, we believe that the implementation of an English version, that is our short-term goal, would face less problems than the Greek one, since the morphology of English is much more simpler than the corresponding Greek one.

Maintainability and expandability of our system is a very crucial point. In general, maintaining and updating template systems is hard, especially when the number of templates is too large. Nevertheless, as it has been already underlined, a concrete component of a letter may be common in different thematic categories. It is possible, therefore, to expand our system with a new category by using some already existing components and defining only a few new ones. Our short-term research focuses on simplifying the insertion of a new thematic category model as more as possible.

Finally, our long-term research will be the extension of our system by integrating work in style identification with the view of achieving automatic business letter categorization in terms of their written style and tone properties.

Acknowledgement

This work was granted by the Hellenic General Secretariat of Research and Technology in cooperation with the Department of Electrical and Computer Engineering of the University of Patras under the contract EPET II-715. The views, opinions, and/or findings contained in this paper are those of the authors and should not be construed as an official HGSRT position, policy, or decision, unless so designated by other official documentation.

References

[1] Allen J. Natural Language Understanding. 2nd Edition, The Benjamin/Cummings Pub. Co., 1995.

[2] Ashley A. *A Handbook of Commercial Correspondence*, Oxford University Press, 1992.

[3] Bateman J., E. Maier, E. Teich, & L. Wanner "Towards an Architecture for Situated Text Generation", in *Proceedings of the ICCICL*, Penang, Malaysia, 1991.

[4] Brettos T. & A. Agalianou-Brettou *Commercial Correspondence*, Eugenidis Pub., 1984, (in Greek).
[5] Coch J. & R. David "Representing Knowledge for Planning Multisentential Text", in *Proceedings of the 4th Conference on Applied Natural Language Processing*, 203-204, 1994.
[6] Goldberg E., N. Drieger & R. Kittredge "Using Natural Language Processing to Produce Weather Forecasts", *IEEE Expert*, 9(2), pp. 45-53, 1994.
[7] Hovy E. *Generating Natural Language under Pragmatic Constraints*, Ph.D. Thesis, Yale University, 1987.
[8] Hovy E. "Language Generation: Overview", in Cole R. *et al.* (eds.) *Survey of the State of the Art in Human Language Technology*, available in http://www.cse.ogi.edu/CSLU/HLTsurvey/, 1995.
[9] Kukich K. *Knowledge-Based Report Generation: A Knowledge-Engineering Approach*, Ph.D. Thesis, University of Pittsburg, 1983.
[10] Lang L. *Letter Writing: A practical guide to effective communication*, HarperCollins Publisher, 1994.
[11] Michos S., E. Stamatatos, N. Fakotakis & G. Kokkinakis "An Empirical Text Categorizing Computational Model Based on Stylistic Aspects", in *Proceedings of the 8th International Conference on Tools with Artificial Intelligence*, pp. 71-77, 1996.
[12] Michos S. & E. Stamatatos "*Dialogos-EPET Project: Requirements Analysis*", Technical Report No. 7.1.1, University of Patras, 1995, (in Greek).
[13] Reiter E., C. Mellish & J. Levine "Automatic Generation of Technical Documentation", *Applied Artificial Intelligence*, 9(3), pp. 259-287, 1995.
[14] Springer S., P. Buta & T. Wolf "Automatic Letter Composition for Customer Service", in R. Smith & C. Scott (eds.) *Innovative Applications of Artificial Intelligence 3*, pp. 67-83, 1991.

Using Fuzzy Logic in ITS-Course Generation

R. Nkambou
Département d'informatique
Université de Moncton
Moncton, NB E1A 3E9, Canada

Abstract

The object of this paper is to show how fuzzy logic has been used in the course building process. This process is based on the curriculum modeling approach we proposed, and exploits several knowledge sources such as target-public knowledge and training requirements. By using these parameters, a fuzzy algorithm generates a course adapted to the given target public that can produce required knowledge. The obtained course can be edited by the designer through graphical interfaces and can be delivered by an object oriented intelligent tutoring system (ITS).

1 Introduction

Industrial training is time consuming and expensive. For instance, IBM US spends 2 billion dollars a year on training including 1 billion dollars for employee salary; Each year, the US government spends more than 20 billion dollars on professional training [1]. Part of this training cost is related to the instructional design (curriculum and course development) and to the teaching process. Thus, a system that permits to rapidly build a course according to some needs could contribute to decrease these costs. Researches have been made to facilitate this process; Systems such as ID2 [2], AGD [3] have been specified to that effect. These systems offer a set of tools that are used in the instructional design process. However, the course building process still remains an explicit task left to the instructional designer.

In this paper, we presents a fuzzy approach in order to automate the course building process. Before the presentation of the approach, we will give a brief description of the curriculum model on which the course generation process is based.

2 A model of ITS curriculum

A modelling approach called CREAM (Curriculum REpresentation and Acquisition Model) [4] has been proposed for curriculum representation in an ITS. In this model, a curriculum is a structured representation of the subject matter in terms of capabilities, instructional objectives and pedagogical resources (learning materials). Achievement of instructional objectives contributes to the acquisition of capabilities. This achievement is supported by pedagogical resources through learning activities (exercises, demonstrations, problems, simulations...). CREAM implements domain, pedagogical and didactic aspects of a subject matter through a network organization of capabilities, of instructional objectives defined on these capabilities and of pedagogical resources supporting the accomplishment of instructional objectives. Using these three knowledge structures, we construct a *pedagogical model* of a curriculum that contains particular links between their elements.

2.1 Formal definition

A *labeled relation* [6] is a couple (R, ψ) where R is a relation and $\psi : R \longrightarrow E$ is a function. The set E is the set of labels. For instance, in the case where R is an *analogy relation* we take $E = \{definition, structural, functional\}$.

Given a description of a domain in term of capabilities, the capability model consists of: The set $\mathcal{C}$ of capabilities; The partition $(\mathcal{C}_i)_{i\in I}$ of $\mathcal{C}$ induced by the capability categories; The family $(\mathcal{E}_i)_{i\in I}$ of evaluation vocabulary; $\mathcal{E}_i$ being the current vocabulary for capabilities of type i; The set $\mathcal{R}_c = \{\mathcal{A}, \mathcal{G}, \mathcal{A}_b, \mathcal{A}_g, \mathcal{D}\}$ denoting the relations existing among the capabilities and The function $\psi_c : \mathcal{A}\cup\mathcal{G}\cup\mathcal{A}_b\cup\mathcal{A}_g\cup\mathcal{D} \longrightarrow E_c$ that associates a label to a given link between $\mathcal{C}$ elements.

Therefore, the capability model ($\mathcal{M}_c$) is the 6-uple $(\mathcal{C}, (\mathcal{C}_i)_{i\in I}, (\mathcal{E}_i)_{i\in I}, \mathcal{R}_c, E_c, \psi_c)$.

In the same way, the objective model ($\mathcal{M}_o$) is the 4-uple $(\mathcal{O}, \mathcal{R}_o, E_o, \psi_o)$ and the resource model ($\mathcal{M}_r$) is the 4-uple $(\mathcal{R}, \mathcal{R}_r, E_r, \psi_r)$ [5]

Fuzzy relation: Let P be the product set of n sets and M a totally odered set. A n-ary fuzzy relation Q is a fuzzy subset of P that take its values in M. Thus, there is a function $\mu : P \longrightarrow M$ so that $Q = \{(x \mid \mu(x)) \mid x \in P\}$, where $\mu(x)$ expresses the appartenance degree of x to the set P.

1082-3409/97 $10.00 © 1997 IEEE

Pedagogical model of the curriculum The Pedagogical model ($\mathcal{T}$) associated to a domain is the 10-uplet $(\mathcal{C}, \mathcal{O}, \mathcal{R}, (\mathcal{C}_i)_{i\in I}, R_1, R_2, R_3, \tau, \mu_1, \mu_2)$ where: $\mathcal{C}$ is the set of capabilities defined in the capability model; $\mathcal{O}$ is the set of objectives defined in the objective model; $\mathcal{R}$ is the set of didactic resources defined in the resource model; $(\mathcal{C}_i)_{i\in I}$ is the partition of C corresponding to capability categories; $R_1 \subset (\mathcal{C} \times \mathcal{O})$ is the prerequisite relation between a capability and an objective; $R_2 \subset (\mathcal{O} \times \mathcal{C})$ is the contribution relation; $R_3 \subset (\mathcal{O} \times \mathcal{R})$ is the relation that connectes objectives to resources; The function $\mu_1 : \mathcal{C} \times \mathcal{O} \longrightarrow [0,\ 1]$ is the function that associates a entry level to a prerequisite link (k, o). It is defined as follow:

$$\mu_1(k,o) = \begin{cases} \beta_{N(k)}(\text{label}(k,o)) & \text{if } (k,o) \in R_1 \\ 0 \quad \text{otherwise} \end{cases}$$

where $\beta_{N(K)}$ is the function that allows to switch from qualitative labels to quantitative values [5]. The function $\mu_2 : \mathcal{O} \times \mathcal{C} \longrightarrow [0,\ 1]$ associates the contribution weight of an objective o to a capability k and the function $\tau : \mathcal{O} \times \mathcal{R} \longrightarrow [0,\ 1]$ associates a label corresponding to the weight of a resource r for an objective o.

The fuzzy prerequisite relation ($\underline{\sigma}_1$) is defined as $\{(x \mid \mu_1(x)) \mid x \in \mathcal{C} \times \mathcal{O}\}$, the fuzzy contribution relation ($\underline{\sigma}_2$) as $\{(x \mid \mu_2(x)) \mid x \in \mathcal{O} \times \mathcal{C}\}$ and the fuzzy objective-resource relation ($\underline{\sigma}_3$) as $\{(x \mid \tau(x)) \mid x \in \mathcal{O} \times \mathcal{R}\}$.

2.1.1 Some access functions

Contribution of an objective $o \in \mathcal{O}$:$\Lambda(o) = \{k \in \mathcal{C} \mid \mu_2(o,k) > 0\}$ Objectives with capability $k \in \mathcal{C}$ as prerequisite: $\Lambda^*(k) = \{o \in \mathcal{O} \mid \mu_1(k,o) > 0\}$ Objectives that produce capability k: $\Gamma(k) = \{o \in \mathcal{O} \mid \mu_2(o,k) > 0\}$ Prerequisites of objective o: $\Gamma^*(k) = \{k \in \mathcal{C} \mid \mu_1(k,o) > 0\}$ Associated resources of o: $\bar{w}(o) = \{r \in \mathcal{R} \mid \tau(o,r) > 0\}$

A curriculum $\mathcal{K}$ associated to a given domain is defined by the 4-uplet $(\mathcal{M}_c, \mathcal{M}_o, \mathcal{M}_r, \mathcal{T})$ where: $\mathcal{M}_c$ is the capabitity model, $\mathcal{M}_o$ is the objective model, $\mathcal{M}_r$ is the resource model and $\mathcal{T}$ is the pedagogical and didacticl model.

3 Course generation process

To generate a course from one or several curricula built according to the networks indicated above, we consider the following parameters: a final state corresponding to the description of the course to be generated (training requirements). This state (D) can be expressed either as a set of objectives that the learner should achieve, or as set of capabilities to be acquired by the student. A starting point corresponding to the knowledge state of the targetted public. We represent this state as a vector (P) whose elements are couples *(capacity, level of mastery)*. We think that a good cognitive analysis of a domain can allow to identify and to classify categories of students with a general idea on their knowledge. The resulting course will be adjusted and adapted by the *Planner* to a particular student by taking into account the interaction between the student and the ITS.

The process of course generation consists in considering D and P and the curriculum knowledge structure as arguments of a fuzzy algorithm that will allow to define a course which is relevant for the concerned public. The choice of objectives is carried out by applying heuristic rules introduced into the system and which consider several parameters: the links between capabilities and objectives (prerequisite or contribution), D and P. We defined three possible heuristics: *General inclusion heuristic* which consists in including all the selected objectives in the course; *Random choice heuristic* which consists in choosing a certain number of objectives according to their contribution value to the capability we want to obtain; *Evaluation of complexity heuristic* consists in evaluating the complexity of the subgraphs rooted at each of the objectives we are considering. It permits to choose the objective with the highest probability of acquiring the considered capability.

3.1 Formal definition of heuristics functions

Let consider $\mathcal{K} = (\mathcal{M}_c, \mathcal{M}_o, \mathcal{M}_r, \mathcal{T})$, a curriculum associated to a domain. Let $H1$ be the general inclusion heuristic, $H2$, the random choice heuristic and $H3$ the evaluation of complexity heuristic. We have the following definitions: $H_1 \ : \ 2^{\mathcal{O}} \times \mathcal{C} \longrightarrow 2^{\mathcal{O}}$

$$(E,k) \longmapsto H_1(E,k) = \{o \in E \mid \mu_2(o,k) \neq 0\}$$

For $E \subset \mathcal{O}, k \in \mathcal{C}$ and $\xi_1, \xi_2 \in [0,\ 1]$. Let consider the set $\mathcal{A}_{E,k}(\xi_1,\xi_2) = \{o \in E \mid \xi_1 \leq \mu_2(o,k) < \xi_2\}$. If there is no ambiguity, we write $\mathcal{A}(\xi_1,\xi_2)$ instead of $\mathcal{A}_{E,k}(\xi_1,\xi_2)$.

$$H_2(E,k) = \begin{cases} \text{an arbitrary element}^1 \text{ of } \mathcal{A}(0.7,1) \\ \qquad \text{if } \mathcal{A}(0.7,1) \neq \emptyset \\ \text{an arbitrary subset of cardinality } 2\ ^1 \\ \qquad \text{of } \mathcal{A}(0.3,0.7) \text{if } \mathcal{A}(0.7,1) = \emptyset \\ \qquad \text{and } \text{card}(\mathcal{A}(0.3,0.7)) > 1 \\ \mathcal{A}(0,0.3) \quad \text{otherwise} \end{cases}$$

For $E \in \mathcal{O}, k \in \mathcal{C}$. Let note by $\mathcal{W}_E$ the set $\{o \in E \mid \mu_2(o,k) > 0.7\}$:

$$H_3(E,k) = \begin{cases} \emptyset & \text{if } \mathrm{card}(\mathcal{W}_E) \leq 1 \\ \text{an element } o \in \mathcal{W}_E & \\ \quad \text{that minimize } \textit{derived(o)} & \text{otherwise} \end{cases}$$

derived (o) is a function that returns the *complexity degree* of the objective o for the current target public. At the present time, the parameter we consider for the computation of this degree is the depth of the graph associated to the objective o relatively to the current target public. The detail of the algorithm of this function is given in [5].

3.2 Fuzzy algorithms of the course generation process

Let us denote by D the course description, by P the target public to be considered, by H the heuristic function to be considered and by $\mathcal{K} = (\mathcal{M}_c, \mathcal{M}_o, \mathcal{M}_r, \mathcal{T})$ the curriculum to be considered.

We put foward two main approaches for course generation process: Generating a course by using a training requirement (course description) expresses as a set of desired capabilities (in the first approach), or as a set of instructional objectives (in the second approach).

3.2.1 First approach: Course description is a set of desired capabilities

In this approach, the generation process operates in four main stages

1. marking of $\mathcal{T}$: The aim of this subprocess is to distribute target public knowledge in the pedagogical structure ($\mathcal{T}$). This distribution consists of two phases: the assignment of a state to prerequisite links in $\mathcal{T}$ and then the marking of $\mathcal{T}$ capability nodes relatively to the target public knowledge. Let E_1 be the set of marks of a prerequisite relation and E_2 the set of marks that qualify the state of a capability for a target public. We consider that $E_1 = \{notAquired, partiallyAcquired, acquired\}$ and $E_2 = \{notMastered, partiallyMastered, Mastered\}$.

   - *Marking of prerequisite links (function ϱ_1).*
     $\varrho_1(\mathcal{T}, P)$
     For all $(k,o) \in R_1$, mark (k,o) with *notAcquired*
     For each $(k,n) \in P$
       For each $(k,o) \in R_1$
         if $(\mu_1(k,o) \geq \beta(n))$
         then mark (k,o) with *acquired*
         else mark (k,o) with *partiallyAcquired*

     The function φ that associate a mark to a prerequisite link (k,o) is define as:

     $$\varphi : R_1 \longrightarrow E_1$$
     $$(k,o) \longmapsto markof(k,o)$$

   - marking capabilities in $\mathcal{T}$
     ϱ_2 ($\mathcal{T}_{d_1}$)
     For all $k \in \mathcal{C}$
     $\mathcal{O}_k = \{o \in \mathcal{O} \mid (k,o) \in R_1\}$
       if $((\forall\ o \in \mathcal{O}_k)\ [\varphi(k,o)$ = *acquired*])
       then mark k with *matered*
       else if (there exist at least one
         $o \in \mathcal{O}_k$ suchthat $\varphi(k,o)$=*acquired*)
         then mark k with *partiallyMastered*
         else mark k with *notMastered*

     The function γ that associated a mark $\gamma(k)$ to a capability k is define as :

     $$\gamma : \mathcal{C} \longrightarrow E_2$$
     $$k \longmapsto markof(k)$$

   N.B.: The structure obtained after the previous two operations on $\mathcal{T}$ is called *Dynamic pedagogical model* and is noted by $\mathcal{T}_d$.

2. Reduction of D: This reduction removes from the course description, all capabilities on which the target public has reach a satifactory level, that are capabilities that are marked with the label *mastered* in $\mathcal{T}_d$ (after the first stage of the generation process). The reduction process is carried out by the function ς_1 defined as:

   $$\varsigma_1 \quad : \quad 2^{\mathcal{C}} \longrightarrow 2^{\mathcal{C}}$$
   $$D \longmapsto D'$$

   with

   $$D' = D - \{k \in D \mid \gamma(k) = mastered\}$$

3. Generation of the subset E of objectives apt to produce D' (function ϑ): This function uses the dynamic pedagogical model obtained after the first stage, the new course description obtained

[1] In the implementation, the arbitrary choice is realized with the random number generator

after the second stage and the current heuristic funtion, and go through a fuzzy reasonning in order to build relevent objectives of the course.

$\vartheta\ (\mathcal{I}_d, D', H)$
$E = \emptyset$
For each $x \in D'$
 $I = \Gamma(x)$;
 if ($I = \emptyset$) then problem: there is no objective apt to produce x
 else $E' = \emptyset$
  For each $y \in I$
   $E' = E' \cup \{y\}$
   $J = \{k \in \Gamma^*\ (y)\ |\ (\gamma(k) = notMastered)$
     or $(\varphi(k, y) = notAcquired)\ \}$
  if ($J \neq \emptyset$) then $E' = E' \cup \vartheta(\mathcal{I}_d, J, H)$
 $E = E \cup H(E', x)$

4. Building a course graph $\mathcal{G}_c$ from E by exploiting the objective model ($\mathcal{M}_o$): The set of instructional objectives obtained after the previous stage is used for the course graph building by exploiting links define in the objective model of the current curriculum.

3.2.2 Second approach: Course description is a set of instructional objectives

This approach also consist of four stages. As stages 1 and 4 are the same as in the first approach, we will only define the stages 2 and 3.

- Stage 2: reduction of D (function ς_2): This function removes in the course description all objectives that can be considered as achieved by the target public. This is done by analyzing the pedagogical model of the curriculum relatively to the contribution links.

$$\varsigma_2:\ 2^{\mathcal{O}} \longrightarrow 2^{\mathcal{O}}$$

$$D \longmapsto D' = D - \{o \in \mathcal{O} | \forall k \in \Lambda(o),\ \gamma(k) = mastered\}$$

- Stage 3: extension of D' (function ϕ): This function extends the course description by adding new objectives obtained through a heuristic reasoning on the dyanamic pedagogical model obtained after the first stage. The resulting set of objectives will serves for the course building. $\phi\ (\mathcal{I}_d, D', H)$
$E = D'$
For each $o \in D'$
 For each k in
$\{x \in \Gamma^*(o)\ |\ \gamma(x) \neq mastered\}$
   $E = E \cup H(\Gamma(k),\ k)$

At the end of the course graph generation process, the course structuration begins. This structuration process deals with the determination of course objectives categories (global, intermediate or terminal). The process is based on prerequisites relationship between selected instructional objective and perform the course graph in order to produce a tree-like structure. The obtained structure is then proposed to the designer through a graphical interface, and he can bring all modifications he wants.

4 Conclusion

A fuzzy system for course generation have been proposed. This system is based on a formal knowledge modelling of the subject-matter. Two generation approaches have been described and each of them exploits heuristic functions in the choice of the course content according to the target group knowledge. We believe that our approach is the framework of new generation authoring systems for the individualized course development, and contributes to decrease the cost relied to this process. Our futur works deal with the development of a course development laboratory that will allow an instructional designer to easy customize and simulate the delivering of courses.

References

[1] T. Murray, B.P. Wools, "Design and implementation of an intelligent multimedia tutor," *AAAI'93 tutorial*, 1993.

[2] M. D. Merrill, "An integrated model for automating instruction design and delivery," *Automating instructional design: concept and issues*, pp. 147-190, Educational Technology Publications, 1993.

[3] G. Paquette, F. Crevier, C. Aubin, E. Bleicher, "AGD: knowledge modeling in an instructional design support system", *Proceedings of the world Conference on educational multimedia (ED-Media)*, 1996.

[4] R. Nkambou, G. Gauthier, "Un modèle de représentation du curriculum dans un STI", *Proceedings of third international conference on Intelliegent Tutoring System*, pp. 420-429, Springer-Verlag, 1996.

[5] R. Nkambou, *Modélisation des connaissances de la matière dans un système tutoriel intelligent: modèles, outils et applications*, Ph.D. Thesis, U. of Montreal, 1996.

[6] A. Kaufmann, *Introduction à la théorie des sous-ensembles flous*, Masson et Cie, 1975.

Session C.2

Vision and Pattern Recognition

Session Chair:
Jason Wang, New Jersey Institute of Technology, USA

Large Scale Pattern Recognition System using Hierarchical Neural Network and False-Alarming Nodes

Bong-Su Kang*, Sung-Il Chien*, Kil-Taek Lim*, and Jin-Ho Kim**
* Dept. of Electronics, Kyungpook National. Univ., Taegu, 702-701, Korea
** Dept. of Electronics, Kyung-Il Univ., Kyung-San City, 712-701, Korea

Abstract

In this paper, a hierarchical neural network was studied for the large scale pattern recognition problem such as the multilingual character recognition. The hierarchical neural network is made of the preclassification and the fine recognition modes. We constructed clusters for the preclassification mode using self-organizing feature map(SOFM) learning and performed modifying steps for reducing the number of clusters. The clusters contain patterns that have the similar characteristics. We adopted the multi-layer perceptron(MLP) networks to the corresponding clusters for the fine recognition mode. And we proposed the use of false-alarming nodes in the output layer of the MLP network, which could be constructed on error-prone negative examples quite similar to the patterns of the selected cluster but actually belonging to different nearby clusters through SOFM's topology-preserving mapping. The proposed system could be successfully adopted for recognizing the large number of printed Korean/Chinese characters database as well as IRIS database.

1. Introduction

The hierarchical neural network systems have been used in the large scale pattern recognition problems[1-3]. Large scale means that there are a large number of object classes to be recognized and much variation expected for each class. This results in many similar confusing patterns as well as large size of database, which usually act as a great burden to a simple structured network. Thus, it is more efficient to solve the large scale problem using the hierarchical neural network rather than using the simple structured one.

Our proposed hierarchical system for pattern recognition is composed of the preclassification mode and the fine recognition mode. The preclassification mode is introduced to divide the input patterns into the set of clusters that have similar elements. The fine recognition mode that follows employs a small scale network for a selected cluster.

We constructed the set of clusters by self-organizing feature map(SOFM)[4-6] learning and prepared secondary merging and modifying procedures. The clusters constructed by SOFM learning contain the elements that have the similar characteristics each other. The neighboring clusters have the property of topology-preserving, roughly meaning that similar patterns are gathered into a part of output SOFM nodes. But the initial size of clusters was required to be very large enough to represent the distributional characteristics of large number of classes and patterns into the output layer of SOFM network, and thus we adopted the second cluster merging and modifying procedure that modifies the output node distribution and also reduces the number of clusters. The cluster modifying procedure is based on the cluster information of every trained patterns.

The multi-layer perceptron(MLP)[7-8] network was used for fine recognition system for a selected cluster. The MLP network has a simple structure but its performance is found to be excellent compared to the others. Finally, we propose the false-alarming nodes in the output layer of the MLP network for rejecting similar patterns that does not belong to the original cluster. For training the false-alarming node in an MLP network for each cluster, negative examples[9-12] could be gathered from the neighboring clusters ordered around the selected cluster due to topology-preserving property of SOFM. Classifying experiments of the proposed system were performed on the IRIS database[13] and mixed Korean/Chinese characters database.

2. Hierarchical Neural Network System

The structure of the proposed hierarchical neural network recognition system is now described in Fig. 1. The input pattern selects the cluster that has the most similar characteristics by the Euclidean distance measure. This selected cluster contains the several elements that look alike to one another, and now the pattern recognition task needs to be performed only for them. The MLP network adopted for the selected cluster is operated to identify each class for the small set of patterns. In this step, it also determines whether the input pattern has selected the desired cluster or not. For this task, the additive false-alarming nodes are added in the output layer.

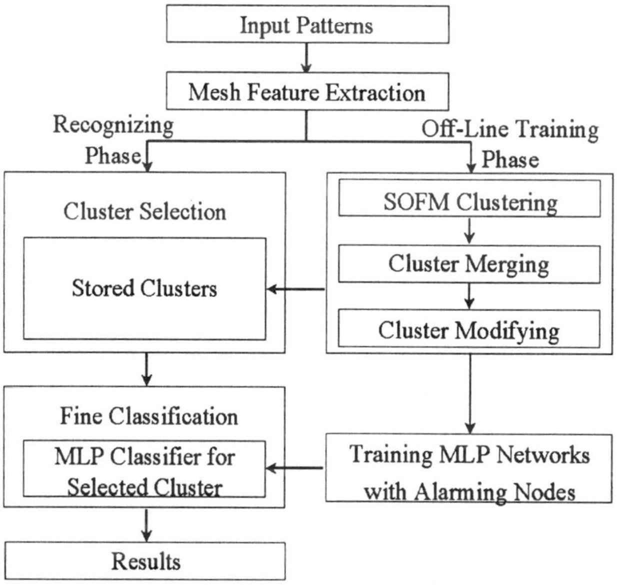

Fig. 1. Recognition and off-line training procedure of the proposed hierarchical system.

2.1. SOFM clustering

Fig. 2 shows the typical structure of SOFM network employing 2D output node structure. One of main characteristics of SOFM network is topology-preserving property[4]. Similar patterns are ordered closely on SOFM output node plane and the spatial distance between the two nodes can act as similarity measure of the input patterns assigned to those nodes. The initial output size of SOFM network should be determined by considering the number of classes to be recognized. If its size is chosen to be too small, SOFM network cannot be trained to map the distributional characteristics of input pattern onto output 2-D space properly. Otherwise, if the size is too lavishly large, the network becomes too inefficient in terms of the speed or the computation involved. However, it is preferable to construct a little large-sized SOFM network and to merge its clusters into small-sized network to avoid oversimplifying the input distribution.

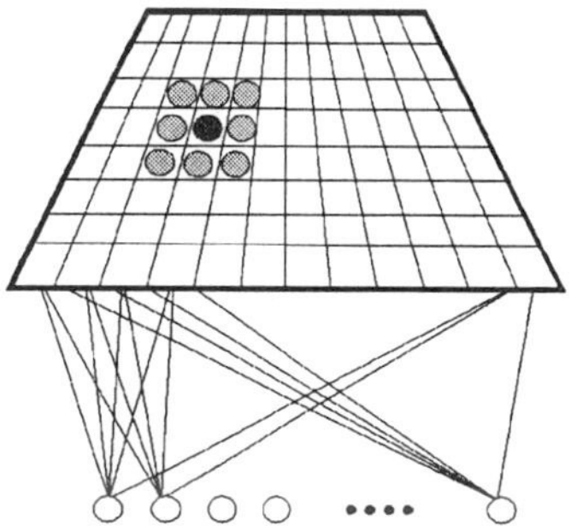

Fig. 2. The structure of SOFM network.

2.2. Cluster merging

The cluster merging process is given as follows after training the SOFM network by formal weight updating rule[4]. This procedure is simply done by merging the 3×3 neighboring clusters and averaging their weight vectors. As described in the previous sections, the clusters in SOFM output are topology-preserved. Thus, the merged clusters still preserve the same topological characteristics of SOFM clusters. The weight vector for a merged cluster is calculated by averaging the weight vectors of the nine neighboring clusters.

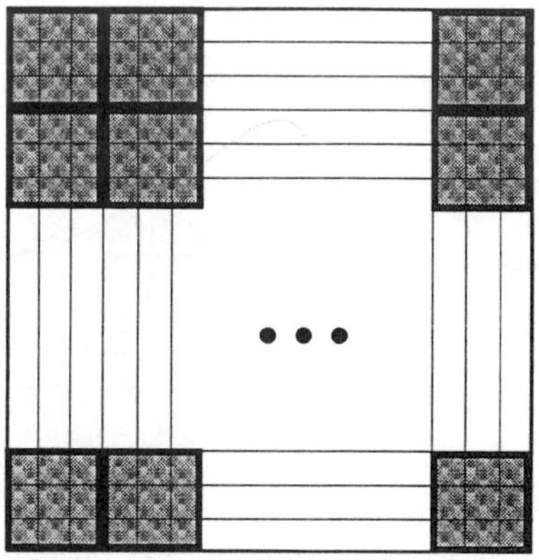

Fig. 3. Cluster merging using the topology-preserving characteristic.

2.3. Cluster modifying

In fact, the cluster merging procedure is somewhat unnatural, since there is a chance of merging the patterns that are not so close. To solve this problem, the cluster modifying procedure is introduced here. This procedure also can reduce the variance values of clusters, which will be detailed later by using numerical examples.

When a pattern $\mathbf{X}$ is given again as an input, it selects the most similar cluster C_1. The target cluster C_T of this present pattern has been already known from the previous clustering procedures. If C_1 and C_T are the same, there is no further change. If C_T is not correspondent with C_1, the reference weight vector of the most similar cluster $\mathbf{W}_1$ is modified as

$$\mathbf{W}_1(t+1) = \mathbf{W}_1(t) + \alpha[\mathbf{X} - \mathbf{W}_1(t)] \quad (1)$$

and we determine that $\mathbf{X}$ belongs to C_1. This does not involve large reshuffling of SOFM but slightly redistribute the input patterns.

2.4. Fine recognition system

The MLP network learned by BP is very simple in structure but is quite excellent in its recognition capability. In this paper, an MLP version adopting alarming nodes is used for fine recognition mode. The critical errors occurring in our hierarchical recognition system are found to be mainly due to the errors of preclassification mode: cluster selection mode. If an input pattern selects a wrong cluster, the final recognition result is simply unacceptable. However, the output peak still produces higher value and this false alarm cannot be easily detected and corrected. Thus, we proposed the use of the false-alarming nodes in the output layer of the MLP network. Obtaining negative or false alarm examples that are very close to one class but still representing the other classes is not an easy task. For instance, for face detection problem, they[10] first constructed an classifier using positive examples only, then intensively tested it against real situation, and gathered negative examples that produced classification errors. Negative examples are then used for retraining the classifier for better results. For our case, due to the SOFM network's topology-preserving property, the patterns of neighboring clusters around a cluster happen to be quite similar to those of that cluster and can be used as negative samples giving false alarm to the MLP classifier attached to that cluster.

2.4.1. Proposed method 1. The first approach in the fine recognition mode is shown in Fig. 4(a). Suppose that the number of classes involved in a cluster is N, this network has $N+1$ nodes in the output layer. In training step, N output nodes are activated when corresponding

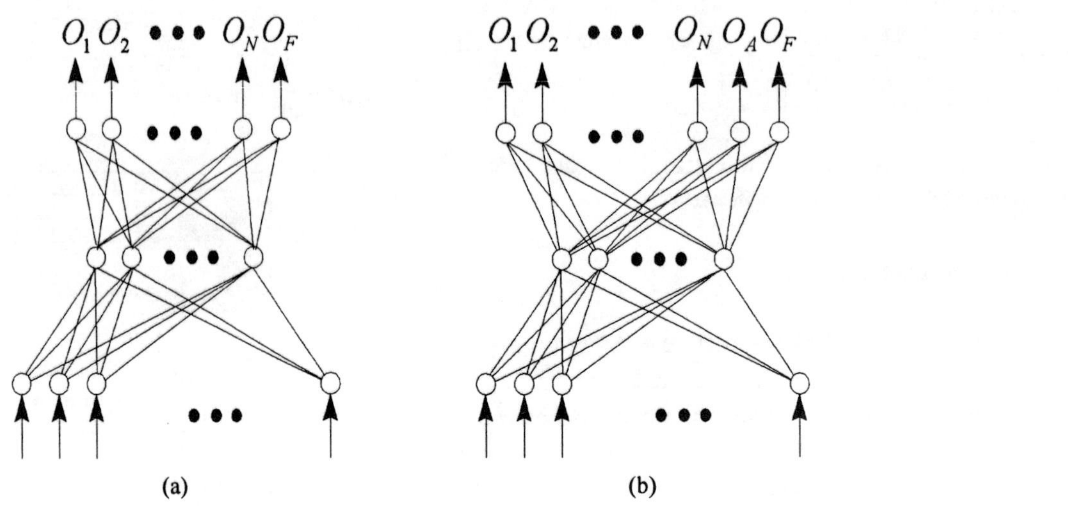

Fig. 4. MLP networks containing (a) false-alarming node(proposed method 1), O_F and (b) accepting and false-alarming nodes(proposed method 2), O_A and O_F.

input patterns are entered into the network and the false-alarming node O_F is not activated. The negative examples for activating the false-alarming node O_F are obtained from the neighborhoods of the present cluster. When one of such negative example happens, O_F is set to one and the remaining class assigning nodes O_1 to O_N are set to zero. When a positive example is trained, only its corresponding node among O_1 to O_N is set to one. In the recognition step, the selected cluster is rejected when the output value of O_F has the largest value.

2.4.2. Proposed method 2. Fig. 4(b) is a second approach using the two alarming nodes, the accepting node O_A and the false-alarming node O_F. For the system recognizing N classes, it needs $N+2$ output nodes. The positive examples are used for activating the corresponding node out of N output nodes and the accepting node O_A at the same time. O_A can be estimated from the class assigning nodes O_1 to O_N and this means redundancy has been introduced in output coding. The question why such redundancy is useful will be further detailed later in section 3.2.3. using the relevant examples. The negative example activates the false-alarming node O_F as in the proposed method 1. In recognition step, the output values of O_A and O_F are compared at first. If the output value of O_F is larger than that of O_A, the system will conclude that false alarm happens. Otherwise, we accept the recognition result of node and switched to find the maximum among O_1 to O_N.

3. Experimental Results

3.1. IRIS database

To compare our proposed hierarchical neural network with a simple MLP network, we first used well-known IRIS database, whose input dimension is four and which has three output classes, each having 50 patterns[13].

We had built simple MLP networks with more than one hidden node. They had been trained by 75 patterns, 25 patterns each class, and could recognized correctly 72 or 73 patterns out of 75 testing patterns not included in training. Next, we tested the proposed system. SOFM network of original 100 output nodes had been compressed into 16 clusters by secondary clustering modification. As the fine recognition mode, an MLP network with two hidden nodes for each cluster had been built. Since there are small number of patterns, no alarming node has been used here.

The summarizing results are included in Table 1. For our SOFM-MLP case, no classification error occurs. As the number of hidden nodes in the simple MLP network increases, its recognizing ability also improves. However for large scale pattern recognition problems that usually have very complicated input distribution, this simple strategy of changing the number of hidden nodes would not be believed to be always promising.

Table 1. Classification results for IRIS database

	Simple MLP network with			Hierarchical Neural network
	2 hidden nodes	3 hidden nodes	4 hidden nodes	
Trained Data(75)	75/75	75/75	75/75	75/75
Tested Data(75)	72/75	72/75	73/75	75/75

3.2. Korean/Chinese characters database and feature space generated

We had used 1,000 classes of Korean characters and 1,800 classes of Chinese characters. Four types of font variations for each class are introduced so that a total of 11,200 Korean/Chinese characters are used as a training set. Sample examples of them are shown in Fig. 5 (a) and (b). In many cases, Korean and Chinese characters are mixed in one paragraph or even a sentence. So, separating or classifying system for mixed database is very needed for actual OCR environments. As a testing database that will evaluate our proposed system rigorously, we needed to gather 29 types of font variations per each class, i.e., 29,000 characters for Korean characters and 34 types of variations per each class, i.e., 61,200 characters. A total of 90,200 characters were used as testing database. For the input of both the preclassification and the fine recognition modes, the 256(16×16) dimensional mesh feature[14] has been extracted from a size-normalized character image.

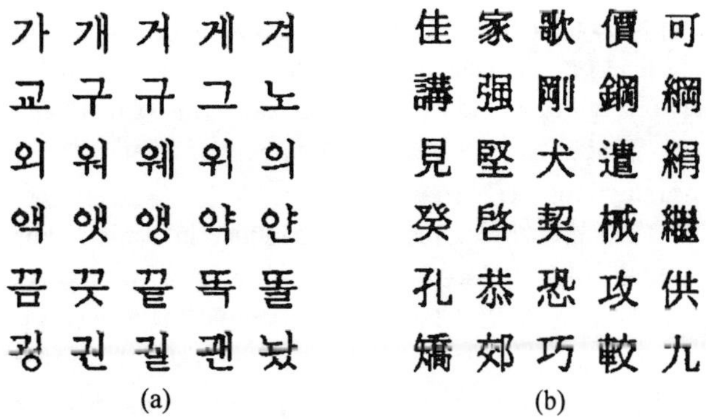

Fig. 5. Sample examples of (a) Korean characters and (b) Chinese characters.

3.2.1. Clustering and modifying procedures.

3.2.1.1. SOFM clustering. The initial size of output nodes has been determined as 55×55(3,025) large enough to include 2,800 classes to be recognized. The resulting map of the clusters is shown in Fig. 6. The distribution of the clusters is roughly separated between Korean and Chinese characters. This means that the global shapes of Korean characters are different from those of Chinese characters. However, there are a group of characters of both languages that are quite similar to one another. These situations are reflected as mixed clusters including both Korean and Chinese characters in Fig. 6.

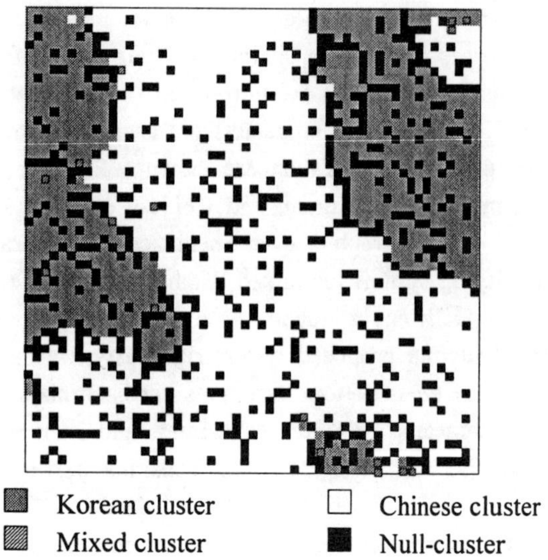

Fig. 6. Distribution of SOFM clusters.

Fig. 7 represents the distance map of all other clusters from an arbitrarily chosen cluster. The neighboring clusters are located nearer than the clusters located much farther from the cluster, and this provides us with the reason that the neighboring clusters will be gathered into a super cluster, which will be detailed in the following section. This is also the reason why the negative examples that might bring out confusion or classification error could be obtained from the neighboring clusters of the chosen cluster.

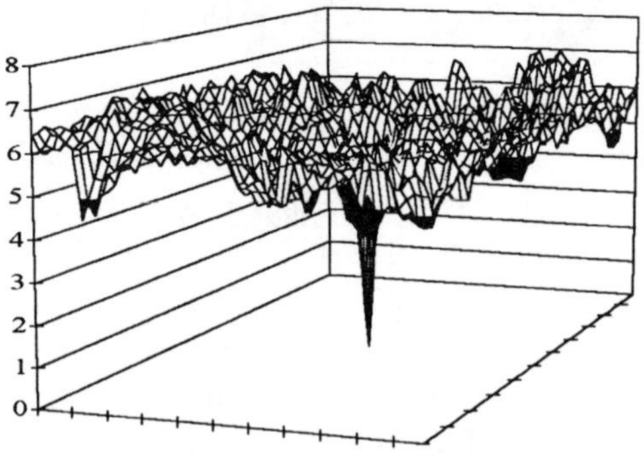

Fig. 7. Clusters' distance map from an arbitrary cluster.

3.2.1.2. Cluster merging and modifying. By the procedure of merging and modifying the clusters, we had reduced SOFM clusters into 19×19(361) clusters. Fig. 8 describes the resultant distribution map of final clusters. The shape of final distribution map of the clusters(Fig. 8) almost follows that of the initial SOFM clusters(Fig. 6). The following Fig. 9 shows that the modifying procedure is indeed required.

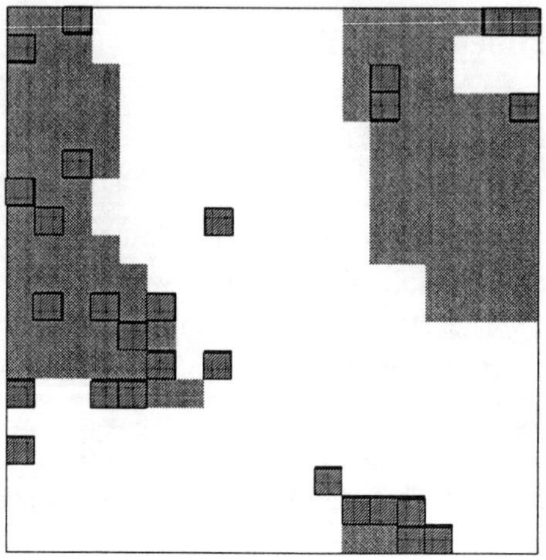

Fig. 8. Distribution of clusters after merging and modifying.

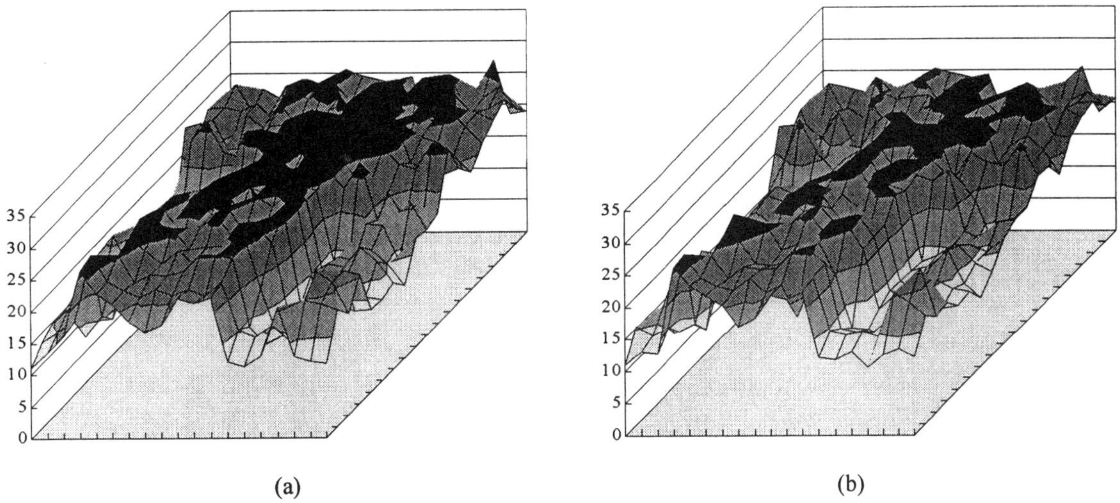

Fig. 9. MSE plot of input features vector for the clusters (a) before modifying and (b) after modifying.

Input training feature vectors belonging to a cluster were gathered and we calculated mean square errors(MSE) of these vector components with respect to a weight components, since the weight vector of SOFM network act as a mean vector for those clustered input vectors. The two plots represent the MSE values for input feature vectors belonging to a cluster for all the clusters arranged in 2-D grids. The two plots look similar at first glance, but actually the values of second plot(Fig. 9(b)) are in the average sense somewhat less than those of the first plot. For instance, black areas represent the values larger than 25.0 and we observe that these areas shrink down in the second plot. Numerically speaking, while the average of such MSE values for all unmodified clusters was 20.9, that for all modified ones was 19.9.

3.2.2. Fine recognition mode. We adopted the MLP classifier for each clustered group of characters as the fine recognition mode. The number of classes to be recognized in one cluster was founded to be about 14 on average. Thus, the number of weighting links was {14 × (No. of hidden nodes+1)}+{(No. of hidden nodes) × (No. of input nodes+1)}. For example, if the numbers of input and hidden nodes are 256 and 8 respectively, the number of weighting links is 2182. In the case of LVQ3, this is estimated to be above 3584 at least. Thus, we constructed total 361 MLP classifiers for fine recognition and the small number of weights are quite useful for reducing the overall size of our system.

The negative examples or false alarm patterns that might be very close to a given cluster and possibly lead to classification error in this paper were gathered from its neighboring clusters. The characters in Fig. 10(b) are some examples of such negative examples to positive examples in a cluster(Fig. 10(a)). We found that they become more quite similar to one another when we use feature space description with reduced dimension.

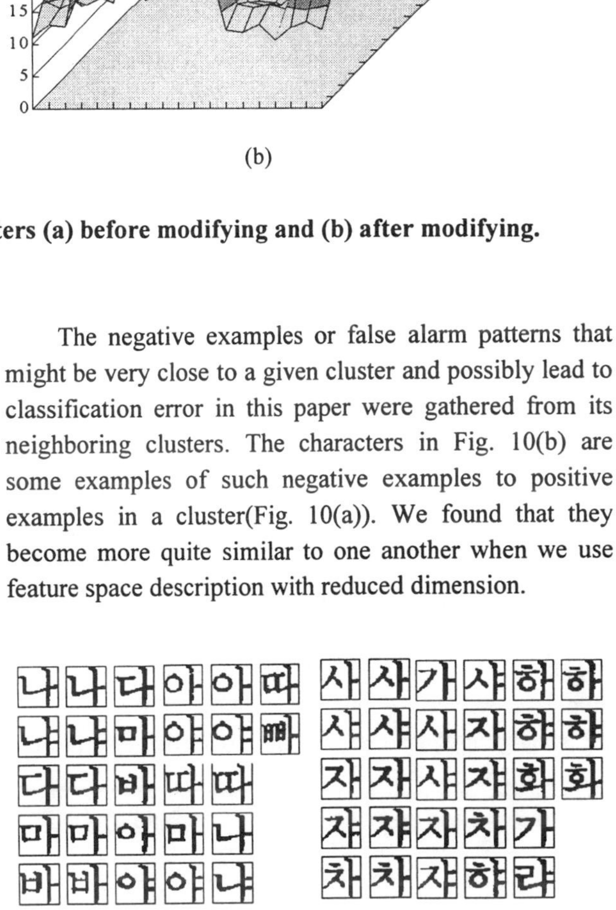

(a) (b)

Fig. 10. (a) Positive examples in one cluster and (b) some negative examples of (a).

3.2.3. Final recognition phase and experimental results. We had examined the performance of our proposed system using about 90,200(29,000 Korean and 61,200 Chinese) characters. For comparative study of fine recognition mode, we compared our proposed systems with general MLPs without alarming nodes. Once training SOFM and their corresponding MLPs were successfully achieved, we then switched to the recognition phase as described in Fig. 1. The extracted input feature vector is forwarded to the SOFM network, which produces three best-matched candidate clusters and three MLP classifiers will be activated for final class assignment. For a system with no false-alarming or accepting nodes, we compare the maximum peaks of the three classifiers and choose the highest peak and its labeled class will be our recognition result. In MLPs with only false-alarming node(proposed method 1), the classifiers producing the highest peak in false-alarming node(O_F) are simply rejected and the highest peak in the remaining classifier will be checked for final class assignment as in the general MLP case. All classifiers can be rejected but this seldom occurs. In MLPs with false-alarming and accepting nodes(O_A and O_F), we first check O_A and O_F, and if the O_F is bigger, the classifier will be rejected. Otherwise, we check the remaining class assigning nodes(O_1 to O_N), and we determine the final class as in the general MLPs. The final classification results are introduced in Fig. 11. The proposed method 2 performs the best in the overall classification as well as in individual Korean and Chinese characters. So far, we could not present concrete theoretical foundation why adopting O_A actually including redundant information has increased classification performance. This experimental result provides us with some morale for using redundant output coding scheme such as error correcting codes, but for conclusive remarks, further theoretical and experimental work should be advanced. Anyhow, we forward some examples of correcting misclassification of the general MLP by adopting false-alarming node and their results are included in Table 2.

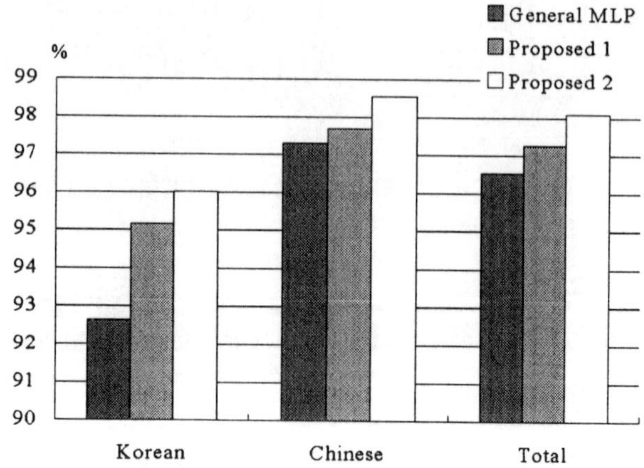

Fig. 11. Comparison the general MLP and the two proposed systems.

Table 2. Examples of the corrected errors

Tested Char.	Results: Without Alarming Node	Results: With Alarming Nodes	Corrected Results
件	**仲(0.99)**	Rejected	仲 → 件
	件(0.99)	**件(0.91)**	
	任(0.55)	Rejected	
호	**支(0.99)**	Rejected	支 → 호
	호(0.99)	**호(0.67)**	
	초(0.98)	표(0.16)	
괴	**져(0.98)**	Rejected	져 → 괴
	괴(0.98)	**괴(0.95)**	
	피(0.65)	Rejected	
刀	云(0.93)	Rejected	方 → 刀
	刀(0.93)	**刀(0.91)**	
	方(0.98)	尤(0.13)	

The input pattern '件' in the first raw of Table 2 has been recognized as '仲' in the first selected cluster with the highest output value 0.99 by the system without alarming nodes. However, this cluster actually did not contain that pattern even though one node of the attached MLP produces very high output value. The proposed the MLP network with alarming nodes could overcome such problem as follows. The first selected cluster's MLP classifier was rejected by false-alarming node, but the second candidate cluster's classifier correctly recognized this one as '件'. In the other cases, we can explain the results similarly.

4. Conclusion

In this paper, the hierarchical neural network based systems have been studied to deal with the large scale pattern recognition problem. For preclassification mode, the set of clusters has been constructed by SOFM learning and its secondary modifying procedures. Inside the cluster thus obtained, the patterns look quite similar to one another and the patterns of the neighboring clusters are still similar to those of the center cluster by topology-preserving property, as is achieved by SOFM learning. The MLP network with false-alarming nodes is employed for fine recognition of each selected cluster. The false-alarming node trained on negative examples from the neighboring clusters is proposed and found to be useful for enhanced performance by resolving the similar and thus confusing patterns often occurring in large scale pattern recognition problem into rejection status. Experiments on Korean/Chinese characters database have demonstrated that the proposed system performs well for a large scale pattern recognition problem.

References

[1] S. I. Chien, "Hangul(Korean) and English OCR System Using Multiple Hypotheses Driven Neural Nets," *Korean-French Character Recognition Workshop*, Seoul, pp.37-52, Sep. 1994.

[2] J. H. Kim, K. K. Kim, and S. I. Chien, "Korean and English Character Recognition system Using Hierarchical Classification Neural Network," *IEEE International Conference on System, Man, and Cybernetics*, Vancouver, vol.1, pp.759-764, Oct. 1995.

[3] A. Itawa, H. Kawajiri, and N. Suzumura, "Classification of Hand-printed Digits by a Large Scale Neural Network "CombNETII"," *IJCNN*, Singapore, vol.1, pp.1021-1026, Nov. 1991.

[4] T. Kohonen, "The Self-Organizing Map," *Proc. IEEE*, vol.78, no.9, pp.1464-1480, Sep. 1990.

[5] N. R. Pal, J. C. Bezdek, and E. C.-K. Tsao, "Generalized Clustering Networks and Kohonen's Self-Organizing Scheme," *IEEE Trans. on Neural Networks*, vol.4, no.4, pp.549-557, July 1993.

[6] J. A. Kangas, T. Kohonen, and J. T. Laaksonen, "Variants of Self-Organizing Maps," *IEEE Trans. on Neural Networks*, vol.1, no.1, pp.93-99, Mar. 1990.

[7] B. Widrow and M. A. Lehr, "30 years of Adaptive Neural Networks: Perceptron, Madaline, and Backpropagation," *Proc. IEEE*, vol.78, no.9, pp.1415-1441, Sep. 1990.

[8] R. P. Lippmann, "An Introduction to Computing with Neural Nets," *IEEE ASSP Mag.*, pp. 4-22, Apr. 1987.

[9] A. Frosini, M. Gori, and P. Priami, "A Neural Network-Based Model for Paper Currency Recognition and Verification," *IEEE Trans. on Neural Networks*, vol.7, no.6, pp.1482-1490, Nov. 1996.

[10] K. K. Sung and T. Poggio, "Example-Based Learning for View-Based Human Face Detection," *MIT A. I. Memo*, no.1521, pp.1-20, Dec., 1994.

[11] S. H. Lin, S. Y. Kung, and L. J. Lin, "Face Recognition/Detection by Probabilistic Decision-Based Neural Network," *IEEE Trans. on Neural Networks*, vol.8, no.1, pp.114-132, Jan. 1997.

[12] J. Cao, M. Ahmadi, and M. Shridhar, "Recognition of Handwritten Numerals with Multiple Feature and Multistage Classifier," *Pattern Recognition*, vol.28, no.2, pp.153-160, 1995.

[13] M. Nadler and E. P. Smith, *Pattern Recognition Engineering*, John Wiley & Sons Pub., New York, pp.341-345, 1993.

[14] K. Miyahara and F. Yoda, "Printed Japanese Character Recognition Based on Multiple Modified LVQ Neural Network," *ICDAR*, Tsukuba, pp.250-253, 1993.

Use of Hopfield Neural Network for Complex Image Registration

Zhebin Qian Jie-gu Li
Institute of Image Processing and Pattern Recognition
Shanghai Jiao Tong University
Shanghai 200030, China

Abstract

This paper presents an image registration method based on a two-dimensional Hopfield Neural Network, where the problem of image matching is treated with the minimization of the energy function of the Hopfield neural network. The input data used for registration are the locations of the corner points extracted from the images. In order to improve and expedite the matching process, a fast block-based algorithm is put forward, together with the laboratory results obtained, which show the effectiveness of the algorithm.

I. Introduction

In many visual intelligent systems, such as robotics, criminal recognition, and autonomous navigation, etc., image registration techniques are used to recognize and locate the objects by matching the object image acquired at real time with the fiducial image stored in the system originally. Usually, the fiducial image occupies a greater pixel area than the object image. In order to perform this kind of work, these have been employed different methods based on statistical studies, such as calculating the sum of the difference of the pixel gray values of two images or the maximum correlation of their pixel gray values. But in some actual cases, the object image acquired at real time may be distorted by many factors, such as resolution difference, geometric error, different emission angles of the light source, strong noise, etc., which exert tremendous influence on the gray value distribution of the object image , and thus may lead to mismatching.

To overcome the disturbance stated above, registration system constructed on the basis of image feature matching is more stable than statistical comparison of the gray value distributions. Here, corner points are used as the image features to be matched. However, in doing so, a new problem will crop up, that is none of the feature extraction algorithm now available is capable of avoiding data missing or false alarming, especially under the influences of distortion factors. Therefore matching work has to be done with two graphs where the point distribution are not exactly the same. A two-dimensional Hopfield Neural Network[1] is chosen to solve such problem.

In this paper, an interesting-point-based neural network algorithm(IPBNNA)[2][3] is introduced, which implements the function of judging whether the object scene exists in the fiducial image, formulating the correspondence of the IPs in both images, and finally finding the location and orientation of the object in the fiducial image. The algorithm is started computation, a fast and more efficient algorithm is put to use, which is based on blocking.

II. Interesting-Point-Based Hopfield Neural Network Matching Algorithm

A. *Extraction of Interesting Points*

A comparative study among the methods for corner point extraction has been made.[4] Finally, the interesting point(IP) method proposed by Moravec is taken into consideration. The IPs are defined as points in the image that have high variance in all directions, or salient points in the two images which can be more easily matched than any other point in the image. These points generally occur at the corners and edge terminals of the object in the image.

The operator used here is called the interesting operator, which can find the variance in the horizontal, vertical, and both diagonal directions for each point in the image. The minimum of these values is then chosen as the variance for that point. The variance equations for each direction are given below:

Horizontal displacement(HD)=

$$\sum_{x=-\lceil (W+1)/2\rceil}^{\lceil (W+1)/2\rceil} \cdot \sum_{y=-\lceil W/2\rceil}^{\lceil W/2\rceil} [g(x,y)-g(x,y+1)]^2$$

Vertical displacement(VD)=

$$\sum_{x=-\lceil W/2\rceil}^{\lceil W/2\rceil} \cdot \sum_{y=-\lceil (W+1)/2\rceil}^{\lceil (W+1)/2\rceil} [g(x,y)-g(x+1,y)]^2$$

Diagonal Displacement(DD－135)=

$$\sum_{x=-\lceil W/2\rceil}^{\lceil W/2\rceil} \cdot \sum_{y=-\lceil W/2\rceil}^{\lceil W/2\rceil} [g(x,y)-g(x+1,y+1)]^2$$

Diagonal Displacement(DD-45)=

1082-3409/97 $10.00 © 1997 IEEE

$$\sum_{x=-\lceil W/2 \rceil}^{\lceil W/2 \rceil} \cdot \sum_{y=-\lceil W/2 \rceil+1}^{\lceil W/2 \rceil+1} [g(x,y) - g(x+1, y-1)]^2$$

Where W is the size of the operator window, the function g(x, y) refers to the gray level value at that point in the image. The smallest value of VD, HD, DD-45, DD-135, called the interest operator value, is taken as the variance for that point.

To reduce the number of IPs , a threshold relevant to the average of the whole image after operator processing is used. Usually at regions of high variance a large number of IPs are found in a cluster. To have distinct features scattered, the point having the local maximal variance in each local region(a window of size 9×9) is chosen as the IP.

In the following discussion, it is assumed that the fiducial image has N IPs, and the object scene has M. Obviously, the latter just corresponds to a small part of the former, so N is much greater than M.

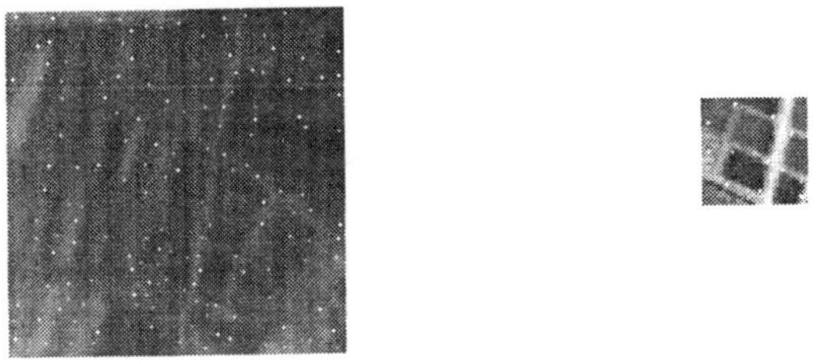

Fig. 1
Fiducial Image and Object image with extracted interesting points

B. *Two-dimensional Binary Hopfield Neural Network*

In this section, it is shown that the point correspondence problem can be formulated as an optimization task where a cost function(energy equation) representing the constraints on the stereo solution is minimized. It is also shown that the minimization problem can be mapped onto a Hopfield neural network such that the cost energy function is the same as the Lyapunov function of the network, with the synaptic interconnection weights between the neurons representing the constraints imposed by the correspondence problem. The Lyapunov function represents the collective behavior of the network. When the network is at its stable state the energy function is said to be at its local minimum. The basic principle of the neural networks is to make a cooperative decision based on the simultaneous input of a whole community of neurons in which each neuron receives information through giving information to every other neuron. This information is used by each neuron to force the network to converge to a stable state in order to make a decision.

A two-dimensional binary Hopfield network is used to find the correspondence between the IPs in the fiducial and object images. The network is represented as an N×M array of neurons. The state of each neuron (on or off) in the network represents a possible match among the IPs in both images. Figure(2) shows the 2-D network and the connection weights between its neurons. The matching process is characterized as minimizing an energy function given by

$$E = -\sum_{i=1}^{M} \cdot \sum_{k=1}^{N} \cdot \sum_{j=1}^{M} \cdot \sum_{l=1}^{N} C_{ikjl} \cdot V_{ik} \cdot V_{jl} + \sum_{i=1}^{M} (1 - \sum_{k=1}^{N} V_{ik})^2 + \sum_{k=1}^{N} (1 - \sum_{i=1}^{M} V_{ik})^2 \qquad (1)$$

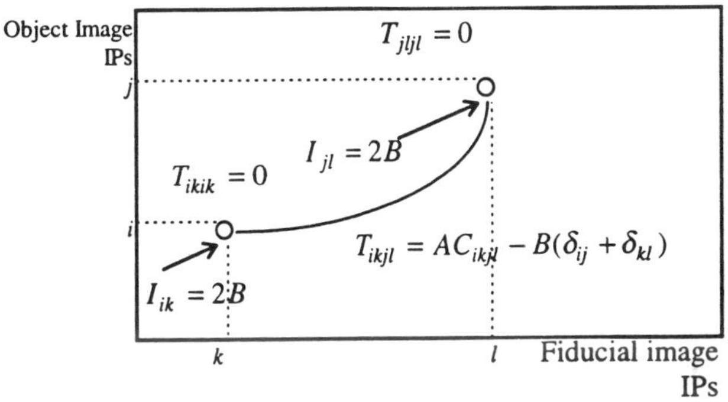

Fig 2. The 2-D Binary Hopfield Neural Network

V_{ik} is analogous to a binary state variable of a neuron, and takes value 1 when the ith feature point in the scene image matches the kth feature point in the fiducial.

Expression(1) is equivalent to minimizing a Hopfield-style energy function given by

$$E = -\frac{1}{2} \sum_{i=1}^{M} \sum_{k=1}^{N} \sum_{j=1}^{M} \sum_{l=1}^{N} T_{ikjl} V_{ik} V_{jl} + \sum_{i=1}^{M} \sum_{k=1}^{N} I_{ik} V_{ik} \qquad (2)$$

where by a simple manipulation it can be shown that expression(2) is equivalent to expression(1) with

$$T_{ikjl} = AC_{ikjl} - B\delta_{ij} - B\delta_{kl} \qquad (3)$$

and

$$I_{ik} = 2B \qquad (4)$$

where δ_{ij} =1 only if i=j and 0 otherwise, similarly $\delta_{kl} = 1$ if k=l and 0 otherwise. The expression for the compatibility measure C_{ikjl} is given by

$$C_{ikjl} = \frac{2}{1 + e^{\lambda(X-\theta)}} - 1 \qquad (5)$$

where X is

$$X = \omega_1 \Delta d + \omega_2 \Delta D \qquad \omega_1 > 0, \omega_2 > 0 \qquad (6)$$

$$\Delta d = \sqrt{(\Delta X_{ij} - \Delta X_{kl})^2 + (\Delta Y_{ij} - \Delta Y_{kl})^2}$$

$$\Delta D = \sqrt{(\Delta X_{ik} - \Delta X_{jl})^2 + (\Delta Y_{ik} - \Delta Y_{jl})^2} \qquad (7)$$

$$\begin{cases}\Delta X_{ij} = X_i - X_j \\ \Delta Y_{ij} = Y_i - Y_j\end{cases}, \begin{cases}\Delta X_{kl} = X_k - X_l \\ \Delta Y_{kl} = Y_k - Y_l\end{cases},$$

$$\begin{cases}\Delta X_{ik} = X_i - X_k \\ \Delta Y_{ik} = Y_i - Y_k\end{cases}, \begin{cases}\Delta X_{jl} = X_j - X_l \\ \Delta Y_{jl} = Y_j - Y_l\end{cases} \quad (8)$$

As seen from the energy equation, the matching process tries to satisfy the constrains globally in a parallel manner to find the matching nodes. The local compatibility measures provide excitory and inhibitory supports for matching local features. The dynamics of the network is characterized as a stochastic process that will arrive at a stable state when the energy function(1) is at its minimum.

The algorithm is summarized in the following steps.

Step 1: The initial states of neurons are set 1 or 0 depending on the degree of match between the corresponding feature points:

$$V_{ik} = \begin{cases}1 & if\left|f_i - f_j\right| < \theta \\ 0 & \text{otherwise}\end{cases} \quad (9)$$

where θ is the threshold used to determine if the ith feature f_i matches the jth feature f_i.

Step 2: Randomly pick up a node (i, k).

Step 3: Calculate its input :

$$H_{ik}(t) = \sum_{j=1}^{N1}\sum_{l=1}^{N2} T_{ikjl} V_{jl}^t + I_{ik}$$
$$= \sum_{j=1}^{N1}\sum_{l=1}^{N2} (A \cdot C_{ikjl} - B \cdot \delta_{ij} - B \cdot \delta_{kl}) V_{jl}^t + 2B \quad (10)$$

Step 4: Decide the new state of each neuron according to the following rules:

$$\begin{array}{ll} V_{ik} \to 1 & \text{if } H_{ik}(t) > 0.5 \\ V_{ik} \to 0 & \text{if } H_{ik}(t) > -0.5 \\ V_{ik} \to no \text{ change} & \text{if } -0.5 \le H_{ik}(t) \le 0.5 \end{array} \quad (11)$$

Step 5: Count the changes of the states, if there is no change after a number of iterations, stop and go to 6) otherwise repeat the process from 2).

Step 6: Output the final states of neurons V_{ik}, which will be the final matches between the fiducial feature and the input features.

III. The Fast Block-Based Algorithm

The longest distance between any two IP(i) and (j) in the object image is the length of the diagonal, this distance keeps nearly invariant in any image, which consists of the base for the cost function. However, many couples of IPs(k) and (l) in the fiducial image are obviously longer than that length. since the fiducial image is much larger in size than the object image with the same definition. In the above algorithm, the neurons corresponding with points (i)(j)(k)(l) will still equally be computed in each iteration, though they are useless to the correct matches at all. So, not only will such redundant computation be cost, but also will it produce many multiple mismatches to the few IPs in the object image.

For the situation of large fiducial image and small object image, a fast improved algorithm is put forward here, which is based on blocking. The simple description of this method is

a) According to the size of object image, fiducial image is divided into several blocks ,

b) Then each block uses Hopfield Neural Network to go on with the correspondence of IPs;

c) Based on a criteria and degree of each correspondence, we can judge whether the scene exists in the fiducial image, and if so, in which block it is contained, and we can also determine the location of the object.

The output of the neural network are pairs of matched nodes for the object scene, the location can be obtained in the following method

i) For each block, the transformation for all of its matched nodes is tabulated in a 3-dimensional buffer(Hough accumulator);

ii) A nearest -neighbor clustering method is then used to find all the points in the cluster;

iii) For each block(hypothesis), an average transformation is obtained from all the points within this cluster.

For each pair of matched nodes in the block its coordinate transformation is tabulated in a 3-D accumulator. This accumulator behaves like the Hough transform, the correct matched pairs will form the largest cluster in the transformation space*(θ, tx, ty)* and the false matched pairs will be scattered , resulting in several smaller clusters. The accumulator is examined to find the location of the largest value to be used as the center of the cluster. If there is no peak every point is considered as a separate cluster, or if the peak is lower than the threshold, the block is not considered as containing the object. The part having the highest peak is considered as the location of the object.

Of course, it is not optimal that the image is simply divided into average parts equal to the object image, because the location may be at any position of the image, and may overlap several such equal blocks, but only a small part is just in each block so the matches are scattered.

Assumed that the size of the fiducial image is Xn×Yn, the size of the object image is Xm×Ym. Let a window of (2Xm-1)×(2Ym-1) in size slides in the fiducial image with the step of Xm×Ym, it can be found that wherever the object locates, the window in a certain step will fully contain it. So blocking can be considered as such a window sliding on the fiducial image. The overlay of the whole image obviously needs such $\lceil Xn/Xm \rceil \times \lceil Yn/Ym \rceil$ windows, but part of the window near the border exceeds the limit of image, or the size of the window is less than (2Xm-1)×(2Ym-1). In practice, we design the sliding window as

$(2\times\lceil Xn/\lfloor Xn/Xm\rfloor\rceil-1)\times(2\times\lceil Yn/\lfloor Yn/Ym\rfloor\rceil-1)$ in size and the step is $\lceil Xn/\lfloor Xn/Xm\rfloor\rceil\times\lceil Yn/\lfloor Yn/Ym\rfloor\rceil$, so the windows near the border will avoid exceeding the limit of image and only $\lfloor Xn/Xm\rfloor\times\lfloor Yn/Ym\rfloor$ windows can overlay the whole big image.

Though adjacent windows are overlapping nearly half of each other, and the whole image is overlaid nearly twice, the computation is not increased, but reduced heavily instead. The reason is that the complexity of the neural network is nonlinear, when the number of the IPs is large in the dimension of the fiducial image, the number of iterations increase greatly; when the number of the IPs drops, the number of iterations decreases dramatically.

In our experiments, 100 couples of object and fiducial images are processed in order to locate the small object in the fiducial image. The size of object pictures is 36×36, and that of fiducial map is 160×160. First the direct match between the two images are performed by IPBNNA. Then by blocking the fiducial map, 9 blocks are matched with the real-time object image in turn. The results of the experiments prove both algorithms are working well, however, as shown Table 1, the blocking process reduces the cost of time efficiently, without loss of performances. Examples of fiducial image and object image are shown as Fig. (3).

Table I Efficiency of Blocking Algorithm

Processing one Couple / size (image and block)	Counts of iteration loops	Average time-costing of processing a couple
160×160	11	261s
80×80(×9)	1.65	57s

IV Conclusion

In vision, many problems can be modeled as minimizing a cost function. In this paper, object registration is formulated as a Hopfield neural network based on IPs, which executes the minimization of a cost function. More, it is proven by the experiments that reasonable blocking and process of the large image will improve the efficiency in the process of matching and reduce the unnecessary multiple mismatches.

Reference

[1]J.J. Hopfield, D.W. Tank, Neural Computation of Detection in Optimization Problems. Biological Cybernetics, vol.36, 1985, pp.141-152.

[2]N.M. Nasrabadi, C.Y. Choo, Hopfield Network for Stereo Vision Correspond, IEEE Trans. Neural Network, vol.NN-3, no.1, 1992, pp.5-13.

[3]N.M. Nasrabadi, W. Li, Object Recognition by a Hopfield Neural Network, IEEE Trans. Systems, Man, and, Cybernetics, vol.SMC-21, no.6,1991, pp.1523-1535.

[4]Y.M. Zhao, J.G. Li, Neural Network matching Algorithm Using Interesting Points(in Chinese), Pattern Recognition and artificial Intelligence, vol.8, Dec., 1995, pp.313-319.

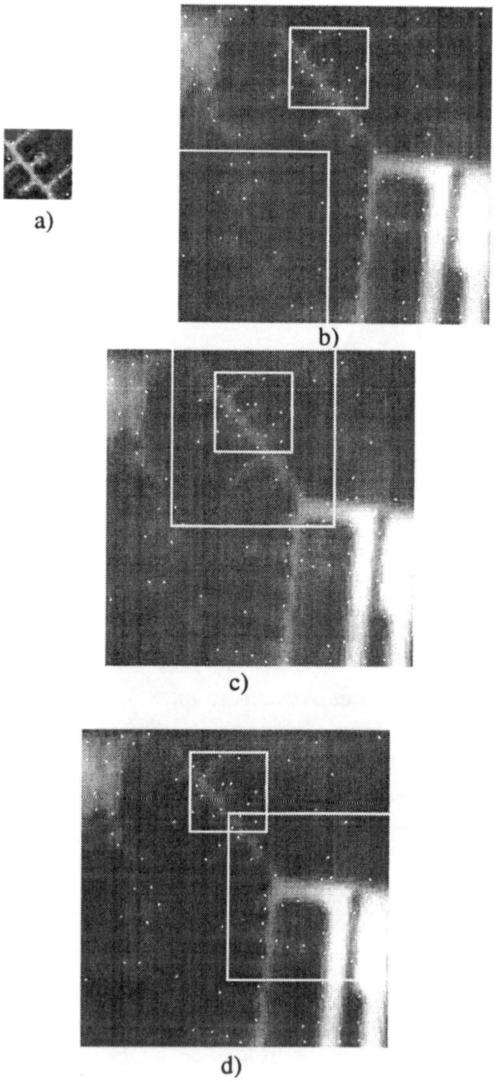

a)object image
b),d) No results in some blocks c) Correct location in Correct Block
Fig.3 Blocking-based Matching

Adaptive Window Algorithm with Four-Direction Sizing Factors for Robust Correlation-Based Tracking

Si-Hun Sung Sung-Il Chien
Department of Electronic Engineering
Kyungpook National University
Taegu, Korea

Mun-Gab Kim Joon-Nyun Kim
Special Product Division
Daewoo Heavy Industries Ltd.
Changwon, Korea

Abstract

In this paper, we propose the Adaptive Window Algorithm with Four-Direction Sizing Factors(AWA-FSF) for robust correlation-based tracking in complex cluttered environments. When size and shape of moving object have been changed, the correlator often accumulates walk-off error. A success of correlation-based tracking largely depends on choosing suitable window size and position and thus transferring the proper reference image to the next frame. Since the AWA-FSF is capable of adjusting a reference image size more rapidly and properly, we can minimize the influence of complex background and clutter. In addition, we can finely tune the center point of the reference image repeatedly after main tracking process. Thus we have increased stability and reliability of correlation-based image tracking. We tested performance of the AWA-FSF using 45 real image sequences made of over 3400 images and had the satisfied results for most of them.

1 Introduction

Correlation-based tracking[1-3] acquires a reference image from the previous frame and looks for the most similar area to the reference image for estimating the object position in the current frame. Although the correlator is said to be robust against the cluttered noise, its real application has some limitations, too. Usually, it is desirable that searching area should be chosen to be small due to its large computation involved. Another one is its tendency to accumulate walk-off error especially when the object of interest is changing in size, shape, or orientation from frame to frame.

If walk-off error accumulation proceeds beyond a certain critical point, correlation-based tracking can be unsuccessful. It is quite important that the size and position of a window should be precisely determined to guarantee that a proper reference image can be transferred to the next frame. In order to increase a correlation reliability, correlation-based tracking is usually expected to have high occupancy rate of an object, which means that the window encloses the object properly. For this, it is quite desirable that the window can adjust its size as circumstances of the object have been under change.

Concept of an adaptive window could be found in stereo matching, too. In case of stereo matching, the disparity boundaries are sharp for the smaller window but the computed disparity becomes noisy. The larger window means that the computed disparity becomes smoother but the disparity boundaries can be blurred. So, noise and boundary sharpness have a relationship of trade-off. Kanade and Okutomi[4] determined the adaptive window size using local intensity and disparity patterns to minimize uncertainty in the disparity computed at each point. Lotti and Giraudon[5] made four non-centered adaptive windows associated to each image point in the thresholded edge image.

In correlation-based tracking, the adaptive window studies based on estimating an object size are not much reported in the technical literature. To automatically adapt the reference area, Hughes and Moy[3] designed edge walking algorithm for the boundary detection to operate on a segmented binary image. This algorithm scans the binary image in a raster fashion looking for illuminated pixels. Once an illuminated pixel has been found, the edge walking algorithm searches for further illuminated pixels connected to the initial pixel. They used the boundary detection for estimating the size of an object and thus the size of window that will enclose the object. Similarly, Montera et al.[1] determined an object region though expanding from the inner point of an object to outer in the image. To yield the boundary of the object, they searched for the areas where pixel values vary from above the threshold to below the threshold. However, we expect that both methods are difficult to be applied to tracking non-homogeneous cluttered background and large objects sometimes having internal edges.

1082-3409/97 $10.00 © 1997 IEEE

Adaptive window without a proper sizing magnitude can hardly accommodate itself to environment variations when a window size is much larger or smaller than an object size or an object size is abruptly changed. To adjust a window size more rapidly and efficiently, this paper proposed the Adaptive Window Algorithm with Four-Direction Sizing Factors(AWA-FSF). The AWA-FSF defines eight districts: four side districts and four corner districts, and determines four window sizing directions and four sizing factors using the extracted mutual information obtained from the relation of a corner district and a side district. As we know, some edge operators may extract valuable information useful for successful tracking. We employed the modified Prewitt operator to generate edge images used in our tracking.

The proposed AWA-FSF has been adapted to our modified correlation method intended for accomplishing image tracking in the highly cluttered environments, which we call the Centroid-Compensated Correlator(CCC). Here, we append the centroid method to finely tune the result of the correlation when clutter components as well as object components are simultaneously contained in the tracking window and centroid compensation moves the matched point further to the location of an object which occupies usually larger area than the clutter components inside the window we consider. Additionally, as basic tracking image set, we adopt the use of the Positive Difference of Edges(PDOE) modified from a previous difference procedure using the absolute value. The detailed description of the CCC and the PDOE is beyond the viewpoint of this paper. Thus we briefly introduce the CCC and the PDOE in section 2. In section 3, we present the structure and the procedure of the proposed AWA-FSF. Then in section 4 we provide experimental results which clearly demonstrate the advantage of the AWA-FSF. Finally, section 5 gives a summary along with discussion.

2 Applied Image Tracker Architecture

The image tracking block diagram we propose is described in Fig. 1. The overall system is largely divided into the PDOE, the CCC, the AWA-FSF, and a recursive updating loop. First, we acquire the background-reduced image using the PDOE as tracking feature and then track the object by applying the CCC. Finally, the AWA-FSF generates a reference image region with tightly enclosing the object for tracking in the next frame. For the consecutive tracking the size and position of the reference image will be suitably updated.

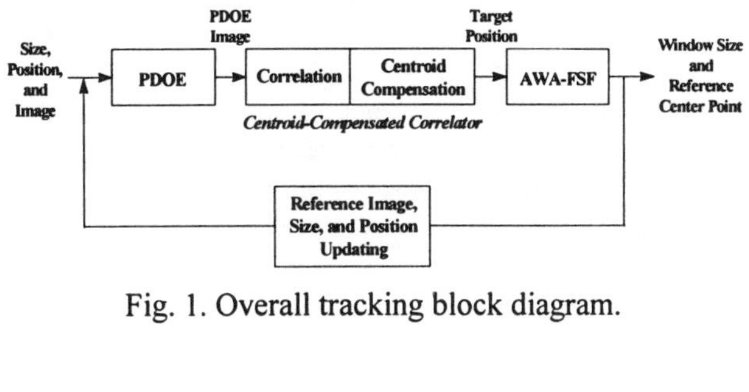

Fig. 1. Overall tracking block diagram.

2.1 Positive Difference of Edges(PDOE) for Feature Extraction

2.1.1 Edge Finding Procedure of the PDOE

There are many kinds of edge operator such as Sobel, Prewitt, Laplacian, and so on. The Sobel operator usually produces many minute edge components, but in case of image tracking, the minute edge found in background can bring undesirable effects. We thus selected the Kirsch operator which is the modified version of the Prewitt operator[6]. The Kirsch operator produces little minute edge components and its local averaging tends to reduce also the effects of noise. We can further reduce computation time through implementing only with summation.

2.1.2 Difference Procedure of the PDOE

The PDOE conceptually has spatial and temporal motion components as shown in Fig. 2. We can express the PDOE image $DE_n(i,j)$ in the current frame such that

$$DE_n(i,j) = \begin{cases} E_n(i,j) - E_{n-1}(i,j), & \text{if } E_n(i,j) > E_{n-1}(i,j) \\ 0, & \text{Otherwise} \end{cases} \quad (1)$$

where $E_n(i,j)$ is an edge image at point (i,j) in the current frame and $E_{n-1}(i,j)$ is one in the previous frame. The PDOE removes negative components from the difference of two edge images. As shown in Fig. 3, the PDOE can detect motion components much better than the difference method just using an absolute value.

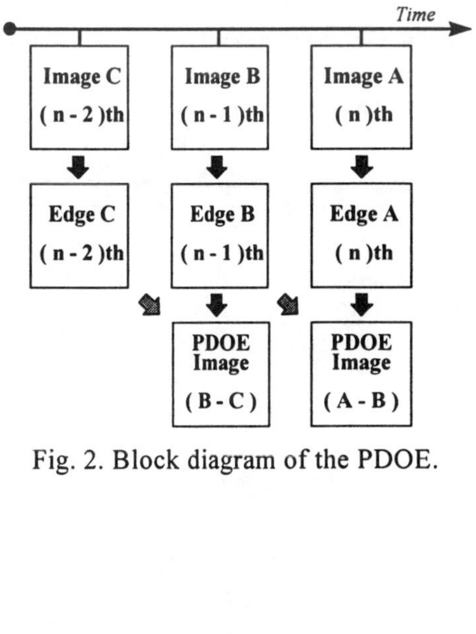

Fig. 2. Block diagram of the PDOE.

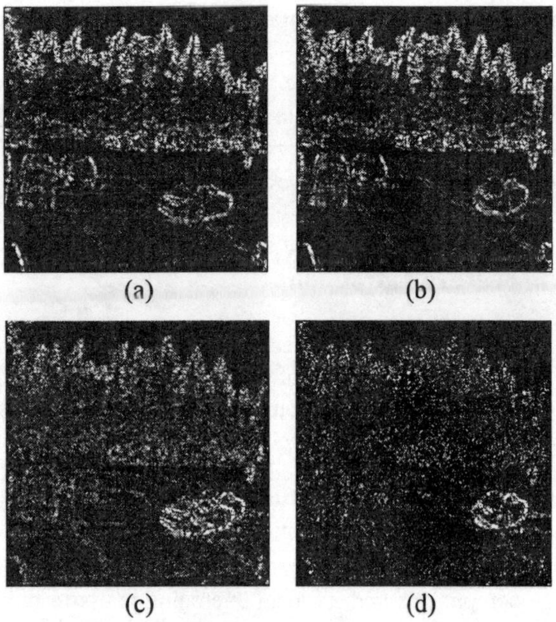

Fig. 3. Image information extracting using two real images: (a) Edge image in the previous frame, (b) Edge image in the current frame, (c) Absolute difference of edge images, and (d) PDOE image.

2.2 Centroid-Compensated Correlator(CCC)

The CCC is a robust image tracker against complex cluttered environment. Correlation-based tracking is a method which looks for the most similar area to the reference image acquired from the previous frame for estimating the object position in the current frame. However, correlation often accumulates the walk-off error. To compensate the error of correlation-based tracking, we sequentially append the centroid method to modify output of correlation.

In case that clutter components are partially included in a reference image, the correlation peak position might be deviated from the center of the object to the clutter part and this is found to be harmful for the correlator. However, the clutter components are usually weak and occupy small region inside the matched window determined by a previous correlator. Thus the centroid position calculated from the window region can be correctly shifted toward the center of object that might not be located at the center of the window. Thus our Centroid-Compensated Correlator is found to be quite useful for overcoming strong cluttered environments and occlusion effects and to prevent the tracker from accumulating the walk-off error severely. Meanwhile, the time consumption added due to the centroid compensation is not so prohibitive because the centroid method is only applied to the small region already decided by the correlator.

3 Adaptive Window Algorithm with Four-Direction Sizing Factors(AWA-FSF)

Fig. 4 describes an overall block diagram of our proposed AWA-FSF architecture. A feature set used for adjusting an adaptive window is the PDOE image previously described. The AWA-FSF needs mainly several steps: the adaptive window setting, the direction of sizing estimation in corner and side, the sizing factor determination, and the window size determination and the reference center point relocation. Here, the adaptive window can expand or shrink independently in four sizing directions, each side having a sizing magnitude derived from each sizing factor. In Fig. 4, we present several sizing parameters: DS_S is a direction of sizing in the side, DS_C is a direction of sizing in the corner, and DS_{CS} is a direction of sizing obtained from converting a corner effect to the corresponding side direction. Additionally, ΔSF indicates a sizing factor that will be used for determining final window size change in pixel unit.

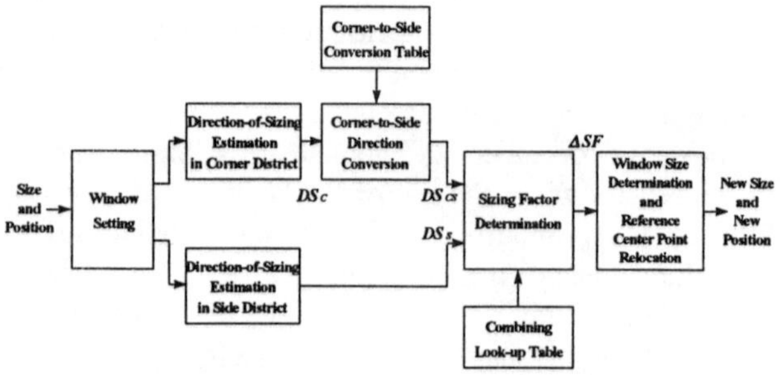

Fig. 4. Overall block diagram of the AWA-FSF.

3.1 Setting Adaptive Window

For adaptively controlling window size and relocating the center point, we now construct three regions: inner region, middle region, and outer region. First, we define the outside boundary of the middle region as the previous window given by the previous Centroid-Compensated Correlator. We design the inner region needed for extracting information within an object boundary and the extended outer region for obtaining useful clues about background information. The extracted information from a middle region will be used as criterion for determining whether pixels in the middle region are part of the object or not. Thus in order to extract more accurate information near the object boundary, the area of the middle region is fixed to be smaller than those of the others.

Second, eight overlapped districts consisting of four side districts and four corner districts are then defined. The direction of sizing in a side, DS_S, will act as a dominant parameter in finally determining a sizing direction of the window. A corner district will evaluate the edge distribution to provide a relevant corner sizing direction, which will be decomposed to the two corresponding side directions. For this, its area is designed to be similar to that of a side district. Finally, each district has been divided into three sub-districts: inner zone(I), middle zone(M), and outer zone(O), which are not overlapped. Actually, the statistical information from these zones will be used to identify various situations leading to the determination of the suitable directions of sizing, which will be detailed in the following sections.

Fig. 5 describes a layout of the left side district of four side districts and a layout of the top right corner district of four corner districts. The remaining side and corner districts will be defined similarly.

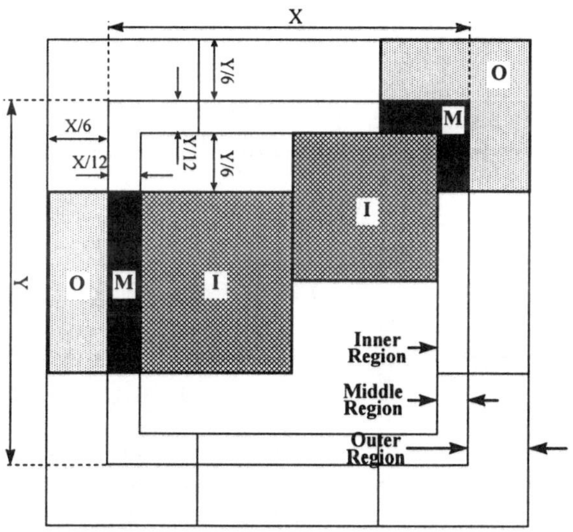

Fig. 5. The layout of the left side district and that of the top right corner district.

3.2 Determining Direction of Sizing

Here, we should estimate a direction of sizing by comparing the extracted statistical information such as means and variances from three zones in each district. A direction of sizing is not the permanent direction but the temporary direction for finally generating the sizing factor ΔSF. The detailed flow chart of determining direction of sizing in a district is shown in Fig. 6, where μ_I, μ_M, and μ_O are means of gray levels in inner zone, middle zone, and outer zone. σ_I^2, σ_M^2, and σ_O^2 are variances of those zones. A positive direction of sizing denotes that the window size should be increased and a negative direction of sizing denotes that the window size should be decreased. The determining procedure of sizing magnitude will be detailed later in section 3.4. The AWA-FSF can perform independently for the corner and the side in adjusting a window size.

We heuristically have made four conditions to control the direction of sizing. Condition I represents the situation of decreasing a window size in which an absolute difference between a mean of inner zone and that of middle zone is larger than an absolute difference between a mean of middle zone and that of outer zone and Condition II represents the opposite situation. In addition, for reducing the boundary sensitivity around the middle zone, we set a marginal range α as 20% of μ_M in Conditions I and II. Condition III plays a role in providing an additional information when the mean value is insufficient to determine a direction of sizing. In the side district, we found that they do not need the marginal range. At later stage, DS_S will dominantly determine a window direction of sizing at later stage and thus we append Condition IV for fine adjustment.

Two corner districts select a sharing side as a sizable region only when the neighbor corner districts have the same signs, that is, DS_Cs. Table 1 is the corner-to-side conversion table which determines the sizable sides by the corner districts. On the contrary, a side district determines a direction of sizing DS_S without considering DS_Ss of neighboring side districts.

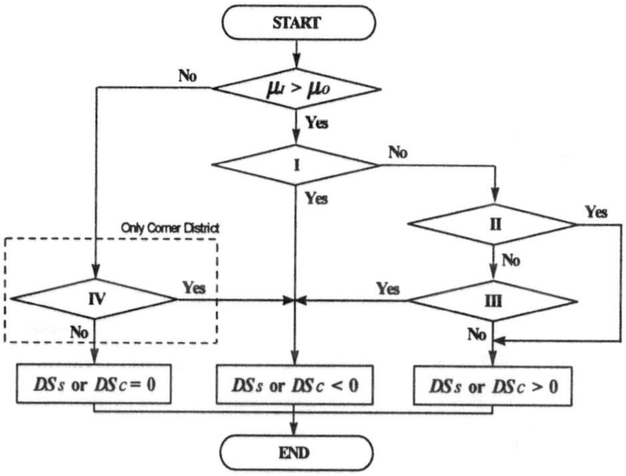

Conditions :

$$\text{I} : |\mu_M - \mu_I| > |\mu_M - \mu_O| + \alpha\mu_M$$

$$\text{II} : |\mu_M - \mu_O| > |\mu_M - \mu_I| + \alpha\mu_M$$

$$\text{III} : \sigma_I^2 > \sigma_O^2 \text{ or } \sigma_M^2 > \sigma_O^2$$

$$\text{IV} : \sigma_I^2 > \sigma_O^2 \geq \sigma_M^2$$

Fig. 6. Flow chart of determining direction of sizing.

Table 1. Corner-to-side conversion table. We choose a DS_{CS} by the corner districts with respect to mutual relation with two neighbor corner districts only when their DS_C s are the same signs. '–' denotes 'don't care'.

		Location of Neighbor Corner District			
		Top Left	Top Right	Bottom Left	Bottom Right
Location of Corner District	Top Left	–	Top	Left	–
	Top Right	Top	–	–	Right
	Bottom Left	Left	–	–	Bottom
	Bottom Right	–	Right	Bottom	–

3.3 Determining Sizing Factor

The AWA-FSF should act adaptively for size variation of a moving object in the complex circumstances. In order to perform sizing more efficiently, a sizing factor that will determine the final window size in pixel unit by also considering the size of the previous window, which will be detailed in section 3.4, is estimated here for each side of the window.

Based on the Window Sizing Direction

Determining a sizing factor also considers the directions of window sizing. If the window fails to enclose the whole part of an object by lavishly reducing its size, the tracker might lose some valuable information and this leads to quite undesirable situation. On the other hand, increasing a window size is more tolerant against sizing error, since the window still encloses a whole object information. This consideration is reflected on Table 2. The magnitude of positive ΔSF representing an increasing window is fixed to be twice as large as that of negative ΔSF representing a decreasing window. This fact means that our window system is designed to be generous in expanding, but somewhat cautious in shrinking.

Based on Mutual Relation with Neighbor Districts

We have to consider the mutual relation between DS_{CS} which is the converted direction of sizing from corner information and DS_S which is the direction of sizing only from side information. If potentially determined directions of sizing differ from each other, we assume that the window boundary is located on the border between the object and background components. We then conclude the DS_S as a window sizing direction by ignoring the result of a corner district, since we found that an object exists more frequently in a side district rather than in a corner district. Meanwhile, if the DS_{CS} that is potentially determined by the two neighbor DS_C s is the same as the DS_S, we assume that an object size is much larger than the window size or is much smaller than the window size. To rapidly adjust a window size in case of the same directions of sizing, the sizing factor is generated twice as large as that in the other cases.

Table 2 summarized the combining look-up table for heuristically determining the sizing factor based on mutual relation with the DS_S and the DS_{CS} and also on inward and outward weighting discussed in previous section 3.3.1.

Table 2. Combining look-up table. Sizing factor determination is based on mutual relation with the DS_S of a side district and the DS_{CS} obtained from the two neighboring corner districts.

Direction-of-Sizing By Side District	Direction-of-Sizing By Neighbor Corner Districts	Sizing Factor ΔSF
$DS_S < 0$	$DS_{CS} > 0$	-1
$DS_S < 0$	$DS_{CS} < 0$	-2
$DS_S > 0$	$DS_{CS} < 0$	$+2$
$DS_S > 0$	$DS_{CS} > 0$	$+4$

3.4 Evaluating Window Sizing Magnitude with Sizing Factor

Here, we also consider the size of the previous window, since it is desirable that the final magnitude of sizing should be to some degree proportional to the size of the previous window. First, we determine that the basic sizing unit S_{B_k} is given by

$$S_{B_k} = \max(1, \frac{S_k}{50}) \qquad \text{for } k = V, H \tag{2}$$

where S_k shown in Fig. 7 is a vertical(V) or horizontal(H) size of a window size in the previous frame. We now put the center of coordinates at the center of window. Then we eventually evaluate a window sizing magnitude ΔS_i for varying the window size in each window sizing direction. ΔS_i now defined in pixel unit is evaluated by

$$\Delta S_i = \Delta SF_i \times S_{B_k} \quad \text{for } i = T, B, L, R; \quad \text{for } k = V, H \tag{3}$$

where

$$\Delta SF_i \in \{ -2, -1, +2, +4 \}. \tag{4}$$

Finally, we can obtain new window center point and new window sizes in four side directions from the center point. New window positions S_T', S_B', S_L', and S_R' from a center point are

$$S_i' = S_i + \mathrm{sgn}(S_i) \times \Delta S_i \quad \text{for } i = T, B, L, R \tag{5}$$

where

$$\mathrm{sgn}(x) = \begin{cases} +1, & \text{if } x > 0 \\ -1, & \text{if } x < 0 \end{cases} \tag{6}$$

and S_i is the coordinate value of the window position before the window sizing procedure. Thus we can find the finely tuned new window center point for acquiring the reference image that will be used for the next frame.

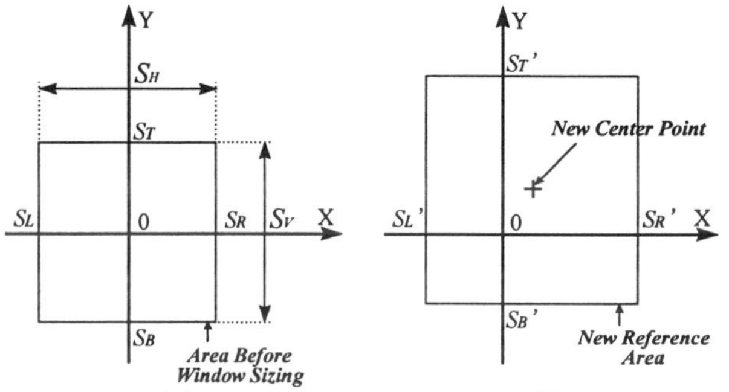

(a) (b)

Fig. 7. Reference window boundary and center point relocation for the more finely tuned reference image: (a) Before window sizing procedure and (b) After window sizing procedure by the AWA-FSF.

3.5 Example of the Proposed AWA-FSF

For easy understanding, we include a conceptual example of the AWA-FSF operation in Fig. 8. First, we determined each direction of sizing from four side districts and four corner districts. The dotted arrows show directions of sizing in each district. Fig. 8(a) shows that a corner district determines the DS_C without considering the results of neighbor corner districts. Actually, we show the DS_{CS} contributed from corner districts to the relevant side directions in Fig. 8(b). For instance, the DS_C of the top left corner district is the same as that of the top right corner district and we can conclude that the window should be increased upward for the top side.

In the meantime, one side district does not care about the results of the others. The DS_S by each side district is now available as shown in Fig. 8(c). Then we determine the window sizing factors using directions of sizing generated by side districts and by neighbor corner districts based on Table 2. We obtain the window sizing directions as well as the sizing factors in four sides, as is described in Fig 8(d). In this example, sizing factors are $+4$ on the top side, -2 on the bottom side, -1 on the left side, and $+2$ on the right side. The center point is relocated to a new position as in Fig. 8(e). In this way, the AWA-FSF can correct the walk-off error introduced by a tracking process and provide a new window that follows and encloses an object efficiently.

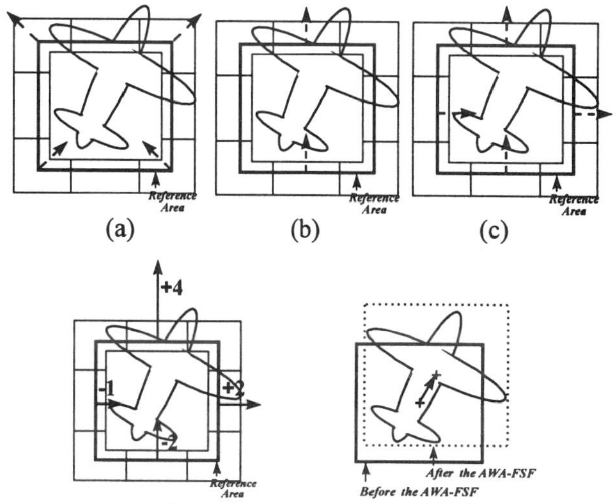

(a) (b) (c) (d) (e)

Fig. 8. Conceptual example of the proposed AWA-FSF: (a) DS_Cs without considering neighbor corner districts in corner districts, (b) DS_{CS}s in corner districts, (c) DS_Ss in side districts, (d) Window sizing directions and sizing factors based on combining DS_{CS} and DS_S as shown in (b) and (c), and (e) Fine tuning effect of the center point of window by the AWA-FSF.

4 Experimental Results

We have applied our proposed method based on the AWA-FSF presented in this paper to real image sequences. We compare the performance of our method having sizing factors described so far with that of adaptive window tracker whose window size is variable by just 1 pixel, $\Delta S_i \in \{-1, +1\}$ in (3), and that of another variant adaptive window tracker without sizing factors in which ΔS_i is determined as $\Delta S_i \in \{-S_{B_k}, +S_{B_k}\}$, i.e., $\Delta SF \in \{-1, +1\}$. When we actually performed tracking experiments based on fixed size window method for many cases in which the size of an object undergoes rapid change, the tracking failed so often that we did not include these experimental results. For objective comparison, the initial position and size of the adaptive windows are set to be the same. We present the results in Fig. 9 and Fig. 10. These experimental results show that the tracker with the AWA-FSF performs better than the others.

The dotted rectangle in these figures is the tracking result obtained from the Centroid-Compensated Correlator before window adjusting by the AWA-FSF. Meanwhile, the solid rectangle is the reference image region adjusted by the AWA-FSF that will be passed to the next frame. We can present some advantages: capability to correct walk-off error by suitably shifting the center point, enhancing stability and reliability by rapidly and tightly adjusting the reference window and so forth.

4.1 Object in the Air

Fig. 9 shows a tracking result that our method is applied to an aircraft going across a ridge whose size has been largely changed from frame to frame. The initial window size is intentionally chosen to be much larger than the object size to verify an initial window sizing speed. We found that dense clouds and ridges in the sequence consisting of 27 real images often bring walk-off error to a basic correlator. Referring to Fig. 9(e) and Fig. 9(f), the adaptive window with just 1-pixel sizing variable and without sizing factors could not properly adapt the window size to the target size. The AWA-FSF, however, accomplishes tightly adjusting the window size to the target size.

4.2 Object on the Ground

Fig. 10 shows the experimental results for an image sequence of the car run along the road overgrown with trees. There are so many vertical clutter components, i.e., trees and road lamp. As shown in Fig. 10(e), in horizontal direction the adaptive window without sizing factors and the AWA-FSF look like having a similar performance. However, vertical window size variation in Fig. 10(f) shows a difference in performance. The AWA-FSF could tightly adjust a window size in 12 frames. The adaptive window without sizing factors stabilizes in 24 frames, and 1-pixel variable window in 39 frames.

5 Conclusion

This paper presented an image tracking architecture employing the centroid compensation and the AWA-FSF for enhancing stability of correlation-based tracking in the cluttered surroundings. The centroid compensation provides our tracker with the capability of modifying the result of the correlation-based tracking to the real center of an object when weak clutter components exist within a window. When the initial window size happens to be much larger than the object size at the onset of tracking, the AWA-FSF could generate enough window sizing magnitudes to remove background components and to increase the occupancy rate of the object components in the reference image. Generally, the window sizing speed of the AWA-FSF is found to be over three times as fast as that of the just 1-pixel sizable adaptive window.

By virtue of the proposed AWA-FSF capable of adjusting window size more rapidly and properly by generating sizing factors in four directions, we could achieve benefit of minimizing influence of complex background and clutter in correlation-based tracking process. In addition, this method can more finely tune the size of the reference image and the reference position repeatedly after the main tracking routine has been terminated. Besides this advantage, we could obtain circumstantial judgment of a moving object: rotation, advance or retreat, and other moving patterns and this history information can be useful for aim-point estimation and other related applications. Since the AWA-FSF can tightly adjust window size around object, computation time for correlation could be optimized. Our experimental results have demonstrated a clear advantage of the AWA-FSF over the adaptive window without sizing factors on 45 sequences composed of more than 3400 real images.

Reference

[1] D. A. Montera, S. K. Rogers, D. W. Ruck, and M. E. Oxley, "Object tracking through adaptive correlation," *Optical Engineering*, Vol. 33, No. 1, pp. 294-302, Jan. 1994.

[2] R. L. Brunson, D. L. Boesen, G. A. Crockett, and J. F. Riker, "Precision trackpoint control via correlation track referenced to simulated imagery," *Proc. SPIE Acquisition, Tracking, and Pointing VI*, Vol. 1697, pp. 325-336, Apr. 1992.

[3] A. D. Hughes and A. J. E. Moy, "Advances in automatic electro-optical tracking systems," *Proc. SPIE Acquisition, Tracking, and Pointing IV*, Vol. 1697, pp. 353-366, Apr. 1992.

[4] T. Kanade and M. Okutomi, "A Stereo Matching Algorithm with an Adaptive Window: Theory and Experiment," *IEEE Trans. on Pattern Anal. Mach. Intell.*, Vol. 16, No. 9, pp. 920-932, Sep. 1994.

[5] J. L. Lotti and G. Giraudon, "Adaptive window algorithm for aerial image stereo," *12th International Conference on Pattern Recognition*, Vol. 1, pp. 701-703, Oct. 1994.

[6] D. H. Ballard and C. M. Brown, *Computer Vision*, pp. 75-88, Prentice-Hall, 1982.

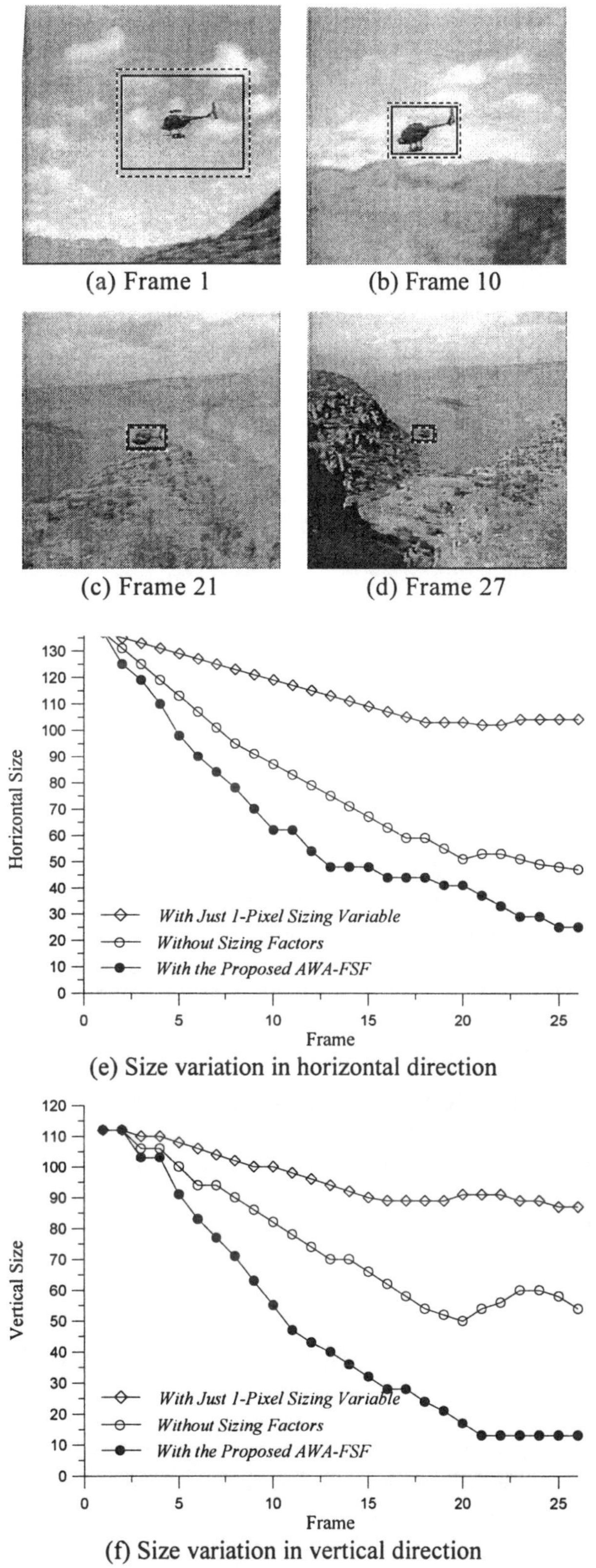

Fig. 9. Test image sequence that aircraft goes over a ridge.

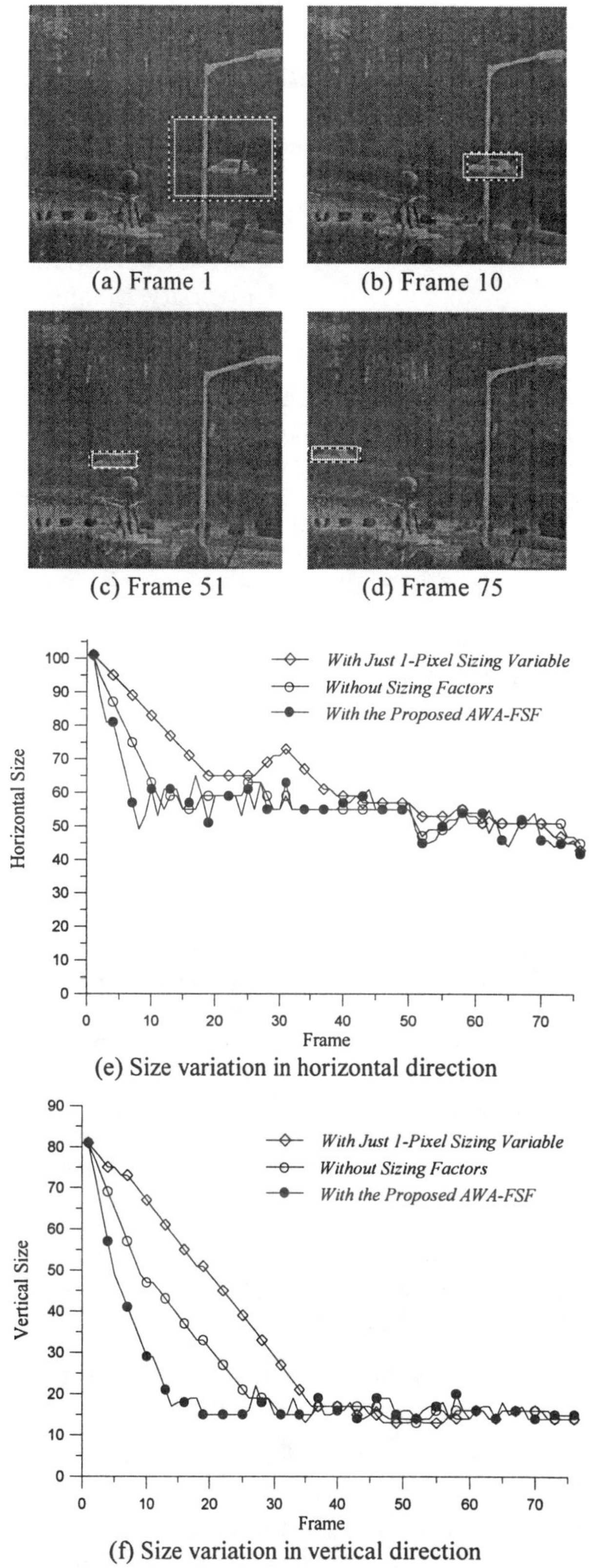

Fig. 10. Test image sequence that target is occluded by vertical clutter components.

Scientific Data Classification: A Case Study*

Gung-Wei Chirn[†] Jason T. L. Wang[‡] Zhiyuan Wang

Department of Computer and Information Science
New Jersey Institute of Technology
University Heights, Newark, NJ 07102, USA

Abstract

Scientific data classification is the activity of determining whether or not an unlabeled scientific object belongs to an existing class. It is an important operation in the management of scientific databases. In this paper we present a case study for scientific data classification. Specifically, we develop a tool for DNA sequence classification. The tool works by generating and matching gapped fingerprints of DNA sequences. Experimental results obtained by applying our tool to classifying a set of Alu sequences demonstrate the good performance of the tool. While the reported research focuses on DNA classification, our techniques should generalize to any domain (e.g. multimedia) where data are naturally represented as sequences.

1 Introduction

Data classification is an important problem in many AI applications [1, 3, 8, 14, 15, 22, 24]. Given an unlabeled object, a classifier makes predictions as to whether or not the object belongs to a particular class. This paper focuses on scientific domains and presents a case study for scientific data classification.

Specifically, we develop a tool for DNA sequence classification. Given an unlabeled sequence S, the tool makes predictions as to whether or not the sequence belongs to a particular class $\mathcal{C}$. Many computer-assisted techniques have been proposed for constructing classifiers from a database of labeled DNA sequences. In general, these techniques can be categorized into the following three classes:

- consensus search – this approach takes a collection of sequences of the class $\mathcal{C}$ and generates a "consensus" sequence which is then used to identify sequences in uncharacterized DNA [9];
- inductive learning/neural networks – this approach takes a set of sequences of the class $\mathcal{C}$ and a set of sequences not in $\mathcal{C}$ and then, based on these sequences and using learning techniques, derives a rule that determines whether the unlabeled sequence S belongs to $\mathcal{C}$ or not [10, 13, 16];
- sequence alignment – this approach aligns the unlabeled sequence S with members of $\mathcal{C}$ using an existing tool such as FASTA [12] and assigns S to $\mathcal{C}$ if the resulting alignment score is sufficiently high.

In this paper we present a new tool for calculating scores to classify DNA sequences. Section 2 gives an overview of the classification algorithm used in the tool. Section 3 details a technique, called *fingerprint* technique [4, 20], used in the classification algorithm. Section 4 reports some experimental results. We conclude the paper in Section 5.

2 Classification Algorithm

Our approach works by first randomly selecting a set $\mathcal{B}$ of sequences of the class $\mathcal{C}$, referred to as "base data." Then we take another set of sequences of $\mathcal{C}$, referred to as "positive training data," and calculate, for each positive training sequence, a score with respect to the base sequences. The minimum score thus obtained is called the positive lower bound, denoted L_p. Next, we take a set of sequences not in $\mathcal{C}$, referred to as "negative training data," and again calculate, for each negative training sequence, a score with respect to the base sequences. The maximum score thus obtained is called the negative upper bound, denoted U_n.

Let $B_{high} = \max\{L_p, U_n\}$ and $B_{low} = \min\{L_p, U_n\}$ (see Fig. 1). When classifying the unlabeled sequence S, we calculate S's score with respect to the

*This work was supported by the U.S. National Science Foundation under Grant Numbers IRI-9224602 and IRI-9531548.

[†]Present address: Bioinformatics Pre-Clinical R&D, Hoffmann-La Roche Inc., 340 Kingsland Street, Nutley, NJ 07110-1199, USA.

[‡]Contact author; email: jason@village.njit.edu.

1082-3409/97 $10.00 © 1997 IEEE

base sequences, denoted c. If $c \geq B_{high}$, then S is classified to be a member of $\mathcal{C}$. If $c \leq B_{low}$, then S is classified not to be a member of $\mathcal{C}$. If $B_{low} < c < B_{high}$, then the "no opinion" verdict is given.

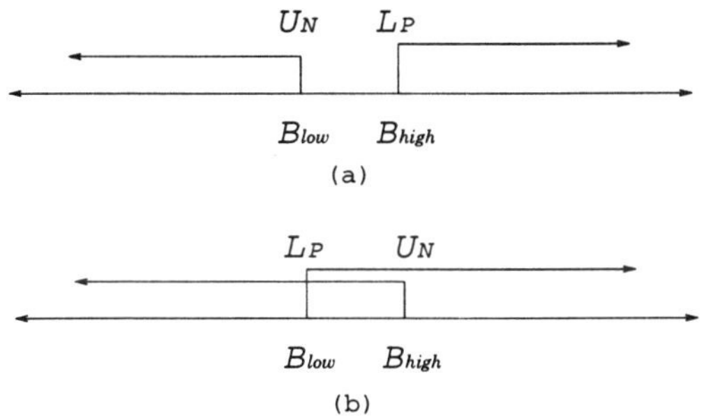

Fig. 1. Illustration of the parameters B_{low} and B_{high} for cases (a) $U_N \leq L_P$ and (b) $U_N > L_P$.

The proposed tool uses the fingerprint technique [4, 20] to process the base sequences and calculate scores for the training and unlabeled sequences. We describe the fingerprint technique in detail in the next section. To demonstrate the utility of our approach, we apply it to classifying Alu sequences (see Fig. 2 for an example) [7]. We then compare our tool with FASTA, the Alu classifier currently used in the scientific community, and evaluate the precision rates obtained from the two tools. Our results show that the proposed tool is better than FASTA in terms of the number of correct classifications.

```
>HSU14568 Human Alu-Sb subfamily consensus
  sequence
GGCCGGGCGCGGTGGCTCACGCCTGTAATCCCAGCACTTTGG
GAGGCCGAGGCGGGCGGATCACGAGGTCAGGAGATCGAGACC
ATCCTGGCTAACACGGTGAAACCCCGTCTCACTAAAAATACA
AAAATTAGCCGGGCGTGGTGGCGGGCGCCTGTAGTCCCAGCT
ACTCGGGAGGCTGAGGCAGGAGAATGGCGTGAACCCGGGAGG
CGGAGCTTGCAGTGAGCCGAGATCGCGCCACTGCACTCCAGC
CTGGGCGACAGAGCGAGACTCCGTCTCAAAAAAAA
```

Fig. 2. An example Alu sequence. The string following > is the title of the Alu sequence. The sequence is composed of nucleotides adenine (A), thymine (T), cytosine (C), and guanine (G).

3 Fingerprint Technique

Our tool uses a hash-based fingerprint technique to calculate the score of a sequence. Fingerprints have been used by many workers in different domains. For example, Califano and Rigoutsos [4] used them to find the best alignment between two DNA sequences. Wang *et al.* applied them to performing information retrieval in digital libraries [18].

Given the set $\mathcal{B}$ of base sequences, we store their fingerprints into a number of ***fingerprint files*** as follows. Let S be a sequence in $\mathcal{B}$. We take every contiguous substring (or ***segment***), denoted by Seg, of length n from S and generate gapped fingerprints from Seg. Each fingerprint is a substring of Seg that always begins with the segment's first nucleotide. The lengths of the fingerprints range from 2 to $n-1$. The number of gaps in a fingerprint is bounded by a parameter gap.

Next, for each fingerprint f of length k, $2 \leq k \leq n-1$, we use a hash function h_k to hash f into a fingerprint file $\mathcal{F}_k$. In $\mathcal{F}_k$, f is associated with a pair of integers (x, y). This pair serves as the position marker for f, where x indicates that f is generated from a segment of the xth sequence in $\mathcal{B}$ and y means that the first nucleotide of f occurs at the yth position in that sequence.

Example 1.
Consider the following three base sequences: S_1 = ACGTTGCA, S_2 = ACCAGTG, S_3 = CGGACTA. Suppose the length of segments is 6. Then, for example, we obtain the following segments from S_1: ACGTTG, CGTTGC and GTTGCA.

Now consider the segment Seg = ACGTTG taken from S_1. Suppose $gap = 2$. Then, we can generate the following 3-nucleotide gapped fingerprints from Seg: ACG (0 gap); AGT (1 gap at position 2), ACT (1 gap at position 3); ATT (1 gap at position 2 and 1 gap at position 3), AGT (1 gap at position 2 and 1 gap at position 4) and ACT (1 gap at position 3 and 1 gap at position 4). Table 1 shows all gapped fingerprints generated from the segment ACGTTG.

Let f = XYZ be a fingerprint of length 3. Suppose the hash function h_3 is $h_3(f) = (num(\texttt{X}) \times 4^2 + num(\texttt{Y}) \times 4^1 + num(\texttt{Z})) \bmod 7$, where $num(\texttt{X})$ is X's ASCII value minus 64. Figure 3 shows the fingerprint file $\mathcal{F}_3$ for the three base sequences S_1, S_2 and S_3. Thus, for example, in bucket 1 in $\mathcal{F}_3$, GGA(3, 2) means that the fingerprint GGA is generated from S_3 and it starts from the 2nd position in S_3.
End of Example

When calculating the score of a sequence S (whether it is a training or an unlabeled sequence), we segment S in the same way as for the base sequences and generate fingerprints from the resulting segments. We then hash the fingerprints, using the same hash functions as for the base sequences. When a match between S's fingerprint and a base sequence's fingerprint occurs, we give one score to an appropriate position in the base sequence. The result is a histogram of scores on the base sequences. Figure 4 summarizes the algorithm.

	2-nucleotide fingerprints	3-nucleotide fingerprints
0 gap	AC	ACG
1 gap	AG	ACT AGT
2 gaps	AT	ACT AGT ATT

	4-nucleotide fingerprints	5-nucleotide fingerprints
0 gap	ACGT	ACGTT
1 gap	ACGT AGTT ACTT	ACGTG AGTTG ACTTG
2 gaps	ACGG ATTG ACTG AGTG	

Table 1. Gapped fingerprints (of lengths 2, 3, 4, 5, respectively) generated from the segment ACGTTG (the segment length is 6 and $gap = 2$).

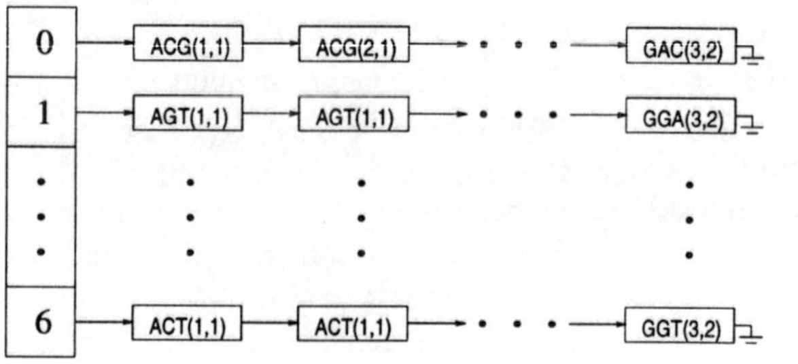

Fig. 3. The fingerprint file $\mathcal{F}_3$ for the three base sequences in Example 1. Note that some entries are duplicate (e.g., AGT(1, 1) in bucket 1); they represent fingerprints with different numbers of gaps.

Input: A sequence S, a set $\mathcal{B}$ of base sequences and $\mathcal{B}$'s fingerprint files.
Output: A histogram of scores on the base sequences in $\mathcal{B}$.
/* Let $\mathcal{F}$ contain all fingerprints generated from S. */
for each fingerprint f in $\mathcal{F}$ **do**
  begin
    /* Let the length of f be k. */
    hash f using h_k and probe into the fingerprint file $\mathcal{F}_k$;
    for each match between f and a fingerprint $\hat{f}$ in $\mathcal{F}_k$ **do**
      begin
        /* Let the position marker associated with $\hat{f}$ be (i, q). */
        /* Suppose the first nucleotide of f occurs at the pth position in S. */
        add one score to the position $q - p + 1$ in the ith base sequence in $\mathcal{B}$;
      end;
  end;

Fig. 4. Algorithm Scoring.

Example 2.
Suppose we are given a sequence S = CGATGCAT. Figure 5 shows the histogram obtained after matching S's fingerprints with the fingerprints of the base sequences in Example 1.
End of Example

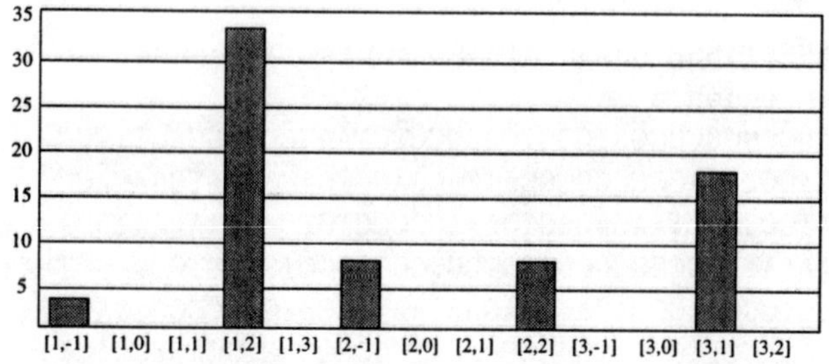

Fig. 5. This histogram is obtained after processing the sequence S in Example 2. The y-axis shows scores. Each $[i, q]$ on the x-axis represents the qth position in the ith base sequence, i.e. S_i, in Example 1.

Let B be a base sequence in $\mathcal{B}$ and let p be a position in B, $1 \leq p \leq |B|$. Let $score(B[p])$ represent the total scores added to the position p after applying the algorithm Scoring to the given sequence S and the base sequences in $\mathcal{B}$. The score of B, denoted $score(B)$, is defined to be

$$score(B) = \max\{score(B[p]) | 1 \le p \le |B|\}.$$

The score of S with respect to the base sequences, denoted $score(S)$, is defined to be

$$score(S) = \frac{\max\{score(B) | B \in \mathcal{B}\}}{|S|} \times 100.$$

4 Experimental Results

The algorithms for the proposed tool were implemented in C on a Sun SPARCstation 20 running the operating system Solaris version 2.4. We compared the relative performance of the tool by applying it to classifying Alu sequences [7]. 327 Alu sequences were used in the experiments, among which 100 were used as base sequences, 100 were used as positive training sequences, and the other 127 were treated as unlabeled test sequences. The lengths of these sequences ranged from 76 bp to 379 bp. In constructing non-alu data, we randomly generated 1,200 sequences that retained the correct nucleotide frequencies using the simulation programming package SIMSCRIPT [11]. Among them, 100 were used as negative training sequences and the other 1,100 were also treated as unlabeled test sequences. The lengths of these sequences ranged from 100 bp to 240 bp. We fixed the segment length at 8 and gap at 0. Table 2 summarizes the parameters and default values used in the experiments.

Parameter	Value	Description
$\lvert\mathcal{B}\rvert$	100	Number of base sequences (Alu)
$NumTest$	1,227	Number of unlabeled test sequences (Alu & non-Alu)
n	8	Segment length used in our tool
gap	0	Number of gaps allowed in our tool

Table 2. Experimental parameters and their default values used in performance analysis.

The metrics used to evaluate the effectiveness of our classification algorithm are precision rates (PR) and no-opinion rates (NR), where

$$PR = \frac{NumCorrect}{NumTest} \times 100\%$$

and

$$NR = \frac{NumNoOpinion}{NumTest} \times 100\%$$

$NumCorrect$ is the number of test sequences classified correctly, $NumNoOpinion$ is the number of test sequences obtaining the "no opinion" verdict, and $NumTest$ is the total number of test sequences, 1,227 in our case. (A test sequence S in a class $\mathcal{C}$ is said to be classified correctly by an algorithm if S is determined to belong to $\mathcal{C}$ by that algorithm.)

Table 3 shows the classification results and the B_{high} and B_{low} values obtained by the proposed tool. For comparison purposes, we also list the results obtained from the Alu classifier FASTA [12] currently used in the Whitehead Institute of MIT. This tool aligns a given unlabeled DNA sequence S with the sequences in the Alu library maintained in the Whitehead Institute and classifies S as an Alu if the resulting alignment score is greater than or equal to a preset threshold. (The threshold used is 100.) Otherwise, S is classified as a non-Alu sequence. The tool does not give the "no opinion" verdict. The experimental results show that our tool is better than FASTA.

	Our Tool	FASTA
PR	99.21%	98.2%
NR	0.0%	—
B_{high}	68	—
B_{low}	65	—

Table 3. Classification results for the two studied classifiers.

We also conducted a series of experiments to examine the impact of the parameter values on the performance of the proposed tool. To avoid the mutual influence of parameters, in each experiment we only varied one parameter's values, with the other parameters being fixed and having the values as shown in Table 2. Figures 6 - 11 summarize the results.

We see from the figures that our tool behaves quite stably with varying $|\mathcal{B}|$. The number of the base sequences has little impact on the performance of the tool. No trend is evident with regard to n and gap used in the tool. However, programs using a short segment (e.g., $n = 5$) and a small gap (e.g., $gap = 0$) run much faster than programs using a long segment (e.g., $n = 9$) and a large gap (e.g., $gap = 4$).

In sum, to achieve good performance, one should use sufficiently many (e.g., 100) sequences as base, positive training and negative training data when constructing the classifier. Using short segments (e.g., with $n = 5$) without gaps is good, as it requires less running time and space while achieving an acceptably high precision rate.

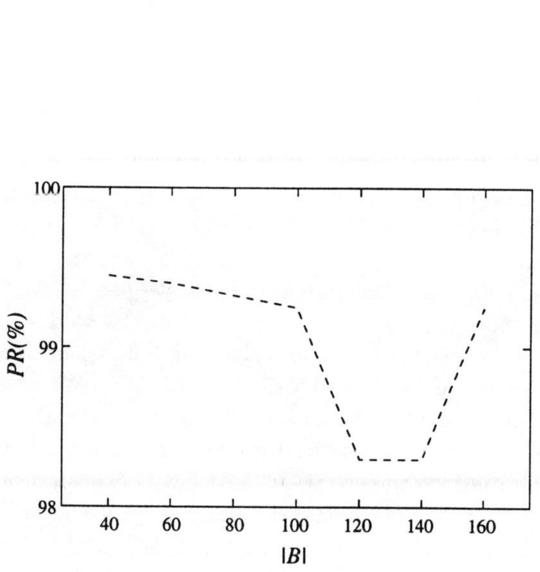

Fig. 6. PR as a function of $|\mathcal{B}|$.

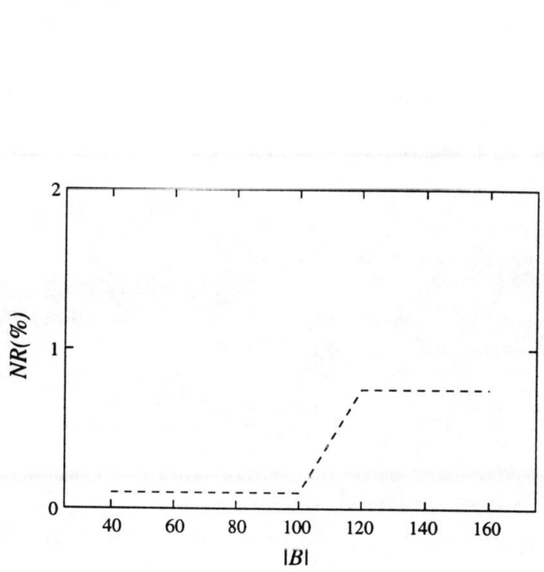

Fig. 9. NR as a function of $|\mathcal{B}|$.

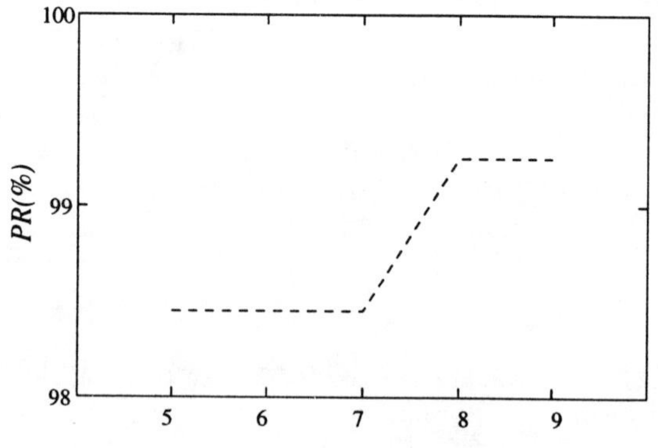

Fig. 7. PR as a function of n.

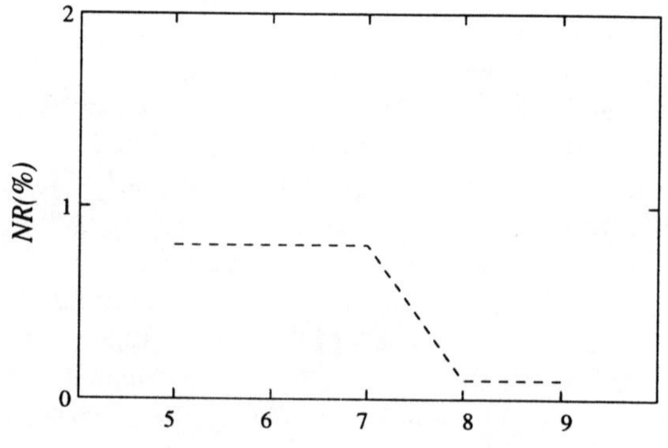

Fig. 10. NR as a function of n.

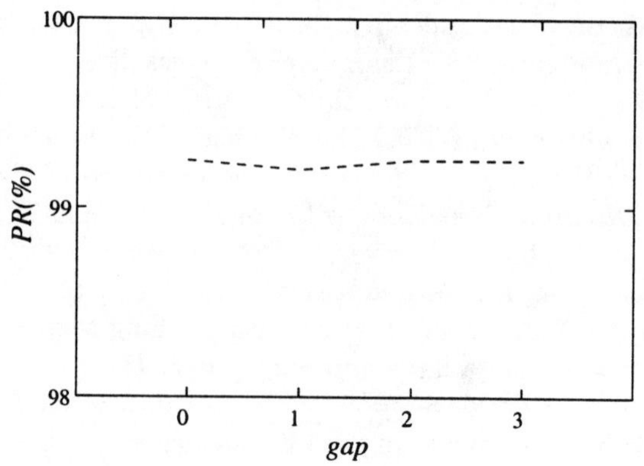

Fig. 8. PR as a function of *gap*.

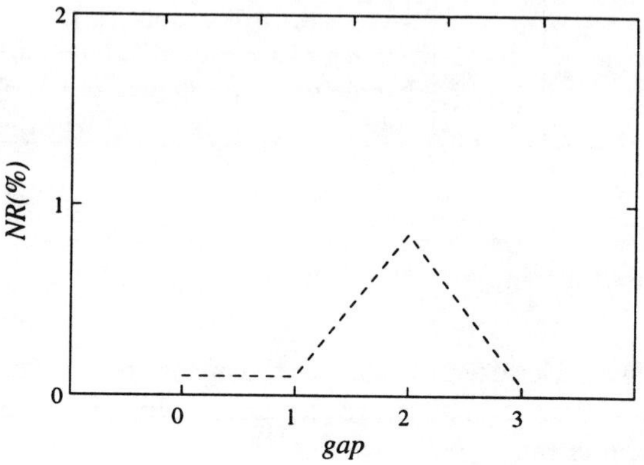

Fig. 11. NR as a function of *gap*.

5 Conclusion

In this paper we presented a case study for scientific data classification. Specifically, we developed a tool for DNA sequence classification. The tool generated and matched gapped fingerprints of DNA sequences. To demonstrate the utility of the proposed tool, we applied it to classifying Alu sequences and compared the results with those obtained from the FASTA classifier currently used in the Whitehead Institute of MIT. Our experimental results showed that the proposed tool is better than FASTA.

The proposed tool runs fast. It took about 20 minutes to train the tool by hashing 100 base, positive and negative training sequences and calculating the positive lower bound and negative upper bound. It took 8 seconds to classify a given unlabeled sequence. Currently, we are incorporating the tool into a visualization toolbox for pattern matching and discovery in scientific [5, 19, 23] and document databases [17, 21]. The executable software packages of the toolbox are available from the authors. A companion email server is established [6], which can be accessed by sending a blank email with the word HELP on the subject line to discover@village.njit.edu (for details, please visit the web site at http://www.cis.njit.edu/jason/help.html).

Acknowledgments

The authors thank Dr. Steve Rozen at the Whitehead Institute of MIT for providing FASTA classification results. Thanks are also to Professor Dennis Shasha of New York University and Dr. Bruce Shapiro of the National Institutes of Health for helpful discussions and to Dr. Peter Yianilos of the NEC Research Institute for his pointing out a relevant paper in the field.

References

[1] R. Agrawal, S. Ghosh, T. Imielinski, B. Iyer, and A. Swami. An interval classifier for database mining applications. In *Proceedings of the 18th International Conference on Very Large Data Bases*, pages 560–573, Vancouver, Canada, Aug. 1992.

[2] S. F. Altschul, W. Gish, W. Miller, E. W. Myers, and D. J. Lipman. Basic local alignment search tool. *Journal of Molecular Biology*, 215:403–410, 1990.

[3] L. Breiman, J. H. Friedman, R. A. Olshen, and C. J. Stone. *Classification and Regression Trees.* Wadsworth International Group, Belmont, CA, 1984.

[4] A. Califano and I. Rigoutsos. FLASH: A fast look-up algorithm for string homology. In *Proceedings of the 1st International Conference on Intelligent Systems for Molecular Biology*, pages 56–64, Bethesda, MD, July 1993.

[5] C.-Y. Chang and J. T. L. Wang. Scientific data mining: A case study. In *Proceedings of the 8th International Conference on Software Engineering and Knowledge Engineering*, pages 100–107, Lake Tahoe, Nevada, June 1996.

[6] G.-W. Chirn. *Pattern Discovery in Sequence Databases: Algorithms and Applications to DNA/Protein Classification.* PhD thesis, Department of Computer and Information Science, New Jersey Institute of Technology, Newark, NJ, USA, 1996.

[7] J.-M. Claverie and W. Makalowski. Alu alert. *Nature*, 371:752, 1994.

[8] U. Fayyad, D. Haussler, and P. Stolorz. KDD for science data analysis: Issues and examples. In *Proceedings of the 2nd International Conference on Knowledge Discovery and Data Mining*, pages 50–56, Portland, Oregon, Aug. 1996.

[9] M. S. Gelfand. Prediction of function in DNA sequence analysis. *Journal of Computational Biology*, 2:87–115, 1995.

[10] H. Hirsh and M. Noordewier. Using background knowledge to improve inductive learning of DNA sequences. In *Proceedings of the IEEE Conference on Artificial Intelligence for Applications*, March 1994.

[11] P. J. Kiviat, H. M. Markowitz, and R. Villanueva. *SIMSCRIPT II.5 Programming Language.* CACI, Los Angeles, CA, 1983.

[12] D. J. Lipman and W. R. Pearson. Rapid and sensitive protein similarity searches. *Science*, 227:1435–1441, 1985.

[13] D. Loewenstern, H. Hirsh, P. Yianilos, and M. O. Noordewier. DNA sequence classification using compression-based induction. Technical Report 95-04, DIMACS Tech. Report, Rutgers University, April 1995.

[14] J. R. Quinlan. Induction of decision trees. *Machine Learning*, 1:81–106, 1986.

[15] J. R. Quinlan. *C4.5: Programs for Machine Learning.* Morgan Kaufmann Publishers, Inc., San Mateo, CA, 1993.

[16] J. W. Shavlik, G. G. Towell, and M. O. Noordewier. Using knowledge-based neural networks to refine existing biological theories. In *Proceedings of the 2nd International Conference on Bioinformatics, Supercomputing and Complex Genome Analysis*, pages 377–390, 1993.

[17] J. T. L. Wang and C.-Y. Chang. Fast retrieval of electronic messages that contain mistyped words or spelling errors. *IEEE Transactions on Systems, Man, and Cybernetics*, 27(3):441-451, June 1997

[18] J. T. L. Wang and C.-Y. Chang. Fast retrieval of electronic documents in digital libraries. In *Proceedings of the 7th IEEE International Conference on Tools with Artificial Intelligence*, pages 208–215, Herndon, Virginia, Nov. 1995.

[19] J. T. L. Wang, G. J. S. Chang, G.-W. Chirn, C.-Y. Chang, W. Wu, and F. Aljallad. A visualization tool for pattern matching and discovery in scientific databases. In *Proceedings of the 8th International Conference on Software Engineering and Knowledge Engineering*, pages 563–570, Lake Tahoe, Nevada, Jun. 1996.

[20] J. T. L. Wang, G.-W. Chirn, T. G. Marr, B. A. Shapiro, D. Shasha, and K. Zhang. Combinatorial pattern discovery for scientific data: Some preliminary results. In *Proceedings of the 1994 ACM SIGMOD International Conference on Management of Data*, pages 115–125, Minneapolis, Minnesota, May 1994.

[21] J. T. L. Wang and P. A. Ng. TEXPROS: An intelligent document processing system. *International Journal of Software Engineering and Knowledge Engineering*, 2(2):171–196, June 1992.

[22] J. T. L. Wang, B. A. Shapiro, D. Shasha, K. Zhang, and C.-Y. Chang. Automated discovery of active motifs in multiple RNA secondary structures. In *Proceedings of the 2nd International Conference on Knowledge Discovery and Data Mining*, pages 70–75, Portland, Oregon, Aug. 1996.

[23] J. T. L. Wang, K. Zhang, K. Jeong, and D. Shasha. A system for approximate tree matching. *IEEE Transactions on Knowledge and Data Engineering*, 6(4):559–571, August 1994.

[24] X. Wang, J. T. L. Wang, D. Shasha, B. Shapiro, S. Dikshitulu, I. Rigoutsos, and K. Zhang. Automated discovery of active motifs in three dimensional molecules. In *Proceedings of the 3rd International Conference on Knowledge Discovery and Data Mining*, pages 89-95, Newport Beach, California, Aug. 1997.

Session D.1

Optimization Problem Solving Tools

Session Chair:
Nikolaos G. Bourbakis, SUNY at Binghamton, USA

Improving the Performance of Weighted Lagrange-Multiplier Methods for Nonlinear Constrained Optimization*

Benjamin W. Wah, Tao Wang, Yi Shang, and Zhe Wu

Center for Reliable and High Performance Computing
Coordinated Science Laboratory
University of Illinois at Urbana-Champaign
Urbana, IL 61801, USA
URL: `http://manip.crhc.uiuc.edu`

Abstract

Nonlinear constrained optimization problems can be solved by a Lagrange-multiplier method in a continuous space or by its extended discrete version in a discrete space. These methods rely on gradient descents in the objective space to find high-quality solutions, and gradient ascents in the Lagrangian space to satisfy the constraints. The balance between descents and ascents depends on the relative weights between the objective and the constraints that indirectly control the convergence speed and solution quality of the method. To improve convergence speed without degrading solution quality, we propose an algorithm to dynamically control these relative weights. Starting from an initial weight, the algorithm automatically adjusts the weights based on the behavior of the search progress. With this strategy, we are able to eliminate divergence, reduce oscillations, and speed up convergence. We show improved convergence behavior of our proposed algorithm on both nonlinear continuous and discrete problems.

1 Introduction

Many applications in engineering, decision science and operation research are formulated as optimization problems. The *constrained nonlinear optimization problems* studied here take the following form.

$$\begin{aligned} &\textit{Minimize} && f(X) \\ &\textit{subject to} && g(X) \le 0 \quad X = (x_1, x_2, \ldots, x_n) \\ & && h(X) = 0 \end{aligned} \tag{1}$$

where X is a vector of real numbers in continuous problems or a vector of discrete numbers in discrete problems, $f(X)$ is an objective function, $g(X) = [g_1(X), \cdots, g_k(X)]^T$ is a set of k inequality constraints, and $h(X) = [h_1(X), \cdots, h_m(X)]^T$ is a set of m equality constraints. Note that f, g, and h can be either continuous or discrete functions.

The problem defined in (1) can be solved by a large number of existing approaches [2] that can be classified into local and global searches. Local-search algorithms include gradient descent, Newton's method, conjugate-gradient method, and Lagrange-multiplier method. Starting from some initial point, they stop at a local minimum. Since the local minima found by local-search methods may be much worse than the global minimum for nonlinear problems, global-search methods have been studied to perform both global search and local refinement. The global-search component goes through the possible search space and identifies some promising points for regions that may have good solutions, whereas the local-refinement component uses these promising points as starting points and employs a local-search algorithm to find local minima.

In this paper, we focus on the Lagrange-multiplier method as a local-search method to find satisfiable solutions and show how its convergence speed can be improved.

2 Lagrange-Multiplier Methods

Lagrange-multiplier methods introduce Lagrange multipliers to gradually resolve constraints iteratively. It is an exact method that optimizes the objective $f(X)$ to meet the Kuhn-Tucker conditions [2].

Since Lagrangian methods cannot directly deal with inequality constraints $g_i(X) \le 0$ in general cases, we transform inequality constraints into equality constraints by adding slack variables z_i, which results in $p_i(X) = g_i(X) + z_i^2 = 0$. The corresponding *Lagrangian function* and *augmented Lagrangian function*

*Research supported by National Science Foundation Grant MIP 96-32316 and National Aeronautics and Space Administration Contract NAG 1-613.

Proc. IEEE International Conference on Tools with Artificial Intelligence, 1997.

1082-3409/97 $10.00 © 1997 IEEE

are defined as follows.

$$\mathcal{L}(X,\lambda,\mu) = f(X) + \lambda^T h(X) + \mu^T p(X) \quad (2)$$

$$L(X,\lambda,\mu) = f(X) + \lambda^T h(X) + ||h(X)||_2^2 + \mu^T p(X) + ||p(X)||_2^2 \quad (3)$$

where $\lambda = [\lambda_1, \cdots, \lambda_m]^T$ and $\mu = [\mu_1, \cdots, \mu_k]^T$ are two sets of Lagrange multipliers, and $p(X) = [p_1(X), \cdots, p_k(X)]^T$. We use the augmented Lagrangian function in this paper since it provides better numerical stability. After simplification [2], the augmented Lagrangian function becomes

$$L_z(X,\lambda,\mu) = f(x) + \lambda^T h(X) + ||h(X)||_2^2 + \sum_{i=1}^{k} \left[max^2(0, \mu_i + g_i(X)) - \mu_i^2\right] \quad (4)$$

2.1 Continuous Lagrangian Methods

For continuous problems, we assume that in (1), every variable x_i $(i = 1, 2, \cdots, n)$ takes a value from R, and that $f(X)$, $g(X)$ and $h(X)$, as well as their derivatives, are continuous functions.

According to classical optimization theory [2], the following set of equations can be used to find local and global extrema of (4):

$$\nabla_X L_z(X,\lambda,\mu) = 0 \qquad \nabla_\lambda L_z(X,\lambda,\mu) = 0$$
$$\nabla_\mu L_z(X,\lambda,\mu) = 0 \quad (5)$$

These conditions are necessary to guarantee the (local) optimality to the solution of (1) and (3). Because a local minimum of the Lagrangian function $L_z(X,\lambda,\mu)$ is a local minimum in the original-variable (X) space and a local maximum of $L_z(X,\lambda,\mu)$ in the Lagrange-multiplier (λ and μ) space, it can be obtained by solving the following dynamic system of equations:

$$\frac{d}{dt}X(t) = -\nabla_X L_z(X(t),\lambda(t),\mu(t))$$
$$\frac{d}{dt}\lambda(t) = \nabla_\lambda L_z(X(t),\lambda(t),\mu(t)) \quad (6)$$
$$\frac{d}{dt}\mu(t) = \nabla_\mu L_z(X(t),\lambda(t),\mu(t))$$

which perform descents in the original-variable space of X and ascents in the Lagrange-multiplier space of λ and μ. The dynamic system evolves over time t, and reaches equilibrium where all gradients vanish.

2.2 Discrete Lagrangian Methods (DLM)

For discrete optimization problems, all the variables x_i $(i = 1, 2, \cdots, n)$ take discrete values (e.g., integers). Given Lagrange multipliers λ and μ, we define the change in the Lagrangian function $L_z(X,\lambda,\mu)$ in the discrete variable space to achieve the maximum decrease in $L_z(X,\lambda,\mu)$ as follows [3]:

$$\Delta_X L_z(X,\lambda,\mu) = \delta_X \quad (7)$$

where $L_z(X \ominus \delta_X, \lambda, \mu)$[1] is the minimum value among all $L_z(Y,\lambda,\mu)$ for Y sufficiently close to X.

Having defined $\Delta_X L_z(X,\lambda,\mu)$, we seek discrete saddle points.[2] The iterative equations are as follows.

$$X(k+1) = X(k) \ominus \Delta_X L_z(X(k),\lambda(k),\mu(k))$$
$$\lambda(k+1) = \lambda(k) + c_1 h(X(k)) \quad (8)$$
$$\mu_i(k+1) = \mu_i(k) \begin{cases} + c_2 g_i(X(k)) \\ \quad \text{if } \mu_i(k) + g_i(X(k)) > 0 \\ - c_2 \mu_i(k) \\ \quad \text{if } \mu_i(k) + g_i(X(k)) \le 0 \end{cases}$$

where c_1 and c_2 are positive real numbers controlling how fast the Lagrange multipliers change. For brevity, the proofs showing the correctness of DLM and (8) are omitted here [3].

3 Convergence Speed of Lagrangian Methods

We show in this section that the convergence speed and/or the solution quality can be affected by an additional weight w in the objective part of the Lagrangian function. This results in a new Lagrangian function as follows,

$$L_o(X,\lambda,\mu) = w\, f(x) + \lambda^T h(X) + ||h(X)||_2^2 + \sum_{i=1}^{k} \left[max^2(0, \mu_i + g_i(X)) - \mu_i^2\right] \quad (9)$$

where $w > 0$ is a static weight on the objective. When $w = 1$, $L_o(X,\lambda,\mu) = L_z(X,\lambda,\mu)$, which is the original Lagrangian function.

In general, adding a weight to the objective changes the Lagrangian function, which in turn may cause the dynamic system to settle at a different local minimum with different solution quality. This is especially true when the local minimum is on the boundary of a feasible region. In this section we show that the solution quality and convergence time can be influenced greatly by the choice of the initial weight.

Starting from initial point $(X(0),\lambda(0),\mu(0))$, (6) is used to find local minima satisfying the constraints

[1] $\ominus$ is an operator for changing one point in discrete space into another with δ value. An example of $\ominus$ is the exclusive-OR operator.

[2] We look for saddle points in discrete space because the first-order conditions defined in (5) do not exist in discrete space.

where L_z is replaced by L_o.

$$\begin{aligned}\frac{d}{dt}X(t) &= -\nabla_X L_o(X(t), \lambda(t), \mu(t)) \\ \frac{d}{dt}\lambda(t) &= \nabla_\lambda L_o(X(t), \lambda(t), \mu(t)) \\ \frac{d}{dt}\mu(t) &= \nabla_\mu L_o(X(t), \lambda(t), \mu(t))\end{aligned} \tag{10}$$

We solve this dynamic system using an ordinary differential equation solver *LSODE*[3] and observe a search trajectory $(X(t), \lambda(t), \mu(t))$. When a local minimum is on the boundary of the feasible region (which is true for most problems studied), the dynamic equation approaches it from both inside and outside of the feasible region. We observe four possible behaviors of the search trajectory.

- The trajectory converges without oscillations;
- The trajectory gradually reduces its oscillations and eventually converges;
- The trajectory oscillates within some range but never converges;
- The magnitude of oscillations increases, and the trajectory eventually diverges.

Obviously, the first two cases are desirable, and the other two are not. Moreover, we would like to reduce the amount of oscillations and improve convergence time by proper control of w.

To illustrate the first behavior, consider the following simple example.

$$\begin{aligned}&\textit{Minimize} \quad x^2 \\ &\textit{subject to} \quad x \le -10\end{aligned} \tag{11}$$

When we start from the initial point $X(t=0) = -20$ with $\mu(t=0) = 0$ using $w = 1$, we obtain a trajectory without oscillations, as shown in Figure 1.

To illustrate the last three behaviors (divergence, oscillations without convergence, and reduction of oscillations until convergence), consider Problem 2.3 in [1]. We set $X(t=0)$, the initial point at $t=0$, at the middle of the search space, and $\lambda(t=0) = \mu(t=0) = 0$. The total time used for *LSODE* is $t_{max} = 10^5$, which is divided into small units of $\Delta t = 1.0$, resulting in a maximum of 10^5 iterations ($= t_{max}/\Delta t$). The stopping condition for (10) is

$$||dX(t)/dt||^2 + ||d\lambda(t)/dt||^2 + ||d\mu(t)/dt||^2 \le \delta \tag{12}$$

[3] *LSODE* is a solver for first-order ordinary differential equations, a public-domain package available from http://www.netlib.org.

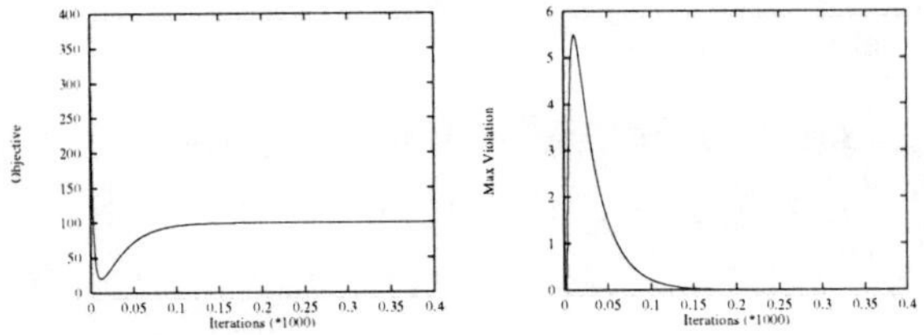

Figure 1: Objective function and maximum violation converge without oscillations.

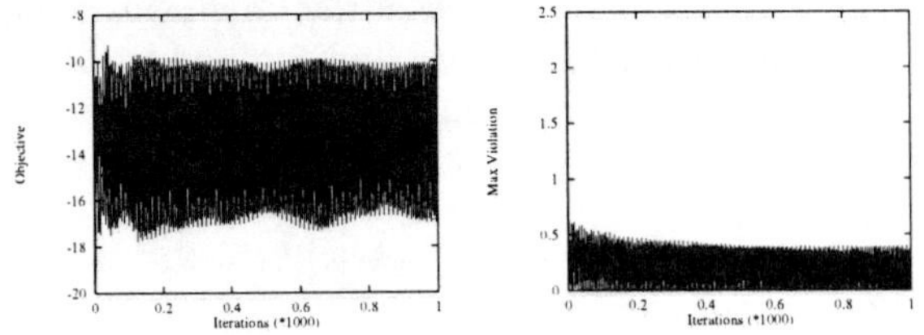

Figure 2: Objective function and maximum violation oscillate.

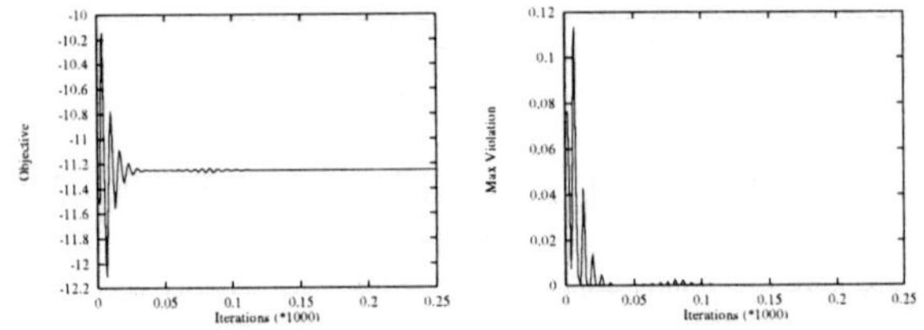

Figure 3: Objective function and maximum violation converge after oscillations subsided.

where $\delta = 10^{-25}$ in our experiments. The dynamic system stops when it converges or when it reaches the maximum number of iterations.

When $w = 1$, (10) diverges quickly into infinity, meaning that the original Lagrangian method governed by (6) will diverge. If we scale the objective by 10 (*i.e.*, $w = 1/10$), then $f(X(t))$ oscillates within the range -17 and -10, while the maximum violation $v_{max}(t)$ is between 0 to 0.4, as shown in Figure 2. Here, $v_{max}(t)$ at time t is defined as

$$v_{max}(t) = \max_{\substack{1\le i\le m,\\ 1\le j\le k}} \{|h_i(X(t))|, \max[0, g_j(X(t))]\} \tag{13}$$

If we further reduces w to $1/15$, then the oscillations are reduced, and the trajectory eventually converges (see Figure 3).

To understand the effect of w on convergence, we randomly generated 20 starting points $X(t=0)$ uniformly distributed in the search space of Problem 2.3 with all Lagrange multipliers $\lambda(t=0) = \mu(t=0) = 0$. For each starting point, we tried different static weight w. In addition, for cases that converged, we report the average convergence time and the solution quality.

Table 1: Effect of w on convergence time and solution quality for Problem 2.3.1 in [1]. (The convergence behavior is measured by three integers: the number of diverged trajectories, the number of oscillating trajectories, and the number of converged trajectories.)

Weight w	Converge Behavior	Average Time(sec.)	Average Solution
1	20/0/0	-	-
1/3	20/0/0	-	-
1/5	0/20/0	-	-
1/7	0/20/0	-	-
1/9	0/20/0	-	-
1/11	0/10/10	-	-
1/15	0/0/20	2.88	−12.67
1/30	0/0/20	1.72	−12.67
1/60	0/0/20	1.76	−12.67
1/150	0/0/20	1.87	−12.67
1/500	0/0/20	1.98	−12.67
1/1000	0/0/20	2.20	−12.67
1/10000	0/0/20	3.90	−12.67
1/100000	0/0/20	2875.1	−12.67

Table 1 shows the results. When $w \leq \frac{1}{3}$, the trajectory diverges for every starting point. When w is between $\frac{1}{5}$ and $\frac{1}{9}$, the trajectories always oscillate without convergence. For $w = \frac{1}{11}$, half of the trajectories finally converge, and the remaining oscillate. When $w \leq \frac{1}{15}$, all the trajectories converge. For cases that converge, the number of oscillations gradually reduces to zero as w is reduced. Hence, it is possible to eliminate all the oscillations at the expense of longer convergence time (e.g. 2875.1 seconds). The convergence behavior when $w = \frac{1}{30}$ seems to be good because both the number of oscillations and the convergence time are small.

The examples here illustrate that the convergence behavior can be affected dramatically by the choice of w. Moreover, the best choice is problem-instance dependent and cannot be selected a priori. Hence, we will propose a scheme to adapt w dynamically so that the convergence behavior is robust and predictable, irrespective of the choice of the static w.

4 Dynamic Weight Adaptation

In this section, we propose a strategy to adapt weight w based on the behavior of the dynamic system (10) (both continuous and discrete versions) in order to obtain high-quality solutions with short convergence time.

4.1 General Weight-Adaptation Strategy

Figure 4 outlines the algorithm. Its basic idea is to first estimate the initial weight $w(t = 0)$ (Step 1),

```
1.  Set control parameters:
        time interval Δt
        initial weight w(t = 0)
        maximum number of iterations i_max
2.  Set window size N_w = 100 or 10
3.  j := 1          /* j is the iteration number */
4.  while j ≤ i_max and stopping condition is unsatisfied do
5.      advance trajectory by Δt to get to (X_j, λ_j, μ_j)
6.      if trajectory diverges then
            reduce w; restart the algorithm by going to Step 2
        end if
7.      record data for calculating performance metrics
8.      if ((j mod N_w) == 0) then
9.          compute performance metrics
10.         change w based on rules in Figure 5
        end if
11. end while
```

Figure 4: Framework of a new dynamic weight-adaptation algorithm

measure the performance metrics of the search trajectory $(X(t), \lambda(t), \mu(t))$ periodically, and adapt $w(t)$ to improve convergence time or solution quality.

Let t_{max} be the total (logical) time for the search, and t_{max} be divided into small units of time Δt so that the maximum number of iterations is $t_{max} / \Delta t$. Further, assume a stopping condition if the search were to stop before t_{max} (Step 4). Given a starting point $X(t = 0)$, we set the initial values of the Lagrange multipliers to be zero, *i.e.*, $\lambda(t = 0) = \mu(t = 0) = 0$. Let (X_i, λ_i, μ_i) be the point of the ith iteration, and $v_{max,i}$ be its maximum violation defined in (13).

To monitor the progress of the search trajectory, we divide time into non-overlapping windows of size N_w iterations each (Step 2). In each window, we compute some metrics to measure the progress of the search relative to that of previous windows. For the mth window ($m = 1, 2, \cdots$), we calculate the average (or median) of $v_{max,i}$ over all the iterations in the window,

$$\bar{v}_m = \frac{1}{N_w} \sum_{j=(m-1)N_w+1}^{mN_w} v_{max,j} \tag{14}$$

and the average (or median) of the objective $f_i(X)$.

$$\bar{f}_m = \frac{1}{N_w} \sum_{j=(m-1)N_w+1}^{mN_w} f_j(X) \tag{15}$$

During the search, we apply an algorithm to solve the dynamic system (10), and advance the trajectory by time interval Δt in each iteration in order to arrive at point (X_j, λ_j, μ_j) (Step 5).

At this point, we test whether the trajectory diverges or not (Step 6). Divergence happens when

$v_{max,j}$ is larger than an extremely large value (e.g. 10^{20}). If it happens, we reduce w by a large amount, say $w \Longleftarrow w/10$, and restart the algorithm. In each iteration, we also record some statistics, such as $v_{max,j}$ and $f_j(X)$, that will be used to calculate the performance metrics for each window (Step 7).

At the end of each window or every N_w iterations (Step 8), we decide whether to update w based on the performance metrics (14) and (15) (Step 9). Currently, we use the averages (or medians) of maximum violation $v_{max,i}$ and objective $f_j(X)$. In general, other application-specific metrics can be used, such as the number of oscillations of the trajectory in nonlinear continuous problems. Based on these measurements, we adjust w accordingly (Step 10).

In the next subsection, we discuss the specific weight-adaptation algorithm in Step 10 for continuous and discrete problems.

4.2 Dynamic Weight Adaptation for Continuous and Discrete Problems

To understand how weights should be updated in Step 10, we examine all possible behaviors of the resulting search trajectory in successive windows. We have identified four possible cases.

First, the trajectory does not stay within a feasible region, but goes from one feasible region to another through an infeasible region. During this time, the maximum violation $v_{max,i}$ is zero when the trajectory is in the first feasible region, increased when it travels from the feasible region to an infeasible region, and decreased when going from the infeasible region to the second feasible region. No oscillations will be observed because oscillations normally occur around a local minimum in one feasible region, as explained in Section 3. In this case, no change of w is required.

Second, the search trajectory oscillates around a local minimum of a feasible region. This can be detected when the number of oscillations in each window is larger than some threshold. Figures 2 and 3 show two typical types of oscillations. To determine whether the oscillations will subside eventually, we compute $\bar{v}_m - \bar{v}_{m+1}$, the difference of the average values of the maximum violation $v_{max,i}$, for two successive windows m and $m+1$. If the difference is not reduced reasonably, then we assume that the trajectory does not converge, and w is then updated.

Third, the search trajectory moves very slowly within a feasible region. This happens when w is very small, and the constraints dominate the search process. As a result, the objective value is improved very slowly and may eventually converge to a poor value. This situation can be identified when the trajectory

Given performance measurements for the mth window
- average (or median) of the maximum violation: $\bar{v}_m$
- average (or median) of the objective: $\bar{f}_m$
- number of oscillations: NO_m

and application-specific constants $\alpha_0, \alpha_1, \beta_0, \beta_1, \delta, \epsilon$

1. Increase weight $w \Longleftarrow w/\alpha_0$ **if**
   - $(c_{1,1})$ $\bar{v}_{m-1}, \bar{v}_m < \delta$
   - $(c_{1,2})$ $\beta_0|\overline{f}_{m-1}| > \overline{f}_{m-1} - \overline{f}_m > \beta_1|\overline{f}_{m-1}|$
2. Decrease weight $w \Longleftarrow \alpha_1 w$ **if**
   - $(c_{2,1})$ $\bar{v}_m \geq \delta$
   - $(c_{2,2})$ $\bar{v}_{m-1} - \bar{v}_m \leq \beta_0 \bar{v}_{m-1}$
   - $(c_{2,3})$ $NO_m \geq \epsilon$

Figure 5: Weight-adaptation rules for continuous and discrete problems (Step 10 of Figure 4).

remains within a feasible region in two successive windows, and there is little improvement in the objective. Obviously, we need to increase w in order to speed up the improvement of the objective. If the objective remains unchanged, then the trajectory has converged, and no further modification of w is necessary.

Finally, the trajectory does not oscillate when it is started from a point in a feasible region, but rather goes outside the feasible region and then converges to a point on the boundary of the feasible region (see Figure 1 for example). In this case, a large w on the objective makes it more difficult to satisfy the constraints, causing the trajectory to move slowly back to the feasible region. At this time, it is desirable to reduce w to accelerate convergence. This situation happens frequently in some cases, such as QMF filter-bank design problem [5], and appropriate decrease of w will greatly shorten the convergence time.

Given the four convergence behaviors, Figure 5 shows a comprehensive weight-adaptation algorithm for both continuous and discrete problems. Scaling factors $0 < \alpha_0, \alpha_1 < 1$ represent how fast w is updated. Because we use numerical methods to solve the dynamic system defined in (10), a trajectory in window m is said to satisfy all the constraints when $v_m < \delta$, where δ is related to the convergence condition and the required precision. Parameters $0 < \beta_0, \beta_1 < 1$ control, respectively, the degrees of improvement over the objective and the reduction of the maximum violation. Note that when comparing values between two successive windows $m-1$ and m, both must use the same weight w; otherwise, the comparison is not meaningful because the terrain may be totally different. Hence, after adapting w, we should wait at least two windows before changing it again.

Weight w should be increased (Rule 1) when we observe the third convergence behavior. In this case,

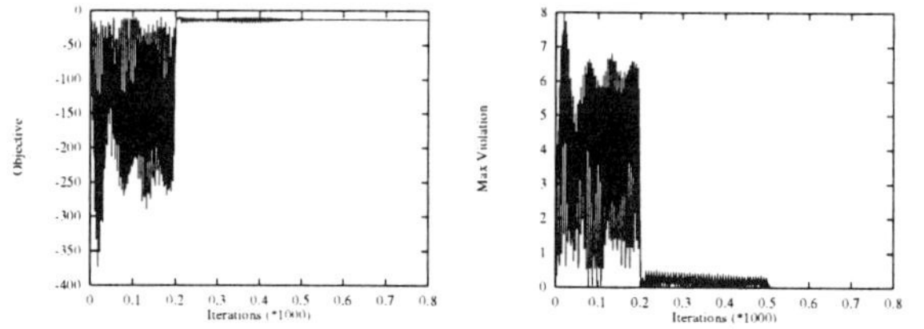

Figure 6: Objective function and maximum violation first oscillate and then converge using dynamic-weight adaptation.

the trajectory is within a feasible region, and the objective is improved in successive windows. Weight w will be increased when the objective does not improve fast enough in a feasible region, until an upper-bound improvement is reached.

Weight w should be decreased (Rule 2) when we observe the second convergence behavior (the trajectory oscillating around a local minimum) or the fourth convergence behavior (the trajectory moving slowly back to the feasible region). Weight w will be decreased when the trajectory oscillates, and the trend of the maximum violation does not decrease.

5 Illustrations of the Dynamic Weight-Adaptation Strategy

In this section, we illustrate our weight-adaptation algorithm using nonlinear continuous optimization problems, which include a set of benchmark problems [1, 4]. After some experimentation, we pick the time unit $\Delta t = 1$ in *LSODE*, and set the window size to be $N_w = 100$.

Recall in Figure 2 that the trajectory oscillates when $w = \frac{1}{10}$ for Problem 2.3 in [1]. Figure 6 shows the resulting trajectory and the maximum violation when the dynamic weight-adaptation algorithm is applied on the same problem. We started with $w(t=0) = \frac{1}{5}$, $\alpha_0 = \alpha_1 = \frac{1}{2}$, $\delta = 10^{-8}$, $\beta_0 = 10^{-2}$, and $\beta_1 = 10^{-3}$. In the first window (first $N_w = 100$ iterations), the average $\bar{v}_1 = 4.11$, which increases slightly to $\bar{v}_2 = 4.2$ in the second window. In addition, $\bar{v}_2 \geq \delta$ and $NO_2 \geq 5$. According to Rule 2 in Figure 5, w is updated to $\frac{1}{10}$. This change in w leads to significant reduction in the maximum violation in the third window. Weight w remains unchanged between the third and the fifth windows. At the end of the fifth window, the maximum violation changes very little. Hence, the algorithm reduces w to $\frac{1}{20}$, making the trajectory converges quickly.

To illustrate the improvement due to dynamic-weight adaptation, we apply the algorithm on the same problem studied in Table 1 from 20 randomly generated starting points. Table 2 shows the results, indicating the convergence of the search trajectory for each initial weight w. For cases that converge using static weights, dynamic-weight adaptation can reduce the convergence time, especially when the choice of the initial weight is poor. For instance, when the initial weight is $\frac{1}{100000}$, the search converges with the final weight in the range $[\frac{1}{6250}, \frac{1}{781.25}]$ and an average convergence time of 3.85 sec., much less than that the 2875.1 sec. required before. If the initial weight chosen is good (e.g. $w = \frac{1}{60}$), then the algorithm is able to maintain the original weight during the search and gets good convergence behavior. This shows the stability and robustness of our dynamic weight-adaptation algorithm, irrespective of the choice of the initial weight.

Table 2: Effects of weight adaptation on convergence time and solution quality for Problem 2.3.1 in [1]

Starting Weight w	Final Weight Range $[w_l, w_u]$	Avg. Converge Time (sec.)	Average Solution
1	1/20	19.14	−13.55
1/3	1/15	10.70	−12.67
1/5	1/20	43.36	−12.67
1/7	[1/28,1/14]	27.43	−12.67
1/9	1/18	19.97	−12.67
1/11	1/22	4.22	−12.67
1/15	1/15	2.88	−12.67
1/30	1/30	1.72	−12.67
1/60	1/60	1.76	−12.67
1/150	1/150	1.87	−12.67
1/500	[1/500,1/1000]	1.95	−12.67
1/1000	[1/1000,1/500]	2.15	−12.67
1/10000	[1/5000,1/625]	3.34	−12.67
1/100000	[1/6250,1/781.25]	3.85	−12.67

6 Experimental Results

In this section we show further experimental results in applying our dynamic weight-adaptation algorithm to both nonlinear continuous and discrete optimization problems. We also compare our results to those obtained by Lagrangian methods with static weights.

6.1 Nonlinear Continuous Benchmark Problems

These constrained benchmark problems [1] were derived from a variety of engineering applications. We selected five problems (with identifiers 2.6, 3.4, 4.6, 5.4 and 6.4) from different classes to test our algorithm. In each problem, we randomly generated 20 starting points $X(t=0)$ uniformly distributed in its search range, and set the initial values for the Lagrange multipliers to be zero ($\lambda(t=0) = \mu(t=0) = 0$). For

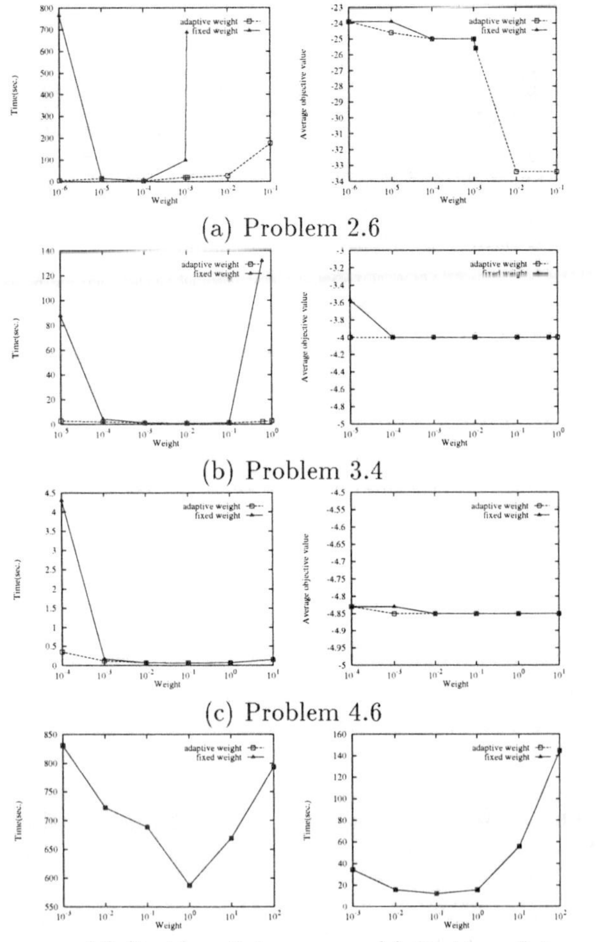

(a) Problem 2.6

(b) Problem 3.4

(c) Problem 4.6

(d) Problem 5.4

(e) Problem 6.4

Figure 7: Comparison of the Lagrangian method with static weights and the adaptive Lagrangian method in terms of convergence time and solution quality.

each starting point, we applied the Lagrangian method using both static weights and dynamically changed weights under the same convergence condition defined in (12). Hence, the Lagrangian method stopped when it either reached the maximum iteration count i_{max} or satisfied the convergence condition.

We chose the static weights in the range between 10^{-6} to 10^{2}, which were also used as initial weights $w(t=0)$ in the dynamic algorithm. The weights were chosen from a wide range in order to test the robustness of our weight-adaptation algorithm. We would like our algorithm to adjust the weight so that the search will converge faster with a solution that is at least as good as that with static weights. In our experiments, we used the following control parameters: time unit $\Delta t = 1$, window size $N_w = 100$, $\alpha_0 = \alpha_1 = \frac{1}{2}$, $\delta = 10^{-8}$, $\beta_0 = 10^{-2}$, and $\beta_1 = 10^{-3}$.

We used two performance metrics, convergence time and solution quality, in our experiments, where convergence time was measured by the average convergence time (in seconds) from 20 starting points, and solution quality was measured by the average objective value when the search converged.

From the experimental results shown in Figure 7, we have the following observations. First, different problems require different ranges of static weights in order to get fast convergence. For example, Problem 2.6 (Figure 7a) converges the fastest using $w = 10^{-4}$, whereas Problem 5.4 (Figure 7d) converges the fastest using $w = 1$. These weights differ by four orders of magnitude. Hence, it is difficult to choose a good static weight for a given problem instance in advance.

Second, our dynamic weight-adaptation algorithm outperforms the Lagrangian method with static weights. For example, in Problem 2.6 (Figure 7a), the Lagrangian method with a static weight is unable to converge (either diverge or oscillate forever) when $w = 10^{-2}$ or larger. However, our dynamic weight-adaptation algorithm can detect this misbehavior and adjust w to allow the search to converge in 27.62 seconds on the average. Likewise, the Lagrangian method with static weight $w = 10^{-6}$ converges using an average of 765.0 seconds, but the dynamic algorithm converges using an average of 5.64 seconds and with the same solution quality. These results show that our weight-adaptation algorithm is robust and insensitive to the initial weights $w(t=0)$ in comparison with the Lagrangian method with a static weight. In fact, our dynamic algorithm can get even better solutions in shorter time when the initial weight is small.

Third, when all the constraints are equality constraints, w is unchanged in the dynamic algorithm, resulting in the same performance for both methods. This is shown in Problem 5.4 (Figure 7d). In some cases, w is unchanged in the dynamic algorithm when there are both inequality and equality constraints, such as Problem 6.4 (Figure 7e). This happens when the Lagrange multipliers already take care of the balance between the objective and the constraints.

6.2 Nonlinear Integer Programming

To test the dynamic weight-adaptation strategy, we selected three problems 2.3, 2.6 and 3.4 from the benchmark collection [1]. We first transformed them to discrete integer programming problems, and then randomly generated 20 discrete starting points with initial values of Lagrange Multipliers to be zero. For each starting point, we applied the Lagrangian method using both static weights and dynamically changed

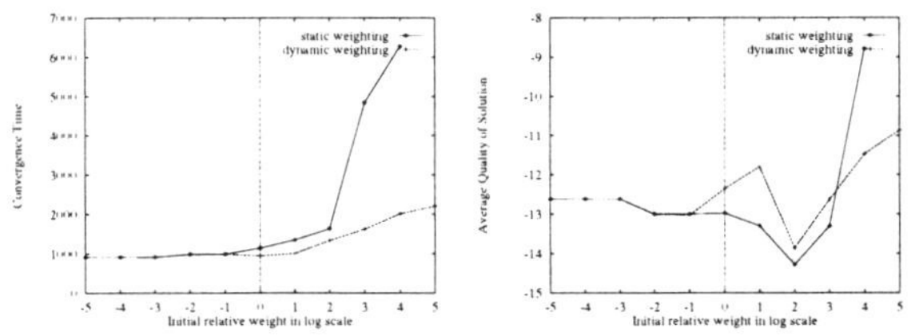

(a) Problem 2.3

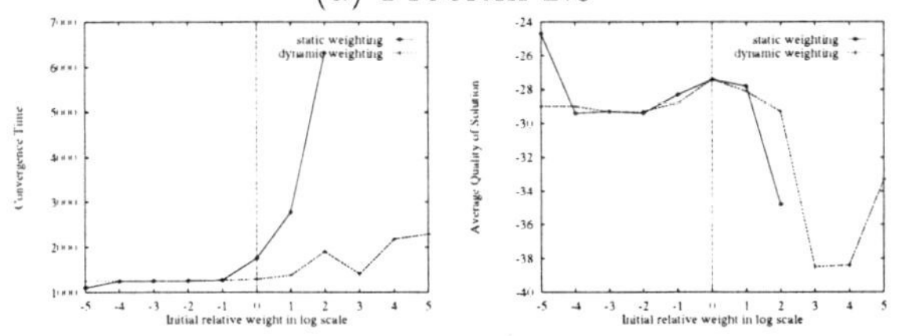

(b) Problem 2.6

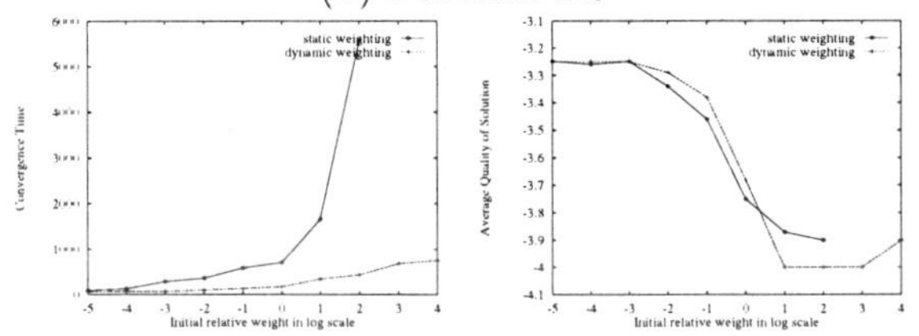

(c) Problem 3.4

Figure 8: Comparison of the Lagrangian method with static weights and the adaptive Lagrangian method in terms of convergence time and solution quality for discrete benchmark problems

weights. We stopped the search when the convergence condition was satisfied or the maximal number of iterations was reached.

The initial weight w was in the range of $[10^{-5}, 10^{5}]$, which was large enough to test the robustness of our adaptive Lagrangian method. The parameters for our algorithm were: window size $N_w = 320, \alpha_0 = 0.8, \alpha_1 = 0.5, \delta = 10^{-8}, \beta_0 = 10^{-3}$, and $\beta_1 = 10^{-4}$.

As is in continuous problems, we use both convergence time and solution quality as our performance metrics, where convergence time is measured by the average convergence time from 20 starting points, and solution quality is measured by the average objective value when the search converges. Figure 8 shows the comparative results. Our dynamic weight-adaptation algorithm improves a lot in convergence time over the algorithm with static weights. When weight w is larger than 100.0 for Problem 2.6, the Lagrangian method with static weights was unable to converge even after 10 hours. In contrast, our dynamic weight-adaptation algorithm converged in less than 1 hour for all different initial weights.

7 Conclusions

In this paper we have studied and evaluated an efficient weight-adaptation algorithm for Lagrangian methods, which adjusts the relative weights between the objective and the constraints based on statistics collected during the search. We have applied the adaptive method to both continuous and discrete constrained optimization problems. (Due to space limitations, we are not able to show results on designing QMF filter banks and multiplierless QMF filter banks.) In both cases, the adaptive method always converges in much shorter time with either the same or better solution. Our results show that the adaptive method is robust, works for both continuous and discrete problems, and exhibits consistent and good convergence behavior.

References

[1] C. A. Floudas and P. M. Pardalos. *A Collection of Test Problems for Constrained Global Optimization Algorithms*, volume 455 of *Lecture Notes in Computer Science*. Springer-Verlag, 1990.

[2] D. G. Luenberger. *Linear and Nonlinear Programming*. Addison-Wesley Publishing Company, 1984.

[3] Y. Shang and B. W. Wah. A discrete lagrangian-based global-search method for solving satisfiability problems. *J. of Global Optimization*, (accepted to appear) 1997.

[4] B. W. Wah and Y.-J. Chang. Trace-based methods for solving nonlinear global optimization problems. *J. of Global Optimization*, 10(2):107–141, March 1997.

[5] B. W. Wah, Y. Shang, T. Wang, and T. Yu. Global optimization of QMF filter-bank design using NOVEL. In *Proc. Int'l Conf. on Acoustics, Speech and Signal Processing*, volume 3, pages 2081–2084. IEEE, April 1997.

Prime Implicant Computation Using Satisfiability Algorithms

Vasco M. Manquinho, Paulo F. Flores, João P. Marques Silva, Arlindo L. Oliveira
Cadence European Laboratories
IST/INESC
1000 Lisboa, Portugal
vmm@calvin.inesc.pt, {pff,jpms,aml}@inesc.pt

Abstract

The computation of prime implicants has several and significant applications in different areas, including Automated Reasoning, Non-Monotonic Reasoning, Electronic Design Automation, among others. In this paper we describe a new model and algorithm for computing minimum-size prime implicants of propositional formulas. The proposed approach is based on creating an integer linear program (ILP) formulation for computing the minimum-size prime implicant, which simplifies existing formulations. In addition, we introduce two new algorithms for solving ILPs, both of which are built on top of an algorithm for propositional satisfiability (SAT). Given the organization of the proposed SAT algorithm, the resulting ILP procedures implement powerful search pruning techniques, including a non-chronological backtracking search strategy, clause recording procedures and identification of necessary assignments. Experimental results, obtained on several benchmark examples, indicate that the proposed model and algorithms are significantly more efficient than other existing solutions.

1 Introduction

Given a propositional formula φ in Conjunctive Normal Form (CNF), denoting a boolean function f, the problem of computing a minimum-size assignment (in the number of literals) that satisfies f is referred to as the ***minimum-size prime implicant problem***. Minimum-size prime implicants find application in many areas including, among others, Automated Reasoning, Non-Monotonic Reasoning and Electronic Design Automation. Moreover, interest on computing minimum-size prime implicants of boolean functions has motivated extensive research work (see for example [8, 9], which include comprehensive bibliographic references.).

In this paper we describe an Integer Linear Program (ILP) formulation for computing minimum-size prime implicants of boolean functions described by Conjunctive Normal Form (CNF) formulas. The proposed ILP model, first introduced in [14], significantly simplifies the one originally described in [9]. Moreover, we propose two new algorithms for solving ILPs where the variables have boolean domains (01-ILPs). Both algorithms are based on propositional satisfiability (SAT). The first one generalizes the SAT-based ILP algorithm originally described in [2], whereas the second one describes a branch and bound ILP procedure built on top of a SAT solver. For both algorithms the GRASP SAT solver [12, 15] is used. Preliminary results, obtained on several satisfiable instances of the DIMACS benchmarks [6], indicate that the proposed model and algorithms can be used for computing minimum-size prime implicants for several classes of boolean functions. Furthermore, we show that widely used ILP algorithms, most of which are based on linear-programming (LP) relaxations [7], may be inadequate for computing minimum-size prime implicants. This result strongly suggests using dedicated ILP algorithms for solving the minimum-size prime implicant problem. Finally, we note that the proposed ILP algorithms, implement powerful search pruning techniques commonly used in SAT algorithms, which include a non-chronological backtracking search strategy, clause recording procedures and identification of necessary assignments.

The paper is organized as follows. In Section 2 the notational framework used throughout the paper is introduced. Afterwards, we describe the ILP model for computing minimum-size prime implicants of boolean functions described with CNF formulas. This model is based on the one proposed in [9], but significantly reduces the number of variables as well as the size of their domains. Consequently, the worst-case size of the search space becomes drastically reduced, and hence a smaller search space is expected for most practical examples. In Section 4 we describe two new SAT-based ILP algorithms and illustrate how the identification of prime implicants can be iterated. The procedure proposed in this paper for iterating prime implicants by increasing size is provably more efficient than the one described in [9]. The different algorithms are experimentally evaluated in Section 5. Finally, Section 6 concludes the paper suggesting potential improvements to the proposed model and algorithms.

1082-3409/97 $10.00 © 1997 IEEE

2 Definitions

The paper follows the definitions introduced in [12, 14], in particular for the organization of the GRASP SAT algorithm which is described in Section 4. In general, a propositional formula φ in CNF denotes a boolean function $f : \{0, 1\}^n \rightarrow \{0, 1\}$, where each clause ω is a sum of literals, and a literal l is either a variable x_i or its complement x_i'. For a search-based algorithm for SAT, a ***conflict*** is said to be identified when all literals of at least one clause are assigned value 0. The GRASP SAT [12] algorithm implements several techniques for pruning the amount of search based on the ***diagnosis*** of conflicts identified during the search.

A clause $\omega = (l_1 + \ldots + l_k)$ denotes a constraint which can also be viewed as a linear inequality, $l_1 + \ldots + l_k \geq 1$. We use this alternative representation when appropriate. Furthermore, since a literal $l = x_i'$ can also be defined by $l = 1 - x_i$, we shall in general use this latter representation when viewing clauses as linear inequalities.

3 Prime Implicant Computation Using Integer Programming

Given a description of a Boolean function in CNF, it is straightforward to formulate the computation of the minimum-size prime implicant as an integer linear program [9]. In this paper we show how to simplify the formulation proposed in [9], thus allowing for a significant reduction in the worst-case search space. This improved model was first described in [14].

Given a CNF formula φ, which is defined on a set of variables $\{x_1, \ldots, x_n\}$, with p clauses $\{\omega_1, \ldots, \omega_p\}$, and which denotes a Boolean function $f : \{0,1\}^n \rightarrow \{0, 1\}$, apply the following transformation.

1. Create a new set of boolean variables $\{y_1, \ldots, y_{2n}\}$, where y_{2i-1} is associated with literal x_i, and y_{2i} is associated with literal x_i'.
2. For each clause $\omega = (l_1 + \ldots + l_m)$, replace each literal l_j with y_{2k-1} if $l_j = x_k$, or with y_{2k} if $l_j = x_i'$.
3. For each pair of variables, y_{2i-1} and y_{2i}, require that at most one is set to one. Hence, $y_{2i-1} + y_{2i} \leq 1$.
4. The set of inequalities obtained from steps 2. and 3. can be viewed as a single set of inequalities $\boldsymbol{A} \cdot \boldsymbol{y} \geq \boldsymbol{b}$. Furthermore, define the cost function to be,

$$\min \sum_{j=1}^{2n} y_j \tag{1}$$

5. The complete ILP formulation is thus defined as follows:

$$\begin{array}{ll} \min & \sum_{j=1}^{2n} y_j \\ \text{s.t.} & \boldsymbol{A} \cdot \boldsymbol{y} \geq \boldsymbol{b} \end{array} \tag{2}$$

It is clear that the solution of (2) denotes a minimum-size prime implicant of the original CNF formula φ, and from [9] we have,

Proposition 1. Given a CNF formula φ and associated boolean function f, the solution of the optimization problem (2) is a minimum-size prime implicant of f.

The proposed ILP model is based on the one described in [9]. However, the model proposed in [9] associates an integer variable λ_i with each inequality created from each original clause ω_i. As we showed above, such integer variables are unnecessary and only increase the worst-case search space. Indeed, for the ILP model of (2), the worst-case search space is,

$$2^{2n} = 4^n \tag{3}$$

whereas for the ILP model of [9], the worst-case search space is,

$$4^n \cdot \prod_{i=1}^{p} |\omega_i| \tag{4}$$

where $|\omega_i|$ denotes the number of literals of clause ω_i, and represents the least upper bound on the integer variable λ_i associated with clause ω_i and introduced in the ILP model of [9]. Consequently, the worst-case search space for the ILP model we propose in this paper is provably less than for the model proposed in [9]. We should note that for both models, and for a search-based ILP algorithm, a straightforward arrangement of the order of the decision variables leads to a worst-case search space of 3^n (since only 3 assignments are possible for each of the n pairs of variables), but unfortunately this information cannot in general be made available to the ILP solver.

The construction of the ILP model (2) will be illustrated with the following CNF formula:

$$\varphi = (x_1 + x_2 + x_3) \cdot (x_1' + x_2') \cdot (x_1' + x_3') \tag{5}$$

First, we start by creating a new set of variables $\{y_1, y_2, y_3, y_4, y_5, y_6\}$, and associate y_{2i-1} with each χ_i and y_{2i} with each x_i'. Consequently, from (5) the following modified CNF formula φ' is obtained:

$$\varphi' = (y_1 + y_3 + y_5) \cdot (y_2 + y_4) \cdot (y_2 + y_6) \tag{6}$$

For each clause, simple algebraic manipulation yields

an equivalent inequality:

$$\begin{aligned} y_1 + y_3 + y_5 &\geq 1 \\ y_2 + y_4 &\geq 1 \\ y_2 + y_6 &\geq 1 \end{aligned} \tag{7}$$

The next step is to require that at most one variable of each pair of variables y_{2i-1}, y_{2i} can be set to one, which yields:

$$\begin{aligned} y_1 + y_2 \leq 1 &\Leftrightarrow -y_1 - y_2 \geq -1 \\ y_3 + y_4 \leq 1 &\Leftrightarrow -y_3 - y_4 \geq -1 \\ y_5 + y_6 \leq 1 &\Leftrightarrow -y_5 - y_6 \geq -1 \end{aligned} \tag{8}$$

Thus allowing for a given variable x_i not to be assigned. Equations (7) and (8) define the set of inequalities $\boldsymbol{A} \cdot \boldsymbol{y} \geq \boldsymbol{b}$. The next step is to identify the cost function, which minimizes the number of variables assigned value one, i.e. the number of variables x_i with an assigned value. Finally the resulting ILP model becomes:

$$\begin{array}{ll} \text{min} & y_1 + y_2 + y_3 + y_4 + y_5 + y_6 \\ \text{s.t.} & \boldsymbol{A} \cdot \boldsymbol{y} \geq \boldsymbol{b} \end{array} \tag{9}$$

One solution to the integer linear program (9) is, for example, $x_1 = 0$ and $x_2 = 1$.

4 Search Algorithms for Solving ILPs

In [2] P. Barth described how to solve ILPs using a propositional satisfiability algorithm. However, the ILP algorithm described in [2] is based on the Davis-Putnam [5] procedure, which has been shown to be particularly inefficient for a large number of instances of SAT [12].

In this section we describe two different algorithms for solving ILPs associated with instances of the minimum-size prime implicant problem. Both are based on SAT algorithms. The first algorithm follows P. Barth's approach, whereas the second builds a branch and bound procedure on top of a SAT engine. The two algorithms use the GRASP SAT algorithm described in [12], which includes several powerful pruning techniques for reducing the amount of search associated with instances of SAT. Among the pruning techniques included in GRASP, the following have been shown to be particularly significant:

- GRASP implements a ***non-chronological backtracking*** search strategy[1]. This backtracking strategy potentially permits skipping over large portions of the decision tree for some instances of SAT.
- GRASP utilizes selective ***clause recording*** techniques. During the search process, and as conflicts are diagnosed, new clauses are created from the causes of the conflicts. These clauses represent implicates of the boolean function associated with the CNF formula, and are often referred to as *nogoods* [11]. Newly recorded clauses are then used for pruning the subsequent search. Moreover, bounds on the size of recorded clauses can be imposed, thus preventing an excessive growth of the resulting CNF formula.
- In most practical situations, instances of SAT can have highly structured CNF representations. The intrinsic structure of these representations can be exploited by GRASP, after diagnosing the causes of conflicts, by identifying ***necessary assignments*** required for preventing conflicts from being identified during the search.
- In addition, other pruning techniques can be straightforwardly applied to SAT algorithms. In particular, and as described in [13], several techniques commonly used in algorithms for different variations of the set covering problem [4].

4.1 SAT-Based Linear Search Algorithm

The first ILP algorithm follows P. Barth's ILP algorithm [2] and was first described in [14]. Let us consider the cost function (1). The possible values assumed by the cost function for the different assignments to the variables in the set $\{y_1, \ldots, y_{2n}\}$ range from 0, when all variables are assigned value 0, to $2n$, when all variables are assigned value 1. Note however, that for the minimum-size prime implicant problem a trivial upper bound is n, since for any pair of variables y_{2i-1}, y_{2i} at most one can be assigned value 1. P. Barth's [2] approach consists of applying the following sequence of steps, starting from an upper bound of $k = n$ on the value of the cost function:

1. Create a new inequality $\sum y_j \leq k$. This inequality basically requires that a computed solution must have no more than k literals assigned value 1.
2. Solve the resulting instance of satisfiability. (Note that the resulting instance of satisfiability is defined on linear inequalities, but modifying most SAT algorithms for handling this generalization is straightforward.)
3. If the instance of SAT is satisfiable decrement k (i.e. specify a new value for the cost function) and go back to step 1. Otherwise, report that the solution to the ILP is $k + 1$.

Note that this ILP algorithm allows for any SAT algorithm to be used as the underlying SAT testing engine, provided the algorithm is modified to handle linear inequalities. The proposed ILP algorithm is illustrated in

1. Some variations of this strategy are also commonly referred to as ***dependency-directed backtracking*** and ***backjumping*** [10].

```
int min_prime(φ)
{
    k = n;
    while (k ≥ 0) {
        φ = φ ∪ {∑y_j ≤ k};
        status = solve_sat(φ);
        φ = φ − {∑y_j ≤ k};
        if (status == SATISFIABLE) {
            k = ∑y_j;
            --k;
        } else { ++k; break; }
    return k;
}
```

Figure 1: SAT-based linear search algorithm

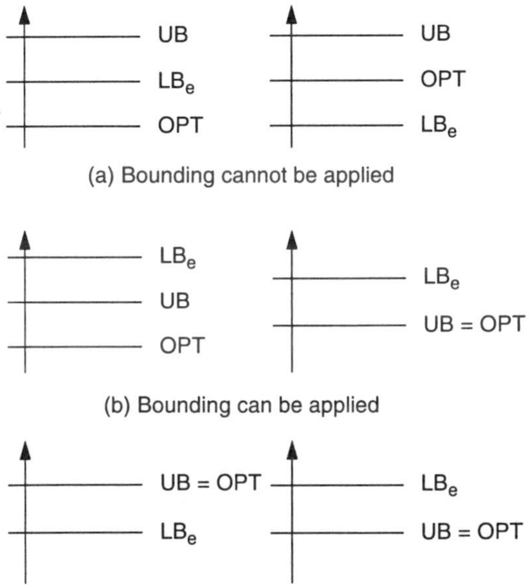

(a) Bounding cannot be applied

(b) Bounding can be applied

(c) UB cannot decrease

Figure 2: Using bounding in the ILP algorithm

Figure 1. For our particular case, the solve_sat function call invokes the GRASP SAT algorithm [12].

4.2 SAT-Based Branch and Bound Algorithm

A different algorithmic organization consists of using a variation of the branch and bound procedure [7], where upper bounds to the cost function (1) are identified and lower bounds to the current set of variable assignments are estimated. In our implementation, we have used the lower bound estimation procedures described in [4].

The operation of bounding for the proposed procedure is illustrated in Figure 2. Let UB denote the lowest *computed* upper bound on the solution of (2), LB_e denote an *estimated* lower bound on the solution of (2) and OPT denote the solution of (2). If the estimated lower bound is less than the already computed upper bound (as shown in Figure 2-(a)), then the search cannot be bound since it may still be possible to reduce the value of the upper bound. Clearly, the search can be bound whenever the estimated lower bound to the value of (1) is larger than or equal to the existing upper bound to the value of (1), as illustrated in Figure 2-(b). Finally, observe that Figure 2-(c) denotes the conditions after which the upper bound will no longer be updated during the search.

Moreover, since the branch and bound procedure is embedded in the SAT algorithm, every pruning technique used by the SAT algorithm can also be used in solving the ILP. This is particularly useful whenever a constraint of (2) becomes unsatisfied. Consequently, the branch and bound procedure consists of the following steps:

1. Initialize the upper bound to highest possible value. (Valid ILPs must correspond to instances of the minimum-size prime implicant problem.)
2. If no decision can be made (i.e. a solution to the constraints has been identified), then compute an upper bound on the minimum value of the cost function of the ILP formulation. Update current upper bound and issue a conflict to guarantee that the search is bound. Otherwise, branch on a given decision variable (i.e. make decision assignment).
3. Apply boolean constraint propagation [16]. If a conflict is reached, then diagnose conflict, record relevant clauses, and proceed with the search process or backtrack if required.
4. Estimate lower bound. If this value is larger than or equal to the current upper bound, then issue a conflict, diagnose the conflict, backtrack, and continue the search from step 2.

The pseudo-code for the algorithm is shown in Figure 3. Observe that the proposed branch and bound SAT-based ILP algorithm has the following main differences with respect to the linear search ILP algorithm:

- No clauses involving the cost function are created. The exception occurs when the estimated lower bound is no less than the computed upper bound. In this situation a clause involving some of the literals in the cost function is temporarily created, thus causing the search procedure to backtrack. (See [12] for details of the backtrack search SAT algorithm.)
- Lower bounding procedures are required. As mentioned earlier, the lower bounding procedures of [4] are used, but lower bounding procedures based on ***linear-programming relaxations*** or ***Lagrangian relaxations***

```
int bsolo(φ)
{
    _UB = ∞;
    while (TRUE) {
        if (Solution_found() ||
             Decide() != DECISION) {
            Update_UB();
            Issue_UB_based_conflict();
        }
        while (Deduce() == CONFLICT) {
            if (Diagnose() == CONFLICT) {
                return _UB;
            }
        }
        while (Estimate_LB() ≥ _UB) {
            Issue_LB_based_conflict();
            if (Diagnose() == CONFLICT) {
                return _UB;
            }
        }
    }
}
```

Figure 3: SAT-based branch and bound algorithm

can also be used [3, 7]. Clearly, the tightness of the lower bounding procedure is crucial for the efficiency of the branch and bound procedure.

4.3 Extensions to the Basic ILP Algorithms

One extension to the proposed ILP algorithms is the ability to incrementally enumerate prime implicants by increasing size [9]. The procedure proposed in [9] basically recreates the search for each new prime implicant to be computed. Clearly, this solution can introduce significant and unnecessary computational overhead. One possible improvement is based on the SAT-based linear search ILP algorithm of Figure 1, and is organized as follows:

1. Keep a stack of pairs of computed solutions and associated upper bound values *k*.
2. Use the current top of the stack to find the next minimum-size prime implicant.
3. For a given solution-upper bound pair *k*, apply the algorithm of Figure 1 until the next optimal solution is found. For this new optimal bound, enumerate all solution assignments.
4. As soon as a given pair solution-upper bound yields no more solutions, pop the stack and go back to step 2. Repeat until stack of solution-upper bound pairs becomes empty.

Since for each prime implicant size only part of the search space is visited, the above algorithm ensures a better worst-case time complexity than the algorithm of [9].

5 Experimental Results

In this section we include experimental results of two tools for computing minimum-size prime implicants, *min-prime* [14] and *bsolo*. *min-prime* is based on linear search through the possible values of the cost function as described in Section 4.1, whereas *bsolo* uses the SAT-based branch and bound algorithm as described in Section 4.2. We also compare these two SAT-based ILP algorithms with other ILP solvers, *lp-solve* [3], *opbdp* [2], and the commercial optimization tool ***CPLEX***. Moreover, the binate covering tool *scherzo* [4] is also evaluated, since minimum-size prime implicant computation can also be viewed as a restricted form of the binate covering problem. For this purpose we selected a set of satisfiable instances of the DIMACS benchmarks [6], from most of the available classes of instances. The CPU times, obtained on a SUN 5/85 machine with 64 MByte of physical memory, are shown in Table 1 and Table 2, where Table 2 includes the results for the SAT-based algorithms. For each benchmark and for each tool 3000 seconds of CPU time were allowed. Column **min** indicates the size of the minimum-size prime implicant, when this size is known. (Observe that for some of the benchmarks the minimum size prime implicant is still unknown.) Table 3 and Table 4 include the upper bound on the minimum size prime implicant computed by each algorithm for each benchmark. When each tool terminates, it reports the minimum size prime implicant if it was identified, otherwise the lowest computed upper bound is reported provided at least one upper bound was identified. For the results shown, whenever a tool quits earlier than 3000 sec, then the tool exceeded the available virtual memory (i.e. 64 MByte).

As can be concluded, general-purpose ILP solvers, such as *CPLEX* and *lp-solve*, may be inadequate for computing minimum-size prime implicants. Similarly, despite the very promising results as an algorithm for solving binate covering problems [4], *scherzo* performs particularly poorly when computing minimum-size prime implicants. The three SAT-based ILP solvers can handle a large number of benchmarks and, in general, *min-prime* and *bsolo* perform better and are more robust than *opbdp*, which is unable to find the solution on a larger number of instances. For the JNH benchmarks, *opbdp* performs better because the amount of search is similar and the overhead of the underlying GRASP SAT algorithm is larger. One key drawback of *min-prime* derives from using an ILP layer around the SAT algorithm which creates large additional clauses. For the minimum-size prime implicant

Benchmark	min	*CPLEX*	*lp-solve*	*scherzo*
aim-50-1_6-y1-1	50	116.50	> 3,000	2.33
aim-50-2_0-y1-2	50	109.50	> 3,000	5.65
aim-50-3_4-y1-3	50	62.90	377.10	0.57
aim-50-6_0-y1-4	50	26.90	96.80	0.73
aim-100-1_6-y1-2	100	> 3,000	> 3,000	> 1,000
aim-100-2_0-y1-3	100	> 3,000	> 3,000	691.57
aim-100-3_4-y1-4	100	> 3,000	> 3,000	35.47
aim-100-6_0-y1-1	100	294.30	> 3,000	2.78
aim-200-1_6-y1-3	200	> 3,000	> 3,000	> 345
aim-200-2_0-y1-4	200	> 3,000	> 3,000	> 1,705
aim-200-3_4-y1-1	200	> 3,000	> 3,000	> 3,000
aim-200-6_0-y1-2	200	> 3,000	> 3,000	619.38
ii8a1	54	63.30	786.90	0.98
ii8b2	—	> 3,000	> 3,000	> 3,000
ii8c2	—	> 3,000	> 3,000	> 3,000
ii8d2	—	> 3,000	> 3,000	> 3,000
ii8e2	—	> 3,000	> 3,000	> 3,000
jnh1	92	> 3,000	> 3,000	70.00
jnh7	89	> 3,000	> 3,000	5.35
jnh12	94	2,529	> 3,000	3.07
jnh17	95	873.90	> 3,000	17.28
ssa7552-038	—	> 3,000	> 3,000	> 223

Table 1: CPU times on selected benchmarks

Benchmark	min	*opbdp*	*min-prime*	*bsolo*
aim-50-1_6-y1-1	50	0.09	0.05	0.07
aim-50-2_0-y1-2	50	0.64	0.02	0.04
aim-50-3_4-y1-3	50	0.40	0.08	0.18
aim-50-6_0-y1-4	50	0.48	0.07	0.17
aim-100-1_6-y1-2	100	> 3,000	0.09	0.22
aim-100-2_0-y1-3	100	42.45	0.17	0.45
aim-100-3_4-y1-4	100	0.81	0.47	1.08
aim-100-6_0-y1-1	100	0.18	0.32	0.52
aim-200-1_6-y1-3	200	> 3,000	0.22	0.76
aim-200-2_0-y1-4	200	> 3,000	0.83	2.60
aim-200-3_4-y1-1	200	41.84	4.32	2.31
aim-200-6_0-y1-2	200	4.59	3.58	2.76
ii8a1	54	1.93	861.53	3.51
ii8b2	—	> 3,000	> 3,000	> 3,000
ii8c2	—	> 3,000	> 3,000	> 3,000
ii8d2	—	> 3,000	> 3,000	> 3,000
ii8e2	—	> 3,000	> 3,000	> 3,000
jnh1	92	2.24	17.96	11.39
jnh7	89	0.45	9.06	2.88
jnh12	94	0.12	0.58	1.10
jnh17	95	0.30	2.53	2.13
ssa7552-038	—	> 3,000	> 1,205	> 500

Table 2: CPU times on selected benchmarks

problem, these additional clauses involve *all* variables in the problem representation. Hence, conflicts involving this clause necessarily lead to chronological backtracking[2], and so the most useful features of GRASP cannot be exploited. Finally, we note that *bsolo* tends to be a more efficient search algorithm than *min-prime*, as the experimental results suggest.

From the obtained experimental results, it can also be concluded that the computation of the minimum-size prime implicant can be a particularly hard problem for specific sets of instances. This is the case, for example, with the ii8 and ssa7552 benchmarks.

2. In such a situation, each conflict involves *all* variables and so backtracking is necessarily chronological, to the most recent decision assignment [12].

6 Conclusions

In this paper we describe a new model and algorithms for computing minimum size prime implicants of boolean functions. The model is based on an ILP formulation and the proposed algorithms are built on top of existing SAT solvers. To our best knowledge *min-prime* and *bsolo* are the first SAT-based ILP algorithms that incorporate conflict diagnosis techniques [12] in solving optimization problems. Both *min-prime* and *bsolo* incorporate several powerful search-pruning techniques which are known to be particularly useful for SAT algorithms, in particular the non-chronological backtracking strategy, clause (nogood) recording procedures, and identification of necessary

Benchmark	min	*CPLEX*	*lp-solve*	*scherzo*
aim-50-1_6-yl-1	50	50	—	50
aim-50-2_0-yl-2	50	50	—	50
aim-50-3_4-yl-3	50	50	50	50
aim-50-6_0-yl-4	50	50	50	50
aim-100-1_6-yl-2	100	—	—	—
aim-100-2_0-yl-3	100	—	—	100
aim-100-3_4-yl-4	100	—	—	100
aim-100-6_0-yl-1	100	100	—	100
aim-200-1_6-yl-3	200	—	—	—
aim-200-2_0-yl-4	200	—	—	—
aim-200-3_4-yl-1	200	—	—	—
aim-200-6_0-yl-2	200	—	—	200
ii8a1	54	54	54	54
ii8b2	—	388	474	—
ii8c2	—	629	668	—
ii8d2	—	588	—	—
ii8e2	—	653	—	—
jnh1	92	93	—	92
jnh7	89	90	—	89
jnh12	94	94	—	94
jnh17	95	95	—	95
ssa7552-038	—	1449	1450	—

Table 3: Computed upper bounds

Benchmark	min	*opbdp*	*min-prime*	*bsolo*
aim-50-1_6-yl-1	50	50	50	50
aim-50-2_0-yl-2	50	50	50	50
aim-50-3_4-yl-3	50	50	50	50
aim-50-6_0-yl-4	50	50	50	50
aim-100-1_6-yl-2	100	100	100	100
aim-100-2_0-yl-3	100	100	100	100
aim-100-3_4-yl-4	100	100	100	100
aim-100-6_0-yl-1	100	100	100	100
aim-200-1_6-yl-3	200	—	200	200
aim-200-2_0-yl-4	200	—	200	200
aim-200-3_4-yl-1	200	200	200	200
aim-200-6_0-yl-2	200	200	200	200
ii8a1	54	54	54	54
ii8b2	—	—	379	379
ii8c2	—	—	525	525
ii8d2	—	—	540	540
ii8e2	—	—	494	494
jnh1	92	92	92	92
jnh7	89	89	89	89
jnh12	94	94	94	94
jnh17	95	95	95	95
ssa7552-038	—	1452	1448	1448

Table 4: Computed upper bounds

assignments.

As the results given in the previous section clearly show, the proposed algorithms, *min-prime* and *bsolo*, are by far the most competitive for the set of benchmarks considered. Thus, for these classes of benchmarks either *min-prime* or *bsolo* would be the option of choice. Moreover, as the experimental results show, the branch and bound SAT-based ILP algorithm *bsolo* is in general more efficient than the SAT-based linear search ILP algorithm.

Despite the promising results given in the previous section, more work needs to be done before an ILP algorithm can be used for solving instances of the minimum-size prime implicant problem which have a practical impact. Furthermore, observe that even though both the minimum size prime implicant problem and the binate covering problem have similar formulations, the algorithms for solving each problem should have different organizations, as the experimental results of *min-prime* [14], *bsolo* and *scherzo* [4] clearly suggest.

As mentioned earlier, one key bottleneck of the proposed *min-prime* algorithmic solution is the ILP layer around GRASP. The repeated addition of large clauses to the CNF formula reduces the ability of GRASP for backtracking non-chronologically and in several cases causes GRASP to always backtrack chronologically. In contrast, with *bsolo*, since no large clauses are created, non-chronological backtracking can in general be exercised.

One other improvement to the proposed algorithmic framework consists of iterating the computation of prime implicants by increasing size. This requires implementing the procedure described in Section 4.3. Its usefulness depends on the target number of prime implicants. If all prime implicants are required, this approach clearly becomes impractical when the total number of prime implicants is exponential on the number of variables.

Finally, other realizations of the SAT-based branch and bound ILP algorithm can be envisioned and used for computing minimum-size prime implicants. These other realizations utilize different bounding procedures. We are currently experimenting with bounding procedures based on LP-relaxations [3, 7] and on Lagrangian relaxations [1, 7].

References

[1] R. K. Ahuja, T. L. Magnanti and J. B. Orlin, *Network Flows: Theory, Algorithms, and Applications*, Prentice-Hall, 1993.

[2] P. Barth, "A Davis-Putnam Based Enumeration Algorithm for Linear Pseudo-Boolean Optimization," Technical Report MPI-I-95-2-003, Max-Planck-Institut für Informatik, January 1995.

[3] M. R. C. M. Berkelaar, UNIX^{TM} Manual Page of lp-solve. Eindhoven University of Technology, Design Automation Section, 1992.

[4] O. Coudert, "On Solving Covering Problems," in *Proceedings of the Design Automation Conference*, June 1996.

[5] M. Davis and H. Putnam, "A Computing Procedure for Quantification Theory," *Journal of the Association for Computing Machinery*, vol. 7, pp. 201-215, 1960.

[6] D. S. Johnson and M. A. Trick (eds.), *Second DIMACS Implementation Challenge*, DIMACS Series in Discrete Mathematics and Theoretical Computer Science, 1993. DIMACS benchmarks available in ftp://Dimacs.Rutgers.EDU/pub/challenge/sat/benchmarks/cnf.

[7] G. L. Nemhauser and L. A. Wolsey, *Integer and Combinatorial Optimization*, John Wiley & Sons, 1988.

[8] T. Ngair, "A New Algorithm for Incremental Prime Implicant Generation," in *Proceedings of the International Joint Conference on Artificial Intelligence*, 1993.

[9] C. Pizzuti, "Computing Prime Implicants by Integer Programming," in *Proceedings of International Conference on Tools with Artificial Intelligence*, November 1996.

[10] S. J. Russell and P. Norvig, *Artificial Intelligence: A Modern Approach*, Prentice-Hall, 1994.

[11] T. Schiex and G. Verfaillie, "Nogood Recording for Static and Dynamic Constraint Satisfaction Problems," in *Proceedings of the International Conference on Tools with Artificial Intelligence*, pp. 48-55, 1993.

[12] J. P. M. Silva and K. A. Sakallah, "Conflict Analysis in Search Algorithms for Propositional Satisfiability," in *Proceedings of the International Conference on Tools with Artificial Intelligence*, November 1996.

[13] J. P. M. Silva and A. L. Oliveira, "Improving Satisfiability Algorithms with Dominance and Partitioning," in *International Workshop on Logic Synthesis*, May 1997.

[14] J. P. M. Silva, "On Computing Minimum Size Prime Implicants," in *International Workshop on Logic Synthesis*, May 1997.

[15] J. P. M. Silva, GRASP source code, available from ftp://algos.inesc.pt/pub/users/jpms/soft/grasp/.

[16] R. Zabih and D. A. McAllester, "A Rearrangement Search Strategy for Determining Propositional Satisfiability," in *Proceedings of the National Conference on Artificial Intelligence*, pp. 155-160, 1988.

Cooperation of LP Solvers for Solving MILPs

Christine SOLNON
LISI - Université Claude Bernard and INSA de Lyon
43, bd du 11 novembre 1918 - Bat. 710
69622 Villeurbanne Cedex - France
e-mail: csolnon@lisihp1.univ-lyon1.fr

Abstract

A standard approach to solve Mixed Integer Linear Programs is to perform a global branch and bound search through all possible combinations. Due to the hardness of the problem, this search must be closely controlled by a constraint solver which uses constraints to prune the search space in an a priori way.

In this paper, we define a new domain reduction solver which uses in a cooperative way a set of Linear Programming solvers. The idea is to compute the actual range of values of the integer variables with respect to the continuous relaxation of the problem, and then narrow these domains to the closest integer interval. This narrowing is iteratively performed until a fixed point is reached where all domains are bound by integer values which belong to the continuous relaxation of the problem. This fixed point corresponds to a new partial consistency, which is stronger than the continuous relaxation and allows us to solve MILPs more efficiently.

1 Motivations

MILPs (Mixed Integer Linear Programs) have many industrial applications such as network design, crew scheduling, resource allocation or cutting stock problems. The general form of a MILP is displayed in figure 1.

$$\begin{array}{lll} \text{minimize} & \sum_{j=1}^{n} c_j x_j & \\ \text{subject to} & \sum_{j=1}^{n} a_{ij} x_j \leq b_i & \forall i \in 1..m \\ & l_j \leq x_j \leq u_j & \forall j \in 1..n \\ & x_j \text{ integral} & \forall x_j \in X_{int} \end{array}$$

Figure 1: General form of a MILP

In this MILP, X_{int} is the subset of variables that are constrained to have integer values. When dropping these integrality restrictions, the resulting linear program —called the continuous relaxation— can easily be solved (by using the simplex algorithm for instance). However, when integrality constraints must be taken into account, the problem becomes much harder (NP-complete).

A standard approach to solve MILPs is to perform a global branch and bound search [14] (also called branch and relax search in [11]). The idea is to solve a relaxation of the MILP and then, if some of the relaxed constraints are not satisfied, to split the MILP into sub-MILPs on which this process is repeated.

The relaxation step is performed at each node of the search in order to detect infeasibility and prune the search space in an a priori way. Most of the time, this relaxation step is performed by a Linear Programming solver (LP solver) which verifies that the continuous relaxation of the MILP is feasible. LP solvers are usually based on the Simplex algorithm[1] and can efficiently solve linear programming problems over the reals and the rationals[2] [8]. However, LP solvers are not able to take into account integrality constraints. These constraints are checked a posteriori, when the search tries to assign an integer value to a variable. As a consequence, many branches of the search tree are tediously explored while some integer variables cannot take integer values any more. In order to partially take into account integrality constraints, and reduce the search space, two main local techniques have been proposed : preprocessing and probing techniques, and domain reduction techniques.

Preprocessing and probing techniques

The main idea of preprocessing [21] is to consider each constraint, together with the lower and upper bounds of its variables, and
- drop the constraint if it is redundant,
- detect inconsistency if the constraint is infeasible or
- tigthen bounds on the variables if the constraint becomes infeasible when the variable is moved to that bound.

If after processing every constraint some variables have been fixed or some bounds have been improved, this process is repeated.

[1]The interior point algorithm, which is in average more efficient for solving large-scale linear programs, is not widely employed in branch and bound searches as it is less incremental than the simplex algorithm.

[2]However, LP solvers are not complete with floating point numbers, due to rounding errors.

1082-3409/97 $10.00 © 1997 IEEE

Probing techniques [21] are used to look ahead one step further : a variable is temporarily set to one of its bounds and then preprocessing techniques are performed. If the problem becomes infeasible, then this value can be discarded ; if some other variable becomes fixed then a new constraint can be derived that tightens the continuous relaxation ; if a constraint becomes redundant, then its formulation can be tightened by coefficient reduction. Such probing techniques are usually performed on binary variables (0-1 variables) only.

Preprocessing and probing techniques have been incorporated in MINTO, a Mixed INTeger Optimizer [20]. The results indicate that these techniques can be very effective and can enhance the performance of a branch and bound search on many MILPs. However, on some MILPs these techniques are less effective and the performances are significantly degraded [14].

Domain reduction techniques

The idea of domain reduction is to successively use each constraint to reduce the domains of its variables until no reduction can be performed for any of the constraints. This fixed point corresponds to some local consistency, usually an approximation of arc-consistency [2]. In order to obtain stronger consistencies (like path-consistency), one can go one step further and look ahead to the remaining possible values of the variables and check whether the constraint can be satisfied with these values.

Domain reduction techniques are widely used to solve constraint satisfaction problems over finite domains (e.g., in CHIP [10], CC(FD) [12] and clp(FD) [9]) and over the reals (e.g., in Newton [3], Interlog [15] and Prolog IV [17]).

Berenger and De Backer defined in [4, 5] a cooperative solver which combines a solver based on domain reduction techniques with a LP solver. The domain reduction solver sends to the LP solver every new integer bound it has inferred, while the LP solver checks for the consistency of the continuous relaxation of the problem, within the bounds sent by the domain reduction solver. Such a cooperation allows them to solve some MILPs more efficiently, both in size of the search tree and time.

Local versus global techniques

Domain reduction techniques as well as basic preprocessing and probing techniques restrict their attention to information in a single constraint at a time. These local checks are computationally efficient but are not always very effective.

Some advanced preprocessing techniques that exploit information from more than one constraint at a time have been proposed [21]. These techniques take advantage of special substructures to reformulate them and tighten the continuous relaxation. They are more effective than basic local preprocessing but, as a counterpart, computationally less efficient.

In this paper, we define another global technique which tightens the continuous relaxation but which is not problem-specific as in advanced preprocessing techniques. The idea is to use LP solvers to narrow the variables domains. Indeed, LP solvers have a global view of the set of linear constraints and are able to compute the actual domains of the integer variables with respect to the continuous relaxation. These computed domains are then narrowed to the closest integer interval. This narrowing is performed until a fixed point is reached where all the domains are bound with integer values which belong to the continuous relaxation of the MILP. This fixed point corresponds to a new partial consistency, called Linear Integer Bounding (LIB) consistency. LIB-consistency is stronger than the continuous relaxation. It partially takes into account integrality constraints and is more effective to reduce the search space. As a counterpart, LIB-consistency is also more expensive to perform. However, first experimentations show that on many examples it allows us to solve MILPs more than twice faster.

2 Notations

The general MILP of figure 1 will be denoted by the triple (X_{int}, C, z) such that X_{int} is the set of integer variables, C the set of linear constraints (linear inequations and variables bounds) and z the objective function to be minimized :

$$\begin{aligned} C = \; & \{ \textstyle\sum_{j=1}^{n} a_{ij}x_j \leq b_i \,, \quad \forall i \in 1..m \} \cup \\ & \{ l_j \leq x_j \leq u_j \,, \qquad \forall j \in 1..n \} \\ z = \; & \textstyle\sum_{j=1}^{n} c_j x_j \end{aligned}$$

The inequations that define the variables bounds are integrated within the set of linear constraints C. We shall note $D_C(x_i)$ the domain associated with a variable x_i in a set of constraints C, i.e., $D_C(x_i) = [l_i..u_i]$ if the constraint $l_i \leq x_i \leq u_i$ belongs to C.

Let v be a real value, we shall note :

- $\lceil v \rceil$ the smallest integer value such that $v \leq \lceil v \rceil$,
- $\lfloor v \rfloor$ the greatest integer value such that $\lfloor v \rfloor \leq v$.

3 Definition of LIB-consistency and LIB-narrowing

We propose to partially take into account integrality constraints in order to tighten the continuous relaxation and reduce the search space. The idea is to check that the bounds of each integer variable are integer values which belong to the set of solutions of the continuous relaxation of the problem. In other words, each facet of the hyper-box defined by the bounds of the integer variables must have a non empty intersection with the polyhedron defined by the continuous relaxation of the MILP. More formally, this partial consistency, called Linear Integer Bounding (LIB) consistency, is defined as follows :

1082-3409/97 $10.00 © 1997 IEEE

Definition of LIB-consistency :

The MILP (X_{int}, C, z) is LIB-consistent if for each integer variable $x_j \in X_{int}$ such that $D_C(x_j) = [l_j..u_j]$,

1. the bounds l_j and u_j are integer values,
2. $C \cup \{x_j = l_j\}$ is feasible over the reals,
3. $C \cup \{x_j = u_j\}$ is feasible over the reals.

When solving a MILP, the domains of the integer variables are often much larger than the convex polyhedron defined by the continuous relaxation of the MILP, so that the problem is not LIB-consistent. In this case, one has to narrow some domains until the MILP becomes LIB-consistent. This narrowing has to be performed without removing any integer solution. More formally, a LIB-narrowing is defined as follows :

Definition of LIB-narrowing :

A LIB-narrowing of a MILP (X_{int}, C, z) is a MILP (X_{int}, C', z) such that :

1. $\forall x_i \in X_{int}, D_{C'}(x_i) \subseteq D_C(x_i)$,
2. C' and C have the same set of integer solutions,
3. (X_{int}, C', z) is LIB-consistent.

4 LIB-narrowing algorithm

LIB-narrowing is performed by the fixpoint algorithm —adapted from the Waltz algorithm [22]— described in figure 2. In this algorithm, Q contains the set of integer variables to be narrowed. When starting narrowing, Q is set to X_{int}. At each iteration, an integer variable x_i is extracted from Q and its associated LP solvers $min[x_i]$ and $max[x_i]$ respectively compute its lower and upper bounds l_f and u_f with respect to the continuous relaxation of the MILP[3]. If the corresponding integer interval $[\lceil l_f \rceil..\lfloor u_f \rfloor]$ is strictly included within the current domain of x_i, then these new bounds are added to C and the set Q of variables to be narrowed is re-initialized to $X_{int} - \{x_i\}$.

This process is repeated until either the continuous relaxation of the MILP becomes inconsistent, or a fixed point is reached (when Q is empty). Termination is ensured as there is a finite number of variables, the domains of which are finite : at each iteration, either a variable is removed from Q and no domain is changed, or the set Q of variables to be narrowed increases but the domain of an integer variable is reduced.

Proposition 1 : The set of constraints returned by `LIB-narrowing(`C`)` has the same set of integer solutions as C.

[3]Each LP solver is based on the Simplex algorithm. The implementation of LP solvers is discussed in section 5.

function `LIB-narrowing`(C: a set of constraints)
returns a set of constraints
  $Q \leftarrow X_{int}$
  while $Q \neq \emptyset$ **and** C is feasible over the reals **do**
    extract from Q an integer variable x_i
    such that $D_C(x_i) = [l_i..u_i]$
    $u_f \leftarrow max[x_i].optimize(C)$
    $l_f \leftarrow min[x_i].optimize(C)$
    if $l_i < \lceil l_f \rceil$ **or** $\lfloor u_f \rfloor < u_i$
    then
      $C \leftarrow C \cup \{\lceil l_f \rceil \leq x_i \leq \lfloor u_f \rfloor\}$
      $Q \leftarrow X_{int} - \{x_i\}$
    end if
  end while
  return(C)
end `LIB-narrowing`

where $min[x_i]$ and $max[x_i]$ are two LP solvers such that the function $optimize(C)$ of $min[x_i]$ (resp. $max[x_i]$) returns the minimum (resp. maximum) value of x_i w.r.t. the set of constraints C.

Figure 2: LIB-narrowing algorithm

Indeed, the algorithm only adds to C constraints like $\lceil l_f \rceil \leq x_i \leq \lfloor u_f \rfloor$. These constraints remove solutions over the reals such that $l_f \leq x_i < \lceil l_f \rceil$ or $\lfloor u_f \rfloor < x_i \leq u_f$. As these intervals do not contain any integer value, their suppression does not cut off any integer solution.

Proposition 2 : The set of constraints returned by `LIB-narrowing(`C`)` is either LIB-consistent, or inconsistent over the reals.

Indeed, the algorithm returns a set of constraints that is consistent over the reals when the set Q of variables to be narrowed is empty. As a consequence, during the last sequence of iterations, for each integer variable $x_i \in X_{int}$, we have $u_i = \lfloor u_f \rfloor$ and $l_i = \lceil l_f \rceil$. In other words, the bounds u_i and l_i of x_i are integer values which belong to the set of solutions of the continuous relaxation of the problem.

5 Implementation issues

LIB-narrowing has been implemented in a cooperative way. The program is composed of a monitor, which manages the set Q of variables to be narrowed, and for each integer variable $x_i \in X_{int}$, two LP solvers $min[x_i]$ and $max[x_i]$ which respectively are in charge of computing the lower and upper bounds of x_i.

Each LP solver $min/max[x_i]$ uses the simplex algorithm to compute the optimal value of x_i with respect to the current set of linear constraints. The computed optimal value is sent to the monitor, which constrains it to an integer value and then forwards it (if necessary) to all other LP solvers. Hence, each $min/max[x_i]$ solver receives numerous new bounds computed by other LP solvers, and has to update consequently the optimal value of x_i.

The key point concerns the way of handling these new bounds. Obviously, one cannot simply add to the simplex a new constraint, each time a new bound is received. Hence, we use *a simplex with explicit bounds* [8, 13] so that the new bounds are simply incorporated by modifying the corresponding bounds in the simplex. In some cases, these modifications lead to a simplex which is still in feasible form, and no further computations are needed. However, if the modified simplex is no longer in feasible form, some iterations have to be performed. In this case, we perform *a dual optimization* [8] so that the new bound is computed in an incremental way : usually, the new optimal value is very close to the last computed one and only few dual iterations are needed to reach the new optimum.

The simplex algorithm is complete over real and rational numbers, but not over floating point numbers, due to rounding errors. In order to minimize these rounding errors, we use a *revised simplex algorithm* which is numerically more stable [8, 18]. However some rounding errors can still occur. In a pragmatic way, we add (resp. subtract) a small value $\epsilon = 1.10^{-6}$ to each upper (resp. lower) bound computed by a LP solver. This practical solution actually prevents nearly all rounding errors. However, from a theoretical point of view, the only correct solution would be to use rational numbers.

LIB-narrowing is performed at each choice point of the search and the state of each LP solver has to be restored after each backtrack. A first solution would be to save the whole state of each solver at each choice point. This solution requires too much memory to be practical. Therefore, we only save the upper and lower bounds of each integer variable, and incrementally re-compute after each backtrack the state of the LP solver by a dual optimization of the simplex.

A prototype has been implemented in C. We used for the implementation of the LP solvers some modules of the `lp_solve` system [6].

6 Application of LIB-narrowing

We evaluate in this section the effectiveness and efficiency of LIB-narrowing : we solve MILPs by a branch and bound procedure and we compare the results obtained when the relaxation step is performed by a LIB solver (which verifies that the set of constraints is LIB-consistent) with the results obtained when the relaxation step is performed by a simple LP solver (which verifies that the continuous relaxation is consistent). This LP solver is implemented with the same algorithm as the LP solvers of the LIB solver, i.e., a revised dual simplex with explicit bounds.

6.1 Branch and bound algorithm

We compare the LP and LIB solvers for solving MILPs. We use in both cases the branch and bound search algorithm described in figure 3.

function `branch-and-bound`(X_{int}, C, z)
returns the solution of the MILP (X_{int}, C, z)
  Solution $\leftarrow \infty$
  $Q \leftarrow \{(X_{int}, C, z)\}$
  while $Q \neq \emptyset$ **do**
    extract from Q a MILP (X_{int}, C', z)
    if `relax`$(C' \cup \{z < Solution\})$=true
    then
      let $\{v_1, \ldots, v_n\}$ be the solution
      that minimizes z w.r.t. C'
      if $\forall x_i \in X_{int}$, v_i is an integer
      then
        /* *an integer solution has been found* */
        Solution $\leftarrow$ value of z corresponding
          to $\{v_1, \ldots, v_n\}$
      else
        /* *creation of 2 new sub-MILPs* */
        choose a variable $x_i \in X_{int}$
        such that v_i is not an integer
        $C'_{low} \leftarrow C' \cup \{x_i \leq \lfloor v_i \rfloor\}$
        $C'_{up} \leftarrow C' \cup \{x_i \geq \lceil v_i \rceil\}$
        $Q \leftarrow Q \cup \{(X_{int}, C'_{low}, z), (X_{int}, C'_{up}, z)\}$
      end if
    end if
  end while
  return(*Solution*)
end `branch-and-bound`

Figure 3: Branch and bound search algorithm

In this algorithm, Q is the set of MILPs to be solved. When starting the optimization, Q only contains the initial MILP. At each iteration, a MILP is extracted from Q. If its relaxation is consistent and the corresponding optimal solution does not meet all integrality constraints, then the MILP is splitted into two new sub-MILPs that are added to Q. In the current implementation, this set Q is organised as a stack, in a last-in/first-out strategy corresponding to a depth first exploration of the search tree.

Upon each iteration, the `relax` function is used to check that a relaxation of the selected MILP is feasible. This function depends on the solver chosen :

- when the LP solver is used, `relax`(C) returns "true" if the set of constraints C is feasible over the reals,
- when the LIB solver is used, `relax`(C) first LIB-narrows the variables domains by the domain reduction algorithm of figure 2, and then returns "true" if the resulting set of constraints is feasible over the reals.

The LIB and LP solvers are successively compared when using the two following heuristics for choosing the variable x_i to be splitted at each iteration :

- `max-fract` chooses the variable x_i such that v_i is the value the fractional part of which is the closest to 0.5, i.e., x_i is the variable that has the largest integer infeasibility.
- `min-dom` chooses the variable x_i that has the smallest domain, i.e., the variable which should "first-fail".

6.2 Test set

We compare the LIB and LP solvers on problems extracted from the test set of real-world MILPs described in [7]. These problems are respectively described in figure 4 by means of the number of variables over the reals (R), the number of general integer variables (I), the number of binary integer variables (B) (the domains of which are {0,1}), the number of constraints (C) and the solution of the MILP.

Some of these MILPs (egout, p0033, pp08a, pp08aCUTS, rgn and stein27) only involve binary integer variables. Hence, these problems have not been solved with the `min-dom` heuristic (as all domains contain two values). The p0033-10 problem is the same problem than p0033 but where the domains of the variables have been relaxed to $\{0, ..., 10\}$.

6.3 Results

Figures 5 and 6 respectively display the results obtained when using the `max-fract` and the `min-dom` heuristic. Each figure successively displays the number of choice points, the number of dual simplex iterations and the cpu time (in seconds, on a HP 715/100 station). For each of these criteria, the first column indicates the results obtained when using the LIB solver,

Problem	Variables R	I	B	C	Optimal solution
bell3a	62	32	39	123	878 430
bell5	36	28	30	91	8 966 406
egout	94	0	55	98	568
flugpl	6	11	0	17	1 201 500
gt2	0	164	24	29	21 166
p0033	0	0	33	14	3 089
p0033-10	0	19	14	14	2 455
pp08a	176	0	64	136	7 350
pp08aCUTS	176	0	64	246	7 350
rgn	80	0	100	24	82
stein27	0	0	27	118	18

Figure 4: Problems description

the second when using the LP solver and the third one gives the ratio between the LP and the LIB solvers. The fourth array gives results for the harder problems that were not solved after more than 30 minutes of cpu time. For these problems, the execution has been stopped at 30 minutes of cpu time and we display the best solution found and the difference between the value of the best solution found and the optimal value (as a percentage of the optimal value).

On these examples, one can remark that LIB narrowing actually tightens the continuous relaxation and drastically reduces the number of performed choice points. However, the results are not uniform and the effectiveness of LIB-narrowing depends on the MILP considered and the heuristic used : on some problems, like bell3a with the max-fract heuristic or flugpl with the min-dom heuristic, LIB-narrowing is very effective and allows one to perform more than 200 times less choice points ; on other problems, like egout or p0033, it reduces the number of performed choice points by a factor of nearly 100 ; finally, on the two problems rgn and stein27, it is not so effective and the LIB solver only performs five times less choice points than the LP solver.

However, there is a trade off between efficiency and effectivity. Indeed, if the LIB solver is actually effective to prune the search space, it is also more expensive than a simple LP solver : at each choice point, the LIB solver usually performs successive dual optimizations while the LP solver only performs one. Each dual optimization itself requires successive iterations of the Simplex. Hence, at each choice point, the LIB solver performs an average of more than 100 iterations while the LP solver only performs 4 iterations. As a consequence, the overall efficiency of LIB narrowing depends on its degree of effectivity : when LIB-narrowing reduces the number of choice points by more than 100 times, the number of performed iterations is more than twice less. However, on the rgn and stein27 problems, on which LIB narrowing is not so ef-

Number of choice points :

Problem	LIB	LP	$\frac{LP}{LIB}$
bell3a	4 407	892 414	202.5
p0033	28	4 276	152.7
p0033-10	509	52 641	103.4
egout	384	33 090	86.2
flugpl	212	17 513	82.6
rgn	460	2 450	5.3
stein27	520	2 604	5.0

Number of simplex iterations :

Problem	LIB	LP	$\frac{LP}{LIB}$
bell3a	437 781	4 530 351	10.3
p0033	6 225	20 956	3.4
p0033-10	89 143	248 644	2.8
egout	67 923	76 393	1.1
flugpl	36 859	40 922	1.1
rgn	516 617	91 979	0.2
stein27	230 994	30 806	0.1

Cpu time, in seconds :

Problem	LIB	LP	$\frac{LP}{LIB}$
bell3a	1 192.9	6 165.3	5.2
p0033	2.4	7.1	3.0
p0033-10	33.5	83.0	2.5
egout	100.8	158.4	1.6
flugpl	10.4	18.2	1.8
rgn	245.6	42.1	0.2
stein27	417.9	73.7	0.2

Problems stopped at 30 mn cpu time :

Problem	LIB		LP	
	last solution	gap (%)	last solution	gap (%)
bell5	8969078	0.1	9377729	4.6
pp08a	8290	6.5	9760	25.4
pp08aCUTS	7930	7.9	9130	24.2
gt2	101266	378.4	103520	389.1

Figure 5: Results with the **max-fract** heuristic

Number of choice points :

Problem	LIB	LP	$\frac{LP}{LIB}$
bell5	11 788	1 487 699	126.2
flugpl	31	15 003	484.0
bell3a	2 991	122 667	41.0
p0033-10	593	28 344	47.8

Number of simplex iterations :

Problem	LIB	LP	$\frac{LP}{LIB}$
bell5	755 969	11 429 974	15.1
flugpl	6 344	28 789	4.5
bell3a	144 373	1 215 710	8.4
p0033-10	53 755	126 252	2.4

Cpu time, in seconds :

Problem	LIB	LP	$\frac{LP}{LIB}$
bell5	1 692.4	10 892.4	6.4
flugpl	2.4	15.2	6.3
bell3a	409.3	1 498.7	3.7
p0033-10	21.7	42.3	2.0

Problem stopped at 30 mn cpu time :

Problem	LIB		LP	
	last solution	gap (%)	last solution	gap (%)
gt2	106 378	402.6	135 468	540.0

Figure 6: Results with the **min-dom** heuristic

fective and only performs 5 times less choice points, the LIB solver is not efficient and performs 5 times more iterations.

Cpu time essentially depends on the number of iterations performed. Hence, for the rgn and stein27 problems LIB narrowing is five times slower, whereas for all other problems, it is twice or more faster (even 6 times faster for the bell5 and flugpl problems with the `min-dom` heuristic).

In general, the `min-dom` heuristic is more efficient than the `max-fract` one, for both the LIB and LP solvers. However, the improvement is slightly more important for the LIB solver than for the LP one. This could be explained by the fact that LIB narrowing dynamically narrows domains during the resolution.

Finally, one can remark that for harder problems like gt2 or pp08a, that have been stopped after 30 minutes of cpu time, the best solution found with the LIB solver is better than the one found with the LP solver.

7 Related works

Branch and cut approaches

Branch and cut approaches are often used to solve MILPs. The idea is to add, at each step of the search, some new linear constraints which cut off the current optimal solution of the continuous relaxation, but which do not remove any integer solution. The key point in this approach is to compute "good" cuts, i.e., cuts that are as close as possible to the convex hull of all integer solutions. In the general case, this appears to be as hard as the resolution of the MILP. However, on some specific problems with restricted types of constraints, this approach allows one to solve MILPs efficiently (see for example CLP($\mathcal{PB}$) [1]). A critical point of the branch and cut approach lies in the fact that, when adding cuts, the MILP becomes larger and typically harder to solve.

The LIB-narrowing algorithm defined in this paper can be viewed as a branch and cut approach : each domain reduction cuts off some solutions over the reals while preserving the integer ones. These cuts can be deduced independently from the kind of constraints and are rather easily computed, provided that one uses an incremental simplex algorithm. Moreover, these cuts can be taken into account in a straightforward way without increasing the size of the simplex (i.e., the number of constraints), provided that one uses a Simplex with explicit bounds.

Domain narrowing and basic preprocessing techniques can also be viewed as branch and cut approaches. In these techniques, the cuts are deduced in a local way, by considering each constraint separately. These cuts are more easily computed but, as a counterpart, they are less effective.

Non linear problems over the reals

We define in [19] an active bounding linear solver, based on a similar cooperative architecture as the LIB solver. This solver cooperatively uses a set of LP solvers to compute the actual range of values of variables with respect to some linear constraints. This cooperative linear solver is integrated with a domain reduction solver into a concurrent architecture. This concurrent cooperative system —named `CCC`— is used to solve over the reals mixed sets of constraints (containing linear equations and inequations and non-linear equations).

8 Further works

When using a constraint solver to prune a search tree, a major efficiency issue lies in the choice of the completeness of the solver : one has to break the tie between the larger cost of a more complete solver and the smaller search space that such a solver can give rise to. Hence, if LIB-propagation drastically reduces the search space, it is also very expensive, both in time and space. However, first experimentations show that it can solve MILPs more efficiently than a simple LP solver.

A major interest of this approach lies in the fact that it could be parallelized in a straightforward way : each LP solver $min/max[x_i]$ can run independently, and only has to communicate to the other solvers the computed optimal values. Hence, we intend to implement the LIB-narrowing algorithm on a parallel machine, in order to compare such a AND-parallelism with the more usual OR-one (which consists in exploring different branches of the search tree in parallel) [16].

Thanks to Jean-Marc Fouet, Simone Pimont and Michel Rueher for reading successive versions of this paper.

References

[1] P. Barth and A. Bockmayr. Finite domain and cutting plane techniques in CLP($\mathcal{PB}$). In Leon Sterling, editor, *Proceedings of ICLP'95*, pages 133–147, Kanagawa, Japan, 1995. MIT Press.

[2] F. Benhamou. Interval Constraint Logic Programming. In Andreas Podelski, editor, *Constraint Programming: Basics and Trends*, volume 910 of *LNCS*, pages 1–21. Springer-Verlag, 1995.

[3] F. Benhamou, D. McAllester, and P. Van Hentenryck. CLP(Intervals) Revisited. In *Proceedings of ILPS'94*, pages 124–138, Ithaca, NY, USA, 1994.

[4] H. Beringer and B. De Backer. Combinatorial problem solving in constraint logic programming with cooperative solvers. In C. Beierle and L. Plume, editors, *Logic Programming: formal methods and practical applications*. Elsevier Science Publisher, 1994.

[5] H. Beringer and B. De Backer. Cooperative solvers and global constraints: the case of linear arithmetic constraints. In *ILPS Workshop*, 1996.

[6] M. Berkelaar. lp_solve. Technical report, available at `ftp://ftp.es.ele.tue.nl/pub/lp_solve`, 1996.

[7] R.E. Bixby, E.A. Boyd, and R.R. Indovina. MIPLIB: a test set of real-world mixed integer programming problems. *SIAM News*, 25(2):16, 1992. (available at ftp://softlib.cs.rice.edu/pub/miplib).

[8] V. Chvatal. *Linear Programming.* W.H. Freeman and Co, 1983.

[9] D. Diaz. *Etude de la compilation des langages logiques de programmation par contraintes sur les domaines finis: le système clp(FD).* PhD thesis, INRIA, 1995.

[10] M. Dincbas, P. Van Hentenryck, H. Simonis, A. Aggoun, T. Graf, and F. Berthier. The constraint logic programming language CHIP. In *Proceedings of the International Conference on Fith Generation Computer Systems*, 1988.

[11] P. Van Hentenryck. Constraint solving for combinatorial search problems. In *PPCP'95: Conference on Principles and Practice of Constraint Programming.* MIT Press, 1995.

[12] P. Van Hentenryck., V. Saraswat, and Y. Deville. Design, implementation and evaluation of the constraint language cc(FD). In *PPCP'95: Conference on Principles and Practice of Constraint Programming.* MIT Press, 1995.

[13] C. Holzbaur. A specialized, incremental solved form algorithm for systems of linear inequalities. Technical Report TR-94-07, University of Vienna, 1994.

[14] E. Johnson, G. Nemhauser, and M. Savelsbergh. Progress in integer programming: an exposition. Research report, Georgia Institute of Technology, 1997.

[15] O. Lhomme. Consistency techniques for numeric CSPs. In R. Bajcsy, editor, *Proceedings of the 13th IJCAI*, pages 232–238, Chambéry, France, 1993. IEEE Computer Society Press.

[16] B. Mans and C. Roucairol. Performances des algorithmes branch and bound parallèles à stratégie meilleur d'abord. Research Report RR-1716, INRIA, 1992.

[17] PrologIA. PrologIV — Constraint inside (handbook of PrologIV). Technical report, PrologIA, Parc Technologique de Luminy, Case 919, 13288 Marseille Cedex 09, France, 1996.

[18] P. Refalo and P. Van Hentenryck. CLP($\mathcal{R}_{lin}$) revised. In *ICLP'96: Joint International Conference on Logic Programming.* MIT Press, 1996.

[19] M. Rueher and C. Solnon. Concurrent cooperating solvers over reals. *Journal of Reliable Computing, Kluwer academic publishers*, 3(3), 1997.

[20] M. Savelsbergh and G. Nemhauser. Functional description of MINTO, a Mixed INteger Optimizer. Technical Report COC-91-03A, Georgia Institute of Technology, 1993.

[21] M.W.P. Savelsbergh. Preprocessing and probing techniques for mixed integer programming problems. *ORSA Journal on Computing*, 6:445–454, 1994.

[22] D.L. Waltz. Generating semantic descriptions from drawing of scenes with shadows. Technical Report AI-TR-271, MIT Cambridge, 1972.

Extending EGENET with Lazy Constraint Consistency

Peter Stuckey and Vincent Tam

Department of Computer Science,
University of Melbourne, 3052
Parkville, Australia.
{pjs,vtam}@cs.mu.oz.au

Abstract

Constraint satisfaction problems (CSPs) occur widely in real-life applications such as bin-packing, planning and scheduling. EGENET, a neural network simulator based on the min-conflict heuristic, has had remarkable success in solving hard CSPs such as hard graph-colouring problems. Consistency techniques such as arc consistency have been extensively used to improve the search behaviour of complete search methods, by removing values and combinations of values that cannot take part in any solution. They are not typically used for stochastic search methods such as EGENET. In this paper we show how to efficiently incorporate consistency methods in EGENET. This improves the convergence behaviour of EGENET and also makes it able to detect insoluble CSPs. We compare the improved EGENET against the original version and versions incorporating state-of-art consistency techniques such as AC-4 or PC-4.

1 Introduction

A *constraint satisfaction problem* (CSP) consists of a set of variables $\{X_1, \cdots, X_n\}$, each of which has a *domain* D_{X_i} of possible values, and a set of constraints $\mathcal{C}$ limiting the combination of values for a subset of variables. The task is to find a *valuation*, that is an assignment of values $v_1 \in D_{X_1}, \cdots, v_n \in D_{X_n}$ to the variables $X_1, \cdots, X_n$, written $(X_1 = v_1, \ldots X_n = v_n)$ satisfying the constraints $\mathcal{C}$. CSP's occur in a large number of applications, such as computer vision, planning, resource allocation, scheduling and temporal reasoning. But CSP's are, in general, NP-complete. Thus, all known algorithms designed to solve any CSP will necessarily require exponential time in the worst case.

GENET [14] is a neural network simulator based on the min-conflict heuristic, specifically designed to solve CSPs. It uses a randomised local search and a heuristic learning rule to search for solutions. It has had remarkable success in solving some hard instances of binary CSPs such as hard graph-colouring problems [7]. Davenport *et. al.* [3] extended GENET with the "illegal" and "atmost" constraints to handle the car-sequencing problem with similarly encouraging results. Lee *et al.* [8, 9] further extended the original GENET with a generic constraint representation scheme to obtain EGENET, a system to handle general, binary and non-binary, constraints.

Because EGENET is a randomised search method, it is not guaranteed to find a solution, even if one exists. For an insoluble CSP, it will search forever unless limited by some resource such a CPU time or number of iterations. In such cases, resource exhaustion indicates that the algorithm has not found a solution, but does not guarantee that a solution does not exist. Hence EGENET cannot detect insoluble CSPs.

Complete search methods, as opposed to random search methods such EGENET, are an alternate approach to solving CSPs. Complete search methods systematically explore the search space until a solution is found. When they fail to find a solution, the CSP is insoluble. But when the CSP is tight[1] or the problem size is large, complete search methods can be very slow [2] due to their algorithmic nature. Complete search methods are often augmented with consistency techniques such as AC-4 [11] and PC-4 [4] which improve the search efficiency by eliminating of redundant values or compound labels from the search space. Consistency techniques have been successfully applied to a number of real-life applications [10, 1] and integrated into the search procedure of existing constraint solving systems such as CHIP [5] and ILOG [6].

In this paper, we propose new "lazy" consistency techniques for EGENET, where consistency is checked

[1] A CSP has few solutions over a large search space.

1082-3409/97 $10.00 © 1997 IEEE

on the fly. We introduce constraint handling nodes into EGENET as a method for implementing lazy consistency. The concept of constraint handlers provide a unified and flexible scheme for extending EGENET. The new model of EGENET not only detects insoluble CSPs but also improves convergence of EGENET on soluble CSPs by moving search away from inconsistent values. Our improved model of EGENET compares favourably against the original model and the original model combined with the state-of-art consistency techniques such as AC-4 [11] or PC-4 [4] on a number of general CSPs.

This paper is organised as follows. Section 2 briefly reviews EGENET. A new kind of consistency checking on-demand called lazy consistency is defined and discussed in detail in Section 3. Section 4 describes the architecture and convergence procedure of the new EGENET model. We present and analyse our preliminary empirical results in Section 5.

2 EGENET

Lee *et al.* [8] proposed EGENET, an extension of GENET to handle arbitrary (non-binary) constraints. EGENET is, like GENET, a min conflict search with heuristic learning, but it differs from GENET in the representation of constraints and the learning rules. In EGENET there are two types[2] of nodes: *variable nodes* and *constraint nodes*. Each variable X_i in a CSP is represented by a variable node[3] with its associated domain, instead of a cluster of nodes as in the GENET model. The *state* of a variable node X_i is defined to be its current value assignment $(X_i = v_i)$.

Each constraint node denotes a constraint c in the CSP. Let $vars(c)$ be the set of variables occurring in constraint c. A constraint node c is connected to a variable node X_i if the variable $X_i \in vars(c)$. A constraint c, where $vars(c) = \{X_1, \ldots, X_k\}$, is considered as a mapping from valuations of the form $X_1 = v_1, \ldots, X_k = v_k$ to non-negative numbers (penalty value)[4]. In essence, we consider each constraint as a scoring function which returns a zero or positive integer for the current valuation of the variables involved in that constraint. If the constraint c holds for $X_1 = v_1, \ldots, X_k = v_k$ then $c(X_1 = v_1, \cdots, X_k = v_k) = 0$. Otherwise, if the constraint c does not hold for the valuation $X_1 = v_1, \ldots, X_k = v_k$, then $c(X_1 = v_1, \cdots, X_k = v_k) > 0$. The constraint c maps valuations to a penalty value, which is 0 if the constraint is satisfied. For example, the penalty value for an inequality $X > 0$, where X is a variable in a CSP, under valuation θ may be defined as: 0 if X's value under θ is greater than 0, and $p(1 - X)$ otherwise, where p is a (positive) penalty multiplier. The penalty value for a conjunction of constraints is defined as the sum of the penalties for each constraint.

[2] In [9] a third type of node is added, this extension is orthogonal to the results of this paper

[3] We abuse terminology by naming a variable (a constraint) node by its variable (constraint) name

[4] We use positive penalties instead of the negative penalties used in the original EGENET model.

Figure 1 shows the constraint network and the EGENET network of a binary CSP with three variables X, Y and Z each with domain $\{1, 2, 3\}$, and a set of constraints $\{X > 1, X < Y, X \neq Z, Y < Z\}$. The variables X, Y and Z are represented by variable nodes. Each variable nodes is initially set to a random element of the domain of the variable. The current assignment $(X = 1, Y = 2, Z = 3)$ can be read from these nodes.

The first constraint node $X > 1$ is connected to the variable node X. The binary constraint $X < Y$ is represented by the second constraint node, and is connected to variable nodes X and Y. Each constraint node shows the penalty value of the corresponding constraint for the current variable assignment. For instance, the penalty value of the constraint $X > 1$ for the current variable assignment is $+1$.

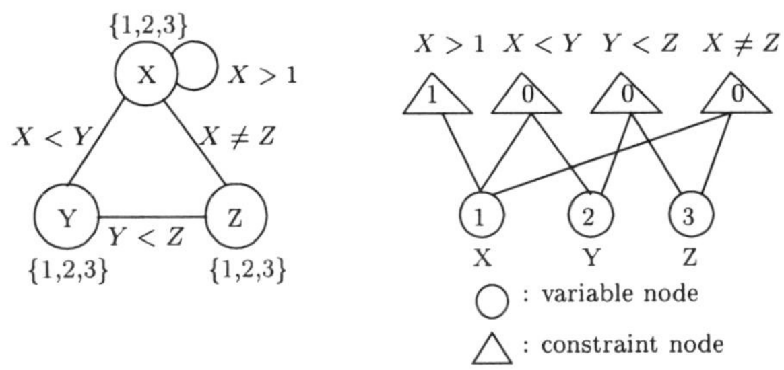

Figure 1: The constraint network and the EGENET network of an example CSP.

Each value v in the domain of variable X_i has an *input* value defined as the sum of penalty values of all the constraint nodes involving variable X_i when $X_i = v$. A positive input indicates the value is involved in the violation of certain constraints. When the sum of inputs for the current variable assignments is zero, the network state represents a solution.

EGENET executes a network convergence procedure as follows. Given a variable node X_i with current state v_i, the input value is calculated for each value $v \in D_{X_i}$. The value v with minimum input is the new state for X_i. In the case of ties, if the old state v_i has minimum input then it remains the state of the node, otherwise one of values with minimum input is chosen randomly.

repeat
  update all variable nodes in parallel asynchronously until no repair occurs
  if (sum of inputs for the network state is zero)
    terminate with success
  else
    activate heuristic learning
until (CPU time or convergence cycle limit is exceeded)

The convergence procedure of EGENET is shown above. The heuristic learning rule in EGENET is left unspecified intentionally since application of domain knowledge can help to design good learning rules for specific problems. For example, one heuristic rule is to increase the penalty multiplier of a violated constraint by 1.

The example CSP shown in Figure 1 is insoluble. When the CSP is insoluble as in this example, EGENET fails to detect the unsatisfiability of the CSP since the minimisation search never finds a solution. Values for variables which cannot take part in a solution are never discovered. Instead, minimisation search and heuristic learning for updating penalties continues forever. As a result, EGENET simply runs forever unless a given resource such as CPU time or convergence cycles is exhausted. In the next section, we discuss "lazy" consistency techniques which extend EGENET to detect and use inconsistency information.

3 Lazy Consistency

Tsang [13] states that the concept of consistency is rooted from the idea of problem reduction which serves to reduce a CSP to an easier and equivalent[5] problem and recognise insoluble CSPs. These concepts are defined to identify redundant values or compound labels. In the past, a number of sophisticated consistency techniques such as AC-4 [11] and PC-4 [4] have been proposed to improve the search efficiency of complete search methods. All these consistency techniques have been successfully applied to a number of real-life applications [10, 1] and forms of consistency reasoning are integrated into the search procedures of existing constraint solving systems such as CHIP [5] and ILOG [6].

In this section, we introduce *illegal* constraints, briefly review the conventional concepts of *node*, *arc* and *path* consistency and then discuss our "lazy" notion of consistency which is more efficient and suitable for EGENET.

Consistency methods discover illegal combinations. An *illegal combination*, denoted $illegal(X_1 = v_1, X_2 = v_2, \ldots, X_k = v_k)$, is a constraint which disallows the simultaneous assignment of values $v_1, v_2, \cdots, v_k$ to the variables $X_1, X_2, \cdots, X_k$ respectively. An *illegal constraint* over variables $X_1, X_2, \ldots, X_k$, denoted $illegal(X_1, X_2, \cdots, X_k)$, is a set of illegal combinations on variables $X_1, \cdots, X_k$, treated as their conjunction.

In subsequent discussion, we use $\mathcal{C}_X$ to refer to the conjunction of all the unary constraints on variable X, we use $c_{X,Y}$ to refer to a particular binary constraint on variables X and Y, and we use $\mathcal{C}_{X,Y}$ to refer to the conjunction of all the binary constraints on variables X and Y.

3.1 Node, Arc and Path consistency

The definitions of *node*, *arc* and *path consistency* [10] of a CSP are given below. Node consistency simply demands that every value in the domain of a variable does not conflict with any unary constraint on that variable.

Definition 1 (Node consistency of a CSP)
A CSP is **node consistent** *iff* $\forall X_i\ (\forall v \in D_{X_i} : \mathcal{C}_{X_i}(X_i = v) = 0)$.

A value v for variable X_i for which the node consistency condition does not hold can be removed from the domain of X_i. For example, for the CSP shown in Figure 1, $\mathcal{C}_X = X > 1$, and $C_X(X = 1) = 1$. Hence the value 1 in the domain of variable X is not node consistent and can be removed.

Arc consistency states that for every constrained pair of variables X_i and X_j, for every element in the domain of X_i there is a supporting value in the domain of X_j so the binary constraints between X_i and X_j are satisfied, and vice versa.

Definition 2 (Arc consistency of a CSP)
A CSP is **arc consistent** *iff* $\forall X_i, X_j (\forall v \in D_{X_i} (\exists u \in D_{X_j} : \mathcal{C}_{X_i,X_j}(X_i = v, X_j = u) = 0))$.

Similarly, a value v for variable X_i for which the the arc consistency condition does not hold can be removed from the domain of X_i. In the example CSP,

[5] Two CSPs are equivalent if they have the same sets of variables and same sets of solutions [13].

$\mathcal{C}_{X,Y} = X < Y$, and the value 3 for variable X is such that, for all $u \in D_Y$, $\mathcal{C}_{X,Y}(X = 3, Y = u) > 0$. Hence 3 can be removed from the domain of X.

In a constraint graph of a binary CSP, the length of a path is n if the path goes through $n+1$ nodes. If every path of length 2 is path consistent, the constraint graph is path consistent [13]. Hence, we only consider path consistency of length 2. Three variables are path consistent if for every pair of values for X_i and X_k there is a supporting value in the domain of X_j so that the binary constraints between X_i and X_j and between X_j and X_k are simultaneously satisfied.

Definition 3 (Path consistency of a CSP with path length = 2)
A CSP is **path consistent** *iff* $\forall X_i, X_j, X_k \; (\forall v \in D_{X_i}, \forall w \in D_{X_k} (\exists u \in D_{X_j} : \mathcal{C}_{X_i,X_j}(X_i = v, X_j = u) = 0 \wedge \mathcal{C}_{X_j,X_k}(X_j = u, X_k = w) = 0))$.

Given a pair of values for variables $X_i = v$ and $X_k = w$, if there is no supporting value $u \in D_{X_j}$, then we can add the illegal combination $illegal(X_i = v, X_k = w)$ since the assignments are path inconsistent. Taking the example CSP illustrated in Figure 1. The valuations $(X = 2, Z = 1), (X = 2, Z = 2)$ and $(X = 2, Z = 3)$ can be identified as illegal by a path consistency algorithm such as PC-4, since for each of these tuples, $\forall u \in D_Y \; \mathcal{C}_{X,Y} > 0 \vee \mathcal{C}_{Y,Z} > 0$. When used in conjunction with arc consistency, path consistency can reduce the domains of variables. For example, the value 2 in the domain of variable X can be removed by an arc consistency algorithm since there does not exist a value u in the domain of Z such that $\mathcal{C}_{X,Z}(X = 2, Z = u) = 0$ (where $\mathcal{C}_{X,Z} = X \neq Z \wedge illegal(X = 2, Z = 1) \wedge illegal(X = 2, Z = 2) \wedge illegal(X = 2, Z = 3)$). Hence, the CSP is insoluble since there is no value left in the domain of variable X.

The space and time complexity of an algorithm for achieving node consistency is $O(nd)$, where n is the number of variables in the CSP and d is the maximum size of the domains. Achieving arc or path consistency is much more computationally expensive. The time complexity for AC-4 is $O(d^2e)$ and that for PC-4 is $O(n^3d^3)$, where e is the number of binary constraints in the CSP. Because of the computational cost, using arc consistency and/or path consistency on a reasonably large CSP may not be practical. In particular, there are many problems which EGENET can solve quickly in their original form. The overhead of using consistency methods for these problems outweighs any possible benefit in the EGENET search. Hence, we propose "lazy" notion of consistency more suitable for EGENET in the following paragraphs.

3.2 Lazy Consistency for EGENET

Because of the randomised search, EGENET may never visit large parts of the search space (unlike complete search methods which may eventually visit all the search space). Hence full arc consistency or path consistency is not necessarily beneficial to EGENET. Instead we would like the consistency to be relevant to the current position in the search.

The first idea is to only consider those values of variables which are relevant to the search for a solution in EGENET at its present position. We call this "value laziness". In term of the EGENET network, we only consider the values appeared in the current network state $(X_1 = v_1, \ldots, X_n = v_n)$. For the moment we restrict ourselves to binary constraints. We are now ready for the first lazy consistency concept:

Definition 4 *(Lazy arc consistency of a CSP and valuation $(X_1 = v_1, \ldots, X_n = v_n)$)*
A CSP is **lazy arc consistent** *for valuation* $(X_1 = v_1, \ldots, X_n = v_n)$ *iff*

$$\forall X_i, X_j \; (\exists u \in D_{X_j} \; \mathcal{C}_{X_i,X_j}(X_i = v_i, X_j = u) = 0).$$

Lazy arc consistency seeks a support value ($\exists u \in D_{X_j}$) for the current variable assignment ($X_i = v_i$) with respect to all the binary constraints $\mathcal{C}_{X_i,X_j}$ on the related variables X_i and X_j. Lazy arc consistency only checks arc consistency with respect to the current variable assignments held in EGENET. Hence, it is targeted to help the EGENET in its current search position and a great deal of arc inconsistency that exists in the problem, in areas where the search never visits does not need to be considered. Thus we obtain the benefits of arc consistency without paying the full cost.

The second idea is rather than treating all the constraints on a pair of variables together as one constraint, we can treat the constraints on a pair of variables separately. In EGENET, the network consists of individual constraint nodes. For each constraint node, we can ask whether the current variable assignments satisfy that particular constraint, that is $c(X_1 = v_1, \ldots, X_k = v_k) = 0$. Hence, treating the constraints on a set of variables independently accords better with the EGENET network structure. We call this "constraint laziness".

Definition 5 *(Lazy arc constraint consistency of a CSP and valuation $(X_1 = v_1, \ldots, X_n = v_n)$)*
A CSP is **lazy arc constraint consistent** *for valuation* $(X_1 = v_1, \ldots, X_n = v_n)$ *iff*

$$\forall c_{X_i,X_j} \; (\exists u \in D_{X_j} \; c_{X_i,X_j}(X_i = v_i, X_j = u) = 0).$$

Lazy arc constraint consistency seeks a *support* value ($\exists u \in D_{X_j}$) for the current variable assignment with respect to each binary constraint c_{X_i,X_j} on X_i and X_j individually. It is a weaker form of lazy arc consistency, but accords better with the EGENET network structure.

Taking the CSP as shown in Figure 1 and the valuation $(X = 3, Y = 1, Z = 2)$. When we consider $X = 3$ and the single constraint $X < Y$, lazy arc constraint consistency will remove this label from the domain of variable X since there does not exist a value in the domain of variable Y which can satisfy the constraint $X < Y$ for this value of X. Applying lazy arc consistency to this CSP will also get the same result since the single constraint $X < Y$ is the only binary constraint between the variables X and Y.

Lazy arc constraint consistency is a more natural formulation for EGENET since each constraint node corresponds exactly to a particular constraint in the CSP. Since EGENET supports both binary and non binary constraints, we can generalise the notion of lazy arc constraint consistency to lazy constraint consistency for constraints of any arity.

Definition 6 *(Lazy constraint Consistency of a CSP and valuation $(X_1 = v_1, \ldots, X_n = v_n)$)*
A constraint c with $vars(c) = \{X_1, \ldots, X_k\}$ together with variable $X_j, 1 \leq j \leq k$ is **lazy constraint consistent** *with respect to valuation $(X_1 = v_1, \ldots, X_n = v_n)$ iff*

$$\exists u \in D_{X_j}\ c(X_1 = v_1, \ldots, X_j = u, \ldots, X_k = v_k) = 0.$$

A CSP is **lazy constraint consistent** *for valuation $(X_1 = v_1, \ldots, X_n = v_n)$, if each constraint c in the CSP and variable X_j in $vars(c)$ is lazy constraint consistent.*

If for some constraint c and variable X_j the valuation is not lazy constraint consistent, then we can add information that the valuation on the remaining variables $X_1 = v_1, \ldots, X_{j-1} = v_{j-1}, X_{j+1} = v_{j+1}, \ldots, X_k = v_k$ is an illegal combination. Obviously, lazy arc constraint consistency is just a special case of lazy constraint consistency.

It is straightforward to define an algorithm that checks lazy constraint consistency for a constraint and variable and the current valuation $X_1 = v_1, \ldots, X_n = v_n$ and builds illegal combinations in the cases that it is violated.

The failure in finding a support for a constraint results in the generation of a new *illegal* combination to penalise a valuation from being selected in the future network states. An illegal combination on a single variable $illegal(X = v)$ can be used to remove the value v from the domain of X. We consider that all illegal combinations for a particular set of variables $X_1, \ldots, X_k$ are maintained as a single *illegal* constraint.

Clearly lazy arc consistency can be implemented using lazy constraint consistency by creating a single constraint combining all the constraints involving a pair of variables X and Y. Similarly, we can define a notion of lazy path consistency notion using lazy constraint consistency.

Definition 7 *(Lazy path Consistency of a CSP for valuation $(X_1 = v_1, \ldots, X_n = v_n)$)*
A CSP is **lazy path consistent** *iff for each pair of constraints c_1 and c_2 and variable $X_j \in vars(c_1) \cap vars(c_2)$ the constraint $c_1 \wedge c_2$ is lazy constraint consistent for variable X_j and valuation $(X_1 = v_1, \ldots, X_n = v_n)$.*

In essence, path consistency simply considers a conjunction of two constraints which share a common variable and detects whether the conjunction is lazy constraint consistent.

If we detect a conjunction of constraints $c_1 \wedge c_2$ which are not lazy constraint consistent for variable X_j, we can add an illegal combination $illegal(X_1 = v_1, \ldots, X_{j-1} = v_{j-1}, X_{j+1} = v_{j+1}, \ldots, X_n = v_n)$. For example, for the CSP illustrated in Figure 1, the constraint $X < Y \wedge Y < Z$ and variable Y is not lazy constraint consistent with $(X = 2, Y = 2, Z = 3)$. We can add the illegal combination $illegal(X = 2, Z = 3)$. Note that both constraints $X < Y$ and $Y < Z$ are lazy constraint consistent for variable Y and this valuation.

Clearly we can generalise lazy path consistency to consider 3 or more constraints sharing a common variable simultaneously.

4 A New Model for EGENET

In order to support lazy consistency, we add a new type of node to EGENET, *constraint handling nodes.* A constraint handling node (CH node) takes as input the output of constraint nodes, together with a variable and may produce illegal combinations.

Figure 2 shows the new EGENET network structure of the example CSP shown in 1, together with some constraint handling nodes. The network structure is basically the same as the network structure of the original model, except that a number of constraint handling nodes are added to perform lazy constraint consistency checking.

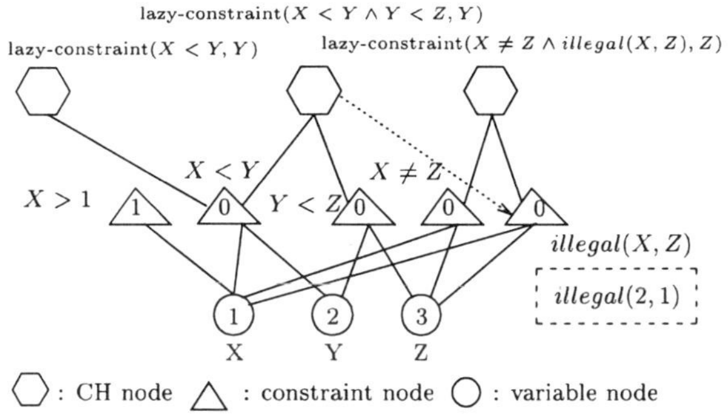

Figure 2: The new EGENET network of an example CSP.

The left CH node connects to the constraint node for $X < Y$. It in effect implements lazy arc consistency for the values of X with respect to the constraints on X and Y. This CH node will only generate new $illegal(X = v)$ combinations when it detects a label v in the domain of variable X which is inconsistent with all the values in the domain of Y. These new "$illegal(X = v)$" constraints will trigger the removal of the values from the domain of variable X in the convergence procedure of the new EGENET model.

The middle CH node performs lazy constraint consistency on the conjunction of constraints $X < Y$ and $Y < Z$ for variable Y. Hence it implements lazy path consistency. It will add $illegal(X = u, Z = w)$ combinations to the network, in the $illegal(X, Z)$ constraint. If each possibility for Y gives a positive penalty value then the pair for X and Z is path inconsistent.

The right CH node performs lazy constraint consistency on $X \neq Z \wedge illegal(X, Z)$ for variable Z, in effect performing lazy arc consistency for the variable pair X and Z since it examines the conjunction of all binary constraints over X and Z. It generates $illegal(X = v)$ combinations, which will remove values from the domain of X.

In general, lazy arc consistency can be implemented in the new EGENET model, by connecting a constraint handling node to all the binary constraints on X and Y, for each of the variables X and Y. These nodes will remove arc inconsistent values discovered during the EGENET search.

Similarly, lazy path consistency can be implemented by creating a lazy constraint node for each pair of constraints, and each variable that they share. Because this node will produce illegal combinations, an initially empty illegal constraint for the appropriate variables should be present in the network. Lazy path consistency will be of little benefit to EGENET unless it is combined with lazy arc consistency to remove values from the domain of variables.

Figure 3 illustrates the general structure of the resulting EGENET networks for checking lazy arc and lazy path consistency.

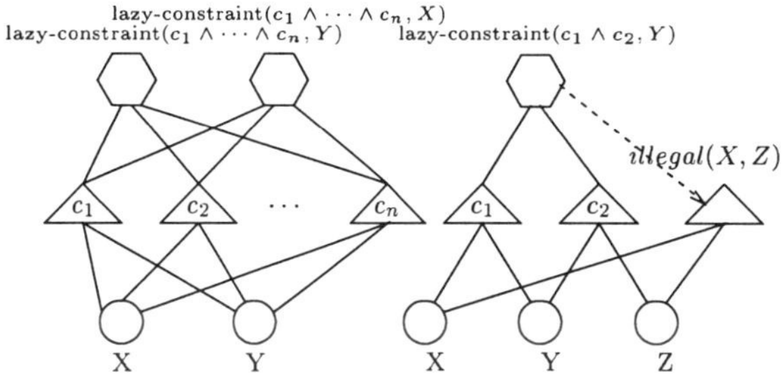

Figure 3: General approach to implementing lazy arc and path consistency.

In building a network including lazy consistency checking, our aim is to add the checking without substantially impacting on the speed of calculation for variable updates. Lazy arc consistency does not do so, since in calculating the input for a variable X we must evaluate all constraint nodes involving X in any case. For binary constraints, if there are n constraints involving X there can be at most n CH nodes involving X. Hence the amount of work required in calculating one variable update cannot increase more than a constant factor.

However, full lazy path consistency computation is expensive. For each variable there can be one CH node for each pair of constraints in which the variable appears. Clearly there can be n^2 consistency checks for a variable X involved in n constraints. This increase in work required for a variable update is unacceptable. To avoid this problem we randomly choose only one pair of constraints on a variable X to be checked in each convergence cycle. This limits the amount of extra work required at each step significantly. Because of the large number of convergence cycles it does allow the detection of path inconsistencies.

4.1 New Convergence Procedure

We need to modify the convergence procedure of EGENET to handle constraint handling nodes. The new convergence procedure, with the integration of lazy consistency techniques, can improve the search efficiency by identifying redundant values or compound labels, and detect unsatisfiability of CSPs.

The new network convergence procedure is basically the same as the convergence procedure of the original EGENET discussed in Section 2. We only have to modify the part for calculating the input for a value (**input**).

```
input(X, v)
   input := 0
   S := nodes above node X
   while (S ≠ ∅)
      remove node n from S
      if (n.type = CH ∧ n.var = X) then
         execute_ch(n, X, v)
      elseif (n.type = constr) then
         S := S ∪ nodes above n
         penalty := calc_penalty(n)
         if (n is unary ∧ penalty > 0) then
            D_X := D_X − {v}
            if (D_X = ∅) then
               signal "the CSP is unsatisfiable"
               terminate with failure
            endif
            return largest integer
         endif
         input += penalty
      endif
   endwhile
   return input
```

```
execute_ch(n, X_j, v)
   let {X_1, ..., X_k} = vars(n)
   if (v is the first value in the domain of X_j)
      then inconsistent(n) := true
   endif
   if (sum of nodes connected to n = 0)
      then inconsistent(n) := false
   endif
   if (inconsistent(n) ∧ v is the last value in the
      domain of X_j)
      then add illegal(X_1 = v_1, ..., X_{j-1} = v_{j-1},
         X_{j+1} = v_{j+1}, ..., X_k = v_k)
   endif
```

During the update of variable X the input for each value v in the domain of X is calculated using **input**(X, v). The **calc_penalty**(n) function returns the penalty value of a constraint or intermediate node n for the current variable assignments. It can be efficiently implemented using the values at its child nodes.

The **execute_ch**(n, X, v) function provides lazy constraint consistency checking for a CH node n. It is an implementation of lazy constraint consistency where the looping over values is external. It makes use of a global array variable *inconsistent* for keeping information over successive multiple calls during variable update.

Node consistency is enforced by using unary constraints or illegal combinations "$illegal(X_i = v)$" generated by CH nodes to eliminate values from the domain of variables. There is no extra cost since the penalty value for these constraints needs to be calculated in any case. After the removal of a node inconsistent value, the algorithm checks whether the domain of variable X is empty. When this happens, it will signal the unsatisfiability of the CSP and terminate with failure. This gives the new EGENET model the capability to detect the unsatisfiability of a CSP.

An example execution of the network illustrated in Figure 2 is as follows. Updating variable X, we calculate the input for value 1. Examining the $X > 1$ node we find the value is node inconsistent and it is removed from the domain of X. For value 2 we obtain penalty 0 from $X > 1$, penalty 1 from $X < Y$, penalty 0 from $X \neq Z$ and penalty 0 from $illegal(X, Z)$, for a total of 1. For value 3 we obtain penalty 0 from $X > 1$, penalty 2 from $X < Y$, penalty 1 from $X \neq Z$ and penalty 0 from $illegal(X, Z)$, for a total of 3. None of the CH nodes involve X so they are ignored. The minimum input is for value 2, so X is set to this.

Updating Y we make the following calculations:

Y	$X < Y$	$Y < Z$	*input*	$X < Y \wedge Y < Z$
1	2	0	2	2
2	1	0	1	1
3	0	1	1	1

Because one value for the node $X < Y$ is 0, the CH node above has not detected an inconsistency. But all values for $X < Y \wedge Y < Z$ are positive, hence this CH node generates $illegal(X = 2, Z = 3)$. which is added to the illegal constraint for X and Z. Y stays at value 2 since it is a minimal input value.

Updating Z we make the following calculations:

Z	$Y < Z$	$X \neq Z$	$ill(X, Z)$	*input*	$X \neq Z \wedge$ $ill(X, Z)$
1	3	0	1	4	1
2	2	1	0	3	1
3	1	0	1	2	1

Because all values for $X \neq Z \wedge illegal(X, Z)$ are positive, the CH node generates $illegal(X = 2)$. Z stays at value 3 since it is the minimal input value.

Updating X results in the removal of the value $X = 2$ using the generated illegal combination. So X must take the value 3. Updating Y generates $illegal(X = 3)$ from the leftmost CH node. When X is next updated the inconsistency is reported.

5 Computational Experiments

To demonstrate the efficiency of lazy consistency for EGENET, we have built a prototype implementation of EGENET with GCC version 2.7.2 on Digital Unix version 3.2F. We compare the benchmarks with the original EGENET on randomly generated and real-life binary CSPs on a DEC AlphaServer 8400 running at 300Mhz. The CPU time is measured in seconds. All the data are averages over 10 runs. We compare against various modifications of EGENET. EGENET-AC is the EGENET algorithm with a preprocessing step of AC-4 which is used to remove arc inconsistent values from the domains of variables, then EGENET is executed on the resulting equivalent CSP. EGENET-LA stands for an EGENET network implementing lazy arc consistency as illustrated in Figure 3. EGENET-PC is EGENET with a preprocessing step of first path consistency via PC-4 and then arc consistency via AC-4. EGENET is executed on the resulting CSP with reduced domains. EGENET-LP is EGENET with both lazy path consistency and lazy arc consistency. In each convergence cycle only one pair of constraints per variable are checked for path consistency. Illegal combinations that are generated are kept in a single illegal constraint. All constraints on a pair of variables (including *illegal* constraints) are checked for lazy arc consistency in each convergence cycle.

For arc consistency, the figures in square brackets denote the average number of arc inconsistent values detected and removed by the version. For path consistency, two figures are given in square brackets. The first figure is the average number of arc inconsistent values, and the second one is the average number of path inconsistent tuples (illegal combinations) identified by the algorithm. A "*" symbol is used to denote the occurrence of resource exhaustion in the network, and an exclamation mark is used to mean that the model detects unsatisfiability of the CSP, and a question mark indicates running out of memory in the preprocessing stage.

We compare the various consistency approaches with the original EGENET model on real-life examples of binary CSPs from the radio link frequency assignment problems (RLFAP) [12], and on a set of hard random binary CSPs. These random binary CSPs gives us a more objective testbed to evaluate the performance of the improved models.

Radio Link Frequency Assignment Problems (RLFAP)

The radio link frequency assignment problems are real-life examples of binary CSPs coming from military applications. The problem is to assign frequencies (values) to radio links (variables). There are eleven instances which involve different optimisation criteria. In these problems, there are only two types of binary constraints between a pair of variables X_i and X_j as: $|X_i - X_j| > k$ or $|X_i - X_j| = k$, where k being a positive integer. The number of possible values for k are limited. We examine the first four RLFAP problems. The convergence cycle limit for all these benchmarks is $1,000,000$.

Figure 4 shows the results of using EGENET, EGENET-LA, EGENET-AC and EGENET-LP on the RFLAP problems. The second and third columns give the number of variables and constraints in each problem.

EGENET-LA and EGENET-LP perform better than the original EGENET when the problem is difficult (Prob. 4). This is because both of them deduce useful information to remove redundant values or tuples, which can help the convergence procedure of EGENET to avoid unpromising network states which can never lead to a solution. This illustrates the advantages of lazy consistency for EGENET when the problem is soluble. EGENET-LA performs the best among all the models. For these problems lazy arc consistency discovers exactly the right amount of useful information to improve the search. The extra information uncovered by EGENET-LP does not further improve the search, but adds extra cost to the convergence procedure.

When the problem is easy, as in the first three cases, both EGENET-LA and EGENET-LP do not find information that removes values from the domain of variables. But their timings are not much larger than that of the original EGENET. This shows that lazy consistency methods do not add much cost to the convergence procedure.

EGENET-AC cannot solve any of the problems except the smallest due to space consumption, since the AC-4 algorithm uses space to improve speed. It does not seem very applicable to large real-life problems.

Prob.	nvar.	nctr.	EGENET	EGENET-LA	EGENET-AC	EGENET-LP
1	916	5548	107.7s	121.0s[0]	?	117.7s[0,138.5]
2	200	1235	7.550s	8.042s[0]	253.3[0]	8.192s[0,29.5]
3	400	2760	28.15s	30.45s[0]	?	30.79s[0,67]
4	680	3967	33663s	7953s[1348]	?	15436s[1367,71640]

Figure 4: Results for RFLAP problems.

Even in the second case where it returns an answer, EGENET-AC performs the worst among the models. This shows that the cost for full arc consistency may be very high, dominating the time to find a solution.

Hard Random Binary CSPs

We experimented with random binary CSPs of size 10×10: that is 10 variables each with a domain of size 10. Two parameters, $P1$ and $P2$ are involved in the generation of these random binary CSPs. $P1$ is the percentage that two variables are constrained in a CSP, and $P2$ is the percentage of legal compound labels for any binary constraint between two variables in the CSP. Five cases are generated for each combination of $(P1, P2)$ in the hardest region[6], $50 \geq P1 \leq 90, 10 \geq P2 \leq 50$. For each case, we ran all the algorithms ten times and calculate the medians. All the figures reported for these random binary CSPs are averages of the 5 medians over the total 50 runs for each data point. The convergence cycle limit for all these benchmarks is set at $100,000$. A "$*$" symbol or exclamation mark, means that all the test cases exhibit the same phenomenon indicated by that particular symbol. When a fraction x/n appears before a symbol, it means x out n cases exhibits the phenomenon indicated by the symbol. For the remaining $n - x$ cases, the algorithm succeeds in finding a solution.

Figure 5 shows the results of EGENET, EGENET-LA, EGENET-AC, EGENET-LP and EGENET-PC on a set of hard random binary CSPs. In general, both EGENET-LA and EGENET-LP better the original EGENET when the problem is insoluble. When the problem is soluble, the timing statistics of EGENET-LA and EGENET-LP do not differ significantly from those of the original EGENET. This again illustrates how lazy consistency methods do not add much extra cost to the convergence procedure.

EGENET-LP performs the best in all the cases since it can deduce additional useful information to improve the search, compared to lazy arc consistency. EGENET-LA performs very closely to EGENET-AC when the problem is insoluble. This shows the computation cost of lazy consistency is very low for the total $100,000$ convergence cycles compared to the full cost of arc-consistency on these small-size CSPs.

For soluble CSPs, as in the cases when $(P1 = 50, P2 = 40), (P1 = 50, P2 = 50)$ and $(P1 = 60, P2 = 50)$, EGENET-LA is faster than EGENET-AC. This is because EGENET-LA does not need to pay the whole cost for enforcing full arc-consistency, part of which may not be relevant to the search in EGENET. This demonstrates the advantages of lazy consistency method as compared to the conventional consistency methods on these random CSPs.

Moreover, EGENET-LP betters EGENET-PC on all instances of these small-sized CSPs since it avoids all the path inconsistent variable assignments only revelant to the current position in the search without paying any extra computation expense to enforce path consistency to other parts of the search space which may never be visited by the EGENET search.

[6]We mean the region where $P1$ is large and $P2$ is small, that is there are few or no solutions for any generated CSPs.

Acknowledgements

The authors wish to thank Edward Tsang and Andrew Davenport for their suggestion of useful references. This research project is supported by a small grant from the Australian Research Council.

References

[1] C. Bessière, E. Freuder, and J.-C. Régin. Using inference to reduce arc consistency computation. Technical report, University of New Hampshire, 1995.

[2] A. Davenport. A comparison of complete and incomplete algorithms in the easy and hard regions. Technical report, Department of Computer Science, University of Essex, 1995.

[3] A. Davenport, E. Tsang, C. Wang, and K. Zhu. GENET: A connectionist architecture for solving constraint satisfaction problems by iterative improvement. In *Proceedings of AAAI'94*, 1994.

	P1 = 50				
P2	EGENET	EGENET-LA	EGENET-AC	EGENET-LP	EGENET-PC
10	115.8s (*)	0.003s[52.8] (!)	0.009s[63.6] (!)	0.017s[57.4, 54.3] (!)	0.247s[57.8, 658.8](!)
20	112.4s (*)	0.017s[52.6] (!)	0.000s[70.6] (!)	0.014s[52.1, 105.2](!)	0.382s[76.8, 765.0] (!)
30	108.2s (*)	77.81s[27.9] (4/5*)	72.00s[31.8] (4/5*)	0.110s[55.3, 263.9](!)	0.574s[75.2, 835.0] (!)
40	0.103s	0.082s[0.5]	0.103s[1.8]	0.065s[0.5, 31.1]	0.928s[2.0, 220]
50	0.010s	0.014s[0.0]	0.023s[0.0]	0.010s[0.0, 0.9]	0.968s[2.4, 272.4]
	P1 = 60				
P2	EGENET	EGENET-LA	EGENET-AC	EGENET-LP	EGENET-PC
10	138.8s (*)	0.010s[59.9] (!)	0.003s[74.0] (!)	0.015s[57.8,55.5](!)	0.308s[72.6,1020] (!)
20	135.2s (*)	0.007s[53.7] (!)	0.007s[69.8] (!)	0.010s[58.5,106.0](!)	0.480s[73.6,1239] (!)
30	131.3s (*)	48.22s[47.7] (2/5*)	44.52s[51.0] (2/5*)	0.057s[56.7,231.5](!)	0.728s[75.0,1233] (!)
40	100.5s (4/5*)	107.2s[2.0] (4/5*)	99.30s[2.4] (4/5*)	0.388s[46.4,450.4](4/5!)	1.055s[73.0,1224.8] (4/5!)
50	0.034s	0.028s[0.0]	0.045s[0.0]	0.027s[0.0,5.1]	1.393s[1.7,104.7]
	P1 = 70				
P2	EGENET	EGENET-LA	EGENET-AC	EGENET-LP	EGENET-PC
10	159.2s (*)	0.005s[59.7] (!)	0.003s[76.4] (!)	0.012s[62.2,60.3] (!)	0.350s[74.4,1314] (!)
20	155.3s (*)	0.014s[57.9] (!)	0.003s[79.4] (!)	0.002s[59.4,109.1] (!)	0.570s[75.8,1697] (!)
30	150.8s (*)	30.43s[56.5] (1/5*)	27.72s[66.0] (1/5*)	0.043s[61.6,246.1] (!)	0.832s[77.0,1675] (!)
40	144.6s (*)	151.5s[3.6] (*)	139.2s[3.6] (*)	0.352s[61.8,606.9] (!)	1.270s[74.8,1523] (!)
50	2.892s (1/5*)	29.72s[0.6] (1/5*)	28.90s[0.8] (1/5*)	0.590s[12.9,236.7] (1/5!)	1.867s[17.4,320.6] (1/5!)
	P1 = 80				
P2	EGENET	EGENET-LA	EGENET-AC	EGENET-LP	EGENET-PC
10	185.5s (*)	0.005s[65.3] (!)	0.000s[67.2] (!)	0.000s[67.9,61.4] (!)	0.409s[65.6,1857] (!)
20	180.8s (*)	0.007s[61.0] (!)	0.009s[79.8] (!)	0.003s[61.2,117.8] (!)	0.653s[70.6,2496] (!)
30	174.5s (*)	0.193s[69.9] (!)	0.017s[83.0] (!)	0.038s[61.9,241.6] (!)	0.982s[78.8,2396] (!)
40	167.1s (*)	168.7s[3.2] (*)	161.2s[3.2] (*)	0.240s[63.6,583.7] (!)	1.445s[81.8,2036] (!)
50	96.32s (3/5*)	99.35s[0.6] (3/5*)	95.22s[0.6] (3/5*)	1.110s[39.6,694.9] (3/5!)	2.165s[78.8,1901] (3/5!)
	P1 = 90				
P2	EGENET	EGENET-LA	EGENET-AC	EGENET-LP	EGENET-PC
10	206.8s (*)	0.002s[68.0] (!)	0.002s[70.8] (!)	0.000s[64.1,57.5] (!)	0.465s[72.6,2368] (!)
20	201.0s (*)	0.007s[63.5] (!)	0.014s[80.0] (!)	0.000s[64.3,111.5] (!)	0.757s[79.2,3339] (!)
30	193.5s (*)	0.170s[70.9] (!)	0.017s[79.2] (!)	0.033s[65.7,270.1] (!)	1.095s[81.2,3170] (!)
40	185.3s (*)	181.0s[7.4] (*)	172.5s[7.4] (*)	0.167s[66.7,563.8] (!)	1.605s[77.4,2710] (!)
50	177.4s (*)	183.3s[0.8] (*)	175.9s[0.8] (*)	1.035s[66.6,1092.2] (!)	2.377s[85.2,2237] (!)

Figure 5: Results for 10 × 10 Random Binary CSPs

[4] C. Han and C. Lee. Comments on mohr and herderson's path consistency algorithm. *Artificial Intelligence*, 36:125 – 130, 1988.

[5] P. V. Hentenryck. *Constraint Satisfaction in Logic Programming.* The MIT Press, 1987.

[6] ILOG. *Introduction to ILOG Solver Version 3.0.* The ILOG Company. http://www.ilog.fr/Press/english/Solver_3.html.

[7] D. Johnson, C. Aragon, L. McGeoch, and C. Schevon. Optimization by simulated annealing: an experimental evaluation; part ii, graph coloring and number partitioning. *Operations Research*, 39(3):378 – 406, 1991.

[8] J. Lee, H. Leung, and H. Won. Extending GENET for Non-Binary CSP's. In *Proceedings of IEEE 7th Int. Conf. on Tools with Artificial Intelligence*, 1995.

[9] J. Lee, H. Leung, and H. Won. Towards a more efficient stochastic constraint solver. In *Proceedings of Principles and Practice of Constraint Programming (CP96)*, 1996.

[10] A. Mackworth. Consistency in networks of relations. *Artificial Intelligence*, 8:99 – 118, 1977.

[11] R. Mohr and T. Henderson. Arc and path consistency revisited. *Artificial Intelligence*, 28:225 – 233, 1986.

[12] S. Tiourine, C. Hurkens, and J. K. Lenstra. An overview of algorithmic approaches to frequency assignment problems. Technical report, Eindhoven University of Technology, August 1995.

[13] E. Tsang. *Foundations of Constraint Satisfaction.* Academic Press, 1993.

[14] C. Wang and E. Tsang. Solving satisfaction problems using neural-networks. In *Proceedings of IEEE 2nd Int. Conf. on Artificial Neural Networks*, 1991.

Session D.2

Evolutionary Computation

Session Chair:
Nick Gessler, University of California at Los Angeles, USA

Fuzzy Approaches to Acquiring Experimental Knowledge in Cultural Algorithms

Robert G. Reynolds and ChanJin Chung
Dept. of Computer Science
Wayne State University
Detroit, Michigan 48202
reynolds@cs.wayne.edu jcc@cs.wayne.edu

Abstract
Self-adaptation has been widely used in Evolutionary Computational models. Angeline [1] defines three distinct adaptive levels, which are: population, individual, and component level. Cultural algorithms have been shown to provide a framework in which to model self-adaptation at all of these levels. Here, we examine the role that different forms of knowledge can play in the self-adaptation process at the population level for evolution-based function optimizers. An acceptance function using a fuzzy inference engine is employed to select acceptable individuals for forming the generalized knowledge in the belief space. Evolutionary programming is used to implement the population space. The results suggest that the use of a cultural framework can produce substantial performance improvements in execution time and accuracy for a given set of function minimization problems.

1 Introduction

Evolutionary Computation (EC) methods have been successful in solving many diverse problems in search and optimization due to the unbiased nature of their operations which still perform well in situations with little or no domain knowledge [5]. However, there can be considerable improvement in EC's performance when acquired problem solving knowledge during evolution is used to bias the problem solving process in order to identify patterns in their performance environment [10,11,3]. These patterns are used to influence the generation of candidate solutions, promote more instances of desirable candidates, or to reduce the number of less desirable candidates in the population.

Adaptive evolutionary computation takes place when an EC system is able to incorporate such knowledge into its representation and operators in order to facilitate the pruning and promoting activities mentioned above. These adaptations can take place at three different scales: the population level, the individual level, and the component level [1]. At the population level, aspects of the system parameters that control all elements of the population can be modified. At the individual level, aspects of the system that control the action of specific individuals can be modified. Component level adaptive ECs dynamically alter how the individual components of each individual will be manipulated independently.

In human societies, culture can be viewed as a vehicle for the storage of information that is globally accessible to all members of the society and that can be useful in guiding their problem solving activities. As such, groups that are able to support a cultural tradition can use their cultural heritage as a mechanism in which to bias the generation of individuals on at least a phenotypic level by facilitating the production of phenotypes that are promising in a given environment on the one hand and deterring the production of phenotypes that are less likely to be productive on the other. Cultural Algorithms have been developed in order to model the evolution of the cultural component of an evolutionary computational system over time as it accumulates experience [10,11]. As a result, cultural algorithms can provide an explicit mechanism for global knowledge and a useful framework within which to model self-adaptation in an EC system.

In this study, the population component of the Cultural Algorithm will be Evolutionary Programming(EP) and the global knowledge that has been learned by the population will be expressed as normative and situational knowledge. A fuzzy inference engine is used to calculate the acceptance function. Three influence functions are developed based on normative and/or situational knowledge in the belief space. Three population only EP systems are tested in order to compare results with cultured EPs.

1082-3409/97 $10.00 © 1997 IEEE

2 EP and Self-Adaptation

Evolutionary Computation can be generally described by the following equation using Fogel's notation [6]:

$$\mathbf{x}^{t+1} = s(v(\mathbf{x}^t))$$

where $\mathbf{x}^t$ is the population of solutions at iteration t under a specified representation, $v(\ )$ is the variation operator to be applied to generate new solutions, and $s(\ )$ is the selection operator that determines which candidate solution will survive in the next population $\mathbf{x}^{t+1}$. The following is the basic EP algorithm. There are many variations of EP according to the different v as described in the subsections from 2.2.

2.1 A basic EP Algorithm

This is a basic EP algorithm skeleton [5] which will be the same for all other EP versions.

(1) Generate an initial population of p candidate solutions for n parameters into $x_{[1..p,1..n]}$ at random.

(2) Assess the performance for each parent solution using the given objective (evaluation, or performance) function f.

(3) Generate p new offspring solutions from $x_{[1..p,1..n]}$ by applying the variation operator, v. Now there are $2p$ solutions in the population.

(4) Assess the performance score of each offspring using the given objective function f.

(5) For each individual, select c competitors at random from the population of $2p$ size. Next, conduct pairwise competitions between the individual and the competitors. This procedure can be described as: For each x_i, $i = 1,\cdots,2p$, the number of wins, w_i is assigned according to:

$$w_i = \sum_{t=1}^{c} w_i^* \qquad w_i^* = \begin{cases} 1, & \text{if } f(x_i) \le f(x_o) \\ 0, & \text{otherwise} \end{cases}$$

where $o \neq i$, the index for a opponent $o = truncate(2pu+1)$. $truncate(x)$ denotes the greatest integer less than or equal to x, c is the number of competitions, and $u \sim U(0,1)$, uniform random variable.

(6) Select the p solutions that have the greatest number of wins (w_i) to be the parents for the next generation.

(7) The process returns to step 3 unless the available execution time is exhausted or an acceptable solution has been discovered.

Step (5) and (6) are procedures for the selection operator s usually used in EP. This is called as tournament selection mechanism.

2.2 Component level Self-Adaptation mechanism

Schwefel [12] devised a method for Evolution Strategies to self-adapt σ which can be used to calculate mutation step sizes. This method can be represented as:

$$\mathbf{X}^{t+1} = s(v(\mathbf{X}^t))$$

where X is a composite structure of both real number x and σ. In this paper we use the following notation to represent this structure: $\mathbf{X} = \langle x, \sigma \rangle$. Here, we denote jth parameter value for ith individual as simply $x_{i,j}$, and also jth σ value for ith individual as simply $\sigma_{i,j}$. Variation operator in this method was defined as follows. For all components, $i = 1,\cdots,p$ and $j = 1,\cdots,n$

$$x_{p+i,j} = x_{i,j} + \sigma_{i,j} \cdot N_{i,j}(0,1)$$

$$\sigma_{p+i,j} = \sigma_{i,j} \cdot \exp(\tau' \cdot N_{i,j}(0,1) + \tau \cdot N_{i,j}(0,1))$$

where $N_{i,j}(0,1)$ is a realization of a Gaussian normal deviate for the jth parameter of the ith individual. $x_{p+i,j}$ is an offspring of $x_{i,j}$ before selection. The offspring's step size is a lognormal perturbation of the parent's step size. The global factor $\tau' \cdot N_{i,j}(0,1)$ allows for an overall change of the mutability, whereas $\tau \cdot N_{i,j}(0,1)$ allows for individual changes of the step sizes. Recommended setting for the parameters τ and τ' is $\tau' = (\sqrt{2\sqrt{n}})^{-1}$, $\tau = (\sqrt{2n})^{-1}$.

2.3 Individual level Self-Adaptation mechanism

Here we developed an individual level self-adaptive EP which can be represented as:

$$\langle \mathbf{X}, \mathbf{age} \rangle^{t+1} = s(v(\langle \mathbf{X}, \mathbf{age} \rangle^t))$$

where age_i means the age for the individual i. This represents an survival count for an individual. When an individual is produced by applying the mutation operation, the age is set to zero. After tournament selection, if an individual survives, the count is increased by one. If the survival count reaches the number of individuals in the population, then the counter is re-initialized as one. The reason for this is that if the age of an individual is old, that means the individual might be trapped in a local optima. In order to escape it, larger perturbation may be required. If we incorporate this idea of the age information into Schwefel's self-adaptive method, the variation operator is, for all components $i = 1,\cdots,p$ and $j = 1,\cdots,n$:

$$x_{p+i,j} = x_{i,j} + \sigma_{i,j} \cdot age_i \cdot N_{i,j}(0,1)$$

$$\sigma_{p+i,j} = \sigma_{i,j} \cdot \exp(\tau' \cdot N_{i,j}(0,1) + \tau \cdot N_{i,j}(0,1))$$

3 Cultural Algorithms and How to Culture EP

Cultural Algorithms (CA) are computational models that consist of a social population and a belief space. The experience of individuals selected from the population space by the *acceptance function* is used to generate problem solving knowledge that resides in the *belief space*. The belief space stores and manipulates the knowledge acquired from the experience of individuals in the population space. This knowledge can control the evolution of the population component by means of the *influence* function. Each basic CA component and its relationships are depicted in figure 1 where **X** is a population; *s* is a selection operator; *v* is a variation operator; *f* is the performance function; *B* is the belief space; *Accept* is the acceptance function; *Adjust* is a belief space operator that adjusts or updates the belief space knowledge, *B*; and *Influence* is a set of influence functions to be used to influence the variation operator *v*. *Accept* and *Influence* together represent the communication protocol for a Cultural Algorithm.

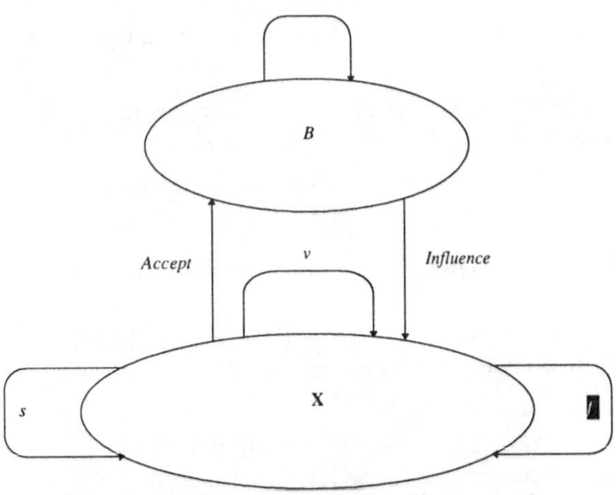

Figure 1 Cultural Algorithm Framework

The evolution of the population **X** can be represented in terms of Cultural Algorithms as [3]:

$$\mathbf{X}^{t+1} = s(v(\mathbf{X}^t, Influence(Adjust(B^t, Accept(\mathbf{X}^t))))).$$

Note that the results of the influence function can influence any of the self-adaptive strategies, depending on the type of self-adaptation in the population.

There are two basic categories of knowledge that we will consider: *normative* and *situational.* Normative knowledge, expressed here in intervals, provides standards for individual behavior and guidelines within which individual adjustments can be made. Situational knowledge provides a set of exemplar cases that are useful for the interpretation of specific individual experience. While there are other types of knowledge that can be contained within a cultural system, these two forms were selected because they are viewed to be fundamental to the operation of cultural systems.

3.1 Belief space structure

The formal syntax of the belief space, *B*, defined in this study is a pair structure $< E, N_{[1..n]} >$, where *E* is a set of exemplars, in this case best individuals, that constitute the situational knowledge. The normative component, *N*, is a set of interval information for each *n* parameter. Each of the *N* intervals in the belief space is represented as a triple$< I, L, U >$. *I* denotes the closed *interval*, that is a continuous set of real numbers *x* represented as a numeric pair:

$$I = [l,u] = \{x | l \le x \le u\}$$

l(lower bound) and *u* (upper bound) are initialized by the given domain values. L_j represents the performance score of the lower bound *l* for parameter *j*. U_j represents the performance score of the upper bound *u* for parameter *j*. They are initialized as -∞ and +∞, respectively.

3.2 Acceptance functions

The acceptance function selects individuals who will impact the formation of the current belief space. A number of different classes of acceptance functions can be employed. One class of functions is static in nature and use only information about the absolute ranking (top 10%, top 20%, top 30%, top 40%, and top 50% of individuals in the population), or the relative ranking (above average individuals) to select the individuals to be used to update the belief space. For example, if the top 20% rule is applied, then just the top 20% individuals impact the belief space in each generation

A second class of functions, called as "modified-top20%" is also static in nature but uses temporal information about the number of generations used so far to determine the number of individuals accepted at time(generation number) *t*. The number of individuals who will impact the current belief space, α, is decided by the following function:

$$\alpha = p \cdot \beta + \lfloor p \cdot \beta / t \rfloor$$

where *p* is the size of the population and *t* is the current generation number. If 0.2 is used for *β*, this is similar to selecting the top 20%. However, it will select more than that in the beginning of the search process and gradually reduce the number as the process proceeds. As in simulated annealing, more information is pumped into the belief space at the onset than at the end.

However, we cannot be certain as to the amount of adjustment that is necessary. In order to address the problem, a third class of acceptance function is suggested. Similar to human culture, it would be desirable to increase the current acceptance percentage;

if many individuals are performing worse than before, it would be desirable to decrease the current acceptance percentage. How can we design something like this? Actually, people are living in an uncertain world. Everything is a matter of degree. Therefore, the goal here is to make the acceptance functions more flexible by employing a fuzzy logic controller.

Previous research in the area of computational intelligence suggests that two basic kinds of information are useful in guiding the selection of individuals by the acceptance function. For example, in Simulated Annealing the modifications made to an individual are a function of the time step or number of generations [2]. On the other hand, the performance (absolute or relative) of the current population can also be an important factor in determining step sizes as suggested by Rechenberg in Evolution Strategies [12]. Here, the number of acceptable individuals is determined by a fuzzy acceptance function whose inputs are the degree of the individual success-ratio, and the current time step, as shown in figure 2.

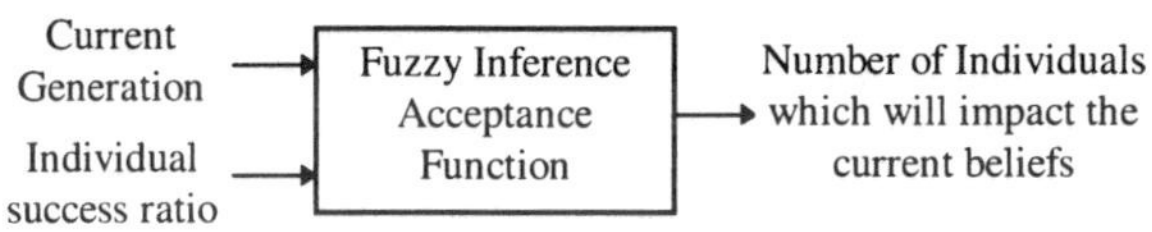

Figure 2 Fuzzy Inference Acceptance Function

The antecedent membership functions here use linear functions for the fuzzification process. The functions are given in figures 3 and 4. In this process, a set of input parameters, current generation number and success ratio are mapped into one or more degrees of membership, e.g. II (initial), MM (middle), and FF (final); LO (low), ME (medium), and HI (high).

After the fuzzification, the inference rules shown in the rule base in table 1, are evaluated by combining their degrees of membership to form output strengths. The consequent membership function for each output strength is shown in figure 5.

The basic intuition used to design the fuzzy inference rules in table 1 is that if the current generation is early on in the evolution process (II) and the success ratio is low (LO), then accept a medium number, around the top 30% (BB) of individuals from the population. If the current generation is early on (II) and the success ratio is high (HI), then accept a larger number of individuals from the population around 40% (CC). If the current generation is near the end of the evolution process (FF) and the success ratio is low (LO), then accept a smaller number, around top 20% (AA) of individuals from the population. If the current generation is near the end (FF) and the success ratio is high (HI), then accept a medium number of individuals from the population, around 30% (BB).

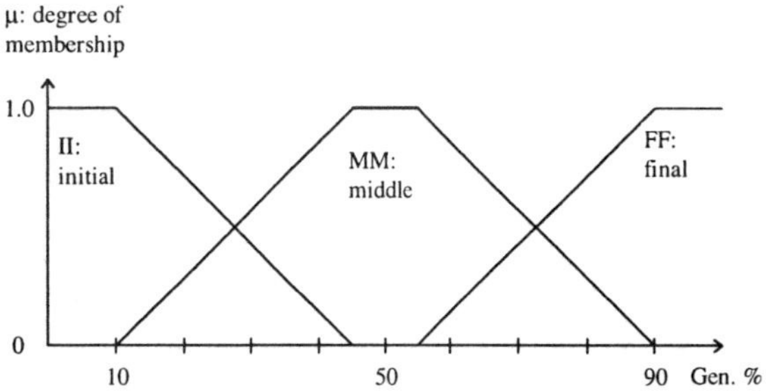

Figure 3 Membership functions for Current Generation

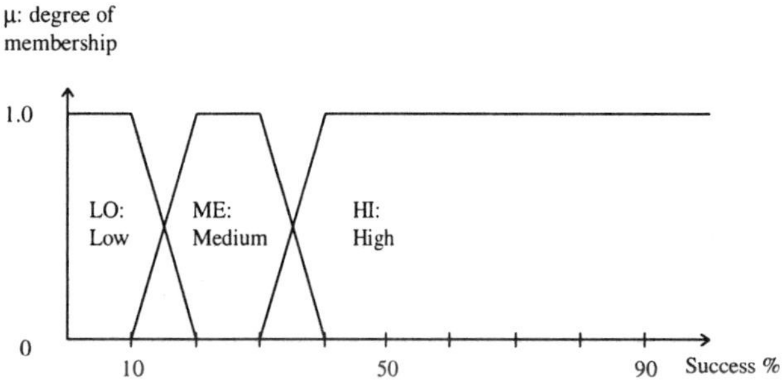

Figure 4 Membership fns for Success Ratio

	LO	ME	HI
II	BB (Rule1)	BB (Rule2)	CC (Rule3)
MM	AA (Rule3)	BB (Rule4)	BB (Rule5)
FF	AA (Rule6)	AA (Rule7)	BB (Rule8)

Table 1 Fuzzy Inference Rules

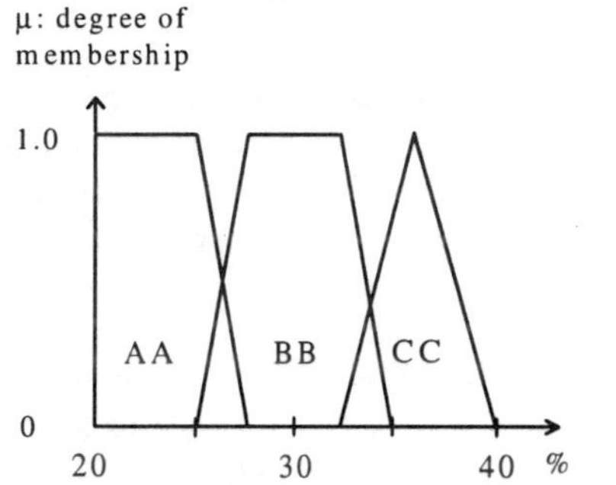

Figure 5 Membership fns for no. of individuals

3.3 Adjusting the belief space

Here, the situational knowledge consists of the current and previous best individuals found so far. That is, $E = \{\vec{E}^t, \vec{E}^{t-1}\}$, and this knowledge is updated by the following rule:

$$\vec{E}^{t+1} = \begin{cases} \vec{x}^t_{best} & if \quad f(\vec{x}^t_{best}) < f(\vec{E}^t) \\ \vec{E}^t & otherwise \end{cases}$$

where $\vec{x}^t_{best}$ denotes the best individual (solution parameter vector) in the population at time t.

The normative knowledge component in the belief space, N, is updated as follows. The parameter values for individuals selected by the acceptance function are used to calculate the current acceptable interval for each parameter in the belief space. The idea is to be conservative when narrowing the interval and be progressive when widening the interval. Therefore, we can formulate the interval update rule as follows. Here, i corresponds to the accepted individual with the lowest value for parameter j, and k is the accepted individual with the highest value for parameter j. For the left boundary and its score for parameter j:

$$l_j^{t+1} = \begin{cases} x_{i,j}^t & if\ x_{i,j}^t \le l_j^t \ or\ f(x_i^t) < L_j^t \\ l_j^t & otherwise \end{cases}$$

$$L_j^{t+1} = \begin{cases} f(x_i) & if\ x_{i,j} \le l_j^t \ or\ f(x_i) < L_j^t \\ L_j^t & otherwise \end{cases}$$

where the ith individual affects the lower bound for parameter j. l_j^t represents lower limit for parameter j at generation t and L_j^t denotes the performance score for it. For the right boundary and its score for parameter j:

$$u_j^{t+1} = \begin{cases} x_{k,j} & if\ x_{k,j} \ge u_j^t \ or\ f(x_k) < U_j^t \\ u_j^t & otherwise \end{cases}$$

$$U_j^{t+1} = \begin{cases} f(x_k) & if\ x_{k,j} \ge u_j^t \ or\ f(x_k) < U_j^t \\ U_j^t & otherwise \end{cases}$$

where kth individual affects the upper bound for parameter j. u_j^t represents upper limit for variable j at generation t and U_j^t denotes the performance score for it.

3.4 Cultured EP algorithm

Below is the pseudocode for a basic "cultured" EP algorithm. Steps (3) and (8), shown in bold characters, are the procedures added to the basic EP algorithm. Notice that step (4) is where the self-adaptation process takes place.

(1) Select an initial population of p candidate solutions from a uniform distribution within the given domain for each parameter from 1 to n.

(2) Assess the performance score of each parent solution by the given objective function f.

(3) Initialize the belief space with the given problem domain and candidate solutions. The structure of the belief space is given in 3.1.

(4) Generate new p offspring solutions by applying the variation operator, v as modified by the influence function, *Influence*. Now there are $2p$ solutions in the population.

(5) Assess the performance score of each offspring solutions by the given objective function f.

(6) For each individual, select c competitors at random from the population of $2p$ size. Conduct a pairwise competitions between the individual and the competitors.

(7) Select the p solutions that have the greatest number of wins to be parents for the next generation.

(8) Update the belief space by accepting individuals using the acceptance function in 3.2. The belief space update rule is described in 3.3.

(9) The process proceeds to step 4 unless the available execution time is exhausted or an acceptable solution has been discovered.

4 Cultured EP versions

The belief space knowledge can influence the evolutionary operator v, variation, in two ways: (1) determining the size of the changes, step size (2) and determining the direction of change, e.g. increase or decrease the current value. Four different instantiations of cultural algorithms are produced by using these different influence functions.

4.1 CAEP(Ns)

This version uses only normative knowledge for deciding the step size of mutation. For all components $i = 1,\cdots,p$ and $j = 1,\cdots,n$

$$x_{p+i,j} = x_{i,j} + size(I_j) \cdot N_{i,j}(0,1)$$

where $size(I_j)$ represents the size of the belief interval for the parameter j.

4.2 CAEP(Ns+S$_d$)

This version uses both normative knowledge to determine the step size, and situational knowledge to determine the direction as shown in the following, for all components $i = 1,\cdots,p$ and $j = 1,\cdots,n$

$$x_{p+i,j} = \begin{cases} x_{i,j} + |size(I_j) \cdot N_{i,j}(0,1)| & if\ x_{i,j} < E_j \\ x_{i,j} - |size(I_j) \cdot N_{i,j}(0,1)| & if\ x_{i,j} > E_j \\ x_{i,j} + size(I_j) \cdot N_{i,j}(0,1) & otherwise \end{cases}$$

If an individual's parameter value is less than that of the current best, then the absolute value of the calculated step size, $size(I_j)$, is added to the current parameter value. If an individual's parameter value is greater than that of the current best, then the absolute value of the step size, $size(I_j)$, is subtracted from the current parameter value. If an individual's parameter value is equal to that of the current best, then $size(I_j) \cdot N_{i,j}(0,1)$ is just added to the current parameter value. In this case the direction of mutation will be random.

4.3 CAEP(N$_{sd}$)

This version uses only normative knowledge to regulate for both mutation step size and direction. The basic idea behind this version is to perturb small in a random direction when the parameter value of a parent is in the acceptable range; otherwise perturb according to the current belief range found toward the left or right boundary of the current range in the belief space. For all components $i = 1,\cdots,p$ and $j = 1,\cdots,n$

$$x_{p+i,j} = \begin{cases} x_{i,j} + \left|size(I_j) \cdot N_{i,j}(0,1)\right| & \text{if } x_{i,j} < l_j \\ x_{i,j} - \left|size(I_j) \cdot N_{i,j}(0,1)\right| & \text{if } x_{i,j} > u_j \\ x_{i,j} + \beta \cdot size(I_j) \cdot N_{i,j}(0,1) & \text{otherwise} \end{cases}$$

where l_j and u_j means the current lower limit and upper limit in the belief space for the parameter j respectively. β is set to 0.2.

5 Implementation

The level of self-adaptation supported for each of the implemented systems described above is given in table 2. One of our goal will be to determine the level of self-adaptation that is most effective in solving different classes of optimization problems.

Self-adaptive level	System Name
Component Level	Schwefel's self-adaptive EP
Individual Level	Individual level self-adaptive EP
Population Level	CAEP(Ns), (Ns+Sd), (Nsd): with 8 different acceptance functions

Table 2 Implemented Systems

For a fair comparison, we use the same population size (p=40), the same maximum number of function evaluations, the same number of maximum generations, and same number of tournament competitions (c=40). Also evolution starts from the same initial population for each problem. The initial sigma used for Schwefel's self-adaptive EP was 5.0.

We investigate how the different self-adaptation mechanisms and knowledge types affects their relative problem solving performance on 34 different function minimization problems. The problem specification is shown in Table 3 and Figure 6. The selected functions represent a broad spectrum of function optimization problems and reflect different degrees of complexity [2,4,8,9,12]. The first column in Table 3 gives the identification number of the function in this study and the second column gives the name of the function. The third column specifies the search space(domains) S. The fourth column gives the best known solution to each problem. The fifth column, n, provides the numbers of parameters or dimensionality used. The last column gives the maximum number of generation used.

6 Test Results and Conclusions

Table 4 shows the average success percentage of 15 runs for all 34 test cases for three CAEP systems using different acceptance functions. The fuzzy acceptance function worked best for the CAEP(Nsd) system, though it did not improve CAEP(Ns) and CAEP(Ns+Sd).

	Ns	Ns+Sd	Nsd
top10%	52.3%	59.9%	53.8%
top20%	45.6%	56.8%	81.5%
mod. top20%	45.9%	57.0%	81.9%
top30%	43.3%	52.7%	81.6%
top40%	38.8%	50.4%	79.9%
above median	34.4%	49.0%	73.0%
above average	37.6%	47.8%	78.1%
fuzzy	43.3%	54.8%	**84.2%**

Table 4 Average Success % for each CAEP system with different acceptance functions

Table 5(a)(b) shows detailed comparisons for each test case between population-only EPs and CAEP(Ns), CAEP(Ns+Sd), and CAEP(Nsd) with fuzzy acceptance functions. In Table 5, the first value in a cell gives the average CPU time taken, in milliseconds, to completion. Completion occurs if either the solution is found or the upper bound on the number of generations computed by the difficulty metric has been reached. The solution is said to be reached when 6 significant digits of the optimum are found. Otherwise, the process continues until the maximum number of generations is reached. The second value in parenthesis gives the percentage of the 15 runs that found the global minimum. The mean best solution value for the function at the maximum number of time step is given as the third value. The best system is shown in bold characters in the table. The best performer was selected based on the success ratio, that is the number of successful runs that found the solution. In case of a tie, first the mean best solution is used to break the tie. If there is still a tie, then the average completion time is used to make the choice.

The results show that one of the fuzzy cultured system, CAEP(Nsd) performed the best in 30 out of 34 optimization problems. Using a static acceptance function, the best system success ratio was 81.9% which was achieved by CAEP(Nsd)-modified-top20%. By using fuzzy acceptance function, here we have achieved the best success ratio which is 84.2%. This is due to the fact that since the CAEP(Nsd)-Fuzzy system uses normative knowledge produced via the generalization of experience, the fuzzy function provides more guidance to it in directing the generalization process than the others by picking the most appropriate number of individuals based upon the experience of the population.

Also based upon the above results, higher levels of self-adaptation appear to give better results in general, if knowledge is appropriately used. That is, a system with component level self-adaptation showed the lowest success ratio (49.9%); a system with individual level self-adaptation showed the median success ratio (52.3%); while systems with population level self-adaptation exhibited the highest average success ratio (61.3%).

The results in general demonstrate that the use of a cultural framework for self-adaptation in EP can produce substantial performance improvements as expressed in terms of CPU time, the percentage of finding global minima, and mean best. Also the use of fuzzy acceptancc function with CAEP(Nsd) system exhibits the best performance with a success ratio of 84.2% for a given 34 function minimization problems. Figure 7 shows an instance of the dynamic relationship between mutation success ratio and the number of individuals calculated from the fuzzy acceptance function for Ackley function (Function No. 9) with 30 parameters. When the individual mutation success ratio was high, a larger number of individuals more than top 20% was accepted to update the belief space. After generation number 950, when it found the near optimal point, it used just top 20% of individuals to impact the belief space. By allowing flexibility in the number of individuals included over time in the belief space, the resultant generalizations were less subject to error.

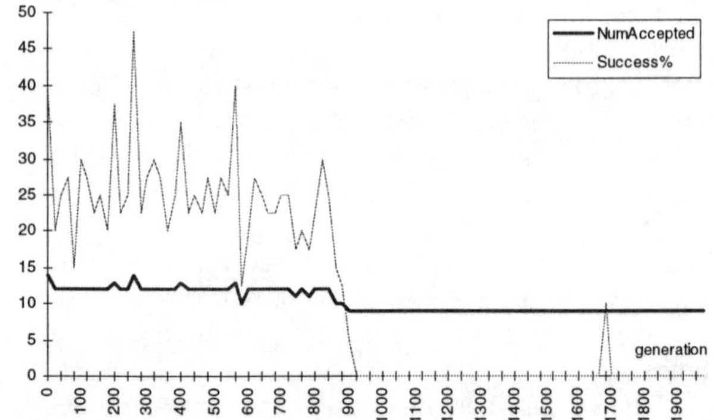

Figure 7 An instance of mutation success ratio and number of individuals calculated from Fuzzy Acceptance Function for Function No. 9 (Ackley)

References

[1] Peter A. Angeline, "Adaptive and Self-Adaptive Evolutionary Computation," in *Computation Intelligence*, Eds. Marimuthu Palaniswami, et. al., IEEE Press, New York, 1995, pp. 152-163.

[2] O. Bohachevsky, M.E. Johnson and M. L. Stein, "Generalized Simulated Annealing for Function Optimization," *Technometrics* 28(3), pp. 209-217

[3] ChanJin Chung, *Knowledge-Based Approaches to Self-Adaptation in Cultural Algorithms*, Ph.D. thesis, Wayne State University, 1997

[4] De Jong, K. A., *The analysis of the behavior of a class of genetic adaptive systems,* Doctoral dissertation, Univ. of Michigan, Ann Arbor

[5] David B. Fogel, *Evolutionary Computation: Toward a New Philosophy of Machine Intelligence*, IEEE Press, Piscataway, NJ, 1995

[6] David B. Fogel, "Using Fitness Distributions to Design More Efficient Evolutionary Computations," in *Proceedings of ICEC'96*, pp. 11-19.

[7] Hoffmeister, and T. Bäck, "Genetic Algorithms and Evolution Strategies: Similarities and Differences," Technical Report No. SYS-1/92, Systems Analysis Research Group, University of Dortmund, Dept. of Computer Science, Dortmund, Germany.

[8] K. Koon, and A. V. Sebald, "Some Interesting Test Functions for Evaluating Evolutionary Programming Strategies," in *Proceedings of the 4th Conference on EP*, 1995, pp.269-280

[9] Zbigniew Michalewicz, *Genetic Algorithms + Data Structures = Evolution Program*, (Second, Extended Edition,) Springer-Verlag, Berlin Heidelberg New York, 1994 (1st edition, 1992)

[10] Robert G. Reynolds, *An adaptive computer model of the evolution of agriculture for hunter-gatherers in the valley of Oaxaca, Mexico*, Doctoral dissertation, Univ. of Michigan, Ann Arbor, 1979

[11] Robert G. Reynolds, "An Introduction to Cultural Algorithms," in *Proceedings of the 3rd Annual Conference on Evolutionary Programming*, Sebald, A.V.; Fogel, L.J. (Editors), River Edge, NJ, World Scientific Publishing, 1994, pp. 131-139.

[12] Hans-Paul Schwefel, *Evolution and Optimum Seeking*, John Wiley & Sons, Inc., 1995

$f_1(x) = \sum_{i=1}^{n} x_i^2$ $\qquad f_2(x) = 100(x_1^2 - x_2)^2 + (1 - x_1)^2$

$f_3(x) = \sum_{i=1}^{5} \lfloor x_i \rfloor$

$f_4(x) = \sum_{i=1}^{n} i \cdot x_i^4$ $\qquad f_4'(x) = \sum_{i=1}^{n} [i \cdot x_i^4 + N(0,1)]$

$$f_5(x) = 1 \Big/ 0.002 + \sum_{j=1}^{25} \frac{1}{j + \sum_{i=1}^{2} (x_i - a_{ij})^6}$$

$$f_6(x) = x_1^2 + 2x_2^2 - 0.3\cos(3\pi x_1)\cos(4\pi x_2) + 0.3$$

$$f_7(x) = \sum_{i=1}^{n} \left[x_i^2 - 10\cos(2\pi x_i) + 10\right]$$

$$f_8(x) = 100(x_1^2 - x_2)^2 + (1 - x_1)^2 + 90(x_4 - x_3^2)^2 + (1 - x_3)^2 + 0.1\left((x_2 - 1)^2 + (x_4 - 1)^2\right) + 19.8(x_2 - 1)(x_4 - 1)$$

$$f_9(x) = -20\exp(-0.2\sqrt{1/n \cdot \sum_{i=1}^{n} x_i^2}) - \exp(\frac{1}{n}\sum_{i=1}^{n} \cos 2\pi x_i) + 20 + e$$

$$f_{10}(x) = \left[1 + (x_1 + x_2 + 1)^2 (19 - 14x_1 + 3x_1^2 - 14x_2 + 6x_1x_2 + 3x_2^2)\right] \cdot \left[30 + (2x_1 - 3x_2)^2 (18 - 32x_1 + 12x_1^2 + 48x_2 - 36x_1x_2 + 27x_2^2)\right]$$

$$f_{11}(x) = \left(4 - 2.1x_1^2 + \frac{x_1^4}{3}\right)x_1^2 + x_1x_2 + (-4 + 4x_2^2)x_2^2$$

$$f_{12}(x) = -\cos(x_1)\cos(x_2)e^{-(x_1-\pi)^2-(x_2-\pi)^2}$$

$$f_{13}(x) = -5\sin(x_1)\sin(x_2)\sin(x_3)\sin(x_4)\sin(x_5) - \sin(5x_1)\sin(5x_2)\sin(5x_3)\sin(5x_4)\sin(5x_5)$$

$$f_{14}(x) = \sum_{i=1}^{30}\left(\sum_{j=1}^{5}(ja_i^{j-1}x_{j+1}) - \left[\sum_{j=1}^{6}(a_i^{j-1}x_j)\right]^2 - 1\right)^2 + x_1^2, \quad a_i = \frac{i-1}{29}$$

$$f_{15}(x) = \frac{1}{2}\sum_{i=1}^{n}(x_i^4 - 16x_i^2 + 5x_i)$$

$$f_{16}(x) = \frac{1}{4000}\sum_{i=1}^{n} x_i^4 - \prod_{i=1}^{n} \cos(x_i \big/ \sqrt{i}) + 1$$

$$f_{17}(x)=\sum_{i=1}^{11}\left(a_i-\frac{x_1(b_i^2+b_ix_2)}{b_i^2+b_ix_3+x_4}\right)^2 \qquad f_{18}(x)=0.26(x_1^2+x_2^2)-0.48x_1x_2$$

$$f_{19}(x)=(x_1^2+x_2^2-2x_1)^2+0.25x_1$$

$$f_{20}(x)=-\sum_{i=1}^{n}\sin(x_i)\cdot\sin^{2m}\left(\frac{i\cdot x_i^2}{\pi}\right),\ m=20$$

$$f_{21}(x)=[1.5-x_1(1-x_2)]^2+[2.25-x_1(1-x_2^2)]^2+[2.625-x_1(1-x_2^3)]^2$$

$$f_{22}(x)=-\sum_{i=1}^{m}c_i\left(e^{-\|\bar{x}-A(i)\|^2/\pi}\cos(\pi\cdot\|\bar{x}-A(i)\|^2)\right),\ m=5$$

$$f_{23}(x)=\sum_{i=1}^{n}10^{i-1}x_i^2 \qquad f_{24}(x)=\sum_{i=1}^{n}\left(\sum_{j=1}^{i}x_j\right)^2$$

$$f_{25}(x)=\sum_{i=1}^{n}|x_i|+\prod_{i=1}^{n}|x_i| \qquad f_{26}(x)=\max_i\{|x_i|,\ 1\le i\le n\}$$

$$f_{27}(x)=\sum_{j=1}^{10}\left(e^{(-0.1jx_1)}-e^{(-0.1jx_2)}-x_3\left[e^{(-0.1j)}-e^{(-j)}\right]\right)^2$$

$$f_{28}(x)=\sum_{i=1}^{5}i\cos[(i+1)x_1+i]\cdot\sum_{i=1}^{5}i\cos[(i+1)x_2+i]$$

$$f_{29}(x)=a(x_2-bx_1^2+cx_1-d)^2+e(1-f)\cos(x_1)+e$$

$$f_{30}(x)=x_1^2+x_2^2-\cos(18x_1)-\cos(18x_2)$$

Figure 6 Function Test Cases

Fn	Fn Name	S	$f(x^*)$	n	*max. gen.*
1	Sphere	$[-5.12, 5.12]^n$	0	30	650
2	Rosenbrock	$[-6.0, 6.0]^n$	0	2	440
3	Step	$[-5.12, 5.12]^n$	-3.00000E+01	5	275
4	De Jong f4 w/o noise	$[-1.28, 1.28]^n$	0	30	650
4'	f4 with noise	$[-1.28, 1.28]^n$	0	30	650
5	Shekel's foxholes	$[-65.536, 65.536]^n$	9.98004E-01	2	440
6	Bohachevsky	$[-6.0, 6.0]^n$	0	2	320
7	Rastrigin	$[-5.12, 5.12]^n$	0	5	800
8	Colville	$[-10.0, 10.0]^n$	0	4	2120
9	Ackley	$[-32.0, 32.0]^n$	0	3	380
9'	Ackley'	$[-32.0, 32.0]^n$	0	30	2000
10	Goldstein-Price	$[-2.0, 2.0]^n$	3.00000E+00	2	320
11	6 hump camel back	$[-3.0, 3.0]^n$	-1.03160E+00	2	320
12	Easom	$[-100.0, 100.0]^n$	-1.00000E+00	2	320
13	Floudas	$[0.0, \pi]^n$	-6.00000E+00	5	800
14	Watson	$[-2.0, 2.0]^n$	2.28800E-03	6	3080
15	Koon's F3	$[-5.0, 5.0]^n$	-1.174985E+02	3	290
15'	Koon's F3	$[-5.0, 5.0]^n$	-1132.575	30	1100
16	Griewank	$[-600.0, 600.0]^n$	0	3	380
16'	Griewank	$[-600.0, 600.0]^n$	0	30	2000
17	Kowalik	$[-1.0, 1.0]^n$	3.0750E-04	4	2120
18	Matyas	$[-10.0, 10.0]^n$	0	2	320
19	Zettl	$[-2.0, 2.0]^n$	-3.7910E-03	2	320
20	Michalewicz	$[0.0, \pi]^n$	-4.68700E+00	5	800
21	Beale	$[-5.0, 5.0]^n$	0	2	320
22	Langerman	$[0.0, 10.0]^n$	-1.40000E+00	5	800
23	Ellipsoid	$[-5.12, 5.12]^n$	0	30	1100
24	Quadratic	$[-5.12, 5.12]^n$	0	30	1100
25	Schwefel 2.22	$[-10.0, 10.0]^n$	0	30	650
26	Schwefel 2.21	$[-100.0, 100.0]^n$	0	30	650
27	Box	$[-10.0, 10.0]^n$	0	3	560
28	Subert	$[-10.0, 10.0]^n$	-186.73	2	1160
29	Branin RCOS	[-5,10][0,15]	0.397887	2	1160
30	Rastrigin2D	$[-3.0, 3.0]^n$	-2.0	2	440

Table 3 Characteristics of Test Functions Used

Fn	Schwefel	Age	Ns-Fuzzy	Ns+Sd-Fuzzy	Nsd-Fuzzy
1	18078 (0%) 3.20010e+00	16730 (0%) 1.90861e+00	14288 (0%) 1.80092E+02	12987 (0%) 1.28607E+02	**4058 (100%)** **3.34982E-28**
2	3848 (13%) 3.14361e-03	2543 (73%) 7.26822e-06	2896 (93%) 1.49939E-07	**1007 (100%)** **2.04634E-24**	1184 (80%) 3.10322E-04
3	662 (100%) -3.00000e+01	538 (100%) -3.00000e+01	395 (100%) -3.00000E+01	**178 (100%)** **-3.00000E+01**	250 (100%) -3.00000E+01
4	19980 (0%) 4.81895e-01	17681 (0%) 1.35881e+00	14628 (0%) 9.66245E+01	13200 (0%) 2.61174E+01	**2413 (100%)** **4.87725E-49**
4'	12782 (80%) -9.47151e+00	10520 (100%) -8.26850e+00	18152 (0%) 9.57791E+01	16810 (0%) 2.68846E+01	**505 (100%)** **-2.06122E+01**
5	4515 (26%) 2.05698e+00	4766 (13%) 2.58555e+00	1917 (100%) 9.98004E-01	**838 (100%)** **9.98004E-01**	2753 (53%) 1.72564E+00
6	522 (100%) 0.00000e+00	827 (100%) 3.25622e-18	412 (100%) 0.00000E+00	195 (100%) 0.00000E+00	**176 (100%)** **0.00000E+00**
7	10372 (0%) 4.11250e+00	9027 (0%) 4.90847e+00	8827 (0%) 1.19912E+01	8143 (0%) 6.57734E+00	**3690 (73%)** **2.65322E-01**
8	23152 (0%) 5.17213e-01	22905 (0%) 1.33899e+00	31736 (0%) 3.98696E-01	**10526 (93%)** **4.98909E-07**	18315 (13%) 2.96171E-02
9	1462 (100%) -1.43982e-16	3290 (86%) 4.31225e-07	3108 (100%) 1.27710E-15	636 (100%) -1.43982E-16	**476 (100%)** **-1.43982E-16**
9'	64164 (0%) 9.82107e+00	62732 (0%) 1.68277e+01	72688 (0%) 2.06006E+01	53502 (0%) 2.04807E+01	**10016 (100%)** **3.64558E-15**
10	542 (100%) 3.00000e+00	1007 (100%) 3.00000e+00	426 (100%) 3.00000E+00	348 (100%) 3.00000E+00	**166 (100%)** **3.00000E+00**
11	**288 (100%)** **-1.03163e+00**	381 (100%) -1.03163e+00	2468 (7%) -1.03153E+00	451 (93%) -1.03162E+00	446 (100%) -1.03163E+00
12	760 (100%) -1.00000e+00	1636 (93%) -9.33333e-01	2859 (0%) -1.96022E-01	1848 (87%) -8.83025E-01	**388 (100%)** **-1.00000E+00**
13	2064 (100%) -6.00000e+00	2738 (100%) -6.00000e+00	4215 (100%) -6.00000E+00	880 (100%) -6.00000E+00	**428 (100%)** **-6.00000E+00**
14	47331 (0%) 1.26697e-02	45240 (0%) 7.39157e-03	42113 (0%) 1.04234E-01	**40594 (0%)** **4.06865E-03**	41128 (0%) 4.25991E-03
15	677 (100%) -1.17499e+02	1029 (100%) -1.17499e+02	1101 (100%) -1.17499E+02	348 (100%) -1.17499E+02	**253 (100%)** **-1.17499E+02**
15'	31332 (0%) -1.02217e+03	29077 (0%) -1.02964e+03	24984 (0%) -4.94748E+02	23155 (0%) -4.94748E+02	**8876 (73%)** **-1.14671E+03**
16	3532 (13%) 1.73105e-01	3756 (0%) 5.41692e+00	3511 (0%) 6.96466E-02	3490 (0%) 3.06521E-02	**5338 (40%)** **3.33903E-03**
16'	66490 (0%) 7.46768e+00	62728 (0%) 1.59646e+02	54863 (0%) 6.19296E+02	50806 (0%) 3.79962E+02	**14682 (93%)** **1.31185E-03**
17	16762 (73%) 3.31013e-04	10528 (93%) 3.07495e-04	13440 (100%) 3.07487E-04	**2255 (100%)** **3.07486E-04**	24021 (93%) 3.07504E-04
18	418 (100%) 3.55255e-37	584 (100%) 1.78986e-16	490 (100%) 2.02092E-34	**208 (100%)** **9.74551E-87**	170 (100%) 2.03766E-72
19	406 (100%) -3.79124e-03	548 (100%) -3.79124e-03	308 (100%) -3.79124E-03	139 (100%) -3.79124E-03	**133 (100%)** **-3.79124E-03**
20	8656 (20%) -4.44493e+00	9817 (0%) -4.48755e+00	9206 (0%) -3.60545E+00	8016 (33%) -4.53824E+00	**5188 (46%)** **-4.65253E+00**
21	566 (100%) 3.84244e-29	828 (100%) 6.98197e-14	601 (100%) 1.02781E-29	**234 (100%)** **0.00000E+00**	204 (100%) 1.89512E-32
22	10505 (13%) -9.36576e-01	6415 (53%) -1.20349e+00	9212 (33%) -1.15634E+00	3961 (73%) -1.34805E+00	**1295 (93%)** **-1.46433E+00**
23	32698 (0%) 1.25032e+20	30337 (0%) 2.21663e+19	25994 (0%) 1.53549E+22	23636 (0%) 1.36121E+16	**11225 (100%)** **1.43173E-34**
24	33782 (0%) 1.69160e+02	31535 (0%) 6.33179e+01	27474 (0%) 4.29892E+04	24874 (0%) 9.47704E+03	**6056 (100%)** **2.12213E-46**
25	31025 (0%) 9.15488e+00	28810 (0%) 1.12656e+01	25252 (0%) 5.87449E+09	22885 (0%) 4.76373E+07	**8606 (100%)** **8.41713E-23**
26	30641 (0%) 3.20302e+01	28516 (0%) 6.31121e+01	24578 (0%) 8.34362E+01	22535 (0%) 8.34362E+01	**13444 (100%)** **3.48532E-11**
27	793 (100%) 2.28949e-14	**1026 (100%)** **4.95900e-15**	612 (100%) 4.98217E-10	565 (100%) 2.22045E-10	443 (100%) 9.02567E-12
28	**512 (100%)** **-1.86731e+02**	656 (100%) -1.86731e+02	11300 (0%) -1.86127E+02	11138 (0%) -1.86469E+02	9574 (26%) -1.86678E+02
29	**436 (100%)** **3.97887e-01**	809 (100%) 3.97887e-01	4390 (73%) 3.97899E-01	1868 (87%) 3.97888E-01	3430 (80%) 3.97894E-01
30	1979 (60%) -1.95156e+00	2086 (66%) -1.95963e+00	1278 (100%) -2.00000E+00	553 (100%) -2.00000E+00	**282 (100%)** **-2.00000E+00**
ms %	14169 (49.9%)	13284 (52.3%)	13521 (44.3%)	10671 (54.9%)	**5871** **(84.2%)**
#w	3	1	0	8	**22**

Table 5 Results between population-only systems and CAEP systems with fuzzy acceptance function

A Genetic Approach to the Attitude Control of an Inverted Pendulum System

Kyung-Jae Ha
Kyungnam University, Korea
Visiting Scholar at the Wayne State University

Hak-Man Kim
Korea Electrotechnology Research Institute, Korea

Abstract

In this paper we present a genetic approach to the optimal Linear Quadratic Regulator (LQR) problem. A design of the optimal LQR depends on choosing weighting matrices. One must carry out a trial-and-error process to choose the proper weighting matrices in general. It is not a trivial problem. We show new possibility using the Genetic Algorithm (GA) to find the proper weighting matrices and hence to obtain the optimal control gain.. We apply the approach to the attitude control of an inverted pendulum system, which is known as the LQR problem. We perform the computer simulations on the system with a 50[cm] long inverted pendulum and obtain good results.

1. Introduction

The control system design for such an inverted pendulum is known as the LQR problem. The optimal LQR is possibly the most important result of modern control and widely used technique of linear control systems [1]. The design of the optimal LQR is to find the control gain, K which minimizes the performance index. The behavior of the optimal LQ controller is determined by the choice of two weighting matrices Q and R within the performance index. However, it is not a trivial problem to decide them. One must carry out a trial-and-error process to choose the proper weighting matrices in general. One way to begin the process is to use weights that normalize the variables with respect to their largest permissible[1]. Obviously this method does not even guarantee that the specification can be met, even by the optimal system.

In this paper we employ a genetic algorithm(GA) to find the best weighting matrices. The GA is a class of a probabilistic algorithm which begins with a population of randomly generated candidates and evolves towards a solution by applying genetic operators, modeled on genetic processes occurring in nature[2]. The GA has been used in various optimization problems including optimal control problems [3][4]. We perform the computer simulation on two cases of a 50[cm] long inverted pendulum system.

2. The GA approach to the optimal LQR

The design of the optimal LQR is to find the control gain, K such that the performance index (1) is minimized for the system represented by (2).

$$J = \frac{1}{2}\sum_{k=0}^{\infty}[x^T(k)Qx(k) + u^T(k)Ru(k)] \quad (1)$$

$$x(k+1) = A_d x(k) + B_d u(k) \quad (2)$$

The control law that minimizes J is given by linear-state feedback.

$$u(k) = -Kx(k) \quad (3)$$

$$S - A_d^T S A_d + A_d^T S B_d (R + B_d^T S B_d)^{-1} B_d^T S A_d - Q = 0 \quad (4)$$

$$K = (R + B_d^T S B_d)^{-1} B_d^T S A_d \quad (5)$$

Weighting matrices in (1) must be decided by the designer's choice. Then, K in equation (5) can be obtained by solving the Riccati equation (4). However, it is not a trivial problem to find the optimal K since the control performance depends on choosing weighting matrices. In this paper, weighting matrices are decided by the genetic search to obtain the best K for the optimal LQR design. To apply the GA, we constitute a chromosome with diagonal elements of Q and R matrices, as shown in Fig.ure 1.

The procedure to obtain the best weighting matrices and gain by using the GA is as follows.

STEP 1: Set the initial population randomly.
STEP 2: Solve the Riccati equation (4) and get the control gain K with respect to each chromosome.
STEP 3: Evaluate the fitness of each chromosome using the performance index (1). If the termination condition is satisfied, then go to STEP 6.
STEP 4: Reproduce the next generation.
STEP 5: Alter chromosomes with crossover and mutation operators. Go to STEP 2.
STEP 6: Determine the best weighting matrices and the best control gain.
STEP 7: End

1082-3409/97 $10.00 © 1997 IEEE

		Q				R	
q_{11}	q_{22}	....	q_{mm}	r_{11}	r_{22}	....	r_{nn}

Fig.1 **Chromosomal representation of Q,R matrices.**

3. Application to an inverted pendulum system

Figure 2 shows an inverted pendulum system, which is the rail-cart type. We carried out two computer simulations on two cases. The first simulation was the observation of the pendulum angle and cart moving distance from the starting time with initial pendulum angle 5°. The other one was carried out with disturbance in the form of pulse wave whose magnitude is 5° after 5 seconds from starting time.

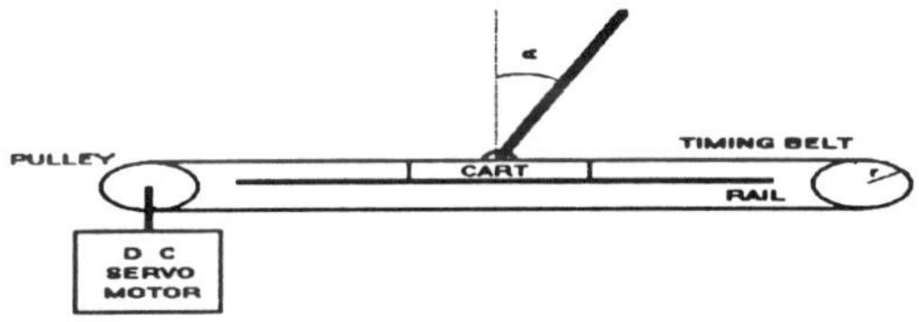

Fig 2 **An inverted pendulum system.**

There can be a little difference between the linearized simulation model and the actual system. So, we added white noises in two simulations to consider the unstable aspect of the actual system due to modeling error. The population size was chosen to be 100, and the probabilities of the crossover and mutation are pc=0.3, pm=0.05 respectively. We set sampling period of 0.01[sec].

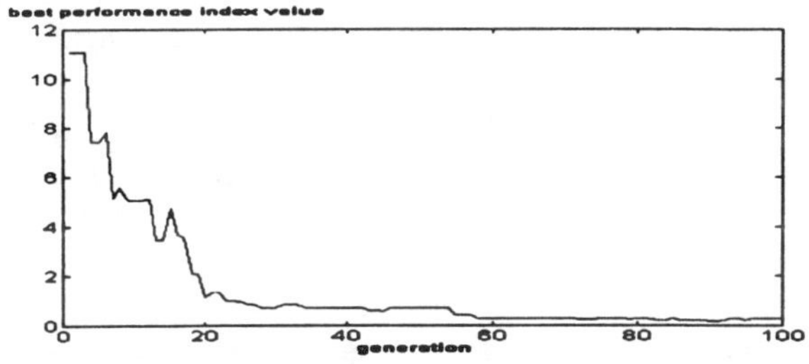

Fig.3 **Minimum performance index of each generation.**

The computer-generated results presented in this paper were obtained using the MATLAB software package, the SIMULINK files. Figure 3 shows the transition of the minimum performance index value of each generation. The best performance index value was found at the 91th generation. We used Q, R and K obtained at the 91th generation for two computer simulations. The results are shown in Figure 4 and 5 respectively and as shown in the figures the pendulum system is controlled well.

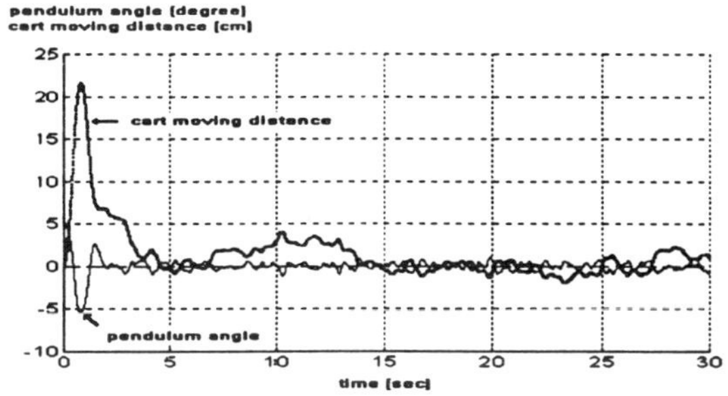

Fig.4 **The result of simulation 1.**

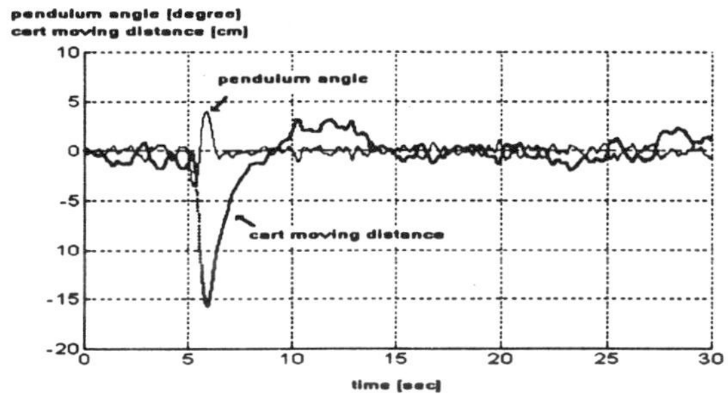

Fig.5 **The result of simulation 2.**

5. Conclusion

In this paper, we presented a new approach to the optimal LQR design using the GA. For the optimal LQR design, one must begin with the choice of proper weighting matrices Q, R by trial-and- error in general. Because this is not trivial problem, we applied the GA to obtain them. For the approach, we constituted a chromosome with diagonal elements of weighting matrices and applied GA to find the best ones and then the best control gain of the LQR for an inverted pendulum system. The results of two cases of computer simulations were very satisfactory.

References

[1] Pierre R. Belanger, Control Engineering - Modern Approach, Saunders College publishing, 1995.

[2] David E. Goldberg, Genetic Algorithms in Search, Optimization & Machine Learning, Addison-Wesley Publishing Company, Inc., 1989.

[3] Z. Michalewics et al., "Genetic Algorithms and Optimal Control Problems" Proc. of the 29th Conf. on Desision and Control", pp. 1664-1666, Dec. 1990.

[4] R.A Hull et al., "Performance Enhancement of a Missile Autopilot via Genetic Algorithm Optimization Techniques", Proc. of the American Control Conf., pp. 1680-1684, 1994.

...aborative Knowledge Acquisition with a Genetic Algorithm

Vladimir Estivill-Castro
Neurocomputing Research Centre
Faculty of Information Technology, QUT
P.O. Box 2434 Brisbane, Qld, 4001
Australia

Abstract

Inductive inference techniques that allow symbolic representation of the acquired knowledge facilitate knowledge validation, revision and understanding by human experts. EVOPROL v 1.1(EVOlutionary PROpositional Logic) is an inductive, efficient, versatile system for supervised learning of logic rules using a genetic algorithm. EVOPROL contributes to computer assisted knowledge acquisition because it allows discovery of flexible and/or alternative rules from examples. The approach presented here integrates sources of knowledge and establishes collaboration between the genetic searcher and the human expert.

1 Introduction

Building an expert system involves *Knowledge Acquisition*; that is, the process of eliciting, analyzing, and interpreting the knowledge that human experts use when solving problems and transforming this knowledge into a suitable machine representation. Experience has shown that this process is both difficult and time consuming and it is often a major bottleneck in the production of expert systems. Programs that induce knowledge from a set of preclassified examples constitute one approach to avoiding the difficulties associated with acquiring knowledge from domain experts. For the process of knowledge acquisition, knowledge representation by logical rules has the very important feature that knowledge is explicit for human understanding and thus, rules contribute to synthesizing knowledge verifiable by human experts. A practical, learning algorithm must employ heuristics to search the space of possible hypotheses consistent with the data. Because of its simplicity and efficiency, Quinlan's ID3 [12] algorithm for induction of rules represented as a decision tree has gained widespread popularity in the machine learning community. ID3 search for decision trees is essentially a hill-climbing approach guided locally by an information theoretic measure. Also, ID3's decision trees allows for little flexibility. For example, different rules with near-by accuracy are hard to obtain. Alternative rules for describing a concept from a different set of attributes are natural in many applications [15]. Since genetic algorithms are less sensitive to local optima, they have been used as an alternative to conduct the search (for example, the AQ algorithm for learning logic rules has been adapted for genetic search [1]).

EVOPROL v. 1.1(EVOlutionary PROpositional Logic) is an inductive and supervised learning system of logic rules using a genetic algorithm for searching the space of theories explaining the set of examples. The system is similar in spirit to BEAGLE [7] and GABIL [5] and other genetic algorithms for inducing logic rules [1, 3, 6, 10]. However, the rules generated by EVOPROL are always logic rules with logical connectives such as AND, OR and NOT. This approach results in more intelligible rules because, as opposed to BEAGLE, EVOPROL does not mix data types. As opposed to GABIL and other systems [3], we can handle both continuous and discrete attributes. We will show that our approach is computationally more efficient than other GA-based inductive learners. EVOPROL has a precise strategy to simplify rules. This feature makes EVOPROL efficient and productive since the induced rules are easier to understand. The tool presented in this paper facilitates knowledge elicitation. Its genetic search allows a more robust and flexible search of the space of rules, as well as the generation of alternative rules for the same concept.

EVOPROL intends to be a tool to improve the process of knowledge elicitation and knowledge acquisition. Therefore, its spirit differs from inductive learning systems in that the source of knowledge is not restricted to examples. It can be used as other inductive learners, but on early stages of knowledge elicitation, both knowledge sources (training data sets and human experts) are available. Thus, the tool integrates human participation in the inference from examples beyond setting initial parameters for the artificial learner. EVOPROL's follows the approach that knowledge elicitation and machine learning are different but complementary [14]. However, as opposed to the Knowledge Factory [14], EVOPROL retains some roles for the knowledge engineer. The system is based on genetic search, that allows human control, deletion of rules, modification of weights and production of alternative rules, as well as human participation in the specialization and generalization of rules.

Section 2 provides a glimpse at the logic language used by EVOPROL to induce rules. Here we explain how EVOPROL handles continuous and discrete attributes. Section 3 describes the use of genetic algorithms in EVOPROL. In particular, it describes the encoding of rules and it explains fitness evaluation. Section 4 compares EVOPROL to previous systems for machine learning including those based on genetic algorithms. Section 5 illustrates the collaborative knowledge elicitation integrated in EVOPROL. We present some final remarks in Section 6.

2 Rule-based classification

Supervised learning concentrates in extracting decision criteria from samples of solved cases that would be applicable to new data. Our interest is that the extracted knowledge be represented as decision-making rules amendable to human understanding. EVOPROL induces logic rules as `if-then` statements (if the antecedent holds, the object should be labeled with the class label in the consequent). The antecedent is a logic expression constructed from nested combinations of atomic predicates using the logical connectives $\wedge$ (AND), $\vee$ (OR) and $\neg$ (NOT). Conjunction and disjunction are treated as binary while negation is unary.

EVOPROL's predicates are constructed from the attribute-vectors describing examples and possible new cases in two fundamental ways.

1.- If the values of attribute A_i range in a small discrete domain $D = \{d_1, \ldots d_t\}$, then the grammar of EVOPROL includes $A_i\_d_j$ as a predicate symbol (for $j = 1, \ldots, t$). For example, the predicate symbols SEX_MALE and SEX_FEMALE will be included for the attribute sex. The meaning of this predicate symbols is naturally that $A_i\_d_j(x)$ evaluates to true if and only if x is an object with value d_j on attribute A_i. For example, SEX_FEMALE(*Marie_Curie*) is true while SEX_FEMALE(*Albert_Einstein*) is false.

2.- When the possible values of attribute A_i constitute a continuous domain D, the grammar includes the predicates VERY_*LOW_A_i, NORMAL_A_i and VERY_*HIGH_A_i (where the regular expression a^* denotes 0, 1 or any finite number of repetitions of the symbol a). The meaning of these predicates will constitute a fuzzy partition of the domain D. The intended meaning is that a predicate like VERY_VERY_LOW_HEIGHT(x) is true for an interval of values of the attribute height that are smaller than those values in the interval of the domain on which VERY_LOW_HEIGHT(x) is true. For every value $d \in D$ of the continuous attribute A_i there is always one predicate that evaluates to true. The predicates are linearly ordered. However, the boundary between two consecutive intervals of the continuous domain is non-deterministically defined (more on this later).

As presented here, EVOPROL expresses concepts in a logic language that has the expressivity of first order logic formula with only unary predicates and allowing just one variable in a formula. This is equivalent to propositional calculus; however, this is the common framework for most Machine Learning systems where examples are in attribute-vector format.

3 Rules as chromosomes

In EVOPROL, searching for good classifiers for a class is performed via a genetic algorithm. Fixed length character strings have been found to present difficulties for some problems in artificial intelligence where the desired solution is hierarchical and where the size of the solution is unknown in advance [5, 11]. Thus, rather than using a mechanism to represent logic rules as fixed length strings [3, 9], we take the approach of operating in structures that represent individuals by their parse tree [7, 11].

In EVOPROL, a genetic algorithm will explore the set of rules for a class by manipulating a population of encoded rules with a common consequent. In fact, EVOPROL v 1.1 represents antecedents as trees where the internal nodes are binary nodes with pointers to their children and a pointer to its parent (the parent pointer in the root is void). Internal nodes to represent NOT are unnecessary because, by De Morgan's Laws applied to logic expressions, we can place the necessary negations at the leaves (leaves encode predicates). Binary nodes store whether they are a conjunction (using 1 for $\wedge$) or a disjunction (using 0 for $\vee$) in one bit. The rank of a node n is the number of nodes in the subtree rooted at n. The rank is recorded for efficient implementation of crossover operators because the rank of n is one more than the number of links of the subtree rooted at n.

The leaves of the tree encode predicates and their negations as binary strings. For a discrete attribute A_i (categorical or ordered) with domain $D = \{d_1, \ldots, d_t\}$, we use $\lceil \log_2 t \rceil$ bits to encode the predicate $A_i\_d_j$ as the value of $j - 1$ in binary. Thus, a leaf for the predicate $A_i\_d_j$ stores the pair of integers

$(i-1, j-1)$ as two binary strings with gray coding.

For a continuous attribute A_i, the predicate VERY_^{j}LOW_A_i is represented as a pair of integers $(i-1, -(j+1))$ where each of the integers is coded in binary (note that in this case the second integer is always negative). The predicate NORMAL_A_i is represented as the pair of integers $(i-1, 0)$ and the predicate VERY_^{j}HIGH_A_i is represented by the pair $(i-1, j+1)$. In each pair, the two integer entries of the pair are encoded with gray coding.

Evaluation of an antecedent on an object x is simple and can be defined recursively once the leaves are evaluated. Predicates for continuous attributes correspond to a discretization of the domain of values dependent on two parameters $\rho \in (0,1]$ and $\tau \in [0, \rho/2)$ specified by the user of EVOPROL before the execution of a generic search. Let A_i be continuous and let μ_i and σ_i the observed mean and standard deviation in the values of attribute A_i among the sample (or training set). Then, the value x_{ik} of attribute A_i for the k-th example x_k is normalized by the transformation

$$z_{ik} \leftarrow \frac{x_{ik} - \mu_i}{\sigma_i}. \quad (1)$$

With this normalization, the variable z_{ik} has mean 0 and variance 1.

The domain of z is partitioned in intervals of $\rho\sigma_i$ units. The *deterministic interval predicate* for NORMAL_A_i is the question: $z \in [-\rho/2, \rho/2]$? Thus, NORMAL_A_i(x) is true if the i-th attribute of x, when normalized by transformation (1) results in a value in the interval $[-\rho/2, \rho/2]$. That is, the value of the i-th attribute of x_k is a normal value if it is not more than $\rho\sigma/2$ units from the observed mean in the examples.

Similarly, the deterministic interval predicate for VERY_^{j}LOW_A_i is the question: $z \in [-\rho(j+1) - \rho/2, -\rho(j) - \rho/2]$?

However, the parameter τ adds an amount of nondeterminism to the boundaries of the intervals in the discretization. If $z \in [a,b]$? is the question corresponding to an interval, then EVOPROL replaces this question by $z \geq a + Y_l$ and $z \leq b + Y_h$? where Y_l and Y_h are independent random variables that are real valued and uniform in $[-\tau, \tau]$ and which are sampled every time the predicate is evaluated. Thus, near the boundary of the interval, the predicate may evaluate to true once and, when evaluated again on the same point near the boundary, it may evaluate to false. This makes, the boundaries of continuous predicates distinct or blurred (as regulated by τ) and allows regulated tolerance for noise in data sets.

The fitness of an encoded rule ϕ is a function of the error rate incurred by ϕ in classifying the sample data. The error rate for a rule is a measure of the agreement of the consequent of the rule and the class label in the inspection of each example. Thus, for each example in the training set, there are four possibilities: (TT) example classified correctly as member of the class, (FF) example classified correctly as outside the class, (TF) example miss-classified as outside the class, and (FT) example miss-classified as member of the class.

The fitness of a rule is then evaluated as follows. For each correct evaluation of an example, (a match with the decision provided by the class label of the example) the rule accumulates positive points, while for each incorrect evaluation of an example, the rule receives negative points. The performance of the rule is a weighted average of the two types of positive points and of the two types of negative points.

If the fitness function is a direct estimation of the error rate difficulties occur. For example, when we have a large training set but only a few examples of the class we are trying to find a rule for. In this case, the other examples are negative examples for the class. A rule that always answers FALSE will get a high performance just because it answers correctly on the large number of negative examples. This difficulty was observed in other learners using genetic algorithms [3, 5].

EVOPROL solves this problem using weights that are in correlation with the proportion of positive examples in the training set. These weights are denoted ω_{TT}, ω_{TF}, ω_{FT} and ω_{FF}. Also these weights allow the user to adjust the search to take into account misclassification costs and attribute testing costs [13]. The formula for evaluating the fitness F of a rule ϕ in a training set TR is

$$\begin{aligned} F(\phi) = \quad & \gamma^* \times & \{\omega_{TT} \times (\sharp \text{ of TT matches}) \\ & & -\omega_{TF} \times (\sharp \text{ of TF mismatches}) \\ & & -\omega_{FT} \times (\sharp \text{ of FT mismatches})\} \\ & +\gamma^- \times & \{\omega_{FF} \times (\sharp \text{ of FF matches})\} \\ & & -\omega_{OR} \times \mathit{Rank}(\phi), \end{aligned}$$

where,

$$\gamma^* = \frac{\sharp \text{ of examples in } TR}{\sharp \text{ of positive examples in } TR},$$

$$\gamma^- = \frac{\sharp \text{ of examples in } TR}{\sharp \text{ of negative examples in } TR}$$

and ω_{OR} is a weight that benefits shorter rules.

We now present the genetic operations. The conclusion of each rule is transmitted to the offspring untouched, both during crossing and during mutation.

The crossing step selects probabilistically subtrees (subexpressions) from the parents and just exchanges these subtrees. The subtrees may not be proper subtrees. The crossover generates offsprings that are syntactically and semantically valid because entire subexpressions are swapped [7, 11].

The mutation operator is just a traversal of the tree (the genotype). With very low probability the components of the tree are modified. Every bit may be negated. Thus, a node with an $\vee$ (OR) can reverse to an $\wedge$ (AND). At the leaves, instead of evaluating the fifth attribute we may now evaluate another attribute whose gray coding is at Hamming distance one (because one bit is reversed). The predicate VERY_HIGH may change to VERY_VERY_HIGH or VERY_LOW, also by the reversal of only one bit. Mutation applied to a link may replace the root node of that link by one of the subexpressions.

The simplification of rules in EVOPROL is another aspect that deserves clarification. An immediate benefit of simplification is shorter and more understandable equivalent expressions for hypotheses consistent with the data. Simplification is required because the same logical concept has equivalent encodings. Simplification of constant expressions was addressed in BEAGLE [7] and its need was identified elsewhere [11]. EVOPROL addresses simplification effectively. For example, without simplification EVOPROL produced the following rule for the Iris data.

IF (NORMAL_PETAL_LENGTH (x) *OR* HIGH_PETAL_LENGTH (x)) *OR*
((LOW_SEPAL_LENGTH(x) *AND* VERY_HIGH_SEPAL_LENGTH (x))
OR NORMAL_PETAL_LENGTH (x))
THEN VERSICOLOR.

However, the subexpression LOW_SEPAL_LENGTH (x) *AND* VERY_HIGH_SEPAL_LENGTH (x) is always *false* because, for all x, the **petal length** can not have a very high value and a low value (these predicates correspond to disjoint intervals in the partition of the domain of this attribute). Thus, we have a subexpression *false OR* NORMAL_PETAL_LENGTH(x). This is equivalent to simply NORMAL_PETAL_LENGTH(x). Finally using the fact that $\phi \vee \psi \vee \phi$ is logically equivalent to $\phi \vee \psi$ the apparently complex rule is simply

IF NORMAL_PETAL_LENGTH(x) *OR* HIGH_PETAL_LENGTH(x)
THEN VERSICOLOR.

EVOPROL solves simplification because antecedents can be simplified by the criteria of minimizing the number of literals. Thus, simplification is performed by standard methods used in logic circuit design (for example, *Incremental Consensus*). However, we do believe that simplification is responsible for EVOPROL computational efficiency. It liberates the user of specifying a target language free of redundancy (a task that may require considerable insight into the problem and good judgement). Other approaches to learning based on genetic algorithms, but utilizing a parameterized representation in the form of parse trees have faced problems of exploring redundant and/or invalid solutions. EVOPROL automatically simplifies chromosomes repeatedly after a few generations (typicly after four or five). In this way, EVOPROL achieves three goals. First, trees may have redundant branches (that serve as memory for the disruptive effects of genetic operators). Second, the search keeps a regulated focus on canonical genotypes. Third, the process to assure the first two objectives is computationally efficient.

4 A comparison

In the comparison presented in this section EVOPROL does not use any human guidance.

4.1 Power of elicitation

The parse tree structure of EVOPROL is similar to that of BEAGLE [7]. However, BEAGLE handles symbolic values as numbers. Our first comparison uses the data set of flags used to illustrate BEAGLE [7]. The data set has the encoding of general and flag information for 194 countries. The target concept is those countries where the official language is Spanish. EVOPROL obtained the following rules.

Antecedent for the consequent THEN LANGUAGE_SPANISH(x)	Correct		Errors	
	TT	FF	FT	TF
IF ZONE_SW(x)	8	165	8	13
IF RELIGION_CATHOLIC(x)	20	153	20	1
IF RELIGION_CATHOLIC(x) AND BLUE_PRESENT(x)	16	163	10	5
IF RELIGION_CATHOLIC(x) AND BLACK_ABSENT(x)	18	160	13	3
IF RELIGION_CATHOLIC(x) AND LOW_NUMBER_OF_BARS(x)	17	163	10	4
IF RELIGION_CATHOLIC(x) AND NORMAL_POPULATION(x)	19	156	17	2
IF RELIGION_CATHOLIC(x) AND NORMAL_POPULATION(x) AND BLUE_PRESENT(x)	16	166	7	5
IF RELIGION_CATHOLIC(x) AND NORMAL_POPULATION(x) AND[BLACK_ABSENT(x) OR NORMAL_NUMBER_OF_CIRCLES(x)]	17	165	8	4

Table 1. Logic rules inferred by EVOPROL. Rules are shown in order of complexity.

One first important aspect of EVOPROL's output is the production of alternative rules that suggest attributes that are relevant for the classification. EVOPROL clusters the most accurate rules. It does not ask the user to review the entire population of rules and can present them sorted by order of accuracy or by order of complexity. BEAGLE produces 4 rules.

Antecedent for the consequent THEN LANGUAGE_SPANISH(x)	Correct		Errors	
	TT	FF	FT	TF
$((white \leq population) - religion)$	20	160	13	1
$(landmass \leq 2.5)$	20	145	28	1
$((zone \leq 2.6) < (((zone \geq 2.0) \geq gold) < area))$	21	141	32	0
$((quarters + stripes) > 2.0)$	17	124	49	4

Table 2. Rules inferred by BEAGLE are shown in order of accuracy.

The second rule in BEAGLE is obtained by making the attributes population, religion and white unavailable for classification; thus, alternative rules based on other features are generated. For EVOPROL, elimination of the attributes population, religion and white in the training set resulted in rules shown next.

Antecedent for the consequent THEN LANGUAGE_SPANISH(x)	Correct		Errors	
	TT	FF	FT	TF
ZONE_NE(x)	3	169	4	18
ZONE_NE(x) AND NORMAL_AREA(x)	2	173	0	19
ZONE_NE(x) AND GREEN_ABSENT(x)	3	169	4	18
LAND_MASS_SOUTH_AMERICA(x) OR[(ZONE_NW(x) AND TOP_LEFT_COLOR_BLUE(x)]	8	165	8	13

Table 3. Rules inferred by EVOPROL in order of complexity. (some attributes have been eliminated).

We find these results illustrative of the capabilities of EVOPROL in two aspects. We focus on the human understanding of rules first; that is the cognitive aspect. For example, consider the most accurate BEAGLE rule. What does it mean to verify that the population (in millions) is larger than the boolean value (0 or 1) of the presence of white in the flag and to subtract the encoding for religion? Note that the rule depends heavily on the encoding. Perhaps we could infer that `religion` is relevant for whether a country is Spanish speaking. However, this fact is most explicit in the set of EVOPROL's rules. With EVOPROL, we clearly confirm that Catholic religion is relevant and highly indicative of Spanish speaking countries. Descriptive interpretation of BEAGLE's third rule is a challenge. Thus, although BEAGLE's rules are interesting relations between attributes with correlation to the goal concept, EVOPROL's rules allow better and easier human understanding and manipulation.

The second aspect is classification accuracy. All of the rules generated by EVOPROL (Tables 1 and 3) are more accurate than the second best rule by BEAGLE and also some rules are more accurate that BEAGLE's most accurate rule.

A second comparison involves the well-known breast cancer data set used for evaluating the performance of several inductive learning algorithms, but in particular, for two inductive learners using genetic algorithms [3, 5].

EVOPROL induced rules from a random subset of 200 cases, and the accuracy of the inferred rule was tested on the unseen cases. The system was run on 10 different random training sets (and in many cases, it converged to the same rule). Some of the rules are presented in Table 4.

Antecedent for the consequent THEN RECURRENCE(x)	Accuracy	
	Train	Test
IF DEGREE_MALIG_3(x)	73%	70%
IF DEGREE_MALIG_3(x) OR INV_NODES_3TO5(x)	71%	71%
IF DEGREE_MALIG_3(x) OR INV_NODES_3TO5(x) OR INV_NODES_9TO11(x)	71%	71%
IF DEGREE_MALIG_3(x) AND [TUMOR_SIZE_30TO34(x) OR NODE_CAPS(x) OR DEGREE_MALIG_2(x)]	80%	71%

Table 4. Rules are shown in order of complexity.

Again, we find the results illustrative of the power of EVOPROL for inductive inference in several aspects. On the aspect of accuracy, EVOPROL shows performance at the levels reported in the literature [3, 4, 5]. EVOPROL's rules classify accurately new examples, even in the presence of noise.

The quest for rules as short as possible has been emphasised many times [4]. This is mainly for two reasons: shorter rules usually do not overfit the data; however, also shorter rules are easier to communicate, validate or apply by human experts. We refer to Clark and Niblett's approach [4] to evaluate the complexity of the knowledge structure induced by different algorithms. The complexity of a decision tree is the number of nodes (including leaves) in the tree. For the CN2 and AQ family, the complexity is the number of selectors in the final rule list and rule set respectively. Measuring the complexity for EVOPROL's rules as the number of nodes (terms) in the tree encoding the rule, shows that the rules in Table 4 have complexity 1, 3, 3, 5, 5, 7 and 7, respectively. The representative of decision trees had complexities of 122 (for no pruning) and 44 (for pruning), while AQR had complexity 208 [4]. CN2 had complexities 28 at 90% threshold, 20 at 95% threshold and 4 at 99% threshold [4].

4.2 Efficiency

EVOPROL is coded in C. Three executions with the breast data (200 cases) with population size 50 and for 100 generations required always less than 20 seconds, on a PC-486. Newbool [3] requires a population of 1000 individuals for this data set and at least 20 minutes on a Sparcstation. For the Trains data set (10 cases), EVOPROL's 16 independent runs on a 486-PC resulted on an average running time of 1.40 seconds per run (with a 99% confidence interval of ±0.28), the longest running time was 2.80 seconds and the shortest 0.90 seconds. EVOPROL achieved 100% classification accuracy with 80 generations in each of the 16 runs. While for this data set, the parallel implementation of GA-SMART [9] used a multiprocessor of 16 transputers, 12 minutes and 170 generations to achieve equivalent results. We were not forced to limit generations or population size as in the case of GABIL [5]. Thus, with respect to other geneticly-based tools, we are confident that EVOPROL is more efficient.

With respect to other paradigms for inductive inference we have used CN2 [4] as a benchmark. We obtained the following run-time comparisons (in seconds) between CN2 [1] and EVOPROL for three computer platforms (we were unable to port CN2 to IRIX 6.0). For this direct comparison the training set was the full data-set of breast-cancer data. The results are averages over 10 runs with 95% confidence intervals and are illustrative of EVOPROL's efficiency.

	CN2	EVOPROL
Toshiba PC-486 (LINUX)	7.0s ± 0.02	14.8s ± 1.44
IPXstation (SUN/OS)	3.0s ± 0.01	6.7s ± 1.09
Power Challenge (IRIX)		4.7s± 0.52

4.3 Other aspects

EVOPROL does not require a domain theory to help its search (as in the case of SIA01 [1]) and does not limit the form of rules (as also is the case of SIA01 [1]). It allows flexible manipulation of the rules. The user may remove conditions, and restrictions or modify individuals in a population and explore their evolution further with EVOPROL. This means that EVOPROL does not require special genetic operators for adding conditions [1, 5] or making rules more general or more specific. EVOPROL provides two mechanisms to achieve the objectives these types of operators are usually put in place for. The first mechanism is implicit and consists of adjusting the weights of the fitness evaluation. The other mechanism is explicit and involves defining a logic expression that will be constantly joined (with an AND for specialization or with an OR for generalization) to evey individual of the population.

5 The spirit of EVOPROL

We now use the data set of flags to illustrate how EVOPROL's search is guided by the human user, rather than fully guided with initial parameters for genetic operators whose role must be adjusted [5].

The first aspect is a facility to construct, edit and test rules in the target language. The user can construct rules interactively. For illustration consider the construction of the first rule of Table 1. The user is required to indicate that is using the predicate for attribute **zone** (EVOPROL displays attribute names for the data set). After this, EVOPROL presents the possible options (in this case `NW`, `SE`, `SW` and `NE`). The user will select `SW` and the system will automaticly build a rule with this predicate as the antecedent:

$$\text{IF ZONE\_SW}(x) \text{ THEN LANGUAGE\_SPANISH}(x). \quad (2)$$

Similarly, to build the second rule in Table 1, the user indicates the attribute **religion**. EVOPROL will offer the alternatives (as defined by the description of the data set); namely, **Catholic**, **Other_Christian**, **Muslim**, **Buddhist**, **Hindu**, **Ethnic**, **Marxist**, **Others**. Selection of the first option builds the rule:

$$\text{IF RELIGION\_CATHOLIC}(x) \text{ THEN LANGUAGE\_SPANISH}(x). \quad (3)$$

Thus, the user can input knowledge in the form of rules. Besides their logic form shown earlier, EVOPROL can display the parse tree as well as a list of terms resulting from post-order traversal of the parse tree. This later format is useful to see how rules are evaluated non-recursively using a stack.

User constructed rules can be inserted into an initial population of the genetic algorithm for developing new variants. Moreover, the rules of an initial population of a second search may be resulting rules from a first search slightly edited or modified by the user.

For example, the two rules above are the result of a genetic search on the flags data set. EVOPROL's meta-information of the classification produces output that is very similar to the first two lines of Table 1. Indication of the accuracy and types of missclassification is given. The user may notice that while the first rule has 13 false negatives the second rule has only 1. This suggest that a combination of the antecedent of the rules may lead to a more accurate rule. After building the rules (alternatively, from the output of a first genetic search), the user indicates the rules to be combined with AND. Thus, with Rule (2) and Rule (3) above, the user obtains the rule:

$$\text{IF ZONE\_SW}(x) \text{ AND RELIGION\_CATHOLIC}(x) \quad (4)$$
$$\text{THEN LANGUAGE\_SPANISH}(x). \quad (5)$$

This is a user controlled specialization since the antecedent is more restrictive. Alternatively, the user may want to generalize the rules when combining them with a disjunction:

$$\text{IF ZONE\_SW}(x) \text{ OR RELIGION\_CATHOLIC}(x) \quad (6)$$
$$\text{THEN LANGUAGE\_SPANISH}(x). \quad (7)$$

The user may test the accuracy of this new rules, and EVOPROL offers such a menu option. The user may be satisfied with Rule (4-5), since this specialization has improved the accuracy to 92% (Rule (6-7) has 85%

[1] Version publicly distributed on `http://www.cs.utexas.edu/users/pclark/software.html#cn2`.

accuracy). Note that Rule (4-5) is the collaborative effort of the genetic search in the data set and the user's suggestion to combine two rules. This is a collaborative knowledge acquisition effort. EVOPROL offers other interesting capabilities for enhancing this.

EVOPROL can report to the user what are the examples that are miss-classifyed. For Rule (4-5), this facility reports that the two countries that do not speak Spanish but are classified as so are Brazil and French Polynesia, while the 13 countries that do speak Spanish but are ruled out by Rule (4-5) are Colombia, Costa-Rica, Cuba, Dominican Republic, El Salvador, Guatemala, Honduras, Mexico, Nicaragua, Panama, Puerto-Rico, Spain and Venezuela. This information may prompt the user's domain knowledge to edit and refine the rule; for example, most of the Spanish speaking countries miss-classifyed are in Central America. However, the attribute `landmass` has only the values `N_America`, `S_America`, `Europe`, `Asia` and `Oceania`. One alternative is to extend the granularity of this attribute and relabel the attribute vector of each example accordingly. This illustrates that EVOPROL's spirit can lead to refinements in the language for knowledge representation. Never the less, EVOPROL offers also another alternative based on selective genetic search for rule refinement.

The accuracy of Rule (4-5) suggests that specialization was a reasonable approach. Moreover, Rule (3) makes only one false negative error and classifies all Central American countries (which are officially Catholic) as Spanish speaking. This fact can be verifyed interactively by querying EVOPROL for the correctly and incorrectly classified examples for Rule (3). Thus, specialization of Rule (3) should be explored. EVOPROL allows the user to specify a rule with one or more undetermined terms P to be explored by genetic search. For example, the user may construct the following second order logical expression.

IF RELIGION_CATHOLIC(x) AND P
THEN LANGUAGE_SPANISH(x).

After this, the user may ask EVOPROL to infer a logic term to be placed where the undetermined term P is. EVOPROL's genetic search engine has been designed to handle this. Only a population of logic terms is manipulated and when it comes to evaluation of their fitness, they are plugged into the place indicated by P. The genetic engine does not manipulate the determined part of the rule. In our example, EVOPROL's most dominant result for P above is LANDMASS_S_AMERICA(x) *OR* LANDMASS_N_AMERICA(x). The user can display the new formed rule and its classification properties.

Antecedent for the consequent THEN LANGUAGE_SPANISH(x)	Correct		Errors	
	TT	FF	FT	TF
IF RELIGION_CATHOLIC(x) AND [LANDMASS_S_AMERICA(x) OR LANDMASS_N_AMERICA(x)]	19	170	3	2

Note EVOPROL's ability to find what we suspected from our domain knowledge. Alternatively, we may want to use EVOPROL to find a balance between the previous specialization and generalization performed with Rules (2) and (3). Favoring specialization of Rule (3) the user can build the following expression.

IF RELIGION_CATHOLIC(x) AND (ZONE_SW(x) OR P)
THEN LANGUAGE_SPANISH(x).

After this, EVOPROL is used to infer a logic term to be placed where the undetermined term P is. Results of this inference are shown next.

Antecedent for the consequent THEN LANGUAGE_SPANISH(x)	Correct		Errors	
	TT	FF	FT	TF
IF RELIGION_CATHOLIC(x) AND (ZONE_SW(x) OR LANDMASS_N_AMERICA(x) OR [NORMAL_AREA(x) AND HIGH_NUM_HORZ_STRIPES(x)])	19	170	3	2
IF RELIGION_CATHOLIC(x) AND (ZONE_SW(x) OR LANDMASS_N_AMERICA(x) OR [LANDMASS_S_AMERICA(x) AND ZONE_NW(x)])	19	169	4	2
IF RELIGION_CATHOLIC(x) AND (ZONE_SW(x) OR LANDMASS_N_AMERICA(x) OR LANDMASS_S_AMERICA(x) OR [NORMAL_AREA(x) AND ZONE_NW(x)])	20	169	4	1

Table 6. Logic rule derived by genetic search from user suggested specialization (accuracy is over 96%).

6 Final remarks

The knowledge-acquisition and knowledge-base construction phases in the development of expert systems are regarded as time consuming and expensive. The development of EVOPROL has been motivated for this quest for methods for automatic knowledge acquisition. Methods based on inductive learning regard the data set as it main (if not its only) input; and thus, the data set is the source of knowledge. We have shown that EVOPROL offers an effective and efficient system for inductive learning.

Simultaneously, there has been a development of architectures and systems where the principal source of knowledge is the human expert and the computer tools are support tools to the process of knowledge elicitation. The most well-known example is KSS0 [8]. Although the inductive learning algorithm ID3 is part of the tools of KSS0, the human experts are the main source of "knowledge", and the elicitation of knowledge has no influence on the behavior of the artificial learner. Here, we propose a closer level of interaction. Human participation is extended from configuring the initial parameters for the artificial learner (a task appropriate for a Knowledge Engineer) to a collaborative effort during knowledge elicitation.

The collaborative knowledge acquisition is due to EVOPROL's use of genetic search. The collaborative effort provides guidance to both parties. EVOPROL's inference suggest relevant attributes and initial rules. The user suggests patterns for new rules. In a sense, the user is shaping the fitness function adaptively for the benefit of the genetic-search. Most importantly, the user can make explicit its advise to the artificial learner and be naturally involved in directing its inference mechanism.

Because of the flexibility gained with the use of a genetic algorithm, and EVOPROL's design, EVOPROL offers to integrate the two sources of knowledge (the human experts and the data sets). It remains closer to the machine learning approach in that the main source of knowledge is a data set. However, EVOPROL allows the interaction with the user for shaping, generalizing or specializing rules as well as generation of alternative rules. Because of EVOPROL's complementary role with KSS0 [8], it could be easily integrated into KSS0's framework, and its representation and use will facilitate an effective interaction with the user. EVOPROL has been integrated into KEM [2] (a knowledge acquisition tool similar to KSS0 that integrates cognitive structuring techniques like Repertory Grids). In KEM, EVOPROL's initial population can be the output of an inductive learner of the decision-tree family.

References

[1] S. Augier, G. Venturini, and Y. Kodratoff. Learning first order logic rules with a genetic algorithm. U.M. Fayyad and R. Uthurusamy, *Proc. of the First Int. Conf. on Knowledge Discovery and Data Mining* , 21–26, CA, USA, 1995. AAAI Press.

[2] E.I. Benitez-Guerrero. KEM: Herramienta colaborativa de extracción de conocimiento. Master's thesis, Universidad Veracruzana — LANIA, Xalapa, Veracruz, México, January 1997.

[3] P. Bonelli and A. Parodi. An efficient classifier system and its experimental comparison with two representative learning methods on three medical domains. In R.K. Belew and L.B. Booker, *Proc. of the 4th Int. Conf. on Genetic Algorithms*, 288–295, San Mateo, CA, 1991. Morgan Kaufman.

[4] P. Clark and T. Niblett. The CN2 induction algorithm. *Machine Learning*, 3(4):261–283, 1989.

[5] K.A. DeJong, W.M. Spears, and Gordon D.F. Using genetic algorithms for concept learning. *Machine Learning*, 13(2-3):161, November 1993.

[6] S. Endo and A. Ohuchi. Disjunctive form concept learning system based on genetic algorithm. In *Proc. of the IEEE Int. Conf. on Systems, Man and Cybernetics — Intelligent Systems for the 21st Century*, 4696–4701, NY, USA, 1995. IEEE Press.

[7] R. Forsyth. *Machine Learning, Principles and Techniques.* Chapman and Hall Computing, New York, 1989.

[8] B.R. Gaines and K.L.G. Shaw. Eliciting knowledge and trasferring it effectively to a knowledge-based system. *IEEE Transactions on Knowledge and Data Engineering*, 5(1):4–14, February 1993.

[9] A. Giordana and C. Sale. Learning structured concepts using genetic algorithms. In D. Sleeman and P. Edwards, *Proc. of the Ninth Int. Workshop on Machine Learning*, 169–178, San Mateo, CA. USA, 1992. Morgan Kauffman.

[10] C.Z. Janikow. A knowledge-intensive genetic algorithm for supervized learning. *Machine Learning*, 13:189–228, 1993.

[11] J.R. Koza. Concept formation and decision tree induction using the genetic programming paradigm. In H.P. Schwefel and R. Maenner, *Parallel Problem Solving From Nature*, 124–128, Berlin, Germany, 1991. Springer-Verlag.

[12] J.R. Quinlan. Induction of decision trees. *Machine Learning Journal*, 1:81–106, 1986.

[13] P. Turney. Cost-sensitive classification: Empirical evaluation of a hybrid genetic decision tree induction algorithm. *Journal of Artificial Intelligence Research*, 369–409, 1995.

[14] G.I. Webb. Integrating machine learning with knowledge acquisition through direct interaction with domain experts. *Knowledge-based systems*, 9(4):253–266, 1996.

[15] W. Ziarko, R. Golan, and D. Edwards. An application of DATALOGIC/R knowledge discovery tool to identify strong predicate rules in stock market data. In G. Piatetsky-Shapiro, *Proc. of the AAAI 1993 Workshop on Knowledge Discovery in Databases*, 80–101. AAAI Press, 1993.

A New Methodology for Optimizing Evasive Maneuvers Under Uncertainty in the Extended Two-Dimensional Pursuer/Evader Problem

Frank W. Moore
Computer Science Dept.
University of Dayton
300 College Park
Dayton, OH 45469-2160
moore@cps.udayton.edu
(937) 229-3895

Oscar N. Garcia
Dept. of Computer Science &Engineering
303 Russ Engineering Center
Wright State University
Dayton, OH 45435
ogarcia@valhalla.cs.wright.edu
(937) 775-5131

ABSTRACT: Traditional analytic or control-theoretic solutions to the problem of optimizing evasive maneuvers in the extended two-dimensional pursuer/evader problem require the evader to execute specific sequences of maneuvers at precise pursuer/evader distances. These solutions depend upon several pursuer-specific characteristics, and fail to effectively account for uncertainty about the state of the pursuer. This paper describes the implementation of a genetic programming system that evolves optimized solutions to the extended two-dimensional pursuer/evader problem that do *not* depend upon knowledge of pursuer's *current state*. Best-of-run programs execute strategies by which an evader may maneuver to successfully evade a pursuer starting from a wide range of relative initial positions, under conditions where the state of the pursuer is unknown or uncertain.

I. INTRODUCTION

The two-dimensional pursuer/evader problem (Hamalainen and Ehtamo, 1990) is a competitive zero-sum game in which a faster, more agile pursuer is given a limited amount of time to capture an evader as both are traveling across a plane. The game ends favorably for the evader if it manages to stay outside the *capture radius* of the pursuer (the maximum distance at which the pursuer is considered to have captured the evader) for the duration of the encounter. A solution to the two-dimensional pursuer/evader problem must incorporate an *optimized strategy* for maneuvering the evader in a manner that successfully escapes the pursuer, regardless of the initial conditions of the system.

(Moore and Garcia, 1997a) described a genetic programming (GP) system that identifies optimized solutions to the *extended two-dimensional pursuer/evader problem* (E2DPE). Formal evaluation of this system incorporated physical data (including mass) and performance characteristics (such as maximum thrust, maximum turning rate, fuel consumption rate, and drag coefficients) of an F-16C aircraft evader (Lambert and Munson, 1994) and various types of Soviet surface-to-air missile (SAM) pursuers (Cullen and Foss, 1995). Each best-of-run program was evolved against a training population of pursuers of a single SAM type, starting from a variety of positions. Subsequent testing against pursuers of the same type demonstrated that the resulting best-of-run programs were capable of evading a high percentage of pursuers from a large, representative test population. Unfortunately, best-of-run programs optimized against one type of pursuer generally did not perform optimally when tested against other types of pursuers. Subsequent research (Moore and Garcia, 1997b) investigated the impact of uncertainty about the *type* of pursuer in the E2DPE problem, and identified a methodology for evolving programs that exhibit optimized performance against multiple pursuer types, by using training populations that reflect specific probability distributions over those types.

These GP solutions to the E2DPE problem assumed that the evader had total knowledge of the *state* of the pursuer (its relative position, velocity, and acceleration vectors) for the duration of each encounter. The resulting best-of-run programs used selection statements based upon the current relative pursuer/evader distance to execute specific sequences of thrusting and turning commands. In contrast, the research described in this paper investigates the problem of identifying optimized evasion strategies in the E2DPE problem that do *not*

1082-3409/97 $10.00 © 1997 IEEE

depend upon knowledge of the *current state* of the pursuer. The resulting methodology represents an alternative to current analytic and control-theoretic solutions to the E2DPE problem.

II. AN OVERVIEW OF THE EXTENDED TWO-DIMENSIONAL PURSUER/EVADER PROBLEM

As shown in Figure 1, the E2DPE problem models pursuer P and evader E as point masses whose motions across a plane are controlled by thrusting forces (applied in the direction of the velocity vector) and turning forces (applied in a direction that is perpendicular to the velocity vector). Both P and E are affected by drag forces and momentum; instantaneous changes in direction are not possible. Since acceleration (a), force (F), and mass (m) are related by the equation a = F/m, the acceleration of P or E depends on its current mass, as well as the magnitude of the applied thrusting and turning forces. The effects of these forces depend on the current state of P or E. The maximum distance over which P pursues E depends on the type of pursuer. P captures E as soon as the distance between them becomes less than a pursuer-specific capture radius.

Prior to the start of the encounter, the pursuer uses the initial state of the evader to predict an *intercept point.* The pursuer then accelerates at maximum thrust towards the intercept point. If the evader fails to maneuver, the pursuer captures the evader at (or very close to) the intercept point. If the evader maneuvers, the pursuer relies upon the highly effective *proportional navigation* technique (Ball, 1985) to compensate for those maneuvers. Proportional navigation causes the pursuer to accelerate in the direction perpendicular the line-of-sight from the pursuer to the evader; the magnitude of this acceleration is calculated by the equation

$$n_c = N' \, V_c \, (d\lambda/dt)$$

where N' is a unitless designer-chosen gain known as the *effective navigation ratio*, and V_c is the pursuer-evader closing velocity vector (the negative rate of change of the distance from the pursuer to the evader). The time derivative of the line-of-sight angle λ is known as the line-of-sight rate. For practical guidance systems, optimal values for N' range between 3 and 5 (Ramo and Pucket, 1959).

The evader maneuvers by executing specific combinations of thrusting and turning forces in specific sequences. The *optimal strategy* for the evader (Zarchan, 1990) is to maneuver in a manner that maximizes the likelihood of evading the pursuer, regardless of the initial state of the evader and the relative starting position of the pursuer.

Note that by rotating the reference coordinate system at the starting location of the pursuer, the initial pursuer/evader line-of-sight angle λ_0 may be considered constant for all pursuer/evader pairs. For this reason, the only variables necessary to describe the initial

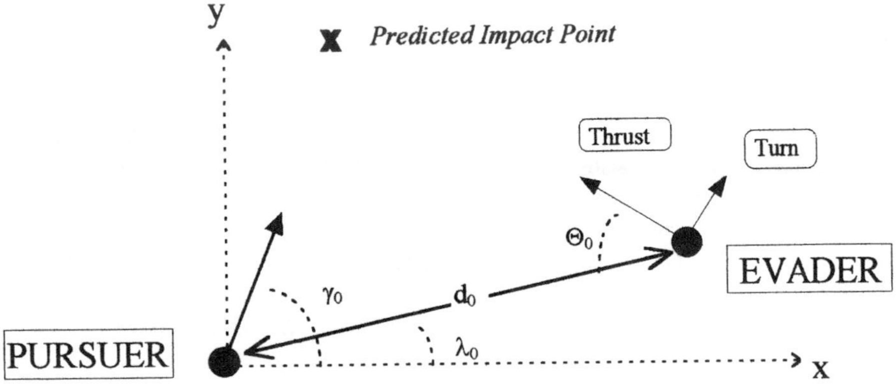

Figure 1. The Extended Two-Dimensional Pursuer/Evader Problem (Initial Conditions).

configuration of each confrontation are the *line-of-sight distance* between the evader and the pursuer, and the *velocity vector* of the evader at the beginning of the encounter.

For each pursuer type, the minimum and maximum effective range of the pursuer defines the range of possible initial line-of-sight distances. The aggregate fitness of a specific program reflects its fitness when evaluated against each of the initial pursuer positions in a specified training population. Optimal evasion programs output commands that assert *thrusting and turning forces* at appropriate moments in order to accomplish maneuvers that optimize evader survivability.

III. PRIOR RESEARCH

A GP solution to the E2DPE problem was successfully implemented (Moore and Garcia, 1997a). During each generation of the GP approach, each member of a population of programs for maneuvering the evader was evaluated against each member of a training population of pursuers. Each GP run optimized maneuvers against a single type of pursuer. Proportional navigation was used by all pursuers. The pursuer and evader had complete knowledge of each other's current state (relative position, velocity, and acceleration). A fitness function was used to qualitatively evaluate the survivability of each evasion program during a simulated encounter; the aggregate fitness of a particular program reflected its overall survivability when independently evaluated against all of the pursuers in the training population. Fitness-proportionate reproduction, together with crossover, was used to create each new generation. Each run was terminated after a fixed number of generations.

A tableau for our GP solution to the original E2DPE problem (Moore and Garcia, 1997a) is shown Figure 2. Cartesian coordinates were used to represent components of position, velocity, and acceleration for both the evader and the pursuer. This simple set of terminals proved to be sufficient to allow the GP system to converge to a solution of this problem. The E2DPE problem fixed the origin of the coordinate system (x = 0, y = 0) at the position of the pursuer. PX and PY thus continually designated the relative displacement from the pursuer to the evader. For each of the functions used by this GP system, an "argument" consists of any syntactically valid composition of functions, variables, and constants that returns a floating-point value in the range [-1.0 ... +1.0].

Function ifDistance is a three-argument selection function: if the current distance between the pursuer and evader is less than the percentage of the pursuer's maximum pursuit distance specified by the absolute value of the first argument, then the second argument is evaluated; otherwise the third argument is evaluated. Functions ifPX and ifPY are two-argument selection functions: ifPX evaluates its first argument if the current x-position of the evader relative to the pursuer is negative; otherwise ifPX evaluates its second argument. Function ifPY is defined similarly for the relative y-position of the evader. Functions ifDistance, ifPX, and ifPY return the value of the evaluated argument.

Functions setThrust and hardTurn are single-argument functions. Function setThrust causes the thrust output of the evader to be set to the percentage of its maximum thrust specified by its argument; for example, setThrust (0.9) will set evader thrust to 90% of its maximum possible value. setThrust ignores the sign of its argument: thrust is assumed to act in the direction of the current evader velocity vector. Function hardTurn causes the evader to execute a turn whose g-force equals the percentage of the maximum allowable turning force of the evader/pilot system specified by its argument; for example, if the maximum turning force is 4 gravities (g's), then hardTurn (0.5) will cause the evader to execute a 2g turn in a direction which is perpendicular and to the right of the current evader velocity vector; the function call hardTurn (-0.5) would result in a 2g evader turn to the left. Both setThrust and hardTurn are assumed to act instantaneously, and both return the value of their input argument.

Fitness cases were identified by two floating-point values ranging from 0.0 to 1.0. The first value, denoted J, identifies the initial line-of-sight distance from the pursuer to the evader. If D_{min} and D_{max} denote the minimum and maximum effective initial distances for the pursuer, then the initial line-of-sight distance d_0 may be calculated as follows:

$$d_0 = D_{min} + (J * (D_{max} - D_{min}))$$

Objective:	Determine an optimized evasion strategy for the Extended Two-Dimensional Pursuer/Evader (E2DPE) problem.
Terminal Set:	***R***, the ephemeral random floating-point constant ranging from -1.0 to 1.0.
Function Set:	ifDistance, ifPX, ifPY setThrust hardTurn
Fitness Cases:	Numerous fitness cases which differ according to the distance from the pursuer to the evader at the start of the encounter, as well as the acute angle between the initial velocity vector of the evader and the line-of-sight vector from evader to pursuer.
Raw Fitness:	The number of encounters during which the distance from pursuer to evader is less than or equal to the capture radius of the pursuer.
Standardized Fitness:	Same as Raw Fitness for this problem.
Hits:	The number of fitness cases that result in capture of the evader prior to the maximum pursuit time of the pursuer. (The encounter is also terminated if the distance between the evader and the pursuer exceeds a pursuer-specific value, at which time the pursuer is considered to have missed the evader.)
Wrapper:	N/A
Parameters:	Population Size M = 100, Maximum Number of Generations G = 21.
Success Predicate:	None.

Figure 2. A Tableau for the State-Dependent Solution to Extended Two-Dimensional Pursuer/Evader Problem

D_{min} and D_{max} depend upon the type of pursuer. The second value, denoted K, identifies the angle that the initial velocity vector of the incoming evader makes with the line-of-sight from the evader to the pursuer. Let Θ_0 denote this angle. If Θ_{min} and Θ_{max} denote the minimum and maximum initial value of Θ, then Θ_0 may be calculated in the following manner:

$$\Theta_0 = \Theta_{min} + (K * (\Theta_{max} - \Theta_{min}))$$

To maintain the relative geometry illustrated in Figure 1 for the pursuer/evader problems addressed by this research, Θ_{min} and Θ_{max} described a range of values between 10 and 80 degrees. For this study, the magnitude of the evader's initial velocity vector (its "speed") was assumed to be the same for each encounter. Thus, each fitness case corresponded to a specific combination of values from sets J and K.

The research described in (Moore and Garcia, 1997a) identified a methodology for evolving optimized evasion strategies (in the form of programs) for a variety of pursuer populations. We began with the two-dimensional problem to reduce the required amount of computation as much as possible. Implicit in the model described above is the assumption that the magnitude of the turning force is independent of the velocity of the evader. Additionally, limitations on the maximum sustainable g-force of the evader were imposed by restricting the magnitude of the evader's turning force; the contribution of thrust to current evader g-force was ignored. We also assumed that the evader stalled if its speed fell below a specified minimum value, resulting in a "capture" for the pursuer. For the purposes of this study, all evaders were assumed to be traveling *inbound* (towards the pursuer) at the start of each confrontation, with lead angle $\gamma_0 > \lambda_0$, as shown in Figure 1. Each best-of-run program represented an optimized evasion technique for a specific type of evader against a specific type of pursuer.

The evader used in (Moore and Garcia, 1997a) was modeled using physical data and performance characteristics of an F-16C aircraft evader, as described in (Stevens and Lewis, 1992). Each pursuer was modeled using physical data and performance characteristics of an SA-6, SA-13, or SA-15 SAM pursuer, in a manner similar to the approach described in

(Klos et al, 1994). Programs were evolved using a training population consisting of a single type of pursuer, starting from a variety of initial positions. Best-of-run programs were evolved for each type of pursuer using a fixed training population of 32 pursuers described by the cross-product of sets J and K:

J = {0.2, 0.3, 0.4, 0.45, 0.5, 0.6, 0.7, 0.8}

K = {2/9, 3/9, 4/9, 5/9}

This combination of values includes several of the most difficult pursuer/evader encounters, which occur when the values for both J_i and K_i are small (denoting small initial pursuer/evader distances and lead angles).

Five separate training runs were performed for each type of pursuer, with each run using a different random number seed during the creation and subsequent evolution of the program population. The particular set of random number seeds used for this study was:

Seed ∈ {0.2, 0.4, 0.6, 0.8, 1.0}

After evolving five best-of-run programs for each type of pursuer, these programs were subsequently tested against a population of 128 pursuers, described by the following set values for J and K:

J = {0.1, 0.15, 0.2, 0.25, 0.3, 0.35, 0.4, 0.45, 0.5, 0.55, 0.6, 0.65, 0.7, 0.75, 0.8, 0.85}

K = {1/9, 2/9, 3/9, 4/9, 5/9, 6/9, 7/9, 8/9}

The results of these tests, showing the number and percentage of successful evasions for each best-of-run program evolved against each type of pursuer, are shown in Figure 3. Note that each entry represents the result of testing a program optimized against a specific type of pursuer, using a test population consisting of the same type of pursuers.

IV. INTRODUCING UNCERTAINTY ABOUT THE STATE OF THE PURSUER

Uncertainty introduces a degree of complexity into the E2DPE problem that is difficult to model using traditional analytical and control-theoretic approaches (Krasovskii and Subbotin, 1988). Techniques for evolving optimized solutions to the E2DPE problem under uncertainty about the *type* of pursuer were examined in (Moore and Garcia, 1997b). In contrast, this study is concerned with determining a methodology for using GP to evolve programs that exhibit optimized performance when the *state* of the pursuer is either unknown or uncertain. "Uncertainty about pursuer state" occurs when the evader is deprived of important information describing the current state of the pursuer. The critical question addressed by this paper is:

Can genetic programming be used to evolve programs that perform near-optimally in situations where the state of the pursuer is either unknown or uncertain?

If so, these programs would represent an alternative to classic analytic and control-theoretic solutions to pursuer/evader problems (Shinar and Steinberg, 1977; Grimm and Well, 1990; Zarchan, 1990; Barron, 1995), which require precise knowledge of the state of the pursuer to identify optimal evasion strategies.

To begin to answer this question, we replaced the selection functions ifDistance, ifPX, and ifPY (as defined in Figure 2) with an ifTime function. In this manner, dependency upon knowledge of the state of the pursuer was eliminated from the programs evolved by the GP

PROGRAM	SA-6	SA-13	SA-15
1 (seed = 1.0)	125 (97.7%)	116 (90.6%)	111 (86.7%)
2 (seed = 0.8)	128 (100%)	115 (89.8%)	113 (88.3%)
3 (seed = 0.6)	128 (100%)	120 (93.8%)	112 (87.5%)
4 (seed = 0.4)	127 (99.2%)	115 (89.8%)	113 (88.3%)
5 (seed = 0.2)	128 (100%)	120 (93.8%)	114 (89.1%)
Average:	127.2 (99.4%)	117.2 (91.6%)	112.6 (88.0%)
Variance:	1.36 (1.06%)	5.36 (4.18%)	1.04 (0.81%)

Figure 3. Test Results for the State-Dependent Solution to the Extended Two-Dimensional Pursuer/Evader Problem

system. ifTime is a three-argument function; if the time elapsed since the beginning of the pursuer/evader encounter is less than the percentage of the maximum duration of the encounter specified by the absolute value of the first argument, then the second argument is evaluated; otherwise, the third argument is evaluated. ifTime returns the value of the evaluated argument. For example, the program fragment

```
(ifTime 0.25 (setThrust 0.7) (hardTurn -0.6))
```

is interpreted as follows: If the time elapsed since the start of the encounter is less than 25% of the maximum encounter duration, set the thrust equal to 70% of the maximum thrust value; otherwise turn to the left at 60% of the maximum turning rate. Note that ifTime requires the evader to know the starting time of the encounter, but does not otherwise depend upon knowledge about the pursuer's current state. The maximum duration of each encounter depends upon the *type* of pursuer, and was assumed during this study to be equal to the time required by the pursuer to traverse from its initial launch position to a distance equal to 125% of its maximum effective range.

Using this new function set, training runs 1-5 were repeated for each type of pursuer, and a new set of programs were optimized for solving the E2DPE problem under conditions in which the current state of the pursuer was unknown. Note that the *type* of pursuer (SA-6, SA-13, or SA-15) was assumed to be known; each pursuer in the training population was assumed to use proportional navigation with an effective navigation ratio N' = 4.

Each best-of-run program was subsequently tested against a large, representative test population of 128 pursuers described by the cross-product of sets J and K, as defined above. Each pursuer in each test population was of the same type as the pursuers in the corresponding training population. The results of these tests are summarized in Figures 4, 5, and 6.

PROGRAM	RESULTS
SA-6 Test 1 (seed = 1.0)	124 (96.9%)
SA-6 Test 2 (seed = 0.8)	128 (100%)
SA-6 Test 3 (seed = 0.6)	126 (98.4%)
SA-6 Test 4 (seed = 0.4)	128 (100%)
SA-6 Test 5 (seed = 0.2)	128 (100%)
Mean = 126.8 (99.1%)	Variance = 2.56 (2.00%)

Figure 4. State-Independent Solutions to the E2DPE Problem: SA-6 Test Results

PROGRAM	RESULTS
SA-13 Test 1 (seed = 1.0)	118 (92.2%)
SA-13 Test 2 (seed = 0.8)	120 (93.8%)
SA-13 Test 3 (seed = 0.6)	120 (93.8%)
SA-13 Test 4 (seed = 0.4)	120 (93.8%)
SA-13 Test 5 (seed = 0.2)	119 (93.0%)
Mean = 119.4 (93.3%)	Variance = 0.64 (0.50%)

Figure 5. State-Independent Solutions to the E2DPE Problem: SA-13 Test Results

PROGRAM	RESULTS
SA-15 Test 1 (seed = 1.0)	113 (88.3%)
SA-15 Test 2 (seed = 0.8)	114 (89.1%)
SA-15 Test 3 (seed = 0.6)	114 (89.1%)
SA-15 Test 4 (seed = 0.4)	114 (89.1%)
SA-15 Test 5 (seed = 0.2)	112 (87.5%)
Mean = 113.4 (88.6%)	Variance = 0.64 (0.50%)

Figure 6. State-Independent Solutions to the E2DPE Problem: SA-15 Test Results

V. ANALYSIS OF TEST RESULTS

Test results clearly demonstrate that the GP system developed during this study was capable of evolving programs that exhibited optimized survivability *without* depending upon knowledge of the pursuer's current state. For SA-6 pursuers, the average fitness of best-of-run programs evolved under conditions of uncertainty about pursuer state differed from that of programs evolved under conditions of certainty by only 0.3%; for SA-13s, this difference was only 1.7%; and for SA-15s, this difference was only 0.6%. In light of the variances indicated in Figure 3, *none* of these differences are considered to be statistically significant. This study demonstrated that certainty about the starting time of the encounter and the type of pursuer provides enough information to the GP system to allow it to produce effective solutions to the E2DPE problems illustrated by Figure 1.

VI. CONCLUSIONS

The GP system described in this paper defines a new methodology for identifying optimized solutions to the E2DPE problem. The advantage of the new methodology is that the resulting evasion programs exhibit optimized performance, *without* requiring information describing the state of the pursuer. The GP methodology used in this project thus provides a medium for automatically creating optimized solutions to a class of difficult strategy optimization problems that may be superior to classical analytic and game-theoretic solutions. As part of on-going dissertation research (Moore, 1997), the methodology established by this study was subsequently extended to integrate the use of countermeasures (such as chaff, flares, and jamming) with maneuvers to further enhance the survivability of the evader under conditions of uncertainty. The dissertation research ultimately defined a genetic programming solution to the three-dimensional missile countermeasures optimization problem.

VII. BIBLIOGRAPHY

Ball, R. E., 1985. The Fundamentals of Aircraft Combat Survivability Analysis and Design, AIAA Education Series, AIAA Inc.

Barron, R. L., 1995. "Reduced-Computation End-Game Steering Laws for Predictive Guidance", in Journal of Guidance, Control, and Dynamics, Vol. 18 No 2, March-April 1995, pp. 306-315, American Institute of Aeronautics and Astronautics, Inc.

Cullen, T. and C. Foss, 1995. Jane's Land-Based Air Defence: 1995-1996, Jane's Information Group, Inc.

Grimm, W. and K. H. Well, 1990. "Modelling Air Combat as Differential Game: Recent Approaches and Future Requirements", in Hamalainen, R. P. and H. K. Ehtamo (eds.), Differential Games -- Developments in Modeling and Computation, Lecture Notes in Control and Information Sciences Vol. 156, pp. 1-13, Springer-Verlag.

Hamalainen, R. P. and H. K. Ehtamo (eds.), 1990. Differential Games -- Developments in Modeling and Computation, Lecture Notes in Control and Information Sciences Vol. 156, Springer-Verlag.

Klos, K., W. Parada and S. Sakamoto, Eidetics International, Inc., 1994. ARENA II Man-in-the-Loop Multi-Mission Air Combat Simulation, Final Report WL-TR-94-3137, Flight Dynamics Directorate, Wright Laboratory, Air Force Materiel Command, Wright-Patterson Air Force Base, OH.

Koza, J. R., 1992. Genetic Programming: On the Programming of Computers by Means of Natural Selection, MIT Press.

Krasovskii, N. N. and A. I. Subbotin, 1988. Game-Theoretical Control Problems, Springer-Verlag.

Lambert, M. and K. Munson (eds.), 1994. Jane's All the World's Aircraft: 1994-1995, Jane's Information Group, Inc.

Moore, F. W., 1997. "A Methodology for Strategy Optimization Under Uncertainty", Ph.D. Dissertation, Computer Science & Engineering, Wright State University.

Moore, F. W. and O. N. Garcia, 1997a. "A Genetic Programming Approach to Strategy Optimization in the Extended Two-Dimensional Pursuer/Evader Problem", in Koza *et al* (eds.), Genetic Programming 1997: Proceedings of the Second Annual Conference, pp. 249-254, Morgan Kaufmann Publishers, Inc.

Moore, F. W. and O. N. Garcia, 1997b. "A Methodology for Strategy Optimization Under Uncertainty the Extended Two-Dimensional Pursuer/Evader Problem", in Santos, E. Jr. (ed.), Proceedings: Eighth Midwest Artificial Intelligence and Cognitive Science Conference, pp. 58-65, AAAI Technical Report CF-97-01, AAAI Press.

Ramo, S. and A. Pucket, 1959. Guided Missile Engineering, McGraw-Hill, pp. 176-180.

Shinar, J. and D. Steinberg, 1977. "Analysis of Optimal Evasive Maneuvers Based on a Linearized Two-Dimensional Model", in Journal of Aircraft, Vol. 14, August 1977, pp. 795-802.

Stevens, B. L. and F. L. Lewis, 1992. Aircraft Control and Simulation, John Wiley and Sons, Inc.

Zarchan, P., 1990. Tactical and Strategic Missile Guidance, Progress in Astronautics and Aeronautics Vol. 124, American Institute of Aeronautics and Astronautics.

Session D.3

Object-Oriented Methodologies for Knowledge Representation and Reasoning

Session Chair:
David Eichmann, University of Iowa, USA

An Object-Oriented Approach to Visual Database[+]

Taehyung Wang and Phillip C.-Y. Sheu
Electrical and Computer Engineering Department
University of California
Irvine, CA 92697

Abstract

As the demand for virtual reality systems increases, a new approach is needed to meet the following requirements: 1) A world consists of a large number of objects; 2) A camera is allowed to move and a world should be displayed in near real-time depending on the position of the camera as well as the angle of its lens; and 3) Minimum effort should be needed when objects are moving. We satisfy these requirements with the following: 1) An object-oriented rendering approach is developed; and 2) An approach based on spatial indexing (specifically R^+-tree) is developed to manage operations to objects (i.e., retrieval, insertion, and deletion) effectively.

Keywords: object-oriented approach, characteristic view, hierarchical storage, and region tree

1. Introduction

In this paper we propose the approaches to retrieving, updating, and displaying a 3-D static or dynamic world which consists of a large number of objects stored in a database. In traditional computer graphics, the major concern is to display a scene accurately without the consideration of secondary storage, and the current spatial database systems do not consider the "visual properties" of objects. Due to the demand for large virtual reality systems, a new methodology is needed to meet the following requirements: 1) A world consists of a large number of objects thus objects have to be stored in a database; 2) A camera is allowed to move and a world should be displayed in near real-time depending on the position of the camera as well as the angle of its lens; and 3) Minimum effort should be needed when objects are moving. To our knowledge, the existing work cannot support the above requirements effectively.

Our approaches to the problems stated in the above can be summarized as follows: 1) Using the concept of object, characteristic views and region trees, an object-oriented rendering approach is implemented. Using this approach the rendering time can be reduced significantly. We show that this approach outperforms other approaches based on preliminary experiments; and 2) An object management approach has been developed to manage a large number of objects in a world with effective spatial indexing.

The remaining of this paper is organized as follows. In Section 2, we discuss the existing work related to the research. Section 3 describes an object-oriented rendering process which consists of an object ordering algorithm. In Section 4, we discuss a method to store 3-D objects in a database and an approach to managing objects with an efficient spatial index scheme. This paper is concluded in Section 5.

2. Background

The paper is related to work exists in two areas: visual database (specifically image database and spatial database) and computer graphics. A major concern of the existing image databases is the storage and retrieval of 2-D images (pictures). One typical approach is to associate each image with some structured attributes or keywords based on which images can be retrieved. Content-based retrieval is a more natural and useful way to retrieve image data; however, it could be a difficult problem for general domains.

Spatial data are the data related to objects that occupy space. A spatial database stores spatial objects

[+] This research is supported in part by NIH under grant number AG-14149 and a UCI Multi-Investigator Faculty Research Grant.

1082-3409/97 $10.00 © 1997 IEEE

represented by spatial data types and spatial relationships among such objects. A spatial database is organized by certain spatial indexing structures and accessed by some spatial access methods. Applications of spatial databases can be found in GIS (Geographic Information Systems), resource and environmental management, agriculture, geology, and CAD.

Compared with the work on image databases and spatial databases, our visual database considers the display of a scene as well as the retrieval and update of graphic data efficiently.

In computer graphics, to generate a 3-D world several processes are required; these include hidden surface removal, shadowing, shading, and texture mapping. Given a set of objects and a view point, it should be determined which objects or which surfaces of objects are invisible. This process is known as hidden surface removal. Shadows improve realism and give useful information about the relationships between objects in a 3-D space. A texture provides depth cues and the appearance of an object's surface. To have an object look real, an image can be mapped to the surfaces of an object. This is known as texture mapping. Each surface's appearance depends on the type of the light source, its property (color, texture, reflection), and its position and orientation with respect to the light source, and the view point. This step is called shading. Previous work on hidden surface removal can be categorized into two approaches: object-precision and image-precision. The object-precision algorithms are performed at the precision with which each object is defined (Note that most algorithms consider a polygon as an "object"). The image-precision algorithms are performed at the resolution of the display device to determine the visibility and the shadows at each pixel. Two most well known algorithms are the Binary Space Partition (BSP) tree algorithm (polygon-precision) and the *z*-buffer algorithm (image-precision). Our approach is an object-oriented approach in the sense that a logical object is considered as a unit based on the observation that the polygons associated with an object typically have the same state and behaviors.

The BSP tree algorithm, developed by Fuchs et. al. [9][10], is efficient in a static environment in which the view point can be changed easily. However a major drawback of this algorithm is that it requires a polygon to be split if the polygon lies in a partitioning plane. Another disadvantage is the expensive cost to reconstruct the BSP tree if an object moves. Toress [18] used auxiliary planes to represent a dynamic scene; however it loses the simplicity of the original BSP tree algorithm. Most extended or applied algorithms for the original BSP tree algorithm deal with polygons [6][18]. If a scene consists of many objects and each object consists of many polygons, the time complexity involved in traversing a BSP tree increases rapidly.

In this paper, we take an object-oriented approach to solve the above problems. The concepts of characteristic views (CVs) and region trees are introduced to solve the hidden surface removal problem with minimum splitting. An R^+-tree approach is employed to search the objects within a view volume and to insert and delete an object efficiently. We combine CVs and region trees with an R^+-tree.

3. An Object-Oriented Rendering Approach

3.1 The OOBSP Tree Algorithm

Since the BSP tree algorithm was introduced, many extended or applied algorithms for the original BSP tree algorithm have been reported. Most of the previous work deal with polygons which are components of polyhedra (objects). If a scene consists of many objects and they are allowed to move, the display cost and the management cost of a BSP tree becomes expensive because the size of the tree become large. The OOBSP (Object-Oriented Binary Space Partition) tree algorithm can more effectively deal with a large number of moving objects.

While most of the previous work deal with each polygon of an object, the OOBSP tree algorithm deals with each object as a unit. When a scene is displayed using a BSP tree, two procedures are needed generally: one is to build a tree and the other is to draw a tree. The purpose of the OOBSP tree algorithm is not only to save the time for building and drawing a tree, but also to simplify the cost of managing the tree in case objects move. The internal nodes of an OOBSP tree are the partitioning planes used to partition a space in order to decide the relative location of each object. Objects are attached to the tree as leaves. When an object is split by a partitioning plane, two new objects are produced: one object lies in the front and the other lies in the back of the plane. Intuitively, compared with the original BSP tree algorithm, the size of a BSP tree can be reduced with the object-oriented approach.

As a simple example, suppose there are three cubes as shown in Figure 1. According to the original BSP tree algorithm, there are 18 nodes in the BSP tree since each polygon must be a node of the tree as shown in Figure 1. Only 5 nodes are required for the object-oriented BSP tree algorithm as shown in Figure 2. In order to build the OOBSP tree, $p1$ is first selected as the partitioning plane whose direction is shown in Figure 2, then object $o1$ is in the front of $p1$ and objects $o2$ and $o3$ are in the back of $p1$ Subsequently we can separate objects $o2$ and $o3$ using another partitioning plane $p2$. Finally, we can obtain the OOBSP tree as shown in Figure 2.

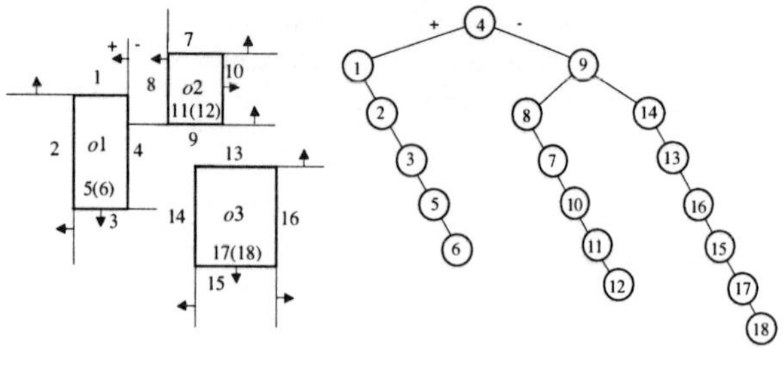

Figure 1. Top view of a scene and the corresponding BSP tree

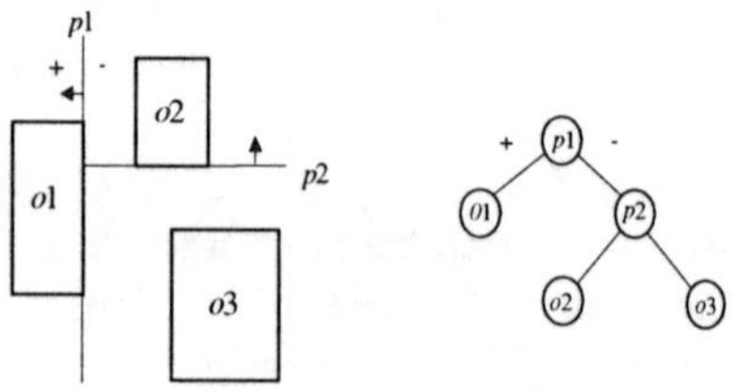

Figure 2. Top view of a scene and the corresponding object-oriented BSP tree

3.2 A Visualization Methodology Using CVs of Objects

The idea of Characteristic Views (CVs) was derived based on the observation that the infinite possible views of a 3-D object can be grouped into a finite number of equivalence classes so that within each class all the views are isomorphic in the sense that they have the same line-junction graphs. The CVs of an object can represent the 3-D object in the 2-D world and can be used in model-based object recognition [2][3][4]. With an arbitrary image of a 3-D object, the exact object corresponding to the image can be recognized by comparing the characteristics of the image with the existing CVs. A CV is a representative of a characteristic view domain (CVD) that is a region of the viewing space of a 3-D object. When the view point is moving within a CVD, the characteristics of the images are not changed. We apply the concept of CV to planar-based 3-D objects. In our method, each CVD has the same set of visible polygons associated with an object. Within a CVD, the visible polygons of an object are not changed.

3.2.1 SPBT Construction for an Object

To create the CVDs of an object, a data structure called *space partitioning binary tree* (SPBT) is introduced where each internal node of the SPBT is associated with a partitioning plane and each leaf node is associated with a subspace corresponding to a CVD. Each CVD of an object corresponds to a subspace of the entire 3-D space. Given an object, we use a space partitioning binary tree (SPBT) to identify the set of CVDs for the given view point. For example, consider the object shown in Figure 3. If the camera (we use the terms "camera" and "view point" interchangeably) is located in area 2, the visible polygons of the object are *a* and *c*.

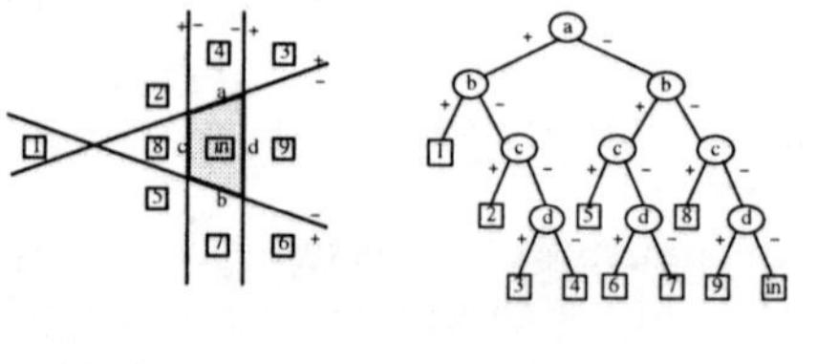

Figure 3. The Space Partitioning Binary Tree for an object

3.2.2 Region Tree

To display a set of objects, we need to obtain an ordering of the objects and draw them from the farthest one to the nearest one. The object space can be divided into a set of regions so that in each region all view points have the same object ordering. Therefore if we store each region together with its associated ordering, the objects can be displayed easily for a given view point. For any two convex objects there is a plane that separates them into two different subspaces. This means we can obtain an ordering between the two objects for any view point. Thus if we can obtain all the partitioning planes for all pairs of objects, we can obtain the ordering of the objects. In order to represent regions of view points, a *region tree* can be defined. It is a binary tree whose internal nodes correspond to a direction of a partition plane and the leaves correspond to the orderings of objects.

We will show an example using the scene shown in Figure 4, which is two-dimensional for simplicity. The example can be easily extended to three-dimensions. Figure 5 shows the partitioning lines and the view regions corresponding to the scene given in Figure 4. After executing the space partitioning algorithm the region tree shown in Figure 6 can be obtained.

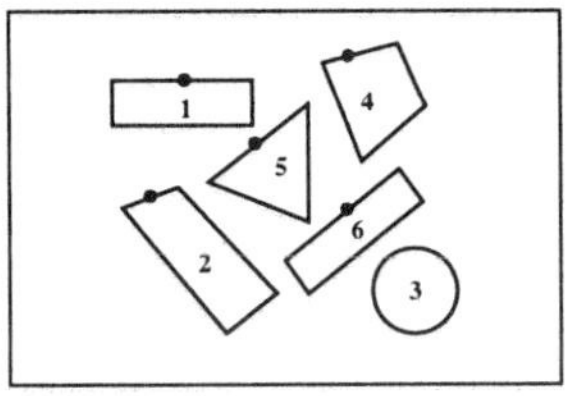

Figure 4. An example scene composed of 6 objects

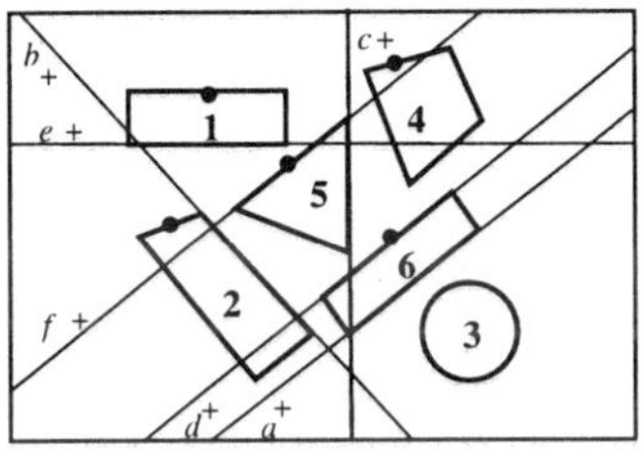

Figure 5. Partitioning lines and view regions for the scene shown in Figure 4

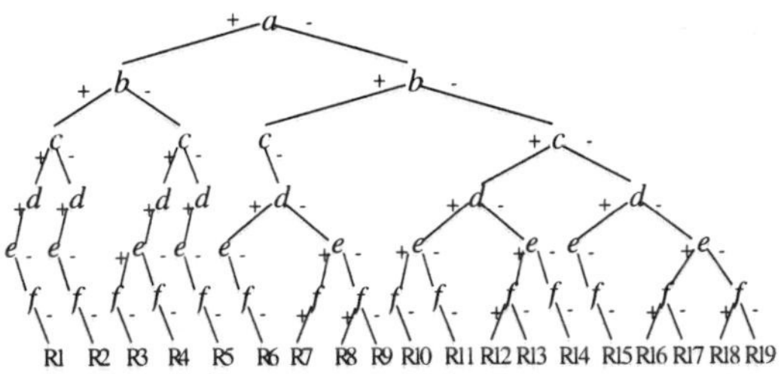

Figure 6. The region tree for the scene of Figure 4

3.2.3 Object Ordering for a Specific View Region

For a specific view region, we can easily obtain an ordering of objects based on the partitioning planes. For each pair of objects, there is a partial ordering between them given a partitioning plane. For example, in Figure 5, object 1 is in the rear of object 3 based on the partitioning plane a if the view point is located in the a+ area. If we collect all these partial orderings in the scene, we can obtain a total ordering of all the objects. To represent the partial orderings, we define a directed graph called *ordering graph*. Each node of the graph represents an object to be displayed and each directed edge represents a spatial relationship (a partial ordering) between two nodes. For instance, if object o_i is in the rear of object o_j for the view point, then a directed edge $<o_i, o_j>$ is added to the graph, where o_i is the tail of the edge and o_j is the head of the edge. The edges in the graph can be easily obtained from the set of partitioning lines and the definition of the view region where the view point is located. Once the graph is constructed, an ordering of all objects can be determined by taking a topological order from the graph.

We will describe some properties of an ordering graph: First, if there exist two edges $<o_i, o_j>$ and $<o_j, o_i>$ for two objects o_i and o_j in the graph, the order of the two objects can be ignored and both edges can be deleted from the graph. This means that we need not consider the order between the two objects because they can be displayed in any order. Second, if there exists a cycle $<o_i, o_j>, <o_j, o_k>, \dots, <o_m, o_i>$ among more than three objects, it is impossible to determine an order among them because we cannot obtain a topological order. In this case, we must remove the cycle by splitting an object in the cycle and modify the graph. This is the case that ordering of objects cannot be obtained without object splitting. Third, if there exists a cycle $<o_i, o_j>, <o_j, o_k>, \dots, <o_m, o_i>$ for the view point, then the reverse cycle $<o_i, o_m>, \dots, <o_k, o_j>, <o_j, o_i>$ also exists for the view points in the opposite side of the view region. Thus, if a cycle is removed, the reverse cycle is also removed.

Let us consider the ordering graph for the view region R1 in our previous example shown in Figure 4. The view region R1 is defined as (a+, b+, c+, d+, e-, f-) by the region tree shown in Figure 6. Since object 3 is located in the front of objects 1, 2, 4, 5 and 6 by line a, edges <1, 3>, <2, 3>, <4, 3>, <5, 3> and <6, 3> are added to the graph. Next, because object 2 is located in the front of objects 3, 4, 5 and 6 by line b, edges <3, 2>, <4, 2>, <5, 2> and <6, 2> are added. By applying these decisions to all the lines repeatedly and deleting two pairs of edges, namely <2, 3>, <3, 2> and <2, 4>, <4, 2>, we can obtain the ordering graph shown in Figure 7(a). In Figure 7(b) to 7(f), we show the procedure to obtain a topological order from the graph. First, we select object 1 which has no incoming edges and remove the node and its outgoing edges from the graph (Figure 7(c)). Next, we select object 5 from the reduced graph shown in Figure 7(c) and remove the node and its outgoing edges (Figure 7(d)). By applying this process repeatedly until no more nodes are left in the graph, we can obtain an ordering of the objects: 1, 5, 4, 6, 3, 2 or 1, 5, 4, 6, 2, 3.

In Figure 8, we show a typical example in which object splitting cannot be avoided. Three objects 1, 2 and 3 are overlapped with each other and cannot be assigned an order for some view regions. For instance, we can simply obtain an ordering of the objects as 3, 2, 1 for any view point in R1 which is defined as (*a*+, *b*+, *c*+). But for a view point in R3 and R6, there are cycles such as <1, 3>, <3, 2>, <2, 1> and <1, 2>, <2, 3>, <3, 1> respectively, see Figure 8(e). In this example, view regions R3 and R6 are in the opposite side of each other.

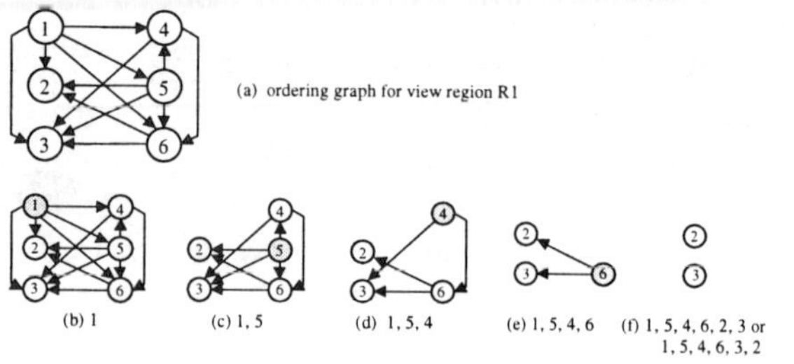

Figure 7. Ordering graph for view region R1

To remove the cycle we must select an object in the cycle and split it into two objects based on the partitioning plane which divides it. Let us assume that we choose object 3 and split it into two objects 31 and 32 by partitioning plane *a* (Figure 9(a)). Then, the set P of partitioning planes is modified in Figure 9(b), but the region tree is not changed. For view region R3, an ordering graph can be obtained as shown in Figure 9(c) and the ordering becomes 32, 2, 1, 31. For view region R6, we can obtain the ordering 31, 1, 2, 32 by reversing the previous ordering.

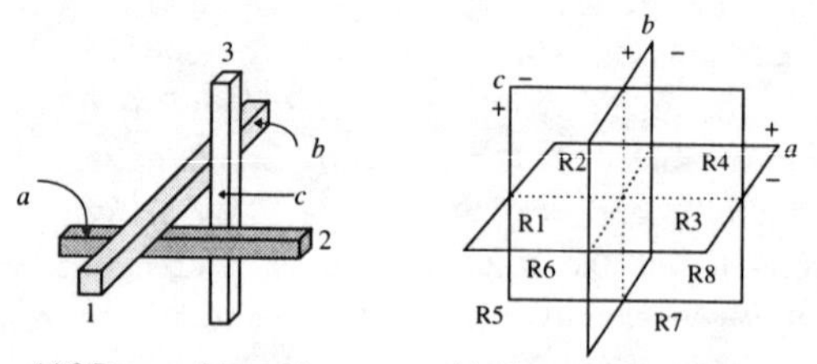

(a) 3-D scene of three objects

(b) 3-D partitioned view regions

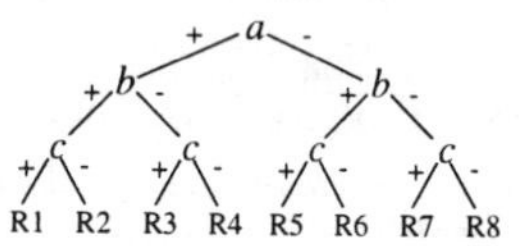

(c) region tree

ID	+	-	split
a	1	2	3
b	1	3	2
c	2	3	1

(d) set P of partitioning planes

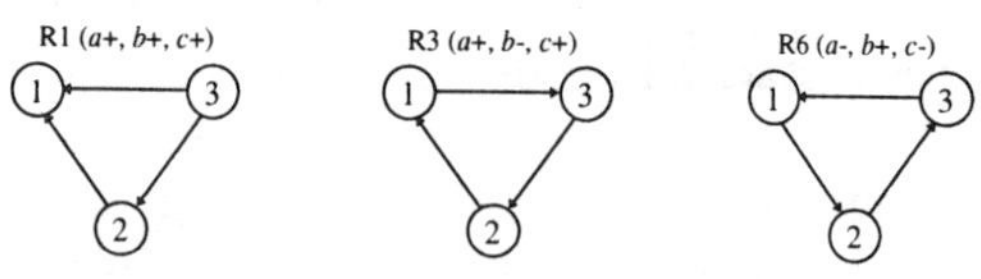

(e) ordering graphs for view regions R1, R3, R6

Figure 8. A 3-D scene requiring object splitting

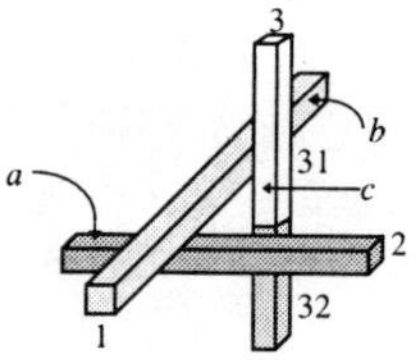

ID	+	-	split
a	1, 31	2, 32	3
b	1	31, 32	2
c	2	31, 32	1

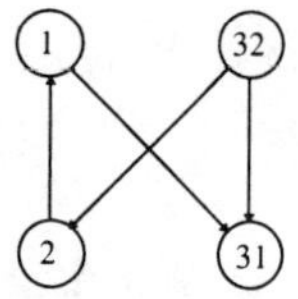

(a) object splitting (b) P (c) modified ordering graph

Figure 9. A 3-D scene after object splitting

3.2.4 Experimental Result

Figure 10 shows a performance comparison among the object-ordering algorithm, the object-oriented BSP tree algorithm, and the original BSP tree algorithm. A cube is employed as an object. The polygons of an object based on a serial order are selected as the partitioning planes in the BSP tree algorithms. As shown in Figure 10 the performance of the object-ordering algorithm is the best because of two factors: object-orientation and minimum splitting.

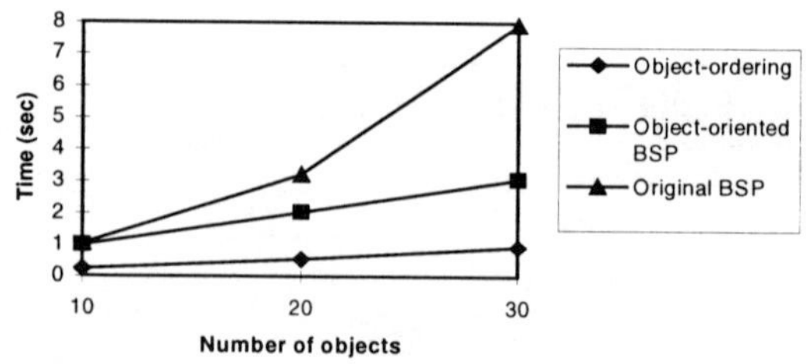

Figure 10. Performance of three algorithms for displaying a scene

4. Object Management

In order to handle multi-dimensional data efficiently, a database system needs an index mechanism that will retrieve data quickly according to their spatial locations. A number of methods have been proposed in the past to handle multi-dimensional data. Cell methods are not efficient for a dynamic environment because the size of a cell must be decided in advance. Quad tress and *k-d* trees are not suitable for handling disk pages.

Because a world consists of a large number of objects and the objects are required to be stored in a database, it is necessary to employ a spatial index mechanism. An R^{+}-tree [14], which is a variant of a R-tree, is suitable for region trees and CVs. Because an R^{+}-tree avoids any overlap among rectangles, it has significantly advantage for searching [8].

4.1 R-Tree

An R-tree [11] is an extension of a B-tree in *k*-dimensions. The data structure is a height-balanced tree. The data objects are stored in the leaf nodes and an intermediate node contains a set of entries each of which contains a pointer to a child node and a rectangle which encloses all rectangles in the lower levels.

A search in an R-tree descends the tree from the root until the object is found in a leaf. Inserting a new object can be done by searching the location and adding the object as a leaf node. A leaf node may split, if an overflow occurs, when the tree is updated. Deleting an object can be done by locating the object and removing it from the associated leaf node. If the number of entries at a leaf node is low, relocation of its entries is necessary.

4.2 R$^+$-Tree

The performance of searching in an R-tree degrades as the amount of *dead space* (i.e. empty space) increases [14]. The concepts of *coverage* and *overlap* are different. Coverage is defined as the area in which a rectangle occupies. Overlap is defined as the total area contained by two or more rectangles. Minimal overlap is more critical than minimal coverage [14]. In an R$^+$-tree no overlap is allowed at the expense of rectangle splitting. Splittings may increase the height of an R$^+$-tree. However [14] showed that better search performance can be obtained using an R$^+$-tree.

4.3 Hierarchical Storage of 3-D Objects

Using the packing algorithm [13] we can build an R$^+$-tree with minimum coverage. After building the tree, the region tree corresponding to each node can be generated. Note that the region tree of a leaf node handles the real objects. On the other hand, the region tree of a non leaf-node handles rectangles.

Given the position of the camera, its view volume can be determined, and the view volume can be considered as a search window. The ordering of search in a node can be obtained using the corresponding region tree at the given view point. The following algorithm, SEARCH, finds all objects in the view volume and their ordering (to be displayed).

Algorithm : **SEARCH** (*R*, *V*)
Input : an R$^+$-tree pointed at a node *R* and a view volume *V*
Output : all objects inside the view volume according to the view point

```
if (R is not leaf)
        /* The ordering of entries is determined by a region tree
        given the view point */
    for each entry (p, BOX) of R  /* p is the pointer to a child */
        if (BOX is overlapped with V)
            SEARCH (CHILD, V ∩ BOX); /* CHILD is the node
            pointed to by p */
else /* R is a leaf */
    check all objects and return those that overlap with V;
```

Figure 11 and 12 show an example for the SEARCH algorithm. Given the view point, the region tree of each entry gives the object ordering. For example, given the view point, the ordering of entries at the root node is 5, 4, 3, 2, and 1. Assume that entries 3 and 1 overlap with the view volume. The child nodes of entry 3 and entry 1 which are overlapped with the view volume are 18, 19, and 6 respectively as shown in Figure 11. Suppose that the order between entry 18 and entry 19 at the view point is 19 and 18. In the same manner the objects belonging to entry 19 can be ordered by the corresponding region tree, for instance, *o*70, *o*69, *o*68, *o*67, and *o*66. The object ordering of entry 18 and entry 6 is *o*65, *o*64, *o*63, *o*62, *o*61 and *o*5, *o*4, *o*3, *o*2, *o*1 respectively. The final object ordering for the view volume is as follows: *o*70, *o*69, *o*68, *o*67, *o*66 *o*65, *o*64, *o*63, *o*62, *o*61 *o*5, *o*4, *o*3, *o*2, and *o*1. In the display stage, clipping is needed after the objects are projected from 3-D to 2-D.

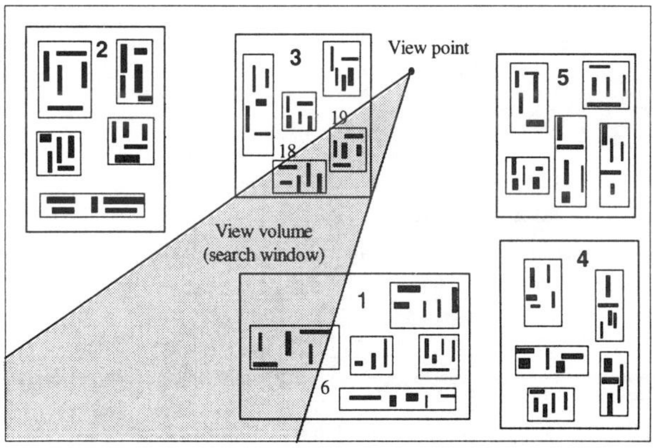

Figure 11. The scene which is decomposed into 5 regions

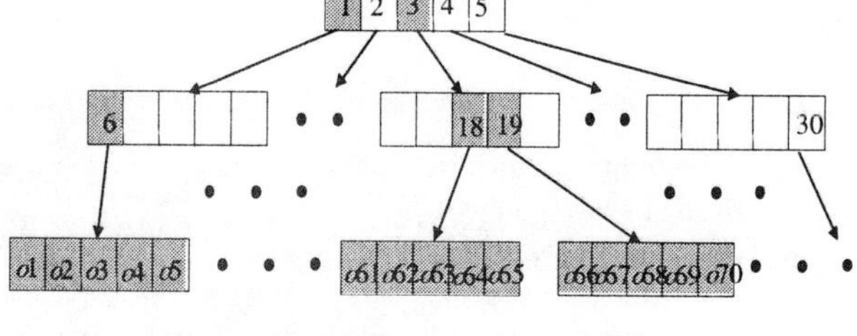

Figure 12. The R^+-tree for the Figure 11

4.3.1 Object Insertion

Inserting a new object into an R^+-tree can be done by searching the R^+-tree and adding the object as a leaf node. The object may be split and added to more than one leaf node because it may be broken according to existing regions. An insertion operation also affects the associated region trees. The affected region trees should be updated. If the number of entries exceeds the maximum number of entries in a node, node-splitting is required to re-organize the tree. In this case, the region trees related to the affected nodes should be modified as well. The following algorithm, INSERT, inserts a new rectangle for a new object into an R^+-tree.

Algorithm: INSERT (*N*, *NR*)
Input : an R^+-tree pointed at a node *N* and a new rectangle *NR*
Output : the new R^+-tree updated after the insertion of *NR*

```
if N is not a leaf {
    for each entry (p, RECT) of N
        if (RECT is overlapped with NR)
            INSERT (Child, NR∩ RECT); // Child is the node
            pointed to by p //
}
else { // N is a leaf //
    add NR in N and ADD_REGION_TREE(N,O);
      if (the number of entries of N in a node exceeds the
            maximum entries)
            split the node to update the tree and build the region
              trees;
}
```

Algorithm: ADD_REGION_TREE(*N*, *O*)
Input : an R^+-tree pointed at a node *N* and a new object *O*
Output : the region tree updated after the insertion of object *O*

```
{
// 1. Using the existing partition lines to compare the new
object with other objects //
for each object in a region tree {
    compare a new object with each object using existing
        partitioning lines;
        obtain pairs whose ordering cannot be determined;
}
// 2. Generate new partition lines //
for each undetermined pairs
        generate new partition lines;

// 3. Insert new lines into a region tree //
for each new line
        insert it into a region tree;
```

4.3.2 Object Deletion

Deleting an object from an R^+-tree can be done by first locating the object to be deleted and then removing it from the leaf node. Because an object may be split into several sub-regions all leaf nodes associated with the object should be deleted. The region tree(s) associated with the object should be updated accordingly. The following algorithm, DELETE, deletes a rectangle which is associated with the object to be deleted from an R^+-tree.

Algorithm : DELETE (*N*, *DR*)
Input : an R^+-tree pointed at a node *N* and a rectangle *DR* to be deleted
Output : the new R^+-tree updated after the deletion of *DR*

```
if N is not leaf {
    for each entry (p, RECT) of N
        if (RECT is overlapped with DR)
            INSERT (Child, DR∩ RECT); // Child is the
                node pointed to by p //
}
else // N is a leaf //
    Delete DR from N and DELETE_REGION_TREE(N, O);
```

Algorithm : DELETE_REGION_TREE(*N*, *O*)
Input : an R^+-tree pointed at a node *N* and an object *O* to be deleted
Output : the region tree updated after the deletion of object *O*

```
// 1. delete the object and compare the remaining objects using
the existing partitioning lines //
delete the object from the set of objects in region tree;
for the remaining objects
    compare pair objects ;

// 2. delete the redundant line from the region tree//
delete the redundant partitioning line from the region tree;
```

5. Conclusion and Future Work

We have developed an object-oriented rendering approach (which includes an object-oriented BSP tree algorithm and a visualization methodology using CVs of objects) and a hierarchical approach for storing and managing 3-D objects. We have accomplished some results for the object-ordering rendering approach whose performance is better than that of any existing work. However, some improvements should be considered. In addition, we need to have a precise performance analysis for searching and updating objects in an R^+-tree.

Using one region tree may not be efficient to build and maintain the object orderings for a scene. The CV algorithm does not consider the method to handle concave objects. If the objects in a scene are allowed to move, the cost of updating the associated region tree can be expensive. The cost of checking cyclic-ordering must be considered as well. Overall the cost of preprocessing is more expensive than that of the BSP algorithm.

The object ordering method has better performance even though the preprocessing cost is relatively high. A major benefit of this algorithm is that it requires the minimum number of object splitting. Some further improvements can be made, however.

Remember that each CVD for an object has a set of visible polygons associated with the view point. Within the same CVD the projected image of an object is different depending on the view point and its angle. Consequently, in the display stage, the projection from a 3-D object to an image is needed. If we have a 2-D image of an object associated with each CVD in advance and image transformation with respect to the view point can be done efficiently, we can get better performance.

In summary, our future tasks for object-oriented rendering include the following: 1) Consider CVs as images and develop an efficient image mapping algorithm; and 2) Obtain analytic and experimental results for searching and updating objects in an R^+-tree.

Reference

[1] Atherton, P., Weiler, K., and Greenberg,D,. "Polygon Shadow Generation," *Proc. SIGGRAPH 78, Computer Graphics* vol. 12, no. 3, pp. 275-281, July 1978.

[2] Chakravarty, I. and Freeman, H., "Characteristic Views as a Basis for Three-Dimensional Object Recognition," SPIE, Vol. 336 pp. 37-45, 1982.

[3] Chen, S. and Freeman H., "On the Characteristic Views of Quadric-Surfaced Solids," Proc. IEEE Workshop on Directions in Automated CAD-Based Vision, pp. 1-10, June 1991.

[4] Chen, S. and Freeman H., "The Primary Set of Characteristic Views of 3D objects," SPIE Proc., Vol. 1570, 1991.

[5] Chin, N., and Feiner, S., "Near Real-Time Shadow Generation Using BSP Trees," *Proc. SIGGRAPH 89, Computer Graphics*, vol. 23, no. 3, pp. 99-106, July 1989.

[6] Chrysanthou, Y., Slater, M., "Computing Dynamic Changes to BSP Trees." Eurographics '92, A. Kilgour and L. Kjelldahl (Editors), Blackwell Publishers, Vol. 11, No. 3, pp. C311-C332, 1992.

[7] Crow, F., "Shadow Algorithms for Computer Graphics," *Proc. SIGGRAPH '77, Computer Graphics*, vol. 11, no. 3, pp. 242 - 248, July 1977.

[8] Faloutsos, C., Sellis, T., and Roussopoulos, N., "Analysis of Object Oriented Spatial Access Methods." *Proc. SIGMOD*, pp.426 - 439, 1987.

[9] Fuchs, H., Kedem Z. M., and Naylor B. F., "On Visible Surface Generation by A Priori Tree Structure," Proc. SIGGRAPH '80, Computer Graphics, Vol. 14, No. 3, pp. 124 - 133, July 1980.

[10] Fuchs, H., Abram, G. D., and Grant, E. D., "Near Real-Time Shaded Display of Rigid Objects," Proc. SIGGRAPH '83, Computer Graphics, Vol. 17, No. 3, pp. 65 - 72, July 1983.

[11] Guttman, A.., "R-Trees: A Dynamic Index Structure for Spatial Searching," *Proc. ACM SIGMOD*, pp. 47--57, June 1984.

[12] Kanjilai P.P., *Adaptive prediction and predictive control,* Peter Peregrinus Ltd., U.K., 1995.

[13] Roussopoulos, N., and Leifker D., "Direct Spatial Search on Pictorial Databases Using Packed R-trees," *Proc. ACM SIGMOD*, pp. 17 - 31, May 1985.

[14] Sellis, T., Roussopoulos, N., and Faloutsos, C. "The R^+-Tree: A Dynamic Index for Multi-Demensional Objects," *Proc. VLDB.*, pp. 507 - 518, 1987.

[15] Sklansky, J. and Siedlecki, W. "Large-scale Feature Selection," *Handbook of Pattern Recognition and Computer Vision,* ed. by C.H. Chen, L.F. Pau, P.S.P. Wang, World Scientific, Singapore, vol. pp. 61 - 123, 1993.

[16] Swain, M., and Ballard, D. "Color Indexing," *International Journal of Computer Vision,* vol. 7, pp. 11 - 32, 1991.

[17] Thibault, W. and Naylor, B., "Set Operations on Polyhedra Using Binary Space Partitioning Trees," Proc. SIGGRAPH '87, Computer Graphics, Vol. 21, No. 4, pp. 153 - 162, July 1987.

[18] Torres, E., "Optimization of the Binary Space Partition Algorithm (BSP) for the Visualization of Dynamic Scenes." Eurographics '90, C.E. Vandoni and D.A. Duce (Editors), Elsevier Science Publishers B.V. North-Holland, pp. 507 - 518, 1990.

Object-Oriented Constraint Programming Environment NeMo+ and its Applications

V. Telerman

AI Laboratory
Institute of Informatics Systems
Novosibirsk, Russia 630090

V. Sidorov, D. Ushakov

Novosibirsk Division
Russian Reasearch Institute of AI
Novosibirsk, Russia 630090

Abstract

A constraint programming environment NeMo+, *which is implemented on a base of a so-called subdefinite models approach is presented. Subdefinite models are a variety of constraint programming techniques.* NeMo+ *includes a high-level object-oriented declarative language for specification of data types and constraints. The method of subdefinite models is briefly reviewed in the first part of the paper. The* NeMo+ *architecture and the* NeMo+ *language are presented in second part. The* NeMo+ *main capabilities in solving some problems and benchmarks are considered in the rest of the paper.*

1 Introduction

One of the most promising lines of development of a computer science is a constraint programming (CP) paradigm [22]. Constraints are the normal language of discource for many high-level applications. For large scale applications such as geografic information systems, CAD/CAM, and shedulling, the efficient processing and management of large sets of constraints is very important.

The greatest amount of work in CP is done in the context of Logic Programming (the so-called Constraint Logic Programming, or CLP) and are represented, for example, by systems like Prolog III [6], CLP(R) [8], CLP(BNR) [3], CHIP [22], clp(BFD) [5], ILOG-solver [16], Newton [1], etc. An important advantage of the CLP techniques is a solid theoretical foundation, which enables one to define classes of problems to be solved and to evaluate formally the quality of the resulting solutions.

On the other hand, already in the early eighties A. S. Narin'yani proposed the so-called method of subdefinite models (or SD-models, for short) which was mainly intended for processing partially known (or subdefinite) information [12, 13]. This method may be regarded as a synthesis of frame-based methods of knowledge representation [10], interval calculations [11], and Tyugu computational models [20]. As became clear later, the method of SD-models is a variety of constraint programming which is based on the local consistency algorithm [18].

The idea of local constraint satisfaction was proposed in [9] for binary constraints on finite domains. In SD-models such local constraint satisfaction algorithm has been applied to finite domains as well as to continuous ones [13], and to some structured domains as sets [12] or records [14]. Independently of SD-models approach the idea of local consistency was extended to interval constraints for finite domains in [22, 16, 5] and reals in [3, 7]. Recently some authors ([4, 21, 2]) have proposed frameworks for integrating interval constraint solving on reals and integers with traditional local consistency methods for finite domains constraints. The last three approaches are very close to the SD-models approach.

The main difference between SD-models and the other approaches is that SD-models are not implemented into Logic Programming paradigm. Hence, the resolution method or terms unification are lacking in the SD-models implementations. One can consider the SD-models apparatus as a purely constraint satisfaction technique that can be used for solving a wide class of problems.

One of the most successful applications based on SD-models is the *UniCalc* interval solver of mathematical problems [17] and the constraint project manager *Time-Ex* [15]. The main feature of the method of SD-models is that it uses a single algorithm of constraint propagation to process data of different types. This allows one to solve a mix of constraints including e.g., set, Boolean, integer and real variables.

In the most advance manner, the SD-models technique was implemented in the constraint programming environment *NeMo+*. In this paper we examine a constraint programming environment *NeMo+*, and its applications to solving problems. *NeMo+* differs from other systems in this class, the authors are aware of, in the following properties:

1. An extended set of predefined data types which may have finite as well as infinite domains of values, such as sets, Boolean, intervals of integer and real, multiintervals, etc.

2. Availability of high-level facilities for specification of problem-oriented constraints and data types. *NeMo+* is not just a comprehensive and extensible C++ library which supports solution of systems of constraints. It also includes a high-level language for specification of systems of constraints. This language is a purely declarative one and allows one to describe

1082-3409/97 $10.00 © 1997 IEEE

a system of constraints (SD-model of a problem) as a collection of formulas. Object-oriented properties of the *NeMo+* language are used to define the structure of a model and to define problem-oriented data types and constraints from the base ones. In addition, the language includes sophisticated means for controlling the constraint propagation process.

3. Use of the single data-flow algorithm to satisfy systems of constraints.

The first part of the paper briefly reviews the method of SD-models. The second part describes the architecture of *NeMo+* and the main capabilities of the model specification language. The third part presents two applications of the *NeMo+* environment. In the fourth part some tables illustrating efficiency of *NeMo+* in some benchmarks are presented.

2 Subdefinite Models Technique

Formal justification of the method of SD-models may be found in [18]. Here we only recall some basic notions needed to understand better the following chapters.

Subdefinite models (SD-models) in fact determine a certain common technique for the representation and solution of constraint satisfaction problems (CSP) in any subject domains and in any classes of problems.

Suppose we have an object v with an associated set X of admissible values, which will be called its *universe*. The main idea of subdefiniteness is that with the object v we associate not only one exact value but a set of values from its universe. The process of computations within a certain class of objects can be organised as a gradual choice of more and more definite values for these objects.

The *subdefinite extension* (SD-extension) of the universe X is any finite system of sets $^*X$ with the following properties:

$$1.\ \emptyset \in {}^*X; \quad 2.\ X \in {}^*X; \quad 3.\ \forall {}^*x, {}^*y \in {}^*X \quad {}^*x \cap {}^*y \in {}^*X.$$

It is obvious, that we can put several SD-extensions in correspondance to each universe X. The class of all possible SD-extension of the universe X will be denoted by SD(X). Let X_0 be any finite subset of X.

The simplest SD-extension is the SD-extension X_0^{Single}, which can be obtained by adding two special elements to the set X_0: undefined ($\{X\}$) and contradiction ($\{\emptyset\}$).

The maximal SD-extension (X_0^{Enum}) is the set of all subsets of X_0 plus X.

In the case when X is a lattice it is possible to define such types of SD-extensions of X as *intervals* and *multiintervals* [19].

The *subdefinite representation* $^*[\xi]$ of any set $\xi \subseteq X$ in the SD-extension $^*X$ is the minimal subset from $^*X$ which contains ξ, namely,

$$^*[\xi] = \bigcap_{\xi \subseteq {}^*\psi \in {}^*X} {}^*\psi.$$

Property 3 from the definition of an SD-extension guarantees that for any set $\xi \subseteq X$ its SD-representation is *unique*.

To define dependences between objects in SD-models, we construct SD-extensions of functions over them.

Let $^*X_i$ for $i = 1, \ldots, m+1$ be SD-extensions of universes X_i correspondingly. The SD-extension of a function $f : X_1 \times \cdots \times X_m \to X_{m+1}$ is a function $^*f : {}^*X_1 \times \cdots \times {}^*X_m \to {}^*X_{m+1}$, such that

$$^*f({}^*x_1, \ldots, {}^*x_m) = {}^*[\{f(x_1, \ldots, x_m) \mid x_i \in {}^*x_i\}].$$

Assume that there is a relation $r(x_1, \ldots, x_n)$ defined in the subject domain, which determines a subset of values in the Cartesian product $X_1 \times \cdots \times X_n$.

The functions f_i $(i = 1, \ldots, n)$ are called an interpretation functions for the relation r if $x_i = f_i(x_1, \ldots, x_{i-1}, x_{i+1}, \ldots, x_n)$, on the set $r(x_1, \ldots, x_n)$.

For example, the equation $x + y = z$ may be interpreted by the following three functions:

$$z := x + y; \qquad x := z - y; \qquad y := z - x;$$

In the sequel, we will consider only such functionally interpretable relations, and will call them *constraints.*

A *subdefinite model* (SD-models) M consists of the four sets $(V, C, W, CORR)$, where

– V is the set of SD-objects from a given subject domain;

– C is the set of constraints defined on SD-objects from V;

– W is the set of assignment functions;

– $CORR$ is the set of correctness check functions.

With each SD-object, we associate a subdefinite type, thus defining its set of admissible values and its set of operations, the initial subdefinite value, the assignment function, and the correctness check function.

The *assignment function* is a function of two arguments which is computed for each attempt of assignment of a new value to the SD-object and determines its new value depending on the current and the assigned values. The *correctness check function* is a unary predicate which verifies that the value of an SD-object v is admissible.

The CSP in SD-models is described as a set of objects and a set of constraints on these objects. We assign a universe and a kind of an SD-extension to each object.

The algorithm of computations implemented in SD-models is a highly parallel data-driven process. Modification of the values of some variables in the common memory automatically results in calling and executing those constraints for which these variables are arguments. The process halts when the network stabilizes, i.e., execution of constraints does not change the objects of the model.

The result of the algorithm is either SUCCESS, in which case the current values of the variables will point to possible values of objects of the model, or FAILURE, which signals that during the execution of the algorithm the value of one of the variables is invalid.

As it was shown in [18], if all the assignment functions work as a set intersection operations and all the correctness functions check that the SD-value of the corresponding object do not become empty, then the constraint satisfaction algorithm in SD-models converges, and the output values of objects for the same input values do not depend on the strategy of choosing the next constraint for interpretation.

3 Constraint Programming Environment NeMo+

3.1 Architecture of NeMo+

SD-models in fact determine a certain common technique for representation and solution of CSP in any subject domains and in any classes of problems. In the most advance manner this technique was implemented in the constraint programming environment *NeMo+*.

The main feature of *NeMo+* is its two-level architecture. The first (basic) level consists of a C++ library which has a set of predefined data types and constraints, as well as a universal (i.e. applicable to any data types) constraint satisfaction algorithm. The second level contains the language for specification of CSPs, which makes it possible to give high-level descriptions of user problems in terms of the subject domain.

In the most general form the architecture of *NeMo+* is shown in Fig. 1.

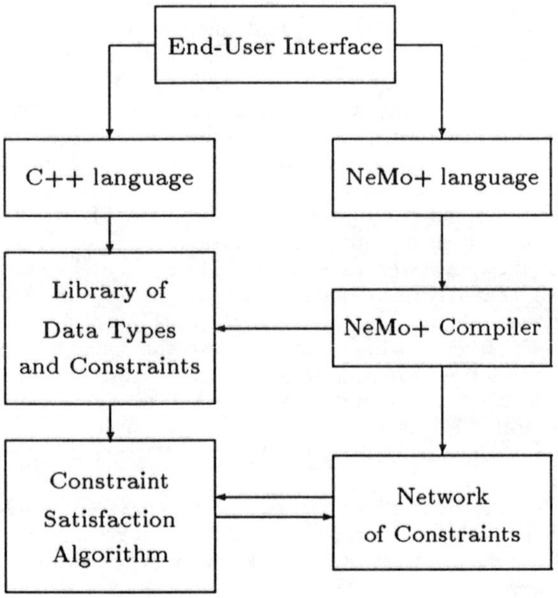

Fig. 1. The architecture of NeMo+.

The object-oriented approach was used in the implementation of all components of *NeMo+*. The *NeMo+* language is used to structure the statement of the problem and to define problem-oriented data types and constraints. A new data type is described as a class of objects whose components are linked by a certain set of constraints. The user may define his own constraints over these; these new constraints are in fact parameterized sets of simpler, which are eventually built of basic constraints.

The compiler transforms the high-level specification of the problem into a network containing just the basic data types and constraints. This network preserves the structure of the original object-oriented description of the problem. This makes it possible to control the constraint propagation process more flexibly and efficiently. For instance, one can simultaneously activate or block groups of semantically related (referring to one object) constraints.

The library of basic data types and constraints is implemented as a system of C++ classes. This library can be extended in two ways. Firstly, the user can describe a new notion in the *NeMo+* language which is then compiled and placed in the library. If the means provided by the language are insufficient, or if the user wants to implement a problem-oriented constraint more efficiently, C++ entry points may be used.

At present *NeMo+* uses one constraint satisfaction algorithm which has two peculiarities. Firstly, it is applied to an object-structured network of constraints. Secondly, this network may contain variables of different types.

The ability to specify problems in terms of their subject domains increases significantly efficiency of application of any software technology. In the *NeMo+* environment this ability is provided within the language of specification of SD-models. The knowledge representation language of *NeMo+* represents a combination of the object-oriented approach and the paradigm of constraint programming. In the *NeMo+* language both internal semantics of the objects and all aspects of interaction between them are described by relations and constraints. Only those properties of the object-oriented approach are used which support knowledge structuring, including construction of an hierarchy of notions, inheritance and incapsulation.

3.2 NeMo+ language

The main features of the *NeMo+* language are the following:

1. The language has a rather broad set of built-in basic types: integer, real, character, boolean, string, and their subdefinite extensions (Single, Enum, Interval, Multiinterval).

2. Abstract data types are supported (for example, *number* is integer or real). An abstract data type is refined when the computational network is generated (e.g., *number* may be transformed into an integer interval or a real multiinterval depending on the environment of the variable of this type).

3. There are two kind of generic data types in the language: *set*, and *array*.

4. It allows the user to define new data types, functions, and constraints.

5. The language allows one to specify extensional constraints as a tabular relation.

6. The language is object-oriented, i.e., it is possible to describe for each data type its own constraints (its own submodel), or to describe a submodel for each

variable; there is also a mechanism of inheritance for constraints and the structure of data types (classes).

7. The language provides the means for controlling the process of computations, such as **if** and **alternate**. Both are not operators, but rather special constructions allowing one to change the network during computations.

8. The language supports modular program development (creation and use of libraries).

3.2.1 Data types in the *NeMo+* language

Due to object-oriented nature of the knowledge representation language of *NeMo+*, we can define new data types (classes) from existing ones, with possible inheritance of properties. Each data type has a certain structure (a set of data components, or slots) and a so-called "active part." The active part of a type is some submodel reflecting interdependencies between the slots of this type. For instance, in the data type *Triangle* the active part of the type may contain constraints reflecting the sine theorem, the cosine theorem, and various formulas computing area, perimeter of a triangle, etc.

There are two important facilities which significantly enhance the type construction system: abstraction-concretisation and inheritance. Abstraction means that when we define a type we can omit a specific kind of subdefiniteness for objects of this type. Such an abstract type may be concretised when it is used, by defining one of the SD-extensions defined in section 1.

Fig. 2 presents the inheritance lattice for abstract data types of the *NeMo+* language. Abstract types define their interface as operations applicable to some abstract entity (for instance, = and ! = for *any*, *min* and *max* for *scalar*, +, −, ∗ and / for *number*, *mod* and *fact* for *int*, etc.).

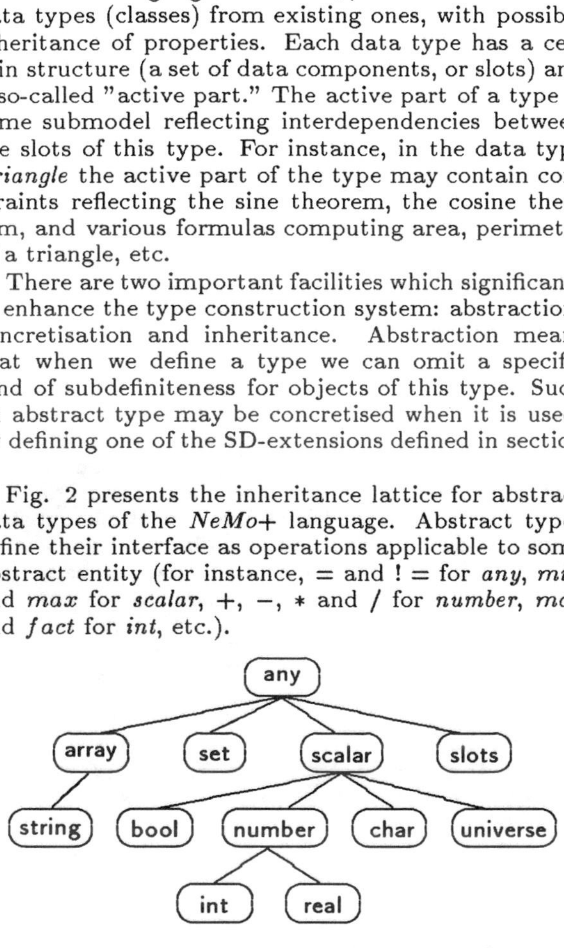

Fig. 2. Inheritance lattice for abstract classes

Thus, the types *int*, *real*, *bool* and others in the *NeMo+* language are abstract data types as well as *any*, or *numbers*. Each of these types has several possible SD-extensions: Single and Interval (for all types), Enum (only for discrete types) and multiinterval (only for numerical types). Examples of such types are *Interval int, Multiinterval real, set of Enum int.* Abstract types enable us to have, for example, just one addition constraint instead of manipulating a large set of such constraints, in which we consider various combinations of reals and integers.

An *universe* is an abstract type defined by enumeration of possible values. For instance, the universe *fruits* may be given in the following form:

```
class fruits; universe {apple,orange,lemon};
end;
```

The *NeMo+* language allows us to have data aggregates. To this end, the language has two built-in generic types: *set* and *array*.

All of *NeMo+* arrays are one-dimensional. A two-dimensional array may be represented as a one-dimensional array in which each element is a one-dimensional array as well.

There is a binary operation for arrays: "take element." Like any other binary operation, it is interpreted in three directions: to the array, to the index and to the result.

Suppose, for example, that an SD-model has a constraint $x = m[i]$, where x is a real interval equal to $[-2.5, 5.5]$, m has the type *array* [5] *of interval int*, and the index i is declared as an integer interval equal to $[2, 5]$. If the elements of the array m have the values $m = \{[-10, 10], [15, 20], [-5, 5], [7, 8], [-3, 10]\}$, then after interpretation of this constraint the index i will equal the interval $[3, 5]$. This happens because the variable x cannot be equal to the element $m[2]$. An even stronger refinement of i occurs if it is represented by an enumeration rather than an interval. In this case the new value of i will be the set $\{3, 5\}$.

In the description of a new user-defined type we can define its ancestors, slots and the active part (as an internal model). The derived type inherits all the properties of its ancestors (slots and active part) and the set of operations defined over them, but redefinition of the inherited information is not allowed.

For instance, a triangle data type may contain three sides, and three angles as slots, and the sine, and cosine theorems, as active part. The triangle type in Cartesian coordinates may be declared as a successor of the type *Triangle* with three new slots (planar coordinates of the vertices):

```
class DecartTriangle : Triangle;
  slots (A, B, C: Point);
  Distance(A,B)=c; Distance(B,C)=a;
  Distance(C,A)=b;
end;
```

It is assumed here that *Distance* is a real function defined earlier which calculates the distance between two points.

3.2.2 Constraints in the NeMo+ language

Constraints in *NeMo+* constitute an hierarchical system whose lowest level consists of basic constraints, i.e. constraints written in C++.

NeMo+ constraints are subdivided into three syntactic groups: functions, infix and prefix constraints.

Functions are parameterized sets of constraints with a distinguished result. For instance, a function computing the distance between two points can be declared as follows:

```
function Distance( a, b : Point ) : real;
  (a.x - b.x)^2 + (a.y - b.y)^2 = Result^2;
end;
```

Here *Result* is a distinguished name denoting a real variable in which the result returned by the function is stored.

Infix constraints can be either binary or n-ary. The use of n-ary infix constraints makes it possible to reduce significantly the size of internal representation of the model in the form of a network of constraints.

Let us consider, for example, the equation `y = x1 + x2 + x3 + x4`. Using the n-ary operator `"+"`, we obtain: `y = +(x1,x2,x3,x4)`, but in the case of the infix `"+"` the result is the following:

```
Tmp1 = +(x1, x2); Tmp2 = +(Tmp1,x3);
y = +(Tmp2, x4);
```

Each infix constraint has a priority in accordance with which the corresponding expressions are parsed.

In real problems we often have to deal with constraints defined extensionally (by enumerating all tuples, or the sets of values satisfying this constraint). Each extensional constraint is most conveniently represented by a table in which the number of columns coincides with the number of arguments of the constraint, and each row has one possible set of the values of its arguments. There are many examples of such constraints: timetables (transport or classes), technical tables, interest rates, etc.

The specification of a tabular constraint in the *NeMo+* language looks as follows:

```
table Name( arg1:type1, arg2:type2, ... )
  from "File"; end;
```

Here *File* defines the name of the file describing the table. The description of the table has a natural form: in each row we indicate the values of arguments of the constraint *Name*. The number of columns corresponds to the number of arguments of the tabular constraint. The number of rows of the table is not limited. Declarative semantics of a tabular constraint is as follows. Each table defines a relation on the Cartesian product of the universes of its arguments. Each relation is defined by an explicit enumeration of all tuples of values which satisfy it. The operational semantics of the tabular constraint is defined as the intersection of the Cartesian product of subdefinite values of the arguments with this relation.

The language provides special constructions allowing run-time modification of the network of constraints: **if**, and **alternate**.

A conditional constraint is different from the traditional conditional operators of conventional programming languages. Since the tested condition may have three values (*true, false*, and *undefine*), a conditional constraint may contain three parts: **then**, **else**, and **undef**. Initially the SD-model contains the condition and the **undef**-part (if it is not omitted). If the condition becomes *true* during interpretation of the SD-model, the **then**-part is added to the SD-model, and if the condition becomes *false*, the **else**-part is added. In both cases, the **undef**-part is deleted. Example:

```
if x=0 then y^3=z; else y=x; undef y=0; end;
```

The specifier of alternatives makes it possible to organize an automated case analysis during the interpretation of a computational network. Each case is a subset of constraints defined over the objects of the SD-model. The specifier offers the interpreter to test all the alternatives in turn, one by one. The specifier of alternatives has the lowest priority among all constraints of the SD-model. Example:

```
alternate x = 0; or x > 0; or x < 0; end;
```

The language has one more construction that makes the level of model specification higher: the loop operator **forall**. This operator is different from the similar operators of conventional programming language: it is elaborated at the compilation phase. Thus, its only purpose is to make the specification of the model more compact. For instance, the operator

```
forall i : [1,4]; x[i] <> y[i+1]; end;
```

transforms after compilation to the following fragment:

```
x[1] <> y[2];    x[2] <> y[3];
x[3] <> y[4];    x[4] <> y[5];
```

4 Applications of the NeMo+

4.1 Arithmetic puzzles

To demonstrate some capabilities of the *NeMo+* environment, consider one of the well-known class of problems: the crypt-arithmetic puzzles.

Let us consider the following puzzle: a multiplication on two numbers for which it is necessary to find "digits for A and asterisk (*)" substitutions satisfying this equation. The leftmost digits are not equal to zero, each asterisk is not equal to A, and values of different asterisks may be equal one to another.

```
          * A * * *   // N[], first
  x       * A * * *   // M[]
         ----------
        A * * * * *   // t[1][], s[1]
      * A * * * *     // t[2][], s[2]
    * * A * *   *     // t[3][], s[3]
  * * * A * *         // t[4][], s[4]
* * * * A *           // t[5][], s[5]
-------------------
* * * A * * * * * *   // R[]
```

0 c_9 c_8 c_7 c_6 c_5 c_4 c_3 c_2 0   // carries-out of addition

There exist various complementary representations for this puzzle. We represent it in the following form. The two multiplicands and the result will be represented by one-dimensional arrays (N, M, and R) of integer numbers, and the intermediate multiplication results (inner asterisks) by a two-dimensional array (t). In addition, we need to define two kinds of carries: multiplication carries as a two-dimensional array ct, and addition carries as c_i, where i is the index of the corresponding column ($R[i]$) whose computation results in the carry. The columns are numbered from right to left.

The complete text of the model in *NeMo+* looks as follows:

```
uses "opr";
  class Digit : int;  This = [0,9]; end;
  class Arr5;  array [5]  of Digit; end;
  class Arr6;  array [6]  of Digit; end;
  class Arr10; array [10] of Digit; end;
  class ArrArr5_5;  array [5]  of Arr5; end;
  class ArrArr5_6;  array [5]  of Arr6; end;
main  Uarr;
  N, M : Arr5;  t : ArrArr5_6;  R : Arr10;
  A : Digit with This = [2,8]; end;
  first : int;  s : Arr5;  ct : ArrArr5_5;
  N[4]=A; M[4]=A; R[7]=A; r[10]=[1,8];
  ct[1][5]=A; M[1]<>1; M[3]<>1; M[5]<>1;
  first = N[1]+10*N[2]+100*N[3]+10^3*N[4]+
        10^4*N[5];
  forall i : [1,5];
    t[i][6] > 0; t[i][7-i] = A;
//  s[i] - number, obtained from the row i:
    s[i] = t[i][1]+10*t[i][2]+10^2*t[i][3]+
    10^3*t[i][4]+10^4*t[i][5]+10^5*t[i][6];
    M[i]*first = s[i];
    M[i]*N[1]=10*ct[i][1]+t[i][1];
    M[i]*N[2]=10*ct[i][2]+t[i][2]-ct[i][1];
    M[i]*N[3]=10*ct[i][3]+t[i][3]-ct[i][2];
    M[i]*N[4]=10*ct[i][4]+t[i][4]-ct[i][3];
    M[i]*N[5]=10*ct[i][5]+t[i][5]-ct[i][4];
  end;
  c2,c3,c4,c5,c6,c7,c8,c9 : int
                          with This=[0,4]; end;
  c2=[0,1]; c3=[0,2]; c4=[0,3];
  c6=[1,4]; c8=[0,3]; c9=[0,2];
  r[1]  = t[1][1];
  r[2]  = t[1][2]+t[2][1] - 10*c2;
  r[3]  = t[1][3]+t[2][2]+t[3][1]+c2-10*c3;
  r[4]  = t[1][4]+t[2][3]+t[3][2]+t[4][1]+
        c3 - 10*c4;
  r[5]  = t[1][5]+t[2][4]+t[3][3]+t[4][2]+
        t[5][1]+c4 - 10*c5;
  r[6]  = 5*a + c5 - 10*c6;
  r[7]  = t[2][6]+t[3][5]+t[4][4]+t[5][3]+
        c6 - 10*c7;
  r[8]  = t[3][6]+t[4][5]+t[5][4]+c7 - 10*c8;
  r[9]  = t[4][6] + t[5][5] + c8 - 10*c9;
  r[10]= t[5][6] + c9;
  forall j:{1..3,5}; A<>N[j]; A<>M[j]; end;
  forall j:{1..5};      A <> t[1][j]; end;
  forall j:{1..4,6};    A <> t[2][j]; end;
  forall j:{1..3,5,6}; A <> t[3][j]; end;
  forall j:{1,2,4..6}; A <> t[4][j]; end;
  forall j:{1,3..6};    A <> t[5][j]; end;
  forall j:{1..10};     A <> R[j]; end;
  R[1]+10*R[2]+100*R[3]+10^3*R[4]+10^4*R[5]+
  10^5*R[6]+10^6*A+10^7*R[8]+10^8*R[9] =
  s[1]+10*s[2]+100*s[3]+10^3*s[4]+
  10^4*(s[5]-10^5*(t[5][6]+c8));
  exact(first,M[3],M[5]);
end;
```

We also define in our model the integer numbers (*first*, *s*[1] – *s*[5], and *r*) corresponding to each line of the puzzle. We encounter the problem of integer overflow, since the result is a 10-digit number which does not fit even in the long integer format of a 16-bit computer. This is why we did not need the second number (corresponding to the line M), and the last but one constraint involves only nine of the ten digits R plus the carries.

The last constraint *exact* indicates the variables for which complete analysis of all values is carried out if the exact result is not found after the calculations are complete. This constraint has the lowest priority, and so it is executed last.

The problem in question has two solutions:

$$N_1 = 95308; \quad M_1 = 75396; \quad R_1 = 7185841968;$$
$$N_2 = 87246; \quad M_2 = 67829; \quad R_2 = 5917808934;$$

These solutions were found on a Pentium 133 computer in 2.78 CPU seconds. The number of backtracks was equal to 133.

4.2 Scheduling problem

Consider now a problem which allows one to combine successfully intensional and extensional relations in one model. The problem is stated as follows.

Mr. X lives in town A and is planning to go to town B for shopping. There are trains going between A and B according to a known timetable. The shop to which Mr. X is going lies in 10 *to* 15 *minutes from the railway station of B. The shop is open from* 10 *to* 7 *p.m. and is closed for lunch from* 2 *p.m. to* 3 *p.m. Immediately on arriving at B, Mr. X intends to visit the shop, and then return to the railway station of B and go back with the next train. Mr. X does not like to wait for the train for more than half an hour; frankly speaking, he would like to minimize the waiting time. Which train should Mr. X choose to go for shopping to B?*

In this problem we use train timetables in which time is divided into hours and minutes. If we represent time by real numbers, we have the problem of converting one hour into a real fraction. In this case, for instance, 30 minutes look as the number 0.5. Therefore, it is better to represent time by integer numbers. In order not to increase the number of columns in tables (with hours and minutes written separately), we use some "absolute" values: time in minutes relative to 0 hours.

Thus, we define the class *Time* with three slots (*Hours*, *Minutes*, and *Abs*), with the corresponding constraint and two infix constraints "=" and "+":

```
class Time;
  slots( Hours, Minutes, Abs : int );
  Hours = [0,23];    Minutes = [0,59];
  Abs = Hours * 60 + Minutes;
end;
inf "="(t1,t2 : Time) : bool;
  t1.Abs = t2.Abs;
end;
inf "+"(t:Time; d:int): Time;
  t.Abs + d = Result.Abs;
end;
```

The timetables are defined in a rather natural manner (up to the remarks concerning time). For example, a fragment of the train timetable between A and B (the file "ab.tab") looks as follows:

```
// departure time    arriving time  (in Abs)
       362                455
       442                536
       ...                ...
       1179               1269
       1316               1410
```

Now we can define the corresponding SD-model. In the *NeMo+* language, this model looks as follows:

```
uses "opr";
instrumental "table.dll";
table AB( d, a : int) from "ab.tab";end;
table BA( d, a : int) from "ba.tab";end;
main Schedule;
  t1, t2, t3, t4, t5, t6, t7 : Time;
  t_wait : int with This = [0,30]; end;
  AB( t1.Abs, t2.Abs );
  t2 + [10,15] = t3;
  t3 + [20,30] = t4;
  t3.Hours >= 10;
  t4.Hours <= 18;
  (t4.Hours<=13)\/(t3.Hours>=15);
  t4 + [15,20] = t5;
  t5 + t_wait = t6;
  BA( t6.Abs, t7.Abs );
  minimize(t_wait);
end;
```

As a result of computing this model in *NeMo+*, we obtain the following result:

```
t_wait = 0;
          // Hours  Minutes    Abs
t1 = Time( 14,     44,        884          );
t2 = Time( 16,     18,        978          );
t3 = Time( 16,     [32,33],   [992,993]    );
t4 = Time( 17,     [2,3],     [1022,1023]  );
t5 = Time( 17,     22,        1042         );
t6 = Time( 17,     22,        1042         );
t7 = Time( 18,     56,        1136         );
```

This solution was found on a Pentium 133 computer in 0.02 CPU seconds without using of backtracking.

5 Benchmarks

In this section we discuss how some benchmarks are solved with the *NeMo+* environment.

Integer Benchmarks. Let us consider the following well known problems.

Zebra. The problem, proposed by Lewis Carroll.

Cryptarithmetic puzzles. We consider two problems: $SEND + MORE = MONEY$ (Send) and $DONALD + GERALD = ROBERT$ (Donald).

Queens. Place N queens on a $N \times N$ chessboard so that there is no pair of queens threatening each other.

Square. Place the numbers $\{1, 2, \ldots, n^2\}$ into the $n \times n$ board so that the sums of numbers in each row, column and main diagonal are equal. To exclude symmetrical solutions we assume that $M(1,1) < M(1,n) < M(n,1), M(1,1) < M(n,n)$, where M is a mapping from $\{1,\ldots,n^2\}$ to $\{1,\ldots,n\} \times \{1,\ldots,n\}$.

The following three problems are taken from [3].

$\sum\prod$. Find integers $x_1, x_2, \ldots, x_N$ such that $\sum_{i=1}^{N} x_i = \sum_{i=1}^{N} i$, and $\prod_{i=1}^{N} x_i = \prod_{i=1}^{N} i$. To exclude symmetrical solutions we assume that $x_1 \leq x_2 \leq \cdots \leq x_N$.

Pythagor. Find integer values from $\{1, 2, \ldots, 100\}$ such that the equation $\sum_{i=1}^{N} x_i^2 = x_{N+1}^2$ is true. To exclude symmetrical solutions we assume that $x \leq y$ in the first case, and $x \leq y \leq w$ in the second.

The table below summarizes the results. The first column gives the problem name and its size if needed. The ff word indicates the use of the first fail principle heuristic. The last column gives the running time for *NeMo+* in seconds. These time were measured on a PC Pentium 133 MHz with 16 MB of RAM. N_V, N_C, N_S, N_F are the numbers of variables, constraints, found solutions ("first" means finding the first solution) and fails respectively.

Problem	N_V	N_C	N_S	N_F	Time
Zebra ff	28	22	1	5	0.01
Send ff	20	18	1	1	< 0.01
Donald ff	29	19	1	6	0.03
Queens 8 ff	22	33	92	375	1.53
Queens 10 ff	28	64	724	5285	29.48
Queens 12 ff	34	89	first	1	0.06
Queens 16 ff	46	151	first	14	0.28
Square 3 ff	9	9	1	6	0.01
Square 4 ff	16	11	880	21871	127.75
$\Sigma\Pi$ 9	9	11	2	445	0.75
$\Sigma\Pi$ 12	12	14	22	7355	17.71
Pythagor 2	6	6	52	86	0.83
Pythagor 3	8	8	573	2331	18.58

Boolean Benchmarks. Now we consider a set of traditional Boolean benchmarks [5]. Instead of Boolean variables we use integer ones with domain $[0, 1]$.

Schur. Put the integers $\{1, 2, \ldots, N\}$ in three boxes so that for any $x, y \in \{1, 2, \ldots, N\}$ x and $2x$ are placed in different boxes and if x and y are placed in the same box than $x + y$ is placed in a different box.

Pigeon. Put N pigeons in M holes with at most 1 pigeon per hole.

Queens. Boolean version of the $N-$Queens problem described above.

All results are summarized in the following table.

Problem	N_V	N_C	N_S	N_F	Time
Schur 13	39	135	18	179	0.44
Schur 14	42	156	0	179	0.49
Pigeon 6/6	36	13	720	719	0.74
Pigeon 8/7	56	16	0	5039	5.41
Queens 8	64	43	92	391	0.81
Queens 10	100	55	724	5904	15.90
Queens 12	144	67	first	37	0.17
Queens 16	256	91	first	1208	6.54

6 Conclusion

The paper examines an object-oriented constraint programming environment *NeMo+*. This system allows one to describe at a high level and to solve CSPs which may include at the same time different data types related to finite and continuous domains. In addition, it provides well-developed means for definition of problem-oriented data types and constraints, as well as for structuring the description of the problem.

The *NeMo+* environment is intended, first of all, to solve problems described by large and heterogeneous systems of constraints. These problems arise, for instance, in the area of CAD/CAM applications. *NeMo+* makes it possible to design complex technical devices by representing them in the form of an hierarchy of objects (in the sense of the relationship "part-whole") with semantics expressed by systems of constraints. In this class of applications constraints are often defined by tables of values. *NeMo+* provides advanced means to define tabular constraints which are the most natural way of linking parameters of different types. At present we are working (jointly with DASSAULT) on applying *NeMo+* technology to solve a number of applied problems in the design of automobiles and airplanes.

The current implementation of *NeMo+* uses one common algorithm of constraint satisfaction for heterogeneous systems. In the future we plan to incorporate in the system a number of specialized techniques which can be used to solve efficiently some particular kinds of CSP. For example, the interval constraint solver *Unicalc*, which is intended to solve purely numerical problems, contains a number of algorithms which combine methods of classical and interval mathematics, as well as the methods of computer algebra with constraint propagation. We plan to integrate some of these algorithms in the *NeMo+* environment.

References

[1] Benhamou F., McAllester D., Van Hentenryck P. "CLP(Intervals) Revisited", *Proceedings of ILPS-94*, Ithaca, NY, 1994, 124 – 138.

[2] Benhamou F. "Heterogeneous Constraint Solving", *Proceedings of the fifth International Conference on Algebraic and Logic Programming*, LNCS 1139, Springer-Verlag, 1996, 62 – 76.

[3] Benhamou F., Older W.J. "Applying Interval Arithmetic to Real, Integer and Boolean Constraints", *Journal of Logic Programming*, 1997.

[4] Caseau Y., Puget J.-F. "Constraints on Order Sorted Domains", *Proceedings ECAI'94 Workshop on Constraints Satisfaction Issues raised by Practical Applications*, Amsterdam, August 1994.

[5] Codognet P., Diaz D. "Boolean Constraint Solving Using clp(FD)", *Proc. of the International Logic Programming Symposium*, 1993, 525 – 539.

[6] Colmerauer A. "An introduction to Prolog III", *Comm.ACM*, 33(7),1990, 69 – 90.

[7] Hyvonen E. "Constraint Reasoning Based on interval Arithmetic: the tolerance propagation approach", *Artificial Intelligence*, V.58, 1992, 71 – 112.

[8] Jaffar J., et al. "The CLP(R) language and system", *ACM Transactions on Programming Languages and Systems*, 14(3), 1992, 339 – 395.

[9] Mackworth A.K. "Consistency in Networks of Relations", *Artificial Intelligence*, vol. 8, (1977), 99 – 118.

[10] Minsky M. "A framework for representation", *AI Memo*, No 306, MIT Cambridge, 1974.

[11] Moore R.E. *Interval Analysis*, Prentice Hall, Englewood Cliffs, NJ, 1996.

[12] Narin'yani A.S. "Subdefinite Set – a Formal Model of Uncompletely Specified Aggregate", *Proc. of the Symp. on Fuzzy Sets and Possibility Theory*, Acapulco, 1980.

[13] Narin'yani A.S. "Subdefiniteness and Basic Means of Knowledge Representation", *Computers and Artificial Intelligence*, Bratislawa, **2**, No.5, 1983, 443 – 452.

[14] Narin'yani A.S., Telerman V.V., Dmitriev V.E. "Virtual data-flow machine as vehicle of inference/computations in knowledge bases", *Artificial Intelligence II: methodology, systems, applications*, ed. by Ph.Jorrand and V.Sgurev, North-Holland, 1987, 149–154.

[15] Narin'yani A.S., Borde S.B., Ivanov D.A. "Subdefinite Mathematics and Novel Scheduling Technology", *Artificial Intelligence in Engineenring*, **11**, Elsevier Science Limited, 1997.

[16] Puget J.-F. "A C++ Implementation of CLP", *Tech. Report*, Ilog, January 1994.

[17] Shvetsov I., Semenov A., Telerman V. "Application of Subdefinite Models in Engineering", *Artificial Intelligence in Engineenring*, **11**, Elsevier Science Limited, 1997, 15 – 24.

[18] Telerman V., Ushakov D. "Subdefinite Models as a Variety of Constraint Programming", *Proc. of the Intern. Conf. Tools of Artificial Intelligence (ICTAI'96)*, Toulouse, 1996.

[19] Telerman V., et al. "Interval and Multiinterval Extensions in Subdefinite Models", *International Conf. on Interval Methods and Computer Aided Proofs in Science and Engineering (INTERVAL'96)*, Wurzburg, 1996, 131 – 132.

[20] Tyugu E. "Solving problem on computational models", *J. Computational Mathematics and Math. Phys.*, vol. 10, 1970, 716 – 733.

[21] van Emden M.H. "Value constraints in the CLP scheme", *Proc. of the ILPS-95, Workshop on Interval Constraints*, Portland, Oregon, 1995.

[22] Van Hentenryck P. *Constraint Satisfaction in Logic Programming*, Logic Programming Series, The MIT Press, Cambridge, MA, 1989.

An Object-Based Methodology for Knowledge Representation in SGML

Robert. L. Kelsey
Los Alamos National Laboratory *
New Mexico State University

Roger. T. Hartley
New Mexico State University

Robert. B. Webster
Los Alamos National Laboratory

Abstract

An object-based methodology for knowledge representation and its Standard Generalized Markup Language (SGML) implementation is presented. The methodology includes class, perspective, domain, and event constructs for representing knowledge within an object paradigm. The perspective construct allows for representation of knowledge from multiple and varying viewpoints. The event construct allows actual use of knowledge to be represented. The SGML implementation of the methodology facilitates usability, structured, yet flexible knowledge design, and sharing and re-use of knowledge class libraries.

1 Introduction

An object-based methodology for knowledge representation uses objects of classes as its fundamental representational building block. The overall concept of using objects as a building block is not unlike what is done in object-oriented analysis (OOA) and design (OOD) [3] [2]. Each of these decomposes knowledge into manageable units called objects. It is natural to decompose knowledge into objects and objects are modular enough to allow for changes and extensions within the representation.

This methodology is a design methodology (not a representation system) for designing domains of knowledge. Knowledge representation systems often skip the step of designing the knowledge that the system represents. As a result, knowledge representation systems are difficult to use. It may be possible that knowledge designed using this methodology can later be put into existing knowledge representation systems.

*The Los Alamos National Laboratory strongly supports academic freedom and a researcher's right to publish; therefore, the Laboratory as an institution does not endorse the viewpoint of a publication or guarantee its technical correctness.

This methodology includes the use of perspectives and events. Perspectives allow for the representation of knowledge from multiple viewpoints. This can increase the detail of the knowledge and put the knowledge in additional context. Events allow for the representation of actual use of the knowledge along with the knowledge itself.

The use of Standard Generalized Markup Language (SGML) to implement the methodology adds structure, but maintains flexibility. Also, SGML facilitates the sharing and re-use of knowledge through it portability and constructs. A less obvious, but important aspect of the SGML implementation is its added usability. A growing familiarity of markup languages helps make the SGML implementation of the methodology more usable. The following sections describe the methodology (briefly) and the SGML implementation. More detail about the methodology can be found in [7].

2 Methodology background

2.1 Introduction

Knowledge is represented in the methodology using three different constructs: the class, the domain, and the event. A class is a template or prototype that describes an object or collection of objects. Once a class is defined it is an available resource for creating a domain of knowledge. A domain is a specific focus of knowledge. Classes are instantiated for use in a domain. Instantiation causes specific instances or objects of those classes to become available for use. This is why the domain can be focused, because only the classes of interest or pertinence need be instantiated. An event is a construct for representing examples of actual use of the knowledge in a domain.

1082-3409/97 $10.00 © 1997 IEEE

2.2 Class

There are two types of classes possible in the methodology, agent and non-agent. Although the types are not formally designated in notation, the distinction is useful for determining interactions of and between objects of classes. Others (particularly Schank [11]) have used the same distinction in representation, calling agent objects actors. Agent objects of a class act on or initiate actions on other objects of both agent and non-agent classes. Non-agent objects of a class are essentially inanimate objects.

A class consists of three parts: attributes, methods, and perspectives. An attribute is a property or characteristic that helps describe an object of a class. An attribute has a name or identifier and a value. It may also have a list of potential or limiting values. The value of an attribute is assigned at the time an object is instantiated from a class and can be changed by methods of the object.

A method determines the behavior of an object of a class. A method is an allowed operation on an object. Objects interact with one another through methods and limiting the methods available can constrain interaction between objects. A method has a name or identifier, a list of arguments (if any), and the operation content. The operation content is how a method goes about doing what it does. This may be represented in a variety of ways including rules, pseudocode, or even a program. A method is not available for use until an object is instantiated from a class.

A perspective defines how or in what way an object of a class may be viewed. Some attributes may be important to one perspective while not important to another perspective. Thus, a particular perspective is defined by grouping the attributes and methods in a class that are pertinent to the perspective. Similar to a method, a perspective on an object is defined in that object's class and limits or constrains the available views. Each attribute and method in a class has a list of perspectives with which it is associated.

The name or identifier and the definition of a perspective go in the class that possesses that perspective or view. There is also a list of classes that are a part of this class's perspective. A perspective can be considered to be how one object of a class views the other objects in a domain.

2.3 Domain

A domain is where objects of classes are instantiated for use. At instantiation, objects are created and named and values within the parts of an object are assigned. Only the knowledge necessary for a particular application need be defined in a domain. A domain has a name and a list of objects contained within the domain. An object (within the domain definition) has a name or identifier, the name of the class from which it was instantiated, and if it is an agent object, the perspective with which it is viewing the rest of the domain.

2.4 Event

A domain of objects can contain or represent knowledge and maybe even how the knowledge is used, but it cannot necessarily represent actual examples of use. An event is specifically designed for representing an example use of knowledge. An event has a name or identifier and consists of four parts: a before state, a method, an after state, and an agent. A state is a snapshot of an object containing the values of an object's attributes. A method is the name of the method causing the change in state from before to after. An agent is the name of the agent object instigating the method to change the state.

A single event represents only two objects, the agent object and the object being acted upon by the agent object. Additionally, only the object attributes that change values from before to after state are listed within the states. This is in keeping with the spirit of only representing what is necessary.

3 SGML background

3.1 Introduction

The Standard Generalized Markup Language (SGML) is an ISO standard for the description of documents [6]. This standard describes technology for facilitating text interchange in documents [12], but the technology has many potential uses. SGML is used to describe the structure and organization of a document, or more specifically, the structure and organization of the content of a document. As a result, the format of the content of a document and the content of a document are two separate things. In short, SGML enables the design and implementation of document structure and the associated notation for marking the content of a document.

Although SGML was originally designed for the publishing of both paper and electronic documents, it has been exploited for use in other areas including enterprise management, engineering, product life cycle, and multi-media. Any application that must process and manage information may benefit from SGML. SGML can help enable applications that use indexing and retrieval of information, cross reference of information, modification and revision of information, and multiple display formats.

3.2 SGML components

There are three components or parts to an SGML document [1]. The first component is the SGML declaration which determines the formal syntax and any optional features to be used within documents. These are the rules for designing a document type definition (DTD) and for validating the conformance of a DTD and an associated document.

The second component is the document type definition (DTD) which is a rule set for a class or group of documents. The rules in a DTD describe the notation for marking the content pieces of a document and how those pieces relate to one another. Some example classes of documents are project plans, memos, and technical reports. Each of these classes of documents has its own style and format.

The third component is an instance of a document which is an actual document containing content and markup. For example, a memo document may contain content like who the memo is to, who the memo is from, and a message. Markup for this document will label or tag those corresponding parts as the to, the from, and the message.

3.3 SGML DTD

There are four constructs used in creating a DTD: the element, the attribute, the entity, and the comment [8]. Note that the attribute construct should not be confused with the attributes of a class discussed previously. The DTD is a grammar that defines the parts to a document, their structure, and their notation in terms of the four constructs mentioned previously.

An element construct can be thought of as a container [8]. Any information that is to be contained must have an element defined to hold the information. For example, the message portion of a memo document will have a message element. There may also be to and from elements. These elements hold and contain the content of the message portion, to portion, and from portion (respectively) of the memo document.

An attribute construct is attached to an element construct and is used to provide further detail about the element. For example, the message element may have an attribute called security type. The security type attribute designates whether the message is unclassified, sensitive, or classified. An attribute construct may be thought of as a modifier of the element construct.

An entity construct is used to contain portions of document content that are repeated throughout the document. By defining an entity, content is defined once, but can be used many times. In this way, an entity is like a macro or an include file. If the content changes, it must only be changed in one place. A comment construct is used to express comments or notes that are not part of the document content and not meant for the end user to see.

4 Implementing the methodology

Implementing the object-based methodology in SGML involves creating a DTD that maps the methodology constructs and their parts into SGML constructs. The following sections describe the SGML constructs for the three methodology constructs and their parts. In the following sections note that when the word attribute is used it refers to the attribute part of the class construct in the methodology. An SGML attribute for an SGML element will be referred to as SGML attribute or SGML attribute construct. Names of the created SGML constructs (and example values) are shown in boldfaced sans serif type. Names and values in the examples in figures are shown in proper SGML notation. The (uncommented) DTD created for the object-based methodology is in Appendix A.

4.1 The class element

The class construct becomes an element called **class**. The three parts to a **class** (attributes, methods, and perspectives) each become elements as well. Contained within the **class** element are the elements called **attribute**, **method**, and **perspective**. The **attribute** element may contain an element called **potvals**. The **potvals** element contains a list of potential values that an **attribute** may possess. The **class** and **attribute** elements each have an SGML attribute construct attached to them called **name**. In both, the **name** holds the name of the **class** and the name of the **attribute**, respectively.

The **method** element may contain the elements called **args** and **content**. The **args** element contains a list of arguments (if any) to the **method**. (Any elements that contain lists may use an additional markup called **li** to designate an individual list item.) The **content** element contains the operation content of the **method**. The **method** element also has an SGML attribute construct attached to it called **name** which holds the name of the **method**. The **method** and **attribute** elements each have an additional SGML attribute construct attached to them called **perspect**. In both, **perspect** holds a list of perspectives with which the **method** and **attribute** (respectively) are associated and/or grouped.

The **perspective** element may contain an element called **def**. The **def** element contains the definition of the **perspective**. There are two SGML attribute constructs attached to the **perspective** element called **name** and **classes**. **Name** holds the name of the **perspective** and **classes** holds a list of classes that are observed within this **perspective** or view.

4.2 The domain element

The domain construct becomes an element called **domain**. The **domain** element may contain an element called **instance**. **Instance** refers to an object being instantiated from a **class**. The **domain** element has an SGML attribute construct attached to it called **name** which holds the name of the domain. The **instance** element has three SGML attribute constructs attached to it called **classname, name**, and **perspect**. **Classname** holds the name of the **class** from which the **instance** or object is being instantiated. **Name** holds the name of the **instance** or object. **Perspect** holds the name of the **perspective** this **instance** or object uses to view the rest of the domain. Within the **instance** element is an element called **attval**. The **attval** element contains the actual value of an **attribute** of the **instance** or object. The **attval** element has an SGML attribute construct attached to it called **name**. **Name** holds the name of the particular **attribute** in the **class** to which this value is assigned.

4.3 The event element

The event construct becomes an element called **event**. The **event** element may contain four elements called **befstate, meth, aftstate**, and **agent**. The **befstate** element contains information about the before state. The **meth** element contains the name of the **method** causing the change in state. The **aftstate** element contains information about the after state. The **agent** element contains the name of the agent object that instigated the **method** to change the state. The **event** element has an SGML attribute construct attached to it called **name** which holds the name of the **event**.

5 An AI example

To illustrate how the SGML implementation is used and what it looks like, a classic problem from artificial intelligence (AI) will be presented. The blocks world is one of the classic problems in AI [9] [10] [13] and comes from a collection of problems known as microworlds [10]. Microworld problems have limited knowledge domains and appear to need intelligence to solve.

The blocks world contains a table, blocks, and a robot arm. The robot arm manipulates the blocks into different arrangements on the table, such as stacks of blocks. The blocks world is a good example to illustrate this methodology and the SGML implementation because it is a narrow domain of knowledge, but contains enough to exercise most of the methodology's constructs.

Note that the figures illustrating each of the constructs use the notation and markup as defined by the SGML DTD created for the methodology. If this research was about document construction and not knowledge representation, then the examples shown in the figures would be known as document instances. The markup language has an opening and closing tag for each element defined in the DTD. An opening tag is delimited by the < and > symbols while a closing tag is delimited by the </and > symbols. The name of the element defined in the DTD appears between the tag delimiters. If the element has an SGML attribute construct attached to it, then the value for the SGML attribute appears (in quotes) in the opening tag of the element.

5.1 Class definitions

The blocks world has three classes of objects which are table, block, and robot arm. The **class** for table is the simplest because it contains no attributes or methods. In this domain of knowledge, the table is merely a physical object where the blocks may be located. Defining more than this in the **class table** is extraneous and irrelevant. The **class robot-arm** has one **attribute** named **holding**. The **holding attribute** contains the knowledge of whether the robot arm is holding a block and if so, which block. The **holding attribute** may have potential values of **NULL** (meaning not holding a block) or a block's identification (**ID**).

The **class robot-arm** is an agent **class**, so it contains a **perspective** named **stacking** whose view of the domain includes the **classes** of **table** and **block**. The definition of the **perspective** is **the typical view of the blocks world**. Figure 1 shows the **class** definitions for **table** and **robot-arm**.

```
<class name="table"></class>

<class name="robot-arm">
<attribute name="holding">
<potvals>
<li>NULL
<li>an ID
</potvals>
</attribute>

<perspective name="stacking"  classes="table block">
<def>
the typical view of the blocks world
</def>
</perspective>
</class>
```

Figure 1: Class definition for classes table and robot-arm.

The **class block** has three attributes named **ID**, **location**, and **covered**. All three attributes are grouped into a perspective (**perspect**) named **stacking**. The **ID** is a block's identification. The **location** is a block's current location and has potential values of **table** or an **ID** (meaning on top of a block). The **attribute covered** indicates whether a block is on top of this block and if so, which block (is on top) and has potential values of **NULL** (meaning not covered) or an **ID** of a block. Figure 2 shows the definition for the **class block**.

```
<class name="block">
<attribute name="ID"  perspect="stacking"></attribute>
<attribute name="location"  perspect="stacking">
<potvals>
<li>table
<li>an ID
</potvals>
</attribute>
<attribute name="covered"  perspect="stacking">
<potvals>
<li>NULL
<li>an ID
</potvals>
</attribute>
<method name="pickup"  perspect="stacking">
<content>
IF robot-arm.holding is NULL THEN
  IF covered is NULL THEN
    location := robot-arm
    robot-arm.holding := ID
  ELSE
    error "block covered"
ELSE
  error "arm is holding"
</content>
</method>
<method name="putdown"  perspect="stacking">
<args>
<li>locale
</args>
<content>
IF robot-arm.holding not NULL THEN
  IF locale = an ID THEN
    IF locale.location = an ID THEN
      error "stack too high"
    ELSE
      location := locale
      robot-arm.holding := NULL
  ELSE
    location := locale
    robot-arm.holding := NULL
ELSE
  error "not holding block"
</content>
</method>
</class>
```

Figure 2: Class definition for the class block.

The **class block** has two methods which are **pickup** and **putdown**. Both of these methods are grouped into a perspective (**perspect**) named **stacking**. The **method putdown** has an argument named **locale** which is the location of where the robot arm will put down a block. The operation **content** of each of the methods is shown in pseudocode. Although these methods sound more like methods for the robot arm, they are methods in the **class block** because these are operations on a block. Actually, putting the methods in the **class robot-arm** was tried. The result was that it did not seem to matter. The methods can be put in either **class**, but it is important to select and use one convention consistently. One possible advantage to having these methods in the **class block** is that they act as a constraint. These are the only operations allowed on a block. The **content** of the methods is also shown in Figure 2.

5.2 Domain and event definitions

An example **domain** for the blocks world contains a **table** object named **table1**, a **robot-arm** object named **robot-arm1**, and four **block** objects named **blockA**, **blockB**, **blockC**, and **blockD**. The name of the **domain** is **blocks-world1**. The object **robot-arm1** is instantiated with the value **NULL** for its **attribute holding**. **Robot-arm1** is an agent object and views the rest of the **domain** from the **stacking** perspective (**perspect**). The four **block** objects are each instantiated with the values of their respective names for the **attribute ID** and the values **table1** and **NULL** for the attributes **location** and **covered**, respectively. Figure 3 shows the definition of the **domain blocks-world1**.

An example **event** named **event1** illustrates **blockA** being picked up by **robot-arm1**. The **befstate** shows **blockA**'s **location** to be on **table1** and **robot-arm1** is not holding a block. The **meth pickup** of **blockA** is executed. The **aftstate** shows **blockA**'s **location** to be **robot-arm1** and **robot-arm1** is holding **blockA**. The **agent** instigating the method is **robot-arm1**. Figure 3 shows the definition of the **event event1**.

5.3 Another perspective

The SGML implementation of the methodology allows for easy extension to the existing knowledge. Suppose that in addition to the **stacking perspective** of the blocks world there is a perspective to teach a child to spell. In this new perspective the blocks may be alphabet blocks and words are spelled by placing the blocks next to each other. This new perspective is named **spelling** and will add attributes and methods to the existing **class block**. Also, the labels of which attributes belong to which perspectives will change.

In the **class block** there are two new attributes called **rightside** and **leftside** which may have potential values of **NULL** (meaning no block present to the particular side) or a block's identification (**ID** of block on the particular side). These two attributes belong within the perspective (**perspect**) **spelling**. The **attribute ID** and the **method pickup** are added to the **perspect spelling** and continue to also remain in the

```
<domain name="blocks-world1">
<instance classname="table" name="table1">
</instance>
<instance classname="robot-arm" name="robot-arm1" perspect="stacking">
<attval name="holding">NULL</attval>
</instance>
<instance classname="block" name="blockA">
<attval name="ID">A</attval>
<attval name="location">table1</attval>
<attval name="covered">NULL</attval>
</instance>
<instance classname="block" name="blockB">
<attval name="ID">B</attval>
<attval name="location">table1</attval>
<attval name="covered">NULL</attval>
</instance>
<instance classname="block" name="blockC">
<attval name="ID">C</attval>
<attval name="location">table1</attval>
<attval name="covered">NULL</attval>
</instance>
<instance classname="block" name="blockD">
<attval name="ID">D</attval>
<attval name="location">table1</attval>
<attval name="covered">NULL</attval>
</instance>
</domain>
```

```
<event name="event1">
<befstate>
blockA.location = table1
robot-arm1.holding = NULL
</befstate>
<meth>
blockA->pickup
</meth>
<aftstate>
blockA.location = robot-arm1
robot-arm1.holding = blockA
</aftstate>
<agent>
robot-arm1
</agent>
</event>
```

Figure 3: Definitions for the domain blocks-world1 and the event event1.

perspect stacking. There is one new method named **putbeside** which may have no arguments (put on the table) or two arguments, an **ID** and a **side** (of a block). The **method putbeside** is grouped within the **perspect spelling** and allows blocks to be placed beside one another. Note that knowledge to actually spell is not represented. Figure 4 shows the definition of **class block** (method content not shown) with the added **perspect spelling**. Only the changes and extensions are shown, otherwise the definition is the same as in Figure 2.

In the **class robot-arm** is the added **perspective spelling** with its definition (**def**) **setting blocks side by side for spelling words**. The list of classes within this perspective are **table** and **block**. The changes and extensions to the **class robot-arm** are also shown in Figure 4.

```
<class name="block">
<attribute name="ID" perspect="stacking spelling">
</attribute>
...
<attribute name="rightside" perspect="spelling">
<potvals>
<li>NULL
<li>an ID
</potvals>
</attribute>
<attribute name="leftside" perspect="spelling">
<potvals>
<li>NULL
<li>an ID
</potvals>
</attribute>
<method name="pickup" perspect="stacking spelling">
...
</method>
...
<method name="putbeside" perspect="spelling">
<args>
<li>NULL
<li>an ID
<li>side
</args>
</method>
</class>
```

```
<class name="robot-arm">
...
<perspective name="spelling" classes="table block">
<def>
setting blocks side by side for spelling words
</def>
</perspective>
</class>
```

Figure 4: Definitions of class block and robot-arm with the added perspective spelling.

5.4 Potential reasoning

Lines of reasoning are possible using perspectives and events. Different perspectives on the same object and the same perspective on different objects may suggest useful comparisons and contrasts. Gentner [5] describes comparisons of objects and domains based on literal similarity, analogy, and abstraction which are derived from the mappings of objects, object attributes, and relations between objects. Consider the example of the blocks world with the two different perspectives **stacking** and **spelling**. These are two different views of the same sets of objects. It is fairly simple to observe that a stack of blocks laid down will look like a line of blocks side by side, but can a reasoning mechanism make this observation? Perspectives may help facilitate this type of reasoning.

Events may be useful for another potential line of reasoning. Consider the **event event1** from Figure 3. Suppose the method (**meth**) was left blank. Given the before state (**befstate**), after state (**aftstate**), and class definitions (with method contents) it may be possible to infer the method (**meth**) executed to change the state. Actually, given any two of the three (**befstate**, **meth**, **aftstate**), the third may be inferred with the help of the class definitions and their method contents. It may be possible to make other inferences by including the **agent** with the other **event** elements.

Although not discussed in this paper, the methodology and its SGML implementation have the ability to create classes using the concepts of inheritance and aggregation/disaggregation. More detail about these concepts is discussed in [7]. Using inheritance and aggregation/disaggregation relationships can allow for additional lines of reasoning.

6 Other features

There are some other features to the methodology that are made available by the SGML implementation. One of these features is the ability to share and re-use knowledge. Part of this is facilitated by the notion of containing knowledge in classes and part of it is facilitated by SGML. Class libraries of common knowledge may be created and distributed in an SGML form. A class can be defined within an entity construct in a DTD. This will allow the class to be included and used in other knowledge domains by referencing the defined entity. That fact that SGML is very portable will also contribute to the sharing of knowledge.

Another feature is the potential ease of use of creating representations using SGML. The increasing popularity of the World Wide Web (WWW) has increased the use and understanding of markup and tagging languages. Using SGML to implement the methodology exploits this growing familiarity with markup languages. In fact, in order to make the creation of knowledge (in SGML) easier and quicker for testing the methodology, an Emacs mode for the Free Software Foundation's GNU Emacs [4] was developed. The mode has control-key sequences defined for all the methodology constructs and their associated tags. Additionally, a knowledge domain and the DTD for the methodology can be checked (within Emacs) against a validating SGML parser. In the future, code will be added to the Emacs mode to reason across some of the knowledge.

7 Conclusions

The object-based methodology and its SGML implementation complement each other. Together they provide a structured, yet flexible means of representing knowledge. The available constructs allow knowledge to be limited and focused to a specific problem or application area. Only the pertinent knowledge need be represented. Should the focus later change, the existing knowledge can be easily changed and/or extended.

The perspective and event constructs add detail to the knowledge being represented. Perspectives allow for the representation of multiple and varying viewpoints. Events allow for the representation of actual knowledge use. Both these constructs may facilitate new lines of reasoning over the knowledge domain.

Additionally, the SGML implementation helps make the knowledge more usable and portable. SGML documents can be interchanged independent of hardware and software and there is no proprietary format [12]. Also, by using the SGML entity construct, class libraries of common knowledge can be created, shared, and re-used.

More research is yet to be done on exercising the methodology and its SGML implementation on more complex knowledge domains. The limits of the methodology in what types of knowledge it may represent must be identified. Also, it should be compared to other representation schemes and systems. More research must also be done to further understand and implement the potential reasoning mechanisms in the methodology including reasoning with perspectives and events.

References

[1] Liroa Alschuler. *ABCD...SGML A User's Guide To Structured Information.* International Thomson Computer Press, Boston, MA, 1995.

[2] Grady Booch. *Object-Oriented Analysis and Design with Applications.* Addison-Wesley Publishing Company, Menlo Park, CA, second edition, 1994.

[3] Peter Coad and Edward Yourdon. *Object-Oriented Design.* Yourdon Press, Englewood Cliffs, NJ, 1991.

[4] Free Software Foundation, Boston, MA. *GNU Emacs Lisp Reference Manual,* 2.4 edition.

[5] Dedre Gentner. *Readings in Cognitive Science A Perspective from Psychology and Artificial Intelligence,* chapter 3.2, Structure-Mapping: A Theoretical Framework for Analogy, pages 303–310. Morgan Kaufmann Publishers, Inc., San Mateo, CA, 1988.

[6] International Organization for Standardization, Geneva. *ISO 8879:1986 Information processing - Text and office systems - Standard Generalized Markup Language (SGML),* October 1986.

[7] Robert L. Kelsey, Roger T. Hartley, and Robert B. Webster. An object-based methodology for knowledge representation. Technical Report LAUR 97-1598, Los Alamos National Laboratory, Los Alamos, NM, 1997.

[8] Eve Maler and Jeanne El Andaloussi. *Developing SGML DTDs From Text to Model to Markup.* Prentice Hall PTR, Upper Saddle River, NJ, 1996.

[9] Elaine Rich and Kevin Knight. *Artificial Intelligence.* McGraw-Hill, Inc., New York, NY, second edition, 1991.

[10] Stuart J. Russell and Peter Norvig. *Artificial Intelligence A Modern Approach.* Prentice Hall, Englewood Cliffs, NJ, 1995.

[11] Roger C. Schank and Robert P. Abelson. *Scripts Plans Goals and Understanding An Inquiry Into Human Knowledge Structures.* Lawrence Erlbaum Associates, Publishers, Hillsdale, NJ, 1977.

[12] Eric van Herwijnen. *Practical SGML.* Kluwer Academic Publishers, Boston, MA, second edition, 1994.

[13] Patrick Henry Winston. *Artificial Intelligence.* Addison-Wesley Publishing Company, Reading, MA, second edition, 1984.

A DTD for the methodology

```
<!ELEMENT kr - - (class*, domain*, event*)>
<!ELEMENT class - - (attribute*, method*, perspective*)>
<!ELEMENT domain - - (instance*)>
<!ELEMENT attribute - - (potvals? | instance?)>
<!ELEMENT method - - (args?, content?)>
<!ELEMENT args - - (li+)>
<!ELEMENT content - - (#PCDATA)>
<!ELEMENT perspective - - (def)>
<!ELEMENT instance - - (attval*)>
<!ELEMENT potvals - - (li+)>
<!ELEMENT attval - - (#PCDATA)>
<!ELEMENT def - - (#PCDATA)>
<!ELEMENT li - o (#PCDATA)>
<!ELEMENT event - - (befstate?, meth?, aftstate?, agent?)>
<!ELEMENT befstate - - (#PCDATA)>
<!ELEMENT meth - - (#PCDATA)>
<!ELEMENT aftstate - - (#PCDATA)>
<!ELEMENT agent - - (#PCDATA)>
<!ATTLIST class name NAME #REQUIRED
          inherit NAME #IMPLIED>
<!ATTLIST attribute name NAME #REQUIRED
          perspect NAMES #IMPLIED>
<!ATTLIST method name NAME #REQUIRED
          perspect NAMES #IMPLIED>
<!ATTLIST perspective name NAME #REQUIRED
          classes NAMES #IMPLIED>
<!ATTLIST instance classname NAME #REQUIRED
          name NAME #REQUIRED
          perspect NAMES #IMPLIED>
<!ATTLIST attval name NAME #REQUIRED>
<!ATTLIST domain name NAME #REQUIRED>
<!ATTLIST event name NAME #REQUIRED>
<!ATTLIST kr name NAME #REQUIRED>
```

Session E.1

Hybrid Knowledge Representation and Reasoning

Session Chair:
Ioannis Hatzilygeroudis, CTI, Greece

Combining Multiple Representations in a Spatial Reasoning System[1]

Brandon Bennett, Anthony G. Cohn and Amar Isli
University of Leeds, Leeds LS2 9JT, UK
{brandon,agc,isli}@scs.leeds.ac.uk

Abstract

We examine a variety of representations for storing and reasoning about spatial information and distinguish between quantitative *representations grounded in numerical coordinate systems and* qualitative *representations, based on a high-level conceptual vocabulary for the description of spatial situations. We suggest that qualitative languages, can add powerful functionality to spatial information system, which have traditionally processed only quantitative data.*

Trade-offs between expressive power, computational tractability and 'naturalness' are considered for several qualitative formalisms. We explain how a significant class of topological relations can be described by a 1st-order language and how these can be encoded into 0-order intuitionistic logic to yield an effective reasoning algorithm. We discuss ways of combining qualitative and quantitative information within a coherent architecture and describe an implementation of a hybrid spatial information system, incorporating three types of spatial information: quantitative data-structures are employed in a database of polygonal regions; a qualitative relational language is used to express high-level queries; intuitionistic propositional logic is used to compute the inferences needed to answer these queries.

1. Introduction

There is increasing demand for computer systems which can carry out complex manipulations of spatial information. These include CAD systems, Geographical Information Systems (GIS) and many graphics related applications. We believe that to meet ever more sophisticated requirements, such software will need to be able to handle information of a *qualitative* nature. In characterising information as 'qualitative', we mean that it is in the form of facts stated in terms of logical formulae whose constituent expressions correspond to high-level non-numerical concepts. In the case of spatial information, this vocabulary will consist of names of regions or objects and spatial relations which may hold between these entities. It may additionally contain logical operators such as Boolean connectives and quantifiers.

There are several reasons why qualitative information may be needed in a spatial information system. One is that, in certain cases, only partial information may be available. For example, we may know that some region is *disconnected* from another without knowing the precise geometry of both regions. Although it may be possible to capture this kind of information in terms of combinations of equations and inequalities between polynomials of numerical coordinates, the resulting representation would be highly complex and moreover would be dependent on the particular coordinate system and data structures employed. A qualitative representation allows information to be stored directly in terms of 'facts', so the fact that regions a and b are disconnected might be stored simply as '$\mathsf{DC}(a,b)$'. Even if all the spatial data stored by a system is in the form of precise geometrical coordinates, mechanisms for extracting and manipulating qualitative relationships between data objects are necessary for many tasks that a system might be expected to perform. The most obvious function of this kind is to answer queries containing qualitative spatial relations ('Find all forests that are *next to* a marsh'). We may also wish to stipulate or to check that the spatial objects in the system obey certain general constraints, which are most naturally specified in qualitative terms. For example we might wish to specify that a certain terrain-type may only be found as *part of* some particular type of region.

The domain of qualitative spatial concepts is extremely wide, so this paper focuses primarily on *topological* relations holding between spatial *regions*.[2] These might either be 2D regions, perhaps corresponding to countries or areas of some particular terrain type, or 3D regions, which could correspond to the volume occupied by some physical body such as a ball or a robot. Regions need not be 'one-piece' — a region can be composed of multiple disconnected parts (e.g. the Greek islands).

The stipulation that qualitative information is non-numerical requires some clarification. Spatial relations which would intuitively be regarded as qualitative in nature can often be defined analytically, in terms of arithmetical and other operations on quantitative data. For example, whether two triangles *overlap* can be characterised by a Boolean combination of inequalities involving the coordinates of the corner points of the triangles. However, despite the possibility of such a definition we still regard 'overlapping' as a qualitative relation because it abstracts quantitative data in a conceptually interesting way, which is *relevant* to high-level descriptions.[3]

As we shall see, there are many very different formalisms which can be used to represent qualitative spatial information and each has its own advantages and shortcomings. Because of this there are good reasons

[1] This work was supported by EPSRC grant GR/K65041.

[2] Other non-topological aspects of qualitative information that have been studied include orientation [29], distance [21] and shape [11, 30]. These and more are covered in [20] and [12].

[3] See [35] for further discussion of the nature of qualitative representations.

1082-3409/97 $10.00 © 1997 IEEE

why one might want to use more than one qualitative representation within a single computer system. It is also clear that for many applications one will need to deal with quantitative as well as qualitative information. This paper aims to suggest ways in which both these kinds of hybridisation can be incorporated within a flexible architecture for spatial information systems.

The remainder of the paper is organised as follows: In the next section, we consider possible representations of topological relations in a number of quite distinct logical languages. We look at the set-theoretic language of general topology, the 1st-order RCC theory [26], an equational algebraic language and finally at 0-order modal and intuitionistic encodings. We survey what is known about the computational complexity of reasoning with these representations, noting that the intuitionistic encoding yields an effective decision procedure for a reasonably expressive spatial language.

Section 3 examines the relationship between qualitative and quantitative information. Much of the functionality of spatial information systems involves the manipulation of quantitative data; and to fully exploit the power of qualitative reasoning we believe that systems will need to be able to integrate and translate between the two kinds of information. This approach is illustrated in section 4, where we describe a prototype implementation which operates with a combination of both quantitative and qualitative data. The system also exhibits a second type of hybridity in that the user can express qualitative queries in an easy-to-understand relational vocabulary but the internal reasoning mechanism employs the intuitionistic encoding of spatial information in order to compute inferences effectively.

2. Representations for Reasoning about Topological Relations

Many formal languages could be used to represent and reason about topological relationships and the relative worth of such a language can be assessed according to a number of different (and often conflicting) criteria. Three principal considerations are: what is the expressive power of the language? how closely does the representation fit with the concepts and structures which we find most natural for describing these relationships? and, how easy is it to determine logical entailments holding among expressions of the language? More briefly these can be called *expressiveness*, *naturalness* and *tractability*.

If a language has limited expressive power, its value will depend upon how significant is the class of relationships which can be expressed. This of course depends upon the kind of information one wants to represent; but it is clear that in our everyday descriptions of physical situations certain topological relationships are much more frequently employed than others. Figure 1 shows eight relationships between pairs of regions which seem to be of special importance — these are: Dis-Connection, External Connection, Partial Overlap, Tangential Proper Part, Non-Tangential Proper Part and Equality. The notations used for these relations are given under the diagrams. The part relations, being asymmetric, have inverses denoted, Ri. As will be explained below, this set of relations figures prominently in the 'RCC' theory of spatial relations [26] and will be referred to as 'RCC-8'. The same relation set[4] has independently been identified as significant in the context of GIS [15, 14, 10].

Evidently, any pair of regions must be related by exactly one of the relations in RCC-8. Such a relation set is *jointly exhaustive and pairwise disjoint* (JEPD). Certain disjunctions of these relations are also useful in describing spatial configurations in more general terms: for instance two regions are discrete $(\mathsf{DR}(x,y))$ if they are either disconnected or externally connected; one region is a proper part of another $(\mathsf{PP}(x,y))$ if it is either a tangential or a non-tangential proper part; a region is part $(\mathsf{P}(x,y))$ of another if it is either a proper part or the two regions are equal.

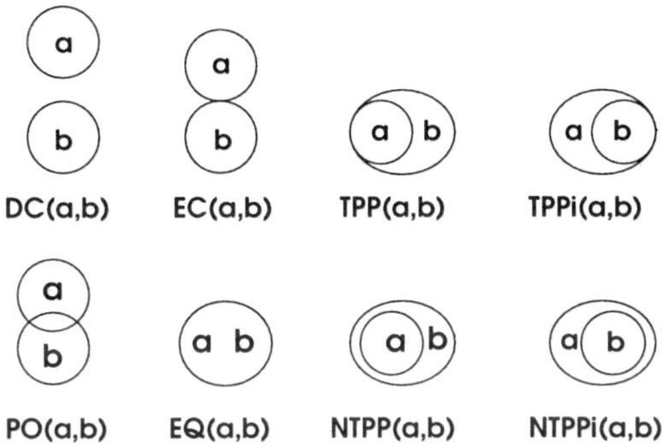

Figure 1: 8 Base Relations in the RCC Theory

As well as identifying significant topological relations, we must also examine the kinds of entity that we want to refer to and between which the relations can be asserted. Topological relations can sensibly be regarded either as holding between material objects of some kind or as holding between abstract regions, which may or may not be occupied by physical matter. In this paper we shall take the latter, more-abstract approach. This has the advantage of avoiding various difficulties associated with a materialistic interpretation — specifically, there is clearly an interaction between material properties (such as solidity) and possible topological relationships (e.g. distinct solid bodies cannot overlap).

For present purposes the dimensionality of regions is not important, since we will only be concerned with topological inferences valid in arbitrary dimensions. Of course it would be desirable to be able to specify the dimensionality of a region or at least constrain all regions to be (say) two or three dimensional. This would mean that further inferences could be made. The problem of characterising dimension in a region-based representation is considered in [17] and [4].

If a logical system is to be used as a formal representation for reasoning about familiar spatial concepts it ought to at least provide an efficient means of validating inferences involving the kinds of relation depicted in figure 1. Thus we now examine how a simple example argument involving three of these relations could

[4] Actually [13] has distinguished slight differences in their possible interpretations.

be represented in three different formal languages. We shall consider the following inference:[5]

$$\frac{\begin{array}{l} a \text{ is a non-tangential part of } b \\ b \text{ is discrete from } c. \end{array}}{a \text{ is disconnected from } c}$$

Note that the relation 'x is discrete from y' ($\mathsf{DR}(x, y)$) is intended to be more general than 'x is disconnected from y'. The latter states that x and y do not touch at any point, whereas the former states that they do not overlap. Thus discrete objects may or may not touch. The distinction between overlapping and connection makes the argument more subtle than the kind of reasoning that can be represented in classical Boolean logic. The following subsections describe a number of more complex logical representations within which the required inference procedures can be formulated.

2.1. Point-Set Topology

Point-set topology is a highly developed body of mathematical theory founded directly upon set-theory. To represent the argument using the symbolism of point-set topology one must first decide how the informal notion of region and the relations between regions should be represented in the precise formal notation of this theory. One possibility is to use the following interpretation:[6]

- A *region* is identified with an *open* set of points.
- Regions are *connected* if their *closures* share at least one point.
- Regions *overlap* if they share at least one point.

There is also a dual interpretation where regions are identified with *closed* sets — these are connected if they share a point and overlap if their *interiors* share a point.

At the level of what one might call 'naturalistic' topological relations such as shown in figure 1, the question of whether regions are taken as open or closed — i.e. as including their boundaries or not — has no real significance as long as we can distinguish the interior points of a region from *boundary* points, which may or may not be considered part of the region. Each of the relations shown in figure 1 can be described in terms of the sets of points making up each region together with some means of distinguishing interior points from boundary points.[7]

Assuming that a region is an open set of points, a non-tangential part of a region is a sub-region whose closure is part of the larger region. Similarly, regions are discrete (i.e. do not overlap) if they share no points (if their closures share points they are discrete but in external contact). Thus our example argument would be formalised as follows:

$$\frac{\begin{array}{l} c(X) \subseteq Y \\ \neg\exists p[p \in Y \wedge p \in Z] \end{array}}{\neg\exists p[p \in c(X) \wedge p \in c(Z)]}$$

where $c(\ldots)$ satisfies appropriate axioms for a topological closure function (see e.g. [23, p.129]). The inference is valid as long as X, Y and Z are open.

The language of set-theory augmented with an axiomatised closure function provides an extremely expressive formalism for describing spatial relationships. However as a calculus for actually reasoning about such relations it is not an effective tool. This is because of the enormous complexity of the task of verifying inferences in such a rich language. Even if we can get by with a 1st-order axiomatisation of set-theory, once we have added the interior function axioms and representations of a number of topological facts we will have a fairly sizable 1st-order theory. Unless we can come up with some special purpose reasoning mechanisms[8] for this type of theory, testing validity of inferences will thus be undecidable; and even finding a proof for a valid inference may be impossible in practice. Thus, the language of set-theoretical topology is very expressive but highly intractable. It is also rather unnatural in that it is based on concepts of interior and closure, which do not correspond to everyday vocabulary.

2.2. 1st-Order Theories

It is apparent that natural descriptions of geographical and other kinds of spatial situation do not normally make use of the full expressivity of the language of point-set topology. The subtle distinction between open and closed sets of points is not one that enters into everyday talk about the arrangements of physical objects or the configurations of regions on a map. Indeed, most of our vocabulary for describing such situations does not even make explicit reference to *points* as constituents of regions; rather we employ properties and relations that apply directly to regions (or in some cases to physical bodies). This suggests it might be possible to build a spatial theory based on individual objects

[5] In this example we employ the relation 'non-tangential part' (NTP) rather than the RCC-8 relation of 'non-tangential *proper* part' (NTPP). The relation NTP can be defined by $\mathsf{NTP}(x, y) \equiv_{def} \forall z[\mathsf{C}(z, x) \rightarrow \mathsf{O}(z, y)]$. It coincides with NTPP in all cases except for a special case involving the universal region, u. Specifically, NTP(u, u) is true, whereas NTPP(u, u) is false: every region is connected to the universe, so according to the definition every region is also an NTP of the universe; but on the other hand no region is a *proper* part of itself, including the universe. Thus NTP is not totally disjoint from EQ but the simplicity of the NTP definition makes its use more convenient than NTPP for many purposes.

[6] This interpretation is very similar to that suggested for the RCC theory in [26].

[7] Consideration of intuitive properties of 'regions' may suggest the further requirement that regions correspond only to *regular* open (or closed) sets — that is sets that are equal to the interior of their closure. Irregular sets have certain properties which may seem contrary to our natural concept of a region: in 2D, irregular closed regions may include isolated points or 1-dimensional spikes, whilst irregular open regions may have 1-dimensional 'cracks' or missing isolated points. However, the types of inference we deal with in this paper do not depend on a restriction to regular sets.

[8] This is essentially what [15, 14, 10] have done: their representation is semantically based on sets of points, but inference is achieved by precomputed *composition tables*. As a sole means of computing inferences, composition tables are rather inflexible: for a given set of relations that one wishes to represent, the composition table must be precomputed and even then the only inferences that can be verified are those which follow from relational composition. Special purpose mechanisms for reasoning about spatial change have also been investigated — e.g. in terms of the notion of *closest topological distance* [16] or *continuity networks* [12].

or regions and high-level relationships, which would be more in keeping with our 'common-sense' conception of topological configurations and perhaps also more tractable than the language of point-set topology.

This is the approach taken by [26], who, building on earlier work of Clarke [8, 9], have developed a 1st-order theory of spatial regions and relationships between them. The basic RCC theory employs just one primitive dyadic relation, $\mathsf{C}(x, y)$, read as 'x connects with y' (i.e. $\mathsf{C}(x, y)$ is the negation of $\mathsf{DC}(x, y)$), which is axiomatised to be reflexive and symmetric. Individuals are intended to be interpreted as denoting spatial regions. A large number of relations (including all those shown in figure 1) and other spatial properties can be defined in terms of C. For example $\mathsf{P}(x, y)$, meaning 'x is part of y', can be defined as $\mathsf{P}(x, y) \equiv_{def} \forall z[\mathsf{C}(z, x) \rightarrow \mathsf{C}(z, y)]$ and the *proper* part relation $\mathsf{PP}(x, y)$ is $\mathsf{PP}(x, y) \equiv_{def} \mathsf{P}(x, y) \wedge \neg\mathsf{P}(y, x)$. The relation '$x$ overlaps y', is then defined by $\mathsf{O}(x, y) \equiv_{def} \exists z[\mathsf{P}(z, x) \wedge \mathsf{P}(z, y)]$ and $\mathsf{DR}(x, y)$ is simply the negation of $\mathsf{O}(x, y)$. The relation of external connection is defined by $\mathsf{EC}(x, y) \equiv_{def} \mathsf{C}(x, y) \wedge \neg\mathsf{O}(x, y)$. By continuing this series of definitions all the RCC-8 relations can be defined starting from only the C primitive ([26] gives a complete set of definitions). We can also define the non-tangential part relation employed in our example argument by $\mathsf{NTP}(x, y) \equiv_{def} \forall z[\mathsf{C}(z, x) \rightarrow \mathsf{O}(z, y)]$.

The RCC theory also contains (quasi-)Boolean operations which can be used to denote regions formed by the sums, intersections and complements of regions. These operations are not truly Boolean because the domain of the RCC theory does not contain a *null* element. Thus, for example, the intersection of two discrete regions does not exist, so the quasi-Boolean operations are not total functions on the domain of regions.

By making use of its defined relations, the language of the RCC theory allows a very straightforward representation of the argument which is very close to its statement in natural language; and, if we replace the NTP, DR and DC relations by their definitions then the inference is very straightforward, involving only a universal instantiation, the observation that O is symmetric and an application of *modus tolens.*

$$\frac{\mathsf{NTP}(a, b) \quad \mathsf{DR}(b, c)}{\mathsf{DC}(a, c)} \qquad\qquad \frac{\forall x[\mathsf{C}(x, a) \rightarrow \mathsf{O}(x, b)] \quad \neg\mathsf{O}(b, c)}{\neg\mathsf{C}(a, c)}$$

Thus although the 1st-order, region-based formalism is less expressive than the point-set representation, the former seems more natural and is certainly more tractable. Nevertheless, 1st-order reasoning is in general undecidable; so as a practical calculus a 1st-order representation is still far from ideal. In fact some results of [19] strongly suggest that no completely adequate 1st-order theory of spatial regions including Boolean functions and the connection relation can be constructed; and moreover that any theory covering this domain (e.g. a 2nd-order theory) must be undecidable. The basis of these results is a demonstration that such a theory could be used to encode 1st-order arithmetical expressions; and 1st-order arithmetic is known to be undecidable.

2.3. An Equational Representation

In considering the use of point-set topology as a description language for spatial relationships the most obvious representations involve 1st-order set theory into which an *interior* operator is introduced. We now present an equational description language which contains Boolean operators and the interior operator but no quantifiers. This is a purely algebraic representation in which the constants denoting regions need not necessarily be considered as sets of points; however, identifying them with open sets is a very natural interpretation. It is perhaps surprising that all the RCC-8 relations can be represented without the use of quantification. In order to achieve this it is most convenient to start by defining a slightly different set of relations, which will be called RCC-7. This is the set {DC, DR, P, Pi, NTP, NTPi, EQ}, for which equational definitions are given in table 1. (Note that unlike RCC-8 it is neither jointly exhaustive nor pairwise disjoint.) The second column of the table gives an alternative representation using *order* constraints instead of equations.[9]

RCC	Set Equation	Order Constraints
$\mathsf{DC}(x, y)$	$i(\overline{x}) \cup i(\overline{y}) = U$	$x \leq i(\overline{y})$
$\mathsf{DR}(x, y)$	$\overline{x \cap y} = U$	$x \leq \overline{y}$
$\mathsf{P}(x, y)$	$\overline{x} \cup y = U$	$x \leq y$
$\mathsf{Pi}(x, y)$	$x \cup \overline{y} = U$	$y \leq x$
$\mathsf{NTP}(x, y)$	$\overline{x} \cup i(y) = U$	$x \leq i(y)$
$\mathsf{NTPi}(x, y)$	$i(x) \cup \overline{y} = U$	$y \leq i(x)$
$\mathsf{EQ}(x, y)$	$(\overline{x} \cup y) \cap (x \cup \overline{y}) = U$	$x \leq y,\ y \leq x$

Table 1: The RCC-7 relations defined in terms of set equations and the interior operator

A much larger set of relations can be characterised in terms of arbitrary conjunctions composed of RCC-7 relations and their negations. For example, the relation $\mathsf{EC}(x, y)$ is equivalent to $\mathsf{DR}(x, y) \wedge \neg\mathsf{DC}(x, y)$. There are a total of $3^7 = 2187$ expressions of this form (each RCC-7 relation is either asserted, negated or not mentioned); however, because of entailments among the RCC-7 set equations many of these are equivalent. The number of distinct relations definable in this way is 171 and includes all relations mentioned so far and almost half of the $2^8 = 256$ relations which are disjunctions of the RCC-8 relations. Moreover, consistency of sets of facts involving the 171 relations can be efficiently tested (see section 2.5 below). Some of the relations definable in this way may be regarded as illegitimate because the set-equation definitions do not require the regions to be non-empty, whereas in the RCC theory, regions cannot be empty. A region x is empty if $\overline{x} = U$ so non-emptiness can be enforced by the negation of such an equation. If we add this *non-null* constraint[10] for each of the two regions involved in a relation then the number of distinct relations which can be defined is 115.[11]

[9] The ubiquity of order constraints in spatial information has been explored by [28] but this formulation will not be further examined in the present paper.

[10] More details on non-null constraints can be found in [3, 5]

[11] A slightly larger class of RCC relations has recently been identified as a maximal tractable subclass by [27]. We are currently investigating the relationship between the two classes.

This analysis illustrates a general methodology in representing systems of relations. Consideration of some knowledge domain will often lead to the classification of the relationship between two objects into some JEPD set of relations (such as RCC-8 or Allen's 13 relations between temporal intervals [1, 2]). To represent partial knowledge or to represent constraints in this domain we will want to reason with *disjunctions* of these basic JEPD relations. But naïve inference with such disjunctions will lead to exponential computational complexity. This is because each disjunctive fact is true in a number of alternative situations; and, given a set of disjunctive facts, the total number of possible situations satisfying these facts is obtained by multiplying the numbers of disjuncts in each fact. To show that a given relation is a consequence of such a set of facts, one has in effect to show that the relation must hold in each of these possible situations. Clearly, for a large number of disjunctive facts, the number of alternative situations will be extremely large and the computation time needed to check an entailment will be approximately proportional to this number. However, analysis of the underlying structure of constraints in terms of which the relations can be defined may lead to an alternative formulation in which a large number of relations can be defined without the use of disjunctions. By using this disjunction free representation one can construct a mechanism for efficient computation of inferences. (The analysis of Allen's interval relations by [34] and its subsequent refinement by [25], where the relations are re-represented in terms of equations and inequalities involving their end-points, is an example of this approach.)

2.4. 0-Order Representations

The equational analysis described in the last section provides a disjunction free representation for a large set of spatial facts. However, in order to reason with this representation we still need a procedure for determining inferences among the disjunction-free facts. As these facts take the form of equations one might expect this procedure to operate directly on these equations. Indeed, equational reasoning has been investigated in some detail by researchers into automated reasoning techniques. However, in the case of the spatial constraints under consideration, a rather more indirect approach has been taken to the reasoning problem. This is based on the further transformation of set equations into 0-order (propositional) formulae.

Investigation of 0-order logics, which are normally thought of as representing propositional reasoning, has revealed correspondences between entailment in these systems and in certain algebraic theories. In particular, any entailment amongst set equations involving the interior operator (i.e. equations such as those of table 1) is mirrored by an entailment between corresponding 0-order formulae of the language $S4$ obtained from the set equations by a simple translation procedure [33, 5]. A similar but slightly more complex correspondence allows spatial relations to be translated into formulae of the intuitionistic propositional calculus, $\mathcal{I}$, [31, 3]. This latter translation has been found most suitable as a basis for effective automated reasoning and has been used to implement a topological reasoning algorithm using the Prolog programming language [3].

Table 2 gives sets of intuitionistic formulae corresponding to topological relations (including the RCC-8 relations). Each relation is actually associated with two kinds of formulae: a model constraint and a set of entailment constraints (this extension of $\mathcal{I}$ we term $\mathcal{I}^+$). To test whether a set of facts formed from such relations is consistent one first forms two sets of formulae: $\mathcal{M}$, consisting of all the model constraints; and $\mathcal{E}$ containing all the entailment constraints associated with these relations. Then, if no formula in $\mathcal{E}$ is a logical consequence of the set $\mathcal{M}$ (according to established rules of inference for intuitionistic logic), the original set of topological relations is consistent (otherwise it is inconsistent). The pair $\langle \mathcal{M}, \mathcal{E} \rangle$ can be regarded as a description of a topological situation. A situation description $\langle \mathcal{M}', \mathcal{E}' \rangle$ is a logical consequence of $\langle \mathcal{M}, \mathcal{E} \rangle$ if either $\langle \mathcal{M}, \mathcal{E} \rangle$ is itself inconsistent or the following conditions hold: each formulae in $\mathcal{M}'$ is entailed by the set $\mathcal{M}$; and for each $\phi \in \mathcal{E}'$, the set $\mathcal{M} \cup \phi$ entails at least one formula in $\mathcal{E}$.

Relation	*Model Con.*	*Entailment Constraints*
DC(x,y)	$\sim x \vee \sim y$	$\sim x, \ \sim y$
EC(x,y)	$\sim(x \wedge y)$	$\sim x \vee \sim y, \sim x, \ \sim y$
PO(x,y)	—	$\sim(x \wedge y), \ x \Rightarrow y, \ y \Rightarrow x, \sim x, \sim y$
TPP(x,y)	$x \Rightarrow y$	$\sim x \vee y, \ y \Rightarrow x, \sim x, \sim y$
TPPi(x,y)	$y \Rightarrow x$	$\sim y \vee x, \ x \Rightarrow y, \sim x, \sim y$
NTPP(x,y)	$\sim x \vee y$	$y \Rightarrow x, \sim x, \sim y$
NTPPi(x,y)	$\sim y \vee x$	$x \Rightarrow y, \sim x, \sim y$
EQ(x,y)	$x \Leftrightarrow y$	$\sim x, \sim y$
NTP(x,y)	$\sim x \vee y$	$\sim x, \sim y$
DR(x,y)	$\sim(x \wedge y)$	$\sim x, \ \sim y$
C(x,y)	—	$\sim x \vee \sim y, \sim x, \sim y$
EQ$(x,$sum$(y,z))$	$x \Leftrightarrow (y \vee z)$	$\sim x, \sim y, \sim z$

Table 2: Some RCC relations defined in $\mathcal{I}^+$

Details of why this works are beyond the scope of the present paper (they are fully described in [3]). However, it is worth noting that each of the formulae employed in the encodings of the RCC-8 relations corresponds directly to an RCC-7 relation. In fact the $\mathcal{I}^+$ representation can be obtained by a simple syntactic transformation of the equational representation which was given in table 1. Bennett's use of *model* and *entailment* constraints to represent the RCC-8 relations also corresponds directly to our characterisation in terms of assertions and negations of the RCC-7 relations; and the non-null constraints appear in the $\mathcal{I}^+$ encoding as entailment constraints of the form $\sim x$. Because our running example argument involves only positive RCC-7 relations it can be formulated simply in terms of an entailment between model constraints and is justified by the following valid intuitionistic inference.[12]

$$\frac{\begin{array}{c}\sim a \vee b \\ \sim(b \wedge c)\end{array}}{\sim a \vee \sim c}$$

[12]Strictly speaking we need also to verify that each of the 'non-null' entailment constraints, $\sim a$ and $\sim c$, associated with DC(a,c), when added to the model constraints derived from NTP(a,b) and DR(b,c), entails one of the entailment constraints, $\sim a$, $\sim b$ and $\sim c$, derived from those formulae. But this is trivial.

2.5. Complexity

Because 0-order intuitionistic logic is decidable, Bennett's encoding of spatial relations into this formalism provides a decision procedure for reasoning about these relations. By analysing the intuitionistic sequents which arise from this encoding, [24] has shown that the consistency of sets of RCC-8 relations can be computed in polynomial time. In fact the problem is in the class NC, which means that it can be computed in polylogarithmic time on polynomially many processors — in other words, parallel processing can be exploited to speed up computation. The same method can be extended to a larger class of relations including all those representable in terms of conjunctions of RCC-7 relations and their negations, without increasing the complexity. [6] gives a tractable algorithm based on special purpose inference rules for a fragment of intuitionistic logic. This can be used to test the consistency of n RCC-8 relations in $O(n^3)$ time.

Other complexity results for spatial reasoning are given in [18], which considers the *realisability* of a set of relations by a set of simply-connected *planar* regions. Drawing on results of [22] about the recognition of realisable string graphs, [18] conclude that testing realisability is NP-hard. This shows that reasoning about connected regions in the plane is harder than the general topological reasoning covered by Bennett's encoding.

3. Qualitative Representations and Quantitative Data

A purely qualitative spatial information system would be based on a qualitative representation of spatial and other properties of objects and would provide an inference mechanism for determining whether any given qualitative fact follows from some set of such facts. This system could be used to answer queries relative to a qualitative database. However, a qualitative reasoning system need not be employed in isolation from coordinate-based geometrical information and other kinds of numerical data. Indeed, for many useful functions, numerical information is essential. Moreover, as we shall explain, the combination of qualitative and quantitative representations promises to be a powerful tool in system design. It also enables useful and novel program functionality based on two possible interfacing procedures: one in which the truth of a qualitative fact can be tested with respect to a quantitative database; and the other in which a set of qualitative facts is generated from a quantitative database.

In current computer systems, representation of spatial information is based almost entirely on numerical coordinates and parameters. Nevertheless, a high proportion of tests made on this data (e.g. in conditional statements of the form '`if` *test* `then` *command*') are actually used to test qualitative relations between data objects. For example, we may wish to test whether two line segments cross. This is a qualitative relationship between the segments. To determine whether a qualitative relationship such as this holds between entities an algorithm is needed which will operate on numerical data-structures so as to extract the required information. In many cases — including the case of the crossing line segments – this can be achieved by formulating the relationship in terms of a Boolean combination of equalities and inequalities involving the coordinates of points; in other cases more complex iterative routines will be required.

Writing such algorithms will generally be straightforward for a competent programmer; but, as large systems are developed, problems may emerge. There is potentially infinite variety in the form that spatial data can take, so a large number of similar algorithms operating on slightly different types of data must be written. (The *object-oriented* paradigm of computer programming can help overcome this problem but only if great care is taken in establishing a hierarchical organisation of data-types — even then it may be difficult to integrate new, unforeseen data-types neatly into an existing structure.) More seriously, the heterogeneity of data objects means that apparently equivalent properties of different data-types may diverge in extreme cases and this can lead to coding errors which are difficult to identify.

Even disregarding potential coding problems, it is clear that, whilst it may be possible, on a case-by-case basis to devise an algorithm to extract specific qualitative information, when needed, from quantitative data-structures, it would be far preferable to have a general purpose method of testing all qualitative relationships which one may encounter. A qualitative representation, whose interpretation is linked in a precise way to the content of quantitative data-structures can go some way towards providing this capability. The idea is that the qualitative representation would be based upon a number of primitive relational and functional expressions and each of these primitives would be associated with an appropriate algorithmic operation on quantitative data. A small number of primitives means there are fewer primitives to implement which is an advantage (provided that the primitives are not unduly complicated to implement of course). Also it should be noted that there may be a tradeoff between the number of primitives and the ease of defining "higher level" concepts and indeed the efficiency in interpreting these defined relations.

Given such an interpretation of the primitives, any complex expression in the qualitative language would then be evaluated by combining these primitive operations in accordance with the semantics of logical operators. Constructing this evaluation mechanism may be very difficult (or even impossible) depending on the nature of the primitives and logical operations involved; but once achieved it provides a general purpose procedure for evaluating a large (probably infinite) class of qualitative expressions. The representation can thus function directly as a query language as well as being used internally for program control.

In fact a limited version of this approach is already found in nearly all computer programs. Whenever one defines some basic qualitative tests (as functions returning Boolean values) and then uses Boolean combinations of these tests in conditional statements, a simple qualitative language is being used. To move from this limited capability to the use of a fully-fledged qualitative representation, one must identify a vocabulary of primitives and logical operators sufficient to represent any qualitative fact in some particular conceptual domain. The problem for the programmer then, rather than being 'how can I code an algorithm to test whether this relationship holds?', becomes 'how can I express this relationship in terms of my qualitative language?'. This architecture has the advantage that evaluation of qualitative tests is independent of the particular data structures used to store quantitative data in the system, except in so far as operations corresponding to the primitives must be coded.

It is perhaps surprising that a complex domain of qualitative facts can be described by means of just a few primitives; but this is just what is done in analytic geometry, where all relations are reduced to polynomial equations/inequalities of coordinates. Moreover, it is known that the whole theory of Euclidean geometry can be formalised in terms of the single ternary relation 'points x and y are equidistant from point z' [32]. Similarly, it is very likely that the connection relation, $\mathsf{C}(x, y)$, can serve as the only primitive in a region-based (non-metrical) theory of topology. Given these observations one may be puzzled that, even when working in a circumscribed conceptual domain such as that of geometrical relationships, a programmer will often find that to test a qualitative relationship (that has not been encountered before) seems to require an entirely new algorithm, which cannot be easily constructed from simple basic operations. This does not necessarily stem from incompetence of the programmer (although it is true that by implementing a powerful and flexible set of primitive operations a great deal of programming time and code complexity can be avoided); rather, the reason is that in an ordinary programming language the only logical operations which can be used to combine test procedures are the Boolean operators. But to express an arbitrary geometrical condition in terms of the equidistance relation will in general require quantification and set theory.

This brings us to a considerable obstacle: unless we are very careful, even a very modest logical vocabulary can give rise to a highly intractable language. In particular, a language which allows quantification over a potentially infinite domain of entities (i.e. a 1st-order language) will be undecidable unless, by taking account of the meanings of the specific vocabulary of the language, some special-purpose decision procedure can be found. Even where a decision procedure can be found, the time taken to evaluate a qualitative test may increase exponentially with the amount of information to be taken into account. This will make the language unsuitable for representing large amounts of data.

However, for many uses it may be that although, the database of quantitative geographical information may be very large, the qualitative tests/queries that the system will be required to evaluate will be relatively simple. The time taken to evaluate a qualitative query will be a function of both the amount of quantitative information stored and the complexity of the query. Retrieving information from the quantitative database will typically take time which increases only polynomially in the size of the database (in most cases retrieval times will increase linearly or as some small power of the database size). Thus, even if the query-answer-time increases exponentially with query complexity this may be acceptable as long as all queries have complexity below a certain level. Also, on receiving a qualitative query it would be possible for the system to estimate the maximum time required to return an answer.

There is another simple but potentially very useful way that a qualitative reasoning system can interface with quantitative data. Rather than interpreting qualitative relations in terms of numerical data, it may often be useful to go the other way round: i.e. take a database of quantitative information and extract from it a set of qualitative facts which constitute all the high-level information required for some purpose. Based on this idea a sophisticated and flexible architecture can be envisaged, in which quantitative data can be transparently combined when required with qualitative data, allowing queries to be addressed to a hybrid information source containing both quantitative and qualitative data.

3.1. The Boolean Algebra of Half-Planes

We now propose a mathematical framework for determining the qualitative RCC-8 relations holding between polygonally specified regions in a quantitative, spatial database of 2-dimensional regions. Our approach is based on what may be called the Boolean Algebra of half-planes. An element of this algebra is a Boolean combination of half-planes. These half-planes may be either open or closed. They may be represented either by two distinct points lying on its boundary or by the three constants, a, b and c in the equation $ax+by+c=0$ of its boundary. An additional data bit is required to specify whether the half-plane is open or closed. In addition to the usual Boolean operations of union, intersection, complement and subtraction we introduce an operator $c(X)$, whose value is the topological closure of the set X.

A term in this algebra denotes a *generalised polygon*, which may be an ordinary polygon, or a set of such polygons, or a half plane or some combination of these. The algebra can represent both open and closed regions but the RCC theory does not make such a distinction. For the purpose of computing RCC-8 relations we identify regions with the closures of the terms used to express them and assume the interpretation given in section 2.1 above. Testing whether a term denotes an empty region plays a crucial role in our algorithm. We transform it into a normal form (analogous to DNF for propositional logics) consisting of a union of intersections of half-planes. This term corresponds to an empty region iff each of these intersections is empty. Because half-planes are convex subsets of the plane we make use of Helly's theorem [7] which ensures that an intersection of 2D convex regions is empty iff any three of the regions involved have an empty intersection. If the objects are half-planes, this just means solving a number of systems of three linear inequalities in two variables which can be done by a straightforward arithmetical test.

The half-plane algebra enables the RCC-8 relation between two regions denoted by terms, R_1 and R_2 to be determined by a sequence of tests for the emptiness of certain algebraic combinations of R_1 and R_2:

1. If $(c(R_1) \cap c(R_2)) = \emptyset$ then $\mathsf{DC}(R_1, R_2)$
2. Otherwise, if $(c(R_1) - c(R_2)) = \emptyset$ then
   a) if $(c(R_2) - c(R_1)) = \emptyset$ then $\mathsf{EQ}(R_1, R_2)$.
   b) otherwise, if $(c(R_1) \cap c(\overline{R_2})) = \emptyset$ then $\mathsf{NTPP}(R_1, R_2)$, otherwise $\mathsf{TPP}(R_1, R_2)$.
3. Otherwise, if $c(R_2) - c(R_1) = \emptyset$ then if $(c(R_2) \cap c(\overline{R_1})) = \emptyset$ then $\mathsf{NTPPi}(R_1, R_2)$, otherwise $\mathsf{TPPi}(R_1, R_2)$.
4. Otherwise, if $\overline{c(\ \overline{(R_1)} \cap c(R_2)\ )} = \emptyset$ then $\mathsf{EC}(R_1, R_2)$, otherwise $\mathsf{PO}(R_1, R_2)$.

4. A Prototype Application

In section 2 we described a number of formalisms for representing topological relationships and section 2.5 gave some complexity results which demonstrate that reasoning with sets of these relations can be performed effectively. However, the details of how these languages could be exploited in a genuine practical application are by no means obvious. We now briefly describe a prototype system which is being developed in order to explore possible ways to exploit qualitative spatial reasoning.

A topological reasoning algorithm based on the intuitionistic encoding has been implemented within a larger 'spatial AI' system being developed as part of EPSRC project GR/K65041 on 'Logical Theories and Decision Procedures for Reasoning about Physical Systems'.[13] The system contains a database of geographical information in the form of polygon data and also contains qualitative data in the form of topological relations between named regions. Some of these named regions are identified directly with polygons in the geometrical database, whereas for others the geometry is not precisely known but only constrained by the qualitative topological relations. The topological relationships determined by the quantitative data can also be computed by means of the Boolean half-plane algebra and thereby accessed by the topological reasoning mechanism. This allows queries to be addressed to the combined qualitative and quantitative database. Such a capability is (as far as we know) not available in any other system.

Figure 2 shows a screen-dump of the current prototype. Most of the code is written in (SICStus) Prolog but a Tcl/Tk sub-process is used to create the GUI. The main window at the top includes a simple cartographical display, whose geometry is determined by a database giving the coordinates and terrain type of a number of triangular regions. Some of this data is shown in the bottom left window. The bottom right window presents a database of qualitative relations between regions. (In this example all the regions have in fact been fully described metrically in the cartographical display but this need not be the case in general). In the figure we see that the 'Evaluate Query' function has just been used to find that '`ec(forest,desert)`' is inconsistent with the qualitative database. Such queries are answered by means of the consistency checking algorithm [3] which determines whether a relation is consistent with, inconsistent with or a necessary consequence of the database.

[13] More information about this project can be found on the web at `http://www.scs.leeds.ac.uk/ctcs/raps.html`.

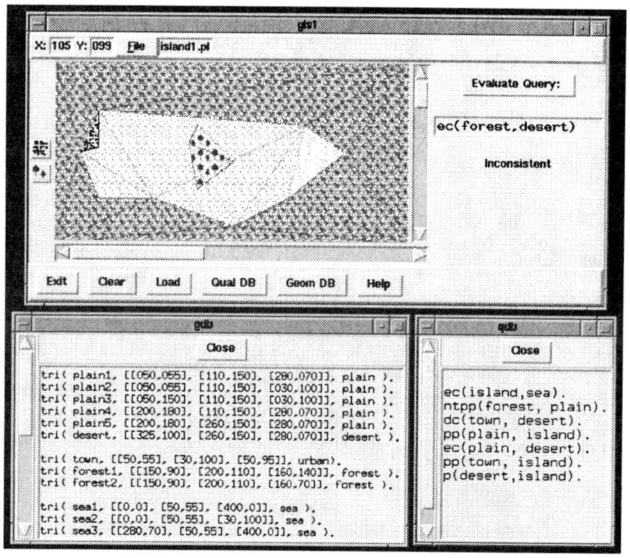

Figure 2: The current prototype system

5. Conclusion

We have motivated the use of qualitative representations in spatial information systems and shown that, even if we restrict attention to the domain of topological relations, a wide variety of different formalisms can be used, each with its own strengths and weaknesses. We have suggested the relation set RCC-8 as providing a very natural partition of possible topological relations, suitable for incorporation into the vocabulary of a user interface such as a query answering system; and have explained, by means of an encoding into 0-order intuitionistic logic, an effective decision procedure for these relations can be obtained. These two representations form a hybrid system able to exploit the best features of each formalism.

We have also considered the interface between qualitative and quantitative information and specified an algorithm for translating the former into the latter using a Boolean Algebra of Half-Planes. This allows one to answer high-level qualitative queries with respect to a quantitative database or even with respect to a hybrid database containing both types of information.

Enhancing and extending our system presents many possibilities for further research. We wish to improve both expressive power and efficiency and this may involve further exploration of ways in which different representations can be combined together. Our development of interfaces between qualitative and quantitative data is still at an early stage and will certainly give rise to further challenges. For instance, we have focused largely on translating quantitative to qualitative data; but one can also envisage many situations where one might want to go from qualitative to quantitative information: i.e. find a possible geometrical configuration satisfying some qualitative conditions on its constituent regions.

[1] J F Allen. An interval-based representation of temporal knowledge. In *Proceedings 7th IJCAI*, pages 221–226, 1981.

[2] J F Allen. Maintaining knowledge about temporal intervals. *Communications of the ACM*, 26(11):832–843, 1983.

[3] B. Bennett. Spatial reasoning with propositional logics. In J Doyle, E Sandewall, and P Torasso, editors, *Principles of Knowledge Representation and Reasoning: Proceedings of the 4th International Conference (KR94)*, San Francisco, CA., 1994. Morgan Kaufmann.

[4] B Bennett. Carving up space: steps towards construction of an absolutely complete theory of spatial regions. In L.M. Pereira J.J. Alfres and E. Orlowska, editors, *Proceedings of JELIA'96*, pages 337-353, 1996.

[5] B Bennett. Modal logics for qualitative spatial reasoning. *Bulletin of the Interest Group in Pure and Applied Logic (IGPL)*, 1996.

[6] Brandon Bennett. *Logical Representations for Automated Reasoning about Spatial Relationships.* PhD thesis, School of Computer Studies, The University of Leeds, 1997.

[7] V. Chvátal. *Linear Programming.* W.H. Freeman and Company, New York, 1983.

[8] B L Clarke. A calculus of individuals based on 'connection'. *Notre Dame Journal of Formal Logic*, 23(3):204–218, July 1981.

[9] B L Clarke. Individuals and points. *Notre Dame Journal of Formal Logic*, 26(1):61–75, 1985.

[10] E Clementini, J Sharma, and M J Egenhofer. Modeling topological spatial relations: strategies for query processing. *Computers and Graphics*, 18(6):815–822, 1994.

[11] A G Cohn. A hierarchcial representation of qualitative shape based on connection and convexity. In A Frank, editor, *Proc COSIT95*, LNCS, pages 311–326. Springer Verlag, 1995.

[12] A G Cohn. Calculi for qualitative spatial reasoning. In J Pfalzgraf J Calmet, J A Campbell, editor, *Artificial Intelligence and Symbolic Mathematical Computation*, volume 1138 of *LNCS*, pages 124–143. Springer Verlag, 1996.

[13] C Dornheim. Vergleichende analyse topologischer ansaetze des qualitativen raeuml ichen siessens. Studienarbeit, fachereich informatik, Universitaet Hamburg, 1995.

[14] M Egenhofer. Reasoning about binary topological relations. In O Gunther and H J Schek, editors, *Proceedings of the Second Symposium on Large Spatial Databases, SSD'91 (Zurich, Switzerland). Lecture Notes in Computer Science 525*, pages 143–160, 1991.

[15] M Egenhofer and R Franzosa. Point-set topological spatial relations. *International Journal of Geographical Information Systems*, 5(2):161–174, 1991.

[16] M J Egenhofer and K K Al-Taha. Reasoning about gradual changes of topological relationships. In A U Frank, I Campari, and U Formentini, editors, *Theories and Methods of Spatio-temporal Reasoning in Geographic Space*, volume 639 of *Lecture Notes in Computer Science*, pages 196–219. Springer-Verlag, Berlin, 1992.

[17] N M Gotts. Formalising commonsense topology: The inch calculus. In *Proc. Fourth International Symposium on Artificial Intelligence and Mathematics*, 1996.

[18] M. Grigni, D. Papadias, and C. Papadimitriou. Topological inference. In C.S. Mellish, editor, *proceedings of the fourteenth international joint conference on artificial intelligence (IJCAI-95)*, volume I, pages 901–906. Morgan Kaufmann, 1995.

[19] A. Grzegorczyk. Undecidability of some topological theories. *Fundamenta Mathematicae*, 38:137–152, 1951.

[20] D Hernández. *Qualitative Representation of Spatial Knowledge*, volume 804 of *Lecture Notes in Artificial Intelligence.* Springer-Verlag, 1994.

[21] D Hernandez, E Clementini, and P Di Felice. Qualitative distances. In W Kuhn A Frank, editor, *Spatial Information Theory: a theoretical basis for GIS*, number 988 in Lecture Notes in Computer Science, pages 45–58, Berlin, 1995. Springer Verlag.

[22] J. Kratochvíl. String graphs ii: recognizing string graphs is np-hard. *Journal of Combinatorial Theory, Series B*, 52:67–78, 1991.

[23] K. Kuratowski. *Introduction to Set Theory and Topology.* Pergamon Press, 2nd edition, 1972.

[24] B. Nebel. Computational properties of qualitative spatial reasoning: First results. In *Procedings of the 19th German AI Conference*, 1995.

[25] B Nebel and H-J Bürckert. Reasoning about temporal relations: a maximal tractable subset of Allen's interval algebra. *Journal of the Association for Computing Machinery*, 42(1):43–66, January 1995.

[26] D A Randell, Z Cui, and A G Cohn. A spatial logic based on regions and connection. In *Proc. 3rd Int. Conf. on Knowledge Representation and Reasoning*, pages 165–176, San Mateo, 1992. Morgan Kaufmann.

[27] Jochen Renz and Bernhard Nebel. On the complexity of qualitative spatial reasoning: a maximal tractable fragment of the Region Connection Calculus. In *Proceedings of IJCAI-97*, 1997.

[28] R Röhrig. A theory for qualitative spatial reasoning based on order relations. In *AAAI-94: Proceedings of the 12th National Conference on AI*, volume 2, pages 1418–1423, Seattle, 1994.

[29] C Schlieder. Reasoning about ordering. In W Kuhn A Frank, editor, *Spatial Information Theory: a theoretical basis for GIS*, number 988 in Lecture Notes in Computer Science, pages 341–349, Berlin, 1995. Springer Verlag.

[30] C Schlieder. Qualitative shape representation. In P Burrough and A M Frank, editors, *Proceedings, GISDATA Specialist Meeting on Geographical Objects with Undetermined Boundaries.* Francis Taylor, 1996.

[31] A. Tarski. Der aussagenkalkül und die topologie [sentential calculus and topology]. *Fundamenta Mathematicae*, 31:103–134, 1938. English translation in A. Tarski, *Logic, Semantics, Metamathematics*, Oxford Clarendon Press, 1956.

[32] A. Tarski and E. W. Beth. Equilaterality as the only primitive notion of Euclidean geometry. *Indagationes Mathematicae*, 18:462–467, 1956.

[33] A. Tarski and J.C.C. McKinsey. Some theorems about the sentential calculi of Lewis and Heyting. *Journal of Symbolic Logic*, 13:1–15, 1948.

[34] P van Beek, H A Kautz, and M Vilain. Constraint propagation algorithms for temporal reasoning: A revised report. In *Proceedings AAAI-86*, Philadelphia, August 1986. Revised version in [35].

[35] D S Weld and J De Kleer, editors. *Readings in Qualitative Reasoning About Physical Systems.* Morgan Kaufman, San Mateo, Ca, 1990.

A Fuzzy Neural Network Approach to Classification Based on Proximity Characteristics of Patterns

K. Blekas* A. Likas‡ A. Stafylopatis*

*National Technical University of Athens
Department of Electrical & Computer Engineering
157 73 Zographou, Athens, Greece
E-mail: kblekas/andreas@cs.ntua.gr

‡University of Ioannina
Department of Computer Science
451 10 Ioannina, Greece
E-mail: arly@cs.uoi.gr

Abstract

A neural network classifier is presented, which is based on geometrical fuzzy sets. Starting from the construction of the Voronoi diagram of the training patterns, an aggregation of Voronoi regions is performed leading to the identification of larger regions belonging exclusively to one of the pattern classes. The resulting scheme is a constructive algorithm that defines fuzzy clusters of patterns. Based on observations concerning the grade of membership of the training patterns to the created regions, decision probabilities are computed through which the final classification is performed. Experimental results concerning several classification problems indicate that the proposed method achieves high classification rates and compares favorably with other well-known approaches.

1. Introduction

Computational intelligence embraces many approaches to pattern recognition that result from the combination of techniques belonging to different fields. In this sense, several models combining fuzzy systems and neural networks have been developed that build efficient pattern classifiers exploiting the particular advantages offered by each technique in a synergistic manner [3, 7, 16, 17]. Most of these methods use the training set to produce geometrical hyperboxes and then compute suitable membership functions in order to specify the desicion boundaries of pattern classes.

A popular approach to the partitioning of the input space given a set of points is based on the construction of *Voronoi diagrams*. A Voronoi diagram, also known as Dirichlet tesselation or Thiessen polygon, is a partition of the pattern space into convex regions. Each of these regions contains points with minimum distance from a specific point (the region generator) compared to their distance from the other points used for the construction of the diagram. Voronoi diagrams have been largely used in pattern recognition problems because they provide a topological division of the pattern space based on the *nearest neighbor* property. This property has been widely exploited in pattern recognition approaches.

The proposed fuzzy neural approach creates fuzzy sets from the Voronoi diagram of the training patterns and builds class boundaries in a statistical manner. Given a set of points in the feature space, the resulting Voronoi diagram can be viewed as a puzzle and the Voronoi regions as the pieces of this puzzle. We can assemble neighboring pieces according to their position and class, in order to appropriately specify the boundaries between classes. This formulation leads to a *reduced Voronoi* diagram where the new broader regions contain more than one adjoining Voronoi regions having the same class label. The resulting aggregate regions are no longer convex and may be considered as fuzzy sets by defining membership functions indicating the degree of belongingness of points of the input space to each region. Each fuzzy set is characterized by a set of hyperplanes (separating the corresponding region from other regions) and a class label.

After constructing the fuzzy sets, decision probabilities are computed based on the density of membership values for each region and the respective performance in the selection of the correct region. Through discretization of the membership axis, a probabilistic function is created that establishes a correspondence between membership values in a specific region and the probability of correct classification. Mapping the above procedure into a neural architecture we are able to obtain an algorithm for the design of fuzzy neural networks for pattern classification.

Voronoi diagrams, with reference to their use in constructing neural network architectures, are briefly discussed in Section 2. Section 3 deals with the construction of the reduced Voronoi diagram, while Section 4 concerns the

1082-3409/97 $10.00 © 1997 IEEE

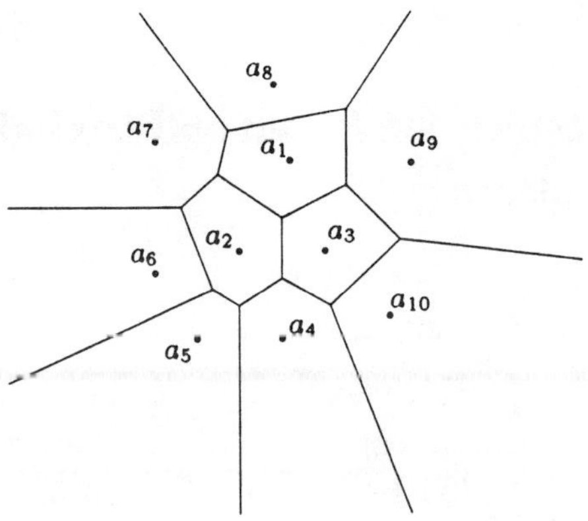

Figure 1. Classical Voronoi diagram

computation of decision probabilities. The architecture of the proposed fuzzy neural classifier is described in Section 5. Experimental results of the application of the proposed scheme and comparisons with other established classification methods are provided in Section 6. Finally, Section 7 contains conclusions and directions for further research.

2. Voronoi Diagrams and Neural Networks

The Voronoi diagram or Dirichlet tesselation is a fundamental concept in computational geometry with many applications. Voronoi diagrams reveal proximity information about a set of given points in a very explicit and computationally useful manner. This makes them applicable to many diverse areas, among which are biology, visual perception and crystallography [1].

Let $D(a, b)$ denote the Euclidean distance between two points a and b in $\Re^d$. Given a finite set $\mathbf{A} = \{a_1, \ldots, a_N\}$ of points in $\Re^d$, a *Voronoi region* V_n $(n = 1, \ldots, N)$ is defined as the set of points:

$$V_n = \{x \in \Re^d \mid D(x, a_n) \leq D(x, a_k) \;\; \forall k \neq n\} \qquad (1)$$

Each Voronoi region V_n contains those points of $\Re^d$ for which the point a_n is the closest. The partition of $\Re^d$ implied by the Voronoi regions $V_1, \ldots, V_N$ is the Voronoi diagram for the set $\mathbf{A}$. Each element of $\mathbf{A}$ is called a *generator* of the Voronoi diagram. A common *boundary* of two Voronoi regions is the perpendicular bisector (hyperplane) of the segment joining the pair of respective generators. Thus, each Voronoi region is defined as the interesection of a finite number of halfspaces determined by the hyperplanes. A point at which boundaries of three or more Voronoi regions meet is called a Voronoi point. An example of a Voronoi diagram in 2-dimensional space is given in Fig. 1.

Several algorithms for the construction of Voronoi diagrams have been proposed. Classical Voronoi diagrams can be constructed by obtaining the convex hull of the given set of points [14, 1, 2] or by incremental insertion of the Voronoi regions [9, 6, 10].

The application of Voronoi diagrams to the design of neural networks has been considered recently. In [13] two neural network construction algorithms for pattern classification are proposed that rely directly or indirectly on the Voronoi tesselation of the input space produced by the given training patterns. A systematic procedure for designing neural networks following the same principle is proposed in [5, 8]. These methods specify the architecture of the neural model based on the construction of corresponding Voronoi diagrams for the training data. They also describe ways to specify the values of the connection weights and thresholds of each node at all layers of the neural architecture. The neural network design is robust and adaptable in order to accomodate new training patterns. It must be noted that these approaches essentially suggest ways to implement a Voronoi diagram using a neural architecture and the classification behaviour of the resulting networks is equivalent to that of nearest neighbor techniques.

In [4] an analogous construction approach was presented which incorporated the idea of fuzzy classification by defining fuzzy decision boundaries for the regions of the tesselation. This scheme is based on an approximate incremental construction of Voronoi diagrams and allows on-line supervised learning using appropriately defined fuzzy membership functions.

3. Reducing the Voronoi regions

Consider a classification problem with d continuous attributes, such that N d-dimensional patterns belong to K distinct classes. By constructing the Voronoi diagram of these generators the d-dimensional feature space is divided into N regions reflecting the *proximity* property.

In pattern recognition we are mostly interested in dividing the input space into a number of regions (clusters) characterized by the same class label. In general, the number of clusters is much smaller than the number of patterns. The Voronoi diagram divides the space into a number of compartments as many as the input patterns, which is not very convenient. Nevertheless, if we managed to join Voronoi regions that are of the same class, we would only consider clusters of patterns. This can be achieved by removing all those hyperplanes (boundaries) of the Voronoi regions that bisect pairs of patterns (generators) belonging to the same class. In this way, the feature space is divided into regions larger than Voronoi regions, where each of these regions is associated with exactly one class label. We shall refer to these major regions as *class regions*, as they come from the union of neighboring Voronoi regions whose generators correspond to the same class. Fig. 2 illustrates such a construction on the 2-dimensional space for a set of 10 input

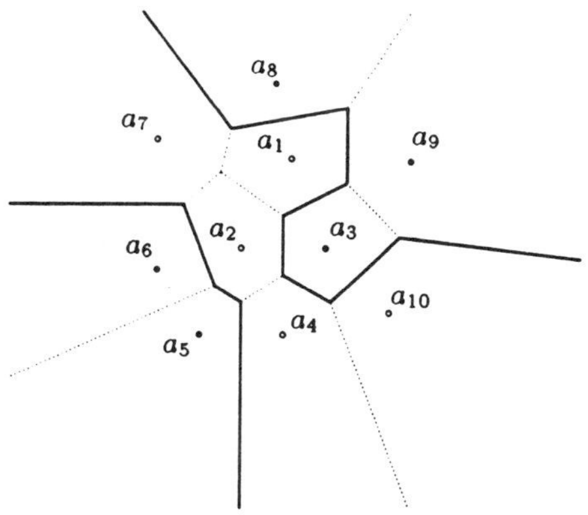

Figure 2. Class regions

points belonging to 2 classes (dotted lines are present in a classical Voronoi diagram).

More specifically, we can define a *class region* as the union of a set of Voronoi regions, such that each region is adjoining (has common boundaries) to at least one other region of the set and their generators belong to the same class. Each class region is characterized by a set of equations that describe the hyperplanes defining class borders. The number of new regions may be equal to or greater than the number K of classes. We only keep large class regions, since small regions containing few generators may be considered as outliers or black holes inside large clusters and therefore they can be ignored.

In fact, the Voronoi diagram can be treated as an undirected graph, where vertices represent generators (or equivalently regions) and edges join vertices corresponding to adjoining Voronoi regions. This graph configuration is equivalent to the construction known as *Delaunay triangulation*. In order to form class regions we start with an arbitrary Voronoi region and mark it as belonging to the first class region. Then we perform a search of the graph structure. The information available from the original construction of the Voronoi diagram is sufficient for performing the search. (Depth-first or breadth-first search could be used.) All regions connected to the starting region and bearing the *same class label* are marked as belonging to the same class region. Neighboring regions bearing a different class label are left unmarked to be included in some subsequent aggregation. A similar procedure is followed from any region marked during the search. When the search is exhausted, i.e. no more Voronoi regions can be included in the current class region, a new unmarked region is selected and the procedure is repeated to construct a new class region, until there are no more unmarked Voronoi regions.

In order to encourage the formation of *nearly-convex* class regions we impose the following restriction during the above aggregation phase. The search can only proceed from the current Voronoi region if the number of neighboring regions bearing the same class label as the current one exceeds a given threshold value λ. If this criterion is not satisfied, the remaining neighboring regions of the current one are left unmarked (independently of their class label) and the search is continued from some other region. The choice of the value of λ is related to the average number of boundaries of a Voronoi region which in turn depends upon the dimension of the feature space. In our implementation, appropriate values of the parameter λ were determined experimentally for the different classification problems considered.

After construction of the reduced Voronoi diagram, it is possible to exploit proximity information for the purposes of classification. In order to formulate the problem as a fuzzy classification problem, we must give an estimation of how much a new pattern belongs to each class region, thus considering class regions as fuzzy sets. When a new input pattern $a = (a_1, \ldots, a_d)$ is presented, an appropriate fuzzy membership value (in $[0, 1]$) is computed. The membership function $\mu_i(a)$ for the ith class region must measure the degree to which the given pattern falls inside or outside the region. This can be considered as a measurement of how far the pattern is situated from all the hyperplanes which define the boundaries of the class region. When the pattern a is in the interior of the region and far from the hyperplanes then the value of $\mu_i(a)$ is large, which means that the point is close to some generator having participated to the formation of that class region. When the pattern falls outside the region then the membership value approaches zero, which means that the point is close to some generator belonging to a different class region.

A function respecting the above guidelines is the average value of the exponential differences between the vertical distances $x_h(a)$ of the input pattern from all hyperplanes h supporting the class region i and the distances l_h of the respective generators from each hyperplane h. (Clearly, within each class region, there is a generator associated with each supporting hyperplane of the region.) It must be noted that the information concerning the distances l_h is already known from the original Voronoi diagram, and is stored for each hyperplane h. The vertical distance $x_h(a)$ of a pattern $a = (a_1, \ldots, a_d)$ from a hyperplane h (described by the equation $\pi_{h1}x_1 + \ldots + \pi_{hd}x_d + \pi_{h,d+1} = 0$) is computed as follows:

$$x_h(a) = \frac{|\sum_{j=1}^{d} \pi_{hj}a_j + \pi_{h,d+1}|}{\sqrt{\sum_{j=1}^{d} \pi_{hj}^2}} \quad (2)$$

Each hyperplane h divides the pattern space into two halfspaces. Consider the quantities $u_{ih}(a)$ which take the values 1 or -1 depending on whether or not the generator corresponding to hyperplane h and belonging to region i is situated in the same halfspace (defined by h) as the pattern a.

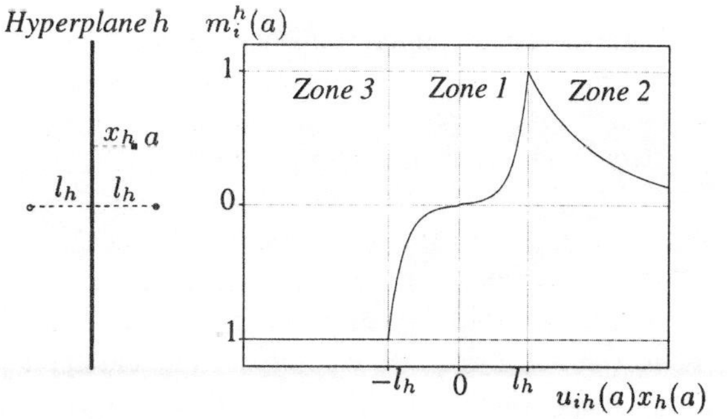

Figure 3. Fuzzy decision boundaries

The membership function of class region i can be computed as follows:

$$\mu_i(a) = \frac{1}{2|H_i|} \sum_{h \in H_i} m_i^h(a) + \frac{1}{2} \tag{3}$$

where H_i is the set of hyperplanes defining class region i (having cardinality $|H_i|$) and m_i^h has the following form :

$$m_i^h(a) = \begin{cases} u_{ih}(a)\exp(\frac{-|x_h(a)-l_h|}{\sigma_1}) & \text{if } x_h(a) \le l_h \\ u_{ih}(a)\exp(\frac{-|x_h(a)-l_h|}{\sigma_2}) & \text{if } x_h(a) > l_h \\ & \text{and } u_{ih}(a) = 1 \\ -1 & \text{otherwise} \end{cases} \tag{4}$$

A graphical representation of Eq. 4 is shown in Fig. 3, which represents m_i^h as a function of the quantity $u_{ih}(a)x_h(a)$. Based on this quantity, we divide the space into three *zones* with respect to the hyperplane h, each zone being characterized by different properties. In the *first zone* the pattern is close to the hyperplane ($x_h(a) \le l_h$) independently of the side of the region border on which it is situated. Starting from the value -1 (when $x_h(a) = l_h$ and $u_{ih}(a) = -1$), the value of m_i^h increases with a steep slope until it reaches the highest value 1 (when $x_h(a) = l_h$ and $u_{ih}(a) = 1$). The *second zone* is related to the case where the pattern and the generator are on the same halfspace but the pattern is far from the hyperplane ($x_h(a) > l_h$ and $u_{ih}(a) = 1$). Although the pattern lies on the good side of the hyperplane with respect to the class region, we must be cautious to avoid circumstances where the pattern is at long distance from the hyperplane and does not belong to the class region. For this reason the value of m_i^h decreases to zero (but with a smoother slope) as the vertical distance $x_h(a)$ from the hyperplane grows. From the above specification it is clear that the value of σ_1 in the first zone must be higher than the value of σ_2 in the second zone to achieve the desired slope. The *third zone* represents the case where the pattern is situated far outside the region of interest and far from the hyperplane h ($x_h(a) > l_h$ and $u_{ih}(a) = -1$). In this case, m_i^h takes its lowest value -1.

It must be noted here that $m_i^h(a)$ does not include precise information about whether or not the pattern is situated inside the class region. Even when the pattern and the generator are in the same halfspace with respect to the hyperplane, we are not aware of what happens with other hyperplanes as we individually examine each hyperplane and not the whole region. After computing all the $m_i^h(a)$ values, we obtain a global estimation of the degree of belongingness of pattern a to the region i through the value of the membership $\mu_i(a)$.

The above membership function takes into account useful proximity information provided by the characteristics of the original Voronoi construction, such as the equations describing hyperplanes, the position of generators relative to hyperplanes and the vertical distances l_h. In addition, it exploits information related to class regions, such as the hyperplanes defining the boundaries of each class region.

4. Computing Decision Probabilities

In the previous sections we have described the first phase of the proposed approach to pattern classification that incorporates the construction of the Voronoi diagram corresponding to the training patterns, the integration of Voronoi regions to a number of class regions and the definition of appropriate membership functions. With this kind of preprocessing the problem of selecting the correct class is transformed to the problem of selecting the correct region. In this section we describe how the membership values of the training patterns are used to construct models providing decision probabilities that a pattern with a given membership value can be assigned to a specific region.

After having computed the membership values corresponding to an input pattern we could perform the classification procedure simply by selecting the class of the region with the maximum membership value. This is what happens in most fuzzy approaches to pattern classification (e.g in the fuzzy min-max network). Unfortunately, this decision scheme does not seem to provide good classification results, since some regions tend to constantly exhibit higher membership values compared to other regions. It seems more effective to evaluate the membership of a given pattern to a region by taking into account the distribution of membership values of the training patterns to this region. This leads to the construction of a probability model for each class region, which provides useful information for the selection of the appropriate region during classification.

The construction of the probability models is based on the search for ranges of membership values that have more chance to lead to the successful selection of a region. More specifically, considering class region i, the interval $[0, 1]$ of membership values is divided into a number L_i of equal-size cells. To each cell v ($v = 1, \ldots, L_i$) we assign a probability value p_i^v computed as the *percentage of the training patterns*

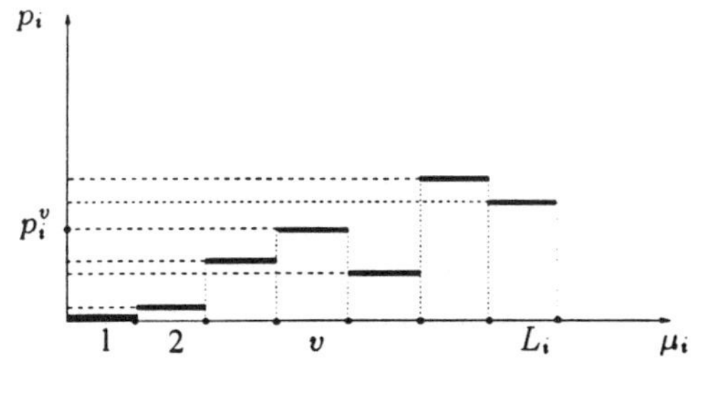

Figure 4. Membership histogram

belonging to region i that have their membership value in the cell v. An example of the above histogram construction is displayed in Fig. 4.

It should be observed that, after the membership values of training patterns to each region have been computed, it is possible to view the classification problem as mapping from the space of membership vectors to the set of classes, $c : (\mu_1, \ldots, \mu_R) \rightarrow \{1, \ldots, K\}$ (where R is the number of class regions and K is the number of classes). Such a mapping can be easily constructed using for example a multilayer perceptron trained by the backpropagation algorithm or any of its variants. Although this approach is intuitively more appealing and exhibited excellent performance on training sets, its performance on the test set was inferior (in all examined datasets) compared with the approach based on the probability model.

5. Neural Network Implementation

In the previous sections we have shown how one can construct fuzzy sets (corresponding to class regions) starting from a Voronoi diagram, as well as how a model of probabilities can be built for each fuzzy set using the distribution of membership values. The proposed construction algorithm can be summarized into the following steps:

1. Construct the classical Voronoi diagram of a set of N patterns $\mathbf{A} = \{a_1, \ldots, a_N\}$, in a d-dimensional space.
2. Reduce the Voronoi diagram into a number of class regions.
3. Discard small class regions and let R be the number of the remaining large class regions.
4. For each pattern a_j, $j = 1, \ldots, N$, compute the membership values $\mu_i(a_j)$, $i = 1, \ldots, R$.
5. For each region i, $i = 1, \ldots, R$, categorize the membership values in a histogram using a number L_i of equal-size cells in $[0, 1]$.
6. Compute selection probabilities p_i^v, $i = 1, \ldots, R$, $v = 1, \ldots, L_i$.

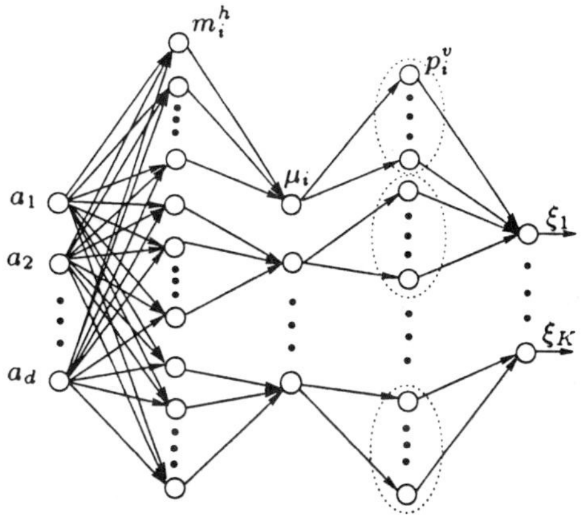

Figure 5. Neural network architecture

In order to use the method for the classification of a new pattern, first the membership values of the pattern to each region i are computed. Then the corresponding probabilities p_i^v are determined (where v represents the cell containing the membership value of the pattern) and the region i with maximum p_i^v is selected. The class of this region is considered as the final classification desicion.

The above desicion approach can be implemented by means of a neural network architecture as illustrated in Fig. 5. The architecture consists of five layers and connections exist only between successive layers. The first layer is the input layer having as many nodes as the dimension of patterns. The nodes in the second layer represent hyperplanes that define class regions. For each class region i there are $|H_i|$ nodes, one for each hyperplane supporting that class. As a hyperplane separates two regions, there will generally be two nodes referring to the same hyperplane (except for hyperplanes supporting small regions that were discarded during construction). Each second layer node computes the value of the function m_i^h for an input pattern using Eq. 4. The third layer contains as many nodes as the number R of class regions. The output of each node i of this layer provides the membership value μ_i of the pattern to the corresponding region as computed in Eq. 3. The connections between nodes of the second and third layer assume binary values 1 or 0 to associate regions with their supporting hyperplanes.

The fourth layer implements the membership histogram. Each region i of the third layer is connected to L_i nodes of the fourth layer corresponding to the cells of the histogram. Each such node v ($v = 1, \ldots, L_i$) fires only in the case where the μ_i value falls inside the corresponding cell and provides the respective probability p_i^v, otherwise the output of the node is zero. This representation allows an efficient implementation of the histogram by means of simple nodes yielding a fixed output on an on-off basis.

The fifth layer embodies one node for each of the K classes. If region i has class label k then the set of L_i nodes of the fourth layer (representing the histogram of region i) is connected to node k of the fourth layer. In other words, the connections between nodes of the fourth and fifth layer take binary values 1 or 0 to associate class regions (histogram cells) with class labels. The output ξ_k of each node k of the last layer is taken equal to the maximum of the outputs (probabilities p_i^v) of the cell nodes connected to that node. Finally, the class k with the maximum ξ_k is the decision of the fuzzy neural classification network.

When a new pattern a is applied to the network, the membership values $\mu_i(a)$ of the pattern to each class region i are initially computed. The computation proceeds by determining the probabilities p_i^v corresponding to the respective histogram cells. The decision of the network is the class of the region with the maximum probability p_i^v, expressed by the quantity ξ_k. As is the case with other neural network designs based on Voronoi diagram information [5, 8, 4], the method has the ability to completely define the neural structure, namely the number of hidden layers and nodes of each layer along with the connection values between nodes of successive layers. The proposed neural architecture incorporates an additional layer with respect to other approaches accounting for the computation of decision probabilities.

6. Experimental results

We have studied the proposed fuzzy neural network classifier on a variety of classification problems, by performing experiments with known datasets, some of which are noisy containing hard examples. In addition we have conducted comparative experiments with many other well-studied classification techniques.

The first dataset we used to train and test our fuzzy neural classifier was the Fisher's Iris dataset. Iris data is a collection of 150 four-dimensional feature vectors in three separate classes, 50 for each class. We considered a training set and a test set of size 75, each of them containing 25 examples of each of the three iris classes. We have also tried the James Cook University Thyroid gland database. Thyroid database contains a set of 215 feature vectors (belonging to one of three classes) that contain 5 continuous attributes. The three classes represent the classification of a patient's thyroid to euthyroidism, hypothyroidism and hyperthyroidism respectively. The database is divided into 150 instances of the first class, 35 instances of the second and 30 of the last class. We used a training set of size 100 (in a manner proportional to the distribution of patterns to classes), while the remaining data set (of size 115) was used for testing.

Another dataset used in our experiments was the synthetic two-class problem taken from Ripley [15]. It is a realistic problem with 1250 2-dimensional patterns that belong to 2 classes, where 250 and 1000 patterns were used for training and testing respectively. Finally, we have also considered the clouds database. Clouds is an artificial collection of 5000 two-dimensional patterns divided into two equal size sets that correspond to two overlapping decision classes. The first 2000 clouds data were handled as the training set while the remaining 3000 data applied to the constructed fuzzy neural classifier for testing. Figs. 6 and 7 provide a graphical representation of the last two datasets.

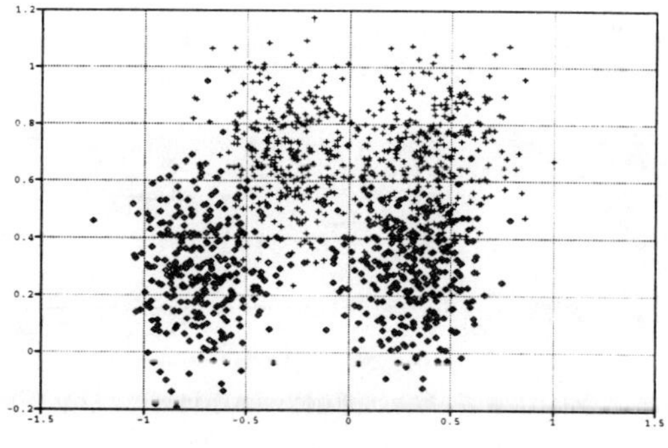

Figure 6. Graphical representation of the synthetic two-class dataset

The parameters in our approach are the number of cells L_i for each class region i and the construction parameter λ, as well as the σ_1, σ_2 values for the membership function (Eq. 4). Although we could select a different value L_i for each region (depending on characteristics of patterns belonging to the region), we have opted for the use of a global value L for all class regions, depending on the difficulty of the considered problem. In the first two problems (iris and thyroid), that are relatively easy, the specification of L was not very critical. For almost all experiments with different values of L ($L \geq 4$) the network achieved the same classification rate on training and testing phases. Moreover, the number of class regions obtained in the case of these two datasets was exactly the same as the number of classes (i.e. $R = 3$), suggesting that the classes in these problems are well separated. Specifically, in the case of the iris dataset a total of 306 hyperplanes were needed for the separation of class regions, where 142, 262 and 208 of these were used to define each one of the three regions respectively. In the thyroid problem the required number of hyperplanes was equal to 676 and the three classes were defined using 527, 386 and 439 hyperplanes repsectively.

The other two datasets (synthetic and clouds) are noisy. As illustrated in Figs. 6, 7 the class boundaries in both problems are not very clear, therefore classification is difficult. The Voronoi diagram in the case of the synthetic problem was reduced to 10 class regions, where only two of

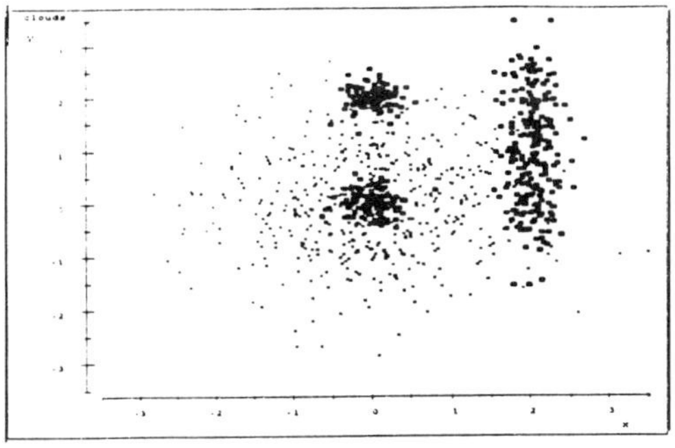

Figure 7. Graphical representation of the clouds dataset

them were big enough including a large number of patterns ($R = 2$). The other eight regions were very small containing only one or two patterns and were rejected as outliers. The two selected class regions were separated with 106 and 112 hyperplanes from a set of 140 hyperplanes of the reduced Voronoi scheme (the difference is due to discarded regions). In the case of the clouds dataset, the number of constructed class regions was equal to 68 out of which we eventually chose only four ($R = 4$). The number of required hyperplanes was 258, 464, 450 and 117 respectively. In this kind of problems, the selection of the parameter L was critical. We observed that in the range of $L = 10, \ldots, 20$ the fuzzy neural network classifier had the same classification behaviour achieving the best classification rate.

In what concerns the effect of the parameter λ on the classification performance the following observations can be made. As stated in Section 3, greater values of λ, lead to more convex and uniform class regions, since the regions are derived from the union of Voronoi regions having at least λ neighboring regions of the same class. The selection of the best value for this parameter depends on the dimension of the pattern space. In the case of the first two examined problems there was a large interval of λ values leading to the construction of exactly the same reduced Voronoi diagrams ($\lambda = 1, \ldots, 9$ for the iris problem and $\lambda = 1, \ldots, 15$ for the thyroid problem) and thus yielding the same best classification rate. As the value of λ was growing, the class regions contained less generators and the number of such regions increased, leading to degradation in the performance of the method. In the last two classification problems the effect of the parameter λ was identical and exhibited the following characteristics. For the first two values ($\lambda = 1, 2$) we obtained similar rates and similar constructed regions. As the value of λ was increased, the network achieved better classification rates attaining the highest values for $\lambda = 3$ and $\lambda = 4$ for the synthetic and clouds problems respectively. Although the number of constructed class regions in these cases was the same as for the previous values of λ, they contained less generators and were characterized by increased generalization capabilities. It must be noted that in all the examined classification problems, when the value of the threshold λ was big enough, the reduced Voronoi scheme was the same as the original Voronoi diagram. Finally, as far as the σ_1, σ_2 parameters are concerened, the appropriate values were determined experimentally and were generally less than 3.

In order to assess the potential of the proposed classifier, we have also applied some other known neural network methods to the same datasets. For that reason we have used the fuzzy min-max classification neural network (FMM), a multilayer perceptron (MLP) trained with the backpropagation algorithm, as well as the learning vector quantization (LVQ) algorithm. We have applied also a simple nearest-neighbor approach (1-NN), which consisted of assigning to a given pattern the class label of its closest training pattern.

The fuzzy min-max classifier [16, 12] is an on-line supervised learning classifier whose operation and training are based on the concept of hyperbox fuzzy sets. The MLP neural network was a single hidden-layer network with a learning rate of 0.09 and a momentum rate of 0.9. The specific LVQ scheme used was the LVQ1 algorithm [11] having a learning rate equal to 0.03. The best results were obtained by considering 6, 6, 6 and 8 centers for the four databases respectively. For these approaches several experiments were conducted using different seed values and taking the best classification rate as the performance measure.

Table 6 summarizes the performance of the proposed classification scheme, denoted RVoD (Reduced Voronoi Diagram), in comparison with the FMM, MLP, LVQ and 1-NN approaches in terms of the classification rate on the test set for the four selected databases. The superiority of the proposed fuzzy neural classifier is apparent. The results indicate that the simple nearest-neighbor scheme (and consequently the approaches based on pure Voronoi diagrams) have been considerably improved so as to outperform the other well-known algorithms.

If we compare our approach to the fuzzy min-max algorithm, we can observe that, in the case of the fuzzy min-max algorithm, the created hyperboxes have only the information of their min and max values along each dimension. The hyperboxes are of finite volume (therefore the technique can be considered as 'local') and their geometrical structure is not so flexible to be able to adapt to strange class boundaries. In the proposed approach, hyperplanes are used to separate classes (therefore the technique can be considered as 'global'), the class regions have in most cases a convex shape and the nearest neighbor criterion is more explicitly taken into account. Apart from the geometrical differences, the FMM algorithm is based on the selection of the hyperbox with the maximum membership value and accept as final

Table 1. Comparative results (classification rates)

Problem	*RVoD*	*FMM*	*MLP*	*LVQ*	*1-NN*
Iris	97.33%	97.33%	94.67%	97.33%	94.67%
Thyroid	98.26%	97.39%	94.78%	95.65%	95.65%
Synthetic	91.14%	90.60%	88.00%	89.50%	85.50%
Clouds	88.27%	84.83%	79.77%	80.13%	84.27%

decision the class of the selected hyperbox. On the other hand the proposed fuzzy neural classifier is able to decide in a more informative manner, since the decision is based on the distribution of the membership values of the training patterns to the constructed regions. Moreover, the proposed method requires no normalization of the feature values of the patterns as is the case with many other approaches.

7. Conclusions

We have proposed a neural network classifier that is based on geometrical fuzzy sets. The approach is based on the construction of Voronoi diagrams in the pattern space and the creation of region aggregates inside the Voronoi puzzle. For the constructed class regions, decision probabilities are computed in terms of the distribution of membership values to these regions. The whole technique can be implemented by means of a five-layer feedforward neural network architecture.

Experimental results concerning several classification problems indicate that the proposed method is effective in terms of the rate of correct classification. Comparisons with other established approaches have shown that the proposed scheme can overcome the difficulties arising from the problem of overlapping classes. Moreover, it has the characteristic of maintaining the powerful geometrical features of the Voronoi structure as well as of creating efficient decision boundaries through the statistical processing of membership values.

This work allows us to further experiment with the use of proximity based approaches to the construction of fuzzy neural classifiers and to discover more efficient techniques in the area of soft decision making. Since the complexity of the construction of Voronoi diagrams becomes high as the dimension of the feature space grows, we are interested in applying effective geometrical algorithms that can suggest neighbors of a given pattern (in the sense of the Voronoi diagram) for large dimensional problems.

References

[1] F. Aurenhammer. Voronoi Diagrams - A Survey of a Funtamental Geometric Data Structure. *ACM Computing Surveys*, 3:345–405, 1991.

[2] C. Barber, D. Dobkin, and H. Huhdanpaa. The Quickhull Algorithm for Convex Hulls. *ACM Transactions on Mathematical Software*, 22:469–483, 1996.

[3] J. Bezdek and S. Pal. *Fuzzy Models for Pattern Recognition*. IEEE Press, 1992.

[4] K. Blekas, A. Likas, and A. Stafylopatis. A Fuzzy Neural Network Approach Based on Dirichlet Tesselations for Nearest Neighbor Classification of Patterns. In *Proc. of IEEE Workshop on Neural Networks for Signal Processing (NNSP '95)*, pages 153–161, 1995.

[5] N. Bose and A. Garga. Neural Network Design Using Voronoi Diagrams. *IEEE Trans. on Neural Networks*, 4:778–787, 1993.

[6] A. Bowyer. Computing Dirichlet Tesselations. *The Computer Journal*, 24:162–166, 1981.

[7] G. Carpenter, S. Grossberg, N. Markuzon, J. Reynolds, and D. Rosen. Fuzzy ARTMAP: A Neural Network Architecture for Incremental Supervised Learning of Analog Multidimensional Maps. *IEEE Trans. on Neural Networks*, 3(5):698–713, 1992.

[8] A. Garga and N. Bose. A Neural Network Approach to the Construction of Delaunay Tesselation of Poinds in R^d. *IEEE Trans. on Circuits and Systems-I: Fundamental Theory and Applications*, 41:611–613, 1994.

[9] P. Green and R. Sibson. Computing Dirichlet tesselations in the plane. *The Computer Journal*, 4:778–787, 1978.

[10] L. Guibas, D. Knuth, and M. Sharir. Randomized incremental construction of Delaunay and Voronoi diagrams. *Algorithmica*, 9:534–560, 1992.

[11] T. Kohonen. The self-organization map. *Proceedings of the IEEE*, 78:1464–1480, 1990.

[12] A. Likas, K. Blekas, and A. Stafylopatis. Application of the Fuzzy Min-Max Neural Network Classifier to Problems with Continuous and Discrete Attributes. In *Proc. of IEEE Workshop on Neural Networks for Signal Processing (NNSP '94)*, pages 163–170, 1994.

[13] D. Murphy. Nearest Neighbor Pattern Classification Perceptrons. *Proceedings of the IEEE*, 78:1595–1598, 1990.

[14] F. Preparata and M. Shamos. *Computational Geometry - An Introduction*. New York: Springer-Verlag, 1985.

[15] B. Ripley. *Pattern Recognition and Neural Networks*. Cambridge University Press, 1996.

[16] P. Simpson. Fuzzy Min-Max Neural Networks-Part 1: Classification. *IEEE Trans. on Neural Networks*, 3(5):776–786, 1992.

[17] L. Tsoukalas and R. Uhrig. *Fuzzy and Neural Approaches in Engineering*. John Wiley & Sons, New York, NY, 1996.

A Metalevel Architecture for Knowledge-Based Neural Network Design

Melanie Hilario, Ahmed Rida, Christian Pellegrini
CUI - University of Geneva
CH-1211 Geneva 4, Switzerland
hilario|rida|pell@cui.unige.ch

Abstract

In this paper, the term 'knowledge-based neural network (NN) design' is used to refer to all efforts at exploiting prior knowledge in neural network configuration and training. A variety of techniques have been proposed for this purpose; SCANDAL provides a workbench for evaluating and integrating these techniques. After a quick overview of three main approaches to NN design, we describe SCANDAL's multi-agent, metalevel architecture as well as its strategies for maximizing the use of domain knowledge. To assess the impact of prior knowledge on NN performance, experiments were conducted comparing knowledge-based techniques with a search-based configuration algorithm. Results show that the use of prior knowledge in neural network design leads to both faster learning and improved generalization. More interestingly, this appears to hold even when domain knowledge and data are deficient; in such cases, knowledge is extracted from the available data and is used both to configure the network and to generate artificial training instances. This leads us to hope that time-consuming iterative search can be avoided even in knowledge-lean domains.

1 Introduction

Early machine learning systems focused mainly on learning from examples until the advent of explanation-based learning, or analytical learning from a given domain theory. Though the utility of explanation-based learning was severely limited by the prerequisite of a complete and correct domain theory, the idea gained ground that prior knowledge could be combined with training instances to remedy the respective shortcomings of empirical and analytical learning. This idea, born in the symbolic community, has been taken up by connectionist researchers who are increasingly exploiting domain knowledge to support neural network configuration and training.

Knowledge-based neural networks (KBNNs) were introduced in the context of hybrid systems which mapped a symbolic domain theory onto a neural network. KBNNs have since been identified with this translational technique, as witnessed by the following definition: "Knowledge-based neural networks are neural networks whose topology and initial connection weights are determined by symbolic knowledge represented in particular formalisms, such as production rules and decision trees." [1]. However, there is now a broad range of techniques for integrating prior knowledge into neural networks, and symbolic-to-connectionist mapping is just a subclass of these. We therefore propose the following generic definition: Knowledge-based neural networks are neural networks which have been designed with the support of prior knowledge, i.e., any information about the task domain or the function to be learned, outside of the training data themselves. This knowledge-level definition dissociates the concept of KBNNs from a specific technique, thus providing a common framework for *knowledge-based neural network design*, a term we shall use to designate all efforts at building prior knowledge into neural networks.

This paper describes an attempt at integrating different strategies for knowledge-based neural network design. Section 2 discusses three main approaches to neural network design, based on the amount of domain knowledge available and the way it is used. All three approaches are represented within the SCANDAL architecture, which is described in Section 3. Section 4 reports on experimental results and Section 5 concludes.

2 Using prior knowledge in NN design

Neural network design can be roughly decomposed into three stages: preprocessing, configuration or the choice of topology, and training. NN design techniques can be situated along an axis representing the amount of domain knowledge available—going from one end where no knowledge is available to the other extreme where domain knowledge forms an an approximately perfect (i.e., almost complete and correct) theory. Between these extremes, a number of intermediate points represent the availability of specific and partial domain knowledge. In this section, we in-

1082-3409/97 $10.00

vestigate a number of NN design techniques in the three main subregions of the (domain) knowledge spectrum—knowledge-intensive, knowledge-primed, and knowledge-free techniques.

2.1 Knowledge-intensive or translational techniques

When prior knowledge is rich enough to form an approximate domain theory, it can be mapped directly onto a neural network using translational techniques. Most often, the source symbolic formalisms are propositional rules, whether categorical as in KBANN [2] and TopGen [3], probabilistic as in BANNER [4], or rules with certainty factors as in RAPTURE [5] and Lacher et al.'s system[6]. Neural networks have also been compiled from decision trees [7] and deterministic finite state automata [8; 9].

Translational methods can be summarized in two steps: map the domain theory onto a neural net, then train the configured network. All rule formalisms, for instance, are translated in basically the same way. Final conclusions of the rulebase are mapped onto output units of the network, intermediate conclusions onto hidden units, and initial facts onto input units. Dependencies among assertions map onto weighted connections between the units. The difference lies in the semantics of the weights of links between rule antecedents and conclusions: depending on the source formalism, they can indicate positive or negative dependencies, certainty factors, measures of probability, degrees of membership, and so on. During the training phase, these techniques are distinguished by the learning algorithms used: while KBANN uses a slightly modified backpropagation procedure, most of the others like TopGen and RAPTURE use dynamic algorithms which add or prune nodes or links during training.

2.2 Knowledge-primed or hint-based techniques

Almost perfect domain theories are hard to come by in real-world applications. The typical situation in neural network design is one in which only partial domain knowledge is available. Though insufficient to completely determine the final neural network structure, such partial knowledge (aka hints) can be used to prime NN design. Hints come in many flavors: some concern the structure of the application task, others involve characteristics of the application domain, and still other express global constraints on the function to be learned, or partial information about its implementation. Approaches based on such hints can be divided into two broad classes—hint-based configuration and hint-based training—depending on the design phase during which prior knowledge is used.

In **hint-based configuration**, any information about the problem domain can be used to determine some aspect of the neural network's structure. The configuration task involves determining the input and output units, the number of hidden layers and units, and the connectivity pattern. Hints can be used to support any of these subtasks. For instance, prior knowledge can be injected as *extra outputs of a neural network.* Practically, this means constraining the network to learn both the original task and a second task related to the first. It has been shown that such hints serve as catalysts, i.e., they accelerate learning speed rather than improve generalization [10]. Prior knowledge can also be formulated as *permanent constraints on connections and weights.* In pattern recognition, for instance, one can encode invariance knowledge by structuring the network in such a way that transformed versions of the same input produce the same output. The best-known technique for doing this is weight sharing—i.e., constraining different connections to have equal weights [11].

In **hint-based training** prior knowledge is incorporated via the training process rather than being wired directly into the network structure. One way to do this is to augment the training set by *generating a sufficiently large number of examples that illustrate the hint.* Abu-Mostafa [12] proposes two ways of doing this. One is by means of duplicate examples: available training examples are copied and modified to express a particular hint. An alternative way is the use of virtual examples; for instance, to reflect the knowledge that the target function is even, a virtual example takes the form $y(x) = y(-x)$ for a particular input x. An alternative to augmenting the number of training instances is to *incorporate more information into each training instance,* as in TangentProp [13]. In this case (as with virtual examples), the objective function used by the learning algorithm is modified to take account of the added information. Other variants of hint-based generation of examples have been used to preset the rolling force in a steel rollmill [14] and to generate error-correcting codes [15].

2.3 Knowledge-free or search-based techniques

At the other extreme, where domain knowledge is scarce or unusable, NN design techniques rely mainly on guided search. These knowledge-free methods can be subdivided into dynamic and static methods. In static configuration the network topology is chosen *before* the training process, whereas in dynamic configuration it is dynamically modified *during* training. Most static configuration methods must rely on iterative generate-and-test in order to find the most appropriate architecture. Dynamic configuration methods can be constructive, i.e., they start with a minimal network structure and progressively add hidden layers or units until network performance is judged satisfactory. Alternatively, destructive methods start from an initially complex model and prune units or links until a stopping criterion is met. Knowledge-free methods do not produce knowledge-based neural networks, but they are included here for completeness, as they are the ultimate fall-back when knowledge-based approaches prove fruitless.

3 Overview of SCANDAL

SCANDAL (Symbolic-Connectionist Architecture for Neural Network Design and Learning) is an experimental workbench for exploring the use of prior knowledge in neural net design. This section describes its architecture and the strategies for building prior knowledge into neural networks.

3.1 Architecture

The architecture consists of a connectionist baselevel and a symbolic metalevel (Fig. 1), each implemented as a set of agents interacting via a distributed platform [16]. The base-level consists of agents which execute decisions taken by metalevel design agents concerning NN configuration and training as well as data preprocessing. At the metalevel, a supervisor receives the application task definition and, on the basis of its knowledge of the domain and of neural networks in general, selects one or several design agents. Each design agent embodies a class of techniques for accomplishing one or several design subtasks. A data preprocessor analyses available data and calls on the competent base level agents as needed: data cleaners fill in missing values or discretize continuous attributes on request, knowledge extractors are symbolic learners such as C4.5 which induce rules for use in subsequent phases of NN design, and artificial data generators are routines which generate training examples from hints expressed as rules or as functional constraints. Several configuration agents are available. A rule compilation agent translates a domain theory expressed as rules into a feedforward network. In the current version, this agent can handle categorical as well as certainty-factor rules. A hint-based configuration agent uses knowledge of related tasks to add extra output units to a network.

Partial knowledge can also be used to improve the training process. For instance, when data deficiency is a problem, the pretraining agent uses knowledge-based artificial examples produced by the data generators to pretrain the network before training on real examples. In knowledge-lean domains, the supervisor has two alternatives: either attempt to exploit domain hints induced from data by the knowledge extractors, or have the search-based agents (e.g. constructive configuration agents) resort to iterative experimentation.

Metalevel design agents are implemented in an object-oriented representation which blends a global ontology with agent-specific rules and methods. The system's ontology provides a unifying framework for domain as well as metalevel knowledge; it is by inspecting this ontology that design agents can access domain knowledge and use it to determine NN structure and development. In addition, base level entities such as network links and weights, nodes and activations, which typically remain invisible in standard simulators, have associated meta-objects which are periodically updated to reflect their current state. Via this dual representation scheme, the internal state of the network remains accessible for explicit reasoning and decision making by the supervisor, the design agents, and the user.

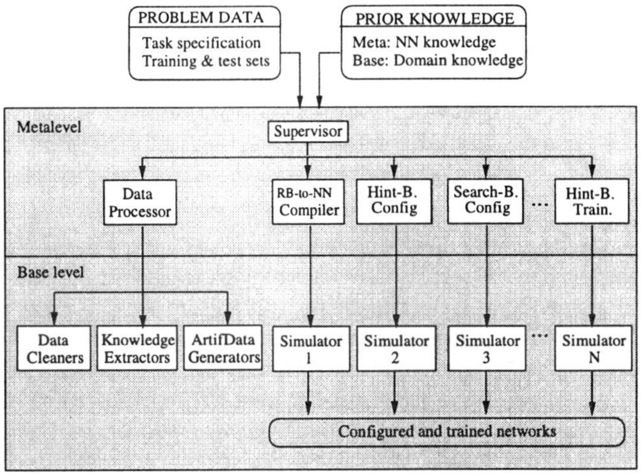

Figure 1: The SCANDAL Architecture

3.2 Strategies for Knowledge Utilization

SCANDAL's basic bias is towards the maximum use of domain knowledge in the different stages of neural network design. Knowledge-based configuration (KBC) consists in using domain knowledge to determine the network's architecture, while knowledge-based training (KBT) integrates domain knowledge into the training process. When background knowledge is insufficient or inaccessible, the system attempts knowledge extraction from data (KEX) to gather hints that might guide the design process. For instance, any rule induction algorithm may be called to generate domain rules for use in subsequent phases. These elementary processes—knowledge extraction from data, knowledge-based configuration, and knowledge-based training—may be combined in four different ways, depending on the adequacy of the knowledge and data available. The four variants of the knowledge-based approach to NN design are summarized in Table 1.

As discussed in Section 2, SCANDAL integrates different techniques for exploiting knowledge during the three phases of NN development. However, in the remainder of this paper, we shall focus on rule-based methods to illustrate knowledge-based NN design: rule induction by C4.5 for KEX, rule mapping onto neural nets for KBC, and rule-based generation of artificial training data for KBT.

Adequate prior knowledge (K) and data (D) → KBC
1. KBC: Compile K into a neural network
2. Train NN on D

Deficient prior knowledge and adequate data → KEX-KBC
1. KEX: Extract K' from D
2. KBC: Compile (K+K') into an NN
3. Train NN on D

Adequate prior knowledge and deficient data → KBC-KBT
1. KBC: Compile K into a neural network
2. KBT: Generate artificial data D' from K
   Pretrain NN on D'
   Train pretrained NN on D

Deficient prior knowledge and data → KEX-KBC-KBT
(in preference to search-based design)
1. KEX: Extract K' from D
2. KBC: Compile (K+K') into NN
3. KBT: Generate D' from (K+K')
   Pretrain NN on D'
   Train pretrained NN on D alone

Table 1: Four strategies for knowledge-based neural network design. KBC stands for knowledge-based configuration, KBT for knowledge-based training, and KEX for knowledge extraction from data.

4 Experimental Results

This section reports on experiments conducted on these four strategies for incorporating knowledge into NN learning. To compare the knowledge-based approach with a state-of-the-art search-based method, the SCANDAL implementation of the Orthogonal Incremental Learning (OIL) algorithm [17] was used. Both approaches were evaluated on several benchmarks from the UCI Machine Learning Repository [18]. All experiments used 10 network initializations, each tested on 10 different permutations of a given dataset. Each experiment thus consisted of 100 training/test runs, each using ten-fold stratified cross-validation. The following subsections present evaluation results for these four strategies in turn.

4.1 Adequate knowledge and data

When both knowledge and data are adequate (in particular when there is an approximate domain theory), the knowledge-based approach is reduced to mapping domain rules onto a neural network, followed by standard training from data. We shall illustrate the effectiveness of this simple approach on two benchmarks. The student loan benchmark contained a relational dataset and rulebase, both of which were rewritten in propositional form. The domain task is to decide, on the basis of 7 features, whether a student is exempted from reimbursing a loan; the 18-rule theory was mapped onto a four-layer 21-6-2-1 neural network. The dataset contains 1000 instances. In the tic-tac-toe endgame benchmark, the task is to determine in which cases player X will win, assuming she played first. The benchmark does not include a domain theory, but it was quite straightforward to define winning endgame configurations in 8 simple rules. However, of the 8 rules which would have defined a complete domain theory, two were purposely eliminated to test the neural network's ability to recover from the lesioned initial theory.

Since prior knowledge is meant to add information value when a dataset is deficient, in this particular case prior knowledge is expected to play a limited role as far as generalization is concerned. This is confirmed by the results shown in Table 2; the knowledge-based and search-based methods attain equivalent mean off-sample accuracy rates. However, the decisive difference lies in the complexity value added by prior knowledge; counting only the number of cycles spent on training the tenured hidden units, KBC is twice as fast as OIL on the second benchmark and 8 times faster on the first. If we take into account the training cycles spent on discarded candidate units, KBC is 22 times faster than OIL on the tic-tac-toe benchmark and 78 times faster on the student loan dataset.

LOANS I=21 N=1000	Accuracy Default=64.3%	Training cycles	
OIL	94.88 ± 0.09	[940]	98
KBC	94.89 ± 0.11		12
TIC-TAC-TOE I=27 N=958	Accuracy Default=64.7%	Training cycles	
OIL	98.50 ± 3.10	[1194]	122
KBC	99.00 ± 1.80		53

Table 2: Results on two benchmarks with adequate knowledge and data. In this and the following tables, I is the number of inputs, N the dataset size. Performance measures are classification accuracy on the test set (mean percentage of cases classified correctly ± the standard deviation) and the number of training epochs. The default accuracy rate is that attained by simply selecting the most frequent class. For the incremental algorithm OIL, training time is represented by the number of training cycles for all candidate hidden units (in brackets), followed by the number of the training cycles for the tenured hidden units alone.

4.2 Deficient knowledge and adequate data

To illustrate the utility of knowledge extraction when there is sufficent data, C4.5 [19] was used to generate rules for two benchmarks which came with no domain theory. In the first, the task is to predict contact lenses prescription (soft, hard, or none) from four features such as age and tear production; in the second, party affiliation is predicted on the basis of a congressman's vote on 17 crucial issues. Rules generated by C4.5 were compiled into a 9-2-3 network for the lenses domain and a 48-2-2 network for the votes domain. Training results are shown in Table 3. The 89.9% accuracy obtained by KEX-KBC on the lenses problem is significantly higher than known previous results which range from 65% accuracy for ID3 and 76.7% for backpropagation to 80.5% for FLARE using prior knowledge and 83.3% for CN2. In the votes domain, KEX-KBC scores 95.6%, as compared with past results: 93.8% for CN2, 95.4% for ID3, 96% for backpropagation, and 94.5% for FLARE using prior knowledge (all past results reported on these two benchmarks are based on [20]). It was also interesting to find out if the inductive method used for knowledge extraction would not have solved these tasks directly; a 10-fold cross-validation run on c4.5 yielded a mean accuracy of 83.3% for lenses and 94% for votes—in both cases lower than the KEX-KBC results.

LENSES I=9 N=24	Accuracy (Default=62.5%)	Training cycles	
OIL	47.03 ± 8.65	[11918]	1101
KEX-KBC	89.93 ± 2.00		3
VOTES I=48 N=435	Accuracy (Default=61%)	Training cycles	
OIL	95.03 ± 0.69	[1725]	277
KEX-KBC	95.60 ± 0.50		12

Table 3: Results on benchmarks with deficient prior knowledge and adequate data.

4.3 Adequate knowledge and deficient data

When prior domain knowledge is available to remedy data deficiency, the combination of knowledge-based configuration and knowledge-based training seems to be the most effective strategy. A network is compiled from domain rules as before; in addition, the same rules are recycled to fulfill another function, the generation of artificial data. These are used to pretrain the network before actual training on the original dataset. This strategy proved appropriate for the Japanese credit screening benchmark, which has a dataset of only 125 instances but includes a domain theory developed in cooperation with domain experts from a Japanese credit company. The original first-order rules were rewritten in propositional form and mapped onto a 25-7-2-1-2 network.

CREDIT I=25 N=125	Accuracy (Default=68%)	Training cycles	
OIL	75.52 ± 2.45	[16692]	2392
KBC	77.05 ± 2.34		36
KBC-KBT	82.42 ± 2.09	[42]	14

Table 4: Results on a benchmark with adequate prior knowledge and deficient data. For KBC-KBT, the number of training cycles includes those for pretraining on artificial data (in brackets), followed by training on the original data.

The results in Table 4 show the improvement added by knowledge-based training to knowledge-based configuration: on average, KBC alone achieves an accuracy of 77% after 36 training epochs whereas KBC-KBT reaches an accuracy to 82.4% in 14 epochs. Of course, the overhead consists of the 42 cycles used to pretrain the network on the knowledge-based examples. This pretraining, which can be seen as a refinement of the weight initializations effected by knowledge-based configuration, seems to improve both generalization and convergence speed during the actual training on the original data. A one-tailed two-sample test on these two variants showed that the improvement in accuracy for this problem is statistically significant at the 0.01 level.

4.4 Deficient knowledge and data

When both knowledge and data are deficient, the SCANDAL strategy is to try the knowledge-based approach anyway, since it is not yet clear under which conditions search-based methods can prove more appropriate. For instance, in the hepatitis benchmark and in a medical application concerning the diagnosis of comas induced by tricyclic antidepressants, both KEX-KBC and KEX-KBC-KBT still attain higher accuracies than OIL, as shown in Table 4.4.

HEPATITIS I=59 N=155	Accuracy (Default=79.4%)	Training cycles	
OIL	83.4 ± 1.8	[5179]	1427
KEX-KBC	85.1 ± 1.3		11
KEX-KBC-KBT	86.1 ± 1.2	[52]	11
TOXIC COMA I=30 N=505	Accuracy (Default=52.5%)	Training cycles	
OIL	55.2 ± 4.4	[10636]	1615
KEX-KBC	60.3 ± 1.4		10
KEX-KBC-KBT	62.3 ± 1.8	[46]	18

Table 5: Results on two problems with deficient knowledge and data.

The hepatitis problem has no available domain knowledge whereas in the coma problem, expert rules are incomplete—they detect the present of antidepressants in isolated form, but not in combination with other toxins. Interestingly, rules extracted by C4.5 proved to be a perfect complement to the expert's rules: induced rules concluded on the absence of antidepressants or their combination with other toxins, but not on their presence in isolation. Both problems are reputedly difficult; for the toxic coma problem, alternative approaches such as maximum entropy probabilistic methods [21] barely bypassed the baseline accuracy, while the best past result for the hepatitis benchmark is 83% accuracy [18]. However, it must be said that the improvement brought by adding KBT to KBC is generally less significant when knowledge is extracted from data than in cases where adequate knowledge from domain experts effectively complete or correct deficient data.

5 Conclusion

The originality of the approach presented in this paper consists in integrating techniques for knowledge-based configuration and knowledge-based training, whereas previous approaches (cf. Section 2) have focused on a specific technique for a single design subtask. Experiments reported in the preceding section show that these different techniques can be combined synergistically to improve neural network performance. These are borne out by the following findings:

- Training time (in terms of number of training cycles) generally decreases as the amount of incorporated prior knowledge increases.
- Generalization power (as measured by off-sample accuracy) generally increases with the amount of knowledge built into a neural network.
- As the size of the dataset increases, the impact of background knowledge on final accuracy diminishes in the sense that a knowledge-free technique will eventually attain accuracy levels comparable to that of a knowledge-based neural network. However, it will do so in a considerably larger number of training epochs (by several orders of magnitude, counting time spent on training pools of candidate hidden units).
- When training data are deficient, the same knowledge that was compiled to configure and initialize a neural net can be recycled to generate artificial examples and obtain higher accuracy levels. More extensive studies will be needed to determine the minimum amount of artificial data needed to obtain significant improvement levels.
- Finally, when both knowledge and data are deficient, knowledge can be extracted from the original data and used both to configure the network and to generate additional training examples. In our experiments, this combination of knowledge extraction with knowledge-based configuration and training led to both higher accuracy and faster learning than search-intensive methods. In particular, rule compilation appears to achieve these effects even when the available rules are far from being approximately complete and correct. Although these findings have to be confirmed by further experimentation, they raise hopes that time-consuming iterative search can be avoided even in knowledge-lean domains.

References

[1] L. M. Fu. Special issue: Knowledge-based neural networks (editorial). *Knowledge-Based Systems*, 8(6):298, 1995.

[2] G. G. Towell and J. W. Shavlik. Knowledge-based artificial neural networks. *Artificial Intelligence*, 70:119–165, 1994.

[3] D. W. Opitz and J. W. Shavlik. Heuristically expanding knowledge-based neural networks. In *Proc. of the 13th IJCAI*, pages 1360–1365, Chambéry, France, 1993. Morgan Kaufmann.

[4] S. Romachandran and R.J. Mooney. Revising Bayesian network parameters using backpropagation. In *Proc. IEEE International Conference on Neural Networks*, pages 82–87, Washington, DC, 1996.

[5] J. J. Mahoney and R. J. Mooney. Combining connectionist and symbolic learning to refine certainty factor rule bases. *Connection Science*, 5(3 & 4):339–393, 1993.

[6] R. C. Lacher, S. I. Hruska, and D. C. Kuncicky. Backpropagatin learning in expert networks. *IEEE Transactions on Neural Networks*, 3:63–72, 1992.

[7] R. P. Brent. Fast training algorithms for multilayer neural nets. *IEEE Transactions on Neural Networks*, 2(3):346–353, 1991.

[8] R. Maclin and J. W. Shavlik. Using knowledge-based neural networks to improve algorithms: refining the Chou-Fasman algorithm for protein folding. In R.S. Michalski, editor, *Machine Learning, Special Issue on Multistrategy Learning*, volume 11, pages 195–215. Kluwer, 1993.

[9] C. L. Giles and C. W. Omlin. Extraction, insertion and refinement of symbolic rules in dynamicallly driven recurrent neural networks. *Connection Science*, 5(3-4):307–337, 1993.

[10] S. C. Suddarth and A. D. C. Holden. Symbolic-neural systems and the use of hints for developing complex systems. *International Journal of Man-Machine Studies*, 35(291-311), 1991.

[11] Y. LeCun, B. Boser, J. S. Denker, et al. Handwritten digit recognition with a back-propagation network. In *Advances in Neural Information Processing, 2*, pages 396–404, San Mateo, CA, 1990. Morgan-Kaufmann.

[12] Y. S. Abu-Mostafa. Hints. *Neural Computation*, 7:639–671, 1995.

[13] P. Simard, B. Victorri, Y. LeCun, and J. Denker. TangentProp—a formalism for specifying selected invariances in an adaptive network. In *Advances in Neural Information Processing, 4* [22], pages 895–903.

[14] M. Röscheisen, R. Hofmann, and V. Tresp. Neural control for rolling mills: incorporating domain theories to overcome data deficiency. In *Advances in Neural Information Processing, 4* [22], pages 659–666.

[15] K. A. Al-Mashouq and I. S. Reed. Including hints in training neural networks. *Neural Computation*, 3:418–427, 1991.

[16] J. C. Gonzalez, J. R. Velasco, and C. A. Iglesias. A distributed platform for symbolic-connectionist integration. In R. Sun and F. Alexandre, editors, *Connectionist-Symbolic Integration: From Unified to Hybrid Approaches*, chapter 10. L. Erlbaum, Montreal, CN, 1997.

[17] V. Vysniauskas, F. C. A. Groen, and B. J. A. Kröse. Orthogonal incremental learning of a feedforward network. In *International Conference on Artificial Neural Networks*, Paris, 1995.

[18] P. M. Murphy and D.W. Aha. UCI repository of machine learning databases. http://www.ics.uci.edu/ mlearn/MLRepository.html, 1991. Irvine, CA: University of California, Dept. of Information and Computer Science.

[19] J. R. Quinlan. *C4.5: Programs for Machine Learning*. Morgan Kaufmann, San Mateo, CA, 1993.

[20] C. Giraud-Carrier. An integrated framework for learning and reasoning. *Journal of Artificial Intelligence Research*, 3:147–185, 1995.

[21] B. Amy, V. Danel, J. Gonzalez, M. Hilario, F. Osorio, V. Rialle, S. Schultz, and J. Velasco. Medical application (final report). Esprit Project MIX Deliverable D16, 1997.

[22] *Advances in Neural Information Processing, 4*. Morgan-Kaufmann, 1992.

Tools and Experiments for Hybrid Neuro-Symbolic Processing

F. Alexandre
CRIN-INRIA
BP 239
F-54506 Vandœuvre

Abstract

Symbolic and connectionist tools are widely used in the Artificial Intelligence (AI) domain. Both approaches report weaknesses to address the full range of capabilities required by this domain, and are often combined one with the other to overcome some limitations, but no extensive efforts have been done to give a wider view of the problem. More precisely, many ad hoc hybrid models were built from symbolic and connectionist tools, but few was said about the choice, integration and combination of such tools. Such was the goal of the European ESPRIT project MIX. We report here the main conclusions of this project, together with its results on a real-world application.

1 Introduction

The idea of combining connectionist and symbolic techniques in so-called hybrid systems is not new. Nevertheless, if we have a look at the state of the art about this topic, one can constat that, up to now, hybrid models have been designed in an *ad hoc* manner, to overcome these or those limitations of a symbolic or a connectionist tool, and that no effort has been made to propose a framework for the automatic design of hybrid models. Given this observation, MIX, a european ESPRIT project, was proposed, in order to study hybridization, develop tools and propose strategies to better understand — and emulate — hybrid models.

Both the connectionist and symbolic domain are very large, including many kinds of approaches, and the risk was to either be too specific or to get lost in these wide areas. We thus selected some representative models within each field, namely multilayer perceptrons, Kohonen maps and prototype based networks from the connectionist part and fuzzy logic, case based, model based and rule based reasoning from the symbolic part.

The first step in our bottom-up approach was then to study what we called "partial hybrids", i.e. numerous possibilities of coupling between each of the selected symbolic tools and each of the selected connectionist tools. These possibilities are numerous for several reasons. First, each model owns a large variety of characteristics on which the coupling can operate. For example, a symbolic model can act on different parameters of a multilayer perceptron, such as its internal parameters (e.g.: learning rate), its architectural parameters (e.g.: number of hidden layers), its external parameters (e.g.:learning corpus), or its activity parameters (e.g.: output). Second, the coupling can be rather loose (e.g.: only one parameter exchange [4]) or rather tight (e.g.: structure or knowledge base exchange [10]), or somewhere in-between. Third, the functional role of the coupling can be manyfold. For example, the function of a symbolic model on a multilayer perceptron can be to tune its learning rate [18], to design its architecture [22], to initialize its weights [9], to build its example bases [18], to facilitate its classification task [18], etc. For each of the selected connectionist and symbolic models, we enumerated a large set of possibilities and retained only those whose information processing interest was clear (See Section 2.1.2). Cooperation between these subtasks allowed us to propose also partial hybrids refering to coupling of more than one symbolic and one connectionist model. Finally, the criterion to select a partial hybrid is only to have a powerful functional role, as discussed in Section 2.

The automatic selection of an appropriate hybrid combination with regard to a task is certainly the core of the hybrid approach, that was never tackled in the past. Therefore, the second step of our work was to propose a unified model representing the second-stage integration of partial hybrids. This aspect will be also discussed in Section 2.

To attain these main goals, a prerequisite was to define a common basis for the implementation of our hybrids and, hence, of their symbolic and connectionist components. On the one hand, one objective of the project was to pay attention to the interface between these heterogeneous models. On the other hand, our project, gathering partners in distant sites throughout Europe and willing to disseminate its results to a wide community needed a generic implementation tool. The nature of the domain itself led to the choice of a distributed artificial intelligence approach.

In this distributed framework, each basic connectionist or symbolic model is considered as an agent and a set of services and communication protocols has been defined to establish an effective dialogue between the models. All the applications mentioned in this paper have been developed on this platform, and most of the time in different sites.

Finally, it was fundamental to assess our work on real-world applications with the evaluation of quantitative and qualitative performance criteria. Three applications were selected in various sectors (namely, the automobile industry, the steel industry and the medical world) concerning various types of information processing (identification, prediction, control and optimization). Today, these three applications have been realized within the MIX framework. Both industrial applications have been successfully transferred to their sectors. The steel industry application will be described in Section 3.

Another objective of the MIX project was to advance the state of the art in connectionist-symbolic integration and to extract more theoretical results from this work. The underlying goal was to decide if the field was mature enough to draw a general methodology for hybridization. These aspects are also discussed in Section 2 below.

2 Main results of the MIX project

The most fundamental results are directly linked to the domain of hybridization itself. They concern partial hybrids, as defined above, their combination for a given application and also, more generally, theoretical foundations of this approach. We present these results here, in that order.

2.1 Results on hybridization

This kind of results are related to the level of partial hybrids. The basic idea is to enumerate and structure the different dimensions of hybridization. The most discriminating dimension is certainly the possible ways in which symbolic and connectionist components are configured in relation to each other. A study of the state of the art made us propose, for one symbolic and one connectionist module, four main configurations that we call integration modes [16].

2.1.1 Four integration modes

In *chainprocessing* mode, the two modules operate in sequence. One is the main processor and is assisted by the other module, acting as a pre or postprocessor. The role of the main processor can be fulfilled by a connectionist module [12] as well as by a symbolic module [11].

In *subprocessing* mode, as in the previous mode, one module is the subcontractor of the other. Here, the difference is that the former is embedded in the latter and has no direct contact with the environment. It is a kind of subroutine, as illustrated in the Innate/Qualms system [4], where an expert system designed for fault diagnosis in a distillation plant subcontracts the task of generating candidate faults to multilayer perceptrons.

In *metaprocessing* mode, one module is the problem solver and the other plays a metalevel role, such as monitoring or control. For example, [13] describes a symbolic problem solver (in the domain of physics) whose successive subgoals are given by a connectionist module, enforcing search control.

In *coprocessing* mode, both modules are equal partners in the problem solving process. Their respective results are mixed in a competitive or cooperative scheme. They can also transmit information one to the other, as illustrated in the Synhesis system [10], for knowledge extraction from the connectionist module to the symbolic one, or knowledge compilation in the reverse direction.

These four integration modes are represented in figure 1

Other dimensions of hybridization can also help to structurate this domain and allow for disambiguation of some cases. The degree of coupling of the symbolic and connectionist modules is one of these dimensions. For example, it can be observed that coupling in the chainprocessing mode is generally loose, whereas subprocessing can lead to tighter coupling.

2.1.2 Functional roles of hybrids

The most important issue in hybridization is that of the functional roles of hybrid models. Beyond the analytical dimensions enumerated above, it is fundamental to wonder about the underlying strategies for the choice of a hybrid integration. We mentioned this point in Section 1 above: among numerous possibilities of coupling, we only selected as valid partial hybrids with an "interesting functional role". We now have to clearly define this criterion. In the hybrid framework, three strategies can be envisaged to pro-

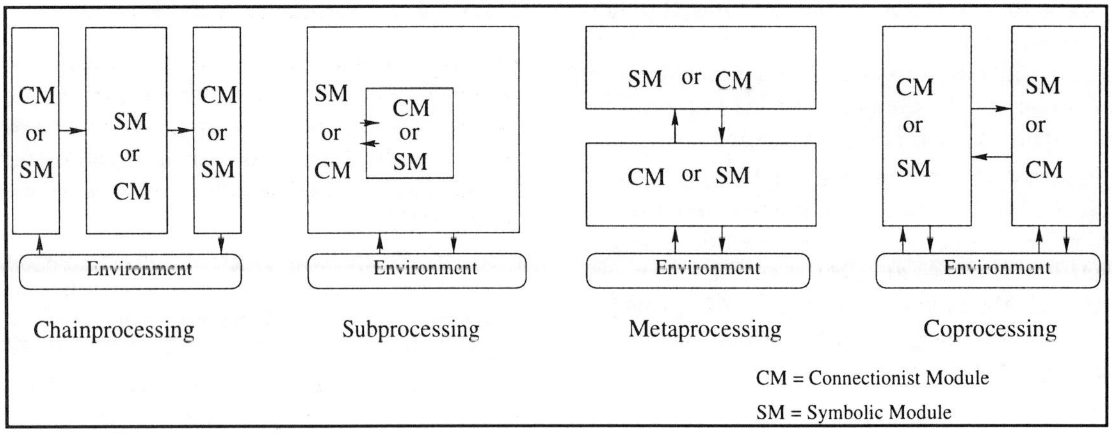

Figure 1: Four integration modes

pose a fruitful combination of a symbolic and a connectionist module.

According to the first strategy, a connectionist module can improve a symbolic one. One possibility for that is to better anchor the symbolic module in the uncertain and incomplete characteristics of real-world data and knowledge. The connectionist approach is a natural way to deal with partial and unreliable data and knowledge. This property has often been offered to the symbolic domain, like in [6], where a connectionist module allows for the expression of uncertain knowledge expressed by physicians, before giving it to a medical expert system. Another possibility for the connectionist module to palliate the weaknesses of a symbolic one is to decrease duration of heuristic search. In this case, the symbolic approach has a skill which is prohibitive with regard to time. Systems like Synhesis [10] or Setheo [11] propose to use associative reasoning of connectionist models to replace long forward-chaining.

In the second strategy, a symbolic module can improve a connectionist one. One possibility is to do this at the level of data processing. Connectionist models are mainly efficient for interpolation tasks, for data with homogeneous probability densities. One way can be thus to divide the input space in typical and atypical regions (i.e. where any interpolation process like generalization can or cannot occur) and to cope with atypical regions thanks to symbolic approaches like case-based reasoning (CBR) or fuzzy logic, better performing on this kind of data. [17] is an example of hybridization where a CBR module is used to process atypical cases whereas a prototypal network represents the regular domains. The other possibility is at the level of connectionist network architecture and internal parameters themselves. Connectionist models are often presented as autonomous adaptative systems. This is true, except for their design, where empirical tricks are often used to decide about their architecture and internal parameters. Attempts have been made to formalize such tricks with a knowledge based approach and can be presented as a contribution of symbolic models to better manipulate — and understand — connectionist ones. Domain knowledge can be related to hints [1], to network initialization [9] or to heuristic search of topology [7].

According to the third strategy, possibilities of cross-fertilization between both modules are envisaged. Either this double way improvement is only the combination of two different one-way improvements mentioned above or, more interestingly, the coupling is tighter than this simple combination. This can be achieved only if the problem can be faced at the same time by both approaches, acting in the coprocessing mode on a shared data and knowledge representation. Synhesis [10] has such characteristics.

From a practical point of view, these results can be summarized as follows: First, a catalogue of coupling schemes with such characteristics as integration modes, level and strength of integration is proposed. On this basis, a set of steps to handle an hybrid application is proposed. Apart from the selection of the better symbolic *and* connectionist model for this task, other models, improving the selected models themselves, must be also looked for. We must also wonder if these selected models can be coupled in a tight combination toward the same goal.

2.2 A unified integration model

A prerequisite for this kind of integration is to have at hand a set of partial hybrids, selected as described in the previous section, each good at dealing with one aspect of the application. Then, another module has to select at each moment the subset of partial hybrids to activate, to solve the current task. We propose that this selection module be itself an hybrid. Consequently, the unified integration model can be globally viewed as a partial hybrid acting in the metaprocessing mode for the choice of the adequate tools, from a set of partial hybrids acting in the coprocessing mode. Each of these partial hybrids can be any combination of symbolic and connectionist modules in any integration mode. In short, our approach has three different levels of choice : (i) choice of the elementary symbolic and connectionist models, (ii) choice of the partial hybrids that improve those models with regard to local aspects of the task, (iii) choice of the partial hybrids that best fit the ongoing task. The former two choices are initially made, to build the global system. The latter is an on-line permanent process.

This latter strategy refers to the very general problem of model selection, which is still today an open problem, addressed by many researchers [5]. It was clearly out of the reach of the MIX project to give a general answer to this problem. Nevertheless, an efficient heuristic approach can be proposed in the framework of hybridization. A training corpus can allow for the creation of a case base, gathering examples together with the performances of each partial hybrid on this example (if applicable). Then, the selection hybrid can be designed as a CBR module, giving an answer from the estimation of performances of each partial hybrid for a new example. These estimations can be performed by a connectionist module acting in the subprocessing mode for the CBR module. Knowing the estimated performances of each partial hybrid (or knowing that it is not applicable), the CBR module can then decide which one(s) to trigger.

The main features of the unified integration model are represented in figure 2.

2.3 Theoretical foundations of hybridization

Up to this point, we have seen that hybridization refers to many domains of intelligent information processing. We briefly discuss them below, as a first theoretical basis of hybridization.

2.3.1 Neuro-Symbolic Integration

The domains which hybridization has to obviously be related to are its mother domains, symbolic and connectionist artificial intelligence (AI). A large part of their history has been devoted to a war between these two paradigms, competing for better modeling human cognitive capabilities. Today, it is widely admitted that these two paradigms have different and complementary strengths [9, 14]. From this remark arises the idea of combining them to benefit from advantages of both : hybridization is one possible strategy of combination of these paradigms, but not the only one.

All possible strategies are gathered within the field of Neuro-Symbolic Integration (NSI) [21] and it is thus interesting to relate hybridization to other strategies [15], like for example the unified approach claiming that connectionist formalism is sufficient to model cognitive tasks, with the help of symbolic AI algorithms (domain of connectionist symbol processing) or theoretical biology (domain of neuronal symbol processing [3]).

Extensive studies of NSI [16] propose that, among these strategies, hybridization is certainly the most mature approach today. Others are certainly very promising, but only hybridization proposes a short term efficient solution of real-world problems.

2.3.2 Combining knowledge and data

Connectionist and symbolic AI are complementary because their competences are respectively related to data and knowledge processing, which are the two major skills of human cognition. In an ideal case, facing a complete domain theory, a knowledge driven solution is sufficient to solve problems in it. Conversely, if no knowledge is available, a data driven method is the only solution. However, it is clear that human cognitive tasks are very rarely situated at these extremes. Only a part of the knowledge and data related to the task is available and thus the selection of the most appropriate method among knowledge and data driven methods is required at each moment. In the MIX project, this gave rise to the unified integration model.

More generally, the AI community is aware of this duality between knowledge and data for the functioning of its tools themselves. The symbolic approach adopts data driven methods to improve their models [8] and the connectionist approach tries to integrate domain-specific knowledge for the design of its networks [22]. This corresponds, in the MIX project, to the partial hybrids and to the strategy to select them as having an interesting functional role : can knowledge (resp. data) be used to improve data (resp. knowledge) driven methods for one aspect of the application?

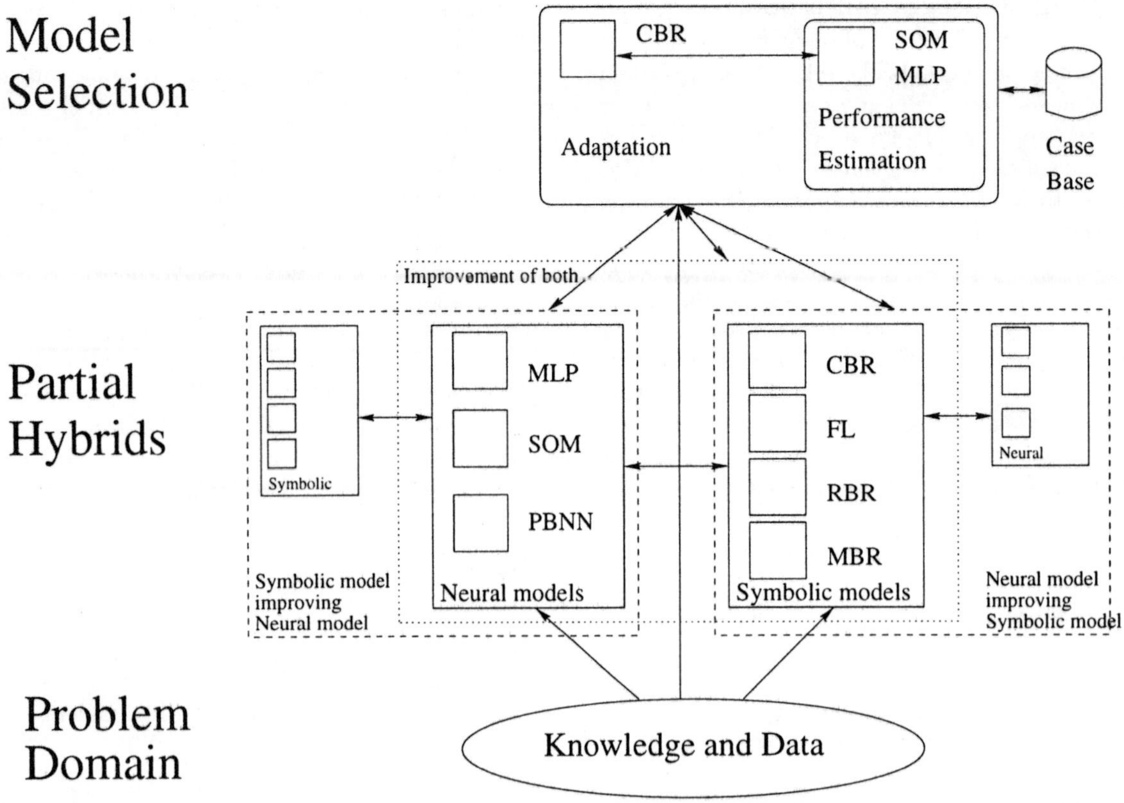

Figure 2: The unified integration model

2.3.3 Meta-learning

What we expressed just above clearly refers to meta-learning, which is a major topic in AI today. It is now widely known that learning about the problem itself is not sufficient and that this adaptive process must also be applied to the processing tools themselves. MIX adopts this strategy at two levels.

First, at the level of partial hybrids, the most common strategies of design are generally concerned with learning to adapt a given tool to the problem with the alternative paradigm. Second, at the level of the selection of the model, this choice is made by learning to estimate performances of each partial hybrid. It is worth noticing here that both levels are also concerned with another domain of machine learning, the multi-strategy learning, since the process is applied to heterogeneous models, using different learning approaches. This then leads to enriching combination of adaptive processes, as described in [17].

2.3.4 About knowledge

Alongside learning, knowledge is certainly the other major concept that hybridization allows to explore with a very original and fruitful manner. Improving data driven and knowledge driven methods one with another means having opportunities to fill in the gap between these two experiences of the world.

Knowledge assimilation is a first possibility when, for example, knowledge is used to design a neural network or to initialize its weights. Interestingly too, is the possibility to extract knowledge from data driven methods, like in the case of rule extraction from neural networks [2]. Basically, the main idea in this domain is that of knowledge exchange and enrichment between the two paradigms.

2.3.5 Cognitive aspects

As a new field of AI, hybridization has also to wonder about its cognitive foundations. We mentioned above that the need for combination between knowledge and data driven approaches arises from the need for modeling human cognitive capabilities. It can thus be suggested that human cognition itself is hybrid. In any case, it is clear that both competencies are present and mixed in most tasks [16].

As a consequence, hybridization could become an approach to better understanding and representing human cognition. In fact, we experienced such ideas during our real-world applications of the MIX project. More precisely, it clearly appeared that experts of the considered domains had a very intuitive sense of our models. They felt thus very comfortable with them and could cope with our tools very easily. We think that cognitive benefits are not of the less important results of our work.

3 The steel roll-mill application

One of the three applications of the MIX project, related to the steel industry, is described here to show how the different concepts presented above have been implemented in a real-world application.

3.1 Presentation

The roll-mill machine, which is at the centre of this study, is in the thin sheet department at the steelmaker Sollac Florange site. Its role is to slightly lengthen the steel band that passes through working rolls in order to stamp the band, print the desired roughness on it and correct possible flatness defects.

Extensive work has been done in the past on this application, yielding data and knowledge about it. Concerning knowledge, Sollac developed (among others) a physical model of the roll-mill and its underlying process. This model, the Roberts's model [20], incorporates theories from various domains such as mechanic, thermic and steel theory. However, physical equation manipulation in such models suffers from inherent limitations. They are effective in giving a qualitative idea of the phenomenon, but are not precise enough to account for the real transformation of the steel and also to be adapted to the specific characteristics of that specific roll-mill. An on-line evaluation of the Roberts's model gives a 25% mean error in the estimation of the presetting rolling force, as a function of the characteristics of the band and of the process.

Concerning data, it must be first underlined that up-to-date computer facilities in the Sollac plant allows access to a very large set of detailed operational examples. These examples are built on the basis of a set of 12 parameters, either desired (e.g: final elongation of the pressed sheet) or measured (e.g: rolling speed, traction force) that have been selected by the steelmakers, because they obviously affect the process. On the basis of such corpus, data driven methods have been tested by one of the MIX partners (INRIA-Lorraine) during the past 5 years. Connectionist models and more precisely multilayer perceptrons (MLP) have been chosen to realize this task. Several MLP configurations were tested [18], depending on the number of hidden layers and the number of neurons per hidden layer. The resulting connectionist architecture, an MLP with two hidden layers of 48 and 24 neurons, has been implemented on line, in the Sollac plant. Its error rate is 17%, which is a rather good improvement with regard to the physical model. That was the status of the application when the MIX project began. We now describe how MIX principles, as presented above, have been applied to this problem.

3.2 Partial hybrids

At the level of partial hybrids, it had to be seen whether each of the symbolic and connectionist approach could be improved by the alternative approach. Our previous experiments were very useful for that.

Concerning the physical model, one of its weaknesses is that its purpose is very general: it is not adapted to the roll-mill on which it has been implemented. A corpus was built to allow an MLP to learn an estimation of the best multiplicative coefficient that adapts the Roberts's output to the actual rolling force. Thus, the physical model output is now:

$$PhysicalOutput = \alpha * RobertsOutput$$

where α is the coefficient estimated by the MLP. This correction leads to a 17.9% physical model error rate.

Concerning the connectionist model, the most expensive part of its design was the empirical search for the better architecture for this application. Now, it is clear that, whatever the change in the application (e.g: production of new kind of steel, extension to other rolling machines), this work has to be done again. This is the reason why we chose to improve the MLP with a Model Based Reasoning approach, whose goal is to automatically find the best architecture for a given problem. More precisely, the Error Model Based approach, proposed by [22], was adapted to this problem. In this model, regression rules are defined to determine the hidden layer size as a function of the training set size and the average test error. In our case, the performances of the MLP were left unchanged, but now this model can easily be extended to other problem configurations.

Finally, another partial hybrid was designed to tackle this problem, and more precisely to handle atypical domains. Fuzzy techniques are already being used successfully in applications faced with the problem of uneven data distribution and are thus very desirable here. Fuzzy rules have been elaborated by a decision tree, namely C4.5 [19]. On the same test corpus as the other partial hybrids, including 3,000 examples, the error rate of this partial hybrid is 18.2%.

To sum up, we have at our disposal three partial hybrids (a physical model hybridized with a MLP, a MLP hybridized with a MBR and a FL module hybridized with a decision tree), each having very close performances on the application (approximately 18% error rate). The question is now to know how to combine these partial approaches to obtain a lower error rate. This is the goal of the integration stage.

3.3 Integration

The main processor of these partial hybrids, acting as a model selection module, is a CBR module. In the course of its operation, this module builds a case base, composed of examples together with the performance of each partial hybrid on each example. As a CBR module, this module has to define several tasks including retrieval (given a case, what are the closest in the case base), adaptation (given these closest cases, which strategy is more appropriate for the current problem) and storage (assimilate this new experience).

To realize these functions, two connectionist modules have been designed, in the subprocessing mode. First, a Kohonen map is built on the basis of the case base, consisting of the association of examples of steel bands (12 parameters) and the corresponding error for each of the partial hybrids (3 parameters). So, for each partial hybrid, a topological mapping of the value of the error with regard to the input space is learned.

Second, a simple perceptron is trained, to learn optimal coefficients α_i such that

$$\alpha_1 * Model_1 + \alpha_2 * Model_2 + \alpha_3 * Model_3 + \alpha_4$$

best approximates the desired output force, for a given example, where $Model_1$, $Model_2$ and $Model_3$ are outputs of partial hybrids corrected by Kohonen estimation of error.

On this basis, a variety of strategies of model selection and combination can be envisaged by the CBR module. We tried some of them, for comparison, on the same corpus (3,000 examples). The best one corresponds to selecting the three closest prototypes, one for each partial hybrid, thanks to the Kohonen module. Each prototype is then corrected by the estimation of its error (Kohonen again) and combined one with another, thanks to the estimation of their relative weights (perceptron model). A 10.5% error rate is measured for this best strategy.

Previous versions of this system have been installed on line in the Sollac plant and the mean error of the rolling force prediction is at the very low rate of 12.5%. The implementation of this latter strategy is now studied by Sollac engineers.

4 Discussion

MIX does not propose a methodology of hybridization, but a framework for hybridization. This framework is methodological, because at the implementation level a common distributed platform has been used to design all our hybrid models. This framework is also conceptual because a grid of analysis of hybrid models has been proposed, together with a general purpose two steps definition for the design of an hybrid model.

Through this experience, we also tried to show that an hybrid approach must be considered as a possible candidate, when a real-world problem is considered. Our framework can be seen as an help to realize such implementations. More theoretical results have been given here as arguments to show the benefits given by this approach. They basically propose exploitation of all kind of information (knowledge or data) available on the problem domain.

Starting from a weak theoretical environment and working on industrial applications, on which knowledge, data and experience of modelization were available, directed our work toward a very practical view of hybridization. On one hand, this is interesting because our two-level framework makes principles of hybridization clearly appear. The first step (partial hybrids) underlines the principles of symbolic-connectionist coupling itself. The second step (integration) explains the necessity of automatically selecting and combining potentials given by each partial hybrid. On the other hand, the MIX project, as a framework for this work, obviously had limitations (in time and in kind of addressed problem classes) that we wish now to tackle.

First, this work lies on three connectionist and four symbolic models. It is clear that this can be extended to other symbolic and connectionist models (as it was done in the roll-mill application with the use of decision trees). Second, this choice of classical tools, together with applications to previously known industrial problems, made us to often choose hybrids with a loose coupling and work on strategies of coupling rather than on improvements of coupling or interfaces. A theory of hybridization should obviously include such capabilities and MIX partners are now willing to continue in those directions.

Acknowledgments

This work was partly funded by the Commission of the European Communities under the ESPRIT Basic Research Project MIX: Modular Integration of

Connectionist and Symbolic Processing in Knowledge Based Systems, ESPRIT-9119.

References

[1] Y. Abu-Mostafa. Learning from hints in neural networks. *Journal of Complexity*, 6:192–198, 1990.

[2] F. Alexandre and J.-F. Remm. Knowledge extraction from neural networks for signal interpretation. In *Proceedings International Conference on ESANN*, Bruges (Belgique), April 1997.

[3] F. Alexandre. Connectionist Cognitive Processing for Invariant Pattern Recognition. In *Proceedings International Conference on Pattern Recognition*, Vienna (Austria), August 1996.

[4] W. R. Becraft, P. L. Lee, and R. B. Newell. Integration of neural networks and expert systems for process fault diagnosis. In *Proc. of the 12 th IJCAI*, pages 832–837, 1991.

[5] P. Brazdil, J. Gama, and R. Henery. Characterizing the applicability of classification algorithms using meta level learning. In F. Bergadano and L. deRaedt, editors, *Machine learning ECML'94*, pages 83–102. Springer Verlag, 1994.

[6] V. Ciesielski, S. Hayes, and B. Kelly. Comparison of an expert system and a hybrid neural network/expert system for a respiratory monitoring problem. In Ron Sun, Lawrence Bookman, and Shashi Shekar, editors, *AAAI-92 Workshop on Integrating Neural and Symbolic Processes—the Cognitive Dimension*, San Jose, California, 1992.

[7] S. Fahlman and C. Lebiere. The cascade-correlation learning architecture. In Touresky, editor, *Advances in Neural Information Processing Systems 2. Proceedings of the 1989 Conference*, pages 524–532, 1989.

[8] N.S. Flann and T.G. Dietterich. A study of explanation-based methods for inductive learning. *Machine Learning*, 4(2):187–226, 1989.

[9] S. I. Gallant. *Neural network learning and expert systems.* MIT Press, 1993.

[10] A. Giacometti, B. Amy, and A. Grumbach. Theory and experiment in connectionist ai: a tighly-coupled hybrid system. In I. Aleksander and J. Taylor, editors, *ICANN*, 1992.

[11] C. Goller. A connectionist control component for the theorem prover setheo. ECAI-94 Workshop on Combining Symbolic and Connectionist Processing, 1994.

[12] R. M. Goodman, J. W. Miller, and P. Smyth. An information theoretic approach to rule-based connectionist expert systems. In D. S. Touretzky, editor, *Advances in Neural Information Processing*, volume 1, pages 256–263, 1989.

[13] M. Gutknecht and R. Pfeifer. An approach to integrating expert systems with connectionist networks. *AI Communications*, 3(3):116–127, September 1990.

[14] M. Gutknecht. The postmodern mind: hybrid models of cognition. *Connection Science*, 4(3 & 4), 1992.

[15] M. Hilario. An overview of strategies for neurosymbolic integration. In Sun and Alexandre, editors, *Proceedings of the IJCAI Workshop on Connectionist-symbolic integration: from unified to hybrid approaches*, Montréal, August 1995.

[16] Y. Lallement, M. Hilario, and F. Alexandre. Neurosymbolic Integration : Cognitive Grounds and Computational Strategies. In M. DeGlas and Z. Pawlak, editors, *Proceedings World Conference on the Fundamentals of Artificial Intelligence*, Paris, July 1995.

[17] M. Malek. A connectionist indexing system for CBR systems. In *Case-Based Reasoning Research and Development : First International Conference on Case-based Reasoning (ICCBR95)*, number 1010 in Lecture Notes in Artificial Intelligence. Springer, 1995.

[18] N. Pican, P. Bresson, and F. Alexandre. Artificial Neural Networks for the Presetting of a Steel Temper Mill. *IEEE Expert Journal, Special Track on Expert Systems in Steel Industry*, 1995.

[19] J. R. Quinlan. *C4.5.* Morgan Kaufmann Publishers, 1992.

[20] W. L. Roberts. An approximate theory of temper rolling. *Iron and steel engineer*, 1972.

[21] R. Sun and F. Alexandre, editors. *Connectionist - Symbolic Integration: from Unified to Hybrid Approaches.* Lawrence Erlbaum Associates, 1997.

[22] V. Vysniauskas, F. Groen, and B. Krose. The optimal number of learning samples and hidden units in function approximation with a feedforward network. In University of Amsterdam, editor, *Technical Report CS-93-15, CSD*, 1993.

Session E.2

Genetic Algorithms and Applications II

Session Chair:
Roland Mittermeir, Universität Klagenfurt, Austria

Toward the Optimization of a Class of Black Box Optimization Algorithms

Gang Wang Erik D. Goodman William F. Punch
Genetic Algorithms Research and Applications Group (GARAGe)
A.H. Case Center and Department of Computer Science
Michigan State University
East Lansing, MI 48824
wanggan1@cps.msu.edu goodman@egr.msu.edu punch@cps.msu.edu

Abstract

Many black box optimization algorithms have sufficient flexibility to allow them to adapt to the varying circumstances they encounter. These capabilities are of two primary sorts: 1) user-determined choices among alternative parameters, operations, and logic structures, and 2) the algorithm-determined alternative paths chosen during the process of seeking a solution to a particular problem. This paper discusses the process of algorithm design and operation, with the intent of integrating the seemingly distinct aspects described above within a unified framework. We relate this algorithmic optimization process to the field of dynamic process control. An approach is proposed toward the optimization of a process for controlling a specific class of systems, and its application to dynamic adjustment of the algorithm used in the search problem. An instance of this approach in genetic algorithms is demonstrated. The experimental results show the adaptability and robustness of the proposed approach.

1 Introduction

Algorithms called Black Box Optimization algorithms ("BBOs") are used to address problems for which domain knowledge is incomplete or unavailable. Although these BBOs are not guaranteed to find the global optimum, especially for NP-complete problems, they are often a useful tool for discovering approximate solutions. Adaptive sampling search methods, particularly, evolutionary computation, have recently become very popular for such uses. They are loosely modeled on the process of evolution in the real world, but they are only paradigms, which means that when given a specific problem, one must fill in a great many details to design and implement the algorithm. Quantitative analysis to discover these details is difficult simply because of the complexity of the problem space. In the typical process of problem solving, adjustment of the algorithms is often done empirically, with limited guidance from theory, rules of thumb, and prior experience.

An algorithmic approach is proposed toward the optimization of BBOs. When applied to Genetic Algorithms (GAs), they provide a more uniform way to formalize the process of designing, implementing, and running a GA-optimization system. The experimental results show the adaptability and robustness of this approach.

2 Issues in algorithm design for black box optimization

In designing algorithms for solving BBO problems, two aspects of algorithm flexibility are involved:

- **External flexibility** of the user-defined structure of the algorithm and parameters, determining the space of possible algorithms to be used. A specific search paradigm includes choices one can make to address a specific problem. For example, with genetic algorithms, one needs to choose (chromosomal) representation, fitness function, genetic operators, selection method, and many control parameters (*e.g.*, probabilities of crossover and mutation). Most BBO algorithms exhibit this sort of flexibility, giving one both the freedom and the responsibility to "tune" the algorithm to the problem at hand. This is called *external flexibility*.

1082-3409/97 $10.00 © 1997 IEEE

- **Internal adaptability** of the logical structure of any particular algorithm to learn about the search space of the optimization problem to be solved. For example, in genetic algorithms, the internal adaptability is reflected in the change in the population of individual solutions with time for better explorating the search space and exploiting the promising area.

The "No Free Lunch" theorem [1] in optimization illustrates that the design of a BBO is itself an optimization problem. If this BBO process is complex enough, which is true for most cases, optimization of external flexibility parameters will be another BBO problem. When the external flexibility parameters are fixed directly by the user based on experience or rules of thumb, it is hard to guarantee that the initial algorithm design is good enough to achieve the desired results.

In [4], external flexibility and internal adaptability were considered explicitly in order to find an optimal algorithm design for solving optimization problems.

Adaptation of control parameters during the problem solving process by evolutionary algorithms has been done previously by several authors ([2][3][14][15][16]). This work can be divided into two primary groups: adaptation on the level of individuals and adaptation of population-wide parameters. In a system implemented by Baeck et al. [14], fine-tuning of control parameters is done with each individual – that is, every individual is associated with a set of control parameters, and the performance of these parameters with the corresponding individuals affects the survival of the parameters themselves.

In Breeding Genetic Algorithms [15], adaptation is done at the population level. In that system, multiple subpopulations with different strategies (control parameters) compete with each other, and populations with better performance increase in size, while populations with poor performance decrease in size. However, there is no recombination or mutation of control parameters associated with the larger or smaller subpopulations produced.

Herdy [16] did very similar work on evolution strategies; in his system, subpopulations with different strategies compete, and higher level strategies combine and mutate with the goal of generating better ones. But there is no exchange of individuals between subpopulations, so they do not take advantage of the individual-level knowledge gained from solving the problem, which is enabled by individual migration.

As we will see in our work, higher level recombination and mutation are used to generate control parameters which are likely better than their predecessors, while lower level migration of individuals makes the performance evaluation on the search processes fair by *sharing* the best knowledge gained so far in solving the problem. This facilitates the emergence of time varying sets of operators, parameters etc, appropriate to the changing phases of problem solution. The work reported here is distinct from other work in these important aspects.

In the following sections, we give a formal description of an optimization process for genetic algorithms and related paradigms; then we return to the proposed approach and discuss the relationship between control of the optimization process and optimal problem solving by an algorithm. With this approach, some of the external flexibilities can be handled in an algorithmic way similar to the internal adaptability in GAs. Therefore, it offers an integrated framework in which to deal with both aspects of flexibility in genetic algorithms.

3 Optimization of an algorithmic problem solving process

In this section, we will cast a GA-based multilevel optimization process into the form of time-invariant state models, and explore the optimization of the performance of those models.

3.1 Algorithmic problem solving process

Following the state model notation in, for example, [5], we shall describe the behavior of a genetic algorithm for a single population as a time-invariant, discrete-time system state model, as follows:

$$X(T+1) = f(X(T), U(T)), T \in 0, 1, \cdots, \infty, X(0) = X_0 \quad (1)$$

- $X = \{x_1, \cdots, x_n\} \in I_n$, the state vector, characterizes the state of the system (which captures its internal adaptability), and for a GA, is the set of all individuals x_i in the population at time (generation) T.

- $U = \{u_1, \cdots, u_r\}$, the input vector which denotes the parameters of the GA (which specify its external flexibility) as a function of time. $U(T)$ represents a complete specification of all previously unspecified parameters – for example, for the single-population simple GA paradigm, specification of crossover operator type and rate, mutation operator type and rate, selection method and fitness scaling (if any), offspring replacement strategy, etc.

Other related subjects concerning the performance of a system in the situation of optimization problem include:

- Function $q(x_i)$, the fitness (or objective function to be optimized) of individual x_i in population $X(T)$.
- Function $Q(X(T)) = \max_{i=1}^{n} q(x_i)$, the maximum fitness of any individual x_i in $X(T)$.
- $X^* \in \{X | X = \{x_1, x_2, ..., x^*, ..., x_n\}\}$, any state which includes an optimal individual x^*.

Note that if $U(T)$ is fixed at $U(0)$, $T \geq 0$, then the system described by f is a finite Markov chain, as described, for example, in [6][7], etc. However, for the systems to be described here, with time-varying operators and parameters, the notation of state models is found more convenient.

Rather than discussing attainment of a global optimum solution x^*, we shall use function $G(U, X_i, X_f, g, \epsilon)$ to denote the probability that system f reaches a state X such that $Q(X)$ is within ϵ of $Q(X_f)$ from initial state X_i, under the control of input $U(T)$, within g generations.

For given constants g, ϵ and optimal solution x^*, we also define a more compact notation, function F, as follows:

$$F(X, U) = \sum_{X_f \ni Q(X_f) = q(x^*)} G_f(U, X, X_f, g, \epsilon) \quad (2)$$

That is, $F(X, U)$ means the probability that system f moves from state X to any state with performance Q within ϵ of the optimum $q(x^*)$ within g generations under the control of U. F captures the idea of how promising the optimization process f is for generating near-optimal solutions beginning from an arbitrary state X.

Unfortunately, it is practically infeasible to determine the forms of functions G and F for many complex BBO approaches. It is therefore useful to define functions E which capture certain properties of function F, for use in evaluation and comparision of multiple optimization processes. Ideally, we seek an $E(X, U)$ which has the following property:
$(\forall X, U_1, U_2)(F(X, U_1) \geq F(X, U_2)) \Leftrightarrow (E(X, U_1) \geq E(X, U_2))$

In section 4.2, we will see how function E is approximated and tested in the system discussed below.

3.2 Measuring the quality of optimization

The goal of the problem solving process can be simply defined as minimizing the following expression for M_0, the measure of the final solution, with Q,X and X^* defined as above.

- $|Q(X(\infty)) - Q(X^*)|$

However, with bounded resources – for example, a maximum number of iterations, T – different optimization processes might give very different results. Therefore, the quality, M_1, of such a bounded optimization process, can be stated in various more practical ways:

> Given a system f with fixed control inputs $U(T)$, starting from $X(0)$,
>
> - **The average time required for system f to produce optimal solution x^*;**
> - **The average time required to produce a near-optimal solution with fitness within ϵ of $q(x^*)$;**
> - **The average distance of the limit of the trajectory $Q(X(T))$ from $Q(X^*)$;**
> - **The average time to produce a solution which recurs in a large number of runs and is potentially a global optimum solution;**
> - **The average time to produce a solution superior to that produced by some other optimization method.**

However, as a problem solver, not only do we need to consider the problem itself, but also the optimal way for solving it. Therefore, given a specific programming paradigm, say, genetic algorithms or genetic programming, the *goal* for optimization of this algorithmic problem solving process at the higher level, is not to optimize $X(T)$ for a fixed $U(T)$, but rather to optimize $U(T)$ so as to minimize the measure M_1. Note that M_1 can have different forms, ideally or practically, as stated above. If M_1 is in the first form listed, we have a typical minimal time problem:

Given an initial population vector $X(0)$ and a target best individual x^*, find an optimal input vector $U(T)$ which changes the state $X(T)$ of the system f from $X(0)$ to state X^*, in minimal time.

A typical procedure in the problem solving process is to manually try a particular function $U(T)$, test its performance by measure M_1, adjust $U(T)$, and repeat until satisfied. Therefore, we have another measure (M_2) to evaluate the cost of this process:

- **Given a system f, the number of tries of input vectors $U(T)$ before measure M_1 is minimized.**

We discuss below an approach to help to minimize measure M_2, thereby increasing the robustness of the optimization process.

3.3 Proposed approach: high level optimizer (HLO)

Given a dynamic system f, with a defined quality measure Q of a state X, input vector $U(T)$, and measure E which characterizes the probability that any state will be transformed to one with $Q(X)$ within ϵ of $q(x^*)$ within time g, define its High Level Optimizer (HLO) as:

1) Initialize m instances of system f with randomly generated input vectors U, $X_i(T+1) = f_i(X_i(T), U_i(T))$, $1 \leq i \leq m$.

2) For each system f_i, run f_i using its control input U_i for a fixed period, then check its performance using measure E.

3) Select among the populations according to their performance measurements $E(X_i, U_i)$, then do recombination and mutation on pairs of U_i.

4) Select some elements of the associated pairs of $X_i(T)$ for exchange;

5) Continue steps 2) and 3) until a stopping criterion is met.

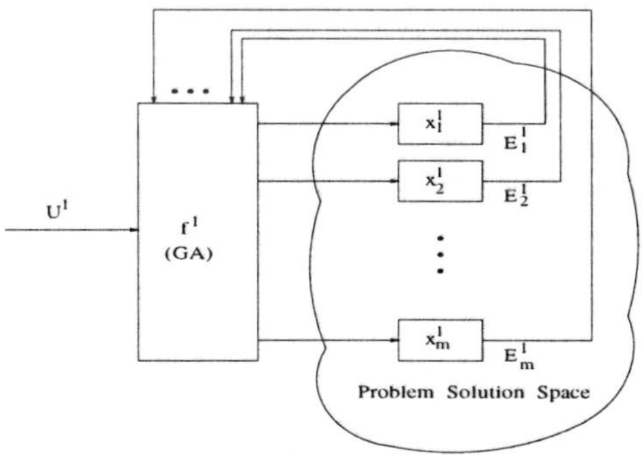

Figure 1: GA configuration

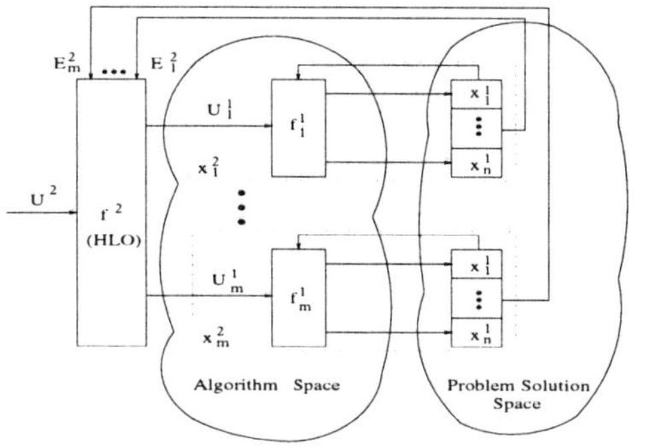

Figure 2: HLO configuration

Our goal in this approach is to improve, in an algorithmic fashion, one or more of the performance measures in $M1$. Of course, the key to actually accomplishing this is the definition of the function E in such a way as to improve F for the particular problem and performance measure at hand. While it is clearly *not* possible to accomplish this in general, it also appears clear that we can find examples of E which are more useful than others for broad classes of significant problems. As we shall see in the following section, another interesting property of this approach is its robustness; that is, it not only tries to minimize measure M_1, but also achieves low values of M_2.

4 DAGA2: Testing the HLO approach on genetic algorithms

DAGA2 (Distributed Adaptive Level-two Genetic Algorithm) [8] is an instance of the HLO approach. In DAGA2, multiple GAs with different parameter settings are supervised and evaluated dynamically. Using higher-level selection and genetic operators, each search process (GA) has a chance to learn better controls from others, thus making it possible for each individual optimization process to improve its M_1.

In DAGA2, control of the optimization process involves the following factors:

- selection operator type and corresponding parameters.

- crossover operator type and crossover probability.

- mutation operator type and mutation probability.

Briefly, DAGA2 first initializes multiple GAs with randomly generated controls, then operates its parallel subpopulations for a fixed number of generations, evaluating the performance of each subpopulation using a "level-two" fitness function E. Each level-two control structure (chromosome) is then, with some probability, subjected to crossover and mutation. Crossover involves fitness-weighted selection of a neighboring level-two chromosome. Migration of level-one chromosomes among neighboring subpopulations is performed at the same interval as the higher-level operations, assuring the benefits of a parallel GA and the distribution of the fitness gains made by any level-one subpopulation among its neighbors. Then the subpopulations, with possibly different individuals and typically better (more fit according to the level-two fitness function) operators/rates, continues to run, and the process is repeated.

The function E for a GA population process might be defined in several ways. Some elements which might be included are:

- best fitness of individuals in the GA population,
- average fitness of individuals in the GA population,
- number of fitness function evaluations,
- diversity measure of the GA population.

Of course, considering some or all of these measures does not allow one to estimate exactly the probability that the algorithm will find the global optimum solution within a particular timeframe. However, for many practical problems, combination of certain of these measures seems to be useful for guiding the selection operation of an *HLO*-based GA scheme, as seen below.

Excellent results from running DAGA2 on a variety of common benchmark functions have been reported elsewhere ([9]). Here we discuss its performance on some simple functions selected to illustrate two aspects of DAGA2 performance: adaptability and robustness.

4.1 DAGA2 adaptability

Adaptability is a very general term, which usually means the capability for a system to adjust its internal structure in order to perform a given task which is newly presented or altered since its previous presentation. If the input vector ($U(T)$) is fixed, then the adaptability of the GA refers to its capability to evolve individual chromosomes with better fitness values. In the case of DAGA2, adaptability is found on two levels – that within the individual GAs on the lower level, and the capability to evolve higher level algorithms (each GAs' external flexibility) for better performance.

To demonstrate simply the capability of DAGA2 to evolve a suitable GA design or a sequence of designs during the course of solving an optimization problem, we run it first on a "Counting Ones" problem, which assigns fitness as the proportion of 1's on the chromosome. It is a very easy problem for a GA with appropriate parameter settings; However, some crucial parameters, probability of mutation(Pm) and probability of crossover(Pc), should be set appropriately based on the chromosome length.

These experiments used a chromosome length of 900, population size at 400. Before running DAGA2 on the problem, we simulated a Simple GA (SGA) within DAGA2, for comparison, by fixing both probability parameters like Pm and Pc and selecting specific operators from a set to use in one single population.

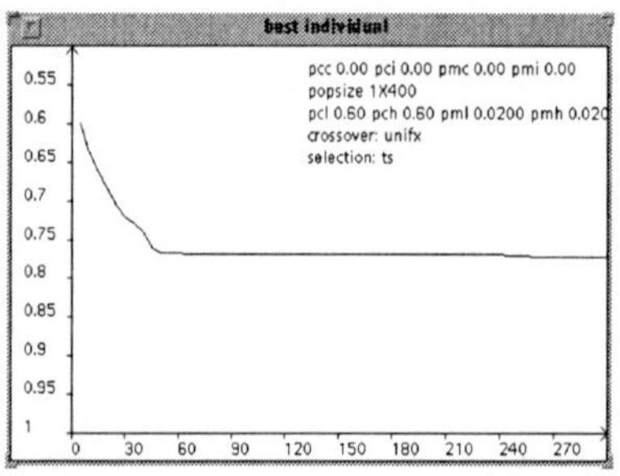

Figure 3: best/gen in experiment 1

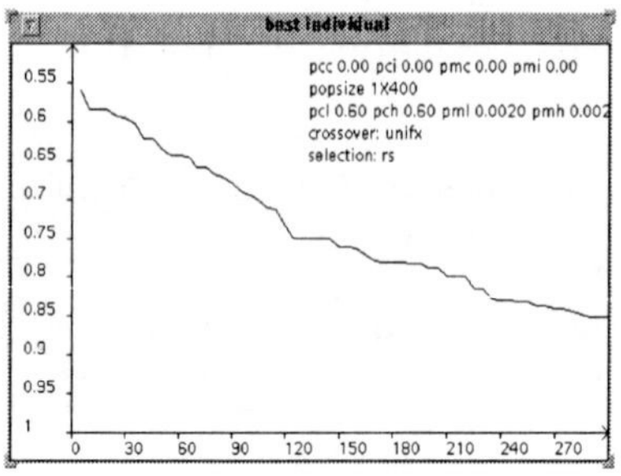

Figure 4: best/gen in experiment 2.

Experiment 1 used tournament selection, uniform crossover and bit-wise mutation, but the mutation rate, Pm, is set too high, at 0.02/bit, for a 900-bit chromosome. It is not surprising that SGA progress ceased at generation 60.

Experiment 2 used roulette wheel selection, uniform crossover and bit-wise mutation. This time, Pm was set appropriately, but with roulette wheel selection, selection pressure was too light; thus, although the SGA continued to make progress, it still had not found the optimal value within 300 generations.

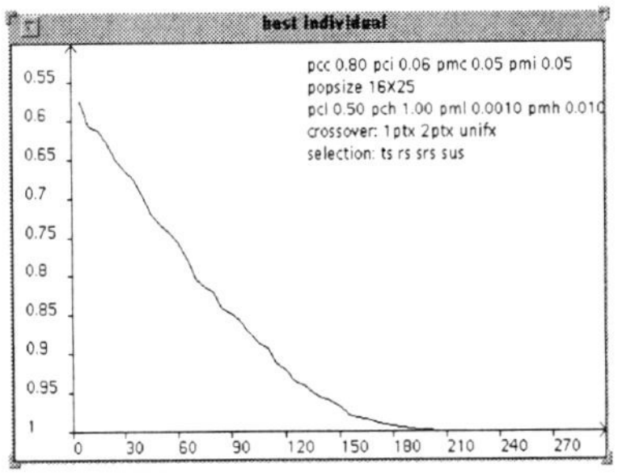

Figure 5: best/gen in experiment 3

Experiment 3 illustrated the use of DAGA2. For this case, available selection methods were tournament selection, roulette wheel selection, stochastic remainder sampling and stochastic universal sampling; available crossover methods were single-point, two-point and uniform crossover; mutation was bitwise. The ranges for Pc and Pm were [0.5, 1.0] and [0.001, 0.01] (per bit), respectively. In this case, the level-two fitness function was defined very simply: the increase in average fitness value in the subpopulation over the previous level-two evaluation plus the average (raw) fitness value in the current subpopulation. The result is that DAGA2 typically found the optimal individual at about generation 220. Other data from that experiment are given below.

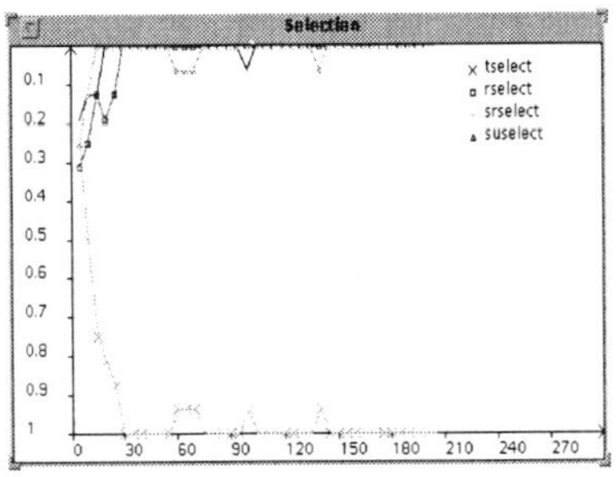

Figure 6: Selection/gen in experiment 3

In all of the figures following, selection/gen means the fraction of subpopulations (i.e., level-2 individuals) using each method of selection, versus generation; crossover/gen means fraction of subpopulations using each crossover method, versus generation. They show that DAGA2 can find "suitable" parameter settings and operators by itself.

In Figure 6, tournament selection soon dominated other selection methods; while in Figure 7, several crossover operators competed; eventually, one-point crossover and uniform crossover were favored.

In Figure 8, the average value of Pc among all sub-

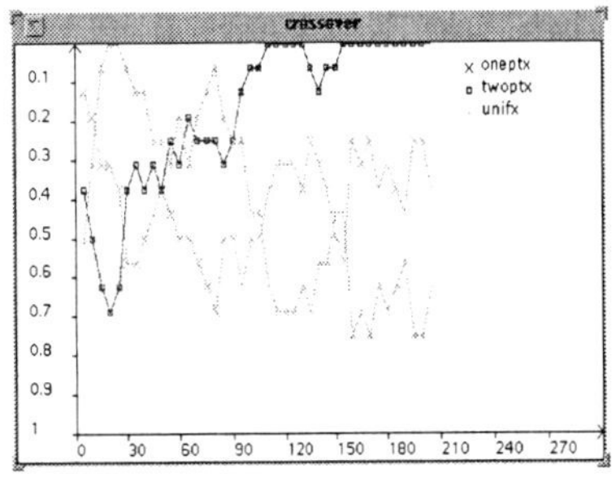

Figure 7: Crossover/gen in experiment 3

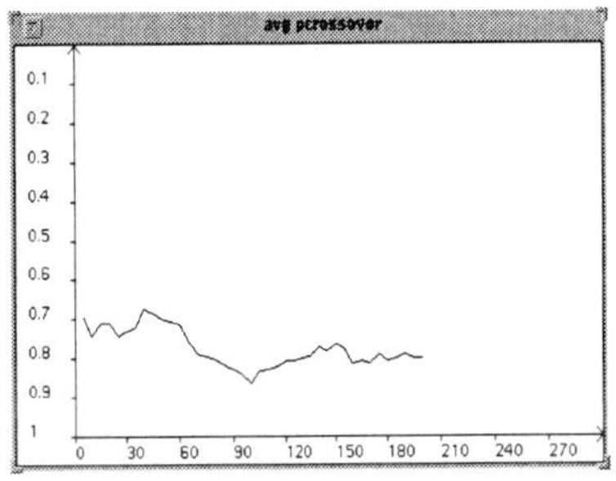

Figure 8: Pc/gen in experiment 3

GAs clustered around 0.8; Figure 9 shows the obvious trace of Pm evolution, by eventually allowing only one or two bit mutation per chromosome. The average of Pm among all subGAs decreased from above 0.005 to around 0.0015 (note that from the schema theorem [10], it is reasonable to assign Pm around 0.0015 if the chromosome length is 900). It should be emphasized that this evolution of upper-level control parameters occurs without user intervention, except to set the search ranges initially. In our experience, DAGA2 was very insensitive to those ranges, even working reasonably well, for example, when they are set to their extremes ([0, 1]).

While Figure 5 - Figure 9 represent a single run, the results of repeated runs with different random seeds closely resembled them, nearly duplicating the operator usage percentage and probability histories.

We have seen in experiment 3 that DAGA2 has the ability to evolve suitable control parameters. Furthermore, the values found by DAGA2 were tested as static settings for an SGA in experiment 4, using tournament selection, uniform crossover, Pm at 0.0015, and Pc at 0.8, which were found to be effective in experiment 3. The result is much better than those in experiments 1 and 2, and even better than that of experiment 3, which is also not surprising. As we see in the definition of DAGA2, control parameters in the subGAs are initialized randomly in a given

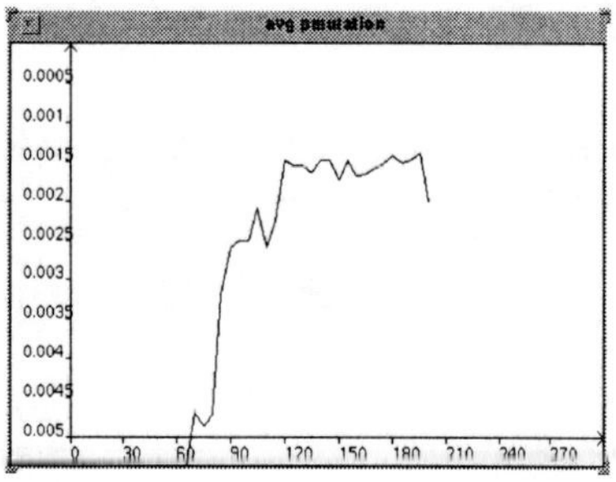

Figure 9: Pm/gen in experiment 3

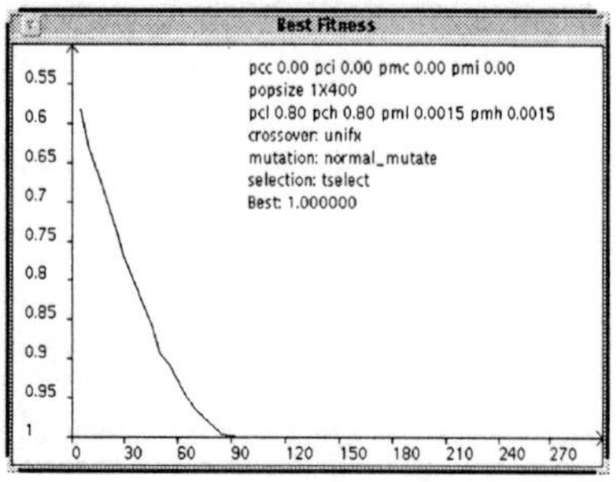

Figure 10: Best/gen in experiment 4

range, so the system always needs some time (generations) to "adjust" to optimal values; thus, it is natural that DAGA2 doesn't behave better than an SGA with suitable parameter settings on this task, which is sufficiently simple task that static values for these settings are appropriate throughout the entire run. As we shall see in other experiments on more difficult problems, for which it is harder to find good parameter settings, or on which static parameter settings and genetic operator choices represent a limitation, DAGA2 performs rather well.

4.2 Robustness of DAGA2 performance

Given a system and a task, one could consider the robustness of the system to be its capacity to achieve a desired value of M_1 given randomly selected values for system inputs ($U(0)$, fixed for all $T \geq 0$), from within a given range of possible values.

Holland described a "Royal Road with potholes" problem at ICGA-93 ([11]), in which he challenged GA methods to complete the assembly of building blocks to level 3 (the penultimate level) of a level-4 problem – i.e., to generate a chromosome with either the first eight or last eight blocks set appropriately. He used a "Cohort GA" ([12]) to attain level 3 with high probability in 10,000 function evaluations. However, we use here the more difficult, level-4 Royal Road simply because we wished to study the robustness of DAGA2 on a problem which was difficult, but in which we could easily visualize the nature of the difficulty.

- **Control of level two DAGA2 process**

For this experiment, DAGA2 was configured so that each subpopulation had 8 (adjacent and diagonal) neighbors. Among level-one subpopulations, DAGA2 used Pm in the range [0.0, 0.002], tournament selection (tourneysize 2), one-point, two-point and uniform crossover, bitwise mutation or multi-bit mutation ([13]), and offspring replacing parents. The range of level-1 crossover values, Pc, is shown in Table 1, as are tr, the number of generations (level 1) between operations at level 2, and Pci, the fraction of a level-1 subpopulation migrated to its neighbors at each interval tr. Probability of mutation of level-2 (control) parameters, Pmc, was 0.3, and crossover probability among parameter strings, Pcc, was 0.8. All runs were terminated when Royal Road level 4 was attained or 60,000 function evaluations were performed.

- **Number of level-two subpopulations**

Most runs were done with 36 subpopulations of 70, because earlier experiments with 5x5 and 4x4 arrays with the same total population size (approximately 2,500 individuals) were much less robust in solving the Royal Road level 4 problem. This is not surprising, both because the smaller number of subpopulations cannot preserve diversity as well even in an ordinary parallel GA, and because doing more evaluations in fewer subpopulations during each interval tr inhibits the rate at which DAGA2 can learn about good parameter settings. That is, with 36 subpopulations and tr=5, DAGA2 performed about 400 level-2 function evaluations during a typical run; with fewer subpopulations, it had much less opportunity to learn about good parameter settings.

- **Level two fitness functions**

The one genuinely difficult decision to make for DAGA2 and any other multi-level evolutionary scheme is the choice of the level-2 fitness function, which expresses what the level two processes are striving to optimize. The goal is a function E which varies monotonically with F, as described above, so it can be used to judge which level-1 GA processes have greater "promise" of attaining a near-optimal solution. It is also among the most important issues to study using a tool like DAGA2. Therefore, in the following experiment, we used DAGA2 with a variety of level-2 fitness functions (these investigations are ongoing).

1) Number of offspring generated with higher

Expt.	*Level2 Params.*	*Succ. Times*	*Avg. Func. Evaluations*
5	6x6x70 *Pc*=[0.2,0.7] *tr*=5 *Pci*=0.07	20/20	47297
6	as in exp. 5 exc. *Pc*=[0.1,0.6]	14/20	36473
7	as in exp. 5 exc. *Pc*=[0.0,1.0]	14/20	34414
8	as in exp. 5 exc. *Pc*=[0.1,0.8]	18/20	43850
9	as in exp. 5 exc. *tr*=8	15/20	52476
10	as in exp. 5 exc. *Pci*=0.05	19/20	46871

Table 1: Results of experiments 5-10, showing attainment of RR level 4 (successes) and average number of function evaluations required, under various DAGA2 level-2 control settings. 6x6x70 means a 6x6 square of subpopulations, each 70 individuals.

fitness than both parents in last *tr* generations

2) (Fitness of best individual) / (number of function evaluations in last *tr* generations)

3) (Number of offspring generated with higher fitness than both parents in last *tr* generations) / (number of function evaluations in last *tr* generations)

Experiment 5 and all others in Table 1 show results with fitness function (3). Experiment 5 was also run with fitness function (1), succeeding 4 of 20 times, with an average of 57,674 function evaluations on successful runs. Fitness function (2) succeeded in 19 of 20 runs, with an average of 36,459 evaluations on successful runs. Measures which reward progress per function evaluation seem likely to produce superior results for many problems when the number of allowable function evaluations is capped, as it was at 60,000 for these runs. We do not yet know whether the greater "exploitation" produced by this per-evaluation pressure increases or decreases the probability of success for this and similar problems given much more generous caps on evaluation numbers.

Experiments on this fitness function constitutes an attempt at optimization at level 3, which is not automated in DAGA2 (that would be in DAGA3). We believe it is important to try to characterize how to define an appropriate function for solving any particular class of problems in the HLO framework.

- **Sensitivity to level 2 parameters**

Experiment 5 showed that DAGA2 could attain Royal Road level four in 20 of 20 runs, in an average of 47,297 function evaluations. DAGA2 is clearly not solving the level 3 problem as efficiently as Holland's Cohort GA, but that is not the goal of this effort; we also do not know how efficiently Holland's Cohort GA would solve the level 4 problem. The other experiments explored the sensitivity of DAGA2's performance to various of its level-2 parameter range settings.

Experiments 6, 7 and 8 vs. 5 showed that altering upper and lower limits (and therefore initial random values) of *Pc* had a negative effect. However, even with no limits on crossover percentage (experiment 7), DAGA2 reached level 4 within 60,000 evaluations in 14/20 runs, demonstrating its insensitivity to this input parameter, and its capacity to evolve a successful optimization algorithm.

Experiment 9 changed *tr* to 8 generations, which had some impact on both success rate and number of evaluations when successful, but success rate remained at 75%.

Experiment 10 decreased *Pci* from 0.07 to 0.05, which reduced the number of migrants to each subpopulation from each of its 8 neighbors at intervals *tr* from 4 to 3. As expected, the influence on the results was very small.

4.3 Discussion

Adaptability and robustness are two closely related issues describing an optimization algorithm's performance on a given range of problems. It is obvious that robustness depends on adaptability. From our experience of applying GAs to various problems, the adapability offered by a classical GA is often not strong enough to achieve adequate performance. At the same time, it shows obvious sensitivity to many aspects of the problem solving process and is not as robust as might be expected.

DAGA2 is intended to address this shortcoming. From the two sets of experiments above, we can see that DAGA2 is able to adjust its internal GAs to appropriate settings during the problem solving process, thus offering a higher level of adaptability to the system. This consequently improves its robustness, which is a very important issue in real-world problem solving.

5 Conclusions

This paper presents a view of function optimization as a two-level optimization process: a lower level representing a black box optimization paradigm, with its internal adaptability for search of the problem space, plus a higher level algorithm which searches the space of external flexibility of the black box paradigm. This search process occurs "on-line" – that is, within a reasonable number of total function evaluations for solution of the low-level optimization problem, rather than as an "off-line" study in preparation for lower-level problem solution.

While many questions remain to be explored, particularly regarding choice of the level-two fitness function appropriate for a given class of problems, DAGA2 appears to be successful in optimizing a particular class of black box optimization algorithms, GAs, in an integrated algorithmic fashion, to solve various interesting problems. This demonstrates the power of the HLO framework presented in this paper. One of our current tasks is to quantify its thereotical and practical ability to boost performance for a given black box optimization algorithm.

References

[1] D.H. Wolpert and W.G. Macready. *No free lunch theorems for search.* Tech. Rep. No. SFI-TR-95-02-010, Santa Fe Institute, Santa Fe, NM, 1995.

[2] T.C. Fogarty, Varying the Probability of Mutation in the Genetic Algorithm, *Proceedings of the Third International Conference on Genetic Algorithms*, Morgan Kaufman, New York.

[3] L. Davis, Adapting Operator Probabilities In Genetic Algorithms, *Proceedings of the Third International Conference on Genetic Algorithms*, Morgan Kaufman, New York.

[4] J.J. Grefenstette. Optimization of control parameters for genetic algorithms. *IEEE Transactions on Systems, Man, and Cybernetics,* SMC-16(1), pages 122-128, 1986.

[5] R. Gabasov and F. Kirillova *The Qualitative Theory of Optimal Processes.* Translated by John L. Casti, Marcel Dekker, Inc. New York, 1976.

[6] K.A. De Jong, W.M. Spears and D.F. Gordon. Using Markov Chains to Analyze GAFOs. *Foundations of Genetic Algorithms*, Morgan Kaufman, New York.

[7] A.E. Nix and M.D. Vose. Modelling genetic algorithms with Markov chains. *Annals of Mathematics and Artificial Intelligence #5*, pages 79-88, 1992.

[8] G. Wang, T. Dexter, E.D. Goodman and W.F. Punch, Optimization Of a GA and Within the GA for a 2-Dimensional Layout Problem. *Proceedings on the First International Conference on Evolutionary Computation and Its Applications*, Russian Academy of Sciences, 1996.

[9] G. Wang, E.D. Goodman and W.F. Punch, Simultaneously Multi-Level Evolutions. GARAGe Technique Report 96-03-01. 1996.

[10] J.H. Holland, *Adaptation in Natural and Artificial Systems.* Ann Arbor: The University of Michigan Press, 1975.

[11] M. Mitchell and J.H. Holland, When Will a Genetic Algorithm Outperform Hill Climbing? *Proceedings of the Fifth International Conference on Genetic Algorithms*, 1993.

[12] John H. Holland, Personal Communications, 1996.

[13] E.D. Goodman, An Introduction to GALOPPS – the Genetic ALgorithm Optimized for Portability and Parallelism System, Release 3.2, *GARAGe Tehnical Report 96-07-01.* 1996.

[14] T. Baeck, F. Hoffmeister, H. Schwefel, A Survey of Evolution Strategies, *Proceedings of the Fourth International Conference of Genetic Algorithms*, pages 2-9, San Diego, 1991.

[15] D. Schlierkamp-Voosen, H. Muhlenbein, Adaptation of Population Sizes by Competing Subpopulations, *Proceedings of International Conference on Evolutionary Computation (ICEC'96)*, pages 330-335, Nagoya, Japan, 1996.

[16] M. Herdy, Reproductive Isolation as Strategy Parameter in Hierarchical Organized Evolution Strategies, *Parallel Problem Solving from Nature (PPSN II)*, Bruxelles, pages 207-217, September 1992.

GA Performance in a Babel-like Fitness Landscape

Hideaki Suzuki
Honda R&D Co., Ltd. Wako Res. Cen.
1-4-1 Chuo, Wako, Saitama 351-01 JPN
h_suzuki@fun.f.rd.honda.co.jp

Yoh Iwasa
Dep. of Biology, Kyushu Univ.
Fukuoka 812-81, JPN
yiwasscb@mbox.nc.kyushu-u.ac.jp

Abstract

The performance of genetic algorithms (GAs) is studied under a babel-like fitness landscape, in which only a one bit sequence is significantly advantageous over the others. Under this landscape, the most dominant process to determine the GA performance is creation of the advantageous sequence, and crossover facilitates the creation, thereby improves the GA performance. We first conduct a computer simulation using the simple GA, and examine the waiting time until domination of the advantageous sequence (T_d). It is shown that crossover with mildly high rate reduces T_d significantly and that the magnitude of this reduction (A_{cross}) is the largest when the mutation rate is an intermediate value. Second, we mathematically analyze the model and estimate the value of A_{cross}. From these observations, we determine implementation criteria for GAs, which are useful when we apply GAs to engineering problems such as having a conspicuously discontinuous fitness landscape.

1: Introduction

Recently in the engineering field, genetic algorithms (GAs) have attracted a great deal of attention as optimization methods [9, 8, 15, 7, 6, 17, 14]. In GAs, each design of an object is typically coded in a gene-like bit sequence and a population of those sequences is prepared. An optimal (or a close to optimal) design is searched for by evolutionary operations including reproduction, natural selection, mutation, and genetic recombination. Among these operations, the most characteristic one is the genetic recombination, or crossover operation. Since GAs without crossover are nothing more than a parallel hill-climbing method, crossover is a key operation to achieve the optimal design in the shortest number of trials. In previous studies, however, crossover's effectiveness in GAs has met with varying degrees of success, depending upon the problem domain and its fitness landscape. We are still far from achieving a complete understanding of GAs, which is important from not only an engineering but also a biological point of view.

Recently, Suzuki [18, 19] proposed an evolutionary programming methodology, MUNCs, in which multiple von Neumann computers with machine language architecture evolve towards the creation of a program that solves a problem prepared in an environmental database. He used GAs for the evolution of MUNCs and found that crossover contributed to the acceleration. Fig. 1 shows the basic evolutionary picture of this system. A sequence of binary bits, which is represented in a row of a binary matrix, codes a program which determines the function of the computer. A part of this bit sequence can constitute an advantageous "schema" which corresponds to a set of machine instructions with an advantageous function, and through the processes shown in Fig. 1(b), those functional schemas appear and dominate the population. Because in MUNCs typical *order*s of those advantageous schemas are rather large, evolution proceeds with a discontinuous picture; long neutral evolutionary periods [10] are punctuated by intermittent short adaptive evolutionary phases during which advantageous schemas spread through the population. In this paper, we use a simpler model and study the acceleration effect by the crossover in MUNCs. We focus on a single advantageous schema and conduct a computer simulation examining the time until an advantageous schema comes to predominate. Taking after MUNCs, the fitness landscape is a babel-like one: an individual enjoys a very high selective advantage if the advantageous schema is present in that individual, and all other sequences without the schema are assumed to be neutral. This very epistatic fitness function makes 'creation' the most dominant process in evolution, and makes crossover a beneficial process

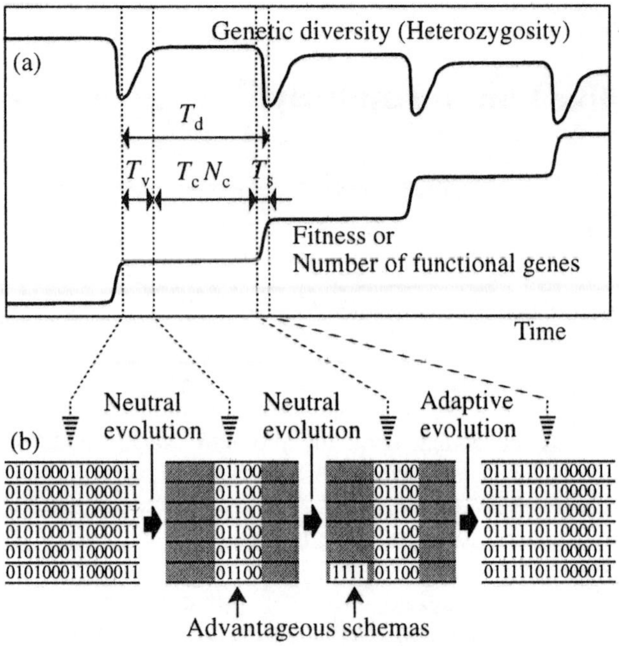

Figure 1 Basic evolutionary picture considered

for faster evolution.

In the following, we first conduct a computer simulation of the GA, and then mathematically analyze it. In the last section, we discuss the implications of the results, in relation to conventional notions about GA mechanisms.

2: Simulation with simple GAs

2.1: The model

Basic assumptions for the model are as follows:

- Individuals are haploid and each individual's genome is represented by a string of a large number of binary (0-1) bits.
- Among all sequences, one sequence (schema), denoted by $[11\cdots1]$, has fitness by far larger than the others, and all the other sequences are of the same fitness level.
- The mating pair is randomly chosen from the sufficiently large population.

The evolutionary speed is measured in terms of the average number of generations from the initial setting until the advantageous schema dominates the population which is called the domination time, T_d. (Here the term 'domination' does not mean that one chromosome completely occupies the population. The precise definition of domination will be given later.) According to the evolutionary picture shown in Fig. 1, evolution proceeds in the following three steps.

Step (i) [Diversification]: Mutation stores diversity in currently useless regions of the genome.

Step (ii) [Creation]: A novel advantageous schema is created in some individual by chance and begins to spread through the population.

Step (iii) [Spread]: The new advantageous schema spreads and dominates the population.

Accordingly, the domination time T_d is decomposed into three parts as follows.

$$T_d = T_v + T_cN_c + T_s, \tag{1}$$

where

T_v = the diversification time defined as the average number of generations taken for the population to store sufficient diversity starting from the initial uniform distribution;

T_c = the creation time defined as the average number of generations between one appearance and the next appearance of the advantageous schema in a sufficiently diverse population;

N_c = the creation number defined as the average number of appearances of the advantageous schema from its absence until it begins to spread;

T_s = the spread time defined as the average number of generations for a novel advantageous schema to spread through the population.

Note that in a finite population, advantageous sequences created have a chance to disappear so that creation and extinction of the advantageous sequence might be repeated many times until its final domination.

Since crossover is a process to randomize the population, T_c decreases and N_c increases with the crossover rate. When the crossover rate is very low, T_c is large and when it is very high, N_c is large. This makes T_d minimum at a moderate crossover rate, and the reduction rate of T_d is studied through the simulation.

Let l be the total number of bits in the sequence, or the number of bits necessary to realize a novel advantageous schema (this is equal to the 'order' of the schema), N be the population size, N_e be the effective population size, s be the selection coefficient of the advantageous schema relative to the other sequences, u be the mutation rate (probability of bit flipping) per locus (bit position) per generation, c be the probability of the crossover point (chiasma) occurring between neighboring binary loci, r be the ratio of the fraction of the population which participates in crossover.

The value of s is taken to be 1 throughout this paper. Two parameters, c and r, specify the crossover rate. When $r < 1$, the population is divided into two parts, the recombining subpopulation and the non-recombining subpopulation. At this time the random mating assumption does not literally hold true but is considered to be approximately valid in that participants in crossover are randomly chosen from the population at each generation. The following simulations are conducted in "few-points major-participants (FPAP)" mode ($c < 0.5$ and $r = 1$) or "many-points minor-participants (MPIP)" mode ($c = 0.5$ and $r < 1$) [20].

The simulation procedure is as follows:

Step 0: [Initial setting] Prepare N sequences of I bits and substitute them with the sequence determined arbitrarily. Hence in this setting, the population has a uniform distribution.

Step 1: [Selection] In proportion to fitness values ($1 + s = 2$ for the advantageous schema and 1 for neutral sequences), select N sequences randomly from the whole population and create copies of them. This makes a new population of sequences for the next generation (the standard process of roulette selection).

Step 2: [Mutation] Choose a binary allele randomly out of all bit sequences and flip it. This modification is repeated so that the number of binary loci subjected to modifications might be approximately equal to NIu.

Step 3: [Crossover] Choose Nr sequences out of the population and pair them randomly. Between each pair, recombine binary strings with the cross-points' occurrence probability being equal to c at every interbit gap. Then, return to Step 1.

Note that $N_e = N$ in the standard roulette selection in Step 1. The generation cycle (recursion of Steps 1~3) is continued until the mean population fitness exceeds 1.5, i.e., until the frequency of the advantageous schema exceeds 0.5 (this is the precise definition of 'domination' in this paper). Through this recursion, the generation number at the time of the first appearance of the $[11\cdots1]$ sequence ($T_v + T_c$) and the generation number at the time of 'domination' (T_d) are measured. The program for the simulation was written in the ANSI-C language and run on a desk-top MIMD computer, Parsytec XPLORER with sixteen Power PCs (80MHz). For each set of parameters, numerical trials were executed fifteen times and the mean values were calculated.

2.2: Results

Fig. 2 shows the results for (a) c-dependence in FPAP mode and (b) r-dependence in MPIP mode. The other parameters are taken to be $I = 20$, $N = N_e = 4096$, and $u = 0.002$. This figure shows that T_d is minimum at an intermediate optimum crossover rate for both modes of crossover. This result is understood as follows. Since both mutation and crossover have a function to create novel sequences, when the mutation rate is not sufficiently high for the mutations to lead to complete randomization of the population, crossover helps create novel sequences of bits and reduces T_c. In the region of lower c/r in Fig. 2(a)/2(b), both T_d and $T_v + T_c$ decrease with c/r. If c/r is too high, however, the created advantageous schemas are destroyed by crossover and cannot spread in the population. This increases N_c and brings about a conspicuous increase in T_d. In the higher c/r region in Fig. 2, $T_v + T_c$ does not increase with c/r, whereas T_d increases markedly.

Since this acceleration is due to the randomization by crossover, the acceleration rate is expected to decrease with the mutation rate u because when u is sufficiently high, sequences are fully randomized by mutation. When u is too low, on the other hand, population diversity is lost and crossover, which is effective only for heterogenous regions of haplotypes, is ineffective. Hence the acceleration rate, defined as

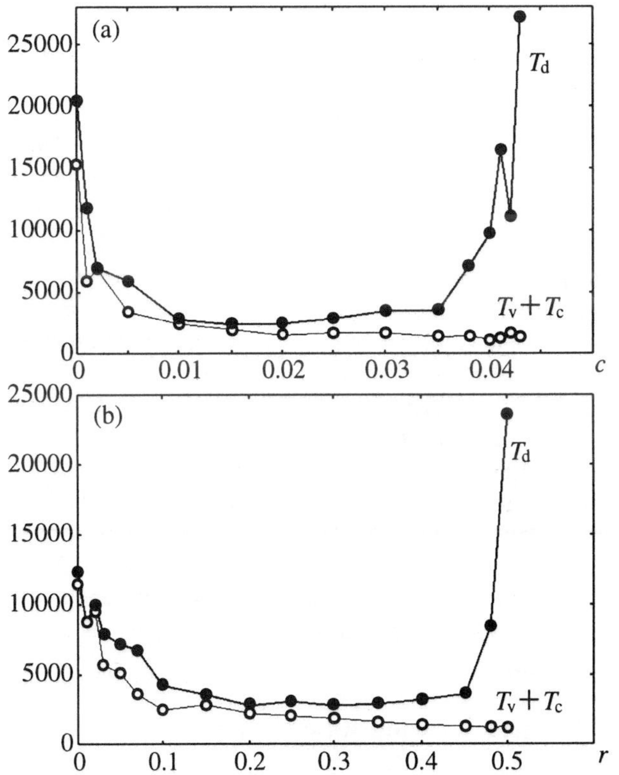

Figure 2 Waiting time until creation/domination of the advantageous sequence as a function of the crossover rate

$$A_{\mathrm{cross}} \equiv \frac{T_{\mathrm{d}}|_{c=0}}{T_{\mathrm{d}}|_{c=0.015}} \text{ (for FPAP-mode)}, \qquad (2)$$

is expected to be maximum at a moderate value of u. The marked points in Fig. 3(a) show the results for this dependence, derived from the simulation. The parameter values are taken to be $I = 12$ and $N = N_e = 500$(○), 2000(●), or 10000(▲). The results for $N = N_e = 500$ or 2000 indicate that A_{cross} is maximum at an intermediate u. Although for $N = N_e = 10000$ the value of A_{cross} monotonically increases with a decrease in u, if we had conducted the simulation in much lower region of u (this cannot accomplished within a practical simulation time), A_{cross} is considered to have the maximum value at an optimal u.

3: Mathematical analysis

Here we mathematically analyze the above model to quantitatively understand the simulation results and to estimate the value of A_{cross} in wide ranges of genetic parameters. Analyses in this section are carried out using the following approximations:

- The 0-1 distribution at the i-th locus is determined only by the parameter q_i, which denotes the frequency of allele 1's, independently of the other loci.
- Selection and mutation supply a new randomly-chosen frequency vector $\{q_i\}$ every generation.
- The spread time T_s is neglected.

Strictly speaking in the present model, the allele distribution is more or less in linkage disequilibrium on account of less than complete recombination, so that there exist some correlations between the loci. However, to incorporate this effect into the analyses is very difficult and we here neglect this correlation as a very rough approximation. The second approximation is valid when $N_e u$ is large enough to make the allele distribution at each locus not inclined to 0 or 1. The third approximation is valid because a large s makes an advantageous sequence which has escaped from the initial danger of extinction spread rapidly until its frequency exceeds 0.5. Although the following formulation is similar to that given in [20], here we improve the accuracy by considering T_v, N_c, and the reduction of heterozygosity caused by the finiteness of the population size.

3.1: Diversification time

Diversification is a process promoted by mutation. Although crossover induces the creation of

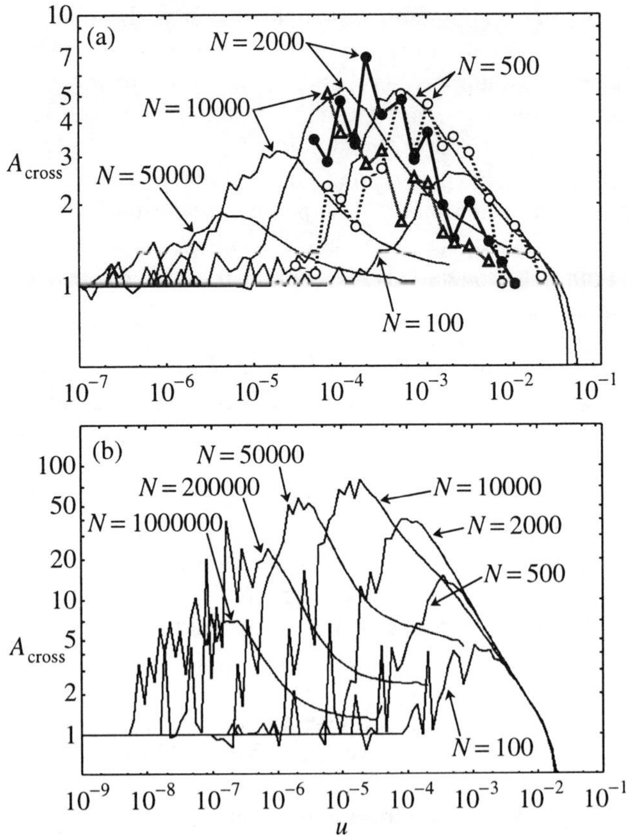

Figure 3 Rate of evolutionary acceleration by crossover as a function of the mutation rate (FPAP mode)

novel sequences, this creation process is based upon currently stored diversity and crossover itself cannot increase the diversity. Therefore, $H^{(t)}$, that is, heterozygosity at generation t, is determined only by mutation and random genetic drift and given by the following equation.

$$H^{(t)} = \frac{2N_e u}{1 + 4N_e u}\left[1 - \exp(-(\frac{1}{N_e} + 4u)\,t)\right], \qquad (3)$$

In the derivation of this equation, approximations $u \ll 1$ and $N_e \gg 1$ are used (see [10] chap. 8). According to this equation, the value of $H^{(t)}$, which is initially 0, gradually approaches the value of $H^{(\infty)}$ with relaxation time $(1/N_e + 4u)^{-1}$. Hence, the diversification time T_v is roughly estimated as

$$T_v = (\frac{1}{N_e} + 4u)^{-1} \qquad (4)$$

3.2: Creation time

Let P_c be the creation probability defined as the probability of at least one advantageous sequence appearing from absence in the population. If we assume that there is no markedly large value of P_c before creation of the advantageous sequence, T_c is approximately given by

$$T_c \sim \{\langle P_c \rangle_{BC}\}^{-1}, \quad (5)$$

where $\langle\ \rangle_{BC}$ denotes the expected value before creation of the advantageous sequence. P_c is formulated with the frequency of the advantageous sequence, x_I. Since the probability of a randomly chosen sequence becoming an advantageous one is equal to x_I, P_c before creation is given by

$$\langle P_c \rangle_{BC} \sim N \langle \Delta x_I \rangle_{BC}, \quad (6)$$

where Δx_I is the increment of x_I from zero per generation.

By lumping neutral sequences, Δx_I by selection, mutation, or crossover per generation is formulated as

$$\Delta x_I^{(\text{sel.})} = \frac{s x_I (1 - x_I)}{1 + s x_I}, \quad (7a)$$

$$\Delta x_I^{(\text{mut.})} = \frac{1}{1 - \prod q_i} [(\prod \{u + (1-2u) q_i\} - \prod q_i) \times (1 - x_I) + \{1 - (1-u)^I\} (\prod q_i - x_I)], \quad (7b)$$

$$\Delta x_I^{(\text{cross.})} = \frac{r \cdot P_{\text{des}} (1 - x_I) (\prod q_i - x_I)}{(1 - \prod q_i)^2}, \quad (7c)$$

where $\prod q_i = \prod_{i=1}^{I} q_i$ is the product of q_is for all loci and P_{des} is the probability of an advantageous sequence being destroyed by recombination with a randomly chosen sequence. These formulas are valid for general situations in which $H^{(\infty)}$ is smaller than 0.5 and q_i is either larger or smaller than 0.5. See Appendix A for the derivations of Eqs. (7b) and (7c), and Appendix B for the detailed expression for P_{des}. Using Eqs. (6) and (7a)~(7c) for which $x_I = 0$ was substituted, $\langle P_c \rangle_{BC}$ is formulated as

$$\langle P_c \rangle_{BC} \cong N [\langle \Delta x_I^{(\text{mut.})} \rangle_{BC} + \langle \Delta x_I^{(\text{cross.})} \rangle_{BC}] = N \left\langle \frac{\prod \{u + (1-2u) q_i\} - (1-u)^I \prod q_i}{1 - \prod q_i} \right\rangle_{BC} + N \left\langle \frac{r \cdot P_{\text{des}} \prod q_i}{(1 - \prod q_i)^2} \right\rangle_{BC}, \quad (8)$$

$\langle X \rangle_{BC}$s in Eq. (8) are evaluated as follows. If there were no selection (i.e., $s = 0$), after the lapse of T_v, namely after the population has stored sufficient diversity at a given parameter condition, the population would be in the equilibrium state wherein each q_i obeys the beta distribution described by

$$h(q) \equiv \frac{\Gamma(4\beta)}{\{\Gamma(2\beta)\}^2} q^{2\beta - 1} (1 - q)^{2\beta - 1}, \quad \beta \equiv N_e u. \quad (9)$$

For the derivation, see [1, 4] for example. Hence, according to the second basic assumption in this section, we can calculate $\langle X \rangle_{BC}$ by using the weight that is the product of $\prod h(q_i)$ and W_{BC}. W_{BC} is the weight for 'Before Creation' defined as the probability of the advantageous sequence not appearing in the population under a given frequency vector $\{q_i\}$. Because the value of W_{BC} changes most drastically around the region where $\prod q_i \sim 1/N$, we have only to formulate W_{BC} precisely around that region. Hence, we assume that $\prod q_i$ (the probability of a randomly chosen sequence being the advantageous one) is very small and that the number of the advantageous sequence in the population (we express it by n_I) obeys the Poisson distribution with average $N \prod q_i$;

$$p(n_I) \equiv (\text{the probability of the number of the advantageous sequence in the population being } n_I) = \frac{(N \prod q_i)^{n_I}}{n_I!} \cdot \exp(-N \prod q_i).$$

Then W_{BC} is given by

$$W_{BC} = p(0) = \exp(-N \prod q_i). \quad (10)$$

The final formula for $\langle X \rangle_{BC}$ is

$$\langle X \rangle_{BC} = \frac{\int_0^1 \cdots \int_0^1 W_{BC} X \prod_i h(q_i) dq_i}{\int_0^1 \cdots \int_0^1 W_{BC} \prod_i h(q_i) dq_i}. \quad (11)$$

We can numerically estimate the value of $\langle X \rangle_{BC}$ by the Monte Carlo method (Appendix C).

3.3: Creation number

The creation number is calculated from the extinction probability z, which is defined as the probability of a newly created advantageous sequence becoming extinct;

$$N_c = \sum_{k=1}^{\infty} k \cdot (\text{probability of the } k\text{-th appearance of the advantageous sequence occasioning the final domination}) = \sum_{k=1}^{\infty} k \cdot z^{k-1} (1 - z) = \frac{1}{1 - z}. \quad (12)$$

In order to formulate z, we assume that the expected frequency of the advantageous schema is very low and that the number of offspring of the advantageous schema has a Poisson distribution with a mean value μ. Then, the population genetic method of the 'branching process' [5, 4] gives the relation

$$z = \exp(-\mu (1 - z)). \quad (13)$$

μ is the expected value of the ratio of x_I at the next generation compared to the current x_I and can be approximately formulated as the product of the frequency ratios for selection, mutation, and crossover;

$$\mu = \left(1 + \langle \frac{\Delta x_I^{(\text{sel.})}}{x_I} \rangle_{\text{AC}}\right)\left(1 + \langle \frac{\Delta x_I^{(\text{mut.})}}{x_I} \rangle_{\text{AC}}\right) \times \left(1 + \langle \frac{\Delta x_I^{(\text{cross.})}}{x_I} \rangle_{\text{AC}}\right), \quad (14)$$

where $\langle \; \rangle_{\text{AC}}$ denotes the expected value immediately after creation of the advantageous sequence. By substituting $x_I = 1/N$ for Eqs. (7a)~(7c), we can derive the detailed formulas for $\langle (\Delta x_I)/x_I \rangle_{\text{AC}}$s (Appendix D). $\langle X \rangle_{\text{AC}}$ is calculated from the similar method to that for $\langle X \rangle_{\text{BC}}$. By use of the assumption of the Poisson distribution, the weight for 'immediately After Creation' W_{AC} is formulated as

$$W_{\text{AC}} = p(1) \propto (\prod q_i) \exp(-N \prod q_i). \quad (15)$$

Then $\langle X \rangle_{\text{AC}}$ is calculated as the weighted average using a weight that is the product of $\prod h(q_i)$ and W_{AC}.

By combining the above formulas, we can calculate the value of N_c as a function of the genetic parameter set. Eq. (13) can be numerically solved by Newton-Raphson's method and $\langle X \rangle_{\text{AC}}$ is estimated numerically by the Monte Carlo method (Appendix C).

3.4: Numerical results

By combining Eqs. (2), (1), (4), (5), and (12) and neglecting T_s, we can calculate the theoretical value of A_{cross} as a function of the genetic parameters. The calculation is also conducted on Parsytec XPLORER. The fine solid lines in Fig. 3 show the results of this estimation of A_{cross} for (a) $I = 12$ and (b) $I = 20$. N_e is taken to be equal to N. (For each value of N, the value of A_{cross} noisily fluctuates in the region of lower u because of limitations of the Monte Carlo estimation method (see Appendix C).)

These results support the notion that there exists an intermediate optimal value of u which maximizes A_{cross}. Fig. 3(a), in which the results from the simple GA simulation are also plotted with marked points, shows that theoretical values agree well with experimental ones, except that when $N = 10000$, the theoretical values are smaller than the experimental ones. This inconsistency comes from the second basic assumption in this section. When $\beta = N_e u$ is low in the GA simulation, the frequency q_is are almost always inclined to 0 or 1 and the distribution of vector $\{q_i\}$ is dependent upon the former values of q_is. Hence, if we neglect this dependence and calculate $\langle X \rangle_{\text{BC}} / \langle X \rangle_{\text{AC}}$ with the weight $\prod h(q_i)$, we underestimate the diversity's reduction effect which causes the advantage of crossover in the region of moderately lower u.

Finally we point out the I-dependence of A_{cross}. As is clear by comparison of Figs. 3(a) and 3(b), the maximum acceleration rate A_{cross} increases geometrically with I. This indicates that the larger the 'order' of the schema to be created, the larger the acceleration effect of crossover is.

4: Discussion

From the study of evolutionary speed, i.e., the mean number of generations until appearance and domination of the advantageous schema, it was found that when the mutation rate is neither too high nor too low, fairly frequent crossover can greatly reduce the time until the domination of an advantageous schema. This acceleration effect was studied under various genetic parameters, and it was found that the acceleration rate is larger with a larger order of the advantageous schema to be created at once. The key point responsible for this result is the babel-like fitness landscape assumed in the model. In this landscape, evolutionary speed is determined by the creation rate of an advantageous schema. Both mutation and crossover can enhance this creation process; hence, when the mutation rate is not sufficiently high for the mutations to lead to complete randomization of the population, crossover can be a beneficial process for faster evolution.

The conventional theory of GAs has been argued based upon the 'building block hypothesis' (BBH) [9] stating that the final solution is achieved through the combination of good component schemas. Many good schemas which are candidates for components of the final solution were considered to spread parallel in 'implicit parallelism' [8], and the crossover operation in GAs has been considered to help combine those component schemas into a single individual to create a more advantageous sequence (Fig. 4(a)).

The implicit parallelism was first doubted by Mitchell *et al.* [15]. They assumed a discontinuous fitness function similar to the present one (they called it 'the royal road function'), studied the GA performance, and found that hitchhiking (they called this 'premature convergence') diminishes the GA performance. Hitchhiking caused by the spread of a very advantageous schema sweeps out the other mildly advantageous schemas, and the population under GA operations could not store many component schemas at once. Although this result made them cast doubt on the implicit parallelism, they studied the GA perfor-

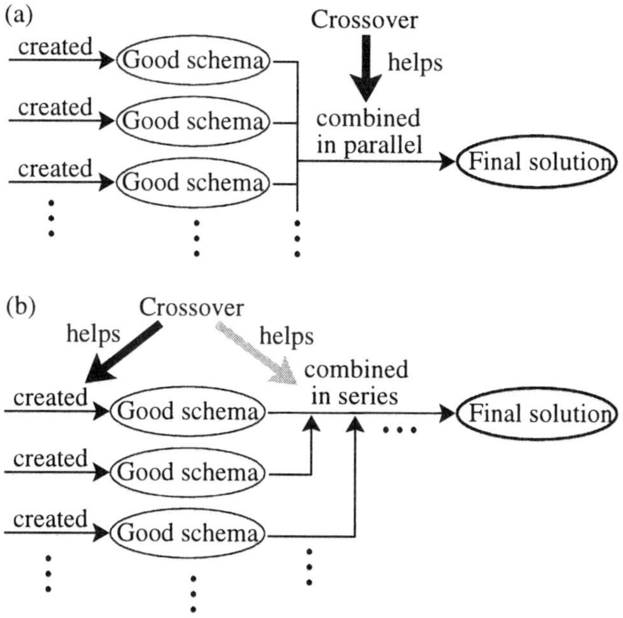

Figure 4 Mechanism of GAs ((a)Conventional and (b)Proposed)

mance focusing on the time necessary for smaller--order schemas to combine to form the larger-order schema and did not examine the influence of crossover on the creation time of the schemas, probably because they had a notion that crossover is useful in combining good schemas.

However, when the fitness landscape is a discontinuous one as a babel-like function or royal road function, evolution proceeds according to the picture shown in Fig. 4(b) rather than that shown in Fig. 4(a). Creation and domination of advantageous component schemas take place not in parallel but serially (one by one). The BBH, if it only asserts that the final solution is made of component good schemas, is valid, and yet in this picture, the primary role of crossover is not to combine created schemas but to create novel schemas. Since this creation (randomization) process is nothing more than that by mutation, when only one good schema is searched for in the bit string, mutation suffices.

Of course, mutation and crossover are not identical operations. The main difference between them is in the workings on established functions. Mutation, which is a blind substitution of bits, destroys the established schemas, whereas crossover, which has no effect on the heterogenous regions of the sequence, can preserve schemas once they are fixed in the population. Accordingly, when we wish to make a very advantageous solution composed of a large number of good schemas, we must keep the mutation rate very low to preserve those schemas. Some investigators have studied this 'error catastrophe' problem in detail [3, 20], and concluded that the mutation rate must be kept low in inverse proportion to the total *order* of good schemas that must be fixed in a population. When the mutation rate is low and the mutations cannot result in complete randomization of the population, crossover helps create novel schemas and can greatly enhance the rate of evolution. The population of sequences that has accumulated many functional schemas can evolve with this creation by crossover which selectively randomizes nonfunctional regions of bit sequences.

These roles and limitations of crossover are the key points in application of GAs to the problem domain with a discontinuous fitness landscape. The implementation rules for genetic parameters in these problems are summarized as follows:

- The mutation rate u must be adjusted to moderate values to enhance evolutionary acceleration by crossover.
- The crossover rate (c or r) must be neither too high nor too low for faster evolution.
- The rate of acceleration by crossover increases geometrically with the order of the advantageous schema to be created at once.

Although these rules are not applicable to all engineering problems for which GAs are used, there exists a class of problems which has a discontinuous fitness function treated here. Genetic programming (GP) using machine language architecture is one such problem. In machine language GP, a program is represented by a very long bit sequence and a functional set of machine codes corresponds to an advantageous schema. As a consequence, evolution typically proceeds with the discontinuous picture shown in Fig. 1, and use of GAs can be a powerful strategy for developing the optimal program in such systems. In [18, 19], GAs were used to create an advantageous function in the program memory and crossover evidently contributed to the acceleration of the creation. Fig. 7 in [19] qualitatively agrees well with Fig. 3 in this paper.

We finish this discussion by pointing out the biological meaning of the above results [20]. In a biological context, the widespread occurrence of sexuality, or genetic recombination in living organisms has been an enigma over the decades [22, 12, 11, 13]. Since Fisher [5] and Muller [16] first proposed the notion that recombination accelerates evolution by combining advantageous mutations which arise separately in different individuals into a single individual, many theoretical population biologists have tested this notion; nevertheless definite evidence of this acceleration effect has not been found because recombination not only creates advantageous combinations but also destroys the created advantageous combinations. The basic picture of the Fisher-Muller theory is the same as that in Fig. 4(a), and in this sense, this theory makes the same argument as the BBH based upon implicit parallelism. When we consider the meaning of recombination in the light of the present results, however, we find that recombination might be useful not because it can spread advantageous genes in parallel but because it can help create a new advantageous combination of genes. Actually in the living world, some advantageous biological functions are achieved by a set of many genes, and the fitness landscape is conspicuously discontinuous in the DNA regions coding those functions [20].

Appendix A: Derivation of the formulas for $\Delta x_I^{(\mathrm{mut.})}$ and $\Delta x_I^{(\mathrm{cross.})}$

To formulate $\Delta x_I^{(\mathrm{mut.})}$, we consider the elementary process of mutation to be divided into the following steps: first we randomly choose a sequence from the population and substitute it for the sequence site A. Next, we flip bits in the sequence with the probability u, and then we put the sequence back into the population. Let A_{bef} denote the event that a sequence chosen for site A is advantageous before mutation and A_{aft} denote the event that the sequence at site A is advantageous after mutation. Hereafter we use the following notations for probability; $P(X)$ is the probability of event X occurring, and $P(X|Y)$ or $P_Y(X)$ are the conditional probability that event X occurs on the condition of event Y occurring. Then, $\Delta x_I^{(\mathrm{mut.})}$ is written as

$$\begin{aligned}
&\Delta x_I^{(\mathrm{mut.})} \\
&= [P(A_{\mathrm{aft}}|A_{\mathrm{bef}})x_I + P(A_{\mathrm{aft}}|\overline{A_{\mathrm{bef}}})(1-x_I)] - x_I \\
&= \frac{P(\overline{A_{\mathrm{bef}}} \wedge A_{\mathrm{aft}})}{P(\overline{A_{\mathrm{bef}}})}(1-x_I) - \{1-P(A_{\mathrm{aft}}|A_{\mathrm{bef}})\}x_I \\
&= \frac{P(A_{\mathrm{aft}}) - P(A_{\mathrm{bef}} \wedge A_{\mathrm{aft}})}{P(\overline{A_{\mathrm{bef}}})}(1-x_I) \\
&\quad -\{1-P(A_{\mathrm{aft}}|A_{\mathrm{bef}})\}x_I \\
&= \frac{P(A_{\mathrm{aft}}) - P(A_{\mathrm{bef}})P(A_{\mathrm{aft}}|A_{\mathrm{bef}})}{1-P(A_{\mathrm{bef}})}(1-x_I) \\
&\quad -\{1-P(A_{\mathrm{aft}}|A_{\mathrm{bef}})\}x_I
\end{aligned}$$

By substituting this formula with $P(A_{\mathrm{aft}}) = \prod\{(1-u)q_i + u(1-q_i)\}$, $P(A_{\mathrm{bef}}) = \prod q_i$ (these are valid on account of the first basic assumption in section 3), and $P(A_{\mathrm{aft}}|A_{\mathrm{bef}}) = (1-u)^I$, we obtain Eq. (7b).

As for crossover, we also consider the elementary crossover process to be divided into the following steps: first we randomly choose two sequences from the population and substitute them for sites A and B, next we recombine these two sequences, and then we put them back into the population. Let $A_{\mathrm{bef}}/B_{\mathrm{bef}}$ denote the event that an original sequence chosen for site A/B is advantageous before crossover and $A_{\mathrm{aft}}/B_{\mathrm{aft}}$ denote the event that the sequence on site A/B is advantageous after crossover. With these symbols, we define the following probabilities:

$$\begin{aligned}
P_{\mathrm{an}} &\equiv P(A_{\mathrm{aft}} \wedge \overline{B_{\mathrm{aft}}}|A_{\mathrm{bef}} \wedge \overline{B_{\mathrm{bef}}}), \\
P_{\mathrm{na}} &\equiv P(A_{\mathrm{aft}} \wedge \overline{B_{\mathrm{aft}}}|\overline{A_{\mathrm{bef}}} \wedge B_{\mathrm{bef}}), \\
P_{\mathrm{nn}} &\equiv P(A_{\mathrm{aft}} \wedge \overline{B_{\mathrm{aft}}}|\overline{A_{\mathrm{bef}}} \wedge \overline{B_{\mathrm{bef}}}).
\end{aligned}$$

$\Delta x_I^{(\mathrm{cross.})}$ is written as

$$\begin{aligned}
&\Delta x_I^{(\mathrm{cross.})} \\
&= r[x_I^2 + (P_{\mathrm{an}} + P_{\mathrm{na}})x_I(1-x_I) + P_{\mathrm{nn}}(1-x_I)^2] - rx_I \\
&= r(1-x_I)[P_{\mathrm{nn}}(1-x_I) - (1-P_{\mathrm{an}}-P_{\mathrm{na}})x_I]. \quad \text{(A.1)}
\end{aligned}$$

First we transform P_{nn};

$$\begin{aligned}
P_{\mathrm{nn}} &= P(A_{\mathrm{aft}} \wedge \overline{B_{\mathrm{aft}}}|\overline{A_{\mathrm{bef}}} \wedge \overline{B_{\mathrm{bef}}}) \\
&= \frac{P(A_{\mathrm{aft}} \wedge \overline{A_{\mathrm{bef}}} \wedge \overline{B_{\mathrm{bef}}})}{P(\overline{A_{\mathrm{bef}}} \wedge \overline{B_{\mathrm{bef}}})} \\
&= \frac{P(A_{\mathrm{aft}} \wedge \overline{A_{\mathrm{bef}}}) - P(A_{\mathrm{aft}} \wedge \overline{A_{\mathrm{bef}}} \wedge B_{\mathrm{bef}})}{P(\overline{A_{\mathrm{bef}}})P(\overline{B_{\mathrm{bef}}})} \\
&= \frac{1}{P(\overline{A_{\mathrm{bef}}})P(\overline{B_{\mathrm{bef}}})}[P(A_{\mathrm{aft}}) - P(A_{\mathrm{aft}} \wedge A_{\mathrm{bef}}) \\
&\quad - P(A_{\mathrm{aft}} \wedge B_{\mathrm{bef}}) + P(A_{\mathrm{aft}} \wedge A_{\mathrm{bef}} \wedge B_{\mathrm{bef}})] \\
&= \frac{1}{(1-P(A_{\mathrm{bef}}))^2}[P(A_{\mathrm{aft}}) - P(A_{\mathrm{bef}})P(A_{\mathrm{aft}}|A_{\mathrm{bef}}) \\
&\quad - P(A_{\mathrm{bef}})P(B_{\mathrm{aft}}|A_{\mathrm{bef}}) + P(A_{\mathrm{bef}})P(B_{\mathrm{bef}}|A_{\mathrm{bef}})].
\end{aligned}$$

Since crossover does not change the values of q_is which determines the probability of a randomly chosen sequence being an advantageous one, $P(A_{\mathrm{aft}}) = P(A_{\mathrm{bef}}) = \prod q_i$. Therefore,

$$\begin{aligned}
P_{\mathrm{nn}} &= \frac{P(A_{\mathrm{bef}})}{(1-P(A_{\mathrm{bef}}))^2}[1 - P(A_{\mathrm{aft}}|A_{\mathrm{bef}}) - P(B_{\mathrm{aft}}|A_{\mathrm{bef}}) \\
&\quad + P(A_{\mathrm{aft}} \wedge B_{\mathrm{aft}}|A_{\mathrm{bef}})] \\
&= \frac{P(A_{\mathrm{bef}})[1 - P(A_{\mathrm{aft}} \vee B_{\mathrm{aft}}|A_{\mathrm{bef}})]}{(1-P(A_{\mathrm{bef}}))^2} \\
&= \frac{P(A_{\mathrm{bef}})P(\overline{A_{\mathrm{aft}}} \wedge \overline{B_{\mathrm{aft}}}|A_{\mathrm{bef}})}{(1-P(A_{\mathrm{bef}}))^2}
\end{aligned}$$

$$= \frac{(\prod q_i)\, P_{\text{des}}}{(1-\prod q_i)^2}. \qquad \text{(A.2)}$$

Here P_{des} is the probability of an advantageous sequence being destroyed by recombination with a randomly chosen sequence formulated as

$$P_{\text{des}} \equiv P(\overline{A_{\text{aft}}} \wedge \overline{B_{\text{aft}}} \mid A_{\text{bef}}). \qquad \text{(A.3)}$$

$1 - P_{\text{an}} - P_{\text{na}}$ is transformed as

$$\begin{aligned}
&1 - P_{\text{an}} - P_{\text{na}} \\
&= 1 - P(A_{\text{aft}} \wedge \overline{B_{\text{aft}}} \mid A_{\text{bef}} \wedge \overline{B_{\text{bef}}}) - P(A_{\text{aft}} \wedge \overline{B_{\text{aft}}} \mid \overline{A_{\text{bef}}} \wedge B_{\text{bef}}) \\
&= 1 - P(A_{\text{aft}} \wedge \overline{B_{\text{aft}}} \mid A_{\text{bef}} \wedge \overline{B_{\text{bef}}}) - P(\overline{A_{\text{aft}}} \wedge B_{\text{aft}} \mid A_{\text{bef}} \wedge \overline{B_{\text{bef}}}) \\
&= P(\overline{A_{\text{aft}}} \wedge \overline{B_{\text{aft}}} \mid A_{\text{bef}} \wedge \overline{B_{\text{bef}}}) + P(A_{\text{aft}} \wedge B_{\text{aft}} \mid A_{\text{bef}} \wedge \overline{B_{\text{bef}}}) \\
&= \frac{P(\overline{A_{\text{aft}}} \wedge \overline{B_{\text{aft}}} \wedge A_{\text{bef}} \wedge \overline{B_{\text{bef}}})}{P(A_{\text{bef}} \wedge \overline{B_{\text{bef}}})} \\
&= \frac{P(\overline{A_{\text{aft}}} \wedge \overline{B_{\text{aft}}} \wedge A_{\text{bef}}) - P(\overline{A_{\text{aft}}} \wedge \overline{B_{\text{aft}}} \wedge A_{\text{bef}} \wedge B_{\text{bef}})}{P(A_{\text{bef}}) - P(A_{\text{bef}} \wedge B_{\text{bef}})} \\
&= \frac{P(\overline{A_{\text{aft}}} \wedge \overline{B_{\text{aft}}} \wedge A_{\text{bef}})}{P(A_{\text{bef}})\,(1 - P(B_{\text{bef}}))} \\
&= \frac{P_{\text{des}}}{1 - \prod q_i}. \qquad \text{(A.4)}
\end{aligned}$$

We can derive Eq. (7c) by substituting Eqs. (A.2) and (A.4) for Eq. (A.1).

Appendix B: Detailed expression for P_{des}

Using the notations defined in Appendix A, P_{des} (Eq. (A.3)) is transformed as

$$\begin{aligned}
P_{\text{des}} &= P_{A_{\text{bef}}}(\overline{A_{\text{aft}}} \wedge \overline{B_{\text{aft}}}) \\
&= 1 + P_{A_{\text{bef}}}(A_{\text{aft}} \wedge B_{\text{aft}}) - P_{A_{\text{bef}}}(A_{\text{aft}}) - P_{A_{\text{bef}}}(B_{\text{aft}}) \\
&= 1 + P_{A_{\text{bef}}}(B_{\text{bef}}) - P_{A_{\text{bef}}}(A_{\text{aft}}) - P_{A_{\text{bef}}}(B_{\text{aft}}).
\end{aligned}$$

Detailed expressions for $P_{A_{\text{bef}}}(A_{\text{aft}})$ and $P_{A_{\text{bef}}}(B_{\text{aft}})$ can be derived from the recursion method established by Suzuki [20]. Let U_i/E_i denote the event that i-th bit pair is unexchanged/exchanged by crossover and A_i/B_i denote the event that leftmost (earlier) i bits on the site A/B are all 1 after crossover. (Note that $A_{\text{aft}}/B_{\text{aft}}$ coincides with A_l/B_l respectively.) Based upon the first basic assumption in section 3, we can set up a recursion formula as

$$\begin{aligned}
&\left[P_{A_{\text{bef}}}(U_i \wedge A_i)\ P_{A_{\text{bef}}}(E_i \wedge A_i)\right] \\
&= \left[P_{A_{\text{bef}}}(U_{i-1} \wedge A_{i-1})\ P_{A_{\text{bef}}}(E_{i-1} \wedge A_{i-1})\right] \\
&\times \begin{bmatrix} 1-c & cq_i \\ c & (1-c)\,q_i \end{bmatrix}. \qquad \text{(B.1)}
\end{aligned}$$

Recursively using Eq. (B.1) from the initial vector

$$\left[P_{A_{\text{bef}}}(U_0 \wedge A_0)\ P_{A_{\text{bef}}}(E_0 \wedge A_0)\right] = \begin{bmatrix} 1 & 0 \end{bmatrix},$$

we can write down a straightforward expression for $P_{A_{\text{bef}}}(U_l \wedge A_l)$ and $P_{A_{\text{bef}}}(E_l \wedge A_l)$ as

$$\begin{aligned}
&\left[P_{A_{\text{bef}}}(U_l \wedge A_l)\ P_{A_{\text{bef}}}(E_l \wedge A_l)\right] \\
&= \begin{bmatrix} 1 & 0 \end{bmatrix} \begin{bmatrix} 1-c & cq_1 \\ c & (1-c)\,q_1 \end{bmatrix} \cdots\cdots \begin{bmatrix} 1-c & cq_l \\ c & (1-c)\,q_l \end{bmatrix}.
\end{aligned}$$

Similarly, the formula for the site B is derived as

$$\begin{aligned}
&\left[P_{A_{\text{bef}}}(U_l \wedge B_l)\ P_{A_{\text{bef}}}(E_l \wedge B_l)\right] \\
&= \begin{bmatrix} 1 & 0 \end{bmatrix} \begin{bmatrix} (1-c)\,q_1 & c \\ cq_1 & 1-c \end{bmatrix} \cdots\cdots \begin{bmatrix} (1-c)\,q_l & c \\ cq_l & 1-c \end{bmatrix}.
\end{aligned}$$

By using these formulas, a detailed expression for P_{des} is derived as

$$\begin{aligned}
&P_{\text{des}} \\
&= 1 + P(B_{\text{bef}}) - P_{A_{\text{bef}}}(A_l) - P_{A_{\text{bef}}}(B_l) \\
&= 1 + \prod q_i - (P_{A_{\text{bef}}}(U_l \wedge A_l) + P_{A_{\text{bef}}}(E_l \wedge A_l)) \\
&\qquad - (P_{A_{\text{bef}}}(U_l \wedge B_l) + P_{A_{\text{bef}}}(E_l \wedge B_l)) \\
&= 1 + \prod q_i \\
&\quad - \begin{bmatrix} 1 & 0 \end{bmatrix} \begin{bmatrix} 1-c & cq_1 \\ c & (1-c)\,q_1 \end{bmatrix} \cdots \begin{bmatrix} 1-c & cq_l \\ c & (1-c)\,q_l \end{bmatrix} \begin{bmatrix} 1 \\ 1 \end{bmatrix} \\
&\quad - \begin{bmatrix} 1 & 0 \end{bmatrix} \begin{bmatrix} (1-c)\,q_1 & c \\ cq_1 & 1-c \end{bmatrix} \cdots \begin{bmatrix} (1-c)\,q_l & c \\ cq_l & 1-c \end{bmatrix} \begin{bmatrix} 1 \\ 1 \end{bmatrix}.
\end{aligned}$$

Appendix C: Monte Carlo estimation of $\langle X \rangle_{\text{AC}}$ and $\langle X \rangle_{\text{BC}}$

In order to calculate $\langle X \rangle_{\text{AC}}$ or $\langle X \rangle_{\text{BC}}$, we need to evaluate

$$\int_0^1 \cdots \int_0^1 Y \prod_i h(q_i)\, dq_i = \int_0^1 \cdots \int_0^1 Y \prod_i dg_i, \qquad \text{(C.1)}$$

where Y is the function of the frequency vector $\{q_i\}$. g is the integral function of $h(q)$ defined by

$$\begin{aligned}
g(q) &\equiv \int_0^q h(q')\,dq' = \frac{\Gamma(4\beta)}{\{\Gamma(2\beta)\}^2} \int_0^q (q')^{2\beta-1} (1-q')^{2\beta-1}\, dq' \\
&= \frac{\Gamma(4\beta)}{\{\Gamma(2\beta)\}^2} \cdot \frac{q^{2\beta}}{2\beta} \cdot F(2\beta, 1-2\beta, 1+2\beta; q)
\end{aligned}$$

$$= \frac{\Gamma(4\beta)}{\{\Gamma(2\beta)\}^2} \cdot \frac{q^{2\beta}}{2\beta} \cdot \sum_{k=0}^{\infty} \frac{(2\beta)_k (1-2\beta)_k}{(1+2\beta)_k} \cdot \frac{q^k}{k!}, \quad (C.2)$$

where

$F(\ )$ is the Gauss' hypergeometric function, and

$(a)_n \equiv a(a+1)\cdots(a+n-1) = \Gamma(a+n)/\Gamma(a)$.

For above derivation see [2, 21] for example. Eq. (C.2) enables us to approximately calculate $g(q)$ by neglecting the higher-order terms of expansion.

Then the numerical estimation of (C.1) is made by the following Monte Carlo method.

Step 1: Randomly choose a real number x within the interval [0,1]. Then calculate $q = g^{-1}(x)$ by use of Newton-Raphson's method or the successive division method.

Step 2: Repeat Step 1 I times and construct a sample vector $\{q_i\} = (q_1, \cdots, q_I)$.

Step 3: With the sample vector $\{q_i\}$, calculate the value of the integrand.

Step 4: Repeat Steps 1~3 16384 (when I = 12) or 131072 (when I = 20) times and calculate the average.

Although the repetition number at Step 4 is fairly large, when u is very low, the above method can make only an incomplete estimation of (C.1). This is because when $\beta = N_e u$ is very low, $g^{-1}(x)$ becomes nearly discontinuous at $x \approx 0.5$ so that qs calculated in Step 1 cannot take intermediate values within a finite number of samplings.

Appendix D: Detailed expressions for $\langle(\Delta x_I)/x_I\rangle_{AC}$s

By substituting $x_I = 1/N$ for Eqs. (7a)~(7c), we can derive the detailed formulas for $\langle(\Delta x_I)/x_I\rangle_{AC}$s as

$$\langle\frac{\Delta x_I^{(\mathrm{sel.})}}{x_I}\rangle_{AC} \sim s,$$

$$\langle\frac{\Delta x_I^{(\mathrm{mut.})}}{x_I}\rangle_{AC} = \langle\frac{1}{1-\prod q_i}[(\prod\{u+(1-2u)q_i\} - \prod q_i)$$

$$\times (N-1) + \{1-(1-u)^I\}(N\prod q_i - 1)]\rangle_{AC},$$

$$\langle\frac{\Delta x_I^{(\mathrm{cross.})}}{x_I}\rangle_{AC} \sim r \cdot \langle\frac{P_{\mathrm{des}}(N\prod q_i - 1)}{(1-\prod q_i)^2}\rangle_{AC}.$$

References

1. Crow, J. F. & Kimura, M. (1970). *An introduction to population genetics theory.* New York: Harper and Row.
2. Erdelyi, A. eds. (1953-55). *Higher transcendental functions. I, II, III.* New York: McGraw-Hill.
3. Eigen, M., Gardiner, W., Schuster, P. & Winkler, R. (1981). The origin of genetic information. *Sci. Amer.* **244,** 88-118
4. Ewens, W. J. (1979). *Mathematical Population Genetics.* New York: Springer-Verlag.
5. Fisher, R. A. (1930). *The Genetic Theory of Natural Selection.* New York: Dover Publications. (2nd Ed. 1958) p. 291
6. Forrest, S. (1993). Genetic algorithms: Principles of natural selection applied to computation. *Science* **261,** 872-878.
7. Forrest, S. & Mitchell, M. (1993). What makes a problem hard for a genetic algorithm? Some anomalous results and their explanation. *Machine Learning* **13,** 285-319.
8. Goldberg, D. E. (1989). *Genetic Algorithms in Search, Optimization and Machine Learning.* New York: Addison-Wesley.
9. Holland, J. H. (1992). *Adaptation in Natural and Artificial Systems.* Boston: MIT Press.
10. Kimura, M. (1983). *The Neutral Theory of Molecular Evolution.* Cambridge: Cambridge Univ. Press.
11. Lloyd, D. G. (1980). Benefits and handicaps of sexual reproduction. *Evol. Biol.* **13,** 69-111.
12. Maynard-Smith, J. (1978). *The Evolution of Sex.* Cambridge: Cambridge Univ. Press.
13. Michod, R. E. & Levin, B. R. (1988). *The Evolution of Sex: An Examination of Current Ideas.* Sunderland, MA: Sinauer Associates.
14. Mitchell, M. (1996). *An Introduction to Genetic Algorithms.* Complex Adaptive Systems series. Boston: MIT Press.
15. Mitchell, M., Forrest, S., & Holland, J. H. (1991). The royal road for genetic algorithms: fitness landscapes and GA performance. Edited by F. J. Varela et al. *Toward a Practice of Autonomous Systems: Proceedings of the First European Conference on Artificial Life.* Cambridge, MA: MIT Press. pp. 245-254.
16. Muller, H. J. (1932). Some genetic aspects of sex. *Amer. Natur.* **66,** 118-138.
17. Otto, S., Feldman, M. W., & Christiansen, F. B. (1994). Some advantages and disadvantages of recombination. Edited by S. Levin. *Frontiers in Mathematical Biology,* Vol. 100 pp. 198-211.
18. Suzuki, H. (1997). Functional Emergence with Multiple von Neumann Computers. Edited by C. Langton & K. Shimohara. *Artificial Life V: Proceedings of the Fifth International Workshop on the Synthesis and Simulation of Living Systems.* Cambridge, MA: MIT Press. pp. 108-115.
19. Suzuki, H. (1997). Multiple von Neumann Computers: An Evolutionary Approach to Functional Emergence. *Artificial Life.* **3,** 121-142.
20. Suzuki, H. (1997). The optimum recombination rate that realizes the fastest evolution of a novel functional combination of many genes. *Theor. Pop. Biol.* **51,** 185-200.
21. Whittaker, E. T. & Watson, G. N. (1958). *A Course of Modern Analysis.* 10th ed. Cambridge, MA.
22. Williams, G. C. (1975). *Sex and Evolution.* Princeton: Princeton Univ. Press.

DCGA : A Diversity Control Oriented Genetic Algorithm

Hisashi Shimodaira
Department of Information and Communication, Bunkyo University
1100 Namegaya, Chigasaki-City, Kanagawa 253, Japan
E-mail: f2610390@ca.aif.or.jp

Abstract

In order to attain the global optimum without getting stuck at a local optimum, the appropriate diversity of the structures in the population needs to be maintained. I propose a new genetic algorithm called DCGA (Diversity Control oriented Genetic Algorithm) to attain this goal. In the DCGA, the structures of the population for the next generation are selected from the merged population of parents and their offspring based on a selection probability, which is calculated using a hamming distance between the candidate structure and the structure with the best fitness value. Within the range of my experiments, the performance of the DCGA is remarkably superior to that of the simple GA and the DCGA seems to be a promising competitor of previously proposed algorithms.

1. Introduction

Genetic algorithms (GA's) are one of promising means for function optimization. Methods for function optimization are required to attain the global optimum without getting stuck at a local optimum. For multimodal functions, because the performance of the simple GA is poor in this point, various researches to improve the performance of the GA have been performed as follows.

Baker [1] observed that premature convergence (convergence to a local optimum) often occurs after an individual or a small group of individuals contributes a large number of offspring to the next generation. Booker [2] mentioned that a large number of offspring for one individual means fewer offspring for the rest of the population and when too many individuals get no offspring at all, the result is a rapid loss of diversity and premature convergence. What is needed to handle premature convergence is to prevent this situation. Baker and Booker explored the methods of selection and crossover, respectively, to achieve this end.

Goldberg [3] proposed a method of sharing function by which the issue is eased allowing the formation of species in niches. This mechanism modifies the reproduction probability of a population member by adjusting the fitness value of the structures according to how many population members occupy a niche of the solution space. The method proved superior, but is computationally expensive, because the distance calculation between the structures has a time complexity $O(N^2)$, where N is the size of the population.

In the paradigm of the simple GA, Srinivas [4] proposed the use of adaptive probabilities of crossover and mutation to realize the twin goals of maintaining diversity in the population and sustaining the convergence capacity of the GA. In his algorithm, the probabilities of crossover and mutation are varied depending on the fitness values of structures. High fitness structures are protected, while structures with subaverage fitness value are totally disrupted. In the simple GA, however, because the selection for reproduction is biased toward selecting the better performing individuals, premature convergence often occurs and is essentially inevitable as indicated in the results of Srinivas.

Eshelman [5] proposed an algorithm employing a highly destructive uniform crossover and the Population-Elitist Selection (PES) method which is cross-generational deterministic rank-based survival selection. In the reproduction stage, two candidate structures are selected for mating. In order to maintain diversity, the hamming distance between them is calculated, and if half that distance does not exceed a difference threshold, they are not mated and deleted from the population. Although the performance is remarkably superior to the simple GA, the algorithm is rather complicated.

In order to achieve the above goal, an essential method to maintain appropriate diversity of the structures in the population during the search so that local search and global search are performed in a balanced way, needs to be developed. In this paper, I propose a new genetic algorithm called DCGA (Diversity Control oriented Genetic Algorithm). In the DCGA, the structures for the next generation are selected from the merged population of parents and their offspring eliminating duplicates based on a selection probability, which is calculated using the hamming distance between the candidate structure and the structure with the best fitness value and is larger for structures with larger hamming distances. Within the range of my experiments, the DCGA outperformed the simple GA and seems to be a promising competitor of the previously proposed algorithms.

This paper describes the DCGA and presents the results of the experiments comparing with the simple GA.

1082-3409/97 $10.00

2. The simple GA

The outline of the simple GA is described to facilitate the later explanation. In the simple GA, the following processing is performed. (1) The number N of individuals in the population is constant and the population is initialized using random numbers. (2) In the reproduction stage, structures are selected from the present population P(t-1) and recombined to form the offspring population C(t), where t is the generation and structure the genotype of an individual. The selection for reproduction (select$_r$) is biased toward selecting the better performing individuals. The recombination is performed using crossover based on probability. A low rate of mutation is used in the recombination stage to maintain population diversity. (3) The selection for survival (select$_s$) is usually unbiased, typically replacing the entire parent population P(t-1) with the child population C(t).

3. DCGA

In order to improve the performance of GA's, the algorithm needs to have ability to robustly explore the solution space to find out the best region containing the global optimum (global search) and to escape from a local optimum when being stuck at it. Attaching greater importance to only current better performing structures may result in premature convergence. On the other hand, a current worse solution may have a greater potential of evolving toward a better future solution to attain the global optimum. The idea motivating my research is to exploit these worse solution instead of discarding them by maintaining the diversity of structures in the population. In addition, it needs to exploit the best solution obtained so far (local search), because it may be in the region containing the global optimum. The DCGA is devised to achieve these twin goals.

The skeleton of the DCGA is shown in Fig.1. The number of structures in the population P(t) is constant and N. The population is initialized using uniform random numbers. In the selection for reproduction select$_r$, all the structures in P(t-1) are paired by selecting two structures without replacement to form P'(t-1). By applying mutation with probability p_m and always applying crossover to the structures of each pair in P'(t-1), C(t) is produced. The mutation rate p_m is constant for all the structures. The structures in C(t) and P(t-1) are merged and sorted in their fitness values order to form M(t). In the selection for survival select$_s$, the structures including the structure with the best fitness value are selected from M'(t) and the population for the next generation P(t) is formed.

The details of the selection for survival select$_s$ are as follows. (1) Duplicate structures in M(t) are eliminated and M'(t) is formed. (2) Structures are selected using the Cross-generational Probabilistic Survival Selection (CPSS) method and P(t) is formed from the structure with the best fitness value in M'(t) and the selected structures. In the CPSS method, structures are selected using random numbers based on a

```
begin;
  t=0;
  initialize population P(t);
  evaluate structures of P(t);
  while (termination condition not satisfied) do;
  begin;
    t=t+1;
    select_r P'(t-1) from P(t-1) by randomly pairing all
      structures without replacement;
    apply mutation with p_m and crossover to each pair
      of P'(t-1) and form C(t);
    evaluate structures in C(t);
    arrange structures of C(t) and P(t-1) in their fitness
      values order and form M(t);
    select_s N structures including the structure with the
      best fitness value from M(t) to form next popul-
      ation P(t) according to the following procedure;
      (1) eliminate duplicate structures in M(t);
      (2) select structures with CDSS or CPSS;
      (3) if the number of selected structures is
          smaller than N, introduce new structures;
  end;
end;
```

Fig.1 Skeleton of DCGA

selection probability defined by the following equation:

$$p_s = \{(1-c)h / L + c\}^{\alpha} \qquad (1)$$

where h is the hamming distance between the candidate structure and the structure with the best fitness value, L the length of the string representing the structure, c the shape coefficient, and α the exponent. If the generated random number is smaller than p_s calculated for a structure, then the structure is selected, otherwise it is deleted. The selection process is performed in the fitness values order of the structures in M'(t) except the structure with the best fitness value. (3) If the number of the structures in P(t) is smaller than N, then new structures generated using random numbers are introduced by the insufficient number. For the traveling salesman problem mentioned later, the hamming distance is calculated considering the order and the reverse order of the city in the structure, because the position of the city does not have a meaning.

The reasons why the above methods are employed in the DCGA are as follows.

Crossover and mutation may side-effectively destroy better performing schemata obtained so far. In the DCGA, because the structure with best performance obtained so far always survives intact into the next generation, the influence of this side-effect is small and large mutation rates can be used and crossover can be always applied. This results in producing offspring which are as different as possible from their parents and examining regions of the search space not yet explored. In fact, the best result was obtained when using the crossover rate equal to 1.0 in the examples mentioned later. On the other hand, in the simple GA, mutation is a background operator, assuring that the crossover has a full range alleles so that the

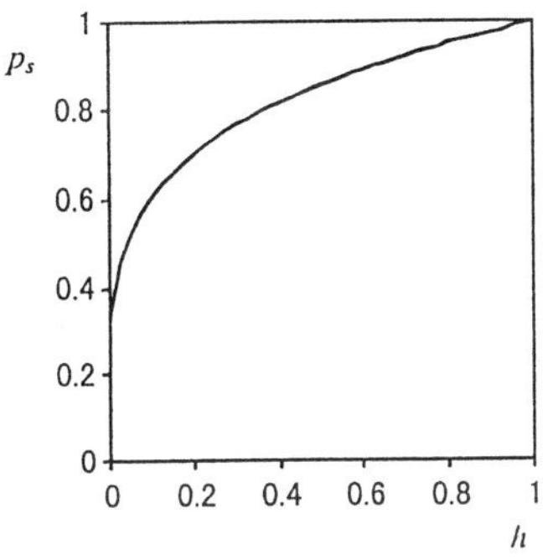

Fig.2 An example curve of Eq.(1) (α=0.225, c=0.0074)

adaptive plan is not trapped on a local optimum [6] and generally small mutation rates are used.

Duplicate structures reduce the diversity of the structures in the population and often cause premature convergence, because the same structures can produce a large number of offspring with the same structure to the next generation. Therefore it is effective to eliminate duplicate structures in order to avoid premature convergence as shown in examples later.

Eq.(1) represents a curve which intersects the two points [h=0, p_s=c^{α}] and [h=L, p_s=1.0] as shown in Fig.2. The curvature of the curve is larger in the region of smaller h, whereas it becomes almost a straight line in the region of larger h. The smaller α becomes, the larger the curvature in the region of smaller h becomes. When α is equal to 1, it becomes a straight line. The larger c becomes, the larger p_s becomes and the curve approaches a horizontal straight line. The selection of structures based on Eq.(1) is biased toward selecting structures with larger hamming distance from the structure with the best fitness value. The degree of the bias is externally adjusted by the values of c and α. The appropriate values need to be explored by trial and error according to the problem. Eq.(1) is very suitable to control the diversity of the structures in the population so as to be in an appropriate condition by externally adjusting the values of c and α.

The structure with the best fitness value obtained so far always survives, because it may be in the region containing the global optimum. Thus the best fitness value for the population can increase monotonously. However, it may be in the region containing a local optimum and the increase of similar structures to it may result in the premature convergence. Therefore, the more similar to the structure with the best fitness value a structure is, the smaller selection probability is applied to it using the CPSS method and the increase of it is restricted. This mechanism may slow the convergence speed to the global optimum, whereas it can be compensated and in fact improved by preventing the solution from getting stuck at a local optimum and stagnating. In this sense, the convergence speed to the global optimum depends upon the diversity of structures in the population. In the DCGA, it can be controlled indirectly by the user through the constants α and c of Eq.(1).

The selection process is performed using the selection probability p_s in the fitness values order of the structures, not considering the fitness values itself. This gives more chances to survive and produce their offspring to current worse structures with the fitness value below the average. In the PES method [5], because the structures are deterministicly selected in their fitness values order, the diversity of structures is often rapidly lost and it results in the premature convergence. The CPSS method can avoid such a situation. The superiority of the CPSS method to the PES method will be demonstrated later.

The introduction of new structures occurs when the iteration proceeds and the diversity of the structures in the population happens to become smaller. This is equivalent to very large mutations introduced into the population and works effectively to restore the diversity automatically.

When the structure is represented by a bit string, binary coding or gray coding is usually used. Caruana [7] suggested that gray coding eliminates the "hamming cliff" problem that makes some transitions difficult when using a binary representation. With the gray coding, the hamming distance between two structures can represent better the degree of their similarity in the phenotype represented by decimal numbers. With the DCGA, because the performance with gray coding is superior to that with binary coding as demonstrated later, it is recommended to use gray coding.

The methods employed in the DCGA can work to escape from a local optimum or avoid premature convergence in the following way.

In the DCGA, structures which survived and the structure with the best fitness value obtained so far can always become parents and produce their offspring. The diversity of the structures in the population is maintained by eliminating duplicate structures and by the selection with the CPSS method. In addition, when the diversity is lost, it can be automatically restored by introducing new structures. Because large crossover and mutation rates are used and diverse structures are maintained in the population, variations of from small to large ranges are applied to each structure. When a small variation is applied to a structure, its neighborhood can be examined to result in the local search. When a large variation is applied to a structure, a region not yet explored can be examined to result in the global search. In such a way, local as well as global searches can be performed in parallel. The structure with the best fitness value obtained so far always survives as a promising candidate to attain the global optimum and its neighborhood can be examined by the local search. On the other hand, because current worse solutions can survive, even if the performance of a structure containing a schema concerning the global optimum is not so high in a stage, this gives the structure a chance by which it can produce an offspring with a fitness value near to the global optimum. This mechanism is similar to that of the simulated annealing (SA) that can escape from a local optimum by accepting a solution based on a probability whose performance is worse than the present solution. In the DCGA, the solution can escape from a local optimum by the similar working to the SA.

With the simple GA, better performing structures can produce multiple offspring. Therefore, schemata for a dominating local optimum can increase rapidly and eventually dominate the population. On the other hand, with the DCGA, the chance for each structure to become a parent is one time in spite of its performance. In addition, the same structures are eliminated and the number of structures similar to the best performing one is restricted by the selection with the CPSS method. Because these can prevent a structure (especially the structure with the best fitness value) or a small group of structures from contributing a large number of offspring to the next generation, the DCGA can avoid premature convergence.

The comparison of the time complexity on the simple GA and the DCGA is as follows. The number of function evaluations in the reproduction selection stage is N times per a generation on both the methods. The amount of computations for the selection for reproduction is almost the same on both the methods. In the survival selection stage, that on the DCGA is much larger than that on the simple GA by the amount of the computations for the processes (1), (2) and (3) in Fig.1. The time complexity on the check for the identity of structures in the process (1) is not so large, because the check needs to be performed among the structures having the same fitness value. That on the distance calculation between the candidate structure and the structure with the best fitness value is $O(N)$. With the CHC [5], that is $O(N/2)$. With the sharing function method [3], that is $O(N^2)$. Therefore, the DCGA requires much smaller computational cost for maintaining the diversity of structures than the sharing function method.

With the simple GA, the parameters to be tuned are N, p_m and p_c, whereas with the DCGA, N, p_m, c and α.

The originality of the DCGA is to have presented a new genetic algorithm in the generation replacement type GA combining the following ideas and to have experimentally proved their effectiveness in attaining the global optimum: in the selection for survival, (1) duplicate structures are eliminated, (2) structures for the next generation are selected based on Eq.(1), and (3) new structures are introduced, if the number of selected structures is smaller than N. It has a salient feature that the diversity of structures in the population (therefore the convergence speed to the global optimum) is externally controlled through the constants of α and c in Eq.(1) so as to be in an appropriate condition according to the objective problem. I believe that these ideas, the CPSS method defined Eq.(1) among others, have not been presented in previous researches as far as I know. The major difference between the DCGA and the CHC [5] is in that the former employs the CPSS method and the latter the PES method. With the PES method, structures for the next generation are deterministicly selected from the merged population of parents and their offspring in their fitness values order. The superiority of the former to the latter will be demonstrated later. Comparing the DCGA with the sharing function method [3], the purpose and the method of realizing the diversity of structures are essentially different. The purpose of the former is to attain the global optimum efficiently, whereas that of the latter is the parallel investigation of many peaks of a multimodal function. The method of the latter is in the paradigm of the simple GA and modifies the reproduction probability of a population member by adjusting the fitness value of the structures according to how many population members occupy a niche of the solution space. In addition, the time complexity on the distance calculation for the former is much smaller than that for the latter as mentioned above.

4. Experimental results

The performance of the DCGA has been tested on various benchmark problems and compared with that of the simple GA, because the simple GA has been treated as the standard measure for comparisons on performance of various GA's. With simple problems, the differences of the performance were small, whereas with complex problems, the differences were large. Therefore, I present the results for the deceptive functions [5], the multimodal functions f6 [8] and the 30-city TSP [9] which are difficult for GA's to optimize.

Each problem has only one global optimum and it was searched by GA's. For both the DCGA and the simple GA, two-point crossover was used. For the DCGA, crossover was always applied to each pair in P'(t-1). For the simple GA, the performance of (1) the roulette selection method using the elitist strategy with or without the fitness scaling, (2) the pure selection method with the fitness scaling proposed by Grefenstette [11], and (3) the stochastic remainder selection method without replacement [4,10] with or without the fitness scaling, was compared. The results by the first one without the fitness scaling (De Jong's standard GA) [11] which showed the best performance are described in the following. For the DCGA, the following three cases of computation conditions were tested in order to examine the effect of the methods (1) and (2) in Fig.1 employed in the survival selection. Case-1: noneliminating duplicate structures and the PES method. Case-2: eliminating duplicate structures and the PES method. Case-3: eliminating duplicate structures and the CPSS method. With the PES method, structures for the next generation are deterministicly selected from M(t) or M'(t) in their fitness values order in the process (2) in Fig.1.

I examined the combination of best-performing parameter values including the population size changing their values little by little. I performed 20 trials per a parameter set changing seed values for the random number generator to initialize the population. The same 20 seed values were used for the trials with each parameter set. The trial was continued until the global optimum was attained by at least one structure (I call this the convergence) or until the maximum number of function evaluation times was reached. The maximum number of function evaluation times was 50,000. The performance was evaluated by the number of instances out of the 20 trials in which the GA converged and the average number of function evaluation times in those trials which converged. (An algorithm performs better on a function if it converged more often, or if it converged the same number of times as its competitor but in fewer evaluation times.). The reason why the number of function evaluation times was used is because the amount of computations for function evaluations is generally larger than that of GA itself. In the following, I present the best result obtained in each case. Table 1 shows the definitions of major symbols used in the following tables.

4.1 Deceptive functions

The Goldberg's order-3 deceptive functions were used. Its structure consists of a 30-bit binary string and the value of the function is the sum of 10 3-bit subfunctions. The subfunctions are defined as in Table 2. The tightly ordered and loosely ordered functions were tested. In the case of the tightly ordered deceptive function, the bits of the subfunction are adjacent (1, 2, 3 for the first subfunction; 4, 5, 6 for the second subfunction, and so forth). In the case of the loosely ordered deceptive function, the first subfunction is located at positions 1, 11, and 21, the second subfunction is located at positions 2, 12, 22, and so forth. The global maximum is 300.

Table 3 shows the best result for the tightly ordered function on the simple GA. Tables 4, 5 and 6 show the best results for the tightly ordered function on the DCGA with case-1,

Table 1 Definitions of major symbols in Tables

B	Gray cording
G	Binary cording
N	Population size
p_m	Mutation rate
p_i	Inversion rate
p_c	Crossover rate
α	Exponent for probability function, Eq.(1)
c	Shape coefficient for probability function, Eq.(1)
NCV	Number of convergence
AVFE	Average number of function evaluation times
SDFE	Standard deviation of function evaluation times
AVEL	Average number of error logarithm (*EL*)
AVBF	Average number of best fitness values
AVNS	Average number of new structures introduced

Table 2 Goldberg's order-3 deceptive function

f(000)=28	f(001)=26	f(010)=22	f(011)=0
f(100)=14	f(101)=0	f(110)=0	f(111)=30

case-2 and case-3, respectively. Table 7 shows the best result for the loosely ordered function on the simple GA. Tables 8, 9 and 10 show the best results for the loosely ordered function on the DCGA with case-1, case-2 and case-3, respectively.

4.2 Multimodal function

The f6 function [8] is as follows:

$$f6 = 0.5 + \frac{0.5 - \sin^2\sqrt{x^2 + y^2}}{[1 + 0.001(x^2 + y^2)]^2} \qquad (2)$$

This function is cylindrically symmetric about the z axis and has the maximum value 1.0 at the origin. Fig.3 shows a section for y=0 including the x and z axes. The points in the search space were coded as Cartesian x and y values in the range -100 to +100 with 22-bit code, respectively. The comparison of gray coding and binary coding was performed. The maximum value to be searched by GA's in the discrete space is the number with eight 9's below the floating point. The error of the best fitness values (f_{max}) obtained in each trial is calculated by the following equation.

$$EL = -\log_{10}(1 - f_{\max}) \qquad (3)$$

For the exact global optimum $EL \cong 8.94$.

Table 11 shows the best results on the simple GA. For the DCGA, Tables 12, 13 and 14 show the best results for case-1, case-2 and case-3, respectively.

4.3 Traveling salesman problem

The Euclidean symmetric 30-city TSP [9] of which global optimum is 420 was tested. The structure was expressed by the path representation. For both the DCGA and the simple GA, the order crossover [9] was used. For the mutation method, the performance with the order-based mutation [14], the position-based mutation, and the inversion was compared. The results by the last one which showed the best performance are described in the following.

Table 15 shows the best results on the simple GA. For the DCGA, Tables 16, 17 and 18 show the best results for case-1,

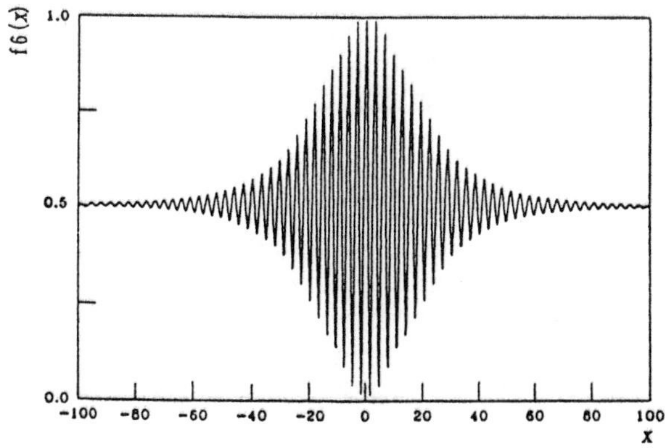

Fig.3 Section of f6 function

Table 3 The best result for tightly ordered deceptive function on simple GA

N	p_m	p_c	NCV	$AVFE$	$SDFE$	$AVBF$
80	0.003	0.6	3	38640	2401	295.4

Table 4 The best result for tightly ordered deceptive function on DCGA with case-1

N	p_m	NCV	$AVFE$	$SDFE$	$AVBF$
90	0.095	20	16880	4782	300.0

Table 5 The best result for tightly ordered deceptive function on DCGA with case-2

N	p_m	NCV	$AVFE$	$SDFE$	$AVBF$
100	0.035	20	6640	2918	300.0

Table 6 The best result for tightly ordered deceptive function on DCGA with case-3

N	p_m	α	c	NCV	$AVFE$	$SDFE$	$AVBF$	$AVNS$
4	0.008	0.49	0.33	20	5018	1940	300.0	242.4

Table 7 The best result for loosely ordered deceptive function on simple GA

N	p_m	p_c	NCV	$AVFE$	$SDFE$	$AVBF$
110	0.0034	0.6	8	75460	14748	297.6

Table 8 The best result for loosely ordered deceptive function on DCGA with case-1

N	p_m	NCV	$AVFE$	$SDFE$	$AVBF$
8	0.085	13	29220	8835	299.1

Table 9 The best result for loosely ordered deceptive function on DCGA with case-2

N	p_m	NCV	$AVFE$	$SDFE$	$AVBF$
4	0.08	20	24928	11001	300.0

Table 10 The best result for loosely ordered deceptive function on DCGA with case-3

N	p_m	α	c	NCV	$AVFE$	$SDFE$	$AVBF$	$AVNS$
4	0.045	0.37	0.8	20	14511	5385	300.0	5.5

Table 11 The best result for f6 function on simple GA

Cord	N	p_m	p_c	NCV	$AVFE$	$SDFE$	$AVEL$
G	70	0.001	0.6	5	30352	8261	3.77
B	30	0.001	0.6	7	7924	2054	4.07

Table 12 The best result for f6 function on DCGA with case-1

Cord	N	p_m	NCV	$AVFE$	$SDFE$	$AVEL$
G	92	0.091	20	25746	6382	8.94

Table 13 The best result for f6 function on DCGA with case-2

Cord	N	p_m	NCV	$AVFE$	$SDFE$	$AVEL$
G	94	0.08	20	22814	6639	8.94

Table 14 The best result for f6 function on DCGA with case-3

Cord	N	p_m	α	c	NCV	$AVFE$	$SDFE$	$AVEL$	$AVNS$
G	12	0.014	0.51	0.235	20	18368	8611	8.94	261.0
B	12	0.014	0.51	0.235	12	20260	9912	7.02	247.8

Table 15 The best result for 30-city TSP on simple GA

N	p_m	p_c	NCV	$AVFE$	$SDFE$	$AVBF$
56	0.09	0.61	7	81048	14866	424.6

Table 16 The best result for 30-city TSP on DCGA with case-1

N	p_i	NCV	$AVFE$	$SDFE$	$AVBF$
110	0.206	10	20174	9830	422.2

Table 17 The best result for 30-city TSP on DCGA with case-2

N	p_i	NCV	$AVFE$	$SDFE$	$AVBF$
120	0.196	20	20298	6029	420.0

Table 18 The best result for 30-city TSP on DCGA with case-3

N	p_i	α	c	NCV	$AVFE$	$SDFE$	$AVBF$	$AVNS$
22	0.097	0.19	0.0	20	19643	6798	420.0	1.1

case-2 and case-3, respectively.

4.4 Summary of the results and discussions

The followings have been experimentally confirmed by these three problems. The performance with case-2 (eliminating duplicate structures) is superior to that with case-1 (noneliminating duplicate structures). In the case of the deceptive functions and the 30-city TSP, the improvement of the performance is remarkable. Therefore, it is obvious that eliminating duplicate structures is very effective to improve the performance for most problems. With the deceptive functions and the f6 function, the performance with case-3 is remarkably superior to that with case-2. With the 30-city TSP, the performance with case-3 is slightly superior to that with case-2. Therefore, it is obvious that the CPSS method is superior to the PES method. According to the results for the f6 function on the DCGA, the performance with gray coding is remarkably superior to that with binary coding. Therefore, it is recommended to use gray coding for the DCGA. It should be noted that with the DCGA, the optimum population size is extremely small and the performance is robust to the changes of the parameter values and the ranges of parameter values with which the global optimum is attained in all trials are considerably wide.

The best results with case-3 show obviously that there exist an optimum population size and an optimum diversity of the structures in the population according to the objective problem. The value of p_{s0} which is p_s for $h = 0$ represents the magnitude of the selection probability and the smaller p_{s0} is, the higher diversity of the structures in the population can be realized. The value of p_{s0} on the best results is 0.58 for the tightly ordered deceptive function, 0.92 for the loosely ordered deceptive function, 0.48 for the f6 function, and 0.0 for the 30-city TSP. It seems that the more difficult the problem is to optimize, the larger the optimum population size becomes. It should be noted that the global optimum can be attained by extremely small structures, if their diversity is appropriately maintained.

In all these three problems, the performance of the DCGA is remarkably superior to that with the simple GA.

It is interesting that how well the DCGA performs comparing with the previous leading methods. The computation conditions in the previous researches are different from each other and some computation conditions and results are not described. Therefore, although exact comparisons of the performance are not impossible, the best results are described in the following for the purpose of conjecturing the differences of the performance.

The results for the deceptive functions are as follows. With the Srinivas's method [4] using the population size of 100 and the upper limit of function evaluation times of 20,000, although the kind of the function used was not described, the 21 trials out of the 30 trials converged. With the CHC [5] using the population size of 50 and the upper limit of function evaluation times of 50,000 for the tightly ordered function, all the 50 trials converged and the average, maximum and minimum numbers of function evaluations to converge were 20,960, 36,297 and 9,933, respectively. With the DCGA using the population size of 4 and the upper limit of function evaluation times of 50,000 for the tightly ordered function, all the 20 trials converged and the average, maximum and minimum numbers of function evaluations to converge were 5,018, 7,684 and 1,834, respectively. With the DCGA using the population size of 4 and the upper limit of function evaluation times of 50,000 for the loosely ordered function, all the 20 trials converged and the average, maximum and minimum numbers of function evaluations to converge were 14,511, 30,216 and 9,173, respectively.

The results for the f6 function are as follows. With the Srinivas's method using a population size of 100, the upper limit of function evaluation times of 20,000 and the convergence threshold value of 0.999 for the function value, the 24 trails out of the 30 trials converged. With the CHC using the population size of 50 and the upper limit of function evaluation times of 50,000, although other computation conditions such as the length of the structure are not described, all the 50 trials converged and the number of function evaluations to converge was on the average 6,496. With the Whitley's method using the population size of 100, the number of 9's below the floating point almost presents a peak at the function evaluation times 4,000 and the maximum value is smaller than 3 [12]. With the DCGA using the population size of 12, gray coding, and the upper limit of function evaluation times of 50,000, all the 20 trials converged and the average, maximum and minimum numbers of function evaluations to converge were 18,368, 42,685 and 6,322, respectively.

The results for the 30-city traveling salesman problem are as follows. With the Srinivas's method using a very large population size of 1,000 and the upper limit of 100,000 function evaluations, the only 7 trials out of the 10 trials converged. With the CHC using the population size of 50 and the upper limit of 50,000 function evaluations, the 29 trials out of the 50 trials converged (convergence rate = 58%) and the number of function evaluations to converge was on the average 24,866. According to this result, it seems that the CHC suffers from the loss of diversity of structures and premature convergence. With the Whitley's method using a very large population size of 1,000 and the upper limit of the function evaluation times of 30,000, all the 30 trials converged [13]. With the DCGA using the population size of 22 and the upper limit of function evaluation times of 50,000, all the 20 trials converged and the average, maximum and minimum numbers of function evaluations to converge were 19,643, 33,838 and 10,362, respectively.

According to the above, the DCGA seems to be especially suitable for problems of which the global optimum is isolated as the deceptive function. It seems that the DCGA outperforms the Srinivas's method for all these three problems. It seems that the DCGA outperforms the CHC remarkably for the deceptive functions and the 30-city TSP. However, it seems that the latter is superior to the former for the f6 function. It should be noted that the optimum population size for the DCGA is extremely small comparing with the these previous methods.

5. Conclusion

Within the range of the above experiments, the following conclusions can be drawn. The methods employed in the DCGA is effective to attain the global optimum. The DCGA has a salient feature that the diversity of structures in the population is externally controlled so as to be in a appropriate condition according to the objective problem. In addition, the optimum population size is extremely small and its performance is robust to the changes of the parameters. The performance of the DCGA is remarkably superior to that of the simple GA. The DCGA may be a promising competitor to the GA's proposed in the previous researches. However, further evaluations of the DCGA on various problems is required before firm conclusions may be drawn. In additional the theoretical analysis of the convergence process of the DCGA is required.

References

[1] Baker, J.E., "Adaptive Selection Methods for Genetic Algorithms", *Proc. of an International Conference on Genetic Algorithms and Their Applications*, Lawrence Erlbaum Associates, 1985, pp.101-111.

[2] Booker, L., "Improving Search in Genetic Algorithms", *Genetic Algorithms and Simulated Annealing*, Morgan Kaufmann, 1987, pp.61-73.

[3] Goldberg, D. E. et al, "Genetic Algorithms with Sharing for Multimodal Function Optimization", *Proc. of the Second International Conference on Genetic Algorithms*, Lawrence Erlbaum Associates, 1987, pp.41-49.

[4] Srinivas, M. et al, "Adaptive Probabilities of Crossover and Mutation in Genetic Algorithms", *IEEE Transactions on Systems, Man and Cybernetics*, Vol.24, No.4, 1994, pp.656-667.

[5] Eshelman, L.J., "The CHC Adaptive Search Algorithm: How to Have Safe Search When Engaging in Nontraditional Genetic Recombination", *Foundation of Genetic Algorithms*, Morgan Kaufmann, 1991, pp.265-283.

[6] Holland, J.H., *"Adaptation in Natural and Artificial Systems"*, MIT Press, 1992, p111.

[7] Caruana, R. et al, "Representation and Hidden Bias: Gray vs. Binary Coding for Genetic Algorithms", *Proc. of 5th Int. Conf. on Machine Learning*, Morgan Kaufman, 1988, pp.153-161.

[8] Schaffer J.D. et al., "A Study of Control Parameters Affecting Online Performance of Genetic Algorithms for Function Optimization", *Proc. of the Third International Conference on Genetic Algorithms*, Morgan Kaufmann, 1989, pp.51-60.

[9] Oliver, I.M. et al, "A Study of Permutation Crossover Operators on the Traveling Salesman Problem", *Proc. of the Second International Conference on Genetic Algorithms*, Lawrence Erlbaum Associates, 1987, pp.224-230.

[10] Goldberg, D.E., "Genetic Algorithms in Search, Optimization & Machine Learning", Addison Wesley, 1989.

[11] Grefenstette,J.J., "Optimization of Control Parameters for Genetic Algorithms", *IEEE Transactions on Systems, Man, and Cybernetics*, Vol.SMC-16, No.1, 1986, pp.122-128.

[12] Davis L., *"Handbook of Genetic Algorithms"*, Van Nostrand Reinhold, 1991.

[13] Starkweather, T. et al, "A Comparison of Genetic Sequencing Operators", *Proc. of the Fourth International Conference on Genetic Algorithms*, Morgan Kaufmann, 1991, pp.69-76.

[14] Shimodaira, H., "DCGA: A Divesity Control Oriented Genetic Algoritm", *Proc. 2nd IEE/IEEE Int. Conf. Genetic Algorithms in Engineering Systems*, 1997, to appear.

Yet Another Genetic Algorithm for Feed-forward Neural Networks

Roman Neruda
Institute of Computer Science
Academy of Sciences of the Czech Republic
PO Box 5, 18207, Prague 8, Czech Republic

Abstract

A functional equivalence property of feed-forward networks has been proposed to reduce the search space of learning algorithms. We summarize previous results describing the form of functional equivalence for one hidden layer perceptron networks and RBF networks with Gaussians. The description of equivalence classes is used in proposition of a genetic learning algorithm which is tested on two simple problems and outperforms the standard genetic learning procedure.

1 Introduction

We consider a feed-forward network to be a tool for computing an approximation of a real function of several real variables which depend on network parameters (weights). A function realized by the network is referred to as *input/output (or I/O) function* of the network. The natural question what functions can be approximated by a given type of network has been solved in the recent years. A so called *universal approximation property* (the possibility to approximate any reasonable (e.g. continuous) function arbitrarily well) was introduced. It has been proven that many common network architectures—including multilayer perceptrons with one hidden layer and RBF networks—posses this property (under certain mild conditions).

Although the theory assures that continuous functions can be approximated by the network, the learning process (i.e. the search for suitable values of network parameters) means usually a non-linear optimization in high dimensional spaces. So, it is sensible to study possibilities of simplifying this problem. One of the choices may be reduction of the size of parameter space by minimizing parameterization redundancy. This can be done by restriction to minimal subsets of weight space containing at least one representative of each class of *functionally equivalent* parameter vectors (i.e., vectors of parameters determining the same input/output function of the network). Hecht-Nielsen [2] pointed out that characterization of functionally equivalent network parameterizations might speed up some learning algorithms. Several authors studied functionally equivalent weight vectors for one hidden layer perceptron-type networks with various activation functions ([9], [1], [4]). In [5], [6] we have characterized the form of functional equivalence of Radial Basis Function networks with Gaussian radial function.

Based on these results we are able to construct a factorization of the whole parameter space into the classes of functionally equivalent network parameterizations. A unique representative—called *canonical parameterization*—is selected from each equivalence class by defining a certain condition that the network parameters have to satisfy. The set of all canonical parameterizations corresponds to minimal search set introduced by Hecht-Nielsen.

In order to take advantage of the description of canonical parameterization we propose a new learning algorithm of the genetic type. The basic idea is that the standard genetic operators are redefined such that they preserve the canonical property of parameterizations. This way, the algorithm is able to search only among canonical parameterizations, which results in much smaller search space and consequently it leads faster learning.

To verify our theoretical considerations we have tested the proposed algorithm on several problems. The results for RBF networks confirm the expecting speedup of canonical genetic learning which is about 100% in comparison to the standard GA.

2 Functional equivalence

From now on we consider two types of neural networks: By the *RBF network* we mean a feed-forward network with one hidden layer containing radial basis function units with a radial function $\psi : \mathcal{R}_+ \to \mathcal{R}$ and a metrics ρ on $\mathcal{R}^n$ (n is the number of input units) and with a single linear output unit. Such a network

1082-3409/97 $10.00

computes the function:

$$f(\mathbf{x}) = \sum_{i=1}^{k} w_i \psi \left(\frac{\rho(\mathbf{x}, \mathbf{c}_i)}{b_i} \right), \quad (1)$$

where $k \in \mathcal{N}$ is the number of RBF units, $w_i \in \mathcal{R}$, $b_i \in \mathcal{R}_+$, $\mathbf{c}_i \in \mathcal{R}^n$.

Here the perceptron network means a feed-forward network with n inputs, one hidden layer containing perceptron units and one linear output unit. This network computes function $f : \mathcal{R}^n \to \mathcal{R}$ of the form:

$$f(\mathbf{x}) = \sum_{i=1}^{k} w_i \psi(\mathbf{v}_i \mathbf{x} + b_i), \quad (2)$$

where $k \in \mathcal{N}$ is the number of hidden units, $w_i, b_i \in \mathcal{R}$, $\mathbf{v}_i \in \mathcal{R}^n$ and $\psi : \mathcal{R} \to \mathcal{R}$ is an activation function.

Definition 1 *A* radial basis function network parameterization with respect to (ψ, n, ρ) *is a sequence* $\mathbf{P} = (w_i, \mathbf{c}_i, b_i;\ i = 1, \ldots k)$, *where k is the number of hidden units and for the i-th hidden unit the vector $\mathbf{c}_i \in \mathcal{R}^n$ describes the centroid while the real numbers b_i and w_i are widths and output weights, respectively (see(1)). If additionally, for every $i = 1 \ldots, k$ $w_i \neq 0$, and for every $i, j \in \{1, \ldots, k\}$ such that for $i \neq j$ either $\mathbf{c}_i \neq \mathbf{c}_j$ or $b_i \neq b_j$, it is called* a reduced parameterization.

Definition 2 *Similarly, a* perceptron network parameterization with respect to (ψ, n) *is a sequence* $\mathbf{Q} = (w_i, \mathbf{v}_i, b_i;\ i = 1, \ldots, k)$ *with the meaning of symbols described by (2). Additionally, if for every $i \in \{1, \ldots, k\}$ $w_i \neq 0$ and every $i, j \in \{1, \ldots, k\}$ $i \neq j$ implies that either $\mathbf{v}_i \neq \mathbf{v}_j$, or $b_i \neq b_j$ and there exists at least one i such that $\mathbf{v}_i = \mathbf{0}$, it is called* a reduced parameterization.

It is clear that a parameterization $\mathbf{P}$ (or $\mathbf{Q}$) determines a unique I/O function of an RBF network according to the formula (1) (or a perceptron network according to (2)).

Definition 3 *Two network parameterizations* $\mathbf{P}$ *and* $\mathbf{P}'$ *are* functionally equivalent *if they determine the same input/output function.*

Definition 4 *Two network parameterizations are called* interchange equivalent, *if $k = k'$ and there exists a permutation π of the set $\{1, \ldots, k\}$, such that for each $i \in \{1, \ldots, k\}$ $w_i = w'_{\pi(i)}$* and *$b_i = b'_{\pi(i)}$* and *$\mathbf{c}_i = \mathbf{c}'_{\pi(i)}$ for RBF network parameterizations, or $\mathbf{v}_i = \mathbf{v}'_{\pi(i)}$ for perceptron network parameterizations.*

We are interested in relationship between the functional equivalence and interchange equivalence. Clearly the later implies the former, so it is the nontrivial reverse implication that is in our focus.

Definition 5 *Let $n \in \mathcal{N}$. Function ψ has a* unique parameterization property *with respect to n, if for every two reduced parameterizations of perceptron networks w.r.t. (ψ, n) (or RBF networks w.r.t. (ψ, n, ρ)) functional equivalence implies interchange equivalence.*

The most general characterization of functions satisfying the unique parameterization property of perceptron networks is due to Kůrková and Kainen [4].

Theorem 1 *Let ψ be bounded, non-constant and asymptotically constant activation function, $n \in \mathcal{N}$. Then, ψ has a unique parameterization property of perceptron networks with respect to n, if and only if it is neither self-affine, nor affinely recursive.*

Many popular activation functions, including logistic sigmoid or Gaussian, are not affinely recursive. On the contrary, polynomials are affinely recursive, so they do not posses the unique parameterization property. Self-affinity requires a finer analysis which is described in the original paper. Roughly speaking, trivial parameter changes such as sign flips also have to be taken into account.

In the case of RBF networks, the standard choice of a radial function is Gaussian and the most popular metrics are those induced by various inner products (such as Euclidean), or the maximum metrics. Our previous results [5] show that the unique parameterization property is satisfied in these cases.

Theorem 2 *Let n be a positive integer, ρ metrics on $\mathcal{R}^n$ induced by an inner product, or a maximum metrics. Then $\gamma(t) = \exp(-t^2)$ has a unique parameterization property of RBF networks.*

Preceding theorems enables to describe a canonical representation of a network computing a particular function easily. One of the possible choices is to impose a condition on a parameterization that weight vectors corresponding to hidden units are increasing in a lexicographic ordering on a parameterization. Represent a parameterization $\{w_i, k_i, \mathbf{c}_i; i = 1, \ldots, k\}$ or $\{w_i, k_i, \mathbf{v}_i; i = 1, \ldots, k\}$ as a vector $\mathbf{p} = \{\mathbf{p}_i, \ldots \mathbf{p}_k\} \in \mathcal{R}^{k(n+2)}$, where $\mathbf{p}_i = \{w_i, b_i, c_{i1}, \ldots, c_{in}\} \in \mathcal{R}^{n+2}$, or $\mathbf{p}_i = \{w_i, b_i, v_{i1}, \ldots, v_{in}\} \in \mathcal{R}^{n+2}$, are weight vectors corresponding to the i-th hidden RBF, or perceptron, unit. Let $\prec$ denotes the lexicographic ordering on

$\mathcal{R}^{n+2}$, i.e. for $\mathbf{p}, \mathbf{q} \in \mathcal{R}^{d+2}$ $\mathbf{p} \prec \mathbf{q}$ if there exists an index $m \in \{1, \ldots, d+2\}$ such that $p_j = q_j$ for $j < m$ and $p_m < q_m$.

Definition 6 *We call a network parameterization* $\mathbf{P}$ *canonical if* $\mathbf{p}_1 \prec \mathbf{p}_2 \prec \ldots \mathbf{p}_k$.

In this terminology, theorems 1 and 2 guarantee that for every network parameterization a canonical parameterization determining the same input-output function exists. Thus, the set of canonical representations corresponds to a minimal search set—parameter space subset containing exactly one representative of each class of functionally equivalent parameterization vectors—proposed in [2].

An important extension of our previous results concerning the approximate version of functional equivalence exists. The strict functional equivalence, as was introduced, may not be a sufficient answer in many problems. Especially when dealing with approximation problems we are interested in the case where two functions realized by networks are not exactly the same but their difference is small. This case is also of a big importance in practical problems when we, by nature, operate with inexact values.

In [7] we have shown that for RBF network parameterizations with bounded and continuous activation function the following holds: Consider the function F_c assigning each canonical parameterization the function realized by the corresponding function. Then, both F_c and F_c^{-1} are continuous and so two close solutions (functions) imply two close parameterizations (and vice versa).

3 Canonical genetic algorithm

In order to take advantage of the previous results a learning algorithm that can operate only on canonical parameterizations is needed. Unfortunately, neither back propagation nor more complicated three step learning algorithms of RBF networks (cf. [3]) are suitable, since the analytical solution obtained in each step of the iterative process cannot in principle be limited to a certain weight space subset. This is not so with genetic algorithm whose operations can be changed to preserve the property of being canonical.

We propose a so-called *canonical GA* that performs a genetic search only among canonial parameterizations. This operates with the strings representing network parameterizations (see Fig. 1) in floating point encoding. Genetic operators of canonical GA have been modified to preserve the canonical property of parameterizations.

The core of canonical GA is standard: In the beginning a population of m canonical parameterizations $\mathcal{P}_0 = \{\mathbf{P}_1, \ldots, \mathbf{P}_m\}$ is generated at random. Having population $\mathcal{P}_i$, the successive population $\mathcal{P}_{i+1}$ is generated by means of three basic genetic operations: *reproduction*, *crossover* and *mutation* that are proposed such that they generate only canonical parameterizations.

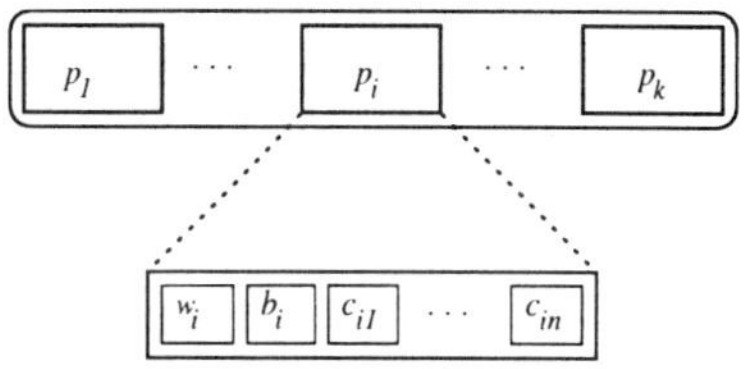

Figure 1: Encoded RBF network parameterization

To generate the *initial population* of canonical parameterizations at random, one has to preserve the property that for each parameterization $\mathbf{P}$ it holds: $\mathbf{p}_s \prec \mathbf{p}_{s+1}$.

The *reproduction* operator represents a probabilistic selection of parameterization $\mathbf{P}_l \in \mathcal{P}_i$ according to the values of objective function $\mathcal{G}(\mathbf{P}_l)$ which is computed by means of the error function (i.e. the sum of distances between the actual and desired output of the network over all of the patterns from the training set).

Thus, we have $\mathcal{G}(\mathbf{P}) = C - \sum_{j=1}^{z} ||f_{\mathbf{P}}(\mathbf{x}_j) - y_j||^2$, where y_j is the desired network output, $f(\mathbf{x}_j)$ represents the actual response of the network when the input $\mathbf{x}_j$ is presented, and C is the maximal error.

For each individual $\mathbf{P}_l$ the value of its objective function $\mathcal{G}(\mathbf{P}_l)$ is computed and then normalized by dividing by the sum of objective function values over all individuals in the population: $p_l = \frac{G(\mathbf{P}_l)}{\sum_{r=1}^{m} G(\mathbf{P}_r)}$. The number p_l then represents the probability with which the parameterization is selected at random. We use the roulette wheel selection together with the elitist mechanism.

The *mutation* operates on two levels—first an element $\mathbf{p}_s$ is chosen randomly as a candidate for mutation. Its neighbors $\mathbf{p}_{s-1}$ and $\mathbf{p}_{s+1}$ then determine the lower and upper border of the range in which the $\mathbf{p}_s$ is changed at random.

The *crossover* operator chooses two parameterizations $\mathbf{P} = (\mathbf{p}_1, \ldots, \mathbf{p}_k)$ and $\mathbf{Q} = (\mathbf{q}_1, \ldots, \mathbf{q}_k)$ in $\mathcal{P}_i$ and generates a new offspring $\mathbf{P}' \in \mathcal{P}_{i+1}$. A position s is found at random and one of the two possible offsprings $(\mathbf{p}_1, \ldots, \mathbf{p}_s, \mathbf{q}_{s+1}, \ldots, \mathbf{q}_k)$ and $(\mathbf{q}_1, \ldots, \mathbf{q}_s, \mathbf{p}_{s+1}, \ldots, \mathbf{p}_k)$ is chosen such that the the resulting parameterization $\mathbf{P}' = (\mathbf{p}'_1, \ldots, \mathbf{p}'_s, \mathbf{p}'_{s+1}, \ldots, \mathbf{p}'_k)$ still satisfies the condition: $\mathbf{p}'_s \prec \mathbf{p}'_{s+1}$.

4 Experiments

In the following we describe our experiments testing the performance of canonical and standard learning algorithms of RBF networks on two problems: the XOR problem and the approximation of $\sin(x) \cdot \sin(y)$ function. The experiments were made on the Pentium 90 PC with 32MB RAM running Linux. The following figures have been obtained by averaging results of 5–10 runs on every task. The program called GARB used in these tests is written in C++ by the author and is publicly available [8].

The first task was a XOR problem defined by four training examples. We used two hidden units in the network, 50 networks in the population and elitist selection for the two best networks. Error values for the first 500 iterations are also plotted on Figure 3, the function realized by the resulting network is shown on Figure 2 . Both algorithms were able to successfully learn the given task quite fast. (cf. Table 1); the canonical algorithm was about two times faster. Running times of both algorithms were roughly identical—about 7 seconds per 1000 iterations.

The second experiment was an approximation of the function $f(x, y) = \sin(x) \cdot \sin(y)$ given by a 10×10 mesh of points regularly taken from a $[0; 2\pi] \times [0; 2\pi]$ square. Again, both algorithms with 50 networks in population and 4 RBF networks were used with the same elitist rate as in the previous experiment. The learning speed is shown on Tables 1 and 2 and Figures 8 and 7.

The performance was similar to the previous experiment: the canonical GA was again about twice faster. The average speed of 1000 iterations was 134 seconds. The resulting network performs function shown on Figure 8.

XOR		
$\mathcal{E}$	canonical	standard
10^{-1}	50	76
10^{-2}	104	268
10^{-3}	443	705
10^{-4}	934	1553
10^{-5}	1075	1988
10^{-6}	1733	4485
10^{-8}	7623	>10000

Table 1: Number of iterations necessary to reach a particular error threshold for XOR

Two sets of experiments were done to test the effect of increasing the population size and increasing the number of RBF units. We first doubled the number

$\sin(x) \cdot \sin(y)$		
$\mathcal{E}$	canonical	standard
10	177	200
5	313	765
3	489	1043
2	1268	—

Table 2: Number of iterations necessary to reach a particular error threshold for $\sin(x) \cdot \sin(y)$

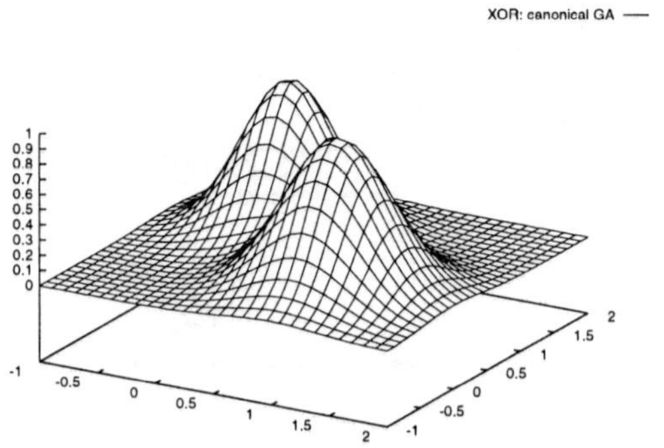

Figure 2: The XOR solution with 2 RBF units found by canonical GA

of networks in the population and tested the learning speed for both the standard and canonical GA. It can be seen from the Figure 4 that there is no relevant performance improvement for either of these algorithm types. On the other hand, of course, the running time for larger populations was twice as big.

In the second comparison we tested several numbers of hidden units between 2 and 16. Figures 5 and 6 show the results. It is worth mentioning that the simplest 2-unit (and "natural") solution showed quite successful and outperformed the 4-unit (or even 8-unit, in one case) solutions. On the other hand, substantial increase of hidden units allowed finer uniform coverage of the space and resulted in better approximation in both cases.

5 Conclusions

We have presented results concerning functional equivalence property for the case of Gaussian RBF networks and one hidden layer perceptron networks. Based on these we have proposed the canonical genetic algorithm for learning feed-forward neural networks. The proposed algorithm has been realized and tested for the case of RBF networks. It has been shown that for small/middle-size tasks the canonical GA is

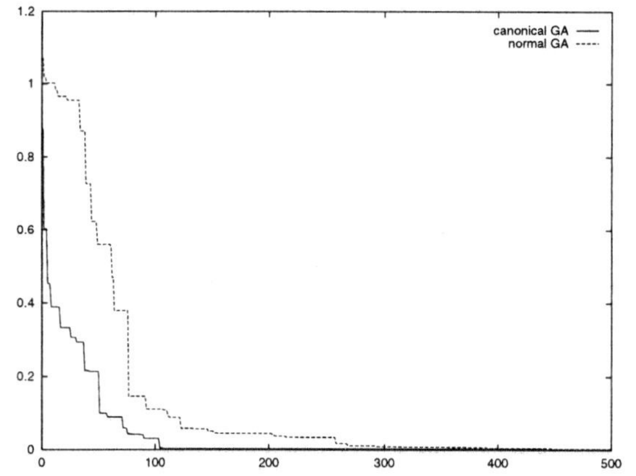

Figure 3: Comparison of the error decrease for the XOR solution with canonical and standard GA

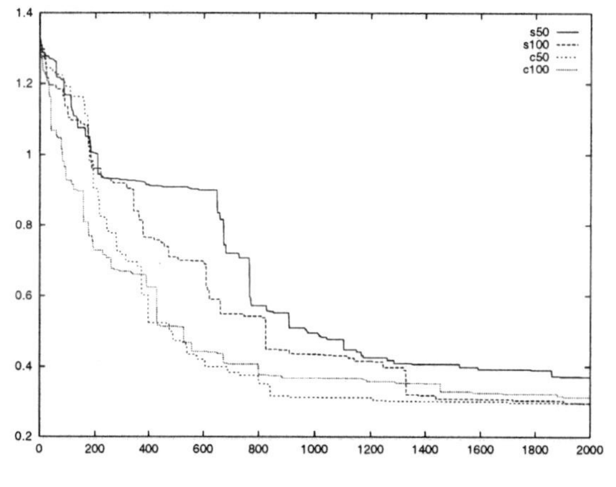

Figure 4: Comparison of error decrease for standard and canonical algorithm with population size of 50 and 100 networks (y scale represents $\log_{10} \mathcal{E}$)

about twice faster in reaching the same error threshold. Moreover, the canonical GA does not show any relevant increase in time for one iteration in comparison to standard GA. Thus, the twice better times hold also in real time.

The interesting comparison would be against the standard learning algorithms of feed-forward networks, such as back propagation. This is one of the directions of our further work. Results by other researchers indicate that genetic learning is usually a bit slower that various gradient descent methods. This slowdown is not caused by a bigger number of iterations needed to reach particular threshold but rather by a bigger time needed for one iteration. On the other hand, genetic algorithms are more suitable for parallelization, as opposed to back propagation-like

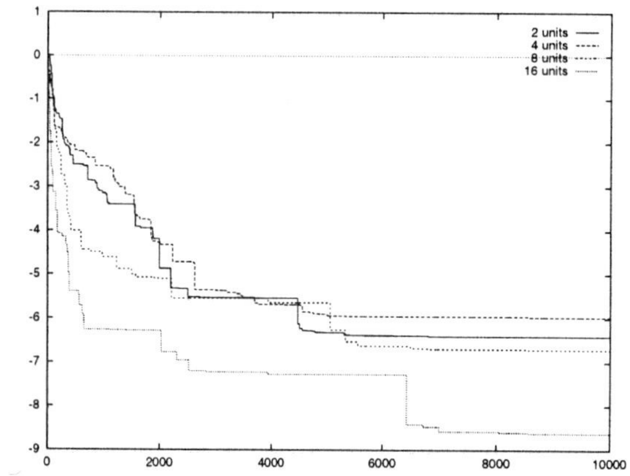

Figure 5: Comparison of the error decrease for the standard GA with a different number of RBF units (y scale represents $\log_{10} \mathcal{E}_S$)

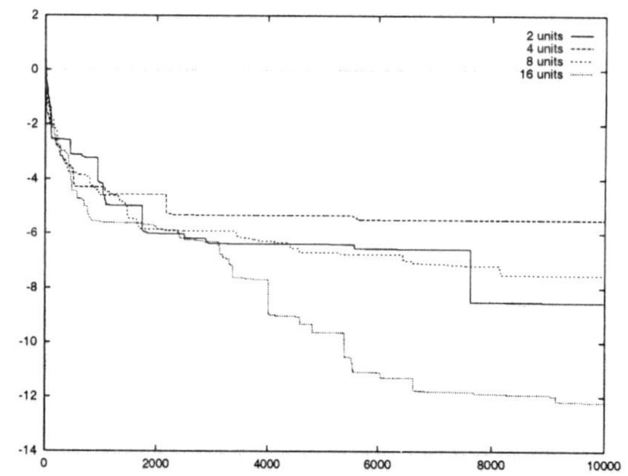

Figure 6: Comparison of the error decrease for the canonical GA with a different number of RBF units (y scale represents $\log_{10} \mathcal{E}_C$)

algorithms that require much more communication. Thus, the parallel implementation of GAs can bring a relevant speedup.

Acknowledgments

This research was partially supported by Grant Agency of the Academy of Sciences of the Czech Republic under grant No. A2030602, by the Grant Agency of the Czech Republic under grant No. 201/95/0976 "HypercompleX", and by the EU Grant No. INCO-COP 96-0195 "ALTEC-KIT".

References

[1] F. Albertini and E.D. Sontag. For neural networks, function determines form. *Neural Networks*, 6:975–990, 1993.

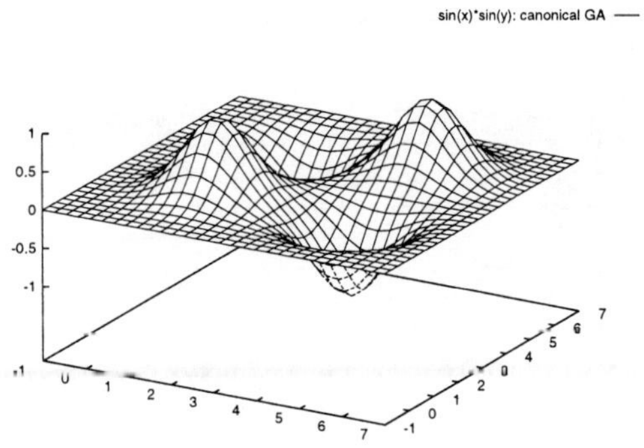

Figure 7: The $\sin(x) \cdot \sin(y)$ solution with 4 RBF units found by canonical GA

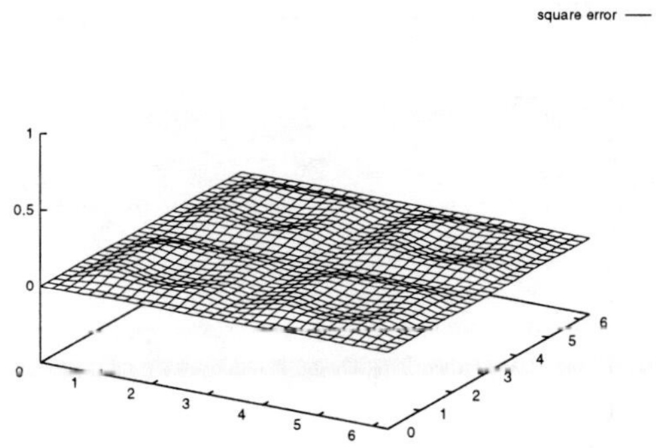

Figure 9: Plot of the square approximation error for the function from previous figure.

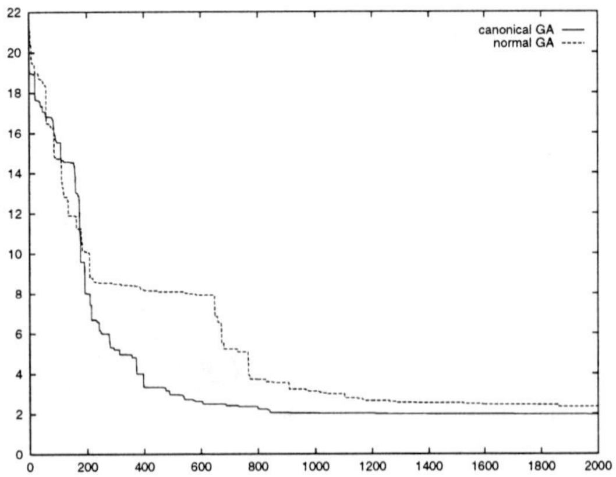

Figure 8: Comparison of error decrease for the $\sin(x) \cdot \sin(y)$ solution with canonical and standard GA

[2] R. Hecht-Nielsen. On the algebraic structure of feedforward network weight spaces. In *Advanced Neural Computers*, pages 129–135. Elsevier, 1990.

[3] K. Hlaváčková and R. Neruda. Radial basis function networks. *Neural Network World*, (1):93–101, 1993.

[4] V. Kůrková and P. Kainen. Functionally equivalent feedforward networks. *Neural Computation*, 6:543–558, 1993.

[5] V. Kůrková and R. Neruda. Uniqueness of the functional representations for the Gaussian basis functions. In *Proceedings of the ICANN'94*, pages 474–477, London, 1994. Springer.

[6] R. Neruda. Functional equivalence and genetic learning of RBF networks. In *Proceedings of the ICANNGA'95*, pages 53–56, Vienna, 1995. Springer Verlag.

[7] R. Neruda. Canonical learning of RBF networks is faster. In *Proceedings of the ICANNGA'97*. Springer, 1997. (in print).

[8] R. Neruda. Genetic learning of RBF networks with GARB. Technical Report V–977, Institute of Computer Science, Prague, 1997.

[9] H.J. Sussmann. Uniqueness of the weights for minimal feedforward nets with a given input-output map. *Neural Networks*, 5(4):589–594, 1992.

Session E.3

Panel Session: Intelligent Agents

Moderator:
Robert Reynolds, Wayne State University, USA

Panelists:
Stefan Covaci, GMD-Fokus, Germany
David Eichmann, University of Iowa, USA
Nick Gessler, University of California at Los Angeles, USA
Don Yu, ITDC Korean Air, USA

Session F.1

Neural Networks

Session Chair:
Don Yu, IDTC Korean Air, USA

VISUAL TARGET TRACKING AND EXTRACTION FROM A SEQUENCE OF IMAGES

N. Bourbakis*+, R. Andel*+ and A.Hall+

** Binghamton University, Center for Intelligent Systems, Engr. School, Binghamton, NY 13902*

+ AirForce Research Lab-at Rome, IRRE Division, Rome, NY 13441

Abstract

This paper presents a methodology for visually tracking and extracting targets from a sequence of images (video). The methodology presented here consists of a combination of algorithms, such as heuristic segmentation, edge detection, thinning, region growing, fractals, feature extraction, graph with attributes, etc., appropriately selected according to the existing situation, such as moving target - still camera, still camera - moving target, moving target - moving camera. The new contribution of this paper is the combination of algorithms in a human like feedback geometric approach of processing low resolution information from consecutive images. Simulated results of the methodology are presented.

Keywords: Visual Target tracking, Feature Extraction, Fractals, Graphs, Processing sequences of images

1. Introduction

Technological advances in artificial intelligence and especially in heuristic search using fractals, pattern recognition and image understanding have provided the opportunity for the development of autonomous systems for Automatic Target Recognition (ATR) from still images [1-9]. ATR in pattern recognition and image understanding based method depends upon resolution for a successful classification. Several of these ATR methodologies can successfully applied to targets detect ion and identification in a sequence of images (video). In particular, Songhua et al. [4] employ the use of a wideband millimeter wave radar to receive high range resolution and extract the target's center. More specifically, they use the high range resolution to extract the target' s features (shape, size, physical structure). Then, they use a heuristic feature extraction technique to detect the target's scattering centers, the number of strong scattering centers, the target's range extent, the range distance between scattering centers and the relative amplitude of the scattering center peaks for the recognition and location of the target in a single frame. A similar ATR radar algorithm was described by them, but on an incoherent low resolution radar. The authors used a semi-fuzzy clustering algorithm to extract the target's feature.

In addition to classical based ATR, researchers have also developed Neural Network based ATR algorithms. The major effort of using ANN algorithms for ATR is to train the neural net with various radar based information related with a specific type of targets, such ships and perform fast classification-recognition of the unknown target received by radar returns. In this type of ATR the training data set is very large, and becomes larger when additional noisy information, such as shift independent, scale, fluctuation, is considered. For these type of ATRs FFT, DMT and CT transformations are needed for the feature extraction and preprocessing, see Min et. al [3]. Most recently, neural nets researchers attempt to overcome with some of the weak points of the neural network ATR approaches, such as fluctuations of echoes, deformation, number of hidden layers and hidden neuron/layer, number and size of neural nets, etc. [1]. The neural net approach seems promisible but has to wait until the VLSI technology is able to support realistic neural nets implementations.

1082-3409/97 $10.00 © 1997 IEEE

The methodology proposed here attempts to visually track and extract the target's features in near real-time by using a human like feedback geometric approach and a limited amount of information (original coordinates, size) available from a sequence of images (video). In particular, the methodology presented here consists of a combination of algorithms, such as heuristic segmentation, edge detection, thinning, region growing, fractals, feature extraction, graphs, etc., appropriately selected according to the existing situation, such as moving target - still camera, still camera - moving target, moving target - moving camera. The new contribution of this method is the combination of algorithms in a human like (heuristic) feedback geometric approach of processing a small amount of information extracted from low resolution data from consecutive images. The human like approach is based on the way that humans maintain and interrelate portions of visual information from sequential views (frames) in order to detect motion and extract features from selected "objects'. In the methodology presented here, we attempt to emulate this human perception by tracking motion of adjacent colors in a sequence of images. Simulated results of the methodology using sequences of images are presented.

2. The Methodology for Visual Target Tracking and Extraction

A classical ATR method may consist of four basic steps: 1) target detection, 2) target tracking, 3) features extraction, and 4) target recognition.
The methodology described by this paper presents only the visual target tracking and features extraction parts from a sequence of images.

2.1. Target's Specs

For any ATR system the target detection part starts with the determination of the targets' specs. More specifically, the specs of a target may vary from a single name (e.g. bus) to a more complex description (e.g. shapes, size, colors, texture, specialized features, etc), or some time something "unknown", which specs does not match with the specs of known targets.
In our case here, we assume that the target's specs are limited to a pair of coordinates (i,j) which point the target at the initial frame. Thus, the goal is to use this limited information (i,j) for the tracking and extraction of a target (T) from a sequence of images. In a future step, our ATR system will accept target's specs and automatically detect the target without the use of initial coordinates [4,6].

2.2. Heuristic based Image Smoothing, Segmentation and Edge-Detection with Thinning

Initially, we apply a heuristic based edge detection - thinning and segmentation method to define and clean the image regions with specific colors [9]. In particular, an image has to be smoothed before an edge detection process in order noise to be removed, especially noise associated with the camera [15].

. Smoothing

During the smoothing process, the color value of a pixel is compared with the color of each its eight neighboring blocks, as shown in figure 1. Note that blocks of pixels are used here instead of single pixels. The average color of a block can be determined by using the neighborhood's membership functions with respect to the center pixel as shown in equation 1.

$$C_{ij,b} = \frac{\sum_{q=p}^{p'} \sum_{s=k}^{k'} \mu_{n_p} \cdot C_{sq}}{\sum_{q=p}^{p'} \sum_{s=k}^{k'} \mu_{n_p}} \qquad (1)$$

where, k,p point to the low left and k', p' to the top right corner pixel in block **b** and **C**sq represents the color vector of a pixel at the location *sp*. This equation evaluates the average color vector of a block **b** with respect to the center i,j of the pixel. For smoothing, the color contrast between the center pixel and all the neighboring blocks must be measured.

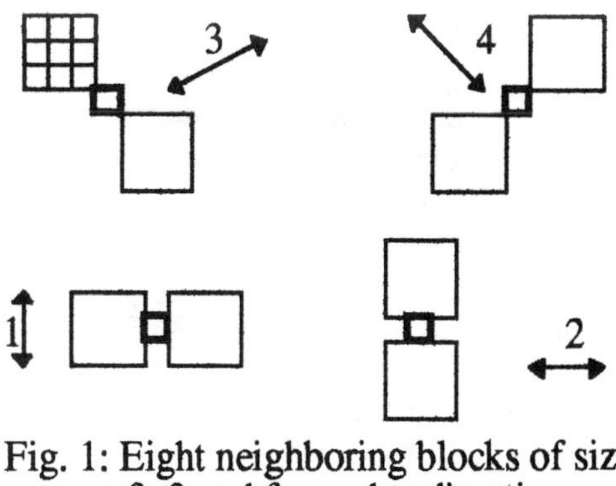

Fig. 1: Eight neighboring blocks of size 3x3 and four edge directions.

. Edge Detection with Thinning

Hue (h) , Intensity (I) and Saturation (s) are important parameters edges in images. These parameters can be computed by using RGB values from the equation (2).

$$x = 0.49R + 0.31G + 0.20B$$
$$y = 0.177R + 0.812G + 0.011B$$
$$z = 0.00R + 0.01G + 0.99B$$
$$l = 116(y/y0)^{1/3}$$
$$a = 500[(x/x0)^{1/3} - (y/y0)^{1/3}] \qquad (2)$$
$$b = 200[(y/y0)^{1/3} - (z/z0)^{1/3}]$$
$$I = l \;;\; s = [(a^2 + b^2)^{1/2}] \;;\; h = \tan^{-1}(a/b)\;;$$

where, x,y,z are color values.

The edge detection algorithm accepts smooth image input, evaluates the four edge directions (fig. 1), defines local maxs by using histogram information, thins the edges and restores the image.

2.3. Region Growing and Chain Coding for Extraction of Target's Regions

When the target's coordinates (i,j) are given their color (v) is defined and a region growing algorithm is applied to determine the shape and the size of the target's color region pointed by the coordinates (i,j).

. The basic steps of the region growing algorithm are:

Define the starting pixel P(i,j);
Create the neighborhood template 3x3 around P(i,j);
Compare the color value (vx) of each neighbor pixel with starting pixel's one (v);
If v≠ vx then define the border pixels and save their coordinates in file and goto the next neighbor pixel;
else continue with the next neighbor pixel;
Repeat the process in a spiral manner;

. The Chain code algorithm is used to select the coordinates from the designated file and converts them into a string S by using the eight directions D={0,1,2,3,4,5,6,7} of the chain code.

$$S = (i,j)\, n_i(d_k) n_j(d_m) \ldots n_r(d_t)$$

where ni, nj, ...,nr ∈ Z represent the number of pixels with the same direction,
dk, dm,...,dt ∈ D represent the chain code directions, and (i,j) represents pairs of coordinates related with the beginning of the string and its substrings if any.

2.4. Target's Region: Shape, Size, Graph and Framing

The target's region (Rc ∈ T) extracted by the region growing algorithm has a specific shape Sh represented by a chain coding string. This particular string is rearranged, by selecting its longest sub-string with the same direction to be at the beginning of Sh∈Rc, as shown in the following example:
original shape
Sh = d1d1d3d3d3d7d7d7d7d7d7d7d7d7d7d7d4...d4
rearranged shape
Sh' = d7d7d7d7d7d7d7d7d7d7d7d4...d4d1d1d3d3d3
The size of a particular target's region is also extracted during the region growing algorithmic process and saved in a file as a number of pixels with the same color.

At this point the methodology creates a graph G(Rc) with attributes for a more robust representation of the region Rc. In particular, a heuristic straight line segment recognition process is used to convert the string Sh' into a sequence of straight line segments, Sh' = L1 L2 L3 L4 ..., as shown below:

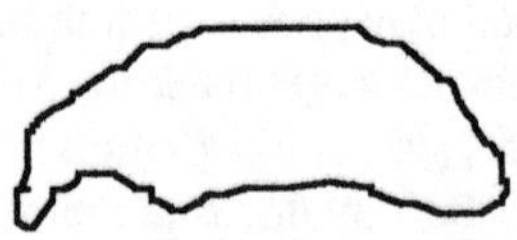

An original shape of a region

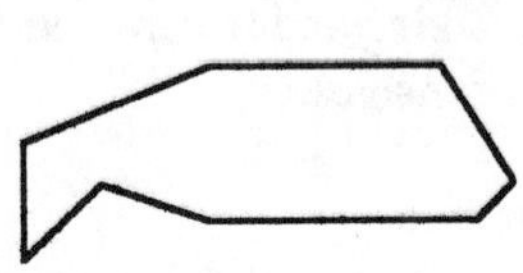

The same shape after the heuristic normalization

At this point, the normalized shape is converted into a graph with attributes

$$G(Rc) = N_1 a^c_{12} N_2 a^c_{23} N_3 \ldots N_k a^c_{k1} N_1 \otimes N_i a^p_{ij} N_j \ldots \otimes N_n a^s_{nm} N_m \ldots$$

where, a graph node N_i represents a straight line segment with the attributes (starting point, orientation, length, curvature); and an arc a_{xij} represents a set relationships among line segments, such as (connectivity (c), parallelism (p), similarity (s), relative magnitude (rm),...).
Finally, a frame around the target's region Rc can be generated. The frame is a rectangular area, which

covers the region Rc ∈ T and additional pixels from the surrounding area. The purpose of this frame is to define a smaller area at the original image frame, which will be used for a quick segmentation and determination of the rest target's parts (regions).

2.5. Tracking and Extraction of Target's Regions in Consecutive Frames

Humans have the ability to detect motion of color regions by comparing them in consecutive views (frames). In particular, the human eye has the ability to approximately maintain a view for 1/10 of a second. This is enough time for the human visual system to compare differences occurred between two or more consecutive views and track the motion of different colors. Then, the visual system extracts the shapes of these regions, synthesizes them into a global shape which represents a moving "object", and attempts to recognize the "object" against to an existing set of relative representations.
We define here the process for tracking moving target 's regions in consecutive frames (images) by emulating the human perception of detecting and tracking motion of adjacent colors in a sequence of images. In particular, the algorithmic steps are:

. Create a frame W(Rc1) around the coordinates (i,j) at the frame f1;
. Apply the heuristic segmentation on the frame W(Rc1);
. Define and extract the shape of a target's region Rc1 with color (v1) by using the coordinates (i,j);
. Generate the graph G(Rc1);
. Move to next frame f2 and develop a new frame W(Rc1) around the coordinates (i,j);
. Apply the heuristic segmentation process on the new frame W(Rc1);
. Search for the region Rc1 by using an S-S or S-D algorithmic procedure;
If Rc1 is found then extract it and generate its graph representation G(Rc1');
Compare the two graphs {G(Rc1),G(Rc1')};
If G(Rc1) is similar to G(Rc1'), then search for an adjacent region Rc2' with color (v2) at the frame f2 and extract its graph G(Rc2');
Go back to frame f1 and search for a region Rc2 with same color v2;
If Rc2 is found then compare their graphs {G(Rc2), G(Rc2')}
if they are similar, then synthesize these two regions into a new one as parts of the target;
. Repeat the process for other adjacent regions;
. When all target's regions have been found, then color them with the same color (vt) defining them as single color target T, generate the target's graph G(T), and create a new frame W(T) for it;
. Go to the next frame f3 searching for the target T;
. Readjust the size of W(T) if the target is moving in depth;
else Rc2' is background; then continue for another adjacent region;
else the Rc1' is background and move the frame W(Rc1) around and repeat the process;

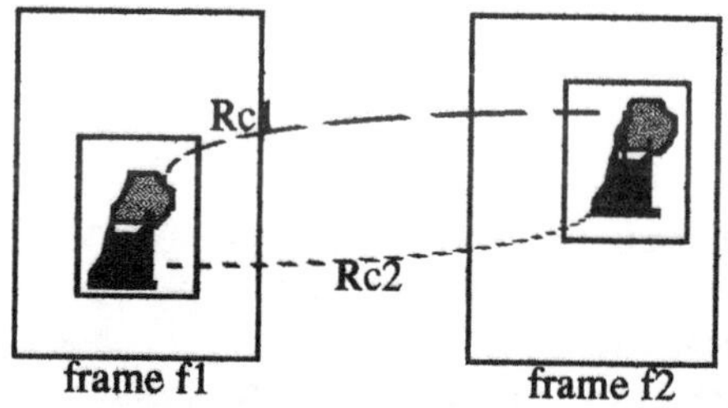

- **Tracking Scenarios**

We examine the methodology to track the regions (or parts) of a target under various scenarios, such as, (a) moving camera-moving target (MCMT), (b) moving camera- still target (MCST), (c) moving target-still camera (MTSC).

. Successive Spirals (SS) for MCMT

In this particular case, both the target and the camera are moving with different velocities (VT, Vc) and in different directions as well, as shown in figure 2.

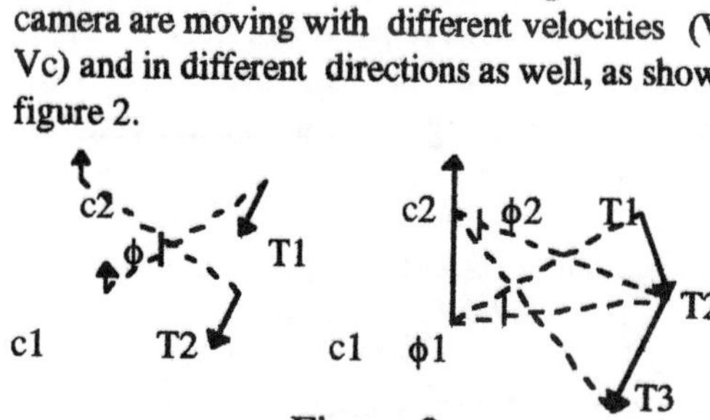

Figure 2.

The basic assumption here is that the target has to appear into two consecutive images (frames) in order to be tracked by the camera. If this assumption is true, then the camera has to rotate itself to the target's direction by an angle ϕi, i=1,2,3... defined by the motion of the target. When the target appears at the first frame (f1), the methodology described here assumes that the target will be automatically detected by another process, or pointed by the user on the frame f1, thus the initial target's coordinates (i0,j0) are saved for the next processing steps. At this point, the methodology extracts the particular region pointed by its specific color value, as mentioned in the previous section. At the second frame (f2) the target will appeared at any position, thus the methodology applies a spiral (Ss) scanning to detect the target at its new position (i1, j1) as shown in figure 3.

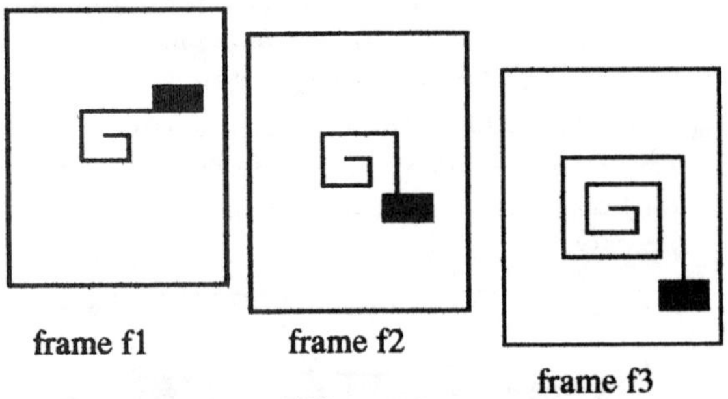

Figure 3.

Since the target is moving, there is always a non zero probability that it will change direction from frame to frame, thus the methodology applies always a spiral detection scanning, starting from the previous (i,j), or the center of the frame (fj, j=2,3,...), to find the target. This proposed target detection approach works based on the target's color under the assumption that the color (v) of the region Rc will not drastically change from a frame fj to the next one fj+1

. Spiral with Successive Diagonals (SDs) for (MTSC), or (MCST).

In these cases, one of the two items used here is moving when the other remains in a fixed position. In particular, there is a case that the camera is still and the target is moving. Here, we assume that the target appears into two consecutive frames f1 and f2 as previously. Thus, the methodology firstly applies a spiral scanning to detect the target at the second frame. At this point the method saves the new co-ordinates (i1,j1) and develops trajectory vector for the motion of the target. Thus, at the next conse-cutive frame f3, the method does not apply a spiral scanning to detect the target, but a diagonal one in smaller area, which requires less scanning steps to find the target, as shown in figure 4.

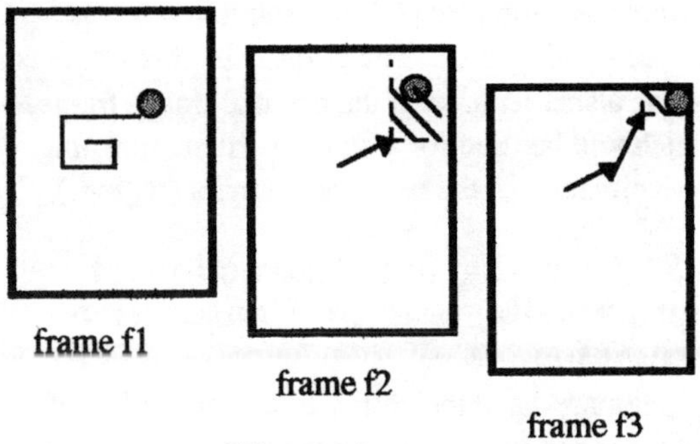

Figure 4.

. Target's region extraction and comparison

In case that the target's region Rc is detected, a region growing algorithm is applied by the methodology to extract the region's characteristics (size, color, shape). These three features are important for the identification of the correct region. Thus, a comparison takes place between the previous region's characteristics and the new ones. Since the color (v) is the same the emphasis is given at the two other features, size and shape. The comparison between two sizes Sz1 and Sz2 is very simple, since by size we mean the number of pixels with the same color (v) . Thus, the methodology subtracts theses sizes $|Sz1-Sz2| \leq \varepsilon$, where ε represents a heuristic acceptance range . Next, the method compares the graphs G(Rc1) and G(Rc2) by using a confidence function f for the graph matching process,

$$f(Ni, aij) = [\ (\#N/\#N') + (\#Nsame/\#N'total) + (\#aij\ same/\#a'ij\ total) + (sub(aij(c))/seq(a'ij(c))) + (\#aij(p)/\#a'ij(p)) + (\#aij(s)/\#a'ij(s))\ ] \leq E$$

where E represents an experimental heuristic parameter.

3. Illustrative Examples

For the illustrative examples, we used sequences of synthetic and grey scale images (4 consecutive frames), a PC pentium 200MHz, and a noisy target of 950 pixels. Note that this methodology works for color sequences images as well. Below the experimental times are presented for a synthetic sequence of images (4 color tank in various positions) and for a sequence of real images (where the moving target is a mini bus on a road). The figures for both examples are given at the end of this paper.

3.1. Synthetic Sequence of Images
. Moving Target - Still Camera

. *Methodology S-Ds*

Results:

Frame f0 = 0 msecs
Frame f1 = 0.35 msecs, spiral
Frame f2 = 0.13 msecs, diagonal
Frame f3 = 0.07 msecs, diagonal

Total = 0.55 msecs

. Moving Camera - Moving Target using previous coordinates

. *Methodology S-Ss*

Results:

Frame f0 = 0 msecs
Frame f1 = 0.35 msecs, spiral
Frame f2 = 0.62 msecs, spiral
Frame f3 = 0.31 msecs, spiral

Total = 1.28 msecs

. Moving Camera - Moving Target using central points

. *Methodology S-Ss*

Results:

Frame f0 = 0 msecs
Frame f1 = 0.0045 msecs, spiral
Frame f2 = 0.49 msecs, spiral
Frame f3 = 2.72 msecs, spiral

Total = 3.21 msecs

3.2. Grey Scale Images
. Moving Target - Still Camera

. *Methodology S-Ds*

Results:

Frame f0 = 0 msecs
Frame f1 = 12.5 msecs, spiral
Frame f2 = 10.5 msecs, spiral
Frame f3 = 10.5 msecs, spiral

Total = 32.5 msecs
(without segmentation)

4. Conclusion and Discussion

In this paper a near real-time methodology for visual tracking and extraction of targets from a sequence of images was presented. This methodology is based on a heuristic human like geometric approach by appropriately combining heuristic segmentation, edge detection, region growing, search (fractals), object extraction and tracking algorithms. The methodology applied on different scenario, such as moving camera-still target, moving target-still camera, and moving camera - moving target. Future work: real-time classification of targets under noisy condition, and fusion of different sensory data, such as IR, radar, thermal.

Acknowledgment

This work is partially supported by the IRR, AFRL-Rome Research Laboratory , 1997

References

[1] S.Grossberg, H>Hawkins and A.Waxman "A special issue of ATR, Neural Network Journal, vol.8,7-8,1995

[2] M.Brown and W.Swonger, "A prospectus for ATR", IEEE-T-AES, 25,3,1989

[3] Min et. al., The second order neural nets for radar ship target recognition, NAE Conf. 1992, pp. 270-277

[4] Songhua et al., "Target discrimination and recognition using high resolution range features", NAE Conf. 1992, pp. 280-286.

[5] Theis, et. al.," Comparison of model based vision statistical based and neural net based ATRs", NAE Conf., 1989, pp. 1733-1739

[6] J.Novak and N.Bourbakis, "A survey on ATR detection and recognition", TR-1993,MV Lab BU-CIS, pages 21.

[7] N.Bourbakis et al., " A comparison among segmentation techniques for ATR", TR-1993, MV Lab, BU-CIS, pages 15

[8] N.Bourbakis, " Knowledge extraction and representation during navigation in unknown environments, IJPRAI, 9,1,1995

[9] A. Mogzadeh and N.Bourbakis, Region growing based segmentation of color images, IAPR Society Pattern Recognition Journal, 30,6,1997

[10] N.Bourbakis and R.Andel, Fusion of color image and sensory data for 3-D space modeling, IEEE I&S-98, May. 1998 CA

[11] N. Bourbakis, A family of SCAN languages, IAPR Society Pattern Recognition Journal to appear

[12] R.Chellapa et. al., Camera calibration, IEEE Symp. on Intelligent Vehicles, MI, 1995

[13] E.Yfantis, J.Jeon, A.Sylakou and N.Bourbakis, An intelligent motion compensation algorithm, Int. Conf. on Intelligent Systems, Boston, MA,July 1997, pp.75-78.

[14] L.Chan and N.Nasrabadi, An application of wavelet based vector quantization in target

recognition, Int. IEEE Symp. on Intelligence and Systems, MD, Nov. 1997,pp.274-281

[15] S.Ghosal and R.Mehtotra, "Detection of composite edges", IEEE T-IP, 3,1,1994.

Simulated Results.

A. Spiral-Diagonal Approach
Target moving-camera fixed

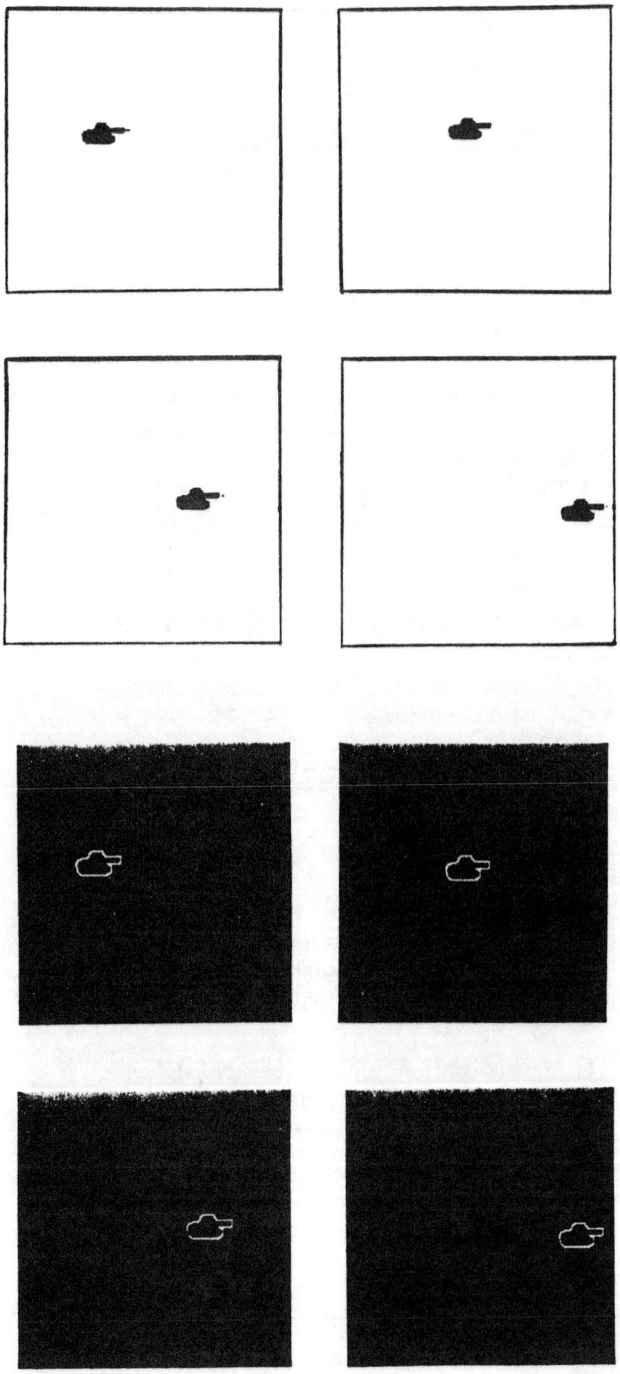

B. Spiral-Spiral Approach
Target moving-camera moving

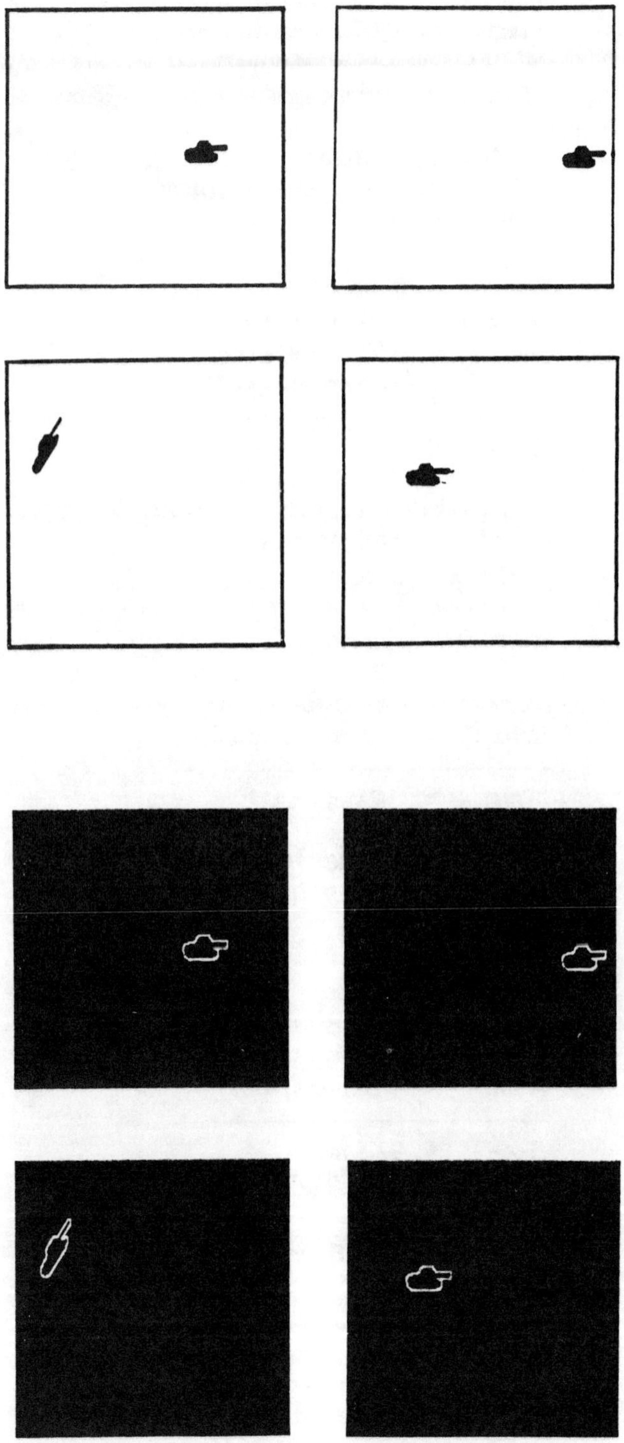

A Real Sequence of Images

First Original Image

Window

Smoothed

Segmented

Target Shape

Window

Segmented

Spiral Search

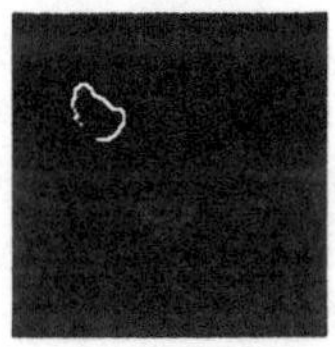

Target Shape

Window

Segmented

Spiral Search

Target Shape

Fuzzy Classification By a CMAC Network

Bai Li
Department of Computing
Nottingham Trent University
Nottingham NG1 4BU
U.K.

Dave Elliman
Department of Computer Science
Nottingham University
Nottingham NG7 2RD
U.K.

Abstract

In this paper we describe a novel application of the CMAC (Cerebellar Model Articulation Controller) neural network. We have identified CMAC as an adaptive fuzzy system that can extract fuzzy rules from training data and use these rules for classifying a unknown input of a class. The extracted fuzzy rules are stored in CMAC's memory table and they do not need to be translated explicitly to be used for classification. We have also discovered that the CMAC's network operations are equivalent to fuzzy operations. This means that the CMAC, which has so far only been recognized as a controller and a function modeller, is in fact also a neuro-fuzzy recognition system.

1. Introduction

There have been many attempts to combine neural networks and fuzzy logic. Neural networks can learn from past experiences, but their ability of dealing with fuzzy linguistic variables is weak. Fuzzy logic can encode expert knowledge in a transparent form as a set of fuzzy production rules with fuzzy linguistic variables, enabling the system to be interrogated and modified. The down side of fuzzy logic is that it often takes a considerable amount of time to design and tune fuzzy rules with fuzzy sets which quantitatively define the fuzzy linguistic variables. The learning ability of neural networks can automate this process and substantially reduce the development time and cost of fuzzy systems. Kosko [6] considered fuzzy rules as data patches, one patch a rule. When fuzzy sets are defined on each coordinate axis, the projections of the rule patches on these axes give the fuzzy rules. Halgamuge & Glesner [5] used a multi-layer perceptron architecture to generate fuzzy systems. They mapped a fuzzy system to a feed-forward neural network. A neuron is described mathematically as an activation function operating on a function of the inputs and connection weights. This function is replaced by the *min* or the *max* function to turn into the neural network into a fuzzy system. The concept of a rule neuron is introduced, conjunction and disjunction rules are implemented as *min* and *max* functions respectively. In short, they elaborately configured a neural network to model the fuzzy sets that are likely to appear in the fuzzy rules to extract. The rule relevant nodes are identified after network training to produce the rules explicitly.

We feel that the above approaches of constructing fuzzy systems by projections of data patches, or by elaborating network structure and weights are less often practical and are limited to simple systems. Simple in the sense that input data has to be clustered in the input space, or uni-modal; fuzzy sets have to be simple enough to be constructed by hand, and the rules have to be simple enough to be spelled out explicitly. This not only requires an enormous amount of effort, but most of all there are so many situations where there are no explicit rules available to describe the data. For instance, there are no explicitly rules to describe the classification benchmark data the two interlocking spirals representing two different classes.

We have looked at the CMAC neural network as a solution to this difficulty. We will describe how a CMAC can be fast-trained, not only to learn to model fuzzy membership functions for the input classes, but also extract the fuzzy rules and behave in the same way as a fuzzy system for recognition.

2. The CMAC Neural Network

The CMAC network was first proposed by Albus in 1975 [1] [2]. The model was based on the structure and the function of the Cerebellum, the part of the brain responsible for muscle control and motor coordination. The functioning of the Cerebellum can be simply described as follows: an input signal to the Cerebellum activates several mossy fibers, each of which touches a Granule cell, and the output of the Cerebellum is the sum of activations of the active Granule cells. The CMAC

1082-3409/97 $10.00

network implements the Cerebellum function as a set of mappings. Several basis functions are defined on the input space, each of which elicits a division of the input space into adjacent lattice cells, and a basis function is non-zero on only one of these cells. An input vector falls into several lattice cells so it contributes to the values stored at the memory locations where the cells are hashed into the CMAC memory table. The weighted sum of values stored at the memory locations forms the output of the CMAC to the input. In order for CMAC to generalize smoothly, the cells for different basis functions are displaced relative to each other, so that only one cell drops out as an input moves parallel to one axis by one cell. Inputs far away from one another have hardly any cells in common and the output for either of them will not affect that of the other. In Figure 1, a 2D input vector *(i,j)* falls into two cells *Be* and *Cf* when *i* falls into *B & C*, and *j* falls into *e & f*.

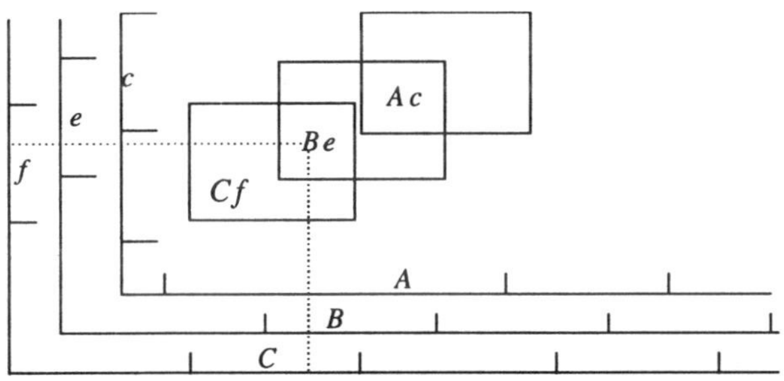

Figure 1.

In the original CMAC, the values stored in the memory table by the input data are modified during training. The error, or the difference between the CMAC output and the desired output, is calculated and a fraction of this is added to each of the values in the memory location addressed. This process is repeated until a satisfactorily small error is achieved. In this paper, we will propose a fast, one-shot training algorithm for CMAC to estimate fuzzy membership functions from input data for recognition.

3. Fuzzy Systems

A fuzzy system comprises of a set of fuzzy facts and fuzzy rules with fuzzy variables. A crisp input is presented to the fuzzy system, the truth values of the crisp input in the fuzzy sets of the input fuzzy variables are computed, and *'anded'*. The result of the *and* operation is the confidence value of the input in the rule's premise and this confidence value is then applied to the conclusion part of the rule. In *min* inferencing, the fuzzy set of the output fuzzy variable in the conclusion part of the rule is clipped off at a height corresponding to the rule premise's computed degree of truth. The clipped fuzzy sets for different rules are then composed. In *sum* composition, the output fuzzy set is constructed by taking the point-wise sum over all of the fuzzy sets of the output fuzzy variables. The output fuzzy set is then defuzzified to produce a crisp output value of the fuzzy system. In *max* defuzzification, one of the variable values at which the fuzzy set has its maximum membership value is chosen as the crisp output value. Rules that have more confidence values to the input contribute greater to the output, and the output is the result of the efforts of all the rules.

4. CMAC as a Fuzzy System

Some researchers [4] have looked at associative memory networks from a fuzzy viewpoint where fuzzy sets are used to implement the basis functions of the networks. The basis functions represent mappings which calculate how close the input is to the center of these basis functions. These associative memory networks differ according to the size, shape and placement of the basis functions in the input space.

CMAC is seen as a distributed associative memory network, distributed in the sense that an input is transmitted by several imprecise basis functions. The effect of the input is thus the sum of values of all the basis functions. If we look at the basis functions along a certain coordinate axis at a time, which is equivalent to slicing the basis functions along one axis of the coordinate space, the effect of the basis functions defined on the overlapping cells can be seen as an approximation of the overall one-dimensional fuzzy set of the input data on that axis. The one-dimensional fuzzy sets on different axes are then *'anded'* or *'ored'* to give the input fuzzy set for the premise of a rule, as shown in Figure 2.

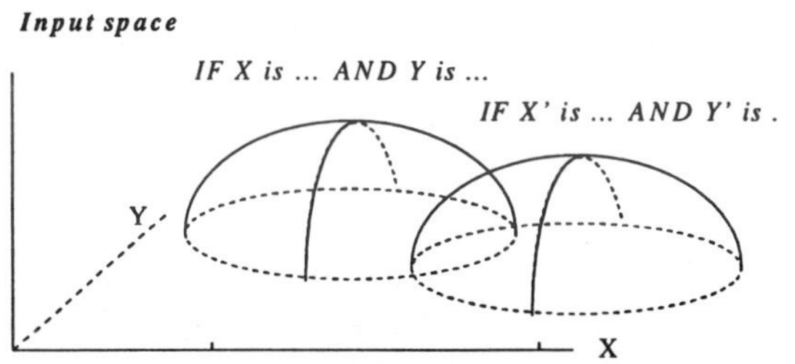

Figure 2.

Having explained how the CMAC models input fuzzy sets for the premises of the rules, we now look at how the CMAC models the output fuzzy sets for the consequences of the rules. The generalization ability of CMAC as a result of overlapping basis functions suggests that inputs close to one another would fall into more common lattice cells, so they will certainly contribute to more similar memory locations addressed by these common lattice cells during training. What this means it that the values stored in memory locations reflect the density of the input data in the input space, or to be more precise, they are in proportional to the density of the input data at any region in the input space. This fact suggests effectively the CMAC's ability to connect input and output, or its ability of extracting the rules bounding the input and the output. We will explain this in some more detail. The fact is that each input/output pair of the training data can be understood as representing an imprecise rule describing the class of the training data. During training, the degree of membership of the input in the input fuzzy set of this rule is distributed into several memory locations addressed by the lattice cells in which the input falls, the values at these locations form a distributed output fuzzy set of the consequence of the rule. The output fuzzy sets of different input/output pairs overlap, which is equivalent to a sum composition of the output fuzzy sets of all the rules describing the class. In summary, the values accumulated by the input data in the CMAC memory table during training form a distributed overall output fuzzy set of the consequence of the rule for the class, as shown in Figure 3.

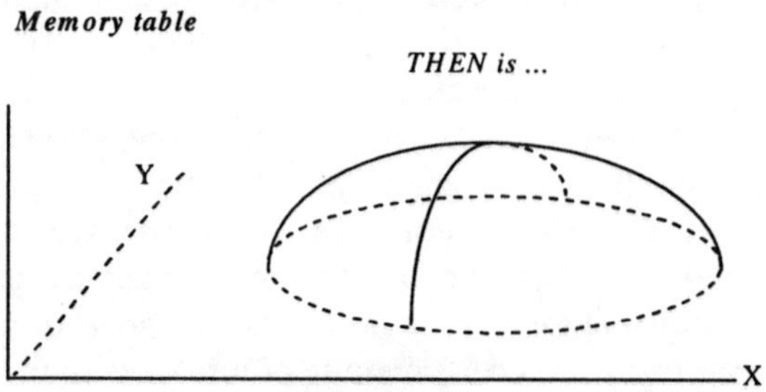

Figure 3.

It is important to note the vital difference between the CMAC as a fuzzy system and the conventional fuzzy systems. In a conventional fuzzy system, the input and the output fuzzy sets of the rules are pre-defined. To produce an output for a given input, the output fuzzy set is either scaled down or clipped off by the degree of membership of the input in the input fuzzy set of the rule premise. The CMAC fuzzy system has no given input nor output fuzzy set, but the network estimates them by adding appropriate values to appropriate memory locations during training.

5. Fuzzy Classification by a CMAC

5.1 One-Shot Training Algorithm

The original CMAC training algorithm modifies the values in memory locations in order to produce the desired output for each input. This is to train the CMAC as a function modeller. To use a CMAC as a classifier the output needs to indicate a specific class. The task of the CMAC is to extract the rules describing the input data and the output, to estimate the output fuzzy sets, which, in this case are the classes. As explained in Section 4 that this can be achieved by adding values to the memory locations addressed by the input data. The overall output fuzzy set built up in CMAC memory table by the training data of a class is the fuzzy set for the class. A different memory table is needed for a different class. Without losing generality, we use two classes in Figure 2. and Figure 3. to illustrate the fuzzy training process. Inputs from each class are hashed to a CMAC memory table representing the class. The overall fuzzy sets for all the classes are built up in the memory tables during training.

5.2 Fuzzy Classification

When comes to classify a unknown input, the lattice cells that the unknown input falls are hashed into all the CMAC memory table. From Section 4 we know that a unknown input which belongs to the training class should share many lattice cells with the training data of the training class. These common cells would have been hashed into memory locations by the training data before classification begins. If we add up the values stored in these common cells, we should get a higher value than that of an input from a different class. In other words, the input should have the maximum membership grade in the fuzzy set for its class. A *winner-takes-all* strategy is then applied to classify the unknown input as belonging to the class in which it achieves the maximum membership degree. This generalizes naturally to classification problems with multi-classes.

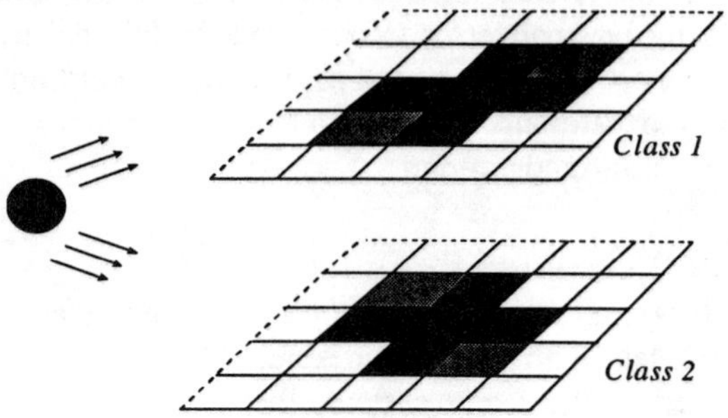

Figure 4.

In Figure 4, a unknown input is hashed to all the memory tables and the outputs of the tables are the degrees of membership of the input in the fuzzy sets of the classes. The input is classified as belonging to the class at which it achieves the maximum membership degree. The output fuzzy membership degree of an input is the sum of values over all the memory locations addressed by the input, which is equivalent to the sum defuzzification of a fuzzy system.

5.3 Comparison

The CMAC classifier is tested against the Bayesian classifiers and a k-nearest neighbour classifier. The testing method chosen was the leaving-one-out method. The classifiers were trained on all but one of the groups, then tested on the group left out. This was repeated with each group being left out. Tests on the CMAC were also made using different basis functions. Fisher's Irish data and the Spiral data are used as the test data. All the classifiers classified these data sets well, except that Bayesian quadratic classifier failed to classify the Spiral data. The Bayesian classifier requires the estimate of a mean vector and a covariance matrix for each class. A posterior probability of the input vector for each class is calculated and the input vector was assigned to the class with the highest value. The estimation of a mean vector and a covariance matrix of a class using statistical and other method is suitable for uni-modal data, which is clustered in one place in the input space. CMAC's memory storage is distributed, the input data is modeled locally (only the basis functions activated by the input contribute to the weight increment during training), so more than one mean vector for a class can be estimated and stored in its memory table. This will enable it to draw decision boundary of arbitrary complexity. The one-shot training gives CMAC the advantage in speed. Experiments showed that the training time for multi-layer perceptron is approximately ten times of that of the CMAC.

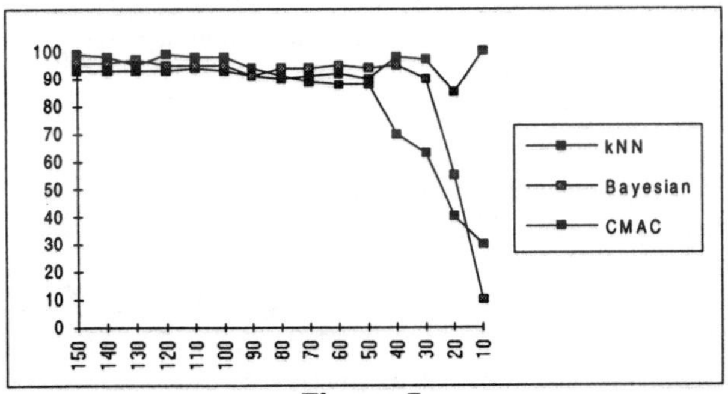

Figure 5.

Figure 5. gives an indication of performance of the CMAC in percentage on Fisher's Irish data, as compared with the performances of Bayesian and k-nearest neighbour classifiers. The horizontal axis represents the sample size. The CMAC is worse than the Normal model on trivial problems, as it has inherent quantization error. However, on more difficult problems, the CMAC out-performs the Normal model, due to the fact that CMAC makes no assumption about the distribution of the data.

6. Conclusion

The CMAC neural network is a fuzzy system which extracts from input data

- *complex rules*
  - some training data cannot be described explicitly by rules, but the CMAC can always estimate the relationship between the input and the output
- *implicit rules*
  - rules learnt are distributed as values in memory tables, there is no need write them down explicitly

The CMAC classifies an input by referring to its memory table. The output is stored in a distributed fashion such that the output of an input at any point in the input space is derived by summing the contents over a number of memory locations. The idea behind our adaptation of CMAC for classification purpose is the CMAC mapping algorithm which converts the similarities in the input data into the degree of overlap between the sets of memory locations where the output values are stored. The fact that CMAC accumulates contributions form different inputs and converts many and overlapping outputs to a single one is equivalent to fuzzy composition and defuzzification.

The CMAC network offers many advantages over other classifiers. It stores and learns information locally so it can form decision boundary of arbitrary complexity. It also performs very simple computation, so its training and recognition time are both very fast.

7. References

[1] Albus J., A New Approach to Manipulator Control, The Cerebellar Model Articulation Controller, *Trans ASME. Jnl. Dyn. Sys. Meas. and Control,* Vol. 63, No. 3, 1975.

[2] Albus J., A Model of the Brain for Robot Control, Part 2: *A Neurological Model*, BYTE, July, 1979.

[3] An P. C., Miller W. T., Parks P. C., Design Improvements in Associative Memories for Cerebellar Model Controllers, *Proceedings of International Conference on Artificial Neural Networks*, Helsinki, North-Holland, Vol. 2, 1991.

[4] Brown M., and Harris C., *NeuroFuzzy Adaptive Modelling and Control*, Prentice Hall International (UK) Limited, 1994.

[5] Halgamuge, S. K., Glesner, M., Neural Networks in Designing Fuzzy Systems for Real World Applications, *International Journal for Fuzzy Sets and Systems*, North Holland, 1994.

[6] Kosko B., *Fuzzy Thinking*, Harper Collins Publishers, 1994.

Pruning Fuzzy ARTMAP Using the Minimum Description Length Principle in Learning from Clinical Databases

Ten-Ho Lin and Von-Wun Soo
Department of Computer Science
National Tsing-Hua University, Hsinchu, Taiwan, R.O.C.
E-mail: soo@cs.nthu.edu.tw

Abstract

Fuzzy ARTMAP is one of the families of the neural network architectures based on ART(Adaptive Resonance Theory) in which supervised learning can be carried out. However, it usually tends to create more categories than are actually needed. This often causes the so called overfitting problem, namely the performance of the networks in test set is not monotonically increasing with the additional training epochs and category creation, for fuzzy ARTMAP. In order to avoid the overfitting problem, Carpenter and Tan [Carpenter and Tan, 1993] proposed a confidence-based pruning method by eliminating those categories that were either less useful or less accurate. This paper proposes yet another alternative pruning method that is based on the Minimal Description Length (MDL) principle. The MDL principle can be viewed as a tradeoff between theory complexity and data prediction accuracy given the theory. We adopted Cameron-Jones' error encoding scheme and Quinlan's modifier for theory encoding to estimate the fuzzy ARTMAP theory description length. A greedy search algorithm of the minimum description length to prune the fuzzy ARTMAP categories one by one is proposed. The experiments showed that fuzzy ARTMAP pruned with the MDL principle gave better performance with far fewer categories created than the original fuzzy ARTMAP and other machine learning systems on a number of benchmark clinical databases such as heart disease, breath cancer and diabetes databases.

(**Subject Area:** Neural Networks; Knowledge Acquisition and Machine Learning)

1. Introduction

Learning and discovery from databases, or data mining, has recently raised much attention in both AI and database community [Frawley et al., 1991] [Agrawal and Psaila, 1995]. The main focus of the research is to induce regularities or rules using the databases as sources of training instances. The task is difficult in that the size of the databases can be potentially very huge and noise and missing data cannot be neglected. This is especially true for many clinical databases where patient records tended to be idiosyncrasy (exception) and imperfect (noisy or missing values).

Fuzzy ARTMAP [Carpenter et al., 1992] is a family of self-organized neural network architectures based on adaptive resonance theory (ART) [Carpenter and Grossberg, 1987] in which supervised learning can be carried out. Roughly speaking, the basic learning mechanism of fuzzy ARTMAP is that creating a new category (neuron unit) when an "unfamiliar" input instance is encountered while updating the connection weights of an old category when a "familiar" input instance with respect to the category is encountered. The level of familiarity is determined by thresholds of so called vigilance value and choice parameters in fuzzy ARTMAP. This learning mechanism makes fuzzy ARTMAP superior to other learning methods in that it can deal with both generalities and exceptions simultaneously.

However, fuzzy ARTMAP tended to create more categories than were actually needed. In many application domains, thousands of categories created in account for the input instances are not uncommon. This is an undesirable feature. Because it is difficult to interpret the learning results of fuzzy ARTMAP in terms of thousands of categories, not to mention that many categories created actually contribute nothing to the prediction accuracy. This belongs to the well

1082-3409/97 $10.00 © 1997 IEEE

known class of overfitting problems that more training efforts paid will not gain performance in testing. To avoid the overfitting problem, Carpenter and Tan [1993] introduced a pruning algorithm based on a so called confidence factor. The confidence factor of a category is a score in terms of a combination of its usage and performance accuracy. Their method not only reduced the network size to one third but also slightly improved the prediction accuracy in a diabetes database. However, the confidence-based pruning algorithm requires a separate training set (known as prediction set) to help learning, and although intuitively acceptable is basically a rule-of-thumb heuristic.

We consider creating a fuzzy ARTMAP category a tradeoff between theory complexity and performance accuracy, namely, creating a category can hopefully increase the performance accuracy but will also increase the complexity of the theory. The Minimum Description Length (MDL) principle [Rissanen, 1983] basically is a Occam's razor that can help to select among competing theories a balance between theory complexity and data prediction accuracy given the theory. The balance selected by the MDL principle is a bias toward a parsimony theory. Besides, the MDL principle has a profound root in information theory [Rissanen, 1983].

Hence we developed a pruning algorithm based on the MDL principle for fuzzy ARTMAP. To evaluate and compare the performance of the new learning scheme, we have done two experiments: 1) using a breast cancer database to compare the performance of the original fuzzy ARTMAP against that of fuzzy ARTMAP with MDL pruning. 2) using a Pima Indian diabetes database to compare the fuzzy ARTMAP performance of the confidence-based pruning against MDL pruning.

In the section 2, we will briefly describe the fuzzy ARTMAP architecture and its learning mechanism. In section 3, we discuss the minimum description length principle and how the it is applied to estimate the theory and data encoding in the fuzzy ARTMAP. In section 4, we describe the MDL-based pruning search algorithm for fuzzy ARTMAP. In section 5, we showed two experiments on different benchmark databases and compared their results. In section 6, we make discussion and conclusion.

2. The fuzzy ARTMAP architecture

Fuzzy ARTMAP is a neural network architecture that performs incremental supervised learning of recognition categories and multidimensional maps of both analog and binary patterns [Carpenter et al., 1992]. It consists of two fuzzy ART [Carpenter, Grossberg, and Rosen, 1991] modules, namely ART_a and ART_b, linked via an inter-ART module, called a *map field* F^{ab} as in Fig. 1. Each field in fuzzy ART, represented as a square in Fig. 1, consists of a set of neurons. The map field F^{ab} links each category to its prediction. In classification tasks, ART_b does nothing more than the identical mapping which directly maps the target vector b into the vector field F_2^b and can be ignored. Each F_2^a node corresponds to a category. The input vectors are preprocessed by a mechanism called *complement coding* where every input vectors is represented by a pair of (a, 1-a), namely, the input pattern a, and its complement 1-a. With the complement coding option, the weight vector w_j^a of a category j can be viewed as a hyperrectangle over the input space under a geometric interpretation. Each category corresponds to a fuzzy inference rule, which tells a prediction is more possible when a input vector falls nearer (or within) the hyperrectangle.

The learning mechanism in fuzzy ARTMAP are conducted at ART_a and map field F^{ab}. It first carries out a vigilance test as following: The category j with the highest value of choice function $T_j = |I \wedge w_j| / (\alpha + |w_j|)$ is chosen, where I is the input vector, $\wedge$ is the fuzzy AND operation, w_j is the weight vector of category j and α is the choice parameter. The chosen category is then tested by the vigilance test $|I \wedge w_j| / |I| > \rho$, where ρ is the vigilance parameter. If it fails the test, the category with the second high choice function is chosen and repeat the procedure above. If the chosen category which passes the vigilance test but predictes a wrong target class, the vigilance parameter is temporary increased and repeat the category choosing and vigilance test process. If the chosen category passes the vigilance test and predicts correctly, it will learn the input vector by updating the weight according to the following formula:

$$W_J^{(new)} = \beta(I \wedge W_J^{(old)}) + (1-\beta) W_J^{(old)} \quad (1)$$

where β is the learning rate. Finally, if no category passes all the tests above, a new category will be created to account for this particular input.

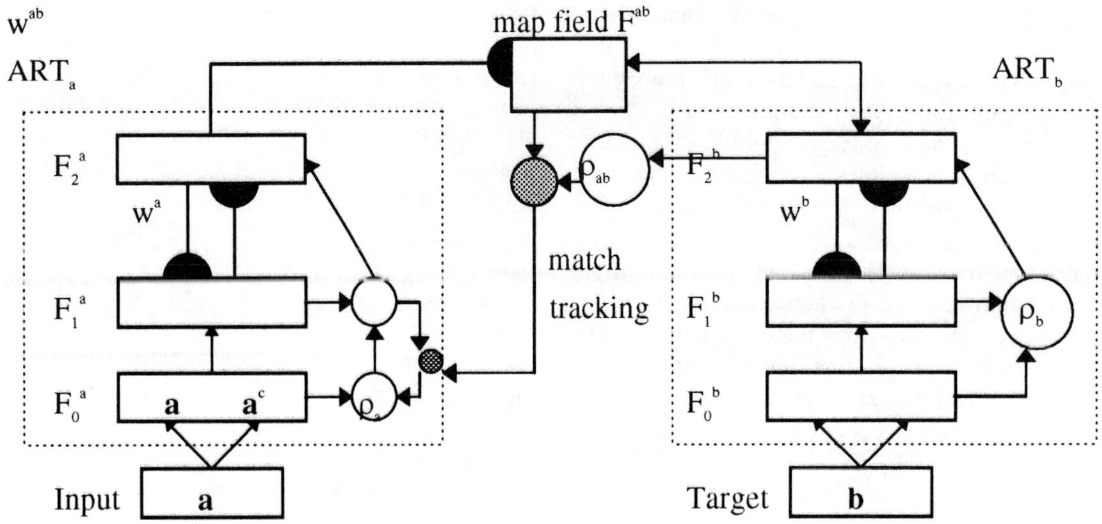

Figure 1: Fuzzy ARTMAP architecture [Carpenter et al., 1992]

3. The MDL principle and fuzzy ARTMAP pruning algorithm

When the learning is done for fuzzy ARTMAP, it enters the pruning phase where we need to decide which unnecessary category to prune away. We will discuss how minimum description length principle is used to guide pruning.

3.1. The Minimum Description Length

Let L(T) denote the number of bits needed to encode the theory T, and L(D|T) denote the number of bits needed to encode the data D with respect to T. L(T) measures the complexity of the theory, and L(D|T) measures how well the theory match the data (fewer bits indicate better fit). The Minimum Description Length principle states that the best theory is the one with the least number of bits required to encode the theory and the data given the theory. In other words, the best theory T is the one that minimizes

$$L(T) + L(D \mid T). \qquad (2)$$

The encoding length of a theory, L(T), for fuzzy ARTMAP is to be discussed in section 3.2 and 3.3. The encoding length of L(D|T) will be discussed in section 3.4.

3.2. Quantization levels of connection weights

To estimate the encoding complexity of theory, L(T), for fuzzy ARTMAP, one needs to know how a quantity of a weight is represented. Carpenter and Tan [1993] suggested the category weights be quantized in terms of nominal rather than numerical values. Quantization level Q is defined as the number of possible values for each category weight. For example, when Q=3, the possible weight values can be expressed as "low", "medium", or "high". There are two quantization methods: quantization by truncation and quantization by round-off. They were found to give similar performance. Quantization by round-off was used in this paper, which is described below:

If all possible values are $V_j = j / (Q-1)$, j=0, 1, ..., Q-1, reduce the weight w to the nearest V_j. Express it mathematically,

$$w^{(quantized)} = \lfloor (Q-1)w + 0.5 \rfloor / (Q-1) \qquad (3)$$

3.3. The description length of Fuzzy ARTMAP

We restrict our research on classification problems, in which the binary target vectors consists of all 0's but only one 1. Hence the ART_b module performs nothing but identical mapping and can be ignored. All we need to estimate is the description length of encoding the ART_a module only. Since ART_a consists of a collection of categories and each category is a vector of connection weight, the problem reduces to how to encode a connection weight. Assume the weights are quantized into Q values. With complement coding and the hyperrectangle interpretation, weights can be expressed in terms of a pair of the lower and upper vectors for categories. For a lower vector not equal to an upper vector, there are $\binom{Q}{2}$ possible combinations. For a lower vector equal to an upper vector, there are Q possible values. So, the description length of a weight is $\binom{Q}{2}+Q=\frac{Q(Q+1)}{2}$. A category consists of M pairs of weights, where M is the number of attributes.

$$M\log(\binom{Q}{2}+Q) \text{ bits.} \quad (4)$$

Assume a fuzzy ARTMAP with N categories which is pruned from the original fuzzy ARTMAP with N_{max} categories. First the number N should be encoded. Because N can be $1,2,\ldots,N_{max}$, it takes $\log N_{max}$ bits to encode the number N. Second, to encode N categories, $N\times M\times\log(\binom{Q}{2}+Q)$ bits are needed. Finally, since the ordering of categories is unimportant, log N! is subtracted from the description length. Therefore, the overall theory coding length L(T) of a fuzzy ARTMAP network is

$$\log N_{max}+N\times M\times\log(\binom{Q}{2}+Q)-\log N!$$

(the length of encoding N_{max} possible categories plus the total length of N categories subtract the information of encoding the ordering of N categories.)

Now we consider the unquantized weights which are difficult to encode because they are arbitrary real numbers between 0 and 1. However, we could assume they are quantized into W values, called *weight precision* which is a threshold parameter. If W is large, it is assumed that more information is on one weight so more categories should be pruned; if W is small, it is assumed that less information is on one weight so fewer categories will be pruned.

3.4. Quinlan's modifier

It was pointed out that traditional methods of applying MDL could lead to poor accuracy in categorical domain [Quinlan, 1994]. Quinlan proposed a modifier to remedy the problem. Quinlan's modifier is a mechanism that improve the MDL selection by restricting candidate theories that tends to perform poorly. Let the probability, or proportion of positives be P(D+), the probability (proportion) of data instances predicted as positives be P(D+|T). The idea is that P(D+|T) should fall between P(D+) ± s.d.(P(D+)), where s.d.(P(D+)) is the standard deviation of P(D+). Assume data instances are independent, and the probability of each data instance being positive is identical. Then the number of positives conforms to the binomial model, so

$$s.d.(P(D+))=\frac{\sqrt{P(D+)(1-P(D+))}}{|D|} \quad (5)$$

The restricting scheme is as follow: let

$$V = |P(D+|T) - P(D+)| / s.d.(P(D+)). \quad (6)$$

If V>1, P(D+|T) is not between P(D+) ± s.d.(P(D+)) and the theory is not likely to match the data, the theory is modified by $\sqrt{V}$ as a penalty. The expression for L(T) above is multiplied by Quinlan's modifier. In one equation, the theory description length of a fuzzy ARTMAP is

$$L(T)=\max(\sqrt{\frac{|P(D+|T)-P(D+)|}{s.d.(P(D+))}},1)\times(\log(N_{max})+NM\log(\binom{Q}{2}+Q)-\log N!) \quad (7)$$

3.4. The description length of data given a theory

In two-class classification problems, encoding data given a theory, namely L(D|T), is equivalent to encoding the errors of the theory [Quinlan, 1994]. We could, therefore, encode the L(D|T) in terms of a function of prediction errors of a theory. However, as pointed out by Quinlan [1994] most description length functions are not monotonically increasing with respect to number of errors. This is because if more than half of data was falsely predicted in two class problems, predictions can be made on the wrong side of the learning system.

Table 1: The experimental results on Wisconsin breast cancer database

Learning systems	Train/Test size	Accuracy	Rules or Instances
C4.5 + MDL	629/70	95.5%	8.5
Fuzzy ARTMAP	629/70	91.86%	13.0
Fuzzy ARTMAP + MDL	629/70	95.57%	4.2

This is an undesirable property because it may prefer a less accurate theory to a more accurate theory when their complexities are the same. Cameron-Jones [1992] has proposed an error encoding scheme that increases monotonically with e, the number of errors. It first defines a code for e=0, then for e=1, 2, etc. Each of these codes is defined by an integer starting with 1 but, since we want no differentiation between theories with the same number e of errors, the encoding length for each theory in the group of the same number of errors is taken to be that of the integer associated with the last theory in the group.

$$\sum_{i=0}^{e}\binom{|D|}{i} \qquad (7)$$

where |D| is the total number of data instances.
To encode this integer, an encoding scheme for arbitrary integer is needed. Rissanen [1983] has claimed that it need

$\log^*(n) + C$ bits

to encode an arbitrary integer n, where C is a constant (and does not matter what number we use in pruning) and

$$\log^*(n) = \log(n)+\log(\log(n))+\log(\log(\log(n)))+\ldots$$

The recursive logarithm function for log*(n) is repeated until the term becomes negative.
Hence the Cameron-Jones' error encoding cost for e errors is

$$\log^*(\sum_{i=0}^{e}\binom{|D|}{i})+C \text{ bits.} \qquad (8)$$

4. Searching for the theory with the minimum description length

The number of possible pruned networks from a fuzzy ARTMAP with N categories is equal to the number of nonempty subsets of N categories, 2^N - 1. This makes exhaustive search of the network with minimum description length almost impossible (there may be thousands of categories in a complex fuzzy ARTMAP, for example, letter recognition benchmark problem in [Carpenter et al., 1992]). We used a greedy algorithm, or a best-first search to search the theory with minimum length. Although this search strategy may found local minimum instead of global minimum, it is a feasible choice due to the time constraint. The search algorithm is described below:

1. Find the description length of the fuzzy ARTMAP L_0.
2. For each category j, assume it is pruned, and find the description length L'(j) according to expression (7) and (9).
3. Find J such that L'(J) = min(L'(j)), i.e. find the category J that decreases the description length most by its pruning.
4. If $L'(j) \geq L_0$, i.e. pruning can no longer decrease description length, or the number of categories are 2, algorithm ends.
5. If $L'(j) < L_0$, prune category J, i.e. prune the corresponding F_2^a node J.
6. Repeat 1 until algorithm ends in step 4.

5. Experimental results

5.1. Wisconsin breast cancer database

The Wisconsin breast cancer database, available via UCI machine learning repository [Murphy and Aha, 1992], was obtained from the University of Wisconsin Hospitals, Madison from Dr. William H. Wolberg. The task is to classify between benign and malignant cases. This database contains 699 instances, of which 458 (66.5%) are benign and 241 (34.5%) are malignant, and 16 missing values. We chose 9 out of 10 attributes (ID number removed) for learning. A fuzzy ARTMAP with missing value treatment using the complement coding strategy can be found in the source program for [Carpenter, 1993]: An input vector $\mathbf{a} = (a_1,\ldots,a_M)$ is turned to $\mathbf{I} = (\mathbf{a}, \mathbf{a}^c) = (a1,\ldots,a_M,a_1^c,\ldots,a_M^c)$ and sent to fuzzy ARTMAP. For known value a_i, $a_i^c = 1-a_i$. For missing value, let $a_i = a_i^c = 1$. This is equivalent to assuming the unknown value fit in the range of every category in that attribute.

Quinlan [1995] used C4.5 with (biased) MDL

Table 2: PID database experiments results (Note that α is the choice parameter; ρ is the vigilance threshold; Q is the quantization level; the question mark ? denotes data are not available; — denotes the parameter is irrelevant or note used; and W is the weight precision. The ##(*20) denotes that the data ## is averaged over 20 voters)

Learning system	α	ρ	Q	Accuracy	# of rules or nodes
ADAP	—	—	—	76.0	100000
C4.5 + MDL	—	—	—	72.4	13.3
Fuzzy ARTMAP	?	?	—	75.9	63.5 (*20)
confidence pruning	?	?	—	78.5	19.6 (*20)
confidence pruning	?	?	5	77.5	19.6 (*20)
Fuzzy ARTMAP	0.2	0.0	—	73.6	75.29 (*20)
confidence pruning	0.2	0.0	—	75.4	18.86 (*20)
MDL pruning, W=5	0.2	0.0	—	75.11	9.90 (*20)
confidence pruning	0.2	0.0	5	72.1	19.90 (*20)
MDL pruning	0.2	0.0	5	72.70	8.20 (*20)
confidence pruning	0.2	0.0	6	72.2	19.08 (*20)
MDL pruning	0.2	0.0	6	74.79	8.27 (*20)
Fuzzy ARTMAP	0.05	0.6	—	73.0	53.91 (*20)
confidence pruning	0.05	0.6	—	72.0	14.56 (*20)
MDL pruning, W=5	0.05	0.6	—	74.74	9.68 (*20)
confidence pruning	0.05	0.6	5	71.5	14.91 (*20)
MDL pruning	0.05	0.6	5	70.16	7.33 (*20)
confidence pruning	0.05	0.6	6	72.5	14.65 (*20)
MDL pruning	0.05	0.6	6	71.36	7.74 (*20)

pruning and achieved 95.5% accuracy by 8.5 rules with 629 training data and 70 testing data. Quinlan used the updated version of data that we used. Another fuzzy ARTMAP simulation with α=0.01, β=1, ρ=0, with the same number of training and test data, was run for 10 trials. It gave 91.86% accuracy by 13.0 rules on average, which is worse than C4.5 + MDL in both performance and number of rules. After MDL pruning with weight precision 5, the accuracy increased to 95.57% by 4.2 rules, which is similar to C4.5 + MDL pruning in accuracy but used about half as many rules. The experimental results are summarized in Table 1.

5.2. Pima Indian Diabetes database

The Pima Indian Diabetes (PID) database, also obtained from UCI machine learning repository is originally owned by National Institute of Diabetes and Digestive and Kidney Diseases. It contains 768 instances, 8 input attributes and 1 target, which represents whether the data shows signs of diabetes according to World Health Organization criteria (i.e., if the 2 hour post-load plasma glucose was at least 200 mg/dl found at any survey examination or during routine medical care). 268 instances of the data are positive, which is 34.9% of the database. There is no missing value instance.

ADAP, a feedforward neural network model, has been applied to PID database using 576 training data and 192 testing data and achieved 76% accuracy by 100000 association units [Smith et al., 1988]. All the following tests used the same training size. The prediction based on 20 voting fuzzy ARTMAP's achieved 75.9% accuracy with average 63.5 (*20) rules, which is very low comparing to 100000 association units of ADAP. With confidence-based pruning, the accuracy could be improved to 78.5% using even fewer rules, 19.6 (*20) [Carpenter, 1993]. Unfortunately, the exact parameters were not listed in the paper, and we couldn't repeated the above results.

In order to compare MDL-based pruning with confidence-based pruning, both techniques were tested under two sets of parameters, α=0.2, β=1, ρ=0 and α=0.05, β=1, ρ=0.6, and different quantization levels. The two sets of parameters have different vigilance values and different number of categories. All simulations are repeated 10 times, with 20 voters. Under these parameters and quantization levels, MDL-based pruning gave slightly better accuracy in about half as many rules. Quantization level 6 gave better accuracy and fewer rules than quantization level 5 in both pruning methods. The results can be found in Table 2.

6. Conclusion

6.1. Summary and discussion

Fuzzy ARTMAP is a powerful neural network model with many useful characteristics, including stability, guaranteed convergence, and online learning. Overfitting avoidance techniques in fuzzy ARTMAP are very important but were seldom addressed.

Fuzzy ARTMAP gave better performance and fewer rules over other machine learning algorithms and neural network models in different benchmark databases learning problems. We found that Fuzzy ARTMAP with MDL-based pruning used fewer categories and often even better performance than fuzzy ARTMAP without MDL pruning. We also found that MDL-based pruning extracted fewer rules and often better accuracy than confidence-based pruning, and need not a separate predicting set.

However, our current greedy search strategy in search of shortest description length theory seems to be problematic in that it may trap in a local optimal. This is due to the execution time of MDL-based pruning. Because computing description length needs to go through all training instances, it takes about the time of a whole training epoch to pruning a single category. In PID database, the original fuzzy ARTMAP has more than 60 categories and the pruned network has less than 10 categories, which means more than 50 categories are pruned, and about the time of 50 epochs is required. It takes a large amount of time in comparison to 10 to 20 epochs that fuzzy ARTMAP usually takes for training. The confidence-based pruning only needs to go through the training data once. This is the reason it didn't look over more thorough search space of all possible networks. However, since fuzzy ARTMAP pruning requires off-line learning, the execution time is not so critical.

6.2. Future work

1. The MDL encoding schemes and Quinlan's modifier are developed based on two-classes (positive and negative) classification. We wish to generalize them to more-than-two classes in the future.
2. The nominal and missing value treatments in fuzzy ARTMAP also need further study.
3. One important and useful property of fuzzy ARTMAP is online learning. Both fuzzy ARTMAP pruning techniques conflict with the concept of online learning, because pruning must be applied after the network is trained. Is it possible for a MDL-based online checking criteria to guide the online learning system in category creation and overfitting avoidance? This is definitely an interesting open problem.

Acknowledgment

This research is supported by the collaboration research project of National Tsing Hua University and Veteran General Hospital under the Grant No. VGHTH 85-008-2.

Reference

Agrawal, R. and Psaila, G. (1995). Active data mining. *Proceedings, First International Conference on Knowledge Discovery and Data Mining*, 216-221. AAAI Press.

Cameron-Jones, R. M. (1992). Minimum description length instance-based learning. *Proceedings 5th Australian Joint Conference on Artificial Intelligence*, (A. Adams and L. Sterling, Eds), Singapore: World Scientific, 368-373.

Carpenter, G. A., and Grossberg, S. (1987). A massively parallel architecture for a self-organizing neural pattern recognition machine. *Computer Vision, Graphics, and Image Processing*, 37, 54-155.

Carpenter, G. A., Grossberg, S., Markuzon, N., Reynolds, J. H., and Rosen, D. B.(1992). Fuzzy ARTMAP: A neural network architecture for incremental supervised learning of analog multidimensional maps. *IEEE Transactions in Neural Networks*, 3, 698-713.

Carpenter, G. A., Grossberg, S., and Rosen, D. B. (1991). Fuzzy ART: Fast stable learning and categorization of analog patterns by an adaptive resonance system. *Neural Networks*, 4, 759-771.

Carpenter, G. A. and Tan, A. H. (1993). Rule extraction, Fuzzy ARTMAP, and medical databases. *Proceedings, World Congress on Neural Networks, Portland, OR* (Vol. I, pp.501-506). Hillsdale, NJ: Lawrence Erlbaum Associates.

Frawley, W. J., Piatetsky-Shapiro, G., and Matheus, C. J. (1991). Knowledge discovery in databases: an overview. *Knowledge Discovery in Databases*, 71-92. AAAI Press / The MIT Press

Gallager, R. G. (1968). *Information Theory and Reliable Communication*. New York: Wiley.

Gennari, J. H., Langley, P., and Fisher, D. (1989). Models of incremental concept formation. *Artificial Intelligence*, 40, 11-61.

Murphy, P. M. and Aha, D. W. (1992) *UCI Repository of machine learning databases* [Machine readable data repository]. Irvine, CA: University of California, Department of Information and Computer Science.

Quinlan, J. R. (1994). The Minimum Description Length principle and categorical theories. *Proceedings 11th International Conference on Machine Learning*, New Brunswick, 233-241. San Francisco: Morgan Kaufmann.

Quinlan, J. R. (1995). MDL and categorical theories (continued). *Proceedings 12th International Conference on Machine*, 464-469. San Francisco: Morgan Kaufmann.

Rissanen, J. (1983). A universal prior for integers and estimation by minimum description length. *Annals of Statistics*, 11, 416-431.

Smith, J. W., Everhart, J. E., Dickson, W. C., Knowler, W. C., and Johannes, R. S. (1988). Using the ADAP learning algorithm to forecast the onset of diabetes mellitus. *Proceedings of the Symposium on Computer Applications and Medical Care*, 261-265. IEEE Computer Society Press.

Zhang, J. (1992). Selecting typical instances in instance-based learning. *Proceedings of the Ninth International Machine Learning Conference*, 470-479. Aberdeen, Scotland: Morgan Kaufmann.

Session F.2

Knowledge Based Systems and Their Applications

Session Chair:
Scott Starks, University of Texas, USA

Feature-based Representation and Indexing of Axisymmetric Parts in Machining Process Planning using Case-Based Reasoning

Wen F. Lu*, Xiaoqing Frank Liu**, Hsin-Chi Chang*, and Lijun Dong**

*Department of Mechanical and Aerospace Engineering
**Department of Computer Science
University of Missouri-Rolla, Rolla, MO 65409

Abstract

A framework of process planning system for machining of axisymmetric parts using case-based reasoning is proposed in this research. It is composed of four major modules: retriever, modifier, simulator and repairer. This paper focuses on the representation, indexing and retrieving of process planning cases. A feature-based representation for parts and processes is presented. An effective similarity metric is developed to measure the similarity between two parts so that the most similar case can be retrieved rapidly and correctly. It is based on the hierarchical representation of part features. In addition, indexing and retrieving mechanisms are discussed in this paper. A prototype based on the proposed representation, indexing and the similarity metric was developed in a Sun workstation using ACIS and 3D-Toolkit from Spatial Technology Inc.

1 Introduction

Process planning is an important activity in CAD/CAM integration. In the past, expert systems have been widely used in the automated process planning system [1][2][3]. However, expert systems are successful only if the domain of applications is well defined and the experts' experience can be translated into rules clearly. Unfortunately, the domain is difficult to define for most of the manufacturing applications, and the knowledge existing in experts' mind is not the form of rules but the past successful process plans. Even though one expert system was built, it is static and hard to change [4]. Besides, the current trend of minimum "time to market" requires that an automated process planning system should be able to advance its own knowledge in response to the rapidly changing markets and manufacturing environments. The ability of learning has thus become critical for such process planning system.

In response to the above challenges, the Case-Based Reasoning (CBR) has been introduced for learning in process planning [5][6]. Using CBR, a process plan of new parts can be generated by retrieving the past similar parts, and then modifying the prior successful plans to match new requirements. It has been recognized that the retrieval mechanism plays an important role in the CBR based process planning system. The key factors affecting the performance of the retrieval mechanism are **representation**, **indexing** and **similarity metric** of parts. A good representation, indexing and similarity metric will enable the system to retrieve the most similar case rapidly and correctly. Therefore, the objective of this paper is to define an appropriate representation and indexing mechanism of parts and process, and an effective similarity metric.

The primary application domain of this study is process planning for axisymmetric parts. Two systems, CAPLAN/CBC [6][7] and PROCASE [5][8], have been developed in this domain. The former assumes that the outlines of a final part can be divided into 3 areas (two rising and a horizontal areas) in the axial direction and each area is machined independently. In practice, these areas are not independent to each other in the machining process. Besides, each geometric feature includes only its dimension in their studies. Precision and material were not considered. In fact, precision and material are two of important factors affecting the selection of cutting tools and process steps in machining process. The latter work, though including the information about material and precision, ignored them while retrieving the most similar case. In addition, the similarity between cases is measured by identifying and counting the shared common features in PROCASE. In this paper, we extend the concept of the feature-based representation [5] to develop an effective indexing mechanism for retrieving similar parts based on a novel similarity metric.

This paper is organized in 7 sections. The framework of the proposed process planning system is first introduced in Section 2. Feature-based representation of parts and processes are discussed in Section 3. Section 4 presents case indexing mechanism. Retrieval techniques and similarity measures are presented in Section 5. One example implemented in a solid modeling environment is given in Section 6. Finally, conclusions are provided in Section 7.

2 Framework

The framework of the feature-based process planning system using case-based reasoning, as shown in Figure 1, is composed of four major components: retriever, modifier, simulator, and repairer. More explanations of these four major components are described in the following.

• The **retriever** searches the plan case base for the "most similar part" according to the similarity metric and uses it as a plan candidate. If the plan is directly applicable to the new part, the parameters of the plan are then instantiated using the simulator. If the plan partially meets the needs of the new part, a modification must be made by the modifier.

• The **modifier** is used to modify the retrieved plan for the new part. The modification is "experience oriented"; that is, either the old experience of modifying a plan or pieces of plans of the old planning cases is used to modify the plan. A set of modification rules are applied to transform a retrieved plan into a new plan that meets requirements of the new part.

• The **simulator** is used to check the feasibility of the plan as well as to assign (instantiate) all the necessary specifications to the plan. If the plan is demonstrated to be correct; that is, the "final product" meets all the specifications listed in the part design, a complete plan is generated. This plan is then stored into the plan case base for future use. If the modified plan fails in simulation, it needs to be repaired.

• The **repairer** is to repair a failed plan utilizing the failure information provided by the simulator. Again, the repaired plan is verified by the simulator. If it is successful, the system presents the successful plan and stores the successful plan in the plan case base. Otherwise, it needs to find the second "most similar plan" and repeat the cycle. The process continues until a successful plan is found or all candidate cases are exhausted.

3 Feature-based representation

3.1 Part representation

In this paper, a feature-based representation is used to represent axisymmetric mechanical parts. Each part is represented by a feature code in the operation. Two key factors affecting the process plan of a part in cutting process are its geometry and material. In order to retrieve the similar parts and their process plans, they should be represented and considered in measuring similarity between parts. Hence, the feature code of one part consists of a main-string and a sub-string which represents geometry and material property, respectively. A main-string is a list of part primitives representing the geometry of one part along the axial direction. Each primitive is represented by a geometric feature class storing its geometric data, such as geometric shape, tolerance, and surface finish. The sub-string represents hardness (HD), heat-treatment (HT) and other material properties. Figure 2 shows an example of part representation.

3.2 Process representation

Each cutting process is expressed as the removal of a geometric feature from the current workpiece. An operation code is used to represent each cutting operation and stored in a plan case. Operation codes are also extended to other non-metal removing processes, such as heat-treatment, clamping, ...etc. Each descendent part results from the application of a cutting operation to its antecedent.

3.3 Case representation

A process plan case is a data file which stores the process plan of a part. A data file contains the procedure of how a raw material is manufactured into the final product. Here, the procedure includes material removal and non-material removal, and each removal step is composed of an antecedent part, a descendent part, and a cutting operation. An example of case representation can be found in Figure 3.

4 Case indexing

One of the powerful capability of a case-based reasoning system is its ability to retrieve similar cases rapidly and accurately from the case base. In this paper, a method called feature-based similarity measurement is developed for case indexing and case retrieval. This method provides an effective similarity function to retrieve the most similar process plan in the proposed domain of application.

Three perspectives of a part are considered in the similarity measurement: geometric shape, material and precision. Geometrical shape is the major consideration in defining the similarity measure since geometrically similar parts normally have similar processing plans. The material property refers to the hardness and heat-treatment of the part. The precision property concerns with the surface finish and tolerance of a specific geometric feature in a part.

Each property plays its role in the matching of two parts. However, they may sometimes conflict with each other. For instance, two parts may have a high geometric shape similarity but very low material similarity. Therefore, a similarity measurement which incorporates the trade-off between three properties was developed. It is based on a hierarchical feature-based part representation, as shown in Figure 4. The root node represents a part using a pair of elements: one element represents its geometry (FS) and the other represents its material property (M). FS is a set of geometric features, F_i (i=1,2,..., n), that comprise the part and M is further decomposed into hardness (HD) and heat-treatment (HT). Each of geometric feature F_i contains the information of its geometric shape (G_i) and its precision value (P_i). The precision property concerns mainly with surface finish (S_1) and tolerance (T_1) of a geometric feature. Thus, a complete specification of a part is

$$(\{(G_1,(S_1,T_1)),\ (G_2,(S_2,T_2)),\ \ldots\},\ \{HD, HT\})$$

This hierarchical representation structure provides the information of what a part is made of, and facilitates the computation of the similarity measurement.

4.1 Geometric feature hierarchy

According to the geometric shape, forty five basic geometric features have been built. They are organized as a tree, shown in Figure 5, based on how they are produced. Each geometric feature is represented as a node in the figure. A node can represent two geometric features which are symmetrical. A child geometric feature can be obtained from its parent geometric feature through a cutting operation. Each node in the tree corresponds to a path from the root, which represents a cutting process from the root. Therefore, the more edges two geometric features share in their paths, the more similar their geometric shapes are. That is, the geometric shape similarity of two geometric features at a lower level should be more similar than those at a higher level. In Figure 5, each geometric feature has two labels: explicit and implicit. An explicit label is used to display and represent a geometric feature while the implicit label is employed to calculate the similarity measure. The geometric shape similarity of two geometric features is calculated in the following two steps.

Step 1) Considering the node location in the tree (first 1–4 digits of the implicit label)

- *If* 1–4 digits of two geometric features are the same → s = 1.0
- *If* 1–3 digits of two geometric features are the same → s = 0.9
- *If* 1–2 digits of two geometric features are the same → s = 0.7
- *If* 1_{st} digit is the same for two geometric features → s = 0.4

Step 2) Considering the symmetrical situation (5_{th} character of the implicit label)

- *If* the characters are the same for two geometric features, or one of them is 'c'
  → similarity measure between two geometric features: S_{geo} = s
- *If* the characters are different for two geometric features (symmetrical case)
  → similarity measure between two geometric features: $S_{geo} = 0.5 \times s$

Therefore, the more digits two geometric features share, the more similar their geometric shapes are, as indicated in Step 1. If two geometric features are symmetric, one geometric feature must be rotated in 180 degree during manufacturing, as considered in Step 2.

4.2 Surface finish matrix

According to the processes and usage of machine tools, the surface finish can be categorized into several surface finish groups ranging from very fine to very rough. If the surface finishes of two geometric features are located in the same group, it usually indicates that the cutting processes and machine tools are the same for those geometric features. In other words, geometric features which have the same surface finish should be more similar than those whose surface finishes are different. The similarity measure of geometric features in terms of surface finish, S_{surf}, can be calculated based on its classification in Figure 6.

4.3 Tolerance matrix

Based on cutting process, tolerance can be divided into several ranges from very tight tolerance to very loose tolerance. Different tolerance groups require different process plans. An example of tolerance similarity measure, S_{tol}, is summarized as the matrix in Figure 7.

4.4 Hardness matrix, and Heat-treatment matrix

A hardness matrix and a heat-treatment matrix are included in Figure 8 and Figure 9.

5 Retrieving

5.1 Similarity metric

With each part indexed with its hierarchical structure described in the previous section, the similarity between two parts can be determined by a similarity metric. The similarity metric is defined as

$$Similarity = \mathbf{W_f}\frac{Simi(P_{si}, G_{si})}{\sum(G_s + G_i)/2} + \mathbf{W_m}\frac{\sum M_{si}}{\sum M_i} \quad (1)$$

This similarity metric is based on the similarity of two hierarchical structures representing two compared parts. This equation includes two terms: the first term represents the geometric comparison between two parts, and the second represents the material comparison. Details are explained as following.

1. $\mathbf{W_f}$ and $\mathbf{W_m}$ are the weighting factors for the geometric features and material, respectively. The summation of these two weights is equal to one. Normally, the geometric features will carry more weight than material since geometric similarity is more important factor for retrieving the most similar part.

2. $Simi(P_{si}, G_{si})$ represents the geometric similarity (including geometric shape, surface finish, and tolerance) of two compared parts. More details are described in next subsection.

3. $\sum(Gs + Gi)/2$ is the average of total number of part primitives in both compared parts. This term is used to normalize the geometric similarity.

4. $\sum M_{si}$ is the summation of hardness similar value and heat-treatment similar value between two parts.

5. $\sum M_i$ is the total number of material factors and is equal to 2 since only hardness and heat-treatment are considered in this paper. The objective of this term is the same as $\sum(Gs + Gi)/2$.

5.2 Geometric similarity algorithm

As described in Section 3.1, a main-string represents the geometry of a part. Comparing the geometries of two parts also means comparing their main-strings. In this paper we extend the concept of finding a longest common subsequence (LCS) of two strings [9][10] to define the value of $Simi(P_{si}, G_{si})$. In their approach, the comparing strings include only characters. If each geometric feature within the main-string is thought as one character, comparing two main-strings will be the same as comparing two strings as in [10]. Based on the hierarchical structure of one part in this research, each geometric feature not only includes the geometric shape, but also includes surface finish and tolerance. Therefore, one matching function is proposed to present the similarity between two geometric features. The abstract of LCS algorithm as well as matching function is described in following. While finding LCS value, the "orders" in which two strings can be compared must be considered. It means that if the ith feature of main-string A compares with the jth feature of main-string B is in an "order", the (i+1)th feature of main-string A can only compare with the (j+m)th feature of main-string B, where m is greater than zero in subsequent "orders". To illustrate the "order" comparison, the following examples are given.

1) IF: *Part A* is composed of one feature, a_1, and *Part B* is also composed of one feature, b_1, **THEN:** the only order in which features of two parts can be compared is: $\{ a_1 \leftrightarrow b_1 \}$.
2) IF: *Part A* includes one feature, a_1, and *Part B* includes two features, b_1 and b_2, **THEN:** two orders in which features of two parts can be compared are: $\{ a_1 \leftrightarrow b_1,\ a_1 \leftrightarrow b_2 \}$.
3) IF: *Part A* includes two features, a_1 and a_2, and *Part B* includes one feature, b_1, **THEN:** two orders in which features of two parts can be compared are: $\{ a_1 \leftrightarrow b_1,\ a_2 \leftrightarrow b_1 \}$.
4) IF: *Part A* includes two features, a_1 and a_2, and *Part B* includes two features, b_1 and b_2, **THEN:** three orders in which features of two parts can be compared are: $\{ a_1 \leftrightarrow b_1 + a_2 \leftrightarrow b_2,\ a_1 \leftrightarrow b_2,\ a_2 \leftrightarrow b_1 \}$.

Based on the above examples, a general geometric similarity algorithm which covers all "order" comparisons between features of two parts is developed and a function called $match()$ is used as a metric to measure the similarity between two features.

Suppose that ***Part A*** is composed of m features, represented by $a_1 a_2 \cdots a_m$, and ***Part B*** is composed of n features, represented by $b_1 b_2 \cdots b_n$, the geometric similarity between these two parts can be computed as follows. Several notations used in the computation are explained first.

1. A_m: ***Part A*** consisting of m features. B_n: ***Part B*** consisting of n features.
2. A_i: The part including only 1–i features of Part A, where $0 < i \leq m$
3. B_j: The part including only 1–j features of Part B, where $0 < j \leq n$
4. $A[i]$: i_{th} feature of ***Part A***, where $0 < i \leq m$
5. $B[j]$: j_{th} feature of ***Part B***, where $0 < j \leq n$
6. $S(A_i, B_j)$: similarity of A_i an B_j.
7. $match(A[i], B[j])$: similarity of i_{th} feature of ***Part A*** and j_{th} feature of ***Part B***.

$$match(A[i], B[j]) = \frac{S_{surf} + S_{tol}}{2} \times S_{geo} \quad (2)$$

The Geometric similarity of A_m and B_n

$$Simi(P_{si}, G_{si}) = S(A_i, B_j), \text{ when } i = m, j = n \quad (3)$$

where, $S(A_i, B_j) =$

$$\begin{cases} max\{S(A_{i-1}, B_{j-1}) + match(A[i], B[j]),\ S(A_{i-1}, B_j), \\ \quad S(A_i, B_{j-1})\}, \quad \text{for } 0 < i \leq m,\ 0 < j \leq n \\ 0, \quad \text{for } i = 0 \text{ or } j = 0 \text{ (one part is empty)} \end{cases} \quad (4)$$

Consequently, the maximum geometric similarity can be calculated by using equation (4).

6 Empirical Results

6.1 An example

The feature library including forty five basic geometric features is shown in Figure 10. Five parts with successful process planning in case base and a new desired part are displayed in Figure 11 by ACIS 3D-Toolkit. The feature codes of these five parts are written as following.

Part a) main-string: pd43-pd08, sub-string: HD 220, HT Norm.

Part b) main-string: pd43-pd78-pd08-px82, sub-string: HD 250, HT Norm.

Part c) main-string: px81-pd02-pd91-pd89-pd18-px82, sub-string: HD 200, HT Norm.

Part d) main-string: px81-pd12-pd72-pd91-pd18-px82, sub-string: HD 200, HT Ann.

Part e) main-string: pd03-pd72-pd91-pd64-pd91-pd28-pd82, sub-string: HD 300, HT Norm.

The feature code of the new desired part is
main-string: px81-pd02-pd91-pd18-px82, sub-string: HD 180, HT Ann.

In this example, both of W_f and W_m are assumed to be 0.65 and 0.35, respectively. In addition, all of tolerances of the new desired part are assumed to be 0.01 (in) and surface finishes are assumed to be 64 (μin). All of tolerances of **Part a** are assumed to be 0.005 (in), and surface finishes are assumed to be 100 (μin). The similarity measure between **Part a** and the new desired part is calculated as follows.

Step 1) Based on equation (4) and Figure 5-7, the geometric similarity, $Simi(P_{si}, G_{si})$, between **Part a** and the new desired part is equal to 0.438.

Step 2) Part a includes two geometric features and the new desired part consists of five geometric features. Therefore, $\sum(G_s + G_i) = 2 + 5 = 7$.

Step 3) Hardness and Heat-treatment are considered in calculation of material similarity.
From the sub-strings of two parts and material similarity matrix in Figures 8 and 9, we have $\sum M_{si} = 0.75 + 0.5 = 1.25$

Step 4) $\sum M_i = 2$, (including 2 items: Hardness and Heat-treatment)

Step 5) Finally, the similarity of **Part a** and the new desired part is equal to 0.300 using equation (1).

Similarly, the similarity between each of other parts and the new desired part can be calculated as

Similarity = 0.081+0.219 = 0.300 for **Part a**,
Similarity = 0.231+0.175 = 0.406 for **Part b**,
Similarity = 0.591+0.219 = 0.810 for **Part c**,
Similarity = 0.520+0.306 = 0.826 for **Part d**,
Similarity = 0.303+0.175 = 0.478 for **Part e**

Therefore, the most similar part is **Part d**. From the similarity values, they provide us two results: First, it is intuitive that **Part c** is the most similar to **new part** and next one is **Part d** based on the geometry from Figure 11. Through our calculation, the value of $\frac{Simi(P_{si},G_{si})}{\sum(G_s+G_i)/2}$, equal to 0.591 for **Part c**, provides us the same result. Second, although **Part c** is the most similar to **new part** from geometry point of view, it does not mean the process plan of **Part c** is the best for the new part. As described earlier, different material properties of parts also affect the cutting process plan. For example, the cutting tools are different for cutting aluminum and cutting steel. In our case, because the heat-treatment of **Part d** is the same as that of **new part**, the similarity for **Part d** is thus greater than the similarity for **Part c**.

Finally, the cutting process of **Part d** can be retrieved from case base and is depicted in Figure 12.

7 Conclusions

It has been demonstrated that CBR can be applied for effective process planning in machining of axisymmetric parts. CBR based process planning system generates a new process plan by retrieving the old cases and then adapting the most similar case. Effective feature-based representation, case indexing and retrieval mechanism have been developed to find out the most similar parts rapidly. The proposed similarity metric has considered geometric shape, tolerance, surface finish, hardness and heat-treatment in the retrieval of similar parts and their process plans, and has been implemented in a Sun workstation using ACIS 3D-Toolkit. One example is given to illustrate the proposed method and evaluation results indicate that it performs very well.

Acknowledgments

This work is supported by the National Science Foundation under Grant Number DMI-9612067.

References

[1] T. C. Chang, *Expert Process Planning for Manufacturing*, Addison-Wesley Publishing Company, Reading, MA, 1990.

[2] L. Alting and H. Zang, "Computer Aided Process Planning: the State-of-art", *International Journal of Production Research*, Vol. 27, No. 4, pp. 553-585, 1989.

[3] Y. P. Cheung and A. L. Dowd, "Artificial Intelligence in Process Planning", *Computer Aided Engineering Journal*, pp. 303-306, August, 1988.

[4] B. Barletta, "An Introduction to Case-Based Reasoning", *AI Expert*, pp. 43-49, August, 1991.

[5] H. Yang, W. F. Lu, and A. C. Lin, "PROCASE: An Intelligent Case-Based process Planning System for Machining of Rotational Parts", *J. of Intell. Manufacturing*, Vol. 5, pp. 411-430, 1994.

[6] H. Muñoz-Avila and J. Hüllen, "Retrieving cases in structured by using goal dependencies", *1st International Conference (ICCBR-95)*, 1995.

[7] H. Muñoz-Avila, J. Paulokat and S. Wess, "Controlling Nonlinear Hierarchical Planning by Case Replay", *Proc. European Workshop on Case-based reasoning (EWCBR-94)*, 1995

[8] H. Yang and W. F. Lu, "Case adaptation in PROCASE: A case-based process planning system for machining of rotational parts", *Artificial Intelligence for Engineering Design, Analysis and Manufacturing*, Vol. 10, pp. 401-419, 1996.

[9] D. S. Hirschberg, "A linear space algorithm for computing maximal common subsequences", *Communications of the ACM*, Vol. 18, No. 6, pp. 341-343, 1975.

[10] P. A. V. Hall and G. R. Dowling, "Approximate string matching", *Computing Surveys*, Vol. 12, No. 4, pp. 381-403, 1980.

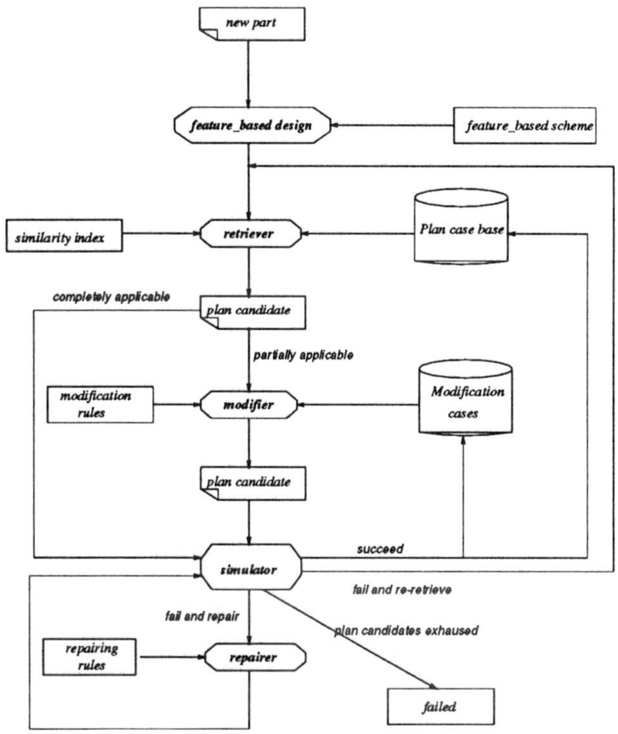

Figure 1. The framework of the system

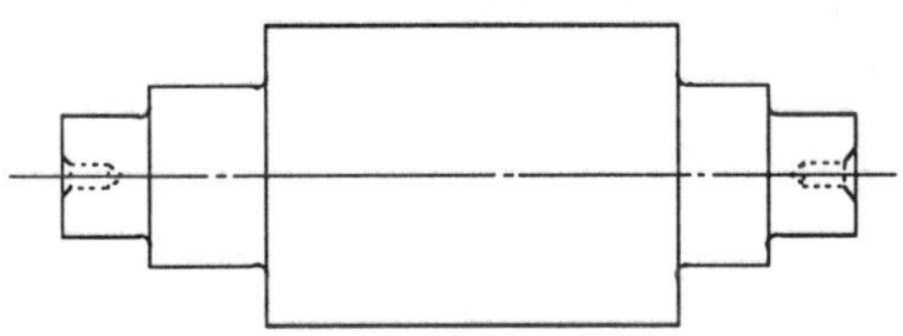

Main-string: PX81_PD12_PD72_PD91_PD78_PD18_PX82
Sub-string: Hardness 220, Heat-treatment Ann.

Figure 2. Part representation

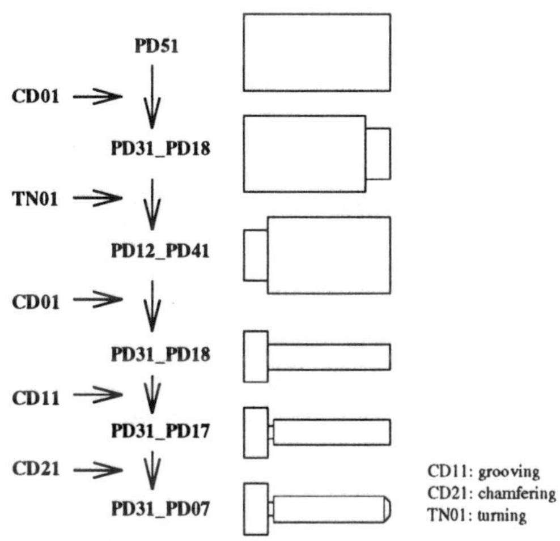

Figure 3. Case representation

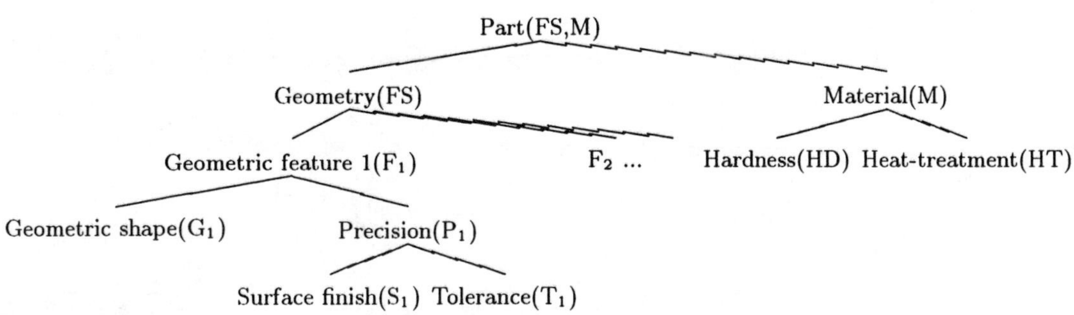

Figure 4. The hierarchical feature-based representation

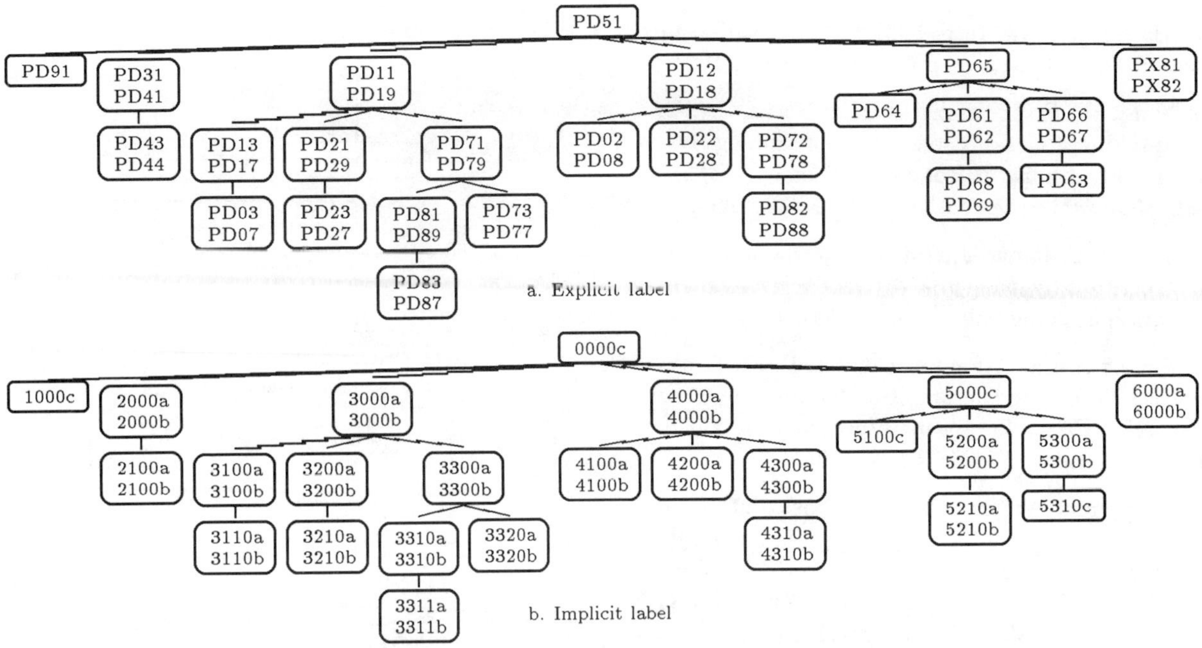

Figure 5. Geometric feature hierarchy

(μ in)	0.5-10	10-200	200-1000
0.5-10	1.0	0.5	0
10-200	0.5	1.0	0.5
200-1000	0	0.5	1.0

Figure 6. Surface finish matrix

(in)	0.0001 -0.0005	0.0005 -0.001	0.001 -0.01	0.01 -0.1
0.0001 -0.0005	1.0	0.75	0.5	0.25
0.0005 -0.001	0.75	1.0	0.75	0.5
0.001 -0.01	0.5	0.75	1.0	0.75
0.01 -0.1	0.25	0.5	0.75	1.0

Figure 7. Tolerance matrix

Brinell hardness number	-100	100 -150	150 -200	200 -250	250-
-100	1.0	0.75	0.5	0.25	0
100 -150	0.75	1.0	0.75	0.5	0.25
150 -200	0.5	0.75	1.0	0.75	0.5
200 -250	0.25	0.5	0.75	1.0	0.75
250-	0	0.25	0.5	0.75	1.0

Figure 8. Hardness matrix

	Norm.	Ann.	Oil-treated
Norm.	1.0	0.5	0.5
Ann.	0.5	1.0	0.5
Oil-treated	0.5	0.5	1.0

Norm.: Normalizing
Ann.: Annealing

Figure 9. Heat-treatment matrix

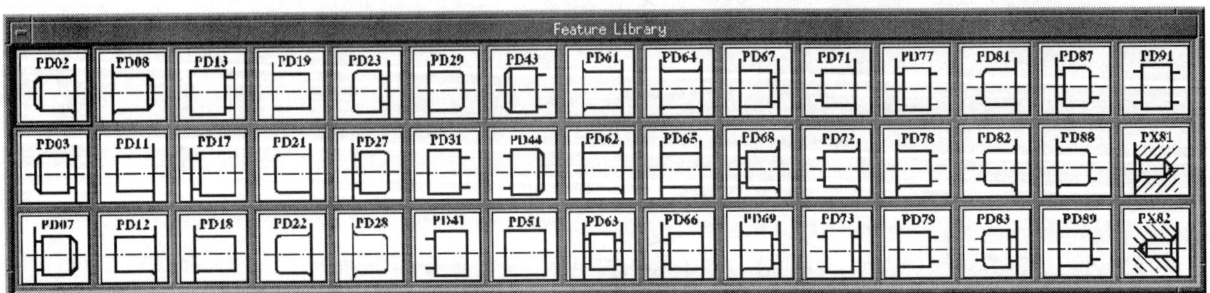

Figure 10. The feature library

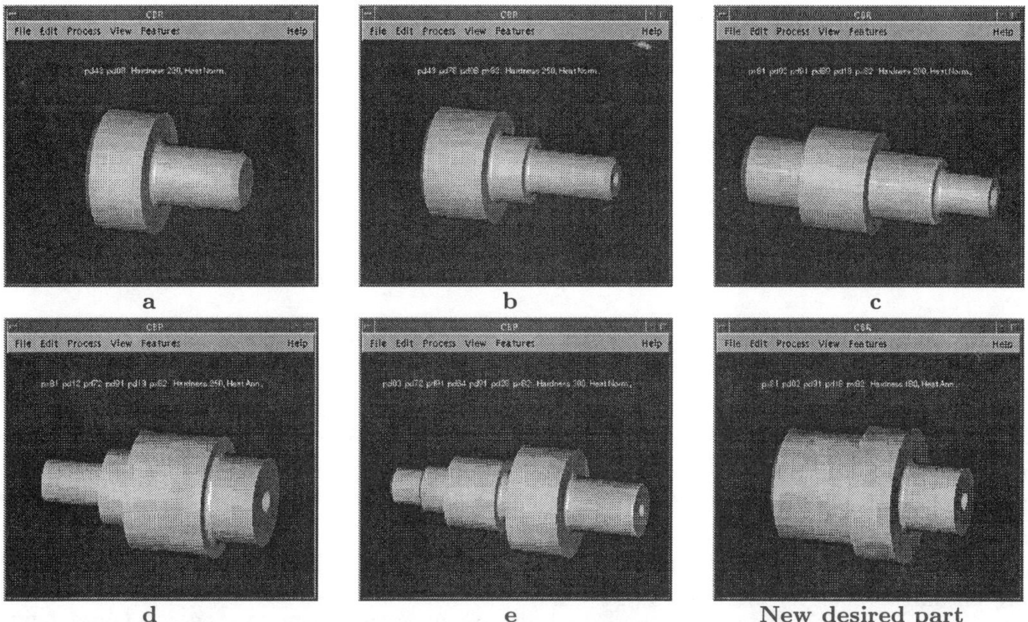

Figure 11. Five cases in case memory and a new desired part

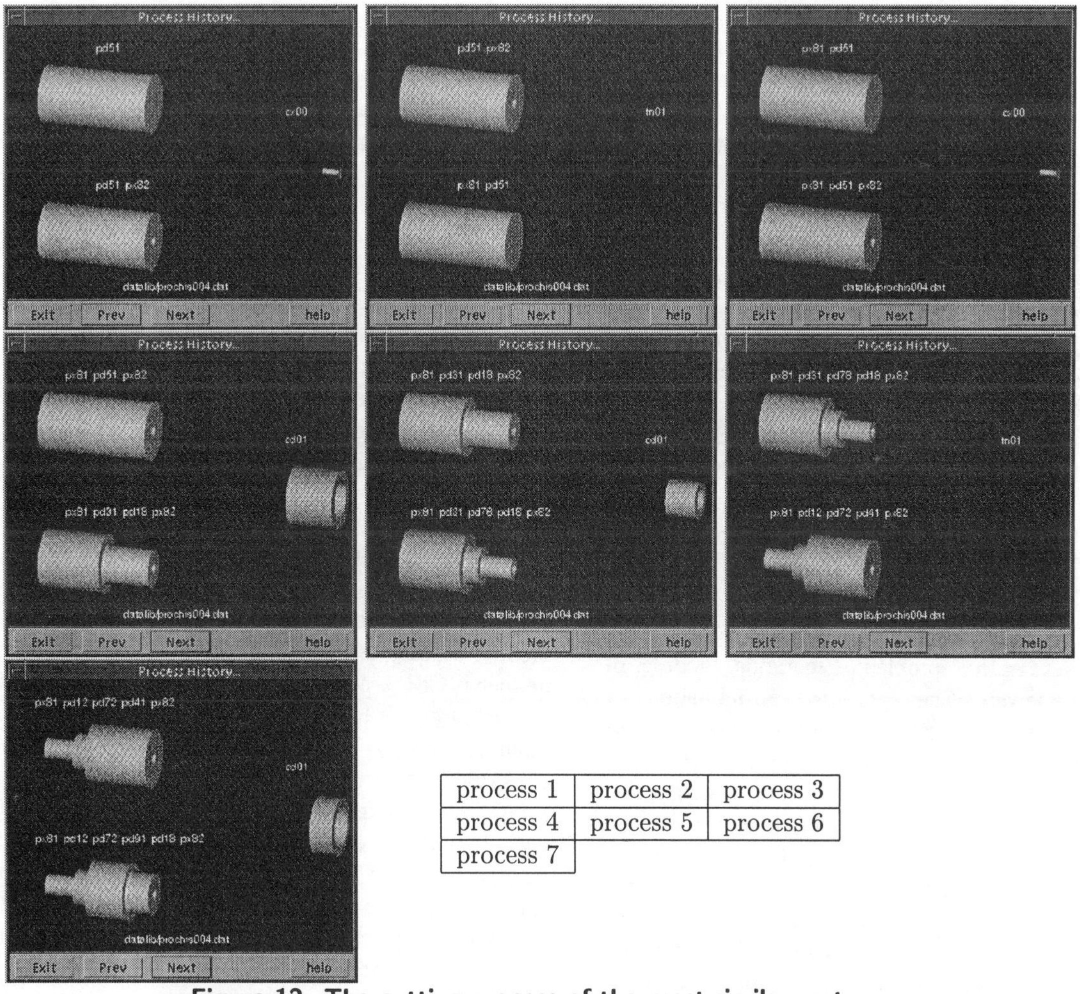

process 1	process 2	process 3
process 4	process 5	process 6
process 7		

Figure 12. The cutting process of the most similar part

CSL (Part I): Modelling General *N*-ary, Logical CSPs

J. C. Tay*, S. Y. Huang** and C. Quek**

*Information Technology Institute
National Computer Board
Singapore

**Intelligent Systems Lab
Nanyang Techological University
Singapore

Abstract

This paper examines and details the motivations and design of a constraint specification language (or CSL) for user-defined constraints. Many approaches to constraint programming are based on as well as extended from the logic programming paradigm. Some of the better known constraint logic programming languages and systems are CLP [9][5], PROLOG III [1] and CHIP [2]. In these languages, unification in conventional logic programming is replaced by constraint satisfaction. Numerical constraints are usually being focused on. The technique of constraint satisfaction is therefore hidden from the user. The motivation for developing CSL is not in adding to the myriad of available constraint programming languages, neither is CSL a complete stand-alone package for solving CSPs (though it has a mode that allows it to do so). Its main purpose, is simpler. CSL serves to enhance the constraint satisfaction aspect of these languages by providing an expressive algebra for describing current definitions of general CSPs as well as extended versions. The descriptions specified in the CSL syntax, are efficiently compiled into data structures that are transparently accessed by algorithms normally associated with only binary CSPs.

1.0 Introduction

In [7], the random problem generation module of APACS was reviewed. There are however, limitations to the scope of problems and type of constraints that could be specified through this representational model [6]. This paper examines the design of a constraint specification language (or CSL) that describes general, logical constraint satisfaction problems (or LCSPs). Essentially, a compiler for CSL will perform the task of translating user-defined constraint logical expressions into a disjunction of binary CSPs, which are then selectively scheduled to external binary CSP algorithms for discovering possible solutions.

Programming with constraints is not new. The generality of the CSP has led to the development of constraint programming languages. These languages provide built-in functions (or predicates) for describing commonly encountered constraints, and help users to solve problems by applying techniques that have been developed in CSP research.

Many approaches to constraint programming are based on as well as extended from the logic programming paradigm. Some of the better known constraint logic programming languages and systems are CLP [9][5], PROLOG III [1] and CHIP [2]. In these languages, unification in conventional logic programming is replaced by constraint satisfaction. Numerical constraints are usually being focused on. The technique of constraint satisfaction is therefore hidden from the user. Characteristics of constraint satisfaction in these languages generally differ on two aspects, namely; *Technique of Constraint Satisfaction* and *Type of Variables Allowed.*

For instance, CLP and PROLOG III uses the simplex method for handling equations and inequalities with numerical variables. CHIP, on the other hand, employs Forward Checking with the heuristic FFP for constraint satisfaction and allows it to handle symbolic, Boolean as well as numerical variables. Other commercially available descendants of CHIP are Charme and PECOS. Both Charme and PECOS are mainly built for handling symbolic but not numerical and Boolean variables.

The motivation for developing CSL is *not* in adding to the myriad of available constraint programming languages, neither is CSL a complete stand-alone package for solving CSPs (though it has a mode that allows it to do so). Its main purpose, is simpler. CSL serves to enhance the constraint satisfaction aspect of these languages by providing an expressive algebra for describing current definitions of general CSPs as well as logically constrained versions (to be described subsequently). The CSL specified script is efficiently compiled into data structures that are transparently accessed by algorithms normally associated with only binary CSPs.

1082-3409/97 $10.00

2.0 Motivations

This section will describe three motivations for the development of CSL.

2.1 Limitations of Random Problem Generation

The random CSP generation module in APACS [7] implements constraints modelled through the Boolean constraint matrix by [6]. This module is employed to create random problem samples in the performance evaluation of binary CSP algorithms. The motivation being that a CSP specified with fixed parameters of n, k, p, and q (where n is the number of variables, k is the domain size and p,q are the parameters for problem tightness) can be varied with constant difficulty to create a sample of size as large as the period of the random number generator. However, in the context of testing algorithms in APACS on more realistic problems such as the Zebra Problem (rather than abstractions such as graph colouring and N-queens), the Boolean constraint matrix specification of CSPs is grossly limited as the following factors reveal:

Explicit enumeration of constraints. The Boolean constraint model [6] requires an explicit enumeration of all allowed (or disallowed) binary compound labels. This is simply impractical when one considers user-definable constraints. For instance, given the constraint $x < y$ for numerical variables x and y. The Boolean constraint model entails that the user specifies every satisfiable binary compound label, $L \in D_x \times D_y$ individually. Obviously, a functional or predicate model for computing the satisfiability would be more suitable for user-defined CSPs.

Space complexity is exponential and not well used. The space complexity of constructing the Boolean constraint matrix in APACS for a CSP with n variables and a domain size of k, is $\Theta(n^2k^2)$. This is a considerable amount even if each constraint set was implemented using bit vectors. In addition, for n number of constraint sets (representing the diagonal elements of M), there are $n \times k \times (k\text{-}1)$ bit locations not used (for the specification of domain values). Therefore, the complexity of *wasted* space in the *best*-case (assuming all constraints are nontrivial) is easily computed to be

$$\Omega(\tfrac{k-1}{nk}) \qquad (2.1.1)$$

and in the *worse*-case (assuming all constraints are trivial) is given as:

$$O(\tfrac{nk-1}{nk}) \qquad (2.1.2)$$

In general, if the tightness of the problem (i.e. number of nontrivial constraints) is denoted by percentage p, then the *average*-case *wasted* space complexity of the Boolean constraint matrix is

$$\Theta((1 - \tfrac{p}{100})(\tfrac{n-1}{n}) + \tfrac{k-1}{nk}) \qquad (2.1.3)$$

Constraint computational cost is excluded. This necessary characteristic of the CSP generated for objective performance evaluation becomes a disadvantage when viewed against the context of describing more realistic CSP models. An alternative is to employ cost variates that conform to some predetermined statistical distribution, but this again, is only an approximation, as far as the accuracy of the statistical model is concerned.

Constraints must necessarily be binary. The structure of the Boolean constraint matrix becomes very complex should it be used to support m-ary constraints. To begin with, the Boolean constraint matrix must be upgraded to a Boolean constraint m-dimensional array, M_m. Therefore, the element $a_{i1xi2x...xim}$ in M_m denotes the constraint set $C_{x1,x2,...,xm}$. If $m = n$, then the space complexity for a CSP with n variables and a domain size of k would be $O(n^n k^2)$. Clearly, this is not practical as the same limitation of (1) persists and the proportion of wasted space of (2) would be compounded if the tightness of the CSP is low.

The four limitations of the Boolean constraint matrix described above when employed for user-defined CSPs clearly indicate the need for an alternative model.

2.2 *N*-ary to Binary CSP Conversion

There is surprisingly not much research effort devoted in the study and the construction of n-ary to binary CSP compilers, even though it has been acknowledged to be possible. The reason as the author believes, stems from the exponential time and space requirements of the straightforward method illustrated in [8, p12-13]. Instead, there is literature reporting on techniques that solve n-ary CSPs directly without conversion (for example, the tree clustering method reviewed by [8]), these are however, not converters per se.

The method of converting a 3-ary to a binary CSP as illustrated in [8] is simple. Consider the constraint $C_{x,y,z}$ in which numerical variables x, y and z have domains of {1,2}. Suppose the constraint $C_{x,y,z}$ dictates that the variables should not all have the same value. Then, to remove this constraint, a new variable W is created to subsume those compound labels in $C_{x,y,z}$. In other words, the domain of W would be {{x/1, y/1, z/2},{x/1, y/2, z/2},{x/1, y/2, z/1},{x/2, y/1, z/2},{x/2, y/1, z/1},{x/2, y/2, z/1}}.

Three new binary constraints are also added; $C_{x,W}$, $C_{y,W}$ and $C_{z,W}$. Each of these new binary constraints, $C_{i,w}$ dictates that the value of variable i must be also be an existing label in the domain of W. Hence, through the creation of W, $C_{x,W}$, $C_{y,W}$ and $C_{z,W}$, the 3-ary constraint can be replaced. The obvious cost of this method admits Tsang ([8]), is that the new variables created will have large domain sizes. In addition, it is also observed that for m number of k-ary constraints, there would be mk binary constraints added, C_{i1}, C_{i2}, ..., C_{ik} for i = 1, 2, ...,m. In effect, the computational cost of checking the ith k-ary constraint is converted to the invariant cost of computing W_i domain and the run-time cost of checking k number of binary constraints, C_{i1}, C_{i2}, ..., C_{ik} for i = 1, 2, ...,m. Indeed, if this method was the only way, then the benefit of conversion is truly questionable. However, through the design of CSL, an alternative method that avoids this cost does exist and that the n-ary to binary CSP conversion can be efficiently constructed. The bottom-line benefit of doing this is to subsume techniques that solve general CSPs directly by employing tried-and-true solvers of classical binary CSPs.

2.3 Representational Limitations of a General CSP

The current definition of a general CSP was given in [8]. The adjective 'general' in the research literature denotes that if the task of a CSP remains the same then two characteristics of a general CSP distinguish itself from other forms (i.e. such as binary CSPs or linear inequalities), in that 1) the variables and their domain need not be purely numerical, and that 2) the arity of the constraints ranges from 1 to n, where n is the total number of variables in the CSP.

This definition of generality is however, controversial. The reason being that the task of the CSP as defined, implicitly maintains that *all* constraints must be satisfied with respect to the labels in the solution tuple. In other words, if the satisfaction of each constraint were to be assigned a propositional symbol P_i, for $1 \le i \le |C|$ where C is the constraint set of the CSP, then the clause

$$P_1 \wedge P_2 \wedge \ldots \wedge P_{|C|}$$

must necessarily be *true* by instantiating values for each variable such that the individual P_i's are *true*. The insolubility of the CSP that is based on the current definition also indicates that there exists at least one proposition P_i that is false and that $\neg P_i$ is *true*. If S is the set of all solution tuples for a given CSP, then the problem is insoluble when

$$\exists P_i \in C \forall S : P_1 \wedge P_2 \wedge \ldots \wedge \neg P_i \wedge \ldots \wedge P_{|C|} \rightarrow \text{true}$$

Common-sense however, would tell us that many daily problems present solutions that depend on the falsity of some proposition P_i. Therefore, a constraint on the truthfulness of each propositional symbol P_i in the above wff would not be able to represent such problems. Similarly, one encounters solutions that are based on the disjunctive satisfiability of the constraint set such that

$$\exists P_i \in C \forall S : (P_1 \wedge P_2 \wedge \ldots \wedge P_{i-1}) \vee P_i \vee (P_{i+1} \ldots \wedge P_{|C|}) \rightarrow \text{tru}$$

The wff above is true if any of the conjuncts in the disjunction is true. However, the current CSP definition requires that all the conjuncts to be simultaneously true. This conjunctive normal form of satisfiability unnecessarily restricts the type of problems that can be represented as CSPs.

Extending the definition of the CSP by treating each constraint as a proposition in a specified wff presents a problem. The current suite of general CSP algorithms and binary CSP techniques all operate with the objective of satisfying each and every constraint. The author proposes the new objective of assigning a true value to a specified wff via the logical satisfaction of each proposition. The research effort in developing new algorithms to solve this new breed of CSPs may be substantial since even simple concepts under the current constraint satisfaction definition break down when logical connectives between constraints are involved. Consider the following CSP:

Example 2.3.1. Z = {x,y,z} D_x= {1,2}, D_y={2,5}, D_z= {3,4} C_{xy}= {{1,2},{1,5}}, C_{xz} ={{1,4}}, C_{yz}= {{5,4},{2,3}} wff1: $S_1 = C_{xy} \wedge C_{yz} \wedge C_{xz}$, wff2: $S_2 = C_{xy} \vee (C_{yz} \wedge C_{xz})$.

Two arbitrary and distinct wffs (1 and 2), S_1 and S_2, based on the CSP in example 2.3.1 are included for discussion. The satisfaction of S_1 is straightforward. The following is the trace using chronological backtracking,

x=1, y=2, z=3
x=1, y=2, z=4
x=1, y=5
x=1, y=5, z=3
x=1, y=5, z=4

The only solution tuple to satisfy S_1 is {x/1, y/5, z/4}. However, in the case for S_2, knowledge of the constraint disjunction would enable CBT to ignore variable z and arrive at a solution with {x=1,y=2} or {x=1,y=5}. The inability of CBT to perform global satisfiability with respect to the logical sentence S_2 prevents it from saving huge computational effort though the eventual derivation of {x/1, y/5, z/4} happens to satisfy S_2 as well. This example is admittedly simple, but with the inclusion of logical clauses involving all three logical connectives, these problems will become increasingly complex. In general, the problem of satisfying the constraint clauses is better known as a decision problem in Boolean logic which is known as the SATISFIABILITY problem [3].

The proof that SATISFIABILITY belongs to the class of NP-complete problems [3, pg 39] is instructive. The transformation of the extended CSP definition to the SAT problem can be achieved in polynomial time, therefore the extended CSP is necessarily NP-complete. Although it has not been proven that NP-complete problems are intractable, knowing that satisfying a problem is NP-complete, reveals that the development of a procedural, polynomial time algorithm for directly solving it is highly impropable.

3.0 Defining the General Logical Constraint Satisfaction Problem (LCSP)

The idea for logical satisfaction of constraints is not new. The industry proven success of constraint programming languages such as CHIPS, PROLOG III and many others have their origins from an underlying logical framework. However, the obvious step of migrating logical satisfaction to the definitions of a general CSP has not been considered. This should not be surprising, when taking into account the mature base of classical binary CSP algorithms and the intense focus on search efficiency as well as the lack of an efficient method for converting *n*-ary CSPs to binary CSPs.

In this section, the formal details for an extended definition of the general CSP will be presented. So that the definition is clear and concise, it will be necessary to introduce additional formal counterparts for many informal notions, such as "constraint clause" and "satisfaction". Once these definitions are well in hand, it will be possible to pursue discussion of CSL primarily at the informal level in later sections, reverting to the formal level only when necessary for clarity and rigour.

Definition 2.1. A truth assignment for a constraint c is a mapping $t{:}c \rightarrow \{T,F\}$. If there exists some applicable compound label L_c, such that c is satisfied, then $t(c) = T|_{L_c}$ and c is "true" under t; if L_c does not exist, then $t(c) = F$, therefore, c is "false". If c is a constraint in C, then c is **a constraint proposition** in C. The constraint proposition c is true under t if and only if there exists an applicable compound label, L_c that satisfies it; the constraint proposition $\bar{c}$ is true if and only if the constraint proposition c is false.

Definition 2.2. A **constraint clause** *cc*, is a disjunction of constraint propositions. It is expressed as elements of a set.

Definition 2.3. A constraint clause *cc*, is **satisfied** when one or more of its constituent constraint propositions is true.

Definition 2.4. A **constraint clause set** *CCS*, is a conjunction of constraint clauses. It is expressed as elements of a set. From example 2.3.1, the constraint clause over S_1 is $\{\{C_{xy}\}, (C_{yz}\}, \{C_{xz}\}\}$ and for S_2, it is $\{\{C_{xy}, C_{yz}\}, \{C_{xy}, C_{xz}\}\}$.

Definition 2.5. A **constraint sentence** *S*, for a constraint clause set *CCS*, is a well-formed formula (or wff) consisting of the constraint clauses in CCS expressed in conjunctive normal form. From example 2.3.1, the constraint sentence for S_1 is $\exists x,y,z \in Z:(C_{xy} \wedge C_{yz} \wedge C_{xz})$ and for S_2, it is $\exists x,y,z \in Z:((C_{xy} \vee C_{yz}) \wedge (C_{xy} \vee C_{xz}))$.

Definition 2.6. A constraint clause set *CCS*, is **satisfied** exactly when every constraint clause $cc \in CCS$ is simultaneously satisfied.

Definition 2.7. A **general logical constraint satisfaction problem** (or LCSP) is a quadruple (*Z*, *D*, *C*, *CCS*) where *Z* is a finite and discrete set of **variables** $\{x_1, x_2, ..., x_n\}$. *D* is a function that maps every variable in *Z* to a set of objects of arbitrary type: $D{:}Z \rightarrow$ finite and discrete set of objects (of any type) and these objects are possible **values** of x_i and the set D_x is the **domain** of x_i; *C* is a finite (possibly empty) set of constraints on an arbitrary subset of variables in *Z*. *CCS* is a constraint clause set over *C*. The **task** in a LCSP is to assign a value to each variable such that the constraint clause set is satisfied.

Definition 2.8. The **solution tuple** of a LCSP is a compound label that satisfies the constraint clause set. This solution tuple is the interpretation that assigns a truth value of 'true' to the constraint sentence wff.

Theorem 2.9. The LCSP is more general than the CSP.
Proof: Given a CSP ~ (*Z*, *D*, *C*), the task is to find a solution tuple that must satisfy all the constraints in *C*. By treating each of the constraints in *C* as a proposition c_i, then the task of finding the solution tuple must assign a 'true' value to the conjunction of these constraint propositions. Therefore, a LCSP ~ (Z_L, D_L, C_L, *CCS*) can be created such that $Z \subseteq Z_L$, $D \subseteq D_L$, $C \subseteq C_L$. And *CCS* is the set $\{\{c_1\},\{c_2\}, ..., \{c_{|C|}\}\}$.

Theorem 2.10. The LCSP decision problem is NP-complete.
Proof: Given a LCSP, Π, it is simple to show that $\Pi \in$ NP. An arbitrary solution tuple can be 'guessed' by assigning values to the variables in Z. This is passed to a nondeterministic algorithm that is able to check in polynomial time whether the constraint clause set can be satisfied. Hence, the LCSP belongs to class 'P'. Since the

LCSP can also be transformed into a SAT problem in polynomial time, (Practically, part II of this paper will show how the SAT problem can be transformed into a LCSP) the LCSP belongs to class NP-complete.

Theorem 2.11. Every LCSP has precisely 1 constraint clause set.

Proof. Given an initial LCSP ~ (Z,D,C,CCS_0). Suppose that additional constraint clause sets, CCS_1, CCS_2, ..., CCS_m where CCS_i is a constraint clause set over C are specified in the problem. Then the task of the LCSP is to discover a solution tuple that will satisfy every constraint clause set CCS_i for $i = 0,1, ...,m$. But this is equivalent to satisfying a constraint sentence of the form $CCS_0 \wedge CCS_1 \wedge ... \wedge CCS_m$ which is itself the constraint clause set $CCS_{0...m} \sim \{\{CCS_0\}, \{CCS_1\}, ..., \{CCS_m\}\}$. Hence $CCS_{0...m}$ is the only constraint clause set in the problem.

3.1 Defining the CSL Algebra

An important part of problem solving is the process of transforming informal word problems into formal entities such as equations, expressions, or algorithms. Another important part of problem solving is the process of transforming these formal entities into solutions by solving equations, simplifying expressions, or implementing algorithms. An algebra should provide tools and techniques to help in describing informal problems in formal terms, and to help in solving the resulting formal problems [4].

The description of problems as CSPs follow the structure of variables, domains and constraints. For the LCSP, one additionally describes in a logical statement how the constraints ought to be satisfied. These informal descriptions however, need to be transformed into formal equations and expressions that would enable algorithms to be built that could solve them. In APACS, the informal word problem of a CSP is directly transformed into the implementational model that is used to solve the problem (i.e. Boolean constraint matrix). For a user-defined LCSP however, one requires an intermediate stage that encapsulates and hides the implementational details of the underlying constraint problem solving system, and provide instead, a set of symbols and operators that can more intuitively express the problem characteristics. For instance, it would be more intuitive to specify for a map colouring problem that

> *x* = **or**(red, green, blue)
> *y* = **or**(red, green)
> x **not_equal_to** y

rather than that of a Boolean constraint matrix N for *x* and *y* in which only the diagonal elements of N are all 0s. The values red, green and blue form the *carriers* of the algebra and =, *or* and *not_equal_to* forms the *operators* of the algebra [4].

Although the primary purpose of CSL is to convert *n*-ary CSPs to binary CSPs, features such as abstract data types and logical operators have been added to allow it to describe LCSPs as well. Though these features are instrumental, it is really the underlying abstract algebra that CSL is based on, that instantiates them. Hence, it is this abstract algebra (adapted from [4, chap 10]), or mathematical framework that will be used in the description of CSL. This will then be followed by the description of the abstract data types and logical operators.

Definition 2.9. The **abstract algebra,** *A* for CSL is described by the following structure:

Carrier: S
Operations:
cons, sent $\in S$
var: $x \rightarrow S$
=: $S \times S \rightarrow S$
op_2: $S \times S \rightarrow S$
op_1: $S \rightarrow S$
print: $x \rightarrow S$

where *cons*, *sent* are constants and x is universally quantified over S.

From the definition, S is the set of domain value types in CSL. For example, Boolean value is an allowed type in CSL that belongs to S. The specification of LCSP variables and their possible domain values are formally described using the ***declaration*** operator *var,* The ***display*** operator, *print,* simply tells the compiler to display meaningful information about variables, constraints and constraint sentences. The display operator constants, *cons* and *sent* are values that represent the constraint and sentence data structures used by the CSL compiler. The ***assignment*** operator, = and the ***type*** operator, **op** are the ones that do the most work and will require more careful treatment.

3.2 The Assignment Statement

According to definition 2.9, the assignment operator is a binary function of the prefix form $=(x, y)$ where $x, y \in S$. The semantics of the assignment operator dictates that the values of the right-hand variable be assigned to the left-hand variable (i.e. y to x). Suppose the values of y are computed from the values of additional variables w and z through some arbitrary binary type operator which is denoted by $\mathbf{op}_{i,j}$, where i is the level of recursion and j is the arity of the operator. Then y can be recursively expanded to give $=(x, \mathbf{op}_{1,2}(w, z))$.

The appropriate instantiation of $\mathbf{op}_{i,2}$ depends on the *type* of its arguments. For instance, if x, w and z are natural numbers then $\mathbf{op}_{i,2}$ could be an element from the set $\{+,\times\}:I\times I\rightarrow I$. Similarly, z can be recursively aggregated from other variables by using another $\mathbf{op}_{2,2}$, such that

$$=(x, \mathbf{op}_{1,2}(w, \mathbf{op}_{2,2}(\ldots\mathbf{op}_{i,2}(\ldots\mathbf{op}_{m,2}(\ldots))))).$$

The semantics of the assignment remains the same. Each $\mathbf{op}_{i,2}$ for i=1,2...m, in the above example, constitutes a level of computation whose result is dependent on the recursive computation of its right hand side argument. Ultimately, x is assigned the computed value of $\mathbf{op}_{1,2}$ over the set of variables in the expression. It can also be easily deduced that an expression involving n number of variables can be expressed using n-1 instances of the binary type operator $\mathbf{op}_{i,2}$. Besides $\mathbf{op}_{i,2}$, the CSL abstract algebra also allows unary operations, $\mathbf{op}_{i,1}$ which are employed in a similar way.

This method of computing the assigned value of a variable (i.e. x), through the recursive computation of binary and unary type operators is called an **assignment operation** in CSL. The corresponding syntax is called the **assignment statement**. In a CSL program, there may be several assignment statements. Each statement uses the algebra of the variable types to express how a variable's value is composed from other variables. At the same time, the nature of the assignment operation as shall be seen, maps a variable to the composed values of the variables in the statement. The overall result of the assignment mechanism allows CSL to 1) precisely represent the constraint computational cost through the algebra of the problem, 2) convert an n-ary constraint to a binary constraint expression, and 3) construct the constraint sentences specified in the CSL program.

The third characteristic of the assignment operation will be described only after the data types of the language have been examined. For now, the formal description of the assignment operation will be provided.

Definition 2.10. For an abstract algebra A in CSL, if t_{i+1} is the (i+1)th recursively computed result of the j-ary type function $\mathbf{op}_{i+1,j}$ where $j\in\{1,2\}$ and v is a variable, then t_i is the computed result of the **binary** type function $\mathbf{op}_{i,2}$ if and only if $=(t_i, \mathbf{op}_{i,2}(v, t_{i+1}))$ and t_i is the result of the **unary** type function $\mathbf{op}_{i,1}$ if and only if $=(t_i, \mathbf{op}_{i,1}(t_{i+1}))$. In both cases, the recursive computation ends when t_{i+1} represents the possible value(s) of a single variable. For instance, if S is the domain of integer numbers, then addition and multiplication are binary and unary operations over the class of S.

Definition 2.11. Given a CSL abstract algebra A, the kth **assignment operation** of values for variable v is computed as $=(v, \mathbf{op}_{i,j})|_k$ where $\mathbf{op}_{i,j}$ is the ith recursively computed j-ary type operation and v is called the **assigned variable**. The parenthesis provides the necessary associativity for applying the operations. For j=2, $\mathbf{op}_{i,j}$ consists of two variables v_1 and v_2. Since each variable v_i constitutes a set of possible domain values, then the total set of values for v by the assignment operation is defined by the mapping $\mathbf{op}_{i,2}$: $v_1\times v_2\rightarrow v$. For j=1, $\mathbf{op}_{i,j}$ consists of a variable v_1 which assigns to v according to the mapping $\mathbf{op}_{i,1}$:$v_1\rightarrow v$.

Example 2.4.1. If S is the set of natural numbers, and x, y, $z\in S$ such that D_x= {1,2,3}, D_y= {1,2} and D_z= {1,2} then to compute $v = x \times y + z$ (following the usual laws of associativity) using the algebra of CSL, we have $=(v, +(z, \times(x, y)))$ which gives v a set of values of the size $|D_x|\times|D_y|\times|D_z|$.

The complexity of the assignment operation in CSL for expressing constraint computational cost incurs in the worse-case, $O(k^n)$ where n is the number of variables and k is the domain size of a given LCSP. In the best-case, this complexity is not incurred at all if no additional expression relating variables is necessary for the LCSP. For instance, in the graph colouring problem, the constraint which specifies that adjacent vertices be coloured differently is sufficient to describe the CSP. However, for constraints of the form $x + y + z < 10$, it is essential that a facility exists that can compute the different values of $(x + y + z)$ so that the satisfaction of the constraint can be attributed to a certain assignment of values to x, y and z. Having said this, there are definite ways that could be employed to improve the algorithm of assignment, but they will be discussed in a later section.

Corresponding to the inequality constraint above, depending on the domain type of the variables x, y and z, there would also be different corresponding operator types for **op**. For example, if x, y and z were *alphanumeric strings*, then instead of '+' and '<', **op** could consist of elements in the set {concat, strlen}. Therefore, the richness of the operators in the instantiated algebra would ultimately determine the ability of the specification language to accurately model the constraint computational cost.

The specification of logical constraint *sentences* in CSL (see definition 2.5) uses the same recursive assignment definition. How this is possible can be fully explained after examining the instantiated algebras in CSL.

3.3 Instantiated Algebras in CSL

There are six instantiations of the CSL abstract algebra. The common ones similarly supported in constraint programming languages are; Integer, Real and Alphanumeric. Another three has been added specifically to test CSL's extendibility and flexibility in problem representation; they are; Complex, Literal and Vector. If I is the domain for integers, R is the domain for real numbers, A is the domain of all alphanumeric strings, C is the domain of complex numbers, L is the domain which consists of true or false propositions, and V is the domain of any tuple of size ≥ 2 consisting of variable types in CSL, then the following gives the instantiated complex number algebra (any comments for a operator is placed on its right hand side, denoted by ';'):

Type *Complex:*

Carrier: C, I, R, Boolean,

Operator:

Add: $C \times C \rightarrow C$	
Mult: $C \times C \rightarrow C$	
Pow: $C \times I \rightarrow C$	;exponential
Neg: $C \rightarrow C$	;negation
Inv: $C \rightarrow C$	;inversion
Conj: $C \rightarrow C$	;conjugation
Mag: $C \rightarrow R$	;magnitude
Arg: $C \rightarrow R$	;argument
==: $C \times C \rightarrow$ Boolean	;equivalence

Each instantiated algebra defines a set of binary and unary operators that are applicable to the respective defined type. As described in the last section, an expression involving operators over a specific type can be specified as a assignment statement in a CSL program. For example, let x, y and z be complex numbers, such that $z = \frac{x}{x+y}$ then in CSL it is specified as =(z,mult(x,inv(add(x, y)))).

The specification of the above assignment statement is the same irregardless of whether x, y and z were integers, reals or complex. The CSL compiler predetermines this at the point when these variables are declared. Similarly if P, Q, R and S were propositional literals, and $R = P \wedge (\neg Q \vee S)$ then in CSL it is specified as =(R,and(P,or(S,not(Q)))).

The resulting value type from an assignment operation such as that above depends on the operator. For instance, the operator '<' for integers accepts integer types but results in a Boolean type. The CSL compiler treats Boolean values of 1 and 0 as literal true and false values. Hence the result of the inequality is of Literal type. This type transformation is done automatically by the compiler.

An important observation gathered from the algebras is that constraints are treated identically as mathematical operators. The only difference is that constraints always produce a result of type Literal (also viewed as Boolean). Since the Literal Algebra provides logical operators, it becomes clear that the assignment statement can similarly be employed to specify constraint sentences. To illustrate how this can be achieved, consider the following example.

Example 2.4.2. Consider the following constraint sentence for inequalities $x + y < 10 \wedge 2x\text{-}y > 3 \wedge \neg\ y=0$. In CSL, this is specified in four assignment statements of the form

=(negY,neg(y))
=(eqn1,<(10,add(x,y)))
=(eqn2,>(3,add(negY,mult(2,x))))
=(obj, and(eqn1,and(eqn2,not(==(0,y)))))

where negY, eqn1, eqn2 and obj are additional variables used to hold the results of the assignments. The values 10, 3, 0, and 2 are integer constants. In the current version of CSL, the constant algebra is still under construction, therefore usually integer type variables that take only these values would be used in place of the constants. For clarity purposes, these integer variables are not employed.

The above example shows how the specification of **constraint sentences** can be seamlessly modelled through algebraic operators, and avoid the necessity of constructing a separate mechanism for doing so. One interesting result of modelling the constraint sentence specification as algebraic operations is that the LCSP can be solved independently (though inefficiently for large problems) of external control strategies. This can be observed by inspecting the values of **obj** in example 2.4.2 above. Here, **obj** will be assigned either true and false values depending on the labels for the variables x, y, and z. Among all compound labels, those that ultimately assign **obj** to literal values of *true* are naturally solution tuples to the LCSP. Practically speaking, there must be some facility to trace the composition of values in order to determine the labels of x, y and z.

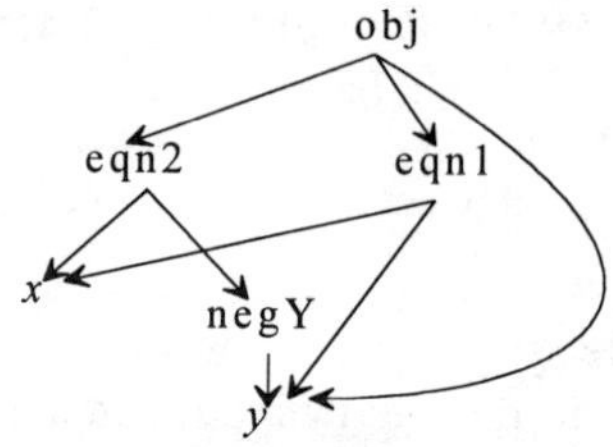

Figure 2.1 Composition of Values in Assignment

Figure 2.1 shows how assigned variables are hierarchically dependent in a non-monotonic manner on the composition of other variables. The directed arcs imply a composition relation on the set of variables. For example, the values of **obj** are ultimately composed from variables **x** and y. This knowledge is however not obvious unless the graph in Figure 2.1 is represented in some form and updated during the assignment operation. A graph that conveys knowledge of composition is formally defined as follows:

Definition 2.12. A **composition digraph** G~(V,E) consists of a set of vertices V which represents variables and a directed edge in this graph is defined by the binary relationship 'composed_of' denoted by the mapping f: $V \times V \rightarrow E$. The binary relation f forms a partial ordering on the nodes of the graph and $\langle V,f \rangle$ is a partially ordered set.

There are 3 common methods of representing information in the composition digraph, creating lists of vertices and edges, creating neighbourhood node lists for each vertex and the adjacency matrix, all of which differ in space complexity by an order that is at most polynomial [3]. The main drawback of these representations however, involves the need to traverse the model to infer composition information. Though efficient algorithms do exist for doing this, the overall system for CSL will become more complex. An alternative solution is to define another algebra that undertakes the intermediate function of collecting composition information. In CSL, this is known as the Composite Algebra.

3.3 The Composite Algebra

The intuitive idea of using a composite algebra to collect composition information is as follows; Given that variables x and y belong to one of the six types defined in the last section such that $x,y \in T$. Supposing there is an operation, $\mathbf{op}_T$ such that $\mathbf{op}_T$: $T \times T \rightarrow T$. Then if

$$=(z, \mathbf{op}_T(x,y)), \qquad (2.2.3.1)$$

the information that z is composed of values from x and y can be kept by using the alternative mapping, $\mathbf{op}_T$: $T \times T \rightarrow Cp$ where Cp subsumes T and is a algebraic type whose domain values basically consist of two slots; Slot A) Composed Value, Slot B) Composition Information.

Slot A stores the actual computed value using $\mathbf{op}_T$ and slot B stores a string involving x and y. In this way, the assignment operation provides the mechanism in which the composition digraph can be incrementally built up for every computed value in the assignment. In other words, if there is another assignment statement that involves z (from 2.2.3.1), such that $=(w, \mathbf{op}_T(u, z))$ where $w, u \in T$, then w would also be a variable of type Cp and CSL would retrieve the composition information from variable z and concatenate that with variable u to form its (i.e. w's) composition information. The composite algebra need not be explicitly defined here because its operators span all the operators of the six previously defined algebras.

4.0 Summary

This paper began with the motivations for building an n-ary to binary CSP conversion system. Firstly, the limitation of the problem generation module in APACS involved its constraint-matrix representational model and space complexity. Secondly, the method of conversion provided by [8] indicated a possible exponential domain size. And thirdly, the current limitations of defined CSPs to allow only conjunctively satisfied constraints. An study of these limitations helped to motivate the formal definition of the LCSP (Logical-CSP), which is a generalisation of the CSP to include logically satisfiable constraints. In addition, the algebra for a constraint specification language is defined that would be used to describe the LCSP. Central to the algebra was the definition of an assignment statement and its operation, which forms the basis for 'compressing' n-ary constraints into binary constraints.

5.0 References

[1] Colmerauer, A., An Introduction to Prolog III, Communications ACM Vol. 33, No 7, July 1990, pg 69-90.

[2] Dincbas, M., van Hentenryck, P., Simonis, H., Aggoun, A., Graf, T., Applications of CHIP to industrial and engineering problems. First International Conference on Industrial and Engineering Applications of AI and Expert Systems, June 1988.

[3] Garey M. R., Johnson D. S., Computers and Intractability : A Guide to the Theory of NP-Completeness, W. H. Freeman and Company, New York, 1979.

[4] Hein J. L., Discrete Structures, Logic And Computability, Preliminary Edition, Jones and Barlett Publishers, Boston, 1994.

[5] Lassez, J-L., McAloon, K., Yap R., Constraint logic programming in options trading, IEEE Expert, Vol. 2, No. 3, 1987, pg 42-50.

[6] A. K. Mackworth, "Consistency in networks of relations," Artificial Intelligence, 8(1):99-118, 1977.

[7] Tay J. C., Quek C., Huang S. Y., "APACS: A Performance Measurement Architecture for Constraint Satisfaction," In the Journal of Expert Systems with Applications, 10(3/4), pp.457-464, Pergamon, UK, 1996.

[8] Tsang, E. P. K., Foundations of Constraint Satisfaction, Computation in Cognitive Science, Academic Press, 1993.

[9] van Hentenryck, P., Constraint satisfaction in Logic Programming, MIT Press, 1989.

CSL (Part II): A compiler for the LCSP

J. C. Tay*, S. Y. Huang** and C. Quek**

*Information Technology Institute
National Computer Board
Singapore

**Intelligent Systems Lab
Nanyang Techological University
Singapore

Abstract

[2] provided a rigorous definition of the CSL algebra as a language to model the general n-ary logical CSP (or LCSP). In the following sections of this paper, the majority of our discussions will focus on design and implementational issues that arose while building a software for compiling the language into executable data structures. The primary objective of the CSL compiler is defined as follows;

To efficiently compile a CSL program (for a user-defined LCSP) into a form that can be solved by binary CSP algorithms.

1.0 Building the CSL Compiler

[2] provided a rigorous definition of the CSL algebra as a language to model the general n-ary logical CSP (or LCSP). In the following sections of this paper, our discussions will now focus on design and implementational issues that arose while building a software for compiling the language into executable data structures. The primary objective of the CSL compiler is defined as follows;

To compile a CSL program (for a user-defined LCSP) into a form that can be solved by binary CSP algorithms through APACS.

1.1 Architectural Design

The architecture of the CSL compiler is shown in Figure 2.1. The connecting edges represent data flow. A CSL program consists of four sections. These sections are ordered for a single-pass compilation. The first program block is the *declaration* section. Program statements in this section are handled by the Declaration Module as seen in the architectural layout. These statements involve the specification of variable names and their domain values. Though each variable is restricted to homogenous domain types, practically, CSL does not impose this because every domain value is type checked and stored using the respective type storing function.

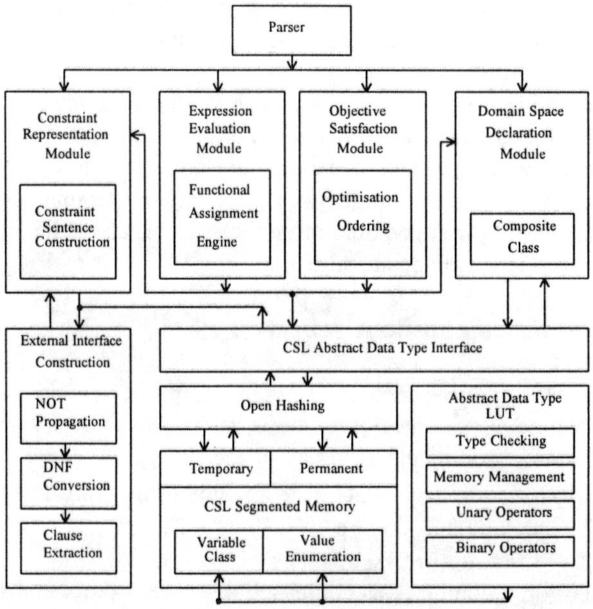

Figure 2.1 Architecture of the CSL Compiler

In fact, the declaration handler accesses each variable type through the CSL abstract data type interface. This interface adds a level of encapsulation by treating each type algebra as a class and each domain value type as an object. The operations on these domain values are interfaces which calls the particular type operations. Some domain types may not have certain operations defined on them, for instance, trigonometric sine is only defined for the Real domain value and is not defined for a complex value. To provide efficient access to the operations for each type of algebra, a look-up table (or LUT) in the main memory is employed. During declaration, the type checking, storage and memory deallocation routines can be accessed very efficiently by storing the pointer to the type location in the LUT with each domain value data structure.

1082-3409/97 $10.00 © 1997 IEEE

The second block of an LCSP specification is the *assignment* section. This section contains all the assignment statements that specify constraint cost and constraint sentences. It is handled by the Expression Evaluation Module as well as the Constraint Representation Module as seen in the architecture. The algorithm for the assignment operation follows its recursive definition (see [2]).

1.2 The Assignment Algorithm

The expression evaluation module handles the computation of a CSL assignment statement. Within the assignment statements, there are binary and unary operators. In order for computational results at each recursive level to be propagated to the assigned variable, they are stored in intermediate CSL variables as well.

Firstly, an encoding scheme for the assignment statement must be defined which will be parsed by the algorithm. The encoding scheme will be a stream of tokens extracted from the statement. Each variable and operator represented by the characters have data structures that implicitly associates them with the corresponding type functions. The simplified assignment algorithm is shown in Figure 2.2. The **GetOperatorFunction** in the algorithm does a linear search in a LUT for the math function corresponding to the token V2. The LUT for math functions in CSL also provides the appropriate arity assignment algorithms represented by **ArityFunction**. For binary operations, the simplified assignment algorithms is shown in Figure 2.3. The algorithm for unary operations is similar, and hence omitted.

```
PROCEDURE AssignmentOperation( V1, TokenStream )
/* Vi is the ith token, TokenStream are the remaining tokens*/
BEGIN
        IF |TokenStream| EQUALS 1 THEN      /* eg =(z,x) */
                V1 <- AssignDomainValues(V2)
        ELSE    /* eg =(z,add(..)..) */
        BEGIN
                MathFunc <- GetOperatorFunction( V2 )
                /* V2 represents the operator */
                /* Based on the arity of MathFunc,
                call the appropriate assignment subfunction */
                ArityFunction( TokenStream, Result,
                MathFunc )
                V1 <- AssignDomainValues( Result )
        ENDIF
END /* of AssignmentOperation */
```

Figure 2.2 Main Assignment Algorithm

```
PROCEDURE Arity2Assignment( TokenStream, Result, MathFunc )
BEGIN
        V1, V2 <- TokenStream
        IF V1 AND V2 EQUALS variables THEN
                Result <- MathFunc( V1, V2 )
        ELSE
        BEGIN
                Tx <- DeclareVariable()
                /* temporary variable Tx */
                TokenStream <- V2
                /* put back V2 into head of stream */
                AssignmentOperation( Tx, TokenStream )
                /* recursive call to assign Tx */
                Result <- DoMatching( MathFunc, V1, Tx )
                /* enumerate and propagate results */
                Tx <- UnDeclareVariable()
                /* free temporary variable */
        ENDIF
END /* of Arity2Assignment */
```

Figure 2.3 Binary Operator Algorithm

1.2.1 Matching Domain Values

The actual computation of values for an arbitrary operator in an assignment statement is conducted by the **DoMatching** function (called in Figure 2.3). For variables v_1 and v_2, and a binary operator called *MathFunc*, the **DoMatching** function essentially forms the set of results obtained from the mapping *MathFunc*: $v_1 \times v_2$.

If P_{v1} and P_{v2} are the partite sets of domain values for v_1 and v_2 respectively, then the basic **DoMatching** corresponds to collecting edges from the complete bipartite graph $K_{|Dv1|,|Dv2|}$. This form of perceiving the operation of **DoMatching** is more significant than simple cross-product because it abstracts the computation of results and provide a 'clean' avenue for introducing problem reduction methods through different bipartite matchings. In other words, the function **DoMatching** is called repeatedly based on a chosen matching method until all the subscribed matchings have been found. The **DoMatching** pseudo-code for binary operators is as follows:

```
PROCEDURE DoMatching( MathFunc, V1, V2 )
BEGIN
        /* E is an edge {e1, e2 }, where e1 is in
        Dv1 and e2 in Dv2 */
        WHILE E <- GetMatchedEdges( Dv1, Dv2, Complete )
        NOT empty DO
        BEGIN
                IF TypeEqual( e1, e2 ) EQUALS true OR
                TypeMixable( e1, e2 ) THEN
                Result_List <- FormComposite( e1, e2,
                MathFunc )
        END
END /* of DoMatching */
```

Figure 2.4 The Matching Algorithm

The function **TypeEqual** in Figure 2.4 checks that two domain values are of the same type before they are sent for computation using *MathFunc*. For instance, it would be an error to add an integer to a vector since their combination is not defined. However, it is possible to add an integer to a complex number resulting in a complex number. The disjunctive condition **TypeMixable** checks for such exceptions. The **FormComposite** function coalesces the computed value from *MathFunc* and the composite information to give a result of type composite.

The pseudo-code for **GetMatchedEdges** is shown in Figure 2.5 below.

```
PROCEDURE GetMatchedEdges( P1, P2, MatchType )
/* Pi: ith Partite set */
BEGIN
        IF MatchType EQUALS Complete THEN
        BEGIN
                e1 <- GetElementFrom( P1 )
                e2 <- GetElementFrom( P2 )
                DoCompleteMatching( P1, P2, e1, e2, true )
        END
        ELSE    /* Other types of matching here */
        ENDIF
END /* of GetMatchedEdges */
```

Figure 2.5 Calling Routine for Matching Algorithm

Currently, the only form of matching in CSL is complete bipartite matching. The algorithm for recursively returning edges in a bipartite graph in which the partite sets correspond to domain values is given as follows:

```
PROCEDURE DoCompleteMatching( P1, P2, e1, e2, MVP_Check )
/* MVP_Check is a flag to check for masked variables */
/* e1 and e2 are the vertices for matched edge */
BEGIN
IF P1 NOT_EQUALS P2 THEN
/* if not operation on same variable */
BEGIN
        WHILE Compatible( e1, e2 ) is FALSE
        BEGIN   IF e2 EQUALS end_of_set THEN
                /* P2 exhausted */
                BEGIN
                P2 <- ResetPointer          /* P2 reset to start */
                e1 <- GetElementFrom( P1 )
                END
                e2 <- GetElementFrom( P2 )
                IF e2 EQUALS end_of_set THEN
                /* call itself when P2 exhausted */
                BEGIN
                DoCompleteMatching( P1, P2, e1, e2,
                MVP_Check ),
                BREAK
                END
                ELSE IF MCP_Check EQUALS true THEN
                /* Check for Masked Variables */
                MCP_Check <- MaskedEquivalence( P1, P2,
                e1, e2 )
                ELSE BREAK
                ENDIF
        ENDWHILE
ELSE    BEGIN
        e1 <- GetElementFrom( P1 )
        e2 <- GetElementFrom( P2 )
        END
ENDIF
return OK
END /* of DoCompleteMatching */
```

Figure 2.6 The Complete Matching Algorithm

Given that the two partite sets P1 and P2 are accessed as lists, then the *worse*-case time complexity for returning all the edges between the sets when P1 and P2 are distinct is $O(|P1||P2|)$. Instead of using dual 'FOR' loops to generate the edges, the algorithm returns for each cycle i (for i=1,2..|P1|) that it is called, |P2| number of edges, resets P2 and then calls itself to increment i to the next cycle. The controlling algorithm **DoMatching** in Figure 2.4 stops calling **DoCompleteMatching** when i = |P1|, because $|P1|\times|P2|$ number of edges would have been received.

The other reason for examining the bipartite matching algorithm is a discovered problem that will significantly affect the efficiency of the assignment operation (and hence, the efficiency of the CSL compiler) if not resolved. The author has termed this problem as the **Masked-variable Constraint Problem** (or **MCP**), which is discussed in the next section. In Figure 2.6, the function **MaskedEquivalence** checks for the existence of the MCP. If it does not exist, then it switches 'itself' off by setting the MCP_Check flag. If it does exist, then the function **MaskedEquivalence** will ensure that only edges that are solutions to this problem are returned.

1.2.2 The Masked-variable Constraint Problem

The MCP presents a possible exponential behaviour in the assignment operation if not resolved. For this reason, it is essential that a section be allocated to its description and solution, though it is seemingly a deviation from our normal course of exposition. The solution to the MCP in the CSL compiler as shall be seen, is very much a part of the assignment operation. To provide an intuitive idea of the MCP, consider the following example:

Example 1.2.2. Consider the following constraint sentence for inequalities; x + y < 10 2x-y > 3 y=0. In CSL, this is specified in four assignment statements of the form

```
=(negY,neg(y))
=(eqn1,<(10,add(x,y)))
=(eqn2,>(3,add(negY,mult(2,x))))
=(obj, and(eqn1,and(eqn2,not(==(0,y)))))
```

From the composition digraph (see Figure 2.7), it can be observed that the variable y is involved in the derivation of 3 variables, eqn1, negY and obj. Similarly, the variable x is involved in the derivation of variables eqn1 and eqn2. Based on the strict idea of complete bipartite matching and the definition of assignment operation then obj would be assigned $|eqn1|\times|eqn2|\times|negY|\times|x|\times|y|$ number of domain values. However, this figure is inherently incorrect simply because x and y are assigned simultaneously different values. In a LCSP, each variable is constrained to be only assigned a single value at a time. From the constraint sentence for the assigned variable obj, this problem is not obvious. The solution is one in which all occurrences of the same variable for a given matching be assigned exactly the same domain value. But first, the existence of the MCP must be established. Identical variables that occur more than once on the composition graph and are assigned different values are called **masked variables**. The correct number of domain values assigned to obj if the MCP exists is |x|× |y|.

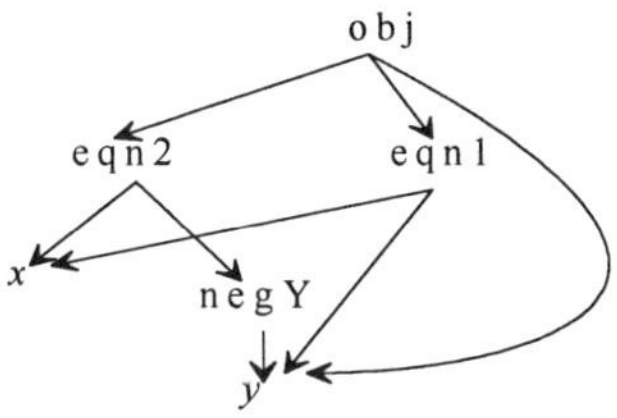

Figure 2.7 Composition of Values in CSL

The simplicity of the solution to the MCP is deceptive. This is because the existence problem presented by the MCP may be very difficult to solve. Therefore, practically speaking, the solution to the MCP existence problem entails searching the composition structure to determine if masked variables exist. As long as a single variable has been found to have been assigned more than 1 value simultaneously, an answer would be found. If the MCP does not exist, the same search needs to be conducted to ensure that all variables that are identical are assigned identical domain values. Either way, the complexity of the existence problem is directly proportional to the search space represented by the composition digraph (Figure 2.7).

If one adopts the composition digraph in Figure 2.7 as the mechanism for storing composition information, then the solution of to the MCP takes worse-case exponential amount of time to discover. To deduce this, consider the trivial case of a single assignment statement of the form

$$=(\mathbf{z}, \mathbf{op_1(v_1...op_i(v_i, ...op_n(w,w) ...)...)}),$$

where z and w are CSL variables and op_i for i=1,2...,n are the operators in the assignment statement (the arities of the operators has been omitted for clarity). In this case, checking for the existence of MCP takes constant time. In this instance of the MCP, there is 1 masked variable and 1 assignment statement, hence it is called a 1 dimensional 1MCP or simply 1/1 MCP. Consider another example of 1/1 MCP; $=(\mathbf{z}, \mathbf{op_1(w, op_2(v_2, ...op_n(x,w))))}$.

In this case, to check the existence of the MCP, the algorithm involves traversing the acyclic composition graph with root z. The worse-case occurs when the masked variable w is furthest from its counterpart as in the above case. The worse-case time complexity is now O(n). Depending on the implementation, for i number of MCPs where i>1, the time complexity differs by at most a constant multiple. However, when considering m/i MCPs, this is equivalent to searching a binary tree that has worse-case time complexity proportional to the number of leaf nodes, that is O(2^n). Repeating each tree search for each ith masked variable compounds the inefficiency.

The inefficiency of the method described above is clearly due to the composition structure employed. The CSL compiler is able to determine the answer to the MCP existence problem in linear time because the composition information in the composition graph is always inherited by the assigned variable. In other words, the domain values of **obj** in example 1.2.2 have got complete information about the composition graph. Checking for the existence of the MCP when given two composite domains simply requires only a linear search through the two composition information strings. This is aided by the fact that MCP detection has been done for every previous assignment statement that composes the current one, hence it is guaranteed that masked variables can only occur in pairs. Hence, the time complexity of the **MaskedEquivalence** function is O(n).

1.3 Constraint Sentence Modelling

The CSL compiler is a single-pass algorithm in that no declaration or assignment statement from a CSL program is accessed more than once. The data structures needed to represent the specified LCSP must be fully developed at the end of the single-pass. To achieve this, the modelling of the constraint sentence of the LCSP must be concurrently carried out during the parsing of the assignment section discussed in the last section. There are two important factors that ensures this concurrency is achievable and sound. It is **sound** when the model of the LCSP generated correctly specifies the logic of the constraint clause set in the CSL program. The two necessary and sufficient lemmas are defined as follows:

Lemma 2.12. All variables specified in the assignment statements must be declared beforehand (besides those assigned variables which can be auto-declared by the Assignment Engine).
Lemma 2.13. Only Constraint operators and Literal values produce domain values of type Boolean.

Lemma 2.12 is complied by enforcing a segmented organisation of the CSL program into declaration, assignment and optimisation sections. Only relevant operators for a section will be pushed onto the command dispatcher stack. Secondly, variables within the assignment statement must be declared beforehand. Declaration of a variable among other things installs the variable name into a hash table and returns a pointer to its location in the CSL segmented memory. Therefore, an undeclared variable cannot be accidentally used without signalling an error.

Lemma 2.13 essentially perceives constraint operators as first-order predicates. This is only natural because one can specify that the result is 'true' when the constraint is satisfied and 'false' when it is not. The constraint predicate model fits nicely into the assignment operations by mapping other types into Literal values. Literal variables are also viewed as constraints which must be satisfied with true and false values. As a result of compliance to the two lemmas, two theorems for all CSL programs can be derived:

Theorem 2.14. Whenever a logical operator (i.e. AND, OR or NOT) occurs in a CSL assignment statement, it *must* involve Literal variables, constraint type operators or variables that are composed of these.

Proof. Lemma 2.12 states that CSL operator can only be correctly applied to a declared CSL variable. Based on this, a logical operator will always be applied to a valid CSL variable. Since logical operators are applicable to only Boolean or Literal values, Lemma 2.13 states that only constraint type operators and Literal variables can produce such types. Hence, whenever a logical connective is encountered in an assignment statement, its arguments can be immediately deduced to be constraints (if Literal variables are treated as constraint as well) or variables composed of constraints.

Theorem 2.15. A constraint sentence specification consists of only logical and constraint operators.

Proof. Lemma 2.13 states that only Literal variables and constraint operators produce Literal values. So such arguments can only be applied to a logical operator. Similarly, only logical operators are juxtaposed among each other as they produce compatible result types. Hence, a constraint sentence specification consists of only logical and constraint operators.

As a result of the two theorems above, one is now able to construct a *logical constraint tree data structure* on-the-fly to represent constraint sentences as the assignment statements are being parsed by the CSL compiler. We begin by defining the concept of a logical constraint tree in the context of CSL programs.

Definition 2.13. A **logical constraint tree** is a tree in which the *leaf* nodes are CSL constraint operators. Sibling nodes of a tree are related to each other conjunctively (the parent is an AND node) or disjunctively (the parent is an OR node). A tree node that has no siblings is negatively related to its parent (called a NOT node).

To construct the logical constraint tree for the constraint sentence simultaneously as the assignment statement is being computed, two additional data structures are needed. Firstly, a **constraint table** that stores pointers to constraints that are encountered during the assignment operations (these can be distinguished from normal operators by their operator type), secondly, a **sentence table** that stores pointers to subtrees that will form the logical constraint tree. The method of constructing the logical constraint tree is quite straightforward. The tree is essentially being built incrementally in a *bottom-up* fashion. Then according to theorems 2.14 and 2.15, the parent nodes of these leaf nodes are necessarily logical operators. Therefore subtrees can be constructed and stored in the sentence table. Subsequently when an overall constraint sentence is specified (such as the one for the assigned variable **obj** in example 1.2.2), CSL will link in the necessary subtrees from the sentence table to form the whole logical constraint tree. To illustrate this bottom-up tree construction process, consider again example 1.2.2 with the additional constraint x > 5 which is disjunctively related to obj through =(obj2, or(obj, >(x,5))).

Figure 2.8 shows the five sequential stages for constructing a logical constraint tree for obj2. The directed edges indicate data flows from and to CSL memory, the constraint table and the sentence table. The declaration section has been omitted for clarity.

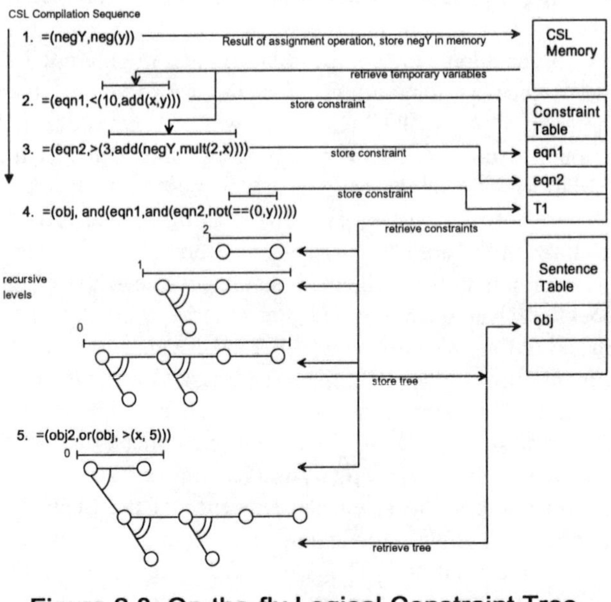

Figure 2.8 On-the-fly Logical Constraint Tree Construction

The CSL compilation process begins at assignment statement 1 and continues progressively downwards to statement 5. Constraints encountered are stored in the constraint table. The leaf nodes for the logical constraint trees have pointers to constraint locations in the table. Assignment statement number 4 shows the incremental construction of the tree using the recursive algorithm of the assignment operation. The resulting tree for obj in statement 4 is then stored in the sentence table. Assignment statement number 5 will retrieve a pointer to this tree and attach it to the left node of the disjunctive tree for obj2. The logical constraint tree for obj2 will form the completed model for the constraint sentence for the CSL program.

2.0 Interfacing CSL to APACS

Up to this stage, the CSL compiler has managed to model an *n*-ary LCSP as a collection of assigned variables and a single encompassing logical constraint tree. If this model was to be directly interfaced to APACS [1], then indeed, the difficulty of the LCSP is as hard as the SATISFIABILITY problem described in [2]. Besides, as mentioned, the algorithms in APACS are geared towards solving binary CSPs whose constraints are only *conjunctively* satisfied. Hence, the current compilation result by CSL so far is still not appropriate for interfacing to APACS.

Knowing that the LCSP decision problem is NP-complete is instructive. It guides one towards techniques that could solve special instances of the more difficult general problem. The LCSP is a general form of the CSP [2]. By converting the constraint sentence in the LCSP from a conjunctive normal form into a disjunctive normal form, one can derive sets of constraints in which the satisfaction of any conjunctive set determines the satisfaction of the overall LCSP. Each conjunctive constraint set defines a set of corresponding variables and domains that can define a CSP with the corresponding variables and domains. In other words, the idea of interfacing CSL to APACS involves two phases:

Phase 1. Convert the constraint sentence of the LCSP into an array of disjunctive binary CSPs, and schedule them to an external client.
Phase 2. Select solvers from APACS to solve a given binary CSP. The satisfaction of any one of the CSPs indicates a solution to the LCSP.

To illustrate the interfacing process, consider the following *general* constraint sentence for an arbitrary LCSP, where *w,x,y* and *z* are CSL variables.

$$\forall w,x,y,z \in Z : \neg\{(C_{xy} \wedge C_{yz}) \vee C_{wx} \wedge (\neg C_{wy} \vee C_{xz})\}$$

The conversion to CNF is as follows:

$$\neg\{(C_{xy} \wedge C_{yz}) \vee C_{wx} \wedge (\neg C_{wy} \vee C_{xz})\}$$
$$\Rightarrow (\neg C_{xy} \wedge \neg C_{wx}) \vee (\neg C_{yz} \wedge \neg C_{wx}) \vee (\neg C_{xy} \wedge C_{wy} \wedge \neg C_{xz})$$

From the resulting DNF clause, one can obtain the following CSPs (the *i*th CSP is denoted by the triple (Z_i, D_i, C_i)) by extracting each conjunctive constraint set starting from the left:

CSP 0: $x, y, w \in Z_0$, $\neg C_{xy}, \neg C_{wx} \in C_0$, $D_0=\{D_x, D_y, D_z\}$
CSP 1: $x, y, z, w \in Z_1$, $\neg C_{yz}, \neg C_{wx} \in C_1$, $D_1=\{D_x, D_y, D_z, D_w\}$
CSP 2: $x, y, z, w \in Z_2$, $\neg C_{xy}, C_{wy}, \neg C_{xz} \in C_2$, $D_2=\{D_x, D_y, D_z, D_w\}$
CSP 4: $x, y, z, w \in Z_3$, $\neg C_{yz}, C_{wy}, \neg C_{xz} \in C_3$, $D_3= \{D_x, D_y, D_z, D_w\}$

The second phase would be to select an algorithm in APACS to solve each binary CSP. A solution to any one of the four constitutes a solution to the LCSP, and the algorithm can halt. A solution for the LCSP cannot be found if and only if all the four CSPs have been determined not to have solutions. The next section will examine the algorithms for converting the logical constraint tree of a LCSP into an array of disjunctive binary CSPs (or simply **disjunctive BCSPs**). This corresponds to phase 1. The interfacing of CSL to APACS corresponds to phase 2.

2.1 Phase 1: Array of Disjunctive Binary CSPs

The conversion of the logical constraint tree into the disjunctive BCSPs is handled by the External Interface Construction Module (see Figure 2.1). There are three stages to this conversion. The explanation provided will be based on two CSL assignment statements of the form

```
=(tmp,or(A,and(B,C)))
=(Z, not(tmp))
```

The logical constraint tree for Z is shown in part (a) of Figure 2.9

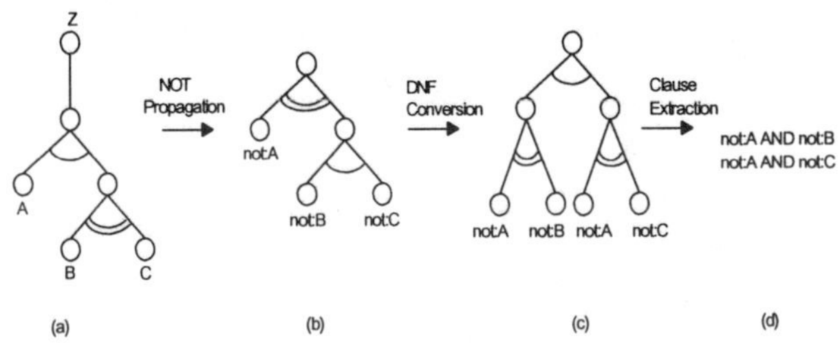

Figure 2.9 Conversion of the Logical Constraint Tree to an Array of Disjunctive Binary CSPs

The first stage of the conversion involves propagating any NOT operators down to the leaf nodes using the following boolean algebraic theorems and axioms for literals *A* and *B*:

1. $\neg(A \vee B) = \neg A \wedge \neg B$ (by DeMorgan)
2. $\neg(A \wedge B) = \neg A \vee \neg B$ (by DeMorgan)
3. $\neg(\neg A) = A$ Axiom

Part (b) of Figure 2.9 shows the result after NOT-propagation. Note that each constraint A, B and C must now contain new information that indicates its overall satisfaction is being based on the dis-satisfaction of the respective constraints. There must be a function that transparently determines the correct type of satisfaction since APACS only allows satisfaction based on true values.

The second stage involves DNF conversion through AND-distribution over OR nodes. The resultant tree is shown in part (c) of Figure 2.9. Notice that some subtrees need to be duplicated. The third and final stage is to traverse the DNF converted tree and extract the constraints under the AND nodes so that they can be subsequently assigned as CSPs. This is shown in part(d) of Figure 2.9. The collection of disjunctive binary CSPs are scheduled one at a time to the Evaluation Control Module of APACS in which a CSP algorithm has been selected to solve it.

2.1.1 Conversion Algorithms

The algorithms for NOT-propagation, DNF conversion and clause extraction are performed on a logical constraint tree structure whose internal nodes represent logical conjunction, disjunction or negation, while its leaf nodes are pointers to constraint functions. Figure 2.9(a) shows an example of such a tree.

```
PROCEDURE NotPropagation( tree, NotConstraintFunc )
/* tree is a pointer to a logical constraint tree and NotConstraintFunc is the function that
changes the satisfiability of a constraint */
BEGIN
IF  RightNode( tree ) EQUALS null AND LeftNode( tree ) EQUALS null THEN
BEGIN
        ConstraintNode <- NotConstraintFunc( tree )
        return
END
IF NodeBranchType( tree ) EQUALS not THEN        /* not(not(A)) */
BEGIN
        tree <- RightNode( tree ) /* Right node as NOT arg */
        return
END
IF NodeBranchType( tree ) EQUALS and THEN/* not(and(A,..)..)*/
BEGIN
        NodeBranchType( tree ) <- or
        NotPropagation( RightNode( tree ),NotConstraintFunc )
        NotPropagation( LeftNode( tree ), NotConstraintFunc )
END
IF NodeBranchType( tree ) EQUALS or THEN /* not(or(A,...)...) */
BEGIN
        NodeBranchType( tree ) <- and
        NotPropagation( RightNode( tree ),NotConstraintFunc )
        NotPropagation( LeftNode( tree ), NotConstraintFunc )
        END
END /* of NotPropagation */
```

Figure 2.10 NOT Propagation Algorithm

The next stage, assuming the tree is now successfully NOT-propagated (i.e. Figure 2.9(b)) is DNF conversion, illustrated in Figure 2.11. The final stage assuming DNF conversion has been successful is the extraction of conjunctive clauses. The pseudo-code for the clause extraction algorithm is shown in Figure 2.12. The result of this algorithm is a linked-list of list of conjunctive constraints. The idea of the clause extraction algorithm is straightforward; recursively search for the first AND node and then recursively collect data from its leaf nodes.

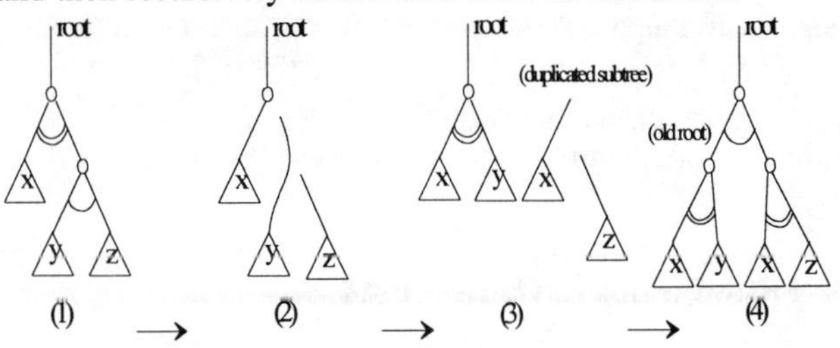

Figure 2.11 AND over OR Distribution Algorithm

```
PROCEDURE ExtractClause( DNFtree, 2DListofConjuncts )
BEGIN
IF BranchNodeType( DNFtree ) EQUALS and OR (RightNode( DNFtree ) EQUALS null
AND LeftNode( DNFtree ) EQUALS null ) THEN BEGIN
        Newlist <- ConstructList()
        GetAllLeafData( DNFtree, NewList )
        2DListofConjuncts <- InsertFrontList( NewList )
END
ELSE BEGIN
        ExtractClause( LeftNode( DNFtree ), 2DListofConjuncts )
        ExtractClause( RightNode( DNFtree ), 2DListofConjuncts )
END
ENDIF /* of ExtractClause */
PROCEDURE GetAllLeafData( tree, ListofData )
BEGIN
IF LeftNode( tree ) EQUALS null AND RightNode( tree ) EQUALS null THEN
        ListofData <- InsertFrontList( ConstraintNode( tree ) )
ELSE BEGIN
        GetAllLeafData( LeftNode( tree ), ListofData )
        GetAllLeafData( RightNode( tree ), ListofData )
END
ENDIF /* of GetAllLeafData */
```

Figure 2.12 The Clause Extraction Algorithm

The two recursive parts are borne by **ExtractClause** and **GetAllLeafData** functions respectively. Through this list of conjunctive constraint clauses, information such as variables and domain sizes are extracted for each clause and a corresponding array of CSPs is constructed.

2.2 Phase 2: Perspective of Roles for Constraint Satisfaction

Essentially, CSL plays the role of compressing n-ary constraints into disjunctive BCSPs, while APACS attempts to solve individual CSPs composed of such binary constraints. The method of compressing n-ary constraints is currently based on matching every value of each variable v_i for $i=1,2,\ldots,n$ with n-1 other variables (see section 1.2.1). When APACS satisfies the binary constraint, the composite information stored in the CSP labels will determine the actual values for each of the n variables. Consider the 3-ary constraint for $A,B,C \in R$, $A\sin(B) < C$. CSL compresses the 3-ary constraint by the mapping

$$T \leftarrow . \circ \sin \; : R \times R$$

and APACS seeks to satisfy the binary constraint T < C by selecting appropriate values for T and C. The resulting solution compound label {T/*u*,C/*v*} can then be expanded using the composition information of *u* to give the values of A and B which have been declared in the CSL program. For instance if *u* is composed of {A/*s*, B/*r*}, then {A/*s*, B/*r*, C/*v*} is the eventual compound label that will satisfy the 3-ary constraint for the LCSP.

3.0 Solving LCSPs using CSL

This section will present an example of LCSP encoded using CSL. The nature of the spanning tree problems has in the past precluded it from being classified as a CSP and is therefore not amenable to algorithms in APACS either. However, if it is defined as a LCSP, the CSL compiler is able to convert the problem into disjunctive BCSPs. The Evaluation Control Module will then schedule a user-selected algorithm with respect to the experimental parameters, and sequentially solve each disjunctive binary CSP. A solution is discovered when one of the CSPs in the array is solved.

3.1 Finding a Spanning Tree

To find a spanning for a graph of the form

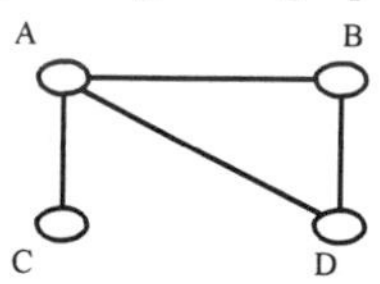

A,B,C and D are nodes

it can be exprcssed as a LCSP by stating that the assignment of a value *i*, to a variable *v* denotes an adjacent edge between variable *v* and *i*. The converse relationship {*i*/*v*} need not be stated as long as all the variables are connected. The semantics of constraints would be twofold:
a. all the variable assignments constitute a single path, and
b. the path has no cycles within it. The corresponding encoding of the above LCSP in CSL is as follows:

```
DECLARATION
        var(Anode,B,C,D)
        var(Bnode,A,D)
        var(Cnode,A)
        var(Dnode,A,B)
        var(nodelist,Anode,Bnode,Cnode,Dnode)
        var(VG,nodelist)
ENDDEC
ASSIGNMENT
        =(tmp1,conn(Anode,Bnode))
        =(tmp2,and(tmp1,conn(Bnode,Dnode)))
        =(c1,not(and(tmp2,conn(Anode,Dnode))))
        =(c2,path(VG))
        =(res,and(c1,c2))
ENDASG
```

Note that the constraint operator **path** checks for part(a) while the assigned variable c1 ensures part(b) of the spanning tree constraint stated above. The variable VG, is a vector whose elements are the variables. Also note that in the declaration section, the domain values correspond to the adjacent nodes of that variable. After DNF conversion and clause extraction, the disjunctive BCSPs and a particular solution is as follows:

```
External Interface Table:
  [CSP 0]: con(2) var(5) dom(3)
  ( VG Anode Bnode Cnode Dnode )
          n:conn( Anode , Dnode )
          path( VG )
  [CSP 1]: con(2) var(5) dom(3)
  ( VG Anode Bnode Cnode Dnode )
          n:conn( Bnode , Dnode )
          path( VG )
  [CSP 2]: con(2) var(5) dom(3)
  ( VG Anode Bnode Cnode Dnode )
          n:conn( Anode , Bnode )
          path( VG )
[CSP 0] Solution Label:  Dnode/B Cnode/A Bnode/A Anode/B VG/nodelist
```

Visually, this solution tuple can be translated as

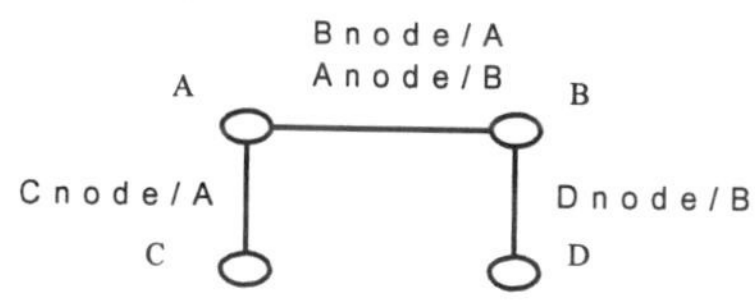

4.0 Summary and Conclusions

This paper has provided a detailed description of the design and construction of the CSL compiler. Its focus was twofold; the assignment algorithm and the solution to the MCP using composite propagating information, and a derivation for the efficient single-pass construction of the logical constraint tree. The conversion of the logical constraint tree into an array of disjunctive binary CSPs was explained through the process of NOT-propagation, DNF conversion and Clause Extraction. Finally, we note that CSL and APACS corporately solves the LCSP but individually plays different roles. Specifically, CSL's role is that of 'compressing' the *n*-ary constraint into a binary form, while APACS satisfies it and derives the solution tuple through the composite information. The given example of a LCSP such as the spanning tree problem serves to demonstrate CSL's current capability.

5.0 References

[1] Tay J. C., Quek C., Huang S. Y., "APACS: A Performance Measurement Architecture for Constraint Satisfaction," In the Journal of Expert Systems with Applications, 10(3/4), pp.457-464, Pergamon, UK, 1996.
[2] Tay J. C., Huang S. Y., Quek C., "CSL (Part I): Modelling General, *N*-ary, logical CSPs," submitted to ICTAI'97.

...t of "IntelligentWorkFlow System" Using Know-how Acquired Based on Work Order

Mikio Sasaki, Tetsuya Mishuku, Akira Takano, Satoshi Tanaka and Akira Maeda
Information Technology R & D Center, Mitsubishi Electric Corp.
msasaki@sy.isl.melco.co.jp

Abstract

In the case of intelligent work that requires sophisticated judgments of experienced worker, if the know-how of experienced workers could be reused, it is expected that even inexperienced workers would be able to perform similar work.

This paper describes "IntelligentWorkFlow System" that uses the know-how of experienced workers by focusing on the sequence of procedures in a work. It stores detail process of work as "work-log", and finds out the "know-how" of work by analyzing the stored work-log. Since this system accumulates the know-how through practical work and its know-how acquisition method doesn't focus on application dependent data, it becomes easy to acquire the know-how without depending on the particular application.

1. Introduction

Accompanying the improved capabilities of computer systems and the introduction of more sophisticated functions for individual software in recent years, computers have come to be used in a wide range of fields. Computer systems are also starting to be applied to intelligent work requiring sophisticated judgments based on human experience, such as tasks involving providing a suitable response to an inquiry regarding a complex problem. What is more, this trend is likely to become even more prominent in the future.

In the case of this type of work requiring judgments and processing based on human experience, if it were possible to reuse the know-how possessed by experienced workers, it is expected that even inexperienced workers would be able to perform similar work. Expert systems and case-based reasoning are examples of technologies that have been proposed to accomplish this [1].

In the case of expert systems, however, it is known to be difficult to have experienced workers describe the knowledge they possess. In the case of systems using case-based reasoning, attributes must be defined that are dependent on the problem region when expressing the examples. As a result, when the system is attempted to be applied to a different application, it is necessary to redefine what attributes are to be used for the new application according to that particular application [2].

In the system that we are examining, the focus is placed on the order of the operations and tasks performed by experienced workers. Information in the form of what type of tasks are appropriate under what circumstances is extracted as used as know-how. When an inexperienced worker attempts to solve a problem, the system provides advice regarding the appropriate tasks to be performed by using this know-how. This system is referred to as IntelligentWorkFlow (abbreviated IWF) system [3].

IWF system has the following characteristics:

- The system is equipped with an know-how acquisition method that is not strongly dependent on the particular application by focusing on the order of work performed by experienced workers, and not the specific attributes associated with a particular task.
- Since know-how is obtained from the work-log of work performed by experienced workers, there is no need to have know-how available in advance.
- Instead of work being performed in a completely automated manner based on the know-how accumulated, workers are provided with support based on that know-how using a dialogue format when performing their work.

2. Approach of IWF System

2.1 Objective of IWF System

In the case of supporting the work performed by a person with a computer, the applications can be classified into three types.

If the order of work performed by a large number of persons for a certain objective is identical and routine, that work can be performed automatically by a computer. This is referred to as "routine work".

On the other hand, since the production of contents and creative activities require the ideas and creativity of individuals, the order of that work can be expected to change significantly each time it is performed, thus making it difficult to automate by computer. This type of work is referred to as "non-routine work".

The last one is referred to as "semi-routine work". "Customer support service" is an example of this kind of work.

In "semi-routine work", the work order itself is not completely different each time. But in each time, the worker should select appropriate choice from multiple number of procedures. So the work order may be partially changed according to the situation. Additionally, we could find the worker's know-how from information that what processing are chosen in which situation.

IWF system is designed to provide support for this type of semi-routine work. Know-how is acquired by focusing on the order of work performed by experienced workers, which in turn is used to provide support for inexperience workers during the course of their work.

2.2 System Overview

Figure. 1 shows the functional overview of IWF system.

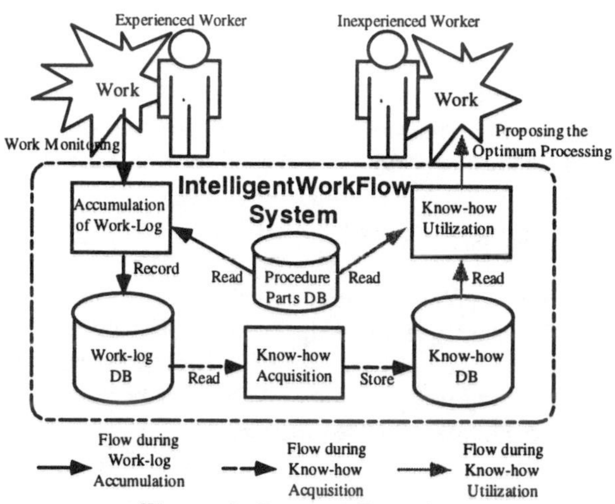

Figure.1 System Overview

Recognizing that the work-log of an experienced worker contains the know-how of that worker, the work performed by experienced workers is first monitored by accumulating in a work-log to accumulate a record of work performed (Flow during work accumulation in Figure. 1).

Next, information considered to be useful when performing the work is extracted from information accumulated by know-how acquisition, and accumulated in the form of know-how (Flow during know-how acquisition in Figure. 1).

Finally, when inexperienced workers are performing that work, the system provides support to those workers by proposing the optimum processing to be performed using that know-how (Flow during utilization of know-how in Figure. 1).

2.3 Procedure parts and Work-log

IWF system records each actual problem solving process as "work-log". Each work-log consists of the sequence of the procedure and its result. Each procedure that constructs work-log is expected as simple and small such like it can be performed mechanically according to a manual. This is referred as a "procedure part". The user selects the required procedure part, executes it and then records the result. The result information shows what happened and how the status changed when a procedure part was processed.

Figure. 2 shows the example of a work-log for inspection work performed when a personal computer has malfunctioned.

Efficient work is considered to be work in the case of

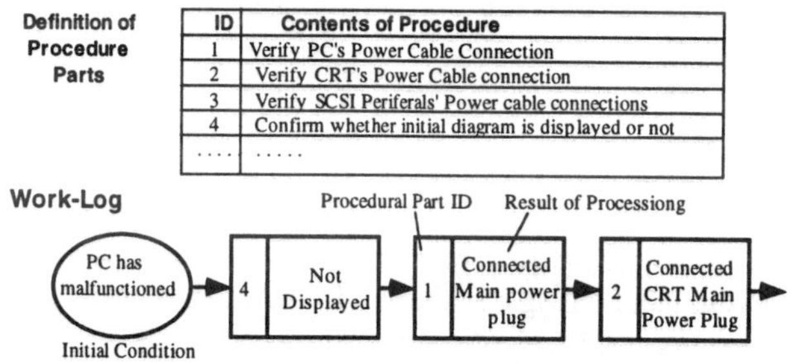

Figure. 2 Example of Procedure parts and Work-log

the work-log achieving the objective of the work in as few steps as possible. In this paper, work-log is expressed in the following form:

$$\textit{Status X}: \ P_1(R_1) \rightarrow P_2(R_2) \rightarrow P_3(R_3) \ldots$$

Status X means initial status, P_n means executed procedure part, and R_n means it's result. For example, *Status X* means "PC has malfunctioned", P_1 is procedure part defined as "Confirm whether initial diagram is displayed or not", R_1 means "Not Displayed" and so on.

In IWF system, although the work-log is accumulated in the "Accumulation of Work-log" step shown in Figure. 1, various accumulation methods can be employed according to the application, such as by monitoring the work with application software or direct input by the user.

3. Organized Information: Know-how

3.1 Definition of Know-how

In IWF system, information that is acquired by organizing procedures is referred to as "know-how". Know-how refers to the expertise used by the system to propose the optimum procedure part when a worker uses a procedure parts to perform work. It is also information that enables the worker to make the best selection when he knows there are a multiple number of processes (procedure parts) that can be applied during the course of solving a problem (Figure. 3).

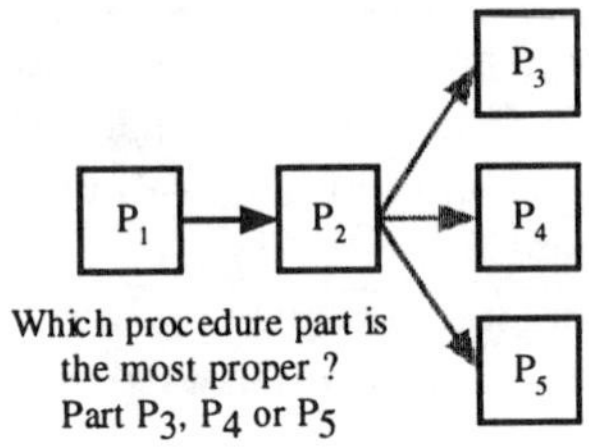

Figure. 3 Case of a Multiple Number of Procedure part Candidates

In order to solve a problem, an experienced worker is conscious of something objective. For example, in the case of responding to inquiries regarding malfunctions, this consists of determining the cause of the malfunction, such as by investigating the power source since it appears to be abnormal, and taking steps to repair the location of that malfunction. A series of tasks are then performed according to that awareness. The objective possessed by a worker is referred to as the "hypothesis".

When processing results are obtained that contradict the hypothesis during the course of the work, the next step is to make a new hypothesis (Figure. 4).

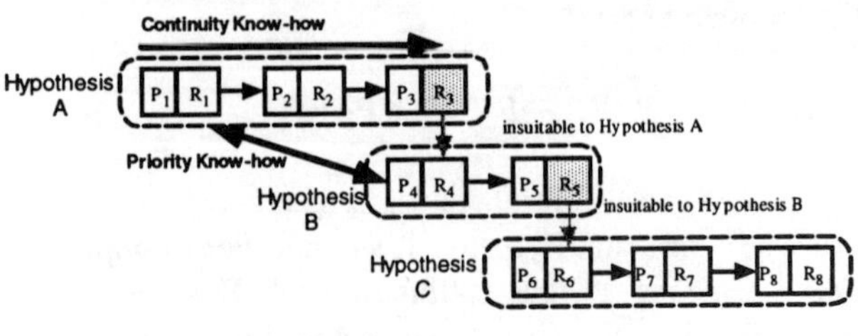

Figure. 4 WorkFlow Based on a Hypothesis

Thus, there are two ways of thinking when selecting a procedure part.

1. Selecting a procedure part in correlation with the previous processing in accordance with the hypothesis.
2. Selecting a procedure part that is in accordance with a new hypothesis as a result of changing the original hypothesis.

In IWF system, these are referred to as "continuity know-how" and "priority know-how", respectively, and defined in the following manner:

Priority know-how
Information in which a certain procedure part was performed preferentially over a certain procedure part.

Continuity Know-how
Information in which a certain procedure part was performed in continuation from a certain procedure part.

This know-how serves as indicators for procedure part selection. Acquisition of know-how is performed in the manner described below.

First, information is extracted relating to the priority relationship between procedure parts corresponding to a given situation during the course of work, and recorded as priority know-how. This is performed for all work-logs to obtain the basic priority relationship between procedure parts.

Moreover, if there are procedure part sequences common to a multiple number of work-logs as determined by observing all the work-logs, the priority know-how of those portions is consolidated to express the connection between procedure parts. This is continuity know-how.

3.2 Priority know-how

Information obtained from a single work-log that defines the priority relationships between procedure parts under various circumstances during the course of work is referred to as "priority know-how". Priority know-how consists of the following information:

- Condition (situation) for using know-how
- Priority between procedure parts

Priority know-how is expressed as follows.

if *Condition A* then

$$P_x > P_y$$

This indicates that the condition for using this know-how is *Condition A*, and procedure part P_x is more suited for the work than procedure part P_y at that time. Although the condition for using the know-how in the form of *Condition A* is not specifically stipulated provided it is an expression that is able to describe the situation, in the present IWF system, it is indicated with the initial status, the procedure part used from that point and the processing result.

3.3 Continuity know-how

When a multiple number of work-logs are accumulated, it becomes possible to detect those procedure parts within those logs that can be used continuously. Information relating to the continuance of a frequently used procedure part, in the form of "procedure part P_x is followed by procedure part P_y", is referred to as continuity information in IWF system. A group of continuous procedure parts that appear in common in a multiple number of work-logs is detected, and stored in the form of continuity know-how.

Continuity know-how is expressed as follows.

if *Condition A* then

$$P_x(R_x) \rightarrow P_y(R_y) > P_z$$

This expression indicates acquired continuity know-how in the case it is observed in numerous work-log groups that procedure part P_x and procedure part P_y are performed continuously in succession in the state of condition A during the course of work performed by an experienced worker. R_x and R_y indicate the respective processing results when procedure part P_x and procedure part P_y were performed.

The condition for use is the same as in the case of priority know-how.

4. Acquisition of Know-how

The flow of know-how acquisition is illustrated in Figure. 5. These processes are performed each time a new work-log is added in the "know-how acquisition" step of Figure. 1.

When a new log is added, the priority relationships between the procedure parts contained in that log are first extracted in the form of priority know-how. Next, the new log is compared with other work-logs that have already been registered, and any mutually coinciding procedure parts are detected.

In the case there is a series of coinciding procedure parts, information is obtained relating to continuous procedure parts from those series to generate continuity know-how.

4.1 Generation and Registration of Priority know-how

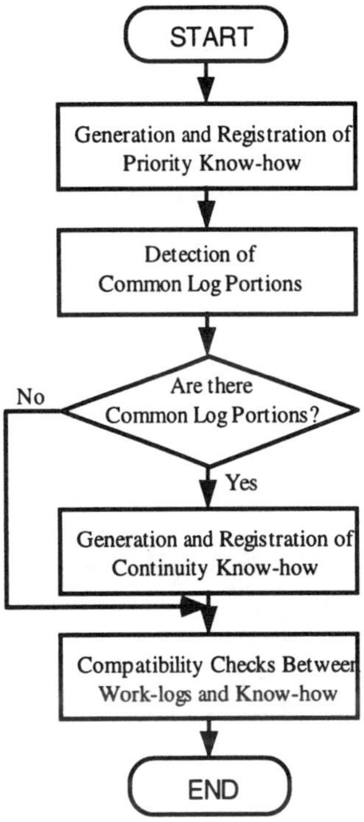

Figure. 5 Flow of Know-how Acquisition

Priority know-how is obtained from the work-log each time an experienced worker performs a new task. For example, in the case the following work-log:

Status X: $P_1(R_1) \rightarrow P_2(R_2) \rightarrow P_3(R_3)$

is obtained, information in the form of "which procedure part was performed preferentially" is used to determine compatibility based on the order of priority between hypotheses. This information enables the priority know-how (1) through (4) shown below to be obtained.

if initial status = *Status X* then

$P_1 > P_2 \ldots$ (1)

$P_1 > P_3 \ldots$ (2)

if initial status = *Status X* and

result of $P_1 = R_1$ then

$P_2 > P_3 \ldots$ (3)

if initial status = *Status X* and

result of $P_1 = R_1$ and

result of $P_2 = R_2$ then

$P_3 > \phi \ldots$ (4)

The initial priority know-how (1) and (2) indicates that "procedure part P_1 is better suited for the work than procedure parts P_2 and P_3 in *Status X*".

In the case identical priority know-how is already registered in the system, that priority know-how is reinforced as a result of having obtained a newly supported work-log.

4.2 Detection of Common Log Portions

A series of work sequences observed to be shared between a multiple number of work-logs is determined to be "continuous" based on the hypothesis, and that common portion is generated in the form of continuity know-how.

Accumulated work-logs are compared and any common portions are detected to generate continuity know-how. For example, in the case of the following two work-logs:

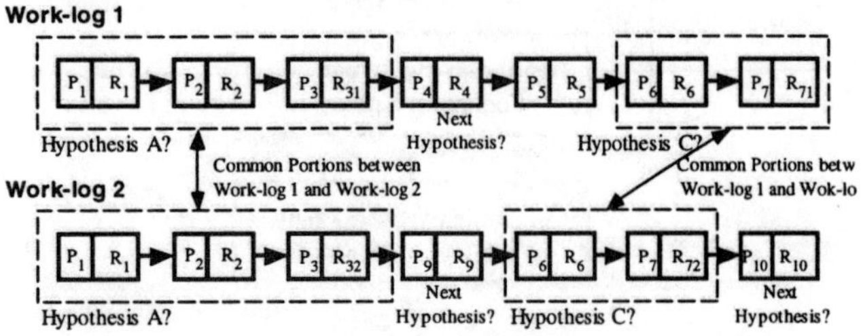

Figure. 6 Detection of Common Portions in Multiple Work-logs

Status X: $P_1(R_1) \rightarrow P_2(R_2) \rightarrow P_3(R_{31}) \rightarrow P_4(R_4) \rightarrow P_5(R_5)$
Status X: $P_1(R_1) \rightarrow P_2(R_2) \rightarrow P_3(R_{32}) \rightarrow P_7(R_7) \rightarrow P_8(R_8)$

the following common portion is detected.

Status X: $P_1(R_1) \rightarrow P_2(R_2) \rightarrow P_3$

Continuity know-how is then generated from this common portion.

4.3 Generation and Registration of Continuity know-how

Continuity know-how is generated from common log portions and stored. In the case that the following common portion is detected,

Status X: $P_1(R_1) \rightarrow P_2(R_2) \rightarrow P_3$

continuity know-how (5) and (6) is obtained as follows.

if initial status = *Status X* then
$P_1(R_1) \rightarrow P_2(R_2) \rightarrow P_3(R_{31}) > P_4$ . . . (5)
$P_1(R_1) \rightarrow P_2(R_2) \rightarrow P_3(R_{32}) > P_7$ . . . (6)

This know-how indicates that it is better to continuously process procedure parts P_1, P_2 and P_3 rather than procedure part P_4 or procedure part P_7 on condition of *Status X*.

In the case identical continuity know-how is already present in the system, it is reinforced as a result of increasing each time. When continuity know-how does not exist in the system, it is registered in the form of new know-how.

4.4 Compatibility Checks Between Work-logs and Know-how

When know-how is acquired from a multiple number of different work-logs, there are cases in which contradictions occur between those work-logs and the know-how. This is considered to occur when, for example, although continuity is recognized between a multiple number of logs and that continuity is obtained in the form of know-how, the use of procedure parts that appears to violate this continuity is found in a work-log that has been newly added.

For example, consider the case in which, in the case of continuity know-how (5) and (6) have previously been obtained and the following work-log:

Status X: $P_1(R_1) \rightarrow P_2(R_2) \rightarrow P_3(R_{31}) \rightarrow P_4(R_4) \rightarrow P_5(R_5)$
Status X: $P_1(R_1) \rightarrow P_2(R_2) \rightarrow P_3(R_{32}) \rightarrow P_7(R_7) \rightarrow P_8(R_8)$

on which the above know-how is based is present in the system, then the following new work-log:

Status X: $P_1(R_1) \rightarrow P_2(R_2) \rightarrow P_5(R_5) \rightarrow P_9(R_9)$

is added resulting in the obtaining of the following priority know-how:

if initial status = *Status X* and
the result of $P_1 = R_1$ and
the result of $P_2 = R_2$ then
$P_5 > P_9$ . . . (7)

This priority know-how (7) is in violation of the above-mentioned continuity know-how (5) and (6). Consequently, continuity know-how (5) and (6) are diminished resulting in the following continuity know-how:

if initial status = *Status X* then
$P_1(R_1) \rightarrow P_2(R_2) > P_3$ . . . (8)

Since the latter portion $P_2 \rightarrow P_3$ of know-how (5) and (6) is invalid as a result of contradicting the above-mentioned priority know-how (7), only the former portion $P_1 \rightarrow P_2$ remains as continuity know-how.

Thus, know-how is acquired while mutually checking compatibility, and there are cases in which that know-how is broken down.

5. Utilization of Know-how

The following describes the manner in which know-how is utilized. This processing is performed in the "Know-how Utilization" step of Figure. 1.

As was indicated in the definition, know-how consists of conditions that indicate under what circumstances that know-how should be used. When using know-how, a comparison is made between the status of work currently being performed, namely which procedure parts are used and what type of situation occurred as a result of their use, and the conditional information possessed by that know-how to obtain coinciding know-how.

Each type of know-how is evaluated and ranked according to frequency and so forth in order to obtain the procedure part to be given the highest priority from know-how that matches with the search conditions. The first procedure part of the hypothesis possessed by that

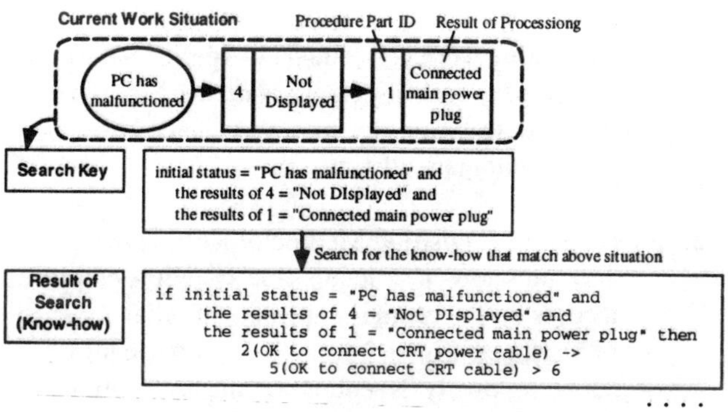

Figure. 7 Searching for Know-how that Matches the Work Situation

know-how is then proposed as the most suitable procedure part. In the case a single procedure part is proposed from multiple know-how, the priority of that procedure part becomes higher. Thus, a multiple number of procedure parts are proposed after rearranging them according to order of priority.

When a procedure part is selected by a user and it is decided to use that continuity know-how, procedure parts to be used are proposed according to the order of the procedure parts within that continuity know-how provided the following does not occur:

- when procedure parts are used to the last procedure part of the continuity know-how, and there is no following procedure part in that hypothesis;
- when the result of using a procedure part differs from that registered in the know-how; and,
- when a procedure part different from the procedure part proposed based on know-how is selected by the user and processed.

In the case any of the above occur, a search is again made of know-how having the current status in its condition portion to determine which know-how can be used. If such know-how is present, a procedure part is proposed based on that know-how.

A search is made of usable know-how corresponding to each situation within the work procedure. The resulting know-how is then used to propose the optimum processing (procedure part) to provide support for the worker when performing a particular task.

6. Prototype System

6.1 Application Target

We are currently developing a prototype IWF system. This prototype system is designed for use at a service center or similar location to provide support when providing advice in response to inquires from customers regarding malfunctions (customer service).

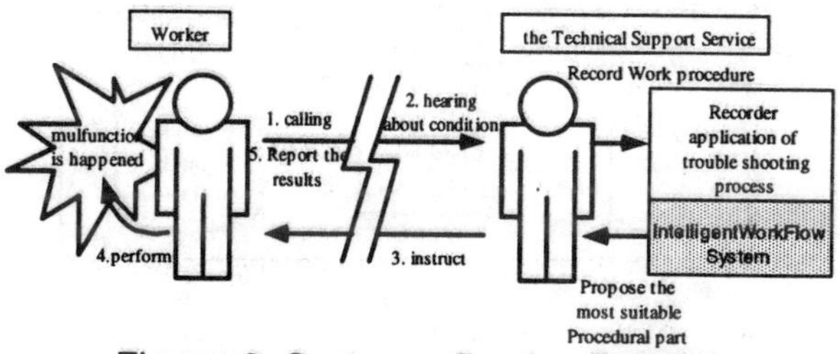

Figure. 8 Customer Service Support

The work flow when responding to customer inquiries during the course of customer service work consists of the following:

1. Customers place telephone calls regarding malfunctions, and service center personnel listen to customers as they explain the circumstances surrounding the malfunction.
2. The cause of the malfunction is determined based on the answers to questions provided by the customer and the customer (or person actually performing the repair work) is instructed of

processing to be performed to correct the malfunction.
3. Processing is performed by the person performing the repairs.
4. The results of that processing are reported to the service center.
5. The process is repeated starting at step 2 until the malfunction is corrected.

The prototype IWF system supports to workers (service center personnel that answer the telephone) at step 2 above. It proposes candidates for suitable process (procedure parts) according to the situation.

6.2 System Configuration

Figure. 9 shows the configuration of the prototype system.

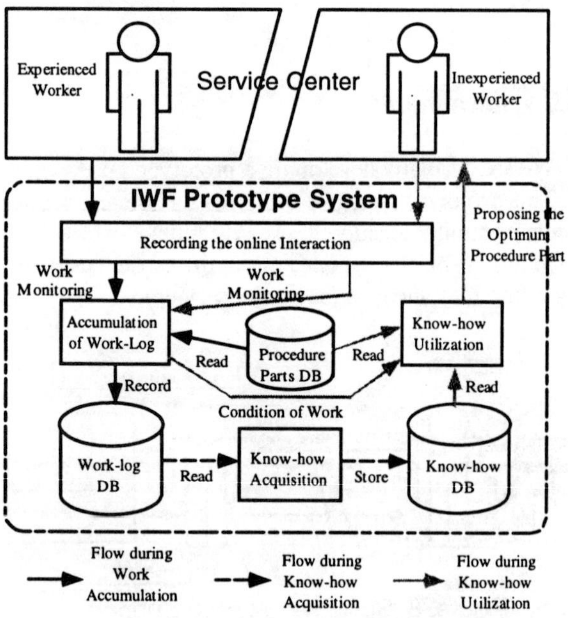

Figure. 9 Prototype System Overview

We developed the front-end application for IWF. This front-end application records the online interaction and make work-log.

The use of this prototype system enables know-how to be obtained as shown in Figure. 7. So even inexperienced workers could refer the efficient know-how of experienced workers.

7. Discussion

7.1 Current Restrictions

The current IWF system has the restrictions described below.

1 Initial Construction of Procedure parts

The procedure parts that compose the work-logs must be defined in advance before work is performed by experienced workers. However, if each procedure part is able to be distinguished using an ID system, the contents do not have to be defined in detail, thus reducing the bother associated with constructing the procedure parts.

2 Work During Initial Acquisition of Know-how

Although IWF system acquires know-how from work-logs it has obtained, if a work-log is incorrect in the initial stages of operation, that know-how may also contain errors. Accordingly, during the initial accumulation of know-how, it is necessary that know-how be acquired using a correct work-log for work performed by an experienced worker.

7.2 Advantages of IWF

IWF system has the following advantages:

1. Acquisition of Know-how from Work-logs

By retaining work performed by experienced workers in the form of a work-log, there is no need to make knowledge descriptions by specialists since know-how is acquired automatically after that point.

2. Independent Acquisition Method of Know-how

Since an know-how acquisition system is employed that focuses on the ordinary attribute of order for each type of work performed, know-how can be acquired without being overly dependent on the application.

3. Elimination of Unnecessary Steps Contained in Work

Unnecessary steps and errors contained in the accumulated work-logs are removed from the know-how as a result of accumulating a large number of correct work-logs. As a result, only the know-how that is used most often remains. The system is therefore able to provide more effective work support than simply using the work-logs alone.

4. Know-how Acquired Even from a Small Number of Work-logs

IWF system is able to acquire know-how and provide support even from a small number of work-logs. However, as was previously mentioned in **7.1**, this is premised on the work being performed effectively by an experienced worker.

7.3 Related Technology

Research related to case-based reasoning technology proposes descriptive formats for various cases and technologies such as high-speed retrieval, and is applied in various applications including design and diagnosis [1]. In these systems, since attributes are defined for case description and those values are used to make a judgment of similarity, a way of processing is strongly dependent on the problem, thus making it difficult to apply the system to a different application. In IWF system, an approach is adopted wherein know-how is extracted from work by focusing on work order to avoid problem-dependent attributes.

In addition, there are limits on the extent to which an appropriate solution can be obtained by correcting a single case only. It has therefore been pointed out that is necessary to use multiple cases [2]. IWF system extracts required information from multiple past work-logs in the form of know-how, and then proposes the necessary processing based on that know-how.

Moreover, there are also products that specifically accumulate, edit and reuse work-logs by recording GUI, such as the operation of software with a personal computer, in the form of script [5]. At present, although the user is required to create effective procedures, and there are still no such products equipped with functions that enable know-how to be extracted from a multiple number of work-logs, these products are worth noting as techniques for work-log description and extraction.

7.4 Future Topics

The following provides a discussion of topics for the future with respect to the restrictions and problems mentioned above.

1. Evaluation and Verification

We first plan to attempt to evaluate and verify that the know-how obtained from the prototype system and proposals made by the system using that know-how are suitable or not. Since the system was developed with the objective of universal way to acquire know-how, evaluations will be made to cover as many types of applications as possible.

2. Acquisition of Know-how Based on Work-log Attributes

Although the current IWF system focuses on the work performed by experienced workers, it is unable to acquire know-how for applications in which the work performed lacks order. In applications such as diagnosis which does not contain any corrective steps, there is little significance in the order of the work performed by people. Instead, there is greater emphasis placed on the attribute values of the status of the object of that work. In order to accommodate these types of applications, we are considering incorporating a system that assigns attributes to the processing contained in a work-log, and then extracts the degree of priority based on those attributes [4]. This expansion system allows the process of solving a problem to accumulated in the form of abstract knowledge.

8. Conclusion

This reported introduces a study conducted to develop a system for extracting order from work-logs and organizing that order in the form of know-how by focusing on the work-logs of experienced workers, along with a description of a prototype of that system.

This system is able to accumulate know-how by having work performed repeatedly instead of describing the know-how of an experienced worker in advance. In addition, the system is used by focusing on the order of work instead of using information associated with a specific application so that the acquisition system itself can be applied in various applications. For the future, we intend to make evaluations based on the prototype system.

9. References

[1]K. Okuda and K. Yamazaki, "Case-Based Reasoning and its Applications", *Journal of Information Processing Society of Japan Vol.31*, No.2, pp.244-254(1990).

[2]S. Kobayashi, "Present and Future of Case-Based Reasoning", *Journal of Japanese Society for Artificial Intelligence*, Vol.7 No4, pp.559-556(1992).

[3]A. Takano, T. Mishuku, M. Sasaki and S. Tanaka, "Intelligentworkflow - a Method For Efficient Trouble Shooting Services by Acquiring and Re-using Procedural Knowledge -", Conference on Agile and Intelligent Manufacturing System, Troy, NY(1996)

[4]T. Mishuku, T. Tsuchida and S. Tanaka, "A Cooperative Scheduling System - CoPlanner - by Interactive Knowledge Acquisition", Proceedings of Sixth International Conference on Data and Knowledge Systems for Manufacturing and Engineering, pp.243-262.

[5]"New Product Report: ScriPlayer-PRO 32", *Nikkei-Byte*, March 1996, Nikkei Business Publications Inc., Tokyo

TED - Turbine Engine Diagnostics
A Practical Application of a Diagnostic Expert System

Ms. Holly Ingham
Dr. Richard Helfman
Mr. Timothy Hanratty
Mr. John Dumer
Mr. Edmund H. Baur

U.S. Army Research Laboratory
AMSRL-IS-CI
Aberdeen Proving Ground, MD 21005

Abstract

TED (Turbine Engine Diagnostics) is a diagnostic expert system to aid the M1 Abrams' mechanic find and fix problems in the AGT-1500 turbine engine. TED was designed to provide the apprentice mechanic the ability to diagnose and repair the turbine engine like an expert mechanic. This paper discusses the reasoning method used in TED, called Procedural Reasoning System (PRS), as well as various design considerations throughout the life of the project. The expert system was designed and built by the U.S. Army Research Laboratory and the U.S. Army Ordnance Center. TED has been fielded to both the active Army and the National Guard.

1. Introduction

Expert Systems development has become the most successful application area of Artificial Intelligence. Numerous systems have been developed and applied in areas ranging from law to forestry to robotics [1],[2],[3]. Many new tools and techniques have been developed that add to the increased interest and success of these expert systems. As an example of some of these tools and techniques being fostered in the area of expert systems, this paper will focus on TED (Turbine Engine Diagnostics), a diagnostic expert system to aid the M1 Abrams' mechanic in finding and fixing problems in the AGT1500 turbine engine. TED was designed and built by the U.S. Army Research Laboratory and the U.S. Army Ordnance Center. Limited fielding was begun in July 1994 to selected National Guard units, and it is currently being fielded to active units of the U.S. Army. TED was designed to provide the apprentice mechanic the ability to diagnose and repair the turbine engine like an expert mechanic.

TED focused on the maintenance of the AGT1500 engine due to the overwhelming repair costs of this engine to the Army. The M1 Abrams tank is the Army's main weapon system, with over 7500 tanks fielded to active and reserve units. The repair costs were noted in a study that concluded, "the maintenance costs of the AGT-1500 engine represents the largest portion of the Army AGT-1500 operation and support (O&S) costs." [4]. Another study determined that in one year, out of a group of 360 engines evacuated to depot, 39% of them were reported as "no evidence of failure" (NEOF). The NEOF condition means that an engine was pulled from the tank, sent back to the depot for repair, but the depot determined there was nothing wrong with the engine. The unnecessary cost related to

1082-3409/97 $10.00 © 1997 IEEE

NEOF conditions was estimated at \$18.2 million annually[5]. The development and fielding of the TED program represents the Army's first successful fielded maintenance system in the area of AI. There are several reasons associated with the success of the TED program: appropriate domain with proper scope, a close relationship with the expert, extensive user involvement, plus others that will be discussed later in this paper.

2. Reasoning in TED

The main diagnostic software in TED is a Windows based expert system shell called Visual Expert™ (formerly Adept) from SoftSell Technology Inc. Visual Expert is based on a reasoning paradigm called Procedural Reasoning System (PRS) [6],[7]. PRS is a visual method of encoding reasoning strategies used by expert problem solvers. The knowledge is represented graphically with semantics suited to the procedural, goal-oriented style of problem solving. PRS is best suited for problems that are both procedural and goal-oriented. A procedural approach uses an ordered step-by step prescription to obtain a desired result, possibly including alternate paths in case of failure. Such an approach is also goal-oriented if some steps are goals to be achieved rather than specific actions to be performed [8].

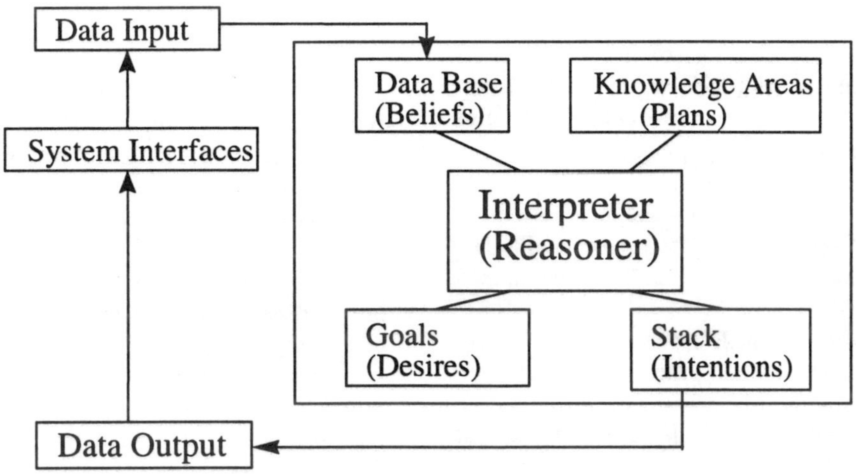

Figure 1 PRS Architecture

PRS is endowed with the attitudes of belief, desire, and intention (See Figure 1). The generalized system is composed of a system database, a set of procedures or plans, an interpreter or inference engine, and a process stack. The database contains the current beliefs of the system. These beliefs could be static properties of the domain or beliefs derived by the system itself as it executes its plans. The plans are descriptions of how to accomplish given goals or to react to certain situations and are represented by declarative procedure specifications. The body of these procedures is represented as a graphical network with sequences of sub-goals to be achieved as well as primitive actions to be accomplished. The interpreter runs the entire system, executing active goals and deciding what course of action to take based on the beliefs the system has at a point in time.

Visual Expert was chosen as the primary tool for development due to TED's need for rapid prototyping, a failed first attempt using a rule-based reasoning system, and the fact that Army TMs closely follow the paradigm of the PRS. Visual Expert uses the concept of visual application creation where development takes place through the manipulation of graphical objects on the screen. This provides an environment that is well suited for rapid prototyping. A program built with Visual Expert is composed of procedures within which there are nodes that are connected via true, false, or unknown arcs. Only one procedure is viewable in its entirety at one time, however, all procedures in the program are viewable by name. This keeps the program environment uncluttered and organized for the programmer. The visual environment was so effective that the subject matter experts (SMEs) assigned to the TED program quickly learned to read the code and some began writing their own code or modifying code written by the knowledge engineers. Visual Expert also provides a debugging environment that further aids the rapid prototype development by shortening the find, fix, and verify time for software problems. Design flaws and/or faulty logic is also much easier to find using a visual based development tool like Visual Expert.

Visual Expert consists of a system database, a display and procedure builder, scripting for application development, an interpreter or inference engine, and a debugger. The display builder is the mechanism by which information is presented to or received from the user. It contains all of the commonly used Microsoft Windows object building tools such as buttons, text boxes, etc. The procedure builder provides the developer the ability to graphically represent a process for solving a problem or performing a task and is the backbone of Visual Expert applications (See Figure 2). "Procedures consist of a series of nodes each containing a set of incoming and outgoing Arc handles. Nodes are connected by arcs showing the sequence of the steps. Information is fired from one node to another through these arcs based on the state of the world. The number and arrangement of the Arc Handles is determined by the node's type" [9].

There are five different node types used to represent steps in a procedure: start, work, case, end, and custom. Work nodes represent the logical flow in a true/false/unknown relationship. Nodes also have several styles: calculation, goal, display, and result. A calculation node performs a mathematical operation, calls a function, or compares variables. A goal node links to another procedure that can solve a problem and return an answer. A result node triggers another procedure, depending on the result of an operation. The display node provides the capability of developing the user interface for a program using the full suite of Microsoft Windows controls. Default displays are provided along with tools to customize displays with text, colors, graphics, shapes, buttons, list boxes, etc. Scripting provides the capability of developing nodes that behave in a way that is particular to a specific application. A script is a collection of statements that define the behavior of a custom node. They can be as simple as a one-line statement that assigns a value to a variable to as complex as containing instructions that perform operations under different conditions.

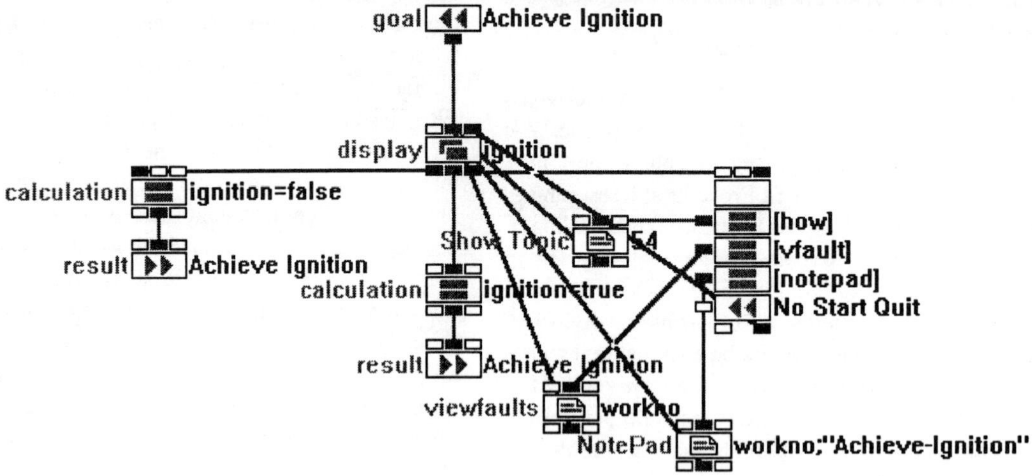

Figure 2 VX Procedure in TED

3. Developmental Issues

The development of any large-scale computer system requires extensive amounts of time and resources. Expert systems are no exception. Careful consideration must be given to a myriad of issues. The following section outlines the critical issues that were part of the TED development process.

The principal reasons for developing an expert system are to disseminate rare or costly expertise and to more effectively and efficiently use the human expert [10]. The selection of an appropriate domain with proper scope is critical to its success. The domain selected should be one that encompasses a problem that is "worthy" of the effort. The specificity within the domain defines the scope of the project. For the TED program, Abrams tank maintenance was quickly identified as the proper domain with special focus on the engine and transmission.

By 1991, several factors were contributing to the selection of tank maintenance as an appropriate domain. In addition to rising maintenance costs, the Army had developed a new funding directive called stock funding of depot level repairables (SFDLR). Essentially, this directive puts the burden of maintenance costs onto the company commander rather than deferring it up the chain, in the hope that overall maintenance costs will be reduced. Finally, the

Army had also developed a new maintenance doctrine in order to maintain a high operational readiness status. Under the new doctrine, when an engine fails, it is pulled from the tank and sent to Direct Support (DS). The tank hull remains at the unit, a new engine is sent forward, and the tank is quickly returned to full operational status.

The TED software engineers quickly established some important guidelines that remain in effect today.

3.1 Establish and Maintain Communication

Software engineers and subject matter experts do not generally speak the same language. Software engineers talk of frames and objects. The subject matter experts for the TED program are M1 tank mechanics. M1 tank mechanics talk of inlet guide vane (IGV) angles and of rotational variable differential transformers (RVDTs). Each needs to learn some of the other's language, but the main effort is on the software engineer to learn the language of the mechanic.

The best way to learn what the user does is to observe the user in his environment. The TED team attended and video taped classes for M1 mechanics. This produced three important benefits. First, it quickly immersed the software engineers into the language of the mechanic. The IGV is located in front of the engine and the angle determines how much air gets through to the turbine blades. Second, it gave an accurate picture of how a mechanic performs his job and how software might improve that job. The TED team noticed during that first session that the original scope of work was too narrow. There was a whole suite of software that could help the mechanic better perform his job. Third, it established a bond between the software engineer and the soldier. Soldiers could sense that the team was serious and that soldier's needs would be given serious attention. They were thus eager to cooperate.

When the aim is to produce software that not only works as planned, but also gets used by the mechanic, then user participation in the development process is critical. The TED team heard many stories from soldiers about equipment that never gets used, and about equipment that is difficult to use for which a small change would have made the item soldier friendly. The TED SME's were assigned full time to the project.

New technology is often met with resistance when it is thrown at an unaware and/or ill-prepared user. Rarely can a user, at the start of a project, envision how technology can improve his job. A system based on initial user expectations will at best be shallow, and may even be useless. The software engineer and the SME are each constantly learning about the other. The software engineer is continually learning about the needs and duties of the mechanic, and the mechanic is learning about the potential impact of new software on his future.

3.2 Rapid Prototyping

A prototype is essential for two-way communication. It allows the user to see and touch what the software engineer envisions for the user. It gives the user the earliest opportunity to comment on his system, and it gives him some clue as to the potential of the project. The user does not always know what technology is available, and the hands-on experience of the prototype is often the best way to educate the user. A prototype serves as a common reference point. Without a prototype, it is difficult to obtain useful feedback. It also shows how well the software engineer understands the user's needs.

3.3 Spiral Model

Boehm's spiral model [11] shown in Figure 3 incorporates an incremental development schema. Successive prototypes are produced that expand upon user requirements. In addition, the software engineer is able to

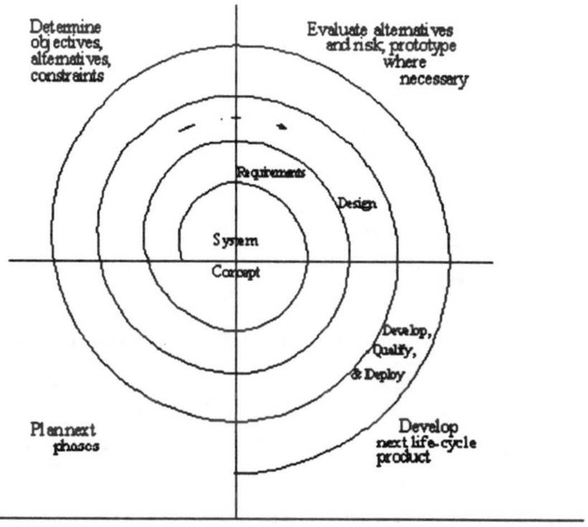

Figure 3 Spiral Model

breakdown complex tasks into smaller components. As each component is developed, it is evaluated against user requirements. The user requirements are re-evaluated as each successive module is developed. Consequently, the user is an integral part of the development team. His input is essential. There are two reasons behind selecting the spiral method for the TED program: rapid changes in PC hardware and software and the need to keep the user in the loop. In 1991, it was obvious that hardware and software for the PC would continue to improve and become more affordable. Computer memory continues to expand and deflate in price. Hard drives continue to get bigger and cheaper. Screen resolution expands and video cards improve. The price of a Pentium system today rivals the price of a 386 system in 1991.

Software follows the same pattern outlined for hardware. Every year, software improves, new products are announced, and existing products offer upgrades at an astounding pace and price. Goals that were impossible or difficult in the past may now be relatively easy tasks. The TED team continues to meet formally once a month to decide on the direction and scope of the project. Unsatisfied goals are re-evaluated, and some may be dropped from the list, while new goals may be added.

4. TED Software Overview

4.1 Design Goals

At about 6 months into the project, the SMEs had established several design goals. These goals were based primarily on each SMEs extensive experience as an M1 mechanic and as an M1 instructor for engine maintenance classes. The SMEs had much previous experience with soldier mechanics-their likes and their dislikes. The following lists the main design goals for the TED software. The software should be:

* accurate,
* easy to use,
* flexible,
* task oriented, and it should
* support multiple levels of expertise

First, the software should be accurate. It need not be perfect, but it should be significantly better at diagnosing faults than the system it is replacing. Otherwise, it will lose soldier respect and it will not be used. Second, it must be easy to use, for otherwise, it will sit on the shelf. Mechanics have favorite stories of diagnostic equipment that does nothing but take up lots of storage space. Third, it must be flexible enough to support a variety of diagnostic styles. For example, some mechanics are thorough and methodical, and a structured step by step approach is best for them. A few have a sixth sense and "know" what is wrong with an engine. They have only limited need for the information in TED and will only use it as an occasional reference. Other soldiers have a mixture of styles. They may know a lot about some parts of the engine, but need guidance on other areas.

The fourth goal is that TED be task oriented and structured in a way that is natural for the soldier. The current Technical Manuals (TMs) have a structure that is difficult to use and to follow. For example, consider a typical task to determine whether excessive metal chips are present. To perform this check, the user must first find the right TM. It's in TM-34. Once in the right TM, the job is to find the right page. Symptom 2, Metal Chips begins on page 3-20. The tasks for Symptom 2, Metal Chips Found, refer to tasks in TM 20-1 and in TM 34-1. However, little information is given as to which page in TM 20-1 or TM 34-1 to turn to. Experts can navigate the TMs, but others find the structure confusing.

The last goal recognizes that mechanics come with different skill levels. Experts need little or no help from TED. Beginners need extensive step by step instructions. A system aimed at just one level of expertise would bore the expert or baffle the beginner.

4.2. Software Selection.

The Army had already chosen the hardware for TED, the Contact Test Set III (a ruggedized 486 PC), which is capable of running Unix, DOS, or Windows. It was clear from the beginning that the project would involve a variety of tasks each needing a specialized software package. It was also clear that no package could run in isolation. Programs would need to exchange information with others. Windows was chosen as the operating system because of its capabilities and its perceived growth potential.

For any software choice, the key is to choose a package that first meets the user's needs, and then, if possible, the programmer's. One choice the programmer must often make is whether to choose commercial off-the-shelf (COTS) packages or whether it is better to write the code himself.

Today COTS packages offer many advantages over code produced in-house. They also have some disadvantages.

The benefits include:

* Cost is reduced by spreading among many.
* External support is available from the developer.
* Code is already written, saving time.
* Technology proliferation offers many selections.

The disadvantages may include:

* The program may not fit the problem.
* Program success is tied to the survivability of the COTS developer.
* Initial code may work but upgrades may not.
* Run-time fees may be high.

The TED team prefers to use COTS software when available and suitable. Whenever such software is not available or suitable, the choice is either to wait until a new product is released or a product upgrade provides the needed functionality, or write the code in-house. For example, the current hypertext package was not chosen until the fall of 1993, and the database was not selected until the fall of 1994. These code decisions are subject to change at each monthly meeting. As the team gathers experience with a package or code, the decision might be to continue as before, to switch from in-house to COTS, (or vice versa), or to switch COTS vendors.

4.3 Soldier Interface.

Users communicate with TED primarily through the mouse, and sometimes through keyboard input. At the top level, TED is menu driven (See Figure 4). At this level, the soldier can choose which module to run. Inside a module, TED can be either soldier driven or data driven. Soldier driven means that TED is in browse mode. This is the equivalent of opening the TM to any section and reading the pages. Browse mode is useful for experts who need little supervision and only occasional help from the TMs.

In data-driven mode, TED first reads its knowledge base (a database of faults previously identified) to determine engine history, and then leads the mechanic through a series of tasks to perform and/or questions to answer. All pertinent information is linked so the user is automatically lead through different sections of the TMs, if necessary. The user can hop out of this mode at any time and jump into browse mode.

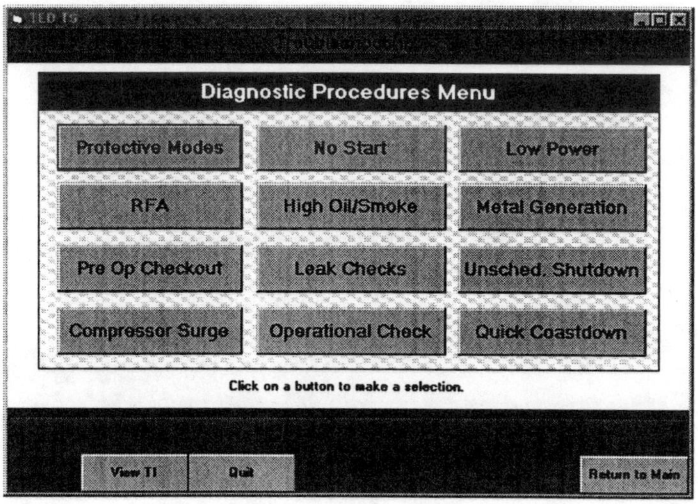

Figure 4 Sample TED Menu

5. TED's Future Direction

As indicated earlier, TED is currently fielded in both the active Army and the National Guard. It is the Army's first successful large-scale application of Expert System technology. Future efforts are concentrated on embedding TED into the tank itself and expanding the scope of diagnostics to other areas of the M1 tank.

The rapid expansion of WEB services also provides an opportunity to create a dynamic diagnostic tool such as TED. A WEB page was designed by the TED team (http://rpstl.arl.mil/ted.html) to act as a reference source and help desk. Current TED information can be found at this WEB site. Every day, new techniques are developed which allow the WEB participant to accomplish so much more through this dynamic environment.

As WEB services improve, on-line diagnostics will become possible. This will provide the mechanic with up-to-date diagnostic capabilities and provide a greater dynamic database to extract/record information that is currently spread by word of mouth or through manual updates. A WEB diagnostic tool for TED is already being researched and a prototype will likely be developed within the next few years. This will in turn, pay off through more efficient diagnostics and smarter mechanics from all locations within the world in contact with each other through the WEB.

REFERENCES

1 De Mukler, R.V., van Noortijkm C., Kerkmeester, H.O., (1989) Knowledge Systems and Law-The JURICAS Project,Proceedings of the Third International Conference on Logic, Informatics, Law (Legal Expert Systems).

2 Mikkonen, Esko & Leinonen, T., (1994) Expert System for Safety Inspection in Logging, IUFRO Div. 3.04.01 meeting. In Miscellaneous Report no. 385. Maine Agr. and For. Exp. Station. Univ. of Maine.

3 Rosenberg, Jerry M., (1986) Dictionary of Artificial Intelligence and Robotics, Wiley, New York

4 Textron Lycoming Internal Memo (1988).

5 Textron Lycoming Internal Memo (1989).

6 Georgeff, M.P. & Lansky, A.L. (1983) Procedural Expert Systems. Proceedings of the Eighth International Joint Conference on AI.

7 Georgeff, M.P. & Lansky, A.L. (1986) A System of Reasoning in Dynamic Domains: Fault Diagnostics on the Space Shuttle. Technical Notes 375, SRI International.

8 Advanced Decision Systems (1988). Procedural Reasoning Systems. Working Paper, TR-ADS-0015, October 1988.

9 Klock, M., Rauch, B., Sperry, S., Himes, A. (1994) Visual Expert Guide. Visual Expert Manual, Version 2.21.

10 Weiss, S.M. & Kulikowski, C.A. (1984) A Practical Guide to Designing Expert Systems. Totowa, NJ: Rowman & Allanheld.

11 Boehm, B.W. (1986). A Spiral Model of Software Development and Enhancement. ACM Software Engineering Notes.

Session G.1

Artificial Intelligence and Software Engineering II

Session Chair:
Arif Ghafoor, Purdue University, USA

Knowledge Refinement to Debug and Maintain a Tablet Formulation System

Susan Craw Robin Boswell*
School of Computer and Mathematical Sciences
The Robert Gordon University
Aberdeen AB25 1HG, UK
Email: smc,rab@scms.rgu.ac.uk

Ray Rowe
ZENECA Pharmaceuticals
Hurdsfield Industrial Estate
Macclesfield
Cheshire SK10 2NA, UK

Abstract

Knowledge refinement tools have commonly been applied to diagnostic applications. This paper considers the refinement of a design application. It explores the differences in knowledge content and problem-solving steps for design rather than diagnosis systems, and investigates additional refinement operators. Although the problem-solving task itself tends to be more complex, this in fact puts more constraints on the results of the problem-solving and so the evidence on which the refinement is based can be more rich. Results are provided for a real tablet formulation system, TFS, *and experience is reported for two types of refinement tasks: debugging to correct faulty problem-solving of an early version of* TFS; *maintenance of* TFS *when the formulation task is altered by a change in company policy.*

1. Introduction

Knowledge refinement is the process of changing knowledge in a knowledge-based system (KBS) in reaction to evidence that the KBS is not producing correct solutions. The KBS is evaluated on tasks provided by an expert. Those where the solutions of the KBS and expert are incompatible provide evidence that the KBS is faulty. The "correct" task-solution pairs can be regarded as training cases for the learning undertaken within the refinement process.

Automated knowledge refinement comprises the following steps. **Blame Allocation** identifies rules or individual conditions which are responsible for the wrong solution. These may be rules which have fired and so are part of the explanation for the solution: **error-causing rules** have fired when they should not have, **wrong-fire** rules have fired but provided the wrong value. However, blame allocation must also identify rules that have not fired but, if they were used, would produce the desired expert solution (**target rules**). **Repair Generation** decides which knowledge changes effect repairs that prevent error-causing rules from firing, allow wrong-fire rules to fire correctly or enable target rules to fire. Of course there will be many changes that achieve similar effects. **Refinement Selection** chooses which potential repairs are likely to be the most effective overall. Selection happens at various stages of the refinement process: which rules are most likely to be to blame for the faulty training case, which repair is most likely to achieve improved problem-solving, which refined knowledge base (KB) appears to achieve the best problem-solving? Selection is therefore based on heuristic knowledge about effective blame allocation or refinement generation, or empirical evidence of the effective problem-solving of refined KBs.

Our application is a rule-based Tablet Formulation System, TFS, implemented in Logica's Product Formulation Expert System shell PFES [16]. TFS is in routine use at Zeneca Pharmaceuticals, where it forms an important stage in the development of tablet formulations for new drugs [15]. Tablet formulation is a complex synthesis task and TFS is one of the few knowledge-based formulation systems in regular commercial use [6]. We are particularly interested in working with TFS because there is considerably less experience both in building and refining such design systems than for the more traditional diagnostic systems.

Section 2 introduces TFS. The KRUST refinement tool is described in Section 3, with TFS-specific details appearing in Section 4. Our experience applying KRUST to TFS is described in Section 5. Related work is considered in Section 6 and Section 7 contains conclusions.

2. The tablet formulation application

The design of a new tablet involves identifying other substances that must be included in the tablet's recipe so that the tablet is manufactured in a robust form, and the desired dosage of drug is delivered and absorbed by the patient. This involves the identification and quantities of in-

*This work was supported by a Robert Gordon University studentship and in part by EPSRC grant GR/L38387

1082-3409/97 $10.00 © 1997 IEEE

ert substances called **excipients** to balance the properties of the drug [15]. Excipients play the role of fillers, binders, lubricants and disintegrants in the tablet. The difficulty of the formulation task arises from the need to select a set of mutually compatible excipients, whilst at the same time satisfying a variety of other constraints.

The input to TFS is a **requirement** comprising the drug name and desired dose, together with the number of fillers to be used. TFS produces a **specification** indicating the desired properties of the tablet and the **formulation** for the tablet:

TFS Requirement

DRUG: Drug-A DOSE: 60 mg
NUMBER OF FILLERS: 2

TFS Specification

FULL-STABILITY: Yes
TARGET-TABLET-WEIGHT: 260mg
START-STRATEGY: Strategy-A
FILLER-CONCENTRATION: 66.9%
DISINTEGRANT-CONCENTRATION: 0.05
TABLET-DIAMETER: 8.73mm
... various other properties ...

TFS Formulation

TABLET WEIGHT: 250mg
FILLERS: Lactose 66.7%
Calcium Phosphate 2.4%
BINDER: Gelatin 4.1%
LUBRICANT: Stearic acid 1.0%
DISINTEGRANT: Croscarmelose 2.1%

We have access to several versions of TFS. **TFS-1A** is an initial version, corresponding to an early stage in development. Its KB is buggy and produced faulty tablet formulations for some tablet requirements. **TFS-1B** is a manually debugged version of TFS-1A. TFS-1B produced correct formulations during its period of usage. **TFS-2** is a manually updated version of TFS-1B that resulted from a paradigm shift in the company's approach to tablet formulation. It also contains further bug repairs. TFS-2 produced correct formulations according to the revised formulation practice during its period of usage. It should be noted that TFS-2 was an update rather than a completely re-engineered system. This evolution of TFS demonstrates the need for debugging and maintenance in the development of a KBS in a commercial environment. Therefore knowledge refinement has a role to play in both the debugging of faulty knowledge and the updating of knowledge to reflect changes in the operational environment.

3. The KRUST tool

Our KRUST refinement tool is unusual in generating many refined KBs and postponing the final choice of a recommended refined KB until it undertakes an empirical evaluation. Figure 1 shows a typical application of KRUST. A set of training cases is available each of which consists of a task and the expert's solution. For TFS, each training case consists of a requirement, a specification and a formulation as described in Section 2. Individual wrongly solved training cases are used to trigger the refinement cycle, but the set of training cases is used to induce new knowledge, reject unsuitable refined KBs, and evaluate the suitable refined KBs in order to select the preferred one, possibly for subsequent refinement with later training cases.

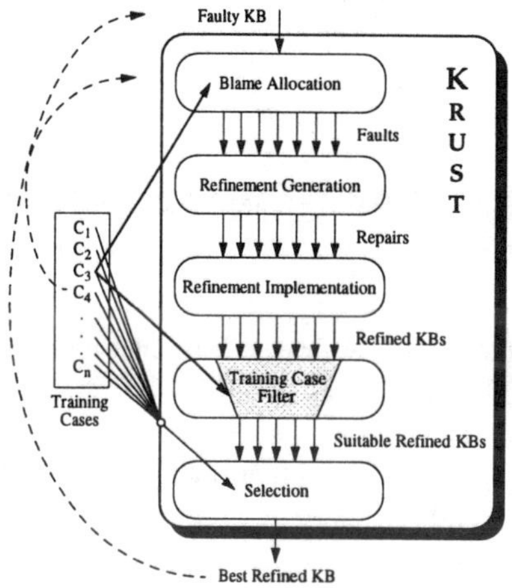

Figure 1. A typical application of KRUST

KRUST is particularly applicable to KBSs where inference provides additional control over the exhaustive deduction assumed in logical theories. It takes account of a rule's position on the execution agenda as well as considering whether the rule's conditions are satisfied or not. Therefore, as well as proposing changes that affect the logical content of the rules, it also suggests knowledge changes that affect how the rule is handled by the control mechanism.

KRUST creates internal models of the KBS's knowledge and its problem-solving (Figure 2). This simulation of the KBS is not used as an efficient replacement of the KBS [3]. Instead it is an aid to guide the refinement process; the refinements are checked using the actual KBS. In this way KRUST reasons about the refinement process in a common knowledge format but does not rely on duplicating all nuances of the KBS.

3.1. Modelling knowledge: the knowledge skeleton

The **knowledge skeleton** is an internal frame-based representation of the KBS's knowledge. It is a general representation of the knowledge, but can be fairly simple since it must faithfully represent only those portions of the knowledge that are pertinent to refinement with KRUST; a language like Ontolingua is unnecessary. KBS validation work

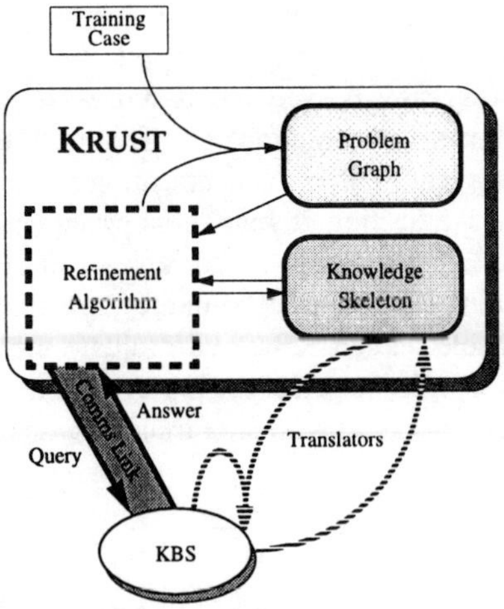

Figure 2. KRUST and KBS processes

also adopts this view [13]. Knowledge that should not be refined (such as procedural code to interact with the user) is duplicated but marked as irrelevant for refinement. A grammar for the relevant knowledge types in the shell's rule format generates a translator that creates a knowledge skeleton for the KB, and reconstructs a refined KB from the original KB and changes in the skeleton, Figure 2.

The knowledge skeleton represents rules as combinations of rule elements. It allows navigation between related pieces of knowledge (rule chains) and assembles additional refinement specific knowledge: which refinement operators are applicable, links to repairs for the rule element. We have evolved an expandable hierarchy of rule elements where a small set of basic rule elements are identified with the various knowledge formats used in several shells. In practice, a rule element conforms to one of a very small set of roles: logical n-ary predicate, variable assignment, numerical test, arithmetic calculation, procedure call.

3.2. Modelling inference: the problem graph

The problem-solving of a KBS is affected by both the knowledge content and the inference engine. Therefore, we have always believed that it is important to consider refinements that alter the way the knowledge is handled by the inference engine, in addition to the more standard changes to the content of the knowledge. Our work with Prolog KBs has always assumed that "the conclusion" is the first solution found and hence has taken account of Prolog's rule order conflict resolution and depth first search [4]. Therefore some refinement operators are concerned with altering the position of rules in the KB. We have extended this idea by developing refinement operators for several shells; specifically CLIPS, PFES and PowerModel (formerly KAPPA).

The **problem graph** is a graphical representation of the problem-solving for a particular training case, that captures the content of the deductions and the structure of the rule firing agenda. Its nodes contain [rule element, deducibility] pairs and the links represent problem-solving. Figure 3 shows the problem graph for the following task-solution pair and simple backward chaining rules when high rule priorities win:

R1: $C \rightarrow -$ (.8)	r2: $G \rightarrow A$ (.8)
R2: $D \rightarrow -$ (.7)	r3: $G \wedge H \rightarrow B$ (.7)
R3: $A \wedge B \rightarrow +$ (.9)	r4: $H \rightarrow C$ (.8)
R4: $D \wedge E \rightarrow +$ (.6)	r5: $I \rightarrow C$ (.7)
r1: $F \rightarrow A$ (.9)	r6: $J \wedge K \rightarrow D$ (.8)

Task: $\neg F \wedge G \wedge \neg H \wedge I \wedge J \wedge K$
Solution: + (the KBS applies R1 and r5 to conclude –.)

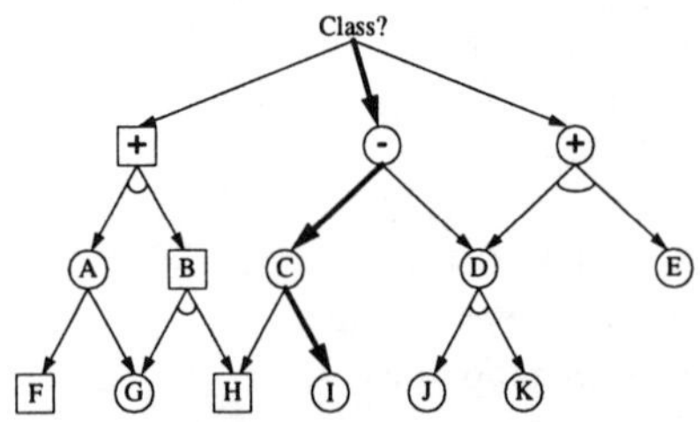

Figure 3. Problem graph for simple ruleset

Each deducible node is shown as a circle and unprovable ones are squares. A node's links are ordered to reflect the decreasing order imposed by conflict resolution and so the solution graph (bold) is the leftmost subgraph whose nodes are deducible. Potential KBS faults are identified in the problem graph as incorrect deductions or wrongly configured links. Repairs express changes to the problem graph as alterations to the knowledge skeleton. Thus, the knowledge skeleton and problem graph indicate the structure and processing of the KBS from which refinements are proposed. We believe this approach can be extended to more complex control mechanisms since Menzies [8] uses a similar abductive model for several problem solving methods.

It may appear that we are trying to create a generic **simulation** for a range of KBSs. This is not the case; the knowledge skeleton and problem graph are simply used to propose possible refinements. KRUST always generates refinements and empirically filters and evaluates them by communicating with the **actual** KBS. Therefore, mismatches between the actual KBS and the internal models result only in proposed refinements that fail and are removed during the empirical filtering, or missed refinements where one of the many other refinements will be selected instead.

4. Using KRUST with TFS

In this section we indicate the updates to KRUST that enable it to model, and so refine, PFES KBSs [2]. Refinement operators are also added to enhance the range of repairs KRUST undertakes for KBSs in PFES, and other shells.

4.1. Communicating with a PC-based KBS

The problem graph is constructed from the knowledge skeleton and answers to queries to the KBS. Originally KRUST and the KBS ran as one process with communication between LISP and Prolog being handled by the POPLOG environment. CLIPS and PowerModel have APIs that allow communication via pipes or RPCs, so KRUST and the KBS run as separate Unix processes, Figure 2. This mechanism was changed to a file-based transfer of messages between the Unix KRUST process and PFES running on a PC. PFES's GUI was replaced by functions that communicated with the message-passing mechanism.

This simple communication was sufficient because few messages were needed since KBS behaviour was extracted from PFES traces. These contain a record of every attempt by the rule interpreter to execute a rule element, together with the result (success or failure) and the bindings for all its variables. The training case trace provides information to construct the problem graph, which is then used for blame allocation and refinement generation.

4.2. Designs as evidence of faults

TFS's formulation task produces a compound answer (Section 2), in contrast to the single result typical of diagnostic systems. Normally, the outputs from different versions of TFS differ at only one or two points, but some training cases can have as many as 12 points of difference. Combining the repairs to fix many differences will lead to a combinatorial explosion. Instead, KRUST automatically determines a chain of dependencies between faults, and attempts to fix the earliest first. A dependency chain is an ordering of the faults from the sequence of rule firings. For those few TFS training cases which exhibit large numbers of errors, it was possible to obtain a few values that are prior to all the others in terms of dependency, and so KRUST focuses its repairs on them.

4.3. New rule elements

Many of the rule elements in PFES KBSs are immediately identified with standard rule elements already used in KRUST's knowledge skeleton and so are easily expressed in the grammar that is used to generate the translators. But PFES rules also apply **agendas**. These are not standard rule execution agendas (e.g. as found in CLIPS), but are used to pass data between rules that generate values and those that subsequently test or filter them. This action is common in constructive KBSs where partial designs must be extended.

Agendas are untyped lists, where items can be read and written to the top or bottom, or directly below another item. Examples of the two most common types in TFS follow.

The **Filler-Agenda** is a list of excipients; their presence on the agenda shows they have passed a stability test:

Snapshot: Cellulose Lactose
PFES Conc:
add <FILLER> to-bottom-of FILLER-AGENDA
PFES Cond: <FILLER> is-on FILLER-AGENDA

The **Property-Agenda** contains a list of pairs comprising an excipient and the value of some mechanical property:

Snapshot: Cellulose 46.2 Lactose 158.8
PFES Conc:
add <FILLER> to-bottom-of PROPERTY-AGENDA
add <STABILITY> to-bottom-of PROPERTY-AGENDA
PFES Conds: <FILLER> is-on PROPERTY-AGENDA
<STABILITY> is-item-after
<FILLER> on PROPERTY-AGENDA

These examples show that PFES agendas behave like attribute-value tuples in working memory and so are similar in behaviour to CLIPS ordered terms. They are translated to KRUST's rule element for ordered terms:

Filler: on-agenda(filler-agenda, <Filler>)
Property: on-agenda(property-agenda, <Filler>)
agenda-anon-attribute(property-agenda,
<Filler>, <Value>)

Notice that conclusions that add items to agendas have different representations in the skeleton, depending on whether the item is an attribute or value. The translator chooses the construction automatically from the context.

We have identified all PFES's rule elements with existing rule elements for KRUST's knowledge skeleton. However, if a KBS rule element does not correspond to existing rule elements, then a new type can be added to KRUST's rule element hierarchy, but new refinement operators must also be defined, based on its parent in the hierarchy.

4.4. New refinement operators

Earlier versions of KRUST concentrated on conservative changes to the knowledge, based on the evidence of a single training case, rather than creating new knowledge. This decision resulted from our desire to investigate how effective knowledge refinement is when few training cases are available; a common scenario with real applications. Therefore, although a refinement operator to create new rules existed, it simply built a rule whose conditions were the training case facts and whose conclusion was the expert's solution. Needless to say the addition of this (very specific) rule was rarely chosen as best in the evaluation of refined KBs!

We have now started to add inductive refinement operators to learn novel pieces of knowledge from a set of training cases. Our experience with TFS has shown that although KRUST has always been able to **identify** these faults, induction is necessary to actually suggest repairs to the knowledge. Our domain expert was very content with KRUST identifying the faults and was happy to volunteer new knowledge for KRUST to incorporate. However we regarded TFS's need for inductive operators as a timely impetus to enhance KRUST's operators!

4.4.1. Acquiring missing database entries

In addition to IF/THEN rules, TFS contains a database of facts about drugs and their interaction with excipients. KRUST treats database entries as rules whose antecedent is always true and suggests refinements in the same way as for rules. New inductive operators are used to add missing facts to the database, but could also be used to create additional conditions for rules.

As an example, suppose TFS wrongly suggests Calcium Phosphate as a filler and KRUST's problem graph identifies the rule chain in Figure 4 as a fault. **Get-Insoluble-Filler** has fired because Calcium Phosphate is (still) on the filler agenda, since **Remove-Excessive-Fillers** has not removed it because the MAX-LEVEL of Calcium Phosphate is missing from the Database. One of KRUST's possible repairs is to supply the database value.

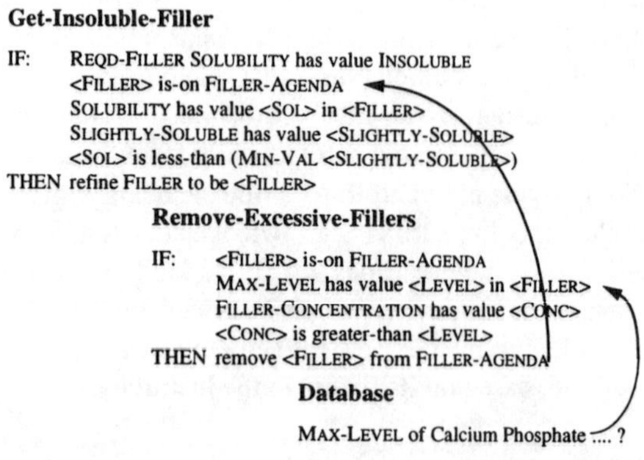

Figure 4. Rule chain for database repair

The remainder of **Remove-Excessive-Fillers** requires the MAX-LEVEL of Calcium Phosphate to be less than the value of FILLER-CONCENTRATION; the value of FILLER-CONCENTRATION can be determined from the trace. KRUST now uses an inductive approach to provide a "best guess" for MAX-LEVEL by using further constraints from a relevant selection from all the training cases:

Positive Examples – training cases (including the current training case) for which TFS wrongly recommends Calcium Phosphate and fails **Remove-Excessive-Fillers** at the same point

Negative Examples – training cases for which TFS correctly recommends Calcium Phosphate and fails **Remove-Excessive-Fillers** at the same point.

The values of FILLER-CONCENTRATION for the positive examples provide a set of upper bounds for the MAX-LEVEL of Calcium Phosphate and KRUST selects the least upper bound. Conversely, the values of FILLER-CONCENTRATION for the negative examples provide a set of lower bounds, and hence a greatest lower bound. The greatest lower bound and least upper bound delimit the new database fact. In this example the most conservative change uses the least upper bound; the most radical change uses the greatest lower bound. Alternatively, the expert could select a value between these two bounds.

4.4.2. Fixing algebraic formulae

TFS contains several algebraic formulae. Again, KRUST has always been able to **identify** rule elements comprising arithmetic calculations as potential faults but has not repaired them. Our experience of these faults in TFS has revealed 2 types. Firstly the conditions under which a formula is applied may be wrong. These faults are repaired with standard KRUST refinement operators including the inductive operator described above (Section 4.4.1.). Secondly, the algebraic formula itself may be wrong. KRUST identifies these faults but currently does not discover a new formula. The expert may wish to volunteer useful information (a new formula or the general format for the formula) but we plan to use positive and negative examples as above to determine a set of points on the curve and then apply a standard curve fitting algorithm.

5. Experience of KRUST with TFS

In this section we describe the faults that have been repaired in TFS. We concentrate on real knowledge engineering issues – the faults occurred in an early version of a real industrial application and the application was modified later in reaction to a real change in company policy. We are therefore not particularly concerned with providing results of the form: "if you randomly select T% of the available data as training data then on average the improved accuracy of the KBS is A% on the (100-T)% remaining data compared to P% prior to learning". We feel that the results here are more important for practising knowledge engineers, since they demonstrate KRUST's effectiveness in a real situation.

5.1. Debugging results

In this section we describe KRUST in its debugging role when it attempts to replicate the manual refinement that has taken place historically developing TFS-1B from TFS-1A. KRUST refines an early (buggy) version TFS-1A and the training cases are provided by a later (assumed correct) version, TFS-1B. Thus TFS-1B, rather than an expert, is playing the part of an oracle. KRUST has access to the knowledge in TFS-1A, the problem-solving of TFS-1A (in the form of traces), and training cases consisting of specifications and formulations produced by TFS-1B. KRUST has no access to traces or knowledge from TFS-1B.

We generated 208 requirements spread evenly through 13 drugs, 10–500mg doses and requiring 1 or 2 fillers. A hierarchical clustering algorithm applied to the TFS-1A traces for these inputs identified 3 types of fault.

Fault 1: incorrect filler The refinement run produced by Case 5 is typical.

Case 5 Input:	Drug-A, 110mg, 1 filler
TFS-1A Output:	Filler Calcium Phosphate 57.3%
TFS-1B Output:	Filler Calcium Carbonate 58.5%

The blame assignment and refinement generation stages produced 61 potential refinements, one of which identified the database value for the MAX-LEVEL of Calcium Phosphate as missing (Example in 4.4.1.). A set of training cases produced the range [12%, 57%] for MAX-LEVEL. The conservative repair, MAX-LEVEL=57% was overridden by the expert's value, 30%. The refined KBs corresponding to each of the refinements were tested by running each on the training case, Case 5. All failed this test except the KB with the repaired database. Note that it would have passed even with the value 57%.

It is at first surprising that filtering the refined KBs using the training case is so effective. Our experience with other KBSs is that many refined KBs survive this filter and require further filtering. The difference here is that the KBS output is a complex formulation and so other changes to the KBS are likely to affect other parts of the formulation for the training case, in addition to the filler. This appears to be an advantage of refining a design system and is in contrast to experience with diagnostic systems, where one difficulty is selecting relevant training cases with which to filter effectively the many refined KBs generated [12].

Fault 2: incorrect quantity of binder Cases 1 and 52 are examples.

Case 1 Input:	Drug-A, 10mg, 1 filler
TFS-1A Output:	Binder Gelatin 4.1%
TFS-1B Output:	Binder Gelatin 2.1%
Case 52 Input:	Drug-G, 210mg, 2 fillers
TFS-1A Output:	Binder Maize-Starch 4.0%
TFS-1B Output:	Binder Maize-Starch 2.0%

The blame assignment and refinement generation stages produced 93 potential refinements for Case 1. One refinement corrects the fault shown in Figure 5 as follows.

```
Update-Formulation
IF:   <BINDER> is-on TABLET-REPORT-AGENDA
      <ADJUSTED-CONC> is-item-after <BINDER> on TABLET-REPORT-AGENDA
THEN set the value of <BINDER> in the FORMULATION to be <ADJUSTED-CONC>

    Set-Binder-Conc
    IF:   BINDER has value <BINDER> in FORMULATION
          <BINDER> has value <CONC> in FORMULATION
          TABLET-WEIGHT has value <TABLET-WEIGHT> in FORMULATION
          TOTAL-CONCENTRATION has value <TOTAL-CONC> in SPECIFICATION
    THEN add <BINDER> to-bottom-of TABLET-REPORT-AGENDA
          <ADJUSTED-CONC> = <CONC> / <TOTAL-CONC>
          add <ADJUSTED-CONC> to-bottom-of TABLET-REPORT-AGENDA
          <WEIGHT> = <ADJUSTED-CONC> * <TABLET-WEIGHT>
          add <WEIGHT> to-bottom-of TABLET-REPORT-AGENDA

        Default-Binder-Level
        IF:   BINDER has value <BINDER> in FORMULATION
        THEN set the value of <BINDER> in the FORMULATION to be 0.04
```

Figure 5. Rule chain for binder level repair

The binder concentration in the FORMULATION will be correctly set from the TABLE-REPORT-AGENDA in **Update-Formulation**, if the ADJUSTED-CONC calculation in **Set-Binder-Conc** is altered. One way of changing this calculation is to alter the value of <CONC>, which was added to the formulation in the conclusion of **Default-Binder-Level**. The back-propagated repair changes the conclusion of **Default-Binder-Level** from 0.04 to 0.02. Again, this repair is the only refined KB to answer the training case, Case 1, correctly.

Fault 3: multiple specification faults Case 183 is typical.

Case 183 Input:	Drug-A, 360mg, 1 filler	
Output:	TFS-1A	TFS-1B
Target Tablet Weight	400mg	450mg
Drug Concentration	9/10	4/5
Filler Concentration	0.0	0.1
... various other discrepancies		

The fault dependency mechanism selected Target Tablet Weight as the independent fault. Moreover, there is only one rule that determines TARGET-TABLET-WEIGHT (in fact, it is responsible for all multiple faults):

1st-Guess-Weight

IF: DRUG has value <D> in FORMULATION

AND <D> has value <DOSE> in FORMULATION

AND <WEIGHT> = round5 $\left(\frac{\text{<DOSE>}}{0.1+0.00221\text{<DOSE>}}\right)$

THEN set value of TARGET-TABLET-WEIGHT in SPECIFICATION to be <WEIGHT>

This is a wrong-fire rule whose action must be corrected. Refinements are generated that make this rule fire correctly; i.e. by setting the correct value for TARGET-TABLET-WEIGHT. The value in <WEIGHT> can be changed by altering the formula, or finding a different value for <DOSE>, or retrieving a different <D> and hence <DOSE>. However, the drug and dose in the formulation are fixed by the input to TFS so cannot be altered. Therefore the only refinement generated is the instruction to repair the algebraic formula. The source of the error has been identified and the proposed curve fitting mechanism (Section 4.4.2.) will implement a repair.

5.1.1. Reaction of the "experts"

Our domain expert has been surprised and encouraged by the success of these refinements. He believes that identifying the missing database entry in Fault 1 and the faulty formula for Fault 3 is very helpful for an expert or knowledge engineer and would be very willing to supply the actual database value or propose a suitable formula for these potential faults.

Another "expert" is TFS-1B; in these experiments its knowledge and formulations take the place of the expert. We have access to the TFS-1B KB and can compare our refined KBs with it. For the Wrong Filler and Wrong Binder Level faults, the repairs that KRUST suggested coincide with the manual updates. For the training case with multiple faults, TFS-1B reveals an additional 1st-Guess-Weight rule for high values of dose; curve fitting would approximate the divergent (cubic) part of the formula.

An inspection of the differences between TFS-1A and TFS-1B revealed that clustering the 208 examples had highlighted all the TFS-1A faults. Therefore the runs above find all the errors. Although it may appear that the repairs are based on single training cases, this is not true; inductive operators require a set of positive and negative training cases.

5.2. Maintenance experience

Our more recent, and incomplete, work investigates the role of refinement for the more difficult maintenance task caused by the change of formulation policy. Now, TFS-1B is the KBS to be refined and TFS-2 is the oracle. We have data from TFS-2 for the original 208 training cases, and we use TFS-1B knowledge and its traces for these cases.

Clustering the TFS-1B cases has identified a class that reveals further debugging changes to the calculation of TARGET-TABLET-WEIGHT. The conditions under which the two TFS-1B formulae apply have changed again. The inductive method in Section 4.4.2. successfully moves the boundary separating the two rules.

Some of the remaining faults found in training cases are due to the paradigm shift. We have been given additional knowledge that supports the changes: excipients have been grouped into 3 classes and excipients in one class are preferred to those in subsequent classes. This is precisely the type of knowledge that KRUST can use with inductive operators to create versions of rules with new conditions relating to the excipient classes.

6. Related work

Many refinement tools are restricted to single shells or languages. Each has concentrated on a particular part of the debugging process. They often select refinements before implementing them as new KBs, so may not detect unintended side-effects. KRUST is unusual in that it generates many refined knowledge bases and tests them empirically.

TEIRESIAS [5] refines MYCIN and other EMYCIN KBSs by assisting the user to browse the potentially faulty knowledge. This approach appears in blame allocation for many more recent, more automated, refinement tools. EITHER [11], FORTE [14], and many other theory revision tools coming from the Machine Learning community, revise Prolog theories. They rely on induction from many examples to replace knowledge that has been removed by their only other refinement operators, rule and rule element deletion. MOBAL [9] acquires and refines knowledge for its own development tool. It contains many knowledge acquisition tools with access to a wide range of knowledge sources. SEEK [7] refines EXPERT KBSs, exploiting the fundamentally numeric format of the rules and conflict resolution strategy, to apply an incremental scoring for potential faults and suitable repairs.

CLIPS-R [10] refines the forward-chaining rules of CLIPS KBSs. Like KRUST it identifies faulty rule elements by working backwards from observed faulty behaviour. But it differs from KRUST in a number of ways. It requires traces containing more information than PFES traces and uses a variety of user-supplied constraints on the correct behaviour of the KBS. It has been applied only to diagnostic systems and it might have difficulty with the generate-and-test mode of design KBSs; e.g. it groups traces sharing an initial sequence of rule firings but these might be overwhelming for a design system.

ODYSSEUS [17] refines Minerva KBSs. A distinctive feature of ODYSSEUS is that the control is explicitly represented as knowledge, and meta-rules allow it to reason about the control strategy and guide the learning of new domain rules. Wilkins' concentration on control supports our belief that inference is an important consideration for refinement, despite it being largely ignored by many refinement tools. Wilkins has also found that specifying meta-level repairs for a **small** set of meta-rule faults is sufficient to solve many refinement problems.

We are lucky to have access to a real KBS application on which to evaluate our refinement tool, especially one containing an archive of versions covering both debugging and maintenance. Many refinement tools rely on corrupted versions of toy applications or simple systems induced from standard machine learning datasets. In particular, it is common for these to have an ample supply of test cases. But in practice, test cases are often scarce and so the field of KBS validation has seen various tools capable of generating test cases with a higher chance of finding faults; e.g. SYCOJET [1]. We believe that refinement tools must make the best use of existing test cases as training data, but if necessary suggest new, complementary test cases [12].

7. Conclusions

We have found that our refinement techniques are equally applicable to design and diagnostic KBSs, since there is nothing fundamentally different about the knowledge content and problem-solving, and so our knowledge skeleton and problem graph models apply. The exploratory nature of design KBSs demands inductive operators, so these are being added to KRUST whilst we continue to develop its ability to cope with real-world systems.

KRUST's speculative approach of generating many potential refinements necessitates effective mechanisms to reject unsuitable repairs. This problem is reduced for design KBSs where the solutions are more complex objects than the single conclusion normally associated with diagnostic applications. Design solutions therefore provide many more constraints on which to evaluate repairs. On the other hand, the complexity of a design demands an understanding of dependencies so that the refinement process can concentrate on underlying faults first.

Access to a real application has provided useful insights into real knowledge engineering issues. TFS is one of the few successful tablet formulation systems because knowledge acquisition is difficult for this complex task. Nevertheless, KRUST found it relatively easy to focus on the various faults. It duplicated the manual refinement from TFS-1A to TFS-1B, and is making progress on the refinement to achieve TFS-2. It is unfortunate that the examples of faulty behaviour that inspired the manual refinement are no longer available, but we use only a few of the abundant test cases generated by our oracles, the various TFS versions.

Acknowledgements

We thank Paul Bentley, Logica, for his assistance with the PFES software interface.

References

[1] M. Ayel and L. Vignollet. SYCOJET and SACCO, two tools for verifying expert systems. *International Journal of Expert Systems: Research and Applications*, 6(3):357–382, 1993.

[2] R. Boswell, S. Craw, and R. Rowe. Knowledge refinement for a design system. In *Proceedings of the European Knowledge Acquisition Workshop (EKAW97)*. Springer, 1997. To Appear.

[3] L. Carbonara and D. Sleeman. Improving the efficiency of knowledge base refinement. In L. Saitta, editor, *Machine Learning: Proceedings of the Thirteenth International Conference*, pages 78–86, Bari, Italy, 1996. Morgan Kaufmann.

[4] S. Craw and P. Hutton. Protein folding: Symbolic refinement competes with neural networks. In A. Prieditis and S. Russell, editors, *Machine Learning: Proceedings of the Twelfth International Conference*, pages 133–141, Tahoe City, CA, 1995. Morgan Kaufmann.

[5] R. Davis. Teiresias. In A. Barr and E. A. Feigenbaum, editors, *The Handbook of Artificial Intelligence Volume 2*, pages 87–101. Morgan Kauffman, Los Altos, CA, 1982.

[6] J. Frank, B. Rupprecht, and W. Schmelmer. Knowledge-based assistance for the development of drugs. *IEEE Expert*, 12(1):40–48, 1997.

[7] A. Ginsberg, S. M. Weiss, and P. G. Politakis. Seek2: A generalized approach to automatic knowledge base refinement. In *Proceedings of the Ninth IJCAI Conference*, pages 367–374, 1985.

[8] T. Menzies. Applications of abduction: Knowledge level modelling. *International Journal of Human-Computer Studies*, 45(3):305–335, 1996.

[9] K. Morik, S. Wrobel, J.-U. Kietz, and W. Emde. *Knowledge Acquisition and Machine Learning*. Academic Press, London, 1993.

[10] P. M. Murphy and M. J. Pazzani. Revision of production system rule-bases. In W. W. Cohen and H. Hirsh, editors, *Machine Learning: Proceedings of the Eleventh International Conference*, pages 199–207, New Brunswick, NJ, 1994. Morgan Kaufmann.

[11] D. Ourston and R. Mooney. Theory refinement combining analytical and empirical methods. *Artificial Intelligence*, 66:273–309, 1994.

[12] G. J. Palmer and S. Craw. The selection of training cases for automated knowledge refinement. In J. Vanthienen and F. van Harmelen, editors, *Proceedings of the 4th European Symposium on the Validation and Verification of Knowledge Based Systems (EUROVAV97)*, pages 205–215, Leuven, Belgium, June 1997.

[13] A. D. Preece, R. Shinghal, and A. Batarekh. Principles and practice in verifying rule-based systems. *Knowledge Engineering Review*, 7(2):115–141, 1992.

[14] B. L. Richards and R. J. Mooney. Refinement of first-order horn-clause domain theories. *Machine Learning*, 19(2):95–131, 1995.

[15] R. Rowe. An expert system for the formulation of pharmaceutical tablets. *Manufacturing Intelligence*, 14:13–15, 1993.

[16] J. Turner. Product formulation expert system. *Manufacturing Intelligence*, 8:12–14, 1991.

[17] D. C. Wilkins. Knowledge base refinement as improving an incorrect and incomplete domain theory. In Y. Kodratoff and R. S. Michalski, editors, *Machine Learning Volume III*, pages 493–513. Morgan Kaufmann, San Mateo, CA, 1990.

Software Development Tool for Object-Oriented Fuzzy Knowledge Systems

Yau-Hwang Kuo and Shiuh-Chu Lee
Institute of Information Engineering, National Cheng Kung University, Tainan, Taiwan, R.O.C

Abstract

Applying fuzzy reasoning concept in an expert system can improve its abilities on approximate reasoning. Embedding object-oriented paradigm into the organization of expert system can additional provide richer knowledge representation and reasoning power. In this paper, a novel Fuzzy Linguistic Object (FLO) model is developed, by which the traditional rule base is replaced by corpus of fuzzy linguistic objects, and the problem solving process is realized by interactions and inheritances among those objects. Based on the proposed model, a three-layered structure including knowledge acquisition layer, object design layer and program design layer is adopted to implement a development tool for fuzzy knowledge systems. In this three-layered structure, user can proceed his design work at any layer, and design information is automatically transformed among layers. Besides, an object simulator is developed to enhance the ability of rapid prototyping. Two case studies have been performed to confirm the functions of the proposed developing tool.

I. Introduction

An ideal software developing tool should base on a powerful design framework which has rich modeling capability on problem domains, and provide sufficient design facilities to aid the progress of design works. In the real world, many sophisticated AI problems are decentralized, vague, and cooperative. Conventional rule-based expert systems could not effectively solve such problems. So, we need a novel modeling framework which meets the following requirements: (a) suitable for decentralized knowledge manipulation; (b) suitable for modeling problem-solving activity realized by multiple independent actors; (c) efficient for representation and manipulation of multiple information types in a modeled system; (d) easy to include more than one reasoning scheme into a modeled system; (e) efficient in manipulation of vague information.

Object-oriented paradigm [1] would be a natural choice to meet the above requirements. Kaindl [2,3] had pointed out that there is a close relationship between object-oriented approach and AI approach. However, there are some problems that should be solved to model sophisticated AI problems by object-oriented modeling approach, including how to embed the approximate reasoning capability into an object-oriented model? how to realize the inheritance process in a vague situation? etc. To make object-oriented paradigm suitable for modeling vague and uncertain cases, fuzzy set theory will be a good choice [4]. Therefore, a modeling framework that integrates object-oriented paradigm and fuzzy logic to model decentralized AI systems or knowledge systems was developed by authors and called FLO model [5]. In this modeling framework, each object represents a fuzzy linguistic variable or a cluster of fuzzy linguistic variables, and fuzzy implications are interpreted as inter-object relationships and executed as passings of vague messages during problem solving. Besides, the FLO modeling framework adopts partial inheritance scheme, where the child object may inherit the properties of parent object partially. Multimedia user interface is also important for new-generation expert systems. Therefore, the FLO model also defines the structure of multimedia FLO to support the design and implementation of multimedia fuzzy knowledge systems. Based on the FLO model, a software development tool with rich design supporting functions is developed and presented in this paper. In this environment, we emphasize on the goals:

(1) full support in the design process of knowledge

1082-3409/97 $10.00 © 1997 IEEE

systems including knowledge acquisition phase, object design phase and program design phase,

(2) sufficient support for rapid prototyping,

(3) having the advantages of maximum flexibility, expandability and user convenience.

To achieve these goals, the development tool is implemented with a three-layered structure, which provides good flexibility and expandability. The first layer, called *knowledge acquisition layer*, functions as the editing environment on acquiring domain knowledge. In this layer, fuzzy rules and structural domain knowledge formulate user knowledge. Multimedia user interface editing is also supported here. The second layer, called *object design layer*, provides object-oriented design and verification facilities on the FLO-based models directly. Object-oriented design notations including class diagram, object interaction diagram, and state transition diagram are applied for both static and dynamic behavior modeling of design systems. An object simulator is embedded in this layer to verify the design correctness even for incomplete or partial designs. An object-view-graph (OVG) model is developed in the object simulator to keep track of runtime status and relationships between objects of the evaluated design system. Functional simulation facilities are also built to make inspection and validation of functional behavior of the evaluated FLO model. Consequently, the goal of rapid prototyping can be easily achieved in the proposed development tool. The third layer, called *program design layer*, functions like a structural C++ program design environment. In general, a user may develop his knowledge system by first expressing the necessary domain entities and rules in the knowledge acquisition layer, and utilizing the multimedia user interface editing facilities for user interface layout. Next, in the object design layer and the program design layer, the user can make additional improvement to object model or program code, or apply the object simulator to validate correctness and evaluate efficiency of the designed system. The translations of design information between the three layers are all performed automatically by the system, and the design work can be proceeded in any layer. Finally, compiling the source codes and linking them with appendant object libraries will generate the desired ready-to-run knowledge system.

II. Fuzzy Linguistic Object Model

We will first illustrate briefly the basic constituent of our framework, the FLO model. It implies not only the object orientation of linguistic variable but also the object orientation of fuzzy inference process.

II.1. Organization of fuzzy linguistic object

In traditional fuzzy information processing, linguistic variables [6] are adopted as basic constituents. However, a linguistic variable can be viewed as an attribute of an object. For example, the linguistic variable *'flyingAbility'* is an attribute of the object *'Eagle.'* Of course, an object may have more than one fuzzy attribute. Such a kind of object is called *Fuzzy Linguistic Object (FLO)*.

The structure of a fuzzy linguistic object is shown in Fig. 1. It includes (1) message exchange interface: Query Processor, Reference Set, and Binding Set, (2) reasoning mechanism: Matcher Set and Conflict Resolver, (3) object information unit: Attributes and Component Set, and (4) Multimedia Interface unit.

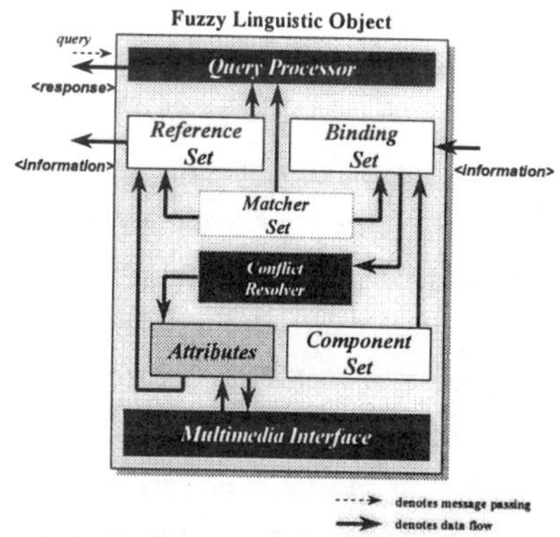

Fig. 1. Structure of fuzzy linguistic object.

(A) Query Processor. It deals with the queries for establishing inference channels from the other linguistic fuzzy objects. If a query is permitted, it constructs a Reference unit with a proper Matcher and responses to the querying fuzzy linguistic object. Then, the two fuzzy linguistic objects establish an inference channel.

(B) Matcher Set. The Matcher Set contains Matchers. A Matcher is an object that deals with the transit of information, where it receives information from one side and transfers it out to another side. A Fuzzy Matcher is a special kind of Matchers that have particular function to deal with fuzzy inference. It encapsulates a fuzzy concept (by the form of membership function) and two action units

for fuzzy inference (a Matching Degree Calculator and an Implication Calculator), as shown in Fig. 2. A Fuzzy Matcher represents a linguistic term and is responsible for all inferencing activities related to this term.

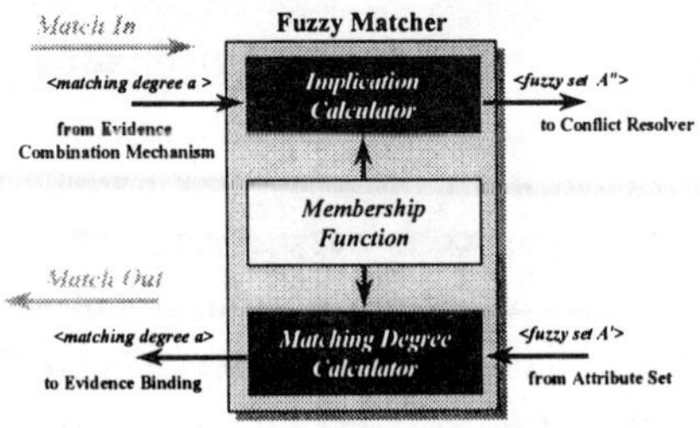

Fig. 2. Structure of Fuzzy Matcher.

The Matching Degree Calculator is activated when the linguistic term A that the Fuzzy Matcher represents appears in the premise statement of the rule being fired. It accepts a fuzzy input A', gets the membership function of A, calculates the matching degree between A and A' by a chosen composition operation, and finally sends the matching degree out. This process is called "match out." The Implication Calculator is activated when the represented term A is denoted in the conclusion statement of the rule being fired. It accepts a matching degree σ from another linguistic object, and then calculates a partial fuzzy conclusion A" for A based on a certain fuzzy reasoning method. This process is called "match in."

By the polymorphism property of object-oriented paradigm, different types of Calculators realize different fuzzy reasoning schemes but have the same invocation interface. Therefore, a FLO model will be able to include more than one fuzzy inference scheme or fuzzy operation types so that has more flexibility to schedule the inference behavior.

(C) Reference Set. This set contains References. A Reference is constructed when an asking for establishing an inference channel is allowed. In the conceptual level, a Reference is a symbol to represent a (fuzzy) concept associated with one attribute of an object. Its meaning is dependent on what type of Matcher is used.

(D) Binding Set. This set contains Bindings. In the conceptual level, a Binding is also a symbol that represents a (fuzzy) concept associated with one attribute of an object, but it differs from a Reference. The Reference is constructed to supply necessary information for inferencing, while the Binding is constructed to make inference. In FLO model, an inference channel is constructed by a (Reference, Binding) pair, and the direction of information flow is from Reference to Binding.

For executing fuzzy reasoning, there are two kinds of Bindings in the Binding Set: Evidence Bindings and Inheritance Bindings, as shown in Fig. 3. Inheritance Bindings deal with the operation of partial inheritance [7] It gets value of an attribute from the parent object, then calculates result based on an inhibiting parameter and an enforcing parameter.

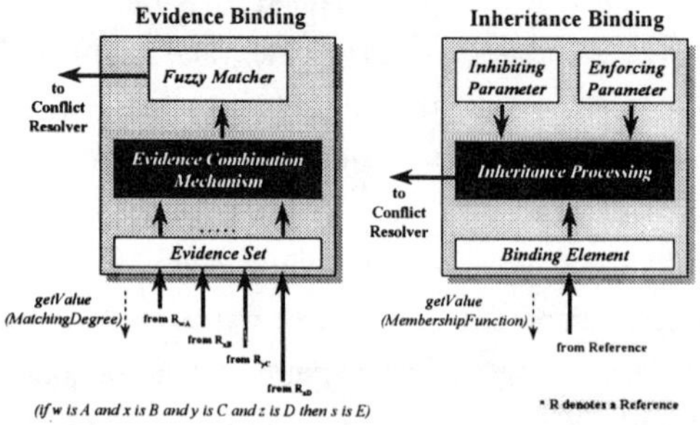

Fig. 3. Structures of Evidence Binding and Inheritance Binding.

An Evidence Binding handles a fuzzy implication relation (fuzzy rule); it gets the matching degrees of premises and calculates a partial conclusion, then sends the partial conclusion to Conflict Resolver. Conflict Resolver gathers all partial conclusions related to the same fuzzy attribute to generate a global conclusion. In an Evidence Binding, the Evidence Set contains a set of basic binding elements to gather the matching degrees of all specified premises.

(E) Attributes. An attribute represents a property of a fuzzy linguistic object. The value in each Attribute unit is updated when a new conclusion related to it arrives from Conflict Resolver, and can be retrieved by References.

(F) Component Set. It is possible that a fuzzy linguistic object is composed of some other fuzzy linguistic objects, which constitutes an aggregation hierarchy. Component Set is the collection of symbols that stand for the component linguistic objects.

(G) Multimedia interface unit. To facilitate interaction with various information sources, such as multimedia user-interface, database, or hardware device sensor, etc., a FLO may acquire attribute values from the multimedia interface unit, or send values to it. Different kinds of FLO may implement different kinds of multimedia interface

mechanism but expose the same software interface, by applying the polymorphism capability of object-oriented paradigm. In our development tool, which will be presented in Section III, we support several kinds of multimedia FLO by providing the MUI class library.

II.2. Inference process of FLO model

Basically the interactions among linguistic objects for problem solving can be distinguished into three different inference types. They are implication, aggregation, and inheritance. Every interaction of any inference type is realized by an inference channel maintained by a (Reference, Binding) pair, as shown in Fig. 4. For the former two inference types, Evidence Bindings are used, while the last inference type adopts Inheritance Bindings.

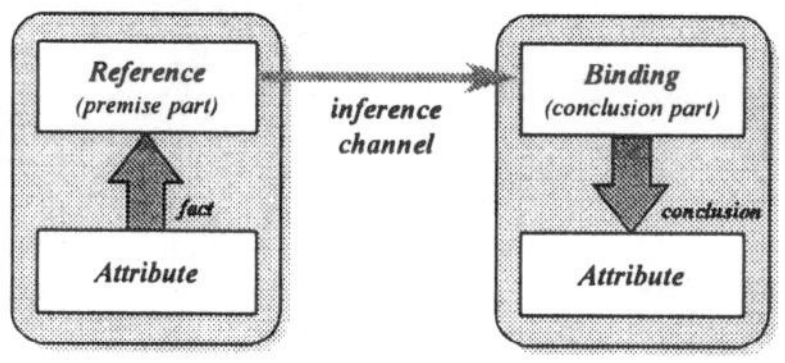

Fig. 4. Inference channel between FLOs.

The (Reference, Binding) inference channels are dynamically established during problem solving. In the initial state, there is no connection among fuzzy linguistic objects. When an interaction for inferencing between two fuzzy linguistic objects is required but the connection has not yet been established, a Binding of the conclusion object will be constructed and then sends a message to Query Processor of the premise object for establishing an inference channel. If the premise object allows this asking, it will construct a Reference with a compatible Fuzzy Matcher and return the address of the Reference to the Binding of conclusion object, then an inference channel between these two fuzzy linguistic objects is constructed. Of course, it is possible that there exist many inference channels between two fuzzy linguistic objects to deal with multiple reasoning relations between them. Once an inference channel is established, it is maintained until the system solves the given problem. The behavior of inference channel follows traditional fuzzy inference concept.

In a FLO model, the direction of inference can be forward chaining, backward chaining, or mix of both. The direction of inference depends on the behavior of (Binding, Reference) pairs. In the process of information transfer between a (Reference, Binding) pair, if Reference sends information to Binding automatically then the inference is forward chaining. On the other hand, if Reference sends information as the response of a request from Binding, then the inference is backward chaining. Of course, backward chaining and forward chaining can be mixed because the encapsulation and polymorphism properties of linguistic objects. The chaining scheme is decided when a model is constructed.

III. Software Development Tool of FLO-based Knowledge Systems

To support the design and implementation of knowledge systems based on FLO model, a three-layered software development tool is developed, and its functional block diagram is shown in Fig. 5. The kernel part of this tool is in the second layer, the object design layer. This layer supports the facilities of object diagram, class diagram and state diagram editing. A simulator for rapid prototyping is also attached. Rambaugh's OID notation, with some extension, is adopted for representing the object model, and the concept of reuse in the large is applied in the management of object model. Because the inference channel can be viewed as a *complex relation* between two FLOs and all inference channels have similar structure, its details can be hidden (and reuse) in the upper-level FLO model. In other words, the object model editor provides a hierarchical organization scheme of FLO model. The state transition diagram editing is used for description of dynamic behavior in a FLO object, which will be referenced in code generation and simulation. Basically, OOExpert is a universal object design environment that can also be employed in the application fields other than knowledge systems. Therefore, a software designer can perform his design with object-oriented paradigm at OOExpert, verify the design by object simulator, and finally generate C++ code for compilation. The code generation is automatically executed in this tool, and of course the designer can further refine the codes at the third layer, the program design layer, as he wants. The functionality of program design layer is similar to existing object-oriented programming tool. To support automatic generation of C++ codes, two class libraries, FLO library and MUI (Multimedia User Interface) library, are developed. Besides code generation, these two libraries are also invoked by FLO and MUI agents when executing object simulation. In other words, the object simulator also employs the characteristic of reusability during simulation.

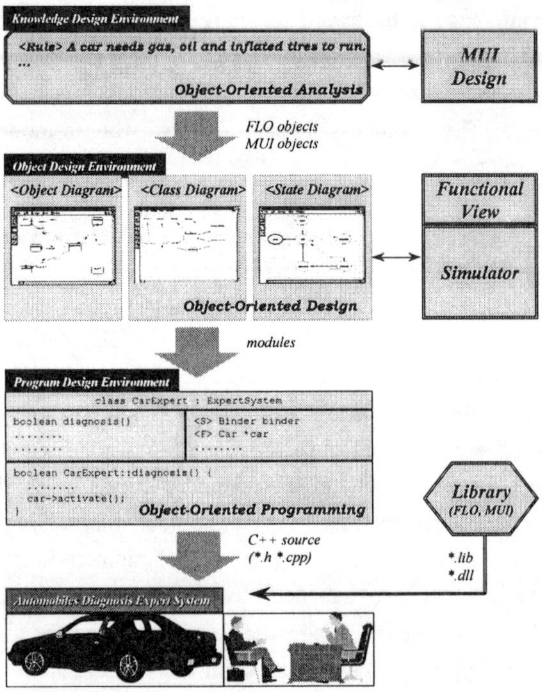

Fig. 5. Software development tool of FLO based knowledge systems.

Besides object diagram based representation, a FLO model can be expressed with a textual rule-like style, which gives users, particularly the users unfamiliar with object-oriented design technique, the convenience that develops the desired knowledge system with traditional manner. To support rule-like design, the first layer, knowledge design layer, is developed and called *Knowledge Expert* which consists of Concept Editor, Schema Editor, Information Editor, and MUI Design Agent. Concept Editor is used to edit the domain-specific concepts and their organization including generalization hierarchy, aggregation hierarchy, and attributes. Schema Editor is adopted for organizing the knowledge structure, for example, the causal relationships. At present, in Knowledge Expert, rules are the major representation scheme. In the future, other schemes such as script can also be adopted. Information Editor binds attributes with appropriate data type. For a fuzzy attribute, the editing facility of membership function is also provided. Fig. 6 illustrates the editing facilities of Knowledge Expert. When a multimedia FLO is expected, the MUI Design Agent is invoked to cooperate with Knowledge Expert for the design of multimedia FLO, as shown in Fig. 7.

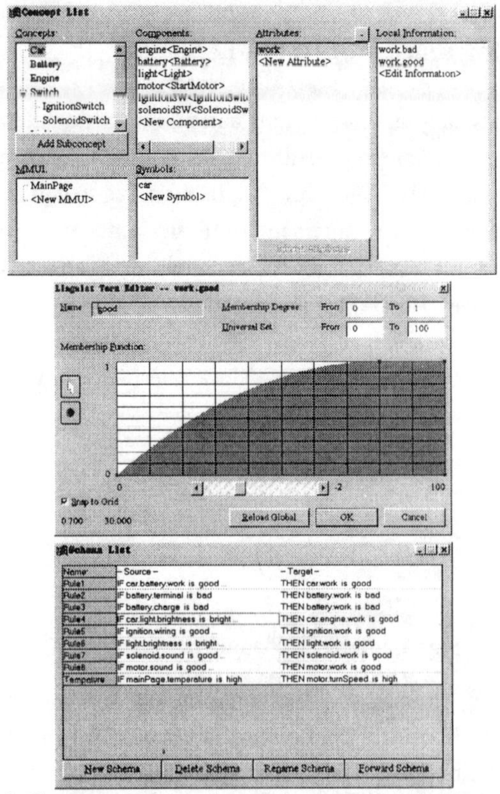

Fig. 6. Concept, Information, Schema Editor in Knowledge Expert.

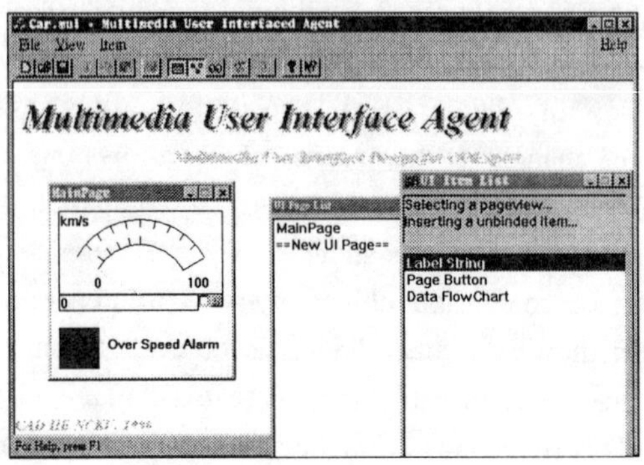

Fig. 7. Multimedia user-interface design agent.

In summary, the operational organization of the whole multimedia object-oriented knowledge system development tool is illustrated in Fig. 8.

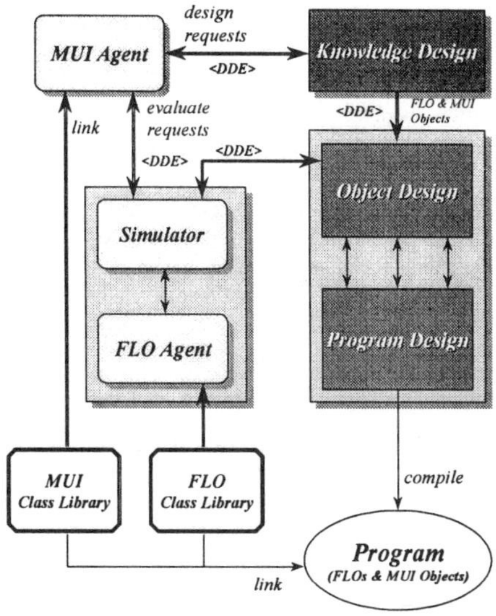

Fig. 8. Operational organization of the development tool.

IV. Object Simulator

IV.1. Functions

To verify the correctness of designs, the development tool also includes an object simulator which can work on object models of the verified designs. By this simulator, users can evaluate a design from the view of its dynamic behavior or high-level functionality. The dynamic behavior to be monitored includes:

(1) creation and deletion of objects;

(2) state transitions of objects in every message passing;

(3) values of attributes in every object during simulation;

(4) sequences of message passings and internal operations of every object during simulation.

The functionality to be evaluated includes rule firing sequence and side effect due to rule firing (for instance, modification of object attributes). Besides, the design errors which could be found in this simulator include incomplete object hierarchy declaration, incomplete object design, incomplete rule design, infinite loop, deadlock, redundancy, circular inheritance, etc. All of the evaluations are dependent on the information in OID description, class diagram, and message execution sequence.

IV.2. Internal organization

The structure of object simulator is shown in Fig. 9, which consists of four major modules: control management unit, data management unit, object behavior retriever, and functional management unit.

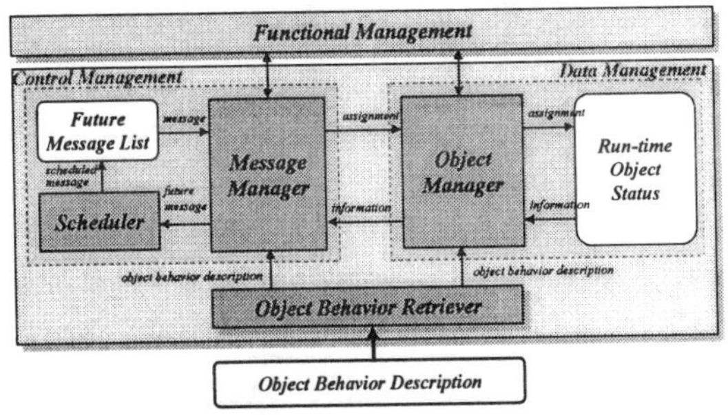

Fig. 9. Internal organization of object simulator.

IV.2.1. Control management unit. This unit handles the control flow of an object when this object receives a message. Control flow includes: (a) what messages and operations will be activated in every state transition of an object, (b) what operations and messages will be driven by a message, and (c) what is the order of the generation of these messages and operations. This unit includes a message manager, a scheduler and a future message list.

Message manager is the main mechanism to process messages. If a message would change the state and information of an object, the message manager will notify the data manager to modify the state and information of that object. If a message generates some operations and messages, the message manager will process and schedule those generated operations and messages. The message manager includes four mechanisms as follows:

(i) Message fetcher: its main functions are (a) getting a message from the future message set, and sending this message to the message processor and (b) determining the source and target objects of the captured message.

(ii) Message processor: this unit processes designated operations in a message including (a) external operation which may generate some special actions to drive some mechanisms, for instance, the MUI, (b) return operation which realizes some actions when the message has been processed, and (c) assignment operation which assign new attribute values generated by the message.

(iii) Succeeding message generating unit: it is the main

mechanism to collect events and messages that will be processed later in the simulator. The succeeding message generating unit includes (a) event processor which is the main mechanism to process events, and (b) succeeding message generator used to collect the messages to be processed later in this simulator.

(iv) Message trace recorder: it is a recorder to record these messages that have been executed in order. User can get the message trace of the simulated object-oriented software by this recorder.

Different orders of message execution would produce different results. When a message is executed by the simulator, it may generate some succeeding messages. Scheduler is a mechanism to schedule these messages.

Future message list collects messages acquired from the scheduler. These messages are stored in a single linked list according to message execution order.

IV.2.2. Data management unit. This unit manages data flow of the simulated object model, including (a) what objects exist at current time step, (b) what is the present state of every object, (c) what information exists in every object at current time step, and (d) what information will be changed in the state transition of every object. This unit consists of an object manager and a run-time object status store.

Object manager is the main mechanism to manage the information and related visibilities of every object in the simulated system. When an object receives a message, it may modify the information and the visibilities of the object.

(1) modification of the state and information of an object: when the message manager processes a message, it may notify the object manager to modify the state and information of objects recorded in the object information recorder of the run-time object status store.

(2) modification of the visibilities of an object: the object manager may modify the parameter visibility and the local visibility of objects recorded in object information recorder of the run-time object status store.

Run-time object status store is a recorder to keep the visibilities, state and information of every object in the simulated object-oriented model. By inspecting the change of state, information and visibilities of objects in the recorder, user can learn the effect to an object when it receives a message.

There are two primary recorders in the run-time object status store including: (1) object view recorder which keeps the visibilities of every object at present and (2) object information recorder which keeps state and attribute values of every object at present.

IV.2.3. Object behavior retriever. It retrieves associated information from the object behavior description to support simulation. The information for simulation includes (a) the object relations, (b) the messages sent on every relation, (c) the succeeding messages of every message, (d) the state transition of every object, (e) the activities of every state in an object, and (f) the visibility of every object.

IV.2.4. Functional management unit. This unit handles the activities of simulation from the aspect of functionality of the simulated system, for example, from the viewpoint of rule firing sequence and side effect. The information handled by this unit includes (a) initialization data for simulation, (b) simulation entry point and breakpoint settings, (c) simulation results (rule firing sequence, updated attributes or objects, etc.), and (d) error messages (infinite rule looping, deadlock, incomplete rule, etc.).

VI. Conclusions and Discussions

With the FLO model, an AI program or knowledge system is organized as a model which consists of a set of interactive fuzzy linguistic objects. Moreover, the problem solving activity is accomplished by the interactions of fuzzy linguistic objects. Therefore, a centralized inference engine and knowledge base are not necessary, i.e., the storage and manipulation of knowledge can thus be decentralized. Such a decentralized knowledge manipulation framework will have advantages of maximizing concurrency in problem solving, maximizing the flexibility on mixing knowledge representation schemes and reasoning strategies, and structurizing the problem solving model. Furthermore, the reusability to increase software productivity can be easily achieved.

The properties of object-oriented paradigm are helpful to model applications requiring decentralized knowledge manipulation. Besides, the concept of uncertain knowledge manipulation should be introduced into object-oriented paradigm to solve real-world problems more effectively and efficiently. This paper embeds the concept of fuzzy logic into object-oriented modeling technology for this purpose. To develop a fuzzy object-oriented modeling framework, some issues must be considered.

First, we must decide the basic constituents in the proposed modeling framework. Obviously, in the object-oriented paradigm, objects are the basic constituents. Therefore, in this paper, we define an object structure, called fuzzy linguistic object, to represent a linguistic variable or a collection of fuzzy linguistic variables.

Second, we must decide the knowledge representation scheme supported by the modeling framework. Based on FLO paradigm, uncertain and decentralized knowledge representation is provided, that is, knowledge is distributed into object associations and internal structure of linguistic objects. Obviously, every linguistic object can organize its internal knowledge in an optimal scheme, which has less constraint than conventional knowledge representation schemes.

Third, we must explore the problem solving behavior of the proposed framework. Single inference strategy or single set of inference operations may be unsatisfactory for solving complex AI problems. Fortunately, different linguistic objects can encapsulate different operators and realize different inference strategies in the same model. The interactions among linguistic objects can also be backward chaining, forward chaining, or mixed mode. Therefore, the proposed framework provides excellent flexibility to develop the inference strategy in reasoning.

Fourth, we must consider how to manipulate uncertain knowledge. In the proposed framework, the linguistic object can contain fuzzy attributes and execute fuzzy implications by message passing. Furthermore, the important property of inheritance in object-oriented paradigm is also extended to a partial inheritance scheme in this paper. Therefore, the manipulation of uncertain knowledge is not difficult.

Finally, we must consider the convenience of implementation for the models designed by using the proposed framework. Software reuse has been seriously considered during the development of this object-oriented framework, so the software productivity could be guaranteed. Based on the proposed framework, a software development tool, which includes knowledge editor, object editor, object simulator, C++ program editor, and multi-media interface editor, is being developed in our laboratory. Users can develop the target applications from high-level knowledge level, object model level, or programming language level. The translations among these levels are automatic.

References:

[1] J. Rumbaugh, M. Blaha, W. Premerlani, F. Eddy and W. Lorensen, Object-Oriented Modeling and Design, Prentice Hall, pp. 1-10, 1991.

[2] Hermann Kaindl, "Object-oriented approaches in software engineering and artificial intelligence," Journal of Object-Oriented Programming, pp. 38-45, January 1994.

[3] Bogdan Czejdo, Christoph F. Eick and Malcolm Taylor, "Integrating Sets, Rules, and Data in an Object-Oriented Environment," IEEE Expert, pp. 59-66, February 1993.

[4] L.A. Zadeh, "Outline of a new approach to the analysis of complex systems and decision processes," IEEE Trans. Syst., Man, Cybern., vol. SMC-3, no. 1, pp. 28-44, 1973.

[5] Shiuh-Chu Lee, Jye-Yuan Lee and Yau-Hwang Kuo, "A framework for object-oriented fuzzy expert systems," Proc. of International Joint Conference of NAFIPS/IFIS/NASA, Dec. 1994, pp. 214-222.

[6] H. -J. Zimmermann, Fuzzy Set Theory and Its Applications, Second Ed., Chap. 9, Kluwer Academic Publishers, Boston, 1991.

[7] Ian Graham, "Fuzzy objects: Inheritance under uncertainty" in Appendix I of OBJECT ORIENTED METHODS, Addison Wesley, pp. 333-365, 1991.

Gathering Requirements from Remote Users

T. Leonard, V. Berzins, LUQI, and M. J. Holden

Luqi@cs.nps.navy.mil

Abstract

We describe a distributed requirements engineering environment using computer aided software engineering tools linked together through the Internet. We created this distributed requirements engineering environment using Microsoft's Personal Web Server (PWS), Microsoft's Open Database Connectivity (ODBC) technology, Netscape Communicator, Microsoft's Internet Explorer, Microsoft's Access97 database, and a set of PERL scripts that are executed by users of the environment to perform database operations. We show how we added basic security features to the Internet accessible database.

1. Introduction

This paper shows how Front Loaded Accurate Requirements Engineering (FLARE) Teams are a means to realize accurate requirements early in project development and a means to ensure that requirements are satisfied in the implementation domain by automated systems [1]. These Teams can use Internet technologies to enhance the effectiveness of the set of CASE tools [2] that they use to manage requirements. Ideally, the set of requirements should be managed throughout the evolution of the system to provide the rationale for the system's behavior [3].

We show how to extend formal and informal specifications with audio and video file representations of requirements [4,5]. This is valuable because video allows developers to quickly gain a conceptual understanding of the problem domain, breaks the mind-numbing monotony often experienced when reading formal textual specifications and graphical diagrams and effectively provides an abstract representation of objects found within specifications.

Additionally, we demonstrate how Internet technologies can help managers improve their task assignment methods by incorporating team members' assessments of the difficulty of implementing software components into the decision process. The products produced by the FLARE Teams are used to make this possible.

2. CASE environment enhancement using internet technologies

The number of computer aided software engineering tools and environments available to assist FLARE Teams is extensive. Queen's University in Kingston, Ontario publishes a partial CASE tool list that has nearly 400 tools listed [6]. Using a small subset of available CASE tools commonly used at the Naval Postgraduate School, we show how to enhance a CASE environment with Internet technologies.

Researchers at the Naval Postgraduate School have developed a CASE tool called Computer-aided Prototyping System (CAPS) [7]. This tool provides a capability to develop prototypes using the prototype system description language (PSDL) [8]. Once completed, CAPS promises to provide a robust environment that will facilitate the management of requirements throughout the life of a system.

By design, the prototypes produced using CAPS are demonstrated to users. Users evaluate the prototypes, and developers use the information obtained from the user's evaluation to refine the requirements of the software system [9]. CAPS would produce the best results if a developer personally presented a prototype to a user, but this would be expensive in terms of travel and set up time, especially if multiple meetings between a developer and user were needed. By using audio and video conferencing techniques over the Internet, similar to those described by Macedonia and Brutzman [10], we can remove this limitation. Additionally, the developer's ability to interact with the user at any time, provided the user has access to an Internet enabled computer with video conferencing capabilities, would enhance the engineering environment created by CAPS and tools similar to it. This enhancement would be achieved by allowing the developer to resolve ambiguous requirements with users while they are still actively involved in the process of developing a prototype or model. It also would reduce the cost of travel by eliminating the requirement of having the developers and users co-located during the presentation of a new or changed prototype. Applications exist on the market that make this possible with a modest, under $1,000.00, investment in additional equipment and software [11,12].

The use of Internet video conferencing to augment a software-engineering environment is available today as are other Internet technologies providing comparable enhancements. One of these additional Internet technologies is "intelligent browsing" [13]. It is now possible for a Software Engineer to use intelligent agents to retrieve information from the Internet [14]. These tools can aid Software Engineers in their efforts to understand the problem domain and to find appropriate solutions to requirements in the implementation domain. Enhanced with intelligent agents and Internet video conferencing, this Software Engineering environment should improve significantly the production of quality software in a timely manner.

3. Augmentation of formal and informal specifications with video

Where appropriate, FLARE Teams will augment requirement specifications with video representations of the requirements. This can be helpful because certain requirements can be better understood by developers if they can observe users during the performance of the activities that generate the requirements [4]. For example, most software developers are not experts in infantry fighting procedures and have no concept of the actual tactics, techniques and procedures used by infantry forces to accomplish their assigned mission. This lack of understanding of the problem domain is further complicated by preconceived ideas formulated by software developers as they are exposed to the entertainment industry's dramatization of infantry soldiers and their fighting techniques. Problem domain objects and concepts such as foxholes, fields of fire, accuracy, timeliness and cover have very specific meanings to infantry soldiers. Typical Software Engineers do not necessarily share these meanings. Software Engineers can represent each of them with formal or informal methods. However, would a Software Engineer located in Silicon Valley, when given a formal or informal representation of the requirements elicited from this problem domain, be able to design a system that would satisfy the needs of the user without direct knowledge of the user's context? The requirements produced from this type of problem domain, a domain that is foreign to most Software Engineers, is an ideal situation to use video to augment requirements. In this section, we show how the addition of a type "video", similar to that of a textual comment, to formal and informal specification and design languages will increase developers understanding of the problem domain.

3.1. The new memory paradigm

In the use of video to augment the representation of requirements, we would like to have easy and quick access to it. The cost of existing magnetic storage has recently dropped to affordable levels, making storage of video on fast hard disk drives feasible. Figure 1 depicts the dramatic reduction in memory prices that have taken place during the ten-year period between 1987 and 1997. It is now economically feasible to augment requirement specifications with video that is retrievable by anyone in the software development group on demand. This capability is the crux of bringing the application domain to the design and implementation domains. Another storage technology, digital versatile disk (DVD), introduced to the masses in 1997, provides additional space to store audio and video files [15].

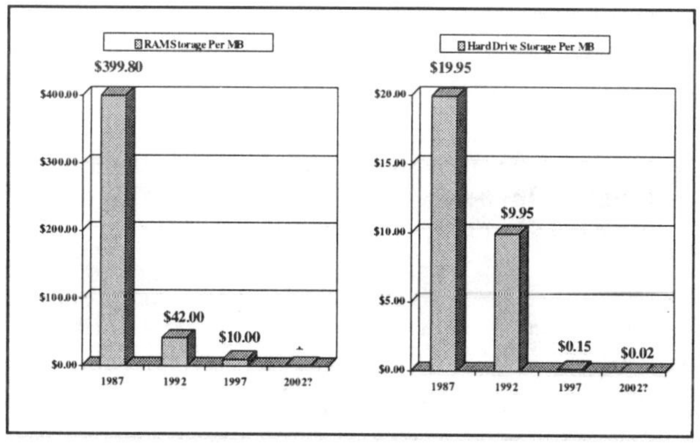

figure 1. Dropping memory prices. In 1987, the cost of secondary magnetic storage, hard drives, was about $20.00 a megabyte (mb) [16: p. 89], and primary memory, random access memory (ram), was about $400.00 a mb [17: p. 309]. In January of 1992 this dropped to about $10.00 a mb for hard drive storage and $42.00 a mb for ram [18: p. 356]. In January of 1997, both types of memory were at an all-time low. hard drive storage sold for about $.15 a mb [19: p. 152], and ram for about $10.00 a mb [20: p. 153]. The prices shown for the year 2002 are based on a 30% yearly reduction in memory prices [21]

The same technology that allows analyzing "a golf swing from up to nine different camera angles" [22] can be used to provide on-demand video to increase software and systems developers' understanding of the problem domain. Adding a type "Video" to specification and design languages provides an easy way to incorporate the use of video into the software engineering process.

3.2. Using video with formal methods

We use the Spec Language [1] to illustrate how FLARE Teams would incorporate video into the development process. This technique requires the representation of the Spec model in HTML format [23] and the use of an Internet browser to access the model. When appropriate, we use comments in Spec models stating that a video clip is available and we hyperlink these comments to video clips. This is attractive because it allows the designer to quickly augment a model with video using comments. Figure 2 shows how to implement this method. When an engineer reads the specification using an Internet browser, the engineer can click on the comment to view a video clip of the object being defined.

```
DEFINITION bunker -- Concept for describing shelters. - - Click
here to view video clip
  INHERIT fortification - - The module "fortification" defines types
security and cover.
.
.
END
```

Figure 2. The bold text on the first line is linked to a video file describing a bunker.

4. Programmer input into the work tasking process

Once designers have identified modules that require implementation, management must produce a programmer work schedule [24]. The products produced by FLARE Teams enable programmers to gain a better understanding of problem domain concepts and objects. This increased understanding makes programmers' input into the module assignment process used by managers more valuable.

Each programmer knows their programming abilities and can estimate the time to complete a programming task. We show how managers can assign tasks to programmers based on these estimates. We use Internet technologies to produce an interactive module evaluation environment where each uncommitted programmer rates unassigned modules by perceived level of difficulty. This process allows managers to produce an optimal programmer work schedule, minimizing the cost of implementing all unassigned modules, measured in terms of time, where a shorter implementation time is better.

We have developed an Internet form that executes a PERL script located on a server to access a Microsoft Access database using Microsoft's ODBC technology to capture programmers' assessments of tasks (Figure 3). [25,26,27,28,29,30]

The method used to gather input requires that each programmer estimate the number of days it would take to implement the module listed on the form. Each programmer is required to repeat the process until they meet one of the following three criteria. They have identified a module that they can implement in minimal time, and the system schedules the programmer to implement it; the programmer has evaluated all modules that have not been scheduled; or management stops the process because they have determined a suitable working schedule.

Once the Send button is pressed, the input provided is automatically transferred to a central location where it is processed. The scheduling process can be automated using techniques similar to those of the Evolution Control System (ECS) [31], incorporating programmer input into the system. The modified ECS can enforce various policies ranging from scheduling a task immediately if a programmer estimates they can complete it in .5 days, to waiting until each programmer has evaluated all modules in an attempt to develop an optimal schedule.

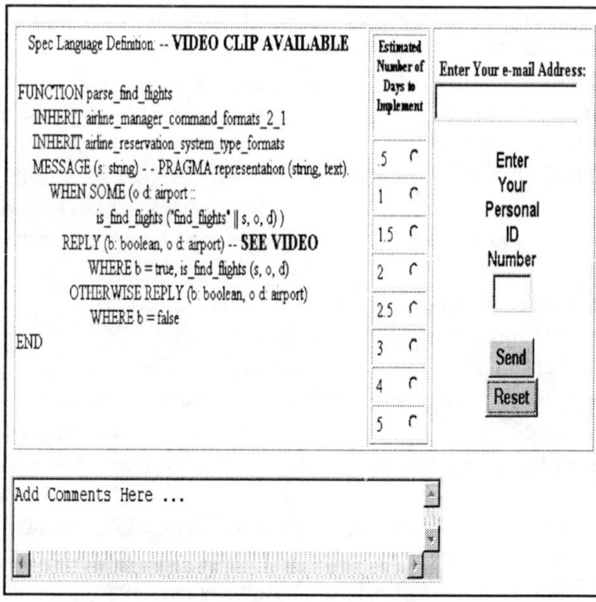

Figure 3. Form used to capture programmers' assessment of the time needed to implement a module. V. Berzins developed the spec language definition [1: p. 424].

This system can be used to assess schedule risk. Modules with a wide variance in programmer estimates are more likely to cause problems than the modules where most of the programmers agree on the time it would take to implement. This system gives managers the ability to base decisions on this information. For example, programmers who continuously have a large variance between estimates and actual implementation time may require additional training on understanding specifications.

Incorporating programmers' assessments into the process also allows management to assign tasks to programmers in a way that takes advantage of each programmer's personal expertise and preferences. Each programmer has one or more classes of problems they can easily solve due to their accumulated experiences and habits. Incorporating their input into the module scheduling process would most likely increase their productivity because they would be assigned modules based on their completion time estimates. Additionally, this system can be utilized to focus recruiting efforts. Consider a situation in which the entire set of programmers rated tasks C, D, and E as taking the maximum allowable time to implement. Management might focus more of their recruiting efforts on finding individuals that rate these tasks as taking less time to implement, thereby increasing the efficiency of the entire organization and minimizing costs.

5. FLARE: a requirements engineering environment

We stated that traditional software engineering environments could be easily enhanced using Internet technologies. We offer evidence for this by introducing a CASE tool called FLARE that uses the technologies presented in Section II to create a distributed requirements engineering environment. FLARE is designed to enhance the software development process by offering a means to inexpensively manage requirements and facilitate communication of requirement related issues between all interested parties in the software development process. The FLARE Team discussed in Section I would use this tool.

5.1. FLARE's components

FLARE is composed of the following programs that use the Internet to exchange information. This coupling produces a synergistic effect by combining the distinct features of each program to produce a requirements engineering environment.

5.1.1. Microsoft's Access 97. An inexpensive database designed to function on Windows 95 or Windows NT, this database makes it relatively easy to manipulate the requirements engineering information entered into the FLARE environment. It also produces reports in HTML format, enabling users of FLARE to easily publish information that has been manipulated by database methods to the Internet. [32]

5.1.2. An access database file. This database file contains the tables, queries, forms, reports, and macros that constitute the management aspects of FLARE. [33]

5.1.3. A set of PERL scripts running on a PWS. Users of the environment access the environment's database by executing PERL scripts located on an Internet server. The PERL scripts are called using FLARE's user interface (Figure 4) that is accessed from an Internet browser.

5.1.4. A set of JavaScript enhanced HTML Files. When accessed with an Internet browser, this set of files creates the user interface for the FLARE environment. The essential elements of these files are embedded JavaScript [34] and Forms [35]. JavaScript enables the pull-down menus found in the user interface to function. The ability to input and transmit information is made possible by using Forms embedded in FLARE's HTML files.

5.1.5. A JavaScript enabled Internet browser. The browser is the shell that the user interface of FLARE runs in. It must be JavaScript enabled to allow the pull-down menus to operate. We used Microsoft's Internet Explorer [32] and Netscape's Communicator [36] to test the user interface.

5.1.6. Microsoft's PWS. We chose this web server to use in the environment because Microsoft freely distributes it.Microsoft's PWS.

5.2. FLARE's user interface

Figure 4 shows the initial user interface of FLARE. Each of the four pull-down menus represents a phase in the software life cycle. Each menu shares the "Mission Needs Statement" option. We chose to include this in each phase to emphasize the needs of the customer. The arrow between the "REQUIREMENTS" and "DESIGN" menus symbolizes communication between the two phases in the form of requirements specifications. The arrow between the "DESIGN" and "IMPLEMENTATION" phases symbolizes communication between the phases in the form of a formal or informal design specification. The arrow between the

"MAINTENANCE" and "REQUIREMENTS" phases symbolizes the transition caused by new or changing requirements. The "TESTING" icon in the center of the interface with arrows radiating in the four directions symbolizes the testing that must be built into each phase of the development cycle.

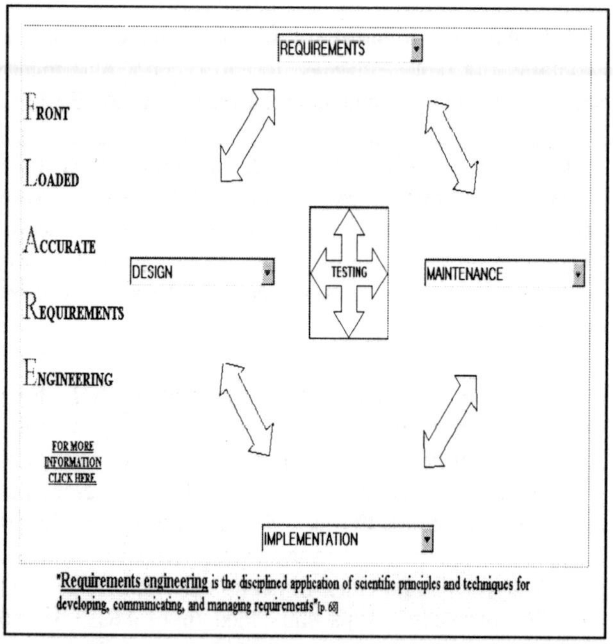

Figure 4. FLARE user interface.

We describe the functionality of each menu option in the following subsections.

5.2.1. Requirements pull-down menu. Enter Requirement: This option allows a Software Engineer to

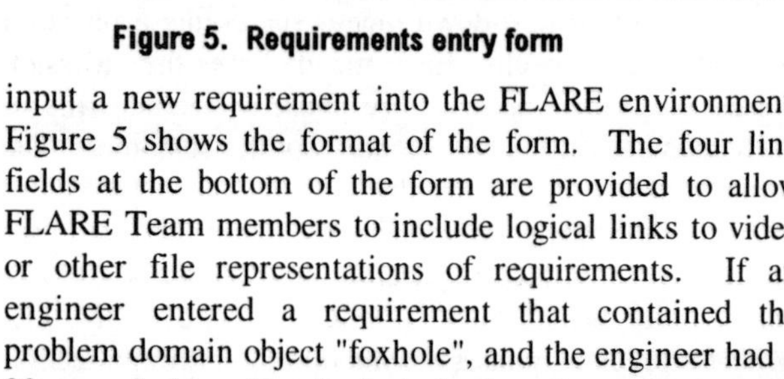

Figure 5. Requirements entry form

input a new requirement into the FLARE environment. Figure 5 shows the format of the form. The four link fields at the bottom of the form are provided to allow FLARE Team members to include logical links to video or other file representations of requirements. If an engineer entered a requirement that contained the problem domain object "foxhole", and the engineer had a 30 second video clip of a foxhole, then the engineer could add a comment in the requirement indicating that a video file of a foxhole was available at link 1. We choose to label these fields 'links" because the FLARE Team could use any file type to augment the requirements.

View Requirements: This option allows engineers to view all approved requirements. Figure 6 shows the HTML page that the database generates automatically when given the "Save as HTML" command found on the menu bar of the Access database.

Ask a Req. Question: This option allows a way to input questions about requirements into the FLARE

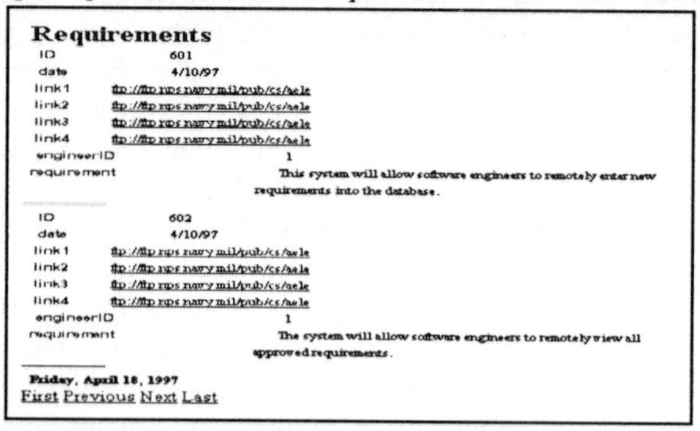

Requirements

ID 601
date 4/10/97
link1 ftp://ftp.nps.navy.mil/pub/cs/sele
link2 ftp://ftp.nps.navy.mil/pub/cs/sele
link3 ftp://ftp.nps.navy.mil/pub/cs/sele
link4 ftp://ftp.nps.navy.mil/pub/cs/sele
engineerID 1
requirement This system will allow software engineers to remotely enter new requirements into the database.

ID 602
date 4/10/97
link1 ftp://ftp.nps.navy.mil/pub/cs/sele
link2 ftp://ftp.nps.navy.mil/pub/cs/sele
link3 ftp://ftp.nps.navy.mil/pub/cs/sele
link4 ftp://ftp.nps.navy.mil/pub/cs/sele
engineerID 1
requirement The system will allow software engineers to remotely view all approved requirements.

Friday, April 18, 1997
First Previous Next Last

Figure 6. Database generated html Page.

system. It is similar in appearance to the form in Figure 5. Upon activation of the send button, the question is automatically imported into the database where a FLARE Team member using the form shown in Figure 7 can answer it.

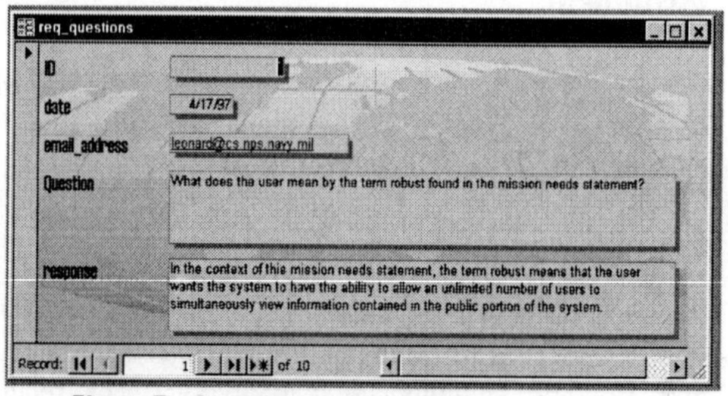

Figure 7. Question response form.

View Requirements Questions: This option allows users to view questions that have been asked along with the answers provided by engineers using the form shown in Figure 7.

We focus on intelligent assistance for organizing questions and answers rather than on intelligent agents for answering questions directly because the domain addressed by the questions has not been accurately formalized - otherwise there would be no need for a requirements determination process. The desired assistance is in locating similar previous questions and the associated answers derived from human expert sources. Our initial approach for providing this assistance is to use a concept similarity lattice to define a distance between questions. This enables computing the nearest neighbors of a given question among the questions previously asked. We are exploring the use of a domain-specific core vocabulary to organize the questions more accurately than would be possible using a generic lexicon. The core vocabulary corresponds to the jargon of the problem domain. Locating repeated words in documents from the application area and filtering out noise words such as articles and prepositions can identify the core vocabulary. This vocabulary must be formalized into a concept hierarchy by knowledge engineers.

Mission Needs Statement: This option allows engineers to review the mission needs statement that prompted the development of the software system.

5.2.2. Design pull-down Menu. Enter Specification: This option allows a Software Engineer to input a specification that satisfies a requirement. Figure 8 shows the format of the form used. Note the fields labeled "Requirement ID." These fields facilitate requirements management. When a specification is entered into the system, the engineer should also enter the requirements that are associated with the specification.

The link fields on the form allow engineers to enter informal design specifications into the FLARE environment. An engineer would enter a comment in the text area of the Specification Entry Form indicating that

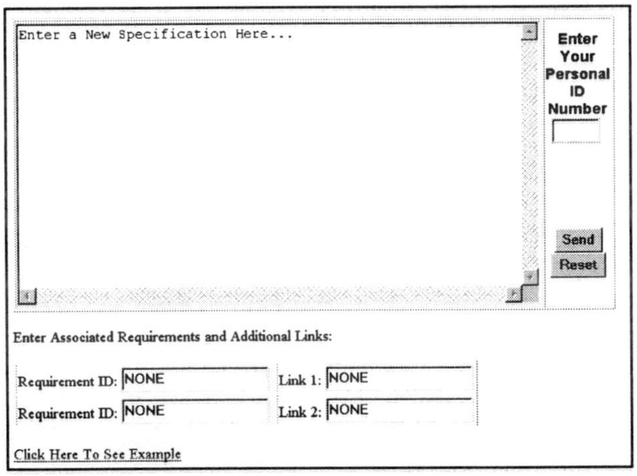

Figure 8. Specification entry form.

a hyperlink to a graphical model or specification exists. An informal specification would likely be in the form of a graphical model such as those found in the Unified Modeling Language [37].

Remaining Menu Options: The menu options View Specifications, Ask a Specification Question, View Specification Questions, and Mission Needs Statement are very similar to those found in subsection B-1 above and do not require further explanation.

5.2.3. Implement pull-down menu. Enter Estimates: The functionality of this option is thoroughly described in Section IV.

Remaining Menu Options: The menu options View Specifications, View Requirements, Ask an Implementation Question, View Implementation Questions, and Mission Needs Statement are very similar to those found in Subsection B-1 above and do not require further explanation.

5.2.4. Maintenance Pull-Down Menu. Enter a Bug Report: This option allows a Software Engineer to input an error found in the implementation into the flare system.

Enter Change Request: This option allows a Software Engineer to input a new or changed requirement into the FLARE environment.

Remaining Menu Options: The menu options View Bug Reports, View Change Requests, Ask a Maintenance Question, View Maintenance Questions, and Mission Needs Statement are very similar to those found in subsection B-1 above and do not require further explanation.

5.3. FLARE database

The database portion of FLARE's environment is implemented with Microsoft's Access database. The conceptual schema for this database is shown in the

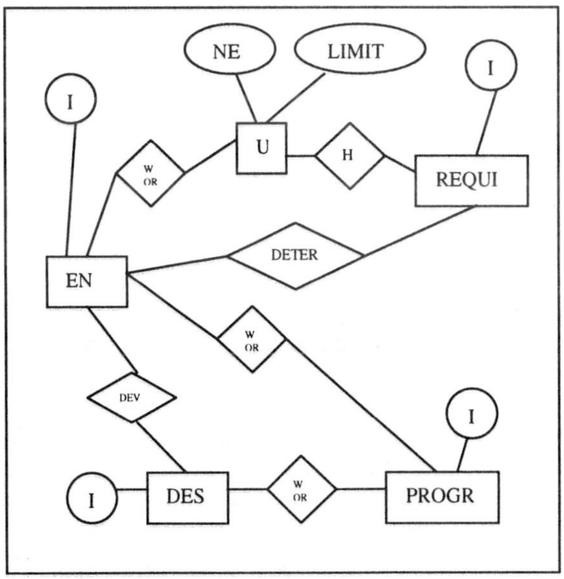

Figure 9. Entity relationship model.

entity relationship model [38] in Figure 9. The data

requirements of the FLARE system are the storage of user needs and limitations, the storage of the required software system capabilities needed by users to solve their problems and the storage of implementation domain information. The required implementation domain information consists of storage of engineer, programmer and design information. FLARE draws a distinction between programmers and engineers because they perform completely different functions and have different responsibilities. This structure supports FLARE Teams by providing a means to manage the information gathered during requirements elicitation. Users have needs, and FLARE Teams are responsible for determining the requirements of software systems that will satisfy these needs. Programmers and other engineers will use the products produced by FLARE Teams stored in the FLARE database to achieve their respective tasks.

5.3.1. Scheduling Algorithm. We developed and implemented a scheduling algo-rithm that automatically assigns tasks to programmers. The algorithm uses programmer's estimates (see Section IV) of the difficulty of translating a design specification module into a programming language implementation. The algorithm uses a greedy strategy [39:p.329]. It picks the lowest estimated time to implement a module and assigns that module to the programmer who made the estimate. The algorithm does not produce optimal results in all cases, yet provides a close approximation; this is acceptable given that the heuristic in which the algorithm determines a schedule is based on imprecise estimates.

6. Security

The initial distributed Internet database application was totally insecure. It was composed of freely available programs that were downloaded from the Internet. We were pleased with the availability of programs that allowed us to quickly create the distributed database environment, but recognize that in the context of security, we are completely at the mercy of the people who developed the components. The products could contain Trojan Horses or undiscovered viruses.

Three of the five components we used have binary files that potentially could contain viruses or Trojan Horses. The PERL library files are too large for us to ensure that they do not contain back doors. The Microsoft products were free of cost, but the licenses specifically state that it is a violation of the license agreements to reverse engineer the code. This makes it impossible for us to make any claims about the security of the system regardless of the security methods that we implement. The application's insecurity made it less than optimal for any purpose other than using it as a teaching or experimentation tool. This section details the steps taken to implement a basic level of security features in the system making it usable by a broader class of people.

We introduced basic security features into the distributed database environment, addressing the four major areas of network security: "Secrecy or Confidentially; Accuracy or integrity; Authenticity; and Availability." [40: p. 202]

6.1. Securing the database

This section shows how we added basic security features to the distributed database environment. The features that we added will keep most unauthorized people from adding, deleting and modifying database records. The features that accomplish this are: identification and authentication; execute, read and write restrictions placed on the server; restricted ftp services, and physical security of the server that has the distributed database located on it. [41]

6.1.1. Identification and authentication. We used a simple database table to implement identification and authentication. In order for users to add, delete, or modify records they must now enter a proper "userID and password" pair. Users must possess a valid userID and password pair to access the database. The userIDs and passwords entered by users should be sent over the Internet encrypted. (Figure 10)

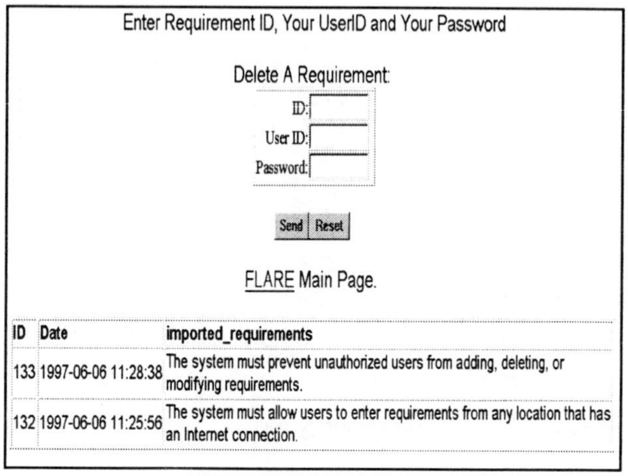

Figure 10. Requirement deletion form with identification and authentication features.

6.1.2. Execute, read and write restrictions. The PWS allows administrators to configure the permissions on directories. We use this to restrict what files users of our

Internet database can read, write, and execute. We use the same procedures Microsoft recommends for users of Active Server Pages.

We placed all HTML files used to provide a portion of the database's user interface in a directory that is readable but does not allow users to write files or execute programs. The directory is readable because users of the system need to read the HTML files in their Internet browsers to display our pages.

We placed all the PERL scripts in a directory that is executable but does not allow users to read or write files. Since the directory is executable, users can execute the PERL scripts that perform the database queries. Read permissions are denied because users do not need to view the scripts to perform database operations. If users were to read the PERL scripts, they could possibly find ways to gain unauthorized access to the data stored in the database or system files.

6.1.3. Restricted FTP services. The PWS has an FTP server. We configured it so that users are not allowed to access the directories containing the database, HTML and PERL script files.

6.1.4. Physical security of the database Server. The computer which stores the environment's files offers no built in security because it is running on Microsoft's Windows 95 operating system. We have placed the computer behind locked doors with limited access. This provides a reasonable level of assurance that unauthorized people will not be able to modify the files stored on the computer. It docs not prevent personnel who routinely work in the area from making unauthorized modifications to the environment's files.

6.2. Additional threats and vulnerabilities

6.2.1. Denial of service attacks. The system does not have any mechanisms to deter or prevent a denial of service attack. Our environment is particularly susceptible to this type of attack. It is not behind a firewall, and it uses the PWS, which has a 64 simultaneous user limit.

6.2.2. Normal hardware failures. The Internet database is stored on magnetic hard drives. A hard drive failure would cause a catastrophic data loss. As usual, backups will mitigate this loss.

6.2.3. Accidental data loss. The database allows authorized users to delete a record accidentally. In addition, the computer that runs the Internet database is used for other purposes than just as a server for our Internet database. Other users of the computer could accidentally delete the database file.

6.3. Countermeasures

We find the most important countermeasures to the threats listed above are an aggressive backup policy and user training. The data stored in the database is the most important element of the distributed environment. Continuous backups using the replication features found in Access are warranted. This countermeasure provides a degree of protection for the other vulnerabilities we listed. User training is an important countermeasure because the system currently allows any user with a valid userID and password pair to delete or modify database records. Users of the system must be trained to limit deletions and modifications, and to take extra care when doing so.

Countermeasures to denial of service attacks are expensive. Firewalls are a way to counter this type of attack [40,41]. Users of the environment should determine when such countermeasures would be cost effective to implement.

7. Conclusions and future work

Matching related statements has other practical and important applications in software engineering, including comparing incoming problem reports to previously received ones to determine whether the reported problem is new or has been reported previously.

As a decision support aid for managers, software engineers and other stakeholders in software development projects, this tool can significantly reduce time spent in preparing and delivering answers to routine questions as well as improve the correlation between stakeholder identified requirements and final production software. The tool and the approach are not limited to the domain of software engineering - any endeavor with frequent interaction between producer and consumer can benefit from its use.

We developed the initial version of a CASE tool FLARE quickly (2 months). FLARE is a requirements engineering environment composed of commercial off the shelf (COTS) software tools tied together by the Internet. Our experience indicates that tools of this kind can be useful for collecting requirements from stakeholders at a variety of physical locations.

FLARE's requirements tracing features could be improved. Even though each requirement receives a unique identification number, FLARE does not automatically track this requirement throughout the development process, rather it relies on engineers "tagging" each new product with the appropriate requirement identification number. Automation of this tagging process would eliminate possibilities of entering incorrect tags, and could potentially allow engineers to look at any object produced in the development process and extract the associated requirement information.

Microsoft's Access database provides the ability to automatically generate HTML files based on the information submitted by the software engineering team. These files are crude. A more sophisticated HTML file generator would be useful.

The greedy strategy used by the module assignment algorithm does not guarantee an optimal solution although it is good enough for initial use. Better algorithms should be explored.

More refined models of who is authorized to modify or delete which parts of the database would help to further improve security with respect to data integrity and protection from data losses.

A demonstration of the FLARE tool can be downloaded from or run directly on the World-Wide Web at URL: http://web.nps.navy.mil/~aeleonar/Welcome.html

8. References

[1] Valetto, G. and Kaiser, G., "Enveloping Sophisticated Tools into Computer-Aided Software Engineering Environments," in Proceedings 7th International Workshop on Computer-Aided Software Engineering, IEEE Computer Soc. Press, Los Alamitos, Calif., 1995, pp. 40-48.

[2] Berzins, V. and Luqi, Software Engineering with Abstractions, Addison-Wesley Publishing Company, Reading, MA, 1991.

[3] Ramesh, B., Powers, T., Stubbs, C. and Edwards, M. "Implementing Requirements traceability: A Case Study," in Proceedings Second IEEE International Symposium on Requirements Engineering, IEEE Computer Soc. Press, Los Alamitos, Calif., 1995, pp. 89-95.

[4] Brun-Cottan F. and Wall, P., "Using Video to Re-Present the User," Communications of the ACM, Vol. 38, No. 5, May 1995, pp. 61-71.

[5] Kaiya, H., Saeki, M. and Ochimizu, K., "Design of a Hyper Media Tool to support Requirements Elicitation Meetings," in Proceedings 7th International Workshop on Computer-Aided Software Engineering, IEEE Computer Soc. Press, Los Alamitos, Calif., 1995, pp. 250-259.

[6] CASE tool index, Queen's University in Kingston, Ontario, available from http://www.qucis.queensu.ca/Software-Engineering/tools.html Internet; accessed 22 March 1997.

[7] Luqi, Ketabchi, M., "A Computer-Aided Prototyping System," IEEE Computer Technology Series, Computer-Aided Software Engineering (CASE), Editor: E. Chikofsky, 1988, pp. 89-95.

[8] Luqi, Berzins, V. and Yeh, R., "A Prototyping Language for Real-Time Software," IEEE Transactions on Software Engineering, Vol. 14, No. 10, October 1988, pp. 1409-1423.

[9] Luqi, "Software Evolution Through Rapid Prototyping," IEEE Computer, May 1989, pp. 13-25.

[10] Macedonia M. and Brutzman, D., "MBone Provides Audio and Video Across the Internet," available from: ftp://taurus.cs.nps.navy.mil/pub/mbmg/mbone.html Internet; accessed 22 March 1997.

[11] Progressive Networks, "Real Audio and Video," available from: http://www.real.com/rvnba.html Internet; accessed 22 March 1997.

[12] Intel, "Internet Video Phone with Proshare Technology," available from: http://connectedpc.com/iaweb/cpc/iivphone/index.htm Internet; accessed 22 March 1997.

[13] O'Leary, D., "The Internet, Intranets, and the AI Renaissance," Computer, January 1997, pp. 71-78.

[14] Autonomy Corporation, "Autonomy Agents," available from: http://www.agentware.com Internet: accessed 23 March 1997.

[15] Poor, A., "DVD and CD-ROM: 21st Century Storage," PC Magazine Online, available from: http://www.pcmag.com/features/cdrom/_open.htm Internet: accessed 23 March 1997.

[16] Computer Mail Order, advertisement, Byte, McGraw-Hill, Peterborough, NH January 1987.

[17] Turner Hall Publishing, advertisement, Byte, McGraw-Hill, Peterborough, NH January 1987.

[18] Nevada Computer, advertisement, Byte, McGraw-Hill, Peterborough, NH January 1992.

[19] Computerlane, advertisement, Byte, McGraw-Hill, Peterborough, NH January 1997.

[20] First Source International, advertisement, Byte, McGraw-Hill, Peterborough, NH January 1997.

[21] Crothers, B., "Memory Prices Creep Back Up," CNET, Inc., available from: http://www.news.com/News/Item/0,4,8426,00.html Internet: accessed 12 May 1997, quoting Handy from Dataquest, available from: http://www.dataquest.com Internet: accessed 12 May 1997.

[22] Toshiba Corp., "A revolution is coming and it will change everything you think about Home Entertainment," available from http://www.toshiba.com/tacp/SD/javahome.html Internet: accessed 23 March 1997.

[23] NCSA, "A Beginner's Guide to HTML," available from: http://www.ncsa.uiuc.edu/General/Internet/WWW/HTMLPrimerAll.html Internet: accessed 23 March 1997.

[24] Luqi, "A Graph Model for Software Evolution," in IEEE Computer Society Press tutorial, Software Merging and Slicing, collected by V. Berzins, May 1995, pp. 202-212.

[25]University of Kansas, "An Instantaneous Introduction to CGI Scripts and HTML Forms," available from: http://www.cc.ukans.edu/info/forms/forms-intro.html Internet: accessed 23 March 1997.

[26] Perl Institute, Online Manual, available from http://www.perl.org/CPAN/doc/manual/html/pod/index.html Internet: accessed 26 May 1997.

[27] ActiveWare, Release Download Page, available from http://www.activeware.com/Download/download.htm Internet: accessed 27 May 1997.

[28] Microsoft Corporation, Access developer web site, available from http://www.microsoft.com/accessdev/docs/bapp97/chapters/ba21_6.htm Internet: accessed 27 May 1997.

[29] Microsoft Corp., Open Database Connectivity, available from http://www.microsoft.com/ODBC/download/DMDownload.htm Internet: accessed 26 May 1997.

[30] Roth, D., Module Description Page, available from http://www.roth.net/odbc/odbc.html#ModDesc Internet: access 28 May 1997.

[31] Badr, S. and Luqi, "Automation Support for Concurrent Software Engineering," Proceeding of the 6th International Conference on Software Engineering and Knowledge Engineering, Jurmala, Latvia, June 1994, pp. 46-53.

[32] Microsoft Corporation, available from: http://www.microsoft.com Internet: accessed 1March 1997.

[33] Leonard, A., "Flare Download Site," available from: http://www.cs.nps.navy.mil/misc/flare/Readme.html Internet: accessed 14 April 1997.

[34] Netscape Corporation, "JavaScript Authoring Guide," available from: http://home.netscape.com/eng/mozilla/Gold/handbook/javascript/index.html Internet: accessed 16 April 1997.

[35] Web Communications, "WWW Fill-Out Forms," available form: http://www.webcom.com/~webcom/html/tutor/forms Internet: accessed 16 April 1997.

[36] Netscape Corporation, available from: http://home.netscape.com Internet: accessed 16 April 1997.

[37] Rational Rose Inc., Unified Modeling Language version 1.0, available from http://www.rational.com/ot/uml/1.0/index.html Internet: accessed 3 April 1997.

[38] Elmasri, R. and Navathe, S. B., Fundamentals of Database Systems, The Benjamin/Cummings Publishing Company, Redwood City, CA 1994.

[39] Cormen, T. H., Leiserson, C. E. and Rivest, R. L., Introduction to Algorithms, MIT Press, Cambridge, 1990.

[40] Russel, D. and Gangemi, G. T. Sr., Computer Security Basics, O'Reilly & Associates, Inc., Sebastopol, CA 1991.

[41] Garfinkel, S. and Spafford, G., Proactical Unix & Internet Security, O'Reilly & Associates, Inc., Sebastopol, CA 1996.

Session G.2

Intelligent User Interface and Scheduling

Session Chair:
Fuad Sobrinho, IISI, Brazil

Data Visualization in the DB-Discover System

Robert J. Hilderman, Liangchun Li, and Howard J. Hamilton
Department of Computer Science
University of Regina
Regina, Saskatchewan, Canada, S4S 0A2
{hilder,lil,hamilton}@cs.uregina.ca

Abstract

The DB-Discover system is a research software tool for knowledge discovery from databases. Utilizing an efficient attribute-oriented induction algorithm based upon the climbing tree and dropping condition methods, called multi-attribute generalization, it generates many possible summaries of data from a database. In this paper, we present the design of the data visualization capabilities of DB-Discover and describe how these capabilities help us manage the summaries generated.

1 Introduction

The design of the data visualization capabilities of the DB-Discover system is presented. *DB-Discover* is a research software tool for knowledge discovery from databases (KDD) developed at the University of Regina from 1992 to date [2]. Data visualization can be used in a KDD system at three stages: (1) to guide discovery, (2) to guide the presentation of the results, and (3) to present the results themselves. Here we focus on the second stage and describe techniques for (1) managing the many possible summaries generated by DB-Discover, and (2) selecting the anomalous (and potentially interesting) summaries among them.

2 The DB-Discover System

The DB-Discover system is based on multi-attribute generalization [4], an enhanced version of a well-known data mining technique called attribute-oriented induction [1]. *Attribute-oriented induction* summarizes data in a database according to user-defined concept hierarchies associated with relevant attributes using techniques which include the dropping condition and climbing tree methods [6]. The *climbing tree method* transforms the data in a database by repeatedly replacing specific attribute values with more general concepts according to user-defined concept hierarchies. A *concept hierarchy* (CH) associated with an attribute in a database is represented as a tree where leaf nodes correspond to actual domain values in the database, intermediate nodes correspond to a more general representation of the domain values, and the root node corresponds to the most general representation of the domain values. The *dropping condition method* transforms the data in a database by removing a condition from a conjunction of conditions, so that the remaining conjunction of conditions is more general.

To facilitate the generation of all possible summaries, *domain generalization graphs* (DGGs) are used to augment CHs and expand the scope of our AOI methods [5, 4]. Informally, a DGG associated with a CH defines a partial order which represents a set of generalization relations for the attribute. A DGG always includes a single source (i.e., the node at the lowest level corresponding to the domain of the attribute) and a single sink (i.e., the node at the highest level corresponding to the most general representation of the domain and which contains the value ANY). The node at each level in a DGG is a general description of the nodes at the same level in the corresponding CH.

When multiple CHs are associated with a single attribute, meaning knowledge about an attribute can be expressed in many different ways, a multi-path DGG can be constructed from the single-path DGGs. We assume that a common name used in the single-path DGGs associated with the attribute represents the same partition of the domain in the associated CHs. Consequently, the like-named nodes can be combined in the multi-path DGG.

A typical discovery task usually involves generalization of a set of attributes, where each attribute is associated with a multi-path DGG. When generalizing a set of attributes, the set can be considered a single attribute whose domain is the cross product of the individual attribute domains. A generalization from this domain is a combination of nodes from the DGGs associated with the individual attributes, taking one node from the DGG for each attribute.

The *generalization state space* consists of all possible summaries which can be generated from the DGGs associated with the set of attributes. This space is more general than a version space [7] because we allow more complex generalizations than value-to-ANY and our summaries contain a relation rather than a single conjunctive description. On the other hand, it is less complete than a Galois lattice [3] because not every possible subset is included in the lattice. The generalization state space is obtained by determining all possible combinations of nodes from the DGGs, and then generating the summary which corresponds to each node combination. The size of the generalization state space depends only on the number of nodes in the associated DGGs; it is not dependent upon the number of tuples in the input relation. For m attributes, a database of n tuples, and an $O(n)$ generalization algorithm, creating all possible summaries requires $O(n \prod_{i=1}^{m} |D_i|)$ time, where $|D_i|$ is the number of nodes in DGG D_i.

3 Data Visualization Capabilities

In the previous section, it was shown that multi-attribute generalization has the potential to generate many summaries, if the number of attributes to be generalized is large or the DGGs associated with the attributes are complex. Our experience in applying data mining techniques to the databases of our commercial partners has shown that domain experts typically perform AOI on a few attributes for which considerable domain knowledge has been accumulated. To assist the domain expert, we propose a tool with a graphical user interface, called DBD-View. *DBD-View* ranks and arranges summaries, according to various user-defined criteria, so that they can be quickly and efficiently analyzed. Our approach is based upon a simple, yet powerful architecture which uses different views for visualizing the summaries generated by a discovery task. In this section, we describe DBD-View and show how it works to manage summaries.

3.1 The Viewspace

The viewspace is a window upon which up to four different views may be placed. The screen snapshot in Figure 1 shows a viewspace that has been filled with a global spatial view (top left), a separate graphs local view (bottom left), a tabular summary view (top right), and a scatterplot global view (bottom right). We describe these views in the sections that follow.

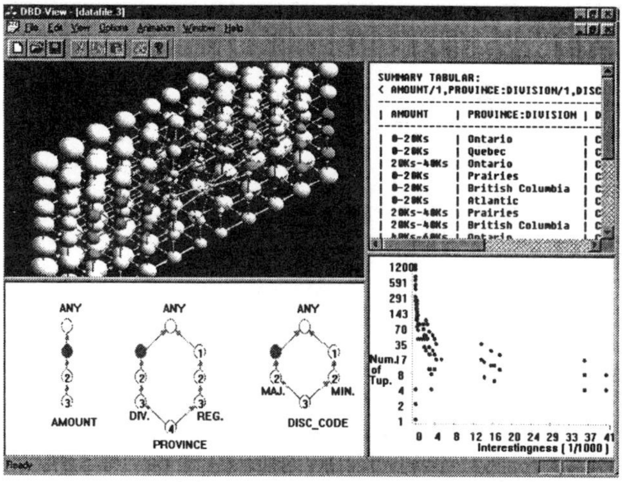

Figure 1. The viewspace showing global, local, and summary views

3.2 The Global View

There are two types of global views which are used to represent the complete generalization state space: a scatterplot global view and a spatial global view. The *scatterplot global view* represents the generalization state space as a two-dimensional graph, where the number of tuples in a summary is plotted against the interestingness of the summary. Figure 2 shows the scatterplot global view of the complete generalization state space for a small discovery task. A summary corresponding to a dot toward the left of the graph is considered less interesting than one toward the right. A summary corresponding to a dot toward the top of the graph contains more tuples than one toward the bottom.

The *spatial global view* represents the generalization state space as a directed graph consisting of nodes of various sizes and colours, connected by edges. The relative size of a node is representative of the number of tuples in the corresponding summary. Similarly, the colour of a node is representative of the interestingness of the corresponding summary. Figure 3 shows the spatial global view of the complete generalization state space for a small discovery task. In this particular example, there is a group of small, dark nodes toward the centre of the graph that are considered most interesting.

The domain expert can utilize the scatterplot and spatial global views to obtain an easy-to-understand,

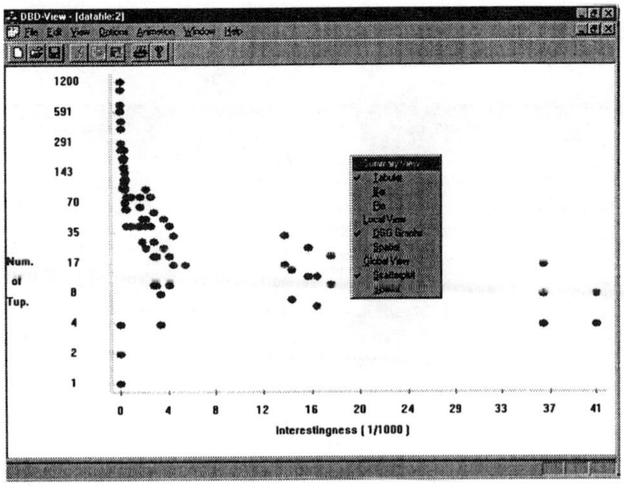

Figure 2. The scatterplot global view

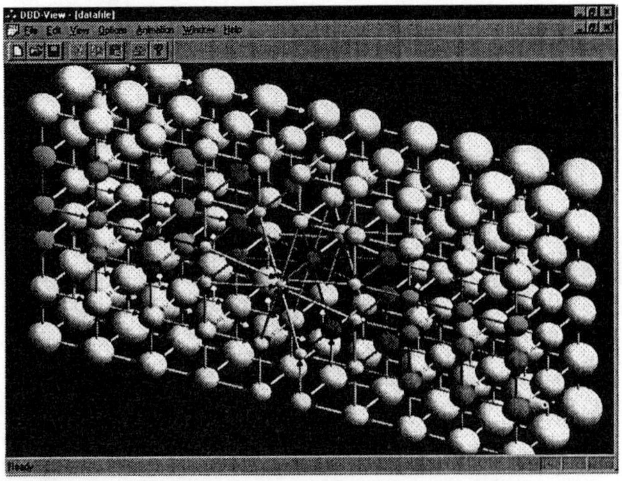

Figure 3. The spatial global view

initial overview analysis of the summaries in the generalization state space. If a particular summary seems interesting, he can left click on a dot (in scatterplot global view) or node (in spatial global view) to make the corresponding summary the active summary. When a summary becomes the *active summary*, the local and summary views are also updated.

3.3 The Local View

There are two types of local views which are used to dissect the generalization state space: a separate graphs local view and a spatial local view. The *separate graphs local view* represents a summary in the generalization state space as a combination of nodes from the DGGs associated with the attributes being generalized. Figure 4 shows the three DGGs from which the summaries in the generalization state space were generated. There is one solid (highlighted) node in each of these DGGs, the combination coinciding with the active summary in the global and summary views.

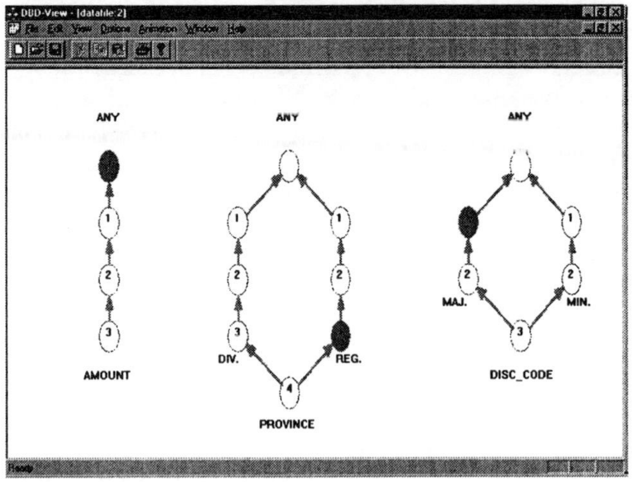

Figure 4. The separate graphs local view

The domain expert can navigate throughout the generalization state space by selecting different combinations of nodes from the separate graphs local view. If a particular summary seems interesting, he can left click one node in each DGG to highlight it and select a new active summary. When a summary becomes the active summary, the global and summary views are updated to coincide with the new local view.

The *spatial local view* represents a logically connected group of summaries in the generalization state space. Figure 5 shows a neighborhood in the generalization state space immediately surrounding the node corresponding to the active summary. The node corresponding to the active summary is the node at the centre of the view, and is called the *current node.* Below the current node are all nodes in the generalization state space from which it is possible to reach the current node by generalizing one attribute up one more level in the associated DGG. These nodes are a more specific representation of the current node. Above the current node, are all nodes in the generalization state space that can be reached from the current node by generalizing one attribute up one more level in the associated DGG. These nodes are a more general representation of the current node. The labels in the nodes identify the attribute that has been generalized (for those nodes below the current node) or will be generalized (for those nodes above the current node).

The domain expert can navigate throughout the generalization state space by selecting a node from the spatial local view. If a particular summary seems in-

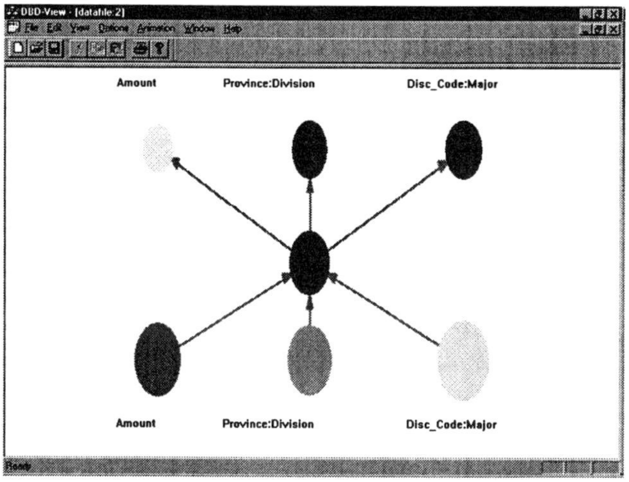

Figure 5. The spatial local view

teresting, he can left click on the corresponding node to highlight it and select a new active summary. The spatial local view is then updated to show the selected node as the current node. The global and summary views are updated to coincide with the new local view.

3.4 The Summary View

The default output format for displaying the summary view is to display it as a table, as shown in Figure 6. Alternative output formats are similar to those in commonly used spreadsheet packages.

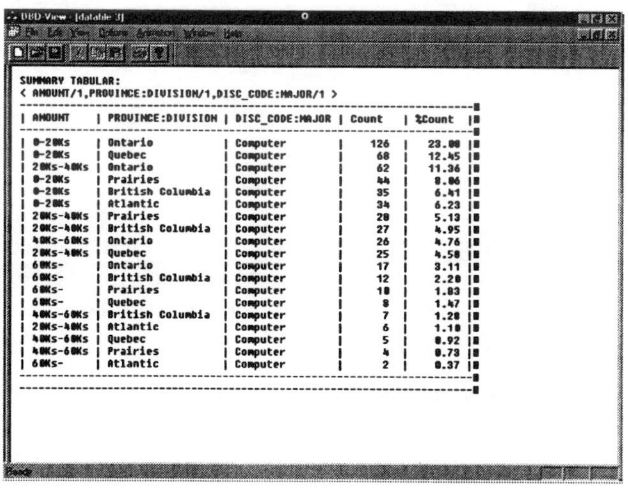

SUMMARY TABULAR:
< AMOUNT/1,PROVINCE:DIVISION/1,DISC_CODE:MAJOR/1 >

AMOUNT	PROVINCE:DIVISION	DISC_CODE:MAJOR	Count	%Count
0-20Ks	Ontario	Computer	126	23.08
0-20Ks	Quebec	Computer	68	12.45
20Ks-40Ks	Ontario	Computer	62	11.36
0-20Ks	Prairies	Computer	44	8.06
0-20Ks	British Columbia	Computer	35	6.41
0-20Ks	Atlantic	Computer	34	6.23
20Ks-40Ks	Prairies	Computer	28	5.13
20Ks-40Ks	British Columbia	Computer	27	4.95
40Ks-60Ks	Ontario	Computer	26	4.76
20Ks-40Ks	Quebec	Computer	25	4.58
60Ks-	Ontario	Computer	17	3.11
60Ks-	British Columbia	Computer	12	2.20
60Ks-	Prairies	Computer	10	1.83
60Ks-	Quebec	Computer	8	1.47
40Ks-60Ks	British Columbia	Computer	7	1.28
20Ks-40Ks	Atlantic	Computer	6	1.10
40Ks-60Ks	Quebec	Computer	5	0.92
40Ks-60Ks	Prairies	Computer	4	0.73
60Ks-	Atlantic	Computer	2	0.37

Figure 6. The tabular summary view

4 Conclusion and Future Work

We have presented the design of the data visualization capabilities of the DB-Discover system. Future work will involve enhancing the data visualization capabilities of DB-Discover. Techniques for displaying and navigating extremely large generalization state spaces are required. Also, techniques for allowing the domain expert to interactively guide a discovery task will be investigated.

References

[1] Y. Cai, N. Cercone, and J. Han. Attribute-oriented induction in relational databases. In G. Piatetsky-Shapiro and W. Frawley, editors, *Knowledge Discovery in Databases*, pages 213–228, Cambridge, MA, 1991. AAAI/MIT Press.

[2] C.L. Carter and H.J. Hamilton. Efficient attribute-oriented algorithms for knowledge discovery from large databases. IEEE Trans. on Knowledge and Data Engineering. To appear.

[3] R. Godin, R. Missaoui, and H. Alaoui. Incremental concept formation algorithms based on galois (concept) lattices. *Computational Intelligence*, 11(2):246–267, 1995.

[4] H.J. Hamilton, R.J. Hilderman, and N. Cercone. Attribute-oriented induction using domain generalization graphs. In *Proceedings of the Eighth IEEE International Conference on Tools with Artificial Intelligence (ICTAI'96)*, pages 246–253, Toulouse, France, November 1996.

[5] R.J. Hilderman, H.J. Hamilton, R.J. Kowalchuk, and N. Cercone. Parallel knowledge discovery using domain generalization graphs. In J. Komorowski and J. Zytkow, editors, *Proceedings of the 1st European Conference on the Principles of Data Mining and Knowledge Discovery*, pages 25–35, Trondheim, Norway, June 1997.

[6] R.S. Michalski. A theory and methodology of inductive learning. In R.S. Michalski, J.G. Carbonell, and T.M. Mitchell, editors, *Machine Learning: An Artificial Intelligence Approach*, pages 83–134. Tioga Publishing Company, 1983.

[7] T.M. Mitchell. *Version Spaces: An Approach to Concept Learning*. PhD thesis, Stanford University, 1978.

Real Time Scheduling with Neurosched

Jean-Michel Gallone, François Charpillet
CRIN-CNRS & INRIA Lorraine,
BP 239, 54506 Vandœuvre-lès-Nancy, France
E-mail: gallone@loria.fr, charp@loria.fr

Abstract

Most of the scheduling problems are NP-Hard. Therefore, heuristics and approximation algorithms must be used for large problems when timing constraints have to be addressed. Obviously these methods are of interest when they provide near optimal solutions and when computational complexity can be controlled. This paper presents such a method based on Hopfield Neural Networks. Scheduling problem are solved in an iterative way, by finding a solution trough the minimization of an energy function. An interesting property of this approach is its capacity to trade-off the quality for computation time. Indeed, the convergence speed of the minimization process can be tuned by adapting several parameters that influence the quality of the results.

1. Introduction

Our aim is to find a schedule of a set of non pre-emptive tasks over a set of processors. Each task T_i is characterized by a given processing time p_i, a time before which T_i cannot begin its execution (R_i the ready time) and a time before which T_i must complete (D_i the deadline). In a real-time context, taking the optimal decision does not consist in computing the schedule with best quality but rather in performing the best trade-off between resource consumption and quality of schedule.

In [2], we proposed scheduling algorithms using Hopfield Neural Networks [5]. Then, we have extended this work by studying the incidence of two kinds of approximation criteria on the processing time and on the success rate [3]. By tuning those two approximation criteria, we have obtained a set of run-time executions of the Hopfield minimization process with different characteristics (quality, efficiency). Each execution is denoted in the anytime terminology as a contract algorithm. Based on this set of algorithms, we built sequences of contract algorithms in order to obtain the best average result of our system for a given computation time. This methodology is based on the performance profiles of the contract algorithms.

2. Performance Profile

The performance profile is in our case a description of the probability to find a result as a function of the approximation parameters. Figure 1 exemplifies performance profiles of several contracts obtained for one class of problems (i.e. problems that have same number of tasks of same temporal window).

The horizontal axis corresponds to the number of iterations, while the vertical axis corresponds to the opposite of the number of violated constraints after a given number of iterations. Theses results have been computed on a corpus of 10 000 problem instances belonging to a given class. The considered class is characterized by problem instances of 20 tasks ; each task has a duration set between 1 and 6 time units and an execution window whose duration is less than twice the task duration ; and an horizon composed of 80 time units. Each problem instance in the corpus has been chosen to be feasible.

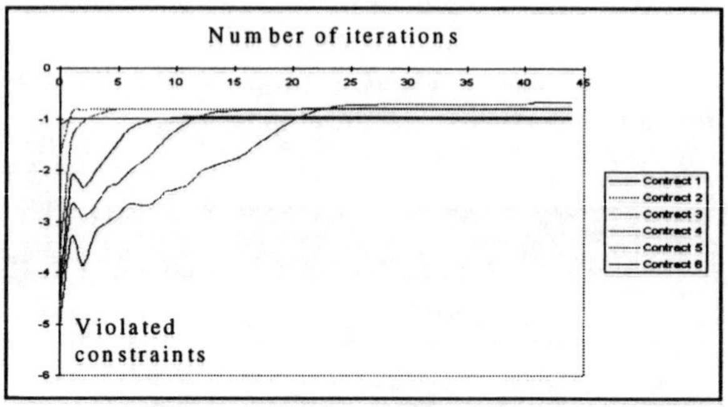

Figure 1: Performance profiles

The anytime behavior of our approach clearly appear on the figure. We can remark that the quality (number of satisfied constraints) is really an increasing function of the time dedicated for the resolution.

3. Conditional Performance Profile

At any time, the optimal policy will determine how to choose the contract that offers the best chance to end before the deadline and to deliver the best result. In order

1082-3409/97 $10.00

to build an optimal sequence, we have to compute conditional performance profiles that define the success rate of a given contract knowing that an other given contract failed to find a solution. Figure 2 illustrates such a conditional performance profile : the vertical axis represents failed contracts, the horizontal axis stands for tested contracts and the darkness of the points on the map states for success rates.

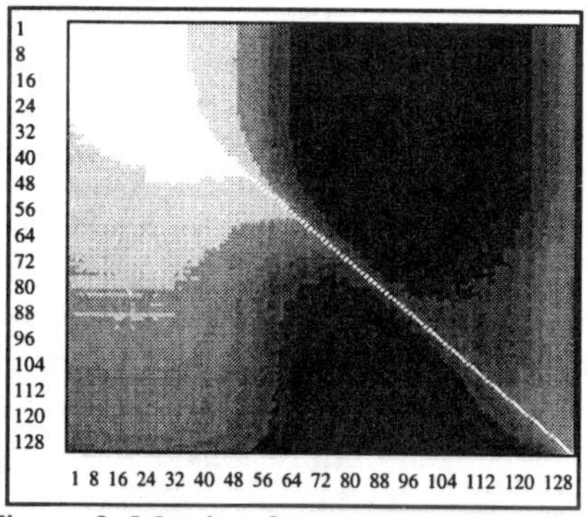

Figure 2: Matrix of success transition

For low values of the convergence speed, the higher you increase the values, the more likely you are to get a good schedule. On the other hand, the higher the convergence speed, the longer the execution time. Thus, for an unknown deadline, the principal difficulty is to find a sequence of contracts that are far enough to improve the actual success rate but close enough to get an answer before the deadline is reached

4. Composition policy

The difficulty come from the a priori uncertainty in the deadline of the problem. The different possible sequences have to be computed so as to dynamically select the best one. Consequently, a good trade-off has to be found to select a contract far enough to give correct result and close enough to give a quick result.

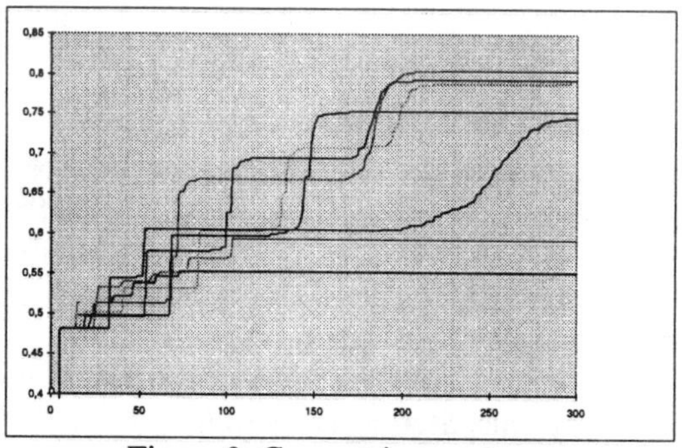

Figure 3: Geometric sequences

Figure 3 exemplifies typical performance profiles obtained by chaining contracts with duration following an geometric progression. We have compared these results with those obtained with arithmetic progression but this did not improved the sucess rate whatever the considered time. Note that a contract can find a solution before its allocated time. This is due to the variance of the duration of a contract depending of the instance of problem for a given class.

5. Conclusion

In this paper, we have presented the Hopfield Artificial Neural Network model and its capability to be used for solving a particular scheduling problem : tasks with release times, deadlines and computation times to be scheduled on several uniform machines. We have validated our approach on a great number of randomly generated examples. Results are better than an efficient scheduling heuristics when no timing constraints exists. Furthermore, It is capable of adapting its behavior when timing constraints are imposed gracefull its anytime property.

This approach can be easily parallelised and even be replaced by a specific hardware system. Thus, it can be on-line used on systems where computation time available for scheduling is very low. A third advantage is the ease of extending the approach. We can easily tackle other classes of problem by adding constraints to the existing network or by modifying the defined constraints.

6. References

[1] Boddy M. and Dean T. Solving Time dependent Planning Problems. Proc. of International joint Conference on Artificial Intelligence, pp. 979-984, 1989.

[2] Gallone J-M. and Charpillet F. Hopfield Neural Network for Scheduling Non Pre-emptive Tasks. 12th European Conference on Artificial Intelligence, pp. 223-227, 1996.

[3] Gallone J.M. and Charpillet F. Composing Approximated Algorithms Based on Hopfield Neural Network for Building a Resource-Bounded Scheduler. IEEE International Conference on Tools with Artificial Intelligence, pp. 445-446, 1996.

[4] Garvey A. and Lesser V. Design-to-time Scheduling, IEEE Transactions on Systems, Man and Cybernetics, Special Issue on Planning, Scheduling and Control, Vol. 23, N_6, 1992.

[5] Hopfield J.J. and Tank D.W. Neural computation of decisions in optimization problems. Biological Cybernetics, 52, pp. 141-152, 1985.

[6] Zilberstein and Russell. Efficient Resource-Bounded Reasoning in AT-RALPH, Proc. first AIPS, pp260, 266, 1992.

Schedular++: Scheduling with Knowledge Objects

Kevin Cai, Xindong Wu and Heinz Schmidt
Department of Software Development, Monash University
900 Dandenong Road, Melbourne, VIC 3145, Australia

Abstract

This paper presents a scheduling system, Schedular++, which integrates logic rules into the object-oriented paradigm. Schedular++ demonstrates the application of knowledge objects to solve a scheduling problem.

1 Introduction

Knowledge objects are an integration of the object-oriented paradigm with logic rules. The class and inheritance features of object-oriented paradigm assist users to describe and define entities more naturally and to emphasize the semantic rather than the syntactic content of applications. The encapsulation and dynamic binding of the object-oriented paradigm make the resultant software more maintainable, adaptable and recyclable. Rule-based programming, however, expresses constraints within and between objects very efficiently in its rules and provides inference power to the system. The proper integration of object-oriented paradigm and rule-based programming provides a flexible and powerful environment, as rule-based components provide facilities for deductive retrieval and pattern matching, and object-oriented components provide a clear intuitive structure for programs in the form of class hierarchies.

Based on the knowledge object concept, this paper designs and develops a scheduling system, Schedular++. The construction of Schedular++ demonstrates that by using an object-oriented representation of knowledge objects, users can be given explicit control of the object hierarchy to customize the system to their particular needs, which includes letting users select among scheduling and other methods. In Schedular++, rules are designed as derivation rules and constraint rules. The purpose of rules is either to restrict object structure and behaviour, or to infer new data from the existing data. Rules are arranged in positions so that object methods are automatically firing up if environment changes are detected by these rules.

2 Schedular++

Scheduling is the allocation of resources over time to perform a collection of tasks [Henke 1994]. It selects among alternative plans and assigning resources and times to the set of activities in the plan. These assignments must obey a set of rules or constraints that reflect the temporal relationships between activities and the capacity limitations of a set of shared resources. The assignments also affect the optimization of a schedule with respect to criteria such as cost, tardiness, or throughput. This section describes a specific scheduling problem and its solution, Schedular++.

Structured design methods guide developers to use algorithms as their fundamental building blocks. A complex scheduling program like Schedular++ would require sophisticated algorithms to process the data if one follows structured design methods. The object-oriented paradigm, however, helps developers exploit the expressive power of object-oriented design and object-oriented programming languages, using classes and objects as basic building blocks. Instead of designing sophisticated algorithms, Schedular++ decomposes entities and their relationships into objects and classes, while using logical rules built inside objects to enhance the description of static and dynamic models of the system, as well as providing inference power to deduce relative complex properties from object data. Since these rules are accessible by users, this implies that users can change some behaviours of objects by configuring different knowledge to objects.

2.1 System Requirements

Telecom manages the telephone network across the entire country. To efficiently manage the network, many fault dispatch centres (FDC) are distributed across the country, and each FDC maintains a team of field workers (called workers here) to fix faults in several of their service suburbs. One of the daily jobs in each FDC is to dispatch workers to fix network faults in each suburb. This includes daily downloading of defect reports from the customer service representatives' (CSR) database (CSR is the operator service where customers call for their telephone defects), and

1082-3409/97 $10.00

schedule workers for the next day.

Consider building an object-oriented system to schedule workers to faults in each FDC. Rules should be incorporated into this system to provide better constraints representation and inference ability to the system.

The following requirements are listed as the basis of the system:

- Every afternoon before workers finish work, this system schedules available workers against existing faults for the next day (ie. one day scheduling only).
- Faults are located scatteredly in suburbs. The urgency of a fault is identified by a priority integer from 1-9, where 9 is the highest priority.
- Higher priority faults should be scheduled before low priority faults.
- At the initiation state, a worker is dispatched from the FDC to a suburb to fix a fault. It takes a fixed amount of time for each worker to travel to a fault.
- A worker starts fixing a fault as soon as he/she reaches it. It takes a fixed amount of time to fix a fault. The worker will then head for another fault.
- A fault in a suburb will be erased after a worker has fixed the fault.
- The schedule report should include fault details assigned to each worker, the time stamp and time taken traveling between different fault sites.

Schedular++ is not a resource optimization program, instead, it is a resource allocation program constrained by business rules specified by users. This reflects the fact that in a rapidly changing business world, the policies and rules of scheduling are reviewed constantly and adjusted according to available time and resources. The following rules are built inside the knowledge objects of Schedular++:

Attraction Rule

To efficiently manage the workers and avoid the situation when all workers are going to one suburb with many faults, while ignoring other suburbs with less faults, a suburb with faults but no workers should be highlighted, so that urgent faults in non-attended suburbs will also be serviced in time.

> If there is no work in a suburb, the attraction generated from faults in this suburb is increased by a certain amount.

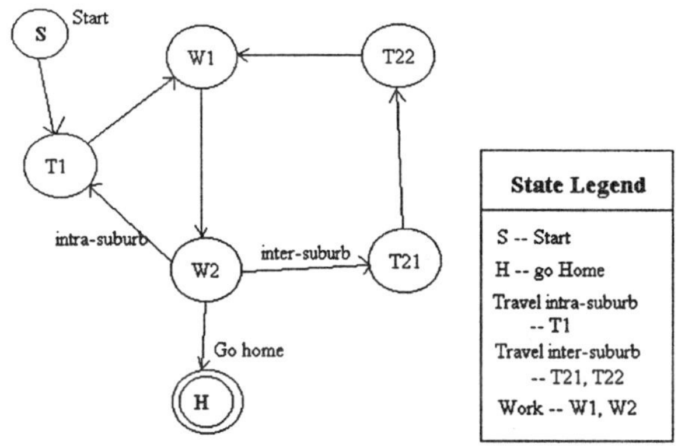

Figure 1: The transition states of a worker object

Selection Rule

At the end of fixing a fault, the worker decides which suburb to go to for the next fault to fix. A fault with a certain severity in the current suburb should be attended before faults with the same severity in other suburbs. Urgent faults should be attended before less urgent faults. If there is no urgent fault in all suburbs, go to the suburb with the most fault attraction.

> If there is one or more remaining urgent faults in the current suburb, then stay in current suburb. If there are urgent faults in other suburbs, then go to the suburb with the most urgent fault. Otherwise, go to the suburb with the most faults attraction.

2.2 System Design

Schedular++ relies on workers who are self-activating to find the most wanted fault (at the end of time ticks) themselves. Therefore the solution is built incrementally (ie. scheduling workers one time tick at a time) and opportunistically (ie. each worker finds the most attractive fault among the remaining faults). A finite state machine (FSM) has been designed to describe the transition states of the worker objects.

In Figure 1, a circle with a symbol in it denotes a distinct state for a worker object at a certain time. Table 1 lists the significance of each transition state.

Worker objects are created at S state, and destroyed at H state. Each worker object has its own state in the FSM as described in Figure 1. No other state, except state W2, needs to select the next state, since there is only one state ahead of the current state. While in state W2, a worker object is facing the selection of a state to go to. The worker can either go to state T1 (ie. to fix a fault in the same suburb as the current

State	Significance
S	A worker starts from FDC, the initiation state of the object life cycle.
T1	Intra-suburb travel. Takes 1 time tick.
T21	First time tick of the inter-suburb travel.
T22	Second time tick of the inter-suburb travel.
W1	First time tick of the working time.
W2	Second time tick of the working time.
H	Go home, the final state of the object life cycle.

Table 1: A worker object's transition states

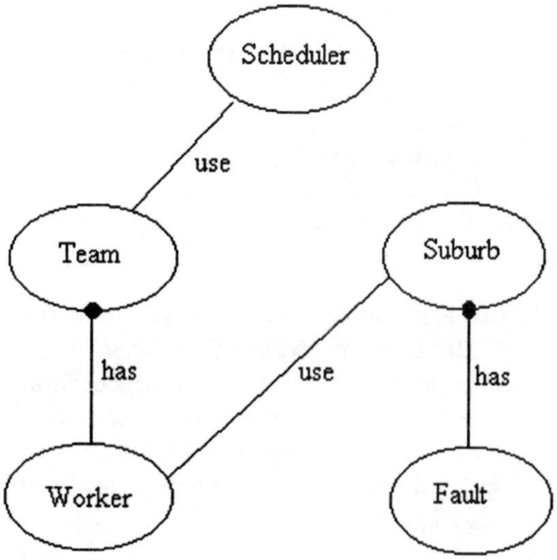

Figure 2: The class diagram of Schedular++

suburb), or go to state T21 (ie. to fix a fault in a different suburb as the current suburb), or go to state H (ie. to go home when his/her maximum working hour is reached). The selection is made as a result of consulting the selection rule embedded in the worker object.

Figure 2 describes all classes and their relationships in Schedular++. Since worker objects are the only group of active objects which move around and hunt for faults, we therefore need to control the pace of hunting and realize the amount of faults left unassigned at a certain time. As a result, a schedular object is designed to send time ticks to all worker objects, and worker objects consult rules at each time tick to decide if they should fire up their move method. To effectively group worker objects together, we make a team object which logically holds all worker objects. Suburb objects are also built to hold all faults and all worker objects in the same suburb.

The scheduling process can be described as the following object interactions (please refer to Figure 1 for state reference):

1. Each suburb object creates fault objects in its region, and worker objects are created at FDC. All worker objects are in S state.
2. The schedular object sends a time tick to the team object, the team object then distributes the time tick to all worker objects.
3. When a worker object receives a time tick, if he/she is not already in W2 state, he/she will step into the next state as described in finite state machine following the current state in the next time tick.
4. If the worker object is already in S or W2 state (ie. at the end of finishing the current fault), he/she is facing the decision of whether he/she should go to T1 (intra-state traveling) or T2 (inter-state traveling). This is actually determined by which suburb he/she should go to for the next time tick.

   To make this decision, the worker object will query the selection rule. The selection rule first ascertains if there are still urgent faults in the current suburb. If there is, the rule returns the current suburb. Otherwise, if there are urgent faults in other suburbs, the rule returns the suburb with the largest number of urgent faults. Otherwise, the rule considers the attractions that the worker object is receiving from all suburbs and determines which suburb has the biggest attraction and returns that suburb. Each suburb object calculates its attraction for this worker object by consulting its embedded attraction rule. The attraction rule indicates that if there is no worker object in this suburb and there is more than one fault object, then the attraction of this suburb should be enlarged by a certain amount.
5. After having decided the next suburb to go to, the move method of the worker object will be fired up and moves the worker object to that suburb. The time of traveling depends on the location of the next fault. If the next fault is in the same suburb as the current one, the worker object will take one time tick to travel. If the next fault is in a different suburb as the current suburb, the worker object will take two time ticks to travel. After traveling to the next fault, the worker object will take the next two following time ticks to fix that fault.

Immediately after the worker object picks up the fault, the fault will be added to his assign list, and then the fault object will be deleted from the suburb.

6. At the time the worker object makes selections via consulting the selection rule (at the end of W2 state), the selection rule checks if the worker's working hour is close to his/her maximum working hour. If so, the worker object will move to H state and finishes the scheduling.
7. After all worker objects finish scheduling, the assign list of each worker object contains all faults assigned to the worker.

2.3 System Implementation

2.3.1 Rules in Schedular++

The object-oriented design breaks down this scheduling problem into many separate smaller problems, therefore the complex scheduling is performed by relatively simple methods. These simple methods allow easy inclusion of rules to alter planning methods in certain circumstances. Because each entity represents such a small part of the overall problem, the rules required for each entity are simple, few in number, and tailored to each object's methods. Almost no interaction occurs between the rules because they are related only to the knowledge objects to which they are attached. The small number and simple form of the rules make it easier for users to enter and change these rules themselves. However, in Schedular++, all rules are hard-coded and only intended to proof the concept of knowledge objects.

Rules in Schedular++ can be divided into two categories, derivation rules and constraint rules. The derivation rules infer new data from the existing data and the constraint rules restrict object's structure and behaviour. In Schedular++, we use a derivation rule (ie. the selection rule for worker objects) to derivate the next suburb for a worker to go, and we use a constraint rule (ie. the attraction rule for suburb objects) to constrain attractions values for the suburb objects.

In Schedular++, rules are designed with the following behaviour:

- Query Rules

Rules are implemented as query rules in Schedular++. This means it can be consulted as many times as you like without any side effect to attributes of the objects. The distinction between a rule and a method in an Schedular++ object is, rules do not change their environment, and methods could update objects attributes.

- Rule-Based Methods

Some methods of objects in Schedular++ are expressed as:

```
IF query-rules THEN action
```

This arrangement makes it possible to fire up object methods if environment changes are detected by these rules.

2.3.2 Knowledge Objects in Schedular++

Worker objects have the selection rule as:

```
RULES SelectionSuburb for Worker
(1) IF there is one or more urgent local
    faults THEN
suburb is the current suburb.
(2) ELSE IF there are urgent faults in other
    suburbs THEN suburb is the suburb with
    the highest attraction from urgent faults.
(3) ELSE
    suburb is the most attractive suburb.
```

The above selection rule is called by the method 'SelectSuburb' in each worker object. The selection rule does not change any attributes of objects, but just advising a suburb for the next move. It is the method 'getJob' to change the location of worker objects.

Suburb objects have the attraction rule as:

```
RULES float Attraction for Suburb
(1) IF No_worker_in_suburb THEN
    Attraction is sumFaultUrgency + 2.
(2) OTHERWISE
    Attraction is sumFaultUrgency.
```

The above attraction rule is called by the method 'hasAttraction'. The method 'hasAttraction' returns the attraction value to a worker object who is comparing attractions from all suburbs. The attraction rule does not change any attributes of objects. It returns the attraction of all faults inside a suburb object relative to a work object.

Further implementation and testing details are omitted in this paper due to size restrictions.

References

[Henke 1994] Henke, A. (1994) Scheduling space shuttle missions: using object-oriented techniques. Stottler henke Assoc Inc, Belmont, CA, USA, *AI Expert*, March 1994, 16–24.

Towards Individualized Information Navigation Tools That Adapt to User Domain Expertise

Kerstin Voigt
Department of Computer Science
California State University, San Bernardino
San Bernardino, CA 92407

Abstract

The navigation of information spaces can be accelerated by restructuring the ways in which the information space is presented to the user. Individuals with little expertise in the browsed subject benefit less from speedy access of material when fast access comes at the expense of the information being moved out of its original context and thereby rendered incoherent. To ensure that users with varying expertise will benefit from individualization it seems necessary to strike user×topic-specific compromises between maximizing access speed and minimizing loss of coherence.

1 Introduction

In this paper, we report on an individualization tool SKIPPER (see [3, 4]). SKIPPER is designed to operate in conjunction with existing information browsers, e.g., Netscape.

More recent developments of SKIPPER have made us keenly aware of the possibility that individualized presentation of information may result in the information's *loss of coherence.* The desired reduction in access cost of an item can result in the information's being presented out of its original context. This in turn can render the information incomprehensible to the user. The body of this paper will suggest ways to consolidate the desires for reduced access cost and information coherence through solving a multi-objective optimization problem that strives to strike a viable compromise between these potentially opposing forces.

1.1 Individualized information access

We view a space of interlinked hypertext documents (e.g., the World Wide Web) as a tree structure. The documents vary in their degree of relevance to the user as indicated by relevance scores (valued between 0 and 1) associated with each document. Assume that a simple information space with associated relevance scores is given as depicted in Figure 1(I). Further assume that in order to access a document, the tree is to be traversed layer-by-layer, from left to right siblings, until the document is found (one can also imagine the children of each node as choices in a hierarchical menu structure). In the example, document F with high relevance 0.8 is relatively costly to access. A customized version of the tree would strive to make F more cheaply accessible. For example, the restructured information space shown in Figure 1(II) is

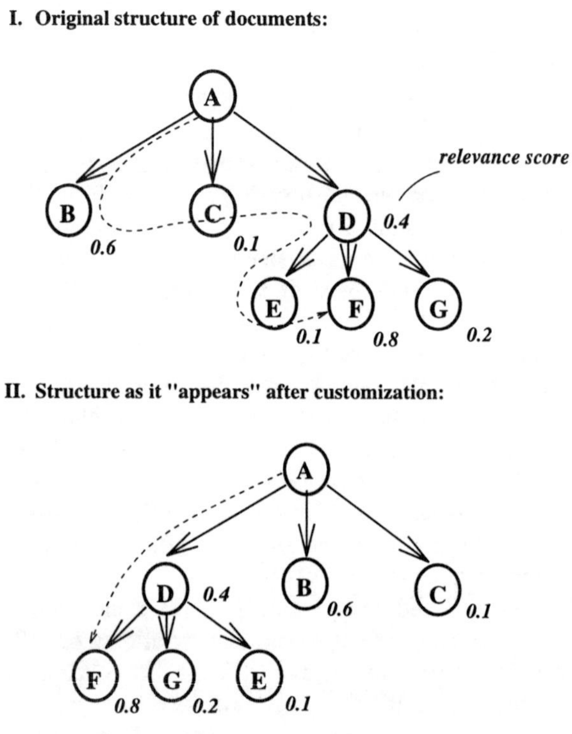

Figure 1: I. Information structure before individualization. II. After individualization, more relevant documents are more cheaply accessible.

more tailored to the needs of a user who regards document F as very relevant, but is less interested in, say, documents C or E. Whether the new document order will affect the *coherence* of document F, however, is another matter. Addressing the latter is one of the distinguishing features of our project.

2 Cost-Model for Information Access

We approach the individualization of information access as a task of optimizing a multi-objective cost function. The following sections will introduce the components of our cost model and formulate the op-

1082-3409/97 $10.00 © 1997 IEEE

timization problem.

The *cost of accessing* an information item (e.g., document F in Figure 1) is a function of the total number of descendents that need to be scanned laterally (left-to-right) for each node on the path from the root to the target document. We compute access cost $AccCost(x)$ as

$$\frac{AccCost(Parent(x))+Posit(x)/Nsibs(x)}{maxdepth-1}$$

(Function $Nsibs(x)$ returns the number of siblings of x, and $Posit(x)$ is the position of x among its siblings.)

Textual information is typically embedded within the context of other information (e.g., introduction, elaboration, follow-up). Information is also usually comprehended best within the intended context. Altering the presentation of information therefore carries the risk of displaying information out of its original context, and thereby compromising its coherence. *Loss of coherence* due to restructuring is measured by

$$CohLoss(x) = \frac{Viols(x)}{Nsibs(x)\times 2^{maxdepth-Depth(x)}}$$

$Viols(x)$ is equal to the number of violated "precedence constraints". Precedence constraints are constraints that must hold between parts of a text for the text to be maximally coherent.

The objective for individualization is to reduce access cost for an item x while preserving coherence. We model the combination of both objectives as the weighted sum $TCost(x)$ defined as

$$TCost(x) = w_1\, AccCost(x) + w_2\, CohLoss(x),$$
$$\text{where } w_1, w_2 \geq 0,\ w_1 + w_2 = 1.0$$

Proper choices for weights $w1$ and w_2 are critical in our approach to individualized information access as explained later.

$Relv(x)$ be the user-specific relevance associated with item x (see also [3]). Then individualizing the information space for the user can be cast as an optimization problem; here we seek to optimize

$$\textstyle\sum_x (TCost(x) - Relv(x))^2 = max.$$

Maximizing the objective function requires that the greater the relevance of an information item is, the more important it is to relocate it to a more cheaply accessibly position within the information structure.

3 Weights From User Expertise

The relative weights w_1 and w_2 play key roles in determining which organization of the information items should be adopted as the basis for individualizing the browser. Excessive weight on access cost (w_1) can lead to information presented in isolation and lacking coherence. Excessive weight on coherence (w_2) may result in insufficient speedup of information access. An appropriate balance needs to be struck, and the most satisfactory setting of weights is expected vary greatly from user to user.

A user's self-rating of expertise in the browsed subject matter translates quite naturally into two relative weights. Selecting lesser levels of expertise translate into a smaller weight for access cost (w_1), and a relatively larger emphasis on coherence (w_2).

On-line adaptation through expertise adjustment. Requiring the user to self-rate his/her levels of expertise is expected to have little detrimental effect on an otherwise user-friendly interface. We believe that it can be most useful to have an "expertise meter" permanently displayed by the information browser. The user is invited to adjust the meter at any point during browsing. Browsing may lead the user from one subject area to another. The user's expertise levels may change relative to the changing information subspaces, and an explicit adjustment to the recorded expertise level is appropriate and necessary for the browser to adapt its presentation the the new performance requirements.

4 Discussion

SKIPPER, the tool to individualize information browsers with the above novel features currently exists as a prototype. We are planning more reality-oriented experimentation with the tool in order to establish its true performance and ultimate user-acceptance of this kind of individualization. Among our questions are: Are users satisfied with the speedup of access to relevant information? Are they willing and able to tolerate the provided levels of information coherence? Do ratings of expertise translate into appropriate weights as suggested above? Will users appreciate the ability of adapting the interface across different portions of the information space? Answers to these questions will also enable us to fine-tune our current cost model.

Acknowledgements

Thanks go to Chetan Prakash for valuable suggestions regarding the cost model and presentation in general.

References

[1] D. Dee-Lucas, "Effects of Overview Structure on Study Strategies and Text Representations for Instructional Hypertext," in *Hypertext and Cognition*, Rouet et. al, (Eds.), Lawrence Erlbaum Associated, 1996.

[2] P. W. Foltz, "Comprehension, Coherence, and Strategies in Hypertext and Linear Text," in *Hypertext and Cognition*, Rouet et. al, (Eds.), Lawrence Erlbaum Associated, 1996.

[3] K. Voigt, "SKIPPER: A tool that Lets Browsers Adapt to Changes in Document Relevance to Its User," *Proceedings of the Sixth International Workshop on Research Issues in Data Engineering*, February 1996, New Orleans, LA.

[4] K. Voigt, "Sacrificing vs. Salvaging Coherence: An Issue for Adaptive Agents in Information Navigation," *AAAI-96 Workshop on Intelligent Adaptive Agents, AAAI-Techreport*, August 1996, Portland, Oregon.

An Intelligent Directory-assistance System using Natural Language Processing and Mapping

Hideki KAWABE, Yoshimi FUKUMURA, Nobuo MUTOH, Hiroaki KARASAWA, and Shigehito IWASE

NTT Information and Communication Systems Laboratories
3-9-11 Midori-cho, Musashino-shi, Tokyo 180 Japan

Abstract

A telephone directory-assistance system has been developed that uses natural language processing and mapping to reduce the time an operator spends looking for requested information. Its address-analysis function has an average response time of 0.15 s with 99% accuracy. Its map-guidance function has a response time of about 3 s for 100 KB of map data. Its search- expansion function decreases operator's keying. Using this system, operators spend an average of 20% less time searching for information.

1. Introduction

When providing a telephone directory-assistance service, operators search a directory for the telephone number corresponding to the given name and address. Some inquiries are more ambiguous in that the name and address do not match those in the directory. In this case, the operator must search for the phone number by using various search assistance techniques. An effective directory-assistance system should reduce the search time, and be independent of an operator's retrieval skills and abilities. We have applied natural language processing and mapping to an on-line directory-assistance system for telephone numbers.

2. Analysis of directory-assistance system

Table 1. Problems and countermeasures.

	Problem	Countermeasure
hearing phase	ambiguous or inaccurate customer recall	search approximately
	slips of the tongue	confirm the inquiry
	incorrect hearing	confirm the inquiry
inputting phase	incorrect keying	correct automatically
	* incorrect separation of inputting address	analyze address using natural language processing
	missing words or incorrect word order in a company name	analyze name using natural language processing
searching phase	* too many results when reducing conditions of inquiry	search expansion to neighboring addresses
	* no notice about searched area	map displaying function

* problems analyzed in this work

First, we analyzed why the operator's search time is sometimes quite long. We found that problems occurred in the hearing phase, the inputting phase and searching phase listed in Table 1. We concentrated on the latter two phases and identified countermeasures to the problems. We developed those that we thought would have the most impact on processing time.

3. Address analysis

An overview of the address analysis method is shown in Fig. 1. First, the address is input using natural language text (in Japanese kana characters). The original input is then analyzed, ignoring the order of the address. Next, the address order is automatically corrected. Any building names are then analyzed. Finally, an address code is generated that can distinguish any address in Japan. The main difference between our system and conventional natural language processing is the functional separation between the morphologic analysis and the semantic analysis. This is done because an address is not a sentence but a series of nouns. This paper assumes the Japanese word order of addresses which is opposite to the English. (The suffix "to"(ト) indicates a prefecture in Japanese.)

(1) morphologic analysis

An operator generally separates the address words using the "space" character such as "トウキョウト シンジュクク ニシシンジュク"(Tokyo-to Shinjuku-ku Nishi-shinjuku). Morphologic analysis ignores these spaces and divides the address into words by referring to a dictionary.

(2) semantic analysis

This process analyzes the relations between words and generates an address-code representing a unique address. The address is automatically rearranged into the standard Japanese address format. And if the end of an address word does not correspond to the beginning, the end is automatically corrected.

(3) intention understanding

If more than one address code is generated by the semantic analysis, the operator must select one. Intention understanding compares the address-codes with the area the customer is calling

1082-3409/97 $10.00

from, and identifies the most likely code.

(4) building-name analysis

If a building name is included in the inquiry, this function divides it into words by referring to a dictionary. It then searches the table of building names using the building name and the address code to get the address code of the building.

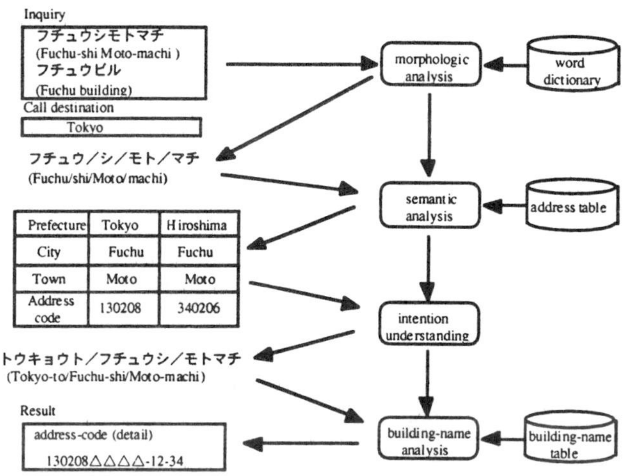

Figure 1. Overview of address-analysis method.

In implementation of this function in a directory-assistance system, the measured response time was about 0.15 s per inquiry, and more than 99% of the test queries were handled correctly.

4. Map guidance

The operator can call up a map covering the area of the address being searched and use the map guidance function as follows.

- If a phone number isn't found for the first input address, operator can simply clickon another likely address displayed on the map.
- If the address of the returned phone number is different from the input address (as sometimes happens with search expansion), the operator can compare the locations of the two addresses to determine if the number is likely to be correct.

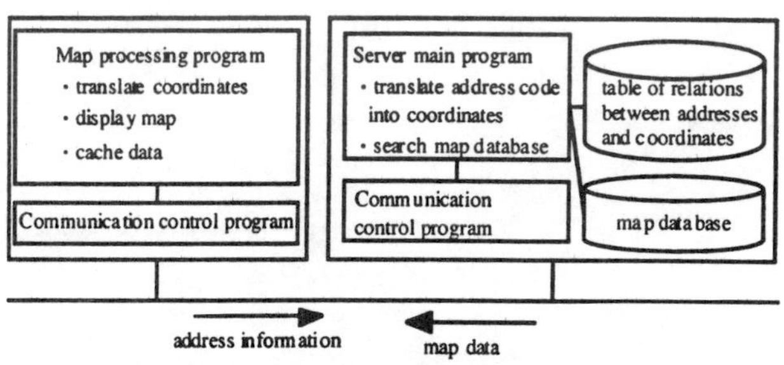

Figure 2. Structure of map-guidance function.

This function has three features: map data division, data caching, and controlled order of display. A mapping system for directory assistance must have a fast response time. The structure of our map guidance function is shown in Fig. 2.

(1) map data division

When map data is divided into a single grid, unnecessary data is sent from the server to the client if the search area is smaller than one block of the grid. Similarly, if the search area covers more than one block, response time will be slow. We thus use several grids of various sizes to divide our maps, so that a block that matches the search area closely can be selected and the response time can be decreased.

(2) data caching in client memory

All map data sent to the client, whether it is displayed or not, is stored in the client's memory. Then if the search area is changed, only the data not already stored in the client's memory must be sent This reduces the data transfer and response times.

(3) control order of display

It is important that the operators can comprehend the displayed map quickly. Therefore, we defined two levels of map data. Area-wide information, such as locality boundaries and railway lines, is displayed first because it is very important for getting an overall perspective. More specific information, such as roads, buildings, and place names, is then displayed.

In implementation of this function in a directory-assistance system, a response time of about 3 s can be achieved for 100 KB of map data per inquiry.

5. Search expansion

When an inquiry is for a company name, the address is usually ambiguous because customers do not know the complete address. The search expansion function thus automatically searches the neighboring areas when a match is not found for the initial address. The implementation of this function in a directory-assistance system enabled operators to answer inquiries more easily.

6. Conclusion

We have developed an intelligent directory-assistance system that reduces the time an operator spends looking for requested information. It uses three functions: address analysis using natural language processing, map guidance using nationwide maps, and search expansion. Using our implemented directory-assistance system, operators spend an average of 20% less time searching.

References

(1) Dumais, S. (1991) Improving the retrieval of information from external sources, *Behavior Research Methods, Instruments & Computers*, 23, pp. 229-236.

(2) Ohyama, M., Iwase, S., and Hashida, Y. : "Directory Assistance System Using a Natural Language", IEEE GLOBECOM'86, pp. 684-688.

Session G.3

Panel Session: Data Mining I

Moderators:
Jaideep Srivastava, University of Minnesota, USA
Bamshad Mobasher, University of Minnesota, USA

Panelists:
Sara Graves, University of Alabama, Huntsville, USA
Mike Pazzani, University of California, Irvine, USA
James Pitkow, Georgia Institute of Technology and Xerox PARC
Padhraic Smyth, University of California, Irvine, USA
Bhavani Thuraisingham, MIRTE Corporation, USA

Session H.1

Intelligent Agents and Applications II

Session Chair:
Moon Kim, Konkuk University, Korea

Java-based Intelligent Mobile Agents for Open System Management

Stefan Covaci, Tianning Zhang, Ingo Busse
GMD FOKUS
Kaiserin-Augusta-Allee 31, 10589 Berlin, Germany

Abstract

Traditional approaches for network and service management are not suitable for heterogeneous, rapidly changing and extending telecommunications environments. This paper discusses the use of Java-based intelligent mobile agents in the field of open system management. It first presents a Java-based mobile agent platform supporting the mobile management agents. Based on the mobility framework, the paper then describes an intelligence platform which supports the specification and processing of management solution knowledge implemented as intelligent mobile agents. The management solutions are viewed as java-based rules, which are organized into a hierarchy by the specialization/generalization relationships among the network situations which the management solutions are developed for. The proposed intelligence paradigm and the associated knowledge processing mechanism offer the advantages of Object-Oriented development in a widely distributed telecommunications environment. The paper introduces an appealing alternative or extension to the current network management solutions.

***Key-words**: Network management, service management, intelligent agents, mobile agents, Java*

1 Introduction

In the traditional approaches of network and service management, i.e. in the field of SNMP[13] and TMN[15]-based management, an agent has a standardized or proprietary interface, providing a fixed functionality, and is running in a specific place. It provides a limited view of the local resources at a remotely accessible management interface. This is used by management applications to monitor the state of the resources or to perform configuration operations via the SNMP or the CMIP protocol.

For several reasons such approaches seem to be insufficient in a dynamically changing, heterogeneous environment which we are facing in the network and service management area today. Here we have to deal with a multi-technology, multi-vendor equipment based environment that is rapidly developing due to technology improvements. This is quite obvious when considering the growing extensions that each vendor defines and offers in addition to the existing management interface standards.

Furthermore, network and service management do not only include the technical supervision of the hardware but it should cover also service and business layer aspects, especially in a multi-domain networked environment, where management systems of different authorities should interact within the open service market. In such a competitive environment a provider must be able to adapt/introduce its services quickly to the demand of the market or of even individual customers.

The current management standards are not flexible enough to build dynamically extensible management solutions.

Another key issue that is not sufficiently addressed in the traditional management frameworks is the support for the acquisition and processing of management expertise. The complexity of modern telecommunications environment means that network and service management have to deal with a large amount of complicated and highly inter-related information, and have to derive management decisions based on very sophisticated expertise. Traditional management approaches focus on the syntactical aspects of the network management information, and rely on the human managers to make management decisions. Lack of enough qualified experts is now becoming a major obstacle in realizing efficient and effective management of global networks and services.

A software design paradigm with support the acquisition and deployment of management knowledge will play a key in the future of telecommunications network management.

Moreover, the management expertise and the related management solutions for specific problems can be acquired or developed anywhere within the global telecommunication market. The same network problems, however, can occur

1082-3409/97 $10.00 © 1997 IEEE

in any remote sites lacking the necessary expertise for maintaining the solutions, and which are also far away from the source of the solutions. There must be therefore a solution for moving the management expertise over the network from its provider to the consumer sites.

To reduce requirement on human expertise and network resources in installing, maintaining and deploying the management expertise, management solutions in the form of autonomous, intelligent mobile entities will play an important role.

The promising approach in this context is the usage of intelligent mobile agents (called IAs hereafter).

An IA is defined as an *autonomous* software entity which, with certain degree of *intelligence*, can *migrate* to and operate in different network nodes to achieve its objectives.

A solution based on IAs has several advantages compared to the traditional management approaches:

- reducing the number of remote interactions and the associated traffic load for realizing the management functionality, via autonomous IA operations,
- reducing the requirement on human intelligence or personnel qualifications during the installation and operation of the management solution, by utilizing the IA intelligence,
- supporting dynamic and flexible management functionality by delegating management solutions *on demand*,
- increasing the fault tolerance and robustness of the management solutions by reducing the dependency of the management operations on the remote network connections,
- enabling, via IA intelligence, mobility and autonomy, a global open service market for network and service management solutions and expertise, where management solutions and expertise can be produced, traded, transported and consumed.

Generally, the computing and communication overhead for management activities can be reduced by putting the agent in place when a specific management action has to be performed, and destroying it when there is no longer a need for it.

Certain management tasks, like gathering usage data and computing/transmission charges, can be located close to the real resources. Then we have only the reduced accounting data that need to be transported. This would reduce the communication overhead and thus the network load.

Such aspects are of major importance in a multi-domain environment where a management solution provider operates the service from a remote site over a wide-area network, which is usually of low bandwidth and has long round-trip time.

Each piece of management software solutions in the managed environment can frequently be outdated, e.g., because a bug was discovered and fixed, or because a new environment requires a different or extended functionality. Using IAs the functionality within an agent can be easily replaced by a new version of the software from a remote site.

The ability to move functionality to several places for execution allows for load balancing and results in a fault tolerant system. IAs can be directed to places with free computing power. In case an agent fails, the functionality can be loaded in a different place on another host. Each host running the agent execution environment can act as a back-up system.

A provider can react flexibly on the changing environment in a customer domain within a Customer Premises Network (CPN) and especially in an intranet management outsourcing scenario [5]. A roaming IA can collect configuration data about the customer domain and return to the provider. Further IAs can be configured and sent to the customer domain according to the equipment installed and with management functionality required, without a manual interaction between the customer and the provider. In case of special fault conditions additional agents for fault analysis/localisation can be sent to the customer domain performing analysis tasks.

2 The Agent Infrastructure

The application of the agent technology has already a history and spreads over many areas [1], including user interface/personal assistance, mobile computing, information retrieval & filtering, data mining, smart messaging, the electronic marketplace, telecommunication services and service / network management. The last area represents a still new application field for agent technology, now rapidly gaining importance in the emerging global Information Infrastructure [11].

The developments of agent technology are currently divided into two separated worlds: static agents and mobile agents.

In the context of static agents, people are focusing on the intelligence aspects of non-mobile agent technology, developing knowledge-based mechanisms for representing and processing application specific expertise and solutions, and for agent co-operations ([6] [8] [23] etc.). The typically used knowledge-based language paradigms have advantages in terms of flexibility, extensibility, reusability, user friendliness and enhanced service support over conventional languages which are typically used in the mobile agent context.

Research and developments in the area of mobile agents focus on the platform for supporting agent migration and management. Agents in this context are usually any program codes in some interpreted imperative languages with strong Internet association. Most important languages in this context are Java, Tcl/Tk or Telescript. The Internet flavour of such languages and the demand for mobile solutions in a distributed global telecommunications environment enable such developments to gain quickly academical and commercial importance. Examples of important platforms developed in this context include the IBM's Aglet [12], Crystaliz's MuBot [3], General Magic's Telescript [10]and Odyssey[9], the Open Group's MOA [21], and GMD FOKUS's JMAF [14].

The separation of static and mobile agents is in fact very *artificial* and was the result of the different backgrounds in which the two technologies emerged. With the distribution and complexity of the telecommunications environment, both mobility and the intelligence based on knowledge processing will be needed for IA-based network and service management solutions.

Basically, the infrastructure supporting the operation of the IAs can be divided into two sub-platforms:

- The *agent intelligence platform* supports the representation and processing of the application specific mobile knowledge. Such mobile knowledge includes the representation of the IAs and the co-operation messages among the IAs.

- The *agent mobility platform* provides the common facilities which will be needed for the management, migration of IAs and the transportation of IA co-operation messages. Such common facilities can include:

  - IA life cycle management (creation, deletion, suspension and activation),
  - IA naming and location services,
  - IA transportation and agent message transportation,
  - security

The agent intelligent platform is in fact the focus of current developments in the area of static agents, while the agent mobility platform falls into the domain of mobile agents. Current standardization in OMG [4], e.g. only addresses the agent mobility platform functionalities.

The agent intelligence platform can be regarded as a client layer of the agent mobility platform, which utilizes the facilities offered by the underlying mobility platform components (figure 1).

Figure 1: The IA Infrastructure

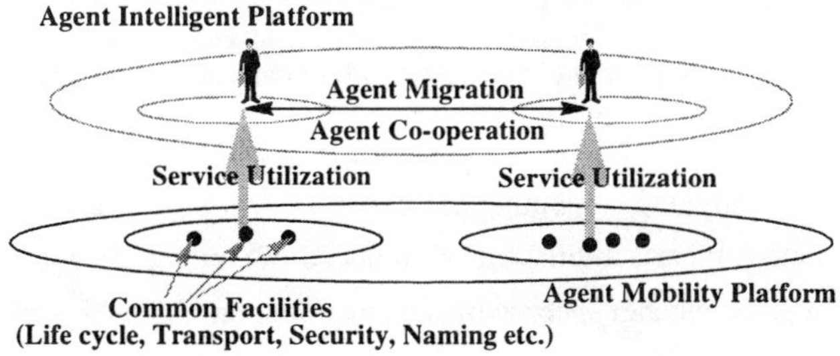

3 The IA Mobility Platform

A suitable support for extensible and mobile agents requires an environment that is available on a number of platforms, because code and state information need to be portable from one execution environment to the next. Java seems to offer a good base for this purpose.

The JavaVM is available on all common computing platforms and provides a machine independent execution environment. It was designed for downloading and executing code from WWW servers so that the basic functionality for moving code is available. A first step for moving the state of objects is provided by the object serialization facility ([19]) currently released by Sun. It allows to stream an object including all referenced objects with minimum effort. Object serialization and the remote method invocation facility [20] allow for passing arbitrary objects from JavaVM to JavaVM between two networked hosts.

Our IA mobility platform is Java-based and makes use of the aforementioned facilities. It has three basic components: agencies, agents and a name server. The IAs discussed in this paper will be a specific type of the agents supported.

Figure 2: IA Mobility Platform

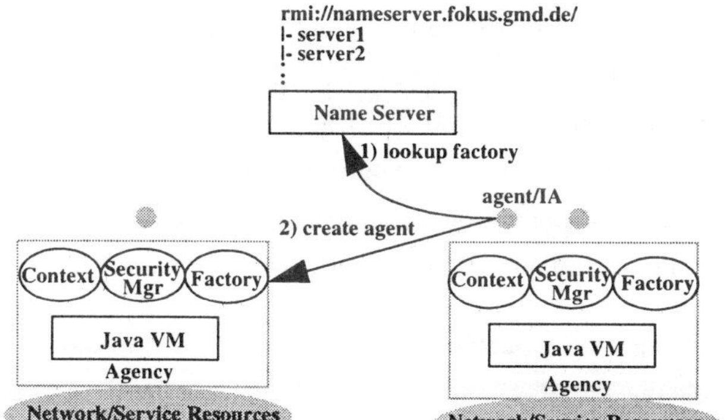

3.1 Agency

An agency has three basic objects: a factory, a context and a security manager.

The *factory object* provides a remote interface. The method *createAgent(Agent)* implements a generic agent factory that is needed to create arbitrary agents from remote or local. Each factory can be uniquely identified with the hostname and the port number. It is registered at the *name server.*

When an agent is created its object reference is stored within the *context object* in order to keep track of all agents at an agency. Then the agent is started within a thread in a separate threadgroup executing the method *run()* of the *agent* object. The *context* then provides the operation facilities to the running agent.

The *security manager object* is based on the extensions of the security feature of JDK 1.1.

3.2 Agent

The class *Agent* implements the behaviour that is common to all agents. It is abstract and cannot be instantiated. Subclass of it specifies the specific behaviour needs to be implemented.

An *agent* has an agent identifier that is globally unique, and which also identifies the current agency for this agent. It has to implement the *runnable interface*, i.e. a method *run()*. Whenever an agent is created or arrives at a new place the *agency* creates a new threadgroup with an initial thread. Within this thread the method *run()* is executed. It implements the behaviour of an *agent.*

The method *move()* allows an *agent* to change the place where it is running. It calls the method *createAgent()* at the factory of the new place and passes itself as the initial state. Then the local entry of the *context* is deleted.

Since the JavaVM does not allow to continue directly upon arrival at the new place, the method *run()* will be entered again from the very beginning. This is a drawback since it slightly complicates the programming of the behaviour within the method *run()*. Practically the method *run()* has to be implemented as a state machine, keeping the current state of execution in an attribute of the agent.

3.3 Name Server

The *name server* provides a directory or naming service. It implements a mapping of URLs to remote object references. The *factory* of an agency is registered at a *name server*. This allows us to use a URL to identify the destination in a *move* operation on a mobile agent.

4 The Intelligence Platform for Agent-based Network and Service Management

To deal with the complexity of managing the emerging telecommunications environment [11], just like in any other areas which provide real challenges to human intelligence, we have to introduce some machinery with needed machine intelligence. Such intelligence can assist or partially replace the human experts in fulfilling their tasks.

It is in this context that the *intelligence* based on management expertise, and its combination with the mobility of agent technology become promising factors for solving network and service management problems.

As discussed above, the intelligence platform is regarded as a client of the mobile agent platform, which makes use of the facilities provided. Within the agent intelligence platform an IA is a subclass of the generic agent class supported by the mobility platform.

Each IA hosts a specific *run()* method which realizes the inference procedure on the management knowledge of the IA. This inference procedure finds out and initiates the appropriate management actions.

4.1 The IA Knowledge Representation

In an open environment, numerous players can contribute to the management solutions with their own experiences and views. A suitable framework supporting such a global and co-operative acquisition of knowledge will therefore determine the success or failure of the IA-based approach. The following characteristics of such a knowledge acquisition framework will play a key role:

- Reusability and Interoperability

The global telecommunications environment encompasses a tremendous number of heterogeneous sub-environments. The success of any solutions in this world depends on their capability of integrating themselves into the operation environments, i.e. the ability to be applied in a wide range of contexts.

Being important in all the scientific areas, *reusability* and *interoperability* provide the dominating requirements in the case of distributed resource management.

Reusability and interoperability in the distributed environment are usually achieved through standardization at different syntactical or semantic levels, and through Object-Oriented constructions.

- Accumulative Construction

To cope with the complexity of the management scenarios, an enormous amount of very complicated knowledge has to be used. Such knowledge can only be derived from profound experiences which have to be collected gradually during the evolution of the resources.

Management however has to be carried out during the whole life cycle of the resources. At the beginning it has to be based on some very primitive management knowledge and operations. As time passes by, new knowledge concerning the deeper inter-relationships between the components of the environment and the detailed behaviour of the components will be obtained, and new management operations can be added due to new requirements and new facilities. All such new knowledge and functionalities have to be gradually integrated into the management stations.

In this sense, accumulative construction of the intelligent management systems is also an important factor in realizing effective management of future networks. The most important technology in this context is the Object-Oriented style of development, which is also the major philosophy of the our IA-based approach for network and service management.

The knowledge for the management IA is the set of *management solutions* that address the problems that can occur in the network. Each management solution can be constructed from two key components:

- the *pre-condition* for the solution, in terms of the network situations that require or support the application/invocation of the solution, and
- the management plan, defined as a pre-defined sequence of management actions, including the generation of new Event Reports.

4.2 The Situation Theory for IA-based Network and System Management

Most of the currently dominating network management frameworks, including the TMN[15] or SNMP[13] based ones, view the managed network environment with its set of resources as a set of managed information entities, as depicted in figure 3.

Figure 3: Network Management View

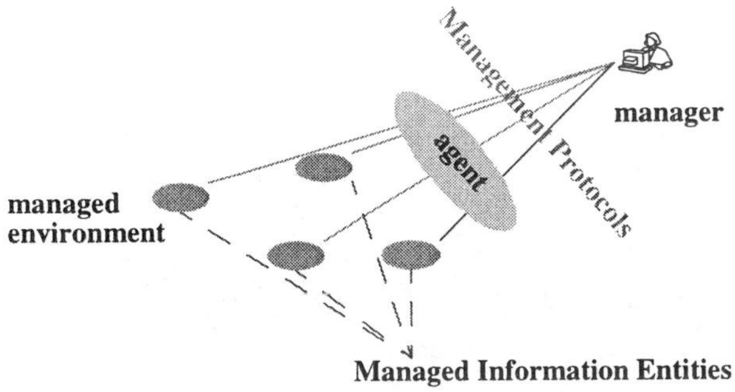

In this context, the managed resources like switches, hosts and processes are controlled by some management agents. Such management agents implement the abstract view of the underlying resources, defined as certain *managed information entities*. Such information entities can be managed or processed by the managing stations or managing processes via standardized management protocols. The protocol (SNMP, or CMIP in case of TMN) and the specification of the managed information (based on either the SMI/ SNMP or the TMN/GDMO [17] specification methodology) determine together the execution environments for any network managing entities including the IAs.

In this paper, we discuss only the TMN/CMIP-based management environment. The framework, however, can be easily adapted to a SNMP-based environment.

In a TMN/CMIP-based environment, the managed information entities are represented as Managed Object (MO) Instances. Each of such MOs can possess the following information capabilities:

- the *attributes*, which contain the status and characteristics information concerning the managed resources,
- management *actions*, which support the management operations upon the underlying resources, and
- the *notifications* with their parameters, which the managed resources can issue to the managers for signalling special events in the network. In the following we will call notifications received by the managers *Event Reports (ERs)* to maintain a simple terminology.

A manager in this context can make the following basic operations on the MOs:

- *get* for obtaining the value of an attribute by providing the Identifier of the attribute
- *set* for setting the value of a MO attribute
- call a management *action* which is supported by the MO
- receive an *ER* from the agent

In such an environment, the *current situation* in the network is characterized by the set of MO instances (with their attribute values) and the generated ERs (with their parameters).

Based on this consideration, we can develop a situation theory for modelling the situations that can occur in the network environment ([22], [23]).

Within this situation theory, a *situation concept* characterizes some possible situations that belong to a specific category and can be used to specify the pre-condition for management solutions.

To test and determine the current situation in the network, we can apply a java method *situation test*, which checks whether the current *situation* in the next work corresponds to a specific *situation concept*.

Some *situation concepts/situation tests* put more restrictions on the possible situations they characterise, and therefore characterise a smaller set of possible real situations. If a situation concept or situation test characterises a subset of situations characterised by a second situation concept/situation test, we say that the first situation concept/situation test is a *specialization* of the second one.

With the specialization relationship, we can derive the hierarchical structuring of the *situation tests* in an Object-Oriented style. Based on the logical operations of the set theory, we can also derive logic operations on situation tests to derive specialized situation tests from more general ones. E.g. the *conjunction (composition)* of a situation test τ and any other situation tests is a specialization of τ.

Intuitively, a specialized *situation concept* contains fewer real situations and can make a closer approximation of the situation in the network. Correspondingly, a specialized *situation test* contains more restrictions on its semantics and can therefore more closely characterize the network situations.

Management plans based on specialized *situation tests* can therefore support safer, and more effective solutions of the current problems in the network. Management plans based on more general situation tests however can be applied in a wider context.

In our Java-based management environment, the pre-condition for a management solutions is specified by the *situation tests* that characterize the network situations for the management actions (management plans).

To get the side-effect free testing of the managed network environment, we restrict the management operations within a *situation test* to the CMIP *get*. With some *approximation*, we can consider the tests as side-effect free. The result of the test composition can be considered as independent of the order in which individual tests are carried out, and is always the specialization of a single test.

A *situation test* in our IA framework is just a boolean Java method which uses only the *get* methods from the CMIP API and any other Java basic methods. This property will be guaranteed by the editing environment for defining IA knowledge.

4.3 The IA Management Solution

As discussed above, a *management solution* consists of a *situation test*, which checks the situation in the environment, and a *management plan* for addressing the corresponding problems in the network by issuing management operations.

Based on the hierarchical structuring of the *situation tests*, we can have also the hierarchical relationship among the management solutions. For building up such a hierarchy of management solutions, we impose the following conventions on the development of management solutions:

- Each management solution will be contained in a separate Java package. Each management solution package for a more specific problem is positioned under the package for a more generic solution.
- The *situation test* within each management solution implies automatically the *situation tests* in all the ancestor (more generic) management solutions.

In this way we build up a hierarchy of management solutions which starts with generic management solutions at the upper part, and grows with specific management solutions positioned under more generic solutions.

The management solutions will be pre-compiled to the Java *class* files. At the time of IA creation, these *class* files will be loaded to build a corresponding hierarchical Java data structure, called the *managementHierarchy*, which contains the management solution classes.

An IA consists of the following key components in addition to the components of the mobile agents:

- the *eventMemory* for holding the set of events collected by the IA during its life time, and which are still relevant for the IA processing,
- the *currentEvent* which is driving the inferencing of the current IA,
- the *managementHierarchy* of management solutions,
- a specific *run()* method for the execution of the IA functionality.

4.4 IA Operation

The IA operation will be realized by the *run()* method which is the same for all the IAs in this context.

Figure 4: IA Operation Environment

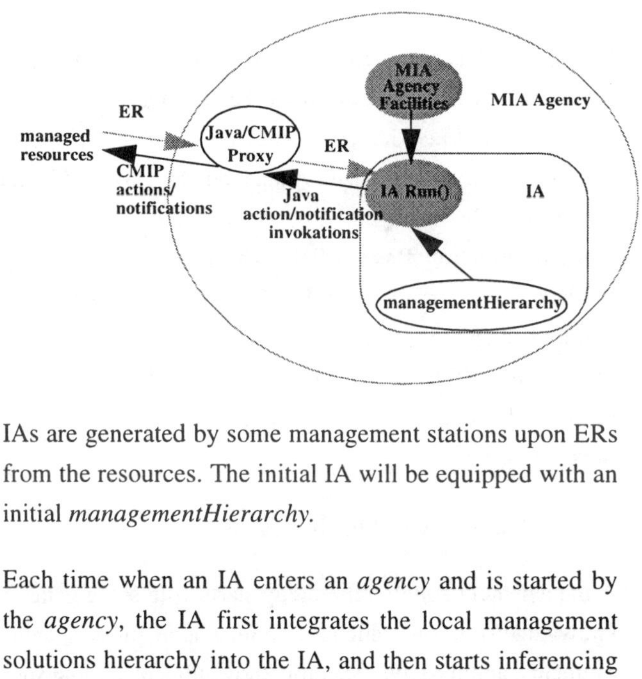

IAs are generated by some management stations upon ERs from the resources. The initial IA will be equipped with an initial *managementHierarchy.*

Each time when an IA enters an *agency* and is started by the *agency*, the IA first integrates the local management solutions hierarchy into the IA, and then starts inferencing on the knowledge hierarchy to find the suitable management operations to be issued to the managed resources via the Proxy.

To update the management solution hierarchy, the IA traverses through the local hierarchy of the Java management solution package file directories, creates an record of each management solution class, and builds up a hierarchy of management solutions (implemented in Java as vector of vectors) to be assigned to the corresponding IA variable.

After the creation of the *managementHierarchy* and the initialization of other variables, the IA starts the traversing of the hierarchy to find a most *specific (specialized)* management solution for the current situation in the network. The traversing will be done in pre-order and started at the root of the hierarchy. At each management solution node the IA will do the following:

1. create and initialize the management solution instance
2. call the *situation test* method
3. if the result of *situation test* is true, and all the children *situation tests* returned false, then call the *management plan*, otherwise continue the traversing of the hierarchy on the next management solution node.

The result of the *managementPlan* method has three possibility:

1. the method returns *null*, and sets the *currentEvent* variable to *null*

In this case the IA will be terminated.

2. the method returns *null*, but sets the *currentEvent* variable to a new ER (one from the *eventMemeory*, or a newly generated one)

In this case the IA will set the hierarchy to the subhierarchy under the current node and restart the process of traversing, based on the intermediate result coded in the new ER.

3. the method returns a new *Agency* address different from the current host

In this case, the IA host sets the *managementHierarchy* to the subhierarchy under the current node and moves the whole IA instance to the new IA Host (figure 5).

In the new network node, the IA first updates the *eventMemory* by adding to it the local events, and then tries to update the hierarchy of management solutions with the local hierarchy of solutions.

To update the management hierarchy, the new IA can also replace those nodes in the IA which are also defined in the local hierarchy (with the same package names) and the descendant nodes of such shared nodes.

After updating the IA knowledge, the IA starts execution just like in the procedure described above.

The advantage with this whole scheme is that each local network node can maintain its proprietary solutions for its local resources. The travelling IA will consider these local solutions even if these are not available in the origin node of the IA.

The pre-order traversing of the management knowledge hierarchy imposes the implicit priorities on the management solutions. This proves to be very useful in the real applications.

Figure 5: IA Execution and Mobility

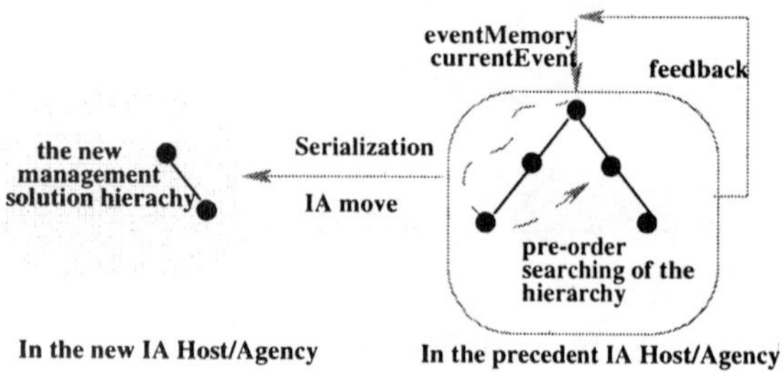

5 Summary

In the above we presented a Java-based mobile agent platform and an intelligent platform for deploying Java-based intelligent and mobile agents in open system management. The combination of mobility and the intelligence based on knowledge processing offers many new possibilities in this context.

The intelligence framework is based on:

- the collection of management solutions in an open global network environment,
- the organization of such management solutions into some global knowledge hierarchies following the application context situations of such solutions,
- using such hierarchies to support the mobile IA in finding out an optimal solution for the problems existing in the networks.

The whole approach has, among others, the following major advantages:

- Automation and delegation of management solutions via mobile, knowledge-based Agents

The management framework enables the delegation of autonomous management solutions. In this way, an enterprise can outsource ([2], [5]) part of the management responsibility and management problems to some specialized management solution providers.

Such outsourcing and the automation of management processes can greatly reduce the complexity and costs within the enterprise for managing the enterprise network resources. With the increasing complexity of broadband telecommunications environments, such reduction of costs will be a major issue in applying any management frameworks.

- Compatibility with existing environments

The approach is designed to be based on the TMN management framework and can easily be adapted to a SNMP environment. Each IA communicates with the managed resources via standardized management protocols and operates on the management view offered by the Management Information Base (MIB). The co-operation among the IAs is realized via TMN Event Reports and Event Forwarding [16] service, instead of novel co-operation languages like KQLM [6]. This approach can therefore be easily embedded in a standard conform network management environment.

- Reusability and Interoperability

A management solution hierarchy starts with some generic knowledge/solutions which are applicable in different environments, and it derives specific knowledge by adding specific information about the individual environment classes. If applied in a different environment, the generic management knowledge in the upper part of the hierarchy will continue to be valid, while the lower part situation knowledge will not be satisfied and will be simply ignored. The result is that the IA with this hierarchy operates also in a new environment, although with some loss of effectiveness.

For the same reason, one management solution hierarchy can be reused in different environments to build there the management systems.

- Accumulative and distributed construction of the global knowledge

When starting to manage an environment with an IA-based framework, we usually use a partial management solution hierarchy to initialize the management functionality. Later, with accumulating experiences and expertise, we can add more specific management solutions with new situation tests and their associated management plans, to improve the performance of the IA system.

Moreover, the management solutions can be developed/ advertised by any players anywhere in the open world. The players can also decide to maintain such solutions only in the proprietary environments, and to ask IAs who visit their sites to use such proprietary solutions instead of the generic ones.

- Standardization of global available management solutions

The hierarchical structuring of the management solutions in the Object-Oriented style enables the standardization of the relatively generic management solutions in various contexts and domains within the upper part of the hierarchy under the root. Such management solutions can be further made available to all users via hierarchical information services like the ITU-T X.500 Directory Services[18].

With these characteristics and possibilities, we expect the approach to provide a realistic management framework for the current and emerging telecommunication networks and services.

6 References

[1] Communication of the ACM Journal, *Intelligent Agent*, Vol.37, No. 7, July 1994.

[2] F. Dotti, S. Covaci, *ODP Viewpoints of Management Outsourcing*, Proceedings of the IEEE /IFIP Network and Management Symposium (NOMS'96), Kyoto, Japan, April 1996.

[3] Crystaliz, *Mobile Unstructured Business ObjecT (MuBot)[TM] Technology - A Fundamental Revolution*, http://www.crystaliz.com/MobileAgents/marketing.html.

[4] Crystaliz, General Magic, GMD FOKUS IBM and The Open Group. *Mobile Agent Facility Specification* (Joint Submission), Draft 5, April 21, 1997.

[5] F. Dotti, *Management Outsourcing in Open Distributed Environments*, Proceedings of the Enterprise Networking Workshop (ENW-96), Dallas, June 1996.

[6] T. Finin, *KQLM as a Agent Communication Language*, Proceedings of the 3rd International Conference on Information and Knowledge Management (CIKM'94), Amsterdam, 1994.

[7] FIPA, *Agent Management*, FIPA'97 Specification Part 1, April 1997.

[8] FIPA, *Agent Communication Language*, FIPA'97 Specification Part 2, April 1997.

[9] General Magic, *Odyssey*, http://www.genmagic.com/agents/odyssey.html.

[10] General Magic, *Telescript Technology: Mobile Agents*, http://www.genmagic.com/Telescript/Whitepapersh/wp4/whitepaper-4.html, 1996.

[11] *The Global Information Infrastructure: Agenda for Cooperation*, http://www.iitf.nist.gov/documents/docs/gii/giiagend.html.

[12] IBM, *IBM Aglets Workbench White Paper*, http://www.trl.ibm.co.jp/aglets/whitepaper.htm.

[13] IETF, *Structure and Identification of Management Information for TCP/IP-based Internets*, RFC 1155, May 1990.

[14] IKV, *JMAF - A Development Kit for Intelligent Mobile Agents*, http://ikv.de/products/fjmaf.html.

[15] ITU-T, Recommendation M.3010, *Principles for a Telecommunications Management Network*, March 1995.

[16] ITU-T, Recommendation X.724, *Information Technology - Open Systems Interconnection - System Management: Event Report Management Function*, 1993.

[17] ITU-T, Recommendation X.722, *Information technology - Open System Interconnection - Structure of Management Information: Guidelines for the Definition of Managed Objects*, January 1992.

[18] ITU-T, Recommendation X.500, *Information technology - Open System Interconnection - The directory: Overview of concepts, models, and services*, November 1995.

[19] Sun Microsystems, Inc., *Java Object Serialisation Specification*, Revision 0.9, May 1996.

[20] Sun Microsystems, Inc., *Java Remote Method Invocation Specification*, Revision 0.9, May 1996.

[21] The Open Group, *Mobile Objects and Agents (MOA) Project*, http://www.opengroup.org/RI/DMO/dmo.htm.

[22] T. Zhang, S. Covaci, *The Semantics of Network Management Information*, Proceedings of the 1996 IEEE INFOCOM Conference, San Francisco, March 1996.

[23] T. Zhang, S. Covaci and Radu Popescu-Zeletin, *Intelligent Agents in Network Management*, Proceedings of the 1996 IEEE GLOBECOM Conference, London, 18-22 November 1996.

Progress : an Approach for Defining and Monitoring Non Deterministic Design-to-Time Methods

François CHARPILLET and Anne BOYER
CRIN-CNRS & INRIA Lorraine,
BP 239, 54506 Vandœuvre-lès-Nancy, France
E-mail: charp@loria.fr, boyer@loria.fr

Abstract

Guaranteed response time is one of the important issues encountered in designing real-time systems. The AI community has developed various approaches to solve this problem, e.g. Anytime algorithms, Approximate processing, Design-to-time Scheduling and Progressive Reasoning. All these approaches rely on a trade-off between run-time and quality of results. In the framework of the ESPRIT projects Nos. 5146 and 7805 REAKT (Real time Knowledge Tool), we have developed a similar approach called PROGRESS (PROGressive REasoning SyStem). PROGRESS manages AI tasks with hard and soft deadlines, provided that competing methods are available for the tasks to be solved. A comparison has been drawn between our model and a conventional algorithm (Earliest Deadline Algorithm) and showed the higher robustness and efficiency of PROGRESS.

1. Introduction

Introducing AI techniques into conventional systems appears as a promising approach to deal with the increasing complexity of real-time applications such as robotics or process control. While real-time systems require predictable and continuous operations, AI techniques rely on time-consuming algorithms, with unpredictable or highly variable performances. Task execution speed is not the only parameter to consider. The ability of the system to react and meet deadlines (timeliness), its ability to stay alert to incoming events (responsiveness) and to reset task priorities according to changes in workload or resource availability (graceful adaptation) are imperative features in a knowledge processing approach to address real-time applications [4].

The European Esprit REAKT Projects (EP 5146 and 7805) come within this scope. The primary objective of those projects was to develop a set of tools and the associated methodology to apply knowledge-based systems in real-time applications [11].

Whereas the conventional real-time approaches are well-suited to domains where the needs and availability of resources are predictable, we propose a method (PROGRESS) for dealing with computational processes with highly variant responses times. Similar paradigms shave been proposed so far such as anytime algorithms [2][14], flexible computation [6], design-to-time [5] and progressive reasoning [12][13]. All of them rely on a trade-off between runtime and result quality. In the field of real time scheduling, some researchers are investigating a similar approach: the *imprecise computation* [9].

This paper describes how our PROGRESS model manages in the REAKT toolkit AI tasks with hard and soft deadlines and multiple competing methods. PROGRESS is close to design-to-time real-time scheduling but it extends this approach to harder real-time constraints. It has been designed as a process which gradually integrates changes and developments in the environment and in the availability of resources.

2. REAKT Architecture

The REAKT architecture extends the blackboard paradigm to deal with real-time applications. It introduces multiprocessing, progressive reasoning and advanced temporal reasoning capacities.

A REAKT application is made up of a community of agents implemented as independent tasks (see figure 1, 2).

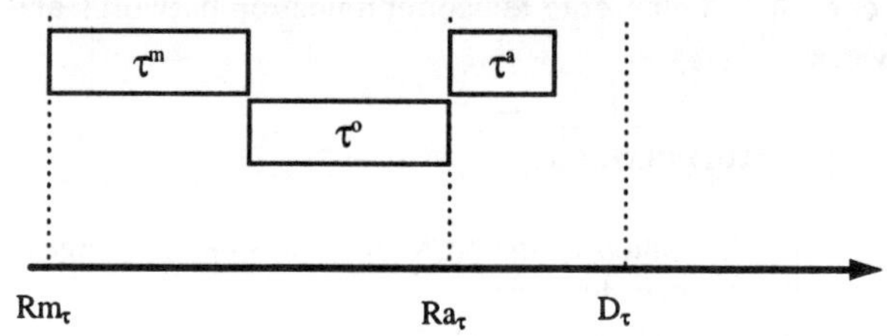

Figure1 - Decomposition of a task

1082-3409/97 $10.00 © 1997 IEEE

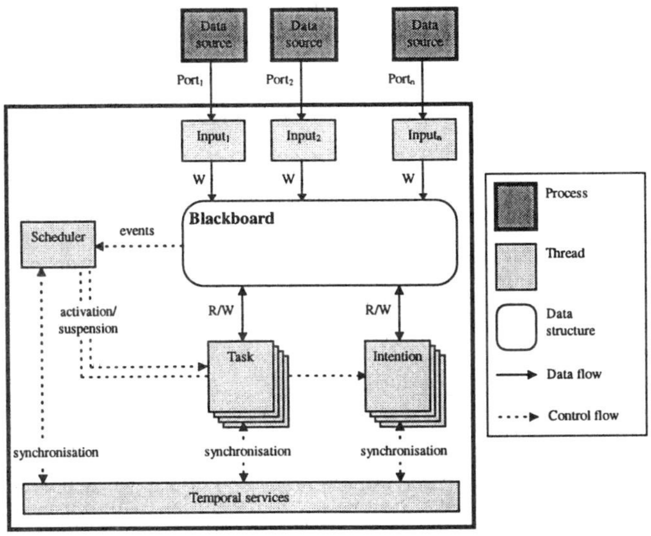

Figure -2- Global architecture of REAKT.

Each task/agent τ is composed of three parts: *mandatory*, *option* and *action* parts (cf. Figure 1) [1]. The mandatory part, activated at Rm_τ, provides a first-level solution; the optional part improves this result, using more complex reasoning mechanisms; the action part is activated before the task deadline D_τ has elapsed, and possibly pre-empts the optional part, and finally uses the best available solution to execute the necessary actions. Important characteristics of a task include its type (*periodic* or *sporadic)*, its temporal characteristics (*period* or *minimum inter-arrival time*, deadline, ...), the name of its *intention structure* [7] that implements the optional part.

A first-level real-time control layer guarantees the response time of the mandatory and action parts of all tasks. It also maximizes the amount of time available for optional second-level activities, in charge of improving the solution quality. For a given task, the basic principle is to execute the mandatory part first, then the optional part, and both to delay the beginning of the action part as much as possible and to execute it before the task deadline. The scheduling algorithm used in the real-time control layer is an adaptation [10] of the *slack-time server* algorithm [8].

Optional parts are made up of subtasks which are either refinements of the mandatory parts, or independent tasks with soft deadlines. The design of optional parts relies on the following assumptions :

- several methods, with various computation times, are available to solve a given subproblem,
- for each method, it is possible to estimate the computation time even inaccurately,
- it is assumed that the longer the time of task execution, the better the result ,
- tasks are supposed to be pre-emptable,
- the response to a given event is computed by a sequence of methods, some of them being time-constrained,
- even if a task is unexpectedly interrupted, a result is available.

Thus, option parts have been implemented as a set of pre-emptable subtasks called intentions, each being organized as a tree of steps, each step being broken down into a set of knowledge Sources or procedures (methods) implementing the set of available methods to solve the same problem. They are sorted by increasing computation time. The faster method is called « first level method» and others are called « higher-level methods ». Thus, an intention represents a set of possibilities to carry out the corresponding optional part. The successful execution of an intention consists in determining step by step a path from the root of the tree to one of its leaves.

Scheduling such intentions is complex and belongs to the generic problem of scheduling non-deterministic dependent sub-tasks. In order to manage deadlines, different policies could be adopted. The first one, derived from design-to-time approach could determine the refinement level of each step when the intention is created. Even if attractive, this policy is not suitable if an accurate prediction of the execution time of methods and computation workload is not available.

Our solution is inspired by the process used to transform contract algorithms into interruptible anytime algorithms. This consists in considering a step as a process obtained by chaining available methods together, from the first level method to the one with the best refinement level. So, at first sight, the execution of a step behaves like an interruptible anytime algorithm. As we do not control the time required for producing the first result with the lower quality, we encourage application developers to design first-level procedures to be as fast and predictable as possible, because a first-level procedure has to be executed to completion to get a minimal result for the step. If not possible, the completion of the corresponding intention is not achieved and the time spent to execute the intention is lost. Thus the main objective of scheduling is to ensure that the first-level methods required to execute an intention can be definitely completed. If no schedule exists, the intention is either discarded (its exception is fired) or kept while computation time is recovered by canceling a less important intention. Based on this model, the purpose of the scheduling algorithm is to determine the existence of a feasible schedule that meets the timing constraints of all steps (by executing at least the first-level method), and find one that maximizes the level of refinement of each steps. Such a schedule satisfies the 0/1 constraint because optional procedures are either completed or discarded. Unfortunately, the general problem of finding such an optimal schedule is NP-complete. This is why we sought a heuristic providing an approximate schedule in polynomial time. Even if not optimal, the schedule we obtain is of good value mainly because our heuristic corrects the drawback of using worst-case computation times.

3. Controlling Progressive Reasoning

Objective and definitions

Let $\{I^1, \ldots, I^N\}$ be a set of N active intentions. An intention I^i is characterized by a weight number w^i (which measures the importance of the intention), a tree of steps, a date of creation and the current step.

Let $\{S^i_1, \ldots, S^i_{N^i}\}$ be the set of steps defining the intention I^i. Each step S^i_j is characterized by a deadline d^i_j, a weight number w^i_j measuring the importance of the step (if not specified, $w^i_j = w^i$), a set of successor nodes in $\{S^i_1, \ldots, S^i_{N^i}\}$ given by the function called succ. A step S^i_j is broken down into several methods: the first-level method procedure M^i_j and the refinement methods $\{O^i_{j1}, \ldots\}$. The computation times of the first-level procedure and refinement procedures are known and are referred to as m^i_j for the computation time of the first-level agent and $\{o^i_{j1}, \ldots\}$ for the computation times of the refinement agents.

Because an intention is a tree of steps, it can be executed in different ways, depending on the chosen path in the tree. A path is a sequence of steps joining the root to a leaf and there are as many possible paths as leaves. Let us select one path per intention. Let S be the set of all the steps of the selected path. A schedule is the sorted sequence of the elements of S with respect to the deadlines. Guaranteeing that all active intentions will be executed, whatever the chosen path in each intention, consists in proving that there exists a feasible schedule of all steps belonging to the chosen paths. The set of all schedules accounting for all the possible paths in all the intentions is called the set of **possible schedules**. If such a schedule is admissible w.r.t. deadlines, the schedule is said **admissible**.

Deadline and release time modifications

Let us now consider the first problem : to prove the existence of an admissible schedule. Referring to the results about dependent tasks scheduling in [3], we extend the process of deadlines, ready-time modifications and the schedulability test.

The tree defining an intention specifies a partial order < between a step and its successors. A step must be completed before one of its successors begins. Then, the given deadline d^i_j of a step S^i_j cannot be completed later than d^i_k of any step S^i_k such that $S^i_k < S^i_j$. Because the minimum time m^i_j required to execute S^i_j is known, we state that the deadline of S^i_j cannot be later than the deadline of S^i_k minus m^i_k. Then, the modified deadline of the step S^i_j is: $d^{i*}_j = \text{Min}\,\{d^i_j, \text{Min}\,\{d^{i*}_k - m^i_k \,/\, S^i_k > S^i_j\}\}$.

The modified deadlines are computed in the worst case because we take into account all possible successors of a step (although only one will be executed). The ready time r^i_j of a step S^i_j is modified in the same way.

Theorem

Let $S=\{S^i_1, \ldots, S^i_{N_i}\}$ be a set of pre-emptable steps and < be a partial order over S. Let $S^*=\{S^{*i}_1, \ldots, S^{*i}_{N_i}\}$ be a set of independent steps such that:

$$m^{*i}_j = m^i_j,$$
$$r^{*i}_j = \text{Max}\,\{r^i_j, \text{Max}\{r^{*i}_k + m^i_k \,/\, S^i_j > S^i_k\}\},$$
$$d^{*i}_j = \text{Min}\,\{d^i_j, \text{Min}\,\{d^{*i}_k - m^i_k \,/\, S^i_k > S^i_j\}\}.$$

S is schedulable if and only if :

For all S^i_a, S^j_b any couple of steps belonging to a same possible schedule such that $r^{*i}_a \leq r^{*j}_b$, $d^{*i}_a \leq d^{*j}_b$, then if $A=\{S^k_c\}$ is the set of steps belonging to the same possible schedule as S^i_a, S^j_b such that $r^{*k}_c \geq r^{*i}_a$, $d^{*k}_c \leq d^{*j}_b$ then

$$\sum_{S^k_c \in A} m^k_c \leq d^{*j}_b - r^{*i}_a$$

The complexity of the schedulability test depends highly on the complexity of the algorithm enumerating all necessary inequations :

$$\sum_{S^k_c \in A} m^k_c \leq d^{*j}_b - r^{*i}_a$$

in which the sum stands for the total duration of the set of steps that can be executed between a release time r^i_a and a deadline d^j_b and belonging to the same possible schedule. If the number of intentions is N and L the number of leaves (paths) per intention, the enumeration requires L^{N-1} iterations. Fortunately, the enumeration of all possible schedules is not necessary because only the worst-case duration is of interest. Let us notice that a possible schedule is made up of partial paths, each one belonging to the intentions with steps having a deadline prior to the one considered in the equations. Among the different partial paths of interest for the equation, only the path with the greatest duration has to be taken into account for a given intention.

Monitoring Progressive reasoning algorithm

The schedulability test given in the previous paragraph neither calculates a schedule nor optimizes the level of refinement allocated to steps. It only proves that an admissible schedule exists. This paragraph describes an algorithm allocating time to the current steps of the active intentions. It is derived from the schedulability test and relies on a local scheduling strategy, that favors the current step of each intention. This algorithm is not optimal as we cannot afford to implement an NP-complete algorithm. *For the sake of simplicity we present in this paper the case with no release-time.*

For all on-going intentions, the algorithm computes the maximum amount of time that can be allocated to each current step, such that all intentions can be completed with respect to the deadlines in the worst case, each step being executed at the lowest refinement level. For this purpose each deadline has to be considered (several deadlines per intention have to be checked). We have to check the correctness of the sum of the worst-case computation times which is needed by each ongoing intention from the current step until the considered deadline. Considering a given deadline d, the worst case computation time to execute a given intention i currently executing a step s, is the maximum execution time to reach a step s', s' having a deadline less or equal to d, and being on a path containing s. As we introduced multiple methods, it makes sense to enlarge the notion of worst case. For a given step, and for a given deadline, there are several interleaved worst cases, depending on the number of refinement levels that are executed for each step. But most cases are of little interest for the scheduling problem. Knowing the level of refinement of future steps is useless, because we do not know the future (i.e. the worst path, considered here, has a low probability to be the one that will be executed). For this reason, the schedulability test consisting of the two following phases is satisfactory:

first phase

```
a schedulability test considering
the first-level parts is executed; if
it fails, among the intentions
involved in the scheduling test, the
one with the lowest importance is
removed; if it succeeds, the second
phase is fired;
```

second phase

```
a schedulability test considering
both first-level and refinement parts
of ongoing steps and first level
only for future steps.
```

Schedulability test algorithm :

Let I be a list containing all the intentions to be scheduled.
Let $Deadl_s$ be a set containing the deadlines of the steps following s in the intention s belongs to.
Let s_i be the current step of the intention i.
Let D be a null-initialized list of deadlines.
Let «current » be the current time.
Let «cumulated» be the cumulated time of all the worst-cases for a given deadline.
Let WC(s,d,n) be a function returning the worst-case computation time needed by an intention to execute the corresponding path starting from s, and finishing by a step s' whose deadline is d', d'≤d ; the step s executing n levels of refinement.

for each i **in** I
  D = D U $Deadl_{si}$
endfor
for each d **in** D
  cumulated = 0
  for each i **in** I
    cumulated = cumulated + WC (s_i,d,1)
  endfor
  if d - current < cumulated
  then test has failed
  endif
endfor

For the first phase of the schedule, the worst-case concerns only the first-level parts of each step. If the test fails, the intention with the lowest importance is removed and the test is redone until it succeeds otherwise there's no more intention.

The second phase of the schedule is dedicated to compute for all intentions, the maximum time that can be allocated to each current step. The schedulability test is applied with :

cumulated = cumulated +WC(si, d, nb_levels(si))

nb_levels(si) is initially set to the maximum number of refinement level for each si. When the schedulability test fails the less important intention is chosen to be approximated (by decreasing the number of refinement level for si). This is the purpose of the following algorithm.

Level Deletion Algorithm
For a given intention i , a given deadline d, and a given cumulated time.
Let nb_levels (s) be a function returning the number of levels planned for the step s.
Let decrease_nb_levels (s) be a function decreasing as a side effect the number of levels planned for step s.

```
while (cumulated > d - current) and (nb_levels (si)>1)
        cumulated = cumulated - WC (si, d, nb_levels (si))
        decrease_nb_levels (si)
        cumulated = cumulated + WC (si,d,nb_levels (si))
endwhile
```

Whenever the two phases have succeeded, the current step of each intention contains the number of levels planned for the execution to come and the steps are scheduled using the Earliest Deadline First algorithm.

Discussion

This heuristic takes advantage of the over-estimation of estimated computation time by favouring current steps while preserving the remaining steps. A first point advocates this approach: deliberating on cases which may not occur is useless. An intention being a tree, the probability to reach a step is function of the number of its alternatives. Therefore it is suitable to put at a disadvantage furthest steps (those that will be probably executed in the future). A second point is related to the chaining of steps. The quality of results produced by intentions depends on the quality of all the steps fired during its execution. As a step uses results produced by previous steps, its quality is related to its entry, i.e. to the quality of results produced by previous steps. Then it is not suitable to refine steps whose previous ones are not. However, let us notice that in some specific cases (we are in the worst-case and there is no remaining time), this strategy leads to a rather inadequate solution quality, the first steps being totally achieved, the last ones being completely approximated.

4. Results

The heuristic presented in previous sections favors the strongest tasks (most important tasks) while avoiding the cancellation of weakest (less important) tasks. In order to measure its efficiency, this approach has been compared with a usual scheduling mechanism, i.e. the earliest deadline (ED) algorithm. Each algorithm (PROGRESS and ED algorithm) has been assessed with a huge number of randomly generated problems. Each problem is characterized by a scenario describing a temporal sequence of events and the tasks involved in this scenario. For each task the triggering conditions are also defined. The structure of each task (the depth and the width of tree) is randomly generated such as the duration of each method, and the deadlines associated to each step.

A qualitative value labels the complexity (in term of timing constraints) of each generated problem. It is a number between 1 and 10 (x-axis of the graphics presented in figures 3, 4 and 5). Thus, the simulation describes the temporal behavior of a problem and makes it possible to measure the most relevant performance criteria: quality of the results and success rate. A successful execution of a task occurs when at least one method per step belonging to a path joining the root of the intention with one of the leaves are completed.

The quality of the results delivered by a given task T is computed from the quality of each step involved. The quality of a step is computed in an objective way as a function of the number of completed methods with respect to the number of available methods (intrinsic measurement). Since, from our experience, we have noticed that first approximate methods contribute more to the global quality than the others, the quality of a step is computed as a logarithmic function of the number of executed methods. Figure 3 exemplifies this notion for a step composed of 10 methods.

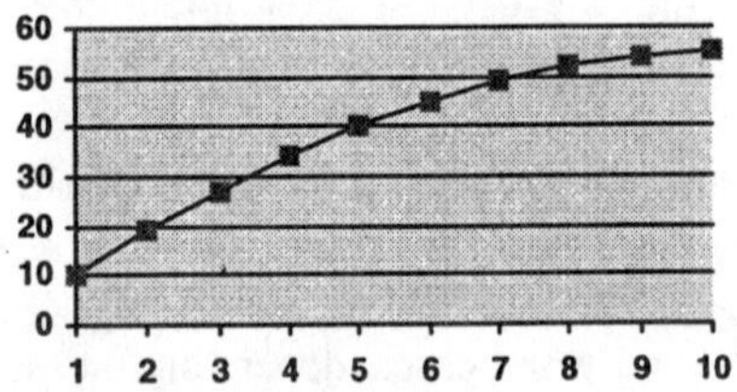

Figure 3. Quality of a step.

The global quality of a task T is computed as the multiplication of the quality of each completed step. The global quality obtained by the system for a given scenario is computed as the weighted sum of the contribution of each task with respect to the quality which could have been obtained without any timing constraints. The success rate of a scenario is the ratio between the number of completed tasks and the total number of triggered tasks during the scenario. This ratio is weighted by the relative importance of each task.

Discussion

PROGRESS always obtains results with better quality than ED algorithm. Its advantage decreases when the timing constraints become stronger because in over-constraints situations, the flexibility of our approach cannot be fulfilled.

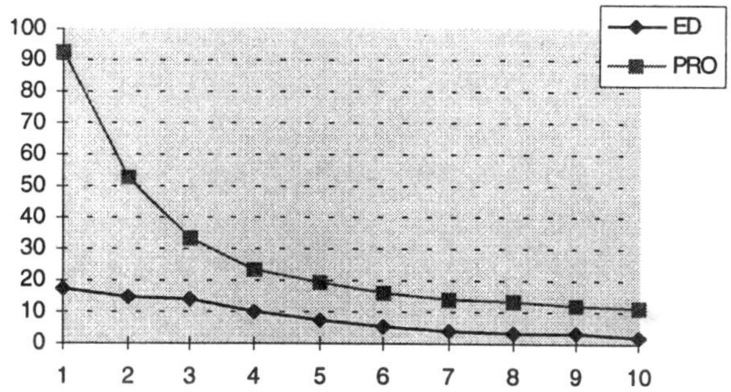

Figure 4. Quality versus complexity

Concerning the success rate, PROGRESS is more efficient than ED algorithm especially in over constraints situations. It could be explained by the capacity of our approach to anticipate the long term requirements of a task.

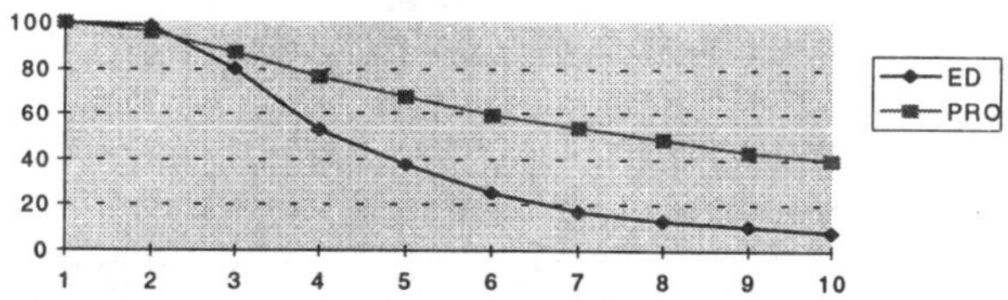

Figure 5. Success rate versus complexity.

5. Conclusion

We have developed a new model termed PROGRESS based on a trade-off between quality versus computation time. This model is a tactical approach and belongs to multiple methods. It is close to the task model TÆMS but extended to generate tasks termed intentions with better real-time behaviour. To trade-off between solution quality versus time, a scheduler has been defined. It is inspired from the process used to transform contract algorithms into interruptible anytime algorithms. The main objective of the scheduling is to ensure that each intention can be completed. Unfortunately, the problem of finding an optimal schedule is NP-complete in general. We paid attention to finding a heuristic that computes approximated schedule in polynomial time.

References

[1] Audsley, Burns, and Welling. Incorporating unbounded algorithms into predictable real-time systems, Technical Report, Universisty of York, UK, 1991.

[2] Boddy and Dean. An Analysis of Time Dependent Planning, in proc. Of 7th AAAI, pp. 49-54, 1988.

[3] Chetto, Silly and Bouchentouf. Dynamic scheduling of Real-Time tasks under precedence constraints, The International Journal of Time-Critical Computing Systems, Vol. 2, No 3, pp.181-4, 1990

[4] Dodhiawala, Sridharan, Raulefs and Pickering. "Real-Time AI Systems: A Definition and An Architecture", in Proc. Of 11th IJCAI, Detroit, 1989.

[5] Garvey and Lesser., "Design-to-time Real-Time Scheduling," IEEE Transactions on Systems, Man and Cybernetics - Special Issue on Planning, Scheduling and Control, Vol. 23, No. 6, 1993.

[6] Horvitz. Reasoning about Beliefs and Actions under Computational Resources Constraints, In Proc. of 1987 Workshop on Uncertainty in Artificial Intelligence, Seattle, Washington, 1987.

[7] Lalanda, Charpillet and Haton. A Real Time Blackboard Based Architecture, in proc. of 10th European Conference on Artificial Intelligence, Vienna (Austria), août 1992.

[8] Lehoczky and Ramos-Thuel. An Optimal Algorithm for Scheduling Soft-Aperiodic Tasks in Fixed-Priority Preemptive Systems, in proc. of IEEE Symposium on Real-Time Systems, 1993.

[9] Liu, Lin, Shih and Yu. "Algorithms for Scheduling Imprecise Computations". IEEE Computer, pp 58-68, 1991.

[10] Mensch and Charpillet. Scheduling in the REAKT kernel: combining predictable and unbounded computations for maximizing solution quality in real-time knowledge based systems, in proc. of RTS&ES'96, Paris, 10-12 Janvier 1996.

[11] Mensch, Kersual, Crespo, Charpillet and Pessi. "REAKT: real-time architecture for time-critical knowledge-based systems". Intelligent Systems Engineering Journal, Autumn 94, pp 153-167.

[12] Mouaddib, Charpillet, Haton. "GREAT: a Model of Progressive Reasoning for Real-Time Systems", in proc. of IEEE International Conference on Tools for AI, 1994.

[13] Mouaddib, Zilberstein. "Knowledge Based anytime computation" in proc. Of IJCAI'95, Montreal.

[14] Zilberstein and Russell. Optimal Composition of Real-Time Systems. Artificial Intelligence, 82(1-2):181-213, 1996.

A Pair of Heterogeneous Agents in a Unique Vehicle for Object Motion

Philippe Morignot
ICS-FORTH STEP-C, Vassilika Vouton, P.O.Box 1385
GR 711 10 Heraklion, Crete, Greece
Phone: +30 81391600 Fax: +30 81391601
E-mail: morignot@ics.forth.gr

Olivier Aycard, François Charpillet[0]
CRIN-CNRS / INRIA-Lorraine, Bat. LORIA, B.P. 239
54500 Vandoeuvre-les-Nancy, France
Phone: +33 3 83592084 Fax: +33 3 83413079
E-mail: {aycard, charp}@loria.fr

Keywords: Intelligent control, hybrid systems.

Abstract

We present a multi-agent architecture for controlling a mobile robot in an unpredictible environment. This architecture has been developed with the objective of coordinating the various competences of the robot (e.g., perception, navigation, planning). The architecture is made up of two agents: the first one specialized for cognitive tasks, the second one dedicated to control of the robot's physical devices. This two-agent architecture guarantees a good robustness of the system, as the navigation modules can run independently of the cognitive ones.

1 Introduction

Being able to design a robot that can both "sense/act" and "reason" at the same time in a coordinated way is a very important goal for both Robotics and AI. In a dynamic and unpredictable environment, a whole spectrum of reactions can be expected from a robot: from a minor bump on its trajectory to avoid an unexpected obstacle, to a major revision of the plan which is intended to carry out a given mission. Moreover, small communication bandwidth and/or low communication speed can limit heplful human intervention: decisions about reactions strictly have to be made onboard. These two requirements of reaction width and of onboard decision making constitute the first step towards the *autonomy* of a robot.

Embedding symbolic computation into robots has been studied by researchers for decades. Fikes, for example, uses a symbolic planner inside the Shakey robot in the early 70's [8]. But apart from the fact that task planning, for example, is an NP-complete problem [4], embedding a reasonably efficient symbolic reasoning capability in a robot leads to difficult architectural issues *per se*: time spent reasoning may be time lost for sensing/reacting. For example, the robot might plan for a task which is already obsolete due to fast changes in the environment — hence making that whole planning session useless, in retrospect.

In another view, Brooks argues that keeping an explicit model of the environment inside a robot may be useless because the robot is *situated* in its environment [3]. (Similarly, living organisms are situated in their natural environment through evolution.) The architecture of robots' software should be thought of as a combinatorial circuit and a time circuitry — both being hand-programmed at design time. However, coupling onboard reasoning with physical moving still seems to be required due to the discrete aspect of robot (re)actions, to the various abstraction levels required for them and to their multiple meanings [5] For example, the robot may act in several ways: navigating to reach some location; navigating to perform bee-like figures to warn other robots; moving objects by pushing them; moving objects by manipulating them with a clamp, with objects having complex uses and functions.

In another view towards adressing architecural issues, it has been proposed to keep the environment's symbolic model inside the robot but to have it run in parallel with sensing/reacting parts [9] [11]. If both activities run on the same processor (even using real-time operating systems), the sensing/reacting capability of the robot is still weakened, but interesting realizations in natural/non-engineered environments have been built [9].

To reinforce this latter view, a paradigm of AI coined *multi-agent* proposes to have problems solved by a a set of autonomous entities (*agents*). The *behavior* of this *society* of *agents* (terms used by analogy with human and animal societies) emerges from the individual activities of these agents and from their mutual interaction [7]. In this paper, we propose a multi-agent architecture for controlling a mobile robot which can reason (e.g., plan) and sense/act at the same time. We first present the design of the multi-agent system. We then present the specific agents for object motion. An implementation on a mobile robot is presented and discussed.

[0]Thanks to Vincent Chevrier for useful comments on earlier drafts of this paper and to the members of the RFIA group for useful discussions. The first author has been supported at CRIN-CNRS/INRIA-Lorraine by an Esprit III contract and at ICS-FORTH by an ERCIM fellowship. The second author has been supported by MSER fellowship from French government. Current address of the first author: GMD FIT.KI, Schloss Birlinghoven, 53754 Sankt Augustin, Germany.

1082-3409/97 $10.00 © 1997 IEEE

2 System Design

Multi-Agent. The mobile robot materializes the agents' society: the behavior of the robot *is* the emerging behavior of this society. Various number of agents of a multi-agent system (or, closely, various number of levels of a unique agent) has been proposed: One [16], two [8], three [9] or n [3]. The system presented in this paper stands between the extreme many-simple-agent approach and the extreme single-complex-agent one: a small number of reasonably complex agents are modeled. We propose (i) an agent architecture, (ii) common component types for agents, (iii) a role for each agent in the society, (iv) a communication protocol for collaboration.

Architecture of One Agent. Each agent is composed of independent modules (*behaviors*), a mechanism for choosing which module to execute next (*controller*) and shared memory (*blackboard*) [10]. A behavior is made up of two parts: *triggering conditions* determine the executability of the behavior, the second part contains the behavior's source code itself.

The controller is a best-first execution cycle on the set of instantaneously-executable behaviors. At each cycle, it checks which behavior is executable (*trigger condition checking*), sorts the executable behaviors by decreasing importance (*agenda management*), and gives control to the most important one (*execution*). It is the behavior's responsibility to give control back to the controller, so as to make the next cycle possible.

At each cycle the executable behaviors that were less important than the executed one are forgotten (hence the term best-first *execution cycle*, for a best-first *search* would keep them). Since all behaviors are considered at each cycle for executability check, a behavior which is declared executable at a given cycle can be declared executable at the next cycle, if its triggering conditions are not affected by the executed behavior.

The sort criterion for evaluating the importance of executable behaviors can be specified in a dedicated part of the shared memory (*control plan*).

An *event* is a record of a change in the shared memory. A memory change can be initiated by the execution of a behavior or by reception of a message from another agent (which, in turn, comes from the execution of its own behaviors). Events, behaviors and other internal objects are stored in another dedicated part of the shared memory.

The controller matches behaviors' triggering conditions against events: This prevents the controller from uselessly polling an unchanged shared memory, hence it reduces the controller's CPU consumption for non-behavioral use.

3 Specialization for Object Motion

For the application of object motion, the presented system is composed of two agents. These agents have heterogeneous semantics and isomorphic structures — hence they play complementary roles in this society. One agent is in contact with the environment through sensors and effectors. It carries out a behavior for action (in a sense similar to *walking*, *running*) or perception (e.g., noticing an open area on the right). Another agent manipulates the interpretation of previous physical behaviors. We informally refer to the former agent as a *physical* agent and to the latter agent as a *cognitive* agent.

The cognitive agent sends action description to the physical agent. The physical agent sends events to the cognitive agent. An event can be perceptual (e.g., open door on the right, stuck) or related to the agent itself (e.g., task performed, low battery).

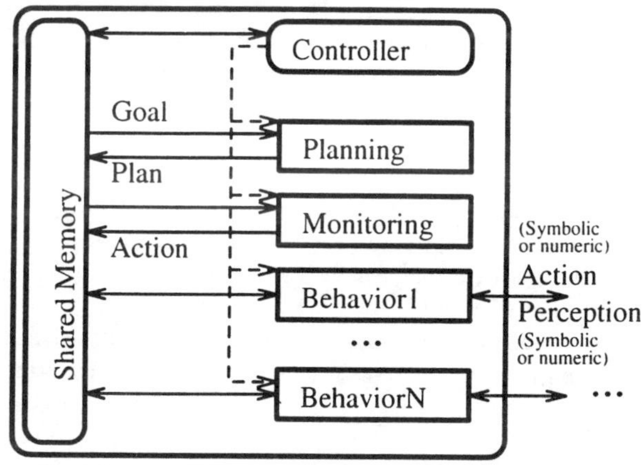

Figure 1: The software architecture of each agent.

To attempt at achieving given task, a mobile robot must anticipate: its intended actions influence the current action. This temporal aspect leads to give at least two behaviors to an agent, as shown in Figure 1: monitoring (i.e., computation about the agent's present) and planning (i.e., computation about the agent's future).

3.1 Cognitive Agent

Task Planning. The triggering condition of this behavior is the presence in the shared memory of a (conjunctive) goal which has no plan satisfying it.

This behavior consists of finding a sequence of action descriptions (a *plan*) that transforms an initial situation description to another in which a given conjunction of *goals* is satisfied. The initial situation description typically is the current situation of the robot, the goals altogether represent a *task* to achieve. This behavior uses a set of descriptions of the actions that the robot can physically perform (see Figure 2). An action is represented as pre-, post-conditions [8] and preservation conditions (i.e., preconditions which must hold *during* the action's execution) [15].

```
(deftemplate (drop ?robot ?object ?location)
   :preservations ((robot ?robot)
                   (height ?object ?height)
                   (at ?robot ?location)
                   (clamp-height ?height))
   :preconditions ((at ?object ?robot)
                   (:not (is-clamp-open)))
   :postconditions ((at ?object ?location)
                    (:not (at ?object ?robot))
                    (:not (is-clamp-open)))
   :location ?location)
```

Figure 2: Description of a **drop** action.

The initial situation description and the goals form an initial plan, which is incrementally improved during the process. The task planner handles partial-ordered partially-instantiated plans: two actions in parallel mean that they are unordered, an uninstantiated variable means that it can be instantiated to more than one constant (the domain of a variable is pruned during the process). Arithmetic equations can be maintained by representing integers as function symbols in actions' pre- and postconditions [13]; this enables to represent limitations on the capacity of the robot.

Task planning is a search in the space of partially-ordered partially-instantiated plans [4]. A best-first search, for example, ensures completeness. A plan is a solution to a given planning problem (i.e., initial plan plus action descriptions) iff it contains no unsatisfied precondition or preservation condition. The satisfaction of a precondition (or, similarly, of a preservation condition) is computed in polynomial time with a modal truth criterion (MTC) [4]. This ensures correctness of the generated plans.

Monitoring. The triggering condition of this behavior is the presence in the shared memory of a plan which contains unexecuted action descriptions.

This behavior attempts at having a plan executed by sending (a simplification of) its *current* action description to the physical agent — this decoupling makes the cognitive agent available for reasoning on other tasks. Such action description is declared executed when a message of successful completion is received from the physical agent. A failure message leads to replanning from the situation just before that action description — this situation is computed by simulating the execution of action descriptions from the initial situation, i.e., adding positive postconditions to it and retracting negative ones from it [8].

An action description can be sent to the physical agent before reception of any message related to the previous action description, if the preservation conditions of one of them do not conflict with the post conditions of the other one, according to the MTC algorithm.

1. If event is **performed-action** and event source is physical agent,
   a. If the current plan has no unexecuted actions.
      Then If there exists at least another plan.
         Then select another plan as current.
         Else exit from this behavior.
   b. Unstack the current action from the current plan.
   c. Send it to the physical agent.
2. If event type is goal and event source is physical agent, store it in the shared memory.
3. If event type is percept and event source is physical agent,
   a. If the event negates a preservation condition of the currently executed action,
      Then stop this action and turn this condition into a goal.
   b. Store it in the shared memory.

Figure 3: Rules for monitoring.

More precisely, this behavior reacts to events (sent by the physical agent), by choosing a plan (step 1.a of Figure 3), taking the current action of that plan (step 1.b) and sending it to the physical agent (step 1.c).

The monitor also filters the perceptual events from the physical agent (step 2). For example, a goal event which is perceived in the environment (e.g., requests from humans) is recognized, which may lead the cognitive agent to plan or replan (see previous paragraph). The monitor also recognizes an self-related event which conflicts with a preservation condition of currently-executed action descriptions (step 3); If so, it turns the threatened preservation condition into a goal (which, again, may lead the cognitive agent to plan or replan).

3.2 Physical Agent

Path Planning. This triggering condition of this behavior is the presence of a motion action description in the shared memory of the physical agent.

This behavior uses a *topographic* map and a *topological* map of the environment. Both maps are stored in the shared memory of the physical agent. The topographic map records fixed obstacles: each point is a binary value can-go/cannot-go — the environment is assumed to be plane. A node of the topological map corresponds to a *salient* location of the topographic map (see Figure 5 for an example). A location is salient iff it can be detected in 2D with precision by the robot's sensors. When the path between two salient locations is unique, an edge is added between these two nodes. The topological map is manually extracted from the topographic map in a preprocessing phase.

Path-planning involves: (1) finding the salient point sp_1 which is the closest to the current location; (2) finding the salient point sp_2 which is the closest one to the goal location; (3) searching for sp_2, starting at sp_1, in the topological map. For example, an A^* search ensures completeness and produces a path from sp_1 to sp_2 which is minimal according to a cost function (e.g., path length).

Navigating. The triggering condition of this behavior is the presence of a primitive motion action description in the shared memory of the physical agent.

The robot has three wheels for translation. Turns can be made by rotating the wheels around a vertical axis (non-holonomic motion). Environment is sensed through a 20-bumper ring (emergency stop) and a 16 sonar/infra-red ring (regular navigation).

Different sensor zones are defined around the robot (e.g., left, front, right); each zone gives a preferred rotation angle and speed for the next cycle; a fuzzy controller merges the different advice (i.e., obstacle avoidance on the left/front/right) to compute the actual values [1]. Navigation stops either (1) when the next salient location is reached (The method for building the topological map from the topographic map guarantees its existence) or (2) when the goal location is estimated to be reached using odometry (Again, the method for building the topological map from the topographic map guarantees the minimal use of this navigation mode.) Salient location detection uses the variation of a sonar/infra-red sensor value between two time points [12] (e.g., open door or corridor on the right).

Grabbing/Dropping. The triggering condition of this behavior is the presence of a grab/drop action description in the shared memory of the physical agent.

A clamp, at the back of the robot, is composed of two parallel bars that move in a horizontal plane (see Figure 4). This clamp can move vertically, can open/close, can detect resistance when closing (hence meaning that an object is being grabbed if $d \neq 0$) and can rotate. (The upper part of the robot is a rotatable turret on which the upper part of the clamp's rail is fixed.)

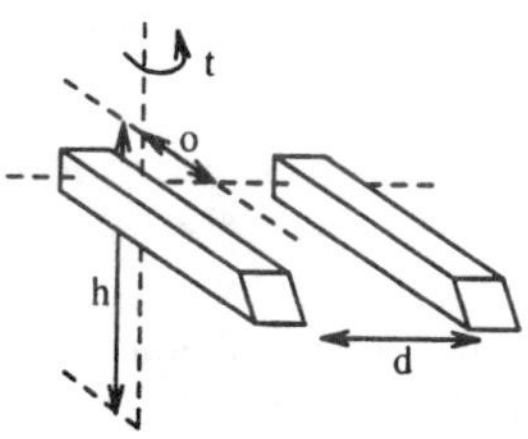

Figure 4: A two-finger clamp rotates (angle t) around the turret's axis (at distance o from the clamp), moves vertically (distance h from the floor, $0 \leq h \leq h_{max}$) and opens/closes (distance d, $0 \leq d \leq d_{max}$).

The plan for grabbing is: (1) move the clamp vertically to reach the target-object's height (the *object's height* refers to the height at which the object should be grabbed, see Figure 2, the actual height of the object usually is higher); (2) open the clamp; (3) close the clamp until resistance is detected; if the clamp is closed and no resistance has been detected on the way, re-open the clamp until $d = d_{max}$, send a warning message to the physical monitor and go to step (3); (4) move the clamp up. *A priori* actions (1) and (2) are unordered.

The plan for dropping is: (1) move the clamp down to reach the target-object's height; (2) open the clamp until $d = d_{max}$; (3) move the clamp down. For safety purposes, the robot with an empty clamp navigates with the clamp in low position $h = 0$. Objects are assumed to have their lower part less wide than d_{max}.

Monitoring. The triggering condition of this behavior is the presence of a plan in the agent's shared memory which contains unexecuted action descriptions. The only difference with the cognitive monitor is that the only filtered percept is the completion or failure of an action — such events are propagated to the cognitive agent.

A plan here either is a structure simpler than these for the cognitive monitor (i.e., sequence of salient locations) or is hand-coded in an action.

4 Experiments

The two-agent architecture has been implemented on a Nomad 200 mobile robot [6]. It is composed of a base and a turret, which can rotate independently. The base is composed of three wheels and is protected by a 20-bumper ring. The turret's horizontal cross-section is an uniform 16-side polygon, with an infrared and ultrasonic sensor on each vertical plane (i.e., on each side of the polygon). The turret also carries a stereo CCD-camera and a pair CCD-camera / laser. An onboard pentium PC under the Linux operating system communicates with the sensors/effectors. It also communicates with the local computer network of the laboratory via a radio link.

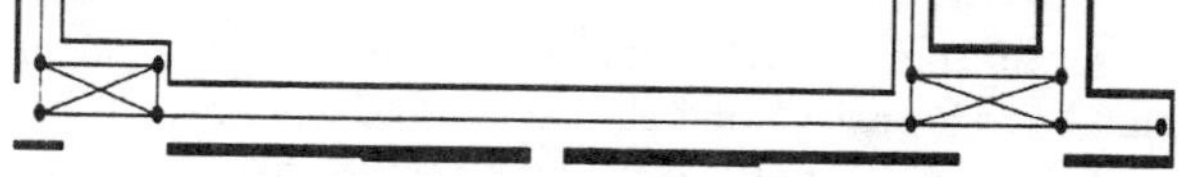

Figure 5: A topographic map. (Nodes and edges of the topological maps are shown as dots and thin lines.)

We tested the two-agent architecture in scenarios where the mobile robot gathers soda cans in an indoor environment (the second floor of the CRIN-CNRS laboratory, see Figure 5). Objects *not* mentionned in the topographic map include: shelves, door frames, fire extinguishers, cardboard boxes and people. This environment has not been engineered for mobile robots in particular.

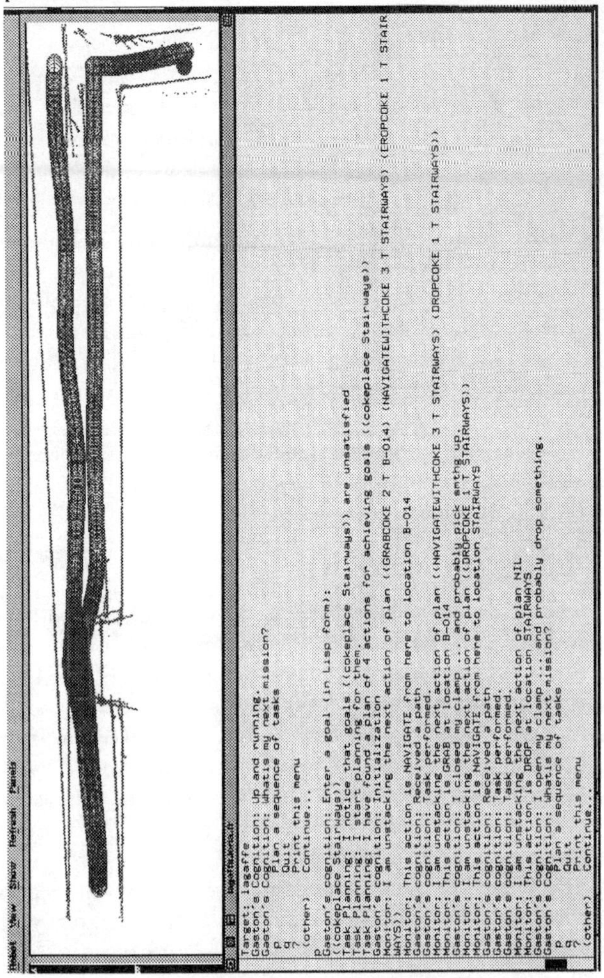

Figure 6: Trace for soda can gathering.

A goal (a mission) is sent on the fly to the cognitive agent: typically, bringing a soda can to some location — the initial locations of the robot and of the can are included in the model of the environment (topographic, topological and symbolic) which is maintained by the robot. Figure 6 and 7 show typical traces of the robot's motion and of the cognitive / physical agents' activity.

5 Discussion

1. Again, our point is not to demonstrate the performance of a particular behavior but to demonstrate the usefulness of a multi-agent architecture for controlling a unique vehicle. However, in cases actually happening in our scenarios in our environment, task planning is faster than action execution (less than one second for task planning [13], several seconds for action execution [1]). But due to the polynomial or exponential complexity of each behavior, opposite observations could be made in close scenarios (e.g., safely moving seven stacked boxes with one intermediate location only (problem known as

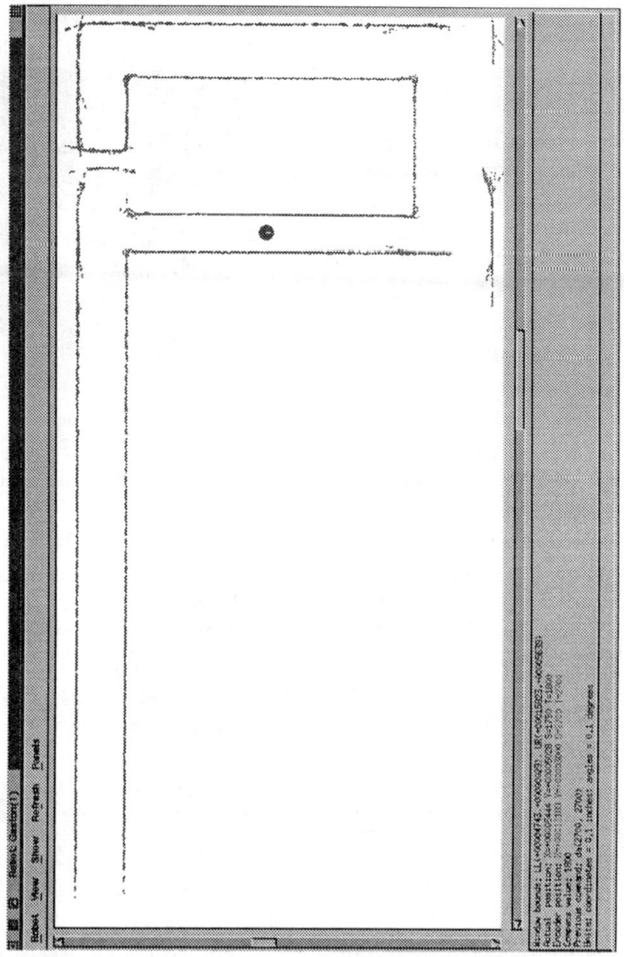

Figure 7: Trace for soda can gathering. (An unexpected obstacle in front of office B-024 leads the robot to go around the stairways.)

the *Towers of Hanoi*)). For the general case, domain-dependent behaviors can be added to each one of the two agents and can mask default-case behaviors (e.g., using priorities in line $1.a.3$ in Figure 3 or in similar lines of the physical monitor).

2. The plans executed by the physical monitor are mostly hand-programmed (except that navigation can require path planning). Extending the best-first execution cycle that currently implements a monitor by using a language such as PRS-Lite [14], for representing such plans or *procedures*, would help expressing the knowledge on use conditions of sensors/effectors and associated behaviors. Thus this would (1) help making these behaviors reusable for instances of our architecture on other robots, (2) improve the *reaction capabilities* while the cognitive agent deliberates (e.g., replans), hence nicely enabling a form of graceful degradation [3].

3. We were not able to find a behavior which was neither cognitive nor physical, so an agent actually refers to a behavior *type*, either cognitive or physical. Now, if an agent refers to a *function* [7], more than two such

agents can be represented in our architecture: each controller acts as an operating system assigning time slices to (aggregations of parts of different) behaviors/agents, their conflicting roles being handled by use of a MTC on their description, or more generally by mutual *negociation*. For example, an "obstacle avoidance" functional agent may involve navigating, path-planning and task planning behaviors, with potential negociation between path-planning and task-planning (e.g., opening a door (which may require fetching keys) vs. taking a longer path to go around it (through another open door)).

Ongoing work involves using Hidden Markov Models for navigation to cope with reflection of sonar/infrared sensors on obstacles [2], and using the stereo CCD-camera for active 3D sensing.

References

[1] Olivier Aycard. A new approach to design fuzzy controllers for mobile robots navigation. In *proceedings of IEEE International Symposium on Computational Intelligence in Robotics and Automation*, pages 68–73, 1997.

[2] Olivier Aycard, François Charpillet, and Jean-Paul Haton. Place Learning and Recognition using Hidden Markov Models. In *proceedings of the IEEE International Conference on Intelligent Robots and Systems*, 1997. To appear.

[3] Rodney Brooks. Intelligence without Reason. In *Proceedings of the International Joint Conference on Artificial Intelligence*, pages 979–984, Detroit, MI, 1991.

[4] David Chapman. Planning for Conjunctive Goals. *Artificial Intelligence*, 32:333–377, 1987.

[5] Raja Chatila. Deliberation and reactivity in autonomous robots. *Robotics and Autonomous Systems*, 16:197–211, 1995.

[6] David Zhu et al. Nomad 200 user s manual. Technical report, Nomadics Technologies Inc., Mountain View, CA, 1996.

[7] Jacques Ferber. *Les Systèmes Multi-Agents: Vers une Intelligence Collective*. InterÉditions, Paris, 1995.

[8] Richard E. Fikes and Nils J. Nilsson. STRIPS: a New Approach to the Application of Theorem Proving to Problem Solving. *Artificial Intelligence*, 2:198–208, 1971.

[9] Erann Gat. Integrating Planning and Reacting in a Heterogeneous Asymchronous Architecture for Controlling a Real-world Mobile Robot. In *Proceedings of the Tenth National Conference on Artificial Intelligence*, San Mateo, CA, 1992. Morgan Kaufmann.

[10] Barbara Hayes-Roth. A Blackboard Architecture for Control. *Artificial Intelligence*, 26:251–321, 1985.

[11] Barbara Hayes-Roth, Karl Pfleger, Philippe Lalanda, Philippe Morignot, and Marko Balabanovic. A Domain-Specific Software Architecture for Adaptive Intelligent Agents. *IEEE Transactions on Software Engineering*, 21(4):288–301, April 1995.

[12] D. Kortenkamp, L. Douglas Baker, and T. Weymouth. Using gateways to build a route map. In *proceedings of the 1992 IEEE International Conference on Intelligent Robots and Systems*, 1992.

[13] Philippe Morignot. Embedded Planning. In Kristian Hammond, editor, *Proceedings of the Second International Conference on A.I. Planning Systems*, pages 128–133, Chicago, IL, 1994.

[14] Karen L. Myers. A Procedural Knowledge Approach to Task-Level Control. In *Proceedings of the Third International Conference on A.I. Planning Systems*, pages **-**, Edimburgh, UK, May 1996.

[15] Edwin Pednault. *The Synthesis of Plans*. PhD thesis, E.E. Dept., Stanford, Palo Alto, California, 1986.

[16] Marcel J. Schoppers. Universal Plans for Reactive Robots in Unpredictible Environments. In *Proceedings of the International Joint Conference on Artificial Intelligence*, pages 1039–1046, 1987.

Enhancing Behavioral Fidelity Within Distributed Virtual Environments

Sheila B. Banks, Eugene Santos Jr., and Martin R. Stytz
Artificial Intelligence Laboratory
Virtual Environments Laboratory
Department of Electrical and Computer Engineering
Air Force Institute of Technology
Wright-Patterson AFB, OH 45433
sbanks@afit.af.mil, mstytz@afit.af.mil, eugene@eng2.uconn.edu

Abstract

For a computer-generated force (CGF) application to be useful in training environments, it must exhibit complex, realistic behavior within the battlespace. To achieve this level of fidelity, it must operate at multiple skill levels and exhibit competency at assigned missions. CGF applications must also have adaptable decisions mechanisms and behaviors even when operating under uncertainty and the application must learn from past experience. Furthermore, simply correct performance of individual entity behaviors is not sufficient. Issues related to complex inter-entity behavioral interactions, such as the need to maintain formation and share information, must also be considered.

To achieve these necessary capabilities, an extensible software architecture, an expandable knowledge base, and an adaptable decision making mechanism are required. Our labs have addressed these issues in the context of the Automated Wingman (AW) project. The AW is based on fuzzy logic, the Common Object DataBase (CODB) software architecture, and a hierarchical knowledge structure. Decision making is founded on multi-layered, fuzzy logic controlled situational analyses combined with adversarial game tree techniques.

1. Introduction

Computer generated forces (CGFs) [5] are software agents that are computer representations of military forces that model human behavior and automatically execute a finite set of actions in response to actions and activities in their environment. CGFs of various complexity have been created for many different platforms [9] and CGFs can serve to augment friendly forces or populate enemy formations. In either role, they improve the fidelity of a distributed virtual environment (DVE) by increasing the number of entities participating in a simulation.

The need for real-time performance combined with realism for training and analysis drives a number of requirements for CGFs. CGF requirements include the need for modifiability, attainment of high fidelity human behavior representations, development of adaptable decision mechanisms and behaviors, and automated incorporation of past reasoning into the decision process. These high level requirements drive additional requirements such as multiple skill levels for classes of entities, graceful degradation of reasoning capability under system stress, an easily expandable modular knowledge structure, and adaptive mission planning. For example, the capability for multiple skill levels would provide pilot behaviors for aircraft entities at different skill levels, such as rookie, expert, and ace levels of pilots within the same battlespace. Additionally, the entity should have a complete set of behaviors for the type of missions it must perform, but not all behaviors for these missions need to be crafted to the same level of fidelity and quality. The CGF should be able to respond acceptably to unforeseen circumstances and deal with uncertain information. In addition to the individual entity requirements, issues related to complex inter-entity behavioral interactions must also be considered. The CGF should exhibit complex, realistic behavior patterns within the battlespace and be able to adaptively change its mission parameters during the course of a mission in response to events. Finally, these capabilities should be embedded in an extensible, explicable software architecture that has well defined locations for reasoning and knowledge storage. Current CGF applications lack the ability to achieve all of these requirements within a single, integrated system.

In this paper, we describe our progress toward achieving a CGF entity that satisfies the requirements presented above. Our CGF architecture is applicable to the development of *any* computer generated force to be operated in complex distributed virtual environments.

Our CGF application is presented by first introducing, in Section Two, the background topics that are relevant to the development of CGFs. Section Three identifies our CGF architecture and the design of an actual CGF, the Automated Wingman (AW). Section Four describes the decision making component of the Automated Wingman within our CGF architecture and Section Five concludes the paper with current research results and suggestions for future improvements.

2. Background

In this section we discuss Distributed Interactive Simulation (DIS), the Common Object DataBase (CODB) architecture, and current aircraft CGF projects in relation to the AW. Presentation of this material is motivated by the need to understand the CGF operational environment, the rationale for the CGF architecture we propose, and the decision-making methodology we employ.

2.1 Distributed Interactive Simulation

Our CGF, the Automated Wingman, operates in a DVE [5] that employs the distributed interactive simulation (DIS) suite of protocols, IEEE 1278-1993 [3]. These protocols enable communication between individual simulator computer systems at distributed locations. DIS achieves an interactive representation of a virtual environment by the interconnection of the distributed hosts. Each host determines what is actually perceived of its entities and only communicates changes in the state of entities for which it is responsible. The DIS approach to DVEs requires participating sites to meet several requirements. These requirements consist of the following: (1) autonomous operation, (2) object and event based simulation, (3) state change information broadcast, and (4) dead reckoning capability. In the DIS protocols, the DVE contains actors and entities that interact through the asynchronous broadcast of event and state information. Stytz presents additional information concerning DIS and DVEs [5].

2.2 Common Object DataBase (CODB)

The Automated Wingman software architecture is founded on the Common Object DataBase (CODB) architecture [6]. The Common Object DataBase is a data-handling architecture that uses structured classes, data containers, and a central runtime data repository to manage and transmit data between application objects. This architecture reduces the coupling in a simulation by reducing the amount of information that a system component object class must maintain about other system component classes. As a result, an application component object must only access the container in the CODB where the information it needs resides.

2.3 Current CGF background and projects

The major structured components of an aircraft CGF include the following: vehicle dynamics, artificial intelligence (AI) reasoning, behavior modeling, and software architecture. CGF vehicle dynamics are important because the CGF should move through the virtual environment accurately whether it is human or computer-controlled. The vehicle dynamics for CGFs should not allow a human to identify it as a CGF by virtue of either exceptionally good or poor dynamic behavior.

The artificial intelligence reasoning component insures that the CGF pursues its goals, responds in a proper, human-like manner based upon its knowledge base, keeps the performance of the CGF within human and sensor limits, develops plans based upon its knowledge base, and manages other tasks. Fielded systems, like TAC-AIR SOAR [9] and ModSAF [1, 2] address these problems at different levels of fidelity. TAC-AIR SOAR, which builds upon the Soar architecture [4] for general intelligence and reasoning, is the most successful of the current aircraft CGFs. However, TAC-AIR SOAR does not accommodate uncertainty in its decision making process.

The central task in knowledge base construction is human behavior modeling. Human behavior modeling is the task of making the behavior and reactions of a CGF seem realistic by developing models that yield a reasonable analog of the output of the human decision-making process. Human behavior modeling requires the acquisition of domain-specific knowledge about human mental models and information brought to the decision-making process, as well as the key factors in the decision process. The human behavior modeling subcomponent of CGFs might normally be considered as part of the artificial intelligence component. However, separating it from the AI reasoning component serves to highlight its importance and the need to make behavior modeling design decisions independently of behavior reasoning mechanism design decisions.

A flexible CGF software architecture ensures that current CGF development efforts are extensible to future CGF requirements. The ability to modify the implemented CGF to include additional behavioral requirements directly depend upon software architecture flexibility.

3. CGF architecture

Our motivation for the development of a general CGF architecture for the AW was to provide a basis for the design of broad classes of CGFs. While each class of CGF has its own unique characteristics and performance requirements, there are many factors common to all classes and these can be successfully abstracted and reused across all classes of CGFs. Our goal is to provide a general architecture for CGFs, which naturally accounts for "variety" in a given type of CGF. Our architecture is based on highly modular components wherein interdependenciesare well-defined and minimized and that allows us to pursue an evolutionary and exploratory approach to knowledge engineering.

3.1 CGF architectural requirements

The architecture we developed is based on several principles [7]. The first is that future architectures should focus on reducing programmer costs, even at the possible expense of marginal runtime processing inefficiencies. The second principle is that the development cycle for a CGF, as in most research and development projects, must include a series of revisions to the requirements. These changes range from changing data formats to introduction of new behaviors into the system. A third principle is that the push to attain improved performance and the strain of meeting delivery deadlines increases the entropy of any design, until the original design concept becomes blurred. The most obvious results of entropy are the use of global variables, global functions, and the disappearance of private data items. A fourth principle is that the components of the airframe model (aerodynamics model, avionics systems, and weapons packages) should be rapidly modifiable. Therefore, these components should be realized as separate objects that have a clean, robust interface to the remainder of the system. The final principle is that expanding system requirements will cause the knowledge base and reasoning system to be modified and adapted to new requirements throughout the life of the project and in the subsequently fielded system. As a result, the knowledge and reasoning components should be structured so that the knowledge base and reasoning system are clearly separated from the remainder of the system.

3.2 CGF component architecture

The essence of the architecture problem domain is the following: given that a need exists to build a CGF, what design architecture and methodology can be applied to take the CGF from concept to implementation, regardless of the type of CGF? Figure 2 presents the baseline architecture and key CGF components that we propose to answer this question. A CGF is essentially comprised of two types of components: a Physical Dynamics Component (PDC) and an Active Decisions Component (ADC). The PDC is made up of the components necessary to model the CGF's physical makeup, such as entity propagation models, sensor models, weapons models, and defensive elements models. The ADC is composed of the components that use the information from the PDC and the DVE to make decisions, and is broken down into three subcomponents: a Strategic Decision Engine (SDE), a Tactical Decision Engine (TDE), and a Critical Decision Engine (CDE). Each of the decision engines operates at a different level of the decision making process and are presented further in Section 3.4.

Although not considered a component equal to the ADC or PDC, the CGF architecture has another important structure. This is the CGF Router, which is the interface between the Distributed Virtual Environment (DVE) and the ADC and PDC.

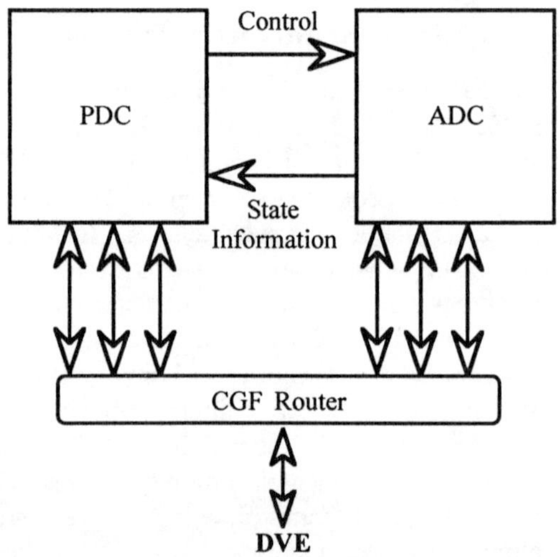

Figure 2. Generic CGF architecture: PDC, ADC, and CGF Router

3.3 Automated Wingman (AW) component architecture

Our AW system architecture (see Figure 3) used the principles in Section 3.1 to refine the CGF architectural definition in Figure 2. Within the architecture we use containers, which are data structures for moving large amounts of structured data between system components, to manage and control inter-component communication. The main CGF components are specified as objects. These objects are the Operator Skills Component (OSC), the Active Decisions Component (ADC), the Physical Dynamics Component (PDC), the Common Object DataBase (CODB), the World State Manager (WSM), and the Environment Database. Each of these

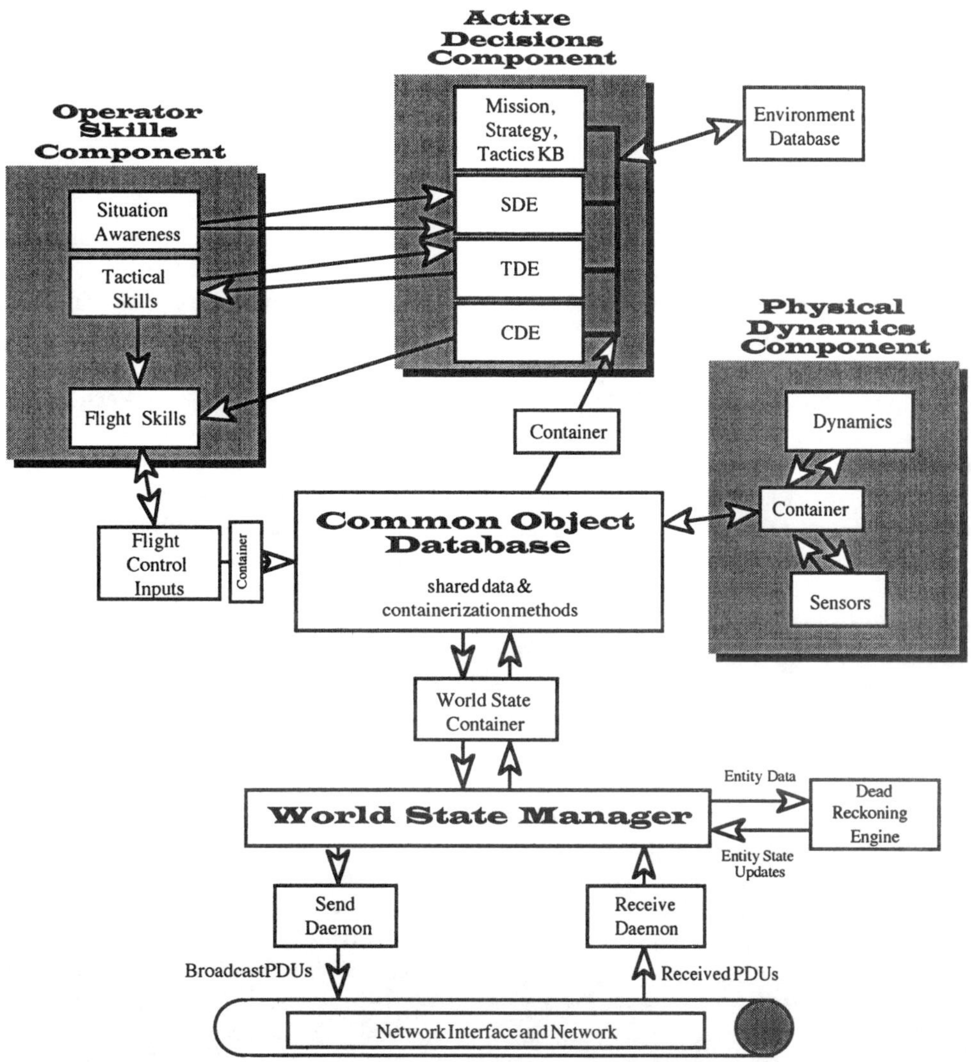

Figure 3. AW system architecture incorporating the Common Object DataBase

objects are, in turn, hierarchically defined as a set of objects that use containers to communicate. The CODB holds all public data and all system components may access the CODB for data from other system components. The World State Manager maintains a complete description of the state of distributed virtual environment as communicated using DIS-formatted PDUs.

3.4 CGF software and decision architecture

The AW architecture consists of three components (Figure 3): an Operator Skills Component (OSC), an Active Decisions Component (ADC), and a Physical Dynamics Component (PDC). The PDC encapsulates all the physical attributes and properties of the CGF. In the AW, this component includes the aerodynamics model, entity-specific properties, aircraft capabilities, weapons load, sensors, damage assessment, and physical status. In addition, the PDC computes physical state changes such as computing the current AW position in the virtual environment. The OSC consists of those portions of the CGF that vary between individual entities within a type and class, and models the skills and ability of the operator of the entity. For an aircraft entity, the components of the OSC include the simulated pilot's ability to maintain situation awareness and to execute tactical and flight skills. The ADC encompasses the intelligent decision making processes and the knowledge necessary to properly drive them, which includes the overall mission, goals and objectives, plan generation, reaction time, and crisis management ability. The ADC must accomplish many of its activities in real-time.

We chose to separate the components of the CGF architecture in this manner to insure that modifications are isolated and will not propagate throughout the system. The PDC only holds the basic entity maneuver information and is completely unaware of the status of the other system components. Likewise, the ADC is solely responsible for decision making and only knows about the physical component's status based upon the data communicated within the system software architecture. The OSC is more closely tied to the ADC than the PDC because the ADC is responsible for computing control outputs for the entity based upon the modeled operator's skills. The OSC describes the operator's ability for the decision making component so that the decision can be appropriately constrained by the pilot's abilities. The division of capabilities between these basic components lessens the system level impact of any changes in the PDC, OSC, or ADC.

The OSC and PDC contain all the information and status required to portray an aircraft model and its operator's ability. The PDC encapsulates the entity state information and the OSC contains a representation for all the operator skill variables. The key aspect of these two components is that these subsystems are completely parameterizable, and hence rapidly reconfigured and reused. We isolate entity control skills in the OSC because this separates the ability to parameterize the operator's capabilities from the decision making mechanisms. This parameterization allows any number of CGFs of a given type to be generated using a given ADC but yet each entity can have its own unique set of operator skills. The OSC models the operator's skills as a hierarchy of capabilities and allows us to compose more complex skills from elementary skills and to compose the higher level skills using a weighting of the appropriate elementary skills. The PDC and OSC do not, however, perform decision making based upon the information they store. The decision making task is solely the responsibility of the ADC.

The ADC contains a fuzzy planner, based upon fuzzy logic [8, 10], that allows certain subgoals to remain unsatisfied but yet allow the supergoal to be satisfied. This decision making flexibility permits a wide variety of possible behaviors and provides decision-making elasticity, allowing the CGF to achieve its mission in the face of uncertainty. Also, the fuzzy approach provides a method for optimization when various subgoals are applicable but only one is desired. This use of fuzzy logic adds another behavioral distinction that can be exploited to create a diverse mix of entities. The ADC is composed of the strategic decision engine (SDE), the tactical decision engine (TDE), and the critical decision engine (CDE).

The SDE is concerned with high level functions such as understanding and implementing mission level goals, communicating with other players, interpreting the surrounding environment, and revising mission goals and subgoals. The SDE handles strategic matters related to accomplishing mission goals by continuously re-evaluating the completion status of mission objectives and re-planning in a deliberative fashion to achieve the objectives. To execute its plans, the SDE then requests the TDE to carry out the near term (tactical) objectives.

The TDE's role is to make decisions about the moment to moment operations of the entity. This entails receiving specific taskings from thc SDE (subgoals), assessing DVE state, and responding to these situations according to the knowledge base of the particular entity. These responses include activities such as determining which maneuvers to make in a given situation, determining when to employ ordnance, and when to implement other application specific elements such as electromagnetic counter measures.

The CDE supplies the survival instinct for the virtual entity and takes over control of the entity in emergency situations where termination of the entity is imminent. The CDE is a purely reactive reasoning system that deals with critical situations the AW might encounter. In operation, the CDE monitors the world state until a critical situation is detected. The CDE then assumes control of the AW until the crisis has passed.

3.5 CGF knowledge hierarchy

The essence of our approach to defining a CGF knowledge hierarchy lies in applying the concept of *separation of concerns* to the domain of CGFs. As defined in the practice of software engineering, applying separation of concerns in a system design means separating the "how" from the "what" in the system. We believe that this technique is useful in creating modular CGFs because it assists in separating an entity's decision making ability from its physical ability. The separation of concerns is also a useful technique for decomposing the entity's decision making process into manageable subcomponents.

We used the concept of separation of concerns to aid in defining and refining the roles of the decision engines. To accomplish this, semantic Areas Of Concern (AOC) were used. An AOC is a question that must be answered to understand the role of a decision engine. The purpose of the AOC is twofold: first, they help the knowledge engineer identify the kinds of knowledge and behaviors to be modeled at the different levels of decision making, and second, they help the software engineer organize the various decision making processes into encapsulated interchangeable modules.

The AOC were established as a result of modeling the considerations that confront a present day war fighter. For example, perhaps the single most fundamental consideration is the mission. From this flows a series of follow-on questions, such as "How do I perform my mission?", and "What is my current task within the

Table 1. Key questions for AOC determination

Decision Engine Component	Key Definitional Questions
SDE	• What's my mission? • How do I perform my mission? • Am I able to accomplish my mission? • What's my current task within the mission? • How do I communicate with other entities and actors? • How do I perceive the outside world? • How do I deal with a lack of appropriate information? • What are the target types that I'm designed for? • What are my responsibilities?
TDE	• What kinds of maneuvers am I capable of? • What kinds of weapons do I know how to use? • How do I choose which maneuver to apply in a given situation? • How do I choose which type of weapon to employ in a given situation? • How do I know when to employ ordnance? • How do I know that the weapon was effective? • How am I aware of my environment? • How does the local DVE state affect my decision making? • What is my tasking within the mission?
CDE	• Am I in any immediate danger? • If I am in danger, what maneuvers do I know how to do to escape the danger? • How would I decide which maneuver to make? • What kinds of countermeasures do I know how to use? • How do I decide when to use a countermeasure?

mission"? To be most useful, the AOC should be as domain independent as possible.

To make the AOC as simple and direct as possible, they are written in a first person perspective from the CGF's point of view. They are designed so that by answering these questions in the context of a specific type of CGF within a specified domain, the bulk of the work for identifying the CGF's behaviors will be accomplished. The key AOC are shown in Table 1.

4. CGF comparative decision mechanism

In addition to the primary decision engines that utilize fuzzy logic as the basis for decision making, the ADC makes use of a comparative decision process to perform "what-if" comparisons. One of the requirements for the Automated Wingman was to be able to choose the "best" maneuver to employ in a real-time engagement. This capability was achieved by modifying a two player, time stepped game tree [11] into a two player, asynchronous game tree (see Figure 4.) This approach allows the CGF to analyze the situation by determining opponent versus AW maneuver combinations, and then scores the resulting, relative orientations of the two aircraft according to what the algorithm expects to happen during the course of a fuzzily determined time period. The algorithm also operates within dynamically determined time constraints based on aircraft positions and velocities as well as expected weapon ranges and velocities. The algorithm analyzes, in a breadth first search, as many maneuver combination as possible within the given time constraints and presents the best possible choice for implementation. The process of selecting the maneuver combination is a discrete choice, not a fuzzy one. We adapted the game tree concept to a dynamic environment so that the CGF could compare and evaluate potential maneuvering decisions with regards to concurrent adversarial maneuvers over time. As a result, the complete ADC decision process requires the integration of multiple fuzzy decisions engines with a non-fuzzy comparative game tree. Our game tree approach is describedbelow.

Game trees are useful a decision mechanism when possible moves between opponents are known and resulting positions can be enumerated. The resulting positions can then be weighed, and decisions made based by selecting the path through the tree that results in the most advantageous weighting. Game trees are not naturally applied to situations where resulting positions between players are anything other than discrete. However, if sets of otherwise non-discrete possible player positions are described in discrete ways, then it is possible to use a game tree to make the best possible

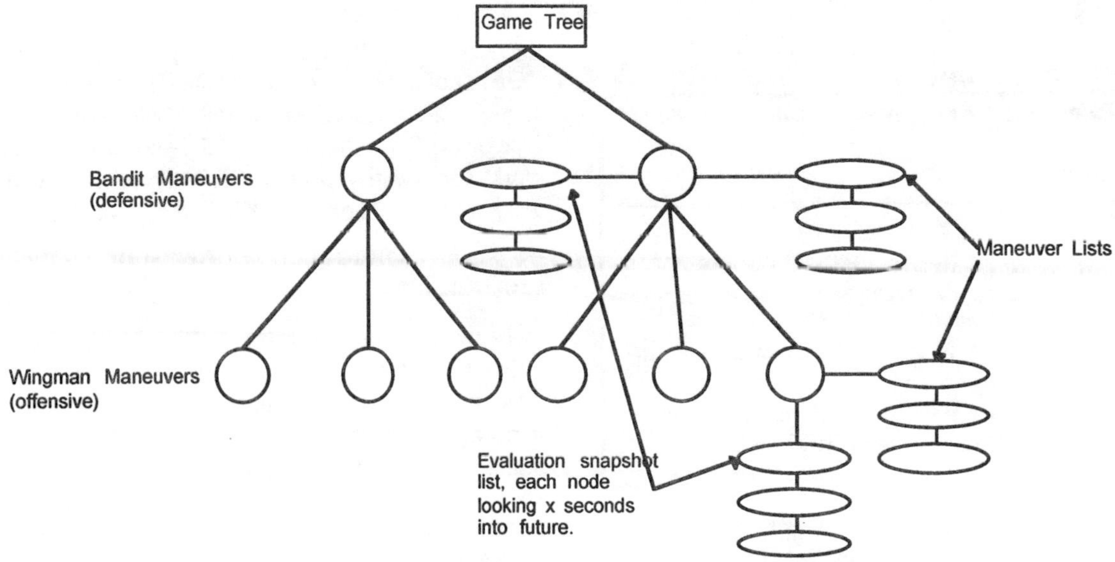

Figure 4. Asynchronous game tree example

choice. We used this technique for the Automated Wingman.

A CGF-type independent knowledge representation for the game tree was developed to represent possible player moves. This representation allows the knowledge to be separated from the algorithm used to act on the knowledge. As a result, we can use the same game tree algorithm for any CGF regardless of its CGF type. We represent the moves, or maneuvers, as directional graphs within a three-dimensional space. We represent the maneuvers in this space by taking the fundamental shape of the maneuver and then rotating and scaling the maneuver using standard formulas, which allows us to achieve any desired permutation of the basic maneuver. We specify the maneuver using x, y, and z coordinates and the values for CGF heading, pitch, and roll. Given these six attributes, it is possible to describe the location and orientation of a CGF with regards to the coordinate system origin. By considering CGF velocity, applying a specific maneuver representation, and then rotating and scaling the maneuver based on the velocity, we can predict the location and orientation of the CGF at a future time.

Given that we used this approach to model maneuver decision making in the highly dynamic and time critical domain of combat aircraft operations, we needed a mechanism to determine the maximum elapsed time that the game tree algorithm could consume while searching for a solution. To establish the maximum time, we calculate the minimum time it would take the AW to intercept the target from the current position. This minimum intercept time is then divided by a user specified value, the result being the maximum allowable time the algorithm can use to make a decision. The user specified divisor prevents the algorithm from consuming the entire time to intercept to make a decision. By giving the user control of this value, it allows flexible scaling of the performance of the CGF's decision making. In addition to the division value, an absolute minimum timing value is also specified in case the calculated decision time is very short (less than one second), this allows the algorithm to override the calculation and use the minimum specified decision time.

The game tree is constructed by using the target's known maneuvers for a defensive approach as the first tier nodes, and then combining all the wingman's maneuvers for an offensive approach as the second tier nodes. As a result, the ply of the basic tree never exceeds two (not including the depth of the evaluation branches discussed in later). Since the algorithm was written to accept any number of maneuvers when constructing the tree, the names of the known maneuvers as well as their data files are established at program startup by an initialization file. The CGF does not accept dynamically defined maneuvers after program start.

To permit it to operate on fuzzy logic variables, the game tree algorithm uses the values of variables defined over fuzzy term sets as iterative multipliers to determine how far ahead the CGF can accurately predict both it's and the opponent's position and orientation. For our tests, the evaluations of the fuzzy values resulted in look-ahead values of one, two, or three seconds. As a result, on each breadth-wise pass through the game tree, an AW with a look-ahead value of three seconds would get to look three seconds into the future of the current maneuver combination. Hence, after two passes of the tree, an AW with a look-ahead of three would be six seconds into the maneuver, whereas an AW with a look-ahead of one would only be two seconds into the maneuver. Thus we are able to establish better foresight performance for an AW with a higher operator skill rating.

By knowing the maneuvers and the aircraft velocities, we can create "snapshots" of future player positions and orientations calculated using the look-ahead value to determine the number of passes through the game tree. These snapshots are then used to represent the discrete player positions required for evaluation of the game tree. Moving breadth-wise through the game tree, player positions are evaluated one maneuver pairing at a time, so long as there is a combination remaining and sufficient time to make the evaluation. A single evaluation involves fuzzifying the coordinate locations, and then allowing the inferencing engine to evaluate all the applicable rules. We use a standard, center of gravity defuzzification technique to derive a player positional score.

5. Future work and conclusions

The AW currently presents a believable but limited portrayal of pilot behaviors within a DVE. Future work should expand the range of behaviors available to the AW. One aspect of this effort should be the design, implementation, and testing of the parameterization of multiple skill levels. Another aspect of the skill levels development activity must be to expand the AW's knowledge base by employing techniques for learning and knowledge-base modeling to provide a capability for achieving multiple levels of CGF ability/skills. However, simply possessing the capabilities for multiple skill levels within the decision component is insufficient for our purposes. A theory for designing entities with multiple skill levels, techniques for reusing skills among multiple skill levels, techniques for degrading skills without reaccomplishing the knowledge-base design, and an approach for modeling skill levels in humans are all required. Based on our results with the AW software and knowledge base architectures, a promising area for research is the investigation of the capability of these architectures to instantiate multiple and differing classes of CGFs.

The Automated Wingman has achieved a basic capability for believable operation within military DVEs and has demonstrated that fuzzy logic in combination with an adversarial game tree approach to decision making can achieve an acceptable range of behaviors for a CGF. The AW is based upon a generic CGF knowledge base and software that permits us to scale the software components and the knowledge base in response to new requirements as well as allowing us to undertake a rapid prototyping approach to CGF development. We have demonstrated the ability to adapt a static game tree to the highly dynamic, asynchronous environment typically found with combat fighter aircraft computer generated forces. The positive results of our initial tests showed that such an asynchronous game tree could in fact perform well in such an environment when the maximum processing time per decision cycle is constrained.

References

[1] Calder, R.B., Smith, J.E., Courtemanche, A.J., Mar, J.M.F., and Ceranowicz, A.Z. "ModSAF Behavior Simulation and Control," *Proceedings of the Third Conference on Computer-Generated Forces and Behavioral Representation*, Orlando, FL, pp. 347-356, 1993.

[2] Ceranowicz, A. "ModSAF Capabilities, A Progress Report," *Proceedings of the Fourth Conference on Computer Generated Forces and Behavioral Representation*, Orlando, FL, pp. 3-8, 4 - 6 May, 1994.

[3] IEEE Std 1278-1993. IEEE Standards Coordinating Committee of the IEEE Computer Society. "IEEE Standard for Information Technology - Protocols for Distributed Interactive Simulation Applications". Technical Report IEEE Std 1278-1993, March 1993.

[4] Laird, J. E., Newell, A., and Rosenbloom, P.S. "SOAR: An Architecture for General Intelligence," *Artificial Intelligence*, Vol. 33, pp. 1-64, 1987.

[5] Stytz, M. R. "Distributed Virtual Environments," *IEEE Computer Graphics and Applications*, Vol. 16, no. 3, pp. 19 - 31, May, 1996.

[6] Stytz, M. R., Adams, T., Garcia, B., Sheasby, S. M., and Zurita, B. "Developments in Rapid Prototyping and Software Architecture for Distributed Virtual Environments," *IEEE Software*, Vol. 14, no. 5, pp. 83-92, Sep. - Oct., 1997.

[7] Stytz, M. R., Banks, S. B., and Santos, E. "Requirements for Intelligent Aircraft Entities in Distributed Environments," *Proceedings of the 18th Interservice/Industry Training Systems and Education Conference*, Orlando, Florida, publication on CD-ROM, 3 - 5 December, 1996.

[8] Schwartz, D. G. "A System for Reasoning with Imprecise Linguistic Information," *International Journal of Approximate Reasoning*, Vol. 8, pp. 463-468, 1991.

[9] Tambe, M., Johnson, W. L., Jones, R.M., Koss, F., Laird, J. E., Rosenbloom, P. S., and Schwamb, K. "Intelligent Agents for Interactive Simulation Environments," *AI Magazine*, Vol. 16, no. 1, pp. 15-40, Spring, 1995.

[10] Zadeh, L. A. "The Concept of a Linguistic Variable and its Application to Approximate Reasoning," *Information Sciences*, Vol. 8, pp. 199-249 and 301-357, 1975.

[11] Giarratano, J. and Riley, G. (1994) *Expert Systems: Principles and Programming*, PWS Kent, Boston.

Session H.2

Machine Learning

Session Chair:
Mike Pazzani, University of California at Irvine, USA

MTLS: A Tool for Extending and Refining Knowledge Bases

Ockkeun Lee
Brightware, Inc.
350 Ignacio Blvd.
Novato, CA 94949
lee@brightware.com

Gheorghe Tecuci
Computer Science Department
George Mason University
Fairfax, VA 22030-4444
tecuci@cs.gmu.edu

Abstract

This paper presents an interactive multistrategy learning system (MTLS) that extends and refines knowledge bases by learning from input examples, discovering new knowledge, and cooperating with a user. The use of the multistrategy learning approach based on plausible justification trees allows MTLS to perform learning tasks that are beyond the capability of a single strategy learning method. A goal-driven knowledge discovery method has been developed and integrated into MTLS to produce additional knowledge needed by the system. MTLS also allows a human expert to guide it to refine and extend the knowledge base. This cooperation between a human expert and the learner enables the system to perform tasks that are intrinsically difficult for an autonomous system. The resulting knowledge base may include new rules discovered from data, as well as revised rules, and new facts learned by analogy. MTLS has been developed as a tool to be used by a domain expert to build a knowledge base to reduce the need of assistance from a knowledge engineer.

1 Introduction

The representation of a real world domain in a knowledge-based system is often incomplete and even partially incorrect, and needs to be improved. Hence, improving a knowledge base (KB) has always been an important research issue in the areas of machine learning and knowledge acquisition. The approach of machine learning and that of knowledge acquisition to improve a knowledge base are complementary in the sense that many of the hard problems in machine learning are significantly easier in knowledge acquisition and vice versa. Consequently, by properly integrating machine learning and knowledge acquisition methods, the knowledge base building process can benefit. Machine learning can facilitate the automation of the knowledge acquisition process and knowledge acquisition can facilitate the interaction with a human expert to acquire knowledge needed by the learning process.

In this paper we present MTLS, a tool for extending and refining knowledge bases that integrates machine learning and knowledge acquisition. MTLS implements the multistrategy learning method based on Plausible Justification Trees (PJT) presented in [9], extending it with goal-driven knowledge discovery of rules, and with cooperative knowledge refinement methods involving a human expert.

2 Learning with a PJT

MTLS is given an incomplete and partially incorrect knowledge base consisting of various kinds of rules and facts, and a set of input examples of a concept. The task of the system is then to determine an operational concept definition representing the input examples, and an improved knowledge base that entails the concept definition.

2.1 Knowledge representation

The KB contains facts and various types of rules represented as Horn clauses without functions. The different types of rules are distinguished by the corresponding operators: examples of concepts (<<), analogical rules (<−−), deductive rules (<=), and inductive rules (<−).

A KB in the area of automobile buying has been created to illustrate the method used in MTLS and a sample of this KB is shown in Table 1. It contains 10 deductive rules (r_1 through r_{10}), 1 analogical rule (r_{11}), and 1 inductive prediction rule (r_{12}). The deductive rule (r_1) states that a car has a good overall value if it has a high value, an above average mechanical review, and satisfying customer test.

2.2 Input examples

The goal of MTLS is to learn the concept (relationship) represented by the input examples, and to improve the KB such that it consistently integrates the information contained in the input. The input consists of a sequence of positive and/or negative examples of a concept or relationship, each example being represented as a conjunction of predicates. Three input examples are presented in Table 2. The head of each positive example is a specific vehicle with a good overall value, and the body of each example is the description of the corresponding vehicle. The negative example (indicated with a negation in its head) describes a vehicle that does not have a good overall value. The examples are assumed to be complete and correct.

1082-3409/97 $10.00 © 1997 IEEE

Table 1: Sample knowledge base.

(r_1) ((overall_value ?x1 good) <= (and (value ?x1 high) (mechanical_review ?x1 above_average) (customer_test ?x1 satisfy)))
(r_2) ((customer_test ?x2 satisfy) <= (and (comfort ?x2 good) (fun_to_drive ?x2 yes)))
(r_3) ((mechanical_review ?x3 above_average) <= (and (performance ?x3 good) (safety ?x3 high) (reliability ?x3 good)))
(r_4) ((value ?x4 high) <= (and (owner_satisfaction ?x4 satisfy) (insurance_cost ?x4 low)))
(r_5) ((owner_satisfaction ?x5 satisfy) <= (and (fuel_efficiency ?x5 economic) (price_retention ?x5 good) (owner_complaints ?x5 low)))
(r_6) ((insurance_cost ?x6 low) <= (insurance_risk ?x6 low))
(r_7) ((performance ?x7 good) <= (acceleration ?x7 fast))
(r_8) ((performance ?x8 good) <= (power ?x8 strong))
(r_9) ((safety ?x9 high) <= (and (breaking_distance ?x9 short) (safety_features ?x9 available) (maneuverability ?x9 good)))
(r_{10}) ((reliability ?x10 good) <= (and (recall_record ?x10 0) (mechanical_trouble ?x10 minor)))
(r_{11}) ((owner_complaints ?x11 ?z) <−− (customer_service ?x11 ?y))
(r_{12}) ((insurance_risk ?x12 low) <− (number_of_door ?x12 four))

(insurance_risk vin_01 low)
(insurance_risk vin_02 low)
(num_of_door vin_03 four)
(maintenance_cost vin_03 low)
(num_of_door vin_04 four)
(insurance_risk vin_06 high)
(maintenance_cost vin_06 low)
(num_of_door vin_07 two)
(maintenance_cost vin_07 low)

(num_of_door vin_01 four)
(num_of_door vin_02 four)
(owner_complaints vin_03 low)
(insurance_risk vin_03 low)
(insurance_risk vin_05 low)
(num_of_door vin_06 two)
(owner_complaints vin_06 low)
(owner_complaints vin_07 low)
(owner_complaints vin_08 low)

(fuel_type vin_01 gas)
(customer_service vin_03 excellent)
(recall_by_manufacture vin_03 none)
(insurance_risk vin_04 low)
(num_of_door vin_05 four)
(customer_service vin_06 excellent)
(insurance_risk vin_07 high)
(customer_service vin_07 excellent)
(maintenance_cost vin_08 low)

2.3 Input understanding

The first step of the learning method is to *understand* the first input example. This is achieved by building a plausible justification tree (PJT) that shows that the input example is a plausible consequence of the knowledge from the KB. A PJT is similar to a proof tree except that the component inference steps may be the result of different types of reasoning. The top of the tree is the head of the example and the leaves are the predicates from the body of the example. The tree shows how the predicates from the body of the example plausibly imply the head of the example.

To determine a most plausible justification of the input example, MTLS conducts a top-down uniform- cost search using a cost function that favors the deductive steps over the non-deductive ones obtained by analogy, inductive prediction, or abduction [9].

As a general strategy, the system always tries to justify a given predicate by deduction (r_1). If it succeeds, then it tries to justify the resulting predicates. However, if it fails, then it tries to justify the predicate first by using analogy, then by using inductive prediction. The PJT in Figure 1 has been built for Example 1 in Table 2 with the KB described in Table 1. It shows that Example 1 is indeed a positive example of the concept "(overall_value ?x good)". The inference steps denoted by "<=" in Figure 1 are the results of deductions. The given target, "(overall_value vin_00 good)," from Example 1 is deductively reduced to "(customer_test vin_00 satisfy)," "(mechanical_review vin_00 above_average)," and "(value vin_00 high)". Since the instantiated predicates in the leaf nodes are not the facts in the input example, the leaves are expanded with other deductive rules (r_2, r_3, and r_4). The node "(owner_complaints vin_00 low)" in Figure 1 expanded from r_5 is justified by analogical inference based on the determination rule r_{11} the level of complaints is determined by the quality of customer service. The node "(insurance_risk vin_00 low)" is justified by using the inductive predication rule r_{12}. MTLS may generate an inductive prediction rule through inductive generalization of concept examples or through discovery from the facts in the KB.

2.4 Generalization of a PJT

Once the PJT in Figure 1 is successfully built, MTLS generalizes the tree, by using a method inspired by the one of [3]. First, each implication is replaced with the least general generalization of all the similar implications that could be obtained from the knowledge that produced it [9]. Then MTLS unifies the generalized implications, and builds a generalized justification tree.

3 Goal-driven knowledge discovery

MTLS may not be able to build a complete PJT of the input example due to the incomplete and partially incorrect KB. The incomplete tree contains at least one unjustified

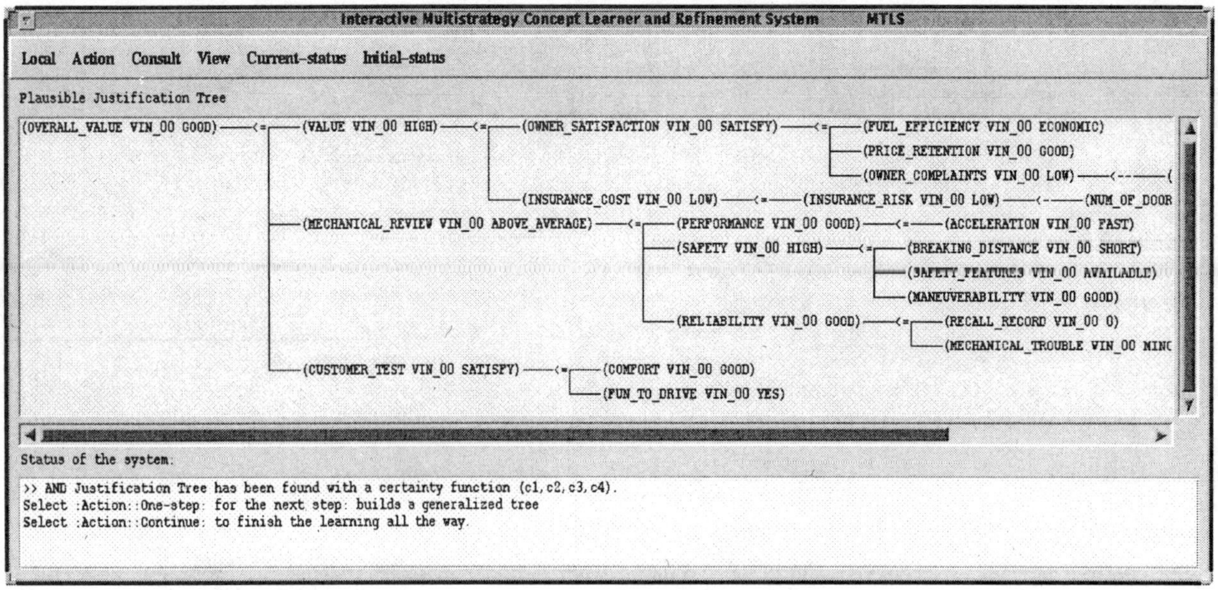

Figure 1: Plausible justification tree as shown in the system.

Table 2: Input examples.

Example 1: ((overall_value vin_00 good) << (and (fuel_efficiency vin_00 economic) (price_retention vin_00 good) (recall_record vin_00 0) (comfort vin_00 good) (customer_service vin_00 excellent) (maneuverability vin_00 good) (breaking_distance vin_00 short) (safety_features vin_00 available) (fun_to_drive vin_00 yes)(num_of_door vin_00 four) (tire vin_00 good_year) (color vin_00 ruby) (mechanical_trouble vin_00 minor) (invoice_less_than vin_00 15000) (acceleration vin_00 fast) (factory_rebate vin_00) (maintenance_cost vin_00 low)))

Example 2: ((overall_value vin_11 good) << (and (fuel_efficiency vin_11 economic) (price_retention vin_11 good) (recall_record vin_11 0) (comfort vin_11 good) (customer_service vin_11 excellent) (maneuverability vin_11 good) (breaking_distance vin_11 short) (safety_features vin_11 available) (fun_to_drive vin_11 yes)(num_of_door vin_11 four) (color vin_11 white) (tire vin_11 firestone)(mechanical_trouble vin_11 minor)(seat_type vin_11 fabric) (power vin_11 strong) (factory_rebate vin_11) (maintenance_cost vin_00 low)))

Example 3: ((not (overall_value vin_12 good)) << (and (fuel_efficiency vin_12 economic) (price_retention vin_12 good) (recall_record vin_12 0) (comfort vin_12 good) (maneuverability vin_12 good) (customer_service vin_12 excellent) (breaking_distance vin_12 short) (safety_features vin_12 available) (fun_to_drive vin_12 yes)(num_of_door vin_12 four) (color vin_12 gold) (tire vin_12 good_year)(fog_light vin_12) (mechanical_trouble vin_12 minor) (acceleration vin_12 fast) (factory_rebate vin_12) (maintenance_cost vin_00 high)))

node, that is, a node that is not implied by the predicates from the body of the example. This unjustified node is the *target* of the discovery process. MTLS will analyze the facts from the KB attempting to discover a rule that imply a generalization of the target predicate.

3.1 Inductive prediction rule

3.1.1. Constructing examples. Suppose that the KB in Table 1 does not contain the inductive prediction rule r_{12}. Then MTLS is not able to justify the target instance "(insurance_risk vin_00 low)." The missing rule can be obtained through inductive learning only if the necessary examples exist. If the examples do not exists, MTLS will construct them. It will first consider the target concept $\mathcal{C}$, "(insurance_risk ?x6 low)," from r_6, which will become the head of a rule to be discovered. Here, the constant "low" is a *value constant* (property) and the constants from the KB that satisfy the variable are *object constants* (instances) of the target concept. Then MTLS identifies vin_01, vin_02, vin_03, vin_04, and vin_05 as instances of vehicles with low insurance risk from the facts in Table 1. Next an example $\mathcal{E}_i$ of $\mathcal{C}$ corresponding to vin_01 is constructed from the KB facts that contain vin_01 as an argument:

((insurance_risk vin_01 low) <<
(and (num_of_door vin_01 four) (fuel_type vin_01 gas)))

Figure 2 illustrates the process of constructing examples with the target, "(insurance_risk vin_00 low)". In general, the system constructs a set of concept examples $\mathcal{E}_i$ of $\mathcal{C}$ in the following form: ($\mathcal{C}_i$ << (and $P_{i1} P_{i2} ... P_{in}$)) where $\mathcal{C}_i$ is an instance of $\mathcal{C}$ that contains i and P_{in} is a predicate from the KB that contains i as an argument. The value constant

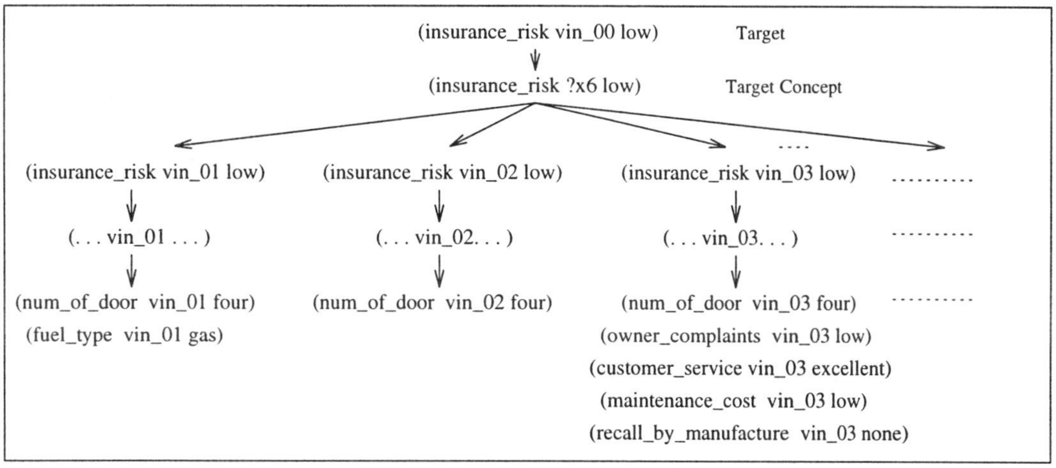

Figure 2: Description of example construction.

in a target concept allows the system to generate both positive and negative examples. The positive examples are the ones generated from the target concept, whereas the negative examples are generated from the same predicate but with different value constants.

3.1.2. Information-based inductive learning. The learning method used in the system is similar to the one used in FOIL [6]. MTLS starts with a clause where the head is the target concept and the body is empty, $(C <\!-\{\})$. Then it selects a first predicate P_1 that best characterizes the set of positive examples $\mathcal{E}_p$ and least characterizes the set of negative examples $\mathcal{E}_n$, according to a *gain* function, $\mathcal{G}$, ([5, 6, 10]). Thus, the discovered rule at this point becomes $(C <\!-P_1)$. Next, the set of positive examples $\mathcal{E}_P$ is reduced to the set $\mathcal{E}_{p1}$ of the positive examples that contain P_1, and the set of negative examples $\mathcal{E}_N$ is reduced to the set $\mathcal{E}_{n1}$ of the negative examples that contain P_1. If $\mathcal{E}_{n1}$ is not empty, the system again selects a predicate P_2 from the reduced sets, $\mathcal{E}_{p1}$ and $\mathcal{E}_{n1}$. The discovered rule becomes (C <– (and $P_1 P_2$)). The process continues until the system finds the property that does not belong to any negative example in the reduced sets. Thus, a discovered rule has the following form: (C <– (and $P_1 P_2 ... P_k$)). Applying this method, MTLS discovered the rule r_{12}, ((insurance_risk ?x low) <– (number_of_door ?x four)), that can be used to justify "(insurance_risk vin_00 low)."

3.2 Plausible determination rule

MTLS can also discover plausible determination rules to justify a predicate Q in a PJT. Such a rule has the form "((Q x z) <–– (P x y))," meaning that P plausibly determines Q [1, 9].

3.2.1. Correlation between facts. To discover a plausible determination rule ((Q x z) <–– (P x y)), MTLS uses a technique similar to the one of [7]. It will analyze the distribution of the y and z values for the different facts in the KB. The possible values of y and z are used as the indices of the rows is and columns js of a two dimensional array A. In this array $A_{i,j}$ indicates the number (X) of instances of x that satisfies y_i and z_j at the same time. To meet the requirement of a plausible determination of the form ((Q x z) <–– (P x y)), the distribution of each row should contain one and only one peak at some column. That is, each row y and column z should contain only one value that represents the number of instances for the corresponding x.

Unlike the approach [7] that selects binary predicates P and Q arbitrarily from the KB, in MTLS, the predicate Q is obtained from a target instance by turning the constants in its argument into variables x and z. This enables MTLS to reduce the search space to the given (Q x z) and the predicates that contain x in their first arguments: (P_1 x y_1), ..., (P_i x y_i).

Each candidate pair for a plausible determination rule, such as ⟨(Q x z), (P_i x y_i)⟩, is tested in accordance with several determination criteria. Namely, for each z, there should be a unique matching y_i, and a set x of at least X constants. Also, the total number of zs should be greater than Z. The values of X and Z are determined by a human expert when the learning environment is set and depend of the domain and the quality of the knowledge pieces available in the KB [2].

3.2.2. An example of discovering a plausible determination rule. Let us assume that X is set to 1 and Z is set to 3. Let us further assume that the plausible determination rule r_{11} is not present in the KB (Table 1) and that the KB contains the sample facts in Table 3. According to the PJT from Figure 1, the instance, "(owner_complaints vin_00 low)," is to be justified and, therefore, becomes the target instance. From the rule, r_5, which created the target instance, the sys-

Table 3: Sample facts in the knowledge base for a determination rule.

(insurance_risk vin_01 low)	(num_of_door vin_01 four)	(fuel_type vin_01 gas)
(insurance_risk vin_02 low)	(num_of_door vin_02 four)	(customer_service vin_03 excellent)
(num_of_door vin_03 four)	(owner_complaints vin_03 low)	(recall_by_manufacture vin_03 none)
(maintenance_cost vin_03 low)	(insurance_risk vin_03 low)	(insurance_risk vin_04 low)
(num_of_door vin_04 four)	(insurance_risk vin_05 low)	(num_of_door vin_05 four)
(insurance_risk vin_06 high)	(num_of_door vin_06 two)	(customer_service vin_06 excellent)
(maintenance_cost vin_06 low)	(owner_complaints vin_06 low)	(insurance_risk vin_07 high)
(num_of_door vin_07 two)	(owner_complaints vin_07 low)	(customer_service vin_07 excellent)
(maintenance_cost vin_07 low)	(owner_complaints vin_08 low)	(customer_service vin_08 excellent)
(maintenance_cost vin_08 low)	(owner_complaints vin_09 high)	(customer_service vin_09 bad)
(owner_complaints vin_10 mid)	(customer_service vin_10 average)	

tem obtains a target concept, "(owner_complaints ?x low)." This concept is further generalized, by turning constants into variables, to "(owner_complaints ?x ?z). Next, MTLS finds all the instances of "(owner_complaints ?x ?z)" in the KB (see Figure 3). Such an instance is "(owner_complaints vin_03 low)". Next it finds all the predicates that have vin_03 as an argument, for example "(insurance_risk vin_03 low)". MTLS will have to check whether any such predicate determines owner_complaints. Applying this method to the facts in Table 3, MTLS produces the following candidate pairs for determinations: ⟨(owner_complaints ?x ?z) (insurance_risk ?x $?y_1$)⟩, ⟨(owner_complaints ?x ?z) (num_of_door ?x $?y_2$)⟩, ⟨(owner_complaints ?x ?z) (customer_service ?x $?y_3$)⟩, ⟨(owner_complaints ?x ?z) (maintenance_cost ?x $?y_4$)⟩ and ⟨(owner_complaints ?x ?z) (recall_by_manufacture ?x $?y_5$)⟩.

For each candidate pair, MTLS first checks the determination criteria. For example, the pair ⟨(owner_complaints ?x ?z), (insurance_risk ?x $?y_1$)⟩ does not qualify because the value of $?y_1$ for each instance is not unique. Indeed, ⟨(owner_complaints vin_03 low), (insurance_risk vin_03 low)⟩ and ⟨(owner_complaints vin_06 low), (insurance_risk vin_06 high)⟩ do not have a unique value of $?y_1$ for the value low of ?z. The second pair, ⟨(owner_complaints ?x ?z), (num_of_door ?x $?y_2$)⟩ does not meet the criteria for the same reason. The third pair ⟨(owner_complaints ?x ?z), (customer_service ?x $?y_3$)⟩, however, meets all the determination criteria and is included as a candidate. The remaining pairs, ⟨(owner_complaints ?x ?z), (maintenance_cost ?x $?y_4$)⟩ and ⟨(owner_complaints ?x ?z), (recall_by_manufacture ?x $?y_5$)⟩, do not satisfy the criteria because the number of instances for each $?y_i$ value is less than X. Therefore, the pair, ⟨(owner_complaints ?z ?y), (customer_service ?x $?y_3$)⟩, becomes the discovered plausible determination rule:

((owner_complaints ?x ?z) <−− (customer_service ?x $?y_3$)).

4 Cooperative knowledge refinement

The general PJT, Tg_1, generalized from the first input example can be further refined with additional input examples and through cooperation with a human expert, as presented in the following.

4.1 Generalization from a new positive example

Consider Example 2 in Table 2. First, the system determines the instance of Tg_1 corresponding to Example 2, and analyzes the leaf predicates and the inference steps from this tree. If the leaf predicates are true and the inference steps are plausible, then the tree is a plausible justification of Example 2. This ends the processing of the current example and the general tree Tg_1 needs not to be changed.

In this case, however, the instantiated tree is not a correct justification of Example 2 because the leaf predicate "(acceleration vin_11, fast)" is not true (see (a) in Figure 4). This leaf node is neither supported by rules in the KB nor by the facts in Example 2. The system's task is to generalize the current justification tree Tg_1 to cover this uncovered positive input example. Therefore, the system uses the deductive rule r_8 (see (b) in Figure 4) from Table 1 as an alternative and builds the correct PJT. That is, the instance, "(performance vin_11 good)," which was not justified by r_7 with Example 2 is now justified by r_8.

Next, the system builds an explanation structure, (c) in Figure 4, which has three general components to be unified. Namely, ?x1 from the general tree Tg_1, ?x2 from the part of the PJT that covers Example 1, and ?x3 from the part of the PJT that covers Example 2. Then the system unifies the connection patterns in the explanation structure and obtains a new general justification tree Tg_2 that covers the justification trees of both Example 1 and Example 2.

Now, suppose that MTLS is not able to provide an alternative rule for a false node (i.e., the KB does not contain rule r_8 and the discovery routine does not provide an alternative rule). In this case, the user must either remove the

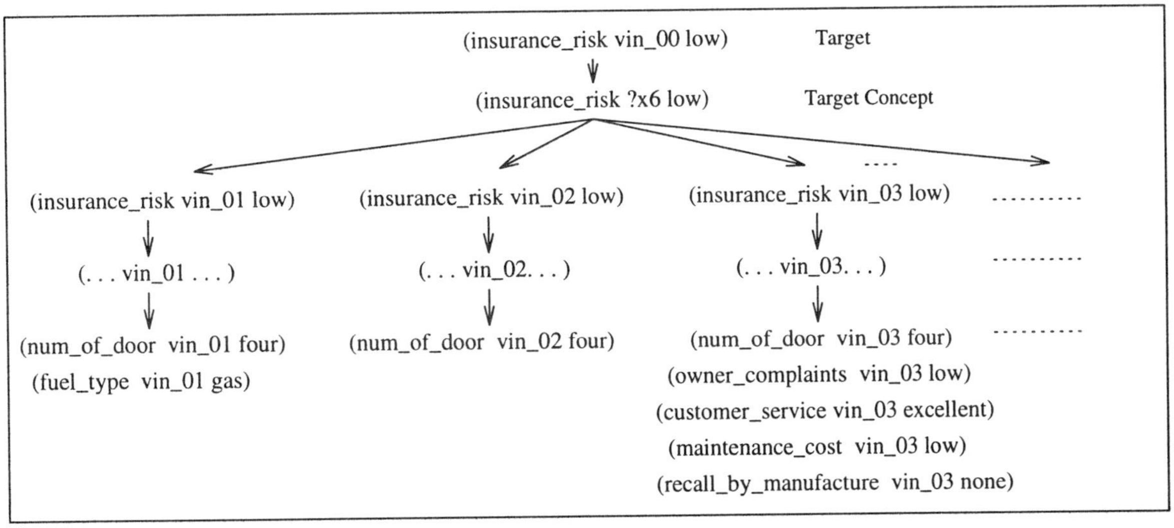

Figure 3: Description of obtaining relevant instances for determination.

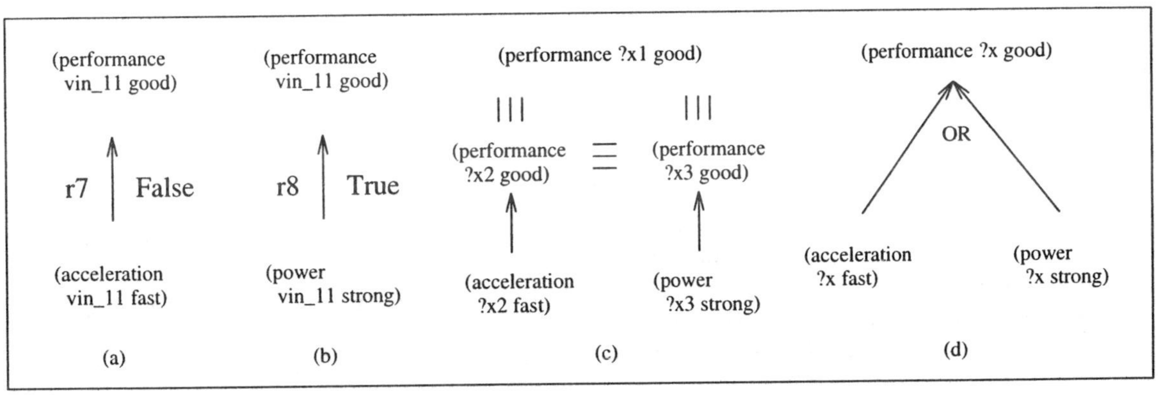

Figure 4: Generalization of a part of Tg_1 to cover example 2.

condition that is not justified by the current example or add an OR condition that allows the input example to be satisfied. To add an OR condition, one must study the features of the input example to identify the one to be added. MTLS provides a dialog interface permitting the user to enter the condition. The details can be found in [2].

4.2 Specialization from a new negative example

Let us now consider the negative input example, Example 3 in Table 2, and the general tree Tg_2 generalized from both Example 1 and Example 2. The system now builds the instance of the tree Tg_2, corresponding to the new input example. Then it analyzes the leaf predicates and the inference steps from this tree, and concludes that this tree leads to a wrong conclusion. In other words, the tree wrongly shows that the current negative input example is a positive example of the concept "(overall_value ?x good)". Therefore, the tree must contain some false leaf predicates or inference steps that need to be detected. Both the general justification tree Tg_2 and the KB should be specialized to no longer contain them. MTLS attempts to find a property common to the positive examples that does not belong to the negative example, and to add it to the PJT as an AND condition. This specializes the PJT to no longer justify the negative example. The rule from the KB the instance of which has been specialized in the PJT, should also be correspondingly specialized.

In considering the input examples in Table 2, the inductive learner would suggest that "(maintenance_cost ?x low)" be added into the current PJT, because it belongs to Example 1 and Example 2, but not to Example 3. Then MTLS will interact with the user to specialize the PJT and the KB with this predicate. The result is a new general tree

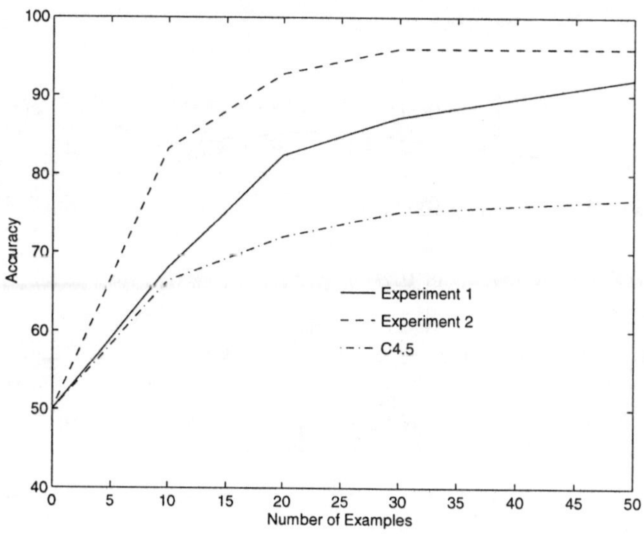

Figure 5: The accuracy of experiments.

Tg_3. If no AND predicate is discovered by MTLS, the system and the user may specialize the PJT by removing an OR condition.

5 Learned knowledge

As mentioned earlier, the goal of the system is to learn the concept represented by the input examples and to improve the KB so as to consistently integrate the information contained in the input. Consequently, MTLS has learned the operational definition of the concept "(overall_value x, good)," represented by the leaves of the justification tree Tg_3:

((overall_value ?x good) <– (and (fuel_efficiency ?x economic) (price_retention ?x good) (comfort ?x good) (customer_service ?x excellent) (maintenance_cost ?x low) (fun_to_drive ?x yes) (or (power ?x strong) (acceleration ?x fast)) (safety_features ?x available) (maneuverability ?x good) (breaking_distance ?x short) (recall_record vin_00 0) (mechanical_trouble ?x minor) (num_of_door ?x four)))

MTLS has also generalized the KB by learning (by analogy) new facts, (owner_complaints vin_00 low), (owner_complaints vin_11 low) and (owner_complaints vin_12 low), and (by empirical generalization) a new rule: ((insurance_risk ?x low) <– (num_of_door ?x four)). Moreover, it has specialized the discovered determination rule to: ((owner_complaints ?x13 low) <– (and (customer_service ?x13 excellent) (maintenance_cost ?x13 low)))

6 Experimental results

MTLS was tested on automobile ratings reported in the 1996 consumer guide [11]. The numeric ratings were converted into symbols. The initial KB was developed from the rating system of the consumer guide that categorizes the rating into several sub-categories. Some abstract subcategories such as the "room comfort" were further explained with more operational definitions, such as the volume of leg room and head room. The KB developed was incomplete and partially incorrect and had to be improved with MTLS.

The training examples in this experiments were obtained from the specifications and detailed rating categories for each automobile reported in the consumer guide. The 119 examples from the consumer guide were divided into three rating levels: high, intermediate, low. Ratings in the upper 40 examples (high) were considered to be positive examples and ratings in the lower 35 examples (low) were considered to be negative examples. There were 44 examples with intermediate ratings, which were imported into the KB as facts. Each input example featured 43 attributes.

In each test, 50 input (training) examples were randomly selected from the total of 75 examples, leaving the remaining 25 examples for testing data. The accuracy was measured against the testing data when the number of input examples reached 10, 20, 30, and 50. This test was repeated 5 times and averaged. For each inconsistency occurred with respect to the input examples, minimum correction was made to refine the PJT.

These tests were performed on the initial knowledge base obtained from the consumer guide (Experiment 1). The result of Experiment 1 was also an the improved knowledge base that contained two refined rules. The same tests were performed with the improved knowledge base (Experiment 2). Also, the same tests were performed with C4.5 [5] without the domain knowledge.

The results show that the accuracy in all three experiments increased with the number of examples. They also show the advantage of using domain knowledge and to interact with the user. Indeed, the performance of MTLS was better than that of C4.5 which does not use of a domain theory and does not interact with its user. A similar result was reported in [4]. The experiments 1 and 2 in the graph also show that the more the KB is complete and correct, the better MTLS performs.

MTLS was also tested with five human subjects to measure the performance from the user's perspective, using the initial knowledge base and 50 randomly selected input data. Each experiment resulted in a different PJT and KB. It was also observed that 80% of the actions occurred within the first 20 input examples. The resulting accuracies of the five human subjects were 80, 84, 76, 85, and 80 out of 100. Within the same environment, C4.5 produced an accuracy of 72%.

MTLS was also tested in the domain of computer workstation allocation and configuration presented in [8] and the geography domain presented in [9].

7 Conclusion and final remarks

In this paper, the MTLS interactive multistrategy learning system was presented. MTLS was implemented using Harlequin Lisp in the UNIX environment and was applied in several domains. The experimental results with MTLS showed that its approach increased the accuracy of the learned rules and led to an improved knowledge base. Therefore, MTLS provides a human expert with a powerful tool for building knowledge-based systems, which may reduce the need of assistance from a knowledge engineer.

Acknowledgments

This research was done in the Learning Agents Laboratory of the Computer Science Department in George Mason University. The research of the LA Lab is supported by the AFOSR grant F49620-97-1-0188, as part of the DARPA High Performance Knowledge Base Program, by the NSF grant CDA-9616478, and by the DARPA contract N66001-95-D-8653

References

[1] T. Davies and S. Russell, "A Logical Approach to Reasoning by Analogy," *Proceedings of the Tenth International Joint Conference on Artificial Intelligence*, 1987.

[2] O. Lee, "Extending and Refining Knowledge Bases with an Interactive Multistrategy Concept Learner," *Ph.D. Thesis*, George Mason University, 1997.

[3] R. Mooney and S. Bennet, "A Domain Independent Explanation Based Generalizer, " *Proceedings of AAAI-86*, Philadelphia, 1986, pp.551-555.

[4] R. Mooney and D. Ourston, "A Multistrategy Approach to Theory Refinement," *Proceedings of the First International Workshop on Multistrategy Learning*, edited by R.S. Michalski and G. Tecuci, Harpers Ferry, W.Va, Nov. 1991.

[5] J. R. Quinlan, *C4.5: Programs for Machine Learning*, Morgan Kaufmann, 1993.

[6] J. R. Quinlan, "Learning Logical Definitions from Relations," *Machine Learning*, Vol. 5, pp 239-266, 1990

[7] W. Shen, "Discovering Regularities from Large Knowledge Bases," *Proceedings of the Eight International Workshop*, San Mateo, CA, Morgan Kaufmann, 1991.

[8] G. Tecuci,"Building Knowledge Bases through Multistrategy Learning and Knowledge Acquisition," *Machine Learning and Knowledge Acquisition: Integrated Approaches*, edited by G. Tecuci and Y. Kodratoff, Academic Press, 1995

[9] G. Tecuci, "An Inference-Based Framework for Multistrategy Learning," *Machine Learning: A Multistrategy Approach*, edited by R. Michalski and G. Tecuci, Morgan Kaufmann, Vol 4, pp. 107-138, 1994.

[10] J. F. Young, *Information Theory*, Published by Wiley Interscience, New York, 1971

[11] Consumer Guide, *Consumer Guide: 1996 Cars*, Published by Publications International, Ltd., 1996

Dimensionality Reduction of Unsupervised Data

M. Dash, H. Liu, J. Yao
Department of Information Systems and Computer Science
National University of Singapore
Kent Ridge, Singapore 119260

Abstract

Dimensionality reduction is an important problem for efficient handling of large databases. Many feature selection methods exist for supervised data having class information. Little work has been done for dimensionality reduction of unsupervised data in which class information is not available. Principal Component Analysis (PCA) is often used. However, PCA creates new features. It is difficult to obtain intuitive understanding of the data using the new features only. In this paper we are concerned with the problem of determining and choosing the important original features for unsupervised data. Our method is based on the observation that removing an irrelevant feature from the feature set may not change the underlying concept of the data, but not so otherwise. We propose an entropy measure for ranking features, and conduct extensive experiments to show that our method is able to find the important features. Also it compares well with a similar feature ranking method (Relief) that requires class information unlike our method.

1 Introduction

In real-world applications the size of a database is usually large. The largeness can be due to the excessive number of features (variables), the huge number of instances (records), or both. For machine learning algorithms to work efficiently one can try to reduce the data size [16]. In this paper we focus on reducing the size by decreasing the number of features. One approach is to determine the relative importance of the features and then select a subset of important features. This can be achieved in various ways, for example, by feature selection [6] or feature extraction [5].

There are a number of feature selection methods [2] that determine the relative importance of the features before selecting a subset of important ones. Examples are Relief [6, 8], POE+ACC [10]. A typical feature selection method tries to choose a subset of features from the original set that is ideally necessary and sufficient to describe the target concept [6]. Target concepts are denoted by class labels. Data with class labels are called supervised data; data without class labels unsupervised. Although original features are selected based on some evaluation function, *these methods require class labels.* Hence, feature selection methods largely fail for unsupervised data.

Feature extraction methods create new features which are uncorrelated and retain as much variation as possible in the database ([16], [5]). One commonly known method is principal component analysis (PCA). Although PCA does not need class labels for extracting the features or Principal Components (PCs), *usually the values of the original features are still needed in order to calculate the PCs since each PC is a function of the original features.* Also, it is difficult to get intuitive understanding of the data *using the extracted features only.*

In practice, we often encounter databases that have large dimensionality and are without class information. Data is normally collected for organizational or book-keeping purposes, and not particularly for machine learning. For example, transactional data does not contain any class information, and it could have a huge number of features. It is often desirable to preprocess the data before applying a knowledge discovery tool [15]. Dimensionality reduction without creating any new feature offers an effective solution to reduce the data size while keeping the original features intact. This helps in obtaining intuitive understanding of the data as one can know the important features for describing the underlying concept. PCA or feature selection methods cannot help much for this type of dimensionality reduction due to the reasons given above. This is a new problem that surfaces as the need for data mining arises. It is also an interesting research problem, and solutions for this will be welcome by both research and industry community who handle data with large dimensionality.

In this paper we attack an unsolved problem, i.e., the problem of determining and choosing the important original features for unsupervised data. An en-

1082-3409/97 $10.00

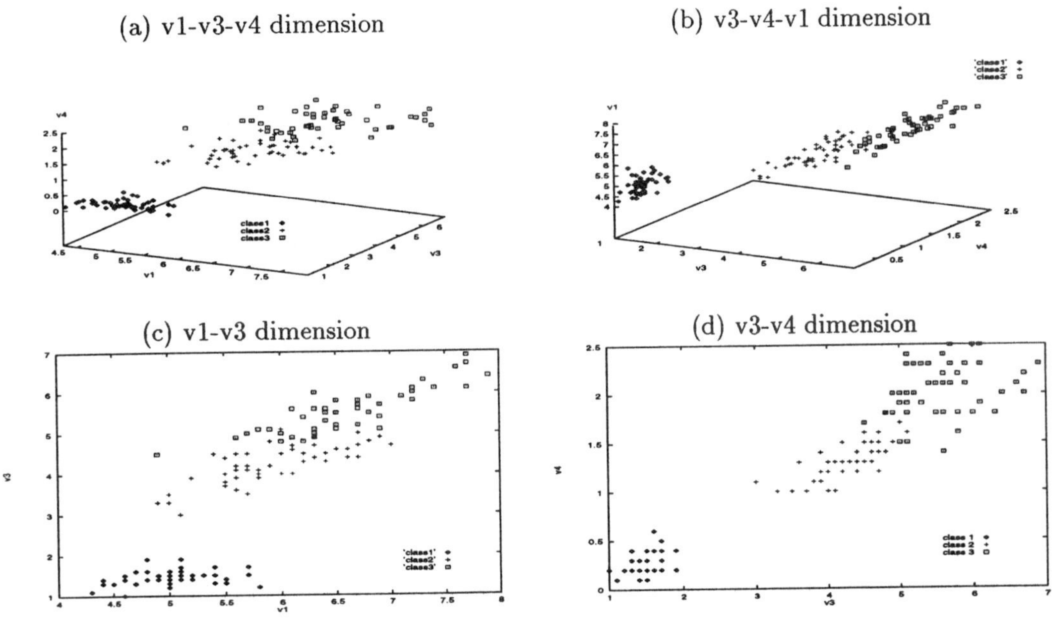

Figure 1: Iris data in different variable dimensional spaces.

tropy measure that determines the importance of the original features with respect to underlying clusters is introduced in the next section. This measure works for both nominal and continuous data types. In Section 3 a sequential backward selection algorithm is given to rank the features in order of their importance, and the problem of determining the threshold (number of features) is also discussed. The experimental study in Section 4 shows that the proposed algorithm is able to find the important features for databases with known important features. It also shows that the performance of the proposed algorithm without using class labels is very close to and sometimes better than that of Relief-F [8] (a generalized version of Relief [6] for multiple class labels) which ranks the original features using the class labels. Experiments with two classifiers show the advantages of feature elimination in unsupervised data. The paper concludes in Section 5 with discussions on the difficulty in finding a threshold to stop selecting features and the complexity of the algorithm.

2 An Entropy Measure for Continuous and Nominal Data Types

In this section we introduce an entropy measure for determining the relative importance of variables. This measure is applicable to both nominal and continuous data types, and does not need class information to evaluate the variables unlike some other entropy measures, for example, information gain measure in ID3 [12].

2.1 Physical Significance

Consider an instance in a dataset, which is described by a set of variables. If the data has distinct clusters, this instance should belong to some cluster, and the instance must be well separated from some instances in other clusters and very close to others in the same cluster. Irrelevant variables have no influence, but relevant ones do, on forming distinct clusters. Our method is based on the observation that removing an irrelevant variable from the variable set may not change the underlying concept of the data, but not so otherwise. Consider a set of N instances in an M dimensional hyper-space, where each instance x_i is represented by a vector of M values (i.e., $x_{i1}, x_{i2}, ..., x_{iM}$). Removing a variable from the original set of variables (i.e., decreasing dimensionality of the hyper-space by one) is to project the data onto the $M-1$ dimensional hyper-space. If the distinctness among the clusters remain after projecting instances from M to $M-1$ dimensions, then the variable is not important for describing the underlying structure of the data.

An Example: The Iris data (summarized in Table 1) has 4 variables in total. Figure 1(a) and (b) show the instances in a 3-dimensional space of subset (v_1, v_3, v_4). Removing variable v_4 is equivalent to projecting the data onto a 2-dimensional plane of subset (v_1, v_3) (Figure 1(c)), and removing variable v_1 is equivalent to projecting the data onto a 2-dimensional plane of subset (v_3, v_4) (Figure 1(d)). By examining the figures, we notice that data in Figure 1(d) for subset (v_3, v_4) displays more distinct clusters than data in Figure 1(c) for subset (v_1, v_3). This implies that variable v_4 is more important than variable v_1. Also, as the clusters in Figure 1(d) for subset (v_3, v_4) are roughly as distinct as the clusters in Figure 1(b) for subset (v_3, v_4, v_1), variable v_1 may be removed if only two variables are allowed. This work is to provide a measure that can capture the difference of two subsets by comparing the distinctness of the underlying clusters.

2.2 The Measure

We wish to find a measure that can determine the irrelevant features. If we start with the complete set of features, the feature removal of which retains the distinctness most among the clusters, should be removed first. Notice that when we remove a feature we project the original data of M dimensions to $M-1$ dimensions, and for M features we create M number of different projections. Hence our task is to compare all these projections and find out the one that retains the distinctness most. We say the data has orderly configurations if it has distinct clusters, and has disorderly or chaotic configurations otherwise. From entropy theory [4], we know that entropy (or probability) is low for orderly configurations, and more for disorderly configurations for the simple reason that there are few orderly configurations compared to disorderly configurations. Thus, if we can measure the entropy content in a data after each projection, then we can determine the feature to remove. Notice that in a dataset entropy should be very low between two instances if they are very close or very far, and very high if they are separated by the mean of all distances. We use a similarity measure (S) that is based on distance, and assumes a very small value (close to 0.0) for very close pairs of instances, and a very large value (close to 1.0) for very distant pairs. For two instances, the entropy measure is $E = -S \log_2 S - (1-S)\log_2(1-S)$ that assumes the maximum value of 1.0 for $S = 0.5$, and the minimum value of 0.0 for $S = 0.0$ and $S = 1.0$ [7].

For a dataset of N instances the entropy measure is given as:

$$\mathbf{E} = -\sum_{i=1}^{N}\sum_{j=1}^{N}(S_{ij} \times \log S_{ij} + (1-S_{ij}) \times \log(1-S_{ij})) \quad (1)$$

where S_{ij} is the similarity value, normalized to [0,1], between the instances x_i and x_j.

When all variables are *numeric* or *ordinal*, the similarity value of two instances is:

$$S_{ij} = e^{-\alpha \times D_{ij}} \quad (2)$$

where D_{ij} is the distance between the instances x_i and x_j, and α is a parameter. If we plot similarity against distance, then the curve will have a bigger curvature for a larger α. The experiments with various values for α suggest that it should be robust for all kinds of datasets, and not just for certain datasets. In this work, α is calculated automatically by assigning 0.5 in equation (2) at which entropy is maximum. This, in fact, produces good results for the tested datasets. Mathematically, it is given as: $\alpha = \frac{-\ln 0.5}{\overline{D}}$ where $\overline{D}$ is the average distance among the instances in a hyperspace. Hence, α is determined by the data and can be calculated easily. Euclidean distance measure is used to calculate the distance D_{ij} between two instances x_i and x_j. In a multi-dimensional space, it is defined as: $D_{ij} = [\sum_{k=1}^{M}(\frac{x_{ik}-x_{jk}}{max_k - min_k})^2]^{1/2}$ where max_k and min_k are the maximum and minimum values for the kth dimension. The interval in the kth dimension is normalized by dividing it by the maximum interval $max_k - min_k$ before calculating the distance.

Similarity for *nominal* variables is measured using the Hamming distance concept. The similarity value of two instances is given as:

$$S_{ij} = \frac{\sum_{k=1}^{M}|x_{ik} = x_{jk}|}{M} \quad (3)$$

where $|x_{ik} = x_{jk}|$ is 1 if x_{ik} equals x_{jk} and 0 otherwise, and M is the number of variables in the subset under consideration.

For mixed data (i.e., both numeric and nominal variables), we can discretize numeric values first before applying our measure [9].

3 Algorithm to Find Important Variables

We use a **Sequential Backward Selection** algorithm [3] to determine the relative importance of variables for **Unsupervised Data (SUD)**. In the algorithm M is the number of variables originally present, and D is the given dataset.

SUD(D)
  T = Original Variable Set
  For $k = 1$ to $M-1$ { /* Iteratively remove variables one at a time */
    For every variable v in T { /* Determine which variable to be removed */
      $T_v = T - v$

Calculate E_{T_v} on D using eqn. 1}

Let v_k be the variable that minimizes E_{T_v}

$T = T - v_k$ /* Remove v_k as the least important variable */

Output v_k }

In each iteration, entropy **E** is calculated after removing one variable from the set of remaining variables. A variable is removed as the least important variable if the set without the variable gives the least entropy. This continues till the importance of all variables is determined. We obtain an ordered list of variables by reversing the order in which they are removed (i.e., the first variable is the most important and the last one is the least important).

As we are interested in dimensionality reduction, naturally we want to know how many variables we should keep for a task. If we know that an application only needs d variables, we can simply choose the first d variables. The automated selection of d is, however, more complicated. We investigated this issue through experiments on a number of datasets with class labels. We ran SUD by removing class labels, and determined the importance levels of all variables. Then we performed 10-fold cross-validation of C4.5 [13] using the subset consisting of the d most important variables, d varies from 1 to M, to obtain average error rates. Two results are shown in Figure 2 and more in Figure 3. They clearly show that increasing d may not improve the performance of the chosen classifier (C4.5) much. But in most cases the performance ceases to improve after a certain point which varies from one dataset to another (in case of the Parity3+3 data, in Figure 3, the performance falls sharply as more variables are added). In order to determine d for any data having class information, one may perform such experiments, and choose d to be the number of variables beyond which the error rate does not fall. If this is not possible, one may use a windowing technique to find d. That is, stop including more variables if the performance does not improve for a few more extra variables. This issue is being investigated in more detail.

4 Experimental Studies

We want to show: (1) SUD can find important variables for continuous and nominal data; and (2) its performance is comparable to a popular feature ranking method that requires class information unlike SUD.

Datasets: a summary of 17 datasets is given in Table 1. Parity3+3 data is a modified version of the original Parity3 data with 3 redundant and 6 irrelevant variables. In the last column of the Table 1 the important variables are shown for the datasets: Iris, Chemical Plant, Non-linear, CorrAL, Monk3, and Parity3+3. For CorrAL, Monk3, and Parity3+3 datasets the target concepts are also known. The important variables for Iris and Chemical Plant are based on the results of other researchers. For Iris data, Chiu [1] and Liu and Setiono [9] conclude that v_3 (petal-length) and v_4 (petal-width) are the most important variables. Both Chemical Plant and Non-linear datasets are taken from Yasukawa and Sugeno's paper [14]. For Chemical Plant data, they conclude that the first 3 variables are important. The Non-linear data has an output or class variable y and two input variables v_1 and v_2, and is defined as: $y = (1 + v_1^2 + v_2^{-1.5})^2, 1.0 \leq v_1, v_2 \leq 5.0$. The other two variables in this dataset are irrelevant. Most datasets, unless specified, can be found in the machine learning repository in the University of California at Irvine.

Method: for part (1) we test SUD over 6 datasets having continuous or nominal variables whose important variables are known. For part (2) we select Relief-F [8] as it is a generalized version of Relief, and also it is quite efficient in ranking the features given the class labels. We run SUD and Relief-F over 15 datasets (Chemical Plant and Non-linear data have continuous class variables, hence, not considered), and obtain the ranking of the features. Then the performance is compared by performing 10-fold cross-validation of C4.5 and OC1 [11] using the subset consisting of the d most important variables, d varies from 1 to M.

Results: we produce the experimental results in Tables 2 and 3, and Figures 3 and 4. In all the experiments with SUD class variables are removed first. Table 2 shows that SUD is able to find the important variables although it assigns high importance to the redundant variables in Parity3+3 and CorrAL. Table 3 shows the order of importance by SUD and Relief-F for 15 datasets with discrete class variables. Figure 3 and 4 compares SUD and Relief-F by performing 10-fold cross-validation of C4.5 (inducing axis-parallel decision trees) and OC1 (producing oblique decision trees) using the subset consisting of the d most important variables, $d = 1...M$. We run OC1 only on continuous data as is suggested in [11]. In each of these graphs average error rates are plotted in the y-axis and the number of variables in the x-axis. It shows that the performance of SUD (without using class variable) is close to and sometimes even better than that of Relief-F (using class variable).

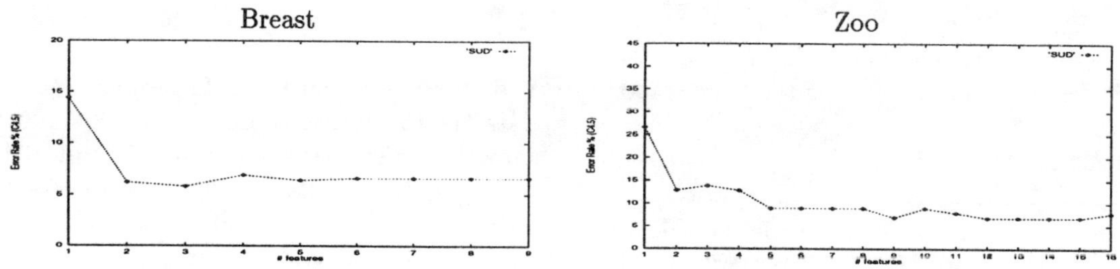

Figure 2: The typical trends of improving performance vs. number of features

Data Set	Data Type	M	N	# Classes	I.V.
Parity3+3	Nominal	12	128	2	{1,7},{2,8},{3,9}
CorrAL	Nominal	6	64	2	1,2,3,4
Monk3	Nominal	6	122	2	2,4,5
Vote	Nominal	16	135	2	NK
Zoo	Nominal	16	74	7	NK
Mushroom	Nominal	22	7125	2	NK
Breast Cancer	Nominal	9	699	2	NK
Lymphography	Nominal	18	148	4	NK
Iris	Continuous	4	150	3	3,4
Bupa	Continuous	6	345	2	NK
New-Thyroid	Continuous	5	215	3	NK
Pima-Diabetes	Continuous	8	768	2	NK
Glass	Continuous	10	214	7	NK
Wine	Continuous	13	178	3	NK
Ionosphere	Continuous	34	351	2	NK
Chemical Plant	Continuous	5	70	∞	1,2,3
Non-linear	Continuous	4	50	∞	1,2

Table 1: Summary of datasets. I.V. – Important Variables, ∞ – Class variable is continuous, NK – Not Known, N and M are defined earlier.

Data set	Important variables	Decreasing order of importance
Iris	3,4	**3**,**4**,1,2
Plant	1,2,3	**3**,**1**,**2**,4,5
Non-linear	1,2	**2**,**1**,3,4
Monk3	2,4,5	**5**,**2**,**4**,1,6,3
CorrAL	1,2,3,4	**3**,6,**1**,**2**,**4**,5
Parity3+3	{1,7},{2,8},{3,9}	**9**,**3**,**8**,**2**,**7**,**1**,4,10,6,5,11,12

Table 2: SUD is able to find important variables for datasets with known important variables.

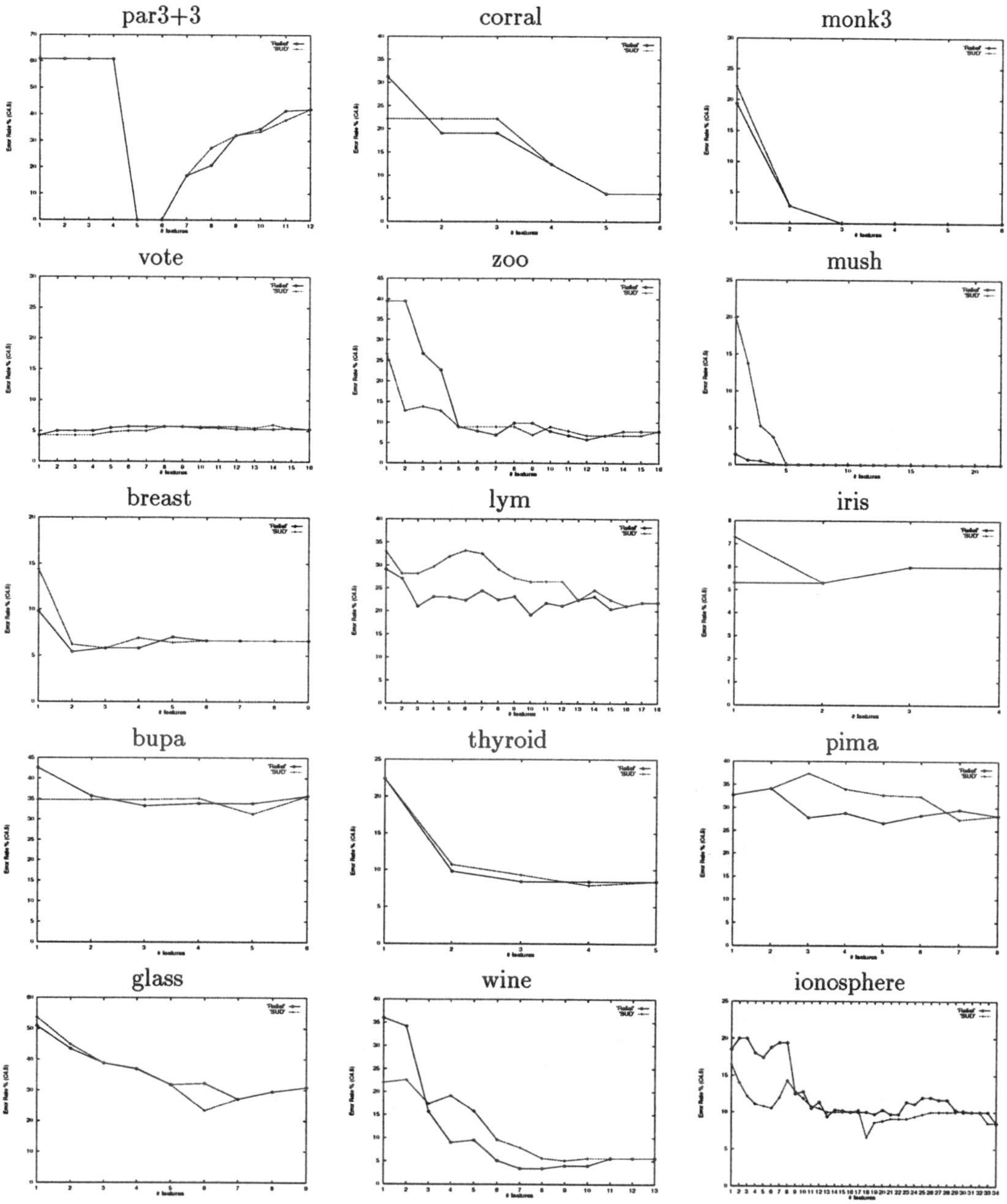

Figure 3: The error rates of 10-fold cross validation of C4.5 using the variables selected by SUD (without class variable) is very close to and sometimes even lower than that using the variables selected by Relief-F (using class variable).

Data	Decreasing order of importance	
	SUD	Relief-F
Par3+3	9,3,8,2,7,1,4,10,6,5,11,12	3,9,7,1,8,2,6,11,12,10,4,5
CorrAL	3,6,1,2,4,5	1,2,6,3,4,5
Monk3	5,2,4,1,6,3	2,5,4,3,6,1
Vote	14,6,5,13,4,12,16,8,7,3,9,15,2,1,10,11	4,3,5,14,11,12,13,8,15,9,10,2,1,6,16,7
Zoo	13,3,4,1,8,16,6,5,2,14,9,10,12,11,15,7	4,3,8,1,13,2,9,10,14,16,12,5,6,7,11,15
Mush	9,3,20,22,5,11,21,2,19,15,14, 1,13,12,4,10,8,7,18,6,17,16	5,20,11,8,19,4,10,22,9,12,13, 21,7,3,2,15,14,18,6,17,16,1
Breast	1,7,3,2,5,6,4,8,9	6,2,3,7,5,1,4,8,9
Lym	18,12,10,13,1,15,11,6,2,16,8,5,17,3,7,4,9,14	2,13,15,10,17,18,5,7,14,11,9,1,3,16,12,6,8,4
Iris	3,4,1,2	4,3,1,2
Bupa	5,3,4,6,1,2	6,5,3,2,4,1
Thyroid	4,5,3,2,1	4,3,1,2,5
Pima	8,1,3,6,5,7,2,4	8,1,2,5,6,4,7,3
Glass	9,7,4,8,3,2,5,6,10,1	7,4,9,3,8,5,2,6,10,1
Wine	7,6,12,9,11,10,5,13,1,4,3,8,2	6,9,1,11,5,7,10,4,12,2,13,3,8
Iono- sphere	13,15,11,9,7,17,19,21,5,3,23,25,27,29,31,33,10 4,6,12,14,8,16,20,18,22,28,26,24,30,32,34,2,1	34,22,33,6,4,8,16,14,21,9,27,15,30,20,29,24,32, 7,12,18,10,11,3,5,28,25,26,19,23,1,31,13,17,2

Table 3: Order of variables by SUD and Relief-F.

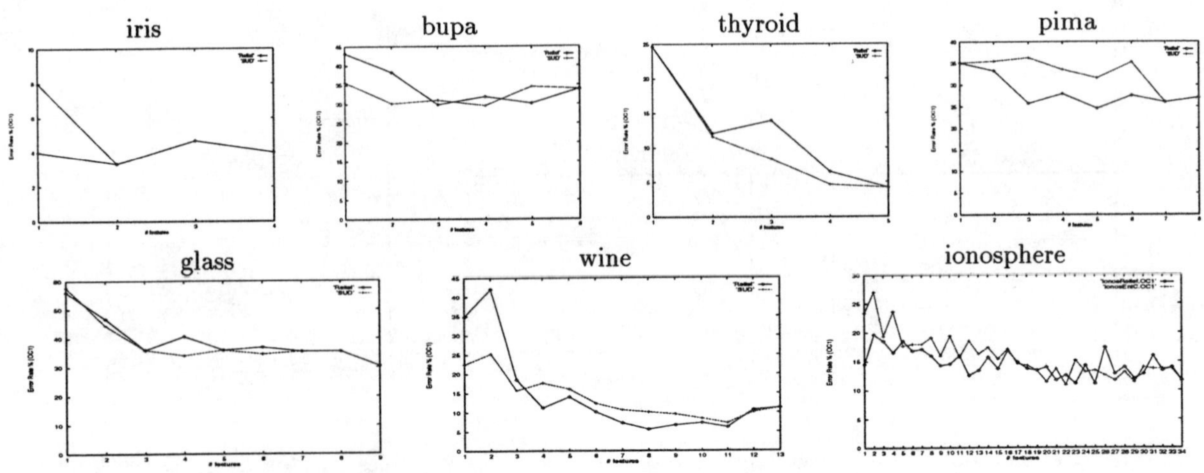

Figure 4: The error rate of 10-fold cross validation of OC1 using the variables selected by SUD (without class variable) is very close to and sometimes even lower than that using the variables selected by Relief-F (using class variable).

5 Discussion and Conclusion

In this paper we focus on solving the unsolved problem of reducing the number of original features for unsupervised data - a problem concerns data with large dimensionality. Neither feature selection methods nor PCA solves this problem directly. An entropy measure is proposed to measure the importance of a variable. The measure is applicable to both numeric and nominal data types. A sequential backward selection algorithm, SUD, is implemented to determine the relative importance among the features. The issue of choosing d important features is also discussed. We carried out two sets of experiments to show that (a) SUD is able to find important features, and (b) it compares well with a feature ranking algorithm that requires class variables unlike SUD.

This paper deals with an interesting problem from both research and industry point of view, and a number of issues are associated with it. Selecting d important features is one and complexity of the algorithm is another. To find a threshold (number of features) to stop selecting is a difficult task as shown by our results in Figures 3 and 4. Although the performances of the classifiers rapidly improve with addition of features, the points (d values), beyond which it no longer improves substantially, vary from one data to another. The graphs also give an insight about how the irrelevant features affect the underlying clustering. Addition of irrelevant features generally do not reduce the distinctness, rather the distinctness becomes stagnant (flat curve). Because of this, determining a robust threshold is difficult. The complexity of our algorithm is $O(M^2N^2)$ where M is the number of features and N is the number of instances. Although this complexity is not very good but one should remember that this method is giving a solution to a problem not yet solved directly.

In conclusion, our method is useful for unsupervised classification and clustering as it helps in removing the irrelevant features. It also helps in getting insight into the data as the important original features are known. Overall, this paper does show convincingly the advantages of feature elimination in unsupervised clustering.

References

[1] S. L. Chiu. Method and software for extracting fuzzy classification rules by subtractive clustering. In *Proceedings of North American Fuzzy Information Processing Society Conf. (NAFIPS'96)*, June 1996.

[2] M. Dash and H. Liu. Feature selection for classification. *Intelligent Data Analysis-An International Journal, http://www.elsevier.com/locate/ida*, 1(3), 1997. forthcoming.

[3] P. A. Devijver and J. Kittler. *Pattern Recognition : A Statistical Approach.* Prentice Hall, 1982.

[4] Johan Diedrich Fast. *Entropy : the significance of the concept of entropy and its applications in science and technology*, chapter The Statistical Significance of the Entropy Concept. Eindhoven : Philips Technical Library, 1962.

[5] I. T. Jolliffe. *Principal Component Analysis.* Springer-Verlag, 1986.

[6] K. Kira and L. A. Rendell. The feature selection problem: Traditional methods and a new algorithm. In *Proceedings of Ninth National Conference on AI*, 1992.

[7] George J. Klir and Tina A. Folger. *Fuzzy Sets, Uncertainty, and Information*, chapter Uncertainty and Information. Prentice-Hall International Editions, 1988.

[8] I. Kononenko. Estimating attributes : Analysis and extension of RELI EF. In *Proceedings of European Conference on Machine Learn ing*, pages 171–182, 1994.

[9] H. Liu and R. Setiono. Chi2: Feature selection and discretization of numeric attributes. In *Proceedings of the 7th IEEE International Conference on Tools with Artificial Intelligence(TAT'95)*, pages 388–391, November 1995.

[10] A. N. Mucciardi and E. E. Gose. A comparison of seven techniques for choosing subsets of pattern recognition. *IEEE Transactions on Computers*, C-20:1023–1031, September 1971.

[11] Sreerama K. Murthy, Simon Kasif, and Steven Salzberg. A system for induction of oblique decision trees. *Journal of Artificial Intelligence Research*, 2:1–32, 1994.

[12] J. R. Quinlan. Induction of decision trees. In *Machine Learning*, pages 81–106. Morgan Kaufmann, 1986.

[13] J. R. Quinlan. *C4.5 : Programs for Machine Learning.* Morgan Kaufmann, San Mateo, California, 1993.

[14] M. Sugeno and T. Yasukawa. A fuzzy-logic-based approach to qualitative modeling. In *IEEE Transactions on Fuzzy system Vol.1, No.1*, February 1993.

[15] Ramasamy Uthurusamy. From data mining to knowledge discovery: Current challenges and future directions. In Usama M. Fayyad, Gregory Piatesky-Shapiro, Padhraic Smyth, and Ramasamy Uthurusamy, editors, *Advances in Knowledge Discovery and Data Mining.* AAAI Press / The MIT Press, 1996.

[16] N. Wyse, R. Dubes, and A. K. Jain. A critical evaluation of intrinsic dimensionality algorithms. In E. Gelsema and L. N. Kanal, editors, *Pattern Recognition in Practice*, pages 415–425. Morgan Kaufmann, 1980.

A Fuzzy Model for Learning And Adaptivity

Robert J. Hammell II
US Army Research Laboratory
ATTN: AMSRL-IS-CI
Aberdeen Proving Ground, MD 21005
rhammell@arl.mil

Thomas Sudkamp
Department of Computer Science
Wright State University
Dayton, OH 45435
tsudkamp@cs.wright.edu

Abstract

Fuzzy models have been designed to represent approximate or imprecise relationships in complex systems and have been successfully employed in control systems, expert systems, and decision analysis. A hierarchical architecture for fuzzy modeling and inference has been developed to learn an initial set of rules from training data and allow adaptation of the rule base via system performance feedback. A general adaptive algorithm is presented and its performance examined for three types of adaptive behavior: continued learning, gradual change, and drastic change. In each of the three types of behavior, the adaptive algorithm has been shown to be able to reconfigure the rule bases to either improve the original approximation or adapt to the new system.

1 Introduction

Fuzzy set theory provides a formal system for modeling complex systems. A system model captures the relationships between the input and output domains. In classical modeling these relationships are expressed as mathematical functions. As systems being modeled become more complex, it is increasingly difficult to develop mathematical models directly from knowledge of the system. This is due to the complexity of interactions within the system as well as an incomplete knowledge of the system operations.

Fuzzy models have been used to model complex systems for which an imprecise or approximate specification is all that is available. A fuzzy model is defined by a set of fuzzy rules that specify a relationship between the input domain(s) and the output domain(s). The earliest applications were led by the research of Mamdani [1] and involved the area of control theory. Fuzzy models have also been successfully applied to many other fields. These include pattern recognition, decision support, approximate reasoning, robotics, natural language and image understanding, machine learning, expert systems, data mining, and others.

In the classical development of fuzzy inference systems, fuzzy rules have been obtained by knowledge acquisition from experts. This paper presents a hierarchical architecture for building a fuzzy model from a set of training examples. The knowledge base of the model consists of two fuzzy associative memories (FAMs). When constructed, one FAM provides a rough approximation of the underlying system while the other refines the model. Originally designed for constructing models with supervised learning, the hierarchical architecture has been modified for modeling adaptive systems. The adaptive capability has been incorporated using rule modification based on system performance feedback. Analysis of the system feedback determines when adaptation is necessary, selects the rules to modify, and appropriately adjusts either or both of the FAMs.

This paper begins with a presentation of the basic information needed to understand fuzzy models followed by a brief introduction to generating fuzzy associative memories from training data. Next, a review of the hierarchical architecture for fuzzy modeling is provided. A description of the adaptive algorithm is then given along with experimental results that demonstrate the ability of algorithm to modify the model based on changes in the underlying system.

2 Fuzzy Models

The input to a fuzzy model consists of the values of a set of variables that describe the state or configuration of the system being modeled. Figure 1 gives a diagram of the components of a two-input, one-output fuzzy model with inputs from the domains U and V and output in W. Fuzzification transforms the input based on the noise in the source of the data or the degree of precision required for the analysis. Defuzzification converts the output from the fuzzy set C produced by the inference system to a singleton c in W.

A fuzzy set represents approximate or vague information over a domain. Figure 2 shows a triangular fuzzy set. The membership function μ for a fuzzy set assigns a grade of membership ranging from 0 to 1 for all elements in the domain. For domain X, a fuzzy set A over X is defined by a

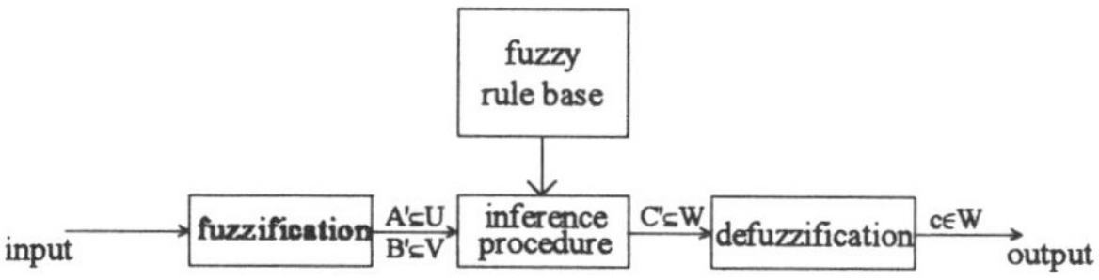

Figure 1. Fuzzy Inference System

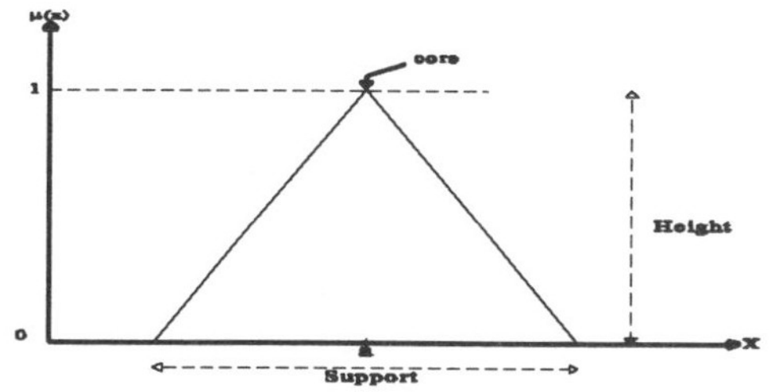

Figure 2. Triangular Fuzzy Set

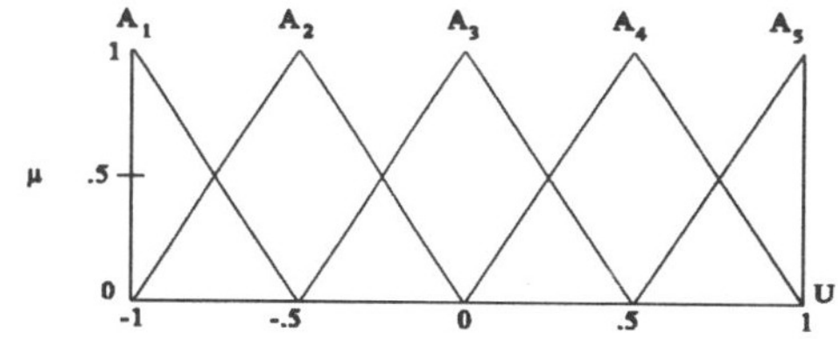

Figure 3. Decomposition of [-1,1]

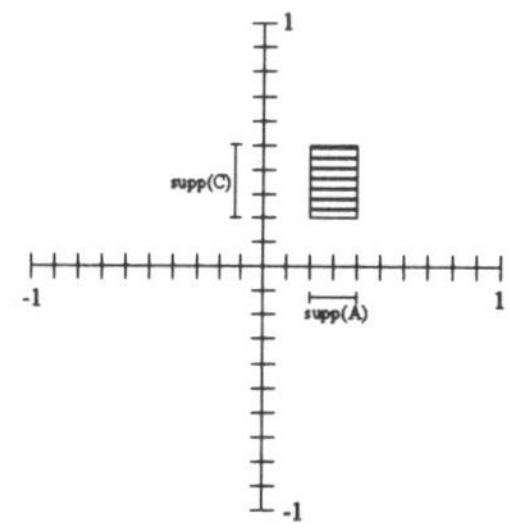

Figure 4. Fuzzy Rule Patch

membership function $\mu_A : X \rightarrow [0,1]$ where $\mu_A(x)$ denotes the membership grade of x in A. The membership grade $\mu_A(x)$ indicates the degree to which x is an element of A or the degree to which x satisfies the predicate A. Triangular fuzzy sets have a unique domain element with membership value 1, referred to as the *midpoint* (shown as the point a in Figure 2).

The domain knowledge of a fuzzy model is encapsulated by a set of fuzzy rules. A fuzzy rule with two antecedents has the form 'if X is A and Y is B then Z is C' where A and B are fuzzy sets over the input domains U and V, respectively and C is a fuzzy set over the output domain W. Thus, a fuzzy rule is used to linguistically represent relationships between domains. For example, 'if speed is ***fast*** and distance is ***medium*** then apply brake ***medium***' is a fuzzy rule that might be used in a brake pressure control system, where ***fast*** is a fuzzy set describing speed, ***medium*** a fuzzy set over distance, and ***medium*** in the consequent a fuzzy set over pressure.

The antecedents and consequents of the rules are determined by the decompositions of the input and output domains, respectively. A decomposition of a domain U is a set of fuzzy sets $A_1, \ldots, A_n$ over U that is assumed to form a fuzzy partition of U. A fuzzy partition satisfies

$$\sum_{i=1}^{n} \mu_{A_i}(u) = 1$$

for every u in U. Figure 3 shows a triangular decomposition of the interval [-1,1] into five fuzzy sets.

The combination of triangular membership functions and the fuzzy partition requirement ensures that any input will have non-zero membership in at most two fuzzy sets (A_i and A_{i+1}), and that the input will have membership of $\geq .5$ in at least one fuzzy set. In this paper, all domains are assumed to be normalized to take values from the interval [-1,1] and the domain decompositions consist of a partition by triangular fuzzy sets.

The region in which a rule provides information for inference is defined by the supports of the fuzzy sets. Figure 4 illustrates the region of influence for the rule 'if X is A then Z is C'. The supports of A and C describe a fuzzy relation patch which bounds the area covered by the rule. This is called the *locality principle* of fuzzy approximation. As more fuzzy sets are used, the region covered by each rule shrinks. Thus, the domain decompositions define the granularity of the approximations.

A fuzzy associative memory (FAM) is an l-dimensional table where each dimension corresponds to one of the input universes. The i'th dimension of the table is indexed by the fuzzy sets that comprise the decomposition of the i'th input domain. Consider a fuzzy model with input domains U and V, and output domain W, as depicted in Figure 1. Let $A_1, \ldots, A_m$ be a partition of U and $B_1, \ldots, B_n$ be a partition of V. A fuzzy rule base for such a system consists of rules of the form 'if X is A_i and Y is B_j then Z is $C_{k_{ij}}$' where $C_{k_{ij}}$ is a fuzzy set over the output domain W. The FAM representing this rule base has the form

	A_1	A_2	...	A_{m-1}	A_m
B_1	$C_{k_{11}}$	$C_{k_{21}}$	...	$C_{k_{(m-1)1}}$	$C_{k_{ml}}$
$\vdots$	$\vdots$	$\vdots$		$\vdots$	$\vdots$
B_n	$C_{k_{1n}}$	$C_{k_{2n}}$	...	$C_{k_{(m-1)n}}$	$C_{k_{mn}}$

where the consequent of a rule with antecedent 'if X is A_i and Y is B_j' is entered in the (i,j)'th position.

A fuzzy rule base consists of a series of rules that trace a fuzzy function from the input domain to the output domain. A one-input one-output system with input domain decomposition $A_1, \ldots, A_7$ and output domain decomposition $C_1, \ldots, C_7$ is used to show the interpretation of fuzzy inference as approximation. A rule base is defined by the 1-dimensional FAM

A_1	A_2	A_3	A_4	A_5	A_6	A_7
C_1	C_2	C_3	C_4	C_3	C_2	C_1

Figure 5 shows the supports of the fuzzy sets in the domain decompositions along the horizontal and vertical axes. The boxed areas indicate the regions in the space that are influenced by each rule. The parabolic shape of the overlapping regions suggests that this may be a fuzzy approximation of the function $f(x) = x^2$.

Fuzzy inference compares the input with the antecedent of a rule to produce the response indicated by that particular rule. The output is obtained by summarizing the responses indicated by each individual rule. As mentioned above, a fuzzy rule 'if X is A then Z is C' represents a functional relationship between input A and output C. The area covered by such a rule is bounded by the supports of A and C. For example, the shaded upper right-hand rectangle in Figure 5 is the region associated with the rule 'if X is A_7 then Z is C_1'.

The role of a fuzzy model is to determine an appropriate output response based on the input to the system. The inference technique determines the degree to which each rule affects the outcome. For the experimental results given in this paper, Mamdani style inference and weighted averaging defuzzification are used to produce the output; this algorithm will be described using a one-input one-output inference system where the domain decompositions are triangular with evenly spaced midpoints. The input universe is subdivided into triangular regions $A_1, \ldots, A_n$ and the output domain is decomposed by the fuzzy partition $C_1, \ldots, C_m$ with associated midpoints $c_1, \ldots, c_m$. The restrictions on the decomposition make inference in such a system very straightforward and efficient. Assume that A_i and A_{i+1} are the two fuzzy sets providing nonzero membership for an input value x with associated FAM entries C_r and C_s, respectively (there will only be two for a one-input system). Using weighted averaging defuzzification, the result z specified by input x is given by

$$z = \frac{\mu_{A_i}(x)c_r + \mu_{A_{i+1}}(x)c_s}{\mu_{A_i}(x) + \mu_{A_{i+1}}(x)} \qquad (1)$$

Rewriting (1) in terms of the midpoints produces

$$z = \frac{x(c_s - c_r) + a_{i+1}c_r - a_i c_s}{a_{i+1} - a_i} \qquad (2)$$

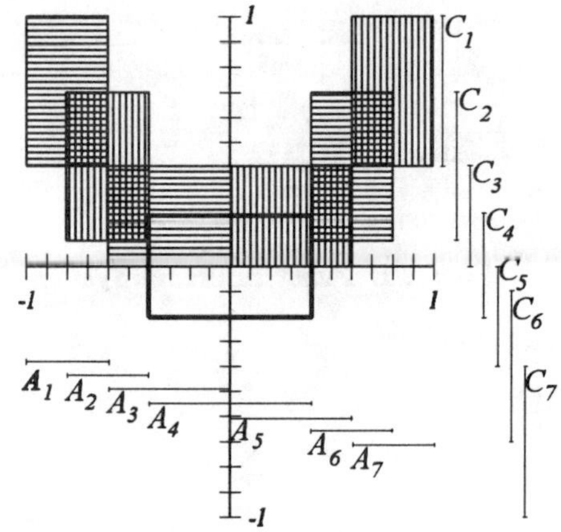

Figure 5. Fuzzy Inference as Approximation

where c_r and c_s denote the midpoints of C_r and C_s respectively. Equation (2) shows that the result is completely determined by the rule base and the midpoints of the triangular decomposition of the domains. As previously mentioned, each of the input and output domains are assumed to be the interval $I = [-1,1]$. When the input is precise, a fuzzy model and weighted-averaging defuzzification defines a real-valued function $\hat{f}: [-1,1]^k \rightarrow [-1,1]^t$ where k and t are the dimensions of the input and output domains respectively.

3 FAM LEARNING

Wang and Mendel [2] introduced an algorithm for generating FAM entries from training data. For a one-input system, the training data consists of a set of input-output pairs $T = \{(x_i, z_i) \mid I = 1, \ldots, k\}$ where x_i is an element from the input domain and z_i is the associated response. The Wang and Mendel algorithm, called FLM, is described below. More detailed examinations of FLM and comparisons with other learning algorithms can be found in [3] and [4].

The FLM algorithm is defined as follows: A training example (x_i, z_i) that has the maximal membership in A_j is selected from T. If more than one example assumes the maximal membership, one is selected arbitrarily. The fuzzy rule 'if X is A_j then Z is C_r' is constructed where the consequent C_r is the fuzzy set in the output domain decomposition in which z_i has maximal membership. If z_i has maximal value in two adjacent regions $(\mu_{C_r}(z_i) = \mu_{C_{r+1}}(z_i) = .5)$, then the consequent C_r is selected.

Example 1: This example illustrates constructing a FAM with FLM 'learning' function $f(x) = x^2$ from training data $T = \{ (-1,1), (-.4,.16), (0,0), (.5,.25), (.7,.49), (1,1) \}$. Note that the training set consists of precise data; each pair has the form

$(x, f(x))$ with no noise introduced into the function value.

The algorithm constructs the approximation $\hat{f}$ from T. In this example, the input and output universes for the FAM are decomposed into the five equally spaced triangular fuzzy regions with midpoints -1, -.5, 0, .5, and 1 as shown in Figure 3. The FLM algorithm produces the FAM

A_1	A_2	A_3	A_4	A_5
C_5	C_3	C_3	C_3	C_5

which provides the approximation $\hat{f}$.

Observe that the x values in both training pairs (.5,.25) and (.7,.49) belong to region A_4 the most. However, since .5 has a higher membership value in this region than .7, the corresponding z value of .25 is used to determine the consequent for the rule 'if X is A_4...'. Also note that training set T completely covers the input regions so no rule base completion is necessary.

The table below examines the approximations $\hat{f}(x)$ provided by the FAM for the original input values from the training set. The last line of the table provides the error in the approximation.

x	-1	-.4	0	.5	.7	1
$z = f(x)$	1	.16	0	.25	.49	1
$\hat{f}(x)$	1	0	0	0	.4	1
$z - \hat{f}(x)$	0	.16	0	.25	.09	0

The generation of a rule with antecedent 'if X is A_j' requires at least one training example with membership .5 or greater in the set A_j. Learning a large number of rules may require a large set of training data, especially with multi-dimensional input. An inference system with five input domains, with each decomposed into five regions, produces a FAM with 3125 rules. If the training set is obtained by sampling an operational system, a suitable training example may not be encountered for all FAM entries. Entries left undefined by FLM are filled using rule base completion ([3],[5]) which is examined in more detail in the next section.

4 Two-Level Architecture

A two-level architecture was designed to enhance the performance of models constructed using supervised learning from training data [6]. Models are constructed using an extension of the FLM algorithm that analyzes the error between the approximating function $\hat{f}$ and the training data. The first step of the FLE (Fuzzy Learning with Error analysis) algorithm is to construct the initial approximation $\hat{f}$ in the standard manner. The second step then re-uses the training

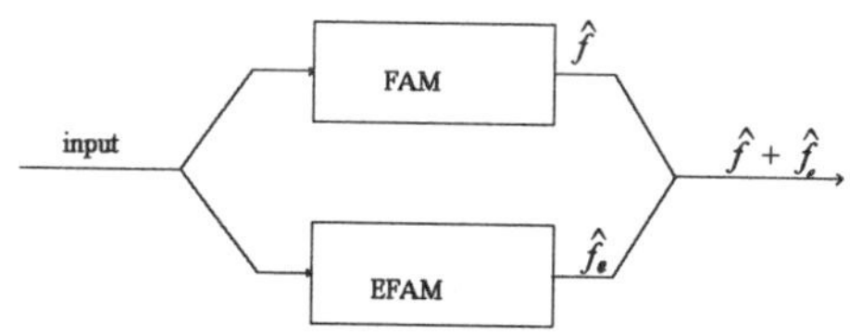

Figure 6. Two-level Architecture

data to refine the approximation. This is done by producing a second FAM that defines a function $\hat{f}_e$ which is used to approximate the error between the training data and $\hat{f}$.

The training set T_e used to learn $\hat{f}_e$ is obtained from the training data T and the initial approximation $\hat{f}$. An element in T_e represents the difference between an original training example and the approximation produced by $\hat{f}$; the training set is $T_e = \{(x_i, z_i - \hat{f}(x_i)) \mid (x_i, z_i) \in T\}$. To define the fuzzy associative memory to approximate the error function, called the EFAM to distinguish it from the original FAM, it is necessary to identify the input and output domains of the error function. The input domain is [-1,1], the same as the approximating function $\hat{f}$. The output of the error function, however, takes values from a smaller interval than the domain of the original FAM. To allow for the largest possible error, the EFAM size is set to one-half of the length of the support of the largest fuzzy set in the FAM output domain decomposition. For an output domain decomposition of 5 equally spaced triangular fuzzy sets, the support of each such fuzzy set is an interval of length .5; the associated EFAM output domain is the interval of [-.25, .25].

Once the domain decompositions have been selected, learning the function $\hat{f}_e$ follows the FLM algorithm using T_e as the training set. The last step in the creation of the EFAM is to use completion to fill in any missing entries.

The approximation produced by the FLE algorithm uses the two FAMs as illustrated in Figure 6. An input x is processed by each of the FAMs. The resulting values $\hat{f}(x)$ and $\hat{f}_e(x)$ are added to produce the single overall system output. Example 2 details the steps of the FLE algorithm by refining the approximation constructed in Example 1.

Example 2: This example shows the process of augmenting a FAM with an EFAM. The FLE algorithm begins by building the approximation $\hat{f}$ from T as in Example 1. The domain decompositions, the training set T, and the resulting FAM are as shown in Example 1.

The second step is to build the training set T_e for the construction of the EFAM. From Example 1, the $(x, \hat{f}(x))$ pairs are (-1,1), (-.4,0), (0,0), (.5,0), (.7,.4) and (1,1). Combining a training example $(x, z) \in T$ with $\hat{f}$ produces the example $(x, z - \hat{f}(x))$. The error training set T_e = { (-1,0), (-.4,.16), (0,0), (.5,.25), (.7,.09), (1,0) }.

To begin the construction of the EFAM, it is necessary to define the output domain and the decompositions. The input domain [-1,1] is decomposed into seven regions. The output domain, however, is set to one-half of the length of the support of the largest fuzzy set in the FAM output domain decomposition. For the input domain decomposition of 5 equally spaced triangular fuzzy sets as used in Example 1, the EFAM output domain is the interval [-.25,.25]. This interval is also decomposed into seven regions.

The EFAM constructed using T_e is

A_1	A_2	A_3	A_4	A_5	A_6	A_7
E_4		E_6	E_4		E_5	E_4

Note that two entries in the EFAM are unfilled; each represents an input for which no action is specified. Overcoming this problem motivates the use of completion algorithms. Completing the EFAM uses the existing rules and interpolation to produce rules for the undefined configurations.

The completion algorithm used in this research is a region growing technique often used in image segmentation [7]. Empty cells in the EFAM that border nonempty cells are filled by extending the values in the neighboring cells. Since the 'growing' only occurs on the boundaries of filled regions, the procedure must be repeated until the entire table is filled. Region growing is the most local of a family of completion algorithms examined in [3].

Using region growing, the completed EFAM is

A_1	A_2	A_3	A_4	A_5	A_6	A_7
E_4	E_5	E_6	E_4	E_4	E_5	E_4

The improvement obtained by incorporating the error function $\hat{f}_e$ into the approximation is shown in the table below. The values in the table provided are the error in the approximation of the function $f(x) = x^2$ using $\hat{f}$ alone and $\hat{f} + \hat{f}_e$ at the training points.

x	-1	-.4	0	.5	.7	1
$z - \hat{f}(x)$	0	.16	0	.25	.09	0
$z - (\hat{f}(x) + \hat{f}_e(x))$	0	.01	0	.25	.02	0

The region growing technique allowed the rule base to be completed so that a reasonable output could be produced for all possible inputs. The completion process for region A_5 was limited to arbitrarily choosing either E_4 or E_5; if E_5 had been picked then the error for $x = .5$ would have decreased to .17 with all other results remaining the same. Also, it should be observed that for input $x = .4$ the approximation used the 'grown' consequent of region A_2, producing a significant decrease in error over the original FAM-only system.

The two-level architecture has been shown to increase the accuracy over the traditional methods of learning fuzzy rules from data ([5],[6]). When restricted to a fixed set of training examples, the FAM-EFAM system produced better approximations than obtainable from a single FAM system regardless of the number of rules in the single FAM. The two-level architecture requires only one additional pass through the training data, maintaining the efficiency of the FAM learning approach. The improved approximations are obtained without additional training instances, making this technique particularly suitable for problem domains in which training data is unavailable or expensive to obtain.

5 Adaptivity

The FAM-based fuzzy inference systems presented so far are static. That is, the design of the system, including the rule generation and domain decomposition, is done off-line and is not changed once the system is put into operation. This produces the obvious disadvantage of prohibiting a fuzzy system from adapting to changes in its environment.

As pointed out in [8], there are basically three sets of fuzzy system parameters that can be manipulated to allow adaptivity: 1) the input and output scaling factors, 2) the membership functions, and 3) the fuzzy rules. The adaptive fuzzy systems herein use the strategy of modifying the fuzzy rules; details of why are presented in [4]. One main reason is that the FLE algorithm provides an excellent platform for rule base adaptivity. Fine grain adaptivity can be achieved by tweaking the error estimation rule base (EFAM). Only when system performance differs greatly from the desired result will the 'original' rule base (FAM) require modification.

Adaptive fuzzy systems using the two-level architecture modify the FAMs based on system performance feedback. The structure of the adaptive fuzzy model, presented in [9], uses a reference model to calculate the desired configuration of the system based on the input that was supplied. The difference between the desired configuration and the actual system configuration provides the error that drives the adaption. A supervisor module analyzes the error and makes the appropriate FAM modifications.

The initial rule bases may be learned from training examples or by knowledge acquisition from domain experts. When the system becomes operational, adaptation may be required. Three basic types of operational system behavior can be identified. One type is when the system does not change at all; in this case there is *continued learning*. Continued learning uses the system feedback as additional training data which will decrease the system error. In the two-level architecture, the majority of the adaptation should be accomplished by modifying the EFAM.

Another type of operational behavior is the *drastic change*. In this case the underlying system changes significantly. An adaptive system must be able to quickly modify all or a good portion of its rules to represent a very different underlying model.

The third type of operational system behavior is a gradual change in the system spread over a period of time, denoted as a ***time warp*** of the system. This type of behavior is the most common for many real systems, such as in the gradual wear of brake system components. For the two-level system, initial small changes would be reflected in EFAM modifications, with FAM rule changes only when the cumulative change is too large for the EFAM structure to accommodate.

The adaptive process begins after the original FAM and EFAM have been constructed and the system is put into operation. The objective was to develop a general algorithm that will modify the rule bases in response to changes in the performance of the underlying system. The AFLE (adaptive FLE) algorithm described in this section makes no assumption of the type change, if any, that will occur.

Design decisions required in producing the adaptive algorithm included establishing:

1. the criteria for adaptation ,
2. the order of the rule base modifications,
3. the rule modification strategy,
4. the completion strategy.

Only the completion strategy will be reviewed here. More details on these design decisions can be found in [10].

Completion is used to assist the rule base to more quickly react to changes in the system. If the operational system undergoes a drastic change, the majority of the rules become obsolete. In this case the new system must be learned from scratch. To accurately rebuild both rule bases would take many inputs. This is especially true for a large EFAM since, as the FAM changed, the EFAM would have to reconfigure for that particular portion of the input domain. The idea behind using completion during adaptation is to throw away many old, inaccurate rules and complete the rule base using the most recent rule modifications. Even in the case of a slowly but continuously changing system, only the last few rule adjustments accurately reflect the current configuration.

A major part of the adaptation step is to determine if rule base completion should be used on the EFAM. The completion process must be carefully controlled since deleting useful rules is undesirable. If the error feedback is small or perhaps decreasing, then the completion algorithm will not be used. If the error feedback suddenly becomes very large or continually increases, the most recent EFAM corrections are used to reconfigure the entire EFAM. A more thorough discussion of the benefit of completion in adaptation can be found in [5].

6 Experimental Results

This section presents results from experimental testing of the AFLE algorithm. To start each test, the FLE algorithm was used to build a system to approximate a target function f:[-1,1] → [-1,1]. The system was then put into simulated operation whereupon the target function either underwent no change, a drastic change, or a gradual change producing a new function f':[-1,1] → [-1,1].

The operation phase consisted of some number of loops through the adaptation process (rule adjustment and completion) with randomly selected input on each loop. After the given number of inputs were processed and used for adaptation, the system was tested to see how well it approximated the 'new' target function. The test consisted of comparing the approximating function $\hat{f} + \hat{f}_e$ with the modified target function f' on a sample of points evenly distributed over the input domain. For the two dimensional functions presented below, the error $|f'(x) - (\hat{f}(x) + \hat{f}_e(x))|$ was obtained at .05 lattice points across the input domain range. The average and maximum error that occur on this set were recorded.

All the experiments discussed in this paper consider two-input systems. Additional experiments with different target functions, both single and multiple input, were run and the results were similar to those reported below.

6.1 Continued Learning

The experiments in this section demonstrate the ability of the AFLE algorithm to continue to learn and improve its performance as additional inputs are received. To provide the continued learning environment, the 'new' function is identical to the initial function. That is, there is no change in the system once it becomes operational.

Table 1 provides the results by 'adapting' $f(x) = x^2 + y^2 - 1$ to $f'(x) = x^2 + y^2 - 1$ in systems with 5 FAM and 25 EFAM regions. This FAM-EFAM configuration was selected because it shows that the average and maximal error may initially increase slightly as indicated in the results for the system originally built with 625 training examples. By 300 online inputs, however, the continued learning process has improved the overall system accuracy. This type of behavior is present in many of the results; a momentary increase in error seems to be caused by an ongoing internal settling of the FAM and/or EFAM rules.

The results from systems with other numbers of EFAM regions and other target functions are similar. The experimental results indicate that the AFLE algorithm can continue to learn and improve performance during on-line operation. While the error values may increase slightly in some cases when the operational phase begins, the rise generally precedes a significant drop in the error rate as inputs continue. Note that no completion occurs in the adaptation process since the error feedback from the reference model is below the threshold needed to trigger this process. Completion during continued learning is not desirable as many of the relevant rules in the EFAM would be discarded.

# Initial Training Examples	Regions	Built for $X^2 + Y^2 - 1$		Number of on-line inputs (after initial training examples)							
				100		300		500		5000	
		Avg Err	Max Err	Avg Err	Max Err	Avg Err	Max Err	Avg Err	Max Err	Avg Err	Max Err
625	5/25	.015	.250	.018	.250	.014	.223	.011	.223	.004	.063
2500	5/25	.008	.083	.007	.083	.007	.083	.006	.083	.004	.023

Table 1. Continued Learning: $x^2 + y^2 - 1$

# Initial Training Examples	Regions	Built for $X^2 + Y^2 - 1$		Number of on-line inputs (after initial training examples)							
				1000		2500		5000		15000	
		Avg Err	Max Err	Avg Err	Max Err	Avg Err	Max Err	Avg Err	Max Err	Avg Err	Max Err
625	5/25	.015	.250	.016	.167	.008	.125	.004	.042	.004	.011
2500	5/25	.008	.083	.014	.167	.007	.125	.004	.042	.003	.011

Table 2. Drastic Change: $(x + \sin y)/2$ to $x^2 + y^2 - 1$

# Initial Training Examples	Regions	Built for $X^2 + Y^2 - 1$		Number of on-line inputs (after initial training examples)							
				1000		2500		5000		15000	
		Avg Err	Max Err	Avg Err	Max Err	Avg Err	Max Err	Avg Err	Max Err	Avg Err	Max Err
625	5/25	.015	.250	.913	2.56	.629	2.56	.776	2.56	.979	2.56
2500	5/25	.008	.083	.932	2.56	.638	2.56	.790	2.56	.962	2.56

Table 3. Drastic Change: $(x + \sin y)/2$ to $x^2 + y^2 - 1$, No Completion

# Initial Training Examples	Regions	Built for $X^2 + Y^2 - 1$		Number of inputs per step							
				10		20		25		30	
		Avg Err	Max Err	Avg Err	Max Err	Avg Err	Max Err	Avg Err	Max Err	Avg Err	Max Err
625	5/15	.018	.250	.013	.181	.015	.268	.015	.158	.012	.080
2500	5/15	.012	.107	.013	.181	.015	.268	.015	.158	.012	.080

Table 4. Gradual Change: $x^2 - y^2$ to $x^2 + y^2 - 1$

6.2 Drastic Change

To test the adaptive capability of the fuzzy inference system in the drastic change scenario, a system was constructed based on one target function and then put into operation based on another. That is, the FAM and EFAM were trained with input-output pairs representing a particular function, but after training ended and on-line operation began, the error for a specific input was computed based on a different target function. This simulated a drastic change in the fuzzy system's environment, thereby testing the ability of the system to adapt to the extent of basically relearning a major portion (if not all) of the rule base.

For example, consider $f(x) = x^2$ 'drastically changed' to $f(x) = x^3$. This means that the model was originally built from training data reflecting $f(x) = x^2$, but as soon as the system went operational, the desired output was changed to $f(x) = x^3$. With the system operational and no adaptation, an input of -1 would result in an error of -2 assuming the system learned x^2 accurately. Thus, the adaptation procedure would be based on an error of -2. After the given number of inputs is processed, $f(x) = x^3$ is used to obtain the average and maximal error for the resulting adapted system.

The results from a 5 FAM and 25 EFAM system adapting from an initial approximation of $f(x) = (x + \sin y)/2$ to $f(x) = x^2 + y^2 - 1$ are shown in Table 2. Results based on 1000, 2500, 5000 and 15000 on-line input values are given. For the system initially built with 625 examples, the maximal error from the adapted system is lower than that of the system directly built for $x^2 + y^2 - 1$ after only 1000 on-line inputs; the average error is only .001 greater. After 5000 inputs, all results are equal or better than those in the 'built for' columns.

The results from the drastic change experiments show that the AFLE algorithm is able to quickly adapt. Employing completion on the EFAM is a significant factor in this success. Table 3 provides results for the same experiment as Table 2 but without using completion during adaptation. Even after 15000 on-line inputs, the adapting systems seem to be hung at a very high error level. This is probably due to severe oscillation in the FAM and EFAM rule changes. Results using other functions were similar, supporting the use of completion in the drastic change scenario.

6.3 Gradual Change

Gradual change is the third type of potential change in an operational system. In this scenario, the system behavior gradually changes from one function to another over time. The classic example of this is a braking system where the components wear and increased pressure is needed to stop within a certain distance for a certain speed. This type of change is perhaps the most realistic for many systems.

Table 4 provides results from using 5 FAM and 15 EFAM systems to follow the time warping of the function $f(x) = x^2 - y^2$ to the function $f'(x) = x^2 + y^2 - 1$ over 10,000 time steps. The total number of online inputs processed in the gradual change situation is the number of time steps multiplied by the number of inputs per step. Thus 10 inputs per step utilize 100,000 online inputs while 20 inputs per step use 200,000, and so on. Note that in the gradual change, only the last few inputs correctly represent the final system.

At 10 inputs/step, the error rates for the adapting system are better than the error rates of the system originally built for $x^2 + y^2 - 1$ with 625 training examples; the errors for the system built with 2500 examples are close. At 20 inputs/step the error rates rise some, but the maximum error begins to fall significantly by 25 inputs/step. At 30 inputs/step all errors from AFLE are equal to or lower than the 'built for' errors.

The results for other systems tested on different functions were similar. Since a gradually changing system represents a 'moving target', the updated approximations were always somewhat behind the current system configuration. The objective of gradual change adaptivity is to reduce the difference between the current system and the model. As before, removal of completion from the algorithm hampered the ability of the systems to follow the moving function.

7 Conclusions

The two-level architecture increases the accuracy over the traditional methods of learning fuzzy rules from data. When restricted to a fixed set of training examples, the FAM-EFAM system produces better approximations than obtainable from a single FAM system regardless of the number of rules in the single FAM. The two-level architecture requires only one additional pass through the training data, maintaining the efficiency of the FAM learning approach. The improved approximations are obtained without additional training instances, making this technique particularly suitable for problem domains in which training data is unavailable or expensive to obtain.

The two-level architecture used in the AFLE algorithm provides an excellent platform for adaptation. The use of the EFAM provides a rule base that can be 'tweaked' for small changes in the system's behavior without upsetting the main FAM rule base. The experimental analysis, especially for gradual change, generally supported the intuition that a smaller number of rules permits faster adaptation.

The experimental analysis revealed the need for completion in both the drastic change and time warp scenarios. The management of the completion process is a complex issue and small variations in starting or stopping the process produced significant differences in experimental results. Further research is being conducted to study the effects of using completion within the AFLE algorithm and the scalabilty of the algorithm to higher dimensional input and output domains.

REFERENCES

1. Mamdani, E. H., "Applications of fuzzy algorithms for simple dynamic plant," *Fuzzy Sets and Systems*, 51(3), 1585-1588, 1974.
2. Wang, L., & Mendel, J. M., "Generating fuzzy rules from numerical data, with applications," Technical Report USC-SIPI-169, Signal and Image Processing Institute, University of Southern California, Los Angeles, 1991.
3. Sudkamp, T., & Hammell II, R. J., "Interpolation, completion, and learning fuzzy rules," *IEEE Transactions on Systems, Man, and Cybernetics*, 24(2), 332-342, 1994.
4. Hammell II, R. J., "A fuzzy associative memory architecture for fuzzy inference and adaptivity," Ph.D. dissertation, Wright State University, Dayton, OH, 1995.
5. Sudkamp, T., & Hammell II, R. J., "Rule base completion in fuzzy models," in *Fuzzy modeling: Paradigms and practice* (W. Pedrycz, ed.), Kluwer Academic Publishers, 1995.
6. Hammell II, R. J., & Sudkamp, T., "A two-level architecture for fuzzy learning," *Journal of Intelligent and Fuzzy Systems*, 3(4), 273-286, 1995.
7. Haralick, R. M., & Shapiro, L. G., "Image segmentation techniques," *Computer Vision, Graphics and Image Processing*, 29, 100-132, 1985.
8. Isomursu, P., & Tauma, T., "A self-tuning fuzzy logic controller for temperature control of superheated steam," *Proceedings of the Third IEEE International Conference on Fuzzy Systems*, Orlando, FL, 1560-1563, 1994.
9. Layne, J. R., & Passino, K. M., "Fuzzy model reference learning control for cargo ship steering," *IEEE Control Systems*, 13(6), 23-34., 1993.
10. Hammell II, R.J., & Sudkamp, T., "An adaptive hierarchical fuzzy model," *Expert Systems With Applications*, 11(2), 125-136, 1996.

Learning Maximal Generalized Decision Rules via Discretization, Generalization and Rough Set Feature Selection *

Xiaohua Hu

Sybase Inc.
77 South Bedford St.
Burlington, MA, USA
xhu@sybase.com

Nick Cercone

Dept. of Computer Science
Univ. of Waterloo, Waterloo
Ont., Canada
ncercone@uwaterloo.ca

Abstract

We present a method to mine maximal generalized decision rules from databases by integrating discretization, generalization and rough sets feature selection. Our method reduces the data horizontally and vertically. In the first phase, discretization and generalization are integrated and the numeric attributes are discretized into a few intervals. Primitive values of symbolic attributes are replaced by high level concepts and some obvious superfluous or irrelevant symbolic attributes are also eliminated. Horizontal reduction is accomplished by merging identical tuples after the substitution of an attribute value by its higher level value in a pre-defined concept hierarchy for symbolic attributes or the discretization of continuous (or numeric) attributes. In the second phase, a novel context-sensitive feature merit measure is used to rank the features, a subset of relevant attributes is chosen based on rough sets theory and the merit values of the features. A reduced table is obtained by removing those attributes which are not in the relevant attributes subset and the data set is further reduced vertically without destroying the interdependence relationships between the classes and the attributes. Rough sets-based value reduction is further performed on the reduced table and all redundant condition values are dropped, finally, tuples in the reduced table are transformed into a set of maximal generalized decision rules. The experimental results on UCI data sets and an actual market database shows that our method can dramatically reduce the feature space and improve the learning accuracy.

*The work was done while the first author was with GTE Labs and the second author with Univ. of Regina

1 Introduction

In order to effectively and efficiently extract rules and understandable forms from these data, we must reduce the data before applying any data mining algorithms. We present a method to mine maximal generalized decision rules from databases by integrating discretization, generalization and rough sets feature selection. Our method reduces the data horizontally and vertically. In the first phase, discretization and generalization are integrated, the numeric attributes are discretized into a few intervals, if it is discretized into one interval, then it is removed. The primitive values of symbolic attributes are replaced by high level concepts and some obvious superfluous or irrelevant symbolic attributes are also eliminated. Horizontal reduction is performed by merging identical tuples after the substitution of an attribute value by its higher level value in a pre-defined concept hierarchy for symbolic attributes or the discretization of continuous (or numeric) attributes. This phase greatly decreases the number of tuples in the databases. In the second phase, a novel context-sensitive feature merit measure is used to rank the features, a subset of relevant attributes is chosen based on rough sets theory and the merit values of the features, a reduced table is obtained by removing those attributes which are not in the relevant attributes subset and data set is further reduced vertically without destroying the interdependence relationships between the classes and the attributes. Then rough sets-based value reduction is performed on the reduced table and redundant condition values are dropped; tuples in the reduced table are transformed into a set of maximal generalized decision rules. The algorithm is incorporated into a prototype system DBROUGH-II and tested on UCI datasets [12] and some actual databases. In Section 2, we illustrate with an example and describe the principle of

1082-3409/97 $10.00 © 1997 IEEE

discretization and generalization. In Section 3, we introduce a novel feature merit measure, which is used to rank the features and present a rough sets based feature selection algorithm which chooses a relevant and important feature subset for the learning task. The algorithm to learn maximal generalized decision rules, DBDeci, is described in Section 4 . The experimental results are shown in Section 5 and in Section 6 we present our discussion and conclusion.

2 Discretization and Generalization

Many applications may contain hundreds to thousands of feature variables. But not all of these feature variables are useful for data mining purposes because most of the time, the data are collected without "mining" in mind. In addition, the existence of numeric data and the primitive values of symbolic attributes create a huge data space determined by the numeric data and primitive symbolic values. To reduce the search space, normally numeric data are discretized and primitive symbolic values are generalized to more abstract concepts. In [2], an attribute-oriented induction method was proposed, which substitutes the primitive data by high level concepts in the concept hierarchies, assuming that the concept hierarchies (permitting the learned rules to be represented in a simple and explicit form) are provided by experts. But there are several drawbacks with this method: (1) its generalization relys on the concept hierarchies; if the attribute is symbolic type, this is appropriate as the distinct number of values for symbolic is limited, but for numeric attributes, concept hierarchies are difficult because of the wide distribution of the values or so many distinct different values, (2) attribute oriented induction uses a threshold T_N (the number of desirable tuples) as the stopping criterion for the generalization. Normally we don't know the desirable value for T_N before the generalization. The choice of T_N has a great effect on the generalized relation. A larger T_N will under-generalize the data, a small T_N will over-generalize the data and introduce many inconsistencies which had not existed before, thus changing the characteristics of the data. Since we want the generalized relation to accurately represent the original data, it is natural to use consistency checking as a stopping criterion instead of the threshold T_N. On the other hand, there are different discretization algorithms in the literature [?]. All of these algorithms just discretize the numeric attributes into some intervals based on some criterion measure without checking whether the numeric attribute is really relevant to the learning concept. Only Chi2 [10], a generalized version of ChiMerge [6] can automatically discretize the numeric attributes as well as removing those irrelevant numeric ones. However, it can't handle symbolic features either. So a natural solution is to integrate symbolic attribute generalization and numeric attribute discretization. Based on this consideration, we proposed a hybird algorithm which integrates Chi2 and attribute-oriented generalization method. The inconsistency criterion is used to specify to what extent the dimensionally reduced data can be accepted. In the algorithm below, for a numeric attribute, based on the inconsistency threshold δ, Chi2 discretizes the attribute into a few intervals. If a numeric attribute is discretized into one interval only without generating more inconsistencies than δ , it simply means that this attribute is not relevant to determine classes according to the χ^2 statistics, hence this attribute is removed. The discretization procedure can automatically discretize the numeric attribute as well as remove those irrelevant ones. For symbolic attributes, the substitution continues as long as it satisfies the inconsistency threshold. For an attribute with no concept hierarchy and many distinct values, even though this atttribute can distinguish the class uniquely, it has no predictive power, thus is removed too. As a result of generalization and discretization, different tuples may become the identical tuples, the redundant tuples are merged. This procedure greatly reduces the number of tuples horizontally.

Algorithm 1 (Discretization & Generalization)

```
1.for  each attribute in the data set {
2.     While (Inconsistency(DataSet) < δ) do {
3.        numeric attribute:
4.            apply Chi2 to discretize the attribute
5.            if the attribute is discretized into one
              interval only, remove it
6.        symbolic attribute:
7.            if there is a concept hierarchy for it
8.             replace the primitive values by high level
               concepts
9.            elseif there is a lot of distinct values for the
                  attribute and no concept hierarchy
                  for it, remove it }
10.    Endwhile }
11.Endfor
```

Example 2.1: Suppose we have a collection of Japanese and America cars with the attributes as **plate#**, **Make_model**, **colour**, **height**, **width** of the car, type of fuel system (**fuel**), engine displacement (**disp**), **weight**, number of cylinders (**cyl**), **power**, presence of turbocharge (**turbo**), compression ratio (**comp**), transmitter (**tran**) and **mileage** depicted in

Table 1 (mileage is the decision attribute) and the concept hierarchy table for the car relation is shown in Figure 1.

{Honda_civic, ..., Honda_acura} ⊂ Honda
{Toyota_tercel,...,Toyota_camry} ⊂ Toyota
{Mazda_323, Mazda_626,..., Mazda_939} ⊂ Mazda
{Toyota , Honda , ..., Mazda } ⊂ Japan(Car)
{Ford_escort,..., Ford_taurus } ⊂ Ford
{Chevrolet_corvette,...,Chevrolet_corsica } ⊂ Chevrolet
{Dodge_stealth,..., Dodge_dynasty } ⊂ Dodge
{Ford, Dodge, ..., Chevrolet } ⊂ USA(Car)
{Japan(Car), ..., USA(Car)} ⊂ Any(Make_model)

Figure 1: Concept Hierarchy Table

The first attribute, "Plate#", is the key of the relation. The key value is distinct for each tuple in the relation. If there is no higher level concept provided for such an attribute in the concept tree, the values of the attribute cannot be generalized, and they should be removed in the generalization. Also, other candidate key attributes or nonkey attributes (like **colour** of the car) can be eliminated under a similar condition. We then examine the remaining attributes and perform generalization for symbolic attributes and discretization for numeric attributes. For symbolic attribute, the primitive value in the attribute is generalized to more abstract level. e.g., ¿from *Mazda 323* to *Mazda*, then to *Japan* for attribute **Make_model**. For a numeric attribute, we apply Chi2 and discretize it into a few interval based on the inconsistency rate. For example, **Weight** of the car is discretized into three intervals [500-800] , [801-1050] and [1051-1500]. Some numeric attributes, for example, **width** is discretized into one interval [63.4-66.6], **height** into [52.4-55.3], which mean that these two attributes are not relevant to the decision attribute **Mileage** based on the χ^2 value, so they are removed. After discretization and generalization, Tabel 2 is obtained.

Suppose there are N tuples in the databases, A_s symbolic and A_n numeric attributes for each tuple, and H levels for each concept tree, the time complexity in the worst case is analyzed as follows: checking the inconsistency rate of data set is $O(N)$, for each symbolic attribute, the time for substituting the lower level concepts by the higher level concepts is N, and the time for checking redundant tuples is $O(NlogN)$. Since the height of the concept tree is H, the time spent on each symbolic attribute is at most $H*(N+NlogN)$. For each numeric attribute, discretization is $O(NlogN)$. Obviously, the upper bound of the total time for processing is $A_s * H * (N + NlogN) + A_n * (N + NlogN)$. In general, A_s, A_n and H are much smaller than N in a large database. Therefore, the time complexity of our approach is $O(NlogN)$ in the worst case.

3 Rough Set Feature Selection

Two kinds of attributes are generally perceived as being unnecessary: attributes that are irrelevant to the target concept, and attributes that are redundant given other attributes. For example, if you include age as well as birth date in your databases, then one of them is redundant as long as you know the other. In real applications, these two kinds of unnecessary attributes are existed in the same time but the latter ones are very hard to deal with because of the interaction between them. In the discretization and generalization phase, we discretized the numeric data and eliminated the very obivious irrelevant features (including those with high distinguishing but low predictive ability). Most of the data reduction is performed horizontally so far, only a small part of the irrelevant attributes are eliminated but there are still a lot of irrelevant and redundant features left in the data. In order to reduce the two kinds of unnecessary attributes to a minimum extent, we have to use feature selection. All the feature selection algorithms fall into two categories : (1) filter approach and (2) wrapper approach. In the filter approach, feature selection is performed as a preprocessing step to induction. Some of the well-known filter feature selection algorithms are FOCUS [1], RELIEF [7] and PRESET [11]. RELIEF is ineffectively dealing with the second feature redundancy. FOCUS is intractable to apply in data mining applications with hundreds or even thousands of features because it selects the minimal subset of features by exhaustively examining all subsets of features. PRESET only works in noise-free domain and is ineffective in dealing with correlated features. In wrapper approach [8], the feature selection is being "wrapper around" an induction algorithm, so that the bias of the operators that define the search and that of the induction algorithm interacts. Even though wrapper approach suffers less from feature interaction, however running time would make the approach infeasible in practice, especially if there are many features, which is very popular in data mining applications. Also we believe that any learning algorithm is biased. Wrapper approach searches for an optimal features subset tailored to a particular algorithm. We intend to keep the algorithm bias as small as possible and would like to find a subset attributes which can generate good results by applying a suite of data mining algorithms. Since our motivation is to build a multi-strategy (or as generic as possible) KDD system, data generalization, discretization and feature selection are served as pre-precessing steps. We focus on an algorithm-independent feature selection. Our goal is very clear: to have a reasonable fast algorithm that can find a relevant subset and eliminate the two kinds of unnecessary attributes effectively.

Plate#	Make_Model	colour	width	height	cyl	door	displace	compress	power	trans	w eight	mileage
BCT89U	Ford escort	silver	63.4	52.4	6	2	Medium	High	high	auto	1020	medium
UYT342	Chevrolet corvette	green	66.3	55.2	4	2	Small	High	medium	manu	890	high
LKIPO8	Chevrolet corvette	brown	64.3	55.3	4	2	Small	High	medium	auto	980	medium
IUTY56	Dodge stealth	green	65.7	66.6	4	2	Medium	Medium	medium	manu	1230	medium
DSA321	Toyota Paso	black	64.9	55.2	4	2	Small	Medium	low	manu	850	high
ERTW34	Ford probe	yellow	65.2	54.5	4	2	Medium	Medium	medium	manu	1500	low
9876T	Chrysler Le B	blue	66.3	52.7	6	4	Medium	Medium	high	auto	1180	medium
UYTHG7	Dodge sprite	light blue	65.9	54.7	6	4	Medium	Medium	high	auto	900	medium
RST45W	Dodge Stealth	red	63.6	53.9	4	2	Medium	Medium	high	auto	1180	medium
RGW45W	Dodge Dayton	light green	65.2	54.7	4	2	Medium	Medium	high	auto	1270	low
78YUTE	Ford escort	black	64.8	53.9	4	2	Medium	High	high	manu	780	high
......	....	.....	..	..	..	....	....	....	....	...	....	...
P0967H	Ford festival	brown	66.1	54.5	4	2	Small	High	medium	auto	850	medium
WEQ546	Toyota corolla	navy	65.7	55.1	4	2	Medium	Medium	medium	manu	900	high
PLMNH7	Mazda 323	yellow	64.9	55.2	4	2	Small	High	low	manu	700	high
QAS453	Dodge Dayton	green	66.6	53.5	4	2	Medium	Medium	medium	manu	1190	medium
PLMJH9	Honda accord	brown	64.8	55.3	4	2	Small	High	high	manu	870	high
PLMJH9	Honda prelude	yellow	65.9	55.3	4	2	Small	High	high	manu	970	high
KNM876	Chevrolet beretta	green	66.1	54.3	6	4	Medium	High	high	auto	1080	medium
IKLO90	Chevrolet cavalier	black	65.7	54.3	6	4	Medium	Medium	high	auto	1100	low
OPL876	Mazda 626	purple	65.9	54.8	4	2	Small	High	medium	manu	980	high
TYUR45	Ford mustang	black	66.2	54.2	4	2	Medium	Medium	medium	manu	1090	medium
0987UO	Dodge dayton	orange	64.3	53.4	4	2	Medium	Medium	medium	manu	1170	medium
UYT789	Chevrolet Corvette	black	63.7	54.8	4	2	Small	High	low	manu	1100	medium

Table 1: Car Relation.

Make_model	cyl	door	displace	compress	power	trans	weight	mileage
USA	6	4	MEDIUM	MEDIUM	HIGH	AUTO	[1051-1500]	LOW
USA	6	2	MEDIUM	MEDIUM	HIGH	MANUAL	[1051-1500]	LOW
USA	6	2	MEDIUM	HIGH	HIGH	AUTO	[801-1050]	MEDIUM
USA	6	4	MEDIUM	MEDIUM	MEDIUM	MANUAL	[801-1050]	MEDIUM
USA	4	2	SMALL	HIGH	MEDIUM	AUTO	[801-1050]	MEDIUM
USA	4	2	MEDIUM	MEDIUM	MEDIUM	MANUAL	[801-1050]	MEDIUM
USA	4	2	MEDIUM	MEDIUM	HIGH	MANUAL	[801-1050]	MEDIUM
USA	6	4	MEDIUM	MEDIUM	HIGH	AUTO	[801-1050]	MEDIUM
USA	4	2	MEDIUM	MEDIUM	HIGH	AUTO	[801-1050]	MEDIUM
USA	4	2	MEDIUM	HIGH	HIGH	MANUAL	[600-800]	HIGH
JAPAN	4	2	SMALL	HIGH	LOW	MANUAL	[600-800]	HIGH
JAPAN	4	2	MEDIUM	MEDIUM	MEDIUM	MANUAL	[801-1050]	HIGH
JAPAN	4	2	SMALL	HIGH	HIGH	MANUAL	[801-1050]	HIGH
JAPAN	4	2	SMALL	MEDIUM	LOW	MANUAL	[801-1050]	HIGH
JAPAN	4	2	SMALL	HIGH	MEDIUM	MANUAL	[801-1050]	HIGH
JAPAN	4	4	MEDIUM	HIGH	MEDIUM	AUTO	[600-800]	HIGH
USA	4	2	SMALL	HIGH	MEDIUM	MANUAL	[801-1050]	HIGH
USA	4	2	SMALL	HIGH	MEDIUM	MANUAL	[600-800]	HIGH

Table 2: A Car Relation After Discretization and Generalization

With these considerations in mind, we proposed a rough set based filter feature selection algorithm.

3.1 Feature Merit Measures

Traditional techniques make use of feature merits based on either the information theoretic or statistics correlation between each feature and the class, or the significant values based on rough set theory [13]. All these measures only consider the single feature's effect on the class distinguishability. But in general, one feature does not distinguish classes by itself; it does so in combination with other features. Therefore, it is desirable to obtain the feature's correlation to the class in the context of other features. Most of the filter approach using the traditional merit measure fails on parity data set, where attributes have a strong interaction. Followed on our earlier work in rough set similarity-based learning [4] and inspried by Hong [3], we propose a feature merit measure to rank the feature in the context of other features. The idea is to assign the contextual merit value based on the component distance of feature weighted by the degree of difference between instances in different classes. The feature merit measure consists of two parts: (1) *Weighted Feature Difference (WFD)* based on the precise unequality of the values of the predictor fields (attributes) and (2) the *Value Difference (VD)* by taking into account the difference of values to evaluate the distinguishability of the two instances.

3.1.1 Weighted Feature Difference (WFD)

The feature difference is based on the precise unequality of the values of the features. A most popular way to compute the feature difference between two instances is to calculate the Euclidean distance between them. Suppose an example in class $D1$ and a counter example in class $D2$ differ in only three features, say C_1 and C_2 and C_3. The distance between the examples is 3. These three features are then the sole contributors in distinguishing the classes of the examples, and hence are "responsible". The inverse of the distance (1/3) which should be shared equally by C_1, C_2 and C_3, i.e., shared in proportion to their component distance (1/9 each in this case). From the pairs of examples in different classes, we obtain merit contributions to the features, so they reflect feature's share of the obligation to seperate the classes in the context of all other features. Based on this philosophy and Hong's work [3], for two instance t_i, t_j, a Feature Differnce WFD_{ij} is defined as $WFD_{ij} = 1/D_{ij}^2$, where $D_{ij} = \sum_{k=1}^{m} d_{ij}^{(k)}$, for a feature C_k, its component distance is

$$d_{ij}^{(k)} = \begin{cases} 1 & \text{if } c_{ki} \neq c_{kj} \\ 0 & \text{otherwise} \end{cases}$$

Where m is the number of features, c_{ki} and c_{kj} are the value of the kth attributes for t_i, t_j in the databases. Here we only need to consider symbolic attributes because the numeric features are already converted into intervals and are treated as symbolic features.

3.1.2 Value-Difference (VD)

Kullback [9] has proposed the following measure for the information content of a value assignment $K(D|C_k = c) = \sum_{d \in D} P(d|c) log(\frac{P(d|c)}{p(d)})$, where c, d represent value assignments of feature C_k, and class D, respectively. The formula can be interpreted as the average mutual information between the events d and c with the expectation taken with respect to the a posterior probability distribution of D. The value difference $VD(c_{ki}, c_{kj})^{(k)}$ is defined as the ratio of their absolute value $K(D|C_k = c_{ki}) - K(D|C_k = c_{kj})$ to the total range of attribute C_k, i.e, $VD(c_{ki}, c_{kj})^{(k)} = \frac{|K(D|C_k = c_{ki}) - K(D|C_k = c_{kj})|}{VD_{max} - VD_{min}}$, where VD_{max}, VD_{min} are the maximum and minimum K values as defined in formula of the attribute C_k.

3.1.3 A Context Sensitive Merit Measure (CM)

In our feature merit measure defined in [4], the difference of the instances in one class D_1 with all the instances in the opposite class $\neg D_1$ are considered. It turns out that the counter examples that are far from the example will only contribute noise to the process, since they would be distinguished from the example easily anyway. Influenced by Hong [3], we first compute the distance to all the counter examples of the opposite class and retain for merit considerations only some fraction of the counter examples that are nearest to the example. This philosophy is similar to that of the K-nearest neighbor shemes. We only retain contribution from the $K = log_2 N2$ nearest counter examples (where $N2$ is the number of the counter examples in the opposite class). Each of the counter examples chosen for the example contribute its $1/D_{ij}$ distributed to the feature in proportion to their component distance, $d_{ij}^{(k)}$. i.e., $d_{ij}^{(k)}/D_{ij}^2$, to the respective merit values of the features. The quantity $1/D_{ij}$ can be viewed as the degree of independence of the distance constituting feature in the given context, or the strength of the context.

The contextual merit CM_k of a feature C_k is defined as $CM_k = \sum_{t_i \in D_1} \sum_{t_j \in \neg D_1} WFD_{ij} \times VD(c_{ki}, c_{kj})^{(k)}$, where WFD_{ij} is $1/D_{ij}^2$ if $t_j \in \neg D_1$ is one of the $K = log_2 N_2$ nearest neighbours of $t_i \in D_1$, otherwise it is 0.

Contextual merits capture relative importance of feature in distinguishing the classes in the context of other features. The notion of context is important here. We take **EXOR(n,m,M)[3]** as an example to show the effectiveness of the merit measure. For EXOR(5,5,500), the feature merits are $CM =$

$(CM_1, CM_2, ..., CM_{10})$=(43 39 56 48 52 || 12 24 31 29 10). (|| is used to seperate the base variables from the random variables). The merit feature can capture the situation where two features are highly correlated. For example, suppose we replace the first random variable C_6 with a copy of the last base variable C_5 so that the modified example data now has two identical columns. The merits of the case are CM=(34 42 35 29 05 || 11 17 15 19 21), the contextual merits of C_5 and C_6 are now the least because duplicated variables must contribute to the distance by the number of duplicity and share the merit component by portion which are that much smaller. Of course as soon as one of these variables is discarded, the merit of the remaining copy of the base variables improves. The next example case illustrates an interesting property of the contextual merit. Let us now replace the first random variable C_6 with the Ex-OR of the first three columns C_1, C_2, C_3. Now the class function can be represented by a simple Ex-Or function of C_4, C_5 and C_6. This modified example produces the following merits CM=(17 22 19 49 55 || 64 22 18 23 24). As can be seen, C_4, C_5, C_6 have larger merit values while C_1, C_2, C_3's merit values are decreased dramatically because C_1, C_2, C_3 are redundant in the presence of C_6.

3.2 Basic Notation of Rough Sets

Rough set theory has been applied in a lot of areas since it was first proposed by Pawlak in early 80's. But the inability to model the uncertain information severely reduce the applicability of rough set approach to the problems which are more probabilistic than deterministic in nature. In the original rough sets model, a strict set inclusion is used to define the lower approximation, which has no tolerance to noise data in the application. However, sets of real-world training examples are almost invariably imprecise. Based on this, Ziarko [15] proposed an Variable Precise Rough Set model (VP-RS). In the VP-RS model, the conditional probability is defined as: $P(D_j|[u_i]_{IND}) = \frac{P(D_j \cup [u_i]_{IND})}{P([u_i]_{IND})} = \frac{card(D_j \cup [u_i]_{IND})}{card([u_i]_{IND})}$, *card* denotes the cardinality of the set

Given a decision table, suppose $\tilde{C} = \{\tilde{C_1}, \tilde{C_2}, ..., \tilde{C_k}\}$ be the collection of equivalence classes induced by attributes C. In the VP-RS model (β is choosen between [0, 0.5) depends on the noise level of the data). :

(1) the β-positive region is $POS_C(D_j) = \cup_{P(D_j|\tilde{C_i}) \geq 1-\beta}\{\tilde{C_i} \in \tilde{C}\}$

(2) the β-boundary region is $BOS_C(D_j) = \cup_{\beta < P(D_j|\tilde{C_i}) < 1-\beta}\{\tilde{C_i} \in \tilde{C}\}$

(3) the β-negative region is $NEG_C(D_j) = \cup_{P(D_j|\tilde{C_i}) \leq \beta}\{\tilde{C_i} \in \tilde{C}\}$

The degree of dependency $K_\beta(C, D)$ in the relationship between the attributes C and attributes D is $K_\beta(C, D) = \frac{card(POS_C(D) + NEG_C(D))}{card(U)}$

The value $K_\beta(C, D)$ is the proportion of these objects in the decision table which can be roughly or definitely assigned into the β-positive and the β-negative regions. It characterizes the abilities to predict the concept D and complement concept $\neg D$ from objects in the decision table. An attribute a is said to be ***dispensable*** in C w.r.t. D if $K_\beta(C - \{a\}, D) = K_\beta(C, D)$; otherwise a is an *indispensable* attribute in C w.r.t D. A subset of condition attributes $B \subset C$ is a *dependent set* in S w.r.t D if there exists a proper subset $E \subset B$ such that $K_\beta(B, D) = K_\beta(E, D)$; otherwise B is an independent set w.r.t D. A relative reduct C' of attributes C is a maximal independent subset of condition attributes w.r.t D. More than one relative reduct may exist for a decision table. Selection of a "best" reduct depends on the optimality criterion associated with the attributes. There are a lot of algorithms developed [5] to find a relative reduct efficiently and effectively. In our experiments [?], we found out that reduct tends to overfit data sets, rules derived from a slightly larger number of attribute than a reduct (minimal subset attributes) tends to have high accuracy. Furthermore, finding just a single reduct of the attributes may be too restrictive for some data analysis problems. Our algorithm computes the feature meirts of all feature and then rank them based on the feature merit values, performs stepwise backward elimination to drop the feature with least merit, then recomputes the features merit. The procedure continues until the dependency relationship (calculated using rough set method) of the feature sets with the classes is still in desirable level. The desired number of features may be more than the reduct (a minimal set) to keep a reasonable distinguishability depending on the problem case, especially when the data is highly noisy. In the algorithm below, if we set $\beta = 0$, then the result is a reduct.

Algorithm 2 (Rough Set Feature Selection)

1. Compute $K_\beta(C, D)$

2. $REDU \leftarrow C$

3. While $K_\beta(C, D) = K_\beta(REDU, D)$ **Do** {

4. Compute the contextual merits CM for all attributes of $REDU$;

5. Sort the set of attributes $REDU$ based on contextual merits;

6. Choose a attribute a_j with the least merit values and $K_\beta(REDU, D) = K_\beta(REDU - \{a_j\}, D)$

7. $REDU \leftarrow REDU - \{a_j\}$ }

8. Endwhile

9. Return $REDU$

Make_model	compress	trans	power	Weight	mileage
USA	MEDIUM	AUTO	HIGH	[1051-1500]	LOW
USA	HIGH	MANUAL	MEDIUM	[1051-1500]	LOW
JAPAN	MEDIUM	AUTO	MEDIUM	[1051-1500]	LOW
USA	HIGH	AUTO	HIGH	[1051-1500]	LOW
USA	MEDIUM	AUTO	MEDIUM	[801-1050]	MEDIUM
USA	HIGH	MANUAL	MEDIUM	[1051-1500]	MEDIUM
JAPAN	MEDIUM	AUTO	HIGH	[801-1050]	MEDIUM
USA	MEDIUM	MANUAL	HIGH	[600-800]	MEDIUM
USA	HIGH	AUTO	MEDIUM	[801-1050]	MEDIUM
USA	MEDIUM	MANUAL	HIGH	[801-1050]	MEDIUM
USA	MEDIUM	AUTO	HIGH	[1051-1500]	MEDIUM
USA	HIGH	MANUAL	MEDIUM	[600-800]	HIGH
JAPAN	HIGH	MANUAL	MEDIUM	[801-1050]	HIGH
JAPAN	MEDIUM	AUTO	MEDIUM	[600-800]	HIGH
JAPAN	MEDIUM	MANUAL	MEDIUM	[600-800]	HIGH

Table 3: Reduced Table

The feature selection algorithm does find a relevant subset of attributes even the attributes have very strong correlation between each other. The complexity of Algorithm 2 (RSFS) is $O(N'^2)$ where N' is the number of tuples left after the generalization and discretization. Normally N' is not very big after generalization and discretization. When the number of example is large, one can use sampling technologies and compute the contextual merits on samples incrementally until the results are stable. Apply this algorithm to Table 2, a relevant attributes subset $REDU = \{Make\_model, compress, trans, weight, mileage\}$ is identified. After removing those attributes *cyl, door, displace* from Table 2 which are not in $REDU$, a much reduced table Table 3 is obtained.

4 Generation of Maximal Generalized Decision Rules

A reduced table can be considered as a set of specific decision rules DEC-RULUS=$\{r_1, r_2, ..., r_n\}$. Each rule r_i corresponds to exact one tuple in the reduced table. Such decision rules can be generalized further by dropping conditions. The process by which the maximum number of condition attribute values are removed without losing essential information is called *value reduction* in rough set theory, and the resulting rules is called *maximal generalized rule*. The *maximal generalized rules* minimize the number of the rule conditions and are optimal because their conditions are non-redundent. Here we propose a new method which simplifies each rule by dropping the redundant conditions. A condition is dropped from a rule r_i, and then rule r_i is checked for consistency with other rules in the rule set DEC-RULES. If rule r_i is inconsistent, then the dropped condition is restored back. This step is repeated until every

Make_model	compress	trans	weight	mileage
			[1051-1500]	LOW
USA		AUTO		MEDIUM
USA	MEDIUM			MEDIUM
		MANUAL	[801-1050]	MEDIUM
	HIGH	MANUAL		HIGH
JAPAN				HIGH
			[600-800]	HIGH

Table 4: Maximal Generalized Decision Rules Table after Value Reduction

condition of the rule r_i has been tested. In summary, we present the algorithm below:

Algorithm 3 (DBDeci–maximal generalized decision rules algorithm)

1. Apply data discretization and generalization algorithm

2. Apply rough set feature selection algorithm

3. Generated the reduced table DECI-RULES by removing those attributes which are not in the selected feature subset obtained at Step 2

4. Simplify each tuple in the reduced table

```
for each tuple r_i in DECI-RULES do {
    M ⟵ |r_i|
    for each condition value a_ij in r_i do {
        Remove a_ij from r_i
        if r_i is inconsistent with any rule r
            in DECI-RULES then
        then put a_ij back to r_i
        endif
    endfor }
endfor }
```

5. Transform the tuples into maximal generalized decision rules for each class in D

Apply DBDeci to Table 3, we get Table 4 after all the redundant condition values for the tuples are dropped. Each tuple is a maximal generalized decision rule. For example, the 4th tuples corresponds to the following maximal generalized decision rule

If (Trans=MANUAL) & (WEIGHT=[801-1050])
    then (Mileage=MEDIUM)

Since the time complexity of step 1 (Discretization and Generalization) is $O(NlogN)$ for N tuples, the complexity of step 2 (Rough Set Feature Selection) is $O(N'^2)$ where N' is the number of tuples left after the generalization and discretization. Suppose there is n tuples (decision rules) with a attribute left after rough set feature selection, finding a maximal generalized rule for each decision rule requires $O(na)$, so finding all maximal generalized rules for n tuples is $O(n^2a)$. The total cost of our algorithm DBDeci is $O(NlogN)$+$O(N'^2)$+$O(n^2a)$.

Dataset	Data Size	Features Orgi/Final	#Concept	C4.5	DBDeci
credit-screening	690	15/11	2	82.75	**88.65**
breast-cancer	699	10/8	7	**96.00**	95.80
glass	214	10/7	7	71.50	**76.56**
heart	920	13/9	2	74.44	**77.43**
hipatitis	155	19/16	2	**83.40**	81.32
horse colic	368	28/19	3	82.4	**84.3**
ionosphere	351	34/25	2	**94.87**	93.45
iris	150	4/2	3	95.33	**98.00**
led	100	7/7	10	63.1	**64.50**
liver-disease	345	6/6	2	**65.3**	76.4
lung-cancer	32	56/30	3	50.00	**54.43**
monk1	432	6/3	2	98.2	**100**
monk2	432	6/6	2	80.4	80.4
monk3	432	6/3	2	96.6	**100.0**
pima	768	8/6	2	74.87	**76.35**
sonar	208	60/53	2	**75.1**	70.34
tictac	958	9/9	2	96.30	**99.20**
vote	435	16/9	2	**99.90**	95.00
wine	178	13/9	3	92.70	**93.90**
zoo	101	17/10	7	93.06	**95.06**
Average				78.50	84.41

Table 5: The Comparison on 20 Datasets

5 Experimental Results

The algorithm DBDeci was integrated into a KDD system DBROUGH-II. DBROUGH-II is an enhanced version of DBROUGH [5]. DBROUGH-II is a suite of data mining tools to discover new patterns and data evolution regulairties. It consists of discrimination (DBClass), decision rule (DBDeci), summarization (DBChar), data evolution regularities algorithms (DBTrend) and so on. The DBROUGH-II system has been used on many real applications such as customer database marketing, city water management system. The number of features varies ¿from dozens to hundreds and number of records from few thousands to several millions. We did some experiments on UCI data sets [12] and a real market database using the induction algorithm C4.5 and DBDeci to compare the classification accuracy. The tests are ran on a SGI workstation running on IRIX release 5.3 operating system and results are shown in Table 5 and 6.

(1) UCI Datasets: 20 data sets from UCI repository databases were chosen. We compared our algorithm with C4.5RULE. We set δ=0.05, β=0.10. 5-fold cross validation was used to measure the classification accuracy. Table 5 shows the results from the experiments described above. On 14 out of 20 datasets, the DBDeci achieves a significant improvement on prediction accuracy over C4.5 Rules. The average prediction accuracy of DBDeci is higher than C4.5RULE.

(2) Customer Market Database: The dataset is confidential. The customer database consumes several gigabytes and contains millions of records. We are helping them to do effective target marketing campaign, need to answer such market questions such as: what is the characteristic of the customer in some areas? what is the difference between customers in different areas? These types of queries typically related to hundreds of features, access thousands even millions of records. 8 market areas were tested. Each data set, 2/3 is used for training and 1/3 for testing. (δ=0.10, β=0.10)

Dataset	Data Size	Features Orgi/Final	C4.5	DBDeci
Market 1	499305	107/45	67.3	73.5
Market 2	160016	107/57	69.4	74.9
Market 3	130345	92/51	72.4	81.9
Market 4	318693	92/46	67.2	75.0
Market 5	176108	124/69	59.4	64.9
Market 6	255675	124/63	60.3	65.7
Market 7	55648	97/53	73.4	80.6
Market 8	45002	97/47	69.3	73.8
Average			67.3	73.8

Table 6: The Comparison on a market database

6 Discussion & Conclusion

In this paper, the discretization, generalization, and rough set based feature selection procedures are integrated as pre-precessing steps for mining maximal generalized decision rules. Discretization merges the values of each numeric attribute, generalization replaces the primitive values by more abstract concepts, thus significantly decreases the numbers of values the attributes can take and reduces the data in a horizontal dimension. The vertical dimensionality reduction is achieved by rough set feature selection that eliminating those unnecessary attributes while keeping the same discriminating power. Theoretical and experimental study shows the advantages of our approach: (1) theoretical foundation, (2) effective and efficient in eliminating irrelevant and redundant features even with strong interaction, (3) feasible for applications with hundreds or thousands of features, (4) tolerant to inconsistencies in the data.

Our algorithm DBDeci can generate maximal generalized decision rules ¿from imprecise data. This capability is important because in practice we seldom have complete and consistent information for the design of intelligent system. The salient feature of the proposed method is that it makes use of the statistical information inherent in the databases. Furthermore, our method can deal with uncertainty, or work with the presence of noise.

Learnability of training set is another important issue in inductive learning. It is associated with uncertainty that exists in the data set. Such data may result in the failure of a learning algorithm in deriving decision rules. We deal with this problem by using an extension of rough set theory. The approximate classification partitions the dataset into the β-positive, β-boundary and β-nagative regions. if β-positive and β-negative region exist, then we can apply rule generation to construct a set of a decision rules for the target concept. Imprecise data are generalized using a rough-sets based approximation technique. Positive, boundary and negative regions of the target concept are defined using statistical information. If the concept is learnable, superfluous attributes are eliminated and rules are generated. Our approach treats each rule as a piece of uncertain evidence, which by itself is of little value with respect to classification but our classficaition procedure combines as many piece of evidence(rules) as possible.

Another novel feature of our algorithm is its use of multiple knowledge rules. The idea is to generate multiple knowledge rules instead of one set of minimum rules to cover all the examples, hoping that the combination of answers of multiple knowledge rules result in better performance. Typically one object is classified with several rules, and the decisions are then combined to obtain the final conclusion. Our algorithm DBDeci contains some amount of redundancy knowledge rules whcih is probably one of the reasons for the successful behaviour. Most popular learning algorithms use a covering strategy during learning. These systems would consider a rule useless if it covered examples that are already covered by other rules. Our method does not follow this way. In our system all potential interesting and useful maximal generalized decision rules are generated even though there are some overlapping of the examples covered by rules and there are negative effects on simplicity and comprehensibility. We believe that system that strives to eliminate redundant rules becomes more sensitive to noise because a small number of rules means that few alternatives existed when classify unseen objects.

References

[1] Almuallim,H. and Dietterich,T.G; Learning boolean concepts in the presence of many irrelevant features. *Artificial Intelligence,* 69(1-2):279-305, 1994

[2] Han,J; Cai,Y; Cercone,N; Knowledge Discovery in Databases: An Attribute-Oriented Approach, *Proceeding of the 18th VLDB Conference,* 335-350, 1992

[3] Hong, S; Use of Contextual Information for Feature Ranking and Discretization, *to appear in IEEE TKDE*

[4] Hu,X; Cercone,N; Rough Set Based Similarity Learning from Databases *Proc. of the 1st KDD Conf,* 1995

[5] Hu. X; Cercone, N; Mining Knowledge Rules from Databases: A Rough Set Approach *Proc. of the 12th International Conf. on Data Engineering (ICDE96),* 1996

[6] Kerber, R; ChiMerge: Discretization of Numeric Attribute, in AAAI-92, 1992

[7] Kira,K; Rendell,L.A; The feature selection problem: Traditional methods and a new algorithm, *In Proc. AAAI-92,* 1992

[8] Kohavi, R; John H; Wrappers for Feature Subset Selection, *to appear in AIJ special issue in relevance,* 1996

[9] Kullback, S; *Information Theory and Statistics,* New York: Dover Publications, 1968

[10] Liu, H; Setiono, R; Chi2: Feature Selection and Discretization of Numerical Attributes, *in Proc. of the IEEE Tools on AI,* 1996

[11] Modrzejewski, M; Feature Selection Using Rough Stes Theory, *in Proc. ECML-93,* 1993

[12] Murphy P.M; Aha D. W; UCI repository of machine learning databases, http://www.ics.uci.edu/ mlearn/MLRepository.html, 1996

[13] Pawlak Zdzislaw; Rough Sets: Theoretical Aspects of Reasoning about Data, Kluwer Academic Publishers, 1992

[14] Quinlan, J.R; 1993, C4.5: Program for machine Learning, Morgan Kaufmann

[15] Ziarko, W; *Variable Precision Rough Set Model.* Journal of Computer and System Sciences, Vol. 46, No. 1, 1993

Session H.3

Knowledge Discovery in Knowledge Based Systems

Session Chair:
Bharghavan Vaduvur, University of Illinois, USA

Web Mining: Information and Pattern Discovery on the World Wide Web *

R. Cooley, B. Mobasher, and J. Srivastava
Department of Computer Science and Engineering
University of Minnesota
Minneapolis, MN 55455, USA

Abstract

Application of data mining techniques to the World Wide Web, referred to as Web mining, has been the focus of several recent research projects and papers. However, there is no established vocabulary, leading to confusion when comparing research efforts. The term Web mining has been used in two distinct ways. The first, called Web content mining in this paper, is the process of information discovery from sources across the World Wide Web. The second, called Web usage mining, is the process of mining for user browsing and access patterns. In this paper we define Web mining and present an overview of the various research issues, techniques, and development efforts. We briefly describe WEBMINER, a system for Web usage mining, and conclude this paper by listing research issues.

1 Introduction

With the explosive growth of information sources available on the World Wide Web, it has become increasingly necessary for users to utilize automated tools in find the desired information resources, and to track and analyze their usage patterns. These factors give rise to the necessity of creating server-side and client-side intelligent systems that can effectively mine for knowledge. *Web mining* can be broadly defined as the discovery and analysis of useful information from the World Wide Web. This describes the automatic search of information resources available on-line, i.e. *Web content mining*, and the discovery of user access patterns from Web servers, i.e., *Web usage mining*.

In this paper, we provide an overview of tools, techniques, and problems associated with both dimensions. We present a taxonomy of Web mining, and place various aspects of Web mining in their proper context. There are several important issues, unique to the Web paradigm, that come into play if sophisticated types of analyses are to be done on server side data collections. These include integrating various data sources such as server access logs, referrer logs, user registration or profile information; resolving difficulties in the identification of users due to missing unique key attributes in collected data; and the importance of identifying user sessions or transactions from usage data, site topologies, and models of user behavior. We devote the main part of this paper to the discussion of issues and problems that characterize Web usage mining. Furthermore, we survey some of the emerging tools and techniques, and identify several future research directions.

*This work was supported in part by NSF grant ASC-9554517

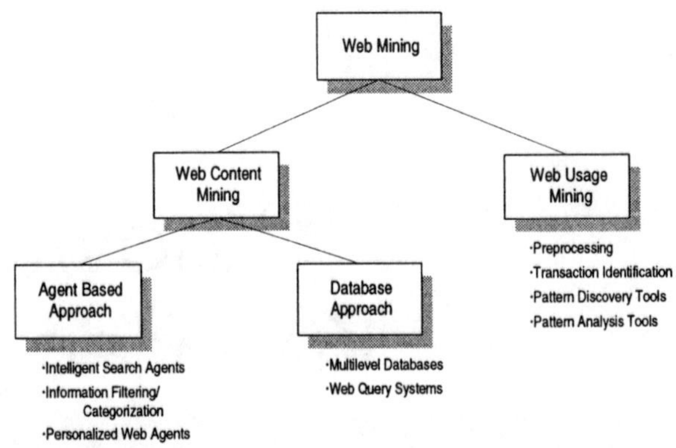

Figure 1: Taxonomy of Web Mining

2 A Taxonomy of Web Mining

In this section we present a taxonomy of Web mining, i.e. Web content mining and Web usage mining. We also describe and categorize some of the recent work and the related tools or techniques in each area. This taxonomy is depicted in Figure 1.

2.1 Web Content Mining

The lack of structure that permeates the information sources on the World Wide Web makes automated discovery of Web-based information difficult. Traditional search engines such as Lycos, Alta Vista, WebCrawler, ALIWEB [29], MetaCrawler, and others provide some comfort to users, but do not generally provide structural information nor categorize, filter, or interpret documents. A recent study provides a comprehensive and statistically thorough comparative evaluation of the most popular search engines [32].

In recent years these factors have prompted researchers to develop more intelligent tools for information retrieval, such as intelligent Web agents, and to extend data mining techniques to provide a higher level of organization for semi-structured data available on the Web. We summarize some of these efforts below.

2.1.1 Agent-Based Approach. Generally, agent-based Web mining systems can be placed into the following three categories:

Intelligent Search Agents: Several intelligent Web agents have been developed that search for relevant information using domain characteristics and user profiles to organize and interpret the discovered information. Agents such as Harvest [6], FAQ-Finder [19], Information Manifold [27], OCCAM [30], and ParaSite [51] rely either on pre-specified domain information about particular types of documents, or on hard coded models of the information sources to retrieve and interpret documents. Agents such as ShopBot [14] and ILA (Internet Learning Agent) [42] interact with and learn the structure of unfamiliar information sources. ShopBot retrieves product information from a variety of vendor sites using only general information about the product domain. ILA learns models of various information sources and translates these into its own concept hierarchy.

Information Filtering/Categorization: A number of Web agents use various information retrieval techniques [17] and characteristics of open hypertext Web documents to automatically retrieve, filter, and categorize them [5, 9, 34, 55, 53]. HyPursuit [53] uses semantic information embedded in link structures and document content to create cluster hierarchies of hypertext documents, and structure an information space. BO (Bookmark Organizer) [34] combines hierarchical clustering techniques and user interaction to organize a collection of Web documents based on conceptual information.

Personalized Web Agents: This category of Web agents learn user preferences and discover Web information sources based on these preferences, and those of other individuals with similar interests (using collaborative filtering). A few recent examples of such agents include the WebWatcher [3], PAINT [39], Syskill & Webert [41], GroupLens [47], Firefly [49], and others [4]. For example, Syskill & Webert utilizes a user profile and learns to rate Web pages of interest using a Bayesian classifier.

2.1.2 Database Approach. Database approaches to Web mining have focused on techniques for organizing the semi-structured data on the Web into more structured collections of resources, and using standard database querying mechanisms and data mining techniques to analyze it.

Multilevel Databases: The main idea behind this approach is that the lowest level of the database contains semi-structured information stored in various Web repositories, such as hypertext documents. At the higher level(s) meta data or generalizations are extracted from lower levels and organized in structured collections, i.e. relational or object-oriented databases. For example, Han, et. al. [56] use a multi-layered database where each layer is obtained via generalization and transformation operations performed on the lower layers. Kholsa, et. al. [25] propose the creation and maintenance of meta-databases at each information providing domain and the use of a global schema for the meta-database. King & Novak [26] propose the incremental integration of a portion of the schema from each information source, rather than relying on a global heterogeneous database schema. The ARANEUS system [40] extracts relevant information from hypertext documents and integrates these into higher-level *derived Web Hypertexts* which are generalizations of the notion of database views.

Web Query Systems: Many Web-based query systems and languages utilize standard database query languages such as SQL, structural information about Web documents, and even natural language processing for the queries that are used in World Wide Web searches. W3QL [28] combines structure queries, based on the organization of hypertext documents, and content queries, based on information retrieval techniques. WebLog [31] Logic-based query language for restructuring extracts information from Web information sources. Lorel [46] and UnQL [7, 8] query heterogeneous and semi-structured information on the Web using a labeled graph data model. TSIMMIS [10] extracts data from heterogeneous and semi-structured information sources and correlates them to generate an integrated database representation of the extracted information.

2.2 Web Usage Mining

Web usage mining is the automatic discovery of user access patterns from Web servers. Organizations collect large volumes of data in their daily operations, generated automatically by Web servers and collected in server access logs. Other sources of user information include *referrer logs* which contain information about the referring pages for each page reference, and user registration or survey data gathered via CGI scripts.

Analyzing such data can help organizations determine the life time value of customers, cross marketing strategies across products, and effectiveness of promotional campaigns, among other things. It can also provide information on how to restructure a Web site to create a more effective organizational presence, and shed light on more effective management of workgroup communication and organizational infrastructure. For selling advertisements on the World Wide Web, analyzing user access patterns helps in targeting ads to specific groups of users.

Most existing Web analysis tools [16, 23, 37] provide mechanisms for reporting user activity in the servers and various forms of data filtering. Using such tools it is possible to determine the number of accesses to the server and to individual files, the times of visits, and the domain names and URLs of users. However, these tools are designed to handle low to moderate traffic servers, and usually provide little or no analysis of data relationships among the accessed files and directories within the Web space.

More sophisticated systems and techniques for discovery and analysis of patterns are now emerging. These tools can be placed into two main categories, as discussed below.

2.2.1 Pattern Discovery Tools. The emerging tools for user pattern discovery use sophisticated techniques from AI, data mining, psychology, and information theory, to mine for knowledge from collected data. For example, the WEBMINER system [12, 36] introduces a general architecture for Web usage mining. WEBMINER automatically discovers association rules and sequential patterns from server access logs. In [11] algorithms are introduced for finding *maximal forward references* and *large reference sequences.* These can, in turn be used to perform various types of user traversal path analysis, such as identifying the most traversed paths thorough a Web locality. Pirolli et. al. [43] use information foraging theory to combine path traversal patterns, Web page typing, and site topology information to categorize pages for easier access by users.

2.2.2 Pattern Analysis Tools. Once access patterns have been discovered, analysts need the appropriate tools and techniques to understand, visualize, and interpret these patterns, e.g. the WebViz system [45]. Others have proposed using OLAP techniques such as data cubes for the purpose of simplifying the analysis of usage statistics from server access logs [15]. The WEBMINER system [36] proposes an SQL-like query mechanism for querying the discovered knowledge (in the form of association rules and sequential patterns). These techniques and others are further discussed in the subsequent sections.

3 Pattern Discovery from Web Transactions

As discussed in section 2.2, analysis of how users are accessing a site is critical for determining effective marketing strategies and optimizing the logical structure of the Web site. Because of many unique characteristics of the client-server model in the World Wide Web, including differences between the physical topology of Web repositories and user access paths, and the difficulty in identification of unique users as well as user sessions or transactions, it is necessary to develop a new framework to enable the mining process. Specifically, there are a number of issues in preprocessing data for mining that must be addressed before the mining algorithms can be run. These include developing a model of access log data, developing techniques to clean/filter the raw data to eliminate outliers and/or irrelevant items, grouping individual page accesses into semantic units (i.e. transactions), integration of various data sources such as user registration information, and specializing generic data mining algorithms to take advantage of the specific nature of access log data.

3.1 Preprocessing Tasks

The first preprocessing task is *data cleaning.* Techniques to clean a server log to eliminate irrelevant items are of importance for any type of Web log analysis, not just data mining. The discovered associations or reported statistics are only useful if the data represented in the server log gives an accurate picture of the user accesses of the Web site. Elimination of irrelevant items can be reasonably accomplished by checking the suffix of the URL name. For instance, all log entries with filename suffixes such as, gif, jpeg, GIF, JPEG, jpg, JPG, and map can be removed.

A related but much harder problem is determining if there are important accesses that are not recorded in the access log. Mechanisms such as local caches and proxy servers can severely distort the overall picture of user traversals through a Web site. Current methods to try to overcome this problem include the use of cookies, cache busting, and explicit user registration. As detailed in [44], none of these methods are without serious drawbacks. Cookies can be deleted by the user, cache busting defeats the speed advantage that caching was created to provide and can be disabled, and user registration is voluntary and users often provide false information. Methods for dealing with the caching problem include using site topology or referrer logs, along with temporal information to infer missing references.

Another problem associated with proxy servers is that of user identification. Use of a machine name to uniquely identify users can result in several users being erroneously grouped together as one user. An algorithm presented in [43] checks to see if each incoming request is reachable from the pages already visited. If a page is requested that is not directly linked to the previous pages, multiple users are assumed to exist on the same machine. In [12], user session lengths determined automatically based on navigation patterns are used to identify users. Other heuristics involve using a combination of IP address, machine name, browser agent, and temporal information to identify users [44].

The second major preprocessing task is *transaction identification.* Before any mining is done on Web usage data, sequences of page references must be grouped into logical units representing Web transactions or user sessions. A user session is all of the page references made by a user during a single visit to a site. Identifying user sessions is similar to the problem of identifying individual users, as discussed above. A transaction differs from a user session in that the size of a transaction can range from a single page reference to all of the page references in a user session, depending on the criteria used to identify transactions. Unlike traditional domains for data mining, such as point of sale databases, there is no convenient method of clustering page references into transactions smaller than an entire user session. This problem has been addressed in [11] and [12].

3.2 Discovery Techniques on Web Transactions

Once user transactions or sessions have been identified, there are several kinds of access pattern mining that can be performed depending on the needs of the analyst, such as path analysis, discovery of association rules and sequential patterns, and clustering and classification.

There are many different types of graphs that can be formed for performing *path analysis*, since a graph represents some relation defined on Web pages (or other objects). The most obvious is a graph representing the physical layout of a Web site, with Web pages as nodes and hypertext links between pages as directed edges. Other graphs could be formed based on the types of Web pages with edges representing similarity between pages, or creating edges that give the number of users that go from one page to another [43]. Most of the work to date involves determining frequent traversal patterns or large reference sequences from the physical layout type of graph. Path analysis could be used to determine most frequently visited paths in a Web site. Other examples of information that can be discovered through path analysis are:

- 70% of clients who accessed `/company/product2` did so by starting at `/company` and proceeding through `/company/new`, `/company/products`, and `/company/product1`;
- 80% of clients who accessed the site started from `/company/products`; or
- 65% of clients left the site after four or less page references.

The first rule suggests that there is useful information in `/company/product2`, but since users tend to take a circuitous route to the page, it is not clearly marked. The second rule simply states that the majority of users are accessing the site through a page other than the main page (assumed to be `/company` in this example) and it might be a good idea to include directory type information on this page if it is not there already. The last rule indicates an attrition rate for the site. Since many users don't browse further than four pages into the site, it would be prudent to ensure that important information is contained within four pages of the common site entry points.

Association rule discovery techniques [1, 48] are generally applied to databases of transactions where each transaction consists of a set of items. In such a framework the problem is to discover all associations and correlations among data items where the presence of one set of items in a transaction implies (with a certain degree of confidence) the presence of other items. In the context of Web usage mining, this problem amounts to discovering the correlations among references to various files available on the server by a given client. Each transaction is comprised of a set of URLs accessed by a client in one visit to the server. For example, using association rule discovery techniques we can find correlations such as the following:

- 40% of clients who accessed the Web page with URL `/company/product1`, also accessed `/company/product2`; or
- 30% of clients who accessed `/company/special`, placed an online order in `/company/product1`.

Since usually such transaction databases contain extremely large amounts of data, current association rule discovery techniques try to prune the search space according to *support* for items under consideration. Support is a measure based on the number of occurrences of user transactions within transaction logs.

Discovery of such rules for organizations engaged in electronic commerce can help in the development of effective marketing strategies. But, in addition, association rules discovered from WWW access logs can give an indication of how to best organize the organization's Web space.

The problem of discovering *sequential patterns* [35, 52] is to find inter-transaction patterns such that the presence of a set of items is followed by another item in the time-stamp ordered transaction set. In Web server transaction logs, a visit by a client is recorded over a period of time. The time stamp associated with a transaction in this case will be a time interval which is determined and attached to the transaction during the data cleaning or transaction identification processes. The discovery of sequential patterns in Web server access logs allows Web-based organizations to predict user visit patterns and helps in targeting advertising aimed at groups of users based on these patterns. By analyzing this information, the Web mining system can determine temporal relationships among data items such as the following:

- 30% of clients who visited `/company/products`, had done a search in Yahoo, within the past week on keyword w; or
- 60% of clients who placed an online order in `/company/product1`, also placed an online order in `/company/product4` within 15 days.

Another important kind of data dependency that can be discovered, using the temporal characteristics of the data, are similar time sequences. For example, we may be interested in finding common characteristics of all clients that visited a particular file within the time period $[t_1, t_2]$. Or, conversely, we may be interested in a time interval (within a day, or within a week, etc.) in which a particular file is most accessed.

Discovering *classification rules* [20, 54] allows one to develop a profile of items belonging to a particular group according to their common attributes. This profile can then be used to classify new data items that are added to the database. In Web usage mining, classification techniques allow one to develop a profile for clients who access particular server files based on demographic information available on those clients, or based on their access patterns. For example, classification on WWW access logs may lead to the discovery of relationships such as the following:

- clients from state or government agencies who visit the site tend to be interested in the page `/company/product1`; or
- 50% of clients who placed an online order in `/company/product2`, were in the 20-25 age group and lived on the West Coast.

Clustering analysis [24, 38] allows one to group together clients or data items that have similar characteristics. Clustering of client information or data items on Web transaction logs, can facilitate the development and execution of future marketing strategies, both online and off-line, such as automated return mail to clients falling within a certain cluster, or dynamically changing a particular site for a client, on a return visit, based on past classification of that client.

4 Analysis of Discovered Patterns

The discovery of Web usage patterns, carried out by techniques described earlier, would not be very useful unless there were mechanisms and tools to help an analyst better understand them. Hence, in addition to developing techniques for mining usage patterns from Web logs, there is a need to develop techniques and tools for enabling the analysis of discovered patterns. These techniques are expected to draw from a number of fields including statistics, graphics and visualization, usability analysis, and database querying. In this section we provide a survey of the existing tools and techniques. Usage analysis of Web access behavior being a very new area, there is very little work in it, and correspondingly this survey is not very extensive.

Visualization has been used very successfully in helping people understand various kinds of phenomena, both real and abstract. Hence it is a natural choice for understanding the behavior of Web users. Pitkow, et al [45] have developed the WebViz system for visualizing WWW access patterns. A *Web path paradigm* is proposed in which sets of server log entries are used to extract subsequences of Web traversal patterns called *Web paths.* WebViz allows the analyst to selectively analyze the portion of the Web that is of interest by filtering out the irrelevant portions. The Web is visualized as a directed graph with cycles, where nodes are pages and edges are (inter-page) hyperlinks.

On-Line Analytical Processing (OLAP) is emerging as a powerful paradigm for strategic analysis of databases in business settings. It has been recently demonstrated that the functional and performance needs of OLAP require that new information structures be designed. This has led to the development of the *data cube* information model [18], and techniques for its efficient implementation [2, 22, 50]. Recent work [15] has shown that the analysis needs of Web usage data have much in common with those of a data warehouse, and hence OLAP techniques are quite applicable. The access information in server logs is modeled as an append-only history, which grows over time. Since the size of server logs grows quite rapidly, it may not be possible to provide on-line analysis of all of it. Therefore, there is a need to summarize the log data, perhaps in various ways, to make its on-line analysis feasible. Making portions of the log selectively (in)visible to various analysts may be required for security reasons.

One of the reasons attributed to the great success of relational database technology has been the existence of a high-level, declarative, query language, which allows an application to express *what conditions must be satisfied by the data it needs*, rather than having to specify *how to get the required data.* Given the large number of patterns that may be mined, there appears to be a definite need for a mechanism to specify the focus of the analysis. Such focus may be provided in at least two ways. First, constraints may be placed on the database (perhaps in a declarative language) to restrict the portion of the database to be mined for, e.g. [36]. Second, querying may be performed on the knowledge that has been extracted by the mining process, in which case a language for querying knowledge rather than data is needed. An SQL-like querying mechanism has been proposed for the WEBMINER system [36]. For example, The query

```
SELECT association-rules(A*B*C*)
FROM   log.data
WHERE  date >= 970101 AND domain = "edu"
  AND support = 1.0 AND confidence = 90.0
```

extracts the rules involving the ".edu" domain after Jan 1, 1997, which start with URL `A`, and contain `B` and `C` in that order, and that have a minimum support of 1 % and a minimum confidence of 90 %.

5 Web Usage Mining Architecture

We have developed a general architecture for Web usage mining which is presented in [13] and [36]. The WEBMINER is a system that implements parts of this general architecture. The architecture divides the Web usage mining process into two main parts. The first part includes the domain dependent processes of transforming the Web data into suitable transaction form. This includes preprocessing, transaction identification, and data integration components. The second part includes the largely domain independent application of generic data mining and pattern matching techniques (such as the discovery of association rule and sequential patterns) as part of the system's data mining engine. The overall architecture for the Web mining process is depicted in Figure 2.

Data cleaning is the first step performed in the Web usage mining process. Some low level data integration tasks may also be performed at this stage, such as combining multiple logs, incorporating referrer logs, etc. After the data cleaning, the log entries must be partitioned into logical clusters using one or a series of transaction identification modules. The goal of transaction identification is to create meaningful clusters of references for each user. The task of identifying transactions is one of either *dividing* a large transaction into multiple smaller ones or *merging* small transactions into fewer larger ones. The input and output transaction formats match so that any number of modules to be combined in any order, as the data analyst sees fit.

Once the domain-dependent data transformation phase is completed, the resulting transaction data must be formatted to conform to the data model of the appropriate data mining task. For instance, the format of the data for the association rule discovery task may be different than the format necessary for mining sequential patterns. Finally, a query mech-

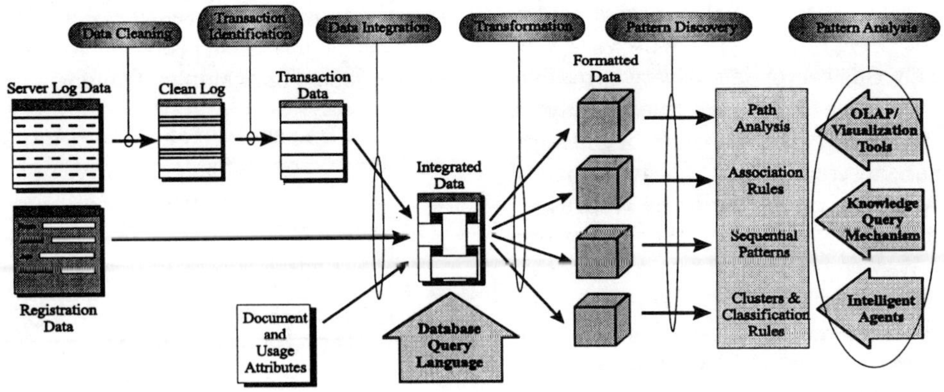

Figure 2: A General Architecture for Web Usage Mining

anism will allow the user (analyst) to provide more control over the discovery process by specifying various constraints. For more details on the WEBMINER system refer to [13, 36].

6 Research Directions

The techniques being applied to Web content mining draw heavily from the work on information retrieval, databases, intelligent agents, etc. Since most of these techniques are well known and reported elsewhere, we have focused on Web usage mining in this survey instead of Web content mining. In the following we provide some directions for future research.

6.1 Data Pre-Processing for Mining

Web usage data is collected in various ways, each mechanism collecting attributes relevant for its purpose. There is a need to pre-process the data to make it easier to mine for knowledge. Specifically, we believe that issues such as instrumentation and data collection, data integration and transaction identification need to be addressed.

Clearly improved data quality can improve the quality of any analysis on it. A problem in the Web domain is the inherent conflict between the analysis needs of the analysts (who want more detailed usage data collected), and the privacy needs of users (who want as little data collected as possible). This has lead to the development of *cookie files* on one side and *cache busting* on the other. The emerging OPS standard on collecting profile data may be a compromise on what can and will be collected. However, it is not clear how much compliance to this can be expected. Hence, there will be a continual need to develop better instrumentation and data collection techniques, based on whatever is possible and allowable at any point in time.

Portions of Web usage data exist in sources as diverse as *Web server logs, referral logs, registration files,* and *index server logs.* Intelligent integration and correlation of information from these diverse sources can reveal usage information which may not be evident from any one of them. Techniques from data integration [33] should be examined for this purpose.

Web usage data collected in various logs is at a very fine granularity. Therefore, while it has the advantage of being extremely general and fairly detailed, it also has the corresponding drawback that it cannot be analyzed directly, since the analysis may start focusing on micro trends rather than on the macro trends. On the other hand, the issue of whether a trend is micro or macro depends on the purpose of a specific analysis. Hence, we believe there is a need to group individual data collection events into groups, called *Web transactions* [12], before feeding it to the mining system. While [11, 12, 36] have proposed techniques to do so, more attention needs to be given to this issue.

6.2 The Mining Process

The key component of Web mining is the mining process itself. As discussed in this paper, Web mining has adapted techniques from the field of data mining, databases, and information retrieval, as well as developing some techniques of its own, e.g. *path analysis.* A lot of work still remains to be done in adapting known mining techniques as well as developing new ones.

Web usage mining studies reported to date have mined for *association rules, temporal sequences, clusters*, and *path expressions.* As the manner in which the Web is used continues to expand, there is a continual need to figure out new kinds of knowledge about user behavior that needs to be mined.

The quality of a mining algorithm can be measured both in terms of how *effective* it is in mining for knowledge and how *efficient* it is in computational terms. There will always be a need to improve the performance of mining algorithms along both these dimensions.

Usage data collection on the Web is incremental in nature. Hence, there is a need to develop mining algorithms that take as input the existing data, mined knowledge, and the new data, and develop a new model in an efficient manner.

Usage data collection on the Web is also distributed by its very nature. If all the data were to be integrated before mining, a lot of valuable information could be extracted. However, an approach of collecting data from all possible server logs is both non-scalable and impractical. Hence, there needs to be an approach where knowledge mined from various logs can be integrated together into a more comprehensive model.

6.3 Analysis of Mined Knowledge

The output of knowledge mining algorithms is often not in a form suitable for direct human consumption, and hence there is a need to develop techniques and tools for helping an analyst better assimilate it. Issues that need to be addressed in this area include usage analysis tools and interpretation of mined knowledge.

There is a need to develop tools which incorporate statistical methods, visualization, and human factors to help better understand the mined knowledge. Section 4 provided a survey of the current literature in this area.

One of the open issues in data mining, in general, and Web mining, in particular, is the creation of intelligent tools that can assist in the interpretation of mined knowledge. Clearly, these tools need to have specific knowledge about the particular problem domain to do any more than filtering based on statistical attributes of the discovered rules or patterns. In Web mining, for example, intelligent agents could be developed that based on discovered access patterns, the topology of the Web locality, and certain heuristics derived from user behavior models, could give recommendations about changing the physical link structure of a particular site.

7 Conclusion

The term *Web mining* has been used to refer to techniques that encompass a broad range of issues. However, while meaningful and attractive, this very broadness has caused Web mining to mean different things to different people [21, 36], and there is a need to develop a common vocabulary. Towards this goal we proposed a definition of Web mining, and developed a taxonomy of the various ongoing efforts related to it. Next, we presented a survey of the research in this area and concentrated on Web usage mining. We provided a detailed survey of the efforts in this area, even though the survey is short because of the area's newness. We provided a general architecture of a system to do Web usage mining, and identified the issues and problems in this area that require further research and development.

References

[1] R. Agrawal and R. Srikant. Fast algorithms for mining association rules. In *Proc. of the 20th VLDB Conference*, pages 487–499, Santiago, Chile, 1994.

[2] S. Agrawal, R. Agrawal, P.M. Deshpande, A. Gupta, J. Naughton, R. Ramakrishna, and S. Sarawagi. On the computation of multidimensional aggregates. In *Proc. of the 22nd VLDB Conference*, pages 506–521, Mumbai, India, 1996.

[3] R. Armstrong, D. Freitag, T. Joachims, and T. Mitchell. Webwatcher: A learning apprentice for the world wide web. In *Proc. AAAI Spring Symposium on Information Gathering from Heterogeneous, Distributed Environments.* 1995.

[4] M. Balabanovic, Yoav Shoham, and Y. Yun. An adaptive agent for automated web browsing. *Journal of Visual Communication and Image Representation*, 6(4), 1995.

[5] A. Z. Broder, S. C. Glassman, M. S. Manasse, and G Zweig. Syntactic clustering of the web. In *Proc. of 6th International World Wide Web Conference*, 1997.

[6] C. M. Brown, B. B. Danzig, D. Hardy, U. Manber, and M. F. Schwartz. The harvest information discovery and access system. In *Proc. 2nd International World Wide Web Conference*, 1994.

[7] P. Buneman, S. Davidson, G. Hillebrand, and D. Suciu. A query language and optimization techniques for unstructured data. In *Proc. of 1996 ACM-SIGMOD Int. Conf. on Management of Data*, 1996.

[8] P. Buneman, S. Davidson, and D. Suciu. Programming constrcuts for unstructured data. In *Proceedings of ICDT'95, Gubbio, Italy*, 1995.

[9] C. Chang and C. Hsu. Customizable multi-engine search tool with clustering. In *Proc. of 6th International World Wide Web Conference*, 1997.

[10] S. Chawathe, H. Garcia-Molina, J. Hammer, K. Irland, Y. Papakonstantinou, J. Ulman, and J. Widom. The tsimmis project: Integration of heterogenous information sources. In *Proc. IPSJ Conference*, Tokyo, 1994.

[11] M.S. Chen, J.S. Park, and P.S. Yu. Data mining for path traversal patterns in a web environment. In *Proceedings of the 16th International Conference on Distributed Computing Systems*, pages 385–392, 1996.

[12] R. Cooley, B. Mobasher, and J. Srivastava. Grouping web page references into transactions for mining world wide web browsing patterns. Technical Report TR 97-021, University of Minnesota, Dept. of Computer Science, Minneapolis, 1997.

[13] R. Cooley, B. Mobasher, and J. Srivastava. Web mining: Information and pattern discovery on the world wide web. Technical Report TR 97-027, University of Minnesota, Dept. of Computer Science, Minneapolis, 1997.

[14] R. B. Doorenbos, O. Etzioni, and D. S. Weld. A scalable comparison shopping agent for the world wide web. Technical Report 96-01-03, University of Washington, Dept. of Computer Science and Engineering, 1996.

[15] C. Dyreson. Using an incomplete data cube as a summary data sieve. *Bulletin of the IEEE Technical Committee on Data Engineering*, pages 19–26, March 1997.

[16] e.g. Software Inc. Webtrends. *http://www.webtrends.com*, 1995.

[17] W. B. Frakes and R. Baeza-Yates. *Information Retrieval Data Structures and Algorithms.* Prentice Hall, Englewood Cliffs, NJ, 1992.

[18] J. Gray, A. Bosworth, A. Layman, and H. Pirahesh. Data cube: A relational aggregation operator generalizing group-by, cross-tab, and sub-totals. In *IEEE 12th International Conference on Data Engineering*, pages 152–159, 1996.

[19] K. Hammond, R. Burke, C. Martin, and S. Lytinen. Faq-finder: A case-based approach to knowledge navigation. In *Working Notes of the AAAI Spring Symposium: Information Gathering from Heterogeneous, Distributed Environments.* AAAI Press, 1995.

[20] J. Han, Y. Cai, and N. Cercone. Data-driven discovery of quantitative rules in relational databases. In *IEEE Transactions on Knowledge and Data Eng.*, volume 5, pages 29–40, 1993.

[21] J. Han, Y. Fu, W. Wang, K. Koperski, and O. Zaiane. Dmql: A data mining query language for relational databases. In *SIGMOD'96 Workshop on Research Issues in Data Mining and Knowledge Discovery (DMKD'96)*, Montreal, Canada, 1996.

[22] V. Harinarayan, A. Rajaraman, and J.D. Ullman. Implementing data cubes efficiently. In *Proc. of 1996 ACM-SIGMOD Int. Conf. on Management of Data*, pages 311–322, Montreal, Canada, 1996.

[23] Open Market Inc. Open market web reporter. *http://www.openmarket.com*, 1996.

[24] L. Kaufman and P.J. Rousseeuw. *Finding Groups in Data: an Introduction to Cluster Analysis.* John Wiley & Sons, 1990.

[25] I. Khosla, B. Kuhn, and N. Soparkar. Database search using informatiuon mining. In *Proc. of 1996 ACM-SIGMOD Int. Conf. on Management of Data*, 1996.

[26] R. King and M. Novak. Supporting information infrastructure for distributed, heterogeneous knowledge discovery. In *Proc. SIGMOD 96 Workshop on Research Issues on Data Mining and Knowledge Discovery*, Montreal, Canada, 1996.

[27] T. Kirk, A. Y. Levy, Y. Sagiv, and D. Srivastava. The information manifold. In *Working Notes of the AAAI Spring Symposium: Information Gathering from Heterogeneous, Distributed Environments.* AAAI Press, 1995.

[28] D. Konopnicki and O. Shmueli. W3qs: A query system for the world wide web. In *Proc. of the 21th VLDB Conference*, pages 54–65, Zurich, 1995.

[29] M. Koster. Aliweb - archie-like indexing in the web. In *Proc. 1st International Conference on the World Wide Web*, pages 91–100, May 1994.

[30] C. Kwok and D. Weld. Planning to gather information. In *Proc. 14th National Conference on AI*, 1996.

[31] L. Lakshmanan, F. Sadri, and I. N. Subramanian. A declarative language for querying and restructuring the web. In *Proc. 6th International Workshop on Research Issues in Data Engineering: Interoperability of Nontraditional Database Systems (RIDE-NDS'96)*, 1996.

[32] H. Vernon Leighton and J. Srivastava. *Precision among WWW search services (search engines): Alta Vista, Excite, Hotbot, Infoseek, Lycos.* http://www.winona.msus.edu/is-f/library-f/webind2/webind2.htm, 1997.

[33] E. Lim, S.Y. Hwang, J. Srivastava, D. Clements, and M. Ganesh. Myriad: design and implementaion of federated database prototype. *Software – Practive & Experience*, 25(5):533–562, 1995.

[34] Y. S. Maarek and I.Z. Ben Shaul. Automatically organizing bookmarks per content. In *Proc. of 5th International World Wide Web Conference*, 1996.

[35] H. Mannila, H. Toivonen, and A. I. Verkamo. Discovering frequent episodes in sequences. In *Proc. of the First Int'l Conference on Knowledge Discovery and Data Mining*, pages 210–215, Montreal, Quebec, 1995.

[36] B. Mobasher, N. Jain, E. Han, and J. Srivastava. Web mining: Pattern discovery from world wide web transactions. Technical Report TR 96-050, University of Minnesota, Dept. of Computer Science, Minneapolis, 1996.

[37] net.Genesis. net.analysis desktop. *http://www.netgen.com*, 1996.

[38] R. Ng and J. Han. Efficient and effective clustering method for spatial data mining. In *Proc. of the 20th VLDB Conference*, pages 144–155, Santiago, Chile, 1994.

[39] K. A. Oostendorp, W. F. Punch, and R. W. Wiggins. A tool for individualizing the web. In *Proc. 2nd International World Wide Web Conference*, 1994.

[40] P. Merialdo P. Atzeni, G. Mecca. Semistructured and structured data in the web: Going back and forth. In *Proceedings of the Workshop on the Management of Semistructured Data (in conjunction with ACM SIGMOD)*, 1997.

[41] M. Pazzani, J. Muramatsu, and D. Billsus. Syskill & webert: Identifying interesting web sites. In *Proc. AAAI Spring Symposium on Machine Learning in Information Access*, Portland, Oregon, 1996.

[42] M. Perkowitz and O. Etzioni. Category translation: learning to understand information on the internet. In *Proc. 15th International Joint Conference on AI*, pages 930–936, Montral, Canada, 1995.

[43] P. Pirolli, J. Pitkow, and R. Rao. Silk from a sow's ear: Extracting usable structures from the web. In *Proc. of 1996 Conference on Human Factors in Computing Systems (CHI-96)*, Vancouver, British Columbia, Canada, 1996.

[44] J. Pitkow. In search of reliable usage data on the www. In *Sixth International World Wide Web Conference*, pages 451–463, Santa Clara, CA, 1997.

[45] J. Pitkow and Krishna K. Bharat. Webviz: A tool for world-wide web access log analysis. In *First International WWW Conference*, 1994.

[46] D. Quass, A. Rajaraman, Y. Sagiv, J. Ullman, and J. Widom. Querying semistructured heterogeneous information. In *International Conference on Deductive and Object Oriented Databases*, 1995.

[47] P. Resnik, N. Iacovou, M. Sushak, P. Bergstrom, and J. Riedl. Grouplens: An open architecture for collaborative filtering of netnews. In *Proc. of the 1994 Computer Supported Cooperative Work Conference, ACM*, 1994.

[48] A. Savasere, E. Omiecinski, and S. Navathe. An efficient algorithm for mining association rules in large databases. In *Proc. of the 21th VLDB Conference*, pages 432–443, Zurich, Switzerland, 1995.

[49] U. Shardanand and P. Maes. Social information filtering: Algorithms for automating "word of mouth". In *Proc. of 1995 Conference on Human Factors in Computing Systems (CHI-95)*, pages 210–217, 1995.

[50] A. Shukla, P.M. Deshpande, J. Naughton, and K. Ramaswamy. Storage estimation for multidimensional aggregates in the presence of hierarchies. In *Proc. of the 22nd VLDB Conference*, pages 522–531, Mumbai, India, 1996.

[51] E. Spertus. Parasite: mining structural information on the web. In *Proc. of 6th International World Wide Web Conference*, 1997.

[52] R. Srikant and R. Agrawal. Mining sequential patterns: Generalizations and performance improvements. In *Proc. of the Fifth Int'l Conference on Extending Database Technology*, Avignon, France, 1996.

[53] R. Weiss, B. Velez, M. A. Sheldon, C. Namprempre, P. Szilagyi, A. Duda, and D. K. Gifford. Hypursuit: a hierarchical network search engine that exploits content-link hpertexxt clustering. In *Hypertext'96: The Seventh ACM Conference on Hypertext*, 1996.

[54] S.M. Weiss and C. A. Kulikowski. *Computer Systems that Learn: Classification and Prediction Methods from Statistics, Neural Nets, Machine Learning, and Expert Systems.* Morgan Kaufmann, San Mateo, CA, 1991.

[55] M. R. Wulfekuhler and W. F. Punch. Finding salient features for personal web page categorization. In *Proc. of 6th International World Wide Web Conference*, 1997.

[56] O. R. Zaiane and J. Han. Resource and knowledge discovery in global information systems: A preliminary design and experiment. In *Proc. of the First Int'l Conference on Knowledge Discovery and Data Mining*, pages 331–336, Montreal, Quebec, 1995.

Knowledge Discovery in Scheme Approximation

Isamu Shioya Takao Miura
SANNO College
Kamikasuya 1573, Isehara, Kanagawa 259-11 JAPAN

Abstract

A scheme in databases can be considered as a knowledge description in database instances. To design schemes of databases is one of knowledge acquisitions. One of deficiencies in database design is there are no unique solutions. In addition, we can not avoid an evolution of the schemes, because of database paradigm. It is useful to employ AI methodologies as machine learning or knowledge discovery in database design. In this paper, we assume ISA hierarchies as a knowledge control, examine the data, and present a knowledge acquisition method to discover or find the difference of type schemes, in a sense of approximation, between a scheme knowledge and a knowledge obtained from database instances.

1 Motivation

A *database design* is a process to clarify, analyze and define what users mean. Since the design phase is inherently non-deterministic, interactive processing should be involved for sophisticated decision supports. Until now we don't establish full methodologies for design and redesign.

The process assumes that the world of interests can be classified *in advance* into a form of scheme, and that data can be manipulated *independent of* problem-domains. By utilizing them, the world of interests is described and manipulated by *sequences of primitive* features provided by data models. This framework is called *database paradigm*[13]. It is the paradigm by which both users and the systems can validate what users intend and how to optimize the way to obtain desired information. The foundation of suitable and efficient processing to massive data is due to the paradigm.

However the paradigm has severe deficiencies, that is, there is no general way to follow changes dynamically that arise very often during life-cycle of databases. The problems come from the inherent properties of the paradigm: we have to determine a database scheme first and *then* populate it. This leads to the fact that scheme descriptions might not model *current* world of interest correctly nor appropriately.

In this paper, we assume ISA hierarchies as knowledge control [6]. We examine the data, and present a knowledge acquisition method to discover, or find the difference of type schemes, in a sense of approximation, between a scheme knowledge and a knowledge obtained from database instances. We present a heuristic method in such a way that a type t is approximated by other types $t_1, .., t_n$, i.e., the interpretation of t can be recovered from the ones of $t_1, .., t_n$.

Section 2 contains definitions of several notions of a data model and some other abstraction techniques used in this work. In section 3 we discuss what *approximation* means and we show our first approach by means of `ISA` hierarchy. In section 4 we develop another approximation techniques that is fully instance-based. Section 5 contains yet another refinement but based on approximated containment. In section 6, we show some discussions. Then section 7 contains experimental results. Finally, we conclude our discussion in section 8.

2 An Instance-based Data Model

We discuss mainly *AIS* data model since the lessons described have wider applicability [12]. An *entity* is a surrogate of an object in the real world so that objects can be captured directly into the computer world independent of representation, properties and characteristic values. We denote a set of entities by $\mathcal{E}$. An *entity type* is an intentional concept to capture common properties among objects, and if an entity e has the properties, we say the entity e has the type t. We denote a set of entity types by $\mathcal{T}$ and a set of entities of a type $t \in \mathcal{T}$ by $\Gamma(t)$. One entity may have more than one types. We assume a special type `@E` which represents all the entities in database instances.

An *association* is a representation of a relationship among objects, so one relationship corresponds to one association. Common properties among associations are captured as *predicates.* Each association of a predicate p among entities $e_1, .., e_n$ is denoted by $p(e_1...e_n)$ or $\widehat{e}$ if p is known in the context. We assume a predicate is assigned to an association and that a predicate has a set of entity types called *defined-types.* If p has $t_1, .., t_n$ as defined types, then $e_i \in \Gamma(t_i)$. The value n is called an *arity* of p. We denote a set of associations of p by $\Gamma(p)$, so $\Gamma(p) \subseteq \Gamma(t_1) \times ... \times \Gamma(t_n)$. Sometimes p is also denoted by p^n.

AIS provides an *attribute* feature (a special predicate) that has functional correspondence between two types. A type may have several attributes.

EXAMPLE 1 Let us consider Asian Racing Horse database as our running example. Here we assume several entity types: Horse, Jockey, Race, Date, Newspaper, Amount-of-Win and some others. Each type may have one of attributes such as `Jockey` carrying `Name, Weight, Age` and `Country` (as the nationality). `Country` is an entity type, which has several sub-types such as `FarEastAsia, WestAsia`. Their meanings are self-explanatory. Also in this example there are 5 predicates:

jockey(Horse,Jockey)
entry(Horse,Jockey,Date,Race)
news(Horse,Jockey,Date,Race,NewsPaper)

1082-3409/97 $10.00 © 1997 IEEE

win(Horse,Jockey,Date,Race,AmountWin)
fun(Horse,Jockey)

where again their meanings are self-explanatory. For instance, `news` means the event has appeared in a newspaper.

As readers see, each entity holds its own types and such model is called an *instance-based* model. AIS data model and many other *semantic* data models (such as Object Oriented models) can be seen as instance-based[3].

Let $\tau(e)$ be a set of types that an entity e has: $\tau(e) = \{t \in \mathcal{T} \mid e \in \Gamma(t)\}$ that is called a *type scheme* of e. Remember an entity e of a type t may have other types. Every $\tau(e)$ is assumed to be finite. All the $\tau(e)$ represent typing information of the database, and we call them a type scheme of a database.

Since we want databases to keep real-world semantics at any time, the type scheme should grow heavily and each entity would carry a lot of characteristics, the description and the manipulation would be complicated. Generally $\tau(e)$ is really not small. When we have a large sets of entities and a huge number of type occurrences of $\tau(e)$, it seems hard to utilize scheme knowledges efficiently since we have to manage $\tau(e)$ individually. Moreover, it is harder to describe and control rules and constraints among types. A systematic management would be hard to obtain unified formalization. Sophisticated constraints such as type hierarchy and type constraints could relieve the situation if they are appropriately defined. We believe knowledge controls over types should be introduced and a unified mechanism for the simplification is indispensable.

EXAMPLE 2 Let us consider some of neighbor areas in Asia as our example. And we will describe type schemes for `Country`. There are 14 countries in Asian area over 7 types (other than `Country` or `@E`).

Country	*Types*
Japan(J)	*Asia, FarEast, Kanji, Pacific*
Taiwan(TW)	*Asia, FarEast, Kanji, Pacific*
Korea(K)	*Asia, FarEast, Kanji, Pacific*
China(C)	*Asia, Kanji*
HongKong(H)	*Asia, Kanji, Pacific, SouthEast*
Philippines(Ph)	*Asia, Pacific, SouthEast*
Singapore(S)	*Asia, Pacific, SouthEast*
Malaysia(M)	*Asia, Pacific, SouthEast*
Indonesia(Is)	*Asia, Pacific, SouthEast*
Thailand(Th)	*Asia, SouthEast*
Australia(A)	*Oceania, Pacific*
NewZealand(NZ)	*Oceania, Pacific*
India(IN)	*Asia, West*
Pakistan(Pk)	*Asia, West*

One of the typical mechanisms to control types is *generalization* or `ISA`. For types t_1 and t_2, t_2 is the generalization of t_1 (or t_1 `ISA` t_2) if $\Gamma(t_1) \subseteq \Gamma(t_2)$ in every database instances. Applying generalization many times, we have the reflexive and transitive closure called `ISA` hierarchy. The hierarchy assures that we can infer `ISA` correctly: by t_1 `ISA` t_2 and t_2 `ISA` t_3 we can imply t_1 `ISA` t_3. Given two types t_1 and t_2, t_2 is called a *direct* generalization of t_1 (or direct `ISA`, direct parent), if t_1 `ISA` t_2 and there exists no t_3 (in a current database scheme) such that t_1 `ISA` t_3 and t_3 `ISA` t_2. Similarly we define direct children.

We always assume the consistency on types and entities keep correct.

EXAMPLE 3 In `ISA` hierarchy of EXAMPLE2, readers can see 9 parents (i.e., direct generalizations) and each type has up to 2 direct generalization. Figure 1 shows (part of) the hierarchy.

Area	*Number*	*Countries*
Asia	*12*	*C,H,In,Is,J,K,M,Ph,Pk,S,TW,Th*
FarEast	*3*	*J,K,TW*
Kanji	*5*	*C,H,J,K,TW*
Oceania	*2*	*A,Nz*
Pacific	*10*	*A,H,Is,J,K,M,Nz,Ph,S,TW*
SouthEast	*6*	*H,Is,M,Ph,S,Th*
West	*2*	*In,Pk*

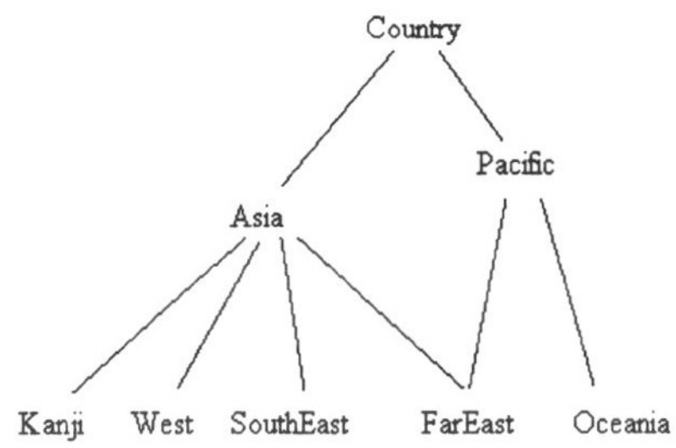

Figure 1: ISA Hierarchy of Asian Countries

3 Type Approximation

Here let us talk about how to detect types that can be approximated by other types, i.e., *type approximation*. By the approximation of a type t by $t_1, .., t_n$, we mean the interpretation $\Gamma(t)$ of t is described mostly by $\Gamma(t_1), .., \Gamma(t_n)$. Then the problems arise: what does the words *description* and *mostly* mean, and how to approximate types.

To see what type approximation means, let us discuss the relationship between `ISA` hierarchy and the approximation in this section. Given a type t, let T_t be all the set of the children: $T_t = \{s \mid s \texttt{ ISA } t\}$. Generally all the union of $\Gamma(s)$ where $s \in T_t$ is a subset of $\Gamma(t)$ by the definition. We say T_t is a *covering* of t, or T_t covers t if the equality holds. When T_t covers t, t can be seen as a *view* that is derivable from T_t by disjunction. In literatures[2, 3, 10, 11], `ISA` has been discussed in the context of covering (and additionally *exclusiveness* among such $\Gamma(s)$). The heart of covering is that all the subtypes constitute a parent t so that t can be approximated.

When $T_t = \{t_1, .., t_n\}$ covers t and t_1 `ISA` t_2, $T_t - \{t_1\} = \{t_2, .., t_n\}$ also covers t. Given a subset T_1 of T_t which covers t, we say T_1 is *non-redundant* with respect to the `ISA` hierarchy if every proper subset of T_1 can't cover t. When $T_t = \{t_1, .., t_n\}$ covers t, it is easy to see that all the set of t' such that t' directly `ISA` t becomes non-redundant.

Assume T_t does not cover t. Very often in database instances, we see t can be covered by other (non-sub) types $s_1, .., s_m$ as well as T_t. This hints us that we might miss other ISA such as s_i ISA t because $\Gamma(s_i) \subseteq \Gamma(t)$ holds in a current database. Database managers might be asked whether they are real ISA or not. The problem is how to get such supplementary types. Clearly it is too bad to exhaust all the types not in the ISA hierarchy rooted at t.

Then here comes our first heuristics. The basic idea is that we utilize ISA hierarchy to obtain candidates. Given an ancestor type type s of t, the interpretation contains the interpretations of both T_t and the candidate supplementary types. Thus, for an ancestor type s, we will search possible descendent types s_t of s (except t and not in T_t) by which t can be covered together with T_t. Figure 2 shows the situation: a type s_t might be a child of t and we might miss the link.

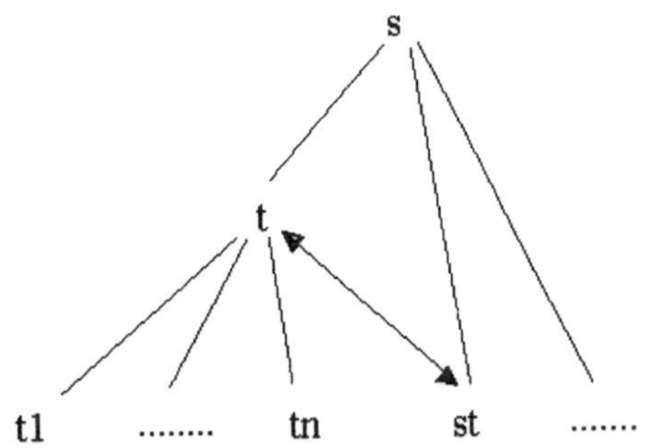

Figure 2: Supplementary Types in ISA Hierarchy

The algorithm proceeds with generation of *candidates*. Let t be a type to be approximated, T_t be all the subtypes of t and V be all the union of their interpretations.

First we will get all the direct parents T_a of t in the ISA hierarchy. For each s in T_a we obtain the direct child c of s where $c \neq t$. Then if $\Gamma(c) \subseteq \Gamma(t)$, then c might be a candidate. In fact, if $\Gamma(c) \cap V = \phi$, then c is one of the answers and we add c to T_t and $\Gamma(c)$ to V. If $\Gamma(c) \cap V \neq \phi$ but $\Gamma(c) \not\subseteq V$, possibly the descendants of c might be answers, so we consider all the direct children as new candidates and we will repeat this process. We note that the result obtained is non-redundant because we don't proceed in the case of $\Gamma(c) \subseteq V$.

If $V = \Gamma(t)$ then t is approximated by T_t. Or if $V \subseteq \Gamma(t)$ and $\frac{|V|}{|\Gamma(t)|} \geq \alpha$, then t is approximated by T_t where $0.0 < \alpha \leq 1.0$. We note $\alpha = 1.0$ means $V = \Gamma(t)$ and α could be seen as *degree of approximation*. We call $\frac{|V|}{|\Gamma(t)|}$ as *approximation ratio* of t.

EXAMPLE 4 In our examples 2 and 3, *Asia* can be approximated by *Kanji*, *West*, *SouthEast* and *FarEast* even if $\alpha = 1.0$. This result hints us to remove a type *Asia* (but to define a *view*) to avoid complexity.

If we give $\alpha = 0.50$, *Pacific* can be described by *FarEast* and *Oceania* with the approximation ratio is 0.50, but readers might say the latter result be erroneous. □

In our heuristic algorithm, a type t is approximated eventually by *descendants* of t so that the interpretation of t could be described by all the unions of the descendants. Such an approximation is called an *interior approximation.* We could think about the opposite direction. That is, a type t is approximated by *ancestors* and the interpretation of t is described by all the intersections of the ancestors. Such an approximation is called an *exterior approximation.*

To obtain an exterior approximation by means of ISA, let V be all the entities and we get all the direct children T_d of t in the ISA hierarchy. For each s in T_d we obtain the direct parent p of s where $p \neq t$. Then if $\Gamma(p) \supset \Gamma(t)$, then p might be a candidate: if $\Gamma(p) \cap V = \phi$ holds additionally, then p is one of the answers and we add p to T_t and replace V by the intersection of $\Gamma(p)$ and V. If $\Gamma(p) \cap V \neq \phi$ but $\Gamma(p) \not\supseteq V$, possibly the ancestors of p might be answers, so we consider all the direct parents as our candidates and we will repeat this process. As readers see, the discussion goes in parallel with interior cases. So we don't discuss any more.

4 Instance-Based Approximation

Since all the instances carry the information correctly, we will examine type schemes of instances one by one and make the approximation by means of such type schemes. Compared to the previous approach, this does neither really seem elegant nor efficient but truly suitable results might be generated. We call this second approach an *instance-based* approximation.

Let us describe our basic idea. Given a type t, each instance e in $\Gamma(t)$ carries its type schemes, i.e., all the types that e has. Then let T_t be the set of s in $\tau(e)$ where some $e \in \Gamma(t)$ has the type s *and* $\Gamma(s) \subseteq \Gamma(t)$: $T_t = \{s | e \in \Gamma(t), s \in \tau(e), \Gamma(s) \subseteq \Gamma(t)\}$. We note all the union of the interpretation of the types in T_t is a subset of $\Gamma(t)$ and T_t might cover t.

The algorithm is simple and easy to understand. Let T_t be all the union of the type schemes of instances of type t, and U and T be empty. For each type r in T_t where $r \neq t$, we examine $\Gamma(r) \subseteq \Gamma(t)$ and $\Gamma(r) \not\subseteq U$. If it is the case, r must be an answer and we add r to T and $\Gamma(r)$ to U. Note U is always included in $\Gamma(t)$. If $\frac{|U|}{|\Gamma(t)|} \geq \alpha$ holds, we completed the approximation. Again we note the result is non-redundant since we skip r such that $\Gamma(r) \subseteq U$.

Similar to the previous discussion, this instance-based approximation is a kind of interior approximations and we can define *exterior* instance-based approximation. In fact, in the definition of T_t, we select a type s where some $e \in \Gamma(t)$ has the type s *and* $\Gamma(s) \supseteq \Gamma(t)$.

EXAMPLE 5 In our examples 2 and 3, *Asia* can be approximated by *Kanji*, *West*, *SouthEast* and *FarEast* with $\alpha = 1.0$. This result is same as the previous one.

If we set $\alpha = 0.60$ in the instance-based approximation, *Kanji* can be described by *FarEast* with the approximation ratio is 0.60. Also *Asia* can be approximated by *Kanji*, *FarEast* and *SouthEast* with the ratio 0.83. The result indicates that one or two types are nearly described by others and it seems better to examine what they really mean. If we change the definition of the concepts, some changes arise to the relevant instances as well as ISA. □

5 Approximation by Containment

In the process of information retrieval, we try to find a set of all the correct answers S_1 but eventually we get another set S_2. To evaluate S_2, we sometimes utilize two criteria: *precision* and *recall*. The first criterion *precision* means how many S_2 contains incorrect answers, i.e., $\frac{|S_2|}{|S_2 \cap S_1|}$, while another criterion *recall* means how many answers S_2 contains, i.e., $\frac{|S_1 \cap S_2|}{|S_1|}$.

In our case, we will proceed with instance-based information (type schemes) and try to find a set of types of which interpretations have good precision and recall ratio. We note that the precision ratio tells us there may be erroneous instances and that the recall ratio tells there may remain other instances to be processed. Such new approach is called *approximation by containment* or *containment approximation*.

The algorithm is similar to the previous one, simple and easy to understand. Let T_t be all the union of the type schemes of instances of type t, and U, T be empty.

For each type r in T_t where $r \neq t$ and $r \neq @E$, we examine $\Gamma(r) \subseteq \Gamma(t)$ and $\Gamma(r) \not\subseteq U$. If it is the case, r must be an answer and we add r to T and $\Gamma(r)$ to U. If both $\Gamma(r) \subseteq \Gamma(t)$ and $\Gamma(r) \subseteq U$ hold, the interpretation of r has already been included. Assume $\Gamma(r) \subseteq \Gamma(t)$ does not hold, and we examine whether the precision $\frac{|V|}{|V \cap \Gamma(t)|}$ is less than or equal α_1 where $V = \Gamma(r) \cup U$. If the case, we add r to T and $\Gamma(r)$ to U. Note some erroneous data would be included at this time within the degree of approximation α_1, so α_1 means precision threshold here.

During the this process, U becomes increasing within α_1 until it contains more than α_2 answers, i.e., $\frac{|V \cap \Gamma t|}{|\Gamma(t)|}$ is greater than α_2, so α_2 represents recall threshold. Again we note the result is non-redundant since we skip r such that $\Gamma(r) \subseteq U$.

Unlike the previous two approximations, this instance-based approximation is neither interior nor exterior but two threshold values define upper/lower bounds of approximation.

EXAMPLE 6 *Asia* is described by *FarEast*, *Kanji*, *SouthEast* and *West* with both precision ratio and recall ratio 1.00.

However, when we assume precision threshold is 1.15 and recall threshold is 0.85, *Pacific* is approximated by *FarEast*, *Oceania* and *SouthEast* with precision ratio 1.10 and recall ratio 1.00. In other words, the three types capture the concept of *Pacific* mostly but not perfectly. The exceptional instance is *Th* which has *SouthEast* type but not *Pacific*, though other *SoutheEast* countries have. □

6 Discussion

To evaluate the results of our approximation, let us define some terms.

'Covering Status' means that a type is approximated fully by only descendants. In this case, `ISA` is designed correctly and effectively and we could consider the type as a kind of *view* not in the definition of a database scheme.

'Non-Covering Status' means that a type is approximated by only descendants but not fully. In this case, `ISA` is designed incorrectly and effectively but still there exist some entities not covered by the descendants. Since we can approximate the type, most of the interpretation is covered by the descendants.

'Missing Status' means that a type is approximated fully by non-descendants and descendants. In this case, `ISA` is designed correctly but becomes covering with other types. Probably we miss some `ISA` definitions and we could consider this fact as an important hint to revisit database schemes.

'ReVisiting Status' means that a type is approximated by non-descendants and descendants but not fully. In this case, `ISA` might be designed correctly with some confusion. Since we can approximate the type by the others, most of the interpretations are covered by the others. This means the concept that the type carries should be re-visited to capture more accurately by using the other types.

In an `ISA`-based approximation, types of covering status mean that the types carry the exact semantics consisting of the semantics of the descendent types in the approximation. In the case, they might be eliminated from database schemes. Types of missing status hint us the lack of `ISA` definitions that are erroneous in the database design. Homonym types show the same sets of the instances have several names, or we might have the duplicate definitions. Finally types in re-visiting status tell us that the types can be approximated independent of the current `ISA` hierarchy, i.e., possibly the database schemes miss the semantics of the real worlds of interests in suitable manner.

By the above consideration, we can say the type approximation tells us essential and important information, or we can obtain design feed-back as follows:

1. Simplifying Definition by Views
   Types of covering status can be represented by others, sometimes they can be replaced by mean of *Views* to avid overhead posed on schemes.

2. Verifying Database Design
   By examining types of covering/non-covering and missing status, database managers can checks whether they are really what they should do.

3. Detecting Missing `ISA`
   We might miss some `ISA` links of types in missing status at the design stages.

4. Detecting Homonyms
   Several types could be determined as identical if they are types of homonym status, and they should be adjusted. We note that it is very hard to find distinct types that are in fact identical while it is easy to see one type plays distinct roles (and it should be divided).

5. Examining Concepts that are ill-captured
   Types of Re-Visiting status can be approximated by other independent of `ISA` hierarchy, that means the hierarchy is not really suitable to model the world. The set of the approximating types hints us when we re-visit the definition of the approximated type.

7 Experimental Results

Here we show experimental results of our approximation algorithms.

7.1 Preliminary

In this experiment, we examine **Nikkei Byte Article Keyword Index** for NIKKEI BYTE magazine from 1985 until 1994 (10 years). The index contains a collection of 2315 articles which contain 2 errors and 2313 articles are processed. Each article record contains titles, volume/number, pages and keywords, and each article is considered as an entity of a type ARTICLE. Here we will regard keywords as types thus an article has several types. There are 196 keywords defined in the index, and 146 keywords among them appear 2792 times in total[1]. Belows are some examples of the index:

(488) GUI based DTP softwares on Unix/Windows:
1992.04:no.98:p.148:Product Report:DTP:GUI:UNIX:Windows

.....

(580) Demonstrating by IBM and MS - OS,Multimedia,Pen:
1991.12:no.93:p.144:Trends:OS Trends:Multimedia:Pen Computer

.....

(666) Page Printer on Windows - PART III Basic Benchmark - Graphics:1991.09:no.90:p.256:Topics:Windows:Printer: Benchmark Test

In this index, the 488-th entry says that the title is **GUI based DTP softwares on Unix/Windows** appeared in volume 1992.04 and number 98 in page 148. The article is classified as **Product Report** and has 4 keywords, DTP, GUI, UNIX and Windows.

In the NIKKEI index, the ISA hierarchy is given as a set of 288 pairs (i.e., direct generalizations) ⟨ keyword, parent ⟩ with 53 direct generalizations of which parents are @E. There are 325 branches of 5 levels where each keyword has up to 5 direct generalization. Next shows a part of the hierarchy.

x86 MicroProcessor:MicroProcessor
A/D Converter:Component
AI:@E
APL:Language
AX:IBM Compatible:Personal Computer
Ada:Language
Apple II:Apple Product:Personal Computer
Apple Product:@E
B16/32:HITACHI Product:Personal Computer
C/C++:Language:Object oriented

In this hierarchy, for instance, **Apple II ISA** both **Apple Product** and **Personal Computer**, and **Apple Product ISA @E**.

Here are summary of the index:

Keywords	*Articles*
1	304
2	44
3	422
4	536
5	341
6	368
7	150
8	75
9	48
10	13
11	9
12	1
13	2
Total	2313
Average	4.35*per article*

Parents	*Count*
1	112
2	77
3	6
4	1
Total	196*kwds*, 288ISA
Average	1.47*per kwd*

[1]Originally the index is in Japanese but it is translated in English in this paper.

7.2 ISA-based Approximation

An ISA-based approximation has been made with the degree of approximation 0.90. You can find the summary in Table 1.

Status	*Numb(ISA)*	*Numb(Inst)*
Covering	47	35
Non − Covering	1	7
Missing	1	18
Re − Visiting	0	5
Total	51	65
Homonym(Covering)	16	13
Homonym(Others)		14

Table 1: Summary of ISA-based and Instance-based

We found many types of Covering status. And most of them seem to have well-defined semantics, for instance, **AppleII** and **Macintosh** constitute **Apple Product**. As described in the previous sections, database managers might examine whether they should be real types or not.

One exceptional type of Non-Covering status is **Database** that is approximates by **Database Management Software** with the approximation ratio 92.4 percent. This means that 92.4 percents of the articles of the type **Database** have also a type **Database Management Software**, and the remaining articles discuss other aspects such as database design and performance efficiency.

All the types of Missing Status are **IBM Compatible**, **Personal Computer** and **OS** where **PC-AT Compatible ISA IBM Compatible**, **Windows-NT ISA Personal Computer** and **Windows-NT ISA OS**. These seem valid so that there might have been erroneous design of ISA hierarchy.

7.3 Instance-based Approximation

An instance-based approximation has been made with the same degree of approximation. We obtain the result in Table 1.

Since we have some allowance of the approximation, some of types of Covering status become decreased and the one of Non-Covering becomes increased. Thus we have 7 types of Non-Covering status since we have examined the instances. For instances the type **CPU** is fully approximated by approximated by **RISC**, **Add-on CPU Board**, **Graphics Processors**, **Co-Processors**, **Micro-Processors** and **TRON**. But also it is approximated by **RISC**, **Add-on CPU Board**, **Graphics Processors**, **Co-Processors** and **Micro-Processors** with the ratio 91.1 percent. In other words, the effect of **TRON** is not really big to determine **CPU**.

All the homonym types obtained are exactly same as the ones in ISA based approximation.

Notable difference arises in 5 types of Re-Visiting status: Five types **OS**, **Software**, **Network**, **Personal Computer** and **Storage Device**. We note all these had been decided to have covering status. In this approximation, by supplying non-descendants, the types of Re-Visiting status are approximated with more than 90 percent ratio, thus their relevant parts of the ISA hierarchy don't seem to model the semantics very well.

7.4 Containment Approximation

As for containment approximation, We made two experiments with the degrees of approximations (1.10, 0.90) and (1.20, 0.80), and we got 68 approximations, while the second, we got 75 approximations.

Below is the summary of the first and the second experiments:

$Status$	$Numb(1st)$	$Numb(2nd)$
$Covering$	32	26
$Non-Covering$	5	11
$Missing$	18	16
$Re-Visiting$	13	22
$Total$	68	75
$Homonym(Covering)$	13	13
$Homonym(Others)$	14	12

There are same trends about Covering and Non-Covering status compared to the previous approximation. That is, the number of types of Covering/N-Covering status becomes decreased since we have *wider* degree of approximation. And so are the cases of Missing status and Homonyms.

8 Conclusion

In this work, we presented a knowledge acquisition method of type scheme in a sense of approximation of ISA hierarchies. It consists of three operators: interior/exterior approximation, ISA-based/instance-based approximations and containment approximation. The type scheme of each database instance falls into two categories: one is the semantics of the instances can be approximated by the scheme in a sense of their operators, other is it should give up the approximation. The essential difference between machine learning and scheme discovery is to capture new concepts. In other words, scheme discovery is to capture *new concepts* in contrast with most of machine leanings or pattern recognition to capture the *reason why*.

Our series of works show how to obtain new database schemes that are suitable for current database instances. We have developed the theories based on a general paradigm [17] from the view point of types [15, 16],predicates [18] and complex objects [19].

Acknowledgment

The authors thank Prof. H.Arisawa (Yokohama National Univ., Japan), Prof. B. Thalheim (Technical Univ. of Cottbus, Germany), Prof. S. Navathe (Georgia Institute of Technology, USA) and Prof. T. Bench-Capon (Univ. of Liverpool, UK) for their encouragement.

References

[1] Agrawal, R., Srikant, R.: Fast Algorithms for Mining Association Rules, *VLDB* (1994), 487-499

[2] Elmasri, R. and Navathe, S.B.: Fundamentals of Database Systems, *Benjamin* (1994)

[3] Hull, R. and King, R.: Semantic Data Modeling, *ACM Computing Surveys* 19-3 (1986)

[4] Han, J., Cai, Y. and Cercone, N.: Knowledge Discovery in Databases : An Attribute Oriented Approach, *VLDB* (1992), 547-559

[5] Han, J. and Fu, Y.: Discovery of Multiple-Level Association Rules from Large Databases, *VLDB* (1995), 420-431

[6] Hamilton, H.J., Hilderman, R.J. and Cercone, N.: Attribute-Oriented Induction Using Domain Generalization Graphs, proc. *ICTAI*, 1996, 246-253

[7] Imielinski ,T. and Mannila, H.: A Database Perspective on Knowledge Discovery, *CACM* 39-11, 1996, 58-64

[8] Ioannidis, Y. and Lashkari, Y.: Incomplete Path Expressions and their Disambiguation, *SIGMOD* (1994), 138-149

[9] Kietz,J.U. and Morik, K.: A Polynomial Approach to the Constructive Induction of Structural Knowledge, *Machine Learning* 14 (1994), 193-217

[10] Kim, W.: Introduction to Object Oriented Databases, *MIT Press* (1990)

[11] Korth, H.F. and Silberschatz, A.: Database System Concepts, *McGraw-Hill* (1986)

[12] Miura, T., Arisawa, H.: Logic Approach of Data Models - *Data Logic, Future Database Systems*, 1990, 228-259

[13] Miura,T: Database Paradigms Towards Model Building, *Object Roll Modelling*, 1994, 228-258

[14] Miura,T. and Shioya, I.: Strategy Control for Database Queries, *Conference and Workshop of DEXA*, 1995, 231-240

[15] Miura, T. and Shioya, I.: Mining Type Schemes in Databases, *Conference and Workshop of DEXA*, 1996, 369-384

[16] Miura, T. and Shioya, I.: Knowledge Acquisition for Classification Systems, proc. *ICTAI*, 1996, 110-115

[17] Miura, T. and Shioya, I.: Paradigm for Scheme Discovery, proc.*CODAS* (1996), 101-108

[18] Miura, T. and Shioya, I.: Differentiation for Scheme Discovery, to appear

[19] Miura, T. and Shioya, I.: On Complex Type Hierarchy, in preparation

[20] Ng, R. and Han, J.: Efficient and Effective Clustering Methods for Spatial Data Mining, *VLDB* (1994), 144-155

[21] Quinlan, R: Induction of Decision Trees, *Machine Learning* 1-1 (1986), 81-106

[22] Quinlan, R: Learning Logical Definition from Rules, *Machine Learning* 5-3 (1990), 239-266

[23] Piatetsky-Shapiro, G. and Frawley, W.J. (ed.): Knowledge Discovery in Databases, *MIT Press* (1991)

Knowledge Discovery in the Legal Domain

John Zeleznikow

Applied Computing Research Institute,La Trobe University, Bundoora, Victoria, Australia, 3083; E-mail: johnz@latcs1.cs.latrobe.edu.au; and

Andrew Stranieri

School of Information Technology and Mathematical Sciences, University of Ballarat, Ballarat, Victoria, Australia, 3353; E-mail: a.stranieri@ballarat.edu.au

ABSTRACT

Whilst cases have been regularly used in building legal case based reasoners, they have rarely been used as a means of automated discovery of legal knowledge. Significant obstacles must be overcome if knowledge discovery techniques are to be applied in the legal domain. In this paper we argue that the use of domain expertise is vital and that an abundance of commonplace cases is necessary. Even with appropriate data, knowledge discovery techniques in law must deal with contradictory cases and use statistical techniques in order to define error and estimate performance. We illustrate these points by describing the use of the cross validation resampling technique, our own error heuristic and the method we use for dealing with contradictions for the training of neural networks in the domain of property proceedings in Australian Family Law.

1: Introduction

[5] define knowledge discovery in database as the *non trivial process of identifying valid, novel, potentially useful understandable patterns in data.* [3] state that in practical applications, data mining is based on two assumptions: 1) The functions that one wants to generalise can be approximated through some relatively simple computational model with a certain level of precision; and 2). The sample data set contains enough information to perform the generalisation. The second condition is a major obstacle in the use of data mining techniques in the legal domain. Despite the fact that artificial intelligence and law researchers have not focussed upon knowledge discovery in database techniques we believe such techniques can be fruitfully applied to analyse legal domains that involve judicial discretion.

[2] views discretion as a power or right conferred upon decision-makers to act according to the dictates of their own judgement and conscience, uncontrolled by the judgement or conscience of others. Few legal reasoning systems have been developed in discretionary domains. [4] applied rule—based reasoning to the discretionary domain of Family Law in Scotland and reported some inadequacies of that approach. Limitations reported there were further confirmed when we built a rule—based system which advised upon marital property division upon divorce [8].

In [13] we reported on the use of neural networks exposed to past cases in family law to predict the outcome of current cases. A full description of the resultant system, Split Up, can be found in [9]. Our experience with the Split Up project led us to conclude that for knowledge discovery in database techniques(KDD) to be applied usefully in legal domains, decisions taken and assumptions made in the selection, pre-processing, transformation and data mining phases of the KDD must be made explicit. In this paper we suggest that commonplace cases are far more appropriate for the selection phase than landmark cases. The transformation phase was performed in Split Up with the use of a hierarchy of attributes, that represents a tree of arguments based on Toulmin's theory of argumentation [10]. The data mining phase was performed with neural networks — the performance of each was verified using a resampling technique known as cross validation.

1082-3409/97 $10.00 © 1997 IEEE

2: Landmark and Commonplace Cases and their significance for knowledge discovery in legal domains

A number of case oriented artificial intelligence paradigms rely on classification. Examples include neural networks, rule induction and statistically oriented case based reasoners. In doing so, these paradigms assume that the experience being modelled has the same context. If the contexts of the cases differ then the expressions used, the factors relevant, and the outcomes of the cases will necessarily mean different things.

[7] incorporates context in her definition of a case for case based reasoning systems. She states that 'a case is a contextualised piece of knowledge representing an experience that teaches a lesson fundamental to achieving the goals of the reasoner'. [12] note that even in non-contentious areas, Kolodner's definition provides scope for considerable problems. They disagree that a case necessarily '...teaches a lesson fundamental to...the reasoner'. Certainly some cases do fit this description. Most notably within law, those decisions from appellate courts which form the basis of later decision and provide guidance to lower courts do provide a fundamental lesson, or normative structure for subsequent reasoning. The common name for such cases are landmark cases.

However, most decisions in any jurisdiction are not landmark cases. Most decisions in any legal system are commonplace. For example, in the last two decades, the number of landmark cases in the Family Court of Australia is in the order of hundreds while the number of commonplace cases is in the order of multiple tens of thousands. Landmark cases will individually have a profound effect on the subsequent disposition of all cases in that domain, whereas commonplace cases will only have a cumulative effect, and that effect will only be apparent over time. Furthermore, the vast majority of

Most legal reasoning systems augment a representation of landmark cases with heuristics used by practitioners of law. Although experts learn these heuristics as a result of constant exposure to commonplace cases there have been few attempts to induce the knowledge directly from case judgments. This is so because: 1) commonplace cases judgments are written reports therefore data about each judgment needs to be extracted manually; and 2) data mining techniques have only recently been developed. We argue that data mining techniques can be useful for gleaning knowledge in legal domains as an abundance of data exists in the form of commonplace cases. Landmark cases are problematical for use in data mining as these decisions are usually contradictory to prior experience

3: Knowledge Discovery in the Split Up system

The Split Up system integrates rule based reasoning with neural networks in architecture that can be described as a partitioned hybrid system. Domain knowledge of legal rules and principles is not modelled as rules. Instead factors that were relevant in determining a percentage split were elicited from experts and from statutes to form a hierarchy of relevant factors. This hierarchy was conceptualised as independent arguments conforming to the structure proposed by [10] whereby every argument has a *claim*, *data*, *warrant*, and *backing* component. Arguments combine to form complex chains because the claim of one argument is a data item for another argument.

Figure 1 depicts three arguments from Split Up, labelled A, B and C. The culminating (right-most) argument, A has, as its claim, the percentage of assets awarded to the husband. This is inferred (using a feed forward neural network represented as a dotted arc) from the contributions of the husband relative to the wife, the future needs of the husband relative to the wife and the wealth of the marriage. These three factors are the data items of the argument. The warrant and backing components of the Toulmin structure are omitted from Figure 1. We sec from this figure that the claim of Argument B is used as a data item for Argument A. The claim of argument B is inferred from its data items with the use of a neural network. The claim of argument C has been inferred from its data items with the use of rule sets and is itself another data item for B. A total of thirty-five arguments are used in Split Up. Twenty of the Split Up argument structures have a feed forward neural network trained with backpropagation of errors as the inference procedure. The remaining argument structures make use of small rule sets.

Neural networks have rarely been used in the legal domain because explanations are difficult to generate and assembling training sets is difficult. We show that connectionism can be useful in law if a series of smaller, networks are used instead of one larger network and if explanations are generated independently of the process used to infer a conclusion. Our approach is hence different from the work of [11] in the KBANN project. KBANN enables a neural network to be initialised with a domain theory. It maps the theory into a neural network, determining its topology and initial weights.

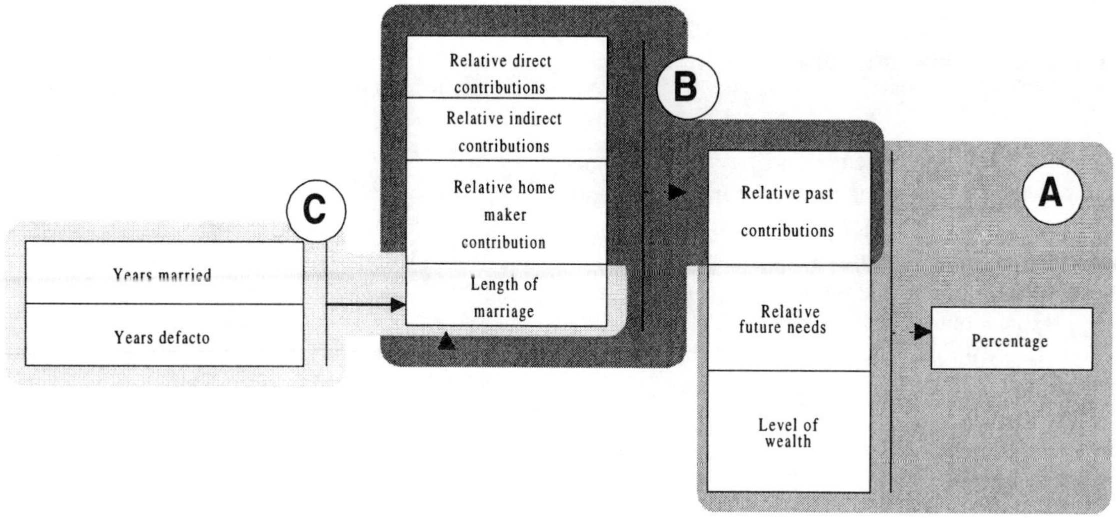

Figure 1 — Tree of factors relevant for a percentage split determination.

The decision as to whether we should use rule sets or neural networks for each argument depended on a classification scheme for classifying legal tasks for determining data mining suitability [9]. The classification scheme which helped us determine which family law tasks were suited to KDD involves the expert's belief about two dimensions: the open textured - well defined axis and a concept we called boundedness.

Data for the Split Up system was initially extracted from four hundred written unreported cases. However many of these were considered unsuitable for the task of data mining the training set. For example we eliminated all cases dealing with the custody of children, since experts believed that litigants often appear to fight about the custody of children when their real aim is to gain a greater share of property. Eventually we used one hundred and three unreported cases were the only issue of conflict was property. The template used for data extraction derived from the hierarchy of arguments depicted in figure 1. Raters extracted data from the cases by reading the text of the judgement and recording values on ninety-four variables.

From our research we have observed that knowledge discovery techniques in law require some manual analysis of the data and the KDD process can only provide support for legal practitioners if commonplace cases are abundant.

We also noted that techniques for dealing with contradictions or outliers must be developed for application in the pre-processing phase. In most legal domains, examples are contradictory if they have different outputs given the same input. Contradictions are to be expected in Family Law, since the weighting of factors can vary between judges and even within the same judge over a period of time. According to [6], contradictory data can severely interfere with the ability of a network to generalise in order to produce accurate outcomes on cases it has not been exposed to during training. For the Split Up project, we considered outputs that differed by a small margin to be contradictions that are allowable. We have implemented a degree of consistency in our method for removing extreme cases, by designing a metric that quantifies the extent to which two outcomes are contradictory.[15]

The data mining phase in Split Up was performed with neural networks. All networks were trained using 5 fold cross validation. The simplest way to define a classifier error is to count the number of examples correctly classified by a neural network however this leads to a measure of network performance which may be too fine-grained for legal applications. A better measure of a network's performance includes an indication of the magnitude of the error. A variation of 5% either way from a judge's decision of the percentage of assets awarded to the wife, is, in our view, a minor error. Although the cut off point for declaring that an error has occurred is necessarily subjective, it was important that a metric be discerned which could be applied consistently to all networks in Split Up.

In [14] we discussed a preliminary evaluation of the Split Up system. In that paper we compared and contrasted the performance of the Split Up system with that of ten domain experts. The system is currently being trialed by a dozen family lawyers and the Family Court of Australia.

4. Conclusion and future research

We have discussed knowledge discovery in the legal domain and indicated how the Split Up system uses neural networks to predict judicial outcomes. We noted that even when using data mining, domain expertise is vital. We illustrated that to perform data mining in a legal domain requires an abundance of commonplace cases.

Knowledge discovery methods in law must deal with contradictory cases. In Split Up extreme contradictions were removed from the data set to train networks. The way we define error and the extent to which error is permitted are issues that impact on KDD in legal domains. In the Split Up system, we defined a metric for determining the magnitude of error and a heuristic for deciding when the error level is acceptable.

One of the prime tasks in the legal domain is negotiation. In [1] we discuss how to use Split Up and knowledge discovery techniques to support negotiation. Following the advice of domain experts, the Split Up system uses ninety-four different attributes. The Split Up architecture provides no mechanism for determining whether the factors are relevant in empirical terms. It is possible that many of the factors declared relevant by our experts do not, in practice, contribute to a prediction. Thus, a family law prediction could possibly be made with only a subset of the factors regarded as relevant by experts. We have applied feature selection techniques using genetic algorithm search to the data used to determine percentage split in the Split Up system

5.References

[1] Bellucci, E. and Zeleznikow, J. 1997. Family—Negotiator: an intelligent decision support system for negotiation in Australian Family Law. *Proceedings of the Fourth Conference of the International Society for Decision Support Systems*, Lausanne, International Society for Decision Support Systems:359-373.

[2] Black, H. C. 1990. *BLACK'S LAW DICTIONARY*, West Publishing Company, St. Paul, Minnesota.

[3] Decker, K. M. and Focardi, S. 1995. *Technology Overview: A Report on Data Mining*. Technical Report 95-02. Swiss Scientific Computing Centre, CSCS-ETH, CH-6928, Manno, Switzerland.

[4] Edwards, L. and Huntley, A. J. K. 1992. Creating a Civil Jurisdiction Adviser. Law, Computers and Artificial Intelligence: 1(1), 5—40.

[5] Fayyad, U., Piatetsky-Shapiro, G. and Smyth, P. 1996a. From data mining to knowledge discovery: An overview. In *Advances in Knowledge Discovery and Data Mining* AAAI/MIT Press: Cambridge, Massachusetts.

[6] Haykin, S. 1994. *Neural Networks: a Comprehensive Foundation*. Macmillan: New York, New York.

[7] Kolodner, J. 1993. *Case based reasoning*. Los Altos: Morgan Kaufmann.

[8] Stranieri, A. and Zeleznikow, J. 1992. SPLIT-UP—Expert system to determine spousal property distribution on litigation in the Family Court of Australia. *Proceedings of Artificial Intelligence Conference (Australia)-92*, Hobart: World Scientific, 51-56.

[9] Stranieri, A., Zeleznikow, J., Gawler, M. and Lewis, B. 1998. A hybrid—neural approach to the automation of legal reasoning in the discretionary domain of family law in Australia. To appear in *Artificial Intelligence and Law*.

[10] Toulmin, S. 1958. *The uses of argument*. Cambridge: Cambridge University Press.

[11] Towell, G. and Shavlik, J. 1994. Knowledge-based artificial neural networks. *Artificial Intelligence* 70(1-2): 119-165.

[12] Zeleznikow, J. Hunter, D. and Stranieri, A. 1997. Using cases to build intelligent decision support systems. Database Applications Semantics — Proceedings of the IFIP Working Group 2.6 Conference. Stone Mountain, Georgia, USA. May 30 - June 2. 1995. Edited by Meersman, R. and Mark, L. Chapman—Hall: 443-460.

[13] Zeleznikow, J. and Stranieri, A. 1995. The Split-Up system: Integrating neural networks and rule based reasoning in the legal domain. *Proceedings of Fifth International Conference on Artificial Intelligence and Law*, ACM:185-194.

[14] Zeleznikow, J. and Stranieri, A. 1997a. Modelling discretion in the Split Upsystem. *PACIS97 The Pacific Asia Conference on Information Systems*, Information Systems Research Management, Queensland University of Technology: 307-320.

[15] Zeleznikow, J. and Stranieri, A. 1997b. Knowledge discovery in the Split-Up project. *Proceedings of Sixth International Conference on Artificial Intelligence and Law*, ACM:89-97.

Fast Similarity Search in the Presence of Longitudinal Scaling in Time Series Databases

Eamonn Keogh

Department of Information and Computer Science
University of California, Irvine
California 92697-3425
eamonn@swim2birds.ics.uci.edu

Abstract

The problem of finding patterns of interest in time series databases (query by content) is an important one, with applications in virtually every field of science. A variety of approaches have been suggested. These approaches are robust to noise, offset translation, and amplitude scaling to varying degrees. However, they are all extremely sensitive to scaling in the time axis (longitudinal scaling). We present a method for similarity search that is robust to scaling in the time axis, in addition to noise, offset translation, and amplitude scaling. The method has been tested on medical, financial, space telemetry and artificial data. Furthermore the method is exceptionally fast, with the predicted 2 to 4 orders of magnitude speedup actually observed. The method uses a piecewise linear representation of the original data. We also introduce a new algorithm which both decides the optimal number of linear segments to use, and produces the actual linear representation.

Introduction

Time series account for a large amount of data stored in databases. A common task with a time series database is to look for an occurrence of a particular pattern within a longer sequence. Such queries have obvious applications in many fields, such as:

- Identifying patterns associated with growth in stock prices.
- Detecting anomalies in an online monitoring system.
- Identifying non-obvious relationships between two time series. For example, a time series recording the sales of ice cream might show peaks in the same places as a time series recording the daily temperature. Such a relationship might be easily detected by simple correlation, but less obvious causal relationships that involve a time lag might be more difficult to discover.
- Hypothesis testing. Here an expert draws a model of a pattern he would expect to find in a database, given his understanding of the domain. Searching for the pattern can help to confirm or deny the original hypothesis, and inspire new ones.

Similarity searching is not a trivial problem. The two primary difficulties are time complexity and defining a similarity measure. The obvious brute force solution to the problem, 'sliding' the shorter query sequence Q against the longer reference sequence R, calculating the error term at each point, is called 'sequential scanning'. Sequential scanning has a time complexity[1] of $O((m-n+1)*n)$ where m is the number of datapoints in R, and n is the number of datapoints in Q. For some of the simple experiments performed for this paper m = 22,627 and n = 1426. Here, sequential scanning requires approximately 30 million operations. For real-world applications we would like to be able to search over much longer time series, ideally in real time.

Sequential scanning typically uses squared error as its similarity measure. This is adequate if an exact match to Q appears in R. However, we do not generally expect to find exact matches to our queries.

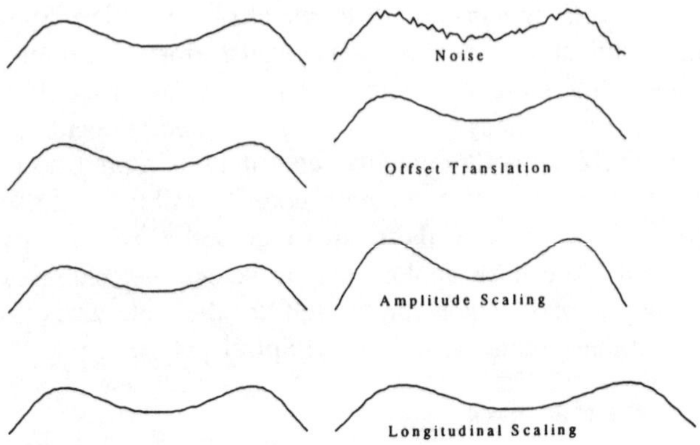

Figure 1: Some of the problems encountered when defining a similarity measure for a time series

We need to allow some degree of fuzziness in our query. While many methods have been proposed which allow some degree of distortion in the y-axis between a query sequence and a potentially matching sub-section of a reference time series, none allows distortion, (i.e. stretching or compressing) in the time axis. The

[1] Note that the worst case is when $n \approx \sqrt{m}$

1082-3409/97 $10.00 © 1997 IEEE

contribution of this paper will primarily be to introduce such a method. In the rest of the paper we shall refer to similarity measures which do *not* allow this elasticity in the time axis, as *lockstep* measures.

Representation

As with most problems in computer science, representation is of key importance. We require a representation that will allow us to define a distance measure that is robust to longitudinal scaling. After examining other possibilities, including Fourier Transforms (Faloutsos et al 1995) and Relational Trees (Shaw and DeFigueiredo 1990, Ehrich and Foith 1976), we decided upon a piecewise liner representation. This representation has many desirable properties, including:

- High rates of data compression. For example, consider Figure 8. The original time series contains 22,627 points. The segmented version of it contains only 38 segments, yet captures most of the essential information.
- Relative insensitivity to noise.
- Intuitiveness and ease of visualization.

The high rate of data compression is of particular importance. As we will see, the computational speedup we achieve will be proportional to the square of compression rate. In addition, it will allow us to search huge time series in main memory without having to swap in and out small sub-sections.

There are many well-known segmentation algorithms in the literature, many of which were pioneered by Pavlidis (1974). It should be emphasized that the distance measures, and search techniques presented in the rest of this paper will work with any segmentation algorithm. For completeness, however, we present a variant of the 'bottom up' algorithm which not only produces a segmentation, but chooses K, the number of segments used to represent the time series.

The decision of how many linear segments to use to approximate a given time series is a very important one. If we choose too small a K, we will lose important features and may fail in our goal of similarity search. On the other hand, if we choose too large a K, we capture all the necessary detail in our time series, but retain redundant information. This is of particular importance because the speedup achieved by the search algorithm presented later in this paper is proportional to the *square* of the compression rate. Approaches in the literature for choosing the correct K range from 'eyeballing' (i.e., manual inspection and choice) to requiring that each segment have its error norm ε less than some threshold (Pavlidis 1973). The problem with the latter approach is that given two time series, A and B, where B is simply A plus noise, it will produce two segmentations, similar in shape, but with the segmentation representing B containing far too many segments. Ideally in this situation we would like the algorithm to produce identical segmentations.

Our segmentation algorithm works in the following manner. We begin by approximating the given time series T (which contains n points), with j linear segments, where $j = \lfloor \frac{n}{3} \rfloor$. At this stage, each segment contains 3 points (we allow the last segment to contain 4 or 5 points if there exists a remainder from $\lfloor \frac{n}{3} \rfloor$). Each segment is the best-fit line through its collection of points, as determined using the classic regression definition $y - \bar{y} = \frac{s_{xy}}{s_x^2}(x - \bar{x})$.

Naturally we don't expect each segment to fit the data perfectly. They will contain some amount of residual error for each point they approximate. This residual error, which is the vertical distance from the best-fit line to the data points, we will call $d_1, d_2 \ldots, d_j$. We define the normalized error e_i, for each segment as: $e_i = \frac{\sum_{m=1}^{j} d_m^2}{j}$

Informally, the measure e_i can be considered a measure of how well the ith segment is approximating its share of the data, normalizing for its length. We note that, in general, the e_i's will display considerable variance. We formally capture this variability by defining the Balance of Error for k segments as: $B_k = std(e_1, e_2, \ldots, e_k)$

The segmentation algorithm begins by merging two neighboring segments to produce a new approximation of the time series with j-1 segments. This process is repeated until we have a single line approximation of the original time series (i.e. j = 1). At this point we have an entire family of linear approximations, one for each value of j from 1 to $\lfloor \frac{n}{3} \rfloor$. Note that we have left two crucial details unspecified :

- What is the criterion for selecting which pair of segments to merge in each iteration?
- Which of the approximations should we actually use?

The criterion for selecting which pair of segments to merge is 'Merge the two segments, which give the minimum value of B_k in the next iteration'. The criterion for selecting which approximation to use is 'Select the model for which B_k was minimized'. The intuition behind this method is as follows. It is known that under certain assumptions, the best approximation for a given function using piecewise polynomials requires that the error norm be equal among all segments (Lawson 1964, Pavlidis 1973). Almost none of these assumptions are true for an arbitrary time series, but as we shall see, balance of error is a useful heuristic. In the first iteration of our algorithm, the balance of error is distributed almost randomly. In each subsequent iteration, the algorithm attempts to redress this. This is possible while the number of segments remaining is greater than the true K. When the number of segments remaining equals K, all segments will have almost equal error norms. In the next iteration two of those segments must be merged, resulting in a larger segment which has a very large error norm.

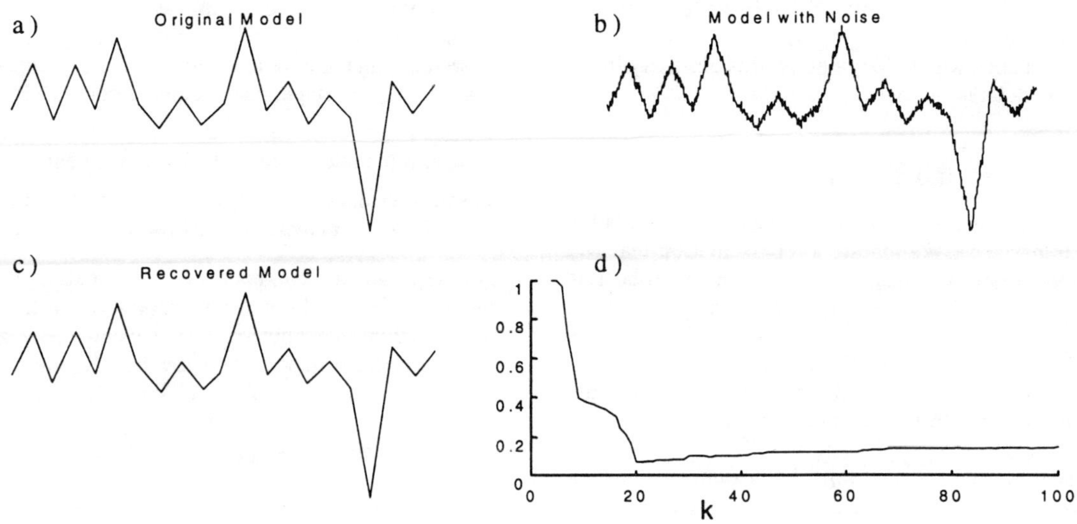

Figure 2: **a)** An artificial time series with a highly linear structure, containing 1000 points. **b)** A noisy version of **a**. **c)** The model recovered by our algorithm. **d)** The Balance of Error, B_k, plotted against k.

To test this algorithm we needed data sets for which the true value of K is not subjective. We built artificial time series containing 1000 points, but with a highly linear structure, as in Figure 2.a. We then added some Guassian[2] noise to the model, as in Figure 2.b, and attempted to reconstruct the original model as in Figure 2c. Figure 2.d shows B_k plotted against k. B_k is clearly minimized at k = 20, which is the correct number of segments in this example.

If the underlying model is truly linear and we have enough data, we can always recover the true model regardless of how much (symmetrically distributed) noise we have. In general, neither of these assumptions holds, so we need to consider what our algorithm will do in these cases. Figure 3 shows the same time series shown in Figure 2.a with various amounts of noise and the models recovered. Given enough noise the algorithm does fail to recover the original model, but appears to degrade gracefully, capturing the overall shape of the underlying time series.

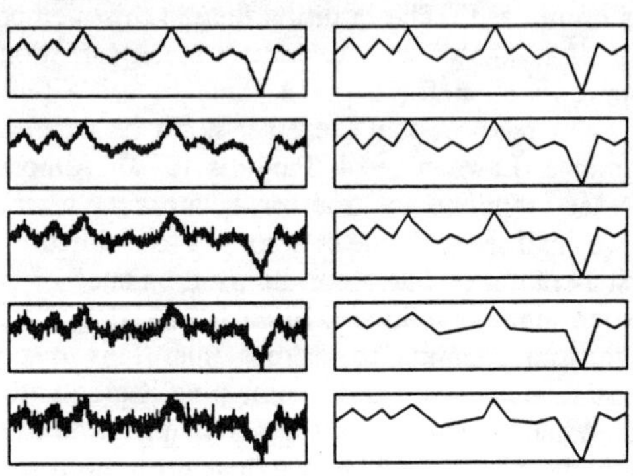

Figure 3: Different amounts of noise added to the same time series shown in Figure 2, and the recovered models.

2 We obtained similar results for other symmetric noise distributions.

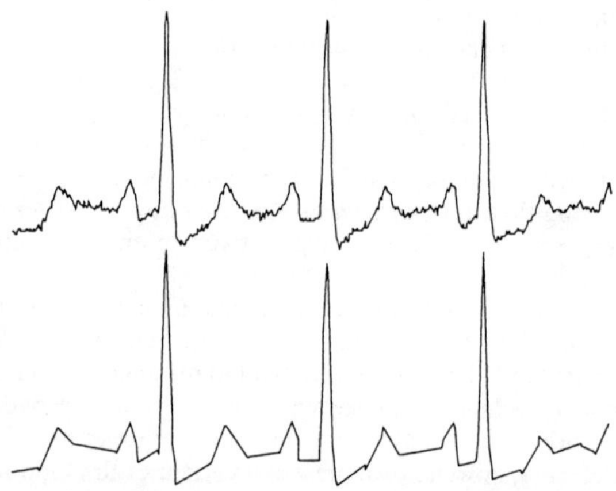

Figure 4: An electrocardiogram containing 512 points, and its 37-segment representation as produced by our algorithm.

Figure 4 shows the results of applying the algorithm to data which is clearly non-linear. Again, the segmented model appears to capture the essential shape of the underlying time series. To avoid confusion throughout the rest of the paper, we will refer to a piecewise-segmented linear representation of a time series as a 'sequence'.

Distance Measures

We begin this section by defining a simple distance measure, which does not possess robustness to longitudinal scaling. Later we will generalize this measure to incorporate longitudinal scaling and compare the two metrics.

A difficulty arises when attempting to compare two sequences represented by piecewise linear segments. In general, the endpoints of the segments do not line up. We solve this problem by projecting every endpoint on each sequence onto the other sequence. We measure the variance of the length of the projected lines, and use this as our distance measure. To get some intuition as to why this makes sense as a distance measure, consider the case where we are comparing two identical sequences. All the projected lines will have the same length, so their variance, and therefore their distance, will be zero. If there is a single feature present in one sequence and not the other, then at least one of the projected lines will be longer (or shorter) than the rest, and the variance and distance will suitably increase. For this measure to work, the two sequences must not cross. This is easily arranged by adding some large constant to all the y-values of one of the sequences.

Note that this measure handles:

- **Noise**. By segmenting the original time series we have 'canceled out' the effects of symmetrically distributed noise. We have also minimized the effects of lone spikes by averaging their effects over 'good' data.
- **Offset translation**. The variance of the projected lines is unaffected by the mean length of those lines, so shifting one of the sequences in the y-axis has no effect on the distance measure.
- **Amplitude Scaling**. There are occasions when we might want amplitude scaling to effect our distance measure, and other occasions when we want to be insensitive to it. In the latter case, we have merely two normalize the two sequences[3] before projecting the lines, and measuring their variance.

This distance measure has the following desirable properties.

$$d(x,y) \geq 0 \quad \forall\, x, y$$
$$d(x,y) = 0 \;\text{ iff }\; x = y$$
$$d(x,y) = d(y,x)$$

Having shown how to compare two sequences of the same length, we need now to consider how to do subsequence matching. This is accomplished in the obvious way. We take the shorter sequence, the Query Q, and 'slide' it along the longer Reference sequence R, as in Figure 5. We anchor the left edge of Q with the left side of every segment in R, then compute the distance between Q, and the appropriate subsection of R. We find the best match by keeping a *best-so-far* variable. This technique, which we call 'Segmented Sequential Scanning' has a time complexity of $O(MN)$, where M is the number of segments used to represent the time series R, and N is the number of segments used to represent the query Q. If c is the *average* number of datapoints represented by each individual segment in both Q and R, then we can rewrite the time complexity as $O((m/c)(n/c))$. This allows easy comparison to the time complexity for classic sequential scanning, and we can see that the speedup achieved is proportional to c^2. The actual value of c is domain dependent. In the experiments used to illustrate this paper it ranged from 6 to 578, giving a theoretical speedup of 36 to 334,084.

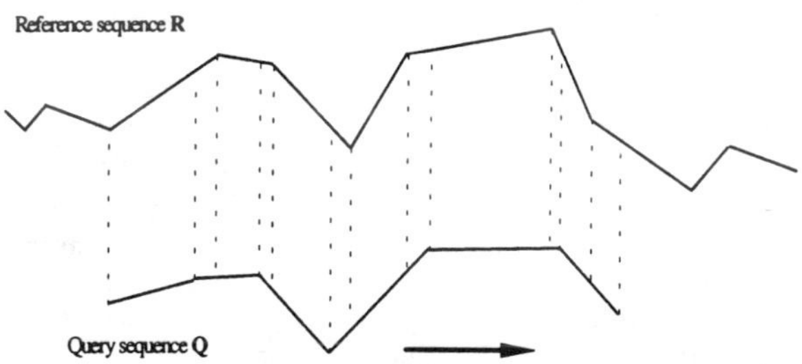

Figure 5: Subsequence matching with the segmented representation is accomplished by 'sliding' **Q**, along **R** and projecting the endpoints of each segment onto its corresponding place in the other sequence. The distance between two sequences is the variance of the projected lines.

3 We need to be careful when normalizing, not to be unduly influenced by a single feature, so rather than use the min and the max, we use the upper and lower quartiles as reference points.

Having defined a *lockstep* distance measure that uses an underlying segmented representation, we will now show a generalized version that allows stretching and shrinking in the time axis. The format for the query now includes two numbers to represent the maximum stretch and the maximum shrink allowed. We will represent this form of query by Q*. In this paper we assume for simplicity that we will allow the template to deform within this interval, without penalty. The more general form where we expect the Q* to be a certain length and penalize longer or shorter potential matches according to some probabilistic model is a simple generalization (Keogh and Smyth 1997, Burl and Perona 1996).

Our approach is based upon the simple observation that although a time series and a stretched version of itself are considered dissimilar to each other, short sub-sections of the time series, and the corresponding sub-sections from the stretched version will appear similar. Figure 6

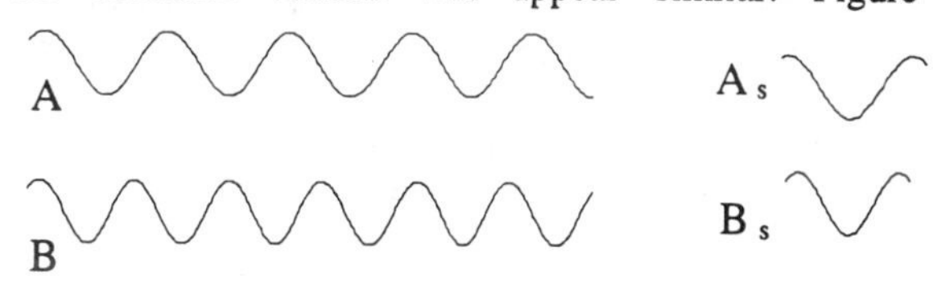

Figure 6: Although **A** and **B** will be considered very dissimilar by *lockstep* distance measures, short sub -sequences such **A$_s$** and **B$_s$** can always be found, which by themselves are arbitrarily similar.

demonstrates this phenomenon.

We will begin, therefore, by extracting two small sub-sections Q_l and Q_r from Q^*, and searching for matches for these sub-queries using the *lockstep* algorithm described above (We will discuss the technique for selecting Q_l and Q_r below). We actually do two searches for each sub-query, one where it has been stretched by the maximum amount allowed, and one where it has been compressed by the maximum amount allowed. The result of this search is used to build a table as shown in Figure 7.

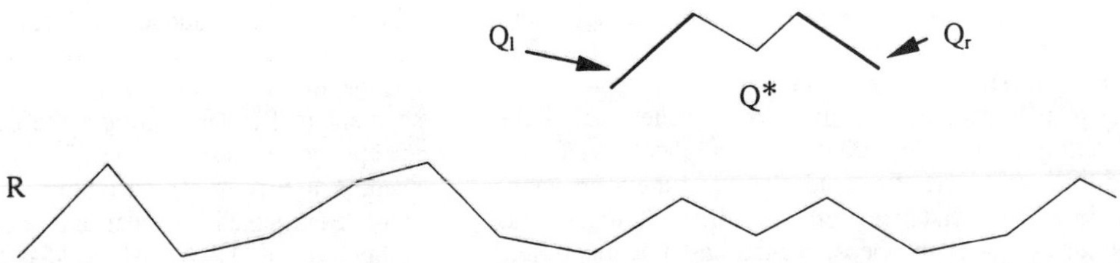

Q_l	.02 | .03	.92 | .91	.23 | .27	.20 | .18	.14 | .15	.82 | .84	.72 | .70	.11 | .09	.30 | .02	.71 | .72	.77 | .75	.21 | .18	.83 | .84	.41 | .43
Q_r	.71 | .72	.21 | .24	.45 | .47	.48 | .43	.53 | .56	.13 | .16	.32 | .35	.46 | .41	.27 | .24	.43 | .41	.12 | .15	.64 | .61	.71 | .73	.12 | .14
X Axis	0	21	43	57	81	99	119	145	161	177	196	220	241	267

Figure 7: The query Q* is decomposed into Q_l and Q_r (show in bold). Both are Q_l and Q_r matched against the reference sequence R, and the results are used to build a table.

Row one shows the goodness of fit of Q_l when aligned with the ith segment in R. Row two shows the goodness of fit of Q_r when aligned with the ith segment in R. Note there are two numbers in each cell, corresponding to the stretched and compressed versions of the templates. Row three contains the x-values of the left side of the ith segment in R. Note that no matter what length a potential overall match to our query is, the contribution of dissimilarity from Q_l and Q_r is bounded between the two values in the corresponding cell in the table.

We will now use this table to guide our search for Q*. First let us consider how to do a brute-force search of the table. We begin by assuming that Q_l is anchored in the first column in row 1 of the table. Given that the length of Q* is variable, the section representing Q_r might be in any one of several contiguous cells in row 2. For each possibility we compress or stretch Q* by an appropriate amount and compare this compressed or stretched query to the sequence R to obtain its goodness of fit. We obtain the appropriate scaling factor by dividing the difference of the values in row 3 of the two columns in question, by the standard length of Q* (Scaling Q* simply corresponds to multiplying its x-values by the scaling factor). Surprisingly, even doing this brute force search, the algorithm is still faster than sequential scanning on the raw data, providing that the average number of points represented by a segment is greater than about 5, and the maximum stretch is less than approximately 200%. Of course, we can avoid this brute force search using a variety of heuristics, including the following:

- Instead of searching left to right, it is better to search the table by anchoring Q_l at the most promising cells first, and keeping a *best-so-far* variable (The most promising cells are identified by looking at the lower of the two values). At every stage of the search we can eliminate all cells which have a minimum value greater than the current *best-so-far*, because they could not be part of an overall match which has a lower dissimilarity than our *best-so-far*. Typically this heuristic alone prunes 95% of the search space.
- Rather than using Q_l as the anchor point for the search, it might be better to use Q_r and search 'backwards'. This would be true if low values for Q_r are rarer than low values of Q_l. A simple test for skewness for each row will tell us the best row to search from.

In addition to the above, we can speed up the search by a careful choice of the segments chosen to represent Q_l and Q_r. By choosing wisely we can ensure that most of the values in the rows 1 and 2 are large, with just a few small values. This will ensure we find low values for *best-so-far* quickly, and can abandon the search early. For all the experiments shown in this paper, we simply use the leftmost segment to represent Q_l and the rightmost segment to represent Q_r. In some cases, however, we may have been better off choosing other segments, based on how often similar angles occur in R, the segments length (longer is better), and the distance between the two segments (further apart is better).

We call this algorithm S7 (Similarity Searching while Shrinking and Stretching using Segmented Sequential Scanning). The time complexity for S7 has two major contributions, the time taken to build the table, and the time taken to search the table. The time taken to build the table is less than or equal to $O(MN)$, the time taken for a *lockstep* search. The time taken to search the table depends on the interval over which Q* may deform and on the structure data itself. In the pathological case where Q* is allowed to stretch over an interval as long as R and all the elements of the table are almost equal, we could be forced to examine the entire table. In general however, working with real data, we found the time needed to search the table is much less than the time need to build the table. The experimental results section below summarizes the empirical results of experiments on various data sets.

Experimental Results

The above algorithm was tested on many data sets from medical, financial and engineering domains. Due to space limitations, we present only a small subset of the results. For each experiment we also ran classic sequential

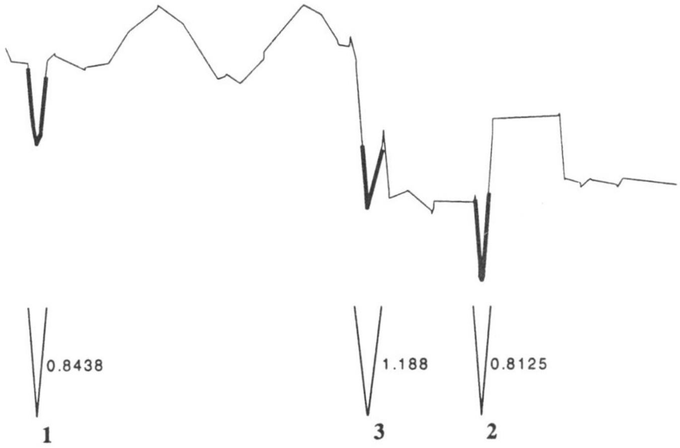

Figure 8: A simple Q* query on a Shuttle sensor. The three best matches are shown, with their scaling factors.

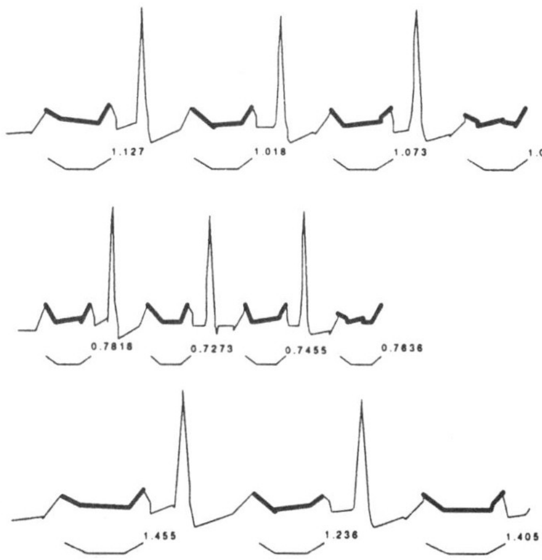

Figure 9: Our algorithm is able to track a particular part of an electrocardiogram, regardless of pulse rate.

scanning as a strawman comparison. Figure 8 shows the result of a simple query on data from a Space Shuttle sensor (Shuttle STS-67 V71H3140B). The original time series has 22,627 points, which our segmentation algorithm transformed into 38 segments. The query Q* is a simple valley, which was allowed to stretch or compress by up to 25%. The three best matches are displayed, together with the amount of scaling necessary to achieve a fit. Surprisingly, one cannot duplicate this result with classic sequencing scanning. If you make the query template narrow enough to find the narrow valleys in the data (Figure 8, **1** and **2**), you are unable to find the wider valley (Figure 8, **3**) and if you make the query template wider, you can find the wider valley, but not the narrow ones.

Figure 9 shows an example of a query on an electrocardiogram. We built a simple three-segment query Q* which can find a certain part of the electrocardiogram. We built the initial template based upon visual inspection of an electrocardiogram recorded at a pulse rate of 70 beats per minute, and defined the limits of scaling based on knowledge of how variable a pulse rate can be. The algorithm easily finds the correct portions of the electrocardiogram, regardless of the patient's pulse rate.

Table 1 shows a comparison of our S7 algorithm vs classic sequential scanning. Note that the speedup achieved greatly depends on the average number of datapoints represented by a segment. The times reported for our algorithm do not include the time needed to segment the data; we assume that this is done off-line.

Related Work

Subsequence matching is a generalization of the much simpler problem of sequence matching. Here both sequences are assumed to be the same length. Agrawal et al. (1995) tackle this problem by dividing up the sequences into windows. Corresponding windows from two time series are compared, and the two time series are said to be similar if enough of these windows are similar. The individual windows are said to be similar if one lies within an envelope of a specified width around another. Each window has its data normalized to remove the effects of amplitude scaling and offset translation. A different approach favored by Berndt and Clifford (1994) uses dynamic time warping. Here two sequences are aligned, then one of them has its x-axis (time parameterization) locally stretched or compressed in order to minimize some distance function. Unfortunately, this technique is computationally very expensive, although it does lend itself to parallelization.

In general, pattern matching on 'raw data' is not feasible because of the sheer volume of data. In addition, raw data may contain spikes, drop-outs or other noise which could

Data Set	Compression Rate Average number points per segment	Sequential scanning (Brute force approach) seconds	S7 seconds
Synthetic data	**32**	**471.2**	**4.8**
Shuttle	**578**	**4101.4**	**1.9**
Electrocardiogram	**61**	**1157.9**	**3.2**
Tree rings	**6**	**17.1**	**5.3**

Table 1

confuse the matching process. A variety of higher-level representations of times series have been proposed, most notably Discrete Fourier Transform. This approach involves performing a Discrete Fourier Transform on the original time series, discarding all but the K most informative coefficients, and then mapping these coefficients into K-dimensional space. The original work by Agrawal, Faloutsos and Swami (1993) only allowed the comparison of two time series of equal length, but was extended by Faloutsos, Ranganathan and Manolopoulos (1994) to include subsequence matching. Here they use a sliding window over the original time series to extract features. This process results in a trail in feature space. These trails are represented by their MBR's (Minimum Bounding Rectangles), and the MBR's are indexed by R*-trees. The method is guaranteed to produce no false hits, but may produce false misses. There are limitations on the shortest possible query (it cannot be shorter than the width of the sliding window). Another problem with the method is that for queries greater than a certain length (the width of the sliding window), the query sequence must be decomposed and the results merged, greatly affecting the speed of the matching. Nevertheless, speedups of 3 to 100 times over sequential scanning are reported.

Others, including, Shatkay and Zdonik (1996) recognize that a piece-wise linear (and higher order) order representation, greatly reduces the required storage and search space for a time series, but fail to suggest a distance measure or search technique.

Summary

We have shown that a piecewise linear representation allows robust sequence matching which is much faster than current techniques. In addition we have presented an algorithm which is the first of which the authors are aware, to allow controlled longitudinal scaling. Some possible extensions and areas for future research include:

- Automating the process of selecting the best possible segments to use as Q_l and Q_r.
- Generalizing linear segments to higher order polynomials.
- Using the algorithm as a tool for learning relationships within, and between time series.
- Allowing non-uniform scaling, perhaps by using dynamic time warping (Brendt and Clifford 1994).

Acknowledgments

I would like to thank Dr. Michael Pazzani for his support and encouragement, and Hagit Shatkay for the electro-cardiogram data. All data mentioned in this paper are available in both original and segmented formats from http://www.ics.uci.edu/~eamonn/timeseries.html.

References

Agrawal, R., Faloutsos, C. and Swami, A. Efficient Similarity Search in Sequence Databases. In Proc. of the Fourth International Conference on Foundations of Data Organization and Algorithms, Chicago, October 1993.

Agrawal, R., Lin, K. I., Sawhney , H. S and Shim, K. Fast Similarity Search in the Presence of Noise, Scaling, and Translation in Times-Series Databases, In VLDB, September 1995.

Berndt, D. J., Clifford, J. Using Dynamic Time Warping to Find Patterns in Time Series. In KDD-94: AAAI Workshop on Knowledge Discovery in Databases. Pages 359-370, Seattle, Washington, July 1994.

Burl, M., Perona, P., Recognition of Planer Class Objects. Proceedings of the 1996 Computer Vision and Pattern Recognition Conference, IEEE Press, 1996.

Cheng, Y. C., Lu, S. Y. Waveform Correlation using Tree Matching: IEEE Conf. PRIP, 1982.

Ehrich, R. W, and Foith, J. P., Representation of Random Waveforms by Relational Trees. IEEE Transactions On Computers, Vol. C-25, NO. 7, July 1976.

Faloutsos, C., Ranganathan, M., Manolopoulos, Y. Fast Subsequence Matching in Time-Series Databases. SIGMOD - Proceedings of Annual Conference, Minneapolis, May 1994.

Hagit, S., Zdonik, S. Approximate Queries and Representations for Large Data sequences. Proc. 12th IEEE International Conference on Data Engineering. Pages 546—553, New Orleans, Louisiana, February 1996.

Keogh, E., Smyth, P., Probabilistic Approach to Fast Pattern Matching in Time Series Databases. To appear KDD-97.

Lawson, C. L., Characteristic Properties of the Segmented Rational Minimax Approximation Problem, Numerical Math., Vol. 6, pp. 293-301. 1964.

Pavlidis, T., Waveform Segmentation Through Functional Approximation, IEEE Transactions on Computers, Vol, C-22, NO. 7 July 1973.

Pavlidis, T., Horowitz, S., Segmentation of Plane Curves, IEEE Transactions on Computers, Vol. C-23, NO 8, August 1974.

Shaw, S. W., DeFigueiredo, R. J. P. Structural Processing of Waveforms as Trees. IEEE Transactions on Acoustics, Speech, and Signal Processing. Vol. 38 No 2 February1990.

Wang, J. T., Zhang, K., Jeong, K and Shasha. A System for Approximate Tree Matching, IEEE Transactions on Knowledge and Data Engineering, 6, no 2 April 1994.

Author Index

Notes

Notes

Notes

IEEE COMPUTER SOCIETY

IEEE Computer Society Publications

The world-renowned Computer Society publishes, promotes, and distributes a wide variety of authoritative computer science and engineering texts. These books are available in two formats: 100 percent original material by authors preeminent in their field who focus on relevant topics and cutting-edge research, and reprint collections consisting of carefully selected groups of previously published papers with accompanying original introductory and explanatory text.

Submission of proposals: For guidelines and information on Computer Society books, send e-mail to cs.books@computer.org or write to the Acquisitions Editor, IEEE Computer Society, P.O. Box 3014, 10662 Los Vaqueros Circle, Los Alamitos, CA 90720-1314. Telephone +1 714-821-8380. FAX +1 714-761-1784.

IEEE Computer Society Proceedings

The Computer Society also produces and actively promotes the proceedings of more than 130 acclaimed international conferences each year in multimedia formats that include hard and softcover books, CD-ROMs, videos, and on-line publications.

For information on Computer Society proceedings, send e-mail to cs.books@computer.org or write to Proceedings, IEEE Computer Society, P.O. Box 3014, 10662 Los Vaqueros Circle, Los Alamitos, CA 90720-1314. Telephone +1 714-821-8380. FAX +1 714-761-1784.

Additional information regarding the Computer Society, conferences and proceedings, CD-ROMs, videos, and books can also be accessed from our web site at http://computer.org/cspress

4/15/97